From **simulations** that place students in the role of campaign manager to **timeline activities**, from **pre- and post-chapter tests** to a fully integrated **Ebook**, MyPoliSciLab brings together an amazing collection of resources for both students and instructors. See a demo now at **www.mypoliscilab.com**!

Here's what's in MyPoliSciLab—

Pre-Test, Post Test, and Chapter Exam.

For each chapter of the text, students will navigate through a pre-test, post-test, and a full chapter exam—all fully integrated with the online Ebook so students can assess, review, and improve their understanding of the material in each chapter.

Ebook.

Matching the exact layout of the printed textbook, the Ebook contains multimedia icons in the margins that launch a wealth of exciting resources.

Chapter Review.

For each chapter, students will find additional resources, such as a complete study guide, learning objectives, a summary, and Web explorations.

Research Navigator™.

This database provides thousands of articles from popular periodicals like *Newsweek* and *USA Today* that give students and professors access to topical content from a variety of sources.

New York Times Online Feed & The New York Times Search by Subject™ Archive.

Both provide free access to the full text of *The New York Times* and articles from the world's leading journalists of the *Times*. The online feed provides students with updated headlines and political news on an hourly basis.

LongmanParticipate.com 3.0

Our well-known and highly respected online tool is now fully updated. Students will find over 100 simulations, interactive timelines, comparative exercises and more—all integrated with the online ebook. Available inside MyPoliSciLab or as a web site alone.

W9-DAS-564

LongmanParticipate.com 3.0
Inside!

Go to www.mypoliscilab.com for a free demo.

The Essentials of American & Texas Government

Continuity and Change

2006 Edition

KAREN O'CONNOR

Professor of Government
American University

LARRY J. SABATO

University Professor and
Robert Kent Gooch Professor of Politics
University of Virginia

STEFAN D. HAAG

Austin Community College

GARY A. KEITH

University of Texas at Austin

PEARSON
Longman

New York San Francisco Boston
London Toronto Sydney Tokyo Singapore Madrid
Mexico City Munich Paris Cape Town Hong Kong Montreal

Executive Acquisitions Editor: Eric Stano
Senior Marketing Manager: Elizabeth Fogarty
Media and Supplements Editor: Kristi Olson
Production Manager: Eric Jorgensen
Project Coordination, Text Design, Art Studio, and
    Electronic Page Makeup: Electronic Publishing Services Inc., NYC
Cover Design Manager: Nancy Danahy
Cover Images: Getty Images, Inc.
Cover Image Montage: Keithley & Associates, Inc.
Photo Research: Photosearch, Inc.
Senior Manufacturing Buyer: Alfred C. Dorsey
Printer and Binder: RR Donnelley & Sons, Co.
Cover Printer: Phoenix Color Corp.

For permission to use copyrighted material, grateful acknowledgment is made to the copyright holders on the pages where the material appears.

Library of Congress Cataloging-in-Publication Data

O'Connor, Karen,
        Essentials of American and Texas government : continuity and change / Karen O'Connor ...
    [et al.].
            p. cm.
        Includes bibliographical references and index.
        ISBN 0-321-36520-8 (paperbound)
            1. United States--Politics and government--Textbooks. 2. Texas--
    Politics and government--Textbooks. I. O'Connor, Karen

JK276.E75 2006
320.473--dc22

                                                        2005012307

Visit us at http://www.ablongman.com

ISBN 0-321-36520-8

12345678910—DOC—08 07 06 05

To Meghan,
who grew up with this book

Karen O'Connor

To my Government 101 students
over the years, who all know that
"politics is a good thing"

Larry Sabato

Brief Contents

ix

APPENDICES

Detailed Contents

xi

Preface

It has happened again. As we prepared this new, essentials version of our bestselling text on American and Texas government, we find ourselves again surprised, challenged, and still riveted by the dramatic changes that continue to take place across our political landscape.

When we first started writing our original American government text over a decade ago, we could never have envisioned that each passing edition would chronicle such dramatic changes in American government and politics. In just over a decade, we experienced 1992's "Year of the Woman" that produced record numbers of women elected to national office, and 1994's "Year of the Angry Male Voter" that produced a Republican revolution in Congress. The editions that followed those years appeared during various phases of the Clinton scandals, including the second impeachment trial of a U.S. president. Next came the 2000 election, the outcome of which did not occur until December and then appeared to many to be decided by a single justice of the U.S. Supreme Court; the terrorist attack of September 11, 2001; and the history-bucking 2002 midterm elections that returned control of both houses of Congress to the Republicans. Little did we realize that, not long after those midterm elections, one of the longest, most expensive, divisive, and impassioned campaigns ever for the presidency was about to get underway. The 2004 national elections were dominated by heated discussion of the preemptive war with Iraq and debates about security and terrorism, the economy, and social issues like same-sex marriage. We saw the emergence of so-called 527s as a powerful (and well-financed) political force, unprecedented "get out the vote" efforts by both Republicans and Democrats, and a closely divided and hotly charged electorate that returned George W. Bush to office for a second term with a majority of the popular votes and a solid win in the Electoral College.

It can never be said that American politics is boring. For every edition of our texts, something unexpected or extraordinary has occurred, giving question to the old adage, "Politics as usual." At least on the national level, there appears to be little that is usual. Politics and policy form a vital, fascinating process that affects all our daily lives, and we hope that this text reflects that phenomenon as well as provides you with the tools to understand politics as an evolutionary process where history matters.

Teaching introductory American government presents special challenges and rewards. It is a challenge to introduce a new discipline to students. It is a challenge to jump from topic to topic each week. Above all, it is a challenge to motivate large and disparate groups of students to master new material and, one hopes, to enjoy it in the process. The rewards of success, however, are students who pay more attention to their government, who participate in its workings as more informed citizens, and who better understand the workings of democracy as practiced in the United States.

We have witnessed some of these rewards in the classroom. With this new book, we hope to offer our experiences in written form. This new, brief and less expensive version of our larger text on American and Texas government should work well in classes that are shorter, where a more inexpensive text is desired, or where instructors want to use a basic text supplemented by diverse readings that amplify specific topics. We believe that students need perspective and motivation; they also need to be exposed to information that will withstand the test of time. Our goal with this text is to transmit just this sort of information while creating and fostering student interest in American politics despite growing national skepticism about government and government officials at all levels. We hope that this brief text will explain the national mood about politics and put it in better context for students, to allow them to understand their role in a changing America.

APPROACH

We believe that one cannot fully understand the actions, issues, and policy decisions facing the U.S. government, Texas government, or the people unless these issues are examined from the perspective of how they have evolved over time. Consequently, the title of this book is *The Essentials of American & Texas Government: Continuity and Change.* In its pages, we try to examine how the United States and Texas are governed today by looking not just at present behavior but also at the Framers' intentions and how they have been implemented and adapted over the years. For example, we believe that it is critical to an understanding of the role of political parties in the United States to understand the Framers' fears of factionalism, how parties evolved, and when and why realignments in party identification occurred.

In addition to questions raised by the Framers, we explore issues that the Framers could never have envisioned, and how the basic institutions of government have changed in response to these new demands. For instance, two centuries ago, no one could have foreseen election campaigns in an age when nearly all American homes contain television sets, and the Internet, fax machines, and even cell phones allow instant access to information. Moreover, increasing citizen demands and expectations have routinely forced government reforms, making an understanding of the dynamics of change essential for introductory students.

Our overriding concern is that students understand their government as it exists today. In order to do so, they must understand how it was designed in the Constitution. Each chapter, therefore, approaches its topic from a combination of perspectives that we believe will facilitate this approach. We have also included a full annotated Constitution of the United States and a new boxed feature, "The Living Constitution," to further increase student understanding and appreciation of the Constitution in our government and everyday lives. (You can read more about these in the "Features" section of this Preface.) In writing this book, we chose to put the institutions of government (Part Two) before political behavior (Part Three). Both sections, however, were written independently, making them easy to switch for those who prefer to teach about the actors in government and elections before discussing its institutions.

Our Texas co-authors have been teaching and participating in Texas politics for more than a quarter of a century. During that time, they have witnessed many changes, not only in politics and government but also in how the subject has been taught. College students need to understand how Texas politics and government work. To this end, the theme of continuity and change lends itself well to the study of Texas politics and government, as students will find in the seven chapters on Texas politics and government. Institutions that were created when Texas was a rural, agrarian state during the late-nineteenth century have survived along with a constitution that was created for a society quite different from that of contemporary Texas. There have also been numerous changes. We doubt that the framers of the 1876 Texas Constitution would recognize that document as it exists today with its more than 400 amendments, but it would not be totally foreign to them either. The continuity that has kept Texas moored to its roots would be evident to them, as would the changes that have been required to make government relevant to the twenty-first century. We hope that students appreciate both as they read about Texas politics and government.

REMAINING CURRENT IN A CHANGING WORLD

In this 2006 Edition of *The Essentials of American & Texas Government: Continuity and Change*, we have retained our basic approach to the study of politics as a constantly changing and often unpredictable enterprise. We discuss the dizzying array of important events that have taken place, with particular attention to developments over the last couple of years. Most importantly, we include in-depth coverage of the 2004 campaign for the presidency and its results. We discuss the issues that were paramount during the long election season, including debates over the war in Iraq, leadership and terrorism, the economy, and issues like same-sex marriage and "moral values." We examine the financing of elections in the wake of campaign finance reform and the emergence of so-called 527 groups, and we include analysis and tallies of both the expenditures and votes for George W. Bush and John Kerry.

In addition, in the policy chapters of the text (Chapter 13: Social and Economic Policy and Chapter 14: Foreign and Defense Policy), we strive to provide coverage of both foreign and domestic policies that have an impact on Americans' daily lives.

Chapter Coverage

Each chapter offers the most up-to-date coverage. **Chapter 1** contains current figures on the changing demographics of the United States and new information on voter turnout. **Chapter 2** includes a full discussion of the Constitutional Convention debate over the question of slavery. **Chapter 3** discusses the state of state budgets, marriage in the federal system, and the issue of access to abortion. **Chapter 4** includes a discussion of obscenity as well as updates on the assault weapons ban, Partial Birth Abortion Ban Act, and the impact of *Lawrence* v. *Texas*. **Chapter 5** has up-to-date coverage of gay rights and of affirmative action. **Chapter 6** includes complete coverage of the membership of the 109th Congress, the 2004 elections, and judicial nominations. **Chapter 7** begins with a vignette on Ronald Reagan's funeral and includes full coverage of the first term of the George W. Bush administration. **Chapter 8** begins with a vignette on Robert Mueller, John Ashcroft, and the Department of Homeland Security. It also includes current figures and data on the federal workforce and coverage of e-government. **Chapter 9** offers coverage on the Supreme Court's 2003-2004 term, William Rehnquist's illness, judicial appointments, and the charateristics of appointees. **Chapter 10** contains recent information on American political knowledge and political behavior in the 2004 election, presents tracking and exit poll data, and evaluates the media coverage of major news events in 2004 and the ways in which politicians use the media. **Chapter 11** begins with a vignette on MoveOn.org and Swift Boat Veterans for Truth, contains current information on party unity, fund-raising, party identification, an exploration of "red and blue" America, and provides up-to-date coverage on interest group activity in the 2004 election. **Chapter 12** features an opening vignette on the 2004 presidential campaigns, with special attention to new campaign finance regulations, 527s, and the advertising strategies utilized by both campaigns, and then examines the highly contentious 2004 presidential election, with current figures on election results, voter turnout, and demographics. **Chapter 13** includes current and complete coverage of welfare policies today, including the new Medicare Prescription Drug Improvement and Modernization Act, and a discussion of the economic policies of the George W. Bush administration and the increasing national debt. **Chapter 14** provides coverage on the continued fighting in Iraq and the presence of the U.S. military overseas, and includes a discussion of the United States' changing role in the world.

Chapter 15 opens with a vignette describing the challenges that projected population changes present for Texas's future. Data on Texas's ethnic groups and officeholders are up-to-date with the most recent projections and election results. **Chapter 16** includes information about recent amendments to the Texas Constitution. **Chapter 17** includes recent coverage on local governments and new features on the Annette Strauss Institute for Civic Participation's efforts to increase political participation by young people and on the creation of regional mobility authorities in the state. **Chapter 18** includes a vignette on the "Ardmore 51" and their efforts to prevent congressional redistricting. Characteristics of the legislature's members include data on the 79th Legislature. The chapter chronicles the rise of partisanship in the Texas House and discusses the activities of the Young Conservatives of Texas (YCT). **Chapter 19** features the reorganization of the health and human services agencies in Texas, and a boxed feature tackles the deregulation of college tuition in Texas. **Chapter 20** has a vignette on Texas Supreme Court Chief Justice Thomas Phillip's resignation in 2004. Boxed features discuss driving while intoxicated in Texas and the evolution of Texas's two supreme courts. **Chapter 21** includes the most recent information on political parties, interest groups, campaigns, and elections in Texas. Boxed features discuss the battle of interest groups over the constitutional amendment to limit medical liability and the rise of Web logs as a new form of media, focusing on the Burnt Orange Report.

FEATURES

This new Essentials Edition of our combined American and Texas government book retained the best features and pedagogy from that larger text.

Historical Perspective

Every chapter uses history to serve three purposes: first, to show how institutions and processes have evolved to their present states; second, to provide some of the color that makes information memorable; and third, to provide students with a more thorough appreciation that our government was born amid burning issues of representation and power, issues that continue to smolder today. A richer historical texture helps to explain the present.

Comparative Perspective

Changes in the Middle East, Russia and Eastern Europe, North America, South America, and Asia all remind us of the preeminence of democracy, in theory if not always in fact. As new democratic experiments spring up around the globe (e.g. Iraq), it becomes increasingly important for students to understand the rudiments of presidential versus parliamentary government and of multiparty versus two-party systems. To put American government in perspective, *Global Perspective* boxes compare issues, politics, and institutions in the United States, with those of both industrialized democracies and non-Western countries such as Russia, Iraq, Egypt, India, Iran, and China.

Pedagogy

We have included many of the pedagogical features from our more comprehensive version of this text to help students become stronger political thinkers and to echo the book's theme of continuity and change.

Preview and Review.   To pique students' interest and draw them into each chapter, we begin each chapter with a contemporary vignette. These vignettes, including the California gubernatorial recall, the Iraqi war protest at the United Nations, and the Supreme Court decision in *Lawrence* v. *Texas* (2003), frequently deal with issues of high interest to students, which we hope will whet their appetites to read the rest of the chapter. Each vignette is followed by a bridge paragraph linking the vignette with the chapter's topics and a road map previewing the chapter's major headings. Chapter summaries at the conclusion of each chapter restate the major points made under each of these same major headings.

Key Terms.   Glossary definitions are included in the margins of the text for all boldfaced key terms. Key terms are listed once more at the end of each chapter, with page references, for review and study.

Special Features.   Throughout the text, in keeping with its theme of continuity and change, there are several boxed features. In addition to standard chapter coverage, we have included features designed to enhance student understanding of the political processes, institutions, and policies of American government:

■ *Annotated Constitution of the United States* Appearing between chapters 2 and 3, this copy of the Constitution is a comprehensive primer on the meaning and context of its most significant articles, sections, and amendments. Students will understand not only what the language of the Constitution says but *why* it was fashioned as it was and how it is relevant today. For instance, students learn everything from why Article I is the longest and most detailed portion of the Constitution to why the "Full Faith and Credit" clause, rarely controversial, now becomes so in the context of gay marriage. The Constitution was annotated here with the significant help of a Constitutional expert, Gregg Ivers, of American University.

■ *The Living Constitution* Appearing in every chapter, these boxes examine the Constitutional context of that chapter's topic. Each box excerpts and explains a relevant portion of the Constitution, analyzes what the Framers were responding to when it was written, and examines how it is still relevant today. For instance, chapter 4 includes a box on the Ninth Amendment, a discussion of the impossibility of enumerating every fundamental liberty and right, and the Supreme Court's ruling—nonetheless—in favor of a host of fundamental liberties since 1965.

■ *On Campus* These boxes, which appear in most chapters, focus in particular on material that we believe will be of great interest to college students. To that end, this feature examines issues of concern on college campuses, as well as issues, events, or legislation that were initiated on college campuses and that had an impact on the larger arena of American politics. For example, chapter 5 describes how college students can help others to attain their civil rights.

■ *Join the Debate* To engage students in critical thinking, foster interest in important issues, and help inspire their participation through involvement in decision making and taking a stand, we developed a *Join the Debate* feature. Current and, we hope, resonant with both instructors and students, this feature introduces provocative issues under debate today and explores those issues by suggesting arguments for and against them. Topics such as chapter 3's "No Child Left Behind Act," chapter 4's "The USA Patriot Act," and chapter 12's "Lowering the Voting Age", accompanied by supporting questions and guidance from the authors, are designed to prompt students to examine various arguments in the debate, consider larger context, and take a position on issues that matter in American government today.

■ *Global Perspective* To put American government in perspective, these boxes compare issues and elements of U.S. politics with other nations. Many of the boxes include comparisons to non-Western nations such as Iran, Iraq, Egypt, India, China, Russia, and Indonesia; some focus on specific issues of particular interest today such as chapter 10's "Al-Jazeera: The CNN of the Arab World?"

■ *Politics Now* These contemporary boxes act as a counterpoint to the text's focus on the "roots of government." Based on current articles, editorials, and moments in time, these boxes are designed to encourage students to think about current issues in the context of the continuing evolution of the American political system. Chapter 5 examines how Native Americans are using diverse ways to reverse the economic adversity of discrimination.

■ *Analyzing Visuals* A feature designed to encourage visual literacy, *Analyzing Visuals* helps students make sense of quantitative and qualitative information presented visually and enables them to get the most out of graphic representations. This feature examines a wide variety of images, including news photographs and political cartoons as well as tables, bar graphs, line graphs, maps, and charts. In addition, students are encouraged to analyze and interpret the visual information themselves, using the introductory captions, pointers, and critical thinking questions provided to guide them. An introductory section, *Analyzing Visuals: A Brief Guide* (see pages xxxii-xxxvi), offers a foundation for analyzing and interpreting different kinds of visuals that students will encounter in the text. In addition to helping students examine the *Analyzing Visuals* features throughout the book, this introduction offers valuable strategies and suggested questions that can be applied to all the visuals in the text as well as those found in daily newspapers, weekly magazines, etc. One of these visual learning features appears in each chapter.

Web Explorations

The end of each chapter contains several links to the World Wide Web through our book-specific Web site. Web Explorations encourage students to learn more and think critically about a specific issue or concept.

MyPoliSciLab and LongmanParticipate.com 4.0   MyPoliSciLab is a state of the art, interactive online solution for your course. Available in CourseCompass, Blackboard, and WebCT, MyPoliSciLab offers students a wealth of simulations, interactive exercises, and assessment tools—all intergrated with the printed text and an online e-book. For each chapter of the text, students can navigate through a pre-test, post-test, chapter review, and a full chapter exam, so they can assess, review, and improve their understanding of the concepts within the chapters. In addition to the online chapter content and assessment, students will have access to LongmanParticipate.com (updated 4.0 version), Longman's best-selling, interactive online tool, which provides over one hundred exercises for students. LongmanParticipate.com (4.0) is also available as a Web site alone.

Throughout the text students will find icons (see page xxxi for samples) in the margins that direct them to relevant simulations, visual literacy exercises and other activities—*all of which appear in both MyPoliSciLab and LongmanParticipate.com 4.0.* Students will know which site to use by looking at the access card that came packaged with this text.

THE ANCILLARY PACKAGE

The ancillary package for *Essentials of American & Texas Government: Continuity and Change, 2006 Edition*, reflects the pedagogical goals of the text: to provide information in a useful context and with colorful examples. We have tried especially hard to provide materials that are useful for instructors and helpful to students.

Instructor Supplements for Qualified College Adopters

Instructor's Manual.   Written by Sue Davis of Denison University. Includes chapter overviews, chapter outlines, learning objectives, key terms, and valuable teaching suggestions for all chapters.

Test Bank.   Written by Paul W. Cooke of Cy-Fair College. Contains hundreds of thoroughly revised and challenging multiple choice, true-false, and essay questions along with an answer key.

TestGen-EQ CD-ROM.   The printed Test Bank is also available through our computerized testing system, TestGen-EQ. This fully networkable, user-friendly program enables instructors to view and edit questions, add their own questions, and print tests in a variety of formats.

MyPoliSciLab and LongmanParticipate.com Faculty Teaching Guide.   Written by Scott Furlong of University of Wisconsin. Contains chapter-by-chapter detailed summaries for each of the sites' interactive activities, as well as a list of concepts covered, recommendations about how to integrate the sites into coursework, and discussion questions and paper topics for every exercise. Instructors may use the table of contents in the front of the guide to locate information on a given activity icon that appears in the margin of their adopted textbook. This guide also provides faculty with detailed instructions and screen shots showing how to use MyPoliSciLab or LongmanParticipate.com, how to register on the sites, and how to set up and use any available administrative features. The introductory chapter describes the numerous additional resources included on the Web sites.

Digital Media Archive Presentation CD-ROM.   This complete multimedia presentation tool provides instructors with the following: a built-in presentation-maker, approximately one hundred photos and 150 figures, graphs, and tables from Longman American government textbooks, forty video clips, and more! All items can be imported into an instructor's existing presentation program, such as PowerPoint®.

Companion Web Site (CW) www.ablongman.com/oconnor. This online course companion provides a wealth of resources for instructors using *Essentials of American & Texas Government: Continuity and Change, 2006 Edition.*

PowerPoint® Presentation.   A lecture outline presentation to accompany all the chapters of this new edition along with complete graphics from the book. See the companion Web site at www.ablongman.com/oconnor to download the presentations.

Interactive American Government Video.   Contains twenty-seven video segments on topics ranging from the term limit debate to Internet pornography to women in the Citadel. Critical thinking questions accompany each clip, encouraging students to "interact" with the videos by analyzing their content and the concepts they address.

Politics in Action Video.   Eleven "lecture-launchers" covering subjects from conducting a campaign to the passage of a bill. Includes narrated videos, interviews, edited documentaries, original footage, and political ads.

American Government Video Program.   Qualified adopters can peruse our additional list of videos for the American government classroom at www.ablongman.com/irc.

Student Supplements for Qualified College Adopters

MyPoliSciLab for American Government with LongmanParticipate.com 4.0.   MyPoliSciLab is a state-of-the-art, interactive online solution for your course. Available in CourseCompass, WebCt, or Blackboard with this text, MyPoliSciLab offers a wealth of simulations, interactive exercises, and assessment tools—all integrated with an online e-book version of this text. For each chapter, students will navigate through a pre-test, post-test, chapter review, and a full chapter exam, allowing them to assess, review, and improve their understanding of key concepts. In addition to the online chapter content, students will have access to LongmanParticipate.com (updated 4.0 version), Longman's best-selling interactive online tool, which offers over one hundred exercises for students. These exercises include:

- ■ Simulations putting students in the role of a political actor;
- ■ Visual Literacy exercises getting students to interpret, manipulate, and apply data in visual form;
- ■ Interactive Timelines enabling students to experience the evolution of an aspect of government;
- ■ Participation activities that personalize politics by either getting students involved (e.g. in a debate) or exploring their own thoughts and opinions about our system;
- ■ Comparative exercises that have students compare aspects of our system to those of other countries.

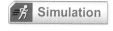

   Students receive feedback at every step, and instructors can track student work through the gradebook feature. The activities for the sites were written and revised by Quentin Kidd, *Christopher Newport University;* and William Field, *Temple University.*

Activities and content that appeared in previous versions of the sites were written by: James Brent, *San Jose State University;* Laura Roselle, *Elon College;* Denise Scheberle, *University of Wisconsin;* B. Thomas Schuman, *University of New Hampshire;* Sharon Spray, *Elon College;* Cara Strebe, *San Francisco State University;* Ruth Ann Strickland, *Appalachian State University;* Kaare Strøm, *University of California, San Diego;* David Tabb, *San Francisco State University;* Paul Benson, *Tarrant County Community College;* Stephen Sandweiss, *Tacoma Community College.*

LongmanParticipate.com is also available as a Web site alone, for instructors who do not wish to use a course management system such as CourseCompass.

A free six-month subscription to MyPoliSciLab or Longman Participate.com is available when access cards to either site are ordered packaged with this text. To find out more about MyPoliSciLab, go to **www.mypoliscilab.com.** To find out more about LongmanParticipate.com go to **www.longmanparticipate.com**.

Companion Web site (CW) www.ablongman.com/oconnor. This online course companion provides a wealth of resources for students using *Essentials of American & Texas Government: Continuity and Change,* including learning objectives, practice tests, vocabulary flashcards, an online glossary, and more.

Study Guide.   Written by John Ben Sutter of Houston Community College. The printed study guide features chapter outlines, key terms, a variety of practice tests, and critical thinking questions to help students learn.

Discount Subscription to the *New York Times*.   A ten-week subscription for only $20! Contact your local Allyn & Bacon/Longman representative for more information.

Discount Subscription to *Newsweek* Magazine.   Students receive twelve issues of *Newsweek* at more than 80% off the regular price. An excellent way for students to keep up with current events.

Culture War? The Myth of a Polarized America.   By Morris P. Fiorina, Stanford University; Samuel J. Abrams, Harvard University; and Jeremy C. Pope, Stanford University. The first book in the "Great Questions in Politics" series, *Culture War? The Myth of a Polarized America* combines polling data with a compelling narrative to debunk commonly believed myths about American politics—particularly the claim that Americans are deeply divided in their fundamental political views.

You Decide! Current Debates in American Politics, 2005 Edition. Edited by John T. Rourke, University of Connecticut, this exciting new debate-style reader examines provocative issues in American politics today—from same-sex marriage and abortion to the Electoral College and the war on terror. The topics have been selected for their currency, importance, and student interest, and the pieces that argue various sides of a given issue come from recent journals, congressional hearings, think tanks, and periodicals. Free when packaged with this text.

Voices of Dissent: Critical Readings in American Politics, Sixth Edition.   Edited by William F. Grover, St. Michael's College, and Joseph G. Peschek, Hamline University, this collection of critical essays goes beyond the debate between mainstream liberalism and conservatism to fundamentally challenge the status quo. Available at a discount when ordered packaged with the text.

American Government: Readings and Cases, Sixteenth Edition. Edited by Peter Woll, Brandeis University, this longtime bestseller offers a strong focus on the major cases and readings that define our thinking about American government and politics. As it has since its first edition, this reader provides a strong, balanced blend of classics that illustrate and amplify important concepts in American government, along with extremely current readings and cases drawn from today's literature. The sixteenth edition continues to put students directly in touch with the great authors and political leaders who have shaped—and are shaping—American government.

Ten Things That Every American Government Student Should Read. Edited by Karen O'Connor, American University. We asked American government instructors across the country to vote for ten things beyond the text that they believe every student should read and put them in this brief and useful reader. Free when ordered packaged with the text.

Choices: An American Government Database Reader.   This customizable reader allows instructors to choose from a database of over 300 readings to create a reader that exactly matches their course needs. Go to *www.pearsoncustom.com/database/choices.html* for more information.

Penguin–Longman Value Bundles.   Longman offers twenty-five Penguin Putnam titles at more than a 60% discount when packaged with any Longman text. A totally unique offer and a wonderful way to enhance students' understanding of concepts in American Government. Please go to *www.ablongman.com/penguin* for more information.

Writing in Political Science, Third Edition.   By Diane Schmidt, This book takes students step-by-step through all aspects of writing in political science. Available at a discount when ordered packaged with any Longman textbook.

Getting Involved: A Guide to Student Citizenship.   By Mark Kann, Todd Belt, Gabriela Copperthwaite, and Steven Horn. A unique and practical handbook that guides students through political participation with concrete advice and extensive sample material—letters, telephone scripts, student interviews, and real-life anecdotes—for getting involved and making a difference in their lives and communities.

Texas Politics Supplement, Fourth Edition.   By Debra St. John, Collin County Community College. A ninety-page primer on state and local government and issues in Texas. Free when shrink-wrapped with the text.

California Politics Supplement, Fourth Edition.   By Pamela Fiber, California State University–Long Beach. A seventy-page primer on state and local government and issues in California. Free when shrink-wrapped with the text.

Florida Politics Supplement.   By John Bertalan, Hillsborough Community College. A fifty-page primer on state and local government and issues in Florida. Free when shrink-wrapped with the text.

ACKNOWLEDGMENTS

Karen O'Connor thanks the thousands of students in her American Government courses at Emory and American University who, over the years, have pushed her to learn more about American government and to have fun in the process. She especially thanks her American University colleagues who offered books and suggestions for this most recent revision—particularly Gregg Ivers and David Lublin. Her former professor and longtime friend and co-author, Nancy E. McGlen, has offered support for more than two decades. Her former students, too, have contributed in various ways to this project, especially John R. Hermann, Paul Fabrizio, Bernadette Nye, Sue Davis, Laura van Assendelft, and Sarah Brewer.

For this edition of the book, Ali Yanus, a brilliant undergraduate, offered invaluable assistance. Her fresh perspectives on politics and ideas about things of interest to students, as well as her keen eye for the typo, have greatly benefited the book. Her unbelievably hard work has made this a much better book.

Larry J. Sabato would like to thank his University of Virginia colleagues and staff, including Joshua Scott, Greg Smith, Matthew Wikswo, and Lawrence Schack.

Particular thanks from both of us go to David Potter of Nanzan University, who prepared the Global Politics features, Stefan Haag of Austin Community College for his help with the Analyzing Visuals features, and Gary Keith of University of Texas at Austin for his help with the Join the Debate features. We would also like to thank our editor Eric Stano, our development editor Barbara Conover, our marketing manager Elizabeth Fogarty, and Lake Lloyd, our production editor at Electronic Publishing Services, Inc. In the end, we hope that all of these talented people see how much their work and support have helped us to write a better book.

For *Stefan Haag* and *Gary Keith*, the chapters on Texas reflect the efforts of more people than the authors listed on the cover. For Stefan Haag, his wife, Patricia, is owed a special debt of gratitude for her understanding and support. Gary Keith thanks his wife, Jacqueline Kerr, for her support, encouragement, and patience. Both of us thank our colleagues at Austin Community College and the University of Texas at Austin for sharing their knowledge and appreciation of Texas politics and government. Learning about, participating in, and writing about Texas politics is always a wild ride! We would also like to acknowledge the assistance of Eric Stano, political science editor, for his support, encouragement, direction, and confidence.

Many of our peers reviewed past editions of the book and earned our gratitude in the process:

Danny Adkinson, *Oklahoma State University*

Weston H. Agor, *University of Texas–El Paso*

James Anderson, *Texas A&M University*

Judith Baer, *Texas A&M University*

Ruth Bamberger, *Drury College*

Christine Barbour, *Indiana University*

Jon Bond, *Texas A&M University*

Stephen A. Borrelli, *University of Alabama*

Ann Bowman, *University of South Carolina*

Gary Brown, *Montgomery College*

John Francis Burke, *University of Houston–Downtown*

Gregory A. Caldeira, *Ohio State University*

David E. Camacho, *Northern Arizona University*

David Cingranelli, *SUNY–Binghamton*

Steve Chan, *University of Colorado*

Richard Christofferson Sr., *University of Wisconsin–Stevens Point*

Clarke E. Cochran, *Texas Tech University*

Anne N. Costain, *University of Colorado*

Cary Covington, *University of Iowa*

Lane Crothers, *Illinois State University*

Abraham L. Davis, *Morehouse College*

Robert DiClerico, *West Virginia University*

Khalil Dokhanchi, *University of Wisconsin–Superior*

John Domino, *Sam Houston State University*

Craig F. Emmert, *Texas Tech University*

Alan S. Engel, *Miami University*

Frank B. Feigert, *University of North Texas*

Evelyn C. Fink, *University of Nebraska–Lincoln*

Scott R. Furlong, *University of Wisconsin–Green Bay*

Christopher P. Gilbert, *Gustavus Adolphus College*

James D. Gleason, *Victoria College*

Sheldon Goldman, *University of Massachusetts–Amherst*

Roger W. Green, *University of North Dakota*

Doris Graber, *University of Illinois at Chicago*

Charles Hadley, *University of New Orleans*

William K. Hall, *Bradley University*

Robert L. Hardgrave Jr., *University of Texas –Austin*

Stacia L. Haynie, *Louisiana State University*

John R. Hermann, *Trinity University*

Marjorie Randon Hershey, *Indiana University*

Cornell Hooton, *Emory University*

Johanna Hume, *Alvin Community College*

Jon Hurwitz, *University of Pittsburgh*

Chip Hauss, *George Mason University/University of Reading*

Joseph Ignagni, *University of Texas–Arlington*

Dennis Judd, *University of Missouri–St. Louis*

Carol J. Kamper, *Rochester Community College*

Kenneth Kennedy, *College of San Mateo*

Donald F. Kettl, *University of Wisconsin*

John Kincaid, *University of North Texas*

Jonathan E. Kranz, *John Jay College of Criminal Justice*

Mark Landis, *Hofstra University*

Sue Lee, *North Lake College*

Brad Lockerbie, *University of Georgia*

Larry Martinez, *California State University–Long Beach*

Lyn Mather, *Dartmouth College*

Steve J. Mazurana, *University of Northern Colorado*

Clifton McCleskey, *University of Virginia*

William P. McLauchlan, *Purdue University*

Joseph Nogee, *University of Houston*

Mary Alice Nye, *University of North Texas*

John O'Callaghan, *Suffolk University*

Bruce Oppenheimer, *Vanderbilt University*

William C. Overton, *Boise State University*

Richard Pacelle, *University of Missouri–St. Louis*

Marian Lief Palley, *University of Delaware*

Richard M. Pious, *Barnard College*

David H. Provost, *California State University–Fresno*

Lawrence J. Redlinger, *University of Texas–Dallas*

Leroy N. Riescelbach, *Indiana University*

David Robertson, *Public Policy Research Centers, University of Missouri–St. Louis*

David Robinson, *University of Houston–Downtown*

David W. Rohde, *Michigan State University*

Frank Rourke, *Johns Hopkins University*

Donald Roy, *Ferris State University*

Ronald Rubin, *City University of New York, Borough of Manhattan Community College*

Bonita A. Sessing-Matcha, *Hudson Valley Community College*

Jocelyn D. Shadforth, *North Central College*

Daniel M. Shea, *University of Akron*

Mark Silverstein, *Boston University*

James R. Simmons, *University of Wisconsin–Oshkosh*

Elliot E. Slotnick, *Ohio State University*

Daniel A. Smith, *University of Denver*

Frank J. Sorauf, *University of Minnesota*

Gerald Stanglin, *Cedar Valley College*

Richard J. Timpone, *SUNY–Stony Brook*

Shirley Anne Warshaw, *Gettysburg College*

James A. White, *Concord College*

Martin Wiseman, *Mississippi State University*

Vincent A. Auger, *Western Illinois University*

Holly Dershem-Bruce, *Dawson Community College*

Finally, we'd also like to thank our peers who reviewed and aided in the development of the current edition:

Myles L. Clowers, *San Diego City College*

John Fobanjong, *University of Massachusetts*

Sean D. Foreman, *Union Institute and University*

Christopher P. Gilbert, *Gustavus Adolphus College*

Donald Roy, *Ferris State University*

Analyzing Visuals: A Brief Guide

The information age requires a new, more expansive definition of literacy. Visual literacy—the ability to analyze, interpret, synthesize, and apply visual information—is essential in today's world. We receive much information from the written and spoken word, but much also comes from visual forms. We are used to thinking about reading written texts critically—for example, reading a textbook carefully for information, sometimes highlighting or underlining as we go along—but we do not always think about "reading" visuals in this way. We should, for images and informational graphics can tell us a lot if we read and consider them carefully. In order to emphasize these skills, this edition of *Essentials of American & Texas Government: Continuity and Change* contains one *Analyzing Visuals* feature in each chapter. The features are intended to prompt you to think about the images and informational graphics you will encounter throughout this text, as well as those you see every day in the newspaper, in magazines, on the Web, on television, and in books. We provide critical thinking questions to assist you in learning how to analyze visuals. Though we focus on a specific visual in each chapter, we encourage you to examine carefully and ask similar questions of *all* the visuals in this text, and those you encounter elsewhere in your study of and participation in American government.

We look at several types of visuals in the chapters: tables, graphs and charts, maps, news photographs, and political cartoons. This brief guide provides some information about these types of visuals and offers a few questions to guide your analysis of each type.

TABLES

Tables are the least "visual" of the visuals we explore. Tables consist of textual information and/or numerical data arranged in tabular form, in columns and rows. Tables are frequently used when exact information is required and when orderly arrangement is necessary to locate and, in many cases, to compare the information. For example, a table presenting changing data regarding Americans' faith in institutions would make time frame comparisons of the data visually accessible.

TABLE 1.3	Faith in Institutions				
Percentage of Americans Declaring They Had a "Great Deal" of Confidence in the Institution					
	1966	1975	1986	1996	2004
Congress	42%	13%	16%	8%	8%
Executive branch	41	13	21	10	25
The press	29	26	18	11	9
Business & industry	55	19	24	23	19
Medicine	73	51	46	45	19

Sources: Newsweek (January 8, 1996): 32; Public Perspective 8 (February/March 1994): 4. Data for 2004: Public Opinion Online.

Here are a few questions to guide your analysis:

- What is the purpose of the table? What information does it show? There is usually a title that offers a sense of the table's purpose.

- What information is provided in the column headings (provided in the top row)? How are the rows labeled?

- Is there a time period indicated, such as January to June 2004? Or, are the data as of a specific date, such as June 30, 2004?

- If the table shows numerical data, what do these data represent? In what units? Dollars a special interest lobby provides to a political party? Percentages of men and women responding in a particular way to a poll question about the president's performance? Estimated life expectancy in years?

- What is the source of the information presented in the table?

CHARTS AND GRAPHS

Charts and graphs depict numerical data in visual forms. The most common kinds of graphs plot data in two dimensions along horizontal and vertical axes. Examples that you will encounter throughout this text are line graphs, pie charts, and bar graphs. These kinds of visuals emphasize data relationships: at a particular point in time, at regular intervals over a fixed period of time, or, sometimes, as parts of a whole. Line graphs show a progression, usually over time (as in Political Party Finances, 1978–2004). Pie charts (such as the distribution of federal civilian employment) demonstrate how a whole (total federal civilian employment) is divided into its parts (employees in each branch). Bar graphs compare values across categories, showing how proportions are related to each other (as

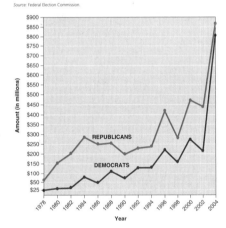

FIGURE 11.3 **Political Party Finances.** Includes totals for national, senatorial, and congressional committees as well as all other reported national, state, and local spending; all presidential, Senate, and House candidates are included. Not included are soft money expenditures. The 2004 amount includes monies spent between January 1, 2003, and June 30, 2004. ■

Source: Federal Election Commission.

FIGURE 8.1 Characteristics and Rank Distribution of Federal Civilian Employees, 2001. ■

Source: Office of Personnel Management, 2001 Fact Book.

in the numbers of women and minorities in Congress). Bar graphs can present data either horizontally or vertically.

Here are a few questions to guide your analysis:

- What is the purpose of the chart or graph? What information does it provide? Or, what is being measured? Usually a title indicates the subject and purpose of the figure.

- Is a time period shown, such as January to June 2004? Or, are the data as of a specific date, such as June 30, 2004? Are the data shown at multiple intervals over a fixed period, or at one particular point in time?

■ What do the units represent? Dollars a candidate spends on a campaign? Number of voters versus number of non-voters in Texas? If there are two or more sets of figures, what are the relationships among them?

■ What is the source? Is it government information? Private polling information? A newspaper? A private organization? A corporation? An individual?

■ Is the type of chart or graph appropriate for the information that is provided? For example, a line graph assumes a smooth progression from one data point to the next. Is that assumption valid for the data shown?

■ Is there distortion in the visual representation of the information? Are the intervals equal? Does the area shown distort the actual amount or the proportion?

FIGURE 6.3 Numbers of Women and Minorities in Congress.

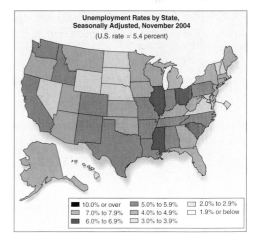

ANALYZING VISUALS: Unemployment Rates by State, November 2004.

MAPS

Maps—of the United States, of particular regions, or of the world—are frequently used in political analysis to illustrate demographic, social, economic, and political issues and trends.

Here are a few questions to guide your analysis:

■ Is there a title that identifies the purpose or subject of the map?

■ What does the map key/legend show? What are the factors that the map is analyzing?

■ What is the region being shown?

■ What source is given for the map?

■ Maps usually depict a specific point in time. What is the point in time being shown on the map?

NEWS PHOTOGRAPHS

If a picture is worth a thousand words, it is no wonder that our newspapers, magazines, and television news broadcasts rely on photographs as well as words to report and analyze the news. Photos can have a dramatic—and often immediate—impact on politics and government. Think about some photos that have political significance. For example, do you remember photos from the September 11, 2001, terrorist attack on the World Trade Center? Visual images usually evoke a stronger emotional response from people than do written descriptions. For this reason, individuals and organizations have learned to use photographs as a means to document events, make arguments, offer evidence, and even in some cases to manipulate the viewer into having a particular response.

Here are a few questions to guide your analysis:

- When was the photograph taken? (If there is no date given for the photograph in its credit line or caption, you may be able to approximate the date according to the people or events depicted in the photo. If the photograph appears in a newspaper, you can usually assume that the shot is fairly current with publication.)
- What is the subject of the photograph?
- Why was the photo taken? What appears to be the purpose of the photograph?
- Is it spontaneous or posed? Did the subject know he or she was being photographed?
- Who was responsible for the photo? (An individual, an agency, or organization?) Can you discern the photographer's attitude toward the subject?
- Is there a caption? If so, what kind of information does it provide? Does it identify the subject of the photo? Does it provide an interpretation of the subject?

POLITICAL CARTOONS

Political cartoons have a long history in America. Some of the most interesting commentary on American politics takes place in the form of political cartoons, which usually exaggerate physical and other qualities of the persons depicted and often rely on a kind of visual shorthand to announce the subject or set the scene—visual cues, clichés, or stereotypes that are instantly recognizable. For example, a greedy corporate executive might be depicted as an individual in professional clothing with paper currency sticking out of his or her pockets. In another cartoon, powdered wigs and quill pens might signal a historical setting. The cartoonist's goal is to comment on and/or criticize political figures, policies, or events. The cartoonist uses several techniques to accomplish this goal, including exaggeration, irony, and juxtaposition. For example, the cartoonist may point out how the results of governmental policies are the opposite of their intended effects (irony). In other cartoons, two people, ideas, or events that don't belong together may be joined to make a point (juxtaposition). Because cartoons comment on political situations and events, you generally need some knowledge of current events to interpret political cartoons.

Here are a few questions to guide your analysis:

■ Study the cartoon element by element. Political cartoons are often complex. If the cartoon is in strip form, you also need to think about the relationship of the frames in sequence.

■ What labels appear on objects or people in the cartoon? Cartoonists will often label some of the elements. For example, a building with columns might be labeled "U.S. Supreme Court." Or, an individual might be labeled "senator" or "Republican."

■ Is there a caption or title to the cartoon? If so, what does it contribute to the meaning or impact of the cartoon?

By permission of Mike Luckovich and Creators Syndicate, Inc.

■ Can you identify any of the people shown? Presidents, well-known members of Congress, and world leaders are often shown with specific characteristics that help to identify them. Jimmy Carter was often shown with an exaggerated, toothy smile. George W. Bush is often shown with large ears, small eyes, and bushy eyebrows—sometimes with a "W." or a "43" label.

■ Can you identify the event being depicted? Historical events, such as the American Revolution, or contemporary events, such as the 2004 presidential election, are often the subject matter for cartoons.

■ What are the elements of the cartoon? Objects often represent ideas or events. For example, a donkey is often used to depict the Democratic Party. Or, an eagle is used to represent the United States.

■ How are the characters interacting? What do the speech bubbles contribute to the cartoon?

■ What is the overall message of the cartoon? Can you determine what the cartoonist's position is on the subject?

Photo courtesy: Eric L. Wheate/Lonely Planet Images

The Political Landscape

WE THE PEOPLE OF THE UNITED STATES, in Order to form a more perfect Union, establish Justice, insure domestic Tranquility, provide for the common defence, promote the general Welfare, and secure the Blessings of Liberty to ourselves and our Posterity, do ordain and establish this Constitution for the United States of America.

These are the words that begin the Preamble to the United States Constitution. Written in 1787 by a group of men we today refer to as the Framers, this document has guided our nation, its government, its politics, its institutions, and its inhabitants for over 200 years.

When the Constitution was written, the phrases "We the People" and "ourselves" meant something very different from what they do today. After all, voting largely was limited to property-owning white males. Indians, slaves, and women could not vote. Today, through the expansion of the right to vote, the phrase "the People" encompasses men and women of all races, ethnic origins, and social and economic statuses—a variety of peoples and interests. The Framers could not have imagined the variety of people today who are eligible to vote.

In the goals it outlines, the Preamble to the Constitution describes what the people of the United States can expect from their government. In spite of the wave of nationalism that arose in the wake of the September 11, 2001, terrorist attacks, some continue to question how well the U.S. government can deliver on the goals set out in the Preamble. Few

CHAPTER OUTLINE

- Government: What It Is and Why We Need It

- Roots of American Government: Where Did the Ideas Come From?

- American Political Culture and the Characteristics of American Democracy

- Changing Characteristics of the American People

- Ideology of the American Public

- Current Attitudes Toward American Government

Americans today classify the Union as "perfect"; many feel excluded from "Justice" and the "Blessings of Liberty," and even our leaders do not believe that our domestic situation is particularly tranquil, as evidenced by the creation of the Department of Homeland Security. Furthermore, recent poll results and economic statistics indicate that many Americans believe their general welfare is not particularly well promoted by their government. Others simply do not care much at all about government, believe that they have no influence in its decision making, or do not see any positive benefits from it in their lives.

If there has been one constant in the United States, it is change. The Framers would be astonished to see the forms and functions the institutions they so carefully outlined in the Constitution have taken on, and the number of additional political institutions that have arisen to support and fuel the functioning of the national government. The Framers also would be amazed at the array of services and programs the government—especially the national government—provides. They further would be surprised to see how the physical boundaries and the composition of the population have changed over the past 200 plus years. And, they might well wonder, "How did we get here?"

It is part of the American creed that each generation should hand down to the next not only a better America, but an improved economic, educational, and social status. In general, Americans long have been optimistic about their nation, its institutions, and its future. Thomas Jefferson saw the United States as the world's "best hope"; Abraham Lincoln echoed these sentiments when he called it the "last, best hope on earth."[1]

IN THIS TEXT, we present you with the tools that you need to understand how our political system has evolved and to prepare you to understand the changes that are yet to come. If you approach the study of American government and politics with an open mind, it should help you become a better citizen. We hope that you learn to ask questions, to become aware of how various issues have come to be important, and to see why a particular law was enacted and how it was implemented. With such understanding, we further hope that you will learn not to accept at face value everything you see on the television news, hear on the radio, or read in the newspaper. Work to understand your government, and use your vote and other forms of participation to help ensure that your government works for you.

We recognize that the discourse of politics has changed dramatically in just the last few years, and that more and more Americans—especially the young—are turned off to politics, especially at the national level. We also believe that a thorough awareness of the workings of government will allow you to question and think about the system—the good parts and the bad—and decide for yourself the advantages and disadvantages of possible changes and reforms. Equipped with such an understanding, we hope you will become better informed and more active participants in the political process.

Every long journey begins with a single step. In this chapter, we will discuss the function and structure of government: what it is and why we need it. After looking at the roots of American government, we will explore American political culture and the characteristics of American democracy, and the changing characteristics of the American people. We will also discuss the political ideologies of the American public and its current attitudes toward American government and toward the role that government plays in people's lives.

GOVERNMENT: WHAT IT IS AND WHY WE NEED IT

THROUGHOUT HISTORY, societies have organized themselves into a variety of governments, small and large, simple and complex, democratic and nondemocratic, elected and nonelected.

Governments, which are made up of individuals and institutions, are the vehicles through which policies are made and affairs of state are conducted. In fact, the term "government" is derived from the Greek for "to pilot a ship," which is appropriate, since we expect governments to guide "the ship of state." Unlike schools, banks, or corporations, the actions of government are binding on all of its citizens, and only governments can legitimately use force to keep order.

government
A collective of individuals and institutions, the formal vehicles through which policies are made and affairs of state are conducted.

Citizens, by law, are members of the political community who by nature of being born in a particular nation or having become naturalized citizens are entitled to all of the freedoms guaranteed by the government. In exchange for these freedoms, citizens must obey the government, its laws, and its constitution. Citizens also are expected to support their governments through exercising their right to vote, paying taxes due, and, if they are eligible, submitting themselves to military service.

citizen
By law, the members of the political community.

politics
The process by which policy decisions are made.

Governments must be discussed in the context of **politics,** the study of what has been called "who gets what, when and how," or more simply, the process of how policy decisions get made. All governments share to greater or lesser degrees the need to provide certain key functions, but to whom they provide these benefits, which benefits they provide, when they provide them, and how they provide them vary tremendously across as well as within nations.

Functions of Government

The Framers of the U.S. Constitution clearly recognized the need for new government. As our opening vignette underscores, in attempting "to form a more perfect Union," the Framers set out several key functions of government that continue to be relevant today. As discussed below, several of the Framers' ideas centered on their belief that the major function of government was creating mechanisms to allow individuals to solve conflicts in an orderly and peaceful manner.

Establishing Justice.   One of the first things expected from governments is a system of laws that allows individuals to abide by a common set of principles. Societies adhering to what is called the rule of law allow for the rational dispensing of justice by acknowledged legal authorities. Thus, the U.S. Constitution created a federal judicial system to dispense justice, and the Bill of Rights specified a host of rights guaranteed to all citizens in an effort to establish justice.

Ensuring Domestic Tranquility.   As we will discuss throughout this text, the role of government in ensuring domestic tranquility is a subject of much debate. In times of crisis, the U.S. government, as well as states and local governments, may take extraordinary measures to contain security threats from abroad as well as within the United States.

Providing for the Common Defense.   The U.S. Constitution calls for the president to be the commander in chief of the armed forces, and the Congress was given the authority to raise an army. The Framers recognized that one of the major purposes of government was to provide for the defense of its citizens, who had no ability to protect themselves from other governments.

Promoting the General Welfare.   When the Framers added "promoting the general welfare" to their list of key government functions, they never envisioned how the involvement of the government at all levels would expand so tremendously. In fact, promoting the general welfare was more of an ideal than a mandate for government. Over time, however, our notions of what the government should do have expanded along with the size of government. Today, a host of mandatory programs

FIGURE 1.1   Allocation of Federal Budget. ■

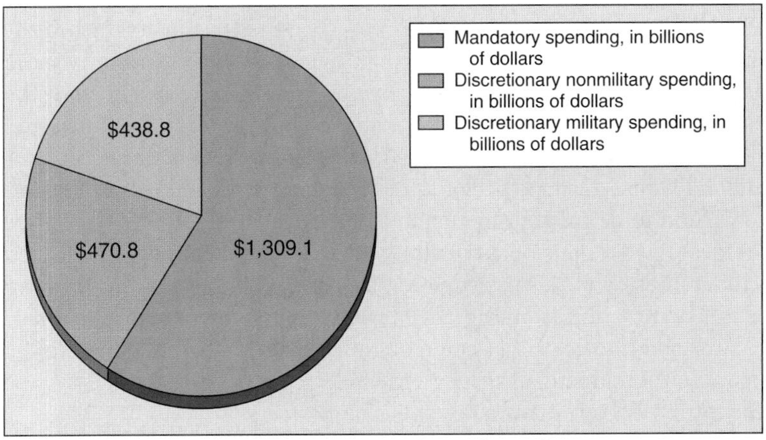

Data for 2005 from http://www.whitehouse.gov/omb/budget/fy2005/pdf/spec.pdf.

designed to promote the general welfare make up a significant proportion of the federal budget, as highlighted in Figure 1.1, although increasing costs of war may soon affect spending on social welfare.

Securing the Blessings of Liberty.   A well-functioning government that enjoys the support of its citizenry is one of the best ways to secure the blessings of liberty for its people. In a free society, citizens enjoy a wide range of liberties and freedoms and feel free to prosper. They are free to criticize the government as well as to petition it when they disagree with its policies or have a grievance.

Taken together, these principal functions of government permeate our lives. Whether it is your ability to obtain a low-interest student loan or to drive a car at a particular age, government has played a major role. Similarly, without government-sponsored research, we would not have cellular telephones or the Internet.

ROOTS OF AMERICAN GOVERNMENT: WHERE DID THE IDEAS COME FROM?

THE CURRENT AMERICAN POLITICAL SYSTEM did not spring into being overnight. It is the result of philosophy, trial and error, and yes, even luck. To begin our examination of why we have the type of government we have today, we look at the theories of government that influenced the Framers who drafted the Constitution and created the United States of America.

Types of Government

As early as Plato and Aristotle, theorists have tried to categorize governments by who participates, who governs, and how much authority those who govern enjoy. As revealed in Table 1.1, a **monarchy** is defined by the rule of one in the interest of all of his or her subjects. In contrast is **totalitarianism**, a system in which the leader exercises unlimited power and individuals have no personal rights or liberties. Generally, these systems tend to be ruled in the name of a particular religion or orthodoxy, an ideology, or a personality cult organized around the supreme leader. **Oligarchies,** while also existing for the benefit of a few, are rare today.

A **democracy,** from the Greek words *demos* (the people) and *kratia* (power or authority), is a system of government that gives power to the people either directly or through their elected representatives. This was the form of government favored by the Framers.

The Reformation and the Enlightenment: Questioning the Divine Right of Kings

In the third century, monarchs throughout Europe began to rule their countries absolutely, claiming their right to govern came directly from God. Thus, since it was God's will that a particular monarch ruled a country, the people in that country had no right to question their monarch's authority or agitate for a voice in their government's operation. In theory, as underscored in Table 1.1, monarchs ruled in the interest of all of their subjects.

The intellectual and religious developments of the Enlightenment and Reformation periods of the sixteenth and seventeenth centuries encouraged people to seek alternatives to absolute monarchies and to ponder new methods of governance. In the late sixteenth century, radical Protestants split from the Church of England (which was created by King Henry XIII when the Roman Catholic Church forbade him to divorce and remarry). These Protestants or Puritans believed in their ability to speak one on one to God and established self-governing congregations. They were persecuted for their religious beliefs by the English monarchy. The Pilgrims were the first group of these Protestants to flee religious

monarchy

A form of government in which power is vested in hereditary kings and queens who govern in the interests of all.

totalitarianism

An economic system in which the government has total control over the economy.

oligarchy

A form of government in which the right to participate is always conditioned on the possession of wealth, social status, military position, or achievement.

democracy

A system of government that gives power to the people, whether directly or through their elected representatives.

TABLE 1.1	Types of Government	
	Whose Interests Are Represented	
Rulers	*The Ruled*	*The Rulers*
Government by one	Monarchy	Totalitarian
Government by a few	Aristocracy	Oligarchy
Government by many	Citizenry	Democracy

Source: Adapted from Albert B. Saye, Merritt B. Pound, and John F. Allums, *Principles of American Government,* 5th ed. (Englewood Cliffs, NJ: Prentice Hall, 1966): 9.

Photo courtesy: Pool/Getty Images
■ Former Iraqi President Saddam Hussein ruled Iraq as a totalitarian state. Here, an imprisoned Hussein was in court to hear the lengthy list of charges against him.

persecution and settle in America. There they established self-governing congregations and were responsible for the first widespread appearance of self-government in the form of a social contract or compact, an agreement between the people and their government signifying their consent to be governed. The Mayflower Compact, deemed sufficiently important to be written while the ship was at sea, reflects this tradition.

Hobbes, Locke, and a Social Contract Theory of Government

Two English theorists of the seventeenth century, Thomas Hobbes (1588–1679) and John Locke (1632–1704), built on conventional notions about the role of government and the relationship of the government to the people in proposing a **social contract theory** of government. They argued that all individuals were free and equal by natural right. This freedom, in turn, required that all men and women give their consent to be governed.

In his now-classic political treatise *Leviathan* (1651), Hobbes argued pessimistically that man's natural state was war.* Government,

social contract theory
The belief that people are free and equal by God-given right and that this in turn requires that all people give their consent to be governed; espoused by John Locke and influential in the writing of the Declaration of Independence.

*The term "man" is used here because only males were considered fit to vote.

he theorized, particularly a monarchy, was necessary to restrain man's bestial tendencies because life without government was but a "state of nature." Without written, enforceable rules, people would live like animals—foraging for food, stealing, and killing when necessary. To escape the horrors of the natural state and to protect their lives, Hobbes argued, people must give up certain rights to government. Without government, Hobbes warned, life would basically be "solitary, poor, nasty, brutish, and short"—a constant struggle to survive against the evil of others. For these reasons, governments had to intrude on people's rights and liberties to better control society and to provide the necessary safeguards for property.

Hobbes argued strongly for a single ruler, no matter how evil, to guarantee the rights of the weak against the strong. Leviathan, a biblical sea monster, was his characterization of an all-powerful government. Strict adherence to Leviathan's laws, however all-encompassing or intrusive on liberty, was but a small price to pay for living in a civilized society.

In contrast to Hobbes, John Locke, like many other political philosophers of the era, took the basic survival of humanity for granted. He argued that a government's major responsibility was the preservation of private property, an idea that ultimately found its way into the U.S. Constitution. In two of his works, *Essay Concerning Human Understanding* (1690) and *Second Treatise on Civil Government* (1689), Locke not only denied the divine right of kings to govern but argued that men were born equal and with natural rights that no king had the power to void. Under Locke's conception of social contract theory, the consent of the people is the only true basis of any sovereign's right to rule. According to Locke, people form governments largely to preserve life, liberty, and property, and to assure justice. If governments act improperly, they break their contract with the people and therefore no longer enjoy the consent of the governed. Because he believed that true justice comes from laws, Locke argued that the branch of government that makes laws—as opposed to the one that enforces or interprets laws— should be the most powerful.

Locke believed that having a chief executive to administer laws was important, but that he should necessarily be limited by law or by the social contract with the governed. Locke's writings influenced many American colonists, especially Thomas Jefferson, whose original draft of the Declaration of Independence noted the rights to "life, liberty, and property" as key reasons to split from England.[2]

Devising a National Government in the American Colonies

The American colonists rejected a system with a strong ruler like the British monarchy as soon as they declared their independence. The colonists also were fearful of replicating the landed and titled system of the British aristocracy. They viewed the formation of a representative form of government as far more in keeping with the ideas of social contract theorists and the colonists' own traditions.

Although the earliest forms of government in the colonies, such as the New England town meeting, where all citizens gather to discuss and decide issues facing the town, utilized **direct democracy,** this tradition soon proved unworkable as more and more settlers came to the New World. Therefore, many town meetings were replaced by mechanisms of **indirect democracy** (this is also called representative democracy), which call for the election of representatives to a governmental decision-making body. The Virginia House of Burgesses, created in 1619, exemplifies this tradition.

Still, many colonists were uncomfortable with the term democracy because it conjured up Hobbesian fears of the people and mob rule. Instead, they preferred the term **republic,** which implied a system of government in which the interests of the people were represented by more educated or wealthier citizens who were responsible to those who elected them. Today, representative democracies are more commonly called republics, and the words democracy and republic often are used interchangeably.

direct democracy
A system of government in which members of the polity meet to discuss all policy decisions and then agree to abide by majority rule.

indirect (representative) democracy
A system of government that gives citizens the opportunity to vote for representatives who will work on their behalf.

republic
A government rooted in the consent of the governed; a representative or indirect democracy.

AMERICAN POLITICAL CULTURE AND THE CHARACTERISTICS OF AMERICAN DEMOCRACY

THE AMERICAN POLITICAL SYSTEM is based on a number of underlying concepts and distinguishing characteristics that sometimes conflict with one another. Taken together, these ideas lie at the core of American political culture. More specifically, **political culture** can be defined as commonly shared attitudes, beliefs, and core values about how government should operate. American political culture emphasizes the values of personal liberty, equality, popular consent and majority rule, popular sovereignty, building civil society, and individualism.

political culture
Commonly shared attitudes, beliefs, and core values about how government should operate.

Personal Liberty

Personal liberty is perhaps the single most important characteristic of American democracy. The Constitution itself was written to assure "life" and "liberty." The Framers intended Americans to be free from governmental infringements on liberties such as religion and speech, and from unreasonable search and seizure (see chapter 4). The addition of the Fourteenth Amendment to the Constitution and its emphasis on equal protection of the laws, and subsequent passage of laws guaranteeing civil rights, further expanded Americans' concept of liberty to include demands for freedom to work or go to school free from discrimination.

personal liberty
A key characteristic of U.S. democracy. Initially meaning freedom from governmental interference, today it includes demands for freedom to engage in a variety of practices free from governmental discrimination.

Comparing Political Landscapes

Equality

Another key characteristic of our democracy is political equality. This emphasis reflects Americans' stress on the importance of the individual. Although some individuals clearly wield more political clout than others, the adage "one person, one vote" implies a sense of political equality for all.

Popular Consent and Majority Rule

popular consent
The idea that governments must draw their powers from the consent of the governed.

Popular consent, the idea that governments must draw their powers from the consent of the governed, is one distinguishing characteristic of American democracy. Derived from Locke's social contract theory, the notion of popular consent was central to the Declaration of Independence. A citizen's willingness to vote represents his or her consent to be governed and is thus an essential premise of democracy.

majority rule
The central premise of direct democracy in which only policies that collectively garner the support of a majority of voters will be made into law.

Majority rule, another core political value, means that the majority of citizens in any political unit should elect officials and determine policies. This principle holds for both voters and their elected representatives. Yet, the American system also stresses the need to preserve minority rights, as evidenced by the myriad protections of individual rights and liberties found in the Bill of Rights.

Popular Sovereignty

popular sovereignty
The right of the majority to govern themselves.

natural law
A doctrine that society should be governed by certain ethical principles that are part of nature and, as such, can be understood by reason.

The notion of **popular sovereignty,** the right of the majority to govern themselves, has its basis in **natural law.** Ultimately, political authority rests with the people, who can create, abolish, or alter their governments. The idea that all governments derive their power from the people is found in the Declaration of Independence and the U.S. Constitution, but the term popular sovereignty did not come into wide use until pre–Civil War debates over slavery. At that time, supporters of popular sovereignty argued that the citizens of new states seeking admission to the union should be able to decide whether or not their states would allow slavery within their borders.

Building Civil Society

civil society
Society created when citizens are allowed to organize and express their views publicly as they engage in an open debate about public policy.

Several of these hallmarks of our political culture also are fundamentals of what many now term **civil society.** This term is used to describe the "nongovernmental, not-for profit, independent nature" of people and groups who are free to express their views publicly and engage in an open debate about public policy.[3] The U.S. government routinely makes grants to nongovernmental organizations, professional associations, civic education groups, religious groups, and women's organizations to encourage this kind of political participation all around the world as a way to export democracy.

AMERICAN UNIQUENESS IN THE WORLD: ARE WE NUMBER ONE?

American uniqueness—or exceptionalism—has been a pervasive theme in American political rhetoric since before the founding. Americans in the nineteenth century routinely described the nation as a City on a Hill—a reference to a passage in the New Testament in which Jesus Christ urges his followers to be an example for the rest of the world. In fact, U.S. foreign policy has for many years been guided by the idea that America is "bound to lead"—in the dual sense that its leadership is both an obligation it owes to the world and an inevitable role, given its strength and abilities.

Throughout this text we will consider, in these brief Global Perspective features, the question of American uniqueness. Study the figure included here, which shows how the United States compares to the rest of the world in a variety of dimensions. Then, you can begin to judge for yourself whether the United States is truly exceptional.

The data seem to reveal that the United States has amassed a tremendous amount of wealth, technology, political stability, human and natural resources, and military might, while at the same time the health and well-being of the American people are merely average.

As you study each chapter of this text, consider whether this situation is a matter of choice or of circumstance. Can the American people, acting privately or through government, change the rankings that we see here, or are they the product of structural forces that are impervious to change?

Questions

1. Is the United States better or worse than you thought in any categories?
2. Do these data accurately reflect how the U.S. is viewed globally?

Sources: Figures are taken from various sources, compiled by Globastat.com. In most cases, the total number of countries listed is 192. The data are from 2001 and 2002.

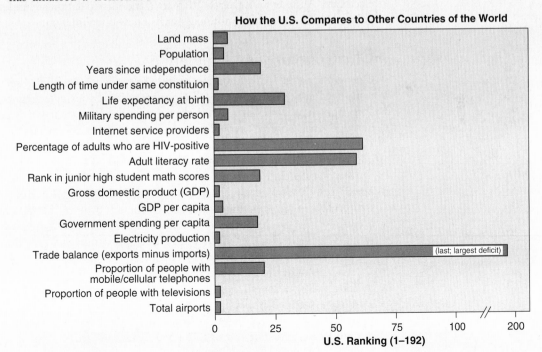

How the U.S. Compares to Other Countries of the World

Individualism

What Are American
Civic Values?

Although many core political values concern protecting the rights of others, tremendous value is placed on the individual. All individuals are deemed rational and fair, and endowed, as Thomas Jefferson proclaimed in the Declaration of Independence, "with certain unalienable rights." Although many view individualism, which holds that the primary function of government is to enable the individual to achieve his or her highest level of development, as a mixed blessing, this concept has been essential throughout American history.

CHANGING CHARACTERISTICS OF THE AMERICAN PEOPLE

AMERICANS HAVE MANY THINGS IN COMMON in addition to their political culture. Most Americans share a common language—English—and have similar aspirations for themselves and their families. Most would rather live in the United States than anywhere else and believe that democracy, with all of its warts, is still the best system. Most Americans highly value education and want to send their children to the best schools possible, viewing an education as the key to success.

Despite these similarities, politicians, media commentators, and even the citizenry itself tend to focus on differences among Americans, in large part because these differences contribute to political conflicts among the electorate. Although it is true that America and its population are undergoing rapid change, this is not necessarily a new phenomenon.

Changing Size and Population

One year after the Constitution was ratified, fewer than 4 million Americans lived in the thirteen states. They were united by a single language and opposition to the king. Most shared a similar Protestant-Christian heritage, and those who voted were white male property owners. The Constitution mandated that each of the sixty-five members of the original House of Representatives should represent 30,000 people.

As revealed in Figure 1.2, as the nation grew with the addition of new states, the population also grew. Although the physical size of the United States has remained stable since the addition of Alaska and Hawaii in 1959, in 2005, there were more than 293 million Americans. In 2005, a single member of the House of Representatives from Montana represented more than 905,000 people.

As a result of this growth, most citizens today feel far removed from the national government and their elected representatives. Members of Congress, too, feel this change. Often they represent diverse constituencies with a variety of needs, concerns, and expectations, and they can meet only a relative few of these people face to face.

FIGURE 1.2   U.S. Population, 1790–2050

Since around 1890, when large numbers of immigrants began arriving in America, the United States has seen a sharp increase in population. The major reasons for this increase are new births and increased longevity, although immigration has also been a contributing factor. ■

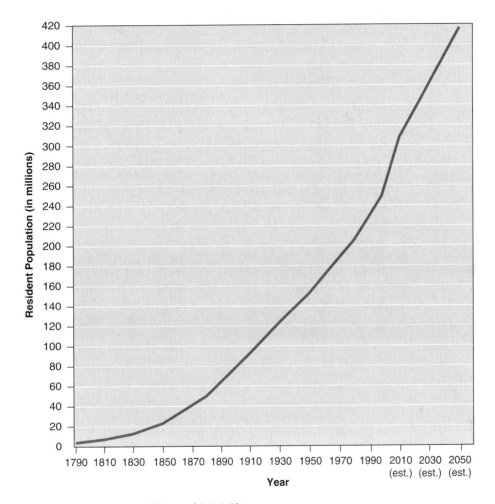

Source: U.S. Census Bureau, *2003 Statistical Abstract of the United States.*

Changing Demographics of the U.S. Population

As the physical size and population of the United States have changed, so have many of the assumptions on which it was founded. Some of the dynamism of the American system actually stems from the racial and ethnic changes that have taken place throughout our history, a notion that often gets lost in debates about immigration policy. Moreover, for the first time, the U.S. population is getting much older.

Visual Literacy

Understanding Who We Are

Changes in Racial and Ethnic Composition.

From the start, the population of America has been changed constantly by the arrival of various kinds of immigrants from various regions to its shores—Western Europeans fleeing religious persecution in the 1600s to early 1700s, Chinese laborers arriving to work on the railroads following the Gold Rush in 1848, Irish Catholics escaping the potato famine in the 1850s, Northern and Eastern Europeans from the 1880s to 1910s, and most recently, Southeast Asians, Cubans, and Mexicans, among others.

Immigration to the United States peaked in the first decade of the 1900s, when nearly 9 million people, many of them from Eastern Europe, entered the country. The United States did not see another major wave of immigration until the late 1980s, when nearly 2 million immigrants were admitted in one year.

Participation

The Debate Over Immigration

While immigration has been a continual source of changing demographics in America, race has also played a major role in the development and course of politics in the United States. As revealed in Figure 1.3, the racial balance in America is changing dramatically. In 2003, for example, non-Hispanic whites made up 68.3 percent of the U.S. population, African Americans 12.7 percent, and Hispanics 13.4 percent, surpassing the number of African Americans in the United States for the first time. Originally, demographers did not anticipate Hispanics would surpass African Americans until 2050. However, in California, Texas, and New Mexico, the Hispanic population is rivaling white, non-Hispanic populations. (See Join the Debate: The Huntington Theory of Hispanization.)

Changes in Age Cohort Composition.

Just as the racial and ethnic composition of the American population is changing, so too is the average age of the population. (See Analyzing Visuals: Changing Age Composition of the United States.) When the United States was founded, the average life expectancy was thirty-five years; by 2003, it was nearly eighty years for women and seventy-four and a half years for men.

As the age profile of the U.S. population has changed, political scientists and others have found it useful to assign labels to various generations. Such labels can be useful in understanding the various pressures put on our nation and its government, because when people are born and the events they experience can have important consequences on how they view other political, economic, and social events. For example, those 76.8 million people born after World War II (1946–1964) often are referred to as Baby Boomers.[4] In contrast, their children, the 50 million who were born in the late 1960s through the mid-1970s, often are called Generation X-ers, the name of an early 1980s punk band and, later, a novel.[5] Those people born from 1977 to 1994 are known as Generation Y.

FIGURE 1.3   Race and Ethnicity in America: 2000 and Beyond. ■

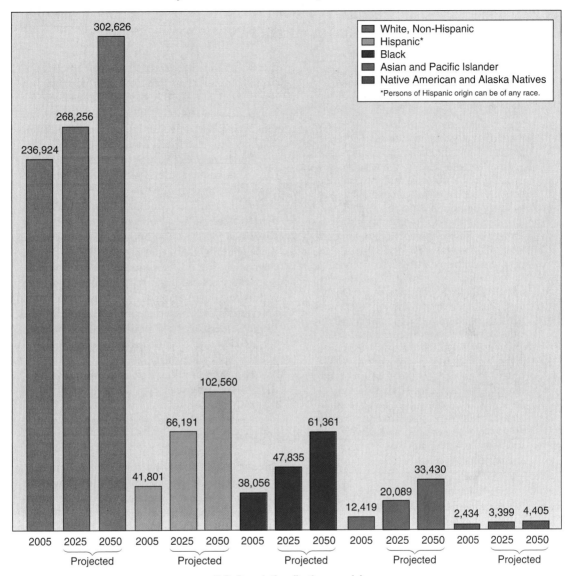

Source: U.S. Census Bureau, *2003 Statistical Abstract of the United States.*

Changes in Family and Family Size.   In the past, large families were the norm (in part because so many children died early) and gender roles were clearly defined. Women did housework and men worked in the fields. Large families were imperative; children were a source of cheap farm labor. Industrialization and knowledge of birth

Join the Debate

THE HUNTINGTON THEORY OF HISPANIZATION

Overview: Many observers of American culture and politics argue that one of the United States' greatest strengths is its ability to absorb and assimilate into the social body the diverse customs and values of different peoples. These commentators highlight the contributions to politics, the arts and sciences, national defense, and the common good by various waves of immigrants—and by those brought against their will during the years of slavery. Traditionalists such as Harvard professor Samuel Huntington contend that the American "melting pot" has been successful in part because, historically, the new Americans have absorbed the fundamental political principles of the United States as their own. Though there are numerous cultures within the country, Huntington insists that there is one shared American culture based on the values espoused in the Declaration of Independence—that is, American political culture is based on the fundamental principles of equality, individual rights, and government by consent. In order for the love of freedom and self-government to be nurtured and maintained, American core principles must be accepted and protected by all citizens.

Huntington argues that during the latter part of the twentieth and into the twenty-first century, there has been a new wave of immigration into the United States unlike any other; he considers immigration from Mexico in particular, and Latin America in general, to be potentially destructive of original American political principles. According to Huntington's highly controversial thesis, this immigration wave is unique in that there is a political agenda within part of the Hispanic community to "reclaim" the lands ceded to the United States after both the Texas war for independence and the Mexican-American War, thus giving Hispanic immigrants a political claim no other group of immigrants have had.

Furthermore, Huntington argues, no other nation has had to contend with a long, contiguous border that immigrants can rather freely cross to maintain familial, economic, and cultural ties, thereby fostering a type of dual national or cultural allegiance (or, at worst, immigrant loyalty to the home country) that can weaken ties to American core values. Finally, he contends, Hispanic immigrants have created linguistic and cultural enclaves within the United States (Los Angeles and Miami, for example) in which there is no need to learn the language, history, and political values of their adopted nation, thus further eroding social and political bonds between citizens.

Huntington raises serious questions with his thesis. Are American core ideals so exceptional that only persons who share those values should be allowed citizenship? Can immigrants whose political and social beliefs differ from or oppose America's core values be assimilated into American society? If not, what corrective policy measures should be implemented? Has American history shown that, ultimately, most immigrants and their descendents embrace the principles that underlie the U.S. Constitution and American political culture?

Arguments for Huntington's Thesis

- **The core political values found in the Declaration of Independence and Constitution**

control methods began to reduce the size of American families by the early 1900s. No longer needing children to work for the survival of the household unit on the farm, couples began to limit the sizes of their families.

16

are essential to maintain freedom and protect rights. It may be that original American principles run the risk of being replaced by ideals that advocate forms of government or politics opposed to liberty, self-government, and individual rights, thus changing the character of the American regime.

■ **American institutions and political culture pursue "Justice as the end of government. . . as the end of civil society."** American ideals can be a guide for all to live together effectively in peace and harmony, rather than an end in themselves. These principles allow most individuals to pursue their unique conception of the American dream, relatively free from interference by the government and others.

■ **A shared language and civic education bind citizens together.** Teaching multiple languages and cultural viewpoints while denying a common civic education and political origin can create competing sources of identity that will weaken citizens' attachments to one another and to their government.

Arguments Against Huntington's Thesis

■ **Historically, certain waves of immigrants were incorrectly thought to be opposed to American values.** Benjamin Franklin expressed concerns that German immigrants could not be assimilated into colonial American life because of their culture and history, and Irish-Catholic immigrants were accused of both giving allegiance to the pope and of being anti-republican in political outlook—fears that proved to be unfounded.

■ **Bilingualism in the Hispanic community does not indicate the creation of competing sources of social and political identity.** According to an opinion poll coordinated by the *Washington Post* in 2000, a mere 10 percent of second-generation Hispanic immigrants rely on speaking only Spanish, which follows the pattern of English language adoption by previous waves of immigration to the United States.

■ **American political culture is more than its Anglo-Protestant core.** A strength of the American experience is its ability to absorb different cultures and values and transform them into one unique political society. It is arguable that it took both the successive waves of immigration and the freeing of the slaves to move the United States toward the realization of the ideals espoused in the Declaration of Independence.

Questions

1. Is this latest wave of immigration truly unique in American history? If so, are core American political values in danger of becoming undermined?
2. Is American political culture more than its core principles and institutions? If so, what other values and institutions add to the United States' claim that it is a true "melting pot?"

Selected Readings

Samuel Huntington. *Who Are We? The Challenges to America's National Identity*. New York: Simon & Schuster, 2004.

Roger Daniels. *Guarding the Golden Door: American Immigration Policy and Immigrants Since 1882*. New York: Hill and Wang, 2004.

In addition, the look of American households has changed dramatically. In 1940, nine out of ten households were "traditional" family households; by 2003, 72.2 percent were two-parent family households, 27.8 percent of all family households were headed by a single parent, and

■ American Muslims celebrate Muslim Day Parade in New York City. From St. Patrick's Day to Chinese New Year celebrations, Americans often honor their immigrant origins.

Photo courtesy: Chris Steele-Perkins/Magnum Photos

more than 25 percent of all households consisted of a single person. Less than one-half of the family households had children under the age of eighteen. Since 1970, the number of female-headed households has more than doubled, from 5.5 million to 12.8 million.

Implications of These Changes

The varied races, ethnic origins, sizes of the various age cohorts, family types, gender roles, and even how marriage is defined have important implications for government and politics. Today, some Americans believe that immigrants (legal and illegal) are flooding onto our shores with disastrous consequences. For example, after the September 11, 2001, terrorist attacks on the World Trade Center and the Pentagon, 83 percent of those polled answered yes to the question "Do you think U.S. immigration laws should be tightened to restrict the number of immigrants from Arab or Muslim countries into the United States?"[6] Opinions such as these often lead to an us versus them attitude.

Demographics also affect politics and government because an individual's perspective influences how he or she hears debates on various issues. Thus, poor and working-class citizens viewed corporate tax breaks quite differently from many wealthy Americans.

These cleavages and the emphasis many politicians put on our demographic differences play out in many ways in American politics. Baby Boomers and the elderly object to any changes in Social Security or Medicare, while those in Generation X vote for politicians who sup-

Simulation

How to Satisfy Aunt Martha

Analyzing Visuals

CHANGING AGE COMPOSITION OF THE UNITED STATES

Between 1990 and 2000, the elderly (age sixty-five and older) increased at a rate similar to those people under eighteen years old because of increased life expectancy, immigration, and advanced medical technologies. By 2040, the elderly will make up nearly the same percentage of the U.S. population as young people. This is a dramatic increase from 1900, when the elderly constituted only 4 percent of the population, and the young were 40 percent of the population. After viewing the bar graph, answer the critical thinking questions presented in the pointer bubbles, using information provided in this chapter. See Analyzing Visuals: A Brief Guide for additional guidance in analyzing graphs.

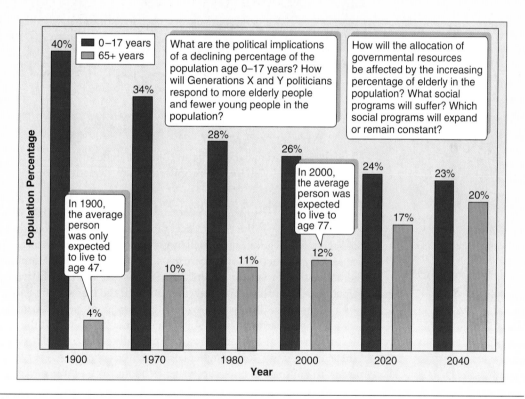

What are the political implications of a declining percentage of the population age 0–17 years? How will Generations X and Y politicians respond to more elderly people and fewer young people in the population?

How will the allocation of governmental resources be affected by the increasing percentage of elderly in the population? What social programs will suffer? Which social programs will expand or remain constant?

In 1900, the average person was only expected to live to age 47.

In 2000, the average person was expected to live to age 77.

Sources: 1900–1980 data from Susan A. MacManus, *Young v. Old: Generational Combat in the 21st Century.* © 1995 by Westview Press, Inc. Reprinted by permission of Westview Press, a member of Perseus Books, L.L.C. 2000 data from Julie Meyer, "Age: 2000," U.S. Census Bureau, C2KBR/01–12, October 2001. Accessed June 30, 2002, http://www.census.gov/population/www/cen2000/briefs.html. 2020–2040 data from U.S. Census Bureau, National Population Projections, Detailed Files, revised November 2, 2000. Accessed June 30, 2002, http://www.census.gov/population/www/projections/natdet-D1A.html.

port change, if they vote at all. Many policies are targeted at one group or the other, further exacerbating differences—real or imagined—and lawmakers often find themselves the target of many different factions.

■ Representative Tom DeLay (R–TX), the House majority whip, and Representative Nancy Pelosi (D–CA), the House minority leader, are both members of the 109th Congress. In the House they stand at opposite ends of the conservative (DeLay) and liberal (Pelosi) spectrum and are two of their parties' most prominent figures.

Photo courtesy: left, Roger L. Wollenberg/Landov; right, Greg Whitesell/UPI Photo/Landov

This diversity can make it difficult to devise coherent policies to "promote the general welfare," as promised in the Constitution.

Ideology of the American Public

political ideology

The coherent set of values and beliefs about the purpose and scope of government held by groups and individuals.

Political ideology is the coherent set of values and beliefs about the purpose and scope of government held by groups and individuals. Most Americans espouse liberalism or conservatism, although a growing number call themselves libertarians. In general, conservatives tend to identify with the Republican Party; liberals usually identify with the Democratic Party.

You probably already have a good idea of what the terms liberal, conservative, and libertarian mean, but you may not be aware that the meaning of these terms has changed dramatically over time. During the nineteenth century, for example, conservatives supported governmental power; in contrast, liberals supported freedom from undue governmental control. Your ideology often is a good predictor of where you stand on a variety of issues as well as how you view the proper role of government.

conservative

One thought to believe that a government is best that governs least and that big government can only infringe on individual, personal, and economic rights.

Conservatives.   **Conservatives** tend to believe that a government is best that governs least, and that big government can only infringe on individual, personal, and economic rights. They want less government, especially in terms of regulation of the economy. Conservatives favor local and state action over federal action, and emphasize fiscal responsibility, most notably in the form of balanced budgets. Conservatives are likely to support smaller, less activist governments and believe that domestic problems like homelessness, poverty, and discrimination are better dealt with by the private sector than by the government. They also tend to be more religious and look to government to regulate some aspects of personal behavior such as abortion or same-sex marriage.

Visual Literacy

Who Are Liberals and Conservatives?

Liberals.   Liberalism is a political view held by those who "seek to change the political, economic, or social status quo to foster the development and well-being of the individual."[7] **Liberals** tend to favor a big government that plays an active role in the economy. They also stress the need for the government to provide for the poor and homeless, to provide a wide array of other social services, and to take an activist role in protecting the rights of women, the elderly, minorities, gays and lesbians, and the environment.

Libertarians.   **Libertarians** tend to believe in the evils of big government and stress that government should not involve itself in the plight of the people or attempt to remedy any social ills. Basically, libertarians, although a very diverse lot, favor a free market economy and an end to governmental intrusion in the area of personal liberties. Generation X-ers are more libertarian in political philosophy than any other age cohort.

liberal
One considered to favor extensive governmental involvement in the economy and the provision of social services and to take an activist role in protecting the rights of women, the elderly, minorities, gays and lesbians, and the environment.

libertarian
One who favors a free market economy and no governmental interference in personal liberties.

Problems with Political Labels

It is important to remember that ideological labels can be quite misleading and do not necessarily allow us to predict political opinions. In a perfect world, liberals would be liberal and conservatives would be conservative. Studies reveal, however, that many people who call themselves conservative actually take fairly liberal positions on many policy issues. In fact, anywhere from 20 percent to 60 percent will take a traditionally conservative position on one issue and a traditionally liberal position on another.[8] (See Table 1.2 to gauge where your political views place you.)

TABLE 1.2   Liberal? Conservative? Libertarian? Chart Your Views on These Issues

| | Government Support of: | | | | |
	Abortion Rights	Environmental Regulation	Gun Control Laws	Poor	Domestic Unions
Conservative	Oppose	Oppose	Oppose	Oppose	Oppose
Liberal	Favor	Favor	Favor	Favor	Favor
Libertarian	Favor	Oppose	Oppose	Oppose	Favor

FIGURE 1.4   Self-Identification as Liberal, Moderate, or Conservative, 1974–2004. ■

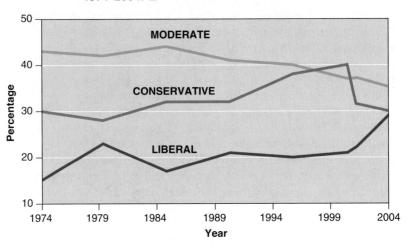

Source: LEXIS/NEXIS.

CURRENT ATTITUDES TOWARD AMERICAN GOVERNMENT

AMERICANS' VIEWS ABOUT AND EXPECTATIONS of government and democracy affect the political system at all levels. It has now become part of our political culture to expect negative campaigns, dishonest politicians, and political pundits who make their living bashing politicians and the political process. How Americans view politics, the economy, and their ability to achieve the **American dream**—an American ideal of a happy and successful life to which many aspire, which often includes wealth, a house, a better life for one's children, and, for some, the ability to grow up to become president—also is influenced by their political ideology as well as by their social, economic, educational, and personal circumstances.

Since the early 1990s, the major sources of most individuals' on-the-air news—the four major networks (ABC, CBS, FOX, and NBC) along with CNN and C-SPAN—have been supplemented dramatically as the number of news and quasi-news outlets has grown exponentially. First there were weekly programs such as *Dateline* on the regular networks. Then came the rapid expansion of cable programming, includ-

American dream
An American ideal of a happy life, which often includes wealth, a house, a better life for one's children, and, for some, the ability to grow up to be president.

ing FOX News, MSNBC, and CNBC—all competing for similar audiences. These networks' news programming has been supplemented by the phenomenal development of the Internet as an instantaneous source of news and rumors about politics.

The competition for news stories, as well as the instantaneous nature of these communications, often highlights the negative, the sensational, the sound bite, and usually the extremes. It's hard to remain upbeat about America or politics amidst the media's focus on personality and scandal, especially because success stories are generally showcased only in State of the Union Addresses or at presidential nominating conventions.

High Expectations

In roughly the first 150 years of our nation's history, the federal government had few responsibilities, and its citizens had few expectations of it beyond national defense, printing money, and collecting tariffs and taxes. The state governments were generally far more powerful than the federal government in matters affecting the everyday lives of Americans (see chapter 3).

As the nation and its economy grew in size and complexity, the federal government took on more responsibilities, such as regulating some businesses, providing poverty relief, and inspecting food. Then, in response to the Great Depression of the 1930s, President Franklin D. Roosevelt's New Deal government programs proliferated in almost every area of American life. Since then, many Americans have looked to the government and politicians for solutions to all kinds of problems.

A Missing Appreciation of the Good

If you don't have faith in America, its institutions, or symbols (and Table 1.3 shows that many of us don't), it becomes even easier to blame

TABLE 1.3   Faith in Institutions

	Percentage of Americans Declaring They Had a "Great Deal" of Confidence in the Institution				
	1966	*1975*	*1986*	*1996*	*2004*
Congress	42%	13%	16%	8%	8%
Executive branch	41	13	21	10	25
The press	29	26	18	11	9
Business & industry	55	19	24	23	19
Medicine	73	51	46	45	19

Sources: Newsweek (January 8, 1996): 32; Public Perspective 8 (February/March 1994): 4. Data for 2004: Public Opinion Online.

the government for all kinds of woes—personal as well as societal—or to fail to credit governments for the things governments do well.

Although all governments have problems, it is important to stress the good they can do. For example, in the aftermath of the Great Depression in the United States, the government created the Social Security Insurance program, which dramatically decreased poverty among the elderly. Government-guaranteed student loan programs make it possible for many students to attend college. And, many Americans enjoy a remarkably high standard of living, much of it due to governmental programs and protections. (See Table 1.4 for quality of life measures.)

Mistrust of Politicians

It is not difficult to see why Americans might be distrustful of politicians when media coverage focuses on corporate and political scandals. However, most local, state, and national legislators are hard working and pride themselves on being able to deliver programs and services to the residents of their districts. Moreover, President George W. Bush got high marks from the American public for his honesty and ability to bring the nation together immediately after the 9/11 attacks.

Voter Apathy

Americans, unlike voters in most other societies, get an opportunity to vote on a host of candidates and issues, but some say those choices are just too numbing. Many citizens opt not to go to the polls, fearing that they lack sufficient information of the vast array of candidates and issues facing them.

TABLE 1.4 How Are Americans Really Doing?			
	1945	*1970*	*2003*
Life expectancy	65.9	70.8	75.4
Per capita income (1999 constant dollars)	$6,367	$12,816	$21,181
Adults who are high school grads	25%[a]	52.3%	84.1%
Adults who are college grads	5%[a]	10.7%	25.6%
Households with phones	46%	87%	94.2%
Households with cable TV	0%	4%	67.5%
Women in labor force	29%	38%	60%
Own their own home	46%	63%	66.9%
Below poverty rate	39.7%[b]	12.6%	11.8%

[a]1940 figure.   [b]1949 figure.

Source: U.S. Census Bureau, *2003 Statistical Abstract of the United States.*

DEEPENING DISAPPROVAL OF U.S. INVOLVEMENT IN IRAQ

Just as Americans' confidence in the institutions of government has fallen, so has global public opinion toward the United States. Although many citizens throughout the world stood solidly with the United States in the aftermath of the September 11, 2001, terrorist attacks, the actions of the United States in Iraq, as well as concerns about globalization, have made Americans and America the target of considerable wrath, even among citizens of normally strong allies. The Spanish electorate's stunning election within days after a terrorist attack of an anti–Iraq War prime minister who pledged to withdraw Spain's troops from Iraq underscores this shift in support for American foreign policy.

Although 67 percent of Americans polled in one 2004 survey expressed their belief that "the U.S.-led war on terrorism [was] a sincere effort to reduce international terrorism," most citizens of other nations did not agree, as is revealed in the figure

shown here. Similarly, in Morocco, Jordan, and Pakistan, George W. Bush's unfavorable ratings are higher than Osama bin Laden's! The majority of those polled in Morocco and Jordan even believe that suicide bombings carried out against Americans in Iraq are justified. Said former Secretary of State Madeleine Albright, "the broad mistrust of American leadership will be difficult to reverse."[a]

Surveys also find that most Western Europeans hold an unfavorable view of President George W. Bush and American foreign policy. Can you think of other reasons why the citizens of other nations distrust the United States? Are these concerns well founded? What might be the consequences of this mistrust of the United States when coupled with Americans' distrust of many political institutions in general?

a Quoted in Susan Page, "Survey Tracks Deepening Distrust Toward U.S.," USA Today (March 17, 2004): 7A.

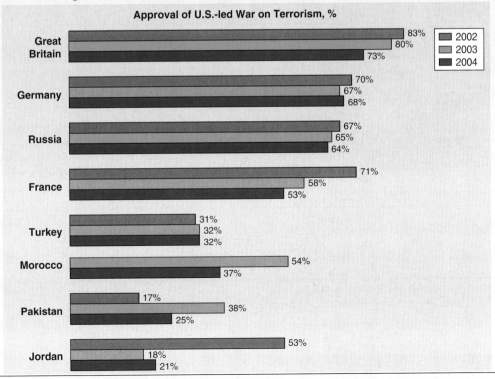

Source: *A Year After Iraq War,* Pew Global Attitudes Project, March 16, 2004.

Photo courtesy: Reuters/Jamal Wilson/Archive Photos

■ Doris "Granny D" Haddock walked 3,200 miles across America to agitate for campaign finance reform in 2000. In 2004, Haddock, along with two friends, drove across the United States in a brightly painted camper. This time, Granny D was trying to motivate single women to vote. Although they make up 46 percent of all women eligible to vote, historically, unmarried women vote in fewer numbers than their married sisters. Underscoring her commitment, also in 2004, she ran unsuccessfully for the U.S. Senate from New Hampshire.

A Census Bureau report examining the reasons given by the millions of eligible voters who stayed home from the polls on Election Day in 2002 showed that being too busy was the single biggest reason Americans gave for not voting. Some commentators have noted that nonvoting may even be a sign of contentment. If things are good, or you perceive that there is no need for change, why vote?

Redefining Our Expectations

Just as it is important to recognize that governments serve many important purposes, it is also important to recognize that government and politics are not static. Politics, moreover, involves conflicts over different and sometimes opposing ideologies, and these ideologies are very much influenced by one's racial, economic, and historical experiences. These divisions are real and affect the political process at all levels. It is clear to most Americans today that politics and government no longer can be counted on to cure all of America's ills. Government, however, will always play a major role. True political leaders will need to help Americans come to terms with America as it is today—not as it was in the past.

SUMMARY

GOVERNMENTS, WHICH ARE MADE UP of individuals and institutions, are the vehicles through which policies are made and affairs of state are conducted. Governments have many functions. In the U.S. context, most are included in the preamble to the Constitution. Governments take many forms depending on the number who rule as well as whose interests are represented.

The American political system was based on several notions that have their roots in classical Greek ideas. The ideas of social contract theorists John Locke and Thomas Hobbes, who held the belief that people are free and equal by God-given right, have continuing implications for our ideas of the proper role of government in our indirect democracy. Key characteristics of the political culture are personal liberty, equality, popular consent and majority rule, popular sovereignty, civil society, and individualism.

Several characteristics of the American electorate can help us understand how the system continues to evolve and change. Chief among these are changes in size, population, and demographics.

Most Americans identify themselves on a traditional conservative-to-liberal continuum, with most believing themselves to be moderates. Outside this continuum, libertarians often hold liberal views on many issues and conservative views on others.

Americans have high and often unrealistic expectations of government. At the same time, they often fail to appreciate how much their government actually does for them. Some of this failure may be due to Americans' general mistrust of politicians, which may explain some of the apathy evidenced in the electorate.

KEY TERMS

American dream, p. 22

civil society, p. 10

citizen, p. 3

conservative, p. 20

democracy, p. 6

direct democracy, p. 9

government, p. 3

indirect (representative) democracy, p. 9

liberal, p. 21

libertarian, p. 21

majority rule, p. 10

monarchy, p. 6

natural law, p. 10

oligarchy, p. 6

personal liberty, p. 9

political culture, p. 9

political ideology, p. 20

politics, p. 4

popular consent, p. 10

popular sovereignty, p. 10

republic, p. 9

social contract theory, p. 7

totalitarianism, p. 6

SELECTED READINGS

Almond, Gabriel A., and Sidney Verba. *Civic Culture: Political Attitudes and Democracy in Five Nations*. Princeton, NJ: Princeton University Press, 1963.

Craig, Stephen C., and Stephen Earl Bennett, eds. *After the Boom: The Politics of Generation X*. Lanham, MD: Rowman and Littlefield, 1997.

Dahl, Robert A. *Polyarchy: Participation and Opposition*. New Haven, CT: Yale University Press, 1971.

Elshtain, Jean Bethke. *Democracy on Trial*. New York: Basic Books, 1995.

Glendon, Mary Ann. *Rights Talk: The Impoverishment of Political Discourse*. New York: Free Press, 1991.

Grossman, Lawrence K. *The Electronic Republic: Reshaping Democracy in the Information Age*. New York: Viking, 1995.

Hobbes, Thomas. *Leviathan*. Richard Tuck, ed. New York: Cambridge University Press, 1996.

Hochschild, Jennifer L. *Facing Up to the American Dream: Race, Class, and the Soul of the Nation*. Princeton, NJ: Princeton University Press, 1995.

Hunter, James Davison. *Culture Wars: The Struggle to Define America*. New York: Basic Books, 1991.

Jamieson, Kathleen Hall. *Dirty Politics: Deception, Distraction, and Democracy*. New York: Oxford University Press, 1992.

Locke, John. *Two Treatises of Government*. Peter Lasleti, ed. New York: Cambridge University Press, 1988.

Putnam, Robert D. *Bowling Alone: Collapse and Revival of the American Community*. New York: Simon and Schuster, 2000.

Skocpol, Theda, and Morris Fiorina, eds. *Civic Engagement in American Democracy*. Washington, DC: Brookings Institution, 1999.

Verba, Sidney, Kay Schlozman, and Henry Brady. *Voice and Equality: Civic Volunteerism in American Politics*. Cambridge, MA: Harvard University Press, 1995.

Zakaria, Fareed. *The Future of Freedom: Illiberal Democracy at Home and Abroad*. New York: Norton, 2003.

WEB EXPLORATIONS

To connect with others who are interested in politics, see
http://www.pbs.org/news/news_government.html

For more on Aristotle and natural law, see
http://www.perseus.tufts.edu/cgi-bin/ptext?doc=Perseus%3Aabo%3Atlg%2C0086%2C035&query=1252a

For more on Thomas Hobbes and John Locke, see
http://www.iep.utm.edu/h/hobmoral.htm and
http://www.utm.edu/research/iep/l/locke.htm

To get a minute by minute update on U.S. population, see
http://www.census.gov/

For more detail on population projections, see
http://www.census.gov/population/www/projections/natsum.html

To learn more about Generation Y, see
http://www.cato.org/research/articles/firey-011203.html

For more information on families and household composition, see http://www.census.gov/population/socdemo/hh-fam/98ppla.txt

For more information on conservatives, see
http://www.conservative.org/

For more information on liberals, see
http://www.turnleft.com/

For more information on libertarians, see
http://www.lp.org/ and http://www.cato.org/

To find out your ideological stance, go to
http://people-press.org/fit/

For more information on the American electorate, see
http://www.census.gov/population/www/socdemo/voting/p20-542.html

2

The Constitution

AT AGE EIGHTEEN, ALL AMERICAN CITIZENS are eligible to vote in state and national elections. This has not always been the case. It took an amendment to the U.S. Constitution—one of only seventeen that have been added since the Bill of Rights was ratified in 1791—to guarantee the franchise to those under twenty-one years of age.

In 1942, during World War II, Representative Jennings Randolph (D–WV) proposed that the voting age in national elections be lowered to eighteen, believing that since young men were old enough to be drafted to fight and die for their country, they also should be allowed to vote. He continued to reintroduce his proposal during every session of Congress, and in 1954, President Dwight D. Eisenhower endorsed the idea in his State of the Union message. Presidents Lyndon B. Johnson and Richard M. Nixon—men who also called upon the nation's young men to fight on foreign shores—echoed his appeal.[1]

By the 1960s, the campaign to lower the voting age took on a new sense of urgency as hundreds of thousands of young men were drafted to fight in Vietnam and thousands of men and women were killed in action. "Old Enough to Fight, Old Enough to Vote," was one popular slogan of the day. By 1970, four states—who under the U.S. Constitution are allowed to set the eligibility requirements for their voters—had lowered their voting ages to eighteen. Later that year, Congress passed legislation lowering the voting age in national, state, and local elections to eighteen.

The state of Oregon, however, challenged the constitutionality of the law in court, arguing that Congress had not been given the authority to establish a uniform voting age in state and local government under the Constitution. The U.S. Supreme Court agreed.[2] The decision from the sharply divided Court meant that those under age twenty-one could vote in national elections but that the states were free to prohibit them from voting in state and local elections. The decision presented the states with a logistical nightmare. States setting the voting age at twenty-one would be forced to keep two sets of registration books: one for voters twenty-one and over, and one for voters under twenty-one.

Jennings Randolph, by then a senator from West Virginia, reintroduced his proposed amendment to lower the national voting age to eighteen.[3] Within three months of the Supreme Court's decision, Congress sent the proposed Twenty-Sixth Amendment to the states for their ratification. The required three-fourths of the states ratified the amendment within three months—making its adoption on June 30, 1971, the quickest in the history of the constitutional amending process.

However, young people never have voted in large numbers. Through 2000, in spite of issues of concern to those under the age of twenty-five, including a possible draft, Internet privacy, reproductive rights, credit card and cell phone rules and regulations, and the continuance of student loan programs, voter turnout among those age eighteen to twenty-four continued to decline. Massive voter registration and voter awareness campaigns by groups such as Rock the Vote and the Hip Hop Action Network and MTV's Choose or Lose Campaign as well as both major political parties helped to reverse this troubling trend in 2004.

THE CONSTITUTION INTENTIONALLY was written to forestall the need for amendment, and the process by which it could be changed or amended was made time-consuming and difficult. Over the years, thousands of amendments have been debated or sent to the states for their approval, but only twenty-seven amendments have successfully made their way into the Constitution. What the Framers came up with in Philadelphia has continued to work, in spite of increasing demands on and dissatisfaction with the national government. Perhaps Americans are happier with the system of government created by the Framers than they realize.

The ideas that went into the making of the Constitution and the ways in which the Constitution has evolved to address the problems of a growing and ever-changing nation are at the core of our discussion in this chapter. First, we will examine the origins of the new nation and the circumstances surrounding the Declaration of Independence and the break with Great Britain. After discussing the first attempts at American government created by the Articles of Confederation, we will examine the circumstances surrounding writing a Constitution and will review the results of the Framers' efforts—the U.S. Constitution. Finally, we will address methods of amending the Constitution.

THE ORIGINS OF A NEW NATION

STARTING IN THE EARLY SEVENTEENTH CENTURY, colonists came to the New World for a variety of reasons. The independence and diversity of the settlers in the New World made the question of how best to rule the new colonies a tricky one. More than merely an ocean separated England from the colonies; the colonists were independent people, and it soon became clear that the Crown could not govern its subjects in the colonies with the same close rein used at home. King James I thus allowed some local participation in decision making through arrangements such as the first elected colonial assembly, the Virginia House of Burgesses, and the elected General Court that governed the Massachusetts Bay colony after 1629. Almost all the colonists agreed that the king ruled by divine right, but English monarchs allowed the colonists significant liberties in terms of self-government, religious practices, and economic organization. For 140 years, this system worked fairly well.[4]

By the early 1760s, however, a century and a half of physical separation, development of colonial industry, and the relative self-governance of the colonies had led to weakening economic ties with—and personal loyalties to—the Crown. By this time, each of the thirteen colonies had drafted its own written constitution, which provided the fundamental rules or laws for each colony. Moreover, many of the most oppressive British traditions—feudalism, a rigid class system, and the absolute authority of the king—were absent in the New World. Land was abundant. Although the role of religion was central to the lives of most colonists, there was no single state church.

Trade and Taxation

mercantilism
An economic theory designed to increase a nation's wealth through the development of commercial industry and a favorable balance of trade.

Mercantilism, an economic theory designed to increase a nation's wealth through the development of commercial industry and a favorable balance of trade, justified Britain's maintenance of strict import/export controls on the colonies. After 1650, for example, Parliament passed a series of navigation acts to prevent its chief rival, Holland, from trading with the English colonies. From 1650 until well into the 1700s, England tried to regulate colonial imports and exports, believing that it was critical to export more goods than it imported as a way of increasing the gold and silver in its treasury. These policies, however, were difficult to enforce and were widely ignored by the colonists, who saw little self-benefit in them. Thus, for years, an unwritten agreement existed. The colonists relinquished to the Crown and the British Parliament the authority to regulate trade and conduct international affairs, but they retained the right to levy their own taxes.

This fragile agreement was soon put to the test. The French and Indian War, fought from 1756 to 1763 on the western frontier of the colonies and in Canada, was part of a global war initiated by the British. In North America, its immediate cause was the rival claims of Great Britain and France for the lands between the Allegheny Mountains and the Mississippi River. When the Treaty of Paris ended this war, the colonists expected that westward migration and settlement could begin in earnest. However, the Crown decreed that there was to be no further westward movement by British subjects. Parliament believed that expansion into Indian territory would lead to new expenditures for the defense of the settlers, draining the already depleted British treasury.

To raise money to pay for the war as well as the expenses of administering the colonies, Parliament enacted the Sugar Act in 1764, which placed taxes on sugar, wine, coffee, and other products commonly exported to the colonies. A postwar colonial depression heightened resentment of the tax. Major protest, however, failed to materialize until imposition of the Stamp Act by the British Parliament in 1765. This law required that all paper items bought and sold in the colonies carry a stamp mandated by the Crown. The tax itself was not offensive to the colonists. However, they feared this act would establish a precedent for the British Parliament not only to regulate commerce in the colonies, but also to raise revenues from the colonists without the approval of the colonial governments. Around the colonies, the political cry "no taxation without representation" became prominent.

Colonists were outraged. Men organized the Sons of Liberty, under the leadership of Samuel Adams and Patrick Henry. Women formed the Daughters of Liberty. Protests against the Stamp Act were especially violent in Boston, where the colonial governor's home was burned by an angry mob, and British stamp agents charged with collecting the tax were threatened. A boycott of goods needing the stamps as well as British imports also was organized.

Photo courtesy: Painting by John Singleton Copley, Museum of Fine Arts, Boston. Reproduced with permission. © 2001, Museum of Fine Arts, Boston. All rights reserved.

■ Today, Samuel Adams (1722–1803), shown here in a painting by John Singleton Copley, is well known for the beer that bears his name. His original claim to fame was as a leader against the British and loyalist oppressors (although he did bankrupt his family's brewery business). As a member of the Massachusetts legislature, he advocated defiance of the Stamp Act. With the passage of the Townshend Acts in 1767, he organized a letter-writing campaign urging other colonies to join in resistance. Later, in 1772, he founded the Committees of Correspondence with members in each colony to facilitate communication and build united resistance to the Crown.

First Steps Toward Independence

Stamp Act Congress
Meeting of representatives of nine of the thirteen colonies held in New York City in 1765, during which representatives drafted a document to send to the king listing how their rights had been violated.

In 1765, the colonists called for the **Stamp Act Congress,** the first official meeting of the colonies and the first step toward a unified nation. Nine of the thirteen colonies sent representatives to a meeting in New York City, where a detailed list of the British Crown's violations of the colonists' fundamental rights was created. Attendees defined what they thought to be the proper relationship between colonial governments and the British Parliament; they ardently believed Parliament had no authority to tax them without representation in that body. In contrast, the British believed that direct representation of the colonists was impractical and that members of Parliament represented the best interests of all the English, including the colonists.

The Stamp Act Congress and its petitions to the king did little to stop the onslaught of taxing measures. In 1767, Parliament enacted the Townshend Acts, which imposed duties on all kinds of colonial imports, including tea. Response from the Sons and Daughters of Liberty was immediate. Another boycott was announced, and almost all colonists gave up their favorite drink in a united show of resistance to the tax and British authority.[5]

Tensions continued to run high, especially after the British sent 4,000 troops to Boston. On March 5, 1770, English troops opened fire on a mob that included disgruntled dock workers, whose jobs had been taken by British soldiers, and members of the Sons of Liberty, who were taunting the soldiers in front of the Boston Customs House. Five colonists were killed in what became known as the Boston Massacre. Following this confrontation, all duties except those on tea were lifted. The tea tax, however, continued to be a symbolic irritant.

In 1773, despite dissent in England over the treatment of the colonies, Parliament passed another tea tax designed to shore up the sagging sales of the East India Company, a British exporter of tea. The colonists' boycott had left that British trading house with more than 18 million pounds of tea in its warehouses. This act granted a monopoly to the financially strapped East India Company to sell the tea imported from Britain. The company was allowed to funnel business to American merchants loyal to the Crown, thereby undercutting other colonial merchants.

When the next shipment of tea arrived in Boston from Great Britain, the colonists responded with the Boston Tea Party, throwing the cargo into the harbor. Similar tea parties were held in other colonies. When news of these actions reached King George, he flew into a rage against the actions of his disloyal subjects. "The die is now cast," the king told his prime minister. "The colonies must either submit or triumph."

King George's first act of retaliation was to persuade Parliament to pass the Coercive Acts in 1774. Known in the colonies as the Intolerable Acts, they contained a key provision calling for a total blockade of Boston Harbor until restitution was made for the tea. Another provision gave royal governors the authority to house British soldiers in the homes of private citizens, allowing Britain to send an additional 4,000 soldiers to patrol Boston.

The Continental Congresses

The British could never have guessed how the cumulative impact of these actions would unite the colonists. Samuel Adams's **Committees of Correspondence** spread the word, and food and money were sent to the people of Boston from all over the thirteen colonies. At the request of the colonial assemblies of Massachusetts and Virginia, all but Georgia's colonial assembly agreed to select a group of delegates to attend a continental congress authorized to communicate with the king on behalf of the united colonies.

The **First Continental Congress** met in Philadelphia, Pennsylvania, from September 5 to October 26, 1774. It was made up of fifty-six delegates from all of the colonies with the exception of Georgia. The colonists had yet to think of breaking with Great Britain; at this point, they simply wanted to iron out their differences with the king. By October, they had agreed on a series of resolutions to oppose the Coercive Acts and to establish a formal organization to boycott British goods. The Congress also drafted a Declaration of Rights and Resolves, which called for colonial rights of petition and assembly, trial by peers, freedom from a standing army, and the selection of representative councils to levy taxes.

King George refused to yield, tensions continued to rise, and a **Second Continental Congress** was deemed necessary. Before it could meet, fighting broke out early in the morning of April 19, 1775, at Lexington and Concord, Massachusetts, with what Ralph Waldo Emerson called "the shot heard round the world." Eight colonial soldiers, called Minutemen, were killed, and 16,000 British troops besieged Boston, marking the beginning of the Revolutionary War.

When the Second Continental Congress convened in Philadelphia on May 10, 1775, delegates were united by their increased hostility to Great Britain. In a final attempt to avert conflict, the Second Continental Congress adopted the Olive Branch Petition on July 5, 1775, asking the king to end hostilities. King George rejected the petition and sent an additional 20,000 troops to quell the rebellion.

The Declaration of Independence

In January 1776, Thomas Paine, with the support and encouragement of Benjamin Franklin, issued (at first anonymously) *Common Sense*, a pamphlet forcefully arguing for independence from Great Britain. *Common Sense* galvanized the American public against reconciliation with England. As the mood in the colonies changed, so did that of the

Committees of Correspondence
Organizations in each of the American colonies created to keep colonists abreast of developments with the British; served as powerful molders of public opinion against the British.

First Continental Congress
Meeting held in Philadelphia from September 5 to October 26, 1774, in which fifty-six delegates (from every colony except Georgia) adopted a resolution in opposition to the Coercive Acts.

Second Continental Congress
Meeting that convened in Philadelphia on May 10, 1775, at which it was decided that an army should be raised and George Washington of Virginia was named commander in chief.

confederation
Type of government in which the national government derives its powers from the states; a league of independent states.

Declaration of Independence
Document drafted by Thomas Jefferson in 1776 that proclaimed the right of the American colonies to separate from Great Britain.

Second Continental Congress. On May 15, 1776, Virginia became the first colony to call for independence, instructing one of its delegates to the Second Continental Congress to introduce a resolution to that effect. This three-part resolution—which called for independence, the formation of foreign alliances, and preparation of a plan of **confederation**—triggered hot debate among the delegates. A proclamation of independence from Great Britain was treason, a crime punishable by death. Although six of the thirteen colonies had already instructed their delegates to vote for independence, the Second Continental Congress was suspended to allow its delegates to return home to their respective colonial legislatures for final instructions. Independence was not a move to be taken lightly.

Still, independence was an option the colonists were seriously considering. Committees were set up to consider each point of the proposal. A committee of five was selected to begin work on a **Declaration of Independence.** The Congress selected Benjamin Franklin of Pennsylvania, John Adams of Massachusetts, Robert Livingston of New York, and Roger Sherman of Connecticut as members. Adams lobbied hard for a Southerner to add balance. Thus, owing to his southern origin as well as his "peculiar felicity of expression," Thomas Jefferson of Virginia was selected as chair.

On July 2, 1776, twelve of the thirteen colonies (with New York abstaining) voted for independence. Two days later, the Second Continental Congress voted to adopt the Declaration of Independence penned by Thomas Jefferson. On July 9, 1776, the Declaration, now with the approval of New York, was read aloud in Philadelphia.[6]

In simple but eloquent language, Jefferson set out the reasons for the colonies' separation from Great Britain. Most of his stirring rhetoric drew heavily on the works of seventeenth- and eighteenth-century political philosophers, particularly the English philosopher John Locke (see chapter 1), who argued that individuals who give their consent to be governed have the right to rebel against a government that violates the rights of its citizens.

It is easy to see the colonists' debt to John Locke. In ringing language, the Declaration of Independence proclaims:

> We hold these truths to be self-evident, that all men are created equal, that they are endowed by their Creator with certain unalienable Rights, that among these are Life, Liberty and the pursuit of Happiness.

The Declaration also justified the colonists' break with the Crown, clarified their notions of the proper form of government, and enumerated the wrongs that the colonists had suffered under British rule. After the Declaration was signed and transmitted to the king, the Revolutionary War waged on, and the Continental Congress attempted to fashion a new united government.

THE FIRST ATTEMPT AT GOVERNMENT: THE ARTICLES OF CONFEDERATION

THE BRITISH HAD NO WRITTEN CONSTITUTION. The delegates to the Second Continental Congress were attempting to codify arrangements that had never before been put into legal terminology. To make things more complicated, the delegates had to arrive at these decisions in a wartime atmosphere. Nevertheless, in late 1777, the **Articles of Confederation,** creating a loose "league of friendship" between the thirteen sovereign or independent states, were passed by the Congress and presented to the states for their ratification.

Articles of Confederation

The compact among the thirteen original states that was the basis of their government. Written in 1777, the Articles were not ratified by all the states until 1781.

Unlike Great Britain's unitary system of government, wherein all of the powers of the government reside in the national government, the national government in a confederation derives all of its powers directly from the states. The Articles of Confederation proposed the following:

- A national government with a Congress empowered to make peace, coin money, appoint officers for an army, control the post office, and negotiate with Indian tribes.
- Each state to retain its independence and sovereignty, or ultimate authority to govern within its territories.
- One vote in the Continental Congress for each state, regardless of size.
- The vote of nine states to pass any measure (a unanimous vote for any amendment).
- The selection and payment of delegates to the Congress by their respective state legislatures.

The Articles were finally ratified by all thirteen states in March 1781.

Problems Under the Articles of Confederation

By 1784, governing the new nation under the Articles of Confederation proved unworkable.[7] Congress rarely could assemble the required quorum of nine states to conduct business. Even when it could, there was little agreement among the states on any policies. To raise revenue to pay off war debts and run the government, various land, poll, and liquor taxes were proposed. But, since Congress had no specific power to tax, all these proposals were rejected. At one point, Congress was even driven out of Philadelphia (then the capital of the new national government) by its own unpaid army.

Although the national government could coin money, it had no resources to back up the value of its currency. Continental dollars were

Photo courtesy: Bettmann/Corbis

■ With Daniel Shays in the lead, a group of farmers and Revolutionary War veterans marched on the courthouse in Springfield, Massachusetts, to stop the state court from foreclosing on farmers' mortgages. Actions such as this prompted quick action to remedy the weaknesses of the Articles of Confederation.

worth little, and trade between states became chaotic as some states began to coin their own money. Congress also had no power to regulate commerce among the states and with foreign nations. As a result, individual states attempted to enter into agreements with other countries, and foreign nations were suspicious of trade agreements made with the Congress of the Confederation.

The draftees of the Articles also made no provision for an executive branch of government that would be responsible for executing, or implementing, laws passed by the legislative branch. Instead, the president was merely the presiding officer at meetings.

In addition, the Articles had no provision for a judicial system to handle the growing number of economic conflicts and boundary disputes among the individual states. Several states claimed the same lands to the west, and Pennsylvania and Virginia went to war with each other.

The Articles' greatest weakness, however, was the lack of creation of a strong central government. States regarded themselves as sovereign entities and were unwilling to give up rights to an untested national government. Consequently, the national government was unable to force the states to abide by the provisions of the Treaty of Paris, signed in 1783, which officially ended the war with Britain.

THE MIRACLE AT PHILADELPHIA: WRITING A CONSTITUTION

ON FEBRUARY 21, 1787, in the throes of economic turmoil and with domestic tranquility gone haywire, the Congress passed an official resolution. It called for a Constitutional Convention to be held in Philadelphia for "the sole and express purpose of revising the Articles of Confederation."

Many of the delegates who gathered in sweltering Philadelphia on May 25, 1787, however, were prepared to take potentially treasonous steps to preserve the union. On the first day the convention was in session, Edmund Randolph and James Madison of Virginia proposed fifteen resolutions creating an entirely new government (later known as the Virginia Plan). Their enthusiasm, however, was not universal. Many delegates, including William Paterson of New Jersey, considered these resolutions to be in violation of the convention's charter, and proposed the New Jersey Plan, which took greater steps to preserve the Articles. These proposals met heated debate on the convention's floor.

The Virginia and New Jersey Plans

The **Virginia Plan** called for a system of government based heavily on the European nation-state model, wherein the national government derives its powers from the people and not from the member states. Its key features included:

Virginia Plan
The first general plan for the Constitution, proposed by James Madison. Its key points were a bicameral legislature, an executive chosen by the legislature, and a judiciary also named by the legislature.

- Creation of a powerful central government with three branches: the legislative, executive, and judicial.
- A two-house legislature with one house elected directly by the people, the other chosen from among persons nominated by the state legislatures.
- A legislature with the power to select the executive and the judiciary.

In general, smaller states such as New Jersey and Connecticut felt comfortable with the arrangements under the Articles of Confederation. These states offered another model of government, the **New Jersey Plan.** Its key features included:

New Jersey Plan
A framework for the Constitution proposed by a group of small states; its key points were a one-house legislature with one vote for each state, the establishment of the acts of Congress as the "supreme law" of the land, and a supreme judiciary with limited power.

- Strengthening the Articles, not replacing them.
- Creating a one-house legislature with one vote for each state with representatives chosen by state legislatures.
- Giving the Congress the power to raise revenue from duties and postal service.
- Creating a Supreme Court appointed for life by the executive officers.

Constitutional Compromises

The most serious disagreement between the Virginia and New Jersey plans concerned state representation in Congress and the North/South division over how slaves were to be counted for purposes of representation and taxation. When a deadlock loomed, Connecticut offered its own compromise. Each state would have an equal vote in the Senate. Again, there was a stalemate.

A committee to work out an agreement soon reported back what became known as the **Great Compromise.** Taking ideas from both the Virginia and New Jersey plans, it recommended:

Great Compromise
A decision made during the Constitutional Convention to give each state the same number of representatives in the Senate regardless of size; representation in the House was determined by population.

- In one house of the legislature (later called the House of Representatives), there should be fifty-six representatives—one representative for every 30,000 inhabitants. Representatives were to be elected directly by the people.

- That house should have the power to originate all bills for raising and spending money.

- In the second house of the legislature (later called the Senate), each state should have an equal vote, and representatives would be selected by the state legislatures.

- In dividing power between the national and state governments, national power was declared supreme.

The Great Compromise ultimately met with the approval of all states in attendance. The smaller states were pleased because they got equal representation in the Senate; the larger states were satisfied with the proportional representation in the House of Representatives. The small states then would dominate the Senate while the large states, such as Virginia and Pennsylvania, would control the House. But, because both houses had to pass any legislation, neither body could dominate the other.[8]

The Great Compromise dealt with one major concern of the Framers—how best to treat the differences in large and small states—but other problems stemming largely from regional differences remained. Slavery was one of the thorniest. Southerners feared that the new national government would interfere with its lucrative cotton trade as well as slavery. Consequently, in exchange for northern support of continuing the slave trade for twenty more years and for a twenty-year ban on taxing exports to protect the cotton trade, southerners consented to a provision requiring only a majority vote on navigation laws, the national government was given the authority to regulate foreign commerce, and the Senate was required to cast a two-thirds vote to pass treaties. The southern states, which made up more than one-third of the new union at that time, would be able to check the Senate's power. The delegates from these states also believed that there would be enough slaves in the United States by 1808 to supply the labor needed for southern agriculture.

Another sticking point concerning slavery remained: how to determine state population for purposes of representation in the House of Representatives. Slaves could not vote, but the southern states wanted them included for purposes of determining population. After considerable dissension, it was decided that population for purposes of representation and the apportionment of direct taxes would be calculated by adding the "whole Number of Free Persons" to "three-fifths of all other Persons." "All other Persons" was the delegates' way of referring to slaves. Known as the **Three-Fifths Compromise,** this highly political deal assured that the South would hold 47 percent of the House—

Three-Fifths Compromise
Agreement reached at the Constitutional Convention stipulating that each slave was to be counted as three-fifths of a person for purposes of determining population for representation in the U.S. House of Representatives.

enough to prevent attacks on slavery but not so much as to foster the spread of slavery northward.

Unfinished Business Affecting the Executive Branch

The Framers next turned to fashioning an executive branch. While they agreed on the idea of a one-person executive, they could not settle on the length of the term of office, nor on how the chief executive should be selected. With Shays's Rebellion still fresh in their minds, the delegates feared putting too much power, including selection of a president, into the hands of the lower classes. At the same time, representatives from the smaller states feared that the selection of the chief executive by the legislature would put additional power into the hands of the large states.

Amid these fears, the Committee on Unfinished Portions, whose sole responsibility was to iron out problems and disagreements concerning the office of chief executive, conducted its work. The committee recommended that the presidential term of office be fixed at four years instead of seven, as had earlier been proposed. By choosing not to mention a period of time within which the chief executive would be eligible for reelection, they made it possible for a president to serve more than one term.

The Framers also created the Electoral College. This system gave individual states a key role, because each state would select electors equal to the number of representatives it had in the House and Senate. It was a vague compromise that removed election of the president and vice president from both the Congress and the people and put it in the hands of electors whose method of selection would be left to the states.

In drafting the new Constitution, the Framers also were careful to include a provision for removal of the chief executive. The House of Representatives was given the sole responsibility of investigating and charging a president or vice president with "Treason, Bribery, or other high Crimes and Misdemeanors." A majority vote would result in issuing articles of impeachment against the president or vice president. The Senate was given sole responsibility to try the chief executive or vice president on the charges issued by the House. A two-thirds vote of the Senate was required to convict and remove the president or vice president from office.

THE U.S. CONSTITUTION

AFTER THE COMPROMISE on the presidency, work proceeded quickly on the remaining resolutions of the **Constitution.** The Preamble to the Constitution, the last section to be drafted, contains

Constitution
The document establishing the structure, functions, and limitations of the U.S. government.

exceptionally powerful language that forms the bedrock of American political tradition. Its opening line, "We the People of the United States," boldly proclaimed that a loose confederation of independent states no longer existed. Instead, there was but one American people and nation.

The simple phrase "We the People" ended, at least for the time being, the question of whence the government derived its power: it came directly from the people, not from the states. The next phrase of the Constitution explained the need for the new outline of government: "in Order to form a more perfect Union" indirectly acknowledged the weaknesses of the Articles of Confederation in governing a growing nation. Then, the optimistic goals of the Framers for the new nation were set out: to "establish Justice, insure domestic Tranquility, provide for the common defence, promote the general Welfare, and secure the Blessings of Liberty to ourselves and our Posterity"; followed by the formal creation of a new government: "do ordain and establish this Constitution for the United States of America." The Constitution was approved by the delegates from all twelve states in attendance on September 17, 1787.

The Basic Principles of the Constitution

The proposed structure of the new national government owed much to the writings of John Locke and the French political philosopher Montesquieu (1689–1755), who advocated distinct functions for each branch of government, called separation of powers, with a system of checks and balances between each branch. The Constitution's concern with the distribution of power between states and the national government reveals the heavy influence of political philosophers, as well as the colonists' experience under the Articles of Confederation.[9] (Table 2.1 compares the major features of the Articles of Confederation and the Constitution.)

federal system
Plan of government created in the U.S. Constitution in which power is divided between the national government and the state governments and in which independent states are bound together under one national government.

separation of powers
A way of dividing power among three branches of government in which members of the House of Representatives, members of the Senate, the president, and the federal courts are selected by and responsible to different constituencies.

Federalism.   The question before and during the Convention was how much power states would give up to the national government. Given the nation's experiences under the Articles of Confederation, the Framers believed that a strong national government was necessary for the new nation's survival. However, they were reluctant to create a powerful government after the model of Britain, the country from which they had just won their independence. Instead, they employed a **federal system,** which divides the power of government between a strong national government and the individual states.

Separation of Powers.   **Separation of powers** is simply a way of parceling out power among the three branches of government. Its three key features are:

TABLE 2.1   Comparing the Articles of Confederation and the Constitution

The United States has operated under two constitutions. The first, the Articles of Confederation, was in effect from March 1, 1781, when Maryland ratified it. The second, the Constitution, replaced the Articles when it was ratified by New Hampshire on June 21, 1788. The two documents have much in common—they were established by the same people (sometimes literally the same exact people, though mostly just in terms of contemporaries). But, they differ more than they resemble each other, when one looks at the details.

	Articles	*Constitution*
Formal name of the nation	The United States of America	Not specified, but referred to in the Preamble as "the United States of America"
Legislature	Unicameral, called Congress	Bicameral, called Congress, divided into the House of Representatives and the Senate
Members of Congress	Between two and seven members per state	Two senators per state, representatives apportioned according to population of each state
Voting in Congress	One vote per state	One vote per representative or senator
Appointment of members	All appointed by state legislatures, in the manner each legislature directed	Representatives elected by popular vote; senators appointed by state legislatures
Term of legislative office	One year	Two years for representatives, six for senators
Term limit for legislative office	No more than three out of every six years	None
Congressional pay	Paid by states	Paid by the federal government
When Congress is not in session	A Committee of States had the full powers of Congress	The President of the United States can call for Congress to assemble
Chair of legislature	President of Congress	Speaker of the House of Representatives; vice president is president of the Senate
Executive	None	President
National judiciary	Maritime judiciary established—other courts left to states	Federal judiciary established, including Supreme Court
Adjudicator of disputes between states	Congress	Supreme Court
New states	Admitted upon agreement of nine states (special exemption provided for Canada)	Admitted upon agreement of Congress
Amendment	When agreed upon by all states	When agreed upon by three-fourths of the states
Navy	Congress authorized to build a navy; states authorized to equip warships to counter piracy	Congress authorized to build a navy; states not allowed to keep ships of war
Army	Congress to decide on size of force and to requisition troops from each state according to population	Congress authorized to raise and support armies
Power to coin money	United States and the states	United States only
Ex post facto laws	Not forbidden	Forbidden of both the states and the Congress
Bills of attainder	Not forbidden	Forbidden of both the states and the Congress
Taxes	Apportioned by Congress, collected by the states	Laid and collected by Congress
Ratification	Unanimous consent required	Consent of nine states required

1. Three distinct branches of government: the legislative, the executive, and the judicial.

2. Three separately staffed branches of government to exercise these functions.

3. Constitutional equality and independence of each branch.

As illustrated in Figure 2.1, the Framers were careful to create a system in which law-making, law-enforcing, and law-interpreting functions were assigned to independent branches of government. On the national level, only the legislature has the authority to make laws; the chief executive enforces laws; and the judiciary interprets them. Moreover, initially, members of the House of Representatives, members of the Senate, the president, and members of the federal courts were selected by and were therefore responsible to different constituencies.

FIGURE 2.1   Separation of Powers and Checks and Balances Illustrated. ■

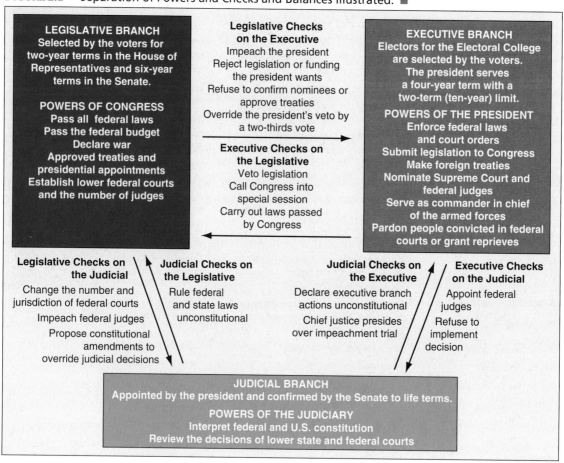

The Framers could not have foreseen the intermingling of governmental functions that has since evolved. Locke, in fact, cautioned against giving a legislature the ability to delegate its powers. In Article I of the Constitution, the legislative power is vested in the Congress. But, the president is also given legislative powers via his ability to veto legislation, and the judiciary has the power to clarify the implementation of legislation through judicial review, a process cemented in 1803 by the Supreme Court decision in *Marbury* v. *Madison*. Therefore, instead of a pure system of separation of powers, a symbiotic, or interdependent, relationship among the three branches of government has existed from the beginning. Or, as one scholar has explained, there are "separated institutions sharing powers."[10]

Checks and Balances.   The separation of powers among the three branches of the national government is not complete. According to Montesquieu and the Framers, the powers of each branch (as well as the two houses of the national legislature and between the states and the national government) could be used to check the powers of the other two branches of government. The power of each branch of government is checked, or limited, and balanced because the legislative, executive, and judicial branches share some authority and no branch has exclusive domain over any single activity. The creation of this system of **checks and balances** allowed the Framers to minimize the threat of tyranny from any one branch. Thus, for almost every power granted to one branch, an equal control was established in the other two branches. The Congress, for example, could check the power of the president and the Supreme Court, and so on, carefully creating balance among the three branches.

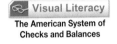

Visual Literacy

The American System of Checks and Balances

checks and balances
A governmental structure that gives each of the three branches of government some degree of oversight and control over the actions of the others.

The Articles of the Constitution

The document finally signed by the Framers condensed numerous resolutions into a Preamble and seven separate articles. The first three articles established the three branches of government, defined their internal operations, and clarified their relationships with one another. The four remaining articles defined the relationships among the states, declared national law to be supreme, and set out methods of amending the Constitution.

Article I: The Legislative Branch.   Article I vests all legislative powers in the Congress and establishes a bicameral legislature, consisting of the Senate and the House of Representatives. It sets out the qualifications for holding office in each house, the terms of office, methods of selection of representatives and senators, and the system of apportionment among the states to determine membership in the House of Representatives. Operating procedures and the formal officers of each house also are described in Article I.

enumerated powers
Seventeen specific powers granted to Congress under Article I, section 8, of the U.S. Constitution; these powers include taxation, coinage of money, regulation of commerce, and the authority to provide for a national defense.

necessary and proper clause
The final paragraph of Article I, section 8, of the U.S. Constitution, which gives Congress the authority to pass all laws "necessary and proper" to carry out the enumerated powers specified in the Constitution; also called the "elastic" clause.

implied powers
A power derived from an enumerated power and the necessary and proper clause. These powers are not stated specifically but are considered to be reasonably implied through the exercise of delegated powers.

One of the most important sections of Article I is section 8. It carefully lists the powers the Framers wished the new Congress to possess. These specified or **enumerated powers** contain many key provisions that had been denied to the Continental Congress under the Articles of Confederation.

Today, Congress often enacts legislation that no specific clause of Article I, section 8, appears to authorize. These laws are justified by a reference to a particular power and a final, general clause of Article I, section 8, known as the **necessary and proper clause.** This clause authorizes Congress to "make all Laws which shall be necessary and proper for carrying into Execution the foregoing Powers." Often referred to as the elastic clause, the necessary and proper clause has been a source of tremendous congressional activity never anticipated by the Framers, as definitions of "necessary" and "proper" have been stretched to accommodate changing needs and times. The clause is the basis for the **implied powers** that Congress uses to execute its other powers.

Article II: The Executive Branch.   Article II vests the executive power, that is, the authority to execute the laws of the nation, in a president of the United States. Section 1 sets the president's term of office at four years and explains the Electoral College. It also states the qualifications for office and describes a mechanism to replace the president in case of death, disability, or removal.

The powers and duties of the president are set out in Article II, section 3. Among the most important of these are the president's role as commander in chief of the armed forces, the authority to make treaties with the consent of the Senate, and the authority to "appoint Ambassadors, other public Ministers and Consuls, the Judges of the supreme Court, and all other Officers of the United States." Other sections of Article II instruct the president to report directly to Congress "from time to time," in what has come to be known as the State of the Union Address. Section 4 provides the mechanism for removal of the president, vice president, and other officers.

Article III: The Judicial Branch.   Article III establishes a Supreme Court and defines its jurisdiction. During the Philadelphia convention, the small and large states differed significantly as to the desirability of an independent judiciary and on the role of state courts in the national court system. The smaller states feared that a strong unelected judiciary would trample on their liberties. In compromise, Congress was permitted, but not required, to establish lower national courts. Thus, state courts and the national court system would exist side by side with distinct areas of authority. Federal courts were given authority to decide cases arising under federal law. The Supreme Court was also given the power to settle disputes between states, or between a state and the national government.

Although some delegates to the convention urged that the president be allowed to remove federal judges, ultimately judges were given appointments for life, presuming "good behavior." And, their salaries, like the president's, cannot be lowered while they hold office. This provision was adopted to ensure that the legislature did not attempt to punish the Supreme Court or any other judges for unpopular decisions.

Articles IV Through VII. The remainder of the articles in the Constitution attempted to anticipate problems that might occur in the operation of the new national government as well as its relations to the states. Article IV begins with what is called the full faith and credit clause, which mandates that states honor the laws and judicial proceedings of the other states. Article IV also includes the mechanisms for admitting new states to the union.

Article V specifies how amendments can be added to the Constitution. The Bill of Rights, which added ten amendments to the Constitution in 1791, was one of the first items of business when the First Congress met in 1789.

Article VI contains the supremacy clause, which asserts the basic primacy of the Constitution and national law over state laws and constitutions. The **supremacy clause** provides that the "Constitution, and the laws of the United States" as well as all treaties, are to be the supreme law of the land. Because of the supremacy clause, any legitimate exercise of national power supersedes any state laws or action, in a process that is called preemption. Without the supremacy clause and the federal court's ability to invoke it, the national government would have little actual enforceable power; thus, many commentators call the supremacy clause the linchpin of the entire federal system.

Article VI also specifies that no religious test shall be required for holding any office. This mandate strengthens the separation of church and state guarantee that was quickly added to the Constitution when the First Amendment was ratified.

The seventh and final article of the Constitution concerns the procedures for ratification of the new Constitution. Nine of the thirteen states would have to agree to, or ratify, its new provisions before it would become the supreme law of the land. (For a discussion of the features common to most constitutions, see Global Perspective: Writing a Constitution.)

supremacy clause
Portion of Article VI of the U.S. Constitution mandating that national law is supreme to (that is, supersedes) all other laws passed by the states or by any other subdivision of government.

Comparing Constitutions

The Characteristics and Motives of the Framers

Fifty-five of the seventy-four delegates ultimately chosen by their state legislatures to attend the Constitutional Convention labored

WRITING A CONSTITUTION: HOW DO WE COMPARE?

There is no such thing as a one-size-fits-all constitution. National constitutions are products of political crises. The American Constitution was written following the Revolutionary War and the failure of the Articles of Confederation to provide a workable governing structure. South Africa wrote its 1996 constitution after the struggle to end apartheid. Russia wrote its 1993 constitution following the breakup of the Soviet Union and the fall of communism. In the Middle East, Iran created a new constitution in 1979 after the shah was forced from power. Similarly, with the end of Saddam Hussein's regime, Iraq is beginning to put a new constitution into place.

The content of these constitutions reflects not only the struggles of the moment but also the country's historical experiences and the influence of ideas about the meaning of good government and the proper relationship between those in power and those whom they rule. These influences often can pull constitutions into different directions, requiring political compromises and creating lengthy and complex documents. The Russian Constitution of 1993 contained 146 articles; as of 2002, the Mexican Constitution had 123 articles.

In spite of these variations, four important features are common to all constitutions. First, most contain a *preamble* that sets forward the principles on which the government is to operate. Although this section often contains a great deal of flowery rhetoric, it also tells us much about the country.

Second, constitutions specify the *organization of the government*. Whereas the United States has a system of checks and balances among the president, Congress, and the courts, the French and Russian constitutions created strong presidents whose powers exceed those of the other two branches.

Third, constitutions *specify individual rights*. The U.S. Constitution does this through its Bill of Rights and other amendments. In some cases, references may also be added to government obligations to citizens. Brazil's 1988 constitution pledged the government to ensure citizens the rights to work and to receive medical care.

Fourth, constitutions provide a means for making *amendments*. In general terms, we can distinguish between rigid constitutional frameworks that are difficult to change and flexible ones. Each has its advantages. Rigid frameworks provide predictability and ensure that if an extremist group achieves power it cannot easily change the rules. Flexible frameworks allow constitutions to remain relevant to the changing requirements of ruling over societies and the changing definitions of human rights. In Canada, both houses of Parliament have to approve an amendment, as do two-thirds of the provinces containing at least one-half the population of the country. In Japan, a two-thirds majority in both houses of the parliament must approve the amendment, and then a majority of the population must do so in a referendum.

We should note that not all constitutions are written. In Great Britain, the constitution is collectively made up of key documents such as the Magna Carta and acts of Parliament. Israeli leaders tried to write a constitution in 1949 shortly after their country's formation but gave up because of deep conflicts between religious and secular groups. Like Great Britain, Israel's constitution is a series of basic laws. Saudi Arabia's constitution is not a written one but a series of royal decrees.

Questions

1. If you were writing a constitution today, what would be the most important influences on your decisions about what you will include?
2. How important is it that constitutions be written?

long and hard that hot summer to produce a final document. Owing to the high stakes of their action, all of the convention's work was conducted behind closed doors. George Washington of Virginia, who was unanimously elected the convention's presiding officer, cautioned delegates to not even reveal details of the convention to their family members.

All of the delegates to the Constitutional Convention were men; hence, they often are referred to as the "Founding Fathers." Most of them were quite young; many were in their twenties and thirties, and only one—Benjamin Franklin, at eighty-one—was very old. (See Analyzing Visuals: Who Were the Framers?) Here, we generally refer to the delegates as the Framers, because their work provided the framework for our new government. The Framers brought with them a vast amount of political, educational, legal, and business experience. It is clear that they were an exceptional lot who ultimately produced a brilliant constitution, or document establishing the structure, functions, and limitations of a government.

However, debate about the Framers' motives filled the air during the ratification struggle and has provided grist for the mill of historians and political scientists over the years. In his *Economic Interpretation of the Constitution of the United States* (1913), Charles A. Beard argued that the 1780s were a critical period not for the nation as a whole, but rather for businessmen who feared that a weak, decentralized government could harm their economic interests.[11] Beard argued that the merchants wanted a strong national government to promote industry and trade, to protect private property, and most importantly, to ensure payment of the public debt—much of which was owed to them.

By the 1950s, this view had fallen into disfavor when other historians were unable to find direct links between wealth and the Framers' motives for establishing the Constitution, and others faulted Beard's failure to consider the impact of religion and individual views about government.[12] In the 1960s, however, another group of historians began to argue that social and economic factors were important motives for supporting the Constitution. In *The Anti-Federalists* (1961), Jackson Turner Main posited that while the Constitution's supporters might not have been the united group of creditors suggested by Beard, they were wealthier, came from higher social strata, and had greater concern for maintaining the prevailing social order than the general public.[13]

In 1969, Gordon S. Wood's *The Creation of the American Republic* resurrected this debate. Wood deemphasized economics to argue that major social divisions explained different groups' support for (or opposition to) the new Constitution. He concluded that the Framers were representatives of a class that favored order and stability over some of the more radical ideas that had inspired the American Revolutionary War and break with Britain.[14]

Analyzing Visuals

WHO WERE THE FRAMERS?

Who were the Framers of the U.S. Constitution? Of the fifty-five delegates who attended some portion of the Philadelphia meetings, seventeen were slaveholders who owned approximately 1,400 slaves. (George Washington, George Mason, and John Rutledge held the greatest number of slaves at the time of the convention.) In terms of education, thirty-one went to college; twenty-four did not. Most of those who did not attend college were trained as business, legal, and printing apprentices. Seven delegates signed both the U.S. Constitution and the Declaration of Independence. After studying the graph and the material on writing and signing the Constitution in this chapter, answer the following critical thinking questions: What is the relationship, if any, between the number of a state's delegates who served in the Continental Congresses and the number of the state's signers of the Constitution? What is the relationship, if any, between a state's population (shown in parentheses in the graph) and the number of the state's signers of the U.S. Constitution? What does that suggest about the conflict between the large states and small states? What is the relationship, if any, between the number of a state's delegates who were slaveholders and the number of the state's signers of the U.S. Constitution? What does that suggest about the conflicts over slavery at the convention?

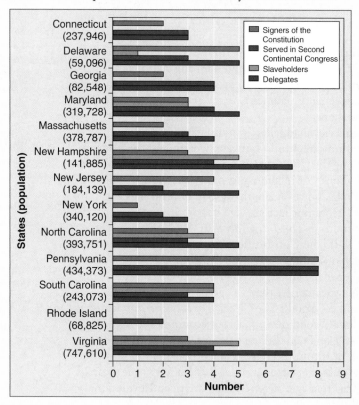

Sources: Clinton Rossiter, *The Grand Convention* (New York: Macmillan, 1966); National Archives and Records Administration, "The Founding Fathers: A Brief Overview," http://www.archives.gov/exhibit_hall/charters_of_freedom/constitution/founding_fathers_overview.html.

THE DRIVE FOR RATIFICATION

THE SECOND CONTINENTAL CONGRESS immediately accepted the work of the convention delegates and forwarded the proposed Constitution to the states for their vote. It was by no means certain that the new Constitution would be adopted. From the fall of 1787 to the summer of 1788, the proposed Constitution was debated hotly around the nation.

Federalists Versus Anti-Federalists

Almost as soon as the ink was dry on the last signature to the Constitution, those who favored the new strong national government chose to call themselves **Federalists.** They were well aware that many still generally opposed the notion of a strong national government. Thus, they did not want to risk being labeled "nationalists." They tried to get the upper hand in the debate by nicknaming their opponents **Anti-Federalists.** Those put in the latter category insisted that they were instead "Federal Republicans" who believed in a federal system. As noted in Table 2.2, Anti-Federalists argued that they simply wanted to protect state governments from the tyranny of a too-powerful national government.[15]

Federalists and Anti-Federalists participated in the mass meetings that were held in state legislatures to discuss the pros and cons of the new plan. Tempers ran high at public meetings, where differences between the opposing groups were highlighted. Fervent debates, often written under pseudonyms such as "Caesar" or "Constant Reader," were published in newspapers, which played a powerful role in the adoption process.

Federalists
Those who favored a stronger national government and supported the proposed U.S. Constitution; later became the first U.S. political party.

Anti-Federalists
Those who favored strong state governments and a weak national government; opposed the ratification of the U.S. Constitution.

TABLE 2.2	Federalists and Anti-Federalists Compared	
	Federalists	*Anti-Federalists*
Who were they?	Property owners, landed rich, merchants of Northeast and Middle Atlantic states.	Small farmers, shopkeepers, laborers.
Political philosophy	Elitist: saw themselves and those of their class as most fit to govern (others were to be governed).	Believed in the decency of the common man and in participatory democracy; viewed elites as corrupt; sought greater protection of individual rights.
Type of government favored	Powerful central government; two-house legislature; upper house (six-year term) further removed from the people, whom they distrusted.	Wanted stronger state governments (closer to the people) at the expense of the powers of the national government; sought smaller electoral districts, frequent elections, referendum and recall, and a large unicameral legislature to provide for greater class and occupational representation.
Alliances	Pro-British, Anti-French	Anti-British, Pro-French

The Federalist Papers

One name stood out from all the rest: "Publius" (Latin for "the people"). Between October 1787 and May 1788, eighty-five articles written under that pen name routinely appeared in newspapers in New York, a state where ratification was in doubt. Most were written by Alexander Hamilton and James Madison. Hamilton, a young, fiery New Yorker born in the British West Indies, wrote fifty-one; Madison, a Virginian who later served as the fourth president, wrote twenty-six; jointly they penned another three. John Jay, also of New York and later the first chief justice of the United States, wrote five of the pieces. These eighty-five essays became known as **The Federalist Papers.**

The Federalist Papers
A series of eighty-five political papers written by John Jay, Alexander Hamilton, and James Madison in support of ratification of the U.S. Constitution.

Forced on the defensive, the Anti-Federalists responded to *The Federalist Papers* with their own series of letters written under the pen names "Brutus" and "Cato," two ancient Romans famous for their intolerance of tyranny. These letters undertook a line-by-line critique of the Constitution.

Anti-Federalists argued that a strong central government would render the states powerless.[16] They stressed the strengths the government had been granted under the Articles of Confederation and argued that these Articles, not the proposed Constitution, created a true federal system. Moreover, they argued that the strong national government would tax heavily, that the Supreme Court would overwhelm the states by invalidating state laws, and that the president eventually would have too much power as commander in chief of a large and powerful army.[17]

In particular, the Anti-Federalists feared the power of the national government to run roughshod over the liberties of the people. They proposed that the taxing power of Congress be limited, that the executive be curbed by a council, that the military consist of state militias rather than a national force, and that the jurisdiction of the Supreme Court be limited to prevent it from reviewing and potentially overturning the decisions of state courts. But, their most effective argument concerned the absence of a bill of rights in the Constitution. James Madison answered these criticisms in *Federalist Nos. 10* and *51*. (The texts of these two essays are printed in Appendices III and IV.)

In *Federalist No. 10*, Madison pointed out that the voters would not always succeed in electing "enlightened statesmen" as their representatives. The greatest threat to individual liberties would therefore come from factions within the government that might place narrow interests above broader national interests and the rights of citizens. While recognizing that no form of government could protect the country from unscrupulous politicians, Madison argued that the organization of the new government would minimize the effects of political factions. The great advantage of a federal system, Madison maintained, was that it created the "happy combination" of a national government too large to be controlled by any single faction, and several state governments that would be smaller and more responsive to local needs. Moreover, he argued in *Federalist No. 51* that the proposed federal government's separation of

You Are James Madison

Photos courtesy: left, Metropolitan Museum of Art, Gift of Henry G. Marquand, 1881 (81.11) © 1987, Metropolitan Museum of Art; center, Colonial Williamsburg Foundation; right, Bettmann/CORBIS

■ Alexander Hamilton (left), James Madison (center), and John Jay (right) were important early Federalist leaders. Jay wrote five of *The Federalist Papers* and Madison and Hamilton wrote the rest. Madison served in the House of Representatives (1789–1797) and as secretary of state in the Jefferson administration (1801–1808). In 1808, he was elected fourth president of the United States and served two terms (1809–1817). Hamilton became the first secretary of the treasury (1789–1795). He was killed in 1804 in a duel with Vice President Aaron Burr, who was angered by Hamilton's negative comments about his character. Jay became the first chief justice of the United States (1789–1795) and negotiated the Jay Treaty with Great Britain in 1794. He then served as governor of New York from 1795 to 1801.

powers would prohibit any one branch from either dominating the national government or violating the rights of citizens.

Ratifying the Constitution

Debate continued in the thirteen states as votes were taken from December 1787 to June 1788, in accordance with the ratifying process laid out in Article VII of the proposed Constitution. Two small states, Delaware and New Jersey, voted to ratify before the large states could rethink the notion of equal representation of the states in the Senate. Pennsylvania, where Federalists were well organized, was also one of the first three states to ratify. New Hampshire became the crucial ninth state to ratify on June 21, 1788. This action marked the beginning of a new nation. But, New York and Virginia, which at that time accounted for more than 40 percent of the new nation's population, had not yet ratified the Constitution. Thus, the practical future of the new nation remained in doubt.

Hamilton in New York and Madison in Virginia worked feverishly to convince delegates to their state conventions to vote for the new government. In New York, sentiment against the Constitution was high. In Albany, fighting resulting in injuries and death broke out over ratification. When news of Virginia's acceptance of the Constitution reached the New York convention, Hamilton finally was able to convince a majority of those present to follow suit by a narrow margin of three votes.

A STUDENT'S REVENGE: THE TWENTY-SEVENTH (MADISON) AMENDMENT

On June 8, 1789, in a speech before the House of Representatives, James Madison stated: "there is seeming impropriety in leaving any set of men without controul to put their hand into the public coffers, to take out money to put into their pockets.... I have gone therefore so far as to fix it, that no law, varying the compensation, shall operate until there is a change in the legislation."

When Madison proposed that any proposed salary increase for members of Congress could not take effect until the next session of Congress, he had no way of knowing that more than two centuries would pass before his plan, now the Twenty-Seventh Amendment, would become an official part of the Constitution. In fact, Madison deemed it worthy of addition only because the conventions of three states (Virginia, New York, and North Carolina) demanded that it be included.

By 1791, when the Bill of Rights was added to the Constitution, only six states had ratified Madison's amendment, and it seemed destined to fade into obscurity. In 1982, however, Gregory Watson, a sophomore majoring in economics at the University of Texas–Austin, discovered the unratified compensation amendment while looking for a paper topic for an American government class. Intrigued, Watson wrote a paper arguing that the proposed amendment was still viable because it had no internal time limit and, therefore, should still be ratified. Watson received a C on the paper.

Despite his grade, Watson began a ten-year, $6,000 self-financed crusade to renew interest in the compensation amendment. Watson and his allies reasoned that the amendment should be revived because of the public's growing anger with the fact that members of Congress had sought to

Photo courtesy: Ziggy Kaluzny/People Magazine Syndication

Gregory Watson with a document that contains the first ten amendments to the Constitution, as well as the compensation amendment ("Article the second: No law varying the compensation for the services of the Senators and Representatives shall take effect until an election of Representatives shall have intervened"), which finally was ratified in 1992 as the Twenty-Seventh Amendment.

raise their salaries without going on the record as having done so. Watson's perseverance paid off.

On May 7, 1992, the amendment was ratified by the requisite thirty-eight states. On May 18, the United States archivist certified that the amendment was part of the Constitution, a decision that was overwhelmingly confirmed by the House of Representatives on May 19 and by the Senate on May 20. At the same time that the Senate approved the Twenty-Seventh Amendment, it also took action to ensure that a similar situation would never occur by declaring "dead" four other amendments.

Sources: Fordham Law Review (December 1992): 497–539, and Anne Marie Kilday, "Amendment Expert Agrees with Congressional Pay Ruling," *Dallas Morning News* (February 14, 1993): 13A.

TABLE 2.3	The Bill of Rights
First Amendment	Freedom of religion, speech, press, and assembly
Second Amendment	The right to bear arms
Third Amendment	Prohibition against quartering of troops in private homes
Fourth Amendment	Prohibition against unreasonable searches and seizures
Fifth Amendment	Rights guaranteed to the accused: requirement for grand jury indictment; protections against double jeopardy, self-incrimination; due process guaranteed
Sixth Amendment	Right to a speedy and public trial before an impartial jury, to cross-examine witnesses, and to have counsel
Seventh Amendment	Right to a trial by jury in civil suits
Eighth Amendment	Prohibition against bail fines, and cruel and unusual punishment
Ninth Amendment	Rights not listed in the Constitution retained by the people
Tenth Amendment	States or people reserve those powers not denied to them by the Constitution or delegated to the national government

Both states also recommended the addition of a series of structural amendments, and a bill of rights.

Adding a Bill of Rights

Once the Constitution was ratified, elections were held. When Congress convened, it immediately sent a set of amendments to the states for their ratification. An amendment authorizing the enlargement of the House of Representatives and another to prevent members of the House from raising their own salaries failed to garner favorable votes in the necessary three-fourths of the states. (See On Campus: A Student's Revenge: The Twenty-Seventh [Madison] Amendment.) The remaining ten amendments, known as the **Bill of Rights,** were ratified by 1791 in accordance with the procedures set out in the Constitution. (For the key features of each amendment, see Table 2.3.) Sought by Anti-Federalists as a protection for individual liberties, they offered numerous specific limitations on the national government's ability to interfere with a wide variety of personal liberties, some of which were already guaranteed by many state constitutions (see chapters 4 and 5).

Bill of Rights
The first ten amendments to the U.S. Constitution.

METHODS OF AMENDING THE CONSTITUTION

THE BILL OF RIGHTS was the first set of amendments to the Constitution. Its quick addition owed its success to a national recognition that the Constitution needed more than what the Framers had been able to agree on. In general, however, the Framers fashioned an amending process that would be relatively immune to the whims of the people. The formal

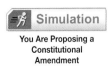

Simulation

You Are Proposing a Constitutional Amendment

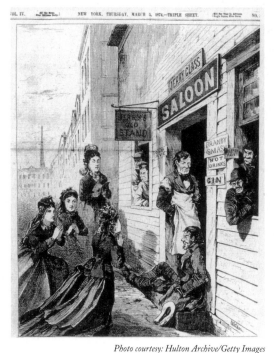

Photo courtesy: Hulton Archive/Getty Images

■ For all its moral foundation in groups such as the Women's Christian Temperance Union (WCTU), whose members invaded bars to protest the sale of alcoholic beverages, the Eighteenth (Prohibition) Amendment was a disaster. Among its side effects was the rise of powerful crime organizations responsible for illegal sales of alcoholic beverages. Once proposed, it took only ten months to ratify the Twenty-First Amendment, which repealed the Prohibition Amendment.

Timeline

The History of Constitutional Amendments

amendment process is a slow one, designed to ensure that the Constitution is not impulsively amended.

Formal Methods of Amending the Constitution

Article V of the Constitution creates a two-stage amendment process: proposal and ratification.[18] The Constitution specifies two ways to accomplish each stage. As illustrated in Figure 2.2, amendments to the Constitution can be proposed by: (1) a vote of two-thirds of the members in both houses of Congress; or, (2) a vote of two-thirds of the state legislatures specifically requesting Congress to call a national convention to propose amendments. The second method has never been used. However, it has served as a fairly effective threat, forcing Congress to consider amendments that might otherwise never have been debated. (The Living Constitution feature discusses the amendment process set out in Article V.)

The ratification process is fairly straightforward. When Congress votes to propose an amendment, the Constitution specifies that the ratification process must occur in one of two ways: (1) a favorable vote in three-fourths of the state legislatures; or, (2) a favorable vote in specially called ratifying conventions in three-fourths of the states.

The Constitution itself was ratified by the favorable vote of nine states in specially called ratifying conventions. The Framers feared that the power of special interests in state legislatures would prevent a positive vote on the new Constitution. Since ratification of the Constitution, however, only one ratifying convention has been called. This occurred when the Twenty-First Amendment, which repealed the Eighteenth (Prohibition) Amendment, was ratified in 1933. Members of Congress correctly predicted that the move to repeal the Eighteenth Amendment would encounter opposition in the statehouses, which were largely controlled by conservative rural interests.

The intensity of efforts to amend the Constitution has varied considerably, depending on the nature of the change proposed. Whereas the Twenty-First Amendment took only ten months to ratify, an equal rights amendment (ERA) was introduced in every session of Congress from 1923 until 1972, when Congress finally voted favorably for it. Even then, years of lobbying by women's groups were insufficient to garner necessary state support. By 1982, the congressionally mandated date for ratification, only thirty-five states—three short of the number required—had

The Living Constitution

The Congress, whenever two thirds of both houses shall deem it necessary, shall propose amendments to this Constitution, or, on the application of the legislatures of two thirds of the several states, shall call a convention for proposing amendments, which, in either case, shall be valid to all intents and purposes, as part of this Constitution, when ratified by the legislatures of three fourths of the several states, or by conventions in three fourths thereof, as the one or the other mode of ratification may be proposed by the Congress.

—Article V

With this article, the Framers acknowledged the potential need to change or amend the Constitution. This article provides for two methods to propose amendments: by a two-thirds vote of both houses of Congress or by a two-thirds vote of the state legislatures. It also specifies two alternative methods of ratification of proposed amendments: by a three-quarters vote of the state legislatures, or by a similar vote in state ratifying conventions.

During the Constitutional Convention in Philadelphia, the Framers were divided as to how frequently or how easily the Constitution was to be amended. The original suggestion was to allow the document to be amended "when soever it shall seem necessary." The Committee on Detail wanted to entrust this authority to the state legislatures; however, others feared that it would give states too much power. James Madison alleviated these fears by suggesting that both Congress and the states have a role in the process.

While it is not unusual to have over one hundred potential amendments introduced in each session of Congress, some, such as banning gay marriage, stopping flag burning, and allowing naturalized citizens to vote are those most often mentioned of late.

However, the failed battles for the Equal Rights Amendment as well as other amendments, including one to prohibit child labor and another to grant statehood to the District of Columbia, underscore how difficult it is to amend the Constitution. Thus, the U.S. Constitution rarely has been amended.

FIGURE 2.2   Methods of Amending the Constitution. ■

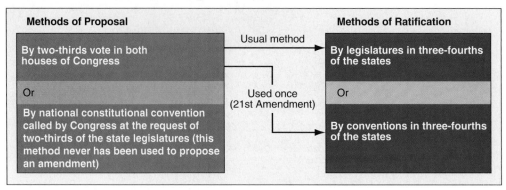

voted favorably on the amendment.[19] More recently, an amendment has been proposed to remove the constitutional requirement that the president of the United States be a natural-born citizen (see Join the Debate: The "Equal Opportunity to Govern" Amendment). Another proposed amendment would restrict marriage to a union between only one man and one woman, thus making same-sex marriage unconstitutional (see Politics Now: The Marriage Amendment).

Informal Methods of Amending the Constitution

The formal amendment process is not the only way that the Constitution has been changed over time. Judicial interpretation and cultural and social change also have had a major impact on the way the Constitution has evolved.

Judicial Interpretation.   As early as 1803, under the leadership of Chief Justice John Marshall, in *Marbury* v. *Madison* the Supreme Court declared that the federal courts had the power to nullify acts of the nation's government when they were found to be in conflict with the Constitution.[20] Over the years, this check on the other branches of government and on the states has increased the authority of the Court and significantly altered the meaning of various provisions of the Constitution, a fact that prompted Woodrow Wilson to call the Supreme Court "a constitutional convention in continuous session." (More detail on the Supreme Court's role in interpreting the Constitution is found in chapters 3, 5, 6, and 10 especially.)

Today, some analysts argue that the original intent of the Framers, as evidenced in *The Federalist Papers* as well as in private notes taken by James Madison at the Constitutional Convention, should govern judicial interpretation of the Constitution.[21] Others argue that the Framers knew that a changing society needed an elastic, flexible document that could conform to the ages.[22] In all likelihood, the vagueness of the document

THE MARRIAGE AMENDMENT

"The union of a man and a woman is the most enduring human institution, honored and encouraged in all cultures and by every religious faith," so spoke President George W. Bush in announcing his initial support of congressional action to amend the Constitution to ban same-sex marriages. He did not endorse a specific amendment, but instead called upon Congress to endorse an amendment in the wake of the specter of the thousands of gay marriages that were conducted in San Francisco, California (and later ruled invalid by that state's Supreme Court).

Members of the House and Senate took up the president's call. In May 2003, Representative Marilyn Musgrave (R–CO) and five co-sponsors introduced a resolution to amend the Constitution to define marriage as a union between a man and a woman. A companion resolution was introduced in the Senate on November 2003 by Senator Wayne Allard (R–CO).

The 2003 resolution calling for a constitutional amendment introduced by Musgrave and Allard read:

> Marriage in the United States shall consist only of the union of a man and a woman. Neither this Constitution nor the Constitution of any state, **nor state or federal law,** shall be construed to require that marital status or the legal incidents thereof be conferred upon **unmarried couples or groups.**

The original proposal went nowhere in Congress, but same-sex couples continued to make progress toward legalized marriage in some states, including Massachusetts. Thus, many members urged the introduction of a new Federal Marriage Amendment. In September 2004, this bill was introduced. Some modifications were made, and the new amendment read:

> Marriage in the United States shall consist only of the union of a man and a woman. Neither this Constitution nor the Constitution of any **State,** shall be construed to require that marriage or the legal incidents

thereof be conferred upon **any union other that the union of a man and a woman.**

Proponents of the new amendment, whose key changes are highlighted above in boldface, moved quickly for a vote as the president of the Human Rights Campaign, the largest gay rights group in the United States, complained that "This is an attempt to change the Constitution from a vessel for freedom to a tool of discrimination. For more than 200 years, the Constitution has been amended to expand individual rights, not restrict them. No matter how you word it, the amendment discriminates against millions of Americans."[a]

The HRC campaign largely fell on deaf ears in both Houses. In the Senate, the amendment was killed for the 108th session in July when a procedural vote to get the resolution to the floor failed. The White House issued a statement noting the president's "disappointment," and urged the House to take up the measure, which it did a few days later. The resolution did come to a floor vote there, but it failed to reach the required 2/3 required on a vote of 227–186.

Although the move for an amendment failed, its backers were heartened by the eleven states, including Ohio and Michigan, that passed constitutional amendments banning same-sex marriage, domestic partnerships, and state recognition of nonmarriage cohabitation arrangements. All of the eleven state bans on same-sex marriage passed by significant majorities, which harbingers well for state support of a constitutional amendment should it be sent to the states for their ratification.

1. How do you think change in language from 2003 to 2004 might affect the eventual adoption or failure of the amendment?
2. Historically, issues about marriage have been left to the states. How appropriate do you think it is to alter the Constitution to take authority over marriage away from the states? Can you think of other instances in which authority has been taken away from the states?

[a]HRC, "HRC: Changing the Constitution Can't be Concealed with Tweaks and Maneuvering," March 22, 2004 press release.

The "Equal Opportunity to Govern" Amendment

Overview: Article II, section 1, clause 5, of the U.S. Constitution declares: "No person except a natural-born citizen, or a citizen of the United States at the time of the Adoption of this Constitution, shall be eligible to the Office of President." Why would the Framers put such a restriction on the qualifications for president of the United States? In a letter to George Washington, John Jay argued that the duty of commander in chief was too important to be given to a foreign-born person—the potential for conflict of interest, danger, and appearance of impropriety in matters of war and foreign policy should not be left to chance. Charles Pinckney, a South Carolina delegate to the Constitutional Convention, expressed concern that foreign governments would use whatever means necessary to influence international events, and he cited the example of Russia, Prussia, and Austria manipulating the election of Stanislaus II to the Polish throne—only to divide Polish lands among themselves. Furthermore, Pinckney contended that the clause would ensure the "experience" of American politics and principles and guarantee "attachment to the country" so as to further eliminate the potential for mischief and foreign intrigue.

The recent election of Austrian-born Arnold Schwarzenegger and of Canadian-born Jennifer Granholm to the governorships of California and Michigan, respectively, has reopened the debate concerning the citizenship requirement for president. Why shouldn't naturalized citizens be eligible for president? Many naturalized citizens have performed great service to their adopted country; both Henry Kissinger (born in Germany) and Madeleine Albright (born in Czechoslovakia) performed admirably as secretary of state, and over 700 foreign-born Medal of Honor recipients have demonstrated patriotism and the willingness to die for the country they embraced. With these viewpoints in mind, in July 2003, Senator Orrin Hatch (R–UT) introduced the "Equal Opportunity to Govern" amendment to strike the natural-born citizen clause from the Constitution. The proposed amendment takes into account the Framers' fear of foreign intervention and of divided loyalty by requiring twenty years of citizenship before naturalized citizens become eligible to run for presidential office.

Is it just that a nation whose fundamental principle is equality of citizens has a constitutional clause that denies some citizens the presidency? Doesn't the Constitution allow the means to adapt to changes in history and social mores, and further to realize the principle of equality of citizens? On the other hand, shouldn't a president be above the appearance of suspicion and divided loyalty? Doesn't the clause help prevent corruption from foreign sources?

Arguments for the "Equal Opportunity to Govern" Amendment

- **The United States is in part built by its immigrant population and they should have a share in all political offices.** America is a nation of immigrants and many of the original Founders were foreign born, notably Alexander Hamilton, who helped shaped Washington's administration and the executive branch. The Constitution allows for naturalized citizens to attain other high political office such as speaker of the House, senator, or Supreme Court justice; why should naturalized citizens be denied the presidency?

- **The natural-born citizen clause has outlived its usefulness.** The Constitution has proved to be durable and the problems that existed in 1787 either have changed or do not exist in the twenty-first century. The amendment process was created to allow for historical and political change, and ratification of the "Equal Opportunity to Govern" amendment will increase the talent pool for presidential nominees, thus increasing the quality and choice of presidential aspirants for the American people.
- **The natural-born citizen clause is discriminatory.** The clause is "un-American" in that it denies equality of opportunity for all American citizens. Naturalized citizens serve in the military, pay taxes, run for local, state, and federal office, endure the same national hardships and crises, and add to the overall quality of American life; thus, naturalized citizens should have the same rights and privileges as the native born.

Arguments Against the "Equal Opportunity to Govern" Amendment

- **Foreign governments still attempt to have undue influence in American politics.** The Framers were correct in assuming foreign governments attempt to manipulate American politics. For example, in 1999, the Democratic National Committee returned over $600,000 in campaign contributions to Chinese nationals attempting to gain influence with the Clinton administration. The clause was meant to be another institutional safeguard against presidential corruption.

- **Running for president is not a right. The office of the President is an institution designed for republican purposes.** The office of the President is an *institution* of government, as is the ability to run for that office. The Framers strongly believed foreign influence within the U.S. government must be restricted (the language was unanimously adopted by the Constitutional Convention) and thus they did not grant a right to run for presidential office.
- **There is no public movement or outcry to remove this clause from the Constitution.** Many constitutional scholars argue the Constitution should be amended only for pressing reasons, and amendments should be construed with a view to the well-being of future generations. Foreign policy and events are too fluid and too volatile to risk undermining the president's foreign policy and commander in chief authority. Until the American people determine otherwise, the clause should remain.

Questions

1. Is the natural-born clause discriminatory? Does it truly deny equality of citizenship and opportunity? If so, shouldn't the Constitution be amended to realize the principle of equality of citizens?
2. Were the Framers wise in their analysis of foreign influence on American politics? Did they create a true institutional barrier to help prevent corruption by foreign governments?

Selected Readings

Akhil Amar. *America's Constitution: A Guided Tour.* New York: Random House, 2004.

was purposeful. Those in attendance in Philadelphia recognized that they could not agree on everything and that it was wiser to leave interpretation to those who would follow them.

Social and Cultural Change. Even the most far-sighted of those in attendance at the Constitutional Convention could not have anticipated the vast changes that have occurred in the United States. For example, although many were uncomfortable with the Three-Fifths Compromise and others hoped for the abolition of slavery, none could have imagined the status of African Americans today, or that Colin Powell or Condoleezza Rice would serve as the U.S. secretary of state. Likewise, few of the Framers could have anticipated the diverse roles that women would play in American society or that women would serve on the Supreme Court. The Constitution has evolved to accommodate such social and cultural changes. Thus, although there is no specific amendment guaranteeing women equal protection of the law, the federal courts have interpreted the Constitution to prohibit many forms of gender discrimination, thereby recognizing cultural and societal change.

Social change has also caused changes in the way institutions of government act. Thus, as problems such as the Great Depression appeared national in scope, Congress took on more and more power at the expense of the states to solve the economic and social crisis. Yale law professor Bruce Ackerman argues that on certain occasions, extraordinary times call for extraordinary measures such as the New Deal that, in effect, amend the Constitution. Thus, congressional passage (and the Supreme Court's eventual acceptance) of sweeping New Deal legislation, which altered the balance of power between the national government and the states, truly changed the Constitution without benefit of amendment.[23]

Advances in technology have also brought about constitutional change. Wiretapping and other forms of electronic surveillance, for example, now are regulated by the First and Fourth Amendments. Similarly, HIV testing must be balanced against constitutional protections, and all kinds of new constitutional questions are posed in the wake of congressional efforts to regulate what kinds of information can be disseminated on the Internet, as well as the executive branch's use of extraordinary means, following September 11, 2001, to prevent additional terrorist attacks. Still, in spite of these massive changes, the Constitution survives, changed and ever changing after more than 200 years.

SUMMARY

THE U.S. CONSTITUTION has proven to be a remarkably enduring document. While settlers came to the New World for a variety of reasons, most remained loyal to Great Britain and considered themselves subjects of the king. Over the years, as new generations of Americans were born on colonial soil, those ties weakened. A series of taxes levied by the King ultimately led the colonists to convene a Continental Congress and to declare their independence.

The Articles of Confederation (1781) created a loose league of friendship between the new national government and the states. Numerous weaknesses in the new government became apparent by 1784. Among the major flaws were Congress's inability to tax or regulate commerce, the absence of an executive to administer the government, and a weak central government.

When the weaknesses under the Articles of Confederation became apparent, the states called for a meeting to reform them. The Constitutional Convention (1787) quickly threw out the Articles of Confederation and fashioned a new, more workable form of government. The Constitution was the result of a series of compromises, including those over representation, over questions involving large and small states, and over how to determine population. Compromises were also made about how members of each branch of government were to be selected. The Electoral College was created to give states a key role in the selection of the president.

The proposed U.S. Constitution created a federal system that drew heavily on Montesquieu's ideas about separation of powers. These ideas concerned a way of parceling out power among the three branches of government, and checks and balances to prevent any one branch from having too much power.

The drive for ratification became a fierce fight between Federalists and Anti-Federalists. Federalists lobbied for the strong national government created by the Constitution; Anti-Federalists favored greater state power.

The Framers wanted a government that would be immune to the whims of the people. Therefore, they designed a two-stage formal amendment process that required approval on the federal and state levels. Formal amendments are not the only way that the Constitution changes. Judicial interpretation, especially by the Supreme Court, also affects the living Constitution, as do social and cultural change.

KEY TERMS

Anti-Federalists, p. 49
Articles of Confederation, p. 35
Bill of Rights, p. 53
checks and balances, p. 43
Committees of Correspondence, p. 33
confederation, p. 34
Constitution, p. 38
Declaration of Independence, p. 34
enumerated powers, p. 44
federal system, p. 40
The Federalist Papers, p. 50
Federalists, p. 49
First Continental Congress, p. 33
Great Compromise, p. 37
implied powers, p. 44
mercantilism, p. 30
necessary and proper clause, p. 44
New Jersey Plan, p. 37
Second Continental Congress, p. 33
separation of powers, p. 40
Stamp Act Congress, p. 32
supremacy clause, p. 45
Three-Fifths Compromise, p. 38
Virginia Plan, p. 37

SELECTED READINGS

Ackerman, Bruce. *We the People.* Cambridge, MA: Belknap, 1991.

Bailyn, Bernard. *The Ideological Origins of the American Revolution.* Cambridge, MA: Belknap, 1967.

Beard, Charles A. *An Economic Interpretation of the Constitution of the United States,* reissue ed. New York: Free Press, 1996.

Bernstein, Richard B., with Jerome Agel. *Amending America,* reissue ed. Lawrence: University Press of Kansas, 1995.

Bowen, Catherine Drinker. *Miracle at Philadelphia.* Boston: Little, Brown, 1986.

Brinkley, Alan, Nelson W. Polsby, and Kathleen M. Sullivan. *New Federalist Papers: Essays in Defense of the Constitution.* New York: Norton, 1997.

Dahl, Robert A. *How Democratic Is the American Constitution?* New Haven, CT: Yale University Press, 2002.

Hamilton, Alexander, James Madison, and John Jay. *The Federalist Papers.* New York: Bantam Books, 1989 (first published in 1788).

Ketchman, Ralph, ed. *The Anti-Federalist Papers and the Constitutional Convention Debated.* New York: Mentor Books, 1996.

Kyvig, David E. *Explicit and Authentic Acts: Amending the U.S. Constitution, 1776–1995.* Lawrence: University Press of Kansas, 1996.

Levy, Leonard W., ed. *Essays on the Making of the Constitution*, 2nd ed. New York: Oxford University Press, 1987.

Main, Jackson Turner. *The Social Structure of Revolutionary America.* Princeton, NJ: Princeton University Press, 1965.

Rossiter, Clinton. *1787: Grand Convention*, reissue ed. New York: Norton, 1987.

Simon, James F., *What Kind of Nation: Thomas Jefferson, John Marshall, and the Epic Struggle to Create a United States.* New York: Simon and Schuster, 2003.

Stoner, James R., Jr. *Common Law and Liberal Theory.* Lawrence: University Press of Kansas, 1992.

Storing, Herbert J. *What the Anti-Federalists Were For.* Chicago: University of Chicago Press, 1981.

Sunstein, Cass R. *Designing Democracy: What Constitutions Do.* New York: Oxford University Press, 2001.

Vile, John R. *Encyclopedia of Constitutional Amendments, and Amending Issues, 1789–1995.* Santa Barbara, CA: ABC-CLIO, 1996.

Wood, Gordon S. *The Creation of the American Republic, 1776–1787*, reissue ed. New York: Norton, 1993.

WEB EXPLORATIONS

For more information on the work of the Continental Congress, see
http://lcweb2.loc.gov/ammem/bdsds/intro01.html

For a full text of the Articles of Confederation, see
http://www.yale.edu/lawweb/avalon/artconfed.htm

For demographic background on the Framers, see
http://www.usconstitution.net/constframedata.html

To compare *The Federalist Papers* with *The Anti-Federalist Papers,* see
http://www.law.emory.edu/FEDERAL/federalist/

For the text of failed amendments to the U.S. Constitution, see
http://www.usconstitution.net/constamfail.html

The Constitution of the United States of America

We the People of the United States, in Order to form a more perfect Union, establish Justice, insure domestic Tranquility, provide for the common defence, promote the general Welfare, and secure the Blessings of Liberty to ourselves and our Posterity, do ordain and establish this Constitution for the United States of America.

ARTICLE I
Section 1.

All legislative Powers herein granted shall be vested in a Congress of the United States, which shall consist of a Senate and House of Representatives.

Article I is the longest and most detailed of any of the articles, sections, or amendments that make up the United States Constitution. By *enumerating* the powers of Congress, the Framers attached limits to the enormous authority they had vested in the legislative branch. At the same time, the allocation of certain powers to Congress ensured that the legislative branch would maintain control over certain vital areas of public policy and that it would be protected from incursions by the executive and judicial branches. Moreover, by clearly vesting Congress with certain powers (for example, the power to regulate interstate commerce), Article I established a water's edge for the exercise of state power in what were now national affairs.

Originally, Article I also contained restrictions limiting the amendment of several of its provisions, a feature found nowhere else in the Constitution. Section 4 prohibited Congress from making any law banning the importation of slaves until 1808, and section 9 prohibited

Congress from levying an income tax on the general population. Neither section is operative any longer. Section 4 expired on its own, and section 9 was modified by passage of the Sixteenth Amendment, which established the income tax (see page 92).

Despite the great care the Framers took to limit the exercise of congressional authority to those powers enumerated in Article I, the power of Congress has grown tremendously since the nation's founding. Under Chief Justice John Marshall (1801–1835), the U.S. Supreme Court interpreted the Constitution to favor the power of the national government over the states and to permit Congress to exercise both its *enumerated* (the power to regulate interstate commerce) and *implied* (the necessary and proper clause) powers in broad fashion. With only the occasional exception, the Court has never really challenged the legislative power vested in Congress to engage numerous areas of public policy that some constitutional scholars (and politicians and voters) believe are the province of the states. Perhaps the only area in which legislative power has diminished over the years has been the war-making power granted to Congress, something that lawmakers, for all their occasional criticism of presidential conduct of foreign policy, have ceded to the executive branch rather willingly.

Section 2.

The House of Representatives shall be composed of Members chosen every second Year by the People of the several States, and the Electors in each State shall have the Qualifications requisite for Electors of the most numerous Branch of the State Legislature.

No person shall be a Representative who shall not have attained to the Age of twenty five Years, and been seven Years a Citizen of the United States, and who shall not, when elected, be an Inhabitant of that State in which he shall be chosen.

The qualifications clause, which sets out the age and residency requirements for individuals who wish to run for the House of Representatives, became the centerpiece of a national debate that emerged during the late 1980s and early 1990s over term limits for members of Congress. In *U.S. Term Limits* v. *Thornton* (1995), the Supreme Court ruled that section 2, clause 2, did not specify any other qualification to serve in the House other than age and residency (as did section 3, clause 3, to run for the Senate). Thus, no state could restrict an individual's right to run for Congress. The Court ruled that any modification to the qualifications clause would have to come through a constitutional amendment.

Representatives and direct Taxes shall be apportioned among the several States which may be included within this Union, according to their respective Numbers which shall be determined by adding to the whole Number of free Persons, including those bound to Service for a Term of Years, and excluding Indians not taxed, three fifths of all other Persons. The actual Enumeration shall be made within three Years after the first Meeting of the Congress of the United States, and within every subsequent Term ten Years, in such Manner as they shall by Law direct. The Number of Representatives shall not exceed one for every thirty Thousand, but each State shall have at Least one Representative; and until such enumerations shall be made, the State of New Hampshire shall be entitled to chuse three, Massachusetts eight, Rhode-Island and Providence Plantations one, Connecticut five, New-York six, New Jersey four, Pennsylvania eight, Delaware one, Maryland six, Virginia ten, North Carolina five, South Carolina five, and Georgia three.

Under the Articles of Confederation, "direct" taxes (such as taxes on property) were apportioned based on land value, not population. This encouraged states to diminish the value of their land in order to reduce their tax burden. Prior to the Constitutional Convention of 1787, several prominent delegates met to discuss—and ultimately propose—changing the method for direct taxation from land value to the population of each state. A major sticking point among the delegates on this issue was how to count slaves for taxation purposes. Southern states wanted to diminish the value of slaves for tax purposes, while northern states wanted to count slaves as closer to a full person. On the other hand, southern states wanted to count slaves as "whole persons" for purposes of representation to increase their power in the House of Representatives, but northern states rejected this proposal. Ultimately, the delegates settled on the "Three-Fifths Compromise," which treated each slave as three-fifths of a person for tax and representation purposes.

At the beginning, the Three-Fifths Compromise enhanced southern power in the House. In 1790, when the 1st Congress convened, the South held 45 percent of the seats, despite a significantly smaller free population than the North. Over time, however, the South saw its power in the House diminish. By the 1830s, the South held just over 30 percent of House seats, which gave it just enough power to thwart norhern initiatives on slavery questions and territorial issues, but not enough power to defeat the growing power of the North to control commercial and economic policy. This standoff between the North and South led to such events as South Carolina Senator John C. Calhoun's doctrine of nullification and secession, which argued that a state could nullify any federal law not consistent with regional or state interests. By the 1850s, the Three-Fifths Compromise had made the South dependent on expanding the number of slaveholding territories eligible for admission to the union and a judicial system sympathetic to slaveholding interests. The Three-Fifths Compromise was repealed by section 2 of the Fourteenth Amendment (see page 90).

When vacancies happen in the Representation from any State, the Executive Authority thereof shall issue Writs of Election to fill such Vacancies.

This clause permits the governor of a state to call an election to replace any member of the House of Representatives who is unable to complete a term of office due to death, resignation, or removal from the House. In some cases, a governor will appoint a successor to fill out a term; in other cases, the governor will call a special election. A governor's decision is shaped less by constitutional guidelines and more by partisan interests. For example, a Democratic governor might choose to appoint a Democratic successor if he or she believes that a Republican candidate might have an advantage in a special election.

The House of Representatives shall chuse their speaker and other Officers; and shall have the sole Power of Impeachment.

Clause 5 establishes the only officer of the House of Representatives—the speaker. The remaining offices (party leaders, whips, and so on) are created by the House.

The House also has the sole power of impeachment against members of the executive and judicial branches. The House, like the Senate, is responsible for disciplining its own members. In *Nixon* v. *U.S.* (1993), the Supreme Court ruled that government officials who are the subject of impeachment proceedings may not challenge them in court. The Court ruled that the sole power given to the House over impeachment precludes judicial intervention.

Section 3.

The Senate of the United States shall be composed of two Senators from each State chosen by the Legislature thereof, for six Years; and each Senator shall have one Vote.

The provision of this clause establishing the election of senators by state legislatures was repealed by the Seventeenth Amendment (see page 93).

Immediately after they shall be assembled in Consequence of the first Election, they shall be divided as equally as may be into three Classes. The Seats of the Senators of the first Class shall be vacated at the Expiration of the second year, of the second Class at the Expiration of the fourth Year, and of the third Class at the Expiration of the sixth Year, so that one third may be chosen every second Year and if Vacancies happen by Resignation, or otherwise, during the Recess of the Legislature of any State, the Executive thereof may make temporary Appointments until the next Meeting of the Legislature, which shall then fill such Vacancies.

Vacancies for senators are handled the same way as vacancies for representatives—through appointment or special election. The Seventeenth Amendment modified the language authorizing the state legislature to choose a replacement for a vacant Senate position.

No Person shall be a Senator who shall not have attained to the Age of thirty Years, and been nine Years a Citizen of the United States, and who shall not, when elected, be an Inhabitant of that State for which he shall be chosen.

The Vice President of the United States shall be President of the Senate, but shall have no Vote, unless they be equally divided.

Clause 4 gives the vice president the authority to vote to break a tie in the Senate. This is the only constitutional duty the Constitution specifies for the vice president. As president of the Senate, the vice president also presides over procedural matters of that body, although this is not a responsibility that vice presidents have really ever shouldered.

The Senate shall chuse their other Officers, and also a President pro tempore, in the Absence of the Vice President, or when he shall exercise the Office of President of the United States.

Clause 5 creates the position of *president pro tempore* (the president of the time), the only Senate office established by the Constitution to handle the duties of the vice president set out in section 3, clause 4.

The Senate shall have the sole Power to try all Impeachments. When sitting for that Purpose, they shall be on Oath or Affirmation. When the President of the United States is tried, the Chief Justice shall preside: And no Person shall be convicted without the Concurrence of two thirds of the Members present.

Judgment in Cases of Impeachment shall not extend further than to removal from Office, and disqualification to hold and enjoy any Office of honor, Trust or Profit under the United States; but the Party convicted shall nevertheless be liable and subject to Indictment, Trial, Judgment and Punishment, according to law.

Just as the House of Representatives has the sole power to bring impeachment against executive and judicial branch officials, the Senate has the sole power to try all impeachments. Unless the president is facing trial in the Senate, the vice president serves as the presiding officer. In 1998, President Bill Clinton was tried on two articles of impeachment (four were brought against him in the House) and found not guilty on each count. The presiding officer in President Clinton's impeachment trial was Chief Justice William H. Rehnquist.

A conviction results in the removal of an official from office. It does not prohibit subsequent civil or criminal action against that individual. Nor does it prohibit an impeached and convicted official from returning to federal office. In 1989, Alcee Hastings, a trial judge with ten years experience on the U.S. District Court for the Southern District of Florida, was convicted on impeachment charges and removed from office. In 1992, he ran successfully for the 23rd District seat of the U.S.

House of Representatives, where he continues to serve as of this writing.

Section 4.

The Times, Places and Manner of holding Elections for Senators and Representatives, shall be prescribed in each State by the Legislature thereof; but the Congress may at any time by Law make or alter such Regulations, except as to the Places of chusing Senators.

The Congress shall assemble at least once in every Year, and such Meeting shall be on the first Monday in December, unless they shall by Law appoint a different Day.

Section 4 authorizes the states to establish the rules governing elections for members of Congress, but Congress has never hesitated to exercise its law-making power in this area when it has believed that improvements were necessary to improve the electoral process. The first such action did not come until 1842, when Congress passed legislation making elections to the House based on single-member districts, not from the general population. By the turn of the twentieth century, Congress had passed legislation establishing additional criteria such as the rough equality of population among districts and territorial compactness and contiguity. Article I, section 4, is one of the three main areas from which Congress derives the power to regulate the electoral process. The other two are the necessary and proper clause of Article I, section 8, clause 3, and section 2 of the Fifteenth Amendment.

Section 5.

Each House shall be the Judge of the Elections, Returns and Qualifications of its own Members, and a Majority of each shall constitute a Quorum to do business; but a smaller Number may adjourn from day to day, and may be authorized to compel the Attendance of absent Members, in such Manner, and under such Penalties as each House may provide.

Each House may determine the Rules of its Proceedings, punish its Members for disorderly Behaviour, and with the Concurrence of two thirds, expel a Member.

Clause 2 gives power to the House and Senate to establish the rules and decorum for each chamber. Expulsion from either the House or the Senate does not preclude a member from running for congressional office again or serving in any other official capacity. In *Powell v. McCormack* (1969), the Supreme Court ruled that the House's decision to exclude an individual from the chamber despite having been elected was different from the expulsion of a sitting representative.

Each House shall keep a Journal of its Proceedings, and from time to time publish the same, excepting such Parts as may in their judgment require Secrecy; and the Yeas and Nays of the Members of either House on any question shall, at the Desire of one fifth of those present, be entered on the Journal.

The *Congressional Record* is the official journal of Congress. Justice Joseph Story, in his much praised scholarly treatment of the U.S. Constitution, *Commentaries on the Constitution* (1833), said the purpose of this clause was "to insure publicity to the proceedings of the legislature, and a correspondent responsibility of the members to their respective constituents." Recorded votes (and yea-or-nay voice votes, if agreed to by one-fifth of the House or Senate), speeches, and other public business are contained in the *Congressional Record*.

Neither House, during the Session of Congress, shall, without the Consent of the other, adjourn for more than three days, nor to any other Place than that in which the two Houses shall be sitting.

Section 6.

The Senators and Representatives shall receive a Compensation for their Services, to be ascertained by Law, and paid out of the Treasury of the United States. They shall in all Cases, except Treason, Felony and Breach of the Peace, be privileged from Arrest during their Attendance at the Session of their respective Houses, and in going to and returning from the same; and for any Speech or Debate in either House, they shall not be questioned in any other Place.

The Twenty-Seventh Amendment, ratified in 1992, now governs the procedures for compensation of members of Congress. From the nation's founding until 1967, Congress had determined the salaries of its members. Then, Congress passed legislation giving the president the responsibility to recommend salary levels for members of Congress, since the president already had the responsibility to recommend pay levels for other federal officials. In 1989, as part of the Ethics Reform Act, Congress established a new system of pay raises and cost-of-living adjustments based on a particular vote.

Clause 1 also protects the right of senators and representatives from criminal prosecution for any "Speech or Debate" made in Congress. This protection stemmed from lessons drawn from the persistent conflicts between the House of Commons and the Tudor and Stuart monarchies in Great Britain, who used their power to bring civil and criminal actions against legislators whose opinions were deemed seditious or dangerous. The 1689 English Bill of Rights contained protection for legislators to conduct their business in Parliament free from such fears, and the Framers believed that such protection was essential for Congress under the Constitution. The Supreme Court has held, however, in *Gravel* v. *U.S.* (1972), that the speech or debate clause does not immunize senators or representatives from criminal inquiry if their activities in the Senate or House are the result of alleged or proven illegal action.

The privilege from arrest clause has little application in contemporary America. The clause applies only to arrests in civil suits, which were fairly common when the Constitution was ratified. The Court has interpreted the phrase "except Treason, Felony or Breach of the Peace"

to make members eligible for arrest for crimes that would fall into that category. For example, a member of Congress is eligible if he or she commits a serious traffic offense, such as drunk or reckless driving, on the way to or from legislative business.

No Senator or Representative shall, during the Time for which he was elected, be appointed to any civil Office under the Authority of the United States, which shall have been created, or the Emoluments whereof shall have been encreased during such time; and no Person holding any Office under the United States, shall be a Member of either House during his Continuance in Office.

Clause 2 prohibits any senator or representative from holding a simultaneous office in the legislative or executive branches. This is one of the least controversial provisions of the Constitution. Indeed, there is no judicial interpretation of its meaning.

The general purpose of this clause is to prevent one branch of government from having an undue influence on another by creating dual incentives. It is also another safeguard in the separation of powers.

Section 7.

All Bills for raising Revenue shall originate in the House of Representatives; but the Senate may propose or concur with Amendments as on other Bills.

The power to raise revenue found in clause 1 is unique to the House of Representatives. In *Federalist No. 58,* James Madison argued that vesting such authority in the House was a key feature of the separation of powers. No bill either raising or lowering taxes may originate in the Senate. Legislation which creates incidental revenue may begin in the Senate, as long as the legislation does not involve taxation.

Every Bill which shall have passed the House of Representatives and the Senate, shall,

before it become a Law, be presented to the President of the United States; If he approve he shall sign it, but if not he shall return it, with his Objections to that House in which it shall have originated, who shall enter the Objections at large on their Journal, and proceed to reconsider it. If after such Reconsideration two thirds of that House shall agree to pass the Bill, it shall be sent, together with the Objections, to the other House, by which it shall likewise be reconsidered, and if approved by two thirds of that House, it shall become a Law. But in all such Cases the Votes of both Houses shall be determined by Yeas and Nays, and the Names of the Persons voting for and against the Bill shall be entered on the Journal of each House respectively. If any Bill shall not be returned by the President within ten Days (Sundays excepted) after it shall have been presented to him, the Same shall be a Law, in like Manner as if he had signed it, unless the Congress by their Adjournment prevent its Return, in which Case it shall not be a Law.

This clause establishes several key features of presidential-congressional relations in the flow of the legislative process. For a bill to become law, it must be passed by the House and Senate, and it must be signed by the president. The Supreme Court has ruled that the veto regulations outlined in this clause serve two purposes. First, by giving the president ten days to consider a bill for approval, clause 2 provides the president with ample time to consider legislation and protects him from having to approve legislation in the wake of congressional adjournment. But clause 2 also provides Congress with a countervailing power to override a presidential veto, a procedure that requires a two-thirds vote in each chamber.

Every Order, Resolution, or Vote to which the Concurrence of the Senate and House of Representatives may be necessary (except on a question of Adjournment) shall be presented to the President of the United States; and before the Same shall take Effect, shall be approved by him, or being disapproved by him, shall be repassed by two thirds of the Senate and House of Representatives, according to the Rules and Limitations prescribed in the Case of a Bill.

Clause 3 covers the presentation of resolutions, not actual legislation. For any resolution to have the force of law, it must be presented to the president for approval. Should the president veto the resolution, Congress may override this veto in the same manner expressed in section 7, clause 2. Resolutions that do not have the force of law do not require presidential approval. Preliminary votes taken on constitutional amendments and other legislative matters covered by clause 3 do not require presentation to the president.

This clause has been the subject of two major Supreme Court decisions dealing with the separation of powers. In *I.N.S.* v. *Chadha* (1983), the Court ruled that the House-only legislative veto, a practice begun during the 1930s to give Congress power to control power delegated to a rapidly expanding executive branch, violated both the bicameralism principles of Article I, section 1, and the presentment clause of section 7, clause 3. At the time, the ruling struck down about 200 legislative vetoes that had been included in various pieces of congressional legislation. In *Clinton* v. *New York* (1998), the Court ruled that the line-item veto passed by Congress to give the president the power to veto specific provisions of legislation rather than an entire bill violated the presentment clause of Article I, section 7, clause 3. The Court claimed that the line-item veto permitted the president to "repeal certain laws," a power that belonged to Congress and not the president.

Section 8.

The Congress shall have Power To lay and collect Taxes, Duties, Imposts and Excises, to pay the Debts and provide for the common Defence and general Welfare of the United States; but all Duties, Imposts and Excises shall be uniform throughout the United States;

To borrow Money on the credit of the United States;

To regulate Commerce with foreign Nations, and among the several States, and with the Indian Tribes;

To establish a uniform Rule of Naturalization, and uniform Laws on the subject of Bankruptcies throughout the United States;

To coin Money, regulate the Value thereof, and of foreign Coin, and fix the Standard of Weights and Measures;

To provide for the Punishment of counterfeiting the Securities and current Coin of the United States;

To establish Post Offices and post Roads;

To promote the Progress of Science and useful Arts, by securing for limited Times to Authors and Inventors exclusive Right to their respective Writings and Discoveries;

To constitute Tribunals inferior to the supreme Court;

To define and punish Piracies and Felonies committed on the high Seas, and Offences against the Law of Nations;

To declare War, grant Letters of Marque and Reprisal, and make rules concerning Captures on Land and Water;

To raise and support Armies, but no Appropriation of Money to that Use shall be for a longer Term than two Years;

To provide and maintain a Navy;

To make Rules for the Government and Regulation of the land and naval Forces;

To provide for calling forth the Militia to execute the Laws of the Union, suppress Insurrections and repel Invasions;

To provide for organizing, arming, and disciplining, the Militia, and for governing such Part of them as may be employed in the Service of the United States, reserving to the States respectively, the Appointment of the Officers, and the Authority of training the Militia according to the discipline prescribed by Congress;

To exercise exclusive Legislation in all Cases whatsoever, over such District (not exceeding ten Miles square) as may, by Cession of particular States, and the Acceptance of Congress, become the Seat of the Government of the United States, and to exercise like Authority over all Places purchased by the Consent of the Legislature of the State in which the Same shall be for the Erection of Forts, Magazines, Arsenals, dock-Yards, and other needful Buildings;—And

Article I, section 8, clause 1, is, in many ways, the engine of congressional power. First, clause 1 gives Congress the power to tax and spend, a power the Supreme Court has interpreted as "exhaustive" and "reaching every subject." Second, in giving Congress the power to provide for the common defense and general welfare, it offers no specific constraint on what Congress may spend public funds for and how much it may spend. Third, section 8 gives Congress complete authority in numerous areas of policy that affect Americans at home and abroad on a massive scale. These powers include the power to regulate interstate commerce (which Congress has relied on to establish federal civil rights law), to make war (a power that Congress, since the end of World War II in 1945, has increasingly deferred to the president), and to establish the federal judicial system.

Clause 1 is often cited by constitutional scholars as an example of how the Constitution constrains legislative power by limiting the powers that Congress may exercise. To a certain extent, this is true. But it is also true that the Court has granted Congress extensive power to legislate in certain areas that bear only a tangential relationship to the specific language of some of the provisions of clause 1. For example, in *Katzenbach* v. *McClung* (1964), the Court turned back a challenge to the constitutionality of the Civil Rights Act of 1964, which Congress had passed under its authority to regulate interstate commerce. The Court ruled that racial discrimination had an adverse effect on the free flow of commerce.

Clause 2 establishes the seat of the federal government—first New York City, now Washington, D.C. The clause also makes Congress the legislative body of the nation's capital, a power that extends to other federal bodies, such as forts, military bases, and other places where federal buildings are located.

To make all Laws which shall be necessary and proper for carrying into Execution the foregoing Powers, and all other Powers vested by this Constitution in the Government of the United States, or in any Department or Officer thereof.

Better known as the necessary and proper clause, this provision of Article I was one of the most contested points between Federalists and Anti-Federalists during the ratification debates over the Constitution. Anti-Federalists feared that the language was too broad and all-encompassing, and, if interpreted by a Supreme Court sympathetic to the nationalist ambitions of the Federalist Party, would give Congress limitless power to exercise legislative authority over state and local matters. In *McCulloch* v. *Maryland* (1819), Chief Justice John Marshall offered what constitutional scholars believe remains the definitive interpretation of the necessary and proper clause. While *McCulloch* certainly did cement the power of Congress in the federal system, the expansive definition given the necessary and proper clause by the Court is also testament to the flexible nature of the Constitution, and why so few amendments have been added to the original document.

Section 9.

The Migration or Importation of such Persons as any of the States now existing shall think proper to admit, shall not be prohibited by the Congress prior to the Year one thousand eight hundred and eight, but a Tax or duty may be imposed on such Importation, not exceeding ten dollars for each Person.

Like the other provisions of the Constitution that refer to slavery, such as the Three-Fifths Compromise, section 9 creates policy governing the institution without ever mentioning the word. The importation clause was a compromise between slave traders, who wanted to continue the practice, and opponents of slavery, who needed southern support to ratify the Constitution. In 1808, Congress passed legislation banning the importation of slaves; until then, Congress used its power to tax slaves brought to the United States.

The Privilege of the Writ of Habeas Corpus shall not be suspended, unless when in Cases of Rebellion or Invasion the public Safety may require it.

Clause 2 is the only place where the writ of *habeas corpus*—the "Great Writ," as it was known to the Framers—is mentioned in the Constitution. Only the federal government is bound by clause 2. The writ may only be suspended in times of crisis and rebellion, and then it is Congress that has the power, not the president.

No Bill of Attainder or ex post facto Law shall be passed.

A bill of attainder is a legislative act punishing a person with "pains and penalties" without the benefit of a hearing or trial. The fundamental purpose of the ban on bills of attainder is to prevent trial by legislature and other arbitrary punishments for persons vulnerable to extra-judicial proceedings. An *ex post facto law* is one passed making a previously committed civil or criminal action subject to penalty. In *Calder* v. *Bull* (1798), the Court ruled that the ban on *ex post facto* laws applied only to penal and criminal actions.

A similar restriction on the states is found in Article I, section 10, clause 1.

No Capitation, or other direct, Tax shall be laid, unless in Proportion to the Census or Enumeration herein before directed to be taken.

This clause, which originally prohibited Congress from levying an income tax, was modified by the Sixteenth Amendment, passed in 1913 (see page 92).

No Tax or Duty shall be laid on Articles exported from any State.

Clause 5 prohibits Congress from levying a tax on any good or article exported from a state to a foreign country or to another state. Many southern states feared that northern members of Congress would attempt to weaken the South's slave-based economy by taxing exports. This clause prohibited such action. Congress may prohibit the shipment of certain items from one state to another—beer and wine, for example—and to other countries.

No Preference shall be given by any Regulation of Commerce or Revenue to the Ports of one State over those of another: nor shall Vessels bound to, or from, one State, be obliged to enter, clear, or pay Duties in another.

Congress is prohibited from making laws regulating trade that favor one state over another. Clause 6 also prohibits Congress from establishing preferences for certain ports or trade centers over others, although it may, under its power to regulate interstate commerce, pass laws that incidentally benefit certain states or maritime outlets. The Supreme Court has ruled that states are not bound by the limitations on Congress expressed in this clause.

No money shall be drawn from the Treasury, but in Consequence of Appropriations made by Law; and a regular Statement and Account of the Receipts and Expenditures of all public Money shall be published from time to time.

Clause 7 serves two fundamental purposes. First, the clause prohibits any governmental body receiving federal funds from spending those funds without the approval of Congress. Once Congress has determined that federal funds are to be spent in a certain way, the executive branch may not exercise any discretion over that decision. Second, by restricting executive control of spending power, the clause firmly reinforces congressional authority over revenue and spending, a key feature of the separation of powers.

No Title of Nobility shall be granted by the United States: And no Person holding any Office of Profit or Trust under them, shall, without the Consent of the Congress, accept of any present, Emolument, Office, or Title, of any kind whatever, from any King, Prince, or foreign State.

This provision is among the first school-taught lessons about the Constitution. To reinforce the commitment to representative democracy, the Framers prohibited a title of nobility from being conferred on any public official. This clause also prohibits any government official from accepting compensation, gifts, or similar benefits from any foreign government for services rendered without the consent of Congress.

Section 10.

No state shall enter into any Treaty, Alliance, or Confederation; grant Letters of Marque and Reprisal; coin Money; emit Bills of Credit; make any Thing but gold and silver Coin a Tender in Payment of Debts; pass any Bill of Attainder, ex post facto Law, or Law impairing the Obligation of Contracts, or grant any Title of Nobility.

This clause denies several powers to the states that were once permissible under the Articles of Confederation, and it emphasizes the Framers' commitment under the Constitution to a strong national government with Congress as the centrifugal force. During the Civil War, the Union relied on this clause in support of its view that the Confederate states had no legal existence but instead were merely "states in rebellion" against the United States.

The restrictions on states passing either bills of attainder or ex post facto laws have come into play at various points in American history. During Reconstruction, several states enacted legislation

prohibiting any individual who aided the Confederacy from entering certain professions or enjoying other benefits available to citizens who remained loyal to the Union. The Supreme Court struck down these laws on the grounds that they violated this clause.

The provision prohibiting states from passing any law "impairing the Obligation of Contracts," better known as the contract clause, has been the subject of considerable litigation before the Supreme Court. The contract clause was intended to bar the states from interfering in private contracts between consensual parties and was considered an important limit on the power of states to restrict the fledgling national economic order of the early republic. Early on, the Court considered many laws that restricted the terms set out in private contracts as unconstitutional. But as the United States became a more industrial society, and as citizen demands grew for government regulation of the economy, the environment, and social welfare benefits, the Court softened its position on the contract clause to permit states to make laws that served a reasonable public interest. A key case involving the contract clause is *Home Building and Loan Association* v. *Blaisdell* (1934). In *Blaisdell,* the Court ruled that a Depression-era law passed by the Minnesota legislature forgiving mortgage payments by homeowners to banks did not violate the contract clause.

No State shall, without the Consent of the Congress, lay any Imposts or Duties on Imports or Exports, except what may be absolutely necessary for executing its inspection Laws: and the net Produce of all Duties and Imposts, laid by any State on Imports or Exports, shall be for the Use of the Treasury of the United States, and all such Laws shall be subject to the Revision and Controul of the Congress.

No state may tax goods leaving or entering a state, although it may charge reasonable fees for inspections considered necessary to the public interest. The restriction on import and export taxes applies only to those goods entering from or leaving for a foreign country.

No State shall, without the Consent of Congress, lay any Duty of Tonnage, keep Troops, or Ships of War in time of Peace, enter into any Agreement or Compact with another State, or with a foreign Power, or engage in War, unless actually invaded, or in such imminent Danger as will not admit of delay.

Clause 3 cements the power of Congress to control acts of war and make treaties with foreign countries. The Framers wanted to correct any perception to the contrary gained from the Articles of Confederation that states were free to act independently of the national government on negotiated matters with foreign countries. They also wanted to ensure that any state that entered into a compact with another state—something this clause does not prohibit—must receive permission from Congress.

ARTICLE II

Section 1.

The executive Power shall be vested in a President of the United States of America. He shall hold his Office during the Term of four Years, and, together with the Vice President, chosen for the same Term, be elected as follows.

In *Federalist No. 70*, Alexander Hamilton argued for an "energetic executive" branch headed by a single, elected president not necessarily beholden to the majority party in Congress. Hamilton believed that a nationally elected president would not be bound by the narrow, parochial interests that drove legislative law-making. The president would possess both the veto power over Congress and a platform from which to articulate a national vision in both domestic and foreign affairs.

Hamilton believed that the constitutional boundaries placed on executive power through the separation of powers and the fact that the president was accountable to a national electorate constrained any possibility that the office would come to resemble the monarchies of Europe. However, most presidential scholars agree that the modern presidency has grown in power precisely because of the general nature of the enabling powers of Article II.

Each State shall appoint, in such Manner as the Legislature thereof may direct, a Number of Electors, equal to the whole Number of Senators and Representatives to which the State may be entitled in the Congress; but no Senator or Representative, or Person holding an Office of Trust of Profit under the United States, shall be appointed an Elector.

Clause 2 established the Electoral College and set the number of electors from each state at the total of senators and representatives serving in Congress.

The Electors shall meet in their respective States, and vote by Ballot for two Persons, of whom one at least shall not be an Inhabitant of the same State with themselves. And they shall make a List of all the Persons voted for, and, of the Number of Votes for each; which List they shall sign and certify, and transmit sealed to the Seat of the Government of the United States, directed to the President of the Senate. The President of the Senate shall, in the Presence of the Senate and House of Representatives, open all the Certificates, and the Votes shall then be counted. The Person having the greatest Number of Votes shall be the President, if such Number be a Majority of the whole Number of Electors appointed; and if there be more than one who have such Majority, and have an equal Number of Votes, then the House of Representatives shall immediately chuse by Ballot one of them for President; and if no Person have a Majority, then from the five highest on the List the said House shall in like Manner chuse the President. But in chusing the President, the Votes shall be taken by States, the Representation from each State having one Vote; A quorum for this Purpose shall consist of a Member or Members from two thirds of the States, and a Majority of all the

States shall be necessary to a Choice. In every Case, after the Choice of the President, the Person having the greatest Number of Votes of the Electors shall be the Vice President. But if there should remain two or more who have equal Votes, the Senate shall chuse from them by Ballot the Vice President.

This provision of section 1 described the rules for calling the Electoral College to vote for president and vice president. Originally, the electors did not vote separately for president and vice president. After the 1800 election, which saw Thomas Jefferson and Aaron Burr receive the identical number of electoral votes even though it was clear that Jefferson was the presidential candidate and Burr the vice presidential candidate, the nation ratified the Twelfth Amendment (see page 88).

The Twelfth Amendment did not resolve what many constitutional scholars today believe are the inadequacies of the Electoral College system. In 1824, the presidential election ended in a four-way tie, and the House of Representatives elected second-place finisher John Quincy Adams. In 1876, Benjamin Harrison lost the popular vote but won the presidency after recounts awarded him an Electoral College majority. But perhaps the most controversial election of all came in 2000, when George W. Bush, who lost the popular contest to Al Gore by approximately 500,000 votes, was named the presidential victor after a six-week court battle over the vote count in Florida. After the Supreme Court ruled against the position of Al Gore that a recount of the Florida popular vote should continue until all votes had been counted, an outcome that would have left the nation without a president-elect for several more weeks, Bush was awarded Florida's electoral votes, which gave him 271, just one more than he needed to win the office. Outraged Democrats pledged to mount a case for Electoral College reform, but, as was so often the case before, nothing happened.

The Congress may determine the Time of chusing the Electors, and the Day on which they shall give their Votes; which Day shall be the same throughout the United States.

No Person except a natural born Citizen, or a Citizen of the United States, at the time of the Adoption of this Constitution, shall be eligible to the Office of President; neither shall any Person be eligible to that Office who shall not have attained to the Age of thirty five Years, and been fourteen Years a Resident within the United States.

This provision of Article II is referred to as the presidential eligibility clause. In addition to setting out the age and resident requirements of presidential aspirants, this clause defines who may *not* run for president—any foreign-born individual who has nonetheless obtained United States citizenship. For example, Michigan Governor Jennifer Granholm, who has lived in the United States since she was four years old, may not run for president because she was born in Canada. The same is true for California Governor Arnold Schwarzenegger, who was born in Austria but has lived in the United States his entire adult life. Judicial interpretation of the presidential eligibility clause has not resolved the question of whether children born to U.S. citizens are eligible to run for president if they meet the residency requirements.

In Case of the Removal of the President from Office, or of his Death, Resignation, or Inability to discharge the Powers and Duties of the said Office, the Same shall devolve on the Vice President, and the Congress may by Law provide for the Case of Removal, Death, Resignation or Inability, both of the President and Vice President, declaring what Officer shall then act as President, and such Officer shall act accordingly, until the Disability be removed, or a President shall be elected.

This presidential succession clause has been modified by the Twenty-Fifth Amendment (see page 98).

The President shall, at stated Times, receive for his Services, a Compensation, which shall neither be encreased nor diminished during the Period for which he shall have been elected, and he shall not receive within that Period any other Emolument from the United States, or any of them.

Presidential compensation, like compensation for members of Congress, may not be increased for the current occupant of the office. The president is not eligible for any other public compensation during time in office. However, the president may continue to receive income such as interest on investments or book royalties.

Before he enter on the Execution of his Office, he shall take the following Oath or Affirmation:—"I do solemnly swear (or affirm) that I will faithfully execute the Office of President of the United States, and will to the best of my Ability, preserve, protect and defend the Constitution of the United States."

Since George Washington's inaugural in 1789, each president has added the phrase "so help me God" to the end of the presidential oath. Although Abraham Lincoln cited the oath to justify his suspension of the writ of *habeas corpus* during the Civil War, no other president has relied on the oath to justify action that stretched the boundaries of executive power. Presidents taking extraordinary action either at home or abroad have relied on either the commander in chief clause of section 2, clause 1, or the provision of section 3 authorizing the president to "faithfully execut[e]" the laws of the United States.

Section 2.

The President shall be Commander in Chief of the Army and Navy of the United States, and of the Militia of the several States, when called into the actual Service of the United States; he may require the Opinion, in writing, of the principal Officer in each of the executive Departments, upon any Subject relating to the Duties of their respective Offices, and he shall have Power to grant Reprieves and Pardons for Offences against the United States, except in Cases of Impeachment.

Section 2, clause 1, establishes the president as commander in chief of the Army and Navy of the United States. In modern times, that authority has extended to the Air Force, the Marines, and all other branches of the armed forces operating under the command of the United States, including state militias, reserve units, and national guards. Article I provides that Congress, and not the president, has the power to declare war. But since World War II, no American president has received or requested a declaration of war to commit the armed forces to military conflicts, including those clearly acknowledged as large-scale war (Korea, Vietnam, the 1991 Persian Gulf War, Afghanistan, and the Iraq War). For these conflicts, the president received congressional *authorization* to use force, but not an Article I declaration.

Clause 1 also implicitly creates the Cabinet by authorizing the president to request the opinion "in writing" of the principal officers of the executive branch. The power to create Cabinet-level offices resides with Congress, not the president.

Presidential power to pardon is broad and limited only in cases of impeachment. Perhaps the most controversial pardon in American political history was President Gerald R. Ford's decision to pardon former President Richard M. Nixon, who resigned his office on August 8, 1974, after news reports and congressional inquiries strongly implicated him in the Watergate scandal. A real possibility existed that President Nixon could be tried on criminal charges as the result of his alleged activities during the Watergate scandal.

He shall have Power, by and with the Advice and Consent of the Senate, to make Treaties, provided two thirds of the Senators present concur; and he shall nominate, and by and with the Advice and Consent of the Senate, shall appoint Ambassadors, other public Ministers and Consuls, Judges of the supreme Court, and all other Officers of the United States, whose Appointments are not herein otherwise provided for, and which shall be established by Law: but the Congress may by Law vest the Appointment of such inferior Officers, as they think proper, in the President alone, in the Courts of Law, or in the Heads of Departments.

The President shall have Power to fill up all Vacancies that may happen during the Recess of the Senate, by granting Commissions which shall expire at the End of their next Session.

Clause 2 describes several powers the president may exercise in conjunction with the advice and consent of the Senate. These powers include the power, upon the approval of two-thirds of the Senate, to make treaties with foreign countries. But the Constitution is silent on the question of whether a president (or Congress) may terminate a treaty by refusing to honor it or simply repealing it outright. When President Jimmy Carter terminated a treaty with China over the objection of Congress, several members sought a judicial resolution of the action; the Court, however, did not decide the case on the merits and offered no resolution on the matter.

The president does not require a two-thirds majority for approval of appointments to the federal judiciary, foreign ambassadorships, Cabinet-level positions, high-ranking positions in non-Cabinet agencies, and high-level military offices. But the fact that the Senate must approve presidential appointments in these areas provides Congress (senators often listen to the constituents of House members on controversial choices) with an important check on presidential power to shape the contours of the executive branch.

The final provision of clause 2 permits Congress to determine whether Senate approval is necessary for lower-level appointments to executive branch or military positions.

A more controversial power related to presidential appointment power is the power of the president to _remove_ officials from public office. The first real confrontation over presidential removal power came after Congress passed the Tenure in Office Act of 1867, a measure intended to prevent President Andrew Johnson from removing officials who had been approved by the Senate. In 1887, Congress repealed the law and returned removal power to the president. In 1926, the Supreme Court finally settled the question of presidential removal power when it ruled in _Myers_ v. _U.S._ that the president had the sole power to remove officials from executive-branch positions. But the Court later ruled in _Humphrey's Executor_ v. _U.S._ (1935) that presidential removal power did not extend to positions that were "quasi-legislative" or "quasi-judicial."

Section 3.

He shall from time to time give to the Congress Information of the State of the Union, and recommend to their Consideration such Measures as he shall judge necessary and expedient; he may, on extraordinary Occasions, convene both Houses, or either of them, and in Case of Disagreement between them, with Respect to the Time of Adjournment, he may adjourn them to such Time as he shall think proper; he shall receive Ambassadors and other public Ministers; he shall take Care that the Laws be faithfully executed, and shall Commission all the Officers of the United States.

The president is required to deliver a State of the Union message to Congress each year. The nation's first two presidents, George Washington and John Adams, delivered their addresses in person. But the nation's third president, Thomas Jefferson, believed that the practice too closely resembled the Speech from the Throne delivered by British royalty. Instead, Jefferson prepared remarks for recitation before Congress by an assistant or clerk of Congress. Every American president after Jefferson followed suit until Woodrow Wilson renewed the original practice after his first year in office. Now, the State of the Union Address is a major

media event, although it is less an assessment of the nation's health and happiness and more a presidential wish-list for policy initiatives and the touting of partisan accomplishments.

The final provision of section 3 authorizing the president to faithfully execute the laws of the United States has proven controversial over the years. Presidents have cited this broad language to justify such far-reaching action as the suspension of the writ of *habeas corpus,* as President Abraham Lincoln did during the Civil War before being rebuffed by the Supreme Court in *Ex parte McCardle* (1867), and the doctrine of executive privilege, which, as asserted by various presidents, permits the executive branch to withhold sensitive information from the public or the other branches of government for national security reasons. The Court has been of two minds about the doctrine of executive privilege. On the one hand, the Court has said in such cases as *New York Times* v. *U.S.* (1971) and *U.S.* v. *Nixon* (1974) that the president has the power to withhold information to protect vital secrets and the nation's security. On the other hand, the Court has said, in ruling against the assertion of executive privilege in these two cases, that only an exceptional and demonstrated case can justify allowing the president to withhold information.

Section 4.

The President, Vice President and all civil Officers of the United States, shall be removed from Office on Impeachment for, and Conviction of, Treason, Bribery, or other High Crimes and Misdemeanors.

Presidential impeachment, like impeachment of the other described offices in section 4, is the responsibility of the House of Representatives. There is no judicial definition to what constitutes a high crime or misdemeanor. Complicating the matter further is that only the House and Senate are given responsibility over the impeachment process. No federal official subject to impeachment may challenge the action in federal court, as the Supreme Court has ruled that the rules governing impeachment are not actionable in court. Only two presidents, Andrew Johnson in 1868 and Bill Clinton in 1998, have ever been impeached. Neither president was convicted by the Senate of the charges brought against them.

ARTICLE III
Section 1.

The judicial Power of the United States, shall be vested in one supreme Court, and in such inferior Courts as the Congress may from time to time ordain and establish. The Judges, both of the supreme and inferior Courts, shall hold their Offices during good Behaviour, and shall, at stated Times, receive for their Services, a Compensation, which shall not be diminished during their Continuance in Office.

Like the power of Congress and the executive branch under Articles I and II, respectively, of the Constitution, the power of the federal judiciary has developed as the result of constitutional silences and ambiguities. Article III establishes only one federal court, the Supreme Court, and leaves to Congress the power to establish "inferior" courts as it deems necessary. Many students are surprised to learn that the power of judicial review was established by Congress, not the Supreme Court. Although the Court did articulate the power of judicial review in *Marbury* v. *Madison* (1803), that decision only applied to the power of the federal courts to review federal laws. The power of the federal courts to review state laws that allegedly trespassed upon the Constitution was established by the Judiciary Act of 1789. But on the fundamental question of what constitutes the foundation and scope of judicial power, there is little doubt that the Court, not Congress, has been the foremost exponent of its own authority. Often, the Court has justified its authority to limit the power of the other branches to regulate its affairs by pointing to other provisions of the Constitution, most notably the supremacy clause of Article VI and section 5 of the Fourteenth Amendment, as well as Article III.

Section 2.

The judicial Power shall extend to all Cases, in Law and Equity, arising under this Constitution, the Laws of the United States, and Treaties made, or which shall be made, under their Authority;—to all Cases affecting Ambassadors, other public Ministers and Consuls;—to all Cases of admiralty and maritime Jurisdiction;—to Controversies to which the United States shall be a Party;—to Controversies between two or more States;—between a State and Citizens of another State;—between Citizens of different States;—between Citizens of the same State claiming Lands under Grants of different States,—and between a State, or the Citizens thereof, and foreign States, Citizens or Subjects.

In all Cases affecting Ambassadors, other public Ministers and Consuls, and those in which a State shall be Party, the supreme Court shall have original Jurisdiction. In all the other Cases before mentioned, the supreme Court shall have appellate Jurisdiction, both as to Law and Fact, with such Exceptions, and under such Regulations as the Congress shall make.

The Trial of all Crimes, except in Cases of Impeachment, shall be by Jury; and such Trial shall be held in the State where the said Crimes shall have been committed; but when not committed within any State, the Trial shall be at such Place or Places as the Congress may by Law have directed.

Section 1 invests the judicial power in "one Supreme Court," but it is in section 2 that we find the source of much of the controversy of the exercise of this power since *Marbury* was decided. By extending the judicial power to all "Cases, in Law and Equity, arising under the Constitution, [and] the laws of the United States," section 2 authorizes the Court to both decide matters of law and, if necessary, mandate a remedy commensurate with the degree of a constitutional violation. For example, in *Swann v. Charlotte-Mecklenburg Board of Education* (1971), the Court ruled that a lower court, having found that a school system had failed to meet

desegregation requirements, had the power to order busing and other remedies to the constitutional violations it found in *Brown* v. *Board of Education* (1954).

Federal judicial power no longer extends to cases involving lawsuits between a state and citizens of another state. This provision was superceded by the Eleventh Amendment.

Section 2 also includes the exceptions and regulations clause. This clause has been used by congressional opponents of some of the Court's more controversial and generally liberal decisions. Although most scholars believe the clause limits the power of Congress to create broad jurisdiction for the courts it creates, others have argued that it permits Congress to strip the federal courts of jurisdiction to hear particular cases. Some opponents of the Court's decisions legalizing abortion, authorizing school busing, and upholding affirmative action have attempted to curb the power of federal courts to rule in such areas by stripping them of jurisdiction in such cases. To date, no president has ever signed such legislation.

Section 3.

Treason against the United States, shall consist only in levying War against them, or in adhering to their Enemies, giving them Aid and Comfort. No Person shall be convicted of Treason unless on the Testimony of two Witnesses to the same overt Act, or on Confession in open Court.

The Congress shall have Power to declare the Punishment of Treason, but no Attainder of Treason shall work Corruption of Blood, or Forfeiture except during the Life of the Person attainted.

Article III defines the only crime mentioned by the Constitution: treason.

ARTICLE IV
Section 1.

Full Faith and Credit shall be given in each State to the public Acts, Records, and judicial Proceedings of every other State. And the

Congress may by general Laws prescribe the Manner in which such Acts, Records and Proceedings shall be proved, and the Effect thereof.

The full faith and credit clause rests on principles borrowed from international law that require one country to recognize contracts made in another country absent a compelling public policy reason to the contrary. Here, this principle, referred to in the law as *comity*, applied to the relationship between the states. For example, a driver's license issued in Ohio is good in Montana. The full faith and credit clause also requires a state to recognize public acts and court proceedings of another state. For the most part, interpretation of the full faith and credit clause has not been controversial. That may well change, as advocates of same-sex marriage have suggested that such a marriage performed in one state must be recognized in another state, as is the case with heterosexual marriage. A constitutional challenge to the clause may well center on the public policy exception recognized in other areas of law.

Section 2.

The Citizens of each State shall be entitled to all Privileges and Immunities of Citizens in the several States.

A Person charged in any State with Treason, Felony, or other Crime, who shall flee from Justice, and be found in another State, shall on Demand of the executive Authority of the State from which he fled, be delivered up, to be removed to the State having Jurisdiction of the Crime.

The extradition clause requires that the governor of one state deliver a fugitive from justice to the state from which that fugitive fled. Congress passed the Fugitive Act of 1793 to give definition to this provision, but the federal government has no authority to compel state authorities to extradite a fugitive from one state to another. A state may, however, sue another state in federal court to force the return of a fugitive.

No Person held to Service or Labour in one State under the Laws thereof, escaping into another, shall, in Consequence of any Law or Regulation therein, be discharged from such Service or Labour, but shall be delivered up on Claim of the Party to whom such Service or Labour may be due.

The fugitive slave clause, which required any state, including those outside the slave-holding states of the South, to return escaped slaves to their owners, was repealed in 1865 by the Thirteenth Amendment. Prior to 1865, Congress passed laws in 1793 and 1850 to enforce the clause, leaving states without power to make concurrent laws on the subject, ensuring that the southern states would always have the Constitution on their side to protect slavery.

Section 3.

New States may be admitted by the Congress into this Union; but no new State shall be formed or erected within the Jurisdiction of any other State; nor any State be formed by the Junction of two or more States, or Parts of States, without the Consent of the Legislatures of the States concerned as well as of the Congress.

The Congress shall have Power to dispose of and make all needful Rules and Regulations respecting the Territory or other Property belonging to the United States; and nothing in this Constitution shall be so construed as to Prejudice any Claims of the United States, or of any particular State.

Section 4.

The United States shall guarantee to every State in this Union a Republican Form of Government, and shall protect each of them against Invasion; and on Application of the Legislature, or of the Executive (when the Legislature cannot be convened) against domestic Violence.

ARTICLE V

The Congress, whenever two thirds of both Houses shall deem it necessary, shall propose Amendments to this Constitution, or, on the Application of the Legislatures of two thirds of the several States, shall call a Convention for proposing Amendments, which, in either Case, shall be valid to all Intents and Purposes, as Part of this Constitution, when ratified by the Legislatures of three fourths of the several States, or by Conventions in three fourths thereof, as the one or the other Mode of Ratification may be proposed by the Congress; Provided that no Amendment which may be made prior to the Year One thousand eight hundred and eight shall in any Manner affect the first and fourth Clauses in the Ninth Section of the first Article; and that no State, without its Consent, shall be deprived of its equal Suffrage in the Senate.

Changes to the Articles of Confederation had required the unanimous approval of the states. But, Article V of the U.S. Constitution offers multiple options—none of which require unanimity—for constitutional change. Article V was quite crucial to the ratification of the Constitution. Federalists who supported the Constitution wanted to ensure that any additions or modifications to the nation's charter would require the approval of more than a simple majority of citizens. This is why any amendment coming out of Congress requires two-thirds of the House and Senate for approval. The same is true for the rule requiring three-fourths of the states to ratify an amendment (either through conventions or state legislative action). Anti-Federalists who either opposed the Constitution or had reservations about key sections of it were soothed by the prospect of an amending process that did not require the unanimous approval of the states.

Since 1789 only twenty-seven amendments have been added to the Constitution, the first fifteen of which were added by 1870. Since 1933, when the nation repealed Prohibition by passing the Twenty-First Amendment, the Constitution has been amended only six times. In the modern constitutional era, efforts to amend

the Constitution have generally centered on unhappiness with Supreme Court decisions (on school prayer, flag burning, school busing, abortion rights) or state court rulings with national implications (such as same-sex marriage) rather than any structural defect in the original Constitution (unlike woman's suffrage or presidential succession) or a seismic political event (the Civil War). To date, none of these efforts have been successful.

ARTICLE VI

All Debts contracted and Engagements entered into, before the Adoption of this Constitution, shall be as valid against the United States under this Constitution, as under the Confederation.

This Constitution, and the Laws of the United States which shall be made in Pursuance thereof; and all Treaties made, or which shall be made, under the Authority of the United States, shall be the supreme Law of the Land; and the Judges in every State shall be bound thereby, any Thing in the Constitution or Laws of any State to the Contrary notwithstanding.

The Senators and Representatives before mentioned, and the Members of the several State Legislatures, and all executive and judicial Officers, both of the United States and of the several States, shall be bound by Oath or Affirmation, to support this Constitution; but no religious Test shall ever be required as a Qualification to any Office or public Trust under the United States.

Article VI made the national government responsible for all debts incurred by the Revolutionary War. This ensured that manufacturing and banking interests would be repaid for the losses they sustained during the conflict. But the most important provisions of Article VI by far are contained in its second and third clauses.

Clause 2 took another major step forward for national power and away from the confederate approach to government structure of the Articles of Confederation. By making "this

Constitution" and all laws made under its authority the "supreme Law of the Land," Article VI created what constitutional scholars call the supremacy clause. The Supreme Court has invoked the supremacy clause on several occasions to rebut challenges mounted by states to its decisions or acts of Congress. Among the more notable decisions by the Supreme Court that have cited the supremacy clause to mandate compliance with a previous ruling is *Cooper* v. *Aaron* (1958). In *Cooper,* the Court cited the supremacy clause in rejecting the argument of Governor Orval Faubus of Arkansas claiming that local schools were not obligated to follow the *Brown* v. *Board of Education* (1954) ruling. The Court said that *Brown* was the law of the land and, as such, all school boards were required to comply with its requirement to desegregate their schools.

Although most Americans rightly point to the First Amendment as the baseline for the guarantee for religious freedom, clause 3 of Article VI contains an important contribution to this principle—the ban on religious tests or qualifications to hold public office. Holders of public office, no matter how great or small, were required to affirm their allegiance to the Constitution and the laws of the United States, but they could not be required to profess a belief in God or meet any other religious qualification. Numerous states nonetheless ignored this requirement until 1961, when the Supreme Court ruled in *Torcaso* v. *Watkins* that states could not administer religious oaths to holders of public office.

ARTICLE VII

The Ratification of the Conventions of nine States, shall be sufficient for the Establishment of this Constitution between the States so ratifying the Same.

Done in Convention by the Unanimous Consent of the States present the Seventeenth Day of September in the Year of our Lord one thousand seven hundred and Eighty seven and of the Independence of the United States of America the Twelfth. IN WITNESS whereof We have hereunto subscribed our Names,

G. WASHINGTON,
Presid't. and deputy from Virginia

Attest
WILLIAM JACKSON,
Secretary

DELAWARE
George Read
Gunning Bedford, Jr.
John Dickinson
Richard Basset
Jacob Broom

MASSACHUSETTS BAY
Nathaniel Gorham
Rufus King

CONNECTICUT
William Samuel Johnson
Roger Sherman

NEW YORK
Alexander Hamilton

NEW JERSEY
William Livingston
David Brearley
William Paterson
Jonathan Dayton

PENNSYLVANIA
Benjamin Franklin
Thomas Mifflin
Robert Morris
George Clymer
Thomas FitzSimons
Jared Ingersoll
James Wilson
Gouverneur Morris

NEW HAMPSHIRE
John Langdon
Nicholas Gilman

MARYLAND
James McHenry
Daniel of St. Thomas Jenifer
Daniel Carroll

VIRGINIA
John Blair
James Madison, Jr.

NORTH CAROLINA
William Blount
Richard Dobbs Spaight
Hugh Williamson

SOUTH CAROLINA
John Rutledge
Charles Cotesworth Pinckney
Charles Pinckney
Pierce Butler

GEORGIA
William Few
Abraham Baldwin

Articles in addition to, and amendment of the Constitution of the United States of America, proposed by Congress and ratified by the Legislatures of the several states, pursuant to the Fifth Article of the original Constitution.

(The first ten amendments were passed by Congress on September 25, 1789, and were ratified on December 15, 1791.)

AMENDMENT I

Congress shall make no law respecting an establishment of religion, or prohibiting the free exercise thereof; or abridging the freedom of speech, or of the press; or the right of the people peaceably to assemble, and to petition the Government for a redress of grievances.

For many Americans, the First Amendment represents the core of what the Bill of Rights stands for: limits on government power to limit or compel religious beliefs, the right to hold political opinions and express them, protection for a free press, the right to assemble peaceably, and the right to petition, through protest or the ballot, the government for a redress of political grievances. But it is also important to remember that the First Amendment, like most of the Bill of Rights, did not apply to state governments until the Supreme Court began to apply their substantive guarantees through the Fourteenth Amendment, a process that did not begin until 1925 in *Gitlow* v. *New York*.

Until then, state and local governments often failed to honor the rights and liberties that Congress, and by extension the national government, was expressly forbidden by the Constitution from withholding. For example, southern states, prior to the Civil War, outlawed pro-abolition literature; numerous states continued to collect taxes on behalf of state-sponsored churches and religious education; newspapers were often forbidden from publishing exposés on industry or political leaders because such speech was considered seditious and thus subject to prior restraint; public protests on behalf of unpopular causes were often banned by state breach of peace laws.

The Supreme Court has recognized other important rights implied by the enumerated guarantees of the First Amendment. These include the right to association, even when such association might come in the form of clubs or organizations that discriminate on the basis of race, sex, or religion, and the right to personal privacy, which the Supreme Court held in *Griswold* v. *Connecticut* (1965) was based in part on the right of married couples to make decisions about contraception, a decision protected by one's personal religious and political beliefs.

AMENDMENT II

A well regulated Militia, being necessary to the security of a free State, the right of the people to keep and bear Arms, shall not be infringed.

Few issues in American politics generate as much emotional heat as the extent to which Americans have a right to keep and bear arms. Supporters of broad gun ownership rights, such as the National Rifle Association, argue that the Second Amendment protects an almost absolute individual right to own just about any small arm that can be manufactured, whether for reasons of sport or self-defense. Proponents of gun control, such as The Brady Campaign to Prevent Gun Violence, argue that the amendment creates no such individual right, but refers instead to the Framers' belief—now outdated—that citizen militias had the right to form in order to protect themselves against other states and, if need be, the national government. Under this view, Congress and the states are free to regulate gun ownership and use as they see fit, provided that the national and state governments are within their constitutional orbit of power to do so.

The Supreme Court has not offered much help on the meaning of the Second Amendment. It has handed down only one case truly relying on the amendment, *U.S.* v. *Miller* (1939). There, a unanimous Court upheld a federal law requiring the registration of sawed-off shotguns purchased for personal use. While the Court rejected the position that the Second Amendment established an individual right to keep and bear arms, it did not close the door on individual gun ownership. This remains the constitutional baseline from which legislative battles over gun control legislation continue to be fought.

AMENDMENT III

No Soldier shall, in time of peace be quartered in any house, without the consent of the Owner, nor in time of war, but in a manner to be prescribed by law.

Among the complaints directed at King George III in the Declaration of Independence was the colonial-era practice of quartering large numbers of troops in private homes. The practice of quartering soldiers, along with the forced maintenance of British standing armies in times of peace without the consent of the colonial legislatures, formed a major component of the political grievances directed at the British Crown. The Third Amendment was intended to protect individuals and their property from the abuse common to the practice of quartering soldiers.

The Supreme Court has never ruled on the meaning of the Third Amendment, making it the only provision of the Bill of Rights to escape such attention. But the Court has referred to the Third Amendment as part of the penumbra of constitutional rights forming the basis for the right of personal privacy established in *Griswold* v. *Connecticut* (1965).

AMENDMENT IV

The right of the people to be secure in their persons, houses, papers, and effects, against unreasonable searches and seizures, shall not be violated, and no warrants shall issue, but upon probable cause, supported by Oath or affirmation, and particularly describing the place to be searched, and the persons or things to be seized.

Although the Fourth Amendment is often discussed in tandem with the Fifth, Sixth, and Eighth Amendments—the other major provisions of the Bill of Rights outlining the criminal due process guarantees of citizens—it shares a similar undercurrent that motivated the adoption of the Third Amendment: to eliminate the practice of British officers from using the general writ of assistance to enter private homes, conduct searches, and seize personal property. British officers had not been required to offer a specific reason for a search or justify the taking of particular items. In most cases, the writ of assistance was used to confiscate items considered to have violated the strict British customs laws of the colonial era.

The twin pillars of the Fourth Amendment, the probable cause and warrant requirements, are a direct reflection of the disdain the Framers had for the Revolutionary-era practices of the British. But, like the First Amendment, the guarantees of the Fourth Amendment did not apply to state and local law enforcement practices until well after the ratification of the Fourteenth Amendment. Until *Wolf* v. *Colorado* (1949), when the Court ruled that the Fourteenth Amendment made the Fourth Amendment binding on the states, evidence seized in violation of the probable cause or warrant requirements could be used against a criminal suspect. The Court's best-known decision on the Fourth Amendment, *Mapp* v. *Ohio* (1961), which established the exclusionary rule, also marked the high-water point in the rights afforded to criminal suspects challenging an unlawful search. Since the late 1970s, the Court has steadily added exceptions to the Fourth Amendment to permit law enforcement officers to engage in warrantless searches and seizures, provided that such practices meet a threshold of reasonableness in the context of the circumstances under which they are undertaken.

AMENDMENT V

No person shall be held to answer for a capital, or otherwise infamous crime, unless on a presentment or indictment of a Grand Jury, except in cases arising in the land or naval forces, or in the Militia, when in actual service in time of War or public danger; nor shall any person be subject for the same offence to be twice put in jeopardy of life or limb; nor shall be compelled in any criminal case to be a witness against himself, nor be deprived of life, liberty, or property, without due process of law; nor shall private property be taken for public use, without just compensation.

The Fifth Amendment, along with the Sixth Amendment, is the legacy of the Star Chamber tactics that figured prominently in the colonial-era system of British justice. By requiring that no person could be held for a "capital, or otherwise infamous" crime except upon indictment by a grand jury, the Fifth Amendment took an important step toward making the criminal indictment process a public function. Along with the public trial and trial by jury guarantees of the Sixth Amendment, the grand jury provision of the Fifth Amendment established that the government would have to make its case against the accused in public. Also, by guaranteeing that no person could be compelled to testify against himself or herself in a criminal proceeding, the Fifth Amendment highlighted the adversarial nature of the American criminal justice system, a feature that is distinct from its British counterpart. "Pleading the Fifth" is permissible in any criminal, civil, administrative, judicial, or investigatory context. *Miranda* v. *Arizona* (1966), one of the most famous rulings of the Supreme Court, established a right to silence that combined the ban against self-incrimination of the Fifth Amendment with the Sixth Amendment's guarantee of the assistance of counsel. The right to silence, unlike the ban against self-incrimination, extends to any aspect of an interrogation.

The Fifth Amendment also forbids double jeopardy, which prohibits the prosecution of a crime against the same person in the same jurisdiction twice, and prevents the government from taking life, liberty, or property without due process of law. This phrase was reproduced in the Fourteenth Amendment, placing an identical set of constraints on the states. The Court has applied all the guarantees of the Fifth Amendment, with the exception of the grand jury provision, to the states through the due process clause of the Fourteenth Amendment. Some constitutional scholars also consider the due process clause of the Fifth Amendment to embrace an equal protection provision when applied to federal cases.

The final provision of the Fifth Amendment prohibits the government from taking private property for public use without just compensation. Litigation on the takings clause, as some scholars refer to this provision, has generally centered on two major questions. The first is what constitutes a taking, either by the government's decision to seize private property or by regulating it to the point where its value is greatly diminished. The second question centers on what the appropriate level of compensation is for owners who have successfully established a taking.

AMENDMENT VI

In all criminal prosecutions, the accused shall enjoy the right to a speedy and public trial, by an impartial jury of the State and district wherein the crime shall have been committed, which district shall have been previously ascertained by law, and to be informed of the nature and cause of the accusation; to be confronted with the witnesses against him; to have compulsory process for obtaining witnesses in his favor, and to have the assistance of counsel for his defence.

The centerpiece of the constitutional guarantees afforded to individuals facing criminal prosecution, the Sixth Amendment sets out eight specific rights, more than any other provision of the Bill of Rights. As with the Fifth Amendment, the core features of the Sixth Amendment build upon the unfortunate legacy of the Star Chamber practices of colonial-era Britain. The very first provision of the Sixth Amendment mandates that individuals subject to criminal prosecution receive "a speedy and public trial"; it then requires that all such trials take place in public, with the defendant informed of the cause and nature of the accusation against him or her. The common theme underlying these sections of the Sixth Amendment, as well as those requiring witnesses for the prosecution to testify in public, allowing the defendant to produce witnesses on his or her own behalf, and securing the assistance of counsel, is that any citizen threatened with the deprivation of liberty is entitled to have the case made against him or her in public. The Fifth Amendment cleared an important initial hurdle to secret justice by requiring the government to produce evidence that did not rely on confessions and self-incrimination; the Fourth Amendment required that any such evidence must be acquired lawfully and with the knowledge of a public magistrate. The Sixth Amendment establishes, in principle, the American criminal justice system as one that is open and public.

Since the vast majority of criminal prosecutions in the United States are undertaken by state and local authorities, the parchment promises of the Sixth Amendment did not extend to most Americans until the Supreme Court began incorporating the guarantees of the Bill of Rights to the states through the Fourteenth Amendment. Perhaps the best-known case involving the Sixth Amendment is *Gideon* v. *Wainwright* (1963), which held that all persons accused of a serious crime are entitled to an attorney, even if they cannot afford one, a rule that was soon extended to cover misdemeanors as well. Three years later, the Supreme Court fused the right to counsel rule established in *Gideon* with the Fifth Amendment ban against self-incrimination to create the principles animating *Miranda* v. *Arizona*. For a long time, the Court had never interpreted the Fifth and Sixth Amendments to mean that individuals had rights to criminal due process guarantees if they did not know about them or could not afford them. Decisions such as *Gideon* and *Miranda* offered a clear departure from this position.

The speedy and public trial clauses only require that criminal trials take place in public within a reasonable amount of time after the period of indictment, and that juries in such cases are unbiased. Americans also often cite the Sixth Amendment as entitling them to a trial by a "jury of one's peers." This is true to the extent individuals are entitled to a trial in the jurisdiction where the crime is alleged to have been committed. It does not mean, however, that they are entitled to a trial by persons of a similar age or background, for example.

AMENDMENT VII

In Suits at common law, where the value in controversy shall exceed twenty dollars, the right of trial by jury shall be preserved, and no fact tried by a jury, shall be otherwise re-examined in any Court of the United States, than according to the rules of the common law.

One feature of the British courts that the Framers sought to preserve in the American civil law system was the distinction between courts of *common law* and courts of *equity*. Common law courts heard cases involving strict legal rules, while equity courts based their decisions on principles of fairness and totality of circumstances. Common law courts featured juries, who were authorized to return verdicts entitling plaintiffs to financial compensation for losses incurred, whereas equity courts relied upon judges to make determinations about appropriate relief for successful parties. Relief in equity courts did not consist of monetary awards, but injunctions, cease-and-desist orders, and so on. The Seventh Amendment carried over this British feature into the Constitution.

In 1938, Congress amended the Federal Rules of Civil Procedure to combine the function of civil common law and equity courts. In cases involving both legal and equitable claims, a federal judge must first decide the issue of law before moving to the equitable relief, or remedy, component of the trial. Judges are permitted to instruct juries on matters of law and fact, and may emphasize certain facts or legal issues to the jury in their instructions to the jury. But the jury alone decides guilt or innocence. In some extraordinary cases, a judge may overturn the verdict of a jury. This happens only when a judge believes the jury has disregarded completely the facts and evidence before it in reaching a verdict.

Congress has also changed the $20 threshold for the right to a trial by jury. The amount is now $75,000. Finally, the Seventh Amendment has never been incorporated to the states through the Fourteenth Amendment.

AMENDMENT VIII

Excessive bail shall not be required, nor excessive fines imposed, nor cruel and unusual punishments inflicted.

For an amendment of so few words, the Eighth Amendment has generated an enormous volume of commentary and litigation since its ratification. This should not be surprising, as the three major provisions of the amendment deal with some of the most sensitive and emotionally charged issues involving the rights of criminal defendants.

The origin of the excessive bail clause stems from the reforms to the British system instituted by the 1689 English Bill of Rights. Having had limited success in preventing law enforcement officials from detaining suspects by imposing outrageous bail requirements, Britain amended previous laws to say that "excessive bail ought not to be required." Much like the British model, the Eighth Amendment does not state what an "excessive bail" is or the particular criminal offense that warrants a high bail amount. The Supreme Court has offered two fundamental rules on the excessive bail clause. First, a judge has the discretion to decide if a criminal offense is sufficiently serious to justify high bail. Second, a judge has the power, under *U.S.* v. *Salerno* (1987), to deny a criminal defendant bail as a "preventative measure." In both such cases, a judge's action must be considered proportionate to the nature of the criminal offense for which an individual stands accused.

Like the excessive bail clause, the excessive fines clause is rooted in the English Bill of Rights. The clause applies only to criminal proceedings, not civil litigation. For example, a tobacco company cannot appeal what it believes is an excessive jury award under this clause. An indigent criminal defendant, however, can challenge a fine levied in connection with a criminal conviction.

The most controversial section of the Eighth Amendment is the clause forbidding cruel and unusual punishments. The absence of such a guarantee from the Constitution was a major impetus for the adoption of the Bill of Rights. While most historians agree that the Framers wanted to prohibit barbaric forms of punishment, including torture, as well as arbitrary and disproportionate penalties, there is little consensus on what specific punishments met this definition. By the late 1800s, the Supreme Court had ruled that such punishments as public burnings, disembowelment, and drawing and quartering crossed the Eighth Amendment barrier. In *Weems* v. *U.S.* (1910), the Court went the additional of step of concluding that any punishment considered "excessive" would violate the cruel and unusual punishment clause. And, in *Solem* v. *Helm* (1983), the Court developed a "proportionality" standard that required punishments, even simple incarceration, to bear a rational relationship to the offense.

The Court has never ruled, however, that the death penalty per se violates the Eighth Amendment. It has developed certain rules and exceptions governing the application of the death penalty, such as requiring a criminal defendant actually to have killed, or attempted to have killed, a victim. It has also ruled that the mentally retarded, as a class, are exempt from the death penalty. But it has also issued highly controversial decisions concluding, for example, that neither racial disparities in the application of capital punishment nor juvenile status at the time the offense was committed violate the Eighth Amendment. Absent a four-year ban on the practice between 1972 and 1976, the death penalty has always been an available punishment in the American criminal justice system.

AMENDMENT IX

The enumeration in the Constitution, of certain rights, shall not be construed to deny or disparage others retained by the people.

A major point of contention between the Federalists and Anti-Federalists was the need for a bill of rights. In *Federalist No. 84*, Alexander Hamilton argued that a bill of rights was unnecessary, as there was no need to place limits on the power of government to do things that it was not authorized by the Constitution to do. Hamilton also argued that it would be impossible to list all the rights "retained by the people." Protecting some rights but not others would suggest that Americans had surrendered certain rights to their government when, in Hamilton's view, the Constitution did nothing of the sort.

Given his well-deserved reputation for unbridled national power, Hamilton's views have often been dismissed as a cynical ploy to sidestep any meaningful discussion of the Bill of Rights and speed along the ratification process. But James Madison, along with Thomas Jefferson, held a much deeper belief in the need for a bill of rights. Madison also believed that the enumeration of certain rights and liberties in the Constitution should not be understood to deny others that exist as a condition of citizenship in a free society. Madison, the primary author of the Bill of Rights, included the Ninth Amendment to underscore this belief.

The Supreme Court has never offered a clear and definitive interpretation of the Ninth Amendment, primarily because it has been wary of giving such general language any substantive definition. The amendment has been cited in such decisions as *Griswold* v. *Connecticut* (1965) and *Richmond Newspapers* v. *Virginia* (1980) along with other constitutional amendments to bolster the case on behalf of an asserted constitutional right. The difficulty in constructing a specific meaning for the Ninth Amendment can be illustrated by the fact that both supporters and opponents of legal abortion have cited it to defend the feasibility of their respective positions.

AMENDMENT X

The powers not delegated to the United States by the Constitution, nor prohibited by it to the States, are reserved to the States respectively, or to the people.

The Tenth Amendment generated little controversy during the ratification process over the Bill of Rights. As the Supreme Court later ruled in *U.S.* v. *Darby* (1941), the Tenth Amendment states a truism about the relationship between the boundaries of national and state power—that the states retain those powers not specifically set out in the Constitution as belonging to the national government. There is little in the history in the debate over the Tenth Amendment to suggest that its language is anything other than declaratory. Indeed, the refusal of the 1st Congress to insert the word "expressly" before "delegated" strongly suggests that James Madison, who offered the most thorough explanation of the amendment during the floor debates, intended to leave room for this relationship to evolve as future events made necessary.

The earliest political and constitutional developments involving the Tenth Amendment tilted the balance of power firmly in favor of national power. Alexander Hamilton's vision for a national bank to consolidate the nation's currency and trading position was realized in *McCulloch* v. *Maryland* (1819), in which the Court held that Article I granted Congress broad power to make all laws "necessary and proper" to the exercise of its legislative power. By no means, however, did *McCulloch* settle the argument over the power reserved to the states. Led by Chief Justice Roger B. Taney, the Court handed down several decisions in the three decades leading up to the Civil War that offered substantial protection to the southern states on the matters closest to their hearts: slavery and economic sovereignty. From the period after the Civil War until the New Deal, the Court continued to shield states from congressional legislation designed to regulate the economy and promote social and political reform. After the constitutional revolution of 1937, when the Court threw its support behind the New Deal, Congress received a blank constitutional check to engage in the regulatory action that featured an unprecedented level of federal intervention in economic and social matters once the purview of the states, one that would last almost sixty years.

Beginning in *New York* v. *U.S.* (1992), however, the Court, in striking down a key provision of a federal environmental law, began to revisit the New Deal assumptions that underlay its modern interpretation of the Tenth Amendment. A few years later, in *U.S.* v. *Lopez* (1995), it invalidated a federal gun control law on the ground that Congress lacked authority under the commerce clause to regulate gun possession. And, in *U.S.* v. *Printz* (1997), the Tenth Amendment explicitly was cited to strike down an important section of the Brady Bill, a congressional law that required states to conduct background checks on prospective gun buyers. Although the Court has not returned to the dual federalism posture on the Tenth Amendment that it built from the years between the Taney Court and the triumph of the New Deal, these decisions make clear that the constitutional status of the states as actors in the federal system has been dramatically strengthened.

citizen from bringing suit against a state in federal court. Citizens may bring lawsuits against state officials in federal court if they can satisfy the requirement that their rights under federal constitutional or statutory law have been violated. The Eleventh Amendment has not been extensively litigated in modern times, but the extent to which states are immune under federal law from citizen lawsuits has reemerged as an important constitutional question in recent years. For example, the Court has said in several cases that the doctrine of sovereign immunity prevents citizens from suing state agencies under the Americans with Disabilities Act of 1990. But as recently as 2003, the Court, in *Nevada* v. *Hibbs,* ruled that the Family and Medical Leave Act of 1993 did not immunize state government agencies against lawsuits brought by former state employees. States are also free to waive their immunity and consent to a lawsuit.

AMENDMENT XI
(Ratified on February 7, 1795)

The Judicial power of the United States shall not be construed to extend to any suit in law or equity, commenced or prosecuted against one of the United States by Citizens of another State, or by Citizens or Subjects of any Foreign State.

The Eleventh Amendment was prompted by one the earliest notable decisions of the Supreme Court, *Chisholm* v. *Georgia* (1793). In *Chisholm,* the Court held that Article III and the enforcement provision of the Judiciary Act of 1789 permitted a citizen of one state to bring suit against another state in federal court. Almost immediately after *Chisholm,* the Eleventh Amendment was introduced and promptly ratified, as the states saw this decision as a threat to their sovereignty under the new Constitution. The amendment was passed in less than a year, which, by the standards of the era, was remarkably fast.

The Eleventh Amendment nullified the result in *Chisholm* but did not completely bar a

AMENDMENT XII
(Ratified on June 15, 1804)

The Electors shall meet in their respective states, and vote by ballot for President and Vice-President, one of whom, at least, shall not be an inhabitant of the same state with themselves; they shall name in their ballots the person voted for as President, and in distinct ballots the person voted for as Vice-President, and they shall make distinct lists of all persons voted for as President, and of all persons voted for as Vice-President, and of the number of votes for each, which lists they shall sign and certify, and transmit sealed to the seat of the government of the United States, directed to the President of the Senate;—The President of the Senate shall, in the presence of the Senate and House of Representatives, open all the certificates and the votes shall then be counted;—The person having the greatest number of votes for President, shall be the President, if such number be a majority of the whole number of Electors appointed; and if no person have such majority; then from the persons having the highest numbers not exceeding three on the list of those voted for as President, the House of Representatives shall choose immediately, by ballot, the President. But in choosing the President, the votes shall be taken by states, the representation from each state having one vote; a quorum for this purpose shall consist of a member or members from two-thirds of the states, and a majority of all the states shall be necessary to a choice. And if the House of Representatives shall not choose a President whenever the right of choice shall devolve upon them, before the fourth day of March next following, then the Vice-President shall act as President, as in the case of the death or other constitutional disability of the President.—The person having the greatest number of votes as Vice-President, shall be the Vice-President, if such number be a majority of the whole number of Electors appointed, and if no person have a majority, then from the two highest numbers on the list, the Senate shall choose the Vice-President; a quorum for the purpose shall consist of two-thirds of the whole number of Senators, and a majority of the whole number shall be necessary to a choice. But no person constitutionally ineligible to the office of President shall be eligible to that of Vice-President of the United States.

The Twelfth Amendment was added to the Constitution after the 1800 presidential election was thrown into the House of Representatives. Thomas Jefferson and Aaron Burr, running on the Democratic-Republican Party ticket, each received seventy-three electoral votes for president, even though everyone knew that Jefferson was the presidential candidate and Burr the vice presidential candidate. This was possible because Article II, section 1, did not require electors to vote for president and vice president separately. The Twelfth Amendment remedied this deficiency by requiring electors to cast their votes for president and vice president separately.

Whether it intended to or not, the Twelfth Amendment took a major step toward institutionalizing the party system in the United States. The 1796 election yielded a president

and vice president from different parties, a clear indication that partisan differences were emerging in a distinct form. The 1800 election simply highlighted the problem further. By requiring electors to make their presidential and vice presidential choices separately, the Twelfth Amendment conceded that a party system in American politics had indeed evolved, an inevitable but nonetheless disappointing development to the architects of the original constitutional vision.

AMENDMENT XIII
(Ratified on December 6, 1865)

Section 1.

Neither slavery nor involuntary servitude, except as a punishment for crime whereof the party shall have been duly convicted, shall exist within the United States, or any place subject to their jurisdiction.

Section 2.

Congress shall have power to enforce this article by appropriate legislation.

The Thirteenth, Fourteenth, and Fifteenth Amendments are known collectively as the Civil War Amendments.

In anticipation of a Union victory, the Thirteenth Amendment was passed by Congress and sent to the states for ratification before the end of the Civil War. The amendment not only formally abolished slavery and involuntary servitude; it also served as the constitutional foundation for the nation's first major civil rights legislation, the Civil Rights Act of 1866. This law extended numerous rights to African Americans previously held in servitude as well as those having free status during the Civil War, including the right to purchase, rent, and sell personal property, to bring suit in federal court, to enter into contracts, and to receive the full and equal benefit of all laws "enjoyed by white citizens." The Thirteenth Amendment overturned the pre–Civil War decision of the Supreme Court in *Dred Scott* v. *Sandford* (1857), which held that

slaves were not people entitled to constitutional rights, but property subject to the civil law binding them to their masters.

In modern times, the Court has ruled that the Thirteenth Amendment prohibits any action that recognizes a "badge" or "condition" of slavery, such as housing discrimination and certain forms of employment discrimination. The Department of Justice also has used the Thirteenth Amendment to file lawsuits against manufacturing sweatshops and other criminal enterprises in which persons are forced to work without compensation.

AMENDMENT XIV
(Ratified on July 9, 1868)

Section 1.

All persons born or naturalized in the United States, and subject to the jurisdiction thereof, are citizens of the United States and of the State wherein they reside. No State shall make or enforce any law which shall abridge the privileges or immunities of citizens of the United States; nor shall any State deprive any person of life, liberty, or property, without due process of law; nor deny to any person within its jurisdiction the equal protection of the laws.

Many constitutional scholars believe the Fourteenth Amendment is the most important addition to the Constitution since the Bill of Rights was ratified in 1791. In addition to serving as a cornerstone of Reconstruction policy, section 1 eliminated the distinction between the rights and liberties of Americans as citizens of their respective states and those to which they were entitled under the Bill of Rights as citizens of the United States. The Republican leadership that drafted and steered the Fourteenth Amendment to passage left no doubt that the three major provisions of section 1, which placed express limits on state power to abridge rights and liberties protected as a condition of national citizenship, were intended to make the Bill of Rights binding upon the states, thus overruling *Barron* v. *Baltimore* (1833). Although the

Supreme Court has never endorsed this view, the selective incorporation of the Bill of Rights to the states during the twentieth century through the Fourteenth Amendment ultimately made the Reconstruction-era vision of the Republicans a reality. The former Confederate states were required to ratify the Fourteenth Amendment to qualify for readmission into the union.

Section 2.

Representatives shall be apportioned among the several States according to their respective numbers, counting the whole number of persons in each State, excluding Indians not taxed. But when the right to vote at any election for the choice of electors for President and Vice President of the United States, Representatives in Congress, the Executive and Judicial officers of a State, or the members of the Legislature thereof, is denied to any of the male inhabitants of such State, being twenty-one years of age, and citizens of the United States, or in any way abridged, except for participation in rebellion, or other crime, the basis of representation therein shall be reduced in the proportion which the number of such male citizens shall bear to the whole number of male citizens twenty-one years of age in such State.

Section 2 established two major changes to the Constitution. First, by stating that representatives from each state would be apportioned based on the number of "whole" persons in each state, section 2 modified theThree-Fifths Compromise of Article 1, section 2, clause 3, of the original Constitution. Note, however, that section 2 still called for the exclusion of Indians "not taxed" from the apportionment criteria. Second, section 2, for the first time anywhere in the Constitution, mentions that only "male" inhabitants of the states age twenty-one or older would be counted toward representation in the House of Representatives and eligible to vote. The Military Reconstruction Act of 1867 had strengthened Republican power in the southern states by stripping former Confederates of the right to vote, a law that, in conjunction with the gradual addition of blacks to the voting rolls, made enactment of the Fourteenth Amendment possible. Section 2 further solidified the Republican presence in the South by eliminating from apportionment counts any person that participated in the rebellion.

Section 3.

No person shall be a Senator or Representative in Congress, or elector of President and Vice President, or hold any office, civil or military, under the United States, or under any State, who, having previously taken an oath, as a member of Congress, or as an officer of the United States, or as a member of any State legislature, or as an executive or judicial officer of any State, to support the Constitution of the United States, shall have engaged in insurrection or rebellion against the same, or given aid or comfort to the enemies thereof. But Congress may by a vote of two-thirds of each House, remove such disability.

Section 3 also reflected the power of the Reconstruction-era Republicans over the South. By eliminating the eligibility of former Confederates for public office or to serve as an elector for president or vice president, the Republicans strengthened their presence in Congress and throughout national politics. This measure also allowed African Americans to run for and hold office in the South, which they were doing by 1870, the same year the Fifteenth Amendment was ratified.

In December 1868, five months after the ratification of the Fourteenth Amendment, President Andrew Johnson declared universal amnesty for all former Confederates. This measure had the effect of returning white politicians and by extension the Democratic Party to power in the South. Republican concern over this development was a major force behind the adoption of the Fifteenth Amendment, which was viewed as an instrument to protect Republican political power by securing black enfranchisement. However, Republican president Ulysses S. Grant, who defeated Johnson in 1868, pardoned all but a few hundred remaining Confederate sympathizers by signing the

Amnesty Act of 1872. Decisions such as these began the gradual undoing of Republican commitment to black civil rights in the South.

Section 4.

The validity of the public debt of the United States, authorized by law, including debts incurred for payment of pensions and bounties for services in suppressing insurrection or rebellion, shall not be questioned. But neither the United States nor any State shall assume or pay any debt or obligation incurred in aid of insurrection or rebellion against the United States, or any claim for the loss or emancipation of any slave, but all such debts, obligations and claims shall be held illegal and void.

Section 4 repudiated the South's desire to have Congress forgive the Confederacy's war debts. It also rejected any claim that former slaveholders had to be compensated for the loss of their slaves.

Section 5.

The Congress shall have power to enforce, by appropriate legislation, the provisions of this article.

By giving Congress the power to enforce the provisions of the Fourteenth Amendment, section 5 reiterated the post–Civil War emphasis on national citizenship and the limit on state power to deny individuals their constitutional rights. Section 5 also extended congressional law-making power beyond those areas outlined in Article I. But the Court has taken a mixed view of the scope of congressional power to enforce the Fourteenth Amendment. In *Katzenbach* v. *Morgan* (1966), for example, the Supreme Court offered a broad ruling on the section 5 power of Congress. It held that Congress could enact laws establishing rights beyond what the Court said the Constitution required, as long as such laws were designed to establish a remedial constitutional right or protect citizens from a potential constitutional violation. In other cases, such as *City of Boerne* v. *Flores* (1997) and *U.S.* v. *Morrison* (2000), the Court ruled that Congress may not intrude upon the authority of the judicial branch to define the meaning of the Constitution or intrude on the power of the states to make laws within their own domain.

AMENDMENT XV
(Ratified on February 3, 1870)

Section 1.

The right of citizens of the United States to vote shall not be denied or abridged by the United States or by any State on account of race, color, or previous condition of servitude.

Section 2.

The Congress shall have power to enforce this article by appropriate legislation.

The Fifteenth Amendment was the most controversial of the Civil War Amendments, both for what it did and did not do. Although the adoption of the Thirteenth and Fourteenth Amendments made clear that blacks could not be returned to their pre–Civil War slavery, enthusiasm for a constitutional right of black suffrage, even among the northern states, was another matter. On the one hand, the extension of voting rights to blacks was the most dramatic outcome of the Civil War. The former Confederate states had to ratify the Fifteenth Amendment as a condition for readmission into the union. On the other hand, the rejection of proposed language forbidding discrimination on the basis of property ownership, education, or religious belief gave states the power to regulate the vote as they wished. And, with the collapse of Reconstruction after the 1876 election, southern states implemented laws created by this opening with full force, successfully crippling black voter registration for generations to come in the region where most African Americans lived. Full enfranchisement for African Americans would not arrive until the passage of the Voting Rights Act of 1965, almost one hundred years after the ratification of the Fifteenth Amendment.

The Fifteenth Amendment also divided woman's rights organizations that had campaigned on behalf of abolition and black enfranchisement. Feminists such as Elizabeth Cady Stanton and Susan B. Anthony were furious over the exclusion of women from the Fifteenth Amendment and opposed its ratification, while others, such as Lucy Stone, were willing to support black voting rights at the expense of woman's suffrage, leaving that battle for another day. The Supreme Court sided with those who opposed female enfranchisement, ruling in *Minor* v. *Happersett* (1875) that the Fourteenth Amendment did not recognize among the privileges and immunities of American citizenship a constitutional right to vote.

AMENDMENT XVI
(Ratified on February 3, 1913)

The Congress shall have power to lay and collect taxes on incomes, from whatever source derived, without apportionment among the several States, and without regard to any census or enumeration.

The Sixteenth Amendment was a response to the Supreme Court's sharply divided ruling in *Pollock* v. *Farmers' Loan & Trust Co.* (1895), which struck down the Income Tax Act of 1894 as unconstitutional. The Court, by a 5–4 margin, held that the law violated Article I, section 9, which prevented Congress from enacting a direct tax (on individuals) unless in proportion to the U.S. Census. In some ways, this was a curious holding, since the Court had permitted Congress to enact a direct tax on individuals during the Civil War. Between the *Pollock* decision and the enactment of the Sixteenth Amendment, the Court approved of taxes levied on corporations, as such taxes were not really taxes but "excises" levied on "incidents of ownership."

Anti-tax groups have claimed the Sixteenth Amendment was never properly ratified and is thus unconstitutional. The federal courts have rejected that view and have sanctioned and fined individuals who have brought such frivolous challenges to court.

AMENDMENT XVII
(Ratified on April 8, 1913)

The Senate of the United States shall be composed of two Senators from each State, elected by the people thereof, for six years; and each Senator shall have one vote. The electors in each State shall have the qualifications requisite for electors of the most numerous branch of the State legislatures.

When vacancies happen in the representation of any State in the Senate, the executive authority of such State shall issue writs of election to fill such vacancies: Provided, That the legislature of any State may empower the executive thereof to make temporary appointments until the people fill the vacancies by election as the legislature may direct.

This amendment shall not be so construed as to affect the election or term of any Senator chosen before it becomes valid as part of the Constitution.

The Seventeenth Amendment repealed the language in Article I, section 3, of the original Constitution, which called for the election of U.S. senators by state legislatures. This method had its roots in the selection of delegates to the Constitutional Convention, who were chosen by the state legislatures. It was also the preferred method of the Framers, who believed that having state legislatures elect senators would strengthen the relationship between the states and the national government, and also contribute to the stability of Congress by removing popular electoral pressure from the upper chamber.

Dissatisfaction set in with this method during the period leading up to the Civil War, especially by the 1850s. Indiana, for example, deeply divided between Union supporters in the northern part of the state and Confederate sympathizers in the southern part, could not agree on the selection of senators and was without representation for two years. After the Civil War, numerous Senate elections were tainted by corruption, and many more resulted in ties that prevented seating senators in a timely fashion. In 1899, Delaware's election was so mired in controversy that it did not have representation in the Senate for four years.

The ratification of the Seventeenth Amendment was the result of almost two decades of persistent efforts at reform. By 1912, twenty-nine states had changed their election laws to require the popular election of senators. In the years before that, constitutional amendments were introduced on a regular basis calling for the popular election of senators. Although many powerful legislators entrenched in the Senate resisted such change, the tide of reform, now aided by journalists and scholars sympathetic to the cause, proved too powerful to withstand. One year after the Seventeenth Amendment was sent to the states for ratification all members of the Senate were elected by the popular vote.

AMENDMENT XVIII
(Ratified on January 16, 1919)

Section 1.

After one year from the ratification of this article the manufacture, sale, or transportation of intoxicating liquors within, the importation thereof into, or the exportation thereof from the United States and all territory subject to the jurisdiction thereof for beverage purposes is hereby prohibited.

Section 2.

The Congress and the several States shall have concurrent power to enforce this article by appropriate legislation.

Section 3.

This article shall be inoperative unless it shall have been ratified as an amendment to the Constitution by the legislatures of the several States, as provided in the Constitution, within seven years from the date of the submission hereof to the States by the Congress.

The Eighteenth Amendment was the end result of a crusade against the consumption of alcoholic beverages than began during the early nineteenth century. A combination of Christian organizations emboldened by the second Great Awakening and women's groups, who believed alcohol contributed greatly to domestic violence and poverty, campaigned to abolish manufacture, sale, and use of alcoholic beverages in the United States. Their campaign was moderately successful in the pre–Civil War era. By 1855, thirteen states had banned the sale of "intoxicating" beverages. By the end of the Civil War, however, ten states had repealed their prohibition laws.

Another wave of anti-alcohol campaigning soon emerged, however, as the Women's Christian Temperance Union, founded in 1874 and 250,000 strong by 1911, and the Anti-Saloon League, founded in 1913, pressed the case for Prohibition. Among the arguments offered by supporters of Prohibition were that the cereal grains used in the manufacture of beer and liquor diverted valuable resources from food supplies and that the malaise of drunkenness sapped the strength of manufacturing production at home and the conduct of America's soldiers in World War I. Underneath the formal case for Prohibition was a considerable anti-immigrant sentiment, as many Prohibitionists considered the waves of Italian, Irish, Poles, and German immigrants unduly dependent on alcohol.

In 1919, Congress passed the Eighteenth Amendment over President Woodrow Wilson's veto. That same year, Congress passed the Volstead Act, which implemented Prohibition and authorized law enforcement to target illegal shipments of alcohol into the United States (mostly from Canada, which, ironically, also mandated Prohibition in most of its provinces during this time) as well as alcoholic beverages illegally manufactured in the United States. Evidence remains inconclusive over just how successful the Eighteenth Amendment was in reducing alcohol consumption in the United States. More certain was the billion-dollar windfall that Prohibition created for organized crime, as well as small-time smugglers and bootleggers.

AMENDMENT XIX
(Ratified on August 18, 1920)

The right of citizens of the United States to vote shall not be denied or abridged by the United States or by any State on account of sex.

Congress shall have power to enforce this article by appropriate legislation.

The two major women's rights organizations of the nineteenth century most active in the battle for female enfranchisement were the National Woman Suffrage Association and the American Woman Suffrage Association. The NWSA campaigned for a constitutional amendment modeled on the Fifteenth Amendment, which had secured African American voting rights, while the AWSA preferred to pursue women's voting rights through state-level legislative initiatives. In 1890, the two organizations combined to form the National American Woman Suffrage Association. By 1919, the NAWSA, the newer, more radical national woman's party, and other activists had secured congressional passage of the Nineteenth Amendment by a broad margin. It was ratified by the states just over a year later.

The Nineteenth Amendment, however, did not free black women from the voting restrictions that southern states placed in the way of African Americans. They and other minorities were not protected from such restrictions until the passage of the Voting Rights Act of 1965.

AMENDMENT XX
(Ratified on February 6, 1933)

Section 1.

The terms of the President and Vice President shall end at noon on the 20th day of January, and the terms of Senators and Representatives at noon on the 3d day of January, of the years in which such terms would have ended if this article had not been ratified; and the terms of their successors shall then begin.

Section 2.

The Congress shall assemble at least once in every year, and such meeting shall begin at noon on the 3d day of January, unless they shall by law appoint a different day.

Section 3.

If, at the time fixed for the beginning of the term of the President, the President elect shall have died, the Vice President elect shall become President. If a President shall not have been chosen before the time fixed for the beginning of his term, or if the President elect shall have failed to qualify, then the Vice President elect shall act as President until a President shall have qualified; and the Congress may by law provide for the case wherein neither a President elect nor a Vice President elect shall have qualified, declaring who shall then act as President, or the manner in which one who is to act shall be selected, and such person shall act accordingly until a President or Vice President shall have qualified.

Section 4.

The Congress may by law provide for the case of the death of any of the persons from whom the House of Representatives may choose a President whenever the rights of choice shall have devolved upon them, and for the case of the death of any of the persons from whom the Senate may choose a Vice President whenever the right of choice shall have devolved upon them.

Section 5.

Sections 1 and 2 shall take effect on the 15th day of October following the ratification of this article.

Section 6.

This article shall be inoperative unless it shall have been ratified as an amendment to the Constitution by the legislatures of three-fourths of the several States within seven years from the date of its submission.

The Twentieth Amendment is often called the lame duck amendment because its fundamental purpose was to shorten the time between the November elections, particularly in a presidential election year, and the starting date of the new presidential term and the commencement of the new congressional session. The amendment modified section 1 of the Twelfth Amendment by moving the beginning of the annual legislative session from March 4 to January 3. This change meant that the newly elected Congress would decide any presidential election thrown into the House of Representatives. It also eliminated the possibility that the nation would have to endure two additional months without a chief executive.

The Twentieth Amendment also modified Article I of the Constitution by placing a fixed time—noon—to begin the congressional session.

AMENDMENT XXI
(Ratified on December 5, 1933)

Section 1.

The eighteenth article of amendment to the Constitution of the United States is hereby repealed.

Section 2.

The transportation or importation into any State, Territory, or possession of the United States for delivery or use therein of intoxicating liquors, in violation of the laws thereof, is hereby prohibited.

Section 3.

This article shall be inoperative unless it shall have been ratified as an amendment to the Constitution by conventions in the several States, as provided in the Constitution, within seven years from the date of the submission hereof to the States by the Congress.

The Twenty-First Amendment repealed the Eighteenth Amendment, which was the first and last time that a constitutional amendment has been repealed. The Twenty-First Amendment is also the only amendment to the Constitution

approved by state ratifying conventions rather than a popular vote.

By the late 1920s, Americans had tired of Prohibition, and the arrival of the Great Depression in 1929 did nothing to lift their spirits. Few public officials, well aware of the extensive criminal enterprises that had grown up around Prohibition and had made a mockery of the practice, attempted to defend Prohibition as a success. Indeed, Franklin D. Roosevelt, in his initial bid for the presidency in 1932, made the repeal of Prohibition a campaign promise. In January 1933, Congress amended the Volstead Act to permit the sale of alcoholic beverages with an alcohol content of 3.2 percent. The ratification of the Twenty-First Amendment in December returned absolute control of the regulation of alcohol to the states. States are now free to regulate alcohol as they see fit. They may, for example, limit the quantity and type of alcohol sold to consumers, or ban alcohol sales completely. The Supreme Court, in *South Carolina* v. *Dole* (1984), ruled that Congress may require the states to set a certain age for the consumption of alcohol in return for participation in a federal program without violating the Twenty-First Amendment.

AMENDMENT XXII
(Ratified on February 27, 1951)

Section 1.

No person shall be elected to the office of the President more than twice, and no person who has held the office of President, or acted as President, for more than two years of a term to which some other person was elected President shall be elected to the office of the President more than once. But this Article shall not apply to any person holding the office of President when this Article was proposed by the Congress, and shall not prevent any person who may be holding the office of President, or acting as President, during the term within which this Article becomes operative from holding the office of President or acting as President during the remainder of such term.

Section 2.

This article shall be inoperative unless it shall have been ratified as an amendment to the Constitution by the legislatures of three-fourths of the several States within seven years from the date of its submission to the States by the Congress.

Thomas Jefferson, who served as the third president of the United States, was the first person of public stature to suggest a constitutional provision limiting presidential terms. "If some termination to the services of the chief Magistrate be not fixed by the Constitution," said Jefferson, "or supplied by practice, his office, nominally four years, will in fact become for life." Until Ulysses S. Grant's unsuccessful attempt to secure his party's nomination to a third term, no other president attempted to extend the two-term limit that had operated in principle. Theodore Roosevelt, having ascended to the presidency after the assassination of William McKinley in 1901, was elected to his second term in 1904. He then sat out a term, and then ran against Woodrow Wilson in the 1912 election and lost.

The first president to serve more than two terms was Franklin D. Roosevelt, and it was his success that inspired the enactment of the Twenty-Second Amendment. In 1946, Republicans took control of Congress for the first time in sixteen years and were determined to guard against such future Democratic dynasties. A year later, Congress, in one of the most party-line votes in the history of the amending process, approved the Twenty-Second Amendment. Every Republican member of the House and Senate who voted on the amendment voted for it. The remaining votes came almost exclusively from southern Democrats, whose relationship with Roosevelt was never more than a marriage of convenience. Ironically, some Republicans began to call for the repeal of the Twenty-Second Amendment toward the end of popular Republican Dwight D. Eisenhower's second term in 1956. A similar movement emerged in the late 1980s toward the end of Republican Ronald Reagan's second term. The American public at large, however, has shown little enthusiasm for repealing the Twenty-Second Amendment.

AMENDMENT XXIII
(Ratified on March 29, 1961)

Section 1.

The District constituting the seat of Government of the United States shall appoint in such manner as the Congress may direct:

A number of electors of President and Vice President equal to the whole number of Senators and Representatives in Congress to which the District would be entitled if it were a State, but in no event more than the least populous State; they shall be in addition to those appointed by the States, but they shall be considered, for the purposes of the election of President and Vice President, to be electors appointed by a State; and they shall meet in the District and perform such duties as provided by the twelfth article of amendment.

Section 2.

The Congress shall have power to enforce this article by appropriate legislation.

Article II, section 2, of the Constitution limits participation in presidential elections to citizens who reside in the states. The Twenty-Third Amendment amended this provision to include residents of the District of Columbia. Since the District was envisioned as the seat of the national government with a transient population, the Constitution afforded no right of representation to its residents in Congress. By the time the Twenty-Third Amendment was ratified, the District had a greater population than twelve states.

In 1978, Congress introduced a constitutional amendment to give the District of Columbia representation in the House and the Senate. By 1985, the ratification period for the amendment expired without the necessary three-fourths approval from the states.

AMENDMENT XXIV
(Ratified on January 23, 1964)

Section 1.

The right of citizens of the United States to vote in any primary or other election for President or Vice President, for electors for President or Vice President, or for Senator or Representative in Congress, shall not be denied or abridged by the United States or any State by reason of failure to pay any poll tax or other tax.

Section 2.

The Congress shall have power to enforce this article by appropriate legislation.

The Twenty-Fourth Amendment continued the work of the Fifteenth Amendment. By abolishing the poll tax, the amendment eliminated one of the most popular tools used by voting registrars to prevent most African Americans and other minorities from taking part in the electoral process. Property ownership and literacy tests as conditions of the franchise extended back to the colonial era and were not particular to any region of the United States. But the poll tax was a southern invention, coming after the enactment of the Fifteenth Amendment. By the fall of Reconstruction in 1877, eleven southern states had enacted poll tax laws. The poll tax was disproportionately enforced against poor African American voters and, in some cases, poor whites.

Congress had begun to debate a constitutional amendment to abolish the poll tax as far back as 1939, but it took the momentum of the civil rights movement to move this process forward. Shortly after the ratification of the Twenty-Fourth Amendment, Congress enacted the Civil Rights Act of 1964, the most sweeping and effective federal civil rights law to date. By the time of ratification of the Twenty-Fourth Amendment, only five states had poll taxes on their books. Spurred on by the spirit of the times, Congress enacted the Voting Rights Act of 1965, which enforced the poll tax ban of the Twenty-Fourth Amendment and also abolished literacy tests, property qualifications, and other obstacles to voter registration. In 1966, in *Harper* v. *Board of Elections,* the Supreme Court rejected a constitutional challenge to the historic voting rights law.

AMENDMENT XXV
(Ratified on February 10, 1967)

Section 1.

In case of the removal of the President from office or of his death or resignation, the Vice President shall become President.

Section 2.

Whenever there is a vacancy in the office of the Vice President, the President shall nominate a Vice President who shall take office upon confirmation by a majority vote of both Houses of Congress.

Section 3.

Whenever the President transmits to the President pro tempore of the Senate and the Speaker of the House of Representatives his written declaration that he is unable to discharge the powers and duties of his office, and until he transmits to them a written declaration to the contrary, such powers and duties shall be discharged by the Vice President as Acting President.

Section 4.

Whenever the Vice President and a majority of either the principal officers of the executive departments or of such other body as Congress may by law provide, transmit to the President pro tempore of the Senate and the Speaker of the House of Representatives their written declaration that the President is unable to discharge the powers and duties of his office, the Vice President shall immediately assume the powers and duties of the office as Acting President.

Thereafter, when the President transmits to the President pro tempore of the Senate and the Speaker of the House of Representatives his written declaration that no inability exists, he shall resume the powers and duties of his office unless the Vice President and a majority of either the principal officers of the executive department or of such other body as Congress may by law provide, transmit within four days to the President pro tempore of the Senate and the Speaker of the

House of Representatives their written declaration that the President is unable to discharge the powers and duties of his office. Thereupon Congress shall decide the issue, assembling within forty-eight hours for that purpose if not in session. If the Congress, within twenty-one days after receipt of the latter written declaration, or, if Congress is not in session, within twenty-one days after Congress is required to assemble, determines by two-thirds vote of both Houses that the President is unable to discharge the powers and duties of his office, the Vice President shall continue to discharge the same as Acting President; otherwise, the President shall resume the powers and duties of his office.

Several tragedies to the men who occupied the offices of president and vice president and the lack of constitutional clarity about the path of succession in event of presidential and vice presidential disability spurred the enactment of the Twenty-Fifth Amendment.

Whether the vice president was merely an acting president or assumed the permanent powers of the office for the remainder of the term upon the death of a president was answered in 1841 when John Tyler became president upon the death of William Henry Harrison, who died only a month after his inauguration. Seven more presidents died in office before the enactment of the Twenty-Fifth Amendment, and in each case the vice president assumed the presidency without controversy. What this amendment answered that the original Constitution did not was the method of vice presidential succession. The vice presidency often went unfilled for months at a time as the result of constitutional ambiguity. Since the enactment of the amendment, there have been two occasions when the president appointed a vice president. Both took place during the second term of President Richard Nixon. For the first time in United States history, the nation witnessed a presidential term served out by two men, President Gerald R. Ford and Vice President Nelson A. Rockefeller, neither of whom had been elected to the position.

The Twenty-Fifth Amendment also settled the path of succession in the event of presidential

disability. This provision of the amendment was prompted by the memories of James Garfield lying in a coma for eighty days after being struck by an assassin's bullet and Woodrow Wilson's bedridden state for the last eighteen months of his term after a stroke. The first president to invoke the disability provision of the Twenty-Fifth Amendment was Ronald Reagan, who made Vice President George Bush acting president for the eight hours while he underwent surgery. The only other time a president invoked this provision came in 2002, when George W. Bush underwent minor surgery and transferred the powers of his office to Vice President Dick Cheney.

The provision authorizing the vice president, in consultation with Congress and members of the Cabinet, to declare the president disabled has never been invoked.

AMENDMENT XXVI
(Ratified on July 1, 1971)

Section 1.

The right of citizens of the United States, who are eighteen years of age or older, to vote shall not be denied or abridged by the United States or by any State on account of age.

Section 2.

The Congress shall have power to enforce this article by appropriate legislation.

The Twenty-Sixth Amendment was a direct response to the unpopularity of the Vietnam War and was spurred by calls to lower the voting age to eighteen so that draft-eligible men could voice their opinion on the war through the ballot box. In 1970, Congress had amended the Voting Rights Act of 1965 to lower the voting age to eighteen in all national, state, and local elections. Many states resisted compliance, claiming that Congress, while having the power to establish the voting age in national elections, had no such authority in state and local elections. In *Oregon* v. *Mitchell* (1970), the Supreme Court agreed with that

view. Congress responded by drafting the Twenty-Sixth Amendment, and the states ratified it quickly and without controversy.

AMENDMENT XXVII
(Ratified on May 7, 1992)

No law, varying the compensation for the services of the Senators and Representatives shall take effect until an election of Representatives shall have intervened.

The Twenty-Seventh Amendment was originally introduced in 1789 during the 1st Congress as one of the original twelve amendments to the Constitution. Only six of the necessary eleven (of thirteen) states had ratified the amendment by 1791. As more states came into the union, the prospect of the amendment's passage only dwindled. No additional state ratified the amendment until 1873, when Ohio approved its addition to the Constitution.

Sometime in the early 1980s, a University of Texas student discovered the amendment and launched an intensive effort to bring it to the public's attention for ratification. The amendment's core purpose, preventing members of Congress from raising their salaries during the terms in which they served, meshed well with another grassroots movement that began during this time, the campaign to impose term limits on members of the House and Senate. Nothing in the nation's constitutional or statutory law prohibited the resurrection of the Twenty-Seventh Amendment for voter approval. In 1939, the Supreme Court had ruled in *Coleman* v. *Miller* that amendments could remain indefinitely before the public unless Congress had set a specific time limit on the ratification process. By 1992, the amendment had received the necessary three-fourths approval of the states, making it the last successful effort to amend the Constitution. The Twenty-Seventh Amendment has not, however, barred Congress from increasing its compensation through annual cost-of-living-adjustments.

3

Federalism

Photo courtesy: Joe Cavaretta/AP/Wide World Photos

IN 2003, RECALLED THE REPUBLICAN GOVERNOR of Nevada, Kenny Guinn (pictured above), the state was "like a casino gambler digging into his life savings just to stay in the game."[1] Like many other states that had built up significant "rainy day funds" during the surplus budget years of the 1990s, Nevada had too, using $135 million of its $136 million fund to keep its budget balanced.

Nevada was not the only state to raid the piggy bank when state expenses rose sharply for post-9/11 security measures and to meet increased demands for state services as unemployment went up, along with the cost of providing health care for the states' poor and aged.

States took a variety of approaches to solving their budget woes. Many enacted new taxes and fees, from increased car registration rates to costs for recording deeds as home sales and mortgage refinancings skyrocketed when mortgage interest rates fell. And, many states raised college and university tuition rates and fees significantly—some by as much as 25 percent! Cities and other local governments similarly looked for new ways to raise revenue, including increased parking fines, better enforcement of trafficking laws, and higher fines for overdue books.

Still, "After three years during which state revenues proved exceedingly dismal, the picture [was] notably—but cautiously—brighter at the end of fiscal 2004," found a report from the National Association of State Budget officers.[2] But, noted its executive director, "the picture is far from rosy. If the states were patients, you could say they are out of intensive care, but they're not out of the hospital yet."³

The woes that many states experienced in 2000, and dramatically after September 11, 2001, vividly illustrate the interrelated nature of the state and national governments in our federal system. In 2003, when two-thirds of the states faced serious budget shortfalls, they pressured Congress to rescue them, which resulted in $20 billion dollars in emergency aid. For states like Nevada, "The $67 million we got from Congress...was a nice little shot in the arm," said its budget administrator.⁴

Some of those dollars went to fund programs mandated by the national government. The federal No Child Left Behind Act creates nationwide educational priorities, for example, but it also requires states to spend billions on standardized testing.⁵ The nationally mandated Medicaid program establishes health coverage for the poor, but it also requires states to spend more than 20 percent of their budgets on Medicaid.⁶

In theory, this kind of federal/state relationship, which attempts to shrink the size of the federal government and return power to state agencies, should create programs that are more tailored to the needs of citizens. Proponents of what is known as the "devolution revolution" argue that state and local governments are closer to their citizens and more able to meet the needs of the region.

■ Among issues behind the move to return power to the states are government regulations affecting the environment. Swimming and fishing restrictions such as these protect people from hazardous lake conditions.

Photo courtesy: Alan Reininger/Contact Press Images

F ROM ITS VERY BEGINNING, the challenge for the United States of America was to preserve the traditional independence and rights of the states while establishing an effective national government. The Framers, fearing tyranny, divided powers between the state and the national governments. At each level, moreover, powers were divided among executive, legislative, and judicial branches. The people are the ultimate power from which both the national government and the state governments derive their power.

Although most of the delegates to the Constitutional Convention favored a strong federal government, they knew that some compromise about the distribution of powers would be necessary. Some of the Framers wanted to continue with the confederate form

FIGURE 3.1 Number of Governments in the United States. ■

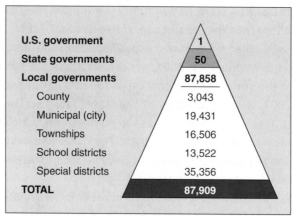

U.S. government	1
State governments	50
Local governments	87,858
County	3,043
Municipal (city)	19,431
Townships	16,506
School districts	13,522
Special districts	35,356
TOTAL	**87,909**

Source: U.S. Census Bureau, http://www.census.gov/govs/www/gid.html.

of government defined in the Articles of Confederation; others wanted a more centralized system, similar to that of Great Britain. Their solution was to create the world's first federal system, in which the thirteen sovereign or independent states were bound together under one national government.

Today, the Constitution ultimately binds more than 87,000 different state and local governments (see Figure 3.1). The Constitution also lays out the duties, obligations, and powers of the states. Throughout history, however, the system and the rules that guide it have been continually stretched, reshaped, and reinterpreted by crises, historical evolution, public expectations, and judicial interpretation. All these forces have had tremendous influence on who makes policy decisions and how these decisions get made.

In this chapter, we will look at the roots of the federal system and the governmental powers under the Constitution created by the Framers. After we explore federalism and how it was molded by the Marshall Court, we will examine the development of dual federalism before and after the Civil War. Following a discussion of cooperative federalism and the growth of national government, we will consider new federalism, especially the movement toward returning power to the states.

THE ROOTS OF THE FEDERAL SYSTEM: GOVERNMENTAL POWERS UNDER THE CONSTITUTION

federal system

System of government where the national government and state governments derive all authority from the people.

THE FRAMERS OF THE CONSTITUTION were the first to adopt a **federal system** of government. This system of government, where the national government and state governments derive all authority from the people, was designed to remedy many of the problems experienced by the Framers under the Articles of Confederation.

The new system of government also had to be different from the **unitary system** found in Great Britain, where the local and regional governments derived all their power from a strong national government. (Figure 3.2 illustrates these different forms of government.) Having been under the rule of English Kings, whom they considered tyrants, the Framers feared centralizing power in one government or institution. Therefore, they made both the state and the federal government

unitary system
System of government where the local and regional governments derive all authority from a strong national government.

FIGURE 3.2   The Federal, Confederation, and Unitary Systems of Government
The source of governmental authority and power differs dramatically in various systems of government. ■

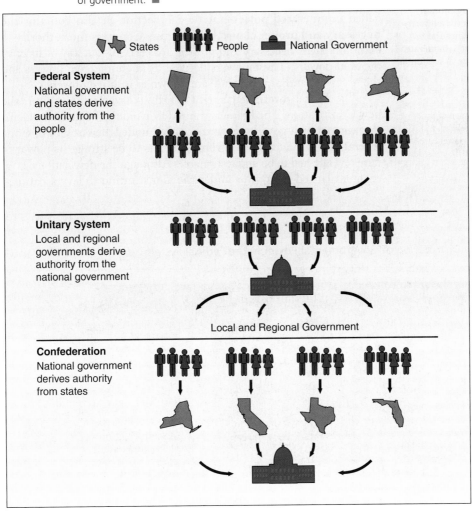

enumerated powers

Seventeen specific powers granted to
Congress under Article I, section 8,
of the U.S. Constitution; these powers include taxation, coinage of
money, regulation of commerce, and
the authority to provide for a
national defense.

necessary and proper clause

The final paragraph of Article I, section 8, of the U.S. Constitution,
which gives Congress the authority
to pass all laws "necessary and
proper" to carry out the enumerated
powers specified in the Constitution;
also called the "elastic" clause.

implied powers

A power derived from an enumerated power and the necessary and
proper clause. These powers are not
stated specifically but are considered
to be reasonably implied through the
exercise of delegated powers.

accountable to the people at large. While the governments shared
some powers, such as the ability to tax, each government was supreme
in some spheres (as depicted in Figure 3.3 and described in the following section).

The federal system as conceived by the Framers has proven tremendously effective. Since the creation of the U.S. system, many other
nations, including Canada, Mexico, and Russia, have adopted federal
systems.

National Powers Under the Constitution

Chief among the exclusive powers of the national government are the
authorities to coin money, conduct foreign relations, provide for an
army and navy, declare war, and establish a national court system. All
of these powers set out in Article I, section 8, of the Constitution are
called **enumerated powers.** Article I, section 8, also contains the
necessary and proper clause, which gives Congress the authority to
enact any laws "necessary and proper" for carrying out any of its enumerated powers. These powers derived from enumerated powers and
the necessary and proper clause are known as **implied powers.**

The federal government's right to tax was also clearly set out in the
new Constitution. The Framers wanted to avoid the financial problems
that the national government experienced under the Articles of Confederation. If the national government was to be strong, its power to
raise revenue had to be unquestionable. Although the new national government lacked the power under the Constitution to levy a national

FIGURE 3.3   The Distribution of Governmental Power in the Federal System. ■

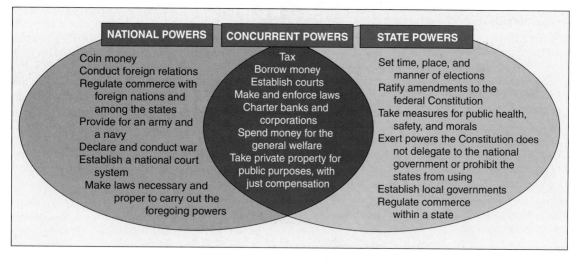

FEDERALISM AROUND THE WORLD

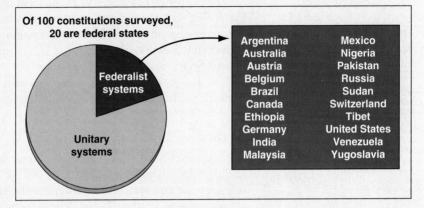

Of 100 constitutions surveyed, 20 are federal states

Federalist systems

Unitary systems

Argentina	Mexico
Australia	Nigeria
Austria	Pakistan
Belgium	Russia
Brazil	Sudan
Canada	Switzerland
Ethiopia	Tibet
Germany	United States
India	Venezuela
Malaysia	Yugoslavia

One of the most fundamental decisions that constitutional framers must make involves choosing between a unitary and a federal framework for organizing political power. In a federal system, political power is firmly divided between the national government and states. In India's federal system, for example, states have jurisdiction over public health, education, and agriculture. In a unitary system, all political power rests with the national government. It may delegate the power to make or implement policies to lesser governmental units such as states, provinces, or cities, but those decisions reside with the national government alone. Great Britain and France are the best-known unitary states.

Around the world there are far more unitary political systems than federal ones. A survey of one hundred constitutions in 2000 found that only twenty were federal states (see the figure). What is immediately obvious is that many of these states are among the world's largest states.

Both systems of governments have their backers. Advocates of federalism assert that it promotes and protects regional/ethnic uniqueness, allows citizens choice, brings citizens closer to their governments, and promotes experimentation. Critics of federalism and those who advocate a unitary system maintain that federalism creates a slow and cumbersome decision-making process, it denies equal treatment to all citizens, and states lack the financial resources to address many of today's problems.

Both federal and unitary political systems around the world have begun to incorporate elements of the other in order to deal effectively with contemporary issues. Unitary systems have undertaken policies to grant subnational regions within their respective countries more autonomy. Spain, which has long confronted strong regional-nationalist sentiment in northern Spain from the Basques and Catalans, has moved to grant increased powers to regional governments and has given them some power over language rights, taxation policy, and other local matters, along with a regional parliament. Federal systems have moved in the opposite direction, incorporating features that promote centralization and uniformity. In Germany, for example, civil service rules are the same in all land (state) governments, and the constitution requires that there be a "unity of living standards" throughout the country.

Questions

1. Which do you think is better suited for solving problems in today's world, a unitary or federal system? Why?
2. Which aspects of the American federal system would you most recommend to a country considering rewriting their constitution? Which feature would you least recommend to them?

Source: Robert Maddex, *Constitutions of the World*, 2nd ed. (Washington, DC: Congressional Quarterly Press, 2000).

income tax, that was changed by the passage of the Sixteenth Amendment in 1913. Eventually, as discussed later in this chapter, this new taxing power became a powerful catalyst for further expansion of the national government.

The addition of Article VI to the federal Constitution underscored the notion that the national government was always to be supreme in situations of conflict between state and national law. The Constitution's **supremacy clause** declares that the U.S. Constitution, the laws of the United States, and its treaties are to be "the supreme Law of the Land; and the Judges in every State shall be bound thereby." This clause has been the subject of much judicial interpretation.

State Powers Under the Constitution

Because states had all the power at the time the Constitution was written, the Framers felt no need, as they did for the new national government, to list and restate the powers of the states. Article I, however, allows states to set the "Times, Places, and Manner, for holding elections for senators and representatives." This article also guarantees each state two members in the Senate and prevents Congress from limiting the slave trade before 1808. Article II requires that each state appoint electors to vote for president, and Article IV contains the **privileges and immunities clause,** guaranteeing that the citizens of each state are afforded the same rights as citizens of all other states. Article IV also provides each state a "Republican Form of Government," meaning one that represents the citizens of the state. It also assures that the national government will protect the states against foreign attacks and domestic rebellion.

It was not until the addition of the **Tenth Amendment** that the states' powers were described in greater detail: "The powers not delegated to the United States by the Constitution, nor prohibited by it to the States, are reserved to the States respectively, or to the people." These powers, often called the states' **reserve** or **police powers,** include the ability to legislate for the public health, safety, and morals of their citizens. Today, the states' rights to legislate under their police powers are used as the rationale for restrictions on abortion, including twenty-four-hour waiting requirements and provisions requiring minors to obtain parental consent. Police powers are also the basis for state criminal laws.

Concurrent and Denied Powers Under the Constitution

As revealed in Figure 3.3, national and state powers overlap. The area where the systems overlap represents **concurrent powers**—powers shared by the national and state governments. States already had the

supremacy clause
Portion of Article VI of the U.S. Constitution that mandates that national law is supreme to (that is, supersedes) all other laws passed by the states or by any other subdivision of government.

privileges and immunities clause
Part of Article IV of the Constitution guaranteeing that the citizens of each state are afforded the same rights as citizens of all other states.

Tenth Amendment
The final part of the Bill of Rights that defines the basic principle of American federalism in stating "The powers not delegated to the United States by the Constitution, nor prohibited by it to the States, are reserved to the States respectively, or to the people."

reserve (or police) powers
Powers reserved to the states by the Tenth Amendment that lie at the foundation of a state's right to legislate for the public health and welfare of its citizens.

concurrent powers
Authority possessed by both the state and national governments that may be exercised concurrently as long as that power is not exclusively within the scope of national power or in conflict with national law.

The Living Constitution

The Powers not delegated to the United States by the Constitution, nor prohibited by it to the States, are reserved to the states respectively, or to the people.

—Tenth Amendment

This amendment to the Constitution—a simple affirmation that any powers not specifically given to the national government are left to the province of the states or to the citizenry—was actually unnecessary and added nothing to the original document. During the ratification debates, however, Anti-Federalists continued to be concerned that the national government would claim powers not intended for it at the expense of the states. Still, during the debates over this amendment, both houses of Congress rejected efforts to insert the word "expressly" before the word delegated. Thus, it was clear that the amendment was not intended to be the yardstick by which to measure the powers of the national government. This was reinforced by comments made by James Madison during the debate that took place over Alexander Hamilton's efforts to establish a national bank. "Interference with the power of the States was no constitutional criterion of the power of Congress."

By the end of the New Deal, the Supreme Court had come to interpret the Tenth Amendment to allow Congress, pursuant to its authority under the commerce clause, to legislate in a wide array of areas that the states might never have foreseen when they ratified the amendment. In fact, until the 1970s, Congress's ability to legislate to regulate commerce appeared to trump any actions of the states. Since the mid-1970s, however, the Court has been very closely divided about how much authority must be reserved to the states vis-à-vis their authority to regulate commerce, especially when it involves regulation of activities of states as sovereign entities. The Court now requires Congress to attach statements of clear intention to tread on state powers. It is then up to the Court to determine if Congress has claimed powers beyond its authority under the Constitution.

power to tax; the Constitution extended this power to the national government as well. Other important concurrent powers include the right to borrow money, establish courts, and make and enforce laws necessary to carry out these powers.

Simulation

You Are a Restaurant Owner

Article I denies certain powers to the national and state governments. In keeping with the Framers' desire to forge a national economy, states are prohibited from entering treaties, coining money, or impairing obligation of contracts. States also are prohibited from entering into "compacts" with other states without express congressional approval. In a similar vein, Congress is barred from favoring one state over another in regulating commerce, and it cannot lay duties on items exported from any state.

Both the national and state governments are denied the authority to take arbitrary actions affecting constitutional rights and liberties. Neither national nor state governments may pass a **bill of attainder,** a law declaring an act illegal without a judicial trial. The Constitution also bars either from passing *ex post facto* **laws,** laws that make an act punishable as a crime even if the action was legal at the time it was committed. (For more on civil rights and liberties, see chapters 5 and 6.)

Relations Among the States

In addition to delineating the relationship of the states with the national government, the Constitution was also designed to provide a mechanism for resolving interstate disputes and to facilitate relations among states. To avoid any sense of favoritism, it provides that disputes between states be settled directly by the U.S. Supreme Court under its original jurisdiction as mandated by Article III of the Constitution (see chapter 10). Moreover, Article IV requires that each state give "Full Faith and Credit…to the public Acts, Records and judicial Proceedings of every other State." The **full faith and credit clause** ensures that judicial decrees and contracts made in one state will be binding and enforceable in another. The Violence Against Women Act, for example, specifically requires states to give full faith and credit to protective orders issued by other states.[7] (See On Campus: Legislating Against Violence Against Women.)

Article IV also requires states to extradite, or return, criminals to states where they have been convicted or are to stand trial. For example, Timothy Reed, an Indian-rights activist, spent five years in New Mexico fighting extradition to Ohio.[8] In 1998, the New Mexico Supreme Court ordered him released from custody in spite of an order from the New Mexico governor ordering his extradition to Ohio. The U.S. Supreme Court found that the Supreme Court of New Mexico went beyond its authority and that Reed should be returned to Ohio.[9]

To facilitate relations among states, Article I, section 10, clause 3, of the U.S. Constitution sets the legal foundation for interstate cooperation in the form of **interstate compacts,** contracts between states that carry the force of law. It reads, "No State shall, without the consent of Congress…enter into any Agreement or Compact with another state." Before 1920, interstate compacts were largely bistate compacts

bill of attainder
A law declaring an act illegal without a judicial trial.

ex post facto **law**
Law passed after the fact, thereby making previously legal activity illegal and subject to current penalty; prohibited by the U.S. Constitution.

full faith and credit clause
Portion of Article IV of the Constitution that ensures judicial decrees and contracts made in one state will be binding and enforceable in any other state.

Visual Literacy
Explaining Differences in State Laws

interstate compacts
Contracts between states that carry the force of law; generally now used as a tool to address multi-state policy concerns.

LEGISLATING AGAINST VIOLENCE AGAINST WOMEN: A CASUALTY OF THE DEVOLUTION REVOLUTION?

As originally enacted in 1994, the Violence Against Women Act (VAWA) allowed women to file civil lawsuits in federal court if they could prove that they were the victim of rape, domestic violence, or other crimes "motivated by gender." VAWA was widely praised as an effective mechanism to combat domestic violence. In its first five years, $1.6 million was allocated for states and local governments to pay for a variety of programs, including a national toll-free hotline for victims of violence that averages 13,000 calls per month, funding for special police sex crime units, and civil and legal assistance for women in need of restraining orders.[a] It also provided money to promote awareness of campus rape and domestic violence and to enhance reporting of crimes such as what is often termed "date rape."

Most of the early publicity surrounding VAWA stemmed from a challenge to one of its provisions. The suit brought by Christy Brzonkala was the first brought under the act's civil damages provision. While she was a student at Virginia Polytechnic Institute, Brzonkala alleged that two football players there raped her. After the university took no action against the students, she sued the school and the students. No criminal charges were ever filed in her case. The conservative federal appeals court in Richmond, Virginia—in contrast to contrary rulings in seventeen other courts—ruled that Congress had overstepped its authority because the alleged crimes were "within the exclusive purview of the states."[b] The Clinton administration and the National Organization for

Photo courtesy: Cindy Pinkston, January 1996

Christy Brzonkala, the original petitioner in *U.S.* v. *Morrison* (2000).

Women Legal Defense and Education Fund (now called Legal Momentum) unsuccessfully appealed this decision to the Supreme Court.

In 2000, five justices of the Supreme Court, including Justice Sandra Day O'Connor, ruled that Congress had no authority under the commerce clause to provide a federal remedy to victims of gender-motivated violence, a decision viewed as greatly reining in congressional power.[c] Thus, today, students abused on campus no longer have this federal remedy.

---

[a] Juliet Eilperin, "Reauthorization of Domestic Violence Act Is at Risk," *Washington Post* (September 13, 2000): A6.

[b] Tony Mauro, "Court Will Review Laws of Protection," *USA Today* (September 29, 1999): 4A.

[c] *U.S.* v. *Morrison*, 529 U.S. 598 (2000).

that addressed boundary disputes. However, more than 200 interstate compacts exist today. Some deal with rudimentary items such as state boundaries, but others help states carry out their policy objectives and play an important role in helping states carry out their functions. In

Participation

Explore Your State Constitution

addition, many modern compacts have as many as fifty signatories.[10] The Drivers License Compact was signed by all fifty states to facilitate nationwide recognition of licenses issued in the respective states.

Relations Within the States: Local Government

Comparing State and Local Governments

Under the provisions of the Constitution, local governments, including counties, municipalities, townships, and school districts, have no independent standing. Thus, their authority is not granted directly by the people, but through state governments, who establish or charter administrative subdivisions to execute the duties of the state government on a smaller scale.

FEDERALISM AND THE MARSHALL COURT

Federalism and the Supreme Court

THE NATURE OF FEDERALISM and its allocation of power between the national government and the states have changed dramatically over the past two hundred years, and these changes are largely due to the rulings of the U.S. Supreme Court. The debate continues today, too, as many Americans, frustrated with the national government's performance on a number of issues, look for a return of more power to the states. Because the distribution of power between the national and state governments is not clearly delineated in the Constitution, over the years the U.S. Supreme Court has played a major role in defining the nature of the federal system.

The first few years that the Supreme Court sat, it handled few major cases. As described in chapter 9, the Supreme Court was viewed as weak, and many men declined the honor of serving as a Supreme Court justice. The appointment of John Marshall as chief justice of the United States, however, changed all of this. In a series of decisions, he and his associates carved out an important role for the Court, especially in defining the nature of the federal/state relationship. Two rulings in the early 1800s, *McCulloch* v. *Maryland* (1819) and *Gibbons* v. *Ogden* (1824), had a major impact on the balance of power between the national government and the states.

McCulloch v. *Maryland* (1819)
The Supreme Court upheld the power of the national government and denied the right of a state to tax the bank. The Court's broad interpretation of the necessary and proper clause paved the way for later rulings upholding expansive federal powers.

McCulloch v. *Maryland* (1819)

McCulloch v. *Maryland* (1819) was the first major Supreme Court decision of the Marshall Court (courts are commonly referred to by the name of the chief justice at the time) to define the relationship between the national and state governments. In 1816, Congress chartered the Second Bank of the United States. (The charter of the First Bank had been allowed to expire.) In 1818, the Maryland state legislature levied a tax requiring all banks not chartered by Maryland (that is, the Second Bank of the United States) to: (1) buy stamped paper from the state on which the Second Bank's notes were to be issued; (2) pay the state $15,000 a year; or, (3) go out of business. James McCulloch, the head cashier of the Baltimore branch of the Bank of the United States, refused to pay the tax, and Maryland brought suit against him. After losing in a Maryland state court, McCulloch appealed his conviction to the U.S. Supreme Court by order of the U.S. secretary of the treasury. In a unanimous opinion, the Court answered the two central questions that had been put to it: Did Congress have the authority to charter a bank? If it did, could a state tax it?

Chief Justice John Marshall's answer to the first question—whether Congress had the right to establish a bank or another type of corporation, given that the Constitution does not explicitly mention such a power—continues to stand as the classic exposition of the doctrine of implied powers and as a reaffirmation of the propriety of a strong national government. Although the word "bank" cannot be found in the Constitution, the Constitution enumerates powers that give Congress the authority to levy and collect taxes, issue currency, and borrow funds. From these enumerated powers, Marshall found, it was reasonable to imply that Congress had the power to charter a bank, which could be considered "necessary and proper" to the exercise of its aforementioned enumerated powers.

Marshall next addressed the question of whether a federal bank could be taxed by any state government. To Marshall, this was not a difficult question. The national government was dependent on the people, not the states, for its powers. In addition, Marshall noted, the Constitution specifically calls for the national law to be supreme. "The power to tax involves the power to destroy," wrote Marshall.[11] Thus,

■ *Gibbons v. Ogden* (1824) opened the waters to free competition. This is the New York waterfront in 1839.

Photo courtesy: I.N. Phelps Stokes Collection, Miriam and Ira D. Wallach Division of Art, Prints, and Photographs, The New York Public Library Astor, Lenox and Tilden Foundations.

the state tax violated the supremacy clause, because individual states cannot interfere with the operations of the national government, whose laws are supreme. The Court's decision in *McCulloch* has far-reaching consequences even today. The necessary and proper clause is used to justify federal action in many areas, including education, health, and welfare. Furthermore, had Marshall allowed the state of Maryland to tax the Second Bank, it is possible that states could have attempted to tax all federal agencies located within their boundaries, a costly proposition that might have driven the federal government into insurmountable debt.

Gibbons v. *Ogden* (1824)

Gibbons v. *Ogden* (1824)

The Supreme Court upheld broad congressional power to regulate interstate commerce. The Court's broad interpretation of the Constitution's commerce clause paved the way for later rulings upholding expansive federal powers.

Shortly after *McCulloch*, the Marshall Court had another opportunity to rule in favor of a broad interpretation of the scope of national power. *Gibbons* v. *Ogden* (1824) involved a dispute that arose after the New York State legislature granted to Robert Fulton the exclusive right to operate steamboats on the Hudson River. Simultaneously, Congress licensed a ship to sail on the same waters. By the time the case reached the Supreme Court, it was complicated both factually and procedurally. Suffice it to say that both New York and New Jersey wanted to control shipping on the lower Hudson River. But, *Gibbons* actually addressed one simple, important question: what was the scope of Congress's authority under the commerce clause? The states argued that "commerce," as mentioned in Article I, should be interpreted narrowly to include only direct dealings in products. In *Gibbons*, however, the Supreme Court ruled that Congress's power to regulate interstate commerce included the power to regulate commercial activity as well, and that the commerce power had no limits except those specifically found in the Constitution. Thus, New York had no constitutional authority to grant a monopoly to a single steamboat operator, an act that interfered with interstate commerce.[12] Like the necessary and proper clause, today the commerce clause is used to justify a great deal of federal legislation, including regulation of highways, the stock market, and even segregation.

DUAL FEDERALISM: THE TANEY COURT, SLAVERY, AND THE CIVIL WAR

dual federalism

The belief that having separate and equally powerful levels of government is the best arrangement.

IN SPITE OF NATIONALIST MARSHALL COURT decisions like *McCulloch* and *Gibbons*, strong debate continued in the United States over national versus state power. It was under the leadership of Chief Justice Marshall's successor, Roger B. Taney (1835–1863), that the Supreme Court articulated the notions of concurrent power and **dual federalism.** Dual federalism posits that having separate and equally powerful state and national governments is the best arrangement. Adherents of this theory typically believe that the national government should not exceed its constitutionally enumerated powers, and, as stated in the Tenth Amendment, all other powers are and should be reserved to the states or the people.

Dred Scott v. *Sandford* (1857) and the Advent of Civil War

During the Taney Court era, the comfortable role of the Supreme Court as the arbiter of competing national and state interests became troublesome when the justices were called upon to deal with the controversial issue of slavery. In cases such as *Dred Scott* v. *Sandford* (1857), the Court tried to manage the slavery issue by resolving questions of ownership, the status of fugitive slaves, and slavery in the new territories.[13] These cases generally were settled in favor of slavery and states' rights within the framework of dual federalism. In *Dred Scott*, for example, the Taney Court, in declaring the Missouri Compromise of 1820 unconstitutional, ruled that Congress lacked the authority to ban slavery in the territories. This decision seemed to rule out any nationally legislated solution to the slavery question, leaving the problem in the hands of the state legislatures and the people, who did not have the power to impose their will on other states.

Photo courtesy: Missouri Historical Society

■ Friends of Dred Scott helped finance a test case seeking his freedom. They believed that his residence in Illinois and later in the Wisconsin Territory, both of which prohibited slavery, made him a free man. After many delays, the U.S. Supreme Court ruled 7–2 that Scott was not a citizen. "Slaves," said the Court, "were never thought of or spoken of except as property."

The Civil War, its Aftermath, and the Continuation of Dual Federalism

The Civil War (1861–1865) forever changed the nature of federalism. In the aftermath of the war, the national government grew in size and powers. It also attempted to impose its will on the state governments through the Thirteenth, Fourteenth, and Fifteenth Amendments. These three amendments, known collectively as the Civil War Amendments, prohibited slavery and granted civil and political rights, including the franchise for males, to African Americans.

The U.S. Supreme Court, however, continued to adhere to its belief in dual federalism. Therefore, in spite of the growth of the national government's powers, the importance of powers of the state governments were not diminished until 1933, when the next major change in the federal system occurred. Generally, the Court upheld any laws passed under the states' police powers, which allow states to pass laws to protect the general welfare of their citizens. These laws included those affecting commerce, labor relations, and manufacturing. After the Court's decision in *Plessy* v. *Ferguson* (1896), in which the Court ruled that state maintenance of "separate but equal" facilities for blacks and whites was constitutional, most civil rights and voting cases also became state matters, in spite of the Civil War Amendments.[14]

The Court also developed legal doctrine in a series of cases that reinforced the national government's ability to regulate commerce. By the 1930s, these two somewhat contradictory approaches led to confusion. States, for example, could not tax gasoline used by federal vehicles,[15] and the national government could not tax the sale of motorcycles to the city police department.[16] In this period, the Court, however, did recognize the need for national control over new technological developments, such as the telegraph.[17] And, beginning in the 1880s, the Court allowed Congress to regulate many aspects of economic relationships, such as outlawing monopolies, a type of regulation or power formerly thought to be in the exclusive realm of the states. Passage of laws such as the Interstate Commerce Act in 1887 and the Sherman Anti-Trust Act in 1890 allowed Congress to establish itself as an important player in the growing national economy.

Setting the Stage for a Stronger National Government

Sixteenth Amendment
Authorized Congress to enact a national income tax.

In 1895, the U.S. Supreme Court found a congressional effort to tax personal incomes unconstitutional, although an earlier Court had found a similar tax levied during the Civil War constitutional. Thus, Congress and the state legislatures were moved to ratify the **Sixteenth Amendment,** although its chief sponsor supported it only because he believed that the national government must be authorized to raise additional funds during a time of war.[18] The Sixteenth Amendment gave Congress the power to levy and collect taxes on incomes without apportionment among the states. The revenues taken in by the federal government through taxation of personal income "removed a major constraint on the federal government by giving it access to almost unlimited revenues."[19] If money is power, the income tax and the revenues it generated greatly enhanced the power of the federal government and its ability to enter policy areas where it formerly had few funds to spend.

Seventeenth Amendment
Made senators directly elected by the people; removed their selection from state legislatures.

The **Seventeenth Amendment,** ratified in 1913, similarly enhanced the power of the national government at the expense of the states. This amendment terminated the state legislatures' election of senators and put their election in the hands of the people. With senators no longer directly accountable to the state legislators who elected them, states lost their principal protectors in Congress. Coupled with the Sixteenth Amendment, this amendment paved the way for a drastic change in the relationship between national and state governments in the United States.

Cooperative Federalism: The New Deal and the Growth of National Government

The era of dual federalism came to an abrupt end in the 1930s. While the ratification of the Sixteenth and Seventeenth Amendments set the stage for expanded national government, the catalyst for dual federalism's demise was a series of economic events that ended in the cataclysm of the Great Depression:

- In 1921, the nation experienced a severe slump in agricultural prices.
- In 1926, the construction industry went into decline.
- In the summer of 1929, inventories of consumer goods and automobiles were at an all-time high.
- Throughout the 1920s, bank failures had become common.
- On October 29, 1929, stock prices, which had risen steadily since 1926, crashed, taking with them the entire national economy.

Despite the severity of these indicators, Presidents Calvin Coolidge and Herbert Hoover took little action, believing that the national depression was an amalgamation of state economic crises that should be dealt with by state and local governments. However, by 1933, the situation could no longer be ignored.

The New Deal

Rampant unemployment (historians estimate it was as high as 40 percent to 50 percent) was the hallmark of the Great Depression. In 1933, to combat severe problems facing the nation, newly elected President Franklin D. Roosevelt (FDR) proposed a variety of innovative programs under the rubric "the New Deal" and ushered in a new era in American politics. FDR used the full power of the office of the president as well as his highly effective communication skills to sell the American public and Congress on a whole new ideology of government. Not only were the scope and role of national government remarkably altered, but so was the relationship between each state and the national government.

The New Deal period (1933–1939) was characterized by intense government activity on the national level. It was clear to most politicians that to find national solutions to the Depression, which was affecting the citizens of every state in the union, the national government would have to exercise tremendous authority.

In the first few weeks of the legislative session after FDR's inauguration, Congress and the president acted quickly to bolster confidence in the national government. Congress passed a series of acts creating new agencies and programs proposed by the president. These new agencies, often known by their initials, created what many termed an alphabetocracy. Among the more significant programs were the Federal Housing Administration (FHA), which provided federal financing for new home construction; the Civilian Conservation Corps

(CCC), a work relief program for farmers and home owners; and the Agricultural Adjustment Administration (AAA) and the National Recovery Administration (NRA), which imposed restrictions on production in agriculture and many industries.

These programs tremendously enlarged the scope of the national government. Those who feared this unprecedented use of national power quickly challenged the constitutionality of New Deal programs in court. And, through the mid-1930s, the Supreme Court continued to rule that certain aspects of the New Deal went beyond the authority of Congress to regulate commerce. The Court's *laissez-faire*, or hands-off, attitude toward the economy was reflected in a series of decisions ruling various aspects of New Deal programs unconstitutional.

FDR and the Congress were outraged. FDR's frustration with the Court prompted him to suggest what ultimately was nicknamed his "Court-packing plan." Knowing that he could do little to change the minds of those already on the Court, FDR suggested enlarging its size from nine to thirteen justices. This would have given him the opportunity to pack the Court with a majority of justices predisposed toward the constitutional validity of the New Deal.

Even though Roosevelt was popular, the Court-packing plan was not. Congress and the public were outraged that he even suggested tampering with an institution of government. Nevertheless, the Court appeared to respond to this threat. In 1937, it reversed its series of anti–New Deal decisions, concluding that Congress (and therefore the national government) had the authority to legislate in areas that affected commerce. Congress then used this newly recognized power to legislate in a wide array of areas, including maximum-hour and minimum-wage laws and regulation of child labor. Moreover, the Court also upheld the constitutionality of the bulk of the massive New Deal relief programs, such as the National Labor Relations Act of 1935, which authorized collective bargaining between unions and employees;[20] the Fair Labor Standards Act of 1938, which prohibited the interstate shipment of goods made by employees earning less than the federally mandated minimum wage;[21] and the Agricultural Adjustment Act of 1938, which provided crop subsidies to farmers.[22]

The New Deal programs forced all levels of government to work cooperatively with one another. Indeed, local governments—mainly in big cities—became a third partner in the federal system, as FDR relied on big-city Democratic political machines to turn out voters to support his programs. For the first time in U.S. history, cities were embraced as equal partners in an intergovernmental system and became players in the national political arena because many in the national legislature wanted to bypass state legislatures, where urban interests usually were underrepresented.

The Changing Nature of Federalism: From Layer Cake to Marble Cake

Before the Depression and the New Deal, most political scientists likened the federal system to a layer cake. Each level or layer of government—national, state, and local—had clearly defined powers and responsibilities. After the New Deal, however, the nature of the federal system changed. Government now looked something like a marble cake: "Wherever you slice through it you reveal an inseparable mixture of differently colored ingredients....Vertical and diagonal lines almost obliterate the horizontal ones, and in some places there are unexpected whirls and an imperceptible merging of colors, so that it is difficult to tell where one ends and the other begins."[23]

The metaphor of marble cake federalism refers to what political scientists call **cooperative federalism,** a term that describes the intertwined relationship among the national, state, and local governments that began with the New Deal. States began to take a secondary, albeit important, cooperative role in the scheme of governance, as did many cities. Nowhere is this shift in power from the states to the national government clearer than in the growth of federal grant programs that began in earnest during the New Deal. The tremendous growth in these programs, and in federal government spending in general, changed the nature and discussion of federalism from "How much power should the national government have?" to "How much say in the policies of the states can the national government buy?" For example, during the 1970s energy crisis, the national government initially imposed a national 55 mph speed limit on the states.

cooperative federalism
The relationship between the national and state governments that began with the New Deal.

Federal Grants and National Efforts to Influence the States

As early as 1790, Congress appropriated funds for the states to pay debts incurred during the Revolutionary War. But, it wasn't until the Civil War that Congress enacted its first true federal grant program, which allocated federal funds to the states for a specific purpose.

Most commentators believe the start of this redistribution of funds began with the Morrill Land Grant Act of 1862, which gave each state 30,000 acres of public land for each representative in Congress. Income from the sale of these lands was to be earmarked for the establishment and support of agricultural and mechanical arts colleges. Sixty-nine land-grant colleges—including Texas A&M University, the University of Georgia, and Michigan State University—were founded or significantly assisted.

As we have seen, Franklin D. Roosevelt's New Deal program increased the flow of federal dollars to the states with the infusion of massive federal dollars for a variety of public works programs, including building and road construction. In the boom times of World War II, even more new federal programs were introduced; by the 1950s and 1960s, federal grant-in-aid programs were well entrenched. They often defined federal/state relationships and made the national government a major player in domestic policy. Until the 1960s, however, most federal grant programs were constructed in cooperation with the states and were designed to assist the states in the furtherance of their traditional responsibilities to protect the health, welfare, and safety of their citizens.

categorical grant
Grant for which Congress appropriates funds for a specific purpose.

Most of these programs were **categorical grants,** ones for which Congress appropriates funds for specific purposes. Categorical grants allocate federal dollars by a precise formula and are subject to detailed conditions imposed by the national government, often on a matching basis; that is, states must contribute money to match federal funds, although the national government may pay as much as 90 percent of the total.

By the early 1960s, as concern about the poor and minorities rose, and as states (especially in the South) were blamed for perpetuating discrimination, those in power in the national government saw grants as a way to force states to behave in ways desired by the national government.[24] If the states would not cooperate with the national government to further its goals, it would withhold funds.

In 1964, the Democratic administration of President Lyndon B. Johnson (LBJ) (1963–1969) launched its Great Society program, which included a War on Poverty. In a frenzy of activity in Washington not seen since the New Deal, federal funds were channeled to states, to local governments, and even directly to citizen action groups in an effort to alleviate social ills that the states had been unable or unwilling to remedy. There was money for urban renewal, education, and poverty programs, including Head Start and job training. The move to fund local groups directly was made by the most liberal members of Congress to bypass not only conservative state legislatures, but also conservative mayors and councils in cities such as Chicago, who were perceived as disinclined to help their poor, often African American, constituencies. Thus, these programs often pitted governors and mayors against community activists, who became key players in the distribution of federal dollars.

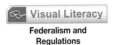

Visual Literacy
Federalism and Regulations

These new grants altered the fragile federal/state balance of power that had been at the core of many older federal grant programs. During the Johnson administration, the national government began to use federal grants as a way to further what federal (and not state) officials perceived to be national needs. Grants based on what states wanted or believed they needed began to decline, while grants based on what the national government wanted states to do to foster national goals increased dramatically. Soon, states routinely asked Washington for help. From pollution to economic development and law enforcement, creating a federal grant seemed like the perfect solution to every problem.[25]

Not all federal programs mandating state or local action came with federal money, however. And, although presidents Richard M. Nixon, Gerald Ford, and Jimmy Carter voiced their opposition to "big government," their efforts to rein it in were largely unsuccessful.

NEW FEDERALISM: RETURNING POWER TO THE STATES

IN 1980, FORMER CALIFORNIA GOVERNOR Ronald Reagan was elected president, pledging to advance what he called a **New Federalism** and a return of power to the states. This policy set the tone for the federal/state relationship maintained since Reagan's presidency. Presidents and Congresses, both Republican and Democrat, have taken steps to shrink the size of the federal government in favor of programs administered by state governments. On the campaign trail in 2000, George W. Bush also seemed committed to this devolution. A struggling economy and the events of September 11, 2001, however, led to substantial growth in the power and scope of the federal government.

New Federalism
Federal-state relationship proposed by Ronald Reagan during the 1980s; hallmark is returning administrative powers to the state governments.

The Reagan Revolution

The Republican Reagan Revolution had at its heart strong views about the role of states in the federal system. While many Democrats and liberal interest groups argued that grants-in-aid were an effective way to raise the level of services provided to the poor, others, including Reagan, attacked them as imposing national priorities on the states. Policy decisions were made at the national level. The states, always in search of funds, were forced to follow the priorities of the national government. States found it very hard to resist the lure of grants, even though many were contingent on some sort of state investment of matching or proportional funds.

Shortly after taking office, Reagan proposed massive cuts in federal domestic programs (which had not become federal functions until the New Deal) and drastic income tax cuts. The Reagan administration's budget and its policies dramatically altered the relationships among federal, state, and local governments. For the first time in thirty years, federal aid to state and local governments declined.[26] Reagan persuaded Congress to consolidate many categorical grants (for specific programs that often require matching funds) into far fewer, less restrictive **block grants**—broad grants to states for specific activities such as secondary education or health services, with few strings attached. He also ended general revenue sharing, which had provided significant unrestricted funds to the states.

block grant
Broad grant with few strings attached; given to states by the federal government for specified activities, such as secondary education or health services.

By the end of the presidencies of Ronald Reagan and George Bush in 1993, most block grants fell into one of four categories: health, income security, education, or transportation. Yet, many politicians, including most state governors, urged the consolidation of even more programs into block grants. Calls to reform the welfare system, particularly to allow more latitude to the states in an effort to get back to the Hamiltonian notion of states as experimental laboratories, seemed popular with citizens and governments alike.

The Devolution Revolution

In 1994, Republicans took over both houses of Congress, and every Republican governor who sought reelection was victorious, while some popular Democratic governors, such as Ann Richards of Texas, lost (to George W. Bush). This Republican sweep was propelled by a campaign document known as the Contract with America.

Participation

Is Federalism Dead and Should It Be?

The contract was a campaign document proposed by then House Minority Whip Newt Gingrich (R–GA) and signed by nearly all Republican candidates (and incumbents) seeking election to the House of Representatives in 1994. In it, Republican candidates pledged to force a national debate on the role of the national government in regard to the states. A top priority was scaling back the federal government, which some commentators called the devolution revolution. Poll after poll, moreover, revealed that many Americans believed the national government had too much power (48 percent) and that they favored their states assuming many of the powers and functions now exercised by the federal government (59 percent).[27]

Following the Republicans' victory in 1994, the majority of the contract's legislative proposals passed the House of Representatives during the first one hundred days of the 104th Congress. This evidence seems to prove that the Contract with America was a great success. However, very few of the contract's proposals, including acts requiring a balanced budget and tax reforms, passed the Senate and became law.

unfunded mandates

National laws that direct states or local governments to comply with federal rules or regulations (such as clean air or water standards) but contain no federal funding to defray the cost of meeting these requirements.

On some issues, however, the Republicans were able to achieve their goals. For example, before 1995, **unfunded mandates,** national laws that direct state or local governments to comply with federal rules or regulations (such as clean air or water standards) but contain no federal funding to defray the cost of meeting these requirements, absorbed nearly 30 percent of some local budgets. Republicans in Congress, loyal to the concerns of these governments, secured passage of the Unfunded Mandates Reform Act of 1995, which prevented Congress from passing costly federal programs without debate on how to fund them.

Republicans also won victory in the area of welfare reform by securing passage of the Personal Responsibility and Work Opportunity Reconciliation Act of 1996, which replaced the existing welfare program with a program known as Temporary Assistance for Needy Families (TANF).

TANF returned much of the administrative power for welfare programs to the states and became a hallmark of the devolution revolution.

In the short run, these and other programs, coupled with a growing economy, produced record federal and state budget surpluses. States were in the best fiscal shape they had been in since the 1970s. According to the National Conference of State Legislatures, total state budget surpluses in 1998 exceeded $30 billion. These tax surpluses allowed many states to increase spending, while other states offered their residents steep tax cuts. Mississippi, for example, increased its per capita spending by 42 percent, while Alaska opted to reduce taxes by 44 percent.[28]

Federalism Under the Bush Administration

On the campaign trail, George W. Bush could not have foreseen the circumstances that would surround much of his presidency. A struggling economy, terrorist attacks on the World Trade Center and the Pentagon, and the rising costs of education and welfare produced state and federal budget deficits that would have been unimaginable only a few years before.

By 2003, many state governments faced budget shortfalls of more than $30 billion. Because state governments, unlike the federal government, are required to balance their budgets, governors and legislators struggled to make ends meet. As illustrated in our opening vignette, however, many states had to make dramatic changes to counter their shrinking coffers. Some states raised taxes, and others cut services, including school construction and infrastructure repairs. By 2004, however, thirty-two states projected surpluses helped by $20 billion in emergency funds from the national government.[29]

The federal government struggled with a $521 billion budget deficit of its own in 2004, with an optimistic $363 billion projected for 2005. However, most remarkable on the federal level was the tremendous expansion of the size and cost of the post-9/11 government. Bush, who campaigned on the idea of limited federal power, found himself asking Congress to create a huge new Cabinet department, the Department of Homeland Security, and federalizing

■ Michigan Democratic Governor Jennifer Grenholm heads a state hard hit by cuts in some federal programs and the loss of jobs.

Photo courtesy: Jerry S. Mendoza/AP/Wide World Photos

THE NO CHILD LEFT BEHIND ACT

Overview: The U.S. Constitution is silent with regard to educating American citizens. Historically, the states have been responsible for educating students because the Ninth and Tenth Amendments give the states and American people the rights and powers not expressly mentioned in the Constitution. For the first 150 years of American history, states assumed this task relatively free from federal interference, but over the last fifty years, declining educational attainment has put education policy at the forefront of the federal domestic policy debate. The most recent federal education plan, the No Child Left Behind Act (NCLB) was signed into law in January, 2002. NCLB was a controversial piece of legislation that gave the national government substantial authority over state educational establishments.

Though many educators and politicians agree on the goals set by NCLB—higher educational standards, greater school accountability, ensuring qualified teachers, closing the gap in student achievement—NCLB is criticized by the two major political parties, even though significant congressional majorities of both parties voted for the act. Republicans complain that NCLB impermissibly allows federal intrusion into the educational rights of states, and Democrats worry that the federal government is not providing enough funding to meet NCLB's strict guidelines. Nevertheless, in practice, both parties seemed to have switched ideological positions in regard to the federal government's role. Though the Republicans in 1996 advocated eliminating the Department of Education and reducing education expenditures, the Bush administration has significantly increased education funding; conversely, Democrats who have traditionally advocated an increased federal role in education, now advocate state's rights (though with increased federal spending as well). Though it is too soon to determine the act's effectiveness, and though there is dramatic new federal involvement in education policy, NCLB is supported by a considerable majority of the American people of all demographics.

In the Information Age, it is imperative that all citizens have the requisite skills to survive and thrive in the new economy. With this in mind, what is the best way to ensure that all can realize their vision of life, liberty, and happiness? What is the best way to ensure a quality education for all Americans? Where does proper authority to educate children lie? How can the federal government determine the best way to educate children in a nation in which there are numerous ethnicities, religions, and cultures, all having differing views on what constitutes education? However, since the federal government in part funds state educational establishments, shouldn't it have a say in how its funds are spent? Since American education achievement lags behind education in other advanced modern democracies, shouldn't school systems and teachers be held accountable, and if so, what is the best way to address this problem?

Arguments for the No Child Left Behind Act

- **NCLB gives state and local school districts the flexibility to meet its requirements.** The law gives states the liberty to define standards and the means to meet and measure them. As long as NCLB guidelines are met, the states are generally free to innovate, educate, and test according to their needs.

- **NCLB is not an unfunded mandate.** The General Accounting Office has ruled that NCLB does not meet the description of an unfunded mandate as defined by the 1995 Unfunded Mandates Reform Act, primarily because state school systems have the option of accepting or rejecting NCLB funding. Federal spending accounts for only 8 percent of all educational expenditures in the United States.
- **NCLB represents federal responsiveness to the needs of parents with children in public schools.** Not only have the states failed to meet the guidelines set forth by various federal policy initiatives, but they have failed the expectations of parents as well. For example, Goals 2000 (1994) mandated a 90 percent high school graduation rate by 2000 and a number one rank in math and science for American students internationally. By 2000, the graduation rate was only 75 percent and American students ranked not first, but nineteenth in math and eighteenth in science.

Arguments Against No Child Left Behind:

- **NCLB requirements force school districts to "teach to the test."** Rather than teaching analytical and creative thinking, the testing requirements force school districts to have students cram for the exam, thus undermining the primary goal of a true education. Educators need to provide a quality education without having to worry about how annual testing will affect their students, schools and careers.
- **NCLB does not distinguish between disabled and non-English speaking students and able English speaking students.** A pri-

mary problem with NCLB is that it combines all students, no matter what level language or other core educational proficiencies. This is an unfair burden on educators in school systems with a disproportionate number of disabled or non-English speaking students, as NCLB's punitive sections assume an able, English-speaking student body.

- **NCLB should be considered an impermissible intrusion on the prerogatives of state educational establishments.** A primary concern of the Founders was excessive federal control over state policy. NCLB further erodes the line separating federal and state authority—if school systems are not addressing the concerns of parents and educational problems, it is the proper duty of the states to address these issues.

Questions

1. Does NCLB place too many guidelines on state educational establishments? If so, what is the best way to ensure higher standards and school accountability?
2. Does NCLB give the federal government too much authority over a policy domain that has traditionally belonged to the states? Since school districts reflect local mores and attitudes, are students best educated based on local guidelines?

Selected Readings

Robert D. Barr. *Saving Our Students, Saving Our Schools: 50 Proven Strategies for Revitalizing At-Risk Student and Low Performing Schools.* Palantine, IL: Iri/Skylight Training & Publishing, 2003

Ken Goodman et al. *Saving Our Schools: The Case for Public Education.* Berkeley, CA: RDR Books, 2004.

thousands of airport security personnel. In addition, the No Child Left Behind Act created a host of federal requirements (see Join the Debate: The No Child Left Behind Act). These requirements have already built frustration among state and local officials, who argue that administering the schools, from class size to accountability testing, should be their responsibility.[30]

This trend of **preemption,** or allowing the national government to override state or local actions in certain areas, is not new. The phenomenal growth of preemption statutes began in 1965 during the Johnson administration. Since then, Congress has routinely used its authority under the commerce clause to preempt state laws. However, until recently, preemption statutes were generally supported by Democrats in Congress and the White House, not Republicans. The Bush administration's use of these laws, therefore, reflects a new era in preemption.

preemption
A concept derived from the Constitution's supremacy clause that allows the national government to override or preempt state or local actions in certain areas.

Simulation
You Are a Federal Judge

The Supreme Court: A Return to States' Rights?

The role of the Supreme Court in determining the parameters of federalism cannot be underestimated. Although Congress passed sweeping New Deal legislation, it was not until the Supreme Court finally reversed itself and found those programs constitutional that any real change occurred in the federal/state relationship. From the New Deal until the 1980s, the Supreme Court's impact on the federal system was generally to expand the national government's authority at the expense of the states.

Beginning in the late 1980s, however, as part of the devolution revolution, the Court's willingness to allow Congress to regulate in a variety of areas waned. Once Ronald Reagan was elected president, he attempted to appoint new justices committed to the notion of states' rights and to rolling back federal intervention in matters that many Republicans believed properly resided within the province of the states and not of Congress or the federal courts.

Mario Cuomo, a former Democratic New York governor, has referred to the decisions of what he called the Reagan-Bush Court as creating "a kind of new judicial federalism." According to Cuomo, this new federalism could be characterized by the Court's withdrawal of "rights and emphases previously thought to be national."[31] In *Webster v. Reproductive Health Services* (1989), for example, a 5–4 decision, the Court first gave new latitude—and even encouragement—to the states to fashion more restrictive abortion laws. Since *Webster*, most states have enacted new restrictions on abortion; spousal or parental consent, informed consent or waiting periods, and bans on late-term abortions are the most common. The Court consistently has upheld the authority of the individual states to limit a minor's access to abortion through imposition of parental consent or notification laws.

Analyzing Visuals

STATE-BY-STATE REPORT CARD ON ACCESS TO ABORTION

According to its concerns, the liberal NARAL Pro-Choice America rates each state and the District of Columbia in fourteen categories, including bans on abortion counseling and procedures such as partial birth abortion, clinic violence, the length of waiting periods, access for minors, and public funding, which it then translates into grades. NARAL gives an A only to states it evaluates as pro-choice on every issue on its agenda. After studying the map, answer the following critical thinking questions: What do the states that receive A's have in common? How might factors such as political culture, geography, and social characteristics of the population influence a state's laws concerning abortion? If a group that opposes abortion, such as the National Right to Life Committee, were to grade the states, would its ratings include the same categories or factors? Explain your answer. See Analyzing Visuals: A Brief Guide for additional guidance in analyzing maps.

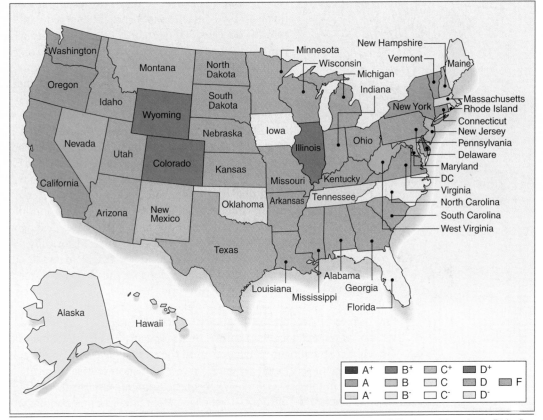

Source: NARAL Pro-Choice America/NARAL Foundation, "Who Decides? A State-by-State Review of Abortion and Reproductive Rights," 2004. Accessed July 1, 2004, http://www.naral.org/yourstate/whodecides/index.cfm. Reprinted by permission.

"I GUESS I JUST HADN'T NOTICED IT BEFORE"

SUPREME COURT OF THE VARIOUS STATES.

OVERRULING OF CONGRESS ON STATE EMPLOYEES RIGHTS

©2000 HERBLOCK

Photo courtesy: Copyright 2000 by Herblock in the Washington Post

And, it also consistently has declined to review most other restrictions, including twenty-four-hour waiting period requirements. In 2000, however, a badly divided (5–4) Supreme Court struck down a Nebraska statute banning partial birth abortion (as discussed in chapter 4). (See Analyzing Visuals: State-by-State Report Card on Access to Abortion.)

The addition of two justices by President Bill Clinton did little to stem the course of a Court bent on rebalancing the nature of the federal system. Since 1989, the Supreme Court has decided several major cases dealing with the nature of the federal system. Most of these have been 5–4 decisions and most have been decided against increased congressional power or in a manner to provide the states with greater authority over a variety of issues and policies.

In *U.S.* v. *Lopez* (1995), for example, which involved the conviction of a student charged with carrying a concealed handgun onto school property, a five-person majority of the Court ruled that Congress lacked constitutional authority under the commerce clause to regulate guns within 1,000 feet of a school.[32] The majority concluded that local gun control in the schools was a state, not a federal, matter.

One year later, again a divided Court ruled that Congress lacked the authority to require states to negotiate with Indian tribes about gaming.[33] The U.S. Constitution specifically gives Congress the right to deal with Indian tribes, but the Court found that Florida's sovereign immunity protected the state from this kind of congressional directive about how to conduct its business. In 1997, the Court decided two more major cases dealing with the scope of Congress's authority to regulate in areas historically left to the province of the states: zoning and local law enforcement. In one, a majority of the Court ruled that sections of the Religious Freedom Restoration Act were unconstitutional because Congress lacked the authority to meddle in local zoning regulations, even if a church was involved.[34] Another 5–4 majority ruled that Congress lacked the authority to require local law enforcement officials to conduct background checks on handgun purchasers until the federal government was able to implement a national system.[35] In 1999, in another case involving sovereign immunity, a slim majority of the Supreme Court ruled that Congress lacked the authority to change patent laws in a manner that would negatively affect a state's right to assert its immunity from suit.[36]

During the 2002 term, however, the Court took an unexpected turn in its federalism revolution.[37] In a case opening states to lawsuits for alleged violations of the federal Family and Medical Leave Act

(FMLA), writing for a six-person majority, Chief Justice William H. Rehnquist rejected Nevada's claim that it was immune from suit under FMLA. Rehnquist noted that the law was an appropriate exercise of Congress's power to combat sex-role stereotypes about the domestic responsibilities of female workers and "thereby dismantle persisting gender-based barriers that women faced in the workplace."[38]

SUMMARY

THE INADEQUACIES OF THE CONFEDERATE form of government created by the Articles of Confederation led the Framers to create a federal system of government that divided power between the national and state governments, with each ultimately responsible to the people. Both the national and state governments have both enumerated and implied powers under the Constitution. The national and state governments share some concurrent powers. Other powers are expressly denied to both governments, although the national government is ultimately declared supreme. The Constitution also lays the groundwork for the Supreme Court to be the arbiter in disagreements between states.

Over the years, the powers of the national government have increased tremendously at the expense of the states. The Supreme Court has played a key role in defining the relationship and powers of the national government through its broad interpretations of the supremacy and commerce clauses.

For many years, dual federalism, which tended to limit the national government's authority in areas such as slavery and civil rights, was the norm in relations between the national and state governments. However, the beginnings of a departure from this ideology became evident with the ratification of the Sixteenth and Seventeenth Amendments in 1913.

The notion of a limited federal government ultimately fell by the wayside in the wake of the Great Depression and Franklin D. Roosevelt's New Deal. This growth in the size and role of the federal government escalated during the Lyndon B. Johnson administration and into the mid to late 1970s. Federal grants became popular solutions for a host of state and local problems.

After his election in 1980, President Ronald Reagan tried to shrink the size and powers of the federal government through what he termed New Federalism. This trend continued through the 1990s, most notably through a campaign document known as the Contract with America. Initially, the George W. Bush administration seemed committed to this devolution, however a struggling economy and the events of September 11, 2001, led to substantial growth in the size of the federal government. Since the Reagan era, the Supreme Court has been willing to limit Congress's authority to legislate in areas it believes are the responsibility of the states.

KEY TERMS

bill of attainder, p. 108
block grant, p. 119
categorical grant, p. 118
concurrent powers, p. 106
cooperative federalism, p. 117
dual federalism, p. 112
enumerated powers, p. 104
ex post facto law, p. 108
federal system, p. 102
full faith and credit clause, p. 108
Gibbons v. *Ogden* (1824), p. 112
implied powers, p. 104
interstate compacts, p. 108
McCulloch v. *Maryland* (1819), p. 110

necessary and proper clause, p. 104
New Federalism, p. 119
preemption, p. 124
privileges and immunities clause, p. 106
reserve (or police) powers, p. 106
Seventeenth Amendment, p. 114
Sixteenth Amendment, p. 114
supremacy clause, p. 106
Tenth Amendment, p. 106
unfunded mandates, p. 120
unitary system, p. 103

SELECTED READINGS

Bowman, Ann O'M., and Richard C. Kearney. *State and Local Government*, 5th ed. Boston: Houghton Mifflin, 2001.

Conlan, Timothy J. *From New Federalism to Devolution: Twenty-Five Years of Intergovernmental Reform.* Washington, DC: Brookings Institution, 1998.

Derthick, Martha. *The Influence of Federal Grants.* Cambridge, MA: Harvard University Press, 1970.

Elazar, Daniel J., and John Kincaid, eds. *The Covenant Connection: From Federal Theology to Modern Federalism.* Lexington, MA: Lexington Books, 2000.

Finegold, Kenneth, and Theda Skocpol. *State and Party in America's New Deal.* Madison: University of Wisconsin Press, 1995.

Grodzins, Morton. *The American System: A View of Government in the United States.* Chicago: Rand McNally, 1966.

Kincaid, John. *The Encyclopedia of American Federalism.* Washington, DC: CQ Press, 2005.

McCabe, Neil Colman, ed. *Comparative Federalism in the Devolution Era.* Lanham, MD: Rowman and Littlefield, 2003.

Nagel, Robert F. *The Implosion of American Federalism.* New York: Oxford University Press, 2002.

Walker, David B. *The Rebirth of Federalism: Slouching Toward Washington*, 2nd ed. New York: Seven Bridges Press, 1999.

Zimmerman, Joseph F. *Interstate Cooperation: Compacts and Administrative Agreements.* New York: Praeger, 2002.

WEB EXPLORATIONS

For a directory of federalism links, see
http://xxx.infidels.org/~nap/index.federalism.html

For more on your state and local governments, see
http://www.statelocalgov.net/

For scholarly works on federalism, see
http://www.temple.edu/federalism and
http://www.cato.org/pubs/journal/cj14n1-7.html
and
http://www.urban.org/Template.cfm?NavMenuID=24&template=/TaggedContent/ViewPublication.cfm&PublicationID=5874

For perspectives on the federal system, see
http://www.usembassy.beusa/usapolitical.htm

For more information on interstate compacts, see
http://ssl.csg.org/compactlaws/comlistlinks.html

For the full text of *McCulloch* v. *Maryland* (1819), see
http://www.landmarkcases.org/mcculloch/home.html

For the full text of *Gibbons* v. *Ogden* (1824), see
http://www.landmarkcases.org/gibbons/legacy.html

For more information on the Great Depression, see
http://newdeal.feri.org/

For more on the devolution revolution, see
http://www.brookings.edu/comm/policybriefs/pb03.htm

To analyze where your state stands relative to other states,
see http://www.taxfoundation.org/statefinance.html

For more information on state abortion restrictions, see
http://www.naral.org/

For more about local gun control initiatives, see
http://www.guncite.com/

Photo courtesy: Bebeto Matthews/AP/Wide World Photos

Civil Liberties

ON FEBRUARY 15, 2003, more than 100,000 demonstrators gathered outside the United Nations (UN) headquarters in New York City to protest the impending U.S.-led war with Iraq. The event was attended by citizens from across the country, including a number of celebrities, from actress Susan Sarandon to activists such as Archbishop Desmond Tutu and Martin Luther King III. However, many of the anti-war demonstrators also protested the barricades that police had set up at the UN's Dag Hammarskjöld Plaza and adjacent streets, which prevented them from moving about freely.

New York City officials argued that the barricades were erected for safety and security reasons. However, protesters, backed by the New York Civil Liberties Union, claimed that the limitations infringed upon their First Amendment right to peaceably assemble. Further, citing the civil rights era march from Selma to Montgomery, Alabama, they argued that a marching protest would have had greater impact than any stationary protest.[1]

Alleged prohibitions on Americans' right to peaceably assemble were not confined to New York City. In St. Louis, students were arrested for carrying protest signs outside a designated protest zone at a speech given by President George W. Bush. On college campuses across the nation, students wishing to express opposition to the Iraq War were confined to free speech zones.[2]

CHAPTER OUTLINE

- The First Constitutional Amendments: The Bill of Rights

- First Amendment Guarantees: Freedom of Religion

- First Amendment Guarantees: Freedom of Speech and Press

- The Second Amendment: The Right to Keep and Bear Arms

- The Rights of Criminal Defendants

- The Right to Privacy

During the war on terrorism and Operation Iraqi Freedom, as in previous times of war, balancing civil liberties with national security has been a difficult and contentious process. President Bush, as evidenced by the USA Patriot Act and its progeny, has indicated that he believes it is necessary to suspend some civil liberties normally enjoyed by citizens. Others, including the American Civil Liberties Union and its affiliates, charge that in a time of war, the United States should be a model of civil liberties protections for the nations we fight against, many of which practice massive civil liberties abuses. The atrocities committed by some members of the U.S. military and U.S. contractors on Iraqi prisoners as well as U.S. citizens held at Guantanamo Bay, Cuba, served to highlight civil liberties abuses.

civil liberties

The personal rights and freedoms that the federal government cannot abridge by law, constitution, or judicial interpretation.

civil rights

The goverment-protected rights of individuals against arbitrary or discriminatory treatment.

Simulation

Balancing Liberty and
Security in a Time of War

WHEN THE BILL OF RIGHTS, which contains many of the most important protections of individual liberties, was written, its drafters were not thinking about issues such as abortion, gay rights, physician-assisted suicide, or many of the personal liberties discussed in this chapter. As a result, the Constitution is nonabsolute in the nature of most civil liberties. **Civil liberties** are the personal rights and freedoms that the federal government cannot abridge, either by law or by judicial interpretation. Civil liberties guarantees place limitations on the power of the government to restrain or to dictate how individuals act. Thus, when we discuss civil liberties such as those found in the Bill of Rights, we are concerned with limits on what governments can and cannot do. **Civil rights,** in contrast, are the goverment-protected rights of individuals against arbitrary or discriminatory treatment. (Civil rights are discussed in chapter 5.)

Questions about civil liberties issues often present complex problems. As illustrated in the opening vignette, we must decide as a society how much infringement on our personal liberties we want to give the police. We must also consider if we want to have different rules for our homes, classrooms, lockers, dorm rooms, or cars. And, do we want to give the Federal Bureau of Investigation (FBI) the right to tap the phones of suspected terrorists or to hold them in jail without access to a lawyer without probable cause? Moreover, in an era of a war on terrorism, it is important to consider what liberties should be accorded to those suspected of terrorism.

In the wake of September 11, 2001, Americans' perceptions about civil liberties and what they are willing to allow the government to do experienced a sea change. The federal government was given unprecedented authority to curtail civil liberties on a scope never before seen. When any political commentators or civil libertarians voiced concerns about the USA Patriot Act and its consequences—the ability to do so being a hallmark of a free society—not only were their voices drowned out by many politicians and other pundits but their patriotism was attacked as well.

Moreover, during the 2001–2002 term of the Supreme Court of the United States, the justices were forced from their chambers for the first time since they moved into the Supreme Court building in 1935. Threats of airborne anthrax closed the Court and several Senate buildings. While the nation was worrying about terrorist attacks from abroad or from within, a quiet revolution in civil liberties continued apace. The five conservative and four moderate Supreme Court justices—who have served together from 1994 through the 2004 term, longer than any other group of justices since 1820—proceeded to make major changes in long-standing practices in a wide range of civil liberties issues.[3] Similarly, the Bush administration continued to advocate new restrictions on civil liberties. Many of the Court's recent decisions, as well as actions of the Bush administration, are discussed in this chapter as we explore the various dimensions of civil liberties guarantees contained in the U.S. Constitution and the Bill of Rights.

In this chapter, we will discuss the Bill of Rights, the reasons for its addition to the Constitution, and its eventual application to the states. After surveying the meaning of one of the First Amendment's guarantees—freedom of religion—we will discuss the meanings of other First Amendment guarantees: freedom of speech, press, and assembly. Following a discussion of the Second Amendment and the right to keep and bear arms, we will analyze the reasons for many of the rights of criminal defendants found in the Bill of Rights and how those rights have been expanded and contracted by the U.S. Supreme Court. Finally, we will discuss the meaning of the right to privacy and how that concept has been interpreted by the Court.

THE FIRST CONSTITUTIONAL AMENDMENTS: THE BILL OF RIGHTS

THE NOTION OF ADDING a bill of rights to the Constitution was not a popular one at the Constitutional Convention. When George Mason of Virginia proposed that such a bill be added to the preface of the proposed Constitution, his resolution was defeated unanimously.[4] In the subsequent ratification debates, Federalists argued that a bill of rights was unnecessary. Not only did most state constitutions already contain those protections, but Federalists believed it was foolhardy to list things that the national government had no power to do.

The insistence of Anti-Federalists on a bill of rights, the fact that some states conditioned their ratification of the Constitution on the addition of these guarantees, and the disagreement among Federalists about writing specific liberty guarantees into the Constitution led to prompt congressional action to put an end to further controversy. This was a time when national stability and support for the new government particularly were needed. Thus, in 1789, Congress sent the proposed Bill of Rights to the states for ratification, which occurred in 1791.

The **Bill of Rights,** the first ten amendments to the Constitution, contains numerous specific guarantees, including those of free speech, press, and religion (see Appendix II for the full text). The Ninth and Tenth Amendments, in particular, highlight Anti-Federalist fears of a too-powerful national government. The **Ninth Amendment,** strongly favored by Madison, makes it clear that this special listing of rights does not mean that others don't exist. The Tenth Amendment reiterates that powers not delegated to the national government are reserved to the states or to the people.

The Incorporation Doctrine: The Bill of Rights Made Applicable to the States

The Bill of Rights was intended to limit the powers of the national government to infringe on the rights and liberties of the citizenry. In *Barron v. Baltimore* (1833), the Supreme Court ruled that the national Bill of Rights limited the actions only of the U.S. government and not of the states.[5] In 1868, however, the Fourteenth Amendment was added to the U.S. Constitution. Its language suggested the possibility that some or even all of the protections guaranteed in the Bill of Rights might be interpreted to prevent state infringement of those rights. Section 1 of the Fourteenth Amendment reads: "No State shall…deprive any person of life, liberty, or property, without due process of law." Questions about the scope of "liberty" as well as the meaning of "due process of law" continue even today to engage legal scholars and jurists.

Until nearly the turn of the twentieth century, the Supreme Court steadfastly rejected numerous arguments urging it to interpret the **due process clause** found in the Fourteenth Amendment as making various provisions contained in the Bill of Rights applicable to the states. In 1897, however, the Court began to increase its jurisdiction over the states.[6] It began to hold states to a **substantive due process** standard whereby state laws had to be shown to be a valid exercise of the state's power to regulate the health, welfare, or public morals of its citizens. Interferences with state power, however, were rare. As a consequence, states continued to pass sedition laws, expecting that the Supreme Court would uphold their constitutionality. These expectations changed

Bill of Rights
The first ten amendments to the U.S. Constitution, which largely guarantee specific rights and liberties.

Ninth Amendment
Part of the Bill of Rights that reads "The enumeration in the Constitution, of certain rights, shall not be construed to deny or disparage others retained by the people."

due process clause
Clause contained in the Fifth and Fourteenth Amendments. Over the years, it has been construed to guarantee to individuals a variety of rights ranging from economic liberty to criminal procedural rights to protection from arbitrary governmental action.

substantive due process
Judicial interpretation of the Fifth and Fourteenth Amendments' due process clause that protects citizens from arbitrary or unjust laws.

dramatically in 1925. Benjamin Gitlow, a member of the Socialist Party, was convicted of violating a New York law that prohibited the advocacy of the violent overthrow of the government. Although Gitlow's conviction was upheld, in *Gitlow* v. *New York* (1925) the Supreme Court noted that the states were not completely free to limit forms of political expression. The Court, instead, argued that certain "fundamental personal rights and liberties" were protected from state impairment by the Fourteenth Amendment's due process clause.[7]

Gitlow, with its finding that states could not abridge free speech protections, was the first step in the slow development of what is called the **incorporation doctrine.** After *Gitlow*, it took the Court six more years to incorporate another First Amendment freedom—that of the press. *Near* v. *Minnesota* (1931) was the first case in which the Supreme Court found that a state law violated freedom of the press as protected by the First Amendment.[8]

As revealed in Table 4.1, not all the specific guarantees in the Bill of Rights have been made applicable to the states through the due process clause of the Fourteenth Amendment. Instead, the Court selectively has chosen to limit the rights of states by protecting the rights it considers most fundamental. This process is referred to as **selective incorporation.**

Selective Incorporation and Fundamental Freedoms

The rationale for selective incorporation, the judicial application to the states of only some of the rights enumerated by the Bill of Rights, was set out by the Court in *Palko* v. *Connecticut* (1937).[9] Frank Palko was charged with first-degree murder for killing two Connecticut police officers, found guilty of a lesser charge of second-degree murder, and sentenced to life imprisonment. Connecticut appealed. Palko was retried, found guilty of first-degree murder, and resentenced to death. Palko then appealed his second conviction, arguing that it violated the Fifth Amendment's prohibition against double jeopardy because the Fifth Amendment had been made applicable to the states by the due process clause of the Fourteenth Amendment.

The Supreme Court upheld Palko's second conviction and the death sentence, thereby choosing not to bind states to the Fifth Amendment's double jeopardy clause. This decision set forth principles that were to guide the Court's interpretation of the incorporation doctrine for the next several decades. The Court found that some protections found in the Bill of Rights are absorbed into the concept of due process only because they are so fundamental to our notions of liberty and justice that they cannot be denied by the states unless the state can show what is called a compelling reason for the curtailment of that particular liberty.

incorporation doctrine
An interpretation of the Constitution that holds that the due process clause of the Fourteenth Amendment requires that state and local governments also guarantee those rights.

selective incorporation
A judicial doctrine whereby most but not all of the protections found in the Bill of Rights are made applicable to the states via the Fourteenth Amendment.

TABLE 4.1 The Selective Incorporation of the Bill of Rights

Amendment	Right	Date	Case Incorporated
I	Speech	1925	*Gitlow* v. *New York*
	Press	1931	*Near* v. *Minnesota*
	Assembly	1937	*DeJonge* v. *Oregon*
	Religion	1940	*Cantwell* v. *Connecticut*
II	Bear arms		Not incorporated (A test has not been presented to the Court in recent history.)
III	No quartering of soldiers		Not incorporated (The quartering problem has not recurred since colonial times.)
IV	No unreasonable searches or seizures	1949	*Wolf* v. *Colorado*
	Exclusionary rule	1961	*Mapp* v. *Ohio*
V	Just compensation	1897	*Chicago, B&O RR Co.* v. *Chicago*
	Self-incrimination	1964	*Malloy* v. *Hogan*
	Double jeopardy	1969	*Benton* v. *Maryland* (overruled *Palko* v. *Connecticut*)
	Grand jury indictment		Not incorporated (The trend in state criminal cases is away from grand juries.)
VI	Public trial	1948	*In re Oliver*
	Right to counsel	1963	*Gideon* v. *Wainwright*
	Confrontation	1965	*Pointer* v. *Texas*
	Impartial trial	1966	*Parker* v. *Gladden*
	Speedy trial	1967	*Klopfer* v. *North Carolina*
	Compulsory trial	1967	*Washington* v. *Texas*
	Criminal jury trial	1968	*Duncan* v. *Louisiana*
VII	Civil jury trial		Not incorporated (Chief Justice Warren Burger wanted to abolish these trials.)
VIII	No cruel and unusual punishment	1962	*Robinson* v. *California*
	No excessive fines or bail		Not incorporated

FIRST AMENDMENT GUARANTEES: FREEDOM OF RELIGION

TODAY, MANY LAWMAKERS AND CULTURAL CRITICS charge that America is becoming a godless nation and worry that the absence of religion in the public schools is having a negative impact on society. Civil libertarians argue that this is far from the case, pointing out that America is one of the most religious nations in the world. According to a 2003 Gallup poll, 65 percent of all Americans belong to a church or synagogue. Many of the Framers were religious men, but they knew what evils could arise if the new nation was not founded with religious freedom as one of its core ideals.

This distaste for a national religion was reflected in the Constitution. Article VI, for example, provides that "no religious Test shall ever be required as a Qualification to any Office or Public Trust under the United States." This simple statement, however, did not reassure those who feared the new Constitution would curtail individual liberty. Thus, the First Amendment to the Constitution soon was ratified to allay those fears.

The **First Amendment** to the Constitution begins: "Congress shall make no law respecting an establishment of religion, or prohibiting the free exercise thereof." This statement sets the boundaries of governmental action. The **establishment clause** directs the national government not to involve itself in religion. It creates, in Thomas Jefferson's words, a "wall of separation" between church and state. The **free exercise clause** guarantees citizens that the national government will not interfere with their practice of religion.

The Establishment Clause

Over the years, the Court has been divided over how to interpret the establishment clause. Does this clause erect a total wall between church and state, or is some governmental accommodation of religion allowed? While the Supreme Court has upheld the constitutionality of many kinds of church/state entanglements, such as public funding to provide sign language interpreters for deaf students in religious schools,[10] the Court has held fast to the rule of strict separation between church and state when issues of prayer in school are involved. In *Engel* v. *Vitale* (1962), the Court first ruled that the recitation in public school classrooms of a twenty-two-word nondenominational prayer drafted by the New Hyde Park, New York, school board was unconstitutional.[11] In 1992, the Court continued its unwillingness to allow organized prayer in public schools by finding unconstitutional the saying of prayer at a middle school graduation.[12] In 2000, the Court ruled that student-led, student-initiated prayer at high school football games violated the establishment clause. But, in 2001, it refused to hear a challenge to a Virginia law that requires students to observe a moment of silence at the start of each school day.[13] Similarly, in 2004, it refused to decide whether "under God" in the Pledge of Allegiance was unconstitutional. In that case, it ruled that a noncustodial father lacked the necessary standing to advance the claim that the pledge advanced religion.[14]

The Court has gone back and forth in its effort to come up with a workable way to deal with church/state questions. In 1971, in *Lemon* v. *Kurtzman*, the Court tried to carve out a three-part test for laws dealing with religious establishment issues. According to the *Lemon* test, a practice or policy was constitutional if it: (1) had a secular purpose;

First Amendment
Part of the Bill of Rights that imposes a number of restrictions on the federal government with respect to the civil liberties of the people, including freedom of religion, speech, press, assembly, and petition.

establishment clause
The first clause in the First Amendment. It prohibits the national government from establishing a national religion.

free exercise clause
The second clause of the First Amendment. It prohibits the U.S. government from interfering with a citizen's right to practice his or her religion.

(2) neither advanced nor inhibited religion; and, (3) did not foster an excessive government entanglement with religion.[15] But, since the early 1980s, the Supreme Court often has sidestepped the *Lemon* test altogether and has appeared more willing to lower the wall between church and state so long as school prayer is not involved.[16] In 1981, for example, the Court ruled unconstitutional a Missouri law prohibiting the use of state university buildings and grounds for "purposes of religious worship." The law had been used to ban religious groups from using school facilities.[17] In 1993, the Court also ruled that religious groups must be allowed to use public schools after hours if that access is also given to other community groups.[18]

In 1995, the Court signaled that it was willing to lower the wall even further. In a 5–4 decision, the majority held that the university violated the free speech rights of a fundamentalist Christian group when it refused to fund the group's student magazine.[19] The importance of this decision was highlighted by Justice David Souter, who noted in dissent: "The Court today, for the first time, approves direct funding of core religious activities by an arm of the state."[20] And, it continues to do so. In 1997, the Court decided that it was constitutional for federally funded public school remedial teachers to provide services to students in parochial schools.[21]

For more than a quarter century, the Supreme Court basically allowed "books only" as an aid to religious schools, noting that the books go to children, not to the schools themselves. In 2000, however, the Court voted 6–3 to uphold the constitutionality of a federal aid provision that allowed the government to lend books and computers to religious schools.[22] And, in 2002, by a 5–4 vote, the Supreme Court in *Zelman* v. *Simmons-Harris* concluded that governments can give money to parents to allow them to send their children to private or religious schools.[23] Building on a line of cases that many critics argue further erode the wall between church and state, the Court now appears willing to support programs as long as they provide aid to religious and nonreligious schools alike, and the money goes to persons who exercise free choice over how it is used.

The Free Exercise Clause

The free exercise clause of the First Amendment proclaims that "Congress shall make no law...prohibiting the free exercise [of religion]." Although the free exercise

■ Rev. Daniel Coughlin, the current House chaplain, is shown here. The chaplain is a powerful reminder that, despite the concerns of some Americans, religion and religious traditions permeate the government. The responsibilities of the House and Senate chaplains include delivering the morning invocation, providing spiritual counsel for members and their families, and holding Bible study groups.

Photo courtesy: Ken Lambert/AP/Wide World Photos

clause of the First Amendment guarantees individuals the right to be free from governmental interference in the exercise of their religion, this guarantee, like other First Amendment freedoms, is not absolute. When secular law comes into conflict with religious law, the right to exercise one's religious beliefs is often denied—especially if the religious beliefs in question are held by a minority or by an unpopular or suspicious religious group. Nonetheless, the Court has made it clear that the free exercise clause requires that a state or the national government remain neutral toward religion.

Many critics of rigid enforcement of such neutrality argue that the government should do what it can to accommodate the religious diversity in our nation. Nevertheless, the Court has interpreted the Constitution to mean that governmental interests can outweigh free exercise rights. In 1990, for example, the Supreme Court ruled that the free exercise clause allowed Oregon to ban the use of sacramental peyote (an illegal hallucinogenic drug) in some Native American tribes' traditional religious services.[24] This decision prompted a dramatic outcry. Congressional response was passage of the Religious Freedom Restoration Act, which reinstated the strict scrutiny, standard of review for laws seen to interfere with religious guarantees. The act required states to show a compelling rationale for their activities to make it harder for states to interfere with how citizens practice their religion. In 1997, however, the Supreme Court ruled that the act was unconstitutional.[25]

Participation
The Courts and School Vouchers

Simulation
You Are a State Legislator

FIRST AMENDMENT GUARANTEES: FREEDOM OF SPEECH, PRESS, AND ASSEMBLY

TODAY, SOME MEMBERS OF CONGRESS criticize the movie industry and reality television shows including *Survivor* and *The Bachelor* for pandering to the least common denominator of society. Other groups criticize popular performers such as Eminem for lyrics that promote violence and that demean women. Janet Jackson's "wardrobe malfunction" as well as Kid Rock's antics at the 2004 Super Bowl, however, launched renewed calls for increased restrictions, the imposition of significant fines on broadcasters, and greater regulation of the airwaves. Today, many civil libertarians believe that the rights to speak, print, and assemble freely are being seriously threatened.[26]

Freedom of Speech and the Press in the United States

A democracy depends on a free exchange of ideas, and the First Amendment shows that the Framers were well aware of this fact.

Comparing Civil Liberties

Historically, one of the most volatile areas of constitutional interpretation has been in the interpretation of the First Amendment's mandate that "Congress shall make no law…abridging the freedom of speech or of the press." Like the establishment and free exercise clauses of the First Amendment, the speech and press clauses have not been interpreted as absolute bans against government regulation. A lack of absolute meaning has led to thousands of cases seeking both broader and narrower judicial interpretations of the scope of the amendment.

Over the years, the Court has employed a hierarchical approach in determining what the government can and cannot regulate, with some items getting greater protection than others. Generally, thoughts have received the greatest protection, and actions or deeds the least. Words have come somewhere in the middle, depending on their content and purpose.

The Alien and Sedition Acts.   When the First Amendment was ratified in 1791, it was considered only to protect against **prior restraint** of speech or expression, or to guard against the prohibition of speech or publication before the fact. However, in 1798, the Federalist Congress enacted the Alien and Sedition Acts, which were designed to ban any criticism by the growing numbers of Democratic-Republicans. These acts made the publication of "any false, scandalous writing against the government of the United States" a criminal offense. Although the law clearly ran in the face of the First Amendment's ban on prior restraint, partisan Federalist judges imposed fines and jail terms on at least ten Democratic-Republican newspaper editors. The acts became a major issue in the 1800 presidential election campaign, which led to the election of Thomas Jefferson, a vocal opponent of the acts. He quickly pardoned all who had been convicted under their provisions, and the Democratic-Republican Congress allowed the acts to expire.

Slavery, the Civil War, and Rights Curtailments.   After the public outcry over the Alien and Sedition Acts, the national government largely got out of the business of regulating speech. But, in its place, the states, which were not yet bound by the Bill of Rights, began to prosecute those who published articles critical of governmental policies. In the 1830s, at the urgings of abolitionists (those who sought an end to slavery), the publication or dissemination of any positive information about slavery became a punishable offense in the North. In the opposite vein, in the South, supporters of slavery enacted laws to prohibit publication of any anti-slavery sentiments. Southern postmasters refused to deliver northern abolitionist papers, which amounted to censorship of the mail.

During the Civil War, President Abraham Lincoln effectively suspended the free press provision of the First Amendment (as well as many other sections of the Constitution). He went so far as to order the

prior restraint
Constitutional doctrine that prevents the government from prohibiting speech or publication before the fact; generally held to be in violation of the First Amendment.

FREEDOM OF THE PRESS

May 3 of each year is World Press Freedom Day. Americans are quite correctly proud of the independent voice exercised by the U.S. press. But, how do press freedoms in the United States compare with those found in other countries? And, just how free is the American press? Global comparisons can be made along three dimensions. First is the legal environment: what rules and regulations govern media content? Second is the political environment: how much political control is exercised over the content of the news media? Third is the economic environment: who owns the media and how are media outlets financed?

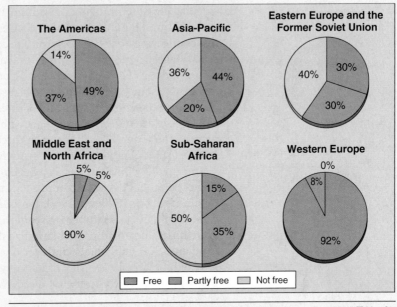

Source: Freedom House, "Global Press Freedoms Deteriorate," and "Freedom of the Press 2004: Table of Global Press Freedom Rankings," both at www.freedomhouse.org/media.

Using these three factors, Freedom House, a nonprofit organization that serves as a watchdog on the relationship between the media and government, issues a report each year on the degree of print, broadcast, and Internet freedom in every country in the world. In 2003 it concluded that the United States was tied for 15th place. Denmark, Iceland, and Sweden were tied for 1st. Close to home, Canada tied for 23rd place and Mexico for 80th. This ranking placed Canada in the free category, which indicates no significant restrictions on the press, and Mexico in the partly free category, which means some media restrictions exist.

Russia, tied for 147th, was judged not to have a free press. The government had nearly complete control of the broadcast media—it passed laws and used financial pressure to restrict critical coverage of its policies.

In general, 2003 was not a particularly good year for freedom of the press. Ten states went down in their ranking and only two—Sierra Leone and Kenya—showed improvement, moving from not free to partly free. As a result of these shifts, 5 percent fewer people enjoyed a free press and 5 percent more lived in countries with no free press at all.

Questions

1. What factors would you look at in judging whether a country had a free press?
2. Are economic, political, or cultural factors most important in making the press free?

139

arrest of the editors of two New York papers who were critical of him. Far from protesting against these blatant violations of the First Amendment, Congress acceded to them. In one instance, William McCardle, a Mississippi newspaper editor who had written in opposition to Lincoln and the Union occupation, was jailed by a military court without having any charges brought against him. He appealed his detainment to the U.S. Supreme Court, arguing that he was being held unlawfully. Congress, fearing that a victory for McCardle would hurt Lincoln's national standing and prompt other similarly treated Confederate editors to follow his lead, enacted legislation prohibiting the Supreme Court from issuing a judgment in any cases involving convictions for publishing statements critical of the United States. Because Article II of the Constitution gives Congress the power to determine the jurisdiction of the Court, the Court was forced to conclude in *Ex parte McCardle* (1869) that it had no authority to rule in the matter.[27]

After the Civil War, states also began to prosecute individuals for seditious speech if they uttered or printed statements critical of the government. Between 1890 and 1900, for example, there were more than one hundred state prosecutions for sedition.[28] By the end of World War I, over thirty states had passed laws to punish seditious speech, and more than 1,900 individuals and over one hundred newspapers were prosecuted for violations.[29] In 1925, however, states' authority to regulate speech was severely restricted by the Court's decision in *Gitlow* v. *New York*.

World War I and Anti-Governmental Speech.

The next major national efforts to restrict freedom of speech and the press did not occur until Congress passed the Espionage Act in 1917. Nearly 2,000 Americans were convicted of violating its various provisions, especially those that made it illegal to urge resistance to the draft or to prohibit the distribution of anti-war leaflets. In *Schenck* v. *U.S.* (1919), the Supreme Court upheld this act, ruling that Congress had a right to restrict speech "of such a nature as to create a clear and present danger that will bring about the substantive evils that Congress has a right to prevent."[30] Under this test, known as the **clear and present danger test,** the circumstances surrounding an incident are important. Anti-war leaflets, for example, may be permissible during peacetime, but they were considered to pose too much of a danger during wartime.

For decades, the Supreme Court wrestled with what constituted a "danger." Finally, in *Brandenburg* v. *Ohio* (1969), the Court fashioned a new test for deciding whether certain kinds of speech could be regulated by the government: the **direct incitement test.** Now, the government could punish the advocacy of illegal action only if "such advocacy is directed to inciting or producing imminent lawless action and is likely to incite or produce such action."[31] The requirement of "imminent lawless action" makes it more difficult for the government to punish speech

Timeline

Civil Liberties and
National Security

clear and present danger test
Test articulated by the Supreme Court in *Schenck* v. *U.S.* (1919) to draw the line between protected and unprotected speech; the Court looks to see "whether the words used" could "create a clear and present danger that they will bring about substantive evils" that Congress seeks "to prevent."

direct incitement test
A test articulated by the Supreme Court in *Brandenburg* v. *Ohio* (1969) that holds that advocacy of illegal action is protected by the First Amendment unless imminent lawless action is intended and likely to occur.

and publication and is consistent with the Framers' notion of the special role played by these elements in a democratic society.

Protected Speech and Publications

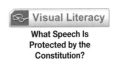

As discussed, the Supreme Court will not tolerate legislation that amounts to prior restraint of the press. Other types of speech and publication are also protected by the Court, including symbolic speech and hate speech.

Prior Restraint.   With only a few exceptions, the Court has made it clear that it will not tolerate prior restraint of speech. In 1971, for example, in *New York Times Co.* v. *Sullivan* (1971) (also called the *Pentagon Papers* case), the Supreme Court ruled that the U.S. government could not block the publication of secret Department of Defense documents illegally furnished to the *Times* by anti-war activists.[32] In 1976, the Supreme Court went even further, noting that any attempt by the government to prevent expression carried "'a heavy presumption' against its constitutionality."[33]

Photo courtesy: UPI Images/Landov

■ Radio personality Howard Stern was suspended by Clear Channel Communications in February, 2004 for "vulgar, offensive, and insulting" content on his syndicated morning show. Stern and critics of the George W. Bush Administration later speculated that his suspension and subsequent firing were actually the result of his anti-Bush rhetoric.

THE USA PATRIOT ACT

Overview: The Declaration of Independence forcefully espouses the principles that all individuals have "certain unalienable rights, that among these are Life, Liberty and the pursuit of Happiness," and that it is government's purpose to guarantee the secure enjoyment of these rights. To assure these liberties, government must necessarily use legitimate police force to ensure safety within its borders, and it must use military force to defend the state from outside aggression.

A considerable problem for democratic peoples in free and open societies is how to define the limits of government intervention in the private sphere. This problem becomes particularly acute during times of national crisis and armed conflict. Establishing the line between the government's constitutional duty to "provide for the common defense" and to "secure the blessings of liberty" is complicated. It becomes even more complex when those who threaten America's national security use the freedom and rights found in the United States as a means through which to wage war. To help defend against those wishing to use the openness of American society for harmful ends, the Uniting and Strengthening America by Providing Appropriate Tools Required to Intercept and Obstruct Terrorism Act of 2001, otherwise known as the USA Patriot Act (USAPA), was signed into law on October 26, 2001, in response to the terrorist attacks on New York City and the Pentagon on September 11, 2001. The purpose of this act is to deter and punish terrorist acts in the United States and around the world, to enhance law enforcement investigatory tools.

The events of 9/11 have thrust the question concerning the balance between liberty and security to the forefront of national discussion, and questions abound regarding the wisdom or folly of the USA Patriot Act. Will the act help defend the United States against terrorist activity, or will it allow the government to abuse its power in the name of national security? Isn't it necessary that government narrow the scope of civil rights and liberties in times of national distress, as has been the case throughout most of American history— for example, when Abraham Lincoln suspended *habeas corpus* in his effort to preserve the United States? Or, conversely, hasn't American history also demonstrated that injustices have been committed in the name of national security—for example, the U.S. government's internment of Japanese American citizens during World War II?

Arguments for the USA Patriot Act

- **The USA Patriot Act allows the government to use new technologies to address new threats.** Those engaged in terrorist activities today use sophisticated technologies. The USAPA allows the government to wage the war on terrorism by using the same and superior technologies to find and prosecute those engaged in terrorism and to help reduce the threat of terrorist attacks.
- **The USA Patriot Act dismantles the wall of legal and regulatory policies erected to limit sharply the sharing of information between intelligence, national security, and law enforcement communities.** Prior policy essentially prohibited various government agencies from communicating and coordinat-

ing domestic and national security activities, thus restricting the flow of valuable information that could prevent terrorist attacks. Now, government agencies can coordinate surveillance activities across domestic and national security policy domains.

- **The USA Patriot Act allows government agencies to use the procedures and tools already available to investigate organized and drug crime.** The Act uses techniques already approved by the courts in investigating such crimes as wire fraud, money laundering, and drug trafficking. These techniques include roving wire taps and judicially approved search warrants, notice of which may be delayed in certain narrow circumstances.

Arguments Against the USA Patriot Act

- **Certain provisions of the USA Patriot Act may violate an individual's right to privacy.** For example, section 216 allows law enforcement officials to get a warrant to track which Web sites a person visits and to collect certain information in regard to an individual's e-mail activity. There need not be any suspicion of criminal activity—all law enforcement authorities need do is to certify that the potential information is relevant to an ongoing criminal investigation.
- **The USA Patriot Act violates the civil rights and liberties of legal immigrants.** The act permits the indefinite detention of immigrants and other noncitizens. The attorney general may detain immigrants merely upon "reasonable grounds" that one is involved in terrorism or engaged in activity that poses a danger to national security, and this detention may be

indefinite until determination is made that such an individual threatens national security.

- **Safeguards to prevent direct government surveillance of citizens have been reduced.** The USA Patriot Act repeals certain precautions in regard to the sharing of information between domestic law enforcement agencies and the intelligence community. These safeguards were put in place during the Cold War after the revelation that the Central Intelligence Agency (CIA) and the Federal Bureau of Investigation (FBI) had been conducting joint investigations on American citizens during the McCarthy era and civil rights movement—including surveillance of Reverend Martin Luther King Jr.—for political purposes.

Questions

1. Does the USA Patriot Act balance liberty with security? If so, how does it strike that balance? If not, what do you think could be done to redress the imbalance?
2. Is the USA Patriot Act a necessary law? If so, what, in your view, can be done to rectify its flaws? If not, what should be done to ensure the security of the United States against terrorist activity?

Selected Readings

Nat Hentoff. *The War on the Bill of Rights—and the Gathering Resistance.* New York: Seven Stories Press, 2003.

Stephen M. Duncan. *War of a Different Kind: Military Force and America's Search for Homeland Security.* Annapolis, MD: United States Naval Institute. 2004.

symbolic speech
Symbols, signs, and other methods of expression generally also considered to be protected by the First Amendment.

Symbolic Speech.   In addition to the general protection accorded to pure speech, the Supreme Court has extended the reach of the First Amendment to **symbolic speech,** a means of expression that includes symbols or signs. In the words of Justice John Marshall Harlan, these kinds of speech are part of the "free trade in ideas."[34]

The Supreme Court first acknowledged that symbolic speech was entitled to First Amendment protection in *Stromberg* v. *California* (1931).[35] There, the Court overturned a communist youth camp director's conviction under a state statute prohibiting the display of a red flag, a symbol of opposition to the U.S. government. In a similar vein, the right of high school students to wear black armbands to protest the Vietnam War was upheld in *Tinker* v. *Des Moines Independent Community School District* (1969).[36]

Burning the American flag also has been held to be a form of protected symbolic speech. In 1989, a sharply divided Supreme Court (5–4) reversed the conviction of Gregory Johnson, who had been found guilty of setting fire to an American flag during the 1984 Republican National Convention in Dallas.[37] As a result, there was a major public outcry against the Court. Unable to pass a constitutional amendment, Congress passed the Federal Flag Protection Act of 1989, which authorized federal prosecution of anyone who intentionally desecrated a national flag. Johnson and his colleagues burned another flag and were again convicted. Their conviction was overturned by the Supreme Court, who held that this federal law "suffered from the same fundamental flaw" as had the earlier Texas state law.[38]

Hate Speech, Unpopular Speech, and Speech Zones.   In the 1990s, a particularly thorny First Amendment area emerged as cities and universities attempted to prohibit what they viewed as offensive hate speech. In *R.A.V.* v. *City of St. Paul* (1992), a St. Paul, Minnesota, ordinance that made it a crime to engage in speech or action likely to arouse "anger," "alarm," or "resentment" on the basis of race, color, creed, religion, or gender was at issue. The Court ruled 5–4 that a white teenager who burned a cross on a black family's front lawn, thereby committing a hate crime under the ordinance, could not be charged under that law because the First Amendment prevents governments from "silencing speech on the basis of its content."[39] In 2003, the Court narrowed this definition, ruling that state governments could constitutionally restrict cross burning when it occurred with the intent of racial intimidation.[40]

Two-thirds of colleges and universities have banned a variety of forms of speech or conduct that creates or fosters an intimidating, hostile, or offensive environment on campus. To prevent disruption of university activities, some universities have created free speech zones that restrict the time, place, or manner of speech. Critics, including the ACLU, charge that free speech zones imply that speech can be limited

on other parts of the campus, which they see as a violation of the First Amendment. They have filed a number of suits in district court, but to date none of these cases has reached the Supreme Court.

Unprotected Speech and Publications

Although the Supreme Court has allowed few governmental bans on most types of speech, some forms of expression are not protected. According to the Court, libel, fighting words, obscenity, and lewdness are not protected by the First Amendment because "such expressions are no essential part of any exposition of ideals, and are of such slight social value as a step to truth that any benefit that may be derived from them is clearly outweighed by the social interest in order and morality."[41]

Libel and Slander.   **Libel** is a written statement that defames the character of a person. If the statement is spoken, it is **slander.** In many nations—such as Great Britain, for example—it is relatively easy to sue someone for libel. In the United States, however, the standards of proof are much more difficult. A person who believes that he or she has been a victim of libel must show that the statements made were untrue. Truth is an absolute defense against the charge of libel, no matter how painful or embarrassing the revelations.

It is often more difficult for individuals the Supreme Court considers to be "public persons or public officials" to sue for libel or slander. *New York Times Co.* v. *Sullivan* (1964) was the first major libel case considered by the Supreme Court.[42] An Alabama state court found the *Times* guilty of libel for printing a full-page advertisement accusing

libel
False written statements or written statements tending to call someone's reputation into disrepute.

slander
Untrue spoken statements that defame the character of a person.

New York Times Co. v. *Sullivan* **(1964)**
The Supreme Court concluded that "actual malice" must be proved to support a finding of libel against a public figure.

Alabama officials of physically abusing African Americans during various civil rights protests. The Supreme Court overturned the conviction and established that a finding of libel against a public official could stand only if there was a showing of actual malice, or a knowing disregard for the truth. Proof that the statements were false or negligent was not sufficient to prove actual malice.

Fighting Words.   In the 1942 case of *Chaplinsky* v. *New Hampshire*, the Court stated that **fighting words,** or words that "by their very utterance inflict injury or tend or incite an immediate breach of peace," are not subject to the restrictions of the First Amendment.[43] Fighting words, which include "profanity, obscenity, and threats," are therefore able to be regulated by the federal and state governments.

These words do not necessarily have to be spoken; fighting words can also come in the form of symbolic expression. For example, in 1968, a California man named Paul Cohen wore a jacket that said "Fuck the Draft. Stop the War" into a Los Angeles county courthouse. He was arrested and charged with disturbing the peace and engaging in offensive conduct. The trial court convicted Cohen, and this conviction was upheld by a state appellate court. However, when the case reached the Supreme Court in 1971, the Court reversed the lower courts' decisions and ruled that forbidding the use of certain words amounted to little more than censorship of ideas.[44]

Obscenity.   Through 1957, U.S. courts often based their opinions of what was obscene on an English common-law test.[45] In *Roth* v. *U.S.* (1957), however, the Court created its own standard of obscenity. To be considered obscene, the material in question had to be "utterly without redeeming social importance." The Court also articulated a new test for obscenity in *Roth*: "whether to the average person, applying contemporary community standards, the dominant theme of the material taken as a whole appeals to the prurient interests."[46]

In many ways, the *Roth* test brought with it as many problems as it attempted to solve. Throughout the 1950s and 1960s, "prurient" remained hard to define, as the Supreme Court struggled to find a standard for judging actions or words. Moreover, it was very difficult to prove that a book or movie was utterly without redeeming social value. In general, even some hardcore pornography passed muster under the *Roth* test.

In light of this evidence and other changes in the political climate, in the 1973 case of *Miller* v. *California*, the Court set out a test that redefined obscenity. To make it easier for states to regulate obscene materials, the justices concluded that lower courts must ask "whether the work depicts or describes, in a patently offensive way, sexual conduct specifically defined by state law." The courts also were to determine "whether the work, taken as a whole, lacks serious literary, artistic, political, or sci-

fighting words
Words that, "by their very utterance inflict injury or tend to incite an immediate breach of peace." Fighting words are not subject to the restrictions of the First Amendment.

entific value. In place of the contemporary community standards gauge used in *Roth*, the Court defined community standards to refer to the locality in question, under the rationale that what is acceptable in New York City might not be acceptable in Maine or Mississippi.[47]

Time and contexts clearly have altered the Court's and, indeed, much of America's perceptions of what works are obscene. But, the Supreme Court has allowed communities great leeway in drafting statutes to deal with obscenity and, even more important, other forms of questionable expression. In 1991, for example, the Court voted 5–4 to allow Indiana to ban totally nude erotic dancing, concluding that the statute furthered a substantial governmental interest, and therefore was not in violation of the First Amendment.[48]

Congress and Obscenity.   While lawmakers have been fairly effective in restricting the sale and distribution of obscene materials, Congress has been particularly concerned with two obscenity and pornography issues: (1) federal funding for the arts; and, (2) the distribution of obscenity and pornography on the Internet.

In 1990, concern over the use of federal dollars by the National Endowment for the Arts (NEA) for works with controversial religious or sexual themes led to passage of legislation requiring the NEA to "[take] into consideration general standards of decency and respect for the diverse beliefs and values of the American public" when it makes annual awards. Several performance artists believed that Congress could not regulate the content of speech solely because it could be offensive; they challenged the statute in federal court. In 1998, the Supreme Court upheld the legislation, ruling that, because decency was only one of the criteria in making funding decisions, the act did not violate the First Amendment.[49]

Monitoring the Internet has proven more difficult for Congress. In 1996, it passed the Communications Decency Act, which prohibited the transmission of obscene materials over the Internet to anyone under age eighteen. In 1997, the Supreme Court ruled in *Reno* v. *American Civil Liberties Union* that the act violated the First Amendment because it was too vague and overbroad.[50] In reaction to the decision, Congress passed the Child Online Protection Act in 1998. The new law broadened the definition of pornography and redefined "visual depiction" to include computer-generated images.[51] The act targeted material "harmful to minors" but applied only to World Wide Web sites, not chat rooms or e-mail. It also targeted only materials used for "commercial purposes."

The ACLU and online publishers immediately challenged the constitutionality of the act, and a U.S. court of appeals in Philadelphia ruled the law was unconstitutional because of its reliance on "community standards" as articulated in *Miller*, which are not enforceable on the Internet. While this case was on appeal to the Supreme Court, Congress enacted the Children's Internet Protection Act, which prohibited public libraries receiving federal funds from allowing minors access to the Web without anti-pornography filters. Meanwhile, in *Ashcroft* v. *Free Speech Coalition* (2002), the Court ruled that Congress had gone too far in a laudable effort to stamp out child pornography.[52] Six justices agreed that the law was too vague because "communities with a narrow view of what words and images are suitable for children might be able to censor Internet content, putting it out of reach of the entire country."[53]

Congressional reaction was immediate. Within two weeks of the Court's decision, lawmakers were drafting more specific legislation to meet the Court's reservations. New regulations were enacted in 2003 as part of an anti-crime bill. In this legislation, Congress further limited the kinds of cyber pornography subject to regulation and allowed those accused of creating and marketing such pornography to "escape conviction if they could show they did not use actual children to produce sexually explicit images."[54] This new law is also under legal challenge.

Freedoms of Assembly and Petition

"Peaceful assembly for lawful discussion cannot be made a crime," Chief Justice Charles Evans Hughes wrote in the 1937 case of *DeJonge* v. *Oregon*, which incorporated the First Amendment's freedom of assembly clause.[55] Despite this clear declaration, and an even more ringing declaration in the First Amendment, the fundamental freedoms of assembly and petition have been among the most controversial, especially in times of war. As with other First Amendment freedoms, the Supreme Court often has become the arbiter between the freedom of the people to express dissent and government's authority to limit controversy in the name of national security.

Because the freedom to assemble is hinged on peaceful conduct, the freedoms of assembly and petition are related directly to the freedoms of speech and of the press. If the words or actions taken at any event cross the line of constitutionality, the event itself may no longer be protected. Absent that protection, leaders and attendees may be subject to governmental regulation and even criminal charges or civil fines.

THE SECOND AMENDMENT: THE RIGHT TO KEEP AND BEAR ARMS

MOST OF THE COLONIES REQUIRED all white men to keep and bear arms, and all white men in whole sections of the colonies were deputized to defend their settlements against Indians and other European powers. These local militias were viewed as the best way to keep order and protect liberty. The Second Amendment was added to the Constitution to ensure that Congress could not pass laws to disarm state militias. This amendment appeased Anti-Federalists, who feared that the new Constitution would cause them to lose the right to "keep and bear arms" as well as an unstated right—the right to revolt against governmental tyranny.

Through the early 1920s, few state statutes were passed to regulate firearms (and generally these laws dealt with the possession of firearms by slaves). The Supreme Court's decision in *Barron* v. *Baltimore* (1833), which refused to incorporate the Bill of Rights to the state governments, prevented federal review of those state laws.[56] Moreover, in *Dred Scott* v. *Sandford* (1857) (see chapter 3),

Photo courtesy: Marcy Nighswander/AP/Wide World Photos

■ President Bill Clinton signs the Brady Bill into law flanked by Vice President Al Gore, Attorney General Janet Reno, and James and Sarah Brady and their children.

Chief Justice Roger B. Taney listed the right to own and carry arms as a basic right of citizenship.[57]

In 1934, Congress passed the National Firearms Act in response to the increase in organized crime that occurred in the 1920s and 1930s as a result of Prohibition. The act imposed taxes on automatic weapons (such as machine guns) and sawed-off shotguns. In *U.S.* v. *Miller* (1939), a unanimous Court upheld the constitutionality of the act, stating that the Second Amendment was intended to protect a citizen's right to own ordinary militia weapons and not unregistered sawed-off shotguns, which were at issue.[58] *Miller* was the last time the Supreme Court directly addressed the Second Amendment. In *Quilici* v. *Village of Morton Grove* (1983), the Supreme Court refused to review a lower court's ruling upholding the constitutionality of a local ordinance banning handguns against a Second Amendment challenge.[59]

In the aftermath of the assassination attempt on President Ronald Reagan in 1981, many lawmakers called for passage of gun control legislation. At the forefront of that effort was Sarah Brady, the wife of James Brady, the presidential press secretary who was badly wounded and left partially disabled by John Hinckley Jr., President Reagan's assailant. In 1993, her efforts helped to win passage of the Brady Bill, which imposed a federal mandatory five-day waiting period on the purchase of handguns.

In 1997, the U.S. Supreme Court ruled 5–4 that the section of the Brady Bill requiring state officials to conduct background checks of prospective handgun owners violated principles of state sovereignty.[60] The background check provision, while important, is not critical to the overall goals of the Brady Bill because a federal record-checking system went into effect in late 1998.

More important to the Brady Bill was its ban on assault weapons. This provision, which prohibited Americans from owning many of the most violent types of guns, carried a ten-year time limit. It expired just before the 2004 elections. Neither the president nor the Republican-controlled Congress made any serious steps toward renewal, causing many to charge that the move was political and prompted by anti-gun interests such as the National Rifle Association, who were major players in the Republican electoral efforts.

THE RIGHTS OF CRIMINAL DEFENDANTS

THE FOURTH, FIFTH, SIXTH, AND EIGHTH Amendments supplement constitutional guarantees against writs of *habeas corpus*, *ex post facto* laws, and bills of attainder by providing a variety of procedural guarantees (often called **due process rights**) for those accused of crimes. Particular amendments, as well as other portions of the Constitution, specifically provide procedural guarantees to protect individuals accused of crimes at all stages of the criminal justice process. As is the case with the First Amendment, many of these rights have been interpreted by the Supreme Court to apply to the states. In interpreting the amendments dealing with what are frequently termed "criminal rights," the courts have to grapple not only with the meaning of the amendments but also with how their protections are to be implemented.

due process rights
Procedural guarantees provided by the Fourth, Fifth, Sixth, and Eighth Amendments for those accused of crimes.

The Fourth Amendment and Searches and Seizures

The **Fourth Amendment** to the Constitution protects people from unreasonable searches by the federal government. Moreover, in some detail, it sets out what may not be searched unless a warrant is issued, underscoring the Framers' concern with possible government abuses.

The purpose of this amendment was to deny the national government the authority to make general searches. Over the years, in a number of decisions, the Supreme Court has interpreted the Fourth Amendment to allow the police to search: (1) the person arrested; (2) things in plain view of the accused person; and, (3) places or things that the arrested person could touch or reach or are otherwise in the arrestee's "immediate control."

In 1995, the Court also resolved a decades-old constitutional dispute by ruling unanimously that police must knock and announce their presence before entering a house or apartment to execute a search. But, said the Court, there may be reasonable exceptions to the rule to account for the likelihood of violence or the imminent destruction of evidence.[61]

Warrantless searches often occur if police suspect that someone is committing or is about to commit a crime. In these situations, police

Fourth Amendment
Part of the Bill of Rights that reads: "The right of the people to be secure in their persons, houses, papers, and effects, against unreasonable searches and seizures, shall not be violated, and no Warrants shall issue, but upon probable cause, supported by Oath or affirmation, and particularly describing the place to be searched, and the persons or things to be seized."

may stop and frisk the individual under suspicion. In 1989, the Court ruled that there need be only a "reasonable suspicion" for stopping a suspect—a much lower standard than "probable cause."[62] Thus, a suspected drug courier may be stopped for brief questioning but only a frisk search (for weapons) is permitted.

In 2001, the Court also ruled on a California policy that required individuals, as a condition of their probation, to consent to warrantless searches of their person, property, homes, or vehicles, thus limiting a probationer's Fourth Amendment protections against unreasonable searches and seizures.[63] The Court did not give blanket approval to searches; instead, a unanimous Court said that a probation officer must have a reasonable suspicion of wrongdoing—a lesser standard than probable cause afforded to most citizens. Searches can also be made without a warrant if consent is obtained, and the Court has ruled that consent can be given by a variety of persons. It has ruled, for example, that police can search a bedroom occupied by two persons as long as they have the consent of one of them.[64]

In situations where no arrest occurs, police must obtain search warrants from a "neutral and detached magistrate" prior to conducting more extensive searches of houses, cars, offices, or any other place where an individual would reasonably have some expectation of privacy.[65] Police cannot get search warrants, for example, to require you to undergo surgery to remove a bullet that might be used to incriminate you, since your expectation of bodily privacy outweighs the need for evidence.[66] But, courts do not require search warrants in possible drunk driving situations. Thus, the police can require you to take a Breathalyzer test to determine whether you have been drinking in excess of legal limits.[67]

Participation

Privacy and Rights of the Accused

Homes, too, are presumed to be private. Firefighters can enter your home to fight a fire without a warrant. But, if they decide to investigate the cause of the fire, they must obtain a warrant before their reentry.[68] In contrast, under the "open fields doctrine" first articulated by the Supreme Court in 1924, if you own a field, and even if you post "No Trespassing" signs, the police can search your field without a warrant to see if you are illegally growing marijuana, because you cannot reasonably expect privacy in an open field.[69]

Cars have proven problematic for police and the courts because of their mobile nature. As noted by Chief Justice William Howard Taft as early as 1925, "the vehicle can quickly be moved out of the locality or jurisdiction in which the warrant must be sought."[70] Over the years, the Court has become increasingly lenient about the scope of automobile searches. In 2002, an unusually unanimous Court ruled that when evaluating if a border patrol officer acted lawfully in stopping a suspicious minivan, the totality of the circumstances had to be considered. Wrote Chief Justice William H. Rehnquist, the "balance between the public interest and the individual's right to personal security," tilts in favor of a "standard less than probable cause in brief investigatory stops."[71]

THE WARTIME RIGHTS OF POLITICAL DETAINEES

In *Federalist No. 47*, James Madison warned against unchecked executive power, which had "affected to render the Military independent of and superior to the Civil Power" and had "deprive[ed them], in many Cases of the Benefits of Trial by Jury." Anxiety about tyranny prompted the Framers to place freedom from arbitrary detention at the core of liberty interests protected by the U.S. Constitution. Still, in the wake of the 9/11 terrorist attacks, Congress passed the Authorization for Use of Military Force, giving the president power to "use all necessary appropriate force" against "nations, organizations, or persons" that he deemed to have "Planned, authorized, committed or aided" in the completion of those attacks.

The president then sent U.S. troops to Afghanistan to subdue al-Qaeda and to quell the supporting Taliban regime. Soon thereafter, members of the U.S.-supported Afghani Northern Alliance captured, among others, two U.S. citizens in Afghanistan, John Walker Lindh and Yaser Hamdi, who were then handed over to U.S. forces. Lindh was charged with conspiring with al-Qaeda to kill U.S. nationals. His confession allegedly was made after he was shackled, naked, and denied food, water, and treatment for an injury. Additionally, he was questioned without a lawyer although his parents had requested that one be appointed for him. Eventually, Lindh cooperated with government investigators, pled to one count of "supplying services as a foot soldier," and was sentenced to up to twenty years in prison.

In sharp contrast, Hamdi, who although a U.S. citizen had spent much of his life in Saudi Arabia, was sent to a U.S. detention facility at Guantanamo Bay, Cuba, then to a U.S. military base in Virginia and finally to a naval brig in South Carolina. The Department of Justice declined to bring any charges against Hamdi and instead designated him an "enemy combatant." At no point was he given access to a lawyer.[a]

In July 2002, Hamdi's father filed suit on his son's behalf, alleging that the government was holding his son in violation of the Fifth and Fourteenth Amendments. A federal judge ordered the United States to allow an attorney to meet with Hamdi in private. The U.S. appealed, Hamdi was held in solitary confinement with no access to his lawyer, and the U.S. Supreme Court accepted the case for review. Hamdi, yet to be charged with a crime, argued that his basic civil liberties as an American citizen were being denied. The U.S. government countered that Hamdi's designation as an enemy combatant justified holding him indefinitely—without formal charges or proceedings—until it decided that access to counsel or other actions were warranted.

In June 2004, the U.S. Supreme Court ruled that "a state of war is not a blank check for the president" to deny basic civil liberties to U.S. citizens held in captivity. The Court went on to say that citizens must be apprised of the charges against them and allowed access to lawyers.[b] Although the Court affirmed the right of the president to detain citizens as enemy combatants, it reiterated that such prisoners must be given the right to challenge their captivity before a neutral fact-finder.

Hamdi was released in October 2004, but as a condition of his release he had to renounce his U.S. citizenship and return to Saudi Arabia.

1. How can the government protect citizens in times of terrorist threats without denying citizens constitutionally guaranteed civil liberties?

2. Should the government be allowed to hold indefinitely noncitizens suspected of being or aiding terrorists? Why, or why not?

---

[a]Lawyers Committee for Human Rights, "Assessing the New Normal: Liberty and Security for the Post September 11 United States," September 2003, 49–50.

[b]*Hamdi et al.* v. *Rumsfeld*, No. 03-6696 (decided June 28, 2004).

Drug Testing. While many private employers and professional athletic organizations routinely require drug tests upon application or as a condition of employment, governmental requirements present constitutional questions about the scope of permissible searches and seizures. In 1989, the Supreme Court ruled that mandatory drug and alcohol testing of employees involved in accidents was constitutional.[72] In 1995, the Court upheld the constitutionally of random drug testing of public high school athletes.[73] And, in 2002, the Court upheld the constitutionality of a Tecumseh, Oklahoma, policy that required mandatory drug testing of high school students participating in any extracurricular activities. Thus, prospective band, choir, debate, or drama club members were subject to the same kind of random drug testing undergone by athletes.[74]

Another question has arisen regarding the constitutionality of compulsory drug testing for pregnant women. In 2001, the Court ruled that the random testing of women for cocaine usage and subsequent reporting of positive tests to law enforcement officials was unconstitutional.[75]

The Fifth Amendment and Self-Incrimination

The **Fifth Amendment** provides that "No person shall be…compelled in any criminal case to be a witness against himself." "Taking the Fifth" is shorthand for exercising one's constitutional right not to self-incriminate. The Supreme Court has interpreted this guarantee to be "as broad as the mischief against which it seeks to guard," finding that criminal defendants do not have to take the stand at trial to answer questions, nor can a judge make mention of their failure to do so as evidence of guilt.[76] Moreover, lawyers cannot imply that a defendant who refuses to take the stand must be guilty or have something to hide.

This right not to incriminate oneself also means that prosecutors cannot use as evidence in a trial any of a defendant's statements or confessions that were not made voluntarily. As is the case in many areas of the law, however, judicial interpretation of the term voluntary has changed over time. In earlier times, it was not unusual for police to beat defendants to obtain their confessions. In 1936, however, the Supreme Court ruled convictions for murder based solely on confessions given after physical beatings unconstitutional.[77] Police then began to resort to other measures to force confessions. Defendants, for example, were "given the third degree"—questioned for hours on end with no sleep or food, or threatened with physical violence until they were mentally beaten into giving confessions.

Miranda v. *Arizona* (1966) was the Supreme Court's response to these creative efforts to obtain confessions that were not truly voluntary. On March 3, 1963, an eighteen-year-old girl was kidnapped and raped on the outskirts of Phoenix, Arizona. Ten days later, police arrested Ernesto Miranda, a poor, mentally disturbed man with a ninth-grade education. In a police station lineup, the victim identified Miranda as her attacker. Police then took Miranda to a separate room and questioned

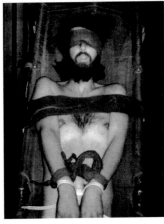
Photo courtesy: AFP/Corbis

■ While the FBI insisted that John Walker Lindh signed away his Miranda rights, his lawyers said he repeatedly asked for counsel and was held incommunicado for fifty-four days, while he was mistreated by authorities. Even if he was Mirandized, if the questioning proceeded without breaks or was accompanied by abuse, or if Lindh was shackled, the courts could have found that his confession was involuntary. Public sentiment, however, ran heavily against Lindh and his claims. Thus, he pled guilty in exchange for a twenty-year prison sentence.

Fifth Amendment
Part of the Bill of Rights that imposes a number of restrictions on the federal government with respect to the rights of persons suspected of committing a crime. It provides for indictment by a grand jury, protection against self-incrimination, and prevents the national government from denying a person life, liberty, or property without the due process of law. It also prevents the national government from taking property without fair compensation.

Miranda v. ***Arizona* (1966)**
A landmark Supreme Court ruling that held the Fifth Amendment requires that individuals arrested for a crime must be advised of their right to remain silent and to have counsel present.

Photo courtesy: Paul S. Howell/Getty Images

■ Even though Ernesto Miranda's confession was not admitted as evidence at his retrial, his ex-girlfriend's testimony and that of the victim were enough to convince the jury of his guilt. He served nine years in prison before he was released on parole. After his release, he routinely sold autographed cards inscribed with what are called the *Miranda* rights now read to all suspects. In 1976, four years after his release, Miranda was stabbed to death in Phoenix in a bar fight during a card game. Two *Miranda* cards were found on his body, and the person who killed him was read his *Miranda* rights upon his arrest.

Miranda rights

Statements that must be made by the police informing a suspect of his or her constitutional rights protected by the Fifth Amendment, including the right to an attorney provided by the court if the suspect cannot afford one.

exclusionary rule

Judicially created rule that prohibits police from using illegally seized evidence at trial.

him for two hours. At first he denied guilt. Eventually, however, he confessed to the crime and wrote and signed a brief statement describing the crime and admitting his guilt. At no time was he told that he did not have to answer any questions or that he could be represented by an attorney.

After Miranda's conviction, his case was appealed on the grounds that his Fifth Amendment right not to incriminate himself had been violated because his confession had been coerced. Writing for the Court, Chief Justice Earl Warren, himself a former district attorney and a former California state attorney general, noted that because police have a tremendous advantage in any interrogation situation, criminal suspects must be given greater protection. A confession obtained in the manner of Miranda's was not truly voluntary; thus, it was inadmissible at trial.

To provide guidelines for police to implement *Miranda*, the Court mandated that: "Prior to any questioning, the person must be warned that he has a right to remain silent, that any statements he does make may be used as evidence against him, and that he has a right to the presence of an attorney, either retained or appointed." In response to this mandate from the Court, police routinely began to read suspects what are now called their **Miranda rights,** a practice you undoubtedly have seen repeated over and over in movies and TV police dramas.

In 2000, in an opinion written by Chief Justice William H. Rehnquist, the Court reaffirmed the central holding of *Miranda*, ruling that defendants must be read *Miranda* warnings. The Court went on to say that, despite an act of Congress stipulating that voluntary statements made during police interrogations were admissible at trial, without *Miranda* warnings, no admissions could be trusted to be truly voluntary.[78]

The Fourth and Fifth Amendments and the Exclusionary Rule

In *Weeks* v. *U.S.* (1914), the U.S. Supreme Court adopted the **exclusionary rule,** which bars the use of illegally seized evidence at trial.[79] Thus, although the Fourth and Fifth Amendments do not prohibit the use of evidence obtained in violation of their provisions, the exclusionary rule is a judicially created remedy to deter constitutional violations. In *Weeks*, for example, the Court reasoned that allowing police and prosecutors to use the "fruits of a poisonous tree" (a tainted search) would only encourage that activity.

In balancing the need to deter police misconduct against the possibility that guilty individuals could go free, the Warren Court decided that deterring police misconduct was most important. In *Mapp* v. *Ohio* (1961), the Warren Court ruled that "all evidence obtained by searches and seizures in violation of the Constitution, is inadmissible in a state court."[80] This historic and controversial case put law enforcement officers on notice that if they found evidence in violation of any constitutional rights, those efforts would be for naught because the tainted evidence could not be used in federal or state trials.

More recently, Congress and the courts have attempted to chip away at the exclusionary rule. They have carved out a variety of limited "good faith exceptions," allowing the use of tainted evidence in a variety of situations, especially when police have a search warrant, and in good faith, conduct the search on the assumption that the warrant is valid—though it is subsequently found invalid. Since the purpose of the exclusionary rule is to deter police misconduct, and in this situation there is no police misconduct, the courts have permitted the introduction at trial of the seized evidence. Another exception to the exclusionary rule is "inevitable discovery." Evidence illegally seized may be introduced if it would have been discovered anyway in the course of continuing investigation.

The Sixth Amendment and the Right to Counsel

The **Sixth Amendment** guarantees to an accused person "the Assistance of Counsel in his defense." In the past, this provision meant only that an individual could hire an attorney to represent him or her in court. Since most criminal defendants are too poor to hire private lawyers, this provision was of little assistance to many who found themselves on trial. Recognizing this, Congress eventually required the federal courts to provide an attorney for defendants who could not afford one. This was first required in capital cases (where the death penalty is a possibility); eventually, attorneys were provided to the poor in all federal criminal cases.[81]

Until the Court's 1963 decision in *Gideon* v. *Wainwright* (1963), criminal defendants were not entitled lawyers in state courts.[82] However, writing for the Court, Justice Hugo Black explained that "lawyers in criminal courts are necessities, not luxuries." Therefore, the Court concluded, the state must provide an attorney to indigent defendants in felony cases. Underscoring the Court's point, Clarence Gideon, who originally acted as his own lawyer, was acquitted when he was retried with a lawyer to argue his case.

In 1972, the Burger Court expanded the *Gideon* rule, holding that "even in prosecutions for offenses less serious than felonies, a fair trial may require the presence of a lawyer."[83] Seven years later, the Court clarified its decision by holding that defendants charged with offenses where imprisonment is a possibility but not actually imposed do not have a Sixth Amendment right to counsel.[84] Thirty years later, the Rehnquist Court expanded *Gideon* even further by revisiting the "actual imprisonment" standard announced in the 1972 and 1979 cases. In 2002, a 5–4 majority held that if a defendant received a suspended sentence and probation for a minor crime but could be sentenced in future if he or she violated the conditions of probation, then the defendant must be provided with a lawyer.[85]

Sixth Amendment
Part of the Bill of Rights that sets out the basic requirements of procedural due process for federal courts to follow in criminal trials. These include speedy and public trials, impartial juries, trials in the state where the crime was committed, notice of the charges, the right to confront and obtain favorable witnesses, and the right to counsel.

The Sixth Amendment and Jury Trials

The Sixth Amendment (and, to a lesser extent, Article III of the Constitution) provides that a person accused of a crime shall enjoy the right to a speedy and public trial by an impartial jury—that is, a trial in which a group of the accused's peers act as a fact-finding, deliberative body to determine guilt or innocence. It also provides defendants the right to confront witnesses against them.

Impartiality is a requirement of jury trials that has undergone significant change, with the method of selecting jurors being the most frequently challenged part of the process. Although potential individual jurors who have prejudged a case are not eligible to serve, no groups can be systematically excluded from serving. In 1880, for example, the Supreme Court ruled that African Americans could not be excluded from state jury pools (lists of those eligible to serve).[86] And, in 1975, the Court ruled that to bar women from jury service violated the mandate that juries be a "fair cross section" of the community.[87]

In 1986, the Court expanded the requirement that juries reflect a fair cross-section of the community. Historically, lawyers had used peremptory challenges (those for which no cause needs to be given) to exclude African Americans from juries, especially when African Americans were criminal defendants. In *Batson* v. *Kentucky* (1986), the Court ruled that the use of peremptory challenges specifically to exclude African American jurors violated the equal protection clause of the Fourteenth Amendment.[88]

In 1994, the Supreme Court answered the major remaining unanswered question about jury selection: can lawyers exclude women from juries through their use of peremptory challenges? The Supreme Court ruled that the equal protection clause prohibits discrimination in jury selection on the basis of gender. Thus, lawyers cannot strike all potential male jurors based on the belief that males might be more sympathetic to the arguments of a man charged in a paternity suit, a rape trial, or a domestic violence suit, for example.

The right to confront witnesses at trial also is protected by the Sixth Amendment. In 1990, however, the Supreme Court ruled that this right was not absolute. In *Maryland* v. *Craig*, the Court ruled that, constitutionally, the testimony of a six-year-old alleged child abuse victim via one-way closed circuit television was permissible. The clause's central purpose, said the Court, was to ensure the reliability of testimony by subjecting it to rigorous examination in an adversarial proceeding.[89]

Eighth Amendment
Part of the Bill of Rights that states: "Excessive bail shall not be required, nor excessive fines imposed, nor cruel and unusual punishments inflicted."

The Eighth Amendment and Cruel and Unusual Punishment

The **Eighth Amendment** prohibits "cruel and unusual punishments," a concept rooted in the English common-law tradition. Prior to the

1960s, however, little judicial attention was paid to the meaning of that phrase, especially in the context of the death penalty.

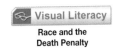

Visual Literacy

Race and the Death Penalty

In the 1960s, the NAACP Legal Defense Fund (LDF), believing that the death penalty was applied more frequently to African Americans than to members of other groups, orchestrated a carefully designed legal attack on its constitutionality.[90] Public opinion polls revealed that in 1971, on the eve of the LDF's first major death sentence case to reach the Supreme Court, public support for the death penalty had fallen to below 50 percent. With the timing just right, in *Furman* v. *Georgia* (1972), the Supreme Court effectively put an end to capital punishment, at least in the short run.[91] The Court ruled that because the death penalty often was imposed in an arbitrary manner, it constituted cruel and unusual punishment in violation of the Eighth and Fourteenth Amendments.

Following *Furman*, several state legislatures enacted new laws designed to meet the Court's objections to the arbitrary nature of the sentence. In 1976, in *Gregg* v. *Georgia*, Georgia's rewritten death penalty statute was ruled constitutional by the Supreme Court in a 7–2 decision.[92] Unless the perpetrator of a crime was fifteen years old or younger at the time of the crime or mentally retarded, the Supreme Court currently is unwilling to intervene to overrule state courts' imposition of the death penalty, even when it appears to discriminate against African Americans.

At the state level, a move to at least stay executions took on momentum when Governor George Ryan (R–IL) ordered a moratorium on all executions in the state of Illinois in March 2000. Ryan, a death penalty proponent, became disturbed by new evidence collected as a class project by Northwestern University students. The students unearthed information that led to the release of thirteen men on the state's death row. Soon thereafter, the governor of Maryland followed suit after receiving evidence that blacks were much more likely to be sentenced to death than whites. Other states, such as Ohio, have made offers of free DNA testing to those sitting on death row.

In addition, before leaving office in January 2003, Governor Ryan commuted the sentences of 167 death row inmates, giving them life in prison instead of death. Ryan also pardoned another four men who had given coerced confessions. This action constituted the single largest anti-death-penalty action since the Court's decision in *Gregg*.

THE RIGHT TO PRIVACY

TO THIS POINT, the rights and freedoms we have discussed have been derived fairly directly from specific guarantees contained in the Bill of Rights. In contrast, the Supreme Court also has given protection to rights not enumerated specifically in the Constitution or Bill of Rights.

right to privacy
The right to be left alone; a judicially created doctrine encompassing an individual's decision to use birth control or secure an abortion.

Although the Constitution is silent about the **right to privacy,** the Bill of Rights contains many indications that the Framers expected that some areas of life were off limits to governmental regulation. As early as 1928, Justice Louis Brandeis hailed privacy as "the right to be left alone—the most comprehensive of rights and the right most valued by civilized men."[93] It was not until 1965, however, that the Court attempted to explain the origins of this right.

Birth Control

Today, most Americans take access to many forms of birth control as a matter of course. This was not always the case. *Griswold* v. *Connecticut* (1965) involved a challenge to the constitutionality of an 1879 Connecticut law prohibiting the dissemination of information about and/or the sale of contraceptives.[94] In *Griswold*, seven justices decided that various portions of the Constitution, including the First, Third, Fourth, Ninth, and Fourteenth Amendments, cast what the Court called "penumbras" (unstated liberties on the fringes or in the shadow of more explicitly stated rights), thereby creating zones of privacy, including a married couple's right to plan a family. Thus, the Connecticut statute was ruled unconstitutional.

Later, the Court expanded the right of privacy to include the right of unmarried individuals to have access to contraceptives. "If the right of privacy means anything," wrote Justice William J. Brennan Jr., "it is the right of the individual, married or single, to be free from unwarranted governmental intrusion into matters so fundamentally affecting a person as the decision to bear or beget a child."[95] This right to privacy was to be the basis for later decisions from the Court, including the right to secure an abortion.

Abortion

Roe v. *Wade* (1973)
The Supreme Court found that a woman's right to an abortion was protected by the right to privacy that could be implied from specific guarantees found in the Bill of Rights applied to the states through the Fourteenth Amendment.

In 1973, the Supreme Court handed down one of its most controversial decisions, *Roe* **v.** *Wade.* Norma McCorvey, already a mother and an itinerant circus worker, was pregnant but unable to care for another child. Texas law allowed abortions only when they were necessary to save the life of the mother. Unable to secure a legal abortion and frightened by the conditions she found when she sought an illegal, back-alley abortion, McCorvey turned to two young Texas lawyers who were looking for a plaintiff to bring a lawsuit to challenge Texas's restrictive statute. Before a final legal decision could be reached, McCorvey gave birth and put the baby up for adoption. Nevertheless, she allowed her lawyers to proceed with the case using her as their plaintiff, under the pseudonym Jane Roe.

When the case came before the Supreme Court, Justice Harry A. Blackmun, a former lawyer at the Mayo Clinic, relied heavily on med-

The Living Constitution

The enumeration in the Constitution, of certain rights, shall not be construed to deny or disparage others retained by the people.

—Ninth Amendment

This amendment simply reiterates the belief of many Federalists who believed that it would be impossible to enumerate every fundamental liberty and right. To assuage the concerns of Anti-Federalists, the Ninth Amendment underscores that rights not enumerated are retained by the people.

James Madison, in particular, feared that the enumeration of so many rights and liberties in the first eight amendments to the Constitution would result in the denial of rights that were not enumerated. So, he drafted this amendment, to clarify a rule about how the Constitution and Bill of Rights were to be construed.

Until 1965, the Ninth Amendment was rarely mentioned by the Court. In that year, however, it was used for the first time by the Court as a positive affirmation of a particular liberty—marital privacy. Although privacy is not mentioned in the Constitution, it was—according to the Court—one of those fundamental freedoms that the drafters of the Bill of Rights implied as retained. Since 1965, the Court has ruled in favor of a host of fundamental liberties guaranteed by the Ninth Amendment, often in combination with other specific guarantees, including the right to have an abortion.

ical evidence to rule that the Texas law violated a woman's constitutionally guaranteed right to privacy, which he argued included her decision to terminate a pregnancy. Writing for the majority in *Roe*, Blackmun divided pregnancy into three stages. In the first trimester, a woman's right to privacy gave her an absolute right (in consultation with her physician), free from state interference, to terminate her pregnancy. In the second trimester, the state's interest in the health of the mother gave it the right to regulate abortions—but only to protect the woman's health. Only in the third trimester—when the fetus becomes potentially viable—did the Court find that the state's interest in potential life outweighed a woman's privacy interests. Even in the third trimester, however, abortions to save the life or health of the mother were to be legal.[96]

Roe v. *Wade* unleashed a torrent of political controversy. From the 1970s through the present, the right to an abortion and its constitutional

■ A once very popular anti-abortion group, Operation Rescue, staged large scale protests in front of abortion clinics across the nation gaining a surprising new member— Norma McCorvey, the "Jane Roe" of *Roe* v. *Wade* (1973). In 1995, she announced that she had become pro-life.

underpinnings in the right to privacy have been under attack by well-organized anti-abortion groups. The administrations of Presidents Ronald Reagan and George Bush were strong advocates of the anti-abortion position, regularly urging the Court to overrule *Roe*. They came close to victory in *Webster* v. *Reproductive Health Services* (1989).[97] In *Webster*, the Court upheld state-required fetal viability tests in the second trimester, even though these tests would increase the cost of an abortion considerably. The Court also upheld Missouri's refusal to allow abortions to be performed in state-supported hospitals or by state-funded doctors or nurses. Perhaps most noteworthy, however, were the facts that four justices seemed willing to overrule *Roe* v. *Wade*.

After *Webster*, states began to enact more restrictive legislation. In the most important abortion case since *Roe*, *Planned Parenthood of Southeastern Pennsylvania* v. *Casey* (1992), Justices Sandra Day O'Connor, Anthony Kennedy, and David Souter, in a jointly authored opinion, wrote that Pennsylvania could limit abortions so long as its regulations did not pose "an undue burden" on pregnant women.[98] The narrowly supported standard, by which the Court upheld a twenty-four-hour waiting period and parental consent requirements, did not overrule *Roe*, but clearly limited its scope by abolishing its trimester approach and substituting the undue burden standard.

While President Bill Clinton was attempting to shore up abortion rights through the appointment of pro-choice judges, Republican Congresses made repeated attempts to ban—for the first time—a specific procedure used in late-term abortions.[99] Although Clinton vetoed this act, many state legislatures passed their own versions. In 2000, the Supreme Court, however, ruled 5–4 in *Stenberg* v. *Carhart* that a Nebraska "partial birth" abortion statute was unconstitutionally vague and therefore unenforceable, calling into question the laws of twenty-nine other states with their own bans on late-term procedures.[100]

By October of 2003, however, Republican control of the White House and both houses of Congress facilitated passage of the federal Partial Birth Abortion Ban Act. Pro-choice groups such as Planned Parenthood, the Center for Reproductive Rights, and the American Civil Liberties Union filed immediate lawsuits challenging the constitutionality of this law. At this writing, three federal district courts have ruled that it is unconstitutional.

Homosexuality

It was not until 2003 that the U.S. Supreme Court ruled that an individual's constitutional right to privacy, which provided the basis for the *Griswold* (contraceptives) and *Roe* (abortion) decisions, prevented the state of Texas from criminalizing private sexual behavior. This monumental decision invalidated the laws of thirteen states, as revealed in

Analyzing Visuals

PARTIAL BIRTH ABORTION BAN

In the photograph, as members of Congress look on, President George W. Bush signs the Partial Birth Abortion Ban Act of 2003 at the Ronald Reagan Building and International Trade Center in Washington, D.C. Standing behind the president are, from left, Speaker of the House Dennis Hastert (R–IL), Senator Orrin Hatch (R–UT), Representative James Sensenbrenner (R–WI), Senator Rick Santorum (R–PA), Representative James Oberstar (D–MN), and Senator Mike DeWine (R–OH). After examining the photograph, answer the following critical thinking questions: Do you think that the photographer is making any specific statement about the civil liberties of American women? Are the members of Congress viewing the signing representative of Congress as a whole? Of the general U.S. public?

Photo courtesy: Pablo Martinez Monsivais/AP/Wide World Photos

Figure 4.1. In *Lawrence* v. *Texas* (2003), six members of the Court overruled a 1986 decision and found that the Texas law was unconstitutional; five justices found it to violate fundamental privacy rights.[101] Justice Sandra Day O'Connor agreed that the law was unconstitutional

FIGURE 4.1   Sodomy Laws in the United States. ■

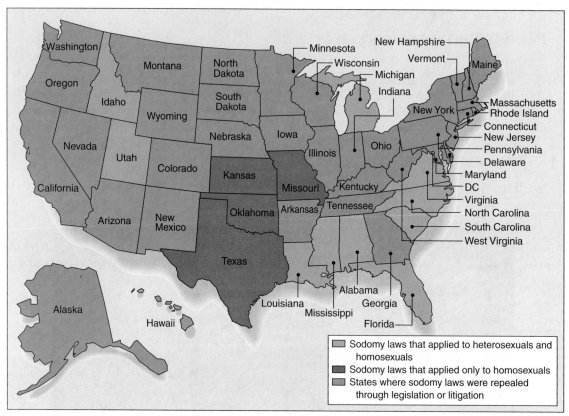

Sodomy laws that applied to heterosexuals and homosexuals

Sodomy laws that applied only to homosexuals

States where sodomy laws were repealed through legislation or litigation

Source: http://www.supremecourtus.gov/opinions/02pdf/02-102.pdf.

but concluded that it was an equal protection violation. (See chapter 5 for a detailed discussion of the equal protection clause of the Fourteenth Amendment.) Although Justice Antonin Scalia issued a stinging dissent charging that "the Court has largely signed on to the so-called homosexual agenda," the majority of the Court was unswayed.[102]

Just three years before, in *Boy Scouts* v. *Dale* (2000), the Court upheld a challenge to the Boy Scouts' refusal to allow a gay man to become a scoutmaster.[103] There, the majority of the Court found that a private club's First Amendment right to freedom of association allowed it to use its own moral code to select troop leaders. While the public largely supported the *Boy Scouts* decision, it also approved of the Court's resolution of the challenge to the Texas sodomy law.[104] A poll taken just before the 2003 ruling showed that the public disagreed with the Court's 1986 decision by a margin of 57 to 38 percent.[105]

While the Court has refused to expand the right to privacy to invalidate state laws that criminalize some aspects of homosexual behavior, in 1996, it ruled that a state could not deny rights to homosexuals simply because they are homosexuals. Thus, as discussed in chapter 6, the Court ruled that the equal protection clause bars unreasonable state discrimination against gays and lesbians.[106]

The Right to Die

In 1990, the Supreme Court ruled 5–4 that parents could not withdraw a feeding tube from their comatose daughter after her doctors testified she could live like that for many more years. Writing for the majority, Chief Justice William H. Rehnquist rejected any attempts to expand the right of privacy into this thorny area of social policy. The Court did note, however, that individuals could terminate medical treatment if they were able to express, or had done so in writing via a living will, their desire to have medical treatment terminated in the event they became incompetent.[107]

In 1997, the U.S. Supreme Court extended that ruling, unanimously stating that terminally ill persons do not have a constitutional right to physician-assisted suicide.[108] But, since that year, Oregon enacted a right-to-die or assisted-suicide law that allows physicians to prescribe drugs to terminally ill patients. In November 2001, however, Attorney General John Ashcroft issued a legal opinion determining that assisted suicide is not "a legitimate medical purpose," thereby putting physicians who follow their state law in jeopardy of federal prosecution.[109] His memo also called for the revocation of physicians' drug prescription licenses, putting the state and the national government in conflict in an area that Republicans historically have argued is the province of state authority. Oregon officials immediately (and successfully) sought a court order blocking Ashcroft's attempt to interfere with implementation of Oregon law.[110] Later, a federal judge ruled that Ashcroft had overstepped his authority on every point.[111] And, in 2005, the U.S. Supreme Court refused to review a Florida State Supreme Court ruling that allowed the husband of a severely brain-damaged woman to remove her feeding tube, effectively ending the woman's life.[112]

SUMMARY

MOST OF THE FRAMERS ORIGINALLY OPPOSED the Bill of Rights. Anti-Federalists, however, continued to stress the need for a bill of rights during the drive for ratification of the Constitution. Thus, during its first session, Congress created a Bill of Rights. Later, the addition of the Fourteenth Amendment allowed the Supreme Court to apply some of the amendments to the states through a process called selective incorporation.

The First Amendment guarantees freedom of religion. The establishment clause, which prohibits the national government from establishing a religion, does not, according to Supreme Court interpretation, create an absolute wall between church and state. The Court generally has adopted an accommodationist approach when interpreting the free exercise clause by allowing some governmental regulation of religious practices.

Historically, one of the most volatile areas of constitutional interpretation has been in the interpretation of the First Amendment's mandate that "Congress shall make no law…abridging the freedom of speech or of the press. Some areas of speech and publication are unconditionally protected by the First Amendment. Among these are prior restraint, symbolic speech, and hate speech. Other areas of speech and publication, however, are unprotected by the First Amendment. These include libel, fighting words, and obscenity and pornography.

The freedoms of peaceable assembly and petition are directly related to the freedoms of speech and of the press. As with other First Amendment rights, the Supreme Court has often become the arbiter between the right of the people to express dissent and government's right to limit controversy in the name of security.

Initially, the right to keep and bear arms was envisioned as one dealing with state militias. Over the years, states and Congress have enacted various gun ownership restrictions, with little Supreme Court interpretation as a guide to their ultimate constitutionality.

The Fourth, Fifth, Sixth, and Eighth Amendments provide a variety of procedural guarantees to individuals accused of crimes. In particular, the Fourth Amendment prohibits unreasonable searches and seizures. The Fifth Amendment guarantees that "no person shall be compelled to be a witness against himself." The Sixth Amendment guarantees "assistance of counsel" and an impartial jury. The Eighth Amendment bans "cruel and unusual punishments."

The right to privacy is a judicially created right carved from the implications of the First, Third, Fourth, Ninth, and Fourteenth Amendments. Statutes limiting access to birth control and abortion rights and banning homosexual acts have been ruled unconstitutional violations of the right to privacy. The Court, however, has not extended privacy rights to include the right to die.

KEY TERMS

Bill of Rights, p. 132
civil liberties, p. 130
civil rights, p. 130
clear and present danger test, p. 140
direct incitement test, p. 140
due process clause, p. 132
due process rights, p. 150
Eighth Amendment, p. 156
establishment clause, p. 135
exclusionary rule, p. 154
Fifth Amendment, p. 153
fighting words, p. 146
First Amendment, p. 135
Fourth Amendment, p. 150
free exercise clause, p. 135
incorporation doctrine, p. 133
libel, p. 145
Miranda rights, p. 154
Miranda v. *Arizona* (1966), p. 153
New York Times Co. v. *Sullivan* (1964), p. 145
Ninth Amendment, p. 132
prior restraint, p. 138
right to privacy, p. 158
Roe v. *Wade* (1973), p. 158
selective incorporation, p. 133
Sixth Amendment, p. 155
slander, p. 145
substantive due process, p. 132
symbolic speech, p. 144

SELECTED READINGS

Abernathy, M. Glenn, and Barbara A. Perry. *Civil Liberties Under the Constitution*, 6th ed. Columbia: University of South Carolina Press, 1993.

Cole, David, and James X. Dempsey. *Terrorism and the Constitution: Sacrificing Civil Liberties in the Name of National Security*, 2nd ed. Washington, DC: First Amendment Foundation, 2002.

Etzoni, Amitai, and Jason H. Mason. *Rights vs. Public Safety after 9/11: America in an Age of Terrorism.* Lanham, MD: Rowman and Littlefield, 2003.

Fiss, Owen M. *The Irony of Free Speech.* Cambridge, MA: Harvard University Press, 1996.

Friendly, Fred W. *Minnesota Rag: Corruption, Yellow Journalism, and the Case That Saved Freedom of the Press.* Minneapolis: University of Minnesota Press, 2003.

Gates, Henry Louis, Jr., ed. *Speaking of Race, Speaking of Sex: Hate Speech, Civil Rights, and Civil Liberties.* New York: New York University Press, 1995.

Greenawalt, Kent. *Fighting Words: Individuals, Communities, and Liberties of Speech.* Princeton, NJ: Princeton University Press, 1995.

Kalven, Harry, Jr. *A Worthy Tradition: Freedom of Speech in America.* New York: Harper and Row, 1988.

Lewis, Anthony. *Gideon's Trumpet,* reissue ed. New York: Vintage Books, 1989.

Lewis, Anthony. *Make No Law: The Sullivan Case and the First Amendment,* reprint ed. New York: Random House, 1991.

Manwaring, David R. *Render unto Caesar: The Flag Salute Controversy.* Chicago: University of Chicago Press, 1962.

O'Brien, David M. *Constitutional Law and Politics, Vol. 2: Civil Rights and Civil Liberties,* 5th ed. New York: Norton, 2002.

O'Connor, Karen. *No Neutral Ground: Abortion Politics in an Age of Absolutes.* Boulder, CO: Westview, 1996.

Regan, Priscilla M. *Legislating Privacy: Technology, Social Values, and Public Policy.* Chapel Hill: University of North Carolina Press, 1995.

Weddington, Sarah. *A Question of Choice.* New York: Grosset/Putnam, 1993.

WEB EXPLORATIONS

To view an original copy of the Bill of Rights, see
http://www.archives.gov/national_archives_experience/charters/bill_of_rights.html

For groups with opposing views on how the First Amendment should be interpreted, see
http://www.au.org/
http://www.pfaw.org/
http://www.aclj.org/

For more information on *Reno* v. *American Civil Liberties Union,* see
http://archive.aclu.org/issues/cyper/trial/appeal.html and http://supct.law.cornell.edu/supct/html/96-126.ZS.html

For other privacy issues, see
http://www.epic.org/ and
http://www.privacy.org/

To compare the different sides of the abortion debate, go to FLITE: Federal Legal Information Through Electronics at http://www.fedworld.gov/supcourt/ and Roe in a Nutshell at
http://hometown.aol.com/abtrbng/roeins.htm

For more on gay rights and recent court cases, see
http://www.infoplease.com/ipa/A0194028.html

To learn more about the right to die movement, see
http://www.hemlock.org/home.jsp

5

Civil Rights

Photo courtesy: Chrystie Sherman/AP/Wide World Photos

THERE IS NO QUESTION that in the 1980s, crime in the United States, and in particular New York City, was out of control and Americans demanded that their governments do something about it. Governments at all levels responded with more police and more prisons. But, now that crime is on the wane and no longer even on Americans' list of top ten concerns, ordinary citizens are asking the question that troubled John Locke and Thomas Hobbes over three centuries ago: how much liberty should you give up to the government in return for safety?

Case after case makes it clear that people of color, whether native or foreign born, are subject to civil rights deprivations at far higher rates than other identifiable groups. On February 4, 1999, for example, Amadou Diallo, a twenty-two-year-old unarmed African immigrant, stood in the vestibule of his apartment building in the Bronx, New York. Four white plainclothes police officers, who were patrolling the neighborhood in an unmarked car, opened fire on him, eventually firing forty-one shots. He died at the scene.[1] There were no witnesses. The four officers, who eventually were charged with second-degree murder, were members of New York City's Street Crimes Unit. This unit was created in the early 1990s by then-Mayor Rudy Giuliani to help lower the crime rate. Known to have targeted blacks, members of the unit admitted to stopping and searching as many as 225,000 citizens since its establishment.[2]

Members of New York City's frightened minority community, African Americans and new immigrants alike, along with liberal activists and everyday citizens, turned their anger on city police and the mayor, who they believed had used overly aggressive, and often racially biased, techniques to reduce crime. In the months after the shooting, citizens from all walks of life—from future Democratic presidential candidate the Reverend Al Sharpton to actress Susan Sarandon to street cleaners—protested at City Hall, and even marched from the federal courthouse over the Brooklyn Bridge and into Manhattan in a procession reminiscent of many 1960s civil rights marches. Over 1,500 protesters were arrested at one demonstration, the largest New York City had seen in twenty-five years.[3] Eventually, all four police officers charged with Diallo's killing were acquitted at trial.

T HE DECLARATION OF INDEPENDENCE, written in 1776, boldly proclaims: "We hold these truths to be self-evident, that all men are created equal, that they are endowed by their Creator with certain inalienable rights." The Constitution, written eleven years later, is silent on the concept of equality. Only through constitutional amendment and Supreme Court definition and redefinition of the rights contained in the Constitution have Americans come close to attaining equal rights. Even so, as the opening vignette highlights, some citizens have yet to experience full equality and the full enjoyment of **civil rights,** or the goverment-protected rights of individuals against arbitrary or discriminatory treatment based on categories such as race, sex, national origin, age, religion, or sexual orientation.

civil rights
The goverment-protected rights of individuals against arbitrary or discriminatory treatment by governments or individuals based on categories such as race, sex, national origin, age, religion, or sexual orientation.

Since the Constitution was written, concepts of civil rights have changed dramatically. The addition of the Fourteenth Amendment, one of three Civil War Amendments ratified from 1865 to 1870, introduced the notion of equality into the Constitution by specifying that states could not deny "any person within its jurisdiction equal protection of the laws." Throughout history, the Fourteenth Amendment's equal protection guarantees have been the linchpin of efforts to expand upon the original intent of the amendment to allow its provisions to protect a variety of other groups from discrimination.

Since passage of the Civil War Amendments, there has been a fairly consistent pattern of the expansion of civil rights to more and more groups. In this chapter, we will first discuss slavery, abolition, and winning the right to vote, 1800–1890. We will then examine African Americans' and women's next push for equality, 1890–1954. These topics lead to an analysis of the civil rights movement and the Civil Rights Act of 1964. After discussing the development of a new women's rights movement, we will present the efforts of other groups to mobilize for rights. Finally, we will explore continuing controversies in civil rights.

SLAVERY, ABOLITION, AND WINNING THE RIGHT TO VOTE, 1800–1890

THE PERIOD FROM 1800 TO 1890 was one of tremendous change and upheaval in America. Despite the Civil War and the freeing of the slaves, the promise of equality guaranteed to African Americans by the Civil War Amendments failed to become a reality. Women's rights activists also began to make claims for equality, often using the arguments enunciated for the abolition of slavery, but they too fell far short of their goals.

Slavery and Congress

As the nation grew westward in the early 1800s, conflicts between northern and southern states intensified over the admission of new states to the union with free or slave status. The first major crisis occurred in 1820, when Missouri applied for admission to the union as a slave state—that is, one in which slavery would be legal. Missouri's admission would have weighted the Senate in favor of slavery and therefore was opposed by northern senators. To resolve this conflict, Congress passed the Missouri Compromise of 1820. The compromise prohibited slavery north of the geographical boundary at 36 degrees latitude. This act then allowed Missouri to be admitted to the union as a slave state. To maintain the balance of slave and free states, Maine was carved out of a portion of Massachusetts.

The First Civil Rights Movements: Abolition and Women's Rights

The Missouri Compromise solidified the South in its determination to keep slavery legal, but it also fueled the fervor of those who opposed slavery. William Lloyd Garrison, a white New Englander, galvanized the abolitionist movement in the early 1830s. Garrison, a newspaper editor, founded the American Anti-Slavery Society in 1833; by 1838, it had more than 250,000 members.

Slavery was not the only practice that people began to question in the decades following the Missouri Compromise. In 1840, for example, Elizabeth Cady Stanton and Lucretia Mott, who were to found the first women's rights movement, attended the 1840 meeting of the World Anti-Slavery Society in London with their husbands. After their long journey, they were not allowed to participate in the convention solely because they were women. As they sat in the balcony apart from the male delegates, they paused to compare their status to that of the slaves they sought to free. They concluded that women were not much better off than slaves, and resolved to meet to address these issues.

The first meeting for women's rights was held in Seneca Falls, New York, in 1848. The 300 people who attended passed resolutions calling for the abolition of legal, economic, and social discrimination against women. All of the resolutions reflected the attendees' dissatisfaction with contemporary moral codes, divorce and criminal laws, and the limited opportunities for women in education, the church, medicine, law, and politics. Ironically, only the call for woman suffrage failed to win unanimous approval.

The 1850s: The Calm Before the Storm

By 1850, much was changing in America—the Gold Rush had spurred westward migration, cities grew as people were lured from their farms, railroads and the telegraph increased mobility and communication, and immigrants flooded into the United States. The woman's movement gained momentum, and slavery continued to tear the nation apart. Harriet Beecher Stowe's *Uncle Tom's Cabin*, a novel that depicted the evils of slavery, further inflamed the country. *Uncle Tom's Cabin* sold more than 300,000 copies in 1852.

The tremendous national reaction to Stowe's work, which later prompted President Abraham Lincoln to call Stowe "the little woman who started the big war," had not yet faded when a new controversy over the Missouri Compromise of 1820 became the lightning rod for the first major civil rights case to be addressed by the U.S. Supreme Court. As discussed in chapter 3, in *Dred Scott* v. *Sandford* (1857), the Court bluntly had ruled that the Missouri Compromise was unconstitutional. Furthermore, the Court went on to add that slaves were not U.S. citizens and therefore could not bring suits in federal court.

The Civil War and Its Aftermath: Civil Rights Laws and Civil War Amendments

The Civil War had many causes, but slavery was clearly a key issue. During the war (1861–1865), abolitionists continued to press for an end to slavery. They were rewarded when President Abraham Lincoln issued the Emancipation Proclamation, which provided that all slaves in states still in active rebellion against the United States would be freed automatically on January 1, 1863. Designed as a measure to gain favor for the war in the North, the Emancipation Proclamation did not free

Thirteenth Amendment
One of the three Civil War Amendments; specifically bans slavery in the United States.

Black Codes
Laws denying most legal rights to newly freed slaves; passed by southern states following the Civil War.

Fourteenth Amendment
One of the three Civil War Amendments; guarantees equal protection and due process of the laws to all U.S. citizens.

Fifteenth Amendment
One of the three Civil War Amendments; specifically enfranchised newly freed male slaves.

all slaves—it freed only those who lived in the Confederacy, which was made up of states that had seceded from the union. Complete abolition of slavery did not occur until congressional passage and ultimate ratification of the Thirteenth Amendment in 1865.

The **Thirteenth Amendment** was the first of the three Civil War Amendments. It banned all forms of "slavery [and] involuntary servitude." Although southern states were required to ratify the Thirteenth Amendment as a condition of their readmission to the Union after the war, most of the former Confederate states quickly passed laws that were designed to restrict opportunities for newly freed slaves. These **Black Codes** prohibited African Americans from voting, sitting on juries, or even appearing in public places. Although Black Codes differed from state to state, all empowered local law-enforcement officials to arrest unemployed blacks, fine them for vagrancy, and hire them out to employers to satisfy their fines.

An outraged Congress enacted the Civil Rights Act of 1866 to invalidate some state Black Codes. President Andrew Johnson vetoed the legislation, but—for the first time in history—Congress overrode a presidential veto. The Civil Rights Act formally made African Americans citizens of the United States and gave the Congress and the federal courts the power to intervene when states attempted to restrict male African American citizenship rights in matters such as voting. Congress reasoned that African Americans were unlikely to fare well if they had to file discrimination complaints in state courts, where most judges were elected. Passage of a federal law allowed African Americans to challenge discriminatory state practices in the federal courts, where judges were appointed for life by the president.

Because controversy remained over the constitutionality of the act (since the Constitution gives states the right to determine qualifications of voters), the **Fourteenth Amendment** was proposed simultaneously with the Civil Rights Act to guarantee, among other things, citizenship to all freed slaves. Other key provisions of the Fourteenth Amendment barred states from abridging "the privileges or immunities of citizenship" or depriving "any person of life, liberty, or property without due process of law," or deny "to any person within its jurisdiction the equal protection of the laws."

Unlike the Thirteenth Amendment, which had near unanimous support in the North, the Fourteenth Amendment (which specifically added the word male to the Constitution for the first time) was opposed by many women because it failed to guarantee suffrage for women.

The **Fifteenth Amendment** was also passed by Congress in the aftermath of the Civil War. It guaranteed the "right of citizens" to vote regardless of their "race, color or previous condition of servitude." Sex was not mentioned.

Women's rights activists were shocked. Abolitionists' continued support of the Fifteenth Amendment, which was ratified by the states

The Living Constitution

*Neither slavery nor involuntary servitude, except
as a punishment for crime whereof the party shall have
been duly convicted, shall exist within the United
States, or any place subject to their jurisdiction.*

—Thirteenth Amendment, Section 1

This amendment, the first of three Civil War Amendments, abolished slavery throughout the United States and its territories. It also prohibited involuntary servitude.

Based on his war powers authority, in 1863, President Abraham Lincoln issued the Emancipation Proclamation abolishing slavery in the states that were in rebellion against the United States. Because Congress was considered to lack the constitutional authority to abolish slavery, after one unsuccessful attempt to garner the two-thirds vote necessary, the proposed Thirteenth Amendment was forwarded to the states on February 1, 1865. The text of the amendment reproduced the words of the Northwest Ordinance of 1787; with its adoption, said one of its sponsors, it relieved Congress "of sectional strifes." Initially, some doubted if any groups other than newly freed African slaves were protected by the provisions of the amendment. Soon, however, the Supreme Court went on to clarify this question by noting: "If Mexican peonage or the Chinese coolie labor system shall develop slavery of the Mexican or Chinese race within our territory, this amendment may safely be trusted to make it void."

In the early 1990s, the Supreme Court was called on several times to construe section 1 of the amendment, especially in regard to involuntary servitude. Thus, provisions of an Alabama law that called for criminal sanctions and jail time for defaulting sharecroppers were considered unconstitutional and Congress enacted a law banning this kind of peonage. More recently, however, the Court has found compulsory high school community service programs not to violate the ban on involuntary servitude. The Court and a host of lower federal and state courts, however, have upheld criminal convictions of those who, for example, psychologically coerced mentally retarded farm laborers into service or who lured foreign workers to the United States with promises of jobs and then forced them to work long hours at little or no pay. Human trafficking, in fact, has been targeted as an especially onerous form of involuntary servitude. The U.S. Department of Justice has undertaken hundreds of investigations in an attempt to end this system.

in 1870, prompted many women's rights supporters to leave the abolition movement to work solely for the cause of women's rights. Twice burned, women's movement leaders Susan B. Anthony and Elizabeth Cady Stanton decided to form their own group, the National Woman Suffrage Association (NWSA), to achieve that goal. (Another, more conservative group, the American Woman Suffrage Association, also was formed.) In spite of the NWSA's opposition, however, the Fifteenth Amendment was ratified by the states in 1870.

Civil Rights, Congress, and the Supreme Court

Congress was clear in its wishes that the rights of African Americans be expanded and that the Black Codes be rendered illegal. The Supreme Court, however, was not nearly so protective of those rights as it interpreted the Civil War Amendments. In the first two tests of the scope of the Fourteenth Amendment, the Supreme Court ruled that the citizenship rights guaranteed by the amendment applied only to rights of national citizenship and not to state citizenship.

Claims for expanded rights and requests for a clear definition of U.S. citizenship rights continued to fall on deaf ears in the halls of the Supreme Court. In 1875, for example, the Court ruled that a state's refusal to let a woman vote did not violate the privileges and immunities clause of the Fourteenth Amendment.[4] The justices ruled unanimously that voting was not a privilege of citizenship.

In the same year, continued southern resistance to African American equality led Congress to pass the Civil Rights Act of 1875, designed to grant equal access to public accommodations. In 1883, however, a series of cases decided by the Supreme Court severely damaged the vitality of the 1875 act.

Civil Rights Cases (1883)

Name attached to five cases brought under the Civil Rights Act of 1875. In 1883, the Supreme Court decided that discrimination in a variety of public accommodations, including theaters, hotels, and railroads, could not be prohibited by the act because it was private, not state, discrimination.

The ***Civil Rights Cases* (1883)** were five separate cases involving the convictions of private individuals found to have violated the Civil Rights Act by refusing to extend accommodations to African Americans in theaters, a hotel, and a railroad.[5] In deciding these cases, the Supreme Court ruled that Congress could prohibit only state or governmental action and not private acts of discrimination. The Court thus seriously limited the scope of the Civil Rights Act by concluding that Congress had no authority to prohibit private discrimination in public accommodations. The Court's opinion in the *Civil Rights Cases* provided a moral reinforcement for racial segregation, as southern states viewed the Court's ruling as an invitation to gut the reach and intent of the Thirteenth, Fourteenth, and Fifteenth Amendments.

In devising ways to make certain that African Americans did not vote, southerners had to avoid the intent of the Fifteenth Amendment. This amendment did not guarantee suffrage; it simply said that states could not deny anyone the right to vote on account of race or color. To exclude African Americans in a seemingly racially neutral way, southern states used three devices before the 1890s: (1) poll taxes (small taxes on the right to vote that often came due when poor African American sharecroppers had the least amount of money on hand); (2) some form of property-owning qualifications; and, (3) literacy or understanding tests, which allowed local voting registration officials to administer difficult reading-comprehension tests to potential voters.

To make certain that these laws didn't further reduce the numbers of poor or uneducated white voters, many southern states added a **grandfather clause** to their voting qualification provisions, granting voting privileges to those who failed to pass a wealth or literacy test only if their grandfathers had voted before Reconstruction. Grandfather clauses effectively denied the descendants of slaves the right to vote.

While African Americans continued to face wide-ranging racism on all fronts, women also confronted discrimination. During this period, married women, by law, could not be recognized as legal entities. Women often were treated in the same category as juveniles and imbeciles, and in many states were not entitled to wages, inheritances, or custody of their children.

grandfather clause
Voting qualification provision that allowed only those whose grandfathers had voted before Reconstruction to vote unless they passed a wealth or literacy test.

THE PUSH FOR EQUALITY, 1890–1954

THE PROGRESSIVE ERA (1890–1920) was characterized by a concerted effort to reform political, economic, and social affairs. Prejudice against African Americans was just one target of progressive reform efforts. Distress over the legal inferiority of African Americans was aggravated by the U.S. Supreme Court's decision in *Plessy v. Ferguson* **(1896).** In *Plessy*, the Court upheld the constitutionality of a Louisiana law mandating racial segregation on all public trains. The majority concluded that the Louisiana law was constitutional. The justices based their decision on their belief that separate facilities for blacks and whites provided equal protection of the laws. After all, they reasoned, African Americans were not prevented from riding the train; the Louisiana statute required only that the races travel separately. Justice John Marshall Harlan was the lone dissenter. He argued that "the Constitution is colorblind" and that it was senseless to hold constitutional a law "which, practically, puts the badge of servitude and degradation upon a large class of our fellow citizens."[6]

The separate-but-equal doctrine enunciated in *Plessy* v. *Ferguson* soon came to mean only separate, as new legal avenues to discriminate against African Americans were enacted into law throughout the South. By 1900, equality for African Americans was far from the promise first offered by the Civil War Amendments. Again and again, the Supreme Court nullified the intent of the amendments and sanctioned racial segregation while the states avidly followed its lead.[7]

Plessy v. *Ferguson* (1896)
Plessy challenged a Louisiana statute requiring that railroads provide separate accommodations for blacks and whites. The Court found that separate but equal accommodations did not violate the equal protection clause of the Fourteenth Amendment.

■ W. E. B. DuBois (second from right in the second row, facing left) is pictured with the original leaders of the Niagara Movement, an early effort to organize African Americans for rights. This 1905 photo was taken on the Canadian side of Niagara Falls. The Niagara reformers—black men seeking solutions to racial discrimination—met in Canada because no hotel on the U.S. side would accommodate them. At that meeting, a list of injustices suffered by African Americans was detailed. Later, many attendees were instrumental in the creation of the NAACP.

Photo courtesy: Photographs and Prints Division, Schomburg Center for Research in Black Culture, New York Public Library, Astor, Lenox, and Tilden Foundations

The Founding of Key Groups

By 1909, major race riots had occurred in several American cities, and progressive reformers were concerned about these outbreaks of violence and the possibility of others. Oswald Garrison Villard, an influential publisher and the grandson of William Lloyd Garrison, called a conference to discuss the problem of "the Negro." Participants soon formally created the National Association for the Advancement of Colored People (NAACP).

The NAACP was not the only new group. The struggle for women's rights was revitalized in 1890 by the merging of the National and American Woman Suffrage Associations into the National American Woman Suffrage Association (NAWSA), devoted largely to securing women's right to vote. The **suffrage movement** was greatly facilitated by the proliferation of women's groups that emerged during the Progressive era. In addition to the rapidly growing temperance movement—the move to ban the sale of alcohol, which many women blamed for a variety of social ills—women's groups were created to seek protective legislation in the form of maximum hour or minimum wage laws for women and to work for improved sanitation, public morals, and education.

NAWSA based its claim to the right to vote largely on the fact that women, as mothers, should be enfranchised. Furthermore, although many members of the suffrage movement were NAACP members, the movement took on racist overtones. Women argued that if undereducated African Americans could vote, why couldn't women?

Having roots in the Progressive movement gave the growing suffrage movement an exceptionally broad base that transformed NAWSA from a small organization of just over 10,000 members in the early 1890s to a true social movement of more than 2 million members in 1917. By 1920, a coalition of women's groups led by NAWSA and the newer, more radical National Woman's Party was able to secure ratification of the **Nineteenth Amendment** to the Constitution. It guaranteed all women the right to vote—fifty years after African American males were enfranchised by the Fifteenth Amendment.

suffrage movement
The drive for voting rights for women that took place in the United States from 1890 to 1920.

Nineteenth Amendment
Amendment to the Constitution that guaranteed women the right to vote.

Photo courtesy: Library of Congress

■ Suffragists demonstrating for the franchise. Parades like this one took place in cities all over the United States.

After passage of the suffrage amendment in 1920, the fragile alliance of diverse women's groups that had come together to fight for the vote quickly disintegrated. Widespread, organized activity on behalf of women's rights did not reemerge until the 1960s. In the meantime, however, the NAACP continued to fight racism and racial segregation. In fact, its activities and those of others in the civil rights movement would later give impetus to a new women's rights movement.

Litigating for Equality

During the 1930s, leaders of the NAACP began to sense that the time was right to launch a full-scale challenge in the federal courts to the constitutionality of the separate-but-equal doctrine of *Plessy* v. *Ferguson* (1896). The NAACP mapped out a long-range strategy that would first target segregation in professional and graduate education.

Test Cases.   The NAACP opted first to challenge the constitutionality of white-only law schools. In 1935, all southern states maintained fully segregated elementary and secondary schools. Colleges and universities also were segregated, but most states did not provide for postgraduate education for African Americans. NAACP lawyers chose to target law schools because they were institutions that judges could well understand, and integration there would prove less threatening to most whites.

Lloyd Gaines, a graduate of Missouri's all-black Lincoln University, sought admission to the all-white University of Missouri Law School in 1936. He was immediately rejected. In the separate-but-equal spirit, the state offered to build a law school at Lincoln (although no funds were allocated for the project) or, if he didn't want to wait, to pay his tuition at an out-of-state law school. Gaines rejected the offer, sued, lost in the lower courts, and appealed to the U.S. Supreme Court.

Photo courtesy: Bettmann/Corbis

■ Here George McLaurin, the plaintiff in one of the LDF's challenges to "separate but equal" doctrine in graduate education, is shown outside of the classroom. This was the university's response when a federal district court ordered his admission into the University of Oklahoma's doctoral program.

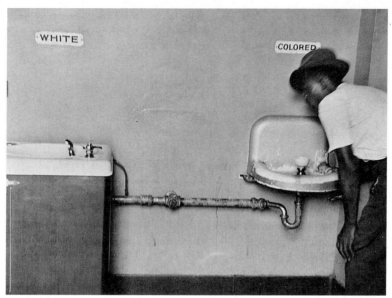

■ Throughout the South, examples of segregation laws abounded. One such law required separate public drinking fountains, shown here. Notice the obvious difference in quality.

Gaines's case was filed at an auspicious time. As you may recall from chapter 3, a constitutional revolution of sorts occurred in Supreme Court decision making in 1937. Before this time, the Court was most receptive to and interested in the protection of economic liberties. In 1937, however, the Court reversed itself in a series of cases and began to place individual freedoms and personal liberties on a more protected footing. Thus, in 1938, Gaines's lawyers pleaded his appeal to a far more sympathetic Supreme Court. NAACP attorneys argued that the creation of a separate law school of a lesser caliber than that of the University of Missouri would not and could not afford Gaines an equal education. The justices agreed and ruled that Missouri had failed to meet the separate-but-equal requirements of *Plessy*. The Court ordered Missouri either to admit Gaines to the school or to set up a law school for him.[8]

Recognizing the importance of the Court's ruling, in 1939 the NAACP created a separate, tax-exempt legal defense fund to devise a strategy that would build on the Missouri case and bring about equal educational opportunities for all African American children. The first head of the NAACP Legal Defense and Educational Fund (often simply called the LDF) was Thurgood Marshall, who later became the first African American to serve on the Supreme Court. Sensing that the Court would be more amenable to the NAACP's broader goals if it was first forced to address a variety of less threatening claims to educational opportunity, Marshall and the LDF brought a series of carefully crafted test cases to the Court.

BROWN V. BOARD OF EDUCATION (1954) AFTER FIFTY YEARS

Overview: It is difficult to overstate the impact of the Supreme Court's decision in *Brown* v. *Board of Education* (1954) on American life. The *Brown* decision was instrumental in making civil rights the highest priority on the domestic policy agenda during the 1950s and 1960s, and it held out the promise of educational equality for all Americans. The Court in *Brown* held "education is perhaps the most important function of state and local governments," and that "In these days, it is doubtful...any child may reasonably be expected to succeed in life if he is denied the opportunity of an education"—which the Court believed is a right that "must be made available to all on equal terms." In order for American society to attain justice, the Court understood segregation had to end and that equal educational opportunity is the key through which all Americans are given the tools to survive and thrive in contemporary society.

After five decades, the results of the *Brown* decision have been mixed. The objective of *Brown* was to create equal educational opportunity; however, there is no constitutional mandate for such a prospect. The Constitution does not speak to education, so that "right" is given to the states to determine, and it follows that with vast discrepancies in wealth and resources between the states, educational establishments will be unequal as well. This problem is exacerbated when fewer funds are allocated to substandard school districts with significant minority populations. Additionally, many members of the middle class, predominately white, have been abandoning the inner cities, leaving poorer, minority populations in underfunded school districts, thus engendering *de facto* segregation. The disparities in education reflect disparities in housing patterns, a problem which is outside the authority of school administrators. Segregation is seen even in "integrated" schools when a disproportionate number of white and Asian Americans are found in advanced-placement classes and a disproportionate number of black and Hispanic Americans are found in remedial and special-needs classes.

A principal effect of *Brown* was to highlight the disparity between the education of majority and minority America. Fifty years later, however, it seems educational segregation may still be the rule rather than the exception. What is the best way to ensure equal educational opportunity for all Americans? Does a diverse classroom necessarily mean a quality education for all? If so, what is the best way to achieve this standard, and if not, what other policy alternatives are available? The 2000 National Assessment of Education Progress (NAEP) shows vast disparities in educational achievement between white and black America. Is segregation the problem, or are there other significant factors as well? What is the best way to ensure a "level playing field" in the education policy domain?

Arguments for the Effectiveness of *Brown*

- ***Brown* has reframed the way Americans view educational integration.** The Court held in *Brown* that education is "necessary for good citizenship" and the only way to make American society more just is to provide all citizens the opportunity for a quality education in order for all to realize their ideal of "the American Dream." Americans now understand that an equal education for all is necessary in order to improve the lives of individuals and to realize fundamental American political principles.

- **_Brown_ signaled the end of racial segregation and helped usher in the civil rights movement.** _Brown_ was instrumental in creating the social context for the Civil Rights Acts of 1957, 1960, and 1964 and the Voting Rights Act of 1965. Though there is work yet to be done, the sum total of this legislation was to help further and partially realize the goals of social equality and equality before the law.
- **_Brown_ set the model for other social justice movements in the United States.** The legal approach by NAACP LDF lawyers has set the standard for other groups pursuing legal and social equality and inclusion. Women's rights, gay rights, disability rights, immigrant rights, and other movements may be said to owe a debt of gratitude to the constitutional interpretation and legal strategies offered by the legal team that argued for _Brown_ and the U. S. Supreme Court.

Arguments Against the Effectiveness of _Brown_

- **Fifty years later, there are still vast disparities in educational attainment between minority and white students.** According to the NAEP, 63 percent of black, inner-city fourth-graders are unable to attain basic proficiency in reading. And, according to black educator Walter Williams, the average black high school graduate has achieved the educational equivalent of a seventh- or eighth-grade mastery of basic subjects and is thus ill prepared to enter the job market or a university.
- **The goal of _Brown_ has yet to be fully realized; instead of educational and social integration, segregation between the races is still a significant problem.** In 2004, approximately 70 percent of African American chil-

dren attend public schools where greater than 50 percent of the student population is black—in Washington, D.C., the student population is 85 percent black. One effect of the _Brown_ decision is "white flight"—the movement of the white middle class out of the inner cities to the suburbs and surrounding country.

- **The _Brown_ decision does not address other problems that affect educational attainment.** _Brown_ does not address other factors understood to affect social and educational achievement. For example, _Brown_ does not address issues such as the effect of high rates of illegitimacy in black communities on educational attainment. In a controversial speech to the NAACP, comedian Bill Cosby took black parents to task for not tending to the education of their children; after all, it is not funding or segregation keeping children from spending time doing their homework, from skipping school, and from reading.

Questions

1. Is integration in educational institutions _the_ solution for academic achievement, or are there other, more significant solutions to help close the learning gap?
2. Will an attempt to realize educational equality across the states violate states' rights and the principle of federalism? What is the best way to ensure this equality?

Selected Readings

Robert Cottrol et al. _Brown_ v. _Board of Education: Caste, Culture and the Constitution._ Lawrence: University Press of Kansas, 2003.

Charles J. Ogletree. _All Deliberate Speed: Reflections on the First Half-Century of Brown_ v. _Board of Education._ New York: Norton, 2004.

The first case involved H. M. Sweatt, a forty-six-year-old African American mail carrier, who applied for admission to the all-white University of Texas Law School in 1946. Rejected on racial grounds, Sweatt sued. The judge gave the state six months to establish a law school or to admit Sweatt to the university. The university then rented a few rooms in downtown Houston and hired two local African American attorneys to be part-time faculty members. Later, the state legislature also authorized $100,000 for a new law school in Austin. It consisted of three small basement rooms, a library of more than 10,000 books, access to the state law library, and three part-time first-year instructors as the faculty. Sweatt declined the opportunity to obtain an education there and instead chose to continue his legal challenge.

Eventually, the Supreme Court handled this case together with another LDF case involving graduate education.[9] The eleven southern states filed an *amicus curiae* (friend of the court) brief, in which they argued that *Plessy* should govern both cases. In a dramatic departure from the past, however, the Harry S Truman administration filed a friend of the court brief urging the Court to overrule *Plessy*. The Court did not overrule *Plessy*, although the justices found that the measures taken by the states in each case failed to live up to the strictures of the separate-but-equal doctrine. The Court unanimously ruled that the remedies to each situation were inadequate to afford a sound education.[10]

In 1950, after these decisions were handed down, the LDF concluded that the time had come to launch a full-scale attack on the separate-but-equal doctrine. The decisions of the Court were encouraging, and the position of the U.S. government and the population in general appeared to be more receptive to an outright overruling of *Plessy*. That challenge came in the form of **Brown v. Board of Education (1954),** four cases involving public elementary or high school systems that mandated separate schools for blacks and whites. In *Brown*, LDF lawyers, again led by Thurgood Marshall, argued that *Plessy's* separate-but-equal doctrine was unconstitutional under the **equal protection clause** of the Fourteenth Amendment. The only way to equalize the schools, argued Marshall, was to integrate them. A major component of the LDF's strategy was to prove that the intellectual, psychological, and financial damage that befell African Americans as a result of segregation precluded any court from finding that equality was served by the separate-but-equal policy.

On May 17, 1954, Chief Justice Earl Warren delivered the fourth opinion of the day, *Brown v. Board of Education*. Writing for the Court, Warren stated: "To separate [some school children] from others…solely because of their race generates a feeling of inferiority as to their status in the community that may affect their hearts and minds in a way very unlikely ever to be undone. We conclude, unanimously, that in the field of public education the doctrine of 'separate but equal' has no place."[11]

Brown was the most important civil rights case decided in the twentieth century.[12] It immediately evoked an uproar that shook the

---

Brown v. Board of Education (1954)
U.S. Supreme Court decision holding that school segregation is inherently unconstitutional because it violates the Fourteenth Amendment's guarantee of equal protection; marked the end of legal segregation in the United States.

equal protection clause
Section of the Fourteenth Amendment that guarantees that all citizens receive "equal protection of the laws."

nation. Some segregationists called the day the decision was handed down Black Monday. The governor of South Carolina denounced the decision, saying, "Ending segregation would mark the beginning of the end of civilization in the South as we know it."[13]

THE CIVIL RIGHTS MOVEMENT

BROWN V. BOARD OF EDUCATION served as a catalyst for change, sparking the development of the modern civil rights movement. Women's work in that movement and in the student protest movement that arose in reaction to the U.S. government's involvement in Vietnam gave women the experience needed to form their own organizations to press for full equality. As African Americans and women became more and more successful, they served as models for other groups who sought equality—Hispanic Americans, Native Americans, homosexuals, the disabled, and others.

■ Seven-year-old Linda Brown lived close to a good public school, but her race precluded her attendance there. When the NAACP LDF sought plaintiffs to challenge this discrimination, her father, a local minister, offered Linda as one of several student plaintiffs named in the LDF's case. Her name came first alphabetically, hence the case name, *Brown* v. *Board of Education* (1954).

Photo source: Carl Iwasaki/TimePix

School Desegregation After *Brown*

One year after *Brown*, in a case referred to as *Brown* v. *Board of Education II* (1955), the Court ruled that racially segregated systems must be dismantled "with all deliberate speed."[14] Many politicians in the South entered into a near conspiracy to avoid the mandates of *Brown II*. In Arkansas, for example, Governor Orval Faubus, who was facing a reelection bid, announced that he would not "be a party to any attempt to force acceptance of change to which people are overwhelmingly opposed."[15] The day before school was to begin, he announced that National Guardsmen would surround Little Rock's Central High School to prevent African American students from entering. Although the federal courts in Arkansas continued to order the admission of African American children, the governor remained adamant. Finally, President Dwight D. Eisenhower sent federal troops to Little Rock to protect the rights of the nine students attending Central High.

In reaction to the governor's outrageous conduct, the Court broke with tradition and

issued a unanimous decision in *Cooper* v. *Aaron* (1958). Each justice signed the opinion individually, underscoring his personal support for the notion that "no state legislator or executive or judicial officer can war against the Constitution without violating his undertaking to support it."[16] The state's actions thus were ruled unconstitutional and its "evasive schemes" illegal.

A New Move for African American Rights

In 1955, soon after *Brown II*, the civil rights movement took another step forward—this time in Montgomery, Alabama. Rosa Parks, the local NAACP's Youth Council adviser, made history when she refused to leave her seat on a bus to move to the back to make room for a white male passenger. She was arrested for violating an Alabama law banning integration of public facilities, including buses. After she was freed on bond, the NAACP urged African Americans to boycott the Montgomery bus system.

The boycott was led by a twenty-six-year-old minister, Reverend Martin Luther King Jr. As it dragged on, Montgomery officials and local business owners began to harass the city's African American citizens. The residents held out, despite suffering personal hardship for their actions. Then, in 1956, a federal court ruled that the segregated bus system violated the equal protection clause of the Fourteenth Amendment. After a year of walking, black Montgomery residents ended their protest when city buses were ordered to integrate. The first effort at nonviolent protest had been successful. Organized boycotts and other forms of nonviolent protest, including sit-ins by college students at segregated restaurants and bus stations, were to follow.

Formation of New Groups

The recognition and respect that the Reverend Martin Luther King Jr. earned within the African American community helped him to launch the Southern Christian Leadership Conference (SCLC) in 1957. Unlike the NAACP, which had northern origins and had come to rely largely on litigation as a means of achieving expanded equality, the SCLC had a southern base and was rooted more closely in black religious culture. The SCLC's philosophy reflected King's growing belief in the importance of nonviolent protest and civil disobedience.

Eventually, the SCLC and the Student Nonviolent Coordinating Committee (SNCC), largely made up of activist college students, dominated the new civil rights movement. While the SCLC generally worked with church leaders in a community, SNCC was much more of a grassroots organization. Always perceived as more radical than the SCLC, SNCC tended to focus its organizing activities on the young, both black and white. In addition to holding sit-ins at segregated facilities, SNCC also led freedom rides, designed to focus attention on segregated public accommodations. Bands of college students and other civil rights activists traveled by bus throughout the South in an effort to force bus stations to desegregate.

While SNCC continued to sponsor sit-ins and freedom rides, in 1963 the Reverend Martin Luther King Jr. launched a series of massive nonviolent demonstrations in Birmingham, Alabama, long considered a major stronghold of segregation. Thousands of blacks and whites marched to Birmingham in a show of solidarity. Peaceful marchers were met there by the Birmingham police commissioner, who ordered his officers to use dogs, clubs, and fire hoses on the marchers. Americans across the nation were horrified as they witnessed the brutality and abuse heaped on the protesters. As the marchers hoped, these shocking scenes helped convince President John F. Kennedy to propose important civil rights legislation.

The Civil Rights Act of 1964

Both the SCLC and SNCC sought full implementation of Supreme Court decisions dealing with race and an end to racial segregation and discrimination. The cumulative effect of collective actions including sit-ins, boycotts, marches, and freedom rides—as well as the tragic bombings and deaths inflicted in retaliation—led Congress to pass the first major piece of civil rights legislation since the post–Civil War era, the Civil Rights Act of 1964. Several events led to the consideration of this legislation.

In 1963, President John F. Kennedy requested that Congress pass a law banning discrimination in public accommodations. Seizing the moment, the Reverend Martin Luther King Jr. called for a monumental march on Washington, D.C., to demonstrate widespread support for far-ranging anti-discrimination legislation. The March on Washington for Jobs and Freedom was held in August 1963, only a few months after the Birmingham demonstrations. More than 250,000 people heard King deliver his famous "I Have a Dream" speech from the Lincoln Memorial. Before Congress had the opportunity to vote on any legislation, however, John F. Kennedy was assassinated on November 22, 1963.

When southern-born Vice President Lyndon B. Johnson succeeded Kennedy as president, he put civil rights reform at the top of his legislative priority list, and civil rights activists gained a critical ally. Thus, through the 1960s, the movement subtly changed in focus from peaceful protest and litigation to legislative lobbying. Its focus broadened from integration of school and public facilities and voting rights to issues of housing, jobs, and equal opportunity.

In spite of strong presidential support and the sway of public opinion, the Civil Rights Act of 1964 did not sail through Congress.

Southern senators, led by South Carolina's Strom Thurmond, a Democrat who later switched to the Republican Party, conducted the longest filibuster in the history of the Senate. For eight weeks, Thurmond led the effort to hold up voting on the civil rights bill, until cloture (see chapter 6) was invoked and the filibuster ended. Once passed, the **Civil Rights Act of 1964:**

Civil Rights Act of 1964
Legislation passed by Congress to outlaw segregation in public facilities and racial discrimination in employment, education, and voting; created the Equal Employment Opportunity Commission.

- Outlawed arbitrary discrimination in voter registration and expedited voting rights lawsuits.
- Barred discrimination in public accommodations engaged in interstate commerce.
- Authorized the Department of Justice to initiate lawsuits to desegregate public facilities and schools.
- Provided for the withholding of federal funds from discriminatory state and local programs.
- Prohibited discrimination in employment on grounds of race, color, religion, national origin, or sex.
- Created the Equal Employment Opportunity Commission (EEOC) to monitor and enforce the bans on employment discrimination.

As challenges were made to the Civil Rights Act of 1964, other changes continued to sweep the United States. African Americans in the North, who believed that their brothers and sisters in the South were making progress against discrimination, found themselves frustrated. Northern blacks were experiencing high unemployment, poverty, discrimination, and little political clout. Some, including Black Muslim leader Malcolm X, even argued that, to survive, African Americans must separate themselves from white culture in every way. These increased tensions resulted in riots in many major cities from 1964 to 1968, when many African Americans in the North took to the streets, burning and looting to vent their rage. The assassination of the Reverend Martin Luther King Jr. triggered a new epidemic of race riots.

THE WOMEN'S RIGHTS MOVEMENT

JUST AS IN THE ABOLITION MOVEMENT in the 1800s, women from all walks of life also participated in the civil rights movement. Women were important members of new groups such as SNCC and the SCLC and more traditional groups such as the NAACP, yet they often found themselves treated as second-class citizens. At one point during a SNCC national meeting, its chair openly proclaimed: "The only position for women in the SNCC is prone."[17] Statements and attitudes like these led some women to found early women's liberation groups that generally were quite radical and small in membership.

The paternalistic attitudes of the Supreme Court, and perhaps society as well, continued well into the 1970s. Said one U.S. Supreme Court justice in 1961: "Despite the enlightened emancipation of women from the restrictions and protections of bygone years, and their entry into many parts of community life formerly considered to be reserved to men, a woman is still regarded as the center of home and family life."[18]

These kinds of attitudes and decisions were not sufficient to forge a new movement for women's rights. Soon, however, three events occurred to move women to action. In 1961, soon after his election, President John F. Kennedy created the President's Commission on the Status of Women. The commission's report, *American Women*, released in 1963, documented pervasive discrimination against women in all walks of life. In addition, the publication of Betty Friedan's *The Feminine Mystique* (1963), led some women to question their status in society.[19] The passage of the Equal Pay Act in 1963 (which guaranteed women equal pay for equal work) and the Civil Rights Act of 1964, which barred discrimination in employment based on sex as well as race (and other factors), motivated women to demand workplace equity. Moreover, in 1966, after the new federal **Equal Employment Opportunity Commission** failed to enforce the Civil Rights Act as it applied to sex discrimination, women activists formed the National Organization for Women (NOW). From its inception, NOW was modeled closely on the NAACP. NOW's first leaders were quite similar to the founders of the NAACP; they wanted to work within the system to prevent discrimination. Initially, most of this activity was geared toward achievement of equality either through passage of an equal rights amendment to the Constitution or by implementation of existing anti-discrimination laws through litigation.

Equal Employment Opportunity Commission
Federal agency created to enforce the Civil Rights Act of 1964, which forbids discrimination on the basis of race, creed, national origin, religion, or sex in hiring, promotion, or firing.

The Equal Rights Amendment

Not all women agreed with the notion of full equality for women. Nevertheless, from 1923 to 1972, a proposal for an equal rights amendment was made in every session of every Congress. Every president since Harry S Truman backed it. By 1972, public opinion favored its ratification, and in response to pressure from NOW, the National Women's Political Caucus, and a wide variety of other feminist groups, Congress voted in favor of the **Equal Rights Amendment** (ERA) by overwhelming majorities (84–8 in the Senate; 354–24 in the House). The amendment provided that:

Equal Rights Amendment
Proposed amendment that would bar discrimination against women by federal or state governments.

> Equality of rights under the law shall not be denied or abridged by the United States or by any state on account of sex.
> The Congress shall have the power to enforce, by appropriate legislation, the provisions of this article.

Within a year, twenty-two states ratified the amendment, most by overwhelming margins. But, the tide soon turned. In 1974 and 1975, the amendment only squeaked through the Montana and North Dakota legislatures, and two states—Nebraska and Tennessee—voted to rescind their earlier ratifications.

By 1978, one year before the deadline for ratification was to expire, thirty-five states had voted for the amendment—three short of the three-fourths necessary for ratification. Efforts in key states such as Illinois and Florida failed as opposition to the ERA intensified. Faced with the prospect of defeat, ERA supporters heavily lobbied Congress to extend the deadline for ratification. Congress extended the ratification period by three years, but to no avail. No additional states ratified the amendment, and three more rescinded their votes.

What began as a simple correction to the Constitution turned into a highly controversial proposal. Even though large numbers of the public favored the ERA, opponents needed to stall ratification in only thirteen states while supporters had to convince legislators in thirty-eight. The success that women's rights activists were having in the courts was hurting the effort. When women first sought the ERA in the late 1960s, the Supreme Court had yet to rule that women were protected by the Fourteenth Amendment's equal protection clause from any kind of discrimination, thus clearly showing the need for an amendment. But, as the Court widened its interpretation of the Constitution to protect women from some sorts of discrimination, the need for the amendment seemed less urgent. The proposed amendment died without being ratified on June 30, 1982.

Litigating for Equal Rights

While several women's groups worked toward passage of the ERA, NOW and several other groups, including the American Civil Liberties Union (ACLU), formed litigating arms to pressure the courts. But, women faced an immediate roadblock in the Supreme Court's interpretation of the equal protection clause of the Fourteenth Amendment.

The Equal Protection Clause and Constitutional Standards of Review.   The Fourteenth Amendment protects all U.S. citizens from state action that violates equal protection of the laws. Most laws, however, are subject to what is called the rational basis or minimum rationality test. This lowest level of scrutiny means that governments must allege a rational foundation for any distinctions they make. As early as 1937, the Supreme Court recognized that certain rights were so fundamental that a very heavy burden would be placed on any government that sought to restrict those rights.[20] When fundamental freedoms such as First Amendment guarantees or **suspect classifications** such as race are involved, the Court uses a heightened standard of review called **strict scrutiny** to determine the constitutional validity of the challenged practices (see Table 5.1). In legal terms, this means that if a statute or

suspect classification
Category or class, such as race, that triggers the highest standard of scrutiny from the Supreme Court.

strict scrutiny
A heightened standard of review used by the Supreme Court to determine the constitutional validity of a challenged practice.

TABLE 5.1 The Equal Protection Clause and Standards of Review Used by the Supreme Court to Determine Whether It Has Been Violated

Type of Classification (What kind of statutory classification is at issue?)	Standard of Review (What standard of review will be used?)	Test (What does the Court ask?)	Example (How does the Court apply the test?)
Fundamental freedoms (including religion, assembly, press, privacy). Suspect classifications (including race, alienage, and national origin).	Strict scrutiny or heightened standard	Is classification necessary to the accomplishment of a permissible state goal? Is it the least restrictive way to reach that goal?	Brown v. Board of Education (1954): Racial segregation not necessary to accomplish the state goal of educating its students.
Gender	Intermediate standard	Does the classification serve an important governmental objective, and is it substantially related to those ends?	Craig v. Boren (1976): Keeping drunk drivers off the roads may be an important governmental objective, but allowing eighteen- to twenty-one-year-old women to drink alcoholic beverages while prohibiting men of the same age from drinking is not substantially related to that goal.
Others (including age, wealth, and mental retardation). standard	Minimum rationality	Is there any rational foundation for the discrimination? restrictions against group homes for the retarded have rational basis.	City of Cleburne v. Cleburne Living Center (1985): Zoning

governmental practice makes a classification based on race, the statute is presumed to be unconstitutional unless the state can prove the law in question is necessary to accomplish a permissible goal and that it is the least restrictive means through which that goal can be accomplished.

During the 1960s and into the 1970s, the Court routinely struck down as unconstitutional practices and statutes that discriminated on the basis of race. "Whites-only" public parks and recreational facilities, tax-exempt status for private schools that discriminated, and statutes prohibiting racial intermarriage were declared unconstitutional. In contrast, the Court refused even to consider the fact that the equal protection clause might apply to discrimination against women. Finally, in 1971, the Supreme Court ruled that an Idaho law granting a male parent automatic preference over a female parent as the administrator of a deceased child's estate violated the equal protection clause of the Fourteenth Amendment.[21] The case was argued by Ruth Bader Ginsburg, as director of the Women's Rights Project of the ACLU; Ginsburg is now an associate Supreme Court Justice.

Timeline
The Struggle for Equal Protection

While the Court did not rule that gender was a suspect classification, it concluded that the equal protection clause of the Fourteenth Amendment prohibited unreasonable classifications based on gender. In *Craig v. Boren* (1976), the Court carved out a new test to be used in examining claims of sex discrimination: "to withstand constitutional challenge,…classifications by gender must serve important governmental objectives and must be substantially related to achievement of those objectives."

Since 1976, the Court has applied the intermediate standard of constitutional review to most claims that it has heard involving gender. It has found that the following kinds of practices violate the Fourteenth Amendment:

- Single-sex public nursing schools.[22]
- Laws that consider males adults at twenty-one years but females at eighteen years.[23]
- Laws that allow women but not men to receive alimony.[24]
- State prosecutors' use of peremptory challenges to reject men or women to create more sympathetic juries.[25]
- Virginia's maintenance of an all-male military college, the Virginia Military Institute.[26]

In contrast, the Court has upheld the following governmental practices and laws:

- Draft registration provisions for males only.[27]
- State statutory rape laws that apply only to female victims.[28]

The level of review used by the Court is crucial. Clearly, a statute excluding African Americans from draft registration would be unconstitutional. But, because gender is not subject to the same higher standard of review that is used in racial discrimination cases, the exclusion of women from the requirements of the Military Selective Service Act was ruled permissible because the government policy was considered to serve "important governmental objectives."[29]

This history perhaps has clarified why women's rights activists continue to argue that until the passage of an equal rights amendment, women will never enjoy the same rights as men. An amendment would automatically raise the level of scrutiny that the Court applies to gender-based claims, although there are clear indications that the women justices on the Court are inclined toward requiring states to show "exceedingly persuasive justifications" for their actions.[30]

Comparing Civil Rights

Statutory Remedies for Sex Discrimination.   In part because of the limits of the intermediate standard of review and the fact that the equal protection clause applies only to governmental discrimination,

WOMEN IN PARLIAMENT

As we have seen in this chapter, the extension of political rights to individuals in a society is often marked by controversy and may occur in stages. In the United States, for example, women were allowed to stand for election in 1788, but not until 1920 and the ratification of the Nineteenth Amendment did they obtain the right to vote. In Canada and Mexico, a reverse process took place. Women received the right to vote with certain restrictions in 1918 and then obtained the right to stand for elected office in 1920, again with certain restrictions. In Mexico, women obtained the right to vote in 1947 and the right to stand for office in 1953. The right of women to stand for election and to vote is not yet universal. In Kuwait, women can do neither. In the United Arab Emirates, the parliament is appointed and neither men nor women have the right to vote or to stand for election.

There can be a significant difference in the right to stand for election and the ability to get elected. If we add up all the members of parliaments around the world and break their membership down by gender, we find that as of May 2004 women hold 15.4 percent of the seats. The percentage is highest in the Nordic countries (Sweden, Norway, Finland, and Iceland) at 39.7 percent and lowest in the Arab world at 6.4 percent. In the Americas, it averages 18.5 percent.

A closer look reveals that, based on election results from 2004, 15.6 percent of the members of the U.S. House of Representatives are women (68 out of 435), and 14 percent of U.S. senators are women (14 out of 100). The table provides us with a picture of how the United States compares with other countries.

Questions

1. What might be some of the reasons that women are not represented in parliaments around the world?
2. What would increase the number of women elected to public office?

Source: Interparliamentary Union, http://www.ipu.org/wmn-e/classif.htm.

Percentage of Women in Lower Houses of Parliament, 2004

Rank	Country	Election year	Seats	Women	% Women	Rank	Country	Election year	Seats	Women	% Women
1	Rwanda	2003	80	39	48.8	50	Suriname	2000	51	9	17.6
2	Sweden	2002	349	158	45.3	60	Equatorial				
3	Denmark	2001	179	68	38.0		Guinea	2004	100	14	14.0
4	Finland	2003	200	75	37.5	75	Lithuania	2000	141	15	10.6
5	Netherlands	2003	150	55	36.7	100	Maldives	1999	50	3	6.0
10	Argentina	2001	256	87	34.0	110	Turkey	2002	550	24	4.4
15	Mozambique	1999	250	75	30.0	115	Iran	2004	290	9	3.1
20	Namibia	1999	72	19	26.4	123	Bahrain	2002	40	0	0.0
25	Switzerland	2003	200	50	25.0	123	Kuwait	2003	65	0	0.0
30	Eritrea	1994	150	33	22.0	123	Saudi Arabia	2001	120	0	0.0

women's rights activists began to bombard the courts with sex-discrimination cases. Many of these cases have been filed under Title VII of the Civil Rights Act, which prohibits discrimination by private (and after 1972 public) employers, or the Equal Pay Act that Congress passed in 1963, which requires employers to pay women and men equal pay for equal work. Nevertheless, a large wage gap between men and women continues to exist. In spite of the fact that the Equal Pay Act is forty years old, women in 2002 earned 77 percent of what men earned. In fact, a study done by the AFL-CIO shows that this discrimination will cost a twenty-one-year-old female college graduate more than one million dollars over her career.[31] (See Figure 5.1.)

Key victories under Title VII include:

- Consideration of sexual harassment as sex discrimination.[32]
- Inclusion of law firms, which many argued were private partnerships, in the coverage of the act.[33]
- A broad definition of what can be considered sexual harassment, which includes same-sex harassment.[34]
- Allowance of voluntary affirmative action programs to redress historical discrimination against women.[35]
- Holding school boards or districts responsible for sexual harassment of students by teachers.[36]

Title IX, which parallels Title VII, greatly expanded the opportunities for women in elementary, secondary, and postsecondary institu-

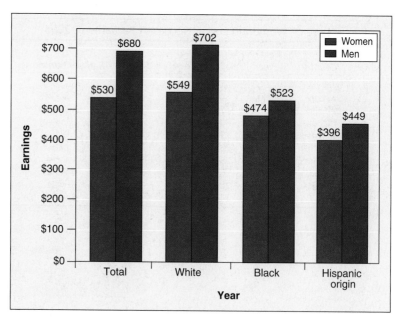

FIGURE 5.1 The Wage Gap, 2002. The Equal Pay Act was passed in 1963; still, women's wages continue to fall short of men's although the gap is closing among all women with the exception of Hispanic women. What factors might account for these inequities? ■

Source: National Committee on Pay Equity.

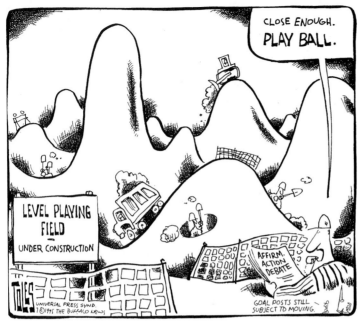

Photo courtesy: TOLES © 1995 The Buffalo News. Reprinted with permission of Universal Press Syndicate. All rights reserved.

tions. It bars educational institutions receiving federal funds from discriminating against female students. Since women's groups, like the NAACP before them, saw eradication of educational discrimination as key to improving other facets of women's lives, they lobbied for it heavily.[37] They have litigated also to make sure that its key provisions are enforced. (See chapter 8 for more on Title IX.)

Title IX
Provision of the Educational Amendments of 1972 that bars educational institutions receiving federal funds from discriminating against female students.

OTHER GROUPS MOBILIZE FOR RIGHTS

AFRICAN AMERICANS AND WOMEN are not the only groups that have suffered unequal treatment under the law. Denial of civil rights has led many other disadvantaged groups to mobilize to achieve greater civil rights.

Hispanic Americans

As noted in chapter 1, Hispanic Americans now are the largest minority group in the United States. Until the 1920s, most Hispanics lived in the southwestern United States. In the decades that followed, large numbers of immigrants from Mexico and Puerto Rico came to the

HELPING OTHERS TO ACHIEVE THEIR CIVIL RIGHTS

Throughout campuses across the nation, students as well as recent graduates are reaching out to help those who, because they cannot speak English, are far less likely to take advantage of a wide array of local, state, and national programs to assist them in fully participating in the political system.

On some campuses, students (and even some faculty and staff) volunteer to assist campus workers who cannot speak English. At Brandeis University, for example, university workers, many of them immigrants in low-paying kitchen, cleaning, or maintenance positions, are paired with students who help them one on one to learn to read and write English. This student-run program, like many others, is "about more than literacy: It's knocking down barriers, a language gap, and the often rigid class and educational divide between students and workers."[a]

In another program, recent college graduates are making two-year commitments to Teach for America. Teach for America participants attend intensive summer institutes to prepare them for the classroom setting, and they are mentored throughout the year in order to be certified as classroom teachers in an expedited fashion. Teach for America participants generally are placed in low-income schools with grave teacher shortages. A program like Teach for America was at the core of Rodney Paige's success in the Houston school system, where he served as superintendent. President George W. Bush was so impressed that he appointed Paige Secretary of Education and directed him to launch the program on a national basis.

Although these new teachers earn what their traditional counterparts make, they are usually recent graduates who might have been more likely to enter higher-paying professions. Lower-performing, often minority, schools, now profit from getting the services of high-quality teachers.

Nearly every study of political participation has noted the importance of education as a predictor of voting. With the kinds of knowledge that both of these programs are imparting to their target audiences, college students are significantly advancing the ability of others to demand full civil rights from their government.

---

[a] Peter Schworm, "Breaking Barriers: At Brandeis, Students and Workers Connect Through ESL Breaking Language, Social Barriers," *Boston Globe* (April 11, 2002): B8.

United States. Mexicans, who quickly became a source of cheap labor, settled in the southwest, where they most frequently were employed as migratory farm workers. In contrast, Puerto Ricans largely moved to New York City. Both groups tended to live in their own neighborhoods, where life was centered around the Roman Catholic Church and the customs of their homeland.

The Hispanic American population continued to grow in the mid-1970s, as immigrants from Cuba as well as several other island and Latin American nations came to the United States seeking a better life. Their problems often were confounded by their need to learn a new language. This language barrier has continued to depress voter registration and voter turnout while contributing to the continued poverty and discrimination suffered by Hispanics.

The earliest push for greater Hispanic rights occurred in the mid-1960s, well before the next major influx of Hispanics to the United States.[38] Like blacks, women, and Native Americans, Hispanic Americans have some radical militant groups, but the movement has been dominated by more conventional organizations, especially those that pursue litigation. These include the Mexican American Legal Defense and Educational Fund (MALDEF) and the Puerto Rican Legal Defense and Educational Fund.

MALDEF was founded in 1968 after members of the League of United Latin American Citizens (LULAC), the nation's largest and oldest Hispanic organization, met with NAACP LDF leaders and secured a $2.2 million start-up grant from the Ford Foundation. It was created to bring test cases to force school districts to allocate more funds to schools with predominantly low-income minority populations, to implement bilingual education programs, to force employers to hire Hispanics, and to challenge election rules and apportionment plans that undercount or dilute Hispanic voting power.

MALDEF has been quite successful in its efforts to expand voting rights and opportunities to Hispanic Americans. In 1973, for example, it won a major victory when the Supreme Court ruled that multimember electoral districts (in which more than one person represents a single district) in Texas discriminated against African Americans and Hispanic Americans.[39]

MALDEF also regularly litigates to alleviate inter-school-district inequalities, which frequently have their greatest impact on poor Hispanic

Photo courtesy: George Rodriguez

■ Vice President of Litigation for the Mexican American Legal Defense and Education Fund, Tom Saenz, defends the rights of "day laborers," people who are employed and get paid on a daily or short-term basis, to work within a safe environment and receive a living wage for a day's work.

children.[40] In 1984, MALDEF filed suit in state court alleging that the Texas school finance policy violated the Texas constitution. In 2004, it entered into a settlement with the state of California in a case brought four years earlier to address, in MALDEF's words, "the shocking inequities facing public school children across the state."[41] Its leaders objected to shorter school calendars for schools where the enrollment was predominantly Hispanic and other poor students.

MALDEF continues to litigate in a wide range of areas of concern to Hispanics. High on its agenda are affirmative action, the admission of Hispanic students to state colleges and universities, health care for undocumented immigrants, and challenging unfair redistricting practices that make it more difficult to elect Hispanic legislators.

MALDEF also continues to be at the fore of legislative lobbying for expanded rights. Since 2002, it has worked to oppose restrictions on legislation concerning driver's license requirements for undocumented immigrants. It won a victory on this issue in California in 2004. MALDEF also focuses on the rights of Hispanic workers and the effects of legislative redistricting on the voting strength of Hispanics.

Native Americans

Native Americans are the first true Americans, and their status under U.S. law is unique. Under the U.S. Constitution, Indian tribes are considered distinct governments, a situation that has affected Native Americans' treatment by the Supreme Court in contrast to other groups of ethnic minorities. And, minority is a term that accurately describes American Indians. It is estimated that there were as many as 10 million Indians in the New World at the time Europeans arrived in the 1400s, with 3 to 4 million living in what is today the United States. By 1900, the number of Indians in the continental United States had plummeted to less than 2 million. Today, there are 2.7 million.

It was not until the 1960s, at the same time women were beginning to mobilize for greater civil rights, that Indians, too, began to mobilize. Like the civil rights and women's rights movements, the movement for Native American rights had a radical as well as a more traditional branch. During this time, many Indians, trained by the American Indian Law Center at the University of New Mexico, began to file hundreds of test cases in the federal courts involving tribal fishing rights, tribal land claims, and the taxation of tribal profits. The Native American Rights Fund (NARF), founded that same year, became the NAACP LDF of the Indian rights movement when the "courts became the forum of choice for Indian tribes and their members."[42]

Native Americans have won some very important victories concerning hunting, fishing, and land rights. They continue to gain access to their sacred places and have filed lawsuits to stop the building of roads and new construction on ancient burial grounds or other sacred spots. Today, these land rights allow Native Americans to play host to a number of casinos across the country, a phenomenon that is explored in Politics Now: Reclaiming Rights. However, Native Americans have not fared particularly well in areas such as religious freedom, especially where tribal practices come into conflict with state law.

Native Americans also continue to fight the negative stereotypes that plague their progress and have found themselves locked in a controversy with the Department of the Interior over its handling of Indian trust funds, which are to be paid out to Indians for the use of their lands. In 1996, several Indian tribes filed suit to force the federal government to account for the billions of dollars it has collected over the years for its leasing of Indian land, which it took from the Indians and held in trust since the late-nineteenth century, and to force reform of the system.[43] As the result of years of mismanagement, the trust, administered by the Department of the Interior, has no records of monies taken in or how they were disbursed. The ongoing class action lawsuit includes 500,000 Indians, who claim that they are owed more than $10 billion. The trial judge found massive mismanagement of the funds, which generate up to $500 million a year, and at one time threatened to hold Secretary of the Interior Gail Norton in contempt. In early 2004, a mediator was appointed to help bring greater resolution to the conflict.[44]

Gays and Lesbians

Until very recently, gays and lesbians have had an even harder time than other groups in achieving fuller rights.[45] Gays, however, have on average far higher household incomes and educational levels than do the other groups, and they are beginning to convert these advantages into political clout at the ballot box and through changes in public opinion. Like African Americans and women early in their quest for greater civil rights, gays and lesbians initially did not fare well in the Supreme Court. In the late 1970s, the Lambda Legal Defense and Education Fund, the Lesbian Rights Project, and Gay and Lesbian Advocates and Defenders were founded by gay and lesbian activists dedicated to ending legal restrictions on the civil rights of homosexuals.[46] Although these groups have won important legal victories concerning HIV/AIDS discrimination, insurance policy survivor benefits, and even some employment issues, they generally were not as successful as other historically legally disadvantaged groups.[47]

In 1993, for example, President Bill Clinton tried to get an absolute ban on discrimination against homosexuals in the armed services, who were subject to immediate discharge if their sexual orientation was discovered. Military leaders and then-Senator Sam Nunn (D–GA) led the effort against Clinton's proposal. Eventually, Clinton and Senate leaders compromised on what was called the "Don't Ask,

RECLAIMING RIGHTS: INDIANS USE DIVERSE WAYS TO REVERSE THE ECONOMIC ADVERSITY OF DISCRIMINATION

Although the U.S. government formally recognizes 107 Indian tribes within California, only fifteen of these owned casinos in 2004. But in the five years that those casinos have been allowed to operate, they have brought in over $5 billion and are expected to increase that amount exponentially in the near future.[a] One tribe, the United Auburn Indian Community, located east of Sacramento, provides an excellent example of how gaming can affect tribal members. And, events similar to those in California are happening within Indian tribes all over the United States, especially where Indians were forced onto reservations.

Under the U.S. Constitution, Indian tribes on tribal lands are treated as foreign nations and are therefore not subject to the laws of the states or the U.S. government—which generally, until recently, have prohibited gambling in most states. In return for settlements of longtime land disputes, in the 1990s many states entered into agreements with tribes, allowing them to build gambling casinos on their reservations in exchange for a portion of the profits. Most tribes have entered into agreements with states to allow them to operate slot machines. Connecticut in 2003, for example, earned more than $400 million in this kind of revenue-sharing agreement.

In California, the United Auburn Indian Community spent $125 million to build the Thunder Valley Casino in 2003 and is expected to earn $300 million in their first year of operations. According to the *Los Angeles Times*, just a year earlier not one of the 250 members of the tribe had ever attended college. Members of the tribe lived in slum conditions, nearly 80 percent did not know how to write a check, and many were unable to afford basic amenities such as running water and kitchen appliances.[b] Some were homeless. Now, the tribe has financial consultants to help its members. All get free medical, dental, and vision care. Special education and tutoring programs are helping the tribe's ninety-three children and their parents become more educated, as well as adjusted to the tremendous changes in their economic status.

All over the nation, tribes are using the money earned from casinos to diversify. Many tribes also sell tobacco on their reservations and in their casinos and spas (which many casinos have added), where they are free from state taxes.[c]

Tribes are even donating to political campaigns of candidates whom they see as predisposed to policies favorable to tribes. The Agua Caliente Band of Cahuilla Indians, who sought to build a theme park and golf practice ranges, donated $7.5 million to political campaigns in just one year alone. During the California governor recall of 2004, Indian tribes contributed over $11 million to candidates, highlighting their political clout. These large expenditures, Indians claim, are legal, because as sovereign nations they are immune from federal and state campaign finance disclosure laws. This issue in all likelihood will be decided by the U.S. Supreme Court as Indians, long one of the most disadvantaged groups politically in the U.S., with the fewest rights, now begin to exercise their political and economic clout.

---

[a] Louis Sahagun, "Tribes Fear Backlash to Prosperity," *Los Angeles Times* (May 3, 2004): B1.

[b] Sahagun, "Tribes Fear Backlash to Prosperity."

[c] Sahagun, "Tribes Fear Backlash to Prosperity."

Don't Tell" policy. It stipulated that gays and lesbians would no longer be asked if they were homosexual, but they were barred from revealing their sexual orientation under threat of discharge from the service.[48]

A shift in the public's views toward homosexuality was signaled by the U.S. Supreme Court's 1996 decision in *Romer* v. *Evans*. In this case, the Court ruled that an amendment to the Colorado constitution that denied homosexuals the right to seek protection from discrimination was unconstitutional under the equal protection clause of the Fourteenth Amendment. In 2000, Vermont became the first state to recognize same-sex civil unions, marking another landmark in the struggle for equal rights for homosexuals. And, in *Lawrence* v. *Texas* (2003), the Court reversed an earlier 1986 ruling by finding a Texas statute that banned sodomy to be unconstitutional.[49] Editorial pages across the country praised the Court's ruling, arguing that the public's view toward homosexuality had changed.[50]

In November 2003, the Massachusetts Supreme Court ruled that denying homosexuals the right to civil marriage was unconstitutional, a ruling many civil rights activists anticipated would take many more years to accomplish. The U.S. Supreme Court later refused to hear this case. Still, in 2004, many conservative groups and Republican politicians made same-sex marriage an issue. Referendums or amendments banning same-sex marriage were placed on eleven state ballots and were passed overwhelmingly by voters.

Disabled Americans

In the aftermath of World War II, many veterans returned to a nation unequipped to handle their disabilities. The Korean and Vietnam Wars made the problems of the disabled all the more clear. When these disabled veterans saw the successes of African Americans, women, and other minorities, they too began to lobby for greater protection against discrimination.[51] In 1990, in coalition with other disabled people, veterans finally were able to convince Congress to pass the Americans with Disabilities Act

Participation

Civil Rights and
Gay Adoption

■ George Lane, the appellant in the 2004 Supreme Court case of *Tennessee* v. *Lane*, crawled up two flights of stairs to get to a court hearing on a misdemeanor charge.

Photo courtesy: Jason R. Davis/AP/Wide World Photos

(ADA). The statute defines a disabled person as someone with a physical or mental impairment that limits one or more "life activities," or who has a record of such impairment. It thus extends the protections of the Civil Rights Act of 1964 to all of those with physical or mental disabilities. It guarantees access to public facilities, employment, and communication services. It also requires employers to acquire or modify work equipment, adjust work schedules, and make existing facilities accessible.

In 1999, the U.S. Supreme Court issued a series of four decisions redefining and significantly limiting the scope of the ADA. The cumulative impact of these decisions was to limit dramatically the number of people who can claim coverage under the act. Moreover, these cases "could profoundly affect individuals with a range of impairments—from diabetes and hypertension to severe nearsightedness and hearing loss—who are able to function in society with the help of medicines or aids but whose impairments may still make employers consider them ineligible for certain jobs."[52] In 2004, however, in *Tennessee* v. *Lane*, the Court ruled that disabled persons could sue states that failed to make reasonable accommodations to assure that courthouses are handicapped accessible (see photo on page 197).[53]

Simply changing the law, while often an important first step in achieving civil rights, is not the end of the process. Attitudes must also change. As history has shown, that can be a very long process and will be longer given the Court's decisions.

CONTINUING CONTROVERSIES IN CIVIL RIGHTS

You Are the Mayor

SINCE PASSAGE OF MAJOR CIVIL RIGHTS legislation in the 1960s and the Supreme Court's continued interest in upholding the civil rights of many groups, African Americans, women, Hispanics, Native Americans, gays and lesbians, and the disabled have come much closer to the attainment of equal rights. Yet, all of these groups still remain far from enjoying full equality under the Constitution in all walks of life.

More than fifty years after *Brown* v. *Board of Education* (1954), the civil rights debate today centers on the question of equality of opportunity versus equality of results. Most civil rights and women's rights organizations argue that the lingering and pervasive burdens of racism and sexism can be overcome only by taking race or gender into account in fashioning remedies for discrimination. They argue that the Constitution is not and should not be blind to color or sex.

The counter-argument holds that if it was once wrong to use labels to discriminate against a group, it should be wrong to use those same labels to help a group. According to this view, quotas and other forms of **affirmative action,** policies designed to give special attention or compensatory treatment to members of a previously disadvantaged group, should be illegal.

affirmative action
Policies designed to give special attention or compensatory treatment to members of a previously disadvantaged group.

Analyzing Visuals

HOW AMERICANS VIEW AFFIRMATIVE ACTION

The following Gallup Poll, taken just before the Supreme Court decided two major affirmative action cases in 2003, queried non-Hispanic whites, blacks, and Hispanics about their opinions regarding affirmative action. Questions regarded not only affirmative action in general, but also affirmative action as it relates to student admissions to a college or university. After studying the charts and reading the material in this chapter on affirmative action, answer the following critical thinking questions: Which group of those who were polled was most supportive of affirmative action? Which was the least supportive? Why do you think the opinions differed so greatly in regard to the question about two equally qualified students applying to a college or university? Is the All category a fair reflection of American views about affirmative action? Why or why not?

Note: N = 1,385 adults nationwide (MoE +/- 3), including, with oversamples, 821 non-Hispanic whites (MoE +/- 4), 241 blacks (MoE +/- 7), and 266 Hispanics (MoE +/- 7). Interviewing was June 12–15, 2003, for non-Hispanic whites, and June 12–18, 2003, for blacks and Hispanics.

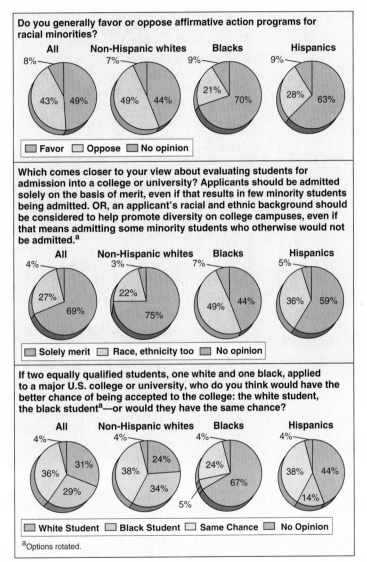

Source: http://www.pollingreport.com/race.htm.

The debate over affirmative action and equality of opportunity became particularly intense during the late 1970s. In 1978, the Supreme Court for the first time fully addressed the issue of affirmative action. In *Regents of the University of California* v. *Bakke* (1978), a sharply divided Court ruled that the use of strict quotas in college admissions activity was inappropriate, however the school was free to "take race into account."[54] Other cases upheld this view until the later 1980s. Then, in a three-month period in 1989, the Supreme Court handed down five civil rights decisions limiting programs and making it harder to prove employment discrimination. In response, Congress passed the Civil Rights Act of 1991, which overruled these decisions. Then, in *Grutter* v. *Bollinger* (2003), the U.S. Supreme Court voted to uphold the constitutionality of the University of Michigan's law school admissions policy, which gave preference to minority applicants.[55] However, in a companion case, the Court struck down Michigan's undergraduate point system, which gave minority applicants twenty points simply because they were minorities.[56]

Taken together, these cases set the stage for a new era in affirmative action in the United States. While the use of strict quotas and automatic points is not constitutional, the Court clearly believes that there is a place for some preferential treatment, at least until greater racial and ethnic parity is achieved.

Race is not the only issue that continues to breed civil rights controversies. Recent developments with two corporations illustrate the reality that discrimination persists in the United States.

Beginning in the mid-1990s, many gay rights activists charged that the Cracker Barrel restaurant chain discriminated against homosexuals by requiring that employees exhibit "heterosexual values" on the job. Following allegations that employees were fired because they were gay and a series of boycotts by gay rights activists, Cracker Barrel adopted a new anti-discrimination policy that included protections for sexual orientation.[57]

More recently, the nation's largest employer, Wal-Mart, has been embroiled in a series of discrimination suits. In the largest class action lawsuit ever brought in the United States, Wal-Mart is charged with gender discrimination for paying women lower wages than men and offering them fewer opportunities for advancement than their male colleagues.[58]

Additionally, nine illegal immigrants who worked as janitors at Wal-Mart are suing it for discriminating against them by paying them lower wages and giving them fewer benefits based on their ethnic origin. Another group of Wal-Mart employees from twenty-one states is also suing the corporation, claiming that executives knowingly conspired to hire illegal immigrants and, in doing so, violated the workers' civil rights by refusing to pay Social Security and other wage compensation benefits.[59] These suits represent a growing trend in discrimination suits filed by immigrants who believe that they have been persecuted following changes in security and immigration law after September 11, 2001.

SUMMARY

WHILE THE FRAMERS AND OTHER AMERIcans basked in the glory of the newly adopted Constitution and Bill of Rights, their protections did not extend to all Americans. When the Framers tried to compromise on the issue of slavery, they only postponed dealing with a volatile question that was later to rip the nation apart. Ultimately, the Civil War was fought to end slavery. Among its results were the triumph of the abolitionist position and adoption of the Thirteenth, Fourteenth, and Fifteenth Amendments. During this period, women also sought expanded rights, especially the right to vote, but to no avail.

Although the Civil War Amendments were added to the Constitution, the Supreme Court limited their application. The NAACP was founded in the early 1900s to press for equal rights for African Americans. Women's groups also were active during this period, successfully lobbying for passage of the Nineteenth Amendment, which assured them the right to vote.

In 1954, the U.S. Supreme Court ruled in *Brown* v. *Board of Education* that state-segregated school systems were unconstitutional. This victory empowered African Americans as they sought an end to other forms of pervasive discrimination. Bus boycotts, sit-ins, freedom rides, pressure for voting rights, and massive nonviolent demonstrations became common tactics. This activity culminated in the passage of the Civil Rights Act of 1964.

After passage of the Civil Rights Act, a new women's rights movement arose. Several women's rights groups were created, and while some sought a constitutional amendment, others attempted to litigate under the equal protection clause and several laws to obtain greater equality.

Building on the successes of African Americans and women, other groups, including Hispanic Americans, Native Americans, gays and lesbians, and the disabled, organized to litigate for expanded civil rights as well as to lobby for anti-discrimination laws. None of the groups discussed in this chapter have yet to reach full equality, and other groups, including immigrants, are seeking to improve their civil rights.

KEY TERMS

affirmative action, p. 198
Black Codes, p. 170
Brown v. *Board of Education* (1954), p. 180
civil rights, p. 167
Civil Rights Act of 1964, p. 184
Civil Rights Cases (1883), p. 172
Equal Employment Opportunity Commission, p. 185
equal protection clause, p. 180
Equal Rights Amendment, p. 185
Fifteenth Amendment, p. 170
Fourteenth Amendment, p. 170
grandfather clause, p. 173
Nineteenth Amendment, p. 175
Plessy v. *Ferguson* (1896), p. 173
strict scrutiny, p. 186
suffrage movement, p. 175
suspect classification, p. 186
Thirteenth Amendment, p. 170
Title IX, p. 191

SELECTED READINGS

Bacchi, Carol Lee. *The Politics of Affirmative Action: 'Women,' Equality and Category Politics.* Thousand Oaks, CA: Sage, 1996.
Eastland, Terry. *Ending Affirmative Action: The Case for Colorblind Justice.* New York: Basic Books, 1997.
Freeman, Jo. *The Politics of Women's Liberation.* New York: Backinprint.com, 2000.
Guinier, Lani. *Who's Qualified?* Boston: Beacon, 2001.
Kluger, Richard. *Simple Justice,* reprint ed. New York: Vintage, 2004.
Mansbridge, Jane J. *Why We Lost the ERA.* Chicago: University of Chicago Press, 1986.
McClain, Paula D., and Joseph Stewart Jr. *"Can We All Get Along?" Racial and Ethnic Minorities in American Politics,* 3rd ed. Boulder, CO: Westview, 2001.
McGlen, Nancy E., et al. *Women, Politics, and American Society,* 4th ed. New York: Longman, 2004.
Nobles, Melissa. *Shades of Citizenship: Race and the Census in Modern America.* Palo Alto, CA: Stanford University Press, 2000.
Reed, Adolph, Jr. *Without Justice for All: The New Liberalism and Our Retreat from Racial Equity.* Boulder, CO: Westview, 1999.

Rodriguez, Clara E. *Changing Race: Latinos, the Census, and the History of Ethnicity in the United States*. New York: New York University Press, 2000.

Rosales, Francisco A., and Arturo Rosales, eds. *Chicano! The History of the Mexican American Civil Rights Movement*. Houston, TX: Arte Publico, 1996.

Verba, Sidney, and Gary R. Orren. *Equality in America: The View from the Top*. Cambridge, MA: Harvard University Press, 1985.

Williams, Juan. *Eyes on the Prize: America's Civil Rights Years, 1954–1965*. New York: Penguin, 1987.

Wilson, William Julius. *The Bridge over the Racial Divide: Rising Inequality and Coalition Politics*. Berkeley: University of California Press, 1999.

WEB EXPLORATIONS

For more on civil rights generally, see
http://www.civilrightsproject.harvard.edu/

For more on abolition, the American Anti-Slavery Society, and its leaders, see
http://www.loc.gov/exhibits/african/afam005.html

For more about the history of Jim Crow in the South, see
http://www.jimcrowhistory.org/

To read the full text of *Brown v. Board of Education* (1954), see
http://caselaw.lp.findlaw.com/cgi-bin/getcase.pl?court=US&vol=347&invol=483

For more about the Montgomery bus boycott and Reverend Martin Luther King Jr., see
http://www.stanford.edu/group/King/about_king/encyclopedia/bus_boycott.html

For more about NOW and the EEOC, see
http://www.now.org
http://www.eeoc.gov/

For more about the Equal Rights Amendment, see
http://www.equalrightsamendment.org/

For more about the ACLU Women's Rights Project, see
http://www.aclu.org/WomensRights/WomensRightsMain.cfm

To learn more about MALDEF, see
http://www.maldef.org/

For more about the Native American Rights Fund, see
http://www.narf.org/

For more about gay and lesbian rights groups, see
http://www.glaad.org/

For more about disability advocacy groups, see
http://www.aapd-dc.org/

Photo courtesy: Larry Downing/Reuters/Corbis

Congress

ON FEBRUARY 6, 2002, Representative Nancy Pelosi (D–CA) broke through a glass ceiling when she was sworn in as the Democratic House whip, becoming the first woman in history to win an elected position in the formal House leadership.[1] The whip position has long been viewed as a stepping stone to becoming the speaker of the House. House Speakers Tip O'Neill (D–MA) and Newt Gingrich (R–GA) were both former whips. As whip, it was Pelosi's responsibility to convince Democratic members of the House to vote together on the full range of bills before the 107th Congress.

First elected to Congress from California in 1986, Pelosi quickly made her mark as an advocate for human rights in China and as an effective fundraiser. Her fund-raising skills and years of experience in the House, in fact, helped her win the hotly contested race for the whip position. As part of the House leadership, she became the first woman to attend critical White House meetings, where, said Pelosi, "Susan B. Anthony and others are with me."[2]

Although the president's party traditionally loses seats in midterm elections, in 2002 House Republicans actually increased their majority. Critics charged that the Democrats lacked a consistent message. Therefore, soon after the election results were in, House Minority Leader Richard Gephardt (D–MO) resigned from his position, leaving Pelosi in line to succeed him. Representative Harold Ford (D–TN), one of the youngest members of the House, threw his hat into the ring to oppose Pelosi's campaign for the leader's position. Ford, a moderate, charged that Pelosi, who already was being referred to by conservatives as a "San Francisco liberal," was simply too liberal to lead the Democrats back to political viability in the 2004 elections. A majority of the members of the Democratic House Caucus, however, did not appear fazed by these charges; Pelosi was elected minority leader by an overwhelming majority of the caucus members. Steny Hoyer (D–MD), who initially had run against Pelosi for the whip position in the 107th Congress, was elected Democratic whip in the 108th Congress.

The election of Pelosi as House minority leader sharply altered the look of power in the House of Representatives. As the leader of all House Democrats, Pelosi automatically is accorded tremendous respect, as well as media attention as the face of Democrats in the House. Thus, more than 150 years after women first sought the right to vote, a woman member of Congress now leads one party in the House of Representatives. The representation of women in Congress has also come a long way since 1917, when Jeanette Rankin (R–MT) became the first woman elected to Congress. Women currently make up over 50 percent of the population but only 15 percent of the members of Congress.[3]

THE FRAMERS' ORIGINAL CONCEPTION of the representational function of Congress was much narrower than it is today. Instead of regarding members of Congress as representatives of the people, those in attendance at the Constitutional Convention were extremely concerned with creating a legislative body that would be able to make laws to govern the new nation. Over time, Congress has attempted to maintain the role of a law- and policy-making institution, but changes in the demands made on the national government have allowed the executive and judicial branches to gain powers at the expense of the legislative. Moreover, although the Congress as a branch of government has experienced a decline in its authority, the power and the importance of individual members have grown. Thus, the public doesn't think much about Congress itself, but somewhat ironically, citizens hold their own elected representatives in high esteem.

The dual roles that Congress plays contribute to this divide in public opinion. Members of Congress must combine and balance the roles of lawmaker and policy maker with being a representative of their district, their state, their party, and sometimes their race, ethnicity, or gender. Not surprisingly, this balancing act often results in role conflict.

In this chapter, we will analyze the powers of Congress and the competing roles members of Congress play as they represent the interests of their constituents, make laws, and oversee the actions of the other two branches of government. We will also see that, as these functions have changed throughout U.S. history, so has Congress itself. We will first examine what the Constitution has to say about Congress—the legislative branch of government. We will then compare the two chambers and consider how their differences affect the course of legislation. After looking at the members of Congress, including how members get elected, and how they spend their days, we will examine the various factors that influence how members of Congress make decisions. We will also examine the law-making function of Congress. Finally, we will discuss the ever changing relationship between Congress and the president, and between Congress and the judiciary.

THE CONSTITUTION AND THE LEGISLATIVE BRANCH OF GOVERNMENT

ARTICLE I OF THE CONSTITUTION describes the structure of the legislative branch of government we know today. As discussed in chapter 2, the Great Compromise at the Constitutional Convention resulted in the creation of an upper house, the Senate, and a lower house, the House of Representatives. Any two-house legislature, such as the one created by the Framers, is called a **bicameral legislature.** Each state is represented in the Senate by two senators, regardless of the state's population. The number of representatives each state sends to the House of Representatives, in contrast, is determined by that state's population.

bicameral legislature
A legislature divided into two houses; the U.S. Congress and the state legislatures are bicameral except Nebraska, which is unicameral.

The U.S. Constitution sets out the formal, or legal, requirements for membership in the House and Senate. House members must be at least twenty-five years of age; senators, thirty. Members of the House must have resided in the United States for at least seven years; those elected to the Senate, nine. Representatives and senators must be legal residents of the states from which they are elected.

Senators were to be elected by state legislatures for six-year terms. The Framers intended for senators to be tied closely to their state legislatures and expected them to represent their states' interests in the Senate. State legislators lost this influence over the Senate with the ratification of the Seventeenth Amendment in 1913, which provides for the direct election of senators by voters. One-third of all senators are up for reelection every two years.

In contrast, members of the House of Representatives are elected to two-year terms by a vote of the eligible electorate in each congressional district. The Framers expected that the House would be more responsible to the people because they were elected directly by them and more responsive to the people because they were up for reelection every two years.

Apportionment and Redistricting

The U.S. Constitution requires that a census, which entails the counting of all Americans, be conducted every ten years. Until the first census could be taken, the Constitution fixed the number of representatives in the House of Representatives at sixty-five. In 1790, then, one member represented 30,000 people. As the population of the new nation grew and states were added to the union, the House became larger and larger. In 1910, it expanded to 435 members, and in 1929, its size was fixed at that number by statute.

Each state is allotted its share of these 435 representatives based on its population. After each U.S. Census, the number of seats allotted to each state is adjusted by a constitutionally mandated process called **apportionment.** After seats are apportioned, congressional districts must be redrawn by state legislatures to reflect population shifts to ensure that each member in Congress represents approximately the same number of residents. This process of redrawing congressional districts to reflect increases or decreases in the number of seats allotted to a state, as well as population shifts within a state, is called **redistricting.** (The effects of redistricting are discussed in chapter 12.)

Constitutional Powers of Congress

The Constitution specifically gives Congress its most important power: the authority to make laws. For example, no **bill** (proposed law) can become law without the consent of both houses. Examples of other constitutionally shared powers include the power to declare war, raise an army and navy, coin money, regulate commerce, establish the federal courts and their jurisdiction, establish rules of immigration and naturalization, and "make all Laws which shall be necessary and proper for carrying into Execution the foregoing Powers." As interpreted by the U.S. Supreme Court, the necessary and proper clause, found at the end of Article I, section 8, when coupled with one or more of the specific powers enumerated in Article I, section 8, has allowed Congress to increase the scope of its authority, often at the expense of the states.

Reflecting the different constituencies and size of each house of Congress (as well as the Framers' intentions), Article I gives special, exclusive powers to each house in addition to their shared role in lawmaking. For example, as noted in Table 6.1, the Constitution specifies that all revenue bills must originate in the House of Representatives. Over the years, however, this mandate has been blurred, and it is not unusual to see budget bills being considered simultaneously in both houses, especially since each must approve all bills in the end.

The House also has the power to impeach: the authority to charge the president, vice president, or other "civil officers," including federal judges, with "Treason, Bribery, or other high Crimes and Mis-

apportionment
The proportional process of allotting congressional seats to each state following the decennial census.

redistricting
The redrawing of congressional districts to reflect increases or decreases in seats allotted to the states, as well as population shifts within a state.

bill
A proposed law.

The Living Constitution

The Congress shall have Power.... To establish an uniform Rule of Naturalization.

—Article I, Section 8

This article reiterates the sovereign power of the nation and places authority to draft laws concerning naturalization in the hands of Congress.

Congress's power over naturalization is exclusive—meaning that no state can bestow U.S. citizenship on anyone. Citizenship is a privilege and Congress may make laws limiting or expanding the criteria. The word *citizen* was not defined constitutionally until ratification in 1868 of the Fourteenth Amendment, which sets forth two kinds of citizenship: by birth and through naturalization. Throughout American history, Congress has imposed a variety of limits on naturalization, originally restricting it to "free, white persons." "Orientals" were excluded from eligibility in 1882. At one time those affiliated with the Communist Party and those who lacked "good moral character" (which was construed to exclude homosexuals, drunkards, gamblers, and adulterers) were deemed unfit for citizenship. Most of these restrictions no longer exist, but they do underscore the power of Congress in this matter.

Congress continues to retain the right to naturalize large classes of individuals, as it did in 2000 when it granted automatic citizenship rights to all minor children adopted abroad as long as both adoptive parents were American citizens. Naturalized citizens, however, do not necessarily enjoy the full rights of citizenship enjoyed by other Americans. Congress at any time, subject only to Supreme Court review, can limit the rights and liberties of naturalized citizens, especially in times of national crisis. In the wake of 9/11, when it was revealed that of the forty-eight al-Qaeda-linked operatives who took part in some sort of terrorist activities against the United States, one-third were lawful permanent residents or naturalized citizens, Congress called for greater screening by the Immigration and Naturalization Service for potential terrorists.

TABLE 6.1   Key Differences Between the House and Senate

Constitutional Differences

House	Senate
Initiates all revenue bills	Offers "advice and consent" on many major presidential appointments
Initiates impeachment procedures and passes articles of impeachment	Tries impeached officials
	Approves treaties
Two-year terms	Six-year terms (one third up for reelection every two years)
435 members (apportioned by population)	100 members (two from each state)

Differences in Operation

House	Senate
More centralized, more formal; stronger leadership	Less centralized, less formal; weaker leadership
Rules Committee fairly powerful in controlling time and rules of debate (in conjunction with the speaker of the House)	No rules committee; limits on debate come through unanimous consent or cloture of filibuster
More impersonal	More personal
Power distributed less evenly	Power distributed more evenly
Members are highly specialized	Members are generalists
Emphasizes tax and revenue policy	Emphasizes foreign policy

Changes in the Institution

House	Senate
Power centralized in the speaker's inner circle of advisers	Senate workload increasing and informality breaking down; threat of filibusters more frequent than in the past
House procedures are becoming more efficient	Becoming more difficult to pass legislation
Turnover is relatively high, although those seeking reelection almost always win	Turnover is moderate

impeachment
The power delegated to the House of Representatives in the Constitution to charge the president, vice president, or other "civil officers," including federal judges, with "Treason, Bribery, or other high Crimes and Misdemeanors." This is the first step in the constitutional process of removing such government officials from office.

demeanors." Only the Senate is authorized to conduct trials of **impeachment,** with a two-thirds vote being necessary before a federal official can be removed from office.

The Senate has the sole authority to approve major presidential appointments, including federal judges, ambassadors, and Cabinet- and sub-Cabinet-level positions. The Senate, too, must approve all presidential treaties by a two-thirds vote.

HOW CONGRESS IS ORGANIZED

EVERY TWO YEARS, a new Congress is seated. After ascertaining the formal qualifications of new members, the Congress organizes itself as

FIGURE 6.1   Organizational Structure of the House of Representatives and the Senate in the 109th Congress. ■

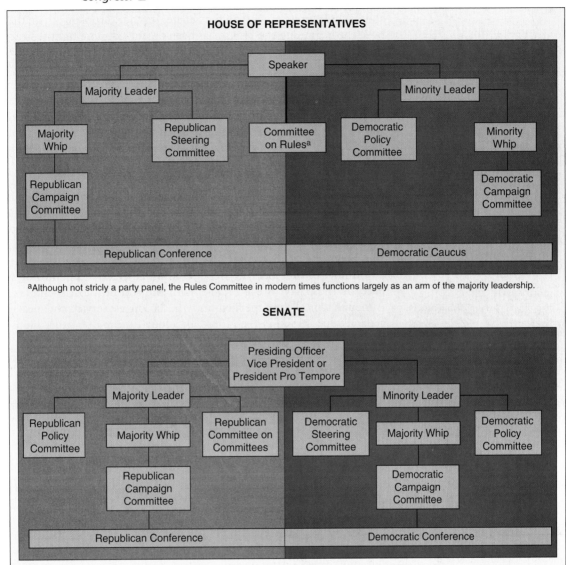

HOUSE OF REPRESENTATIVES

Speaker

Majority Leader

Minority Leader

Majority Whip

Republican Steering Committee

Committee on Rules^a

Democratic Policy Committee

Minority Whip

Republican Campaign Committee

Democratic Campaign Committee

Republican Conference

Democratic Caucus

^aAlthough not stricly a party panel, the Rules Committee in modern times functions largely as an arm of the majority leadership.

SENATE

Presiding Officer Vice President or President Pro Tempore

Majority Leader

Minority Leader

Republican Policy Committee

Majority Whip

Republican Committee on Committees

Democratic Steering Committee

Majority Whip

Democratic Policy Committee

Republican Campaign Committee

Democratic Campaign Committee

Republican Conference

Democratic Conference

Source: Adapted from Roger H. Davidson and Walter J. Olezek, *Congress and its Members,* 6th ed. Washington D.C.: CQ Press, 2002.

it prepares for the business of the coming session. Among the first items on its agenda are the election of new leaders and the adoption of rules for conducting its business. As illustrated in Figure 6.1, each house has a hierarchical leadership structure.

The House of Representatives

Even in the first Congress in 1789, the House of Representatives was almost three times larger than the Senate. It is not surprising, then, that from the beginning the House has been organized more tightly, structured more elaborately, and governed by stricter rules. Traditionally, loyalty to the party leadership and voting along party lines has been more common in the House than in the Senate. House leaders also play a key role in moving the business of the House along. Historically, the speaker of the House, the majority and minority leaders, and the Republican and Democratic House whips have made up the party leadership that runs Congress. This group now has been expanded to include deputy whips of both parties.

The Speaker of the House.   The **speaker of the House** is the only officer of the House of Representatives specifically mentioned in the Constitution. The entire House of Representatives elects the speaker at the beginning of each new Congress. Traditionally, the speaker is a member of the **majority party,** the party in each house with the greatest number of members, as are all committee chairs. (The **minority party** is the party in each house with the second most members.) Although typically not the member with the longest service, the speaker generally has served in the House for a long time and in other House leadership positions as an apprenticeship.

The speaker presides over the House of Representatives, oversees House business, and is the official spokesperson for the House, as well as being second in the line of presidential succession. Moreover, the speaker is the House liaison with the president and generally has great political influence within the chamber. The speaker is also expected to smooth the passage of party-backed legislation through the House.

Other House Leaders.   After the speaker, the next most powerful people in the House are the majority and minority leaders, who are elected in their individual **party caucuses** or **conferences.** The **majority leader** is the second most important person in the House; his or her counterpart on the other side of the aisle (the House is organized so that if you are facing the front of the chamber, Democrats sit on the left side and Republicans on the right side of the center aisle) is the **minority leader.** The majority leader helps the speaker schedule proposed legislation for debate on the House floor. In the past, the leaders of both major parties worked closely with the speaker. More recently, the Republican House leadership rarely consults with the Democratic leaders. (See Politics Now: A Minority Bill of Rights?)

The Republican and Democratic **whips,** who are elected by party members in caucuses, assist the speaker and majority and minority leaders in their leadership efforts. The position of whip originated in the

speaker of the House
The only officer of the House of Representatives specifically mentioned in the Constitution; elected at the beginning of each new Congress by the entire House; traditionally a member of the majority party.

majority party
The political party in each house of Congress with the most members.

minority party
The political party in each house of Congress with the second most members.

party caucus or conference
A formal gathering of all party members.

majority leader
The elected leader of the party controlling the most seats in the House of Representatives or the Senate; is second in authority to the speaker of the House and in the Senate is regarded as its most powerful member.

minority leader
The elected leader of the party with the second highest number of elected representatives in the House of Representatives or the Senate.

whip
One elected leader who keeps close contact with all party members and takes "nose counts" on key votes, prepares summaries of bills, and in general acts as communications link within the party.

Photo courtesy: *Office of the Minority Leader Nancy Pelosi*

■ Nancy Pelosi (D–CA), the House minority leader, reveals a portrait of Representative Mary Norton, which now hangs in the leader's office. Norton (D–NJ), the first Democratic woman elected to Congress and the first woman to chair a standing committee of the House, served from 1925–1951 and sought to establish rights for "blue and pink collar" workers. Her strenuous efforts to enforce fair pay and decent working conditions made a crucial impact on our government.

British House of Commons, where it was named after the "whipper in," the rider who keeps the hounds together in a fox hunt. Party whips— who were first designated in the House in 1899 and in the Senate in 1913—do, as their name suggests, try to "whip" fellow Democrats or Republicans into line on partisan issues. They try to maintain close contact with all members on important votes, prepare summaries of content and implications of bills, get "nose counts" during debates and votes, and in general get members to toe the party line. Whips and their deputy whips also serve as communications links, distributing word of the party line from leaders to rank-and-file members and alerting leaders to concerns in the ranks.

Timeline

The Power of the Speaker of the House

The Senate

The Constitution specifies that the presiding officer of the Senate is the vice president of the United States. Because he is not a member of the Senate, he votes only in the case of a tie.

The official chair of the Senate is the president pro tempore, or pro tem, who generally is the most senior senator of the majority party and presides over the Senate in the absence of the vice president. Once elected, the pro tem stays in that office until there is a change in the

ETHICS AND THE CONGRESS

Overview: Article I, section 5, of the U.S. Constitution gives both chambers of Congress the authority to police the activities and conduct of its members. Because of the nature of congressional office, members enjoy certain protections denied to most Americans—for example, members receive heightened protections for speech, as well as protections against arrest for civil violations during legislative sessions. It's not that members are considered above law; it is simply that the Constitution's framers believed those engaged in law-making, the highest function of representative government, need additional freedoms and protections to carry out their duties. Nevertheless, the Constitution does not speak to ethical norms or provide guidelines for correct behavior during congressional assemblies. Over time, ethical oversight and procedure has been determined by the leadership of the two major political parties, who have taken on the responsibility for supervising the behavior of party and congressional members.

The past two decades have seen high-profile ethical lapses from members of Congress. Two speakers have resigned in disgrace, another member resigned after conviction for having sex with a minor and soliciting child pornography, one more pleaded guilty to mail fraud, and yet another was removed after being convicted of bribery and racketeering.

When it comes to ethical lapses regarding campaign finance and party politics, the Congress is less than forthright in detailing ethical failures. Investigations of members are usually secret, and congressional rules do not allow outsiders to bring charges of malfeasance. Prior to 1997, both major parties used accusations of corruption to score political points, so much so that many observers believed protocol in the House would degenerate into disorder. In 1997, the parties in the House instituted an ethics truce in an attempt to bring order and decorum to the legislative process. The primary problem is the secret nature of investigating ethical transgressions; this helps foster the public perception that Congress hides its accountability and protects morally suspect members.

The nature of political office is such that the American people hold elected representatives to high ethical standards; after all, law ultimately reflects the prevailing morality of legislative bodies. How can the American public ensure representatives are held accountable for bad behavior? Should outside watchdog groups be allowed to bring charges of corruption and wrongdoing, or is the electoral process an adequate safeguard against political malfeasance? Should Congress create an independent regulatory body to ensure members' compliance to ethical standards, or should the parties themselves be held to stricter accountability for their members' behavior? What can be done to reestablish trust between the American people and their elected officials?

Arguments Supporting Congressional Oversight Authority

- **The Framers gave Congress traditional parliamentary rights.** Supreme Court Justice Joseph Story, in his *Commentaries on the Constitution*, states that common law gives legislators the right to define contempt, or unethical behavior, based on the fact that members of Congress have unique competency in determining matters of legislative ethics. Thus, Congress is the "proper and exclusive forum" for determining if ethical breaches have occurred.

- **Congress does respond to unethical behavior by its members.** The Congress is responsive to ethical violations by its members. For example, many members of Congress have resigned in disgrace—in 1995 Senator Bob Packwood (R–OR) resigned due to sexual misconduct, in 1990 Representative Barney Frank (D–MA) was reprimanded for fixing parking tickets for a lover, and in 1991 Senator Alan Cranston (D–CA) was formally reprimanded for his role in the Keating Five savings and loan scandal.
- **Voters are competent to unseat unethical members.** Voters force members to pay attention to ethics or risk losing their seats. For example, Representative Gary Condit (D–CA) was not reelected after his relationship with an intern became public; Representative Dan Rostenkowski (D–IL) was not returned to office amid allegations of fraud and influence peddling.

Arguments Against Congressional Oversight Authority

- **Congress has demonstrated that it cannot be trusted to exercise oversight over its members.** The 1994 Republican Revolution in the House was in part due to the GOP's promise to adhere to strict ethical standards. Of late, rules have been flouted and the Congress has slowly relaxed ethical standards; in the 108th and 109th Congresses, the House relaxed gift rules, giving lobbyists loopholes so they can provide perks—such as dinners, golfing vacations, and tickets to sporting and cultural events—to members as they attempt to gain access, and even removed the head of the Republican Ethics Committee of his overzealousness.
- **An independent regulatory agency acting as a filter between members and the ethics process can ensure fairness in investigatory procedure.** An independent, unbiased, nonpartisan entity can ensure members are treated impartially. An independent entity can also ensure allegations of ethical misconduct are investigated fairly and then make recommendations for disposition of allegations. This will help limit partisan political maneuvering.
- **Allowing private individuals and watchdog groups to request investigations would improve accountability.** Establishing a formal procedure for investigations initiated by the public can help increase congressional accountability by putting members under the watchful eye of public interest groups. Members would be less likely to engage in misbehavior if they knew their actions were being observed by those outside their party.

Questions

1. What can be done to make members of Congress adhere to ethical guidelines?
2. If Congress should not have sole jurisdiction over the policing of its members, what institutions or procedures can be created that fall within the scope of the Constitution?

Selected Readings

Martin and Susan Tolchin. *Glass Houses: Congressional Ethics and the Politics of Venom.* Boulder, CO: Westview, 2001.

Dennis Thompson. *Ethics in Congress: From Individual to Institutional Corruption.* Washington, DC: Brookings Institution Press, 1995.

A MINORITY BILL OF RIGHTS?

It is customary for the party in control of the House of Representatives to limit the minority's ability to amend bills as well as shape the debate on proposed legislation. But Democrats, as the minority party after forty years of control, are charging that Republicans are wielding their power in unfair ways that damage the deliberative process of that body. A scholar from the moderate to conservative American Enterprise said that Democrats' complaints have some merit. "Republicans are at a point now where, reveling in the power they have, they are using techniques to jam bills through even when they don't have to...simply because they can."[a]

In an effort to allow the minority party more input, House Minority Leader Nancy Pelosi proposed a "Minority Bill of Rights," which she pledged to follow should the Democrats regain power in 2005. Among its provisions are calls for:

- *Bipartisan administration of the House.* This would provide for regular consultation between the leaders of both parties concerning scheduling, administration, and operation of the House. This would include a guarantee that the minority party would get at least one-third of committee budgets and office space.

In the past, meetings of minority and majority party leaders were routine, as were meetings between committee chairs and ranking members. Speaker Dennis Hastert rarely meets with Pelosi, and only a few committee chairs consult with ranking minority members. The budget and office space condition was followed in the 108th Congress, and Pelosi says it should be mandatory.

- *Regular order for legislation.* This would require that bills be developed following full hearings and open committee and subcommittee markups, and that members would have at least twenty-four hours to read any bill before it came to a vote. This would also mandate that all floor votes be completed within fifteen minutes.

Republicans have delayed floor votes in order to allow the whips and other leaders to convince members to change their votes. The Republicans held up voting on the Medicare prescription drug bill for nearly three hours, well after midnight, to convince Republican dissidents to change their votes after the leadership appeared headed for defeat. Pelosi also called for regular House-Senate conference committee meetings that would allow minority party members some input into final conference committee legislation.

In the 108th Congress, the Rules Committee frequently rejected amendments from Democrats, often met until one or two o'clock in the morning, then scheduled votes on what it had done for ten o'clock the same morning.

1. Pelosi pledged to apply these rules should she become speaker. Do you think these suggestions should be adopted? Why or why not?
2. Can you think of other suggestions to cure the problems Pelosi seeks to address?

---

[a] Charles Babington, "Pelosi Seeks House Minority 'Bill of Rights,' Hastert Dismisses Democrats' Complaint, Saying GOP Record Is Better Than Foes," *Washington Post* (June 24, 2004): A23.

majority party in the Senate. Since presiding over the Senate can be a rather perfunctory duty, neither the vice president nor the president pro tempore actually performs the task very often. Instead, the duty of presiding over the Senate rotates among junior members of the chamber.

The true leader of the Senate is the majority leader, elected to the position by the majority party. Because the Senate operates without many of the more formal House rules concerning debate, the majority leader is not nearly as powerful as the speaker of the House. The Republican and Democratic whips round out the leadership positions in the Senate and perform functions similar to those of their House counterparts. But, leading and whipping in the Senate can be quite a challenge. Senate rules always have given tremendous power to individual senators; in most cases senators can offer any kind of amendments to legislation on the floor, and an individual senator can bring all work on the floor to a halt indefinitely through a filibuster unless three-fifths of the senators vote to cut him or her off.[4]

Photo courtesy: REUTERS/William Philpott/Corbis

■ Senate Majority Leader Bill Frist (R–TN), left, talks to House Majority Leader Tom DeLay (R–TX) at the 2003 Congress of Tomorrow retreat that brought House and Senate Republicans together.

The Role of Political Parties in Organizing Congress

The organization of both houses of Congress is closely tied to political parties and their strength in each House. For the party breakdowns in the 109th Congress, see Figure 6.2. Parties play a key role in the committee system, an organizational feature of Congress that facilitates its law-making and oversight functions and often sets the congressional agendas.

At the beginning of each new Congress, the members of each party gather in its party caucus or conference. Historically, these caucuses have enjoyed varied powers, but today the party caucuses have several roles, including nominating or electing party officers, reviewing committee assignments, discussing party policy, imposing party discipline, setting party themes, and coordinating media, including talk radio. Conference and caucus chairs are recognized party leaders who work with others who are part of the House or Senate leadership.[5]

Each caucus or conference has specialized committees that fulfill certain tasks. House Republicans, for example, have a Committee on Committees that makes committee assignments. The Democrats' Steering Committee performs this function. Each party also has a congressional campaign committee to assist members in their reelection bids.

FIGURE 6.2   The 109th Congress. ■

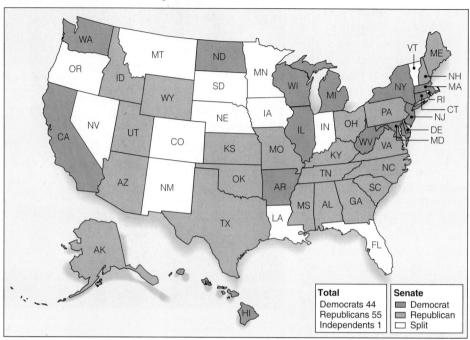

Total
Democrats 44
Republicans 55
Independents 1

Senate
■ Democrat
■ Republican
□ Split

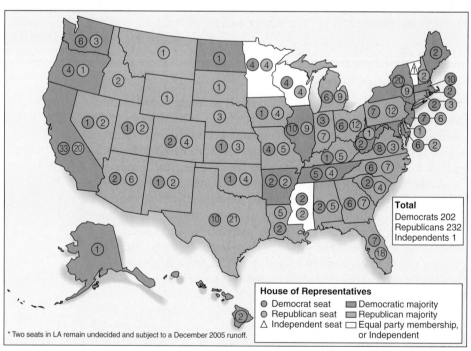

Total
Democrats 202
Republicans 232
Independents 1

House of Representatives
● Democrat seat   ■ Democratic majority
● Republican seat   ■ Republican majority
△ Independent seat   □ Equal party membership,
                          or Independent

* Two seats in LA remain undecided and subject to a December 2005 runoff.

The Committee System

The saying "Congress in session is Congress on exhibition, whilst Congress in its committee rooms is Congress at work" may not be as true today as it was when Woodrow Wilson wrote it in 1885.[6] Still, "The work that takes place in the committee and subcommittee rooms of Capitol Hill is critical to the productivity and effectiveness of Congress."[7]

Committees are especially important in the House of Representatives because of its size. Organization and specialization are critically important, as noted in Table 6.2. The establishment of subcommittees allows for even greater specialization.

TABLE 6.2 Committees of the 109th Congress (with a Subcommittee Example)

Standing Committees

House	Senate
Agriculture	Agriculture, Nutrition, and Forestry
Appropriations	Appropriations
Armed Services	Armed Services
Budget	Banking, Housing, and Urban Affairs
Education and the Workforce	Budget
Energy and Commerce	Commerce, Science, and Transportation
Financial Services	Energy and Natural Resources
Government Reform	Environment and Public Works
Homeland Security	Finance
House Administration	Foreign Relations
International Relations	Health, Education, Labor, and Pensions
Judiciary	Homeland Security and Governmental Affairs
Judiciary Subcommittees	Judiciary
Courts, the Internet, and Intellectual Property	*Judiciary Subcommittees*
Immigration, Border Security, and Claims	Administrative Oversight and the Courts
Commercial and Administrative Law	Immigration, Border Security, and Citizenship
Crime, Terrorism, and Homeland Security	Antitrust, Competition Policy, and Consumer Rights
Constitution	Terrorism, Technology, and Homeland Security
Resources	Crime, Corrections, and Victims' Rights
Rules	The Constitution, Civil Rights, and Property Rights
Science	Full Committee Task Force on Anti-Trust
Small Business	Rules and Administration
Standards of Official Conduct	Small Business and Entrepreneurship
Transportation and Infrastructure	Veterans Affairs
Veterans Affairs	
Ways and Means	

Select, Special, and Other Committees

House	Senate	Joint Committees
Select Intelligence	Special Aging	Economics
	Select Ethics	Printing
	Select Intelligence	Taxation
	Indian Affairs	Library

Types of Committees. There are four types of congressional committees: (1) standing; (2) joint; (3) conference; and, (4) special, or select.[8]

standing committees
Committees to which proposed bills are referred.

joint committees
Committees that includes members from both houses of Congress which conduct investigations or special studies.

conference committees
Joint committees created to iron out differences between Senate and House versions of a specific piece of legislation.

select (or special) committees
Temporary committees appointed for a specific purpose such as a special investigation or study.

1. **Standing committees,** so called because they continue from one Congress to the next, are the committees to which bills are referred for consideration.

2. **Joint committees** are set up to expedite business between the houses and to help focus public attention on major matters, such as the economy, taxation, or scandals. They include members from both houses of Congress who conduct investigations or special studies.

3. **Conference committees** are special joint committees that reconcile differences in bills passed by the House and Senate. The conference committee is made up of members from the House and Senate committees that originally considered the bill.

4. **Select (or special) committees** are temporary committees that are appointed for specific purposes. Generally such committees are established to conduct special investigations or studies and to report back to the chamber that established them.

The House and Senate standing committees listed in Table 6.2 were created by rule. In the 109th Congress, the House has nineteen standing committees, each with an average of thirty-one members. Together, these standing committees have a total of eighty-six subcommittees that collectively act as the eyes, ears, and hands of the House. They consider issues roughly parallel to those of the departments represented in the president's Cabinet.

Although most committees in one house parallel those in the other, the House Rules Committee, for which there is no counterpart in the Senate, plays a key role in the House's law-making process. Indicative of the importance of the Rules Committee, majority party members are appointed directly by the speaker. This committee reviews most bills after they come from a committee and before they go to the full chamber for consideration. Performing a "traffic cop" function, the Rules Committee gives each bill what is called a *rule,* which contains the date the bill will come up for debate and the time that will be allotted for discussion, and often specifies what kinds of amendments can be offered.

Standing committees have considerable power. They can kill bills, amend them radically, or hurry them through the process. In the words of former president Woodrow Wilson, who, as a political scientist, wrote an early seminal work on Congress, once a bill is referred to a committee, it "crosses a parliamentary bridge of sighs to dim dungeons of silence from whence it never will return."[9] Committees report out to the full House or Senate only a small fraction of the bills assigned to them. Bills can be forced out of a House committee by a **discharge petition** signed by a majority (218) of the House membership.

In the 109th Congress, the Senate has sixteen standing committees that range in size from fifteen to twenty-nine members. It also has sixty-eight subcommittees, which allows all majority party senators to chair one. For example, the Senate Judiciary Committee has seven subcommittees, as illustrated in Table 6.2.

In contrast to the House, whose members hold few committee assignments (an average of 1.8 standing and three subcommittees), senators are spread more thinly, with each serving on an average of three to four committees and seven subcommittees. Whereas the committee system allows House members to become policy or issue specialists, Senate members often are generalists. In the 109th Congress, Senator Kay Bailey Hutchison (R–TX), for example, serves on several committees, including Appropriations; Commerce, Science, and Transportation; Veterans Affairs; and Rules. She also serves on even more subcommittees, chairing two of them, and is the vice chair of the Republican Conference.

Senate committees enjoy the same power over framing legislation as do House committees, but the Senate, being an institution more open to individual input than the House, gives less deference to the work done in committees. In the Senate, legislation is more likely to be rewritten on the floor, where all senators can participate and add amendments at any time.

Committee Membership.

Many newly elected members of Congress come into the body with their sights on certain committee assignments. Others are more flexible. Many legislators seeking committee assignments inform their party's selection committee of their preferences. They often request assignments based on their own interests or expertise or on a particular committee's ability to help their prospects for reelection. One political scientist has noted that committee assignments are to members what stocks are to investors—they seek to acquire those that will add to the value of their portfolios.[10]

Representatives often seek committee assignments that have access to what is known as **pork,** legislation that allows representatives to bring money and jobs to their districts in the form of public works programs, military bases, or other programs. Legislators who bring jobs and new public works programs back to their districts are hard to defeat when up for reelection. But, ironically, these are the programs that attract much of the public criticism directed at the federal government in general and Congress in particular. Thus, it is somewhat paradoxical that pork improves a member's chances for reelection or for election to higher office.

discharge petition
Petition that gives a majority of the House of Representatives the authority to bring an issue to the floor in the face of committee inaction.

pork
Legislation that allows representatives to "bring home the bacon" to their districts in the form of public works programs, military bases, or other programs designed to benefit their districts directly.

Pork isn't the only motivator for those seeking strategic committee assignments.[11] Some committees, such as Energy and Commerce, facilitate reelection by giving House members influence over decisions that affect large campaign contributors. Other committees, such as Education and the Workforce or Judiciary, attract members eager to work on the policy responsibilities assigned to the committee even if the appointment does them little good at the ballot box. Another motivator for certain committee assignments is the desire to have power and influence within the chamber. The Appropriations and Budget Committees provide that kind of reward for some members.

In both the House and the Senate, committee membership generally reflects the party distribution within that chamber. For example, at the outset of the 109th Congress, Republicans held a narrow majority of House seats (229) and thus claimed about a 55 percent share of the seats on several committees, including International Relations, Energy and Commerce, and Education and the Workforce. On committees more critical to the operation of the House or to setting national policy, the majority often takes a disproportionate share of the slots. Since the Rules Committee regulates access to the floor for legislation approved by other standing committees, control by the majority party is essential for it to manage the flow of legislation. For this reason, no matter how narrow the majority party's margin in the chamber, it makes up more than two-thirds of the Rules Committee membership.

Committee Chairs.   Committee chairs enjoy tremendous power and prestige. They are authorized to select all subcommittee chairs, call meetings, and recommend majority members to sit on conference committees. Committee chairs may even opt to kill a bill by refusing to schedule hearings on it. They also have a large committee staff at their disposal and are often recipients of favors from lobbyists, who recognize the chair's unique position of power. Personal skill, influence, and expertise are a chair's best allies.

Historically, committee chairs were the majority party members with the longest continuous service on the committee. Committee chairs in the House, unlike the Senate, are no longer selected by **seniority,** or time of continuous service on the committee. Today, the House leadership interviews potential chairs to make certain that candidates demonstrate loyalty to the party, although seniority continues to be a factor.

seniority
Time of continuous service on a committee.

THE MEMBERS OF CONGRESS

MANY MEMBERS OF CONGRESS RELISH their work, although there are indications that the high cost of living in Washington and maintaining two homes, political scandals, intense media scrutiny, the need to tackle hard issues, and a growth of partisan dissension is taking a toll on many members. It is also difficult for members to appease two constituencies—party leaders, colleagues, and lobbyists in Washington, D.C., and constituents at home.[12] (For a representative's typical day among home consitutents and in Washington, D.C., see Table 6.3.)

Running for Office and Staying in Office

Despite the long hours, hard work, and sometimes even abuse that senators and representatives experience, thousands aspire to these jobs every year. Yet, only 535 men and women (plus five nonvoting delegates)

TABLE 6.3 A Day in the Life of a Member of Congress

Typical Member's At-Home Schedule[a]		Typical Member's Washington Schedule[b]	
7:30 a.m.	Business group breakfast, 20 leaders of the business community	8:30 a.m.	Breakfast with former member
8:45 a.m.	Hoover Elementary School, 6th grade class assembly	9:30 a.m.	Committee on Science, Space, and Technology hearing on research and development in the 1990s
9:45 a.m.	National Agriculture Day speech, Holiday Inn South	10:00 a.m.	Briefing by FAA officials for members of Congress who represent families of victims of Pan Am Flight #103
10:45 a.m.	Supplemental Food Shelf, pass foodstuffs to needy families	10:00 a.m.	Energy and Commerce Committee mark-up session on Fairness in Broadcasting
12:00 noon	Community College, student/faculty lunch, speech, and Q & A	12:00 noon	Reception/photo opportunity with telecommunications officials
1:00 p.m.	Sunset Terrace Elementary School, assembly 4th, 5th, 6th graders, remarks/Q & A	12:00 noon	House convenes
(Travel Time: 1:45 p.m.–2:45 p.m.)		12:00 noon	Lunch with personal friend at Watergate Hotel
2:45 p.m.	Plainview Day Care facility owner wishes to discuss changes in federal law	1:30 p.m.	Subcommittee on Science Space Applications hearing
4:00 p.m.	Town Hall Meeting, American Legion	1:30 p.m.	Subcommittee on Health and Environment mark-up session on Trauma Care Systems Planning Act
(Travel Time: 5:00 p.m.–5:45 p.m.)			
5:45 p.m.	PTA meeting, speech, education issues before Congress (also citizen involvement with national associations)	3:00 p.m.	Meeting with officials of the National Alliance for Animal Legislation
6:30 p.m.	Annual Dinner, St. John's Lutheran Church Developmental Activity Center	4:30 p.m.	Meeting with delegates from American Jewish Congress on foreign aid bill
7:15 p.m.	Association for Children for Enforcement of Support meeting to discuss problems of enforcing child support payments	5:00 p.m.	New York University reception
		5:00 p.m.	Briefing by the commissioner of the Bureau of Labor (statistics on the uninsured)
(Travel Time: 8:00 p.m.–8:30 p.m.)		5:30 p.m.	Reception/fundraiser for party whip
8:30 p.m.	Students Against Drunk Driving (SADD) meeting, speech, address drinking age, drunk driving, uniform federal penalties	6:00 p.m.	Reception/fundraiser for fellow member
		6:00 p.m.	"Cajun" reception/fundraiser for Louisiana member
9:30 p.m.	State university class, discuss business issues before Congress	6:00 p.m.	Winetasting reception by New York wine industry
		8:00 p.m.	Back to Capitol Hill for a vote

[a]Craig Shultz, ed., *Setting Course: A Congressional Management Guide* (Washington, DC: American University, 1994), 335.
[b]http://congress.indiana.edu/learn_about/schedule.htm.

actually serve in the U.S. Congress. Membership in one of the two major political parties is almost always a prerequisite for election, because election laws in various states often discriminate against independents (those without party affiliation) and minor-party candidates.

Incumbency also helps members to stay in office once they are elected.[13] It's often very difficult for outsiders to win because they don't have the advantages enjoyed by incumbents, including name recognition, access to free media, the inside track on fund-raising, and districts drawn to favor their reelection.

As illustrated in Analyzing Visuals: Approval Ratings of Congress and Individual Representatives, most Americans approve of their own members of Congress. It is not surprising, then, that from 1980 to 1990, an average of 95 percent of the incumbents who sought reelection won their primary and general election races.[14] More recent elections saw even higher proportions of incumbents returning to office. One study basically concluded that unless a member of Congress was involved in a serious scandal, his or her chances of defeat were minimal.[15] In 2004, only seven members seeking reelection lost. Four were from Texas, where a redistricting plan forced several incumbents to run against each other.

Congressional Demographics

Congress is better educated, richer, more male, and more white than the rest of the United States. In fact, all but three senators are college graduates; 401 representatives share that honor. Over two-thirds of each body also holds advanced degrees.[16]

incumbency
The period during which a persion is in office; incumbency helps a person stay in elected office because of a variety of benefits that go with the position.

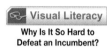
Visual Literacy
Why Is It So Hard to Defeat an Incumbent?

STILL THE BEST CONGRESSIONAL TERM-LIMITING DEVICE.

Analyzing Visuals

APPROVAL RATINGS OF CONGRESS AND INDIVIDUAL REPRESENTATIVES

For many years, political scientists have noted that approval ratings of Congress as an institution are generally quite low, rarely exceeding 50 percent approval. On the other hand, the public's approval rating of its own member tends to be much higher, usually above 50 percent. The line graph demonstrates the discrepancy between these ratings since 1990. After studying the graph and the material in this chapter on the incumbency advantage, answer the following critical thinking questions: Do the data for approval of Congress and approval of one's own representative follow similar trends over the period covered in the figure? What factors do you think account for the differences in the ratings of Congress and of one's own representative? What are the effects of the differences in these ratings?

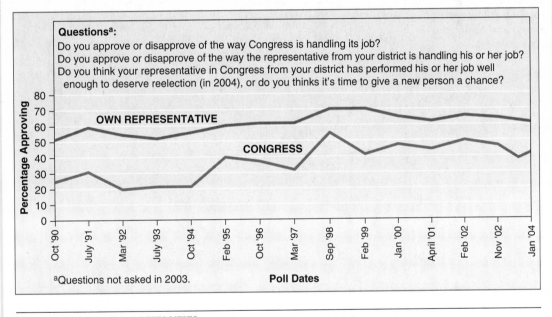

Questions[a]:
Do you approve or disapprove of the way Congress is handling its job?
Do you approve or disapprove of the way the representative from your district is handling his or her job?
Do you think your representative in Congress from your district has performed his or her job well enough to deserve reelection (in 2004), or do you thinks it's time to give a new person a chance?

[a]Questions not asked in 2003.

Source: Data derived from R-Poll, LEXIS/NEXIS.

One hundred seventy members of Congress are millionaires and it took a net worth of at least $3.1 million to be one of the top fifty richest members of Congress. The Senate, in fact, is often called the Millionaires Club and its members sport names including Rockefeller and Kennedy. Twenty-one senators are worth at least $3.1 million. Twenty-nine members of the House have a net worth over that amount.[17]

The average age of senators is sixty. The average age of House members is fifty-four. As revealed in Figure 6.3, the 1992 elections saw a record number of women, African Americans, and other minorities elected to Congress. By the 109th Congress, there were 68 women in the House and 14 in the Senate. In 2005, there were 42 African Americans in the House and one in the Senate. Although Hispanics now outnumber African Americans in the United States, there are but 28 Hispanics in the 109th Congress—26 of them serve in the House of Representatives and two in the Senate. All African Americans and the vast majority of Hispanics are Democrats.

Members of Congress no longer overwhelmingly are lawyers, although lawyers continue to be the largest single occupational group. In the 108th Congress, 275 were former state legislators and 111 were former congressional staffers. The number of veterans has continued to decline since the end of the Vietnam War.[18]

FIGURE 6.3 Numbers of Women and Minorities in Congress. ■

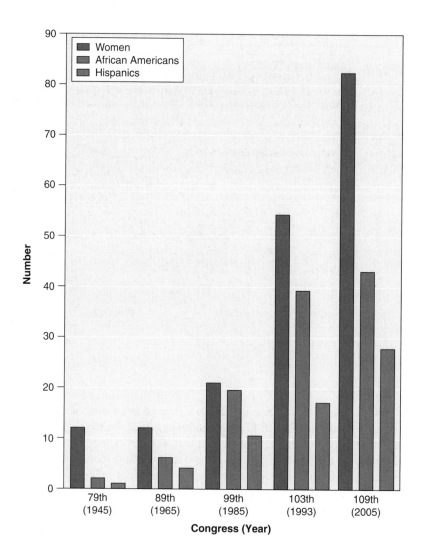

Theories of Representation

Over the years, political theorists have offered various ideas about how constituents' interests are best represented in any legislative body. British political philosopher Edmund Burke (1729–1797), who also served in the British Parliament, believed that although he was elected from Bristol, it was his duty to represent the interests of the entire nation. He reasoned that elected officials were obliged to vote as they personally thought best. According to Burke, representatives should be **trustees** who listen to the opinions of their constituents and then can be trusted to use their own best judgment to make final decisions.

A second theory of representation holds that representatives are **delegates.** True delegates are representatives who vote the way their constituents would want them to, whether or not those opinions are the representative's. Delegates, therefore, must be ready and willing to vote against their conscience or personal policy preferences if they know how their constituents feel about a particular issue. Not surprisingly, members of Congress and other legislative bodies generally don't fall neatly into either category. It is often unclear how constituents feel about a particular issue, or there may be conflicting opinions within a single constituency. With these difficulties in mind, a third theory of representation holds that **politicos** alternately don the hat of trustee or delegate, depending on the issue. On an issue of great concern to their constituents, representatives most likely will vote as delegates; on other issues, perhaps those that are less visible, representatives act as trustees and use their own best judgment.[19]

How a representative views his or her role—as a trustee, delegate, or politico—may still not answer the question of whether or not it makes a difference if a representative or senator is male or female, African American or Hispanic or Caucasian, young or old, gay or straight. Burke's ideas about representation don't even begin to address more practical issues of representation. Can a man, for example, represent the interests of women as well as a woman? Can a rich woman represent the interests of the poor? Are veterans more sensitive to veterans issues?

The actions of the lone Native American who served in the Senate until 2005 underscore the representative function that members play in Congress. Senator Ben Nighthorse Campbell (R–CO), for example, sat on the Committee on Indian Affairs. Earlier, as a member of the

trustee
Role played by elected representatives who listen to constituents' opinions and then use their best judgment to make final decisions.

delegate
Role played by elected representatives who vote the way their constituents would want them to, regardless of their own opinions.

politico
Role played by elected representatives who act as trustees or as delegates, depending on the issue.

■ Democrat Barack Obama (D–IL) on the campaign trail in 2004. Obama is the only African American serving in the Senate.
Photo courtesy: The Register Mail, Mia Algotti/AP/Wide World Photos

THE PARLIAMENT OF THE "UNITED STATES OF EUROPE"

The union of thirteen separate British colonies into the United States and the subsequent expansion into a country of fifty states spanning a continent and beyond is one of the amazing political stories of history. Today, another amazing political story is unfolding. In 1956, six countries in Western Europe—France, Italy, West Germany, Belgium, the Netherlands, and Luxembourg—came together to create the European Common Market. It was an economic union, not a political one, but virtually from the outset some political commentators saw in it the nucleus of a "United States of Europe." Still, for most observers, it was an inconceivable notion that many of the states of Europe, which had fought two long and brutal world wars in the twentieth century and then became the primary battleground for the Cold War, might overcome their differences and voluntarily and peacefully form a single country. Yet, this vision slowly appears to be becoming true.

The process of unification begun in 1956 has passed through several stages. A first expansion in membership occurred in 1973 when Denmark, Ireland, and Great Britain joined the then Common Market. Greece joined in 1981, and Spain and Portugal joined in 1986. In 1994 Austria, Finland, and Sweden became members. Enlargement reached a new milestone in May 2004 when ten new states joined what is today known as the European Union (EU). Even more significant

Distribution of Seats in the European Parliament			
Austria	21	Latvia	9
Belgium	25	Lithuania	13
Cyprus	6	Luxembourg	6
Czech Republic	24	Malta	4
Denmark	16	Netherlands	31
Estonia	6	Poland	54
Finland	16	Portugal	25
France	87	Slovakia	14
Germany	99	Slovenia	7
Greece	25	Spain	64
Hungary	24	Sweden	22
Ireland	15	United Kingdom	87
Italy	87		

than the number of states that joined (increasing membership from fifteen to twenty-five) or the overnight growth of its population (by 20 percent to 450 million) was the identity of the states that joined. Five of the ten were Eastern European states once ruled by communism: the Czech Republic, Slovenia, Slovakia, Poland, and Hungary. Three states had actually been part of the Soviet Union before it collapsed: Latvia, Estonia, and Lithuania. The other two were Malta and Cyprus. The EU was now truly becoming continental in scope and may continue to grow. Turkey hopes to be admitted in the near future, and another round of expansion is set for 2007.

As with the American experience, adding new states (countries) requires making a series of

Comparing Legislatures

House, he successfully fought for legislation to establish the National Museum of the American Indian on the Mall in Washington, D.C. New African American and Hispanic senators are expected to be similarly reactive to issues of racial importance.

HOW MEMBERS OF CONGRESS MAKE DECISIONS

AS A BILL MAKES ITS WAY through the law-making process, members are confronted with the question: "How should I vote?" Mem-

adjustments in how the EU is governed. One significant change was adjusting the size of the legislature, the European parliament. It had 140 members when first created in 1958. With this latest expansion, it now has 787 members. The distribution of seats by country is shown in the table.

Making the European parliament bigger was necessary to ensure that all of the countries belonging to the EU are fairly represented. To reach the goal of bringing the states of Europe together in a democracy, the EU had to answer questions such as the following.

- **How are members to be chosen?** The first answer given was that members should be appointed by their national parliaments. Beginning in 1979, members have been directly elected by the people.
- **Who can vote for members to the European parliament?** The voting age in all countries is eighteen. Even if you are not a citizen of the country you are living in, you may still vote in that country for members of the European parliament provided you are considered a resident of that country. Definitions of residence, however, vary greatly. So do rules governing the right of citizens living abroad to submit absentee ballots in their home country.
- **Who can run for a seat in the European parliament?** Age requirements vary from country to country, ranging from a low of eighteen to a high of twenty-five. Luxembourg also has a ten-year residency requirement.
- **When are elections held?** There is no single day for parliamentary elections. In 1999, the most frequent voting day was Sunday, June 13, but in four countries it was June 10 as Thursday is their traditional voting day.
- **How will the parliament be organized?** Members do not sit as part of country delegations but according to their political affiliation. Among the political groups that can be found in the European parliament are the European People's Party, the Party of European Socialists, the European Liberal Democratic Party, and the Reform Party.
- **How many committees should there be?** Members are assigned to seventeen committees as well as to a number of parliamentary delegations.

Questions

1. How does current and past U.S. experience compare to that of the European Union as to selecting members of the legislature and organizing the legislative body?
2. Would policy making in the United States be improved if Congress and the president worked as partners, rather than as separate, competing powers? Explain your answer.

bers adhere to their own personal beliefs on some matters, but their views often are moderated by other considerations. To avoid making any voting mistakes, members look to a variety of sources for cues.

Party

Members often look to party leaders for indicators of how to vote. Indeed, it is the whips' job in each chamber to reinforce the need for party cohesion, particularly on issues of concern to the party. From 1970 to the mid-1990s, the incidence of party votes in which majorities of

227

the two parties took opposing sides roughly doubled to more than 60 percent of all roll-call votes.[20]

Partisanship still reigns supreme in both houses of Congress. In the 107th Congress, for example, there was perfect party unity on all major votes taken in the House.[21] In the 108th Congress, Democratic senators demonstrated unanimity in filibustering several presidential judicial nominations to the U.S. Courts of Appeals. Although some charged that this was evidence not of party unity but instead of elected officials taking their direction from major liberal special interest groups, there can be no doubt that in both closely divided houses, party reigns supreme.[22]

divided government
The political condition in which different political parties control the White House and Congress.

With Republicans in control of both houses in recent Congresses, many critics charge that the two major parties have pressured their members to take increasingly partisan positions. Surprisingly, in times of **divided government,** when different political parties control the executive and legislative branches, most commentators have noted how rancorous law-making can get. Today, with Congress and the presidency controlled by one party, it seems as though things have only gotten worse.

Party loyalty is not the only reason members vote the way they do. Each party has committees in both houses of Congress that provide extraordinary campaign assistance in the form of funding, political and media consulting, and direct mailing. Members know that if they fail to go along with the party on major votes, they risk this critical campaign support. Similarly, both senators and representatives can be assisted in their reelection bids by having the president (if he is of the same party) or highly popular political leaders come to their states or districts to assist them in their electioneering activities.

Constituents

Constituents—the people who live and vote in the home district or state—are always in the member's mind when he or she is casting a vote.[23] It is rare for legislators to vote regularly against the wishes of their constituencies, particularly on issues of welfare rights, domestic policy, or other highly salient issues such as civil rights, abortion, or war. Most constituents often have strong convictions on one or more of these issues. But, gauging how voters feel about any particular issue often is not easy. Because it is virtually impossible to know how the folks back home feel on all issues, a representative's perception of their preferences is important. Even when voters have opinions, legislators may get little guidance if their district is narrowly divided.

Colleagues and Caucuses

The range and complexity of issues confronting Congress means that no one can be up to speed on more than a few topics. When members must vote on bills about which they know very little, they often turn to colleagues who have served on the committee that handled the legislation. On issues that are of little interest to a legislator, **logrolling,** or vote trading, often occurs. Logrolling frequently takes place on specialized bills targeting money or projects to selected congressional districts. An unaffected member often will exchange a yea vote for the promise of a future yea vote on a similar piece of specialized legislation.

Members may also look to other representatives who share common interests for voting cues. Special interest caucuses created around issues, home states, regions, congressional

Photo courtesy: Dennis Cook/AP/Wide World Photos

■ Melvin Watt, (D–NC) discusses his selection as the new chair of the Congressional Black Caucus at a news conference on Capitol Hill in December 2004. Watt succeeds Elijah Cummings (D–MD) at left.

logrolling
Vote trading; voting yea to support a colleague's bill in return for a promise of future support.

class, or other shared interests facilitate this communication. Prior to 1995, the power of these groups was even more evident, as several caucuses enjoyed formal status within the legislative body and were provided staff, office space, and budgets. Today, however, all caucuses are informal in nature, although some are far more organized than others. The Congressional Women's Caucus, for example, has formal elections of its Republican and Democratic co-chairs and vice chairs, provides staff members detailed to work on issues of common concern to caucus members, and meets regularly to urge its members to support legislation of interest to women.

Interest Groups, Lobbyists, and Political Action Committees

A primary function of most lobbyists, whether they work for interest groups, trade associations, or large corporations, is to provide information to supportive or potentially supportive legislators, committees, and their staffs.[24] Lobbyists and the corporate or other interests they represent, however, are also an important source of campaign contributions. The high cost of campaigning has made members of Congress, especially those without huge personal fortunes, attentive to those who help pay the tab for the high cost of many campaigns. Pressure groups also use grassroots appeals to pressure legislators by urging their members in a particular state or district to call, write, fax, or e-mail their senators or representatives.

They also air television ads supporting their positions. Lobbyists can't vote, but voters back home can and do, and they often respond to calls to lobby for or against particular bills. Many pressure groups also have political action committees to support the campaigns of friendly legislators.

Staff and Support Agencies

Members of Congress rely heavily on members of their staffs for information on pending legislation.[25] Not only do staff members meet regularly with staffers from other offices about proposed legislation or upcoming hearings, but they also prepare summaries of bills and brief members of Congress based on their research and meetings. Especially if a bill is nonideological or one on which the member has no real position, staff members can be very influential.

Congressional committees and subcommittees also have their own dedicated staff to assist committee members. Additional support for members comes from support personnel at the Congressional Budget Office, the Congressional Research Service at the Library of Congress, and the General Accountability Office.

THE LAW-MAKING FUNCTION OF CONGRESS

THE ORGANIZATION OF CONGRESS allows it to fulfill its constitutional responsibilities, chief among which is its law-making function. It is through this power that Congress affects the day-to-day lives of all Americans and sets policy for the future. Proposals for legislation can come from the president, executive agencies, committee staffs, interest groups, or even private individuals. Only members of the House or Senate, however, formally can submit a bill for congressional consideration. Once a bill is introduced by a member of Congress, it usually reaches a dead end. Of the approximately 9,000 or so bills introduced during any session of Congress, fewer than 10 percent are made into law.

How a Bill Becomes a Law

A bill must survive three stages before it becomes a law. It must be approved by one or more standing committees and both chambers, and, if House and Senate versions differ, each house must accept a conference report resolving those differences. A bill may be killed during any of these stages, so it is much easier to defeat a bill than it is to get one passed. The House and Senate have parallel processes, and often the same bill is introduced in each chamber at the same time.

A bill must be introduced by a member of Congress, but, in an attempt to show support for the aims of the bill, it is often sponsored by several other members (called co-sponsors).[26] Once introduced, the bill is sent to the clerk of the chamber, who gives it a number (for example, HR

You Are a Member of Congress

FIGURE 6.4 How a Bill Becomes a Law. ■

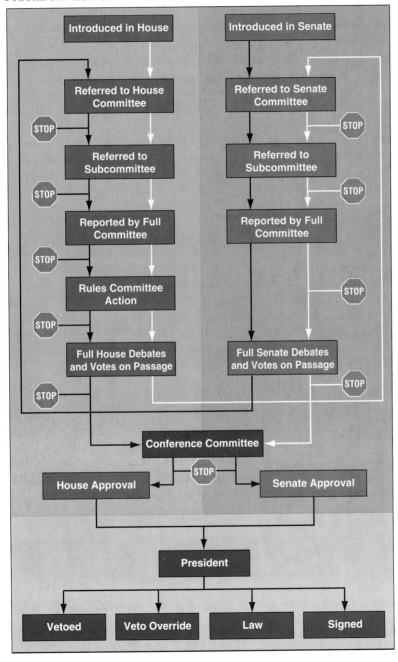

1 or S 1—indicating House or Senate bill number one for the Congress).
The bill is then printed, distributed, and sent by the majority party leadership to the appropriate committee or committees for consideration.

The committee usually refers the bill to one of its subcommittees, which researches the bill and decides whether to hold hearings on it. The subcommittee hearings provide the opportunity for those on both sides of the issue to voice their opinions. Most of these hearings are now open to the public because of the 1970s sunshine laws, which require open sessions. After the hearings, the bill is revised in subcommittee, and then the subcommittee votes to approve or defeat the bill. If the subcommittee votes in favor of the bill, it is returned to the full committee, which then either rejects the bill or sends it to the floor with a favorable recommendation (see Figure 6.4).

The second stage of action takes place on the House or Senate floor. As previously discussed, in the House, before a bill may be debated on the floor, it must be approved by the Rules Committee and given a rule and a place on the calendar, or schedule. (House budget bills don't go to the Rules Committee.) In the House, the rule given to a bill determines the limits on the floor debate and specifies what types of amendments, if any, may be attached to the bill. Once the Rules Committee considers the bill, it is put on the calendar.

When the day arrives for floor debate, the House may choose to form a Committee of the Whole. To expedite consideration of the bill, this allows deliberation with only one hundred members present. Then, the bill is debated, amendments are offered, and a vote is taken by the full House. If the bill passes, it is sent to the Senate for consideration if it was not considered there simultaneously.

Unlike the House, where debate is necessarily limited, given the size of the body, bills may be held up by a hold or a filibuster in the Senate. A **hold** is a tactic by which a senator asks to be informed before a particular bill is brought to the floor. This request signals the Senate leadership and the sponsors of the bill that a colleague may have objections to the bill and should be consulted before further action is taken.

Filibusters, which allow for unlimited debate on a bill (or on presidential appointments), grew out of the absence of rules to limit speech in the Senate. In contrast to a hold, a filibuster is a more formal and public way of halting action on a bill. There are no rules on the content of a filibuster as long as a senator keeps on talking. A senator may read from a phone book, recite poetry, or read cookbooks in order to delay a vote. Often, a team of senators will take turns speaking to keep the filibuster going in the hope that a bill will be tabled or killed. In 1964, for example, a group of northern liberal senators continued a filibuster for eighty-two days in an effort to prevent amendments that would weaken a civil rights bill. Filibusters often are more of a threat than an actual event on the Senate floor, although they are becoming more frequent.

There is only one way to end a filibuster. Sixteen senators must sign a motion for **cloture.** This motion requires the votes of sixty members to limit debate; after a cloture motion passes the Senate floor, members may spend no more than thirty additional hours debating the legislation at issue.

hold
A tactic by which a senator asks to be informed before a particular bill is brought to the floor. This stops the bill from coming to the floor until the hold is removed.

filibuster
A formal way of halting action on a bill by means of long speeches or unlimited debate in the Senate.

cloture
Mechanism requiring sixty senators to vote to cut off debate.

The third stage of action takes place when the two chambers of Congress approve different versions of the same bill. When this happens, they establish a conference committee to iron out the differences between the two versions. The conference committee, whose members are from the original House and Senate committees, hammers out a compromise, which is returned to each chamber for a final vote. Sometimes the conference committee fails to agree and the bill dies there. No changes or amendments to the compromise version are allowed. If the bill is passed, it is sent to the president, who either signs it or vetoes it. If the bill is not passed in both houses, it dies.

The president has ten days to consider a bill. He has four options:

1. He can sign the bill, at which point it becomes law.
2. He can veto the bill, which is more likely to occur when the president is of a different party from the majority in Congress.
3. He can wait the full ten days, at the end of which time the bill becomes law without his signature if Congress is still in session.
4. If the Congress adjourns before the ten days are up, he can choose not to sign the bill, and it is considered "pocket vetoed."

A **pocket veto** allows bills figuratively stashed in the president's pocket to die. To become law, the bill would have to be reintroduced in the next session and go through the process all over again. Because Congress sets its own date of adjournment, technically the session could be continued the few extra days necessary to prevent a pocket veto. Extensions are unlikely, however, as sessions are scheduled to adjourn close to the November elections or the December holidays.

pocket veto
If Congress adjourns during the ten days the president has to consider a bill passed by both houses of Congress, without the president's signature, the bill is considered vetoed.

CONGRESS AND THE PRESIDENT

THE CONSTITUTION ENVISIONED that the Congress and the president would have discrete powers and that one branch would be able to hold the other in check. Over the years, and especially since the 1930s, the president often has held the upper hand. In times of crisis or simply when it was unable to meet public demands for solutions, Congress willingly has handed over its authority to the chief executive. However, legislators retain ultimate legislative authority to question executive actions and to halt administration activities by cutting off funds. Congress also wields ultimate power over the president, since it can impeach and even remove him from office.

The Shifting Balance of Power

The balance of power between Congress and the executive branch has seesawed over time. Today, Congress often finds itself responding to executive branch proposals. Critics of Congress point to its slow and unwieldy nature as well as the complexity of national problems as reasons that Congress often doesn't seem to act on its own.

Congressional Oversight of the Executive Branch

oversight
Congressional review of the activities of an agency, department, or office.

Since the 1960s, Congress has increased its **oversight** of the executive branch.[27] Oversight subcommittees became particularly prominent in the 1970s and 1980s as a means of promoting investigation and program review, to determine if an agency, department, or office is carrying out its responsibilities as intended by Congress.[28] Congressional oversight also includes checking on possible abuses of power by members of the military and governmental officials, including the president.

Key to Congress's performance of its oversight function is its ability to question members of the administration to see if they are enforcing and interpreting the laws as intended by Congress. These committee hearings, now routinely televised, are among Congress's most visible and dramatic actions.

These hearings are not used simply to gather information. Hearings may focus on particular executive branch actions and often signal that Congress believes changes in policy need to be made before an agency next comes before the committee to justify its budget. Hearings also are used to improve program administration. Since most members of House and Senate committees and subcommittees are interested in the issues under their jurisdiction, they often want to help and not hinder policy makers.

congressional review
A process whereby Congress can nullify agency regulations by a joint resolution of legislative disapproval.

Legislators augment their formal oversight of the executive branch by allowing citizens to appeal adverse bureaucratic decisions to agencies, Congress, and even the courts. The Congressional Review Act of 1996 allows Congress to nullify agency regulations by joint resolutions of legislative disapproval. This process, called **congressional review,** is another method of exercising congressional oversight.[29] The act provides Congress with sixty days to disapprove newly announced agency regulations, often passed to implement some congressional action. A regulation is disapproved if the resolution is passed by both chambers and signed by the president, or when Congress overrides a presidential veto of a disapproving resolution.

Foreign Affairs Oversight.   The Constitution divides foreign policy powers between the executive and the legislative branches. The president has the power to wage war and negotiate treaties, whereas the Congress has the power to declare war and the Senate has the power to ratify treaties. The executive branch, however, has become preeminent in foreign affairs despite the constitutional division of powers. This supremacy is partly due to a series of crises and the development of nuclear weapons in the twentieth century; both have necessitated quick decision making and secrecy, which are much easier to manage in the executive branch. Congress, with its 535 members, has a more difficult time reaching a consensus and keeping secrets.

After years of playing second fiddle to a series of presidents from Theodore Roosevelt to Richard M. Nixon, a "snoozing Congress" was "aroused" and seized for itself the authority and expertise necessary to go head-to-head with the chief executive.[30] In a delayed response to Lyndon B. Johnson's conduct of the Vietnam War, Congress passed in 1973 the **War Powers Act** over President Nixon's veto. This act requires presidents to obtain congressional approval before committing U.S. forces to a combat zone. It also requires them to notify Congress within forty-eight hours of committing troops to foreign soil. In addition, the president must withdraw troops within sixty days unless Congress votes to declare war. The president also is required to consult with Congress, if at all possible, prior to committing troops.

The War Powers Act has been of limited effectiveness in claiming a larger congressional role in international crisis situations. Presidents Gerald Ford, Jimmy Carter, and Ronald Reagan never consulted Congress in advance of committing troops, citing the need for secrecy

Photo courtesy: © Larry Downing/Reuters/Corbis

and swift movement, although each president did notify Congress shortly after the incidents. They contended that the War Powers Act was probably unconstitutional because it limits presidential prerogatives as commander in chief. In late 2001, when Congress passed a joint resolution authorizing the president to use force against terrorists, the resolution included language that met War Powers Act requirements and waived the sixty-day limit on the president's authority to involve U.S. troops abroad.

Confirmation of Presidential Appointments.

The Senate plays a special oversight function through its ability to confirm key members of the executive branch, as well as presidential appointments to the federal courts. As discussed in chapters 8 and 9, although the Senate generally confirms most presidential nominees, it does not always do so. A wise president considers senatorial reaction before nominating potentially controversial individuals to his administration or to the federal courts. In the case of federal district court appointments, senators often

■ Condoleezza Rice testifies before the U.S. Senate Foreign Relations Committee during her confirmation hearing to become Secretary of State. The often heated questioning in January of 2005 was fully televised and created such sparring between Rice and some Democratic senators that it was even parodied in a skit on *Saturday Night Live*.

War Powers Act
Passed by Congress in 1973; the president is limited in the deployment of troops overseas to a sixty-day period in peacetime (which can be extended for an extra thirty days to permit withdrawal) unless Congress explicitly gives its approval for a longer period.

TABLE 6.4   The Eight Stages of the Impeachment Process

---

1. **The Resolution.** A resolution, called an inquiry of impeachment, is sent to the House Judiciary Committee. Members also may introduce bills of impeachment, which are referred to the Judiciary Committee.
2. **The Committee Vote.** After the consideration of voluminous evidence, the Judiciary Committee votes on the resolution or bill of impeachment. A positive vote from the committee indicates its belief that there is sufficiently strong evidence for impeachment in the House.
3. **The House Vote.** If the articles of impeachment are recommended by the House Judiciary Committee, the full House votes to approve (or disapprove) a Judiciary Committee decision to conduct full-blown impeachment hearings.
4. **The Hearings.** Extensive evidentiary hearings are held by the House Judiciary Committee concerning the allegations of wrongdoing. Witnesses may be called and the scope of the inquiry may be widened at this time. The committee heard only from the independent counsel in the case of President Bill Clinton.
5. **The Report.** The committee votes on one or more articles of impeachment. Reports supporting this finding (as well as dissenting views) are forwarded to the House and become the basis for its consideration of specific articles of impeachment.
6. **The House Vote.** The full House votes on each article of impeachment. A simple majority vote on any article is sufficient to send that article to the Senate for its consideration.
7. **The Trial in the Senate.** A trial is conducted on the floor of the Senate with the House Judiciary Committee bringing the case against the president, who is represented by his own private attorneys. The Senate, in essence, acts as the jury, with the chief justice of the United States presiding over the trial.
8. **The Senate Vote.** The full Senate votes on each article of impeachment. If there is a two-thirds vote on any article, the president automatically is removed from office and the vice president assumes the duty of the president. Both articles issued against President Clinton, charging him with lying to a grand jury and encouraging a grand jury witness to lie or mislead, were defeated in the Senate.

---

senatorial courtesy
A process by which presidents, when selecting district court judges, defer to the senator in whose state the vacancy occurs.

have a considerable say in the nomination of judges from their states through what is called **senatorial courtesy,** a process by which presidents generally defer selection of district court judges to the choice of senators of their own party who represent the state in which a vacancy occurs.

The Impeachment Process.

As discussed earlier, the impeachment process is Congress's ultimate oversight of the president and of federal court judges. The Constitution is quite vague about the impeachment process, and much of the debate about it concerns what is an impeachable offense. The Constitution specifies that a president can be impeached for treason, bribery, or other "high crimes and misdemeanors." Most commentators agree that this phrase was meant to mean significant abuses of power. In *Federalist No. 65,* Alexander Hamilton noted his belief that impeachable offenses "are of a nature which may with peculiar propriety be denominated political, as they relate chiefly to injuries done immediately to society itself."

House and Senate rules control how the impeachment process operates. (See Table 6.4.) Yet, because the process is used so rarely, and under such disparate circumstances, there are few hard and fast rules. Until 1998, the House had voted to impeach only sixteen federal officials—and only one of those was a president, Andrew Johnson. (Of those, seven were convicted and removed from office and three resigned before the process described above was completed.) Four articles of impeachment against President Bill Clinton were considered in the

House; two of these were sent to the Senate, where the president was found not guilty of the charges contained in both articles.

CONGRESS AND THE JUDICIARY

CONGRESS EXERCISES ITS CONTROL over the judiciary in a variety of ways. It has the constitutional authority to establish the size of the Supreme Court and the structure of the federal court system, and the Senate has the authority to accept or reject presidential nominees to the federal courts. Congress also has the authority to set appellate jurisdiction. Originally, the jurisdiction, or ability of the federal courts to hear cases, was quite limited. Over time, however, as Congress legislated to regulate the economy and even crime, the caseload of the courts skyrocketed.

In 2004, several members of Congress, unhappy by Supreme Court decisions, and even the U.S. Senate's failure to pass a proposed constitutional amendment to ban same-sex marriage, began to push for a bill to prevent federal courts from hearing challenges to the federal Defense of Marriage Act. In the House, the majority leader pledged to promote similar legislation to bar court challenges to the Pledge of Allegiance and other social issues, including abortion. When Congress rears the ugly head of jurisdiction, it is signaling to the federal courts that Congress believes federal judges have gone too far. So, while individual judges can be removed by congressional impeachment, a very cumbersome process, the jurisdiction of all of the federal courts can be expanded or contracted by Congress, at will. Contraction, however, tends to be viewed as merely a threat because it happens so rarely.

SUMMARY

THE SIZE AND SCOPE OF CONGRESS, and demands put on it, have increased tremendously over the years. The Constitution created a bicameral legislature with members of each body to be elected differently, and thus to represent different constituencies. Article I of the Constitution sets forth qualifications for office, states age minimums, and specifies how legislators are to be distributed among the states. The Constitution also requires seats in the House of Representatives to be apportioned by population. The Constitution provides a vast array of enumerated and implied powers to Congress. Some, such as law-making and oversight, are shared by each house of Congress; others are not.

Political parties play a major role in the way Congress is organized. The speaker of the House, the most powerful person in Congress, is traditionally a member of the majority party, and members of the majority party chair all committees. In addition to the party leaders, Congress has a labyrinth of committees and subcommittees that cover the entire range of government policies, often with a confusing tangle of shared responsibilities. Each legislator serves on one or more committees and multiple subcommittees. Most business of Congress is done in committees.

Incumbency is an important factor in winning reelection—as is the kind of representation a member or senator provides to his or her district. A multitude of factors impinge on legislators as they decide policy issues. These include political party, constituents, colleagues and caucuses, interest groups, lobbyists, political action committees, and staff and support agencies.

The road to enacting a bill into law is long and strewn with obstacles, and only a small share of the proposals introduced become law. Legislation must be approved by committees in each house and on the floor of each chamber. Legislation that is passed in different forms by the two chambers must be resolved in a conference before going back to each chamber for a vote and then to the president, who can sign the proposal into law, veto it, or allow it to become law without his signature.

Although the Framers intended for Congress and the president to have discrete spheres of authority, over time, power shifted between the two branches, with Congress often appearing to lose power to the benefit of the president. Still, Congress has attempted to oversee the actions of the president and the executive branch through legislative oversight. Congress also uses congressional review to limit presidential power. Congress also has attempted to rein in presidential power through passage of the War Powers Act, to little practical effect. Congress, through the Senate, possesses the power to confirm or reject presidential appointments. Its ultimate weapon is the power of impeachment and conviction.

Congress exercises its control over the judiciary in a variety of ways. It has the constitutional authority to establish the size of the Supreme Court and the structure of the federal court system. The Senate has the authority to accept or reject presidential nominees to the federal courts. And, Congress can set appellate jurisdiction.

KEY TERMS

apportionment, p. 206
bicameral legislature, p. 205
bill, p. 206
cloture, p. 232
conference committees, p. 218
congressional review, p. 234
delegate, p. 225
discharge petition, p. 219
divided government, p. 228
filibuster, p. 232
hold, p. 232
impeachment, p. 208
incumbency, p. 222
joint committees, p. 218
logrolling, p. 229
majority leader, p. 210
majority party, p. 210
minority leader, p. 210
minority party, p. 210
oversight, p. 234
party caucus or conference, p. 210
pocket veto, p. 233
politico, p. 225
pork, p. 219
redistricting, p. 206
select (or special) committees, p. 218
senatorial courtesy, p. 236
seniority, p. 220
speaker of the House, p. 210
standing committees, p. 218
trustee, p. 225
War Powers Act, p. 235
whip, p. 210

SELECTED READINGS

Bianco, William T., ed. *Congress on Display, Congress at Work.* Ann Arbor: University of Michigan Press, 2000.

Campbell, Colton C., and Paul S. Herrnson. *War Stories from Capitol Hill.* New York: Pearson, 2003.

Davidson, Roger H., and Walter Oleszek. *Congress and Its Members,* 9th ed. Washington, DC: CQ Press, 2003.

Deering, Christopher J., and Steven S. Smith, *Committees in Congress,* 3rd ed. Washington, DC: CQ Press, 1997.

Dodd, Lawrence C., and Bruce I. Oppenheimer, eds. *Congress Reconsidered,* 7th ed. Washington, DC: CQ Press, 2000.

Fenno, Richard F., Jr. *Going Home: Black Representatives and Their Constituents.* Chicago: University of Chicago Press, 2003.

Fenno, Richard F., Jr. *Home Style: House Members in Their Districts,* reprint ed. New York: Longman, 2002.

Gertzog, Irwin N. *Women and Power on Capitol Hill: Recon-structing the Congressional Women's Caucus.* Boulder, CO: Lynne Rienner, 2004.

Hibbing, John R., and Elizabeth Theiss-Morse. *Congress as Public Enemy: Public Attitudes Toward American Political Institutions.* New York: Cambridge University Press, 1996.

King, David C. *Turf Wars: How Congressional Committees Claim Jurisdiction.* Chicago: University of Chicago Press, 1997.

Mayhew, David R. *Congress: The Electoral Connection.* New Haven, CT: Yale University Press, 1974.

Oleszek, Walter J. *Congressional Procedures and the Policy Process,* 6th ed. Washington, DC: CQ Press, 2004.

Polsby, Nelson W. *How Congress Evolves: Social Bases of Institutional Changes.* New York: Oxford University Press, 2003.

Price, David E. *The Congressional Experience: A View from the Hill,* 2nd ed. Boulder, CO: Westview, 2000.

Rosenthal, Cindy Simon, ed. *Women Transforming Congress.* Norman: University of Oklahoma Press, 2003.

Schickler, Eric. *Disjointed Pluralism: Institutional Innova-tion and the Development of the U.S. Congress.* Princeton, NJ: Princeton University Press, 2001.

Swers, Michele. *The Difference Women Make: The Policy Impact of Women in Congress.* Chicago: University of Chicago Press, 2002.

Thurber, James A. ed. *Rivals for Power: Congressional Pres-idential Relations.* Lanham, MD: Rowman and Little-field, 2001.

WEB EXPLORATIONS

To find out who your representative is and how he or she votes, see
http://www.thomas.loc.gov

To learn more about the legislative branch, see
www.senate.gov/
www.house.gov/

To evaluate your own representative, see
http://scorecard.aclu.org/scorecardmain.html

To learn more about the 109th Congress, see
http://clerk.house.gov/

For more on the offices of the Congress, including the speaker of the House and his activities, see
http://speakernews.house.gov/

To get up-to-date data on House leaders, see
http://tomdelay.house.gov/ and
http://democraticleader.house.gov/

For information on specific committees, see
www.senate.gov/
www.house.gov/

7

The Presidency

Photo courtesy: Dennis Brack

WHEN RONALD REAGAN DIED on June 5, 2004, many Americans were able to see, for the first time in recent memory, the grandeur of a presidential state funeral. Americans first in California, and then in Washington, D.C., lined up for hours to pay their respects to the fortieth president of the United States. Reagan was the first president to lie in state in the Rotunda of the Capitol since Lyndon B. Johnson did in January, 1973, and one of only nine American presidents to do so.

The 200 plus years of presidential funerals underscore the esteem with which most Americans accord the office of the president, regardless of its occupant. Just before the first president, George Washington, died, he made it known that he wanted his burial to be a quiet one, "without parade or funeral oration." He also asked that he not be buried for three days; at that time, it was not without precedent to make this kind of request out of fear of being buried alive. Despite these requests, Washington's funeral was a state occasion as hundreds of soldiers, with their rifles held backward, marched to Mount Vernon, Virginia, where he was interred.[1]

When Abraham Lincoln died in 1865 after being wounded by an assassin's bullet, more than a dozen funerals were held for him. Hundreds of thousands of mourners lined the way as the train carrying his open casket traveled the 1,700 miles to Illinois, where he was buried next to the body of his young son, who had died three years earlier. Most presidents' bodies were transported to their final resting place by train, thus allowing ordinary Americans the opportunity to pay their respects as trains traveled long distances. When Franklin D. Roosevelt died in Warm Springs, Georgia, his body was transported to Washington, D.C., and then to Hyde Park, New York, where he, like Washington, was buried on his family's estate.

One of the first things that a president is asked to do upon taking office is to consider his funeral plans. The military alone has a book 138 pages long devoted to the kind of ceremony and traditions that were so evident in the Reagan funeral: a horse-drawn caisson; a riderless horse with boots hung backward in the stirrups to indicate that the deceased will ride no more; a twenty-one-gun salute; a flyover by military aircraft.

The Reagan funeral also created a national timeout from the news of war, and even presidential campaigns were halted in respect for the deceased president. Said one historian, the event gave Americans the opportunity to "rediscover...what holds us together instead of what pulls out apart."[2] This is often the role of presidents, in life or in death.

THE AUTHORITY GRANTED TO THE PRESIDENT by the U.S. Constitution and through subsequent congressional legislation makes it a position with awesome responsibility. The Framers could not possibly have envisioned such a powerful role for the president, nor could they have foreseen the skepticism with which many presidential actions are now greeted in the press, on talk radio, and on the Internet. Presidents have gone into policy arenas never dreamed of by the Framers. Imagine, for example, what the Framers might have thought about President Bush's 2004 State of the Union message, which advocated colonizing Mars and addressed steroid use.

The modern media, used by successful presidents to help advance their agendas, have brought us closer to our presidents and made them seem more human, a mixed blessing for those trying to lead. Only two photographs exist of Franklin D. Roosevelt in a wheelchair—his paralysis was a closely guarded secret. Five decades later, Bill Clinton was asked on national TV what kind of underwear he preferred (briefs). Later, revelations about his conduct with Monica Lewinsky made this exchange seem tame. This demystifying of the president and increased mistrust of government make governing a difficult job.

A president relies on more than the formal powers of office to lead the nation: public opinion and public confidence are key components of his ability to get his programs adopted and his vision of the nation implemented. As political scientist Richard E. Neustadt has noted, the president's power often rests on his power to persuade.[3] To persuade, he not only must be able to forge links with members of Congress, but he also must have the support of the American people and the respect of foreign leaders.

The abilities to persuade and to marshal the informal powers of the presidency have become more important over time. In fact, the presidency of George W. Bush and the circumstances that surround it are dramatically different from the presidency of his father (1989–1993). America is changing dramatically and so are the responsibilities of the president and people's expectations of the person who holds that office. Presidents in the last century battled the Great Depression, fascism, communism, and several wars involving American soldiers. With the Cold War over, until September 11, 2001, there were few chances for modern presidents to demonstrate their leadership in a time of crisis or threat.

The tension between public expectations about the presidency and the formal powers of the president permeate our discussion of how the office has evolved from its humble origins in Article II of the Constitution to its current stature. First, we will examine the roots of and rules governing the office of president of the United States and the constitutional powers of the president. We will then examine the development and expansion of presidential power and a more personalized presidency. After discussing the development of the presidential establishment, we will focus on the president as policy maker. Finally, we will examine presidential leadership and the importance of public opinion.

THE ROOTS OF AND RULES GOVERNING THE OFFICE OF PRESIDENT OF THE UNITED STATES

LIKE MANY OF AMERICA'S POLITICAL INSTITUTIONS, the roots of the presidency date back to the Constitutional Convention. The delegates there quickly decided to dispense with the Articles of Confederation and fashion a new government composed of three branches: the legislative (to make the laws), the executive (to execute, or implement, the laws), and the judicial (to interpret the laws). The Framers had little difficulty in agreeing that executive authority should be vested in one person, although some delegates suggested multiple executives to diffuse the power of the executive branch. Under the Articles of Confederation, there had been no executive branch of government; the eighteen different men who served as the president of the Continental Congress of the United States of America were president in name only—they had no actual authority or power in the new nation. Yet, because the Framers were so sure that George Washington—whom they had trusted with their lives during the Revolutionary War—would become the first president of the new nation, many of their deepest fears were calmed. They agreed on the necessity of having one individual speak on behalf of the new nation, and they all agreed that this one individual should be George Washington.

The manner of the president's election haunted the Framers for some time, and their solution to the dilemma—the creation of the Electoral College—is described in detail in chapter 12. We leave the resolution of that issue aside for now and turn instead to details of the issues the Framers resolved quickly.

Photo courtesy: Ken James/UPI/Landov

Presidential Qualifications and Terms of Office

The Constitution requires that the president (and the vice president, whose major function is to succeed the president in the event of his death or disability) be a natural-born citizen of the United States, at least thirty-five years old, and a resident of the United States for at least fourteen years.

At one time, the length of a president's term was controversial. Four-, seven-, and eleven-year terms with no eligibility for reelection were suggested by various delegates to the Constitutional Convention. The Framers ultimately reached agreement on a four-year term with eligibility for reelection. In the 1930s and 1940s, Franklin D. Roosevelt ran successfully in four elections as Americans fought first the Great Depression and then World War II. Despite Roosevelt's popularity, negative reaction to his long tenure in office ultimately led to passage (and ratification in 1951) of the **Twenty-Second Amendment,** which limits presidents to two four-year terms. A vice president who succeeds a president because of death, resignation, or impeachment is eligible for a total of ten years in office: two years of a president's remaining term and two elected terms.

Removal from Office

During the Constitutional Convention, Benjamin Franklin was a staunch supporter of including a provision allowing for **impeachment,** a process by which to begin to remove an official from office. He noted that "historically, the lack of power to impeach had necessitated

■ The election of Arnold Schwarzenegger as governor of California, as well as that of Jennifer Granholm in Michigan, brought forward again the debate about whether presidents must be natural-born citizens. Many people argue that because the United States is a nation of immigrants, all citizens should have the opportunity to become president.

Twenty-Second Amendment
Adopted in 1951, prevents a president from serving more than two terms or more than ten years in office.

impeachment
The power delegated to the House of Representatives in the Constitution to charge the president, vice president, or other "civil officers," including federal judges, with "Treason, Bribery, or other high Crimes and Misdemeanors." This is the first step in the constitutional process of removing such government officials from office.

recourse to assassination."[4] Not surprisingly, then, he urged the rest of the delegates to formulate a legal mechanism to remove the president and vice president.

The impeachment provision ultimately included in Article II was adopted as a check on the power of the president. As discussed in detail in chapter 6, each house of Congress was given a role to play in the impeachment process to assure that the chief executive could be removed only for "Treason, Bribery, or other high Crimes and Misdemeanors."

The House is empowered to vote to impeach the president by a simple majority vote. The Senate then acts as a court of law and tries the president for the charged offenses. A two-thirds majority vote in the Senate on any count contained in the articles of impeachment is necessary to remove the president from office.

In 1974, President Richard M. Nixon resigned from office rather than face the certainty of impeachment, trial, and removal from office for his role in covering up details about a break-in at the Democratic Party's national headquarters in the Watergate office complex. What came to be known simply as Watergate also produced a major decision from the Supreme Court on the scope of what is termed **executive privilege,** the presidential power to withhold information. In *U.S. v. Nixon* **(1974),** the Supreme Court ruled unanimously that there was no overriding executive privilege that sanctioned the president's refusal to comply with a court order to produce information for use in the trial of the Watergate defendants.

executive privilege
An assertion of presidential power that reasons that the president can withhold information requested by the courts in matters relating to his office.

U.S. v. Nixon (1974)
The Supreme Court ruled that there is no constitutional absolute executive privilege that would allow a president to refuse to comply with a court order to produce information needed in a criminal trial.

Rules of Succession

Through 2005, eight presidents have died in office from illness or assassination. The Framers were aware that a system of orderly transfer of power was necessary; this was the primary reason they created the office of the vice president. To further clarify the order of presidential succession, in 1947, Congress passed the Presidential Succession Act, which lists—in order—those in line (after the vice president) to succeed the president:

1. Speaker of the House of Representatives
2. President pro tempore of the Senate
3. Secretaries of state, treasury, and defense, and other Cabinet heads in order of the creation of their department

Twenty-Fifth Amendment
Adopted in 1967 to establish procedures for filling vacancies in the office of president and vice president as well as providing for procedures to deal with the disability of a president.

The Succession Act has never been used because there has always been a vice president to take over when a president died in office. The **Twenty-Fifth Amendment,** in fact, was added to the Constitution in 1967 to assure that this will continue to be the case. Should a vacancy

The Living Constitution

Whenever there is a vacancy in the office of the Vice President, the President shall nominate a Vice President who shall take office upon confirmation by a majority vote of both Houses of Congress.
—Twenty-Fifth Amendment, Section 2

This clause of the Twenty-Fifth Amendment allows a president to fill a vacancy in the office of vice president by a simple majority of both Houses of Congress. The purpose of this amendment, which also deals with vacancies in the office of the president, was to remedy some structural flaws in Article II. At the time of this amendment's addition to the Constitution in 1965, seven vice presidents had died in office and one had resigned. For over 20 percent of the nation's history there had been no vice president to assume the office of the president in case of his death or infirmity. When John F. Kennedy was assassinated, Vice President Lyndon B. Johnson became president and the office of vice president was vacant. Since Johnson had suffered a heart attack as vice president, members of Congress were anxious to remedy the problems that might occur should there be no vice president.

Richard M. Nixon followed Johnson as president, and ironically, during Nixon's presidency, the office of the vice president became empty twice! First, his first vice president, Spiro T. Agnew, was forced to resign amid allegations of illegal activity as a county executive in Maryland; he was replaced by popular House Minority Leader Gerald R. Ford (R–MI), who had no trouble getting a majority vote in both houses of Congress to confirm his nomination. When Nixon resigned rather than face sure impeachment, Ford became president and selected the former governor of New York, Nelson A. Rockefeller, to be his vice president.

occur in the office of the vice president, the Twenty-Fifth Amendment directs the president to appoint a new vice president, subject to the approval (by a simple majority) of both houses of Congress (see The Living Constitution).

THE CONSTITUTIONAL POWERS OF THE PRESIDENT

Simulation

Presidential Leadership: Which Hat Do You Wear?

THOUGH THE FRAMERS NEARLY UNANIMOUSLY agreed about the need for a strong central government and a greatly empowered Congress, they did not agree about the proper role of the president or the sweep of his authority. In contrast to Article I's laundry list of enumerated powers for the Congress, Article II details few presidential powers. Perhaps the most important section of Article II is its first sentence: "The executive Power shall be vested in a President of the United States of America." Nonetheless, the sum total of his presidential powers, enumerated below, allows him to become a major player in the policy process.

The Appointment Power

To help the president enforce laws passed by Congress, the Constitution authorizes him to appoint, with the advice and consent of the Senate, "Ambassadors, other public Ministers and Consuls, judges of the supreme Court, and all other Officers of the United States, whose Appointments are not herein otherwise provided for, and which shall be established by Law." Although this section of the Constitution deals only with appointments, behind that language is a powerful policy-making tool. The president has the authority to make more than 6,000 appointments to his administration (of which 1,125 require Senate confirmation), and he technically appoints more than 75,000 military personnel.[5] Many of these appointees are in positions to wield substantial authority over the course and direction of public policy. Although Congress has the authority "to make all laws," through the president's enforcement power—and his chosen assistants—he often can set the policy agenda for the nation. And, especially in the context of his ability to make appointments to the federal courts, his influence can be felt far past his term of office.

It is not surprising, then, that selecting the right people is often one of a president's most important tasks. Presidents look for a blend of loyalty, competence, and integrity. Identifying these qualities in people is a major challenge that every new president faces. Recent presidents have made an effort to make their Cabinets and staffs look "more like America" (see Table 7.1).

In the past, when a president forwarded a nomination to the Senate for its approval, his selections traditionally were given great respect—especially those for the **Cabinet,** an advisory group selected by the president to help him make decisions and execute the laws. In fact, until the Clinton administration, the vast majority (97 percent) of all presidential nominations were confirmed.[6]

Cabinet

The formal body of presidential advisers who head the fourteen executive departments. Presidents often add others to this body of formal advisers.

TABLE 7.1	Presidential Teams (Senior Administrative Positions Requiring Senate Confirmation)		
	Total Appointments	Total Women	Percentage Women
Jimmy Carter	1,087	191	17.6%
Ronald Reagan	2,349	277	11.8%
George Bush	1,079	215	19.9%
Bill Clinton	1,257	528	42%
George W. Bush	862[a]	182	21%

[a] As of June 2002.

Sources: "Insiders Say White House Has Its Own Glass Ceiling," *Atlanta Journal and Constitution* (April 10, 1995): A4; and Judi Hasson, "Senate GOP Leader Lott Says He'll Work with Clinton," *USA Today* (December 4, 1996): 8A.

The Power to Convene Congress

The Constitution requires the president to inform the Congress periodically of "the State of the Union," and authorizes the president to convene either or both houses of Congress on "extraordinary Occasions." In *Federalist No. 77*, Hamilton justified the latter by noting that because the Senate and the chief executive enjoy concurrent powers to make treaties, "It might often be necessary to call it together with a view to this object, when it would be unnecessary and improper to convene the House of Representatives." The power to convene Congress was important when Congress did not sit in nearly year-round sessions. Today, this power has little more than symbolic significance.

The Power to Make Treaties

The president's power to make treaties with foreign nations is checked by the Constitution's stipulation that all treaties must be approved by at least two-thirds of the members of the Senate. The chief executive can also "receive ambassadors," wording that has been interpreted to allow the president to recognize the very existence of other nations.

The Senate may require substantial amendment of a treaty prior to its consent. When President Jimmy Carter proposed the controversial Panama Canal Treaty in 1977 to turn the canal over to Panama, for example, the Senate required several conditions to be ironed out between the United States and Panama before approving it.

Presidents often try to get around the "advice and consent" requirement for ratification of treaties and the congressional approval required for trade agreements by entering into an **executive agreement,** which allows the president to enter into secret and highly sensitive arrangements with foreign nations without Senate approval. Presidents have used these agreements since the days of George Washington, and their use has been upheld by the courts. Although executive agreements are

executive agreement
Formal government agreement entered into by the executive branch that does not require the advice and consent of the U.S. Senate.

not binding on subsequent administrations, since 1900 they have been used far more frequently than treaties, further cementing the role of the president in foreign affairs, as revealed in Table 7.2.

The Veto Power

In keeping with the system of checks and balances, the president was given the veto power, but only as a "qualified negative." Although the president was given the authority to veto any act of Congress (with the exception of joint resolutions that propose constitutional amendments), Congress was given the authority to override an executive veto by a two-thirds vote in each house. This **veto power,** the authority to reject any congressional legislation, is a powerful policy tool because Congress usually cannot muster enough votes to override a veto. Thus, in over 200 years, there have been approximately 2,500 presidential vetoes and only about a hundred have been overridden.

veto power
The formal, constitutional authority of the president to reject bills passed by both houses of Congress, thus preventing their becoming law without further congressional action.

The Power to Preside over the Military as Commander in Chief

One of the most important constitutional executive powers is the president's authority over the military. Article II states that the president is

TABLE 7.2 Treaties and Executive Agreements Concluded by the U.S., 1789–2002

Years	Number of Treaties	Number of Executive Agreements
1789–1839	60	27
1839–1889	215	238
1889–1929	382	763
1930–1932	49	41
1933–1944 (F. Roosevelt)	131	369
1945–1952 (Truman)	132	1,324
1953–1960 (Eisenhower)	89	1,834
1961–1963 (Kennedy)	36	813
1964–1968 (L. Johnson)	67	1,083
1969–1974 (Nixon)	93	1,317
1975–1976 (Ford)	26	666
1977–1980 (Carter)	79	1,476
1981–1988 (Reagan)	125	2,840
1989–1992 (Bush)	67	1,350
1993–2000 (Clinton)	209	2,047
2001–2002	21	262

Note: Number of treaties includes those concluded during the indicated span of years. Some of these treaties did not receive the consent of the U.S. Senate. Varying definitions of what an executive agreement comprises and their entry-into-force date make the above numbers approximate.

Source: Harold W. Stanley and Richard E. Niemi, eds., *Vital Statistics on American Politics, 2001–2002* (Washington, DC: CQ Press, 2001): 334.

"Commander in Chief of the Army and Navy of the United States."
Although the Constitution specifically grants Congress the authority to declare war, presidents since Abraham Lincoln have used the commander-in-chief clause in conjunction with the chief executive's duty to "take Care that the Laws be faithfully executed" to wage war (and to broaden various powers).

Modern presidents continually clash with Congress over the ability to commence hostilities. In 1973, Congress passed the **War Powers Act** to limit the president's authority to introduce American troops into hostile foreign lands without congressional approval. President Richard M. Nixon vetoed the act, but it was overridden by a two-thirds majority in both houses of Congress.

Presidents since Nixon have continued to insist that the War Powers Act is an unconstitutional infringement of their executive power. In 2001, President George W. Bush sought, and both houses of Congress approved, a joint resolution authorizing the use of force against "those responsible for the recent [September 11] attacks launched against the United States." This resolution actually gave the president more open-ended authority to wage war than his father received in 1991 to conduct the Persian Gulf War or President Lyndon B. Johnson received after the Gulf of Tonkin Resolution in 1964.[7] In October 2002, after President George W. Bush declared Iraq to be a "grave threat to peace," the House (296–133) and Senate (77–23) voted overwhelmingly to allow the president to use force in Iraq "as he determines to be necessary and appropriate," thereby conferring tremendous authority on the president to wage war. (See Join the Debate: The War Powers Act.)

War Powers Act
Passed by Congress in 1973; the president is limited in the deployment of troops overseas to a sixty-day period in peacetime (which can be extended for an extra thirty days to permit withdrawal) unless Congress explicitly gives its approval for a longer period.

The Pardoning Power

Presidents can exercise a check on judicial power through their constitutional authority to grant reprieves or pardons. A **pardon** is an executive grant releasing an individual from the punishment or legal consequences of a crime before or after conviction, and restoring all rights and privileges of citizenship. Presidents exercise complete pardoning power for federal offenses except in cases of impeachment, which cannot be pardoned. President Gerald R. Ford granted the most famous presidential pardon when he pardoned former President Nixon—who had not been formally charged with any crime—"for any offenses against the United States, which he, Richard Nixon, has committed or may have committed while in office." This unilateral, absolute pardon prevented the former president from ever being tried for any crimes he may have committed. It also unleashed a torrent of public criticism against Ford and questions about whether or not Nixon had discussed the pardon with Ford before Nixon's resignation. Many analysts attribute Ford's defeat in his 1976 bid for the presidency to that pardon.

pardon
An executive grant providing restoration of all rights and privileges of citizenship to a specific individual charged or convicted of a crime.

THE WAR POWERS ACT

Overview: It is difficult to interpret how the Constitution divides war powers between Congress and the president. Over the course of American history, it is the president's office that has assumed considerable constitutional discretion in how the United States engages in war and diplomacy. Though the Constitution gives Congress the authority to declare war, "to make rules for the government and regulation of" military forces as well as provide appropriations to the armed services, it is the president's constitutional jurisdiction over the war power that has steadily increased since the nation's founding. For example, President James Madison would not go to war with Great Britain in 1812 without a war declaration from Congress, yet the last six major American conflicts—in Korea, Vietnam, the Persian Gulf, Kosovo, Afghanistan, and Iraq—were conducted without declarations of war. And, at times, a president has withheld information from Congress. During the Vietnam War, President Richard M. Nixon, for example, authorized bombing neutral Cambodia and Laos without notifying Congress.

The War Powers Act of 1973 was an attempt to rein in the war-making authority of the president by demanding, among other things, that the executive notify Congress when committing the U.S. military to hostile action. The War Powers Act requires the president "in every possible instance" to report to Congress within forty-eight hours after deploying the armed forces to combat; implied is the understanding that the information Congress receives is timely and accurate.

The intelligence information that the president and Congress receive is critically important in determining whether to engage in and support armed conflict. The president's constitutional authority as commander in chief gives him access to significant intelligence resources through which to conduct foreign affairs, but sometimes these sources are flawed. President Bill Clinton, for example, ordered the destruction of a chemical plant in Sudan that he believed produced nerve gas but that may have produced less dangerous pharmaceuticals. More recently, President George W. Bush made the case for invading Iraq in part due to the fear that Iraq possessed, after having displayed the will to use, weapons of mass destruction (WMD). WMDs loomed large in the national debate about whether to intervene in Iraq, and the fact that stockpiles have not been found is problematic for the American public.

According to *Federalist No. 3*, the decision to go to war is one of the most solemn a republic can make. Considering the events of September 11, 2001, should a president, in times of crisis, be limited in his ability to defend the United States? Conversely, should there be additional constitutional constraints on the executive's war-making authority in light of the experience of American history? What can be done to ensure that when the United States goes to war, the war is both necessary and just and is conducted with the least amount of casualties and damage to all parties? How can the American people be sure the information they, the Congress, and the president receive is accurate and timely?

Arguments for the War Powers Act

- **The War Powers Act reflects the will of the American people.** The doctrine of civilian supremacy places ultimate war-making authority with the American people, and the War Powers Resolution reflects the will of the people as expressed through the representative institution of Congress. This support is confirmed by the congressional override of President Nixon's veto.
- **The War Powers Act is an attempt by Congress to restore the balance of shared control of the military with the executive.** The act's stated pur-

pose is to "fulfill the intent of the framers…and insure that the collective judgment of both the Congress and the President will apply to the introduction of United States Armed Forces into hostilities…and to the continued use of such forces." This is an attempt to return to the constitutional principle that waging war is to be shared by both branches of government.

- **The War Powers Act is an additional check on the president's authority as commander in chief.** The act is an attempt to prevent future presidents from engaging in hostilities of questionable importance to U.S. national security and to force deliberation within the government in regard to armed conflict. For example, had Congress known of President Lyndon Johnson's use of faulty or intentionally misleading information to increase U.S. military involvement in Vietnam after the Gulf of Tonkin incident, U.S. involvement in Southeast Asia may have taken a different path, less costly in both lives and expenditures.

Arguments Against the War Powers Act

- **International relations can be so volatile that the president must be able to act quickly without hindrance.** Alexander Hamilton argues that the reasons for war are "infinite" and that the United States must have an institution that can react quickly and with force to defend the United States. He finds this energy in government to be in the executive— and the American executive was created to act quickly without relative interference during exceptional times of crisis.
- **The Supreme Court has upheld an expanded interpretation of the president's authority.** In *U.S. v. Curtiss-Wright* (1936), the Court found that the president and "not Congress has the better opportunity of knowing the conditions which prevail in foreign countries, and especially this is true during times of war. He has

his confidential sources of information…. Secrecy in respect of information gathered by them may be highly necessary and the premature disclosure of it productive of harmful results." Thus, the Court concluded that the president is uniquely responsible in the area of foreign policy and war making.

- **During times of conflict, it is the president's duty to "preserve, protect and defend" the Constitution and thus the country it governs, and it is the executive's prerogative to decide the means to do so.** During extraordinary times, the president must take extraordinary means to defend the state without undue interference from Congress. *Federalist No. 8* argues: "It is the nature of war to increase the executive at the expense of the legislative authority" as this is considered a natural shift in power. A historical example is President Lincoln's use of presidential power during the Civil War and a current example would be the war on terrorism.

Questions

1. Is the War Powers Act unconstitutional? Does Congress have the constitutional right to limit the war-making power of the executive? If so, what implications does this have for U.S. national security?
2. Do the American people have the right and need to specific information and intelligence regarding matters of war and peace? Doesn't the representative principle mean elected officials are charged with making certain decisions without informing the public, especially when that information may be confidential in nature?

Selected Readings

Louis Fisher. *Presidential War Power.* Lawrence: University Press of Kansas, 2004.

John Hart Ely. *War and Responsibility: Constitutional Lessons of Viet Nam and Its Aftermath.* Princeton, NJ: Princeton University Press, 1995.

THE PRESIDENT'S MANY HATS

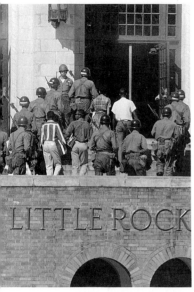

Photo courtesy: John Bryson/Time

■ Chief law enforcer: National Guard troops sent by President Dwight D. Eisenhower enforce federal court decisions ordering the integration of public schools in Little Rock, Arkansas.

Photo courtesy: Mark Reinstein/The Image Works

■ Leader of the Party: Ronald Reagan mobilized conservatives and changed the nature of the Republican Party.

Photo courtesy: Wally McNamee/Folio, Inc.

■ Commander in chief: President George Bush and his wife, Barbara, with troops in the Persian Gulf.

Photo courtesy: Bettman/Corbis

■ Shaper of domestic policy: President Jimmy Carter announces new energy policies. Here, he wears a sweater to underscore that thermostats in the White House were turned down to save energy.

Photo courtesy: Dick Halstead/Getty Images

■ Key player in the legislative process: President Bill Clinton proposes legislation to Congress and the nation.

Photo courtesy: Bettmann/CORBIS

■ Chief of state: President John F. Kennedy and his wife, Jacqueline, with the president of France and his wife during the Kennedys' widely publicized 1961 trip to that nation.

Although the pardoning power normally is not considered a key presidential power, its use by a president can get him in severe trouble with the electorate. Three presidents defeated in their reelection bids—Ford, Carter, and George Bush—all incurred the wrath of the voters for unpopular pardons.

THE DEVELOPMENT AND EXPANSION OF PRESIDENTIAL POWER

EACH PRESIDENT BRINGS TO THE POSITION not only a vision of America, but also expectations about how to use presidential authority. Most presidents find accomplishing their goals much more difficult than they envisioned. After President John F. Kennedy was in office two years, for example, he noted publicly that there were "greater limitations upon our ability to bring about a favorable result than I had imagined."[8] Similarly, as he was leaving office, President Harry S Truman mused about what surprises awaited his successor, Dwight D. Eisenhower, a former general: "He'll sit here and he'll say, 'Do this! Do that!' And nothing will happen. Poor Ike—it won't be a bit like the army. He'll find it very frustrating."[9]

A president's authority is limited by the formal powers enumerated in Article II of the Constitution and by the Supreme Court's interpretation of those constitutional provisions. How a president wields these powers is affected by the times in which the president serves, his confidantes and advisers, and the president's personality and leadership abilities. The 1950s postwar era of good feelings and economic prosperity presided over by the grandfatherly former war hero Dwight D. Eisenhower, for instance, called for a very different leader from the one needed by the Civil War–torn nation governed by Abraham Lincoln.

During that war, Lincoln argued that he needed to act quickly for the very survival of the nation. He suspended the writ of habeas corpus, which allows those in prison to petition to be released, citing the need to jail persons even suspected of disloyal practices. He ordered a blockade of southern ports, in effect initiating a war without the approval of Congress. He also closed the U.S. mails to treasonable correspondence. Lincoln argued that the **inherent powers** of his office allowed him to circumvent the Constitution in a time of war or national crisis. Since the Constitution conferred on the president the duty to make sure that the laws of the United States are faithfully executed, reasoned Lincoln, the acts enumerated above were constitutional. He simply refused to allow the nation to crumble because of what he viewed as technical requirements of the Constitution.

inherent powers
Powers of the president that can be derived or inferred from specific powers in the Constitution.

TABLE 7.3   The Best and the Worst Presidents

Who was the best president and who was the worst? Many surveys of scholars have been taken over the years to answer this question, and virtually all have ranked Abraham Lincoln the best. A 2000 C-SPAN survey of fifty-eight historians, for example, came up with these results:

Ten Best Presidents	Ten Worst Presidents
1. Lincoln (best)	1. Buchanan (worst)
2. F. Roosevelt	2. A. Johnson
3. Washington	3. Pierce
4. T. Roosevelt	4. Harding
5. Truman	5. W. Harrison
6. Wilson	6. Tyler
7. Jefferson	7. Fillmore
8. Kennedy	8. Hoover
9. Eisenhower	9. Grant
10. L. Johnson (10th best)	10. Arthur (10th worst)

Source: Susan Page, "Putting Presidents in Their Place," *USA Today* (February 21, 2000): 8A.

New Deal
The name given to the program of "Relief, Recovery, Reform" begun by President Franklin D. Roosevelt in 1933 designed to bring the United States out of the Great Depression.

Not only do different times call for different kinds of leaders; they also often provide limits, or conversely, wide opportunities, for whoever serves as president at the time. Crises, in particular, trigger expansions of presidential power. The danger to the nation posed by the Civil War in the 1860s required a strong leader to take up the reins of government. Because of his leadership during this crisis, Lincoln is generally ranked by historians as the best president. (See Table 7.3.)

The Growth of the Modern Presidency

Before the days of instantaneous communication, the nation could afford to allow Congress, with its relatively slow deliberative processes, to make most decisions. Furthermore, decision making might have been left to Congress because its members, and not the president, were closest to the people. As times and technology have changed, however, so have the public's expectations of anyone who becomes president. For example, the breakneck speed with which cable news networks and Internet sites report national and international events has intensified the public's expectation that, in a crisis, the president will be the individual to act quickly and decisively on behalf of the nation. Congress often is just too slow to respond to fast-changing events—especially in foreign affairs.

In the twentieth and twenty-first centuries, the general trend has been for presidential—as opposed to congressional—decision making to be more and more important. The start of this trend can be traced to the four-term presidency of Franklin D. Roosevelt (FDR), who led the nation through several crises. This growth of presidential power and the growth of the federal government and its programs in general are now questioned by many critics.

FDR took office in 1933 in the midst of a major crisis—the Great Depression—during which a substantial portion of the U.S. workforce was unemployed. Noting the sorry state of the national economy in his inaugural address, FDR concluded, "This nation asks for action and action now." To jump-start the American economy, FDR asked Congress for and was given "broad executive powers to wage a war against the emergency, as great as the power that would be given to me if we were in fact invaded by a foreign foe."[10]

Just as Abraham Lincoln had taken bold steps on his inauguration, Roosevelt also acted quickly. He immediately fashioned a plan for national recovery called the **New Deal**, a package of bold and controversial programs designed to invigorate the failing American economy (see chapter 3).

Roosevelt served an unprecedented twelve years in office (he was elected to four terms but died shortly after beginning the last one). During this period, the nation went from the economic war of the Great Depression to the real international conflict of World War II. The institution of the presidency changed profoundly and permanently, and new federal agencies were created to implement New Deal programs as the executive branch became responsible for implementing a wide variety of new programs.

Not only did FDR create a new bureaucracy to implement his pet programs, but he also personalized the presidency by establishing a new relationship between the presidency and the people. In his radio addresses, or fireside chats, as he liked to call them, he spoke directly to the public in a relaxed and informal manner about serious issues.

To his successors, FDR left the modern presidency, including a burgeoning federal bureaucracy (see chapter 8), an active and usually leading role in both domestic and foreign policy and legislation, and a nationalized executive office that used technology—first radio and then television—to bring the president closer to the public than ever before.

THE PRESIDENTIAL ESTABLISHMENT

AS THE RESPONSIBILITIES AND SCOPE of presidential authority grew over the years, so did the executive branch, including the number of people working directly for the president in the White House. The vice president and his staff, the Cabinet, the first lady and her staff, the Executive Office of the President, and the White House staff all help the president fulfill his duties as chief executive.

The Vice President

Historically, presidents chose their vice presidents largely to balance— politically, geographically, or otherwise—the presidential ticket, with little thought given to the possibility of the vice president's becoming president. Franklin D. Roosevelt, for example, a liberal New Yorker, selected John Nance Garner, a conservative Texan, to be his running mate in 1932. After serving two terms, Garner—who openly disagreed with Roosevelt over many policies, including Roosevelt's decision to seek a third term—unsuccessfully sought the 1940 presidential nomination himself.

How much power a vice president has depends on how much the president is willing to give him. Jimmy Carter was the first president to give a vice president, Walter Mondale, more than ceremonial duties. In fact, Mondale was the first vice president to have an office in the White House. (It wasn't until 1961 that a vice president even had an office in the Executive Office Building next door to the White House!) The Mondale model of an active vice president has now become the norm.

The Bush/Cheney ticket in 2000 showed an effort to balance the ticket, but in ways different from the past. Most commentators agreed that Dick Cheney was chosen to provide "gravitas"—that is, a sense of national governmental experience, especially in foreign affairs, that Governor Bush neither had nor claimed. The question still exists, however, as to whether the vice presidency is a stepping stone to the presidency. As the 2000 campaign underscored, the vice president of a very popular president at a time of unprecedented economic prosperity, Al Gore, was unable to translate that good will into election for himself.

The Cabinet

The Cabinet, which has no basis in the Constitution, is an informal institution based on practice and precedent whose membership is determined by tradition and presidential discretion. By custom, this advisory group selected by the president includes the heads of major executive departments. Presidents today also include their vice presidents in Cabinet meetings, as well as any other agency heads or officials to whom they would like to accord Cabinet-level status. As a body, the Cabinet's major function is to help the president execute the laws and assist him in making decisions.

As revealed in Table 7.4, over the years the Cabinet has grown. Departments have been added to accommodate new pressures on the president to act in areas that initially were not considered within the scope of concern of the national government. As interest groups, in particular, pressured Congress and the president to recognize their demands for services and governmental action, they often were rewarded by the creation of an executive department. Since each was headed by a secretary who automatically became a member of the president's Cabinet, powerful groups including farmers (Agriculture), business people (Commerce), workers (Labor), and teachers (Education) saw the creation of a department as increasing their access to the president.

The size of the president's Cabinet has increased over the years at the same time that most presidents' reliance on their Cabinet secretaries has decreased, although some individual members of a president's Cabinet may be very influential. Because the Cabinet secretaries and high-ranking members of their departments routinely are subjected to congressional oversight and interest group pressures, they often have divided loyalties. In fact, Congress, through the necessary and proper clause, has the authority to reorganize executive departments, create new ones, and abolish existing ones. For this reason, most presidents now rely most heavily on members of their inner circle of advisers for advice and information, although some presidents remain close to one or two Cabinet secretaries. (Chapter 8 provides a more detailed discussion of the Cabinet's role in executing U.S. policy.)

TABLE 7.4 The U.S. Cabinet and Responsibilities of Each Executive Department

Department Head	Department	Date of Creation	Responsibilities
Secretary of State	Department of State	1789	Responsible for the making of foreign policy, including treaty negotiation
Secretary of the Treasury	Department of the Treasury	1789	Responsible for government funds and regulation of alcohol, firearms, and tobacco
Secretary of Defense	Department of Defense	1789, 1947	Created by consolidating the former Departments of War, the Army, the Navy, and the Air Force; responsible for national defense
Attorney General	Department of Justice	1870	Represents U.S. government in all federal courts, investigates and prosecutes violations of federal law
Secretary of the Interior	Department of the Interior	1849	Manages the nation's natural resources, including wildlife and public lands
Secretary of Agriculture	Department of Agriculture	Created 1862; elevated to Cabinet status 1889	Assists the nation's farmers, oversees food-quality programs, administers food stamp and school lunch programs
Secretary of Commerce	Department of Commerce	1903	Aids businesses and conducts the U.S. Census (originally the Department of Commerce and Labor)
Secretary of Labor	Department of Labor	1913	Runs labor programs, keeps labor statistics, aids labor through enforcement of laws
Secretary of Health and Human Services	Department of Health and Human Services	1953	Runs health, welfare, and Social Security programs; created as the Department of Health, Education, and Welfare (lost its education function in 1979)
Secretary of Housing and Urban Development	Department of Housing and Urban Development	1965	Responsible for urban and housing programs
Secretary of Transportation	Department of Transportation	1966	Responsible for mass transportation and highway programs
Secretary of Energy	Department of Energy	1977	Responsible for energy policy and research, including atomic energy
Secretary of Education	Department of Education	1979	Responsible for the federal government's education programs
Secretary of Veterans Affairs	Department of Veterans Affairs	1989	Responsible for programs aiding veterans
Secretary of Homeland Security	Department of Homeland Security	2002	Responsible for all issues pertaining to homeland security

The First Lady

From Martha Washington to Laura Bush, first ladies (a term coined during the Civil War) have assisted presidents as informal advisers while making other, more public contributions to American society. Until recently, the only formal national recognition given to first ladies was

Photo courtesy: Osamu Honda/AP/Wide World
Photos

■ First Lady Laura Bush addresses the International Women's Day Conference on Afghani women at the United Nations headquarters on March 8, 2002. The first lady called for international support for women who suffered under the oppressive Taliban regime.

Executive Office of the President (EOP)
Establishment created in 1939 to help the president oversee the bureaucracy.

an exhibit of inaugural ball gowns at the Smithsonian Institution. In 1992, in keeping with renewed interest in the varied roles played by first ladies, the Smithsonian launched an exhibit that highlighted the personal accomplishments of first ladies since Martha Washington. The exhibit was built around three themes: (1) the political role of the first ladies, including how they were portrayed in the media and perceived by the public; (2) their contributions to society, especially their personal causes; and, (3) still, of course, their inaugural gowns.

The Executive Office of the President (EOP)

The **Executive Office of the President (EOP)** was established by FDR in 1939 to oversee his New Deal programs. It was created to provide the president with a general staff to help him direct the diverse activities of the executive branch. In fact, it is a mini-bureaucracy of several advisers and offices located in the ornate Executive Office Building next to the White House on Pennsylvania Avenue, as well as in the White House itself, where the president's closest advisers often are located.

The EOP has expanded over time to include several advisory and policy-making agencies and task forces, each of which is responsible to the executive branch. Over time, the units of the EOP have become more responsive to individual presidents rather than to the executive branch as an institution. They often now are the prime policy makers in their fields of expertise as they play key roles in advancing the president's policy preferences. Among the EOP's most important members are the National Security Council, the Council of Economic Advisers, the Office of Management and Budget, the Office of the Vice President, and the U.S. Trade Representative.

The National Security Council (NSC) was established in 1947 to advise the president on American military affairs and foreign policy. The NSC is composed of the president, the vice president, and the secretaries of state and defense. The chair of the Joint Chiefs of Staff and the director of the Central Intelligence Agency also participate. Others such as the chief of staff and White House counsel may attend. The national security adviser runs the staff of the NSC, coordinates information and options, and advises the president.

Presidents can give clear indications of their policy preferences by the kinds of offices they include in the EOP. President George W. Bush, for example, not only moved or consolidated several offices when he became president in 2001, but he quickly sought to create a new Office of Faith Based and Community Initiatives to help him achieve his goal of greater religious involvement in matters of domestic policy.

The White House Staff

The White House chief of staff facilitates the smooth running of the staff and the executive branch of government. Successful chiefs of staff also have protected the president from mistakes and helped implement policies to obtain the maximum political advantage for the president. Other key White House aides include those who help plan domestic policy, maintain relations with Congress and interest groups, deal with the media, provide economic expertise, and execute political strategies.

Although White House staffers prefer to be located in the White House in spite of its small offices, many staffers are relegated to the old Executive Office Building next door because White House office space is limited. In Washington, the size of the office is not the measure of power that it often is in corporations. Instead, power in the White House goes to those who have the president's ear and the offices closest to the Oval Office.

THE PRESIDENT AS POLICY MAKER

WHEN FDR SENT HIS FIRST legislative package to Congress, he broke the traditional model of law-making.[11] As envisioned by the Framers, it was to be Congress that made the laws. Now FDR was claiming a leadership role for the president in the legislative process. Said the president of this new relationship, "It is the duty of the President to propose and it is the privilege of the Congress to dispose."[12] With those words and the actions that followed, FDR shifted the presidency into a law- and policy-maker role. Now not only did the president and the executive branch execute the laws, but he and his aides generally suggested them, too.

The President's Role in Proposing Legislation

From FDR's presidency to the Republican-controlled 104th Congress, the public looked routinely to the president to formulate concrete legislative plans to propose to Congress, which then adopted, modified, or rejected his plans for the nation. Then, in 1994, it appeared for a while that the electorate wanted Congress to reassert itself in the legislative process. In fact, the Contract with America (see chapter 3) was a Republican call for Congress to take the reins of the law-making process. But several Republican Congresses failed to pass many of the items of the contract, and President Bill Clinton's continued forceful presence in the budgetary process made a resurgent role for Congress largely illusory. The same scenario holds true for George W. Bush.

On the whole, presidents have a hard time getting Congress to pass their programs.[13] Passage is especially difficult if the president presides over a divided government, which occurs when the presidency and Congress are controlled by different political parties (see chapter 6). Recent research by political scientists, however, shows that presidents are much more likely to win on bills central to their announced

THE PRESIDENT AS POLICY MAKER: TURNING THE RECOMMENDATIONS OF THE 9/11 COMMISSION INTO LAW

On July 22, 2004, the bipartisan National Commission on Terrorist Attacks Upon the United States (better known as the 9/11 Commission) released its "Final Report" to the public. It called for a complete overhaul of the U.S. intelligence community to create greater responsibility, accountability, and unity among the nation's fifteen intelligence agencies—goals that they deemed essential to improving the nation's ability to gather, share, analyze, and act on intelligence information.

President George W. Bush initially opposed the creation of the 9/11 Commission. But in the end, it provided critical information to the Commission, including direct testimony by President Bush, Vice President Dick Cheney, and then National Security Advisor Condoleezza Rice.

Key figures in both political parties, such as Senators John F. Kerry (D–MA), John McCain (R–AZ), and House Minority Leader Nancy Pelosi (D–CA) urged Congress and the president to turn all forty-one recommendations in the final report into law as quickly as possible. In early October, the Senate overwhelmingly passed a reform bill, but the Republican leadership in the House of Representatives believed that they should take more time to review the report and apply their own expertise to craft the reforms.

Several powerful members of the House contested the Commission's recommendation to transfer control over the bulk of the $40 billion annual national intelligence budget, to a new Director of National Intelligence, who would report directly to the President, and the House Intelligence Committee. Other House Republicans also wanted more restrictions on immigration and expanded powers for law enforcement agencies to counter terrorism. Consequently, Republican leaders had to block a vote on the bill in November 2004 when it could not muster a majority of Republican House members to support the reforms, even after President Bush called Senate leaders to help work out a compromise.

After several more weeks of intense discussions, however, President Bush brokered a compromise deal with Republican House leaders in early December 2004 that left control over intelligence-gathering satellites and reconnaissance aircraft in the hands of the Department of Defense. The White House suggested new language regarding Defense Department control over some intelligence resources, President Bush called on Congress to pass the bill in his weekly radio talk to the nation, while Vice President Cheney phoned several reluctant House Republicans to get their support for the legislation.[a] Finally, on December 7, 2004—the last working day of the 108th session of Congress—the House passed the compromise measure, which the Senate approved the following day and President Bush signed into law. "Some people, including me, were not sure which side of this he [President Bush] was on in the early stages, or whether he might be on both sides of this," noted the senior Democratic member of the House Intelligence Committee, Jane Harmon (D–CA), then "it turned out, in the later weeks, that he and his White House staff were all over this and really helped bring this across the finish line."[b]

Questions

1. Generally, presidents enjoy their greatest success rates right after their election or reelection. Why do you think that passage of this legislation proved so difficult?
2. In legislation directly affecting the structure of the Executive branch, as well as lines of authority to the president, how much weight should Congress pay to his recommendations?

[a]Charles Babington, "House Approves Intelligence Bill," Washington Post (December 8, 2004) A1, A4.

[b]James Kuhnhenn, "House OK's Intelligence Overhaul Bill," Miami Herald (December 8, 2004) http://www.miami.com/mld/miamiherald/news/.

agendas, such as President George W. Bush's victory on the Iraq war resolution, than to secure passage of legislation proposed by others.[14]

Presidents generally experience declining support for policies they advocate throughout their terms. That is why it is so important for a president to propose key plans early in his administration during the honeymoon period, a time when the goodwill toward the president often allows a president to secure passage of legislation that he would not be able to gain at a later period. Even President Lyndon B. Johnson, who was able to get about 57 percent of his programs through Congress, noted: "You've got to give it all you can, that first year…before they start worrying about themselves…. You can't put anything through when half the Congress is thinking how to beat you."[15]

Presidents can also use **patronage** (jobs, grants, or other special favors that are given as rewards to friends and political allies for their support) and personal rewards to win support. Invitations to the White House and campaign visits to the home districts of members of Congress running for office are two ways to curry favor with legislators, and inattention to key members can prove deadly to a president's legislative program. Former Speaker of the House Tip O'Neill (D–MA) reportedly was quite irritated when the Carter transition team refused O'Neill's request for extra tickets to Jimmy Carter's inaugural. This incident did not exactly get the president off to a good start with the powerful speaker.

Another way a president can bolster support for his legislative package is to call on his political party. As the informal leader of his party, he should be able to use that position to his advantage in Congress, where party loyalty is very important. This strategy works best when the president has carried members of his party into office on his coattails, as was the case in the Johnson and Reagan landslides of 1964 and 1984, respectively. In fact, many scholars regard Lyndon B. Johnson as the most effective legislative leader.[16] Not only had he served in the House and as Senate majority leader, but he also enjoyed a comfortable Democratic Party majority in Congress.[17]

patronage
Jobs, grants, or other special favors that are given as rewards to friends and political allies for their support.

The Budgetary Process and Executive Implementation

Closely associated with a president's ability to pass legislation is his ability to secure funding for new and existing programs. A president sets national policy and priorities through his budget proposals and his continued insistence on their congressional passage. The budget proposal not only outlines the programs he wants but indicates the importance of every program by the amount of funding requested for each and its associated agency or department.

Because the Framers gave Congress the power of the purse, Congress had primary responsibility for the budget process until 1930. The economic disaster set off by the stock market crash of 1929, however, gave Franklin D. Roosevelt, once elected in 1932, the opportunity to assert himself in the congressional budgetary process, just as he inserted himself into the legislative process. In 1939, the Bureau of the Budget, which had been created in 1921 to help the president tell Congress how much money it would take to run the executive branch of government, was made part of the newly created Executive Office of the President. In 1970, President Nixon changed its name to the **Office of Management and Budget (OMB)** to clarify its function in the executive branch.

The OMB works exclusively for the president and employs hundreds of budget and policy experts. Key OMB responsibilities include preparing the president's annual budget proposal, designing the president's program, and reviewing the progress, budget, and program proposals of the executive department agencies. It also supplies economic forecasts to the president and conducts detailed analyses of proposed bills and agency rules. OMB reports allow the president to attach price tags to his legislative proposals and defend the presidential budget. The OMB budget is a huge document, and even those who prepare it have a hard time deciphering all of its provisions. Even so, the expertise of the OMB directors often gives them an advantage over members of Congress.

Policy Making Through Regulation

Proposing legislation and using the budget to advance policy priorities are not the only ways that presidents can affect the policy process, especially in times of highly divided government. Executive orders offer the president an opportunity to make policy without legislative approval. Major policy changes have been made when a president has issued an **executive order,** a rule or regulation issued by the president that has the effect of law. While many executive orders are issued to help clarify or implement legislation enacted by Congress, other executive orders have the effect of making new policy. President Harry S Truman ordered an end to segregation in the military through an executive order, and affirmative action was institutionalized as national policy through Executive Order 11246, issued by Lyndon B. Johnson in 1966.

Executive orders have been used since the 1980s to set national policies toward abortion. Ronald Reagan, for example, used an executive order to stop federal funding of fetal tissue research and to end federal funding of any groups providing abortion counseling. Bill Clinton immediately rescinded those orders when he became president. One of George W. Bush's first acts upon taking office was to reverse those Clinton orders.

Like presidents before him, George W. Bush has used executive orders to put his policy stamp on a wide array of important issues. For example, he signed an executive order limiting federal funding of stem

---

Office of Management and Budget (OMB)
The office that prepares the president's annual budget proposal, reviews the budget and programs of the executive departments, supplies economic forecasts, and conducts detailed analyses of proposed bills and agency rules.

executive order
A rule or regulation issued by the president that has the effect of law. All executive orders must be published in the *Federal Register*.

Timeline

"With the Stroke of a Pen:" The Executive Order Over Time

cell research to the sixty or so cell lines already in the possession of scientific researchers.[18] An executive order also was used to allow military tribunals to try any foreigners captured by U.S. forces in Afghanistan or linked to the terrorist acts of 9/11.

PRESIDENTIAL LEADERSHIP AND THE IMPORTANCE OF PUBLIC OPINION

A PRESIDENT'S ABILITY to get his programs adopted or implemented depends on many factors, including his leadership abilities, his personality and powers of persuasion, his ability to mobilize public opinion to support his actions, and the public's perception of his performance.

Presidential Leadership

Leadership is not an easy thing to exercise, and it remains an elusive concept for scholars to identify and measure, but it is important to all presidents seeking support for their programs and policies. Moreover, ideas about the importance of effective leaders have deep roots in our political culture. The leadership abilities of the great presidents—Washington, Jefferson, Lincoln, and Franklin D. Roosevelt—have been extolled over and over again, leading us to fault modern presidents who fail to cloak themselves in the armor of leadership. Americans thus have come to believe that "If presidential leadership works some of the time, why not all of the time?"[19] This attitude directly influences what we expect presidents to do and how we evaluate them.

Political scientist James David Barber believes that there are four presidential character types, based on energy level (whether the president is active or passive) and the degree of enjoyment a president finds in the job (whether the president has a positive or negative attitude) (see Table 7.5). Barber believes that active and positive presidents are more successful than passive and negative presidents. Active-positive presidents generally enjoyed warm and supportive childhood environments and are basically happy individuals open to new life experiences. They approach the presidency with a characteristic zest for life and have a drive to lead and succeed. In contrast, passive-negative presidents find themselves reacting to circumstances, are likely to take direction from others, and fail to make full use of the enormous resources of the executive office.

TABLE 7.5   Barber's Presidential Personalities

	Active	Passive
Positive	F. Roosevelt Truman Kennedy Ford Carter[a] Bush	Taft Harding Reagan
Negative	Wilson Hoover L. Johnson Nixon	Coolidge Eisenhower

[a]Some scholars think that Carter better fits the active-negative typology.

Source: James David Barber, The Presidential Character: Predicting Performance in the White House, 4th ed. (Englewood Cliffs, NJ: Prentice Hall, 1992).

Research by political scientists shows that presidents can exercise leadership by increasing public attention to particular issues. Analyses of presidential State of the Union addresses, for example, reveal that mentions of particular policies translate into more Americans mentioning those policies as the most important problems facing the nation.[20]

The presidency often transforms its occupants. There is an old adage that great crises make great presidents. President Franklin D. Roosevelt's handling of the Great Depression solidified his place in American history, as did Abraham Lincoln's handling of the Civil War. Many critics argue that September 11, 2001, transformed George W. Bush's presidency to the degree that commentators now refer to the pre- and post-9/11 president.[21] President Bush not only cast himself as the strong leader of the United States but has portrayed himself as the worldwide leader in a war against terrorism, transforming himself from the candidate who disavowed interest in or much knowledge of international affairs. His newfound self-confidence was what Americans look for in a time of crisis.

Frequently, the difference between great and mediocre presidents centers on their ability to grasp the importance of leadership style. Truly great presidents understood that the White House was a seat of power from which decisions could flow to shape the national destiny. They recognized that their day-to-day activities and how they went about them should be designed to bolster support for their policies and to secure congressional and popular backing that could translate their intuitive judgment into meaningful action. Mediocre presidents, on the other hand, have tended to regard the White House as "a stage for the presentation of performances to the public" or a fitting honor to cap a career.[22]

■ In 2003, President George W. Bush surprised American troops in Iraq on Thanksgiving Day.

Photo courtesy: Anja Niedringhaus/Pool/Reuters/Corbis

Presidential Personality and the Power to Persuade

In trying to lead against long odds, a president must not only exercise the constitutional powers of the chief executive but also persuade enough of the country that his actions are the right ones so that he can carry them out without national strife.[23] A president's personality and ability to persuade others are key to amassing greater power and authority.

IN THE PUBLIC EYE: PRIME MINISTERS AND PRESIDENTS

Many Americans might find the parliamentary system of government strange. Historically, however, new democratic regimes have had two models to choose from: the American presidential system and the British parliamentary system. The American system is based on a constitution that was the product of political creativity and compromise more than 200 years ago. The U.S. Constitution survives essentially intact, although changes in the way various players interpret its provisions have resulted in dramatic shifts in the balance of power between the legislative and executive branches of government in Washington, D.C., and between the federal government and the states.

In contrast, the British system has no written constitution but is the product of a long series of agreements between the monarchy, feudal lords, the business class, trade unions, and other segments of British society, going back to the thirteenth century. The one principle that has guided British constitutional law for the past two or three centuries is "parliamentary sovereignty"—that is, that the House of Commons (and to an increasingly lesser extent, the House of Lords) governs Britain. The leadership of the House of Commons is determined by the majority party (or coalition of several parties). The British Cabinet is made up of members of Parliament (MPs) who have typically served many terms and have demonstrated their party loyalty. Led by the prime minister, who serves as the head of government, they administer each of the departments in Britain.

Because prime ministers are selected by their respective parties, most of these leaders have considerable experience and moderate temperament (with a few flamboyant exceptions). Their job

security depends on making sure their party remains in the majority, and so they tend to work closely with party regulars. Leaders such as John Major of the United Kingdom and John Howard of Australia are typical in their rather cautious approach to public life. Major's predecessor, Margaret Thatcher, however, ended up alienating both the British public and the Conservative Party leadership, which voted her out of her position as head of the party, and thereby removed her as prime minister without a direct election.

Most democratic systems in the developing world have adopted the presidential system. In many instances this is a result of American influence, whereas in others it represents a concession to those who support authoritarianism rather than democracy. The separate election of a president means that his or her political support is dependent not on the legislature, but instead on personal popularity with the masses. The result is that presidential systems often produce more charismatic and independent personalities, such as populist leaders Hugo Chavez, who became the president of Venezuela in 1998, and Lula da Silva, who became the president of Brazil in 2002.

Questions

1. Does the American style of selecting leaders predispose it to picking certain types of presidents? Are they populist and flamboyant? Are they independent from political parties? Are they seasoned and experienced in national leadership?
2. What aspects of the British parliamentary system might be better than those of the U.S. presidential system?

Presidential personality and political skills often determine how effectively a president can exercise the broad powers of the modern presidency. To be successful, says political scientist Richard E. Neustadt,

Comparative

Comparing Chief Executives

a president not only must have a will for power but must use that will to set the agenda for the nation. In setting that agenda, in effect, he can become a true leader. According to Neustadt, "Presidential power is the power to persuade," which comes largely from an individual's ability to bargain. Persuasion is key, Neustadt says, because constitutional powers alone don't provide modern presidents with the authority to meet rising public expectations.[24]

Going Public: Mobilizing Public Opinion

Even before the days of radio and television, presidents tried to reach out to the public to gain support for their programs through what President Theodore Roosevelt called the bully pulpit. The development of commercial air travel and radio, newsreels, television, and communication satellites have made direct communication to larger numbers of voters easier. Presidents, first ladies, and other presidential advisers no longer stay at home but instead travel all over the world to expand their views and to build personal support as well as support for administration programs.

Direct presidential appeals to the electorate like those often made by recent presidents are referred to as "going public."[25] Going public means that a president goes over the heads of members of Congress to gain support from the people, who can then place pressure on their elected officials in Washington.

The Public's Perception of Presidential Performance

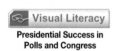

Visual Literacy

Presidential Success in Polls and Congress

Participation

Rate the Presidents

Typically, presidents enjoy their highest level of public approval at the beginning of their terms and try to take advantage of this honeymoon period to get their programs passed by Congress as soon as possible. Each action a president takes, however, is divisive—some people will approve, and others will disapprove. Disapproval tends to have a cumulative effect. Inevitably, as a general rule, a president's popularity wanes, although Bill Clinton, who ended with a higher approval rating than any president in recent history, was a notable exception.

Since Lyndon B. Johnson's presidency, only four presidents have left office with an approval rating of more than 50 percent. (See Analyzing Visuals: Presidential Approval Ratings Since 1938.) Many credit this trend to events such as Vietnam, Watergate, the Iran hostage crisis, the Iran-Contra scandal, and the Iraq War, which have made the public increasingly skeptical of presidential performance. Presidents George Bush, Bill Clinton, and George W. Bush, however, experienced increases in their presidential performance scores during the course of their presidencies. George Bush's rapid rise in popularity occurred after the major and, perhaps more important, quick victory in the 1991 Persian Gulf

Analyzing Visuals

PRESIDENTIAL APPROVAL RATINGS SINCE 1938

Presidents generally have enjoyed their highest ratings at the beginning of their terms and experienced lower ratings toward the end. Presidents George Bush, Bill Clinton, and George W. Bush, however, enjoyed popularity surges during the course of their terms. After viewing the line graph of presidential approval scores and reading the related chapter material, answer the following critical thinking questions about presidential approval: What types of events (domestic or international) tend to boost presidential approval? What do you think enabled George W. Bush to sustain his high approval rating for a relatively long period after the 9/11 terrorist attacks?

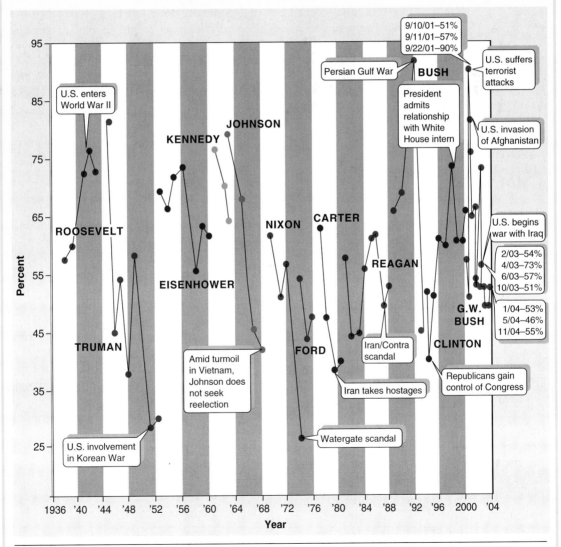

Sources: USA Today (August 14, 2000): 6A. © 2000, USA Today. Reprinted by permission. "President Bush: Job Ratings," and CNN/USA Today/Gallup Poll, PollingReport.com, 2002, accessed November 10, 2002, http://www.pollingreport.com/BushJob.htm. Updated by author.

War. His popularity, however, plummeted as the good feelings faded and Americans began to feel the pinch of recession. In contrast, Bill Clinton's approval scores skyrocketed after the 1996 Democratic National Convention. More interestingly, Clinton's high approval ratings continued in the wake of allegations of wrongdoing in the Oval Office, his eventual admission of inappropriate conduct, and his impeachment proceedings. In fact, when Clinton went to the American public and admitted that he misled them about his relationship with Monica Lewinsky, an ABC poll conducted immediately after his speech showed a 10-point jump in his job approval rating.[26]

Most presidents experience surges in popularity after major international events, but they generally don't last long. Each of the last twelve presidents experienced at least one rallying point based on a foreign event. Before President George W. Bush, who experienced increased popularity for almost a year following 9/11, rallies lasted an average of ten weeks, with the longest being seven months.[27] These popularity surges allow presidents to make some policy decisions that they believe are for the good of the nation, even though the policies are unpopular with the public.

SUMMARY

BECAUSE THE FRAMERS FEARED a tyrannical monarch, they gave considerable thought to the office of the chief executive. Since ratification of the Constitution, the office has changed considerably—more through practice and need than from changes in the Constitution. Distrust of a too-powerful leader led the Framers to create an executive office with limited powers. They mandated that a president be at least thirty-five years old, a natural-born citizen, and a U.S. resident for at least fourteen years, and they opted not to limit the president's term of office. To further guard against tyranny, they made provisions for the removal of the president.

The Framers gave the president a variety of specific constitutional powers in Article II, including the appointment power, the power to convene Congress, and the power to make treaties. In addition, the president derives considerable power from being commander in chief of the military. The Constitution also gives the president the power to grant pardons and to veto acts of Congress.

The development of presidential power has depended on the personal force of those who have held the office. The modern presidency, though, is generally marked by the election of Franklin D. Roosevelt in 1932. As the responsibilities of the president have grown, so has the executive branch of government. FDR established the Executive Office of the President to help him govern. Perhaps the most key policy advisers are those closest to the president: the vice president, the White House staff, some members of the Executive Office of the President, and sometimes, the first lady.

Since FDR, the public has looked to the president to propose legislation to Congress. Through proposing legislation, advancing budgets, and involvement in the regulatory process, presidents make policy.

To gain support for his programs or proposed budget, the president uses a variety of skills, including personal leadership, patronage, and direct appeals to the public. How the president goes about winning support is determined by his leadership and personal style, affected by his character and his ability to persuade. Since the 1970s, however, the American public has been increasingly skeptical of presidential actions, and few presidents have enjoyed extended periods of the kind of popularity needed to help win support for programmatic change.

KEY TERMS

Cabinet, p. 246
executive agreement, p. 247
Executive Office of the President (EOP), p. 258
executive order, p. 262
executive privilege, p. 244
impeachment, p. 243
inherent powers, p. 253
New Deal, p. 254
Office of Management and Budget (OMB), p. 262
pardon, p. 249
patronage, p. 261
Twenty-Fifth Amendment, p. 244
Twenty-Second Amendment, p. 243
U.S. v. *Nixon* (1974), p. 244
veto power, p. 248
War Powers Act, p. 249

SELECTED READINGS

Barber, James David. *The Presidential Character: Predicting Presidential Performance in the White House,* 4th ed. Englewood Cliffs, NJ: Prentice Hall, 1992.

Campbell, Karlyn Kohr, and Kathleen Hall Jamieson. *Deeds Done in Words: Presidential Rhetoric and the Genres of Governance.* Chicago: University of Chicago Press, 1990.

Cooper, Philip J. *By Order of the President: The Use and Abuse of Executive Direct Action.* Lawrence: University Press of Kansas, 2002.

Dallek, Robert. *Hail to the Chief: The Making and Unmaking of American Presidents.* New York: Oxford University Press, 2001.

Daynes, Byron W., and Glen Sussman. *The American Presidency and the Social Agenda.* Upper Saddle River, NJ: Prentice Hall, 2001.

Edwards, George C., III, and Stephen J. Wayne. *Presidential Leadership: Politics and Policy Making,* 6th ed. New York: Bedford Books, 2002.

Greenstein, Fred I. *The Presidential Difference: Leadership Style from FDR to George W. Bush,* 2nd ed. Princeton, NJ: Princeton University Press, 2004.

Kellerman, Barbara. *The Political Presidency: Practice of Leadership from Kennedy Through Reagan.* New York: Oxford University Press, 1997.

Martin, Janet M. *The American Presidency and Women: Promise, Performance, and Illusion.* College Station: Texas A&M Press, 2003.

Neustadt, Richard E. *Presidential Power and the Modern Presidents.* New York: Free Press, 1991.

Pfiffner, James P. *Modern Presidency.* Belmont, CA: Wadsworth, 2000.

Ragsdale, Lyn. *Vital Statistics on the Presidency: Washington to Clinton.* Washington, DC: CQ Press, 1998.

Rossiter, Clinton. *The American Presidency.* Baltimore, MD: Johns Hopkins University Press, 1987.

Skowronek, Stephen. *The Politics Presidents Make: Leadership from John Adams to Bill Clinton.* Cambridge, MA: Harvard University Press, 1997.

Walcott, Charles E., and Karen Hult. *Governing the White House.* Lawrence: University Press of Kansas, 1995.

Warshaw, Shirley Anne. *The Keys to Power: Managing the Presidency,* 2nd ed. New York: Longman, 2004.

WEB EXPLORATIONS

To learn more about specific presidents, see
http://www.nara.gov/nara/president/address.html
For a chronology of the Clinton impeachment proceedings, see http://www.washintonpost.com/wp-srv/politics/special/clinton/timeline.htm
For more on the vice president, see
http://www.whitehouse.gov/vicepresident/
To learn more about presidential pardons, go to
http://jurist.law.pitt.edu/pardons0a.htm
For more on the modern White House, see
http://www.whitehouse.gov/
For more on first ladies, see
http://www.firstladies.org/
To try your hand at balancing the budget, go to
http://www.nathannewman.org/nbs/
For more details on Watergate, see
http://watergate.info/
For more on the White House Project, see
http://www.thewhitehouseproject.org/

8

The Executive Branch and the Federal Bureaucracy

Photo courtesy: Charles Dharapak/AP/Wide World Photos

FREQUENTLY, CRITICS OF THE BUREAUCRACY argue that the maze of administrative regulations, rules, and procedures makes it difficult for individual citizens to obtain government services, from student loans to drivers' licenses. One bureaucrat might tell you to do X; another one will tell you to do Y—after you have stood in the wrong line for an hour or two. But, it is unusual for a major actor in the bureaucracy not to know what other actors are doing.

However, the major governmental reorganization that occurred in the wake of the September 11, 2001 terrorist attacks has caused a number of conflicts over departmental responsibilities. For example, as a part of the reorganization, Congress authorized the creation of a Department of Homeland Security. Under the Homeland Security Act of 2002, the Department alone has the authority to issue threat warnings with the cooperation of several agencies and the White House. These warnings are usually issued by the Department's Secretary; during President Bush's first term, this post was filled by former Pennsylvania Governor Tom Ridge.

But, on May 27, 2004, Attorney General John Ashcroft and FBI Director Robert Mueller called a press conference to ask the public's help in capturing seven suspected terrorists within the United States (see photo, above). In that same press conference they addressed an imminent terrorism threat to the United States. Both men concluded that a terrorist attack on the United States was likely in the next few months. News accounts quickly revealed that Secretary Ridge first heard about Ashcroft's and Mueller's concerns as he watched television along with millions of other Americans. In fact, earlier that day on several morning news shows, Ridge had downplayed any increased risks of terrorist attack.

Lawmakers, whose job it is to oversee the Department of Homeland Security, were irate and said that the comments made by Ashcroft and Mueller undermined efforts of the national government to assure its citizens of their safety. For example, Representative Christopher Cox (R–CA) who chairs the House committee overseeing the Department of Homeland Security remarked, "The reason that Congress created the Department of Homeland Security is that we need to merge the various parts of government responsible for pieces of the war on terrorism into one coordinated effort."[1]

The White House was quick to call a meeting of all of the principals, who then issued a joint statement in an effort to clear the air of conflicting messages. But, to the general public, the issue was not one of conflicting messages. It underscored the common perception that the federal bureaucracy is rife with problems in spite of continued efforts to improve performance and communication that actually have succeeded in some areas.

THE BUREAUCRACY OFTEN IS CALLED the fourth branch of government because of the tremendous power that agencies and bureaus can exercise. Politicians often charge that the **bureaucracy,** the thousands of federal government agencies and institutions that implement and administer federal law and federal programs, is too large, too powerful, and too unaccountable to the people or even to elected officials. Many politicians, elected officials, and voters complain that the bureaucracy is too wasteful. Nevertheless, few critics discuss the fact that laws and policies also are implemented by state and local bureaucracies and bureaucrats whose numbers are proportionately far larger, and often far less efficient, than those working for the federal government.

Although many Americans are uncomfortable with the large role of the federal government in policy making, current studies show that most users of federal agencies rate quite favorably the agencies and the services they receive. Many of those polled by the Pew Research Center as part of its efforts to assess America's often seemingly conflicting views about the federal government and its services were frustrated by complicated rules and the slowness of a particular agency. Still, a majority gave most

bureaucracy
A set of complex hierarchical departments, agencies, commissions, and their staffs that exist to help a chief executive officer carry out his or her duties. Bureaucracies may be private organizations of governmental units.

agencies overall high marks. Most of those polled drew sharp distinctions between particular agencies and the government as a whole, although the federal government, especially the executive branch, is largely composed of agencies, as we will discuss later in this chapter.

Harold D. Lasswell once defined political science as the "study of who gets what, when, and how."[2] It is by studying the bureaucracy that those questions can perhaps best be answered. To understand the role of the bureaucracy, we will first examine the executive branch and the development of the federal bureaucracy. Then, after examining the modern bureaucracy by discussing bureaucrats and the formal organization of the bureaucracy, we will consider how the bureaucracy works. Finally, we will discuss making agencies accountable.

THE EXECUTIVE BRANCH AND THE DEVELOPMENT OF THE FEDERAL BUREAUCRACY

IN THE AMERICAN SYSTEM, the bureaucracy can be thought of as the part of the government that makes policy as it links together the three branches of the national government in the federal system. Although Congress makes the laws, it must rely on the executive branch and the bureaucracy to enforce and implement them. Often, agency determinations are challenged in the courts. Because most administrative agencies that make up part of the bureaucracy enjoy reputations for special expertise in clearly defined policy areas, the federal judiciary routinely defers to bureaucratic administrative decision makers.

German sociologist Max Weber believed bureaucracies were a rational way for complex societies to organize themselves. Model bureaucracies, said Weber, are characterized by certain features, including:

1. A chain of command in which authority flows from top to bottom.
2. A division of labor whereby work is apportioned among specialized workers to increase productivity.
3. Clear lines of authority among workers and their superiors.
4. A goal orientation that determines structure, authority, and rules.
5. Impersonality, whereby all employees are treated fairly based on merit and all clients are served equally, without discrimination, according to established rules.
6. Productivity, whereby all work and actions are evaluated according to established rules.[3]

Bureaucracy in the United States

In 2005, the executive branch had approximately 1.8 million civilian employees employed directly by the president or his advisers or in independent agencies or commissions. The Department of Defense employed an additional 2.3 million in the military. The Postal Service, which is a quasi-governmental corporation not part of the executive branch, has more than 800,000 employees (and is second only to Wal-Mart in total number of employees).[4]

In 1789, conditions were quite different. Only three departments existed under the Articles of Confederation: Foreign Affairs, War, and Treasury. George Washington inherited those departments, and soon, the head of each department was called its secretary and Foreign Affairs was renamed the Department of State. To provide the president with legal advice, Congress also created the office of attorney general. From the beginning, individuals appointed as Cabinet secretaries (as well as the attorney general) were subject to approval by the U.S. Senate but were removable by the president alone. Even the First Congress realized how important it was for a president to be surrounded by those in whom he had complete confidence and trust. (See The Living Constitution.)

Timeline

Evolution of the
Federal Bureaucracy

The Civil War and the Growth of Government

As discussed in chapter 3, the Civil War (1861–1865) permanently changed the nature of the federal bureaucracy. As the nation geared up for war, thousands of additional employees were added to existing departments. The Civil War also spawned the need for new government agencies. A series of poor harvests and distribution problems led President Abraham Lincoln (who understood that you need well-fed troops to conduct a war) to create the Department of Agriculture in 1862, although it was not given full Cabinet-level status until 1889.

After the Civil War, the need for a strong national government continued unabated. The Pension Office was established in 1866 to pay benefits to the thousands of Union veterans who had fought in the war (more than 127,000 veterans initially were eligible for benefits). Justice was made a department in 1870. The increase in the types and nature of government services resulted in a parallel rise in the number of federal jobs.

From the Spoils System to the Merit System

In 1831, describing President Andrew Jackson's populating the federal government with his political cronies, a New York senator commented, "To the victor belong the spoils." From his statement derives the term **spoils system** to describe the firing of public office holders of the defeated political party and their replacement with loyalists of a new administration. Political positions often are referred to as **patronage** positions.

spoils system
The firing of public-office holders of a defeated political party and their replacement with loyalists of the newly elected party.

patronage
Jobs, grants, or other special favors that are given as rewards to friends and political allies for their support.

The Living Constitution

The President . . . may require the Opinion, in writing, of the principle Officer in each of the executive Departments, upon any subject relating to the Duties of their respective Office.

—Article II, Section 2

This clause, along with additional language designating that the president shall be the commander in chief, notes that the heads of departments are to serve as advisers to the president. There is no mention of the Cabinet in the Constitution.

This meager language is all that remains of the Framers' initial efforts to create a council to guide the president. Those in attendance at the Constitutional Convention largely favored the idea of a council, but could not agree on who should be a part of that body. Some actually wanted members from the House and Senate who would rotate into the bureaucracy; most, however, appeared to support the idea of the heads of departments along with the chief justice, who would preside when the president was unavailable. The resulting language above depicts a one-sided arrangement whereby the heads of executive departments must simply answer in writing questions put to them by the president.

The Cabinet of today is totally different from the structure envisioned by the Framers. George Washington was the first to convene a meeting of what he called his Cabinet. Some presidents have used their Cabinets as trusted advisers; others have used them to demonstrate that they are committed to political, racial, ethnic, or gender diversity, and have relied more on White House aides than particular Cabinet members. Who is included in the Cabinet, as well as how it is used, is solely up to the discretion of the sitting president.

Pendleton Act
Reform measure that created the Civil Service Commission to administer a partial merit system. The act classified the federal service by grades, to which appointments were made based on the results of a competitive examination. It made it illegal for federal political appointees to be required to contribute to a particular political party.

This system reached a high-water mark during Abraham Lincoln's presidency. By the time James A. Garfield was elected president in 1880, many reformers were calling for changes. On his election to office, thousands pressed Garfield for positions. This siege prompted Garfield to resolve to reform the civil service, but his life was cut short by the bullets of an assassin who, ironically, was a frustrated job seeker.

Public reaction to Garfield's death and increasing criticism of the spoils system prompted Congress to pass the Civil Service Reform Act in 1883, more commonly known as the **Pendleton Act,** in honor of its sponsor, Senator George H. Pendleton (D–OH). It established the principle of federal employment on the basis of open, competitive exams and created a bipartisan three-member Civil Service Commission, which operated until 1978. Initially, only about 10 percent of the positions in the federal **civil service system** were covered by the law, but later laws and executive orders extended coverage of the act to over 90 percent of all federal employees. This new system was called the **merit system,** one characteristic of Weber's model bureaucracy.

Regulating the Economy and the Growth of Government in the Twentieth Century

As the nation continued to grow, so did the bureaucracy. In the wake of the tremendous growth of big business (especially railroads), widespread price fixing, and other unfair business practices that occurred after the Civil War, Congress created the Interstate Commerce Commission (ICC). In creating the ICC, Congress was reacting to public outcries over the exorbitant rates charged by railroad companies for hauling freight. It became the first **independent regulatory commission,** an agency outside a major executive department. In 1887, the creation of the ICC also marked a shift in the focus of the bureaucracy from service to regulation. Its creation gave the government—in the shape of the bureaucracy—vast powers over individual and property rights.

As discussed in chapter 3, the ratification of the Sixteenth Amendment to the Constitution in 1913 also affected the size of government and the possibilities for growth. It gave Congress the authority to implement a federal income tax to supplement the national treasury and provided an infusion of funds to support new federal agencies, services, and governmental programs.

The bureaucracy continued to grow after the stock market crashed in 1929, ushering in the high unemployment and weak financial markets of the Great Depression. During this era, President Franklin D. Roosevelt created hundreds of new government agencies to regulate business practices and various aspects of the economy. The desperate mood of the nation supported these moves, as most Americans began to change their ideas about the proper role of government and the provision of governmental services. Formerly, most Americans had believed in a hands-off approach; now they considered it the government's job to get the economy going and get Americans back to work.

World War II also prompted an expansion of the federal bureaucracy. Tax rates were increased to support the war, and they never again fell to prewar levels. After the war, this infusion of new monies and veterans' demands for services led to a variety of new programs and a much bigger government. The G.I. (Government Issue) Bill, for example, provided college loans for returning veterans and reduced mortgage

civil service system
The system created by civil service laws by which many appointments to the federal bureaucracy are made.

merit system
The system by which federal civil service jobs are classified into grades or levels, to which appointments are made on the basis of performance on competitive examinations.

independent regulatory commission
An agency created by Congress that is generally concerned with a specific aspect of the economy.

Visual Literacy
The Changing Face of
The Federal Bureaucracy

■ During the New Deal, President Franklin D. Roosevelt suggested and Congress enacted the Emergency Relief Appropriation Act, which authorized the Works Progress Administration (WPA) to hire thousands of unemployed workers to complete numerous public work projects.

Photo courtesy: AP/Wide World Photos

rates to allow them to buy homes. With these programs, Americans became increasingly accustomed to the national government's role in entirely new areas such as affordable middle-class housing, which never would have existed without government assistance.

Within two decades after World War II, the civil rights movement and President Lyndon B. Johnson's war on poverty produced additional growth in the bureaucracy. The Equal Employment Opportunity Commission (EEOC) was created in 1965 (by the Civil Rights Act of 1964), and the Departments of Housing and Urban Development (HUD) and Transportation were created in 1966. These expansions of the bureaucracy corresponded to increases in the president's power and his ability to persuade Congress that new agencies would be an effective way to solve pressing social problems.

Government Workers and Political Involvement

Hatch Act

Law enacted in 1939 to prohibit civil servants from taking activist roles in partisan campaigns. This act prohibited federal employees from making political contributions, working for a particular party, or campaigning for a particular candidate.

As an increasing proportion of the American workforce came to work for the U.S. government as a result of the New Deal recovery programs, many began to fear that the members of the civil service would play major roles not only in implementing public policy but also in electing members of Congress and even the president. Consequently, Congress enacted the Political Activities Act of 1939, commonly known as the **Hatch Act,** in honor of its main sponsor, Senator Carl Hatch (D–NM).

It was designed to prohibit federal employees from becoming directly involved in working for political candidates.

Although presidents as far back as Thomas Jefferson had advocated efforts to limit the opportunities for federal civil servants to influence the votes of others, over the years many considered the Hatch Act too extreme. Critics argued that it denied millions of federal employees First Amendment guarantees of freedom of speech and association and discouraged political participation among a group of people who might otherwise be strong political activists. They also argued that civil servants should become more involved in campaigns, particularly at the state and local level, to understand better the needs of the citizens they serve.

In 1993, in response to criticisms of the Hatch Act and at the urgings of President Bill Clinton, Congress enacted the **Federal Employees Political Activities Act.** This liberalization of the Hatch Act allows employees to run for public office in nonpartisan elections, contribute money to political organizations, and campaign for or against candidates in partisan elections. They still, however, are prohibited from engaging in political activity while on duty, soliciting contributions from the general public, or running for office in partisan elections.

Federal Employees Political Activities Act
1993 liberalization of the Hatch Act. Federal employees are now allowed to run for office in nonpartisan elections and to contribute money to campaigns in partisan elections.

THE MODERN BUREAUCRACY

CRITICS CONTINUALLY LAMENT that the national government is not run like a business. Private businesses as well as all levels of government have their own bureaucratic structures. But, the national government differs from private business in numerous ways. Governments exist for the public good, not to make money. Businesses are driven by a profit motive; government leaders, but not bureaucrats, are driven by reelection. Businesses get their money from customers; the national government gets its money from taxpayers. Another difference between a bureaucracy and a business is that it is difficult to determine to whom bureaucracies are responsible. Is it the president? Congress? The citizenry? Still, governments can learn much from business, and, as discussed in the previous section, recent reform efforts have tried to apply business solutions to create a government that works better and costs less.

The different natures of government and business have a tremendous impact on the way the bureaucracy operates. Because all of the incentive in government "is in the direction of not making mistakes," public employees view risks and rewards very differently from their private-sector counterparts.[5] The key to the modern bureaucracy is to understand who bureaucrats are, how the bureaucracy is organized, and how organization and personnel affect each other. It also is key to understand that government cannot be run like a business. An understanding of these facts and factors can help in the search for ways to motivate positive change in the bureaucracy.

E-GOVERNMENT

In 1992, the White House posted its first Web page. Now all government agencies and bureaus have Web sites and provide a plethora of information to the American public that formerly would have taken numerous trips to the library or even Washington, D.C., to obtain.

By 1998, the Government Paperwork Elimination Act required that federal agencies allow persons transacting business with the government to have the option of submitting information or transacting business with them electronically. It is from this act that you or members of your family now have the option of submitting your tax returns electronically.

In 2002, the Bush administration took additional advantage of changing technologies and the increasing number of Americans' access to it, whether in their homes, at local public libraries, or at Internet cafes. The E-Government Act of 2002 was an effort to mandate that all government agencies use "Internet-based information technologies to enhance citizens' access to government information and services."[a]

According to the E-Gov Web site, E-Gov is not simply about putting forms online; its major purpose is to harness technology to make it easier for citizens to learn more about government services. GovBenefits.gov, for example, has been created so that citizens can find answers to a range of questions dealing with their individual circumstances and will immediately receive a list of government programs that they may be eligible for. Recreation.gov allows individuals to find out about national parks and recreation sites and to make online reservations at those facilities.

The newest addition to the e-government effort under the Bush administration is its eRule-making Initiative. Managed through a cross-agency effort led by the Environmental Protection Agency, this new use of technology is designed to transform "the federal rule-making process by enhancing the public's ability to participate in their government's regulatory decision making."[b] Regulations.gov was launched in 2002 to allow the public to "search, view, and comment on proposed federal regulations open for comment."[c] While the regulatory process almost exclusively involved interest groups and affected industries, this new initiative allows the public to search proposed regulations easily. Agencies are in the process of posting their proposed regulations on this central site, although some agencies still have their own sites. One 2004 study revealed that some agencies had failed to post proposed regulations on the central site, but efforts are being made to remedy these lapses. By 2006, individuals should be able to track and comment on regulations from the 173 rule-making entities of the federal government as each of these units adapts to this new technology.

1. Will the bureaucracy become more responsive to citizens and less captured by special interests as e-government increases?
2. Is there any downside to e-regulations?

---

[a] About E-Gov,
http://www.whitehouse.gov/omb/egov/about_leg.htm.

[b] http://www.regulations.gov.

[c] http://www.regulations.gov.

Who Are Bureaucrats?

Federal bureaucrats are career government employees who work in the executive branch in the Cabinet-level departments and independent agencies that comprise more than 2,000 bureaus, divisions, branches, offices, services, and other subunits of the federal government. There are approximately 1.8 million federal workers in the executive branch, a figure that does not include postal workers and uniformed military personnel. (See Figure 8.1: Number of Federal Employees in the Executive Branch, 1789–2002.) Nearly one-third of all civilian employees work in the Postal Service. The remaining federal civilian workers are spread out among the various executive departments and agencies throughout the United States. Most of these federal employees are paid according to what is called the "General Schedule" (GS). They advance within GS grades and into higher GS levels and salaries as their careers progress.

Participation

Who Wants to Be
a Bureaucrat?

As a result of reforms during the Truman administration that built on the Pendleton Act, most civilian federal governmental employees today are selected by merit standards, which include tests (such as civil service or foreign service exams) and educational criteria. Merit systems protect federal employees from being fired for political reasons.

At the lower levels of the U.S. Civil Service, most positions are filled by competitive examinations. These usually involve a written test, although the same position in the private sector would not. Mid-level to upper ranges of federal positions do not normally require tests; instead, applicants simply submit a resume, or even apply by phone. Personnel departments then evaluate potential candidates and rank candidates according to how well they fit a particular job opening. Only the names of those deemed qualified are then forwarded to the official filling the vacancy. This can be a time-consuming process; it often takes six to nine months before a position can be filled in this manner.

The remaining 10 percent of the federal workforce is made up of persons not covered by the civil service system. These positions generally fall into three categories:

1. Appointive policy-making positions. About 6,000 persons are appointed directly by the president. Some of these, including Cabinet secretaries, are subject to Senate confirmation. These appointees, in turn, are responsible for appointing the high-level policy-making assistants who form the top of the bureaucratic hierarchy.

2. Independent regulatory commissioners. Although each president gets to appoint as many as one hundred commissioners, they become independent of his direct political influence once they take office.

3. Low-level, nonpolicy patronage positions. At one time, the U.S. Postal Service was the largest source of these government jobs. In 1971, Congress reorganized the Postal Service and removed positions such as local postmaster from the political patronage/rewards pool. Since then, these types of positions generally concern secretarial assistants to policy makers.

More than 15,000 job skills are represented in the federal government, and its workers are perhaps the best trained and most skilled and efficient in the world (see Global Perspectives: Who Are the Bureaucrats? Should We Care?). Government employees, whose average age is

Analyzing Visuals

CHARACTERISTICS AND RANK DISTRIBUTION OF FEDERAL CIVILIAN EMPLOYEES

The bar graph depicts the percentage of the federal civilian workforce in several categories: gender, gender and rank, race or ethnicity, disability, age, length of service, and union representation. After reviewing the data displayed in the graph, answer the following critical thinking questions: What do you notice about the percentages of males and females in the lowest (GS-01 through GS-04) and the highest (GS-13 through GS-15) grades? How would you explain the differences in percentages of males and females in those grades? Which racial/ethnic groups are represented in percentages that are greater than their percentages in the population (see the population statistics in the Changes in Racial and Ethnic Distributions section in chapter 1)? What do you think would explain the high percentage of the federal civilian workforce represented by a union?

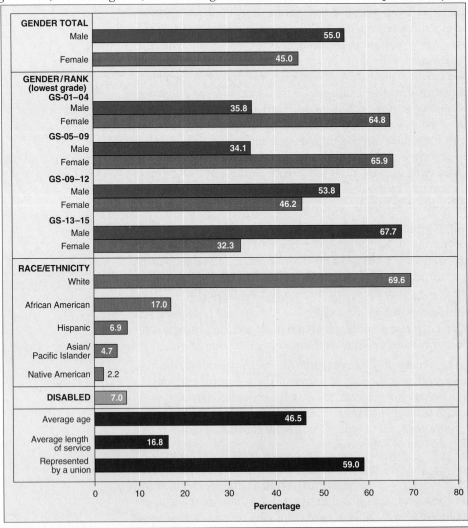

Source: Office of Personnel Management, *2003 Fact Book.*

FIGURE 8.1   Number of Federal Employees in the Executive Branch, 1789–2002. ■

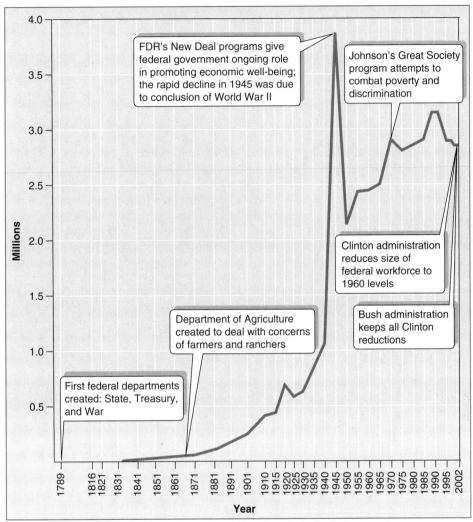

FDR's New Deal programs give federal government ongoing role in promoting economic well-being; the rapid decline in 1945 was due to conclusion of World War II

Johnson's Great Society program attempts to combat poverty and discrimination

Clinton administration reduces size of federal workforce to 1960 levels

Department of Agriculture created to deal with concerns of farmers and ranchers

Bush administration keeps all Clinton reductions

First federal departments created: State, Treasury, and War

Source: Office of Personnel Management, *The Fact Book,* http://www.opm.gov/feddata/03factbk.pdf.

forty-seven, with an average length of service at seventeen years, include forest rangers, FBI agents, foreign service officers, computer programmers, security guards, librarians, administrators, engineers, plumbers, lawyers, doctors, postal carriers, and zoologists, among others.

The diversity of government jobs mirrors the diversity of jobs in the private sector. The federal workforce, itself, is also diverse. As revealed in Analyzing Visuals: Characteristics and Rank Distribution of Federal Civilian Employees, the federal workforce largely reflects the racial and ethnic composition of the United States as a whole, although the employment of women lags behind that of men. Women still make up more than 60 percent of the lowest GS levels but have raised their proportion of positions in the GS 13–15 ranks from 18 percent in 1990 to over 30 percent in 2004.[6]

WHO ARE THE BUREAUCRATS? SHOULD WE CARE?

It is tempting to think of the bureaucracy simply as a machine created by political officials to carry out the laws they have passed and the regulations they have established. In looking at bureaucracy as a machine we tend not to worry about differences among the people who work in the bureaucracy. Civil servants are neutral, competent, and expert. They drive the machine without regard to their personal values. An important line of thought in the study of bureaucracy, known as the representative bureaucracy perspective, argues, however, that to view bureaucracy as a machine is a mistake. Instead, bureaucracy is about people. First, it is about the people within bureaucracy. The different ideas people have about what is right and wrong, the appropriate way to behave, and what—if anything—the government owes the people and the people owe the government inevitably influence how civil servants approach their jobs and the types of decisions they make. Second, it is about the people with whom the bureaucracy interacts. Minority groups may not be well served by the bureaucracy if everyone in it comes from groups with values different from theirs.

From the representative bureaucracy perspective it is extremely important to know who these bureaucrats are in terms of their social, economic, and cultural backgrounds. Systematic comparative data of this type is hard to come by. The table below presents information on the background of high ranking civil servants in Canada and Israel in terms of their social class, level of education, minority status, and gender.

In addition to this comparison, here are some additional observations about how the U.S. bureaucracy compares with others in terms of its representativeness. Most high-ranking civil servants come from middle class backgrounds. Germany is typical of many West European countries with only 11 percent of its bureaucrats coming from working class backgrounds. Pakistan is even lower at 2 percent. Almost everywhere, high ranking civil servants have at least some form of college education. This shared characteristic hides some important differences, however. In the United States, many civil servants graduate from state-supported universities; however, in Great Britain, France, Japan, South Korea, and Greece, to name only a few countries, there has been a long-standing bias for recruiting civil servants from only a few elite universities.

As for ethnic background, in most countries the dominant ethnic group is overrepresented. The United States appears to be an exception, although even here overrepresentation of the dominant ethnic group reappears when total civil service numbers are looked at (63 percent–37 percent). In some countries, specific bureaucratic positions are reserved for people from specific ethnic groups—the practice in Austria, Belgium, and Lebanon. Along with ethnicity, gender is a major dividing line within bureaucracies. Although, in many countries, over 50 percent of civil service is made up of women, rarely are many found in the higher civil service ranks.

Questions

1. How important is it that the U.S. bureaucracy looks like the American population?
2. Which of the background characteristics discussed here do you think is most important for creating a representative bureaucracy?

Backgrounds of Civil Servants in Two Democracies (percentages)

	Social Background		Education		Ethnic Group		Gender	
Canada	Upper	44	High School*	2	Dominant	70	Female	23
	Middle	19	College Grad	34	Minority	30	Male	67
	Working	36	Post College	65				
Israel	Upper	18	High School*	49	Dominant	81	Female	3
	Middle	59	College Grad	28	Minority	19	Male	97
	Working	23	Post College	23				

*This category combines those with a high school diploma and some college. In Israel all of these had some college.
Source: B. Guy Peters, *The Politics of Bureaucracy* (New York: Routledge, 2001), pp. 112-125.

FIGURE 8.2   Federal Agency Regions and City Headquarters. ■

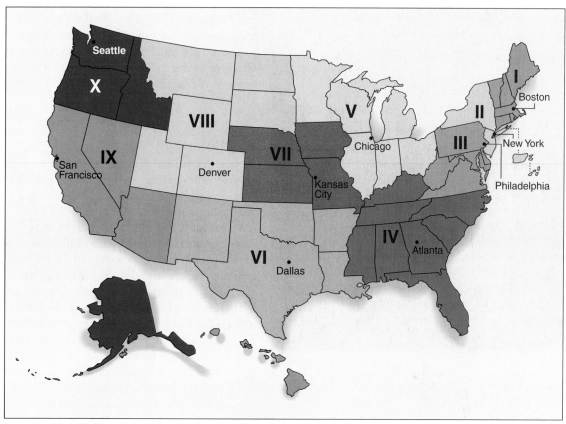

Source: Department of Health and Human Services, http://www.hhs.gov/images/regions.gif.

Comparative

Comparing
Bureaucracies

There are about 326,000 federal workers in the nation's capital; the rest are located in regional, state, and local offices scattered throughout the country. To enhance efficiency, the United States is broken up into several regions, with most agencies having regional offices in one city in that region. (See Figure 8.2.) The decentralization of the bureaucracy facilitates accessibility to the public. Decentralization also helps distribute jobs and incomes across the country.

The graying of the federal workforce is of concern to many. By 2005, "more than two-thirds of those in the Senior Executive Service and large numbers of mid-level managers will be eligible to retire,"[7] taking with them "a wealth of institutional knowledge."[8] Many in government hope that the Presidential Management Fellows (PMF) Program, which was begun in the 1970s to hire and train future managers and executives, will be enhanced to make up for the shortfall in experienced managers that

Photo courtesy: Everett Collection

■ Bureaucrats perform all kinds of jobs. The cast of CBS's *The Agency,* a series about the people who work in the Central Intelligence Agency (CIA), actually can be considered bureaucrats.

the federal government is expected to face soon. Agencies even are contemplating ways to pay the college loans of prospective recruits.[9] At the same time the federal government is trying to recruit and retain federal workers, it is also trying to shrink the number of federal employees by using outside contractors, who are often cheaper and easier to fire.

Formal Organization

Although even experts can't agree on the exact number of separate governmental agencies, commissions, and departments that make up the federal bureaucracy, there are at least 1,149 civilian agencies.[10] A distinctive feature of the executive bureaucracy is its traditional division into areas of specialization. For example, the Occupational Safety and Health Administration (OSHA) handles occupational safety, the Department of State specializes in foreign affairs, the Environmental Protection Agency (EPA) in the environment, and so on. It is not unusual, however, for more than one agency to be involved in a particular issue or for one agency to be involved in myriad issues. In fact, numerous agencies often have authority in the same issue areas, making administration even more difficult. Agencies fall into four general types: (1) Cabinet departments; (2) government corporations; (3) independent agencies; and, (4) regulatory commissions.

department
Major administrative unit with responsibility for a broad area of government operations. Departmental status usually indicates a permanent national interest in that particular governmental function, such as defense, commerce, or agriculture.

The Cabinet Departments.   The fifteen Cabinet **departments** are major administrative units that have responsibility for conducting a broad area of government operations. Cabinet departments account for about 60 percent of the federal workforce. The vice president, the heads of all of the departments, as well as the heads of the EPA, Office of Management and Budget (OMB), Office of National Drug Control Policy, the U.S. Trade Representative, and the president's chief of staff make up his formal Cabinet.

The executive branch departments depicted in Figure 8.3 are headed by Cabinet members called secretaries (except the Department of Justice, which is headed by the attorney general). The secretaries are responsible for establishing their department's general policy and overseeing its

FIGURE 8.3   The Executive Branch. ■

THE PRESIDENT OF THE UNITED STATES

Cabinet

Department of State | Department of the Treasury | Department of Defense | Department of Justice

Department of the Interior | Department of Agriculture | Department of Commerce | Department of Labor | Department of Transportation

Department of Housing and Urban Development | Department of Health and Human Services | Department of Energy | Department of Education | Department of Veterans Affairs | Department of Homeland Security

Independent Agencies and Government Corporations

Advisory Council on Historic Preservation
African Development Foundation
American Battle Monuments Commission
Appalachian Regional Commission
Architectural and Transportation
    Barriers Compliance Board
Arctic Research Commission
Armed Forces Retirement Home
Barry M. Goldwater Scholarship and
    Excellence in Education Foundation
Broadcasting Board of Governors
Central Intelligence Agency
Civil Air Patrol Great Lakes Region
Commission on Civil Rights
Commission of Fine Arts
Committee for Purchase from People
    Who Are Blind or Severely Disabled
Commodity Futures Trading Commission
Consumer Product Safety Commission
Corporation for National Service
Defense Nuclear Facilities Safety Board
Delaware River Basin Commission
Environmental Protection Agency
Equal Employment Opportunity Commission
Export-Import Bank of the U.S.
Farm Credit Administration
Federal Communications Commission
Federal Deposit Insurance Corporation
Federal Election Commission
Federal Emergency Management Agency
Federal Energy Regulatory Commission
Federal Housing Finance Board
Federal Labor Relations Authority
Federal Maritime Commission

Federal Mediation and Conciliation Service
Federal Mine Safety and Health Review Commission
Federal Reserve System
Federal Retirement Thrift Investment Board
Federal Trade Commission
General Services Administration
Harry S Truman Scholarship Foundation
Inter-American Foundation
International Boundary and Water Commission,
    United States and Mexico
International Broadcasting Bureau
Interstate Commission on the Potomac River Basin
James Madison Memorial Fellowship Foundation
Japan–United States Friendship Commission
Marine Mammal Commission
Merit Systems Protection Board
National Aeronautics and Space Administration
National Archives and Records Administration
National Capital Planning Commission
National Commission on Libraries and
    Information Science
National Council on Disability
National Credit Union Administration
National Foundation on the Arts
    and the Humanities
National Labor Relations Board
National Mediation Board
National Performance Review
National Railroad Passenger Corporation (Amtrak)
National Science Foundation
National Transportation Safety Board
Nuclear Regulatory Commission
Occupational Safety and Health Review Commission
Office of Government Ethics

Office of Navajo and Hopi Indian Relocation
Office of Personnel Management
Office of Special Counsel
Overseas Private Investment Corporation
Peace Corps
Pension Benefit Guaranty Corporation
Physician Payment Review Commission
Postal Rate Commission
President's Commission on White House
    Fellowships
President's Committee on Employment
    of People with Disabilities
Railroad Retirement Board
Securities and Exchange Commission
Selective Service System
Small Business Administration
Smithsonian Institution
Social Security Administration
Surface Transportation Board
Susquehanna River Basin Commission
Tennesse Valley Authority
Trade Development Agency
U.S. Arms Control and Disarmament Agency
U.S. Chemical Safety and Hazard
    Investigation Board
U.S. Holocaust Memorial Council
U.S. Information Agency
U.S. Institute of Peace
U.S. International Development
    Corporation Agency
U.S. International Trade Commission
U.S. Postal Service
Woodrow Wilson International Center
    for Scholars

Source: Library of Congress, http://www.loc.gov/global/executive/fed.html.

Join the Debate

THE EPA AND LEAD IN WATER

Overview: Government bureaucracies influence life in the United States in many beneficial and, sometimes, not so beneficial ways. Most are charged with securing the common good and are dedicated to serving the American public. Administrative agencies, however, do not operate in a vacuum—they have mandates from the government and are ultimately subject to congressional, executive, and judicial supervision. The idea of bureaucratic oversight is to ensure that agencies and departments are held accountable for their activities. These administrative units have more or less discretion and freedom of action depending on their mandates. But, though considered expert in their respective policy domains, bureaucracies may receive from the government ill-conceived or poorly researched directives that can interfere with an agency's mission or hinder proper administrative functioning. As with any organization under human control, they also reflect the effect of human foibles and corruption. Nevertheless, because of the unique nature of government bureaucracies in that they can affect the lives of millions, there must be accountability when bureaucracies fail in their mission.

In February 2004, it was revealed that the District of Columbia's drinking water contained dramatically increased levels of lead, which can increase the risk of cancer. The problem affected approximately 23,000 domiciles in the District. It was later determined that the District's Water and Sewer Authority (WASA) neglected to follow the Environmental Protection Agency's (EPA) mandated language when informing citizens of high lead levels in D.C.'s water supply, and that WASA also neglected to do follow-up water testing in areas where lead service pipes had been partially replaced. And, the EPA stands accused of neglecting oversight of WASA by taking too long to notice and act on the violations, some of which occurred in 2002.

Ironically, the increased lead levels were caused by the Army Corps of Engineers' attempt in 2000 to increase the quality of the water supply. The Army Corps of Engineers oversees the Washington Aqueduct that supplies drinking water to the city, while WASA manages operations of the water supply. In 2000, the Army Corps of Engineers sought to improve water quality by switching from chlorine to chloramine (a combination of chlorine and ammonia) to purify water. This change had the unintended effect of further corroding lead pipes and thus increasing the amount of lead in the water supply. Once word of the problem became public, the EPA had the Corps of Engineers replace chloramine with chlorine, and lead levels dropped immediately and significantly.

What is the lesson to be learned from this case? Where does accountability lie—with the EPA, with WASA, or with the Corps of Engineers? With all? All these agencies *were* pursuing a public good: lower lead levels in the water supply that could reduce the risk of cancer for D.C. residents. Should motive and intent be taken into account when determining accountability? On the one hand, doesn't the fact that the water supply was immediately fixed demonstrate bureaucratic accountability? On the other, WASA was demonstrably negligent when informing D.C. residents of the problem by ignoring federal language guidelines in notices, pamphlets, and public service announcements, and WASA was negligent as well for not doing follow-up testing after replacing pipes, as required by EPA guidelines. Additionally, a Cato Institute scholar accused the EPA of bowing to interest-group pressure to replace chlorine with chloramine—pressure that advocated change based on questionable science and experience. Should bureaucracies heed private interests outside government?

Arguments for EPA Accountability

- **Accountability is ultimately the responsibility of the agency in question.** In the end, the parent agency is responsible for ensuring oversight and the proper functioning of all bureaucratic agencies and departments within its purview. Since the EPA is the ultimate authority for protecting the water supply, they should be held accountable.
- **Agencies are accountable for the science and methods used.** If science or methodology has not been scrupulously proved safe or effective, change should not be implemented until the science or methods have been demonstrated to be sound.
- **Government bureaucracies should not be influenced by interest groups.** If it is true that the EPA bowed to the wishes of interest groups—in this case, the environmental lobby—it is not performing its function as intended. Bureaucracies are accountable to the government, not outside interests.

Arguments Against EPA Accountability

- **Those in charge of regulation may sometimes be unaware of mid- and low-level problems.** Many times lower-level bureaucrats hide their actions from superiors in order to protect themselves. It is unreasonable to

expect senior managers to know what is consciously being hidden at lower departmental levels. Those directly culpable should be disciplined accordingly.
- **The EPA was following federal law.** According to National Public Radio, weak federal laws regulating drinking water are to blame for water quality in the United States. What happened in the District of Columbia is to be expected when those engaged in oversight have little knowledge and understanding of, or little concern for, the domain being regulated. Ultimately, bureaucracies are to be held accountable to established law.
- **Bureaucratic efficiency and quality are only as good as current research and science.** The EPA cannot be held accountable for acting on possibly flawed science. The intent behind changing the water purification system in D.C. was to reduce the risk of cancer and affiliated illness. Practice showed the change to chloramine caused increased lead levels, and once the problem was noticed, it was fixed.

Questions

1. What agency or agencies were at fault in the above case study? What would be a means to determine accountability?
2. Should Congress be more diligent in exercising its oversight authority? If so, is the government not ultimately accountable?

Selected Readings

John Burke. *Bureaucratic Responsibility*. Johns Hopkins University Press, 1988.

David Osborne and Peter Plastrik. *Banishing Bureaucracy: Five Strategies for Reinventing Government*. Addison Wesley, 1997.

operations. As discussed in chapter 7, Cabinet secretaries are responsible directly to the president but are often viewed as having two masters—the president and those affected by their department. Cabinet secretaries also are tied to Congress, from which they get their appropriations and the discretion to implement legislation and make rules policy.

Although departments vary considerably in size, prestige, and power, they share certain features. Each department covers a broad area of responsibility generally reflected by its name. Each secretary is assisted by one or more deputies or undersecretaries who take part of the administrative burden off the secretary's shoulders, as well as by several assistant secretaries who direct major programs within the department. In addition, each secretary, like the president, has numerous assistants who help with planning, budgeting, personnel, legal services, public relations, and other key staff functions. Most departments are subdivided into bureaus, divisions, sections, or other smaller units, and it is at this level that the real work of each agency is done. Most departments are subdivided along functional lines, but the basis for division may be geography, work processes, or clientele.

Because many of these agencies were created at the urging of well-organized interests to advance their particular objectives, it is not surprising that clientele groups are powerful lobbies with their respective agencies in Washington. The clientele agencies and groups also are active at the regional level, where the agencies devote a substantial part of their resources to program implementation.

government corporation
Business (such as the U.S. Postal Service) established by Congress that performs functions that could be provided by a private business.

Government Corporations.   **Government corporations** are the most recent addition to the bureaucracy. Dating from the early 1930s, they are businesses established by Congress to perform functions that could be provided by private businesses. The corporations are formed when the government chooses to engage in activities that primarily are commercial in nature, produce revenue, and require greater flexibility than Congress generally allows regular departments. Some of the better known government corporations include Amtrak and the Federal Deposit Insurance Corporation. Unlike other governmental agencies, government corporations charge for their services.

independent executive agency
Governmental unit that closely resembles a Cabinet department but has a narrower area of responsibility (such as the Central Intelligence Agency) and is not part of any Cabinet department.

Independent Executive Agencies.   **Independent executive agencies** closely resemble Cabinet departments but have narrower areas of responsibility. Generally speaking, independent agencies perform service rather than regulatory functions. The heads of these agencies are appointed by the president and serve, like Cabinet secretaries, at his pleasure.

Independent agencies exist apart from executive departments for practical or symbolic reasons. The National Aeronautics and Space Administration (NASA), for example, could have been placed within the Department of Defense. Such positioning, however, could have conjured up thoughts of a space program dedicated solely to military purposes, rather than to civilian satellite communication or scientific exploration. Similarly, the Environmental Protection Agency (EPA) was created in 1970 to administer federal programs aimed at controlling pollution and protecting the nation's environment. It administers all congressional laws concerning the environment and pollution. Along with the Council on Environmental Quality, a staff agency in the Executive Office of the President, the EPA advises the president on environmental concerns, and its head is considered a member of the president's Cabinet.[11] It also administers programs transferred to it with personnel detailed from the Departments of Agriculture, Energy, Interior, and Health and Human Services, and the Nuclear Regulatory Commission, among other agencies. The expanding national focus on the environment, in fact, has brought about numerous calls to elevate the EPA to Cabinet-level status to reinforce a long-term national commitment to improved air and water and other environmental issues.

Photo courtesy: Mark J. Terrill/AP/Wide World Photos

■ Mars Exploration project members speak to the press at NASA's Jet Propulsion Laboratory in Pasadena, California, shortly before the Mars landing of the "rover" named Spirit, in January 2004. While on its mission, the Spirit was able to take more than 30,000 photos of the planet.

Independent Regulatory Commissions. Independent regulatory commissions are agencies that were created by Congress to exist outside the major departments to regulate a specific economic activity or interest. Because of the complexity of modern economic issues, Congress sought to create agencies that could develop expertise and provide continuity of policy with respect to economic issues, since neither Congress nor the courts have the time or talent to do so. Examples include the National Labor Relations Board, the Federal Reserve Board, the Federal Communications Commission, and the Securities and Exchange Commission (SEC).[12]

Older boards and commissions, such as the SEC and the Federal Reserve Board, generally are charged with overseeing a certain industry. Most were created specifically to be free from partisan political pressure. Each is headed by a board composed of five to seven members (always an odd number, to avoid tie votes) who are selected by the president and confirmed by the Senate for fixed, staggered terms to increase

You Are the President of MEDICORP

the chances of a bipartisan board. Unlike executive department heads, they cannot easily be removed by the president.

However, newer regulatory boards are more concerned with how the business sector relates to public health and safety. They often lack autonomy and freedom from political pressures; they are generally headed by a single administrator who can be removed by the president. These boards and commissions, therefore, are far more susceptible to the political wishes of the president who appoints them.

HOW THE BUREAUCRACY WORKS

WHEN CONGRESS CREATES ANY KIND of department, agency, or commission, it is actually delegating some of its powers listed in Article I, section 8, of the U.S. Constitution. Therefore, the laws creating departments, agencies, corporations, or commissions carefully describe their purpose and give them the authority to make numerous policy decisions, which have the effect of law. Congress recognizes that it does not have the time, expertise, or ability to involve itself in every detail of every program; therefore, it sets general guidelines for agency action and leaves it to the agency to work out the details. How agencies execute congressional wishes is called **implementation,** the process by which a law or policy is put into operation.

Historically, political scientists attempting to study how the bureaucracy made policy investigated what they termed **iron triangles,** a term that was used to refer to the relatively stable relationships and patterns of interaction that occurred among federal workers in agencies or departments, interest groups, and relevant congressional subcommittees (see Figure 8.4).

Today, however, iron triangles no longer dominate most policy processes, although some persist, such as the relationships among the Department of Veterans Affairs, the House Committee on Veterans Affairs, and the American Legion and the Veterans of Foreign Wars, the two largest veterans groups. Both individual veterans and organizations such as these continually lobby or are in contact with the federal employees who are responsible for promulgating rules and implementing policies that affect veterans on a daily basis.

Today, many political scientists examining external influences on the modern bureaucracy prefer to examine **issue networks.** In general, issue networks, like iron triangles, include agency officials, members of Congress (and committee staffers), and interest group lobbyists. But, they also include lawyers, consultants, academics, public relations specialists, and sometimes even the courts. Unlike iron triangles, issue networks are constantly changing as members with technical expertise or newly interested parties become involved in issue areas.

implementation
The process by which a law or policy is put into operation by the bureaucracy.

iron triangle
The relatively stable relationship and pattern of interaction that occur among an agency, interest groups, and congressional committees or subcommittees.

issue network
The loose and informal relationship that exists among a large number of actors who work in broad policy areas.

FIGURE 8.4 An Iron Triangle. ■

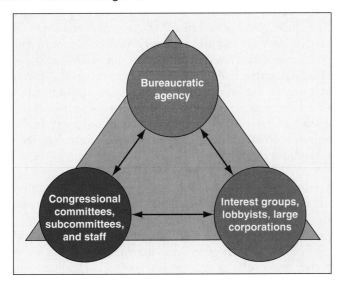

As a result of the increasing complexity of many policy domains, many alliances also have been created within the bureaucracy. One such example is **interagency councils,** working groups that bring together representatives of several departments and agencies to facilitate the coordination of policy making and implementation. Depending on how well these councils are funded, they can be the prime movers of administration policy in any area where an interagency council exists. The U.S. Interagency Council on the Homeless, for example, was created in 1987 to coordinate the activities of the more than fifty governmental agencies and programs that work to alleviate homelessness.

In areas where there are extraordinarily complex policy problems, recent presidential administrations have created policy coordinating committees (PCCs) to facilitate interaction among agencies and departments at the subcabinet level. These PCCs have gained increasing favor post-9/11. For example, the PCC on Terrorist Financing, which includes representatives from the Departments of Treasury, State, Defense, and Justice, along with the CIA and FBI, conducted a study that recommended to the president that he ask the Saudi government to take action against alleged terrorist financiers.[13]

interagency council
Working group created to facilitate coordination of policy making and implementation across a host of governmental agencies.

Making Policy

The end product of all of these decision-making bodies is policy making. Policy making and implementation take place on both formal and informal levels. Practically, many decisions are left to individual government employees on a day-to-day basis. These street-level bureaucrats make policy on two levels. First, they exercise wide discretion in decisions concerning citizens with whom they interact. Second, taken together, their individual actions add up to agency behavior.[14] Thus, how bureaucrats interpret and how they apply (or choose not to apply) various policies are equally important parts of the policy-making process.

Administrative discretion, the ability to make choices concerning the best way to implement congressional or executive intentions, also allows decision makers (whether they are in a Cabinet-level position or at the lowest GS levels) a tremendous amount of leeway. It is exercised through two formal administrative procedures: rule making and administrative adjudication.

Rule Making.   **Rule making** is a quasi-legislative administrative process that results in regulations and has the characteristics of a legislative act. **Regulations** are the rules that govern the operation of all government programs and have the force of law. In essence, then, bureaucratic rule makers often act as lawmakers as well as law enforcers when they make rules or draft regulations to implement various congressional statutes. Some political scientists say that rule making "is the single most important function performed by agencies of government."[15]

Because regulations often involve political conflict, the 1946 Administrative Procedures Act established rule-making procedures to give everyone the chance to participate in the process. The act requires that: (1) public notice of the time, place, and nature of the rule-making proceedings be provided in the *Federal Register*; (2) interested parties be given the opportunity to submit written arguments and facts relevant to the rule; and, (3) the statutory purpose and basis of the rule be stated. Once rules are written, thirty days generally must elapse before they take effect.

Sometimes an agency is required by law to conduct a formal hearing before issuing rules. Evidence is gathered, and witnesses testify and are cross-examined by opposing interests. The process can take weeks, months, or even years, at the end of which agency administrators must review the entire record and then justify the new rules. Although cumbersome, the process has reduced criticism of some rules and bolstered the deference given by the courts to agency decisions. Many Americans are unaware of the opportunities available to them to influence government at this stage. As illustrated in On Campus: Enforcing Gender Equity in College Athletics, women's groups and female athletes testified at hearings held around the country, urging Secretary of Education Rod Paige not to revise existing Title IX regulations. Change could have affected their ability to play sports or receive college athletic scholarships.[16]

Administrative Adjudication.   **Administrative adjudication** is a quasi-judicial process in which a bureaucratic agency settles disputes between two parties in a manner similar to the way courts resolve

administrative discretion
The ability of bureaucrats to make choices concerning the best way to implement congressional intentions.

rule making
A quasi-legislative administrative process that has the characteristics of a legislative act.

regulation
A rule that governs the operation of a particular government program and has the force of law.

You Are a Federal Administrator

administrative adjudication
A quasi-judicial process in which a bureaucratic agency settles disputes between two parties in a manner similar to the way courts resolve disputes.

ENFORCING GENDER EQUITY IN COLLEGE ATHLETICS

In 2004, there were approximately 150,000 female student-athletes, a number up dramatically from 1971, when there were only about 30,000 women participating in collegiate athletics.[a] A major source of that difference? The passage in 1972 of legislation popularly known as Title IX, which prohibits discrimination against girls and women in federally funded education, including athletics programs.

Increased emphasis on Title IX enforcement has led many women to file lawsuits to force compliance. In 1991, in an effort to trim expenses, Brown University cut two men's and two women's teams from its varsity roster. Several women students filed a Title IX complaint against the school, arguing that it violated the act by not providing women varsity sport opportunities in relation to their population in the university. The women also argued that cutting the two women's programs saved $62,000, whereas the men's cuts saved only $16,000. Thus, the women's varsity programs took a bigger hit, in violation of federal law.

A U.S. district court refused to allow Brown to cut the women's programs. A U.S. court of appeals upheld that action, concluding that Brown had failed to provide adequate opportunities for its female students to participate in athletics.[b] In 1997, in *Brown University* v. *Cohen*, the U.S. Supreme Court declined to review the appeals court's decision.[c] This put all colleges and universities on notice that discrimination against women would not be tolerated, even when, as in the case of Brown University, the university had expanded sports opportunities for women tremendously since the passage of Title IX.

Most colleges still provide far fewer opportunities to women, given their numbers in most universities, and enforcement still lags.

In early 2003, after holding hearings on Title IX throughout the United States, a com-

Photo courtesy: Doug Mills/The New York Times

Here, Julie Foudy, captain of the victorious 2004 U.S. Olympic soccer team and former president of the Women's Sports Foundation, lobbies to preserve Title IX.

mission appointed by the Bush administration recommended to the secretary of education that enforcement of Title IX's requirements that provide opportunities for women in athletics be weakened to account for perceived differences in interest in athletics between male and female college students. The recommendation was greeted with protest from women members of the House, who held their own hearings in support of Title IX, and the Bush administration, for the time being, allowed Title IX to stand. Public support for Title IX is quite high. A 2003 Roper poll found that 61 percent of the public viewed Title IX favorably.[d]

---

[a] *Intercollegiate Athletics: Status of Efforts to Promote Gender Equity*, General Accounting Office, October 25, 1996.

[b] *Cohen* v. *Brown University*, 101 F.3d 155 (1996).

[c] 520 U.S. 1186 (1997).

[d] Public Opinion Online, Accession Numbers 0418720 and 0418721.

disputes. Administrative adjudication is referred to as "quasi" (Latin for "seemingly") judicial, because law-making by any body other than Congress or adjudication by any body other than the judiciary would be a violation of the constitutional principle of separation of powers.

Agencies regularly find that persons or businesses are not in compliance with the federal laws the agencies are charged with enforcing, or that they are in violation of an agency rule or regulation. To force compliance, some agencies resort to administrative adjudication, which generally is less formal than a trial. Several agencies and boards employ administrative law judges to conduct the hearings. Although these judges are employed by the agencies, they are strictly independent and cannot be removed except for gross misconduct.

MAKING AGENCIES ACCOUNTABLE

THE QUESTION OF TO WHOM BUREAUCRATS should be responsible is one that continually comes up in any debate about governmental accountability. Should the bureaucracy be answerable to itself? To organized interest groups? To its clientele? To the president? To Congress? Or to some combination of all of these? At times an agency becomes so removed from the public it serves that Congress must step in.

While many critics of the bureaucracy would argue that federal employees should be responsive to the public interest, the public interest is difficult to define. As it turns out, several factors work to control the power of the bureaucracy, and to some degree, the same kinds of checks and balances that operate among the three branches of government serve to check the bureaucracy.

Executive Control

As the size and scope of the American national government, in general, and of the executive branch and the bureaucracy, in particular, have grown, presidents have delegated more and more power to bureaucrats. But, most presidents have continued to try to exercise some control over the bureaucracy, although they often have found that task more difficult than they first envisioned.

Presidents try to appoint the best possible persons to carry out their wishes and policy preferences. Making hundreds of appointments to the executive branch, they have the opportunity to appoint individuals who share their views on a range of policies. Although presidential appointments make up a very small proportion of all federal jobs, presidents usually fill most top policy-making positions.

Presidents, with the approval of Congress, can reorganize the bureaucracy. They also can make changes in an agency's annual budget requests and can ignore legislative initiatives originating within the bureaucracy. As discussed in chapter 7, presidents also can shape policy and provide direction to bureaucrats by issuing **executive orders,** presidential directives to an agency that provide the basis for carrying out laws or for establishing new policies.[17] Even before Congress acted to protect women from discrimination by the federal government, for example, the National Organization for Women convinced President Lyndon B. Johnson to sign Executive Order 11375 in 1967. This amended an earlier order prohibiting the federal government from discriminating on the basis of race, color, religion, or national origin in the awarding of federal contracts, by adding to it the category of "gender." Nevertheless, although the president signed the order, the Office of Federal Contract Compliance, part of the Department of Labor's Employment Standards Administration, failed to draft appropriate guidelines for implementation of the order until several years later.[18]

executive order
A rule or regulation issued by the president that has the effect of law. All executive orders must be published in the *Federal Register*.

Congressional Control

Congress, too, plays an important role in checking the power of the bureaucracy. Constitutionally, it possesses the authority to create or abolish departments and agencies as well as to transfer agency functions. It also can expand or contract bureaucratic discretion.

Congress uses many of its constitutional powers to exercise control over the bureaucracy. These include its investigatory powers. It is not at all unusual for a congressional committee or subcommittee to hold hearings on a particular problem and then direct the relevant agency to study the problem or find ways to remedy it. Representatives of the agencies also appear before these committees on a regular basis to inform members about agency activities and ongoing investigations. In addition, Congress uses its power of the purse to control the bureaucracy, and the Senate's ability to confirm presidential appointments of agency heads and other top officials is an important form of congressional control.

Legislators also augment their formal oversight of the executive branch by allowing citizens to appeal adverse bureaucratic decisions to agencies, Congress, and even the courts. Congressional review, a procedure adopted by the 104th Congress by which agency regulations can be nullified by joint resolutions of legislative disapproval, is another method of exercising congressional oversight. This form of oversight is discussed in greater detail in chapter 6.

Judicial Control

Whereas the president's and Congress's ongoing control over the actions of the bureaucracy is very direct, the judiciary's oversight function is less apparent. Still, federal judges, for example, can directly issue injunctions or orders to an executive agency even before a rule is promulgated formally, giving the federal judiciary a potent check on the bureaucracy. The courts also have ruled that agencies must give all affected individuals their due process rights guaranteed by the U.S. Constitution. On a more informal, indirect level, litigation, or even the threat of litigation, often exerts a strong influence on bureaucrats. Injured parties can bring suit against agencies for their failure to enforce the law and can challenge agency interpretations of the law. In general, however, the courts give great weight to the opinions of bureaucrats and usually defer to their expertise.[19]

Research by political scientists shows that government agencies are strategic. They often implement Supreme Court decisions "based on the costs and benefits of alternative policy choices." Specifically, the degree to which agencies appear to respond to Supreme Court decisions is based on the "specificity of Supreme Court opinions, agency policy preferences, agency age, and *amicus curiae* support."[20]

The development of specialized courts has altered the relationship of some agencies with the federal courts, apparently resulting in less judicial deference to agency rulings. Research by political scientists reveals that specialized courts such as the Court of International Trade, because of their expertise, defer less to agency decisions than do more generalized federal courts. Conversely, decisions from executive agencies are more likely to be reversed than those from more specialized independent regulatory commissions.[21]

SUMMARY

THE BUREAUCRACY PLAYS A MAJOR ROLE in America as a shaper of public policy, earning it the nickname the fourth branch of government. According to Max Weber, all bureaucracies have similar characteristics. These characteristics can be seen in the federal bureaucracy as it developed from George Washington's time, when the executive branch had only three departments—State, War, and Treasury—through the Civil War. Significant gains occurred in the size of the federal bureaucracy as the government geared up to conduct a war. As employment opportunities within the federal government increased, concurrent reforms in the civil service system assured that more and more jobs were filled according to merit and not by patronage. By the late 1800s, reform efforts led to further increases in the size of the bureaucracy, as independent regulatory commissions were created. In the wake of the Depression, many new agencies were created to get the national economy back on course as part of President Franklin D. Roosevelt's New Deal.

The modern bureaucracy is composed of nearly two million civilian workers from all walks of life. In general, bureaucratic agencies fall into four general types: departments, government corporations, independent agencies, and independent regulatory commissions.

The bureaucracy gets much of its power from the Congress delegating its powers. A variety of formal and informal mechanisms have been created to help the bureaucracy work more efficiently. These mechanisms help the bureaucracy and bureaucrats make policy.

Agencies enjoy considerable discretion, but they also are subjected to many formal controls. The president, Congress, and the judiciary all exercise various degrees of control over the bureaucracy.

KEY TERMS

administrative adjudication, p. 292
administrative discretion, p. 292
bureaucracy, p. 271
civil service system, p. 275
department, p. 284
executive order, p. 295
Federal Employees Political Activities Act, p. 277
government corporation, p. 288
Hatch Act, p. 276
implementation, p. 290
independent executive agency, p. 288
independent regulatory commission, p. 275
interagency council, p. 291
iron triangle, p. 290
issue network, p. 290
merit system, p. 275
patronage, p. 273
Pendleton Act, p. 274
regulation, p. 292
rule making, p. 292
spoils system, p. 273

SELECTED READINGS

Aberbach, Joel D., and Bert A. Rockman. *In the Web of Politics: Three Decades of the U.S. Federal Executive.* Washington, DC: Brookings Institution, 2000.

Borrelli, MaryAnne. *The President's Cabinet: Gender, Power, and Representation.* Boulder, CO: Lynne Rienner, 2002.

Brehm, John, and Scott Gates. *Working, Shirking, and Sabotage: Bureaucratic Response to a Democratic Public.* Ann Arbor: University of Michigan Press, 1997.

Derthick, Martha, and Paul J. Quirk. *The Politics of Deregulation.* Washington, DC: Brookings Institution, 1985.

Felbinger, Claire L., and Wendy A. Haynes, eds. *Outstanding Women in Public Administration: Leaders, Mentors, and Pioneers.* Armonk, NY: M. E. Sharpe, 2004.

Goodsell, Charles T. *The Case for Bureaucracy: A Public Administration Polemic.* Chatham, NJ: Chatham House, 1994.

Handler, Joel F. *Down the Bureaucracy: The Ambiguity of Privatization and Empowerment.* Princeton, NJ: Princeton University Press, 1996.

Ingraham, Patricia Wallace. *The Foundation of Merit: Public Service in American Democracy.* Baltimore, MD: Johns Hopkins University Press, 1995.

Kerwin, Cornelius M. *Rulemaking: How Government Agencies Write Law and Make Policy,* 3rd ed. Washington, DC: CQ Press, 2003.

MacKenzie, G. Calvin. *The Irony of Reform: Roots of Political Disenchantment.* Boulder, CO: Westview, 1996.

Osborne, David, and Peter Plastrik. *Banishing Bureaucracy: The Five Strategies for Reinventing Government.* Boston: Addison-Wesley, 1997.

Peters, B. Guy. *The Politics of Bureaucracy,* 5th ed. New York: Routledge, 2001.

Richardson, William D. *Democracy, Bureaucracy and Character.* Lawrence: University Press of Kansas, 1997.

Stivers, Camilla. *Gender Images in Public Administration: Legitimacy and the Administrative State.* Thousand Oaks, CA: Sage, 2002.

Twight, Charlotte. *Dependent on DC: The Rise of Federal Control over the Lives of Ordinary Americans.* New York: Palgrave Macmillan, 2002.

Wilson, James Q. *Bureaucracy: What Government Agencies Do and Why They Do It,* reprint ed. New York: Basic Books, 2000.

WEB EXPLORATIONS

To examine the federal workforce by gender, race, and ethnicity, go to
www.opm.gov/feddata/factbook/

To see federal agency rules and regulations contained in the *Federal Register,* go to
www.gpoaccess.gov/fr/index.html

For more about the IRS and its modernization efforts, see
www.irs.gov

9

The Judiciary

Photo courtesy: Rick Priedman/Corbis

WHEN THE SUPREME COURT AGREED to hear the case of *Lawrence* v. *Texas* in late 2002, many social conservatives were stunned. Although legally, the petitioners only asked the justices to rule on the constitutionality of a Texas statute banning consensual sodomy between same-sex couples, the case had much broader practical implications. If the justices found the statute unconstitutional, the Court would be able to redefine the gay rights movement in the United States and perhaps open the door for equal rights for homosexuals in areas such as marriage and adoption.

Speculation about how the Court would decide the case, and how broad this decision would be, continued until the Court handed down its final decision on June 26, 2003. In this opinion, written by Justice Anthony Kennedy, the Court ruled that the Texas statute violated John Geddes Lawrence's Fourteenth Amendment right to due process of the law, as well as to his right to privacy. This decision also rendered unconstitutional the laws of thirteen other states and established a new national standard for the regulation of private sexual activity, to say nothing of bringing the gay rights struggle into the spotlight for the 2004 election cycle. The decision was celebrated throughout the United States by same-sex couples and supporters of gay rights (see photo, above).

The Supreme Court has not always played such a key role in setting the terms of constitutional debate in American society, nor have its members been able to make such broad legal policy. Today, however, the Court controls the fate of nearly every major policy made on the most significant local, state, and national social issues in our society, including abortion, the death penalty, the extent of the government's involvement in religion, and the scope of its right to resolve competing claims of domestic safety versus individual liberties.

Because the Court has usurped such tremendous policy-making power and is the final word on the meaning of the Constitution, many groups who believe that they cannot achieve policy change through traditional legislative means choose to bring their claims to the judiciary, especially the federal courts. This authority gives the nine men and women who sit on the Supreme Court unprecedented power in American society.

I N 1787, WHEN ALEXANDER HAMILTON WROTE to urge support of the U.S. Constitution, he firmly believed that the judiciary would prove to be the weakest of the three departments of government. In its formative years, the judiciary was, in Hamilton's words, "the least dangerous" branch. The judicial branch seemed so inconsequential that when the young national government made its move to the District of Columbia in 1800, Congress actually forgot to include any space to house the justices of the Supreme Court!

Today, the role of the courts, particularly the Supreme Court of the United States, is significantly different from that envisioned in 1788, the year the national government came into being. What was considered the least dangerous branch is now perceived by many as having too much power, and critics charge that the Framers would not recognize the current federal government, especially the judiciary.

In this chapter, we will first look at the Constitution and the creation of the federal judiciary as well as the Judiciary Act of 1789 and its establishment of the federal judicial system. After considering the American legal system and the concepts of civil and criminal law, we will discuss the federal court system composed of specialized courts, district courts, courts of appeals, and the Supreme Court, which is the ultimate authority on all federal law. Then, we will examine how federal court judges are selected. All appointments to the federal district courts, courts of appeals, and the Supreme Court are made by the president and are subject to Senate confirmation. Our study of the Supreme Court today will make clear that only a few of the millions of cases filed in courts around the United States every year eventually make their way to the Supreme Court through the lengthy appellate process. After an examination of judicial philosophy and decision making and how judicial decision making is based on a variety of legal and extra-legal factors, we will discuss judicial policy making and implementation.

A note on terminology: When we refer to the "Supreme Court," the "Court," or the "high Court" here, we always mean the U.S. Supreme Court, which sits at the pinnacle of the federal and state court systems. The Supreme Court is referred to by the name of the chief justice who presided over it during a particular period (for example, the Marshall Court is the Court presided over by John Marshall from 1801 to 1835). When we use the term "courts," we refer to all federal or state courts unless otherwise noted.

THE CONSTITUTION AND THE CREATION OF THE FEDERAL JUDICIARY

THE DETAILED NOTES JAMES MADISON took at the Constitutional Convention in Philadelphia make it clear that the Framers devoted little time to the writing of, or the content of, Article III, which created the judicial branch of government. The Framers believed that a federal judiciary posed little of the threat of tyranny that they feared from the other two branches. Anti-Federalists, however, were quick to object to a judiciary whose members had life tenure and the ability to interpret what was to be "the supreme law of the land."

The Framers also debated the need for any federal courts below the level of the Supreme Court. A compromise left the final choice to Congress, and Article III, section 1, begins simply by vesting "The judicial Power of the United States…in one supreme Court, and in such inferior Courts as the Congress may from time to time ordain and establish." Although there is some debate over whether the Court should have the power of **judicial review,** which allows the judiciary to review the constitutionality of acts of the other branches of government and the states, the question was left unsettled in Article III—and not finally resolved until *Marbury* v. *Madison* (1803), regarding acts of the national government, and *Martin* v. *Hunter's Lessee* (1816), regarding state law.[1]

Article III, section 1, also gave Congress the authority to establish other courts as it saw fit. Section 2 specifies the judicial power of the Supreme Court (see Table 9.1) and discusses the Court's original and appellate jurisdiction. This section also specifies that all federal crimes, except those involving impeachment, shall be tried by jury in the state in which the crime was committed. The third section of the article defines treason, and mandates that at least two witnesses appear in such cases.

Although it is the duty of the chief justice of the United States to preside over presidential impeachments, this is not mentioned in Article III. Instead, Article I, section 3, notes in discussing impeachment, "When the President of the United States is tried, the Chief Justice shall preside."

judicial review
Power of the courts to review acts of other branches of government and the states.

Comparing Judiciaries

JUDICIAL STRUCTURE AND POWERS

Constitutions are powerful documents. They establish who holds power in governments and where those powers begin and end. But, they are not necessarily unambiguous. Just what does "freedom of the press" mean? If Congress does not declare war, something it has done only five times and not since World War II, were the Korean War, Vietnam War, Persian Gulf War, and Iraq War all unconstitutional? Moreover, even when a constitution is clear as to what is meant by a word or phrase, it is not self-implementing. Some institution must have the binding authority to reach the conclusion that the constitution has been ignored or violated. That institution is the judiciary.

Constitutional democracies have taken two different approaches to creating courts with this power of judicial review. One approach is to give this power to the highest court in the country. The United States, Canada, India, and Australia employ this system. A second approach is to create a separate Constitutional Court, which exists apart from courts that hear criminal cases. Germany, France, Spain, and Greece use this judicial system. We can get a clearer idea of how the U.S. Supreme Court compares with other courts of final constitutional jurisdiction by taking a look at the German and Canadian examples—important points of comparison, since the United States was an important influence on each.

The Supreme Court of Canada has a chief justice and eight junior justices, all of whom are appointed by the governor-in-council. While Canada is an independent country, it is also part of the British Commonwealth, and the governor-in-council represents the British queen or king in Canada. The political reality is that the governor-in-council is a ceremonial figure and the actual selections are made by the prime minister.

The Supreme Court of Canada has both original jurisdiction for some cases and appellate jurisdiction. Most of its cases are heard on appeal, and decisions generally take the form of a single opinion written by the majority. Dissenting and concurrent opinions are also presented. For most of its history, the Supreme Court of Canada took a limited view of its power of judicial review and limited its decisions to questions of federalism. More recently it has begun to render decisions on matters of civil rights. The Supreme Court of Canada also routinely gives "advisory opinions" on important political issues, unlike the U.S. federal courts.

The Constitutional Court of Germany is not part of the regular court system; instead, it is only a court of original jurisdiction on questions of constitutional interpretation. The full Constitutional Court is made up of sixteen justices. In practice, it is divided into two panels of eight justices each. Three justices on each panel must be career judges, and the rest tend to be civil servants, politicians, or law professors. Justices serve a twelve-year term; they cannot be reappointed and must retire at age sixty-eight.

A case comes before the Constitutional Court in three different ways. First, the federal government, a state government, or one-third of the members of the lower house of the German parliament can ask for a court ruling on the constitutionality of a law before it goes into effect. Second, judges hearing a case in the regular court system can refer it to the Constitutional Court if they believe it raises constitutional issues. Third, and by far the most frequent way cases reach the Constitutional Court, petitions are filed by citizens. These cases of alleged violations of constitutional rights are screened by a committee of three justices and only about 3 percent are accepted.

Questions

1. Do you think the United States should create a separate constitutional court? Why or why not?
2. Which system for selecting justices do you think is best, the U.S., Canadian, or German approach? Explain your answer.

TABLE 9.1   The Judicial Power of the United States Supreme Court

The following are the types of cases the Supreme Court was given the jurisdiction to hear as initially specified in the Constitution:

- All cases arising under the Constitution and laws or treaties of the United States
- All cases of admiralty or maritime jurisdiction
- Cases in which the United States is a party
- Controversies between a state and citizens of another state
- Controversies between two or more states
- Controversies between citizens of different states
- Controversies between citizens of the same states claiming lands under grants in different states
- Controversies between a state, or the citizens thereof, and foreign states or citizens thereof
- All cases affecting ambassadors or other public ministers

Had the Supreme Court been viewed as the potential policy maker it is today, it is highly unlikely that the Framers would have provided for life tenure with "good behavior" for federal judges in Article III. This feature was agreed on because the Framers did not want the justices (or any federal judges) to be subject to the whims of politics, the public, or politicians. Moreover, Alexander Hamilton argued in *Federalist No. 78* that the "independence of judges" was needed "to guard the Constitution and the rights of individuals." Because the Framers viewed the Court as quite powerless, Hamilton stressed the need to place federal judges above the fray of politics.

Some checks on the power of the judiciary were nonetheless included in the Constitution. The Constitution gives Congress the authority to alter the Court's jurisdiction (its ability to hear certain kinds of cases). Congress can also propose constitutional amendments that, if ratified, can effectively reverse judicial decisions, and it can impeach and remove federal judges. In one further check, it is the president who (with the "advice and consent" of the Senate) appoints all federal judges.

The Judiciary Act of 1789 and the Creation of the Federal Judicial System

In spite of the Framers' intentions, the pervasive role of politics in the judicial branch quickly became evident with the passage of the Judiciary Act of 1789. Congress spent nearly the entire second half of its first session deliberating the various provisions of the act to give form and substance to the federal judiciary.

The **Judiciary Act of 1789** established the basic three-tiered structure of the federal court system. At the bottom are the federal district courts—at least one in each state—each staffed by a federal judge. If the people participating in a lawsuit (called litigants) are unhappy with the district court's verdict, they can appeal their case to a circuit court. Each

Judiciary Act of 1789
Established the basic three-tiered structure of the federal court system.

The Living Constitution

The Judges both of the supreme and inferior Courts, shall...receive for their Services, a Compensation, which shall not be diminished during their Continuance in Office.

—Article III, Section 1

This section of Article III simply posits the notion that the salaries of all federal judges cannot be reduced during their service on the bench. During the Constitutional Convention, there was considerable debate over how to treat the payment of federal judges. Some believed that Congress should have an extra check on the judiciary by being able to intimidate judges with the threat of reducing their salaries. This provision was a compromise after James Madison suggested that Congress have the authority to bar increases as well as decreases in the salaries of these unelected jurists. The delegates recognized that decreases, as well as no opportunity for raises, could negatively affect the pluses associated with life tenure.

There has not been much controversy over this clause of the Constitution. When the federal income tax was first enacted, some judges unsuccessfully challenged it as a diminution of their salaries. Much more recently, since becoming chief justice, William H. Rehnquist has been a vocal proponent of increased salaries for federal judges, who now earn less than some of their former clerks do as first-year associates in private law firms. As early as 1989, he noted that "judicial salaries were the single greatest problem facing the federal judiciary today." In 2002, not only did Rehnquist note the increased workload of each federal judge and the relative static salary of federal judges, but he also pointed out that while the salaries of those lawyers engaged in private practice has skyrocketed, the salaries of federal judges have stagnated, with judges receiving only small cost-of-living increases. This inequity is making it difficult to attract and retain top-flight judges, especially those who have children to put through college. He believes that inadequate pay undermines the strength of the independent judiciary. More and more federal judges are leaving the bench for more lucrative private practice, which is a relatively recent phenomenon. While $150,000 may sound like a lot to most people, lawyers in large urban practices routinely earn more than double and often triple that amount each year.

■ The Supreme Court held its first two sessions in this building, called the Exchange.

Photo courtesy: Bettmann/Corbis

circuit court initially was composed of one district court judge and two itinerant Supreme Court justices who met as a circuit court twice a year.

The third tier of the federal judicial system fleshed out by the Judiciary Act of 1789 was the Supreme Court. Although the Constitution mentions "the supreme Court," it was silent on its size. In the Judiciary Act, Congress set the size of the Supreme Court at six—the chief justice plus five associate justices. After decades of tinkering with the Court's size, the number of justices was fixed at nine in 1869.

The first session of the Supreme Court, presided over by John Jay, who was appointed chief justice of the United States by George Washington, initially had to be adjourned when a quorum of the justices failed to show up. It later decided only one major case. Moreover, as an indication of its lowly status, one associate justice left the Court to become chief justice of the South Carolina Supreme Court.

In its first decade, the Court—although not yet a truly co-equal branch—took several actions to help mold the new nation. First, by declining to give President George Washington advice on the legality of some of his actions, the justices attempted to establish the Supreme Court as an independent, nonpolitical branch of government. The early Court also tried to advance principles of nationalism and to maintain the national government's supremacy over the states. Finally, in a series of circuit and Supreme Court decisions, the justices paved the way for announcement of the doctrine of judicial review by the third chief justice, John Marshall.[2]

The Marshall Court: *Marbury* v. *Madison* (1803) and Judicial Review

John Marshall was appointed chief justice by President John Adams in 1801, three years after he declined to accept a nomination as associate justice. An ardent Federalist, Marshall has come to be considered the most important justice ever to serve on the high Court. Part of his reputation is the result of the duration of his service and the historical significance of this period in our nation's history.

Marshall, for example, began the practice of issuing opinions on behalf of the Court. For the Court to take its place as an equal branch of government, Marshall strongly believed the justices needed to speak as a Court and not as six individuals. He also claimed for the Court the right of judicial review, from which the Supreme Court derives much of its day-to-day power and impact on the policy process.

In *Federalist No. 78*, Alexander Hamilton first publicly endorsed the idea of judicial review, noting, "Whenever a particular statute contravenes the Constitution, it will be the duty of the judicial tribunals to adhere to the latter and disregard the former." Nonetheless, because the power of judicial review is not mentioned in the U.S. Constitution, the actual authority of the Supreme Court to review the constitutionality of acts of Congress was an unsettled question. But, in **Marbury v. Madison (1803)**, Chief Justice John Marshall claimed this sweeping authority for the Court by asserting that the right of judicial review was a power that could be implied from the Constitution's supremacy clause.[3]

Marbury v. *Madison* arose amid a sea of political controversy. In the final hours of the Adams administration, William Marbury was appointed a justice of the peace for the District of Columbia. But, in the confusion of winding up matters, Adams's secretary of state failed to deliver Marbury's commission. Marbury then asked James Madison, President Thomas Jefferson's new secretary of state, for the commission. Under direct orders from Jefferson, who was irate over the Adams administration's last-minute appointment of several Federalist judges (quickly confirmed by the Federalist Senate), Madison refused to turn over the commission. Marbury and three other Adams appointees who were in the same situation then filed a writ of *mandamus* (a legal motion) asking the Supreme Court to order Madison to deliver their commissions.

Political tensions ran high as the Court met to hear the case. Jefferson threatened to ignore any order of the Court. Marshall realized that he and the prestige of the Court could be devastated by any refusal of the executive branch to comply with the decision. Responding to this challenge, in a brilliant opinion that in many sections reads more like a lecture to Jefferson than a discussion of the merits of Marbury's claim,

Photo courtesy: Boston Athenaeum

■ John Marshall was an ardent Federalist and a third cousin of Democratic-Republican President Thomas Jefferson, whose administration he faced head on in *Marbury* v. *Madison* (1803). Marshall came to the Court with little legal experience and no judicial experience.

Marbury v. Madison (1803)
Supreme Court first asserted the power of judicial review in finding that the congressional statute extending the Court's original jurisdiction was unconstitutional.

Marshall concluded that although Marbury and the others were entitled to their commissions, the Court lacked the power to issue the writ sought by Marbury. In *Marbury* v. *Madison*, Marshall further ruled that the parts of the Judiciary Act of 1789 extending the jurisdiction of the Court to allow it to issue writs were inconsistent with the Constitution and therefore unconstitutional.

Although the immediate effect of the decision was to deny power to the Court, its long-term effect was to establish the principle of judicial review, a power that Marshall concluded could be implied from the Constitution. Said Marshall, writing for the Court, "it is emphatically the province and duty of the judicial department to say what the law is."

Through judicial review, an implied power, the Supreme Court can dramatically exert its authority to interpret what the Constitution means. Since *Marbury,* the Court routinely has exercised the power of judicial review to determine the constitutionality of acts of Congress, the executive branch, and the states.

THE AMERICAN LEGAL SYSTEM

trial courts
Courts of original jurisdiction where a case begins.

THE JUDICIAL SYSTEM in the United States can best be described as a dual system consisting of the federal court system and the judicial systems of the fifty states. Cases may arise in either system. Both systems are basically three tiered. At the bottom of the system are **trial courts,** where litigation begins. In the middle are appellate courts in the state systems and the courts of appeals in the federal system. At the top of each pyramid sits a high court. (Some states call these supreme courts; New York calls its highest court the Court of Appeals; Oklahoma and Texas call their highest state court for criminal cases Courts of Criminal Appeals.) The federal courts of appeals and Supreme Court as well as state courts of appeals and supreme courts are **appellate courts** that, with few exceptions, review on appeal only cases that already have been decided in lower courts. These courts generally hear matters of both civil and criminal law.

appellate courts
Courts that generally review only findings of law made by lower courts.

Jurisdiction

jurisdiction
Authority vested in a particular court to hear and decide the issues in any particular case.

Before a state or federal court can hear a case, it must have **jurisdiction,** which means the authority to hear and decide the issues in that case. The jurisdiction of the federal courts is controlled by the U.S. Constitution and by federal statute. Jurisdiction is conferred based on issues, money involved in a dispute, or the type of offense. Procedurally, we speak of two types of jurisdiction: original and appellate.

original jurisdiction
The jurisdiction of courts that hear a case first, usually in a trial. Courts determine the facts of a case under their original jurisdiction.

Original jurisdiction refers to a court's authority to hear disputes as a trial court and may occur on the federal or state level. More than 90 percent of all cases, whether state or federal, end at this stage.

Appellate jurisdiction refers to a court's ability to review cases already decided by a trial court. Appellate courts ordinarily do not review the factual record; instead, they review legal procedures to make certain that the law was applied properly to the issues presented in the case.

appellate jurisdiction
The power vested in an appellate court to review and/or revise the decision of a lower court.

Criminal and Civil Law

Criminal law is the body of law that regulates individual conduct and is enforced by the state and national governments.[4] Crimes are graded as felonies, misdemeanors, or offenses, according to their severity. Some acts—for example, murder, rape, and robbery—are considered crimes in all states. Although all states outlaw murder, their penal, or criminal, codes treat the crime quite differently; the penalty for murder differs considerably from state to state. Other actions—such as gambling—are illegal only in some states.

criminal law
Codes of behavior related to the protection of property and individual safety.

Criminal law assumes that society itself is the victim of the illegal act; therefore, the government prosecutes, or brings an action, on behalf of an injured party (acting as a plaintiff) in criminal cases. Criminal cases are more often filed in state courts. But, a burgeoning set of federal criminal laws is contributing significantly to delays in the federal courts.

Civil law is the body of law that regulates the conduct and relationships between private individuals or companies. Because the actions at issue in civil law do not constitute a threat to society at large, people who believe they have been injured by another party must take action on their own to seek judicial relief. Civil cases, then, involve lawsuits filed to recover something of value, whether it is the right to vote, fair treatment, or monetary compensation for an item, or service that cannot be recovered.

civil law
Codes of behavior related to business and contractual relationships between groups and individuals.

Each civil or criminal case has a plaintiff, or petitioner, who brings charges against a defendant, or respondent. Sometimes the government is the plaintiff. The government may bring civil charges on behalf of the citizens of the state or the national government against a person or corporation for violating the law, but it is always the government that brings a criminal case. When cases are initiated, they are known first by the name of the petitioner. In *Marbury* v. *Madison*, William Marbury was the plaintiff, suing the defendants, the U.S. government and James Madison as its secretary of state, for not delivering his judicial commission.

Before a criminal or civil case gets to court, much has to happen. Most cases involve a whole series of formal and informal proceedings before a formal trial, and most legal disputes that arise in the United States never get to court. Most individuals accused of criminal conduct plead guilty, often to a lesser charge or in exchange for a guaranteed sentence. Individuals and companies involved in civil disputes also routinely settle their disagreements out of court. Often these settlements are not reached until minutes before the case is to be tried. Many civil cases that go to trial are settled during the course of the trial—before the case can be handed over to the jury or submitted to a judge for a decision or determination of responsibility or guilt.

During trials, judges must often interpret the intent of laws enacted by Congress and state legislatures as they bear on the issues at hand. To do so, they read reports, testimony, and debates on the relevant legislation and study the results of other similar legal cases. They also rely on the presentations made by lawyers in their briefs and at trial. If it is a jury trial, the jury ultimately is the finder of fact, while the judge is the interpreter of the law.

THE FEDERAL COURT SYSTEM

constitutional courts

Federal courts specifically created by the U.S. Constitution or by Congress pursuant to its authority in Article III.

THE FEDERAL DISTRICT COURTS, circuit courts of appeals, and the Supreme Court are called **constitutional** (or Article III) **courts** because Article III of the Constitution either established them (as is the case with the Supreme Court) or authorizes Congress to establish them. Judges who preside over these courts are nominated by the president (with the advice and consent of the Senate), and they serve lifetime terms, as long as they engage in "good behavior."

legislative courts

Courts established by Congress for specialized purposes, such as the Court of Military Appeals.

In addition to constitutional courts, **legislative courts** are set up by Congress, under its implied powers, generally for special purposes. The U.S. Territorial Courts (which hear federal cases in the territories) and the U.S. Court of Veterans Appeals are examples of legislative courts, or what some call Article I courts. The judges who preside over these federal courts are appointed by the president (subject to Senate confirmation) and serve fixed, limited terms.

District Courts

There are currently ninety-four federal district courts staffed by a total of 646 active judges, assisted by more than 300 retired judges who still hear cases on a limited basis. No district court cuts across state lines. Every state has at least one federal district court, and the most populous states—California, Texas, and New York—each have four.

Federal district courts, where the bulk of the judicial work takes place in the federal system, have original jurisdiction over only specific types of cases, as indicated in Figure 9.1. Although the rules governing district court jurisdiction can be complex, cases heard in federal district courts by a single judge (with or without a jury) generally fall into one of three categories:

1. They involve the federal government as a party.
2. They present a federal question based on a claim under the U.S. Constitution, a treaty with another nation, or a federal statute.
3. They involve civil suits in which citizens are from different states, and the amount of money at issue is more than $75,000.[5]

FIGURE 9.1   The Federal Court System. ■

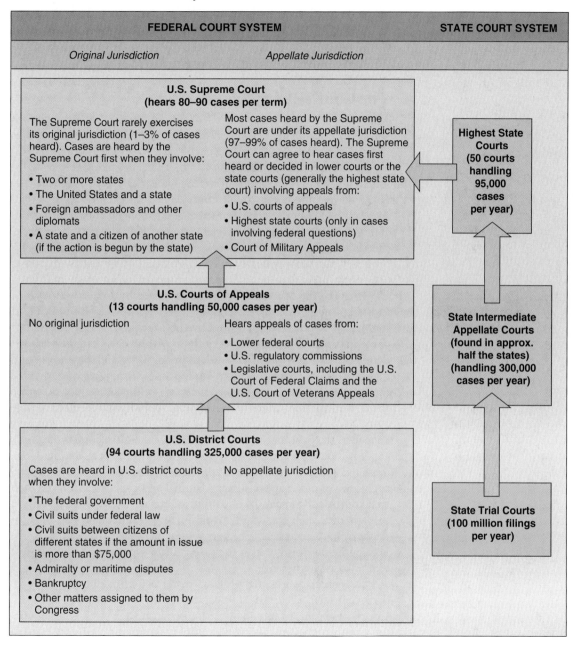

Each federal judicial district has a U.S. attorney, who is nominated by the president and confirmed by the Senate. The U.S. attorney in each district is that district's chief law enforcement officer. The size of the staff and the number of assistant U.S. attorneys who work in each district depend on the amount of litigation in each district. U.S. attorneys, like district attorneys within the states, have a considerable amount of discretion as to whether they pursue criminal or civil investigations or file charges against individuals or corporations.

The Courts of Appeals

The losing party in a case heard and decided in a federal district court can appeal the decision to the appropriate court of appeals. The United States Courts of Appeals (known as the circuit courts of appeals prior to 1948) are the intermediate appellate courts in the federal system and were established in 1789 to hear appeals from federal district courts. There are currently eleven numbered circuit courts. A twelfth, the D.C. Court of Appeals, handles most appeals involving federal regulatory commissions and agencies, including the National Labor Relations Board and the Securities and Exchange Commission. The thirteenth federal appeals court is the U.S. Court of Appeals for the Federal Circuit, which deals with patents and contract and financial claims against the federal government.

Case Overload

In 2005, the courts of appeals were staffed by 167 active judges—assisted by more than eighty retired judges who still hear cases on a limited basis—who were appointed by the president, subject to Senate confirmation. The number of judges within each circuit varies—depending on the workload and the complexity of the cases—and ranges from six to nearly thirty. In deciding cases, judges are divided into rotating three-judge panels, made up of the active judges within the circuit, visiting judges (primarily district judges from the same circuit), and retired judges. In rare cases, all the judges in a circuit may choose to sit together (*en banc*) to decide a case by majority vote.

The courts of appeals have no original jurisdiction. Rather, Congress has granted these courts appellate jurisdiction over two general categories of cases: appeals from criminal and civil cases from the district courts, and appeals from administrative agencies. Once a decision is made by a federal court of appeals, a litigant no longer has an automatic right to an appeal. The losing party may submit a petition to the U.S. Supreme Court to hear the case, but the Court grants few of these requests (see Figure 9.2).

In general, courts of appeals try to correct errors of law and procedure that have occurred in lower courts or administrative agencies. Courts of appeals hear no new testimony; instead, lawyers submit written arguments, in what is called a **brief** (also submitted in trial courts), and then appear to present and argue the case orally to the court.

brief
A document containing the legal written arguments in a case filed with a court by a party prior to a hearing or trial.

The Supreme Court

The U.S. Supreme Court, as we saw in the opening vignette, often is at the center of the storm of highly controversial issues that have yet to

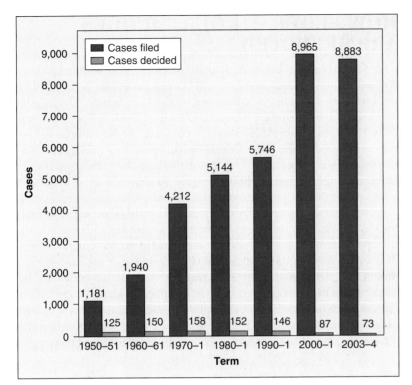

Source: Supreme Court Public Information Office.

FIGURE 9.2 Supreme Court Caseload, 1950–2004 Terms. Cases the Supreme Court chooses to hear represent a tiny fraction of the total number of cases filed with the Court. ■

be resolved successfully in the political process. As the court of last resort at the top of the judicial pyramid, it reviews cases from the U.S. courts of appeals and state supreme courts (as well as other courts of last resort) and acts as the final interpreter of the U.S. Constitution. It not only decides major cases with tremendous policy significance each year, but it also ensures uniformity in the interpretation of national laws and the Constitution, resolves conflicts among the states, and maintains the supremacy of national law in the federal system.

Decisions of any court of appeals are binding on only the district courts within the geographic confines of the circuit, but decisions of the U.S. Supreme Court are binding throughout the nation and establish national **precedents.** This reliance on past decisions or precedents to formulate decisions in new cases is called *stare decisis* (a Latin phrase meaning "let the decision stand"). The principle of *stare decisis* allows for continuity and predictability in our judicial system. Although *stare decisis* can be helpful in predicting decisions, at times judges carve out new ground and ignore, decline to follow, or even overrule precedents in order to reach a different conclusion in a case involving similar circumstances. In one sense, that is why there is so much litigation in America today. Parties know that one cannot always predict the outcome of a case; if such prediction were possible, there would be little reason to go to court.

precedent
Prior judicial decision that serves as a rule for settling subsequent cases of a similar nature.

stare decisis
In court rulings, a reliance on past decisions or precedents to formulate decisions in new cases.

HOW FEDERAL COURT JUDGES ARE SELECTED

THE SELECTION OF FEDERAL JUDGES often is a very political process with important political ramifications because judges are nominated by the president and must be confirmed by the U.S. Senate. During the administrations of Ronald Reagan and George Bush in the 1980s and early 1990s, for example, 553 mostly conservative Republican judges were appointed to the lower federal bench, remolding it in a conservative image (see Figure 9.3). The cumulative impact of this conservative block of judges led many liberal groups to abandon their efforts to achieve their policy goals through the federal courts.

Presidents, in general, try to select well-qualified men and women for the bench. But, these appointments also provide a president with the opportunity to put his philosophical stamp on the federal courts. Nominees, however, although generally members of the nominating president's party, usually are vetted through the senator's offices of the states where the district court or court of appeals vacancy occurs. This process, by which presidents generally defer selection of district court judges to the choice of senators of their own party who represent the state where the vacancy occurs, is known as **senatorial courtesy.**

senatorial courtesy
A process by which presidents, when selecting district court judges, defer to the senator in whose state the vacancy occurs.

Who Are Federal Judges?

Typically, federal district court judges have held other political offices, such as those of state court judge or prosecutor. Most have been involved in politics, which is what usually brings them into consideration for a position on the federal bench.

Photo courtesy: William Philpott/Corbis

■ Senate Majority Leader Bill Frist and the Senate Republican leadership speak to the press before launching a forty-hour "Talkathon" session criticizing the Senate's failure to confirm judicial nominees selected by George W. Bush.

FIGURE 9.3   How a President Affects the Federal Judiciary

This figure depicts the number of judges appointed by each president and how quickly a president can make an impact on the make-up of the Court. ■

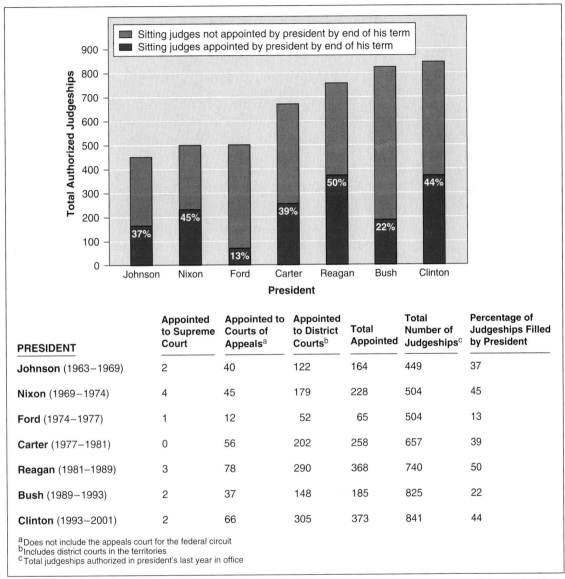

PRESIDENT	Appointed to Supreme Court	Appointed to Courts of Appeals[a]	Appointed to District Courts[b]	Total Appointed	Total Number of Judgeships[c]	Percentage of Judgeships Filled by President
Johnson (1963–1969)	2	40	122	164	449	37
Nixon (1969–1974)	4	45	179	228	504	45
Ford (1974–1977)	1	12	52	65	504	13
Carter (1977–1981)	0	56	202	258	657	39
Reagan (1981–1989)	3	78	290	368	740	50
Bush (1989–1993)	2	37	148	185	825	22
Clinton (1993–2001)	2	66	305	373	841	44

[a] Does not include the appeals court for the federal circuit
[b] Includes district courts in the territories
[c] Total judgeships authorized in president's last year in office

Sources: "Imprints on the Bench," *CQ Weekly Report* (January 19, 2001): 173. Reprinted by permission of Copyright Clearance Center on behalf of Congressional Quarterly, Inc. Bush data compiled by authors from data from the Senate Judiciary Committee.

Increasingly, most judicial nominees have had prior judicial experience. White males continue to dominate the federal courts, but since the 1970s, most presidents have pledged (with varying degrees

Senatorial Confirmation of Judicial Nominations

In May 2004, Senate Republican and Democratic leaders finally agreed to end a lengthy impasse over the confirmations of several judicial nominations to the federal courts made by President George W. Bush. In exchange for a commitment from Senate Democrats not to block twenty-five Bush nominees, the administration agreed not to make any more recess appointments. The Democrats, however, pledged to continue to block the confirmation of seven nominees who they believed are far too extreme to be on the federal bench.

"It's fair, it's balanced," said Senate Majority Leader Bill Frist (R–TN). The Democrats put a different spin on the agreement. Said Charles Schumer (D–NY) who sits on the Senate Judiciary Committee, "The White House waved the white flag here."[a]

This highly publicized dispute began when the Democrats perceived that President Bush was appointing high-profile, very conservative judges to vacancies on the federal courts. Still stinging from what they had perceived as unfair Republican treatment of several Clinton nominees to the federal bench (as well as other positions), the Democrats refused to allow votes to be taken on several nominees as they filibustered, or extended debate, to block the appointment of the few whom they found the most conservative. As the filibusters continued, the frustrated Bush administration appointed two of the most controversial nominees, William H. Pryor Jr. and Charles W. Pickering Sr., while the Senate was in recess. This action allows these men to serve as judges without Senate confirmation until the end of the congressional term. Thus, unlike other federal judges, they do not have a life term. Pryor, a devout Catholic, has characterized *Roe* v. *Wade* as "the worst abomination of constitutional law in our history," while Pickering drew the wrath of Democratic senators and liberal interest groups for his actions to reduce the sentence of a man convicted of burning a cross in the yard of an interracial couple.[b] Pickering's nomination actually had been rejected by the Senate in 2001 when it was controlled by Democrats.

After these appointments, outraged Democrats moved to stop consideration of all judicial nominees, even those who were uncontroversial. And, with an election coming up in November, Republican senators and the administration recognized that many of their selections for the bench might never be confirmed if the White House changed hands in 2005.

In agreeing to allow noncontroversial nominees to be confirmed, however, Senate Democrats continued to block the nominations of the seven most controversial judges, five of whom were nominated to the courts of appeals. As these are seats just one step away from the U.S. Supreme Court, and the most common training ground for Supreme Court nominees, the Democrats believed that they had to take a stronger stand. And, by appearing to compromise with the White House on some nominees, they hoped to make judicial nominations less of an issue in the November elections.

1. Did the Democrats' strategy concerning court of appeals nominees work?
2. Do you think that the selection of federal court judges should be as political as it has become in recent years?

---

[a] Both quoted in Neil A. Lewis, "Deal Ends Impasse Over Judicial Nominees," *New York Times* (May 19, 2004): A19.

[b] Mike Allen and Helen Dewar, "Bush Bypasses Senate on Judge; Pickering Named to Appeals Court During Recess," *Washington Post* (January 17, 2004): A1.

of success) to do their best to appoint more African Americans, Hispanics, women, and other traditionally underrepresented groups to the federal bench (see Analyzing Visuals: Race/Ethnicity and Gender of District Court).

Appointments to the U.S. Supreme Court

Like other federal court judges, the justices of the Supreme Court are nominated by the president and must be confirmed by the Senate. Historically, because of the special place the Supreme Court enjoys in our constitutional system, its nominees have encountered more opposition than district court or court of appeals nominees. As the role of the Court has increased over time, so too has the amount of attention given to nominees. With this increased attention has come greater opposition, especially to nominees with controversial views.

Nomination Criteria

Justice Sandra Day O'Connor once remarked that "You have to be lucky" to be appointed to the Court.[6] Although luck is certainly important, over the years nominations to the bench have been made for a variety of reasons. Some nominees have been friends or political allies of the president. At least three criteria today are especially important: competence, ideology or policy preferences, and pursuit of political support through attention to religion, race, and gender.

Timeline

The Chief Justice of the United States

Competence.   Most prospective nominees are expected to have had at least some judicial or governmental experience. Most have had some prior judicial experience. Through 2005, eight sitting Supreme Court justices had prior judicial experience (see Table 9.2). If Chief Justice Rehnquist's service as associate justice is included, all nine justices enjoyed prior judicial experience.

Ideology or Policy Preferences.   Most presidents seek to appoint to the Court individuals who share their policy preferences, and almost all have political goals in mind when they appoint a justice. Presidents Franklin D. Roosevelt, Richard M. Nixon, and Ronald Reagan were very successful in molding the Court to their own political beliefs. Nixon and Reagan, in fact, publicly proclaimed that they would nominate only conservatives who favored a **strict constructionist** approach to constitutional decision making—that is, an approach emphasizing the original intentions of the Framers.

strict constructionist
An approach to constitutional interpretation that emphasizes the Framers' original intentions.

Analyzing Visuals

RACE/ETHNICITY AND GENDER OF DISTRICT COURT

Traditionally, white males have dominated federal court appointments. Of President Ronald Reagan's 290 appointees to federal district courts, for example, 92.4 percent were white males. Of President Bill Clinton's 305 appointments, however, the percentage of white males was only 52.1 percent. George W. Bush reversed the trend during the first eighteen months of his term; 68.7 percent of his appointees were white males. While most presidents in recent years have pledged to appoint more African Americans, women, and Hispanics to the federal bench, Clinton was the most successful. After reviewing the bar graph to the left, answer the following critical thinking questions: Is there a difference between appointments made by Democratic presidents (Carter and Clinton) and Republican presidents? Which group is most underrepresented in appointments? What factors do presidents consider, in addition to gender and race/ethnicity, in making appointments? Should gender and race/ethnicity be considered by a president?

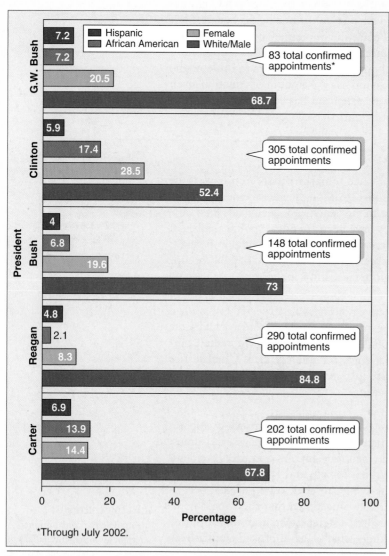

*Through July 2002.

Source: Sheldon Goldman et al., "W. Bush Remaking the Judiciary: Like Father like Son?" *Judicature* 86 (May–June 2003): 304.

TABLE 9.2 The Supreme Court, 2004

Name	Year of Birth	Year of Appointment	Political Party	Law School	Appointing President	Religion	Prior Judicial Experience	Prior Government Experience
William H. Rehnquist	1924	1971/1986[a]	R	Stanford	Nixon	Lutheran	Associate justice U.S. Supreme Court	Assistant U.S. attorney general
John Paul Stevens	1920	1975	R	Chicago	Ford	Nondenom- inational Protestant	U.S. Court of Appeals	
Sandra Day O'Connor	1930	1981	R	Stanford	Reagan	Episcopalian	Arizona Court of Appeals	State legislator
Antonin Scalia	1936	1986	R	Harvard	Reagan	Catholic	U.S. Court of Appeals	
Anthony Kennedy	1936	1988	R	Harvard	Reagan	Catholic	U.S. Court of Appeals	
David Souter	1939	1990	R	Harvard	Bush	Episcopalian	U.S. Court of Appeals	New Hampshire assistant attor- ney general
Clarence Thomas	1948	1991	R	Yale	Bush	Catholic	U.S. Court of Appeals	Chair, Equal Employment Opportunity Commission
Ruth Bader Ginsburg	1933	1993	D	Columbia	Clinton	Jewish	U.S. Court of Appeals	
Stephen Breyer	1938	1994	D	Harvard	Clinton	Jewish	U.S. Court of Appeals	Chief counsel, Senate Judiciary Committee

[a]Promoted to chief justice by President Reagan in 1986.

Pursuit of Political Support from Various Groups.   During Ronald Reagan's successful campaign for the presidency in 1980, some of his advisers feared that the "gender gap" would hurt him. Polls repeatedly showed that he was far less popular with female voters than with men. To gain support from women, Reagan announced during his campaign that should he win, he would appoint a woman to fill the first vacancy on the Court. When Justice Potter Stewart, a moderate, announced his early retirement from the bench, under pressure from women's rights groups President Reagan nominated Sandra Day O'Connor of the Arizona Court of Appeals to fill the vacancy.

Through 2004, only two African Americans and two women have served on the Court. Race was undoubtedly a critical issue in the appointment of Clarence Thomas to replace Thurgood Marshall, the first African American justice. But, President George Bush refused to acknowledge his wish to retain a black seat on the Court. Instead, he

Simulation

You Are Appointing a Supreme Court Justice

announced that he was "picking the best man for the job on the merits," a claim that was met with considerable skepticism by many observers, but meant that he could try to curry favor from African Americans.

Ironically, religion, which historically has been an important issue, was hardly mentioned during the most recent Supreme Court vacancies. Some, however, hailed Clinton's appointment of Ruth Bader Ginsburg, noting that the traditionally Jewish seat on the Court had been vacant since the retirement of Justice Abe Fortas in 1969.

Through 2004, of the 108 justices who served on the Court, almost all have been members of traditional Protestant faiths.[7] Only nine have been Catholic and only seven have been Jewish.[8] Today, however, it is clear that religion cannot be taken as a sign of a justice's conservative or liberal ideology. When Justice William H. Brennan Jr. was on the Court, he and fellow Catholic Antonin Scalia were at ideological polar extremes.

The Supreme Court Confirmation Process

The Constitution gives the Senate the authority to approve all presidential nominees to the federal bench. As detailed later, the Senate's Judiciary Committee investigates the nominees, holds hearings, and votes on its recommendation for Senate action. At this stage, the committee may reject a nominee or send the nomination to the full Senate for a vote. The full Senate then deliberates on the nominee before voting. A simple majority vote is required for confirmation.

Investigation.   As a president begins to narrow the list of possible nominees to the Supreme Court, those names are sent to the Federal Bureau of Investigation before a nomination formally is made. Once the formal nomination is made and sent to the Senate, the Judiciary Committee begins its own investigation. (The same process is used for nominees to the lower federal courts, although such investigations generally are not nearly as extensive as for Supreme Court nominees.)

Lobbying by Interest Groups.   Until recently, interest groups played a minor and backstage role in most appointments to the Supreme Court. Although interest groups generally have not lobbied on behalf of any one individual, in 1981 women's rights groups successfully urged President Ronald Reagan to honor his campaign commitment to appoint a woman to the high Court.

It is more common for interest groups to lobby against a prospective nominee. Even this, however, is a relatively recent phenomenon. In 1987, the nomination of Robert H. Bork to the Supreme Court led liberal groups to launch the most extensive radio, television, and print media campaign against a nominee to the U.S. Supreme Court. These interest groups believed that Bork's actions as the U.S. solicitor general, especially his firing of the Watergate special prosecutor at the request of President Richard M. Nixon, as well as his political beliefs, were abhorrent.

More and more frequently, interest groups also are getting involved in district court and court of appeals nominations. They recognize that these appointments often pave the way for future nominees to the Supreme Court, as was the case with most of the members of the current Court.

The Senate Committee Hearings and Senate Vote.   After hearings are concluded, the Senate Judiciary Committee usually makes a recommendation to the full Senate. Any rejections of presidential nominees to the Supreme Court generally occur only after the Senate Judiciary Committee has recommended against a nominee's appointment. Few recent confirmations have been close; prior to Clarence Thomas's 52–48 vote in 1991, William H. Rehnquist's nomination in 1971 as associate justice (68–26) and in 1986 as chief justice (65–33) were the closest in recent history.

THE SUPREME COURT TODAY

GIVEN THE JUDICIAL SYSTEM'S VAST SIZE and substantial, although often indirect, power over so many aspects of our lives, it is surprising that so many Americans know next to nothing about the judicial system, in general, and the Supreme Court, in particular.

Even today, after the unprecedented attention the Supreme Court received when the fate of the 2000 presidential election was in its hands, nearly two-thirds of those sampled in 2002 could not name one member of the Court; only 32 percent knew that the Court had nine members. In sharp contrast, 75 percent knew that there are three Rice Krispies characters. Sandra Day O'Connor, the first woman appointed to the Court, is the most well-known justice. Still, less than a quarter of those polled could name her.[9] To fill in any gaps in your knowledge of the current Supreme Court, see Table 9.2.

Although much of this ignorance can be blamed on the American public's lack of interest, the Court has also taken great pains to ensure its privacy and sense of decorum. Its rites and rituals contribute to the Court's mystique and encourage a "cult of the robe."[10] Consider, for example, the way Supreme Court proceedings are conducted. Oral arguments are not televised, and deliberations concerning the outcome of cases are conducted in utmost secrecy. In contrast, C-SPAN brings us daily coverage of various congressional hearings and floor debate on bills and important national issues, and Court TV (and sometimes other networks) provides gavel-to-gavel coverage of many important state court trials. The Supreme Court, however, remains adamant in its refusal to televise its proceedings, including public oral arguments, although it now allows same-day audio tapes of oral arguments to be released.

Deciding to Hear a Case

Although more than 9,000 cases were filed at the Supreme Court in its 2003–2004 term, this was not always the norm. As recently as the 1940s, fewer than 1,000 cases were filed annually. Since that time, filings increased at a dramatic rate until the mid 1990s and then shot up again in the late 1990s. The increased number of filings does not mean the Court is deciding more cases. In fact, of the 98,883 petitions it received during the 2003–2004 term, ninety cases were argued and seventy-three signed opinions were issued. The process by which cases get to the Supreme Court is outlined in Figure 9.4.

The content of the Court's docket is, of course, every bit as significant as its size. During the 1930s, cases requiring the interpretation of constitutional law began to take a growing portion of the Court's workload, leading the Court to take a more important role in the policy-making process. At that time, only 5 percent of the Court's cases involved questions concerning the Bill of Rights. By the late 1950s, one-third of filed cases involved such questions; by the 1960s, half did.[11] More recently, 42 percent of the cases decided by the Court dealt with issues raised in the Bill of Rights.[12]

As discussed earlier in the chapter, the Court has two types of jurisdiction (see Figure 9.1). The Court has original jurisdiction in "all Cases affecting Ambassadors, other public Ministers and Consuls, and those in which a State shall be a party." It is rare for more than three or four of these cases to come to the Court in a year. The second kind of jurisdiction enjoyed by the Court is its appellate jurisdiction. The Court is not expected to exercise its appellate jurisdiction simply to correct errors

Photo courtesy: Ken Heinen/Pool/AP/Wide World Photos

■ The Supreme Court in 2004. From left to right: Clarence Thomas, Antonin Scalia, Sandra Day O'Connor, Anthony Kennedy, David Souter, Stephen Breyer, John Paul Stevens, William H. Rehnquist, and Ruth Bader Ginsburg.

FIGURE 9.4 How a Case Goes to the Supreme Court and What
Happens After a Case Is Accepted. ■

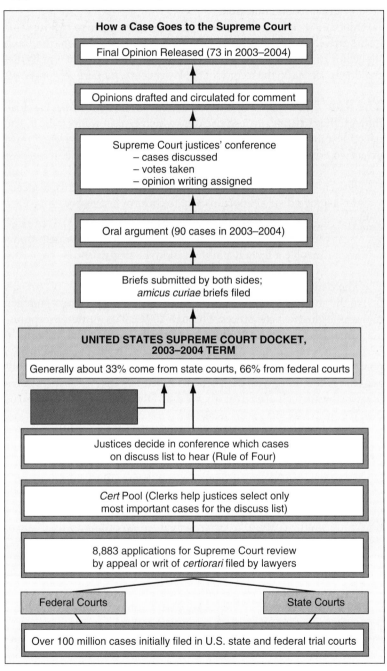

How a Case Goes to the Supreme Court

Final Opinion Released (73 in 2003–2004)

↑

Opinions drafted and circulated for comment

↑

Supreme Court justices' conference
– cases discussed
– votes taken
– opinion writing assigned

↑

Oral argument (90 cases in 2003–2004)

↑

Briefs submitted by both sides;
amicus curiae briefs filed

↑

**UNITED STATES SUPREME COURT DOCKET,
2003–2004 TERM**

Generally about 33% come from state courts, 66% from federal courts

↑

Justices decide in conference which cases
on discuss list to hear (Rule of Four)

↑

Cert Pool (Clerks help justices select only
most important cases for the discuss list)

↑

8,883 applications for Supreme Court review
by appeal or writ of *certiorari* filed by lawyers

Federal Courts   State Courts

Over 100 million cases initially filed in U.S. state and federal trial courts

of other courts. Instead, an appeal to the Supreme Court should be taken only if the case presents important issues of law, or what is termed "a substantial federal question."

Since 1988, nearly all appellate cases that have gone to the Supreme Court arrived there on a petition for a **writ of *certiorari*** (from the Latin "to be informed"), which is a request for the Supreme Court—at its discretion—to order up the records of the lower courts for purposes of review.

writ of *certiorari*
A request for the Court to order up the records from a lower court to review the case.

The Rule of Four.   The Supreme Court controls its own caseload through the *certiorari* process, deciding which cases it wants to hear, and rejecting most cases that come to it. All petitions for *certiorari* must meet two criteria:

1. The case must come either from a U.S. court of appeals, a special three-judge district court, or a state court of last resort.
2. The case must involve a federal question. This means that the case must present questions of interpretation of federal constitutional law or involve a federal statute, action, or treaty.

The clerk of the Court's office transmits petitions for writs of *certiorari* first to the chief justice's office, where clerks review the petitions, and then to the individual justices' offices. Through 2004, all the justices except Justice John Paul Stevens (who allows his clerks great individual authority in selecting the cases for him to review) participated in what is called the *cert* pool.[13] As part of the pool, they review their assigned fraction of petitions and share their notes with each other. Those cases that the justices deem noteworthy are then placed on what is called the "discuss list" prepared by the chief justice's clerks and circulated to the chambers of the other justices. All others are dead listed and go no further unless a justice asks that a case be removed from the dead list and discussed at conference. Only about 30 percent of submitted petitions make it to the discuss list. During one of the justices' weekly conference meetings, the cases on the discuss list are reviewed. The chief justice speaks first, then the rest of the justices, according to seniority. The decision process ends when the justices vote, and by custom, *certiorari* is granted according to the **Rule of Four**—when at least four justices vote to hear a case.

Rule of Four
At least four justices of the Supreme Court must vote to consider a case before it can be heard.

The Role of Clerks.   As early as 1850, the justices of the Supreme Court beseeched Congress to approve the hiring of a clerk to assist each justice. Congress denied the request, so when Justice Horace Gray hired the first law clerk in 1882, he paid the clerk himself. Justice Gray's clerk was a top graduate of Harvard Law School whose duties included cutting Justice Gray's hair and running personal errands. Finally, in 1886, Congress authorized each justice to hire a "stenographer clerk" for $1,600 a year.

Clerks typically are selected from candidates at the top of the graduating classes of prestigious law schools. They perform a variety of tasks, ranging from searching for arcane facts to playing tennis or taking walks with the justices. Clerks spend most of their time researching material relevant to particular cases, reading and summarizing cases, and helping justices write opinions. The clerks also make the first pass through the petitions that come to the Court, undoubtedly influencing which cases get a second look. Just how much help they provide in the writing of opinions is unknown[14] (See Table 9.3 for more on what clerks do.)

In 2005, the nine justices employed a total of thirty-four clerks. This number represents a significant increase over the last forty years and has had many interesting ramifications for the Court. As the number of clerks has grown, so have the number and length of the Court's opinions.[15] And, until recently, the number of cases decided annually increased as more help was available to the justices.

The relationship between clerks and the justices for whom they work is close and confidential, and many aspects of the relationship are kept secret. Clerks may sometimes talk among themselves about the views and personalities of their justices, but rarely has a clerk leaked such information to the press. In 1998, a former clerk to Justice Harry A. Blackmun broke the silence. Edward Lazarus published a book that shocked many Court watchers by penning an insider's account of how the Court really works.[16] He also charged that the justices give their young, often ideological, clerks far too much power.

How Does a Case Survive the Process?

It can be difficult to determine why the Court decides to hear a particular case. The Court does not offer reasons, and "the standards by which the justices decide to grant or deny review are highly personalized and necessarily discretionary," noted former Chief Justice Earl Warren.[17] Political scientists nonetheless have attempted to determine the characteristics of the cases the Court accepts; not surprisingly, they are similar to those that help a case get on the discuss list. Among the cues are the following:

- The federal government is the party asking for review.
- The case involves conflict among the circuit courts.
- The case presents a civil rights or civil liberties question.

TABLE 9.3 What Do Supreme Court Clerks Do?

Supreme Court clerks are among the best and brightest recent law school graduates. Almost all first clerk for a judge on one of the courts of appeals. After their Supreme Court clerkship, former clerks are in high demand. Firms often pay signing bonuses of up to $80,000 to attract clerks to their firms, where salaries start at over $150,000 a year.

Tasks of a Supreme Court clerk include the following:
- Perform initial screening of the 9,000 or so petitions that come to the Court each term
- Draft memos to summarize the facts and issues in each case, recommending whether the case should be accepted by the Court for full review
- Write a bench memo summarizing an accepted case and suggesting questions for oral argument
- Write the first draft of an opinion
- Be an informal conduit for communicating and negotiating between other justices' chambers as to the final wording of an opinion

You Are a Clerk for Supreme Court Justice Judith Gray

- The case involves ideological and/or policy preferences of the justices.
- The case has significant social or political interest, as evidenced by the presence of interest group *amicus curiae* briefs.

amicus curiae
"Friend of the court"; a third party to a lawsuit who files a legal brief for the purpose of raising additional points of view in an attempt to influence a court's decision.

solicitor general
The fourth-ranking member of the Department of Justice; responsible for handling all appeals on behalf of the U.S. government to the Supreme Court.

The Federal Government.   One of the most important cues for predicting whether the Court will hear a case is the position the solicitor general takes on it. The U.S. **solicitor general,** appointed by the president, is the fourth-ranking member of the Department of Justice and is responsible for handling most appeals on behalf of the U.S. government to the Supreme Court. The solicitor's staff resembles a small, specialized law firm within the Department of Justice. But, because this office has such a special relationship with the Supreme Court, even having a suite of offices within the Supreme Court building, the solicitor general often is referred to as the Court's "ninth and a half member."[18] Moreover, the solicitor general, on behalf of the U.S. government, appears as a party or as an *amicus curiae* in more than 50 percent of the cases heard by the Court each term. This special relationship with the Court helps explain the overwhelming success the solicitor general's office enjoys before the Supreme Court. The Court generally accepts 70 to 80 percent of the cases where the U.S. government is the petitioning party, compared with about 5 percent of all others.[19]

Conflict Among the Circuits.   Conflict among the lower courts is apparently another reason that the justices take cases. When interpretations of constitutional or federal law are involved, the justices seem to want consistency throughout the federal court system.

Interest Group Participation.   A quick way for the justices to gauge the ideological ramifications of a particular civil rights or liberties case is by the nature and amount of interest group participation. Richard C. Cortner has noted that "Cases do not arrive on the doorstep of the Supreme Court like orphans in the night."[20] Instead, most cases heard by the Supreme Court involve either the government or an interest group—either as the sponsoring party or as an *amicus curiae*. Liberal groups such as the ACLU, People for the American Way, or the NAACP Legal Defense Fund, and conservative groups including the Washington Legal Foundation, Concerned Women for America, or the American Center for Law and Justice, routinely sponsor cases or file *amicus* briefs either urging the Court to hear a case or asking it to deny *certiorari*. Research by political scientists has found that "not only does [an *amicus*] brief in favor of *certiorari* significantly improve the chances of a case being accepted, but two, three and four briefs improve the chances even more."[21]

Clearly, it's the more the merrier, whether or not the briefs are filed for or against granting review.[22] Interest group participation may highlight lower court and ideological conflicts for the justices by alerting them to the amount of public interest in the issues presented in any particular case.

Hearing and Deciding the Case

Once a case is accepted for review, a flurry of activity begins (see Figure 9.4). Lawyers on both sides of the case begin to prepare their written arguments for submission to the Court. In these briefs, lawyers cite prior case law and make arguments as to why the Court should find in favor of their client.

Simulation
You Are a Young Lawyer

More often than not, these arguments are echoed or expanded in *amicus curiae* briefs filed by interested parties, especially interest groups. (The vast majority of the cases decided by the Court in the 1990s, for example, had at least one *amicus* brief.) Interest groups also provide the Court with information not necessarily contained in the major-party briefs, help write briefs, and assist in practice oral arguments. In these moot-court sessions, the lawyer who will argue the case before the nine justices goes through several complete rehearsals, with prominent lawyers and law professors role playing the various justices.

Oral Arguments.   Once a case is accepted by the Court for full review, and after briefs and *amicus* briefs are submitted on each side, oral argument takes place. Oral argument generally is limited to the immediate parties in the case, although it is not uncommon for the U.S. solicitor general to appear to argue orally as an *amicus curiae*. Oral argument at the Court is fraught with time-honored tradition and ceremony. At precisely ten o'clock every morning when the Court is in session, the Court Marshal, dressed in a formal morning coat, emerges to intone "Oyez! Oyez! Oyez!" as the nine justices emerge from behind a reddish-purple velvet curtain to take their places on the raised and slightly angled bench. The chief justice sits in the middle with the justices to his right and left, alternating in seniority.

Almost all attorneys are allotted one half hour to present their cases, and this allotment includes the time taken by questions from the bench. Although many Court watchers have tried to figure out how a particular justice will vote based on the questioning at oral argument, most find that the nature and the number of questions asked do not help much in predicting the outcome of a case.

The Conference and the Vote.   The justices meet in closed conference once a week when the Court is hearing oral arguments. Since the ascendancy of Chief Justice Roger B. Taney to the Court in 1836, the justices have begun each conference session with a round of handshaking. Once the door to the conference room closes, no others are allowed to enter. The justice with the least seniority acts as the doorkeeper for the other eight, communicating with those waiting outside to fill requests for documents, water, and any other necessities.

Conferences highlight the importance and power of the chief justice, who presides over them and makes the initial presentation of each case. Each individual justice then discusses the case in order of his or her seniority on the Court, with the most senior justice speaking next. Most accounts of the decision-making process reveal that at this point some justices try to change the minds of others, but that most enter the conference room with a clear idea of how they will vote on each case. Although other Courts have followed different procedures, on the Rehnquist Court, through 2004, the justices generally voted at the same time they discussed each case, with each justice speaking only once. Initial conference votes are not final; justices are able to change their minds before final votes are taken.

Writing Opinions.   After the Court has reached a decision in conference, the justices must formulate a formal opinion of the Court. If the chief justice is in the majority, he selects the justice who will write the opinion. This privilege enables him to wield tremendous power and is a very important strategic decision. If the chief justice is in the minority, the assignment falls to the most senior justice in the majority.

The opinion of the Court can take several different forms. Most decisions are reached by a majority opinion written by one member of the Court to reflect the views of at least five of the justices. This opinion usually sets out the legal reasoning justifying the decision, and this legal reasoning becomes a precedent for deciding future cases. The reasoning behind any decision often is as important as the outcome. Under our system of *stare decisis,* both are likely to be relied on as precedent later by lower courts confronted with cases involving similar issues.

In the process of creating the final opinion of the Court, informal caucusing and negotiation then often take place, as justices may hold out for word changes or other modifications as a condition of their continued support of the majority opinion. This negotiation process can lead to divisions in the Court's majority. When this occurs, the Court may be forced to decide cases by plurality opinions, which attract the support of three or four justices. Although these decisions do not have the precedential value of majority opinions, they nonetheless have been used by the Court to decide many major cases.

Justices who agree with the outcome of the case but not with the legal rationale for the decision may file concurring opinions to express their differing approach. Justices who do not agree with the outcome of a case file dissenting opinions. Although these opinions have little direct legal value, they can be an important indicator of legal thought on the Court and are an excellent platform for justices to note their personal and legal disagreements with other members of the Court.

The process of crafting a final opinion is not an easy one, and justices often rely heavily on their clerks to do much of the revision. Neither is the process apolitical. Especially in a closely divided Court, such as the current Court, one vote can be the difference between two very different outcomes.

JUDICIAL PHILOSOPHY AND DECISION MAKING

JUSTICES ARE HUMAN BEINGS, and they do not make decisions in a vacuum. Principles of *stare decisis* dictate that the justices follow the law of previous cases in deciding cases at hand. But, a variety of legal and extra-legal factors have also been found to affect Supreme Court decision making.

Judicial Philosophy, Original Intent, and Ideology

Legal scholars long have argued that judges decide cases based on the Constitution and their reading of various statutes. Determining what the Framers meant—if that is even possible today—often appears to be based on an individual jurist's philosophy.

One of the primary issues concerning judicial decision making focuses on what is called the activism/restraint debate. Advocates of **judicial restraint** argue that courts should allow the decisions of other branches to stand, even when they offend a judge's own sense of principles. Restraintists defend their position by asserting that the federal courts are composed of unelected judges, which makes the judicial branch the least democratic branch of government. Consequently, the courts should defer policy making to other branches of government as much as possible.

Advocates of judicial restraint generally agree that judges should be strict constructionists; that is, they should interpret the Constitution as it was written and intended by the Framers. They argue that in determining the constitutionality of a statute or policy, the Court should rely on the explicit meanings of the clauses in the document, which can be clarified by looking at the intent of the Framers.

Advocates of **judicial activism** contend that judges should use their power broadly to further justice, especially in the areas of equality and personal liberty. Activists argue that it is the courts' appropriate role to correct injustices committed by the other branches of government. Explicit in this argument is the notion that courts need to protect oppressed minorities.[23]

Although judicial activists are often considered politically liberal and restraintists politically conservative, in recent years a new brand of conservative judicial activism has become prevalent. Unlike their liberal counterparts, whose activist decisions often expanded the rights of political and legal minorities, conservative activist judges view their positions as an opportunity to issue a broad ruling that imposes conservative political beliefs and policies on the country at large. (See Join the Debate: Separation of Powers and the Scalia Recusals.)

Some scholars argue that this increased conservative judicial activism has had an effect on the Court's reliance on *stare decisis* and adherence to precedent. Chief Justice William H. Rehnquist, too, has

judicial restraint

A philosophy of judicial decision making that argues courts should allow the decisions of other branches of government to stand, even when they offend a judge's own sense of principles.

judicial activism

A philosophy of judicial decision making that argues judges should use their power broadly to further justice, especially in the areas of equality and personal liberty.

SEPARATION OF POWERS AND THE SCALIA RECUSALS

Overview: The separation of powers is one of the fundamental tenets of the Constitution. Although the lines of authority among the legislative, executive, and judicial branches endlessly shift as the power of each increases or diminishes, each branch must retain its constitutional independence. Once a branch acts in collusion with another, American political theory argues, the door to corruption is opened. When it was learned that Justice Antonin Scalia went duck hunting with Vice President Dick Cheney a few months before the Supreme Court was to review the government's suit to compel the vice president to release documents concerning his secretive Energy Task Force, the question of conflict of interest arose. With this in mind, the Sierra Club filed a motion to formally ask that Justice Scalia recuse (or remove) himself from hearing the case in order to prevent undue influence. Justice Scalia refused to recuse himself and thus proffered an interesting ethical question.

It is historical and common practice for justices to socialize with the political and intellectual classes, and justices regularly recuse themselves if there is a conflict of interest. For example, Justice Ruth Bader Ginsburg favored the position of the National Organization for Women's legal defense fund in a case before the Court and then spoke at NOW's lecture series two weeks later—these types of practices are considered proper.

Additionally, during the last five years, there have been nearly 500 recusals by the justices. Commentary in the *National Law Journal* argues that if a case before the Court involves an institutional issue, a justice's recusal is not necessary when a friend, family member, or acquaintance is involved. Because the issue in *Cheney* v. *U.S. D.C. for the District of Columbia* concerns the separation of powers, the personal and political motives of the parties involved would seem irrelevant. However, public distrust of government, and of the Supreme Court in particular, has been increasing. Therefore, it could be argued, all who act in a political capacity should be meticulous in avoiding the appearance of impropriety or conflict of interest.

Should politicians and judges be held to higher ethical standards than the average citizen? Should members of the Supreme Court be allowed to participate in cases where acquaintances, friends, or family are involved? After all, some justices, such as Justices Sandra Day O'Connor and David Souter, recuse themselves as a matter of course if there is a hint of conflict of interest. Should the other justices be bound to do so as well? Is the issue of the public's trust in government so important that all Supreme Court justices should adhere to the highest ethical standard?

Arguments for Recusal

- **Justices should avoid the appearance of conflict of interest.** The current polarized polit-

noted that while "*stare decisis* is a cornerstone of our legal system…it has less power in constitutional cases."[24]

Models of Judicial Decision Making

Most political scientists who study what is called judicial behavior conclude that a variety of forces shape judicial decision making. Of late, many

ical atmosphere and the American public's distrust of government and its institutions requires highly visible political figures such as Supreme Court justices to adhere to a rigorous ethical code to help the American people maintain confidence in their political and governmental establishments.

- **The principle of separation of powers must be maintained.** Situations may arise in which either intentional or unintentional collusion or influence occurs. The result could be an event or decision that is harmful to the national interest.
- **Justices must remain impartial.** If a justice's personal or political life might intrude on the decision-making process when rendering judgment, basic judicial ethics suggest that recusal is the proper remedy. Fairness and trust demand that a justice maintain impartiality when hearing a case.

Arguments Against Recusal

- **Questioning of judicial integrity may have a partisan basis.** Though oversight of the judiciary is indispensable, many charges against justices are partisan in nature. To bow to partisan pressure would further implicate the Court as being responsive to partisan politics.
- **A recusal impairs the proper functioning of the Court.** When a member of the Court is recused, the number of justices is reduced. One possibility is that the Court's decision

may be evenly split, which effectually means the case is not decided. The Court might fail to reach a decision that could clarify or settle an important constitutional or political question.

- **It is unreasonable to expect justices to recuse themselves because of friendship.** It is the nature of the capital's professional, social, and political structure for justices to have social contact, address conferences and groups, and engage in political life. It is only natural that the justices over time would develop many different relationships outside the Court. To ask for a recusal in every instance in which a justice has a friend or acquaintance before the Court would be disabling.

Questions

1. What is the best way to ensure accountability in the federal judiciary? Should we expect our judges to be scrupulously apolitical?
2. What is the best way to ensure the independence of the judiciary? Are the lines that separate the branches becoming blurred, and is this a problem?

Selected Readings

Jeffrey Shaman et al. *Judicial Conduct and Ethics.* New York: Matthew Bender, 1990.

John T. Noonan, ed. *The Responsible Judge: Readings in Judicial Ethics.* New York: Praeger, 1993.

have attempted to explain how judges vote by integrating a variety of models to offer a more complete picture of how judges make decisions.[25] Many of those models attempt to take into account justices' individual behavioral characteristics and attitudes as well as the fact patterns of the case.

Behavioral Characteristics.   Originally, some political scientists argued that social background differences, including childhood experiences, religious values, education, earlier political and legal careers, and political party loyalties, are likely to influence how a judge evaluates the facts and legal issues presented in any given case. Justice Harry A. Blackmun's service at the Mayo Clinic often is pointed to as a reason that his opinion for the Court in *Roe* v. *Wade* (1973) was grounded so thoroughly in medical evidence. Similarly, Justice Potter Stewart, who was generally considered a moderate on most civil liberties issues, usually took a more liberal position on cases dealing with freedom of the press. Why? It may be that Stewart's early job as a newspaper reporter made him more sensitive to these claims.

The Attitudinal Model.   The attitudinal approach links judicial attitudes with decision making.[26] The attitudinal model holds that Supreme Court justices decide cases according to their personal preferences toward issues of public policy. Among some of the factors used to derive attitudes are a justice's party identification,[27] the party of the appointing president, and the liberal/conservative leanings of a justice.[28]

The Strategic Model.   Some scholars who study the courts are now advocating the belief that judges act strategically, meaning that they weigh and assess their actions against those of other justices to optimize the chances that their preferences will be adopted by the whole Court.[29] Moreover, this approach seeks to explain not only a justice's vote but also the range of forces such as congressional/judicial relations and judicial/executive relations that also affect the outcome of legal disputes.

Public Opinion.   Many political scientists have examined the role of public opinion in Supreme Court decision making.[30] Not only do the justices read legal briefs and hear oral arguments, but they also read newspapers, watch television, and have some knowledge of public opinion—especially on controversial issues.

Whether or not public opinion actually influences some justices, public opinion can act as a check on the power of the courts as well as an energizing factor. Activist periods on the Supreme Court generally have corresponded to periods of social or economic crisis. For example, the Marshall Court supported a strong national government, much to the chagrin of a series of pro–states' rights Democratic-Republican presidents in the early crisis-ridden years of the republic. Similarly, the Court capitulated to political pressures and public opinion when, after 1936, it reversed many of its earlier decisions that had blocked President Franklin D. Roosevelt's New Deal legislation.

The courts, especially the Supreme Court, also can be the direct target of public opinion. When *Webster* v. *Reproductive Health Services* (1989) was about to come before the Supreme Court, the Court was subjected to unprecedented lobbying as groups and individuals on both sides of the abortion issue marched and sent appeals to the Court. Earlier, in the fall of 1988, Justice Harry A. Blackmun, author of *Roe* v. *Wade* (1973), had warned a law school audience that he feared the decision was in jeopardy.[31] This in itself was a highly unusual move; until recently, it was the practice of the justices never to comment publicly on cases or the Court.

Speeches such as Blackmun's put pro-choice advocates on guard. When the Court agreed to hear *Webster*, the pro-choice forces mounted one of the largest demonstrations in the history of the United States—more than 300,000 people marched from the Mall to the Capitol, just across the street from the Supreme Court. In addition, full-page advertisements appeared in prominent newspapers, and supporters of *Roe* v. *Wade* were urged to contact members of the Court to voice their support. Mail at the Court, which usually averaged about 1,000 pieces a day, rose to an astronomical 46,000 pieces per day, virtually paralyzing normal lines of communication.

The Court is also dependent on the public for its prestige as well as for compliance with its decisions. In times of war and other emergencies, the Court frequently has decided cases in ways that commentators have attributed to the sway of public opinion and political exigencies. In *Korematsu* v. *U.S.* (1944), for example, the high Court upheld the obviously unconstitutional internment of Japanese American citizens during World War II.[32] Moreover, Chief Justice William H. Rehnquist has suggested that the Court's restriction on presidential authority in

Photo courtesy: Jodi Buren/Woodfin Camp & Associates

■ The 1989 pro-choice rally in Washington, D.C., was part of an intense lobbying effort to influence the Court's decision in the *Webster* case. Justice Sandra Day O'Connor, viewed as a swing vote on the case, was a particular target of the lobbying.

Youngstown Sheet & Tube Co. v. *Sawyer* (1952), which invalidated President Harry S Truman's seizure of the nation's steel mills, was largely attributable to Truman's unpopularity and that of the Korean War.[33]

Public confidence in the Court, like other institutions of government, has ebbed and flowed. Public support for the Court was highest after the Court issued *U.S.* v. *Nixon* (1974), in which the Court effectively ordered the White House to turn over tapes of Oval Office conversations involving criminal activity.[34] At a time when Americans lost faith in the presidency, they could at least look to the Supreme Court to do the right thing. Although the numbers of Americans with confidence in the courts has fluctuated over time, in 2004, 46 percent of those sampled by Gallup International had a "great deal" or "quite a bit" of confidence in the Supreme Court.[35]

The Supreme Court also appears to affect public opinion. Political scientists have found that the Court's initial rulings on controversial issues such as abortion or capital punishment positively influence public opinion in the direction of the Court's opinion. However, this research further finds that subsequent decisions have little effect.[36]

JUDICIAL POLICY MAKING AND IMPLEMENTATION

As ILLUSTRATED IN THE OPENING VIGNETTE, all judges, whether they recognize it or not, make policy. The primary way federal judges, and the Supreme Court, in particular, make policy is through interpreting statutes or the Constitution. This occurs in a variety of ways. Judges can interpret a provision of a law to cover matters not previously understood to be covered by the law, or they can discover new rights, such as that of privacy, from their reading of the Constitution. They also have literal power over life and death when they decide death penalty cases.

Policy Making

One measure of the power of the courts and their ability to make policy is that more than one hundred federal laws have been declared unconstitutional. Although many of these laws have not been particularly significant, others have.

Another measure of the policy-making power of the Supreme Court is its ability to overrule itself. Although the Court generally abides by the informal rule of *stare decisis,* by one count, it has overruled itself in more than 200 cases.[37] Moreover, in the past few years, the Court has repeatedly reversed earlier decisions in the areas of criminal defendants' rights, women's rights, and the establishment of religion, thus revealing its powerful role in determining national policy. Another measure of the growing power of the federal courts is the degree to which they now handle issues that, after *Marbury* v. *Madison* (1803), had been considered political questions more appropriately left to the other branches of government to decide.

Implementing Court Decisions

President Andrew Jackson, annoyed about a particular decision handed down by the Marshall Court, is alleged to have said, "John Marshall has made his decision; now let him enforce it." Jackson's statement raises a question: how do Supreme Court rulings translate into public policy? In fact, although judicial decisions carry legal and even moral authority, all courts must rely on other units of government to carry out their directives. If the president or Congress, for example, doesn't like a particular Supreme Court ruling, they can underfund programs needed to implement a decision or seek only lax enforcement. **Judicial implementation** refers to how and whether judicial decisions are translated into actual public policies affecting more than the immediate parties to the lawsuit.

> **judicial implementation**
> Refers to how and whether judicial decisions are translated into actual public policies affecting more than the immediate parties to a lawsuit.

How well a decision is implemented often depends on how well crafted or popular it is. Hostile reaction in the South to *Brown* v. *Board of Education* (1954) and the absence of precise guidelines to implement the decision meant that the ruling went largely unenforced for years. The *Brown* experience also highlights how much the Supreme Court needs the support of both federal and state courts as well as other governmental agencies to carry out its judgments. For example, you probably graduated from high school after 1992, when the Supreme Court ruled that public middle school and high school graduations could not include a prayer, yet your own commencement ceremony may have included one.[38]

For effective implementation of a judicial decision, the first requirement is that the members of the implementing population must act to show that they understand the original decision. For example, the Supreme Court ruled in *Reynolds* v. *Sims* (1964) that every person should have an equally weighted vote in electing governmental representatives.[39] This "one person, one vote" decision might seem simple enough at first glance, but in practice it can be very difficult to understand.

The second requirement is that the implementing population must actually follow Court policy. Thus, when the Court ruled that men could not be denied admission to a state-sponsored nursing school, the implementing population—in this case, university administrators and the board of regents of the nursing school—had to enroll qualified male students.[40]

Judicial decisions are most likely to be implemented smoothly if responsibility for implementation is concentrated in the hands of a few highly visible public officials, such as the president or a governor. By the same token, these officials also can thwart or impede judicial intentions. Recall from chapter 5, for example, the effect of Governor Orval Faubus's initial refusal to allow black children to attend all-white public schools in Little Rock, Arkansas.

The third requirement for implementation is that what political scientists call the consumer population must be aware of the rights that a decision grants or denies them. Teenagers seeking an abortion, for example, are consumers of the Supreme Court's decisions on abortion. They need to know that most states require them to inform their parents of their intention to have an abortion or to get parental permission to do so.

SUMMARY

THE JUDICIARY AND THE LEGAL PROCESS—on both the national and state levels—are complex and play a far more important role in the setting of policy than the Framers ever envisioned. Many of the Framers viewed the judicial branch of government as little more than a minor check on the other two branches, ignoring Anti-Federalist concerns about an unelected judiciary and its potential for tyranny. The Judiciary Act of 1789 established the basic federal court system we have today. It was the Marshall Court (1801–1835), however, that interpreted the Constitution to include the Court's major power, that of judicial review.

Ours is a dual judicial system consisting of the federal court system and the separate judicial systems of the fifty states. In each system there are two basic types of courts: trial courts and appellate courts. Each type deals with cases involving criminal and civil law. Original jurisdiction refers to a court's ability to hear a case as a trial court; appellate jurisdiction refers to a court's ability to review cases already decided by a trial court.

The federal court system is made up of constitutional and legislative courts. Federal district courts, courts of appeals, and the Supreme Court are constitutional courts.

District court and court of appeals judges are nominated by the president and subject to Senate confirmation. Senators often play a key role in recommending district court appointees from their home state. Supreme Court justices are nominated by the president and must also win Senate confirmation. Presidents use different criteria for selection, but important factors include competence,

standards, ideology, rewards, pursuit of political support, religion, race, and gender.

Several factors go into the Court's decision to hear a case. Not only must the Court have jurisdiction, but at least four justices must vote to hear the case, and cases with certain characteristics are most likely to be heard. Once a case is set for review, briefs and *amicus curiae* briefs are filed and oral argument scheduled. The justices meet after oral argument to discuss the case, votes are taken, and opinions are written and circulated.

Judges' philosophy and ideology have an extraordinary impact on how they decide cases. Political scientists consider these factors in identifying several models for how judges make decisions, including the behavioral, attitudinal, and strategic models.

The Supreme Court is an important participant in the policy-making process. The process of judicial interpretation gives the Court powers never envisioned by the Framers.

KEY TERMS

amicus curiae, p. 324
appellate courts, p. 306
appellate jurisdiction, p. 307
brief, p. 310
constitutional courts, p. 308
criminal law, p. 307
civil law, p. 307
judicial activism, p. 327
judicial implementation, p. 333
judicial restraint, p. 327
judicial review, p. 300

Judiciary Act of 1789, p. 302
jurisdiction, p. 306
legislative courts, p. 308
Marbury v. *Madison* (1803), p. 305
original jurisdiction, p. 306
precedent, p. 311
Rule of Four, p. 322
senatorial courtesy, p. 312
solicitor general, p. 324
stare decisis, p. 311
strict constructionist, p. 315
trial courts, p. 306
writ of *certiorari*, p. 322

SELECTED READINGS

Abraham, Henry J. *The Judiciary: The Supreme Court in the Governmental Process,* 10th ed. New York: New York University Press, 1996.

Barrow, Deborah J., Gary Zuk, and Gerard S. Gryski. *The Federal Judiciary and Institutional Change.* Ann Arbor: University of Michigan Press, 1996.

Baum, Lawrence. *The Supreme Court,* 8th ed. Washington, DC: CQ Press, 2004.

Baum, Lawrence. *The Puzzle of Judicial Behavior.* Ann Arbor: University of Michigan Press, 1997.

Clayton, Cornell, and Howard Gillman, eds. *Supreme Court Decision-Making: New Institutionalist Approaches.* Chicago: University of Chicago Press, 1999.

Epstein, Lee, et al. *The Supreme Court Compendium,* 3rd ed. Washington, DC: Congressional Quarterly Inc., 2002.

Goldman, Sheldon. *Picking Federal Judges: Lower Court Selection from Roosevelt Through Reagan.* New Haven, CT: Yale University Press, 1997.

Hall, Kermit L., ed. *The Oxford Companion to the Supreme Court of the United States,* 2nd ed. New York: Oxford University Press, 2005.

Lazarus, Edward. *Closed Chambers: The First Eyewitness Account of the Epic Struggles Inside the Supreme Court.* New York: Times Books, 1998.

O'Brien, David M. *Storm Center: The Supreme Court in American Politics,* 6th ed. New York: Norton, 2002.

Perry, H. W. *Deciding to Decide: Agenda Setting in the United States Supreme Court.* Cambridge, MA: Harvard University Press, 1994.

Provine, Doris Marie. *Case Selection in the United States Supreme Court.* Chicago: University of Chicago Press, 1980.

Salokar, Rebecca Mae. *The Solicitor General: The Politics of Law.* Philadelphia: Temple University Press, 1992.

Slotnick, Elliot E., and Jennifer A. Segal. *Television News and the Supreme Court: All the News That's Fit to Air.* Boston: Cambridge University Press. 1998.

Spaeth, Howard, and Jeffrey A. Segal. *Majority Rule or Minority Will: Adherence to Precedent on the U.S. Supreme Court.* New York: Cambridge University Press, 2001.

Sunstein, Cass R. *One Case at a Time: Judicial Minimalism on the Supreme Court,* 2nd ed. Cambridge, MA: Harvard University Press, 2001.

Woodward, Bob, and Scott Armstrong. *The Brethren: Inside the Supreme Court.* New York: Avon, 1996.

WEB EXPLORATIONS

To learn more about the workings of the U.S. justice system, see http://www.usdoj.gov/

To learn more about U.S. federal courts, see http://www.uscourts.gov/UFC99.pdf

To take a virtual tour of the U.S. Supreme Court and examine current cases on its docket, go to www.supremecourtus.gov

To learn about the U.S. Senate Judiciary Committee and judicial nominations currently under review, see http://judiciary.senate.gov/

To examine the major Supreme Court decisions from the past to the present, go to http://supct.law.cornell.edu/supct/index.htm/

To examine the recent filings of the office of solicitor general, go to http://www.usdoj.gov/osg/

10

Public Opinion and the News Media

Photo courtesy: Davis Guttenfelder/AP/Wide World Photos

AS BOMBS RAINED DOWN ON BAGHDAD, Iraq, in March 2003, Americans watched transfixed in the family rooms and dens around the nation. The character of the twenty-four-hour news cycle and a demand for immediate detail and analysis caused a 20 percent spike in viewership as Americans turned to their televisions to watch the war. The 1991 Persian Gulf War had been fought and won in four days and did not provide particularly interesting visuals. Earlier, however, the Vietnam War had been played out in American living rooms with graphic color footage of American soldiers fighting on foreign shores.

But the war in Iraq, or Operation Iraqi Freedom, as it was called, was different from wars before it. Although wars as early as World War II had journalists embedded in the field with troops, this war was brought to Americans in real time as they watched bombs explode over Iraq or followed journalists in the thick of fighting. In fact, one *USA Today* columnist was prompted to question whether it was a war that he was watching or another reality television program.

How news of the war or any other major event is reported can have enormous effects on public opinion. President George W. Bush's administration was mindful of that fact when it decided to allow journalists access to the troops. As all of the major networks and cable news outlets devoted nearly twenty-four hours of coverage each day, their task was facilitated by the journalists assigned to particular military units on land

and at sea. These embedded journalists ate, slept, and observed the war from within the confines of their units (as depicted in the photo at left). In return for this access, they agreed to a set of rules not to print or broadcast certain facts or occurrences that might help the enemy. Geraldo Rivera of Fox News, for example, was removed from his embedded assignment after he allegedly gave away troop locations and movements prior to their proper release times.

More than 600 embedded print and television journalists brought Americans to the theater of war. While many praised this firsthand reporting, some journalists believed that those in the immediate fray were unable to see the big picture, often reported details incorrectly, and were in danger of being swayed by their close association with the men and women of the military with whom they lived. Moreover, some feared that the accounts of embedded journalists were too positive and not adequately critical of war efforts. Most, however, agreed that the majority of the reporting of embedded journalists was quite effective and contributed to wide support for the war in the United States.

Public support for President George W. Bush hovered around the 70 percent mark at the beginning of the Iraq war. And, as the major combat phase of the war wound down, President Bush announced its success from an aircraft carrier in prime time, using the media to show himself as a successful leader. Eventually, public support for the war dipped when Americans saw day after day of violence and the U.S. death toll went over 1,000. Still, the media's repetition of Bush as a war president helped him use that mantle in his reelection bid.

THE NETWORKS, MANY MAJOR NEWSPAPERS, and polling organizations routinely report on and often attempt to gauge public opinion about a wide array of events. Still, many citizens question the fairness or bias of the media in all of its forms as well as the accuracy of public opinion polls. Often, as reported by or even commissioned by the media, polls reveal much about what "the public" is thinking. The complex interactions of the media and public opinion are the focus of this chapter.

First we will describe efforts to influence and measure public opinion. We then will discuss political socialization and other factors that influence opinion formation about political matters. After an examination of how we form political opinions, we will analyze how public opinion is measured. Looking at the news media, we will examine its influence on the public and public opinion. Finally, we will discuss government regulation of the electronic media.

EFFORTS TO INFLUENCE AND MEASURE PUBLIC OPINION

public opinion
What the public thinks about a particular issue or set of issues at any point in time.

FROM THE VERY EARLY DAYS of the republic, political leaders recognized the importance of **public opinion,** what the public thinks about a particular issue or set of issues at any point in time, and they used all of the means at their disposal to manipulate it for political purposes. By the early 1800s, the term public opinion frequently was being used by the educated middle class. As more Americans became educated, they became more vocal about their opinions and were more likely to vote. A more educated, reading public led to increased demand for newspapers, which in turn provided more information about the process of government. As the United States grew, there were more elections and more opportunities for citizens to express their political opinions through the ballot box. As a result of these trends, political leaders were forced more frequently to try to gauge public opinion to remain responsive to the wishes and desires of their constituents.

During World War I, some people argued that public opinion didn't matter at all. But, President Woodrow Wilson argued that public opinion would temper the actions of international leaders. Therefore, only eight days after the start of the war, Wilson created a Committee on Public Information. Run by a prominent journalist, the committee immediately undertook to unite U.S. public opinion behind the war effort. It used all of the tools available—pamphlets, posters, and speakers who exhorted the patrons of local movie houses during every intermission—in an effort to garner support and favorable opinion for the war. In the words of the committee's head, it was "the world's greatest adventure in advertising."[1]

Early Efforts to Measure Public Opinion

public opinion poll
Interview or survey with sample of citizens that is used to estimate the feelings and beliefs of the entire population.

Public opinion polls—interviews or surveys with samples of citizens that are used to estimate what the public is thinking—did not have a significant role until the 1930s, when researchers in a variety of disciplines, including political science, tried to use scientific methods to measure political thought. As methods for gathering and interpreting data improved, survey data began to play an increasingly important role in all walks of life, from politics to retailing.

As early as 1824, one Pennsylvania newspaper tried to predict the winner of that year's presidential contest. Later, in 1883, the *Boston*

Globe sent reporters to selected election precincts to poll voters as they exited voting booths, in an effort to predict the results of key contests. In 1916, *Literary Digest*, a popular magazine, began mailing survey postcards to potential voters in an effort to predict election outcomes. *Literary Digest* drew its survey sample from "every telephone book in the United States, from the rosters of clubs and associations, from city directories, lists of registered voters [and] classified mail order and occupational data."[2] Using data from the millions of postcard ballots it received from all over the United States, *Literary Digest* correctly predicted every presidential election from 1920 to 1932.

Literary Digest used what were called **straw polls,** unscientific surveys gauging public opinion, to predict the popular vote in those four presidential elections. Its polling methods were hailed widely as "amazingly right" and "uncannily accurate."[3] In 1936, however, its luck ran out. *Literary Digest* predicted that Republican Alfred M. Landon would beat incumbent President Franklin D. Roosevelt by a margin of 57 percent to 43 percent of the popular vote. Roosevelt, however, won in a landslide election, receiving 62.5 percent of the popular vote and carrying all but two states.

Literary Digest's 1936 straw poll had three fatal errors. First, its sample was drawn from telephone directories and lists of automobile owners. This technique oversampled the upper middle class and the wealthy, groups heavily Republican in political orientation. Moreover, in 1936, voting polarized along class lines. Thus, the oversampling of wealthy Republicans was particularly problematic because it severely underestimated the Democratic vote.

Literary Digest's second problem was timing. Questionnaires were mailed in early September. The changes in public sentiment that occurred as the election drew closer were not measured.

Its third error occurred because of a problem we now call self-selection. Only highly motivated individuals sent back the cards—a mere 22 percent of those surveyed responded. Those who respond to mail surveys (or today, online surveys) are quite different from the general electorate; they often are wealthier and better educated and care more fervently about issues. *Literary Digest*, then, failed to observe one of the now well-known cardinal rules of survey sampling: "One cannot allow the respondents to select themselves into the sample."[4]

At least one pollster, however, correctly predicted the results of the 1936 election: George Gallup. Gallup had written his dissertation in psychology at the University of Iowa on how to measure the readership of newspapers. He then expanded his research to study public opinion about politics. He was so confident about his methods that he gave all of his newspaper clients a money-back guarantee: if his poll predictions weren't closer to the actual election outcome than those of the highly acclaimed *Literary Digest*, he would refund their money. The

straw poll
Unscientific survey used to gauge public opinion on a variety of issues and policies.

Digest predicted Alfred M. Landon to win; Gallup predicted Roosevelt. Although Gallup underpredicted Roosevelt's victory by nearly 7 percent, the fact that he got the winner right was what everyone remembered, especially given *Literary Digest*'s dramatic miscalculation.

Recent Efforts to Measure Public Opinion

Through the late 1940s, polling techniques became more sophisticated. The number of polling groups also dramatically increased, as businesses and politicians began to rely on polling information to market products and candidates. But, in 1948, the polling industry suffered a severe, although fleeting, setback when Gallup and many other pollsters incorrectly predicted that Thomas E. Dewey would defeat President Harry S Truman.

Nevertheless, as revealed in Figure 10.1, the Gallup Organization, now co-chaired by George Gallup Jr., continues to predict the winners

FIGURE 10.1   The Success of the Gallup Poll in Presidential Elections, 1936–2004

As seen here, Gallup's final predictions have been remarkably accurate. Furthermore, in each of the years where there is a significant discrepancy between Gallup's prediction and the election's outcome, there was a prominent third candidate. In 1948, Strom Thurmond ran on the Dixiecrat ticket; in 1980, John Anderson ran as the American Independent Party candidate; in 1992, Ross Perot ran as an independent. ■

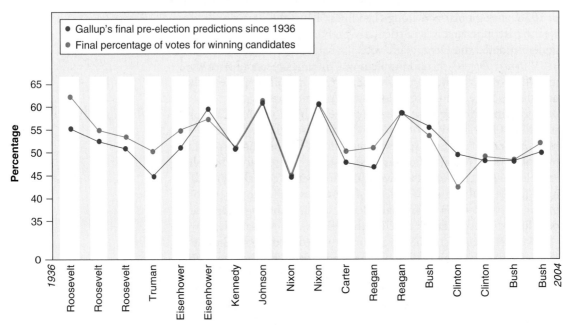

Sources: Marty Baumann, "How One Polling Firm Stacks Up," *USA Today* (October 27, 1992): 13A. 1996 data from Mike Mokrzycki, "Pre-election Polls' Accuracy Varied," *Atlanta Journal and Constitution* (November 8, 1996): A12. 2000 data from Gallup Organization, "Poll Releases" (November 7, 2000). 2004 data from *USA Today* and CNN/Gallup Tracking Poll, USAtoday.com.

of the presidential popular vote successfully. But, as the 2000 presidential election reminded most Americans, it is the vote in the Electoral College—not the popular vote—that ultimately counts. Thus, while George W. Bush's lead in the polls continued to shrink in the final days of 2000 polling, he won a 271–266 vote in the Electoral College. On November 7, 2000, the Gallup Organization announced what turned out to be a major understatement: the election was too close to call. Ultimately, Bush got 48 percent of the popular vote; Gore 49 percent. Still, despite its reputation for accuracy, even the Gallup Organization is not immune from error.

POLITICAL SOCIALIZATION AND OTHER FACTORS THAT INFLUENCE OPINION FORMATION

POLITICAL SCIENTISTS BELIEVE that many of our attitudes about issues are grounded in our political values. We learn these values through **political socialization,** "the process through which an individual acquires his particular political orientations—his knowledge, feeling and evaluations regarding his political world."[5]

political socialization
The process through which an individual acquires particular political orientations; the learning process by which people acquire their political beliefs and values.

For example, try to remember your earliest memory of the president of the United States. It may have been George Bush or Bill Clinton (older students probably remember earlier presidents). What did you think of the president? Of the Republican or Democratic Party? It is likely that your earliest feelings or attitudes were shaped by what your parents thought about that particular president and his party. Your experiences at school and your friends also probably influence your political beliefs today. Similar processes also apply to your early attitudes about the American flag, or the police. Other factors, too, often influence how political opinions are formed or reinforced. These include political events; the social groups you belong to, including your church; your demographic group, including race, gender, and age; and even the region of the country in which you live.

The Family

The influence of the family on political socialization can be traced to two factors: communication and receptivity. Children, especially during their preschool years, spend tremendous amounts of time with their parents; early on they learn their parents' political values, even though these concepts may be vague. One study, for example, found that the most important visible public figures for children under the age of ten were police officers and, to a much lesser extent, the president.[6] Young children almost uniformly view both as "helpful." But, by the age of ten or eleven, children become more selective in their perceptions of the president. By this age, children raised in Democratic households are much more likely to be critical of a Republican president than are those raised in Republican households. In 1988, for example, 58 percent of children in Republican households identified themselves as Republicans, and many had developed strong positive feelings toward Ronald Reagan, the Republican president. Support for and the popularity of Ronald Reagan translated into support for the Republican Party through the 1988 presidential election and also contributed to the decline of liberal ideological self-identification of first-year college students (see Figure 10.2).

School and Peers

Researchers report mixed findings concerning the role of schools in the political socialization process, which affects how individuals perceive events. There is no question that, in elementary school, children are taught respect for their nation and its symbols. Most school days begin with the Pledge of Allegiance, and patriotism and respect for country are important, although subtle, components of most school curricula. Support for flag and country create a foundation for national allegiance

FIGURE 10.2 The Ideological Self-Identification of First-Year College Students

A majority of first-year college students describe themselves as middle of the road; this number has held fairly steady since the early 1990s. The number of students identifying themselves as liberal and far left declined dramatically during the 1970s and early 1980s, while the number of students identifying themselves as conservative and far right increased. ■

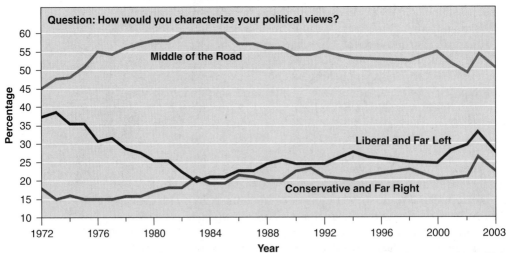

Sources: Reprinted from Howard W. Stanley and Richard G. Niemi, *Vital Statistics on American Politics, 2001–2002* (Washington, DC: CQ Press, 2001), 119. 2003 data from Cooperative Institutional Research Program (CIRP), "The American Freshman: National Norms for Fall 2003" (December 2003).

that prevails despite the negative views about politicians and government institutions that many Americans develop later in life. For example, though many Americans questioned action in Iraq in 2003, large numbers of schoolchildren prepared letters and packages to send to troops in Iraq. Measures such as these, however controversial, help to build a sense of patriotism at a young age.

A child's peers—that is, children about the same age—also seem to have an important effect on the socialization process. Whereas parental influences are greatest from birth to age five, a child's peer group becomes increasingly important as the child gets older, especially as he or she gets into middle school or high school.[7]

High schools also can be important agents of political socialization. They continue the elementary school tradition of building good citizens and often reinforce textbook learning with trips to the state or national capital. They also offer courses on current U.S. affairs. Many high schools impose a compulsory service learning requirement, which some studies report positively affects later political participation.[8] Although the formal education of many people in the United States ends with high school, research shows that better-informed citizens vote more often as adults. Therefore, presentation of civic information is especially critical at the high school level, where it reinforces views about participation.

At the college level, teaching style often changes. Many college courses and texts like this one are designed in part to provide you with the information necessary to think critically about issues of major political consequence. It is common in college for students to be called on to question the appropriateness of certain political actions or to discuss underlying reasons for certain political or policy decisions. Therefore, most researchers believe that college has a liberalizing effect on students. Since the 1920s, studies have shown that students become more liberal each year they are in college. However, students entering college in the 1980s were more conservative than in past years. The 1992 and 1996 victories of Bill Clinton and his equally youthful running mate Al Gore, who went out of their way to woo the youth vote, probably contributed to the small bump in the liberal ideological identification of first-year college students in those years (see Figure 10.2).

The Mass Media

The media today are taking on a growing role as a socialization agent. Adult Americans spend nearly thirty hours a week in front of their television sets; children spend even more.[9] Television has a tremendous impact on how people view politics, government, and politicians. TV talk shows, talk radio, and now even online newsletters and magazines are important sources of information about politics for many, yet the information that people get from these sources often is skewed.

Over the years, more and more Americans have turned away from traditional sources of news such as nightly news broadcasts on the major networks and daily newspapers in favor of different outlets. In 2004, one study estimated that more than 40 percent of those polled regularly learned about the election or candidates from alternative sources such as *The Tonight Show*, *The Late Show*, or *The Daily Show*.[10]

All of the major candidates in the 2004 presidential election also used another form of media to sway and inform voters: the Internet, a form of campaigning that was considered new in 1996. Many political groups had Internet-based exhibits at the 2000 Republican and Democratic National Conventions, and the outcome of the 2000 presidential election was first called online, prompting other forms of media to follow quickly. By the 2004 election cycle, not only had each presidential and most other major and minor campaigns launched their own Internet sites, but all of the major networks and newspapers had their own sites reporting on the election. More than 50 percent of those polled about the 2004 election reported using the Internet to research candidates' positions on the issues.[11]

Social Groups

Group effects—that is, certain characteristics that allow persons to be lumped into categories—also affect the development and continuity of political beliefs and opinions. Among the most important of these are religion, education level, income, and race. Researchers have learned that gender and age also are becoming increasingly important determinants of public opinion, especially on certain issues. Region, too, appears to influence political beliefs and political socialization.

Religion.   Throughout our history, religion has played an extraordinary role in political life. Many colonists came to our shores seeking religious liberty, yet many quickly moved to impose their religious beliefs on others and some made participation in local politics contingent on religiosity. Since political scientists began to look at the role of religion, numerous scholars have found that organized religion influences the political beliefs and behaviors of its adherents. The effects of organized religion are magnified in today's society, as 67 percent of all Americans are members of a church or synagogue. This figure contrasts with that for 1776, when only one in five citizens was a member of such a group.

Through much of the twentieth century, social scientists found that faith-based political activity occurred largely on the left. From the civil rights movement, to efforts to improve the living standards of farmers and migrant workers, to abolition of the death penalty, religious leaders were evident. The civil rights movement, in particular, was led by numerous religious leaders, including Reverend Martin Luther King Jr. and Reverend Andrew Young (who later became mayor of Atlanta, Georgia,

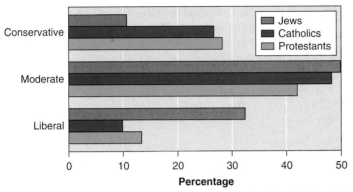

FIGURE 10.3 The Ideological Self-Identification of Protestants, Catholics, and Jews. ▪

Source: Data compiled and analyzed by Alixandra Yanus from National American Election Studies 2002.

and the U.S. ambassador to the United Nations). More recent civil rights leaders include Reverend Jesse Jackson and Reverend Al Sharpton.

In 1972, for the first time, a religious gap appeared in voting and public opinion. Richard M. Nixon's campaign was designed to appeal to what he termed "the Silent Majority," who wanted a return to more traditional values after the tumult of the 1960s. By the 1980s, conservative Christians could take credit for the election of Ronald Reagan. Throughout the 1980s, first the Moral Majority and then the Christian Coalition played increasingly key roles in politics. Today, religion is the single largest predictor of the vote, after party identification. And, regular church-goers have conservative views and vote Republican by a 2 to 1 margin.

In 2004, 56 percent of Americans identified themselves as Protestant, 27 percent as Catholic, 2 percent as Jewish, and 7 percent as other. Only 8 percent claimed to have no religious affiliation. Shared religious attitudes tend to affect voting and stances on particular issues. Catholics as a group, for example, favor aid to parochial schools, while many fundamentalist Protestants support organized prayer in public schools. Protestants, especially fundamentalists, are the most conservative and Jews the most liberal. And, as liberals, Jews tend to vote Democratic,[12] as shown in Figure 10.3. In 2004, for example, John Kerry captured 74 percent of the Jewish vote.[13]

Race and Ethnicity.   Differences in political socialization of African Americans and whites appear at a very early age. Young black children, for example, generally show very positive feelings about the American society and political processes, but this attachment lessens considerably over time. Black children fail to hold the president in the esteem accorded him by white children; indeed, older African American children in the 1960s viewed the government primarily in terms of the U.S. Supreme Court.[14] These differences continue through adulthood.

Race and ethnicity are exceptionally important factors in elections and in the study of public opinion. The direction and intensity of African American opinion on a variety of hot-button issues often are quite different from those of whites. As revealed in Analyzing Visuals: Racial and Ethnic Attitudes on Selected Issues, whites are much more likely to believe that police treat all races fairly than are blacks or Hispanics. Likewise, differences can be seen in other issue areas, including abortion.[15] Other issues, however, such as school vouchers, show much smaller racial dimensions.

Hispanics, Asians/Pacific Islanders, and Native Americans are other identifiable ethnic minorities in the United States who often respond differently to issues than do whites. Generally, Hispanics and Indians hold similar opinions on many issues, largely because so many of them have low incomes and find themselves targets of discrimination. Government-sponsored health insurance for the working poor, for example, is a hot-button issue with Hispanic voters, with 94 percent favoring it.[16] Unlike many other Americans, they also favor bilingual education and liberalized immigration policies. Within the Hispanic community, however, existing divisions often depend on national origin. Generally, Cuban Americans who cluster in Florida and in the Miami–Dade County area, in particular, are more likely to be conservative. They fled from communism and Fidel Castro in Cuba, and they generally vote Republican. In contrast, Hispanics of Mexican origin who vote in California, New Mexico, Arizona, Texas, or Colorado are more likely to vote Democratic.[17]

Gender.   Poll after poll reveals that women hold very different opinions from men on a variety of issues, as shown in Table 10.1. From the time that the earliest public opinion polls were taken, women have been found to hold more negative views about war and military intervention than do men, and more strongly positive attitudes about issues touching on social-welfare concerns, such as education, juvenile justice, capital punishment, and the environment. Some analysts suggest that women's more nurturing nature and their prominent role as mothers lead women to have more liberal attitudes on issues affecting the family or the safety of their children. Research by political scientists, however, finds no support for a maternal explanation.[18]

These differences on political issues have often translated into substantial gaps in the way women and men vote. Women, for example, particularly unmarried women young and old, are more likely to be Democrats, and they often provide Democratic candidates with their margin of victory.[19]

Historically, public opinion polls have also found that women hold more negative views about war and military intervention. However, the gender gap on military issues began to disappear in the late

Analyzing Visuals
RACIAL AND ETHNIC ATTITUDES ON SELECTED ISSUES

Political opinions held by racial and ethnic groups in the United States differ on many issues. In the figure below, the opinions of whites, blacks, and Hispanics are compared on a number of political issues. After studying the bar graph and the material in this chapter on race, ethnicity, and public opinion, answer the following critical thinking questions: What do you observe about the differences and similarities in opinions among the different groups? On which issues do blacks and whites, Hispanics and blacks, and Hispanics and whites have similar or diverging opinions? What factors might explain these similarities and differences?

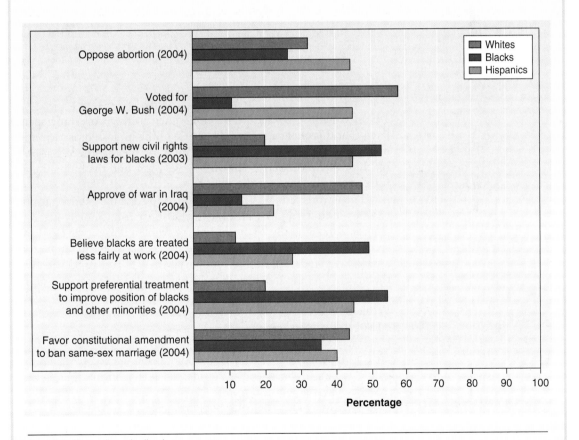

Source: http://nationaljournal.polltrack.

TABLE 10.1   Gender Differences on Political Issues

	Men (%)	Women (%)
Support initial sending of troops to Gulf (1991)	62	41
Support return of Elian Gonzalez to his father (2000)	63	32
Believe crime influences the way they live (2000)	47	66
Favor the death penalty (2000)	72	60
Favor gun control legislation (2000)	55	77
Approve of George W. Bush's handling of the presidency (2002)	85	83
Believe war on terrorism will spread (2002)	24	74
Have a favorable view of Saudi Arabia (2003)	42	23
Favor stricter laws against abortion	35	36
Believe books that contain dangerous ideas should be banned from public libraries (2003)	47	56
Consider prayer important in daily life (2003)	42	60

Sources: Data from CNN/*USA Today* (December 28–30, 1994); Roper Center *Public Opinion Online,* 1998; Gallup Organization, *Washington Post*/ABC Poll (May 7–10, 2000): Harris Poll February 22–March 3, 2001); Harris Interactive 2001, 2002, CBS News; and http://nationaljournal.qpass.com/members/polltrack/2001/issues.htm.

1990s, when the United States intervened in Kosovo. Many speculated that this change occurred because of the increased participation of women in the workforce and the military, the "sanitized nature of much of the war footage" shown on television, and the humanitarian reasons for involvement.[20]

The terrorist attacks of 9/11 appeared to erase the gender gap concerning military affairs, at least in the short run. Shortly after the attacks, although only 24 percent of the women polled (versus 41 percent of the men) favored an increase in defense spending before the attacks, 47 percent voiced their support post-9/11 (versus 53 percent of the men).[21] As the memory of 9/11 has receded, the war in Iraq has resulted in a renewed gender gap in public opinion in foreign affairs. While 62 percent of the men in one poll favored staying in Iraq, only half of the women agreed.[22]

Age.   As Americans live longer, senior citizens are becoming a potent political force. In states such as Florida, to which many northern retirees have flocked seeking relief from cold winters and high taxes, the elderly have voted as a bloc to defeat school tax increases and to pass tax breaks for themselves. As a group, senior citizens are much more likely to favor an increased governmental role in the area of medical insurance and to oppose any cuts in Social Security benefits.

In the future, the graying of America will have major social and political consequences. As we discuss in chapter 12, those between sixty and seventy vote in much larger numbers than do their younger counterparts. Moreover, the fastest-growing age group in the United States is that of citizens over the age of sixty-five. Thus, not only are there more people in this category, but they are more likely to be registered to vote, and often vote conservatively, especially on fiscal matters.[23]

Age seems to have a decided effect on one's view of the proper role of government, with older people continuing to be affected by having lived through the Great Depression and World War II. One political scientist predicts that as Baby Boomers age, the age gap in political beliefs about political issues, especially governmental programs, will increase.[24] Young people, for example, resist higher taxes to fund Medicare, while the elderly resist all efforts to limit it or Social Security. Figure 10.4 reveals differences among four age cohorts on several political issues.

Region.   Regional and sectional differences have been important factors in the development and maintenance of public opinion and political beliefs since colonial times. As the United States developed into a major industrial nation, waves of immigrants with different religious traditions and customs entered the United States and often settled in areas where other immigrants from their region already lived. For example, thousands of Scandinavians settled in Minnesota, and many Irish settled in the urban centers of the Northeast, as did many Italians and Jews. All brought with them unique views about many issues, as well as about the role of government. Many of these regional differences continue to affect public opinion today and sometimes result in conflict at the national level.

One of the most long-standing and dramatic regional differences in the United States is that between the South and the North. Recall that during the Constitutional Convention most Southerners staunchly advocated a weak national government. Nearly a hundred years later, the Civil War was fought in part because of basic differences in philosophy toward government (states' rights in the South versus national rights in the North). As we know from the results of modern political polling, the South has continued to lag behind the rest of the nation on support for civil rights, while continuing to favor return of power to the states at the expense of the national government.

The South also is much more religious than the rest of the nation, as well as more Protestant. Sixty-four percent of the South is Protestant (versus 39 percent for the rest of the nation), and 45 percent identify themselves as born-again Christians. Nearly half of all Southerners believe that "the United States is a Christian country, and the government should

FIGURE 10.4 Group-Identified Voting Patterns in the 2004 Presidential Election. ■

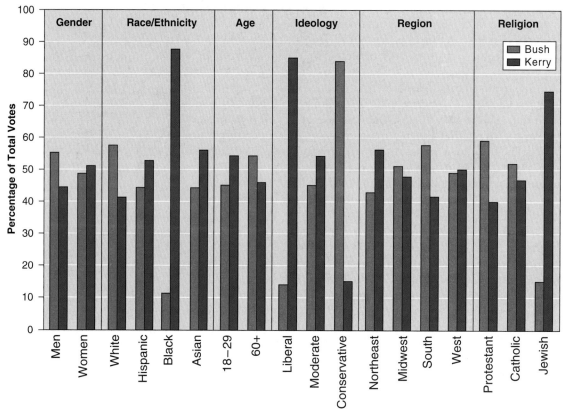

Source: CNN Exit Polls, http://www.cnn.com/election/2004/pages/results/states/us/p/00/epols.0.html.

make laws to keep it that way."[25] Church attendance is highest in the South, where 38 percent report weekly visits. In contrast, only 26 percent of those living in the Midwest and 19 percent of those residing in the West go to church or synagogue on a weekly basis.[26] Given the South's higher churchgoing rates, it is not surprising that the Christian Coalition has been very successful at mobilizing voters in that region.

Southerners also are much more supportive of a strong national defense. They accounted for 41 percent of the troops in the early days of the 1991 Persian Gulf War, even though they made up only 28 percent of the general population.

The West, too, now appears different from other sections of the nation. Some people have moved there to avoid city life; other residents have an anti-government bias. Many who have sought refuge there are staunchly against any governmental action, especially on the national level.

The Impact of Events

Key political events play a very important role in a person's political socialization. You probably have some professors who remember what they were doing on the day that President John F. Kennedy was killed—November 22, 1963. This dramatic event is indelibly etched in the minds of virtually all people who were old enough to be aware of it. Similarly, most college students today remember where they were when they heard of Princess Diana's death, or when they learned about the Oklahoma City bombing. No one old enough to have been aware of the events will ever forget where they were when they first heard about or saw the 2001 attacks on the World Trade Center and the Pentagon. These attacks on American shores evoked a profound sense of patriotism and national unity as American flags were displayed from windows, doors, balconies, and cars. For many Americans, the attacks were life-changing political events.

One has to go back to 1974 to find a political event that similarly affected what people thought about the political process. President Richard M. Nixon's resignation in 1974 made a particular impression on young people, who were forced to realize that their government was not always right or honest. This general distrust of politicians was reignited during the highly publicized investigation of President Bill Clinton and his subsequent impeachment.

The tragedy of 9/11, at least in the short term, had the opposite effect of the Watergate and Clinton scandals. In times of war, the public generally rallies round the flag, which happened after the 1991 invasion of Iraq as well as during the effort to remove the Taliban from Afghanistan in 2001.

Timeline

War, Peace, and
Public Opinion

Political Ideology and Public Opinion About Government

As discussed in chapter 1, an individual's coherent set of values and beliefs about the purpose and scope of government is called his or her **political ideology.** Americans' attachment to strong ideological positions has varied over time. In sharp contrast to spur-of-the-moment responses, these sets of values, which are often greatly affected by political socialization, can prompt citizens to favor a certain set of policy programs and adopt views about the proper role of government in the policy process.

Conservatives generally are likely to support smaller, less activist governments, limited social welfare programs, and reduced government

political ideology
The coherent set of values and beliefs about the purpose and scope of government held by groups and individuals.

Participation

Are You a Liberal or a Conservative?

regulation of business. Increasingly, they also have strong views on social issues such as abortion and same-sex marriage. In contrast, liberals generally believe that the national government has an important role to play in a wide array of areas, including helping the poor and the disadvantaged. Unlike most conservatives, they generally favor activist governments. Most Americans today, however, identify themselves as moderates.

HOW WE FORM POLITICAL OPINIONS

MANY OF US HOLD OPINIONS on a wide range of political issues, and our ideas can be traced to our social group and the different experiences each of us has had. Some individuals (called ideologues) think about politics and vote strictly on the basis of liberal or conservative ideology. Others vote according to party affiliation. Most people, however, do neither. Most people filter their ideas about politics through the factors discussed above, but they are also influenced by: (1) personal benefits; (2) political knowledge; and, (3) cues from various leaders or opinion makers.

Personal Benefits

Most polls reveal that Americans are growing more and more "I" centered. This perspective often leads people to agree with policies that will benefit them personally. You've probably heard the adage, "People vote with their pocketbooks." Taxpayers generally favor lower taxes, hence the popularity of candidates pledging "No new taxes." Similarly, an elderly person is likely to support Social Security increases, while a member of Generation X, worried about the continued stability of the Social Security program, is not likely to be very supportive of federal retirement programs. Those born in Generation Y appear even less willing to support retirement programs. Similarly, an African American is likely to support strong civil rights laws and affirmative action programs, while a majority of nonminorities will not.

Some government policies, however, do not really affect us individually. Legalized prostitution and the death penalty, for example, are often perceived as moral issues that directly affect few citizens. Individuals' attitudes on these issues often are based on underlying values they have acquired through the years.

When we are faced with policies that don't affect us personally and don't involve moral issues, we often have difficulty forming an opinion. Foreign policy is an area in which this phenomenon is especially true. Most Americans often know little of the world around them, and American public opinion is likely to be volatile in the wake of any new information.

Comparative

Comparing Public Opinion

Political Knowledge

Political knowledge and political participation have a reciprocal effect on one another—an increase in one will increase the other.[27] Knowledge about the political system is essential to successful political involvement, which, in turn, teaches citizens about politics and increases their interest in public affairs.[28]

Americans enjoy a relatively high literacy rate, and most Americans (82 percent) graduate from high school. Most Americans also have access to a range of higher education opportunities. In spite of that access to education, however, Americans' level of knowledge about history and politics is quite low. A 2002 Department of Education report found that most high school seniors had a poor grasp of history and that levels of knowledge haven't changed in nearly a decade.[29] Fifty-two percent didn't know that Russia was an ally of the United States in World War II, and 63 percent didn't know that Richard M. Nixon opened diplomatic relations with China. According to the Department of Education, today's college graduates have less civic knowledge than high school graduates did fifty years ago.[30]

In 1925, Walter Lippmann critiqued the American democratic experience and highlighted the large but limited role the population plays. Citizens, said Lippmann, cannot know everything about candidates and issues but they can, and often do, know enough to impose their views and values as to the general direction the nation should take.[31] This generalized information often stands in contrast and counterbalance to the views held by more knowledgeable political elites "inside the Beltway."

As early as 1966, noted political scientist V. O. Key Jr. argued in *The Responsible Electorate* that voters "are not fools."[32] Since then, many political scientists have argued that generalizable knowledge is enough to make democracy work. Research, for example, shows citizens' perception "of the policy stands of parties and candidates were considerably more clear and accurate when the stands themselves were more distinct."[33] In elections with sharp contrasts between candidates—such as the 1964 battle between President Lyndon B. Johnson, who was very liberal on social issues, and Barry Goldwater, who was extremely conservative—voters seem to have clearer liberal-conservative belief systems. Voters in this type of election are also more likely to be aware of important issues and vote along those lines.[34] This phenomenon held true in 2004 when George W. Bush and John Kerry had sharply contrasting views on many issues.

Cues from Leaders

Low levels of knowledge can lead to rapid opinion shifts on issues. The ebb and flow of popular opinion can be affected dramatically (some might say manipulated) by political leaders. Given the visibility of political leaders and their access to the media, it is easy to see the important role they play in influencing public opinion. Political leaders, members of the news media, and a host of other experts have regular opportunities to influence public opinion because of the lack of deep conviction with which most Americans hold many of their political beliefs.[35]

The president, especially, is often in a position to mold public opinion through effective use of the bully pulpit, as discussed in chapter 7.[36] Political scientist John E. Mueller concludes, in fact, that there is a group of citizens—called followers—who are inclined to rally to the support of the president no matter what he does.[37]

HOW PUBLIC OPINION IS MEASURED

PUBLIC OFFICIALS AT ALL LEVELS use a variety of measures as indicators of public opinion to guide their policy decisions. These measures include election results; the number of telephone calls, faxes, or e-mail messages received pro and con on any particular issue; letters to the editor in hometown newspapers; and the size of demonstrations or marches. But, the most commonly relied-on measure of public sentiment continues to be the public opinion survey, more popularly called a public opinion poll. Opinion polls are big news—especially during an election year. However, even the most accurate polls can be very deceiving. In the past sixty years, polls have improved so much that we may be dazzled—and fooled—by their apparent statistical precision.

Creating a Public Opinion Poll

Polling has several key phases: (1) determining the content and phrasing the questions; (2) selecting the sample; and, (3) contacting respondents.

Determining the Content and Phrasing the Questions.   Once a candidate, politician, or news organization decides to use a poll to measure the public's attitudes, special care has to be taken in constructing the questions to be asked. For example, if your professor asked you, "Do you think my grading procedures are fair?" rather than asking, "In general, how fair do you think the grading is in your American Politics course?" you might give a slightly different answer. The wording of the first question tends to put you on the spot and personalize the grading style; the second question is more neutral. Even more obvious differences appear in the real world of polling, especially when interested groups want a poll to yield particular results. Responses to highly emotional issues such as abortion, gay marriage, and affirmative action often are skewed depending on the wording of a particular question.

Selecting the Sample.
Once the decision is made to take a poll, pollsters must determine the universe, or the entire group whose attitudes they wish to measure. This universe could be all Americans, all voters, all city residents, all Hispanics, or all Republicans. In a perfect world, each individual would be asked to give an opinion, but such comprehensive polling is not practical. Consequently, pollsters take a sample of the universe in which they are interested. One way to obtain this sample is by **random sampling.** This method of selection gives each potential voter or adult the same chance of being selected. In theory, this sounds good, but it is actually impossible to achieve because no one has lists of every person in any group. Thus, the method of poll taking is extremely important in determining the validity and reliability of the results.

random sampling
A method of poll selection that gives each person in a group the same chance of being selected.

Most national surveys and commercial polls use samples of 1,000 to 1,500 individuals and use a variation of the random sampling method called **stratified sampling.** Simple random, nonstratified samples aren't very useful at predicting voting because they may undersample or oversample key populations that are not likely to vote. To avoid these problems, reputable polling organizations use stratified sampling based on census data that provide the number of residences in an area and their location.

stratified sampling
A variation of random sampling; census data are used to divide a country into four sampling regions. Sets of counties and standard metropolitan statistical areas are then randomly selected in proportion to the total national population.

About twenty respondents from each primary sampling unit are selected to be interviewed. Generally four or five city blocks or areas are selected, and then four or five target families from each district are used. Large, sophisticated surveys such as the National Election Study and General Social Survey, which produce the data commonly used by political scientists, attempt to sample from lists of persons living in each household. The key to the success of the stratified sampling method is not to let people volunteer to be interviewed—volunteers as a group often have different opinions from those who don't volunteer.

Stratified sampling (the most rigorous sampling technique) generally is not used by those who do surveys reported in the *New York Times* and *USA Today* or on network news programs. Instead, those organizations or pollsters working for them randomly place telephone calls to every tenth, hundredth, or thousandth person or household. If those individuals don't answer, they call the next person on the list.

Contacting Respondents.
After selecting the methodology to conduct the poll, the next question is how to contact those to be surveyed. Television stations often ask people to call in, and some surveyors hit

By permission of Mike Luckovich and Creators Syndicate, Inc.

the streets. Telephone polls, however, are becoming the most frequently used mechanism by which to gauge the temper of the electorate.

The most common form of telephone polls are random-digit dialing surveys, in which a computer randomly selects telephone numbers to be dialed. Because it is estimated that as many as 95 percent of the American public have telephones in their homes, samples selected in this manner are likely to be fairly representative, although the increasing use of cell phones may eventually affect this.

You Are a Polling Consultant

Individual, in-person interviews are conducted by some groups, such as the University of Michigan for the National Election Study. Some analysts favor such in-person surveys, but others argue that the unintended influence of the questioner or pollster is an important source of errors. How the pollster dresses, relates to the person being interviewed, and even asks the questions can affect responses. Some of these factors, such as tone of voice, can also affect the results of telephone surveys.

Political Polls

As polling has become increasingly sophisticated and networks, newspapers, and magazines compete with each other to report the most up-to-the-minute changes in public opinion on issues or politicians, new types of polls have been put into use. Each type of poll has contributed much to our knowledge of public opinion and its role in the political process.

Push Polls.

All good polls for political candidates contain push questions. These questions produce information that helps campaigns judge their own strengths and weaknesses as well as those of their opponents.[38] They might, for example, ask if you would be more likely to vote for candidate X if you knew that candidate was a strong environmentalist. These kinds of questions are accepted as an essential part of any poll, but there are concerns as to where to draw the line. Questions that go over the line result in **push polls,** which are telephone polls with an ulterior motive. Push polls are designed to give respondents some negative or even untruthful information about a candidate's opponent in order to push them away from that candidate toward the one paying for the poll.

Tracking Polls.

During the 2004 presidential election, **tracking polls** were taken on a daily basis by some news organization (see Figure 10.5). These polls allow candidates to monitor short-term campaign developments and the effects of their campaign strategies.

Tracking polls involve small samples (usually of registered voters contacted at certain times of day) and are conducted every twenty-four hours. They usually are combined with some kind of a moving statistical average to boost the sample size and therefore the statistical reliability.[39] Even though such one-day surveys are fraught with reliability problems and are vulnerable to bias, many major news organizations continue their use.

Exit Polls.

Exit polls are polls conducted at selected polling places on Election Day. Generally, large news organizations send pollsters to selected precincts to sample every tenth voter as he or she emerges from the polling place. The results of these polls are used to help the media predict the outcome of key races, often just a few minutes after the polls close in a particular state

push poll
Poll taken for the purpose of providing information on an opponent that would lead respondents to vote against that candidate.

tracking poll
Continuous survey that enables a campaign to chart its daily rise or fall in support.

exit poll
Poll conducted at selected polling places on Election Day.

■ This script provides the general format for a survey conducted by the Council for Marketing and Opinion Research. Note that even in a telephone survey drawn from a random sample, the respondent has the opportunity to self-select out of the sample.

Photo courtesy: Council for Marketing and Opinion Research

CMOR Council for Marketing and Opinion Research

Model Introduction

Hello, my name is _____ and I'm calling from (company). Today/Tonight we are calling to gather opinions regarding (general subject), and are not selling anything. This study will take approximately (length) and may be monitored (and recorded) for quality purposes. We would appreciate your time. May I include your opinions?

Closing

- At the conclusion of the survey, thank the respondent for his/her time.
- Express the desired intention that the respondent had a positive survey experience and will be willing to participate in future market research projects.
- Remind the respondent that his/her opinions do count.

MODEL CLOSING

Thank you for your time and cooperation. I hope this experience was a pleasant one and you will participate in other market research projects in the future. Please remember that your opinion counts! Have a good day/evening.

Alternative: Participate in collecting respondent satisfaction data to improve survey quality.

Thank you very much for taking part in this survey. Because consumers like you are such a valued part of what we do, I'd like you to think about the survey you just participated in. On a scale from 1 to 10 where ten means "it was a good use of my time", and one means "it was not a good use of my time", which number between 1 and 10 best describes how you feel about your experience today? That's all the questions I have. Please remember that your opinion counts! Have a good day/evening.

FIGURE 10.5 A Daily Tracking Poll for the 2004 Presidential Election. ■

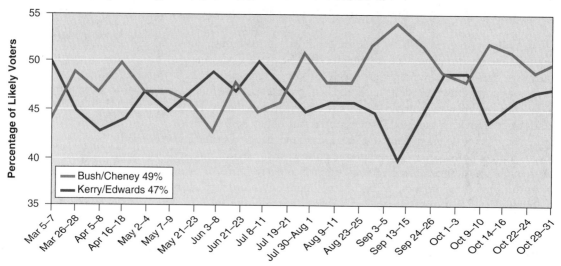

Source: USA Today and CNN/Gallup Poll results, http://www.usatoday.com/news/politicselections/nation/polls/usatodaypolls.htm.

and generally before voters in other areas—sometimes in a later time zone—have cast their ballots. They also provide an independent assessment of why voters supported particular candidates.

In 1980, President Jimmy Carter's own polling and the results of network exit polls led him to concede defeat three hours before the polls closed on the West Coast. Many Democratic party officials and candidates criticized Carter and network predictions for harming their chances at victories, arguing that with the presidential election already called, voters were unlikely to go to the polls. In the aftermath of that controversy, all networks agreed not to predict the results of presidential contests until all polling places were closed.

Exit polls continue to be problematic. In 2000, they led newscasters to inaccurately place Florida in the Gore column, as discussed below. In 2004, mid-afternoon exit poll results were leaked on the Internet, making many believe a Kerry victory was at hand. Whether many Republicans tended to vote later in the day, or Democrats were more willing to be polled, or for other reasons, the exit polls were wrong.

Shortcomings of Polling

The information derived from public opinion polls has become an extremely important part of governance. When the results of a poll are accurate, they express the feelings of the electorate in unique ways and help guide the creation of public policy. However, when the results of a poll are inaccurate, disastrous consequences often result.

Sampling Error.   The accuracy of any poll depends on the quality of the sample that was drawn. Small samples, if properly drawn, can be very accurate if each unit in the universe has an equal opportunity to be sampled. If a pollster, for example, fails to sample certain populations, his or her results may reflect that shortcoming. Often the opinions of the poor and homeless are underrepresented because insufficient attention is given to making certain that these groups are sampled representatively. For example, in the case of tracking polls, if you choose to sample only on weekends or from 5 p.m. to 9 p.m., you may get more Republicans, who tend to have higher incomes and are less likely to be working shift work or multiple jobs. There comes a point in sampling, however, where increases in the size of the sample have little effect on a reduction of the **sampling error** (or **margin of error**), the difference between the actual universe and the sample.

sampling error or margin of error
A measure of the accuracy of a public opinion poll.

All polls contain errors. Standard samples of approximately 1,000 to 1,500 individuals provide fairly good estimates of actual behavior (in the case of voting, for example). Typically, the margin of error in a sample of 1,500 will be about 3 percent. If you ask 1,500 people "Do you like ice cream?" and 52 percent say "yes" and 48 percent say "no," the results are too close to tell whether more people like ice cream than not. Why? Because the margin of error implies that somewhere between 55 percent (52 + 3) and 49 percent (52 − 3) of the people like ice cream, while between 51 percent (48 + 3) and 45 percent (48 − 3) do not. The margin of error in a close election makes predictions very difficult.

Limited Respondent Options.   Polls can be inaccurate when they limit responses. If you are asked, "How do you like this class?" and are given only like or dislike options, your full sentiments may not be tapped if you like the class very much or feel only so-so about it.

Lack of Information.   Public opinion polls may be inaccurate when they attempt to gauge attitudes about issues that some or even many individuals don't care about or about which the public has little information. Most academic public opinion research organizations, such as the National Election Study, use some kind of filter question that first asks respondents whether or not they have thought about the question. These screening procedures generally allow surveyors to exclude as many as 20 percent of their respondents, especially on complex issues like the federal budget. Questions on more personal issues such as moral values, drugs, crime, race, and women's role in society get far fewer "no opinion" or "don't know" responses.

Intensity.   Another shortcoming of polls concerns their inability to measure intensity of feeling about particular issues. Whereas a respondent might answer affirmatively to any question, it is likely that his or her feelings about issues such as abortion, the death penalty, or support for U.S. troops in Afghanistan or Iraq are much more intense than are his or her feelings about the Electoral College or even the preferability of certain types of voting machines.

THE NEWS MEDIA

THE MEDIA HAVE THE POTENTIAL to exert enormous influence over public opinion. Not only can they tell us what is important by setting the agenda for what we will watch and read, but they can also influence what we think about issues through the content and slant of their news stories. The simple words of the First Amendment, "Congress shall make no law…abridging the freedom of speech, or of the press," have shaped the American republic as much as or more than any others in the Constitution. With the Constitution's sanction, as interpreted by the Supreme Court over two centuries, a vigorous and highly competitive press has emerged. This freedom has been crucial in facilitating the political discourse and education necessary to maintain democracy.

The Evolution of Journalism in the United States

Timeline

Three Centuries of
American Mass Media

Journalism—the process and profession of collecting and disseminating the news (that is, new information about subjects of public interest)—has existed in some form since the dawn of civilization.[40] Yet, its practice has often been remarkably uncivilized, and it was much more so at the beginning of the American republic than it is today.

The first newspapers were published in the American colonies in 1690. The number of newspapers grew throughout the 1700s, as colonists began to realize the value of a press free from government oversight and censorship. The battle between Federalists and Anti-Federalists, discussed in chapter 2, played out in various partisan newspapers. Thus, it was not surprising that one of the Anti-Federalists' demands during our country's constitutional debate was to include an amendment guaranteeing the freedom of the press in the final version of the Constitution.

A free press is a necessary component of a democratic society because it informs the public, giving them the information they need to choose their leaders and influence the direction of public policy. In fact, the American media are so important that they have been called the "fourth branch of government" because their influence is often as great as that of the three constitutional branches: the executive, the legislative, and the judiciary. However, this term is misleading because the American media comprise many competing private enterprises.

The Living Constitution

Congress shall make no law . . . abridging the freedom . . . of the press . . .

—First Amendment

The Founders knew that no democracy is easy, that a republic requires a continuous battle for rights and responsibilities. One of those rights is the freedom of the press, preserved in the First Amendment to the Constitution. To protect the press, the Founders were wise enough to keep the constitutional language simple—and a good thing, too. Their view of the press, and its required freedom, was almost certainly less broad than we conceive of the press today.

It is difficult today to appreciate what a leap of faith it was for the Founders to grant freedom of the press when James Madison brought the Bill of Rights before Congress. Newspapers were largely run by disreputable people, since at the time editors and reporters were judged as merely purveyors of rumor and scandal, the reason Madison, as well as Alexander Hamilton and John Jay, published their newspaper articles advocating the ratification of the Constitution, *The Federalist Papers,* under the pseudonym "Publius."

Not much has changed since the Founders instituted the free press. We still have tabloids and partisan publications in which politicians attack each other, and we still rely on the press to give us important political information with which we make voting decisions. The First Amendment declares the priority of free expression. The Founders recognized that all kinds of information would have to be allowed, in order to create as many opportunities for solid information to be reported, the fear being that regulations in response to what offends some people might be the first step on the slippery slope to censorship. In other words, protecting the *New York Times* means protecting the "paparazzi" or else we will have neither. Although the vices and virtues of a free press have not changed, the number of media has, but the simple yet powerful protection the Founders created in the First Amendment made their invention and implementation merely a continuation of a freedom we all enjoy. Still, however, the press can be sued for publishing known nontruths.

During his presidency, George Washington escaped the sort of harsh press scrutiny that presidents experience today, but he detested journalists nonetheless because his battle tactics in the Revolutionary War had been much criticized in print. An early draft of his "Farewell Address to the Nation" at the end of his presidency (1796) contained a savage condemnation of the press.[41] The partisan press eventually gave way to the penny press. In 1833, Benjamin Day founded the *New York Sun*, which cost a penny at the newsstand. Because it was not tied to one party, it was politically more independent than the party papers. The *Sun*, the forerunner of modern newspapers, relied on mass circulation and commercial advertising to produce profit. By 1861, the penny press had so supplanted partisan papers that President Abraham Lincoln announced that his administration would have no favored or sponsored newspaper.

Although the press was becoming less partisan, it was not necessarily becoming more respectable. Mass-circulation dailies sought wide readership, attracting readers with the sensational and the scandalous. The sordid side of politics became the entertainment of the times. One of the best-known examples occurred in the presidential campaign of 1884, when the *Buffalo Evening Telegraph* headlined "A Terrible Tale" about Grover Cleveland, the Democratic nominee.[42] In 1871, while sheriff of Buffalo, Cleveland had allegedly fathered a child. Even though paternity was indeterminate because the child's mother had been seeing other men, Cleveland willingly accepted responsibility, since all the other men were married, and he had dutifully paid child support for years. The strict Victorian moral code that dominated American values at the time made the story even more shocking than it would be today. Fortunately for Cleveland, another newspaper, the *Democratic Sentinel*, broke a story that helped to offset this scandal: Republican presidential nominee James G. Blaine and his wife had had their first child just three months after their wedding.

yellow journalism
A form of newspaper publishing in vogue in the late-nineteenth century that featured pictures, comics, color, and sensationalized, oversimplified news coverage.

In the late 1800s and early 1900s, the era of the intrusive press was in full flower. Pioneered by prominent publishers such as William Randolph Hearst and Joseph Pulitzer, **yellow journalism**—the name strictly derived from printing the comic strip "Yellow Kid" in color—featured pictures, comics, and color designed to capture a share of the burgeoning immigrant population market. These newspapers also oversimplified and sensationalized many news developments. The front-page editorial crusade became common, the motto for which frequently seemed to be: "Damn the truth, full speed ahead."

muckraking
A form of journalism, in vogue in the early twentieth century, concerned with reforming government and business conduct.

After the turn of the twentieth century, the muckrakers—so named by President Theodore Roosevelt after a special rake designed to collect manure[43]—took charge of a number of newspapers and nationally circulated magazines. **Muckraking** journalists searched out and exposed misconduct by government, business, and politicians in order to stimulate reform.[44] There was no shortage of corruption to reveal, of course, and much good came from these efforts. In particular, muckrakers stimulated demands for the increased regulation of public trusts. But, an unfortunate side effect of the emphasis on crusades and investigations was the frequent publication of gossip and rumor without sufficient proof.

The modern press corps may also be guilty of this offense, but it has achieved great progress on another front. Throughout the nineteenth century, payoffs to the press were common. Andrew Jackson, for instance, gave one in ten of his early appointments to loyal reporters.[45] During the 1872 presidential campaign, the Republicans slipped cash to about 300 newsmen.[46] Wealthy industrialists also sometimes purchased investigative cease-fires for tens of thousands of dollars. Examples of such press corruption in the United States are exceedingly rare today.

As the news business grew, its focus gradually shifted from passionate opinion to corporate profit. Newspapers, hoping to maximize profit, were more careful to avoid alienating the advertisers and readers who produced their revenues, and the result was less harsh, more objective reporting. Meanwhile, media barons such as Joseph Pulitzer and William Randolph Hearst became pillars of the establishment; for the most part, they were no longer the anti-establishment insurgents of yore.

Technological advances had a major impact on this transformation in journalism. High-speed presses and more cheaply produced paper made mass-circulation dailies possible. The telegraph and then the telephone made news gathering easier and much faster. When radio became widely available in the 1920s, millions of Americans could hear national politicians instead of merely reading about them. With television—first introduced in the late 1940s, and nearly a universal fixture in U.S. homes by the mid-1950s—citizens could see and hear candidates and presidents. The supplanting of newspapers and magazines as the foremost conduits between politicians and voters had profound effects on the electoral process, as we discuss shortly.

Timeline

Major Technological Innovations that Have Changed the Political Landscape

The U.S. Media Today

The editors of the first partisan newspapers could scarcely have imagined what their profession would become more than two centuries later. The number and diversity of media outlets existing today are stunning. The **print press** consists of many thousands of daily and weekly newspapers, periodicals, magazines, newsletters, and journals. The **electronic media** are radio and television stations and networks, and the Internet.

Readers of daily newspapers among the top fifty markets fell from 58 percent in 1998 to 54 percent in 2003.[47] But, this number conceals more than it reveals: 68 percent of Americans over age sixty-five read daily newspapers, while only 40 percent of readers age eighteen to twenty-four and 41 percent of readers between age twenty-five to

Simulation

You Are the News Editor

print press
The traditional form of mass media, comprising newspapers, magazines, and journals.

electronic media
The broadcast and cable media, including television, radio, and the Internet.

FIGURE 10.6   Distribution of News Source Usage by Individuals

While the dominant, mainstream media outlets are still used by the greatest number of consumers, the only growth areas are ethnic, alternative, and online media. ■

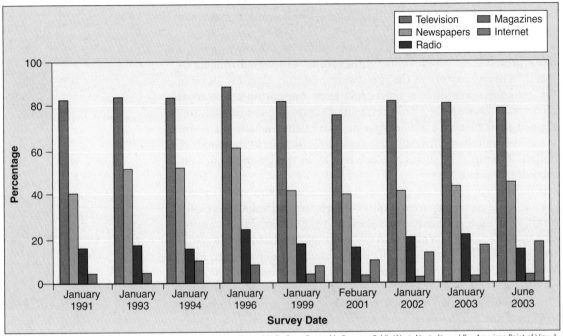

Source: Pew Research Center for the People and the Press, "Strong Opposition to Media Cross-Ownership Emerges: Public Wants Neutrality and Pro-American Point of View," accessed August 13, 2004, http://www.stateofthenewsmedia.org/narrative_overview_audience.asp?media=1.

thirty-four did. In spring of 2004, the Newspaper Association of America sought new methods to retain and grow readership, such as posting content on newspaper Web sites and focusing on local events.[48]

One cause of the newspapers' declining audience is the increased numbers of television sets and cable and satellite television subscribers. In the early 1960s, a substantial majority of Americans reported that they got most of their news from newspapers (see Figure 10.6). Forty years later, 83 percent of Americans claimed to get their news from television, whereas only a little over 50 percent read newspapers. There is, however, an important distinction between network and cable news stations. Network news has lost viewers since 1980, with the loss becoming even steeper after the advent of cable news. Between 2000 and 2004, viewership for all network news programming declined from 45 percent to 35 percent.[49] Cable news has seen an increase in viewership, from 34 percent in 2000 to 38 percent in 2004. This increase is due in large part because of the increased availability of services providing the twenty-four-hour news channels. By 2004, 67 percent of all U.S. households were wired for basic cable, with 18 percent of households using a direct broadcast satellite (such as DirectTV or DISH). Thus, the vast majority of Americans receive cable news in addition to their broadcast stations.[50]

Within the realm of cable news, the two ratings leaders, CNN and Fox News, have begun engaging in *niche journalism*—that is, both stations cater particularly to specific groups of people. The two stations divide audiences by ideology. Fox News increasingly favors a more conservative view and CNN a more liberal one, although the Fox view is much more pronounced.[51] Despite its many drawbacks (such as simplicity, brevity, and entertainment orientation), television news, especially cable news, is "news that matters." It has the power to affect greatly which issues viewers say are important.[52]

Cable and satellite providers also give consumers access to a less glitzy and more unfiltered source of news with C-SPAN. C-SPAN is a basic cable channel that offers coverage of congressional proceedings, major political events, and events sponsored by political groups. It also produces some of its own programming, such as *Washington Journal*, which invites scholars and journalists to speak about topics pertaining to their areas of expertise. C-SPAN expanded its brand to include C-SPAN2 and C-SPAN3, which air academic seminars and book presentations in a series titled *BookTV*. C-SPAN benefits from having no sponsors distracting (with commercials or banners) or possibly affecting what it broadcasts. Because the content of C-SPAN can be erudite, technical, and sometimes downright tedious (such as the fixed camera shot of the Senate during a roll-call vote), audiences tend to be very small, but they are very loyal and give C-SPAN its place as a truly content-driven medium.

Local television reporters often outnumber the national television news corps on the campaign trail. Satellite technology has provided any of the 1,300 local stations willing to invest in the hardware an opportunity to beam back reports from the field. Consequently, local news can tie national events to local issues in ways national network and cable news cannot. It is no surprise, then, that Americans prefer local news to the other two, 42 percent of them watching their local news program for news. This number has, however, dropped from 48 percent in 2000, perhaps because of the increased access to cable news and the subsequent fragmentation of news sources. Unfortunately, however, studies also show that local news, compared to newspapers and network reports, contains the least substantive coverage. National news reports are more likely to criticize and analyze policy positions and candidates than are local broadcasts.[53]

More and more, young people are abandoning traditional media outlets in favor of other sources (see Table 10.2). Although cable news networks still are the most frequently viewed, the Internet and comedy television shows are close behind and gaining ground.[54]

The World Wide Web is an increasingly important source of information. In 2000, 9 percent of Americans claimed to receive news from the Internet, whereas more than 20 percent do now.[55] Of course, few people rely exclusively on the Internet for news, although it is likely

TABLE 10.2   The News Generation Gap

	Age			
	18–29 %	*30–49* %	*50–64* %	*65+* %
Did yesterday				
Watched TV news	40	52	62	73
Local TV news	28	41	49	52
Network evening	17	25	38	46
Cable TV news	16	23	30	35
Morning News	11	16	21	27
Read a newspaper	26	37	52	59
Listened to radio news	34	49	42	29
No news yesterday	33	19	12	12
Watch/listen/read regularly				
Local TV news	46	54	64	69
Cable TV news	23	31	42	38
Nightly network news	19	23	45	53
Network TV magazines	15	22	30	33
Network morning news	16	22	23	31
Call-in radio shows	16	19	20	10
National Public Radio	14	18	15	11
Time/Newsweek/US News	12	13	15	13
Online news 3+ times/week	31	30	24	7

Source: Pew Research Center for the People and the Press, "Public's Habits Little Changed by September 11," June 9, 2002.

in the future that many citizens will use the video components of the World Wide Web to substitute for television news watching or newspaper reading. Already, many major networks and newspapers offer their news online. Major cable news stations, such as CNN, MSNBC, and Fox News, each have their own Web sites that are also used to promote their television programming as well as provide up-to-date news. The *New York Times* and *Washington Post* are available online for free to users who register. Access to older articles requires a fee. Political magazines such as the *National Review* and the *Nation* provide all online content free of charge; like the online newspapers, they earn revenue from advertising through pop-up and banner ads.

Many people wonder if newspapers and television stations currently offering free Web sites are cutting into their own subscription revenues. However, there is very little evidence that this is happening. By and large, the people who use media Web sites are highly informed voters who devour additional information about politics and government and use the Web for updates and supplements to their traditional media services. Indeed, a recent study discovered that out of light, medium, and heavy users of online news sites, heavy users read newspapers the most, while light users read newspapers the least. In short, heavy users, those most interested in the news, will take their news any way they can get it.[56]

The Internet also offers access to foreign news media previously unavailable to most Americans. The British Broadcasting Channel

AL-JAZEERA: CNN OF THE ARAB WORLD?

Few Americans other than those of Arabic descent had heard of al-Jazeera before October 7, 2001. On that day, less than one month following the terrorist attacks on the World Trade Center and the Pentagon, Osama bin Laden spoke to the world for six and one-half minutes. It was not the first time al-Jazeera carried his image or his words, nor would it be the last. In June 1999 it broadcast a ninety-minute interview with him, and several bin Laden tapes have been aired since then. Many have taken these interviews as evidence that al-Jazeera is little more than a mouthpiece for al-Qaeda's anti-American propaganda.

Al-Jazeera means "the island" or "the peninsula" in Arabic. It is an independent station that broadcasts from the tiny oil-rich and Islamic country of Qatar in the Persian Gulf. Qatar is a member of the Organization of Petroleum Exporting Countries (OPEC) and is ruled by a progressive emir (prince) who is pro-Western. The emir allowed American troops to use Qatar as a staging point for the 1991 Persian Gulf War and the Iraqi War. He also funded al-Jazeera when it was founded in 1996. Al-Jazeera emerged out of the failure of a British Broadcasting Corporation (BBC) news service, after a Saudi Arabian–owned radio and television network reportedly terminated its financial support because the news service had aired a documentary about executions in Saudi Arabia.

Al-Jazeera immediately set a course that separated it from its competitors in the region. Most of them were owned either by Middle Eastern governments or by powerful individuals within these countries, and their standard offerings emphasized entertainment and limited news that amounted to state propaganda. Sensitive political and social issues were ignored for fear of the controversy they would create.

In contrast, the trail that al-Jazeera chose to follow was pioneered by Cable News Network (CNN). Like CNN, al-Jazeera focuses its political reporting on two staples. The first is on-the-scene coverage of conflict. Just as CNN was the only television network to broadcast out of Baghdad in the Persian Gulf War, al-Jazeera had a monopoly of live reporting from Kabul during the war in Afghanistan against the Taliban. Three Western news agencies, including CNN, also received permission from the Taliban government in 1999 to establish offices in Afghanistan, but only al-Jazeera did so. Al-Jazeera also covers the Palestinian conflict extensively, receiving heavy criticism from the West for referring to Palestinians killed by Israeli forces as martyrs and showing extensive footage of Palestinian casualties.

The second staple is political talk shows that often feature call-ins from viewers. Among the most popular are *The Opposite Direction,* a live weekly two-hour show modeled after CNN's *Crossfire,* and *Without Frontiers,* in which an individual discusses a current event topic in depth. Shows such as these have often angered Middle Eastern governments where there is little tradition of free press. Libya and Kuwait both threatened to recall their ambassadors to Qatar in protest over critical stories aired by al-Jazeera. Saudi Arabia did so and prohibited al-Jazeera from covering the pilgrimage to Mecca. Saddam Hussein once criticized al-Jazeera's broadcasts as too "pro-American" and expelled two al-Jazeera reporters during the Iraq War because of its coverage. Yasser Arafat criticized al-Jazeera for carrying an interview with Sheikh Ahmed Yassin, head of Hamas and his longtime rival for leadership among the Palestinians.

Not only Arabs appear on al-Jazeera news shows: U.S., British, and Israeli leaders, including President George W. Bush, Prime Minister Tony Blair, Secretary of State Condoleezza Rice have all been interviewed by al-Jazeera.

Questions

1. Take a look at the Web site of al-Jazeera (aljazeera.net). How does its coverage compare with that of American networks?
2. Is the United States better off or worse off in the Middle East because of al-Jazeera?

(BBC) has a Web site entirely devoted to news and available in over forty languages. International newspapers offer online content although usually in their native languages. Al-Jazeera, a major Arabic television news source, has an English-language Web site providing news concerning Arabs and Muslims in the Middle East (see Global Perspective: Al-Jazeera: CNN of the Arab World?). For those many Americans with access to the Internet, these alternative sources of information may shed a different perspective on global issues.

How the Media Cover Politicians and Government

The news media focus much attention on our politicians and the day-to-day operations of our government. In this section, we will discuss coverage of the three constitutionally created branches of government (Congress, the president, and the courts), and show how the tenor of this coverage has changed since the Watergate scandal of the early 1970s.

How the Press and Public Figures Interact.   The type of communication between elected officials or public figures and the media can take different forms. A **press release** is a written document offering an official comment or position on an issue or news event; it is usually printed on paper and handed directly to reporters, or increasingly, released by e-mail or fax. A **press briefing** is a relatively restricted live engagement with the press, with the range of questions limited to one or two specific topics. In a press briefing, a press secretary or aide represents the elected official or public figure, who does not appear in person. In a full-blown **press conference,** an elected official appears in person to talk with the press at great length about an unrestricted range of topics. Press conferences provide a field on which reporters struggle to get the answers they need, and public figures attempt to retain control of their message and spin the news and issues in ways favorable to them.

Covering the Presidency.   The three branches of the U.S. government—the executive, the legislative, and the judicial—are roughly equal in power and authority, but in the world of media coverage the president is first among equals. All television cables lead to the White House, and a president can address the nation on all networks almost at will. Since Franklin D. Roosevelt's time, chief executives have used the office and presidential press conference as a bully pulpit to shape public opinion and explain their actions. The presence of the press in the White House enables a president to appear even on very short notice and to televise live, interrupting regular programming. The White House's press briefing room is a familiar sight on the evening news, not just because presidents use it so often, but also because the presidential press secretary has almost daily question-and-answer sessions there.

Although the president receives the vast majority of the press's attention, much of this focus is unfavorable. Since the advent of televis-

press release
A document offering an official comment or position.

press briefing
A relatively restricted session between a press secretary or aide and the press.

press conference
An unrestricted session between an elected official and the press.

ing press conferences in the 1960s, press coverage of the president has become dramatically more negative. Dwight Eisenhower once opened up a press conference by inviting the press to "nail him to the cross" as they usually did, and this approach suggests the way most presidents approach their formal encounters with the press. A study in the early 1990s found coverage of George Bush's handling of important national problems was almost solely negative.[57] The media have faced a more difficult challenge in covering the administration of George W. Bush, a president who prides himself on the tight-lipped, no leaks nature of his White House. No member of his staff appears on television or in print without prior permission, while Bush himself has held a record low number of press conferences. Bush clearly has tried to control his image by controlling how much the press directly encounters him.

Covering Congress.   The size of Congress (535 members) and its decentralized nature (bicameralism, the committee system, and so on) make it difficult for the media to survey. Nevertheless, the congressional press corps has more than 3,000 members.[58] Most news organizations solve the size and decentralization problems by concentrating coverage on three groups of individuals. First, the leaders of both parties in both houses receive the lion's share of attention because only they can speak for a majority of their party's members. Usually the majority and minority leaders in each house and the speaker of the House are the preferred spokespersons, but the whips also receive a substantial share of air time and column inches. Second, key committee chairs command center stage when subjects in their domain are newsworthy. Heads of the most prominent committees (such as Ways and Means or Armed Services) are guaranteed frequent coverage, but even the chairs and members of minor committees or subcommittees can achieve fame when the time and issue are right. Third, local newspapers and broadcast stations normally devote some resources to covering their local senators and representatives, even when these legislators are junior and relatively lacking in influence. Most office holders, in turn, are mainly concerned with meeting the needs of their local media contingents, since these reporters are the ones who directly and regularly reach the voters in their home constituencies. Coverage of Congress has been greatly expanded through cable channels C-SPAN and C-SPAN2, which provide gavel-to-gavel coverage of House and Senate sessions as well as many committee hearings. For the first time, Americans can watch their representatives in action twenty-four hours a day.

One other kind of congressional news coverage is worth noting: investigative committee hearings. Occasionally, a sensational scandal leads to televised congressional committee hearings that transfix and electrify the nation. In the early 1950s, Senator Joseph R. McCarthy (R–WI) held a series of hearings to root out what he claimed were Communists in the Department of State and other U.S. government agencies, as well as in Hollywood's film industry. The senator's style of investigation, which involved many wild charges made without proof and the smearing and labeling of opponents as Communists, gave rise to the term *McCarthyism*. Congressional investigation became its own subject after the photographs depicting abuse of Iraqi prisoners in Abu Ghraib were released to the press in 2004. Democrats questioned why the Republican majority in both houses refused to perform any real investigation of prison abuse, citing their obvious political alliance with President Bush. In short, Democrats wanted not only an investigation of the abuse but also an investigation of why there had been no investigation.

The Judiciary.   Cloaked in secrecy—because judicial deliberations and decision making are conducted in private—the courts receive scant coverage under most circumstances. However, a volatile or controversial issue, such as abortion, same-sex marriage, or the 2000 presidential election, can change the usual type of coverage, especially when the Supreme Court is rendering the decision. Each network and major newspaper has one or more Supreme Court reporters, people who are usually well schooled in the law and whose instant analysis of court opinions interprets the decisions for the millions of people without legal training. Gradually, the admission of cameras into state and local courtrooms across the United States and the popularity of Court TV are offering people a more in-depth look at the operation of the judicial system. Many judges, however, can use their discretion to keep cameras out of their courtrooms, and the U.S. Supreme Court does not permit televised proceedings or photographs of its sittings.

Even more than the Court's decisions, presidential appointments to the high Court are the focus of intense media attention. As the judiciary has assumed a more important role in modern times, the men and women considered for the post are being subjected to withering scrutiny of their records and even of their private lives. For example, the media's coverage of the Clarence Thomas Supreme Court nomination hearings in 1991 made Thomas a household word.

Investigative Journalism and the Character Issue

The Watergate scandal of the Nixon administration had a profound impact on press conduct. Watergate began a chain reaction that today allows for intense media scrutiny of public officials' private lives and shifted the orientation of journalism away from mere description (providing an account of happenings) and toward prescription—helping to set the campaign's (and society's) agenda by focusing attention on the candidates' shortcomings as well as on certain social problems. After Watergate, people increasingly saw the press as the most powerful agent to keep government accountable through sustaining the constant threat of finding and exposing political corruption.

The sizable financial and personnel investments many major news organizations make in investigative units almost guarantee that they give greater attention to scandals, and that they uncover more of them than in the pre-Watergate years in journalism. Another clear consequence of Watergate has been the increasing emphasis by the press on the character of candidates. The issue of character has always been present in U.S. politics—George Washington was not made the nation's first president for his policy positions but because he was esteemed as the general who won the Revolutionary War. But, rarely if ever has character been such an issue as it has in elections since Watergate. In 2004, the character issue appeared in the form of questions about the major candidates' military service. President George W. Bush's National Guard tenure was examined, while Senator John Kerry's conduct in Vietnam drew significant attention.

The character trend in reporting is supported by certain assumptions held by the press. First, the press has mainly replaced the political parties as the screening committee that winnows the field of candidates and filters out the weaker contenders. (This fact may be another reason to support the strengthening of the political parties. Politicians are in a much better position than the press to provide professional peer review of colleagues who are seeking the presidency.) Second, many journalists believe it necessary to publicize a candidate's foibles that might affect his or her public performance. Third, the press believes that it is giving the public what it wants and expects. Finally, scandal sells papers and attracts television viewers.[59]

In the past, a reporter would think twice about filing a story critical of a politician's character, and the editors probably would have killed the story had the reporter been foolish enough to do so. The reason? Fear of a libel suit. (Recall from chapter 4 that libel is written defamation of character that unjustly injures a person's reputation.) The first question editors would ask about even an ambiguous or suggestive phrase about a public official was, "If we're sued, can you prove beyond a doubt what you've written?"

Such inhibitions were ostensibly lifted in 1964, when the Supreme Court ruled in ***New York Times Co. v. Sullivan*** that simply publishing a defamatory falsehood is not enough to justify a libel judgment.[60] Henceforth, a public official would have to prove "actual malice," a requirement extended three years later to all public figures, such as Hollywood stars and prominent athletes.[61] The Supreme Court declared that the First Amendment requires elected officials and candidates to prove that the publisher either believed the challenged statement was false or at least entertained serious doubts about its truth and acted recklessly in publishing it in the face of those doubts. The actual malice rule has made it very difficult for public figures to win libel cases.

New York Times Co. v. Sullivan (1964)
The Supreme Court concluded that "actual malice" must be proved to support a finding of libel against a public figure.

Are the Media Biased?

Whenever the media break an unfavorable story about a politician, the politician usually counters with a cry of "biased reporting"—a claim that

Participation
Are the Media Biased?

the press has told an untruth, has told only part of the truth, or has reported facts out of the complete context of the event. Who is right? Are the news media biased? The answer is simple and unavoidable: of course they are. Journalists are fallible human beings who inevitably have values, preferences, and attitudes galore—some conscious, others subconscious, but all reflected at one time or another in the subjects selected for coverage or the slant of that coverage. Given that the press is biased, in what ways is it biased and when and how are the biases shown?

For much of the 1980s and 1990s, the argument was that the media are liberally biased because of the sheer number of journalists who lean to the left. Studies showed that professional journalists are drawn heavily from the ranks of highly educated social and political liberals.[62] Journalists are substantially Democratic in party affiliation and voting habits, progressive and anti-establishment in political orientation, and well to the left of the general public on most economic, foreign policy, and social issues (such as abortion, affirmative action, gay rights, and gun control). Indeed, a 2001 survey revealed that, whereas 35 percent of the general public describes themselves as being ideologically conservative, only 6 percent of those in the media would do the same.[63] In addition, dozens of the most influential reporters and executives entered (or reentered) journalism after stints of partisan participation in campaigns or government; studies in the 1980s showed that a substantial majority worked for Democrats.[64]

It seems that much of the more recent media bias is intentional and a response to increasing fragmentation and competition among media. Uncovering media bias may no longer be necessary, since it is no longer something the media (whether the journalists or the corporate executive) wish to hide, but rather something they very intentionally market to gain a competitive edge. A comprehensive study of the news media reports that audiences seek out particular perspectives in the news they consume. While "mainstream, general interests newspapers, network television and local television news" are slowly losing audiences, "online, ethnic and alternative media are growing markedly" and "share the same strength— the opportunity for audiences to select tailored content and, in the case of the Internet, to do it on demand."[65] In order for various media to compete, they have to differentiate themselves from the rest, and their current method of choice is in the bias infused within their content.

Recent survey data show that 27 percent of Democrats watch CNN while only 20 percent of Republicans do. Meanwhile, 29 percent of Republicans, but a mere 14 percent of Democrats, watch Fox News.[66] With cable news becoming a crowded field fighting over audience share, stations have tried to differentiate themselves in order to attract audiences. The trend, however, goes beyond cable news. Forty percent of Democrats watch network news, while only 20 percent of Republicans do. Republicans listen to the radio for news more than Democrats, 20 to 12 percent respectively. This number may even hide the divisions existing among stations—National Public Radio (NPR) typically catering to a more liberal palette and talk radio to a more conservative one. Finally, there is only a small disparity in newspaper reading between Republicans and Democrats (38 to 43 percent respectively). However, like radio, newspapers can be subdivided by ideology; for instance, the *Washington Times* offers more conservative fare than its rival the *Washington Post.*

The Internet now features Web sites openly devoted to ideological rabble rousing and rumor mongering. The right-leaning *Drudge Report* pioneered the spreading of newsworthy rumors during the second Clinton administration and has inspired a Web site, the *Drudge Retort*, devoted to debunking its counterpart's less reliable content. MoveOn.org has established itself as the leading site for liberal activists against the Bush administration. Thousands of individuals host Weblogs—known commonly as "blogs"—that contain daily entries espousing that individual's political opinions and, in some cases, gain a significant following from those with similar political perspectives. These "bloggers" (those who keep blogs) link their sites to sites with ideologically like-minded bloggers, creating a network for those who read daily entries.

The deepest bias most political journalists have is the desire to get to the bottom of a good campaign story—which is usually negative news about a candidate. The fear of missing a good story, more than bias, leads all media outlets to develop the same headlines and to adopt the same slant. In the absence of a good story, news people may attempt to create a horse race where none exists. News people, whose lives revolve around the current political scene, naturally want to add spice and drama, minimize their boredom, and increase their audience. While the horse-race components of elections are intrinsically interesting, the limited time that television has to devote to politics is disproportionately devoted to the competitive aspects of politics, leaving less time for adequate discussion of public policy.

Other human biases are also at work in reporting on politics. Whether the press likes or dislikes a candidate personally is often vital. Richard M. Nixon and Jimmy Carter—both aloof politicians—were disliked by many reporters who covered them, and they suffered from a harsh and critical press. The higher a politician's profile, the more open he or she is to scrutiny, and the more care he or she must take in handling the press.

Some research suggests that candidates may charge the media with bias as a strategy for dealing with the press, and that bias claims are part of the dynamic between elected officials and reporters. If a candidate can plausibly and loudly decry bias in the media as the source of his negative coverage, for example, reporters might temper future negative stories or give the candidate favorable coverage to mitigate the calls of bias.[67]

One other source of bias in the press, or at least of nonobjectivity, is the increasing celebrity status of many people who report the news. In an age of media stardom and blurring boundaries between forms of entertainment, journalists in prominent media positions have

MEDIA BIAS: IS THE NEWS AFFECTED BY AN IDEOLOGICAL BIAS?

OVERVIEW: Throughout the second half of the twentieth century, the national news media made the claim that their journalists had fully developed the professionalism they needed to be objective in their reporting. Journalistic objectivity is the reporting of the facts of an event without imposing a political or ideological slant. The objectivity of journalists is crucial, since the vast majority of Americans rely on the news media for the information they need to make political decisions. To charge bias against the news media, then, is to explode a whole learning model for American citizenship. Rather than allowing American citizens' to make political decisions based on facts, the media would make the decisions for them by either reporting only certain aspects of a story or not reporting the story at all. The media would control what you know or how you know it, making all the political decisions of average Americans merely an outcome of the original bias.

But is there a systemic bias? Conservative critics charge that up to 90 percent of journalists vote Democratic,[a] and that many of the political reporters and analysts are hired not merely because of their political experience but also because of their Democratic experience. For example, ABC News hired former Clinton White House adviser George Stephanopolous to host the Sunday morning political talk show *This Week*. Liberals argue in return that conservatives have no right to talk, since Fox News reports news for conservatives.[b] Moreover, the corporate interests of companies that own the media, regarded as fiscally conservative and strongly hesitant to criticize possible sponsors, operate as much stronger biases than do the personal beliefs of journalists.[c]

The difficulty of proving bias is that it often requires one to believe it exists before one can prove it. While conservative watchdog group Accuracy in Media believes that the media reported stories of Iraqi violence too often, liberal watchdog group Fairness and Accuracy in Reporting believes that media intentionally suppressed stories about Iraqi civilian casualties and prisoner abuse. However, editors have to make decisions on what to report based on newsworthiness and audience demand, not merely their own politics, in order to keep viewers watching or readers reading. Otherwise, editors would simply drive their paper or program into the ground. Therefore, to prove bias, one must disprove alternatives, such as newsworthiness, a standard as frustratingly subjective as bias itself.

Arguments Asserting Media Bias

- **Since journalists have their own personal bias, claims of professional objectivity are absurd.** Journalistic professionalism is a myth sustained only by those who wish to conceal a personal agenda. Even if journalists feel bound to be objective, it is hard to believe that all of them are all of the time, especially when audiences have no other information with which to corroborate stories the media report. Since they are unaccountable, journalists may be fearless in imposing their beliefs on unsuspecting American audiences.
- **Corporate demands for the news media to make profits preclude the reporting of otherwise newsworthy stories.** Huge corporations demand that papers, television programs, and Web sites report only the stories that attract viewers rather than educating them, and that attract sponsors rather than holding them accountable. The result is that tabloid

journalists report on minor scandals and not on Iraqi human rights abuse or threats from corporate mergers, leading to further audience ignorance of important issues.

- **Ideological bias aside, the American media insufficiently report news from other regions of the world.** Americans lack sufficient knowledge about global events. This void is dangerous, since these events directly affect American interests. On television, reports on world news usually come packaged as "Around the World in 80 Seconds," while newspapers typically relegate world news not immediately pertaining to American interests to the back pages. This downplay creates an unfounded bias among audiences that places America at the center of world affairs.

Arguments Denying Media Bias

- **Bias is not systemic but a problem only with particular journalists.** Even if a certain journalist is unprofessional, it does not follow that all journalists are. Accusations of systemic bias could be themselves the product of bias, since the vast majority of journalists have done nothing to lead us to believe that they are somehow politically biased. The practice of uncovering media bias is nothing more than a witch hunt.

- **Bias is a misunderstanding of the niche journalism trend.** Recently, all news media have begun tailoring their content to specific audiences because audiences for news have fractured into tinier and tinier pieces. Some media direct content toward specific ideologies. Calling certain newspapers or cable stations biased is wrong, not because it is not factually true, but because the stations, rather openly, have begun presenting information about matters important to liberals or to

conservatives. That's how the free market works.

- **There are simply too many sources of news for an audience to suffer the influence of media bias.** Perhaps there was once a media bias, when there were only a few television stations and national newspapers from which to derive political information. Now, however, there are dozens of magazines, news Web sites, and smaller circulation newspapers that allow audiences different views of subjects. Bias, in this context, is understood. Audiences merely must learn about opposing positions on an issue and decide for themselves where they stand.

Questions

1. What other kinds of biases might exist in the news media, aside from a regional or ideological one? Do these seriously impact American audiences? If so, how could these biases be corrected without violating the First Amendment?
2. What does it mean for a journalist to be "objective"?

Selected Readings

Shanto Iyengar and Richard Reeves. *Do the Media Govern? Politicians, Voters, and Reporters in America.* Newbury Park, CA: Sage, 1997.

Bernard Goldberg. *Bias: A CBS Insider Exposes How the Media Distort the News.* Washington, DC: Regnery, 2001.

---

[a] According to Accuracy in Media, a conservative watchdog group, http://www.aim.org/static/19_0_7_0_C.

[b] The Pew Research Center for the People and the Press. "News Audiences Increasingly Politicized: Online News Audience Larger, More Diverse," June 8, 2004, http://people-press.org/reports/display.php3?PageID=834.

[c] According to Fairness and Accuracy in Reporting, a liberal watchdog group, http://www.fair.org/media-woes/corporate.html.

unprecedented opportunities to attain fame and fortune, of which they often take full advantage. Already commanding multimillion-dollar salaries, these celebrity journalists can often secure lucrative speaker's fees. Especially in the case of journalists with highly ideological perspectives, close involvement with wealthy or powerful special-interest groups can blur the line between reporting on policy issues and influencing them. Some journalists even find work as political consultants or members of government—which seems reasonable, given their prominence, abilities, and expertise, but which can become problematic when they move between spheres not once, but repeatedly. A good example of this revolving-door phenomenon is the case of Pat Buchanan, who has repeatedly and alternately enjoyed prominent positions in media (as a host of CNN's *Crossfire* and later as a commentator on MSNBC) and politics (as a presidential candidate).

THE MEDIA'S INFLUENCE ON THE PUBLIC

Visual Literacy
The Media and the American Public

HOW MUCH INFLUENCE do the media have on the public? In most cases the press has surprisingly little effect. To put it bluntly, people tend to see what they want to see; that is, human beings will focus on parts of a report that reinforce their own attitudes and ignore parts that challenge their core beliefs. Most people also selectively tune out or ignore reports that contradict their preferences in politics and other fields. Therefore, a committed Democrat will remember certain portions of a televised news program about a current campaign—primarily the parts that reinforce his or her own choice—and an equally committed Republican will recall very different sections of the report or remember the material in a way that supports the GOP position. In other words, most voters are not empty vessels into which the media can pour their own beliefs. This fact dramatically limits the ability of news organizations to sway public opinion.

However, some political scientists argue that the content of network television news accounts for a large portion of the volatility and change in policy preferences of Americans, when measured over relatively short periods of time.[68] These changes are called **media effects.** Let's examine how these media-influenced changes might occur.

media effects
The influence of news sources on public opinion.

First, reporting can sway people who are uncommitted and have no strong opinion in the first place. Second, the media have a much greater impact on topics far removed from the lives and experiences of its readers and viewers. News reports can probably shape public opinion about events in foreign countries fairly easily. Yet, what the media say about domestic issues such as rising prices, neighborhood crime, or child rearing may have relatively little effect, because most citizens have personal experience of and well-formed ideas about these subjects. Third, news organizations can

WHEN THE MEDIA BECOME THE STORY

The purpose of the news media is to cover the news, not to make the news. But, now and then, whether journalists like it or not, they become the story. A classic example, and one that will live for years to come, occurred in September 2004 when CBS news anchor Dan Rather, reporting on *60 Minutes II*, took center stage in the presidential contest in a way he and his network had not intended.

For years, George W. Bush's service in the National Guard during the Vietnam War had percolated in the political system, occasionally becoming news but generally lying below the surface. In 2000, when Bush was campaigning for the presidency, reporters asked about his National Guard posting, by which he avoided military service in Vietnam. This was a product, in part, of the extensive coverage in the 1992 campaign given to Bill Clinton, who rather openly evaded the draft and never served in either the active military or the National Guard during the Vietnam War. Bush insisted in 2000 that he had served honorably and fulfilled all of his obligations, and his Democratic opponent, Al Gore, who had served in Vietnam for a brief period, decided not to make it an issue.

The issue of Bush's military record resurfaced in 2004, however, when John Kerry, a certified war hero from his service in Vietnam, was nominated as the Democrats' presidential candidate. Kerry's service contrasted with Bush's decision not to go to Vietnam. But, attacks by a group named Swift Boat Veterans for Truth and other supporters of Bush's candidacy questioned whether Kerry deserved some of his medals and particularly broadsided Kerry on his anti-war comments to the U.S. Senate and the news media after he returned from Vietnam.

Enter Dan Rather and CBS. Mary Mapes, a producer for *60 Minutes II* and a close associate of Rather, had long been interested—critics say obsessed—with the Bush National Guard episode and had been collecting information for years. Then, Bill Burkett, a Texan who had served in the National Guard about the same time as Bush and knew some of the key players, turned over documents that apparently showed Bush had violated the terms of his National Guard agreement relating to the scheduling of a physical examination and reporting for drill. In a hastily prepared piece, broadcast at a critical juncture in the campaign, Rather reported that "Mr. Bush may have received preferential treatment in the Guard after not fulfilling his commitments." Within hours of the broadcast, conservative bloggers had dissected the documents and were claiming that they were produced on computers unavailable in the early 1970s. As evidence, they cited the small superscript "th" after several unit numbers and a font that appeared to be Times New Roman, a font not in existence at the time.

Initially, Rather and CBS held firm. But, when media reporters from major outlets revealed that the bloggers were right, CBS launched a major investigation headed by former Attorney General Richard Thornburgh, who had served as Republican governor of Pennsylvania in the 1980s. The investigation report indicated that CBS had been negligent and Rather and Mapes had not fulfilled their journalistic obligations in verifying the authenticity of documents provided by Burkett. Several CBS employees lost their jobs; Rather had announced his retirement before the report was released.

What other recent political news stories have or might lead to similar difficulties for journalists?

help tell us what to think about, even if they cannot determine what we think. Indeed, the press often sets the agenda for government or a campaign by focusing on certain issues or concerns.

THE PUBLIC'S PERCEPTION OF THE MEDIA

THE NEWS MEDIA HAVE LONG BEEN SUBJECT to greater public discontent and criticism than other institutions essential to the operation of the American government. When asked in the summer of 2002 how much confidence they had in various institutions, only 11 percent of the public said they had a great deal of confidence in the media. By comparison, 50 percent had a great deal of confidence in the president, and 71 percent felt the same way about the military.[69] The Pew Research Center for the People and the Press, which has been studying public opinion of the media since 1985, found that survey participants when asked to describe the national news media use the words "biased" and "sensational" nearly as often as "good" and "informative."[70] A majority of Americans perceive the media to be politically biased, believe they stand in the way of solving society's problems, and think that they usually report inaccurately and are unwilling to admit mistakes. In a recent survey, Americans found media election coverage biased, but those Americans most likely to report a bias were on the ideological extremes, liberal Democrats reporting a Republican bias and conservative Republicans reporting a Democratic bias.[71] The public perception of the media is as much a function their ideological stance as it is a response to media content.

Despite the obvious displeasure that the majority of Americans express about political bias and sensationalism, credibility ratings for the national news media have remained relatively high. Broadcast news outlets tend to get higher believability ratings than print, with CNN, C-SPAN, and the major networks leading the way. The main exception to the domination of broadcast outlets is the *Wall Street Journal*, which consistently ranks with CNN at the top of credibility polls.

The terrorist attacks of September 11, 2001, caused a temporary shift in the public's attitude toward the media—Americans followed the news more closely and relied heavily on cable network coverage of the attacks and the war on terrorism. Among Americans polled, 69 percent believed that the news media defend America abroad, and the professionalism rating of the news media soared to 73 percent. During this period of extreme stress, however, Americans appeared to have simply united behind their institutions against an unknown threat. After all, the bounce in media popularity was short-lived. By July 2002, less than a year after the attacks, the public's perception and support of the media were essentially the same as pre-9/11 levels. However, Americans continue to value the watchdog role that the media serve, with 59 percent believing that press scrutiny keeps political leaders from doing things they should not do. In addition, a substantial majority thinks that the media's influence is increasing, rather than decreasing.[72]

Numerous polling organizations and scholarly centers (such as the Pew Research Center for the People and the Press) survey voters to gather and analyze public opinion regarding the news media in order to understand why American audiences use the media the way they do and how the media can, then, understand and improve their relationship with their audiences. Several major newspapers and magazines, including the *Washington Post* and the *Boston Globe*, have media critics, who assess how the media are performing their duties. Even Fox News has Fox Newswatch to dissect news coverage. Some nonprofits, such as the Center for Media and Public Affairs in Washington, D.C., conduct scientific studies of the news and entertainment media. Other groups, including the conservative watchdog group Accuracy in Media and its liberal counterpart Fairness and Accuracy in Reporting (FAIR), critique news stories and attempt to set the record straight on important issues that they believe have received biased coverage. All of these organizations have a role in ensuring that the media provide fair and balanced coverage of topics that are of importance to citizens.

Table 10.3 illustrates journalists' perceptions of the problems they face in their field. National journalists cite coverage quality as their

TABLE 10.3 Journalists' Perceptions of Top Problems Facing Journalism

	National		Local	
	1999 %	2004 %	1999 %	2004 %
Quality of Coverage	**44**	**41**	**39**	**33**
Reporting accurately	10	8	10	10
Not relevant/Out of touch	12	7	6	7
Sensationalism	8	8	12	5
Lack of depth/context	—	6	—	4
Reporting objectively/Balance	12	5	6	4
Business and Financial	**25**	**30**	**25**	**35**
Decline in audience/readership	14	9	11	8
Lack of resources/cutbacks	3	8	4	9
Bottom-line emphasis	8	5	7	9
Corporate owners/consolidation	2	5	2	4
Commercial/ratings pressure	6	3	6	4
Loss of Credibility with Public	**30**	**28**	**34**	**23**
Credibility problem	23	22	28	17
Lack of trustworthiness	6	5	8	4
Changing Media Environment	**24**	**15**	**19**	**7**
Too much competition	17	5	15	2
Need to adapt to changes	—	3	—	2
Speed/pace of reporting	—	5	—	2
Ethics and Standards	**11**	**5**	**10**	**6**

Source: Pew Research Center for the People and the Press, May 23, 2004.

primary concern, while local journalists mention business and financial problems just as frequently.

GOVERNMENT REGULATION OF THE ELECTRONIC MEDIA

THE U.S. GOVERNMENT REGULATES the electronic, noncable component of the media. Unlike radio or television, the print media are exempt from most forms of government regulation, although even print media must not violate community standards for obscenity, for instance. There are two reasons for this unequal treatment. First, the airwaves used by the electronic media are considered public property and are leased by the federal government to private broadcasters. Second, those airwaves are in limited supply; without some regulation, the nation's many radio and television stations would interfere with one another's frequency signals. It was not, in fact, the federal government but rather private broadcasters, frustrated by the numerous instances in which signal jamming occurred, that initiated the call for government regulation in the early days of the electronic media.

In 1996, Congress passed the sweeping Telecommunications Act, deregulating whole segments of the electronic media. The Telecommunications Act sought to provide an optimal balance of competing corporate interests, technological innovations, and consumer needs. It appeared to offer limitless opportunities for entrepreneurial companies to provide enhanced services to consumers. The result of this deregulation was the sudden merger of previously distinct kinds of media in order to create a more "multimedia" approach to communicating information and entertainment, such as TimeWarner and Comcast.

In June 2003, the FCC further deregulated media by pushing through a series of reforms that enabled media corporations to own more of different kinds of media in a given media market. However, there was a general public outcry against this deregulation, with legislators receiving angry letters and e-mails demanding Congress stop the FCC.[73] By July, a huge bipartisan majority in both houses of Congress voted to block the FCC policy changes.

Although the Senate voted quickly to reverse the decision, similar legislation was blocked in the House. Community radio station proponent Prometheus Radio Project, along with several advocacy groups, successfully petitioned a stay on the FCC decision at the Third Circuit U.S. Court of Appeals in Philadelphia.

Content Regulation

The government subjects the electronic media to substantial **content regulation** that does not apply to the print media. Charged with ensuring that the airwaves "serve the public interest, convenience, and necessity," the FCC has attempted to promote equity in broadcasting. For example, the **equal time rule** requires that broadcast stations sell campaign airtime equally to all candidates if they choose to sell it to any, which they are under no obligation to do. An exception to this rule is a political debate: stations may exclude from this event less well-known and minor-party candidates.

Until 2000, FCC rules required broadcasters to give candidates the opportunity to respond to personal attacks and to political endorsements by the station. In October 2000, however, a federal court of appeals found these rules, long attacked by broadcasters as having a chilling effect on free speech, to be unconstitutional when the FCC was unable to justify these regulations to its satisfaction.

content regulation
Government attempts to regulate the electronic media.

equal time rule
The rule that requires broadcast stations to sell air time equally to all candidates in a political campaign if they choose to sell it to any.

Prior Restraint

In the United States, only government officials can be prosecuted for divulging classified information; no such law applies to journalists. Nor can the government, except under extremely rare and confined circumstances, impose prior restraints on the press—that is, the government cannot censor the press. This principle was clearly established in *New York Times Co. v. U.S.* (1971).[74] In this case, the Supreme Court ruled that the government could not prevent publication by the *New York Times* of the Pentagon Papers, classified government documents about the Vietnam War that had been stolen, photocopied, and sent to the *Times* and the *Washington Post* by Daniel Ellsberg, a government employee. "Only a free and unrestrained press can effectively expose deception in the government," Justice Hugo Black wrote in a concurring opinion for the Court. "To find that the President has 'inherent power' to halt the publication of news by resort to the courts would wipe out the first Amendment."

These same questions arose once again with regard to the war on terrorism, with national security officials expressing concern about leaks that appeared in the media. Indeed, the issue took on increased controversy when it became apparent that some of the leaks may have come from members of Congress.

Such arguments are an inevitable part of the landscape in a free society. Whatever their specific quarrels with the press, most Americans would probably prefer that the media tell them too much rather than not enough.

SUMMARY

PUBLIC OPINION AND THE NEWS MEDIA are two factors that have a drastic impact on American politics and public policy. Almost since the beginning of the United States, various attempts have been made to influence public opinion about particular issues or to sway elections. Modern-day polling did not begin until the 1930s, however. Over the years, polling to measure public opinion has become increasingly sophisticated and more accurate because pollsters are better able to sample the public in their effort to determine their attitudes and positions on issues.

The first step in forming opinions occurs through a process called political socialization. Our family, school, peers, social groups—including religion, race, gender, and age—as well as where we live, the impact of events, and political ideology all affect how we view political events and issues.

Myriad factors enter our minds as we form opinions about political matters. These include a calculation about the personal benefits involved, degree of personal political knowledge, and cues from leaders.

Measuring public opinion can be difficult. The most frequently used measure is the public opinion poll. Determining the content, phrasing the questions, selecting the sample, and choosing the right kind of poll are critical to obtaining accurate and useful data.

The modern media consist of print press (many thousands of daily and weekly newspapers, magazines, newsletters, and journals) and electronic media (television and radio stations and networks as well as computerized information services and the Internet).

Media coverage of politics has shifted focus from investigative journalism in the Watergate era toward the more recent attention to character issues. Studies have shown that by framing issues for debate and discussion, the media have clear and recognizable effects on voters.

The government has gradually loosened restrictions on the media. The Federal Communications Commission (FCC) licenses and regulates broadcasting stations but has been quite willing to grant and renew licenses and has reduced its regulation of licensees. Content regulations have loosened, with the courts using a narrow interpretation of libel.

KEY TERMS

content regulation, p. 381
electronic media, p. 363
equal time rule, p. 381
exit poll, p. 357
media effects, p. 376
muckraking, p. 362
New York Times Co. v. *Sullivan* (1964), p. 371
political ideology, p. 351
political socialization, p. 341
press briefing, p. 368
press conference, p. 368
press release, p. 368
print press, p. 363
public opinion, p. 338
public opinion poll, p. 338
push poll, p. 357
random sampling, p. 355
sampling error, p. 359
stratified sampling, p. 355
straw poll, p. 339
tracking poll, p. 357
yellow journalism, p. 362

SELECTED READINGS

Alvarez, R. Michael, and John Brehm. *Easy Answers, Hard Choices: Values, Information, and American Public Opinion.* Princeton, NJ: Princeton University Press, 2002.

Broder, David S. *Behind the Front Page*, reprint ed. New York: Simon and Schuster, 2000.

Erikson, Robert S., and Kent L. Tedin. *American Public Opinion: Its Origins, Contents, and Impact*, 6th ed. New York: Longman, 2001.

Hamilton, John Maxwell. *Hold the Press: The Inside Story on Newspapers*, reprint ed. Baton Rouge: Louisiana State University Press, 1997.

Jamieson, Kathleen Hall. *Everything You Think You Know About Politics...And Why You Were Wrong.* New York: Basic Books, 2000.

Jamieson, Kathleen Hall, and Paul Waldman. *The Press Effect: Politicians, Journalists, and the Stories That Shape the Political World.* Oxford, UK: Oxford University Press, 2002.

Kerbel, Matthew Robert. *Remote and Controlled: Media Politics in a Cynical Age,* 2nd ed. Boulder, CO: Westview, 1998.

Manza, Jeff, ed. *Navigating Public Opinion: Polls, Policy, and the Future of American Democracy.* New York: Oxford University Press, 2002.

McChesney, Robert. *The Problem of the Media.* New York: Monthly Review Press, 2004.

Mutz, Diana Carole. *Impersonal Influence: How Perceptions of Mass Collectives Affect Political Attitudes.* New York: Cambridge University Press, 1998.

Norrander, Barbara, and Clyde Wilcox, eds. *Understanding Public Opinion,* 2nd ed. Washington, DC: CQ Press, 2001.

Patterson, Thomas E. *Out of Order: An Incisive and Boldly Original Critique of the News Media's Domination of America's Political Process,* reprint ed. New York: Vintage, 1994.

Sabato, Larry J. *Feeding Frenzy: Attack Journalism and American Politics,* updated ed. Baltimore, MD: Lanahan, 2000.

Starr, Paul. *The Creation of the Media.* New York: Basic Books, 2004.

Warren, Kenneth F. *In Defense of Public Opinion Polling.* Boulder, CO: Westview, 2001.

West, Darrell M. *Air Wars: Television Advertising in Election Campaigns, 1952–1996.* Washington, DC: CQ Press, 2000.

Zaller, John. *The Nature and Origins of Mass Opinions.* New York: Cambridge University Press, 1992.

WEB EXPLORATIONS

To learn more about the Gallup Organization and poll trends, see http://www.gallup.com/

To use NES data sets,
   http://www.umich.edu/~nes/

For the most recent Roper Center polls, see
   http://www.ropercenter.uconn.edu/

To see an example of a nonstratified poll, go to
   http://www.cnn.com/

For examples of nineteenth-century yellow journalism, go to
   http://www.onlineconcepts.com/pulitzer/yellow.htm

To see how the media are diversifying and repackaging themselves through the use of pundits, go to
   www.publicagenda.org/specials/cjrpolls/cjrdec.htm

To see which newspapers, magazines, and networks have a Web presence and how that complements their standard coverage, go to
   www.nationaljournal.com
   www.washingtonpost.com
   www.cnn.com/ALLPOLITICS

To compare news coverage on a particular news story for evidence of political bias, go to
   hometown.aol.com/gopbias/
   and
   new.mrc.org/cyberalerts/1999/cyb19990125.asp#1

11

Political Parties and Interest Groups

Roy Hoffmann
Rear Admiral
Distinguished Service Medal, Silver Star
www.swiftvets.com

Photo courtesy: Swiftvets/AP/Wide World Photos

SOON AFTER THE DEMOCRATIC NATIONAL CONVENTION in July 2004, an interest group calling itself Swift Boat Veterans for Truth aired a television advertisement charging that Democratic presidential nominee John Kerry was lying about his military service record. Most specifically, the ad asserted that Senator Kerry (D–MA) had exaggerated the severity of the wounds that led to his first Purple Heart. Less than a week after this ad hit the airwaves, another organized interest, MoveOn.org, countered the Swift Boat Veterans ad with a commercial attacking the many gaps in President George W. Bush's military record. "George Bush used his father to get into the National Guard," the ad charged, "and when the chips were down, went missing. Now he's allowing false advertising that attacks John Kerry, a man who served with dignity and heroism."[1]

Although personal attacks are not unusual in modern American politics, it is important to ask who these groups are, and how they came to have such substantial influence in the 2004 presidential election. Swift Boat Veterans for Truth is a loose association of Vietnam veterans who first came together in 2000 to attack the military service record of Senator John McCain (R–AZ) during the South Carolina presidential primary.[2] MoveOn.org is an organization founded by a group of Silicon Valley financiers in 1998 to protest the impeachment of President Bill Clinton.

Both groups became major players in American politics following the 2002 campaign finance reform law commonly know as the McCain-Feingold Act. After that law banned all soft money donations from corporations and political action committees to political parties and candidates, political elites began to look for new ways to remain influential players in electoral politics. Groups quickly discovered a loophole in the 2002 law that allows for tax-exempt organizations—known as 527s, for the section of the Internal Revenue Code that governs them—to raise unlimited money for the purposes of voter mobilization and issue advocacy as long as they do not expressly advocate the election of a particular candidate.[3]

This loophole allows 527s to air almost unlimited ads attacking candidates for their character, career choices, or policies, so long as the advertisements never explicitly state, for example, "Vote for John Kerry." MoveOn.org spent more than $62 million during the 2004 election cycle on print, radio, and television ads that both raised questions about members of the Bush administration and voiced support for liberal stances such as legalized same-sex marriage and opposition to outsourcing American jobs. However, even after a slow start, conservative 527s managed to spend more than $70 million on advertisements criticizing John Kerry. In an attempt to maximize their impact, the groups aired most of these ads in America's largest and most contentious media markets.

WHEN JAMES MADISON warned of the dangers of faction in *Federalist No. 10,* he never envisioned the development of political parties, or the role that organized interests would eventually play in politics and policy making. It was not long after the ink was dry on the new Constitution that factions arose concerning the desirability to the new system of government that it created. And, soon after, political parties were formed to reflect those political divisions.

At the most basic level, a **political party** is a group of office holders, candidates, activists, and voters who identify with a group label and seek to elect to public office individuals who run under that label. Notice that the goal is to *win* office, not just compete for it. This objective is in keeping with the practical nature of Americans and the country's historical aversion to most ideologically driven, purist politics. Nevertheless, the group label—also called party identification—can carry with it clear messages about ideology and issue positions. Although these especially exist for minor, less broad-based parties that have little chance of electoral success, they also apply to the Democrats and the Republicans, the two national, dominant political parties in the United States.

In contrast to political parties, **interest groups,** which go by a variety of names—special interests, pressure groups, organized interests,

political party
A group of office holders, candidates, activists, and voters who identify with a group label and seek to elect to public office individuals who run under that label.

interest group
An organized group that tries to influence public policy.

political groups, lobby groups, and public interest groups—are organizations that "seek or claim to represent people or organizations which share one or more common interests or ideals."[4] Distinguished political scientist V. O. Key Jr. tried to differentiate political parties from interest groups by arguing that "interest groups promote their interests by attempting to influence government rather than by nominating candidates and seeking responsibility for the management of government."[5]

In this chapter we trace the evolution of the role of political parties and interest groups in the American political process. First, we will examine the role of *political parties* in the American political process. Then, we will we turn to a discussion of *interest groups*.

POLITICAL PARTIES

POLITICAL PARTIES HAVE EVOLVED CONSIDERABLY and changed form from time to time. Nevertheless, they usually have been reliable vehicles for mass participation in a representative democracy.

The Evolution of American Party Democracy

It is one of the great ironies of the early republic that George Washington's public farewell, which warned the nation against parties, marked the effective end of the brief era of partyless politics in the United States. Washington's unifying influence ebbed as he stepped off the national stage, and his vice president and successor, John Adams, an ally of Alexander Hamilton, occupied a much less exalted position. To win the presidency in 1796, Adams narrowly defeated Thomas Jefferson, Hamilton's former rival in Washington's Cabinet. Before ratification of the Constitution, Hamilton and Jefferson had been leaders of the Federalists and Anti-Federalists, respectively (see chapter 2). Over the course of Adams's single term, two competing congressional party groupings (or caucuses) gradually organized around these clashing men and their principles: Hamilton's Federalists supported a strong central government; the Democratic-Republicans of Thomas Jefferson and his ally James Madison inherited the mantle of the Anti-Federalists and preferred a federal system in which the states were relatively more powerful. In the presidential election of 1800, the Federalists supported Adams's bid for a second term, but this time the Democratic-Republicans prevailed with their nominee, Jefferson, who became the first U.S. president elected as the nominee of a political party (see The Living Constitution).

Jefferson was deeply committed to the ideas of his party, but not nearly as devoted to the idea of a party system. He regarded his party as a temporary measure necessary to defeat Adams and Hamilton. Neither Jefferson's party nor Hamilton's enjoyed widespread loyalty among the citizenry akin to that of today's Democrats and Republicans. Although Southerners were overwhelmingly partial to the Democratic-Republicans and New Englanders to the Federalists, no broad-based party organizations existed on either side to mobilize popular support. Rather, the congressional factions organized around Hamilton and Jefferson were primarily governmental parties designed to settle the dispute over how strong the new federal government would be.[6]

What is sometimes called the second party system began around 1824, when Andrew Jackson ran for president. Around that time, party membership broadened along with the electorate (see Figure 11.1). After receiving criticism for being elitist and undemocratic, the small caucuses of congressional party leaders that had previously nominated candidates gave way to nominations at large party conventions. In 1832, the Democratic Party, which succeeded the old Jeffersonian Democratic-Republicans, held the first national presidential nomination convention. Formed around the charismatic populist President Andrew Jackson, the Democratic Party attracted most of the newly enfranchised voters, who were drawn to Jackson's style. His strong personality helped to polarize politics, and opposition to the president coalesced into the Whig Party. The Whig Party was descended from the Federalists; its early leaders included Henry Clay, the speaker of the House from 1811 to 1820. The incumbent Jackson defeated Clay in the 1832 presidential contest. Jackson became the first chief executive who won the White House as the nominee of a truly national, popularly based political party.

The Whigs and the Democrats continued to strengthen after 1832, establishing state and local organizations almost everywhere. Their competition was usually fierce and closely matched, and they brought the United States the first broadly supported two-party system in the Western world.[7] Unfortunately for the Whigs, the issue of slavery sharpened the many divisive tensions within the party, which led to its gradual dissolution and replacement by the new Republican Party. Formed in 1854 by anti-slavery activists, the Republican Party set its sights on the abolition (or at least the containment) of slavery. After a losing presidential effort by John C. Fremont in 1856, the party was able to assemble enough support primarily from the Whigs and anti-slavery northern Democrats to win the presidency for Abraham Lincoln in a fragmented 1860 vote. In that year, the South voted solidly Democratic, beginning a tradition so strong that not a single southern state voted Republican for president again until 1920.

Democrats and Republicans: The Golden Age.   From the presidential election of 1860 to this day, the same two major parties, the Republicans and the Democrats, have dominated elections in the United States, and control of an electoral majority has seesawed

FIGURE 11.1 American Party History at a Glance

This table shows the transformations and evolution of the various parties that have always made up the basic two-party structure of the American political system. ∎

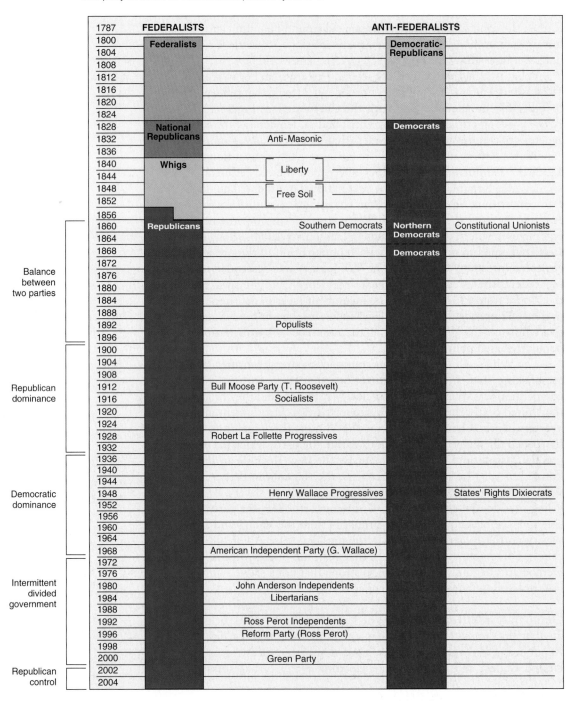

between them. Party stability, the dominance of party organizations in local and state governments, and the impact of those organizations on the lives of millions of voters were the central traits of the era called the Golden Age of political parties.

This era occurred as emigration from Europe (particularly from Ireland, Italy, and Germany) fueled the development of big-city party organizations that gained control of local and state government. These big-city party organizations were called political **machines.** A political machine is a party organization that uses tangible incentives to recruit its members. Machines are characterized by a high degree of leadership control over member activity, and party machines were a central element of life for millions of people in the United States during the Golden Age. For city-dwellers, their party and their government were virtually interchangeable during this time. Party organizations sponsored community events, such as parades and picnics, and provided social services, such as helping new immigrants settle in and giving food and temporary housing to those in immediate need, all in exchange for votes.

machine
A party organization that recruits its members with tangible incentives and is characterized by a high degree of control over member activity.

The parties offered immigrants not just services but also the opportunity for upward social mobility as they rose in the organization. Because they held the possibility of social advancement, the parties engendered intense devotion among their supporters and office holders that helped to produce voter turnouts of 75 percent or better in all presidential elections from 1876 to 1900—startlingly high when compared with the 50 percent to 55 percent turnout from 1900 until the 2004 election, which saw an increase to 59 percent.[8] The strength of parties during the Golden Age also fostered the greatest party-line voting ever achieved in Congress and many state legislatures.[9]

The Modern Era Versus the Golden Age: Is the Party Over?

The modern era seems very different from the Golden Age of parties. Many social, political, technological, and governmental changes have contributed to party decline since the 1920s. Historically, the government's gradual assumption of important functions previously performed by the parties, such as printing ballots, conducting elections, and providing social welfare services, had a major impact. Beginning in the 1930s with Franklin Roosevelt's New Deal, social services began to be seen as a right of citizenship rather than as a privilege extended in exchange for a person's support of a party. Also, as the flow of immigrants slowed dramatically in the 1920s, party organizations gradually withered in most places.

At the same time, in the first two decades of the twentieth century, a **direct primary** system, in which party nominees were determined by the ballots of qualified voters rather than at party conventions, gained

direct primary
The selection of party candidates through the ballots of qualified voters rather than at party nomination conventions.

widespread adoption. Direct primaries removed the power of nomination from party leaders and workers and gave it instead to a much broader and more independent electorate, thus loosening the tie between party nominees and the party organization.

Reforms championed by the Progressive movement, which also flourished in the first two decades of the twentieth century, also contributed to the loss of party influence in the United States. **Civil service laws,** for example, which require appointment on the basis of merit and competitive examinations, removed opportunities for much of the patronage used by the parties to reward their followers.

In the post–World War II era, extensive social changes contributed to the move away from strong parties. Higher levels of education gave rise to **issue-oriented politics,** politics that focuses on specific issues, such as civil rights, tax cutting, or environmentalism, rather than on party labels. Issue politics tends to cut across party lines and encourages voters to **ticket-split,** that is, to vote for candidates of different parties for various offices in the same election (a phenomenon we discuss in greater depth in chapter 12). Another post–World War II social change that has affected the parties is the shift from urban to suburban locales. Millions of people have moved from the cities to the suburbs, where a sense of privacy and detachment can deter the most energetic party organizers. In addition, population growth in the last half-century has created districts with far more people, making it unfeasible to knock on every door or shake every hand.

Politically, many other trends have contributed to the parties' decline. Television, which has come to dominate U.S. politics, naturally emphasizes personalities rather than abstract concepts such as party labels. Other technological advances such as the autodialer, a computer that leaves prerecorded messages on voters' answering machines, have often alienated voters and further eroded precinct organization. It is little wonder that many candidates and office holders who have reached their posts without much help from their parties consider themselves as free as possible of party ties.

The Two-Party System and Third Parties

The two-party system has not gone unchallenged. At the state level, two-party competition was severely limited or nonexistent in much of the country for most of the twentieth century.[10] Even in some two-party states, many cities and counties had a massive majority of voters aligned with one or the other party and thus were effectively one-party in local elections. The spread of two-party competition, while still uneven in some respects, is one of the most significant political trends in recent times, and virtually no one-party states are left.

Third partyism, or the rise of alternative parties based on a single cause neglected by the major parties, has had an important impact on

civil service laws
These acts removed the staffing of the bureaucracy from political parties and created a professional bureaucracy filled through competition.

issue-oriented politics
Politics that focuses on specific issues rather than on party, candidate, or other loyalties.

ticket-split
To vote for candidates of different parties for various offices in the same election.

third-partyism
The tendency of third parties to arise with some regularity in a nominally two-party system.

American politics, even if its existence has been sporadic and intermittent. Third parties find their roots in sectionalism (as did the South's states' rights Dixiecrats, who broke away from the Democrats in 1948); in economic protest (such as the agrarian revolt that fueled the Populists, an 1892 prairie-states party); in specific issues (such as the Green Party's support of the environment); in ideology (the Socialist, Communist, and Libertarian Parties are examples); and in appealing, charismatic personalities (Theodore Roosevelt's affiliation with the Bull Moose Party is perhaps the best case). Many minor parties have drawn strength from a combination of these sources. The American Independent Party enjoyed a measure of success because of a dynamic leader (George Wallace), a firm geographic base (the South), and an emotional issue (civil rights).

Minor-party and independent candidates are not limited to presidential elections. Many also run in congressional elections, and the numbers appear to be growing. In the 2004 congressional elections, for example, more than 850 minor-party and independent candidates ran for seats in the House and Senate—almost eight times as many as in 1968 and nearly three times the number that ran in 1980. A recent study shows that minor-party candidates for the House are most likely to emerge under three conditions: (1) when a House seat becomes open; (2) when a minor-party candidate has previously competed in the district; and, (3) when partisan competition between the two major parties in the district is close.[11]

Above all, third parties make electoral progress in direct proportion to the failure of the two major parties to incorporate new ideas or alienated groups or to nominate attractive candidates as their standard-bearers. Third parties do best when declining trust in the two major political parties plagues the electorate.[12] Usually, though, third parties are eventually co-opted by one of the two major parties, each of them eager to take the politically popular issue that gave rise to the third party and make it theirs in order to secure the allegiance of the third party's supporters. Third parties in the United States, however, are basically akin to shooting stars that appear briefly and brilliantly but do not long remain visible in the political constellation. In fact, the United States is the only major Western nation that does not have at least one significant, enduring national third party (see Global Perspective: The Emergence of New Parties on page 394).

Timeline

Third Parties in American History

Comparative

Comparing Political Parties

The Basic Structure of American Political Parties.   Although the distinctions might not be as clear today as they were two or three decades ago, the two major parties remain fairly simply organized, with national, state, and local branches (see Figure 11.2). The different levels of each party represent diverse interests in Washington, D.C., state capitals, and local governments throughout the nation.

National Committees.   The first national party committees were skeletal and were formed some years after the creation of the presidential

FIGURE 11.2 Political Party Organization in America: From Base to Pinnacle. ■

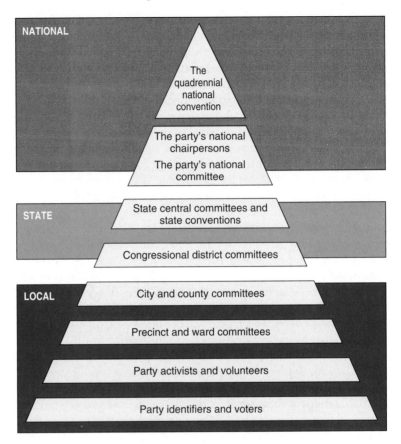

NATIONAL

The quadrennial national convention

The party's national chairpersons

The party's national committee

STATE

State central committees and state conventions

Congressional district committees

LOCAL

City and county committees

Precinct and ward committees

Party activists and volunteers

Party identifiers and voters

national convention

A party conclave (meeting) held in the presidential election year for the purposes of nominating a presidential and vice presidential ticket and adopting a platform.

party platform

A statement of the general and specific philosophy and policy goals of a political party, usually promulgated at the national convention.

nominating conventions in the 1830s. Every four years, each party holds a **national convention** to nominate its presidential and vice presidential candidates. First the Democrats in 1848 and then the Republicans in 1856 established national governing bodies—the Democratic National Committee, or DNC, and the Republican National Committee, or RNC—to make arrangements for the conventions and to coordinate the subsequent presidential campaigns. Although the nomination of the presidential ticket naturally receives the lion's share of attention, the convention also fulfills its role as the ultimate governing body for the party. The rules adopted and the **party platform,** a major statement of each party's basic views on a variety of issues, passed at the quadrennial conclave are durable guidelines that steer the party for years after the final gavel has been brought down.

The key national party official is the chairperson of the national committee. Although the chair is formally elected by the national committee, he or she is usually selected by the sitting president or newly nominated presidential candidate, who is accorded the right to name the individual for at least the duration of his or her campaign. The chair often becomes the prime spokesperson and arbitrator for the party during the four years between elections. He or she is called on to lessen factionalism, negotiate candidate disputes, raise money, and prepare the machinery for the next presidential election. Balancing the interests of all potential White House contenders is a particularly difficult job, and strict neutrality during the presidential primary season is normally expected from the chair.

To serve their interests, the Senate and House party caucuses or conferences in both houses of Congress organized their own national committees. These are loosely allied with the DNC and RNC.

State and Local Parties.   Although national committee activities of all kinds attract most of the media attention, the party is structurally based not in Washington, D.C., but in the states and localities. Except for the campaign finance arena, virtually all governmental regulation of political parties is left to the states, for example, and most elected officials give their allegiance to the local party divisions they know best. Most importantly, the vast majority of party leadership positions are filled at subnational levels.

Visual Literacy

**Political Parties:
State Control and
National Platforms**

The pyramid arrangement of party committees provides for a broad base of support. The smallest voting unit, the precinct, usually takes in a few adjacent neighborhoods and is the fundamental building block of the party. Each of the more than 100,000 precincts in the United States potentially has a committee member to represent it in each party's councils. The precinct committee members are the foot soldiers of any party, and their efforts are supplemented by party committees above them in the wards, cities, counties, towns, villages, and congressional districts.

The state governing body supervising this collection of local party organizations is usually called the state central (or executive) committee. Its members come from all major geographic units, as determined by and selected under state law. Generally, state parties are free to act within the limits set by their state legislatures without interference from the national party, except in the selection and seating of presidential convention delegates.

Party Identifiers and Voters.   Universal party membership does not exist in the United States: the voter pays no prescribed dues; no formal rules govern an individual's party activities; and voters assume no enforceable obligations to the party even when they consistently vote for its candidates. A party has no real control over or even an accurate accounting of its adherents, and the party's voters subscribe to few or none of the commonly accepted tenets of organizational membership, such as regular participation and some measure of responsibility for the group's welfare. Rather, **party identification** or affiliation is an informal and impressionistic exercise whereby a citizen acquires a party

party identification
A citizen's personal affinity for a political party, usually expressed by his or her tendency to vote for the candidates of that party.

THE EMERGENCE OF NEW PARTIES

The American political party system essentially is a two-party system. Occasionally, third parties or independent candidates surface and make a bid to win public office, but for all practical purposes, Americans remain wedded to the Republican and Democratic parties. The same allegiance has not occurred in Western Europe. Here, support for new political parties (those founded since 1960) has been growing steadily over the past four decades at the expense of older established political parties. The emergence of these new parties is tied to voter dissatisfaction with existing parties and the ability of new parties to tap into very specific concerns on the part of citizens.

In the 1960s, new parties received only 3.9 percent of the vote across Western Europe. They were most successful in France and least successful in Great Britain and Ireland. Their percentage of the vote increased to 9.7 percent in the 1970s and to 15.3 percent in the 1980s. In the 1990s, new parties received 23.7 percent of all votes cast in Western Europe—a 19.8 percent increase.

The following table shows growth of support for new parties in selected West European states.

Mean Percentage of Vote Recieved by New Parties

Country	1960s	1970s	1980s	1990s
Finland	1.6	8.2	13.7	22.3
France	16.3	29.1	27.1	41.7
Germany	4.3	0.5	7.5	13.9
Great Britain	0	0.8	11.6	2.3
Italy	9.5	3.3	7.1	66.8
Netherlands	2.3	26.6	44.5	45.9

Even more significant than the growth in support for new parties in Western Europe is the growing support over the past two decades for extremist parties—political parties at the ideological ends of the political spectrum. Those on the political left are most easily identified today as Green Parties. They advocate an aggressive pro-environmental agenda. Those on the political right are more difficult to classify. Many of the most visible ones, such as the National Front in France, advocate strongly nationalistic and anti-immigration policies.

On balance, Greens have not mounted a significant electoral challenge to the traditional ruling parties of Western Europe. But Greens have succeeded in influencing the political agenda in many countries and have become part of governing coalitions in France, Germany, Italy, and Finland. Whereas the appeal of the Greens is fairly even, the appeal of right-wing parties is quite varied. In many countries it is almost totally absent, while in others it has some support. And, in three countries—Austria, Italy, and France—extreme right-wing parties now represent real challenges to traditional parties. Unlike the very democratic Green Parties, right-wing parties bring back memories of fascism and concerns about how willing these parties are to abide by democratic procedures. The following table shows the vote totals for Green and right-wing extremist parties in the same countries profiled above. Because of the newness of many of these parties, data are only from the 1980s and 1990s.

Mean Percentage of Vote Received by Extremist Parties

Country	Green Vote		Right-Wing Vote	
	1980s	1990s	1980s	1990s
Finland	2.7	7.0	0	0.3
France	0.9	8.4	6.7	14.2
Germany	5.1	6.4	0.3	2.5
Great Britain	0.3	0.3	0.1	0
Italy	1.3	2.7	6.6	20.9
Netherlands	1.1	5.6	0.6	1.8

Questions

1. Under what conditions might new parties develop in the United States and get the support they have in Western Europe?
2. Which type of extremist parties do you see as more likely to become electorally successful in the United States, ones on the political left or the political right?

Source: Hans Keman, ed., *Comparative Democratic Politics* (London: Sage, 2002), 134, 137.

label and accepts its standard as a summary of his or her political views and preferences.

On the whole, Americans regard their partisan affiliation as a convenience rather than a necessity. Individual party identifications are reinforced by the legal institutionalization of the major parties. Because of restrictive ballot laws, campaign finance rules, the powerful inertia of political tradition, and many other factors, voters for all practical purposes are limited to a choice between a Democrat and a Republican in almost all elections—a situation that naturally encourages the pragmatic choosing up of sides. About half of the states require a voter to state a party preference (or independent status) when registering to vote, and they restrict voting in a party primary only to registrants in that particular party, making it an incentive for voters to affiliate themselves with a party.[13]

However, although partisan identification is often informal, this does not mean that it is unimportant. The party label becomes a voter's central political reference symbol and perceptual screen, a prism or filter through which the world of politics and government flows and is interpreted. For many Americans, party identification is a significant aspect of their political personality and a way of defining and explaining themselves to others. The loyalty generated by the label can be as intense as any enjoyed by sports teams and alma maters; in a few areas of the country, "Democrat" and "Republican" are still fighting words.

Sources of Party Identification.

As revealed in Table 11.1, Republicans are much more likely to be white, to be male, and to have at least some college education. The sharpest difference between Democrats and Republicans is political ideology. More than half of the Republicans but only 22 percent of the Democrats surveyed by the Gallup Organization say that they are conservative. Democrats are more likely than Republicans to identify themselves as moderate.

Whatever the societal and governmental forces responsible for party identification, the explanations of partisan loyalty at the individual's level are understandably more personal. Not surprisingly, parents are the single greatest influence in establishing a person's first party identification. Politically active parents with the same

Party delegates celebrate at the 2004 Democratic Convention in Boston, Massachusetts.

Photo courtesy: Victoria Arocho/AP/Wide World Photos

TABLE 11.1   Who Identifies with the Republican and Democratic Parties?

	Republicans (Including Independents Who Lean Republican)	Democrats (Including Independents Who Lean Democratic)
Gender		
Male	53%	43%
Female	47%	57%
Age		
18–29	21%	20%
30–49	43%	40%
50–64	19%	21%
65+	15%	18%
Race		
White	93%	75%
Black	3%	19%
Other nonwhite	4%	6%
Education		
Postgraduate degree	12%	13%
Undergraduate degree	14%	11%
Some college	37%	29%
No college	38%	47%
Household Income		
$75,000 and over	22%	15%
$50,000–$74,999	21%	16%
$30,000–$49,999	24%	25%
$20,000–$29,999	12%	14%
Less than $20,000	15%	23%
Region		
East	20%	25%
Midwest	24%	22%
South	33%	31%
West	22%	21%

Source: http://www.gallup.com/poll/releases/pr000728e.asp.

party loyalty raise children who will be strong party identifiers, whereas parents without party affiliations or with mixed affiliations produce offspring more likely to be independents.

Early socialization is hardly the last step in an individual's acquisition and maintenance of a party identity; marriage and other aspects of adult life can change one's loyalty. Gender and race, too, are com-

Photo courtesy: Mary Altaffer/AP/Wide World Photos

■ National security was a prominent theme at both parties' conventions in 2004. Here, delegates hold signs in support of President Bush at the Republican National Convention in New York City.

pelling predictors of party identification. Women and African Americans, for example, are much more likely to identify as Democrats than as Republicans.

Party identification can also be affected by charismatic political personalities, particularly at the national level (such as Franklin D. Roosevelt and Ronald Reagan), cataclysmic events (the Civil War, the Great Depression, the attacks on September 11, 2001), and maybe intense social issues (for instance, abortion and same-sex marriage). Social class is not an especially strong indicator of likely partisan choice in the United States, at least in comparison with Western European democracies. Not only are Americans less inclined than Europeans to perceive class distinctions, preferring instead to see themselves and most other people as members of an exceedingly broad middle class, but other factors, including sectionalism and candidate-oriented politics, tend to blur class lines in voting.

The Roles of Political Parties in the United States

The two-party system has helped organize and resolve social and political conflict for 150 years. Political parties perform many other important roles.

Mobilizing Support and Gathering Power.   Party affiliation is enormously helpful to elected leaders. Therefore the parties aid office holders by giving them room to develop their policies and by mobilizing support for them. When the president addresses the nation and

requests support for his policies, for example, his party's members are usually the first to respond to the call, perhaps by flooding Congress with telegrams urging action on the president's agenda. Moreover, because there are only two major parties, citizens who are interested in politics or public policy are mainly attracted to one or the other party, creating natural majorities or near-majorities for party office holders to command. The party generates a community of interest that bonds disparate groups over time into a **coalition.**

coalition
A group of interests or organizations that join forces for the purpose of electing public officials.

A Force for Stability and Moderation.

The parties encourage stability in the type of coalitions they form. Imagine the constant chaos and mad scrambles for public support that would ensue without the continuity provided by the parties. There are inherent contradictions in these coalitions that, oddly enough, strengthen the nation even as they strain party unity. Franklin D. Roosevelt's Democratic New Deal coalition, for example, included many African Americans and most southern whites, opposing groups nonetheless joined in common political purpose by economic hardship and, in the case of better-off Southerners, in longtime voting habits.

Unity, Linkage, and Accountability.

Parties are the glue that holds together the disparate elements of the fragmented U.S. governmental and political apparatus. The Framers designed a system that divides and subdivides power, making it possible to preserve individual liberty but difficult to coordinate and produce action in a timely fashion. Parties help compensate for this drawback by linking all the institutions of power one to another. Although rivalry between the executive and legislative branches of U.S. government is inevitable, the partisan affiliations of the leaders of each branch constitute a common basis for cooperation, as the president and his allied party members in Congress usually demonstrate daily.

■ One of the last of the big-city party bosses, Chicago Mayor Richard J. Daley (left) controlled a powerful political machine for over twenty-five years. Here, at a 1974 political rally, his son Richard M. Daley displays remarkably similar mannerisms. Assuming a "hereditary mantle," Richard M. Daley has served as mayor of the city since he was elected to the office in 1979.

Photo courtesy: AP/Wide World Photos

The party's linkage function does not end there. Party identification and organization foster communication between the voter and the candidate, as well as between the voter and the office holder. The party connection is one means of increasing accountability in election campaigns and in government. Candidates on the campaign trail and elected party leaders in office are required from time to time to account for their performance at party-sponsored forums, nominating primaries, and conventions.

Political parties, too, can take some credit for unifying the nation by dampening sectionalism. Because parties must form national majorities to win the presidency, any single, isolated region is guaranteed minority status unless it establishes ties with other areas. The party label and philosophy build the bridge that enables regions to join forces; in the process, a national interest, rather than a merely sectional one, is created and served.

The Electioneering Function.

The election, proclaimed author H. G. Wells, is "democracy's ceremonial, its feast, its great function," and the political parties assist this ceremony in essential ways. First, the parties funnel eager, interested individuals into politics and government. Thousands of candidates are recruited each year by the two parties, as are many of the candidates' staff members—the people who manage the campaigns and go on to serve in key governmental positions once the election has been won.

The national, state, and local parties also help raise money for candidates. The contemporary national Republican Party has considerable organizational prowess, surpassing the Democrats in fund-raising by large margins in recent election cycles—usually by at least a two to one ratio, and often considerably higher (see Figure 11.3). Until 2004, Democrats struggled to raise enough money to meet the basic needs of most of their candidates, while Republicans often raised more money than they could spend.[14] In 2004, however, while Republicans still outspent the Democrats in Senate and House races, the Democrats came closer to matching the Republicans than in any other modern election season. Either way, a party or candidate with a considerable financial advantage can daunt opponents. Recent empirical evidence shows that large campaign war chests of incumbents act to deter high-quality challengers from entering political races.[15]

The money raised by both parties is used to support a dazzling variety of party activities and campaign services, including party staff, voter contact in the form of phone centers and mass mailings, media advertising, and campaign staff and training. The Republican and Democratic National Committees, for example, spend millions of dollars for national, state, and local public opinion surveys. In important contests, the party will frequently commission tracking polls—continuous surveys that enable a campaign to chart its daily rise or fall. The information provided in such polls is invaluable in the tense concluding days of an election. Both national parties also operate sophisticated in-house media divisions that specialize in the design and production of television advertisements for party nominees at all levels.

FIGURE 11.3 **Political Party Finances.** ■

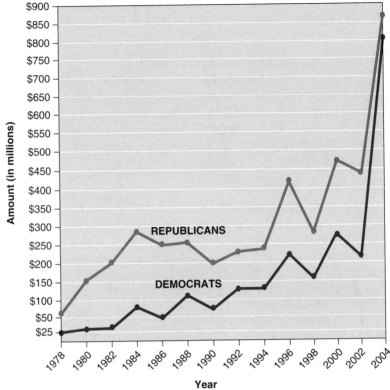

Year

Note: Includes totals for national, senatorial, and congressional committees as well as all other reported national, state, and local spending; all presidential, Senate, and House candidates are included. Not included are soft money expenditures. The 2004 amount includes monies spent between January 1, 2003, and June 30, 2004.

Source: Federal Election Commission.

Policy Formulation and Promotion.   The national party platform is the most visible instrument that parties use to formulate, convey, and promote public policy (see Table 11.2). Every four years, each party produces a lengthy platform, approved by delegates to the presidential nominating conventions, explaining its positions on key issues. Platforms have considerable impact. About two-thirds of the promises in the victorious party's presidential platform have been completely or mostly implemented; even more astounding, one-half or more of the pledges of the losing party find their way into public policy (with the success rate depending on whether the party controls one, both, or neither house of Congress).[16]

The party platform also has great influence on a new presidential administration's legislative program and on the president's State of the Union Address. While party affiliation is normally the single most important determinant of voting in Congress and in state legislatures, the party–vote relationship is even stronger when party platform issues come up on the floor of Congress.[17] Besides mobilizing Americans on a permanent basis, then, the parties convert the cacophony of hundreds of identifiable social and economic groups into a two-part semiharmony

TABLE 11.2   Republican and Democratic 2004 Party Platforms Compared on Key Issues

	Republicans	Democrats
Theme	"A Safer World and a More Hopeful America"	"Strong at Home, Respected in the World"
Afghanistan	"Today, Afghanistan is a world away from the nightmare of the Taliban. ... Women are respected. ... Terror camps are closed."	"Nowhere is the need for collective endeavor greater than in Afghanistan. The Bush Administration badly mishandled the war's aftermath. ...allowing it to become a safe haven for terrorists."
USA Patriot Act	Favors the Patriot Act and hails its accomplishments.	Will strengthen some sections but change provisions that threaten individual rights.
Social Security	Support personal retirement accounts and extensive reform of current system.	Preserve current system.
Education	Supports school choice, increasing charter schools, and vouchers, abstinence education and voluntary prayer in schools.	Support public school choice including magnet and charter schools; oppose vouchers
Labor	Support right-to-work laws.	Support worker's rights to join unions and to organize on a level playing field.
Stem Cell Research	Supports use of adult stem cell and cord blood stem cell research. Prevents use of new embryonic stem cells and federal funding of new embryonic stem cell research.	Calls for federal funding of embryonic stem cell research.
Climate	Oppose Kyoto Protocol and any other mandatory carbon emissions controls.	Argue that the U.S. should be at the forefront of efforts to protect the global environment.
D.C. Statehood	Oppose.	Support D.C. right to self-government and "Congressional representation for the citizen of our nation's capital.
Marriage	Support a "constitutional amendment that fully protects marriage."	Oppose a "Federal Marriage Amendment."
Taxes	Support 2001 and 2003 tax cuts.	Role back tax cuts for those making more than $200,000 a year.
Title IX	"Support a reasonable approach to Title IX that seeks to expand opportunities for women without adversely affecting male athletics."	"We will restore vigorous enforcement ... (of) Title IX."
Cuba	Support trade embargo with and and travel to Cuba.	Support a "policy of principled travel to Cuba..."

Source: 2004 Democratic and Republican Party Platforms.

that is much more comprehensible, if not always on key and pleasing to the ears. The simplicity of two-party politics may be deceptive, given the enormous variety in public policy choices, but a sensible system of representation in the American context might be impossible without it.

Legislative Organization.   In no segment of U.S. government is the party more visible or vital than in the Congress. In this century, the political parties have dramatically increased the sophistication and impact of their internal congressional organizations. Prior to the beginning of every session, the parties in both houses of Congress gather (or caucus) separately to select party leaders (House speaker and minority leader, Senate majority and minority leaders, party whips, and so on) and to arrange for the appointment of members of each chamber's committees. In effect, then, the parties organize and operate the Congress.

To promote their policy positions, the leaders of each party in Congress try to advance legislation to further their interests. Party labels, in fact, have consistently been the most powerful predictor of congressional roll-call voting. In the last few years, party voting has increased noticeably, as reflected in the upward trend by both Democrats and Republicans. A member's party affiliation has proven to be the indicator of his or her votes more than 80 percent of the time in recent years; that is, the average representative or senator sides with his or her party on about 80 percent of the votes that divide a majority of Democrats from a majority of Republicans (see Figure 11.4).

There are many reasons for the recent growth of congressional party unity and cohesion. Some are the result of long-term political trends. Both congressional parties, for instance, have gradually become more ideologically homogeneous and internally consistent. Southern Democrats today are more moderate and much closer philosophically to their northern counterparts than the South's legislative barons of old ever were. Similarly, there are few liberal Republicans left in either chamber of Congress, and GOP House members from all regions of the country are—with a few exceptions—moderately to solidly conservative. As each party became more ideologically homogeneous, rank-and-file members of Congress (especially in the House) delegated

FIGURE 11.4 Congressional Party Unity Scores, 1959–2003

Note how party-based voting has increased conspicuously since the 1970s. ■

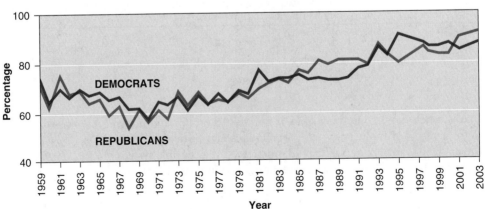

Sources: *Congressional Quarterly Almanacs* (Washington, DC: CQ Press).

to party leaders enhanced powers with which to push through the party's agenda.[18]

INTEREST GROUPS

THE FACE OF INTEREST GROUP POLITICS in the United States is changing as quickly as laws, political consultants, and technology allow. Big business and trade groups are increasing their activities and engagement in the political system at the same time that there is conflicting evidence concerning whether ordinary citizens join political groups. In an influential 1995 essay and a 2000 book, political scientist Robert Putnam argued that fewer Americans are joining groups, a phenomenon he labeled "bowling alone."[19] Others have faulted Putnam, concluding that America is in the midst of an "explosion of voluntary groups, activities and charitable donations [that] is transforming our towns and cities."[20] Although bowling leagues, which were a very common means of bringing people together, have withered, other groups such as soccer associations, health clubs, and environmental groups are flourishing. Older groups such as the Elks Club and the League of Women Voters, whose membership was tracked by Putnam, no longer are attracting members, but this does not necessarily mean that people aren't joining groups; they just aren't joining the ones studied by Putnam.

Why is this debate so important? Political scientists believe that involvement in these kinds of community groups and activities enhances the level of **social capital,** "the web of cooperative relationships between citizens that facilitates resolution of collective action problems."[21] The more social capital that exists in a given community, the more citizens are engaged in its governance and well-being, and the more likely they are to work for the collective good.[22] This tendency to form small-scale associations for the public good, or **civic virtue,** as Putnam calls it, creates fertile ground within communities for improved political and economic development.[23] In studying community involvement in local politics in Italy, for example, Putnam found that good government was a by-product of singing groups and soccer clubs.[24] Thus, if Americans truly are joining fewer groups, we might expect the overall quality of government and its provision of services to suffer.

Although the debate continues over whether America continues to be the nation of joiners that French political philosopher Alexis de Tocqueville found in the 1830s, it is clear that people are reporting more individual acts—many of them designed to pressure policy makers at all levels of government. Newer types of groups have replaced those that were common in the past, and Ladd believes that political scientists trained in the 1960s and 1970s overlook the kinds of contributions made by young people today, such as involvement in voluntary community service work. Young people often don't see participation in

social capital
The myriad relationships that individuals enjoy that facilitate the resolution of community problems through collective action.

civic virtue
The tendency to form small-scale associations for the public good.

Comparing Interest Groups

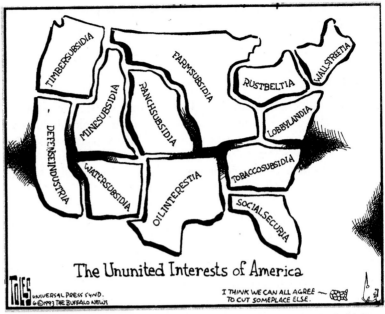

groups such as Habitat for Humanity or working in a soup kitchen as political, but frequently it is.

Interest groups often fill voids left by the traditional political parties and give Americans another opportunity to take their claims directly to the government. Interest groups give the unrepresented or underrepresented an opportunity to have their voices heard, thereby making the government and its policy-making process more representative of diverse populations and perspectives. (See Join the Debate: Limits on Interest Group Participation.)

Why and How Interest Groups Form and Maintain Themselves

Interest groups go by various names: special interests, pressure groups, organized interests, nongovernmental organizations (NGOs), political groups, lobby groups, and public interest groups. Originally, most political scientists used the term "pressure group" because it best described what these groups do. Today, most political scientists use the term interest group or organized interest. David Truman, one of the first political scientists to study interest groups, defines an organized interest as "any group that, on the basis of one or more shared attitudes, makes certain claims upon other groups in society for the establishment, maintenance, or enhancement of forms of behavior that are implied by shared attitudes."[25] Truman further posed what he termed **disturbance theory** to explain why interest groups form.[26] He hypothesized that groups arise, in part, to counteract the activities of other groups or of organized special interests.

Political scientist Robert Salisbury expanded on Truman by arguing that groups form when resources—be they clean air, women's rights, or rights of the unborn, for example—are inadequate or scarce. Unlike Truman, Salisbury stresses the role that leaders, or what he terms "entrepreneurs," play in the formation of groups.[27]

The Role of Leaders.   Interest group theorists frequently acknowledge the key role that leaders play in the formation, viability, and success of interest groups, while noting that leaders often vary from rank-and-file members on various policies. The role of an interest-group leader is similar to that of an entrepreneur in the business world. Leaders of groups must find ways to attract members. As in the marketing of a new product, an interest-group leader must have something attractive to offer to persuade members to join. Potential members of the group must be convinced that the benefits of joining outweigh the costs.

The Role of Patrons and Funding.   All interest groups require adequate funding to build their memberships as well as to advance their policy objectives. Governments, foundations, and wealthy individuals can serve as **patrons,** providing crucial start-up funds for groups, especially public interest groups. Advertising, litigating, and lobbying are expensive. Without financiers, few public interest groups could survive their initial start-up period.

The Role of Members.   Organizations are usually composed of three kinds of members. At the top are a relatively small number of leaders who devote most of their energies to the single group. The second tier of members is generally involved psychologically as well as organizationally. They are the workers of the group—they attend meetings, pay dues, and chair committees to see that things get done. In the bottom tier are the rank and file, members who don't actively participate. They pay their dues and call themselves group members, but they do little more. Most group members fall into this last category.

Groups vary tremendously in their ability to enroll what are called potential members. Economist Mancur Olson Jr. notes that all groups provide some **collective good**—that is, something of value, such as money, a tax write-off, a good feeling, or a better environment, that can't be withheld from a nongroup member.[28] If one union member at a factory gets a raise, for example, all other workers at that factory will, too. Therefore, those who don't join or work for the benefit of the group still reap the rewards of the group's activity. The downside of this phenomenon is called

disturbance theory
Political scientist David B. Truman's theory that interest groups form in part to counteract the efforts of other groups.

patron
A person who finances a group or individual activity.

collective good
Something of value that cannot be withheld from a nongroup member, for example, a tax write-off or a better environment.

LIMITS ON INTEREST GROUP PARTICIPATION

OVERVIEW: The First Amendment to the Constitution guarantees the right to freedom of speech, press, association, and the right to "petition the government for a redress of grievances." These rights are necessary in a democracy because they guarantee that—within the framework of law—the people have their voice heard by the government. Grievances can be political or social in nature, and all citizens have the right to petition the government to have their (sometimes narrow) interest or issue addressed and to express their policy preferences.

Political speech and activity, however, are regulated by law, as are the actions of the government (so as to prevent undue influence and corruption), and the line between constitutional regulation and rights violations is difficult to discern. Additionally, in order for government to fulfill its functions, it must attempt to balance fairly the claims of very diverse competing interests—for example, the legal, economic, and rights claims of both music and video file-sharers and the entertainment industry. Because the framework within which interest groups and government must operate is contentious, regulation is necessary. But, when a group lobbies to change government policy, can the government require full disclosure of the group's activities and finances?

Depending on what is done with the information gathered from interest group disclosure requirements, the government may be acting in the public interest. For example, part of the mandate from the Lobbying Disclosure Act of 1995 is to facilitate public access to information about lobbying groups as well as that about the government's knowledge of their activities. The goal is to allow concerned citizens to verify accountability of both interest groups and government. Thus, government watchdog groups such as OpenSecrets can correlate lobbying activities with perceived government response. Moreover, insisting that groups disclose information allows both the government and the public to know who or what is behind a lobby's agenda. For example, billionaire George Soros has given $7.85 million to interest groups such as MoveOn.org and the Campaign for America's Future to fund political activities. This information is relevant when one tries to discern motive and assign accountability behind an interest's political action.

The political nature of lobby activity may mean interest groups are subject to a high standard of disclosure and scrutiny similar to the demand for transparency in government activity. But what about the right to privacy? Should interest groups have the same right to privacy as individuals? After all, citizens are not required to disclose the reasons behind their votes or why they engage in political activity. Why, then, should interest groups be denied this standard of privacy?

Arguments for Regulating Interest Group Activities

- **Interest groups are not given a constitutional role to make or influence policy.** Though individuals and groups have the right to lobby the government, they have no unrestricted right to do so. Given hundreds if not thousands of interests, the government must have some means to prioritize and determine the legitimacy of various groups. For example, should a local 4H group have the same voice and access to national policy makers as the National Dairy Association?

- **Regulation is necessary to ensure that the public knows why and in what capacity an interest group is acting.** The regulatory mandate of the 1995 Lobbying Disclosure Act is to ensure accountability in the lobbying process. The public needs to know about corruption or misinformation coming from either the government or an interest group. For instance, the Rainbow Push Coalition was implicated in lobbying the City of Chicago to keep a dangerous after-hours dance club open in which a fire subsequently caused twenty-one deaths. The club owners, Rainbow Push, and certain Chicago politicians were known to have a relationship.

- **Regulation of interest groups allows the government to level the playing field.** Research published by the American Political Science Association (APSA) contends inequality and unequal access to wealth harms the American democratic process. APSA implies that wealthier groups have a larger voice and thus more access to policy makers. By regulating interest groups, the federal government can ensure relative equality of access to policy makers.

Arguments Against Regulating Interest Group Activities

- **Government regulation of interest groups may stifle political speech.** For example, the Supreme Court upheld the 2002 Bipartisan Campaign Reform Act's provision prohibiting groups from issue advertising sixty days prior to a general election (see page 448). Many scholars and legal experts believe this is a fundamental violation of political speech rights,

as it is now understood that money gives voice to the political process. To deny groups the right to political advertisement is to deny political speech.

- **Regulation of groups essentially creates approved speech and politics.** By using regulations to determine which groups have the right to lobby the government, the government is in effect establishing which groups are legitimate (in both their activities and speech) and which are not. It is not the government's role to conclude whether one group's political activity and speech are more or less legitimate or important than another group's.

- **Government regulation of interest groups is not necessary.** In an open, pluralistic society, interest groups are subject to market dynamics. Groups that truly represent broad or important interests will have their views heard over those that do not. This economic reality gives voice to the groups deemed by the American people to represent important interests and issues.

Questions

1. Is compelling disclosure of group information a violation of privacy rights? How can a group's privacy rights be reconciled with the public's right to know?

2. What information should interest groups be required to provide? And, to whom should they provide it?

Selected Readings

Kevin Phillips. *Arrogant Capital: Washington, Wall Street, and the Frustration of American Politics.* Boston: Back Bay Books, 1995.

Luigi Graziano. *Lobbying, Pluralism and Democracy.* New York: Palgrave Macmillan, 2001.

the **free rider problem.** As Olson asserts, potential members may be unlikely to join a group because they realize that they will receive many of the benefits the group achieves regardless of their participation. Not only is it irrational for free riders to join any group, but the bigger the group, the greater the free rider problem. Thus, groups need to provide a variety of other incentives to convince potential members to join. These can be newsletters, discounts, or simply a good feeling

The Roots and Development of American Interest Groups

Although all kinds of local groups proliferated throughout the colonies and in the new states, it was not until the 1830s, as communications networks improved, that the first groups national in scope emerged. Many of these first national groups were single-issue groups deeply rooted in the Christian religious revivalism that was sweeping the nation. Concern with humanitarian issues such as temperance (total abstinence from alcoholic beverages), peace, education, and slavery led to the founding of numerous associations dedicated to solving these problems. Among the first of these groups was the American Anti-Slavery Society, founded in 1833 by William Lloyd Garrison.

After the Civil War, more groups were founded. For example, the Women's Christian Temperance Union (WCTU) was created in 1874 with the goal of outlawing the sale of liquor. Its members, many of them quite religious, believed that the consumption of alcohol was an evil injurious to family life because many men drank away their paychecks, leaving no money to feed or clothe their families. Business interests, too, began to play even larger roles in both state and national politics. A popular saying of the day noted that the Standard Oil Company did everything to the Pennsylvania legislature except refine it. Increasingly large trusts, monopolies, business combinations, and corporate conglomerations in the oil, steel, and sugar industries became sufficiently powerful to control many representatives in the state and national legislatures.

By the 1890s, a profound change had occurred in the nation's political and social outlook. Rapid industrialization, an influx of immigrants, and monopolistic business practices created a host of problems including crime, poverty, squalid and unsafe working conditions, and widespread political corruption. Many Americans began to believe that new measures would be necessary to impose order on this growing chaos and to curb some of the more glaring problems. The political and social movement that grew out of these concerns was called the Progressive movement.

In response to the pressure applied by Progressive era groups, the national government began to regulate business. Because businesses had a vested interest in keeping wages low and costs down, more business groups organized to consolidate their strength and to counter Progressive moves.

Not only did governments have to mediate Progressive and business demands, but they also had to accommodate the role of organized labor, which often allied itself with Progressive groups against big business.

The National Association of Manufacturers (NAM) was founded in 1895 by manufacturers who had suffered business reverses in the economic panic of 1893 and who believed that they were being affected adversely by the growth of organized labor. NAM first became active politically in 1913 when a major tariff bill was under congressional consideration. The second major business organization came into being in 1912, when the U.S. Chamber of Commerce was created with the assistance of the Department of Commerce and Labor. (The chamber was created before that department was split into the Department of Commerce and the Department of Labor.)

Until the creation of the American Federation of Labor (AFL) in 1886, there was not any real national union activity. The AFL brought skilled workers from several trades together into one stronger national organization for the first time. As the AFL grew in power, many business owners began to press individually or collectively to quash the unions. As business interests pushed states for what are called open shop laws to outlaw unions in their factories, the AFL became increasingly political. It also was forced to react to the success of big businesses' use of legal injunctions to prohibit union organization. In 1914, massive lobbying by the AFL and its members led to passage of the Clayton Act, which labor leader Samuel Gompers hailed as the Magna Carta of the labor movement. This law allowed unions to organize free from prosecution and also guaranteed their right to strike, a powerful weapon against employers.

Membership in labor unions held steady throughout the early and mid-1900s and then skyrocketed toward the end of the Depression. By then, organized labor began to be a potent political force as it was able to turn out its members in support of particular political candidates. Labor became a stronger force in U.S. politics when the American Federation of Labor merged with the Congress of Industrial Organizations in 1955. Concentrating its efforts largely on the national level, the new AFL-CIO immediately turned its energies to pressuring the government to protect concessions won from employers at the bargaining table and to other issues of concern to its members, including minimum wage laws, the environment, civil rights, medical insurance, and health care.

More recently, the once fabled political clout of organized labor has been on the wane at the national level. Union membership has plummeted as the nation has changed from a land of manufacturing workers and farmers to a nation of white-collar professionals and service workers. Thus, unions no longer have the large memberships or the political clout they once held in governmental circles.

The Rise of the Interest Group State. During the 1960s and 1970s, the Progressive spirit reappeared in the rise of public interest

The Living Constitution

Congress shall make no law respecting...the right of the people peaceably to assemble, and to petition the Government for a redress of grievances.

—First Amendment

This amendment prohibits the national government from enacting laws dealing with the right of individuals to join together to make their voices known about their positions on a range of political issues. There was little debate on this clause in the U.S. House of Representatives and none was recorded in the Senate. James Madison, however, warned of the perils of "discussing and proposing abstract propositions," which this clause was for many years.

The concept of freedom of association, a key concept that allows Americans to organize and join a host of political groups, grew out of a series of cases decided by the Supreme Court in the 1950s and 1960s when many southern states were trying to limit the activities of the National Association for the Advancement of Colored People (NAACP). From the right to assemble and petition the government, along with the freedom of speech, the Supreme Court construed the right of people to come together to support or to protest government actions. First, the Court ruled that states could not compel interest groups to provide their membership lists to state officials. Later, the Court ruled that Alabama could not prohibit the NAACP from urging its members and others to file lawsuits challenging state discriminatory practices. Today, although states and localities can require organized interests to apply for permits to picket or protest, they cannot in any way infringe on their ability to assemble and petition in peaceable ways.

public interest group
An organization that seeks a collective good that will not selectively and materially benefit the members of the group.

groups. **Public interest groups** are organizations "that seek a collective good, the achievement of which will not selectively and materially benefit the membership or activists of the organization."[29] Many Progressive era groups were created to solve the varied problems of new immigrants and the poor. Today, civil rights and liberties groups such as the NAACP and the American Civil Liberties Union (ACLU), environmental groups, good government groups such as Common Cause, peace groups, church groups, groups that speak out for those who cannot (such as children, the mentally ill, or animals), and organizations such as Concerned Women for America are examples of public interest groups. Generally, liberal public interest groups devote themselves to representing the interests of African Americans, women, the elderly, the poor, and consumers, or to working on behalf of the environment. Many of their leaders and members were active in the civil rights and anti–Vietnam War movements of the 1960s.

Simulation
You Are an
Environmental Activist

The civil rights and anti-war struggles left many Americans feeling cynical about a government that they believed failed to respond to the will of the majority. They also believed that if citizens banded together, they could make a difference. Thus, two major new public interest groups—Common Cause and Public Citizen, Inc.—were founded. Common Cause, a good-government group that acts as a watchdog over the federal government, is similar to some of the early Progressive movement's public interest groups. Common Cause effectively has challenged aspects of the congressional seniority system, successfully urged the passage of sweeping campaign financing reforms, and played a major role in the enactment of legislation authorizing federal financing of presidential campaigns. Perhaps more well known than Common Cause is Public Citizen, Inc., the collection of groups headed by Ralph Nader (who later went on to run as a candidate for president in 1996, 2000, and 2004).

Conservative Backlash: Religious and Ideological Groups.

During the 1960s and 1970s, various public interest groups and civil rights and women's rights movements grew and achieved success in shaping and defining the public agenda. Conservatives, concerned by the activities of these liberal groups, responded by forming religious and ideological groups that became a potent force in U.S. politics. In 1978, the Reverend Jerry Falwell founded the first major new religious group, the Moral Majority. The Moral Majority was widely credited with assisting in the election of Ronald Reagan as president in 1980 as well as with the defeats of several liberal Democratic senators that same year. Falwell claimed to have sent 3 to 4 million newly registered voters to the polls.[30]

In 1990, televangelist Pat Robertson, host of the popular television program *The 700 Club*, formed a new group, the Christian Coalition. Since then, it has grown in power and influence. The Christian Coalition played an important role in the Republicans' winning control of the Congress in 1994. In 2004, the group distributed more than 100 million voter guides in churches throughout the United States. The Christian Coalition also lobbies Congress and the White House. The group had the sympathetic ear of President George W. Bush, whom it helped elect. In fact, one of Bush's first moves as president was to create an Office of Faith-Based and Community Initiatives to work with religious groups to effect policy change.

The Christian Coalition is not the only conservative interest group to play an important role in the policy process as well as in elections at

FIGURE 11.5   How NRA Membership Has Fluctuated

The National Rifle Association (NRA), a single-issue interest group, lobbies against any law that would restrict an individual's right to bear arms. NRA membership tends to increase in reaction to proposed gun control legislation or near an election. Interestingly, following the Columbine High School shooting in 1999, in which thirteen people were killed and several others were wounded, membership increased dramatically. Its membership also took a jump after the September 11, 2001, terrorist attacks but then declined. ■

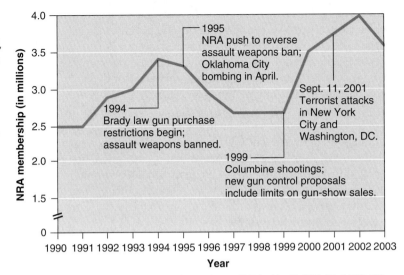

Sources: Genevieve Lynn, "How the NRA Membership Has Risen," *USA Today* (May 18, 2000): 1A. © 2000, USA Today. Reprinted with permission. Updated by the authors.

the state and national level. The National Rifle Association (NRA), an active opponent of gun control legislation, saw its membership rise in recent years (see Figure 11.5), as well as its importance in Washington, D.C. The NRA and its political action committee spent $20 million to help reelect President George W. Bush in 2004. (For a look at how one conservative group's efforts may affect college students, see On Campus: Conservative Student Groups: Speaking Up.)

What Do Interest Groups Do?

Interest groups are involved in myriad activities. They lobby all three branches of government, and engage in grassroots lobbying. They also engage in protest activities, and many are actively engaged in the campaign process, among other activities.

Lobbying.   Most interest groups put lobbying at the top of their agendas. **Lobbying** is the process by which interest groups attempt to assert their influence on the policy-making process. The term lobbyist refers to any representative of a group that attempts to influence a policy maker by one or more of the tactics listed in Table 11.3. Almost all interest groups lobby by testifying at hearings and contacting legislators. Other groups also provide information that decision makers might not have the time, opportunity, or interest to gather on their own.

lobbying
The activities of a group or organization that seeks to influence legislation and persuade political leaders to support the group's position.

Lobbying Congress.   Members of Congress are the targets of a wide variety of lobbying activities: congressional testimony on behalf of a

CONSERVATIVE STUDENT GROUPS: SPEAKING UP

Many conservative college students believe that their voices are being stifled on campuses across the United States. Some charge that there is discrimination by professors and a lack of respect of diverse views in the classroom. Others say that the hiring process favors liberal professors. Some charge a bias in the selection of campus speakers and funding of groups.

A 2002 study by the Center for the Study of Popular Culture revealed that at the nation's top thirty-two universities, Democratic professors greatly outnumbered Republicans. Said Harvey Mansfield, a conservative Harvard political scientist, "We have sixty members in the department of government. Maybe three are Republicans. How could that be just by chance? How could that be fair?"[a]

The Center for the Study of Popular Culture has drafted an Academic Bill of Rights that it is urging colleges and universities to adopt. This document requests institutions of higher learning to "include both liberal and conservative viewpoints in their selection of campus speakers and syllabuses for courses and to choose faculty members 'with a view toward fostering a plurality of methodologies and perspectives.'"[b] It also notes a variety of ways in which students' academic freedom can be compromised, including:

- Mocking national or religious leaders.
- Forcing students to take a particular point of view in assignments.
- Requiring readings that cover only one side of an issue.

Several state legislators have considered enacting legislation suggesting that publicly funded state colleges and universities adhere to this statement of principles. Representative Jack Kingston (R–GA) introduced a nonbinding resolution along these lines in the U.S. House of Representatives, on which the Congress took no action.

University administrators, as well as the American Association of University Professors (AAUP) have been nearly unanimous in their disapproval of the center's proposed Academic Bill of Rights. "The danger of such guidelines," says the AAUP, is that they invite diversity to be measured by political standards that diverge from the academic criteria of the scholarly profession." The AAUP points out that to comply with this Academic Bill of Rights, a professor professing a Nazi philosophy would need to be hired even "if that philosophy is not deemed a reasonable scholarly option within the discipline."[c]

The Center for the Study of Popular Culture is working closely with Students for Academic Freedom, a national coalition of student organizations whose goal is to bring dual viewpoints to campuses; the center also works with College Republicans groups on some campuses. At some schools, including the University of Colorado, students can post alleged discrimination by liberal professors on special student-created Web sites.[d] The University of Texas at Austin has a "Professor Watch List," and Students for Academic Freedom and NoIndoctrination.org allow students from all over the country to post complaints about particular professors. Many professors view this as a form of blacklisting like that which existed in the 1950s when professors who were suspected of being members of or sympathetic to the Communist Party were barred from teaching positions.

1. How do interest groups such as Students for Academic Freedom benefit from working in coalition with other groups?
2. Getting issues on the public agenda is often as important for groups as the actual passage of legislation or rules. How successful have conservative student groups been on your campus in having issues of classroom bias addressed?

[a] Quoted in Yilu Zhao, "Taking the Liberalism Out of Liberal Arts," *New York Times* (April 3, 2004): B9.

[b] Zhao, "Taking the Liberalism Out."

[c] http://www.aaup.org.

[d] Dave Curtin, "Students' Site Solicits Allegations of CU Bias," *Denver Post* (January 20, 2004): A1.

TABLE 11.3   Groups and Lobbyists Using Each Lobbying Technique (Percentage)

| Technique | STATE-BASED GROUPS | | WASHINGTON, DC-BASED GROUPS |
	Lobbyists (n = 595)	Organizations (n = 301)	(n = 175)
1. Testifying at legislative hearings	98	99	99
2. Contacting government officials directly to present point of view	98	97	98
3. Helping to draft legislation	96	88	85
4. Alerting state legislators to the effects of a bill on their districts	96	94	75
5. Having influential constituents contact legislator's office	94	92	80
6. Consulting with government officials to plan legislative strategy	88	84	85
7. Attempting to shape implementation of policies	88	85	89
8. Mounting grassroots lobbying efforts	88	86	80
9. Helping to draft regulations, rules, or guidelines	84	81	78
10. Raising new issues and calling attention to previously ignored problems	85	83	84
11. Engaging in informal contacts with officials	83	81	95
12. Inspiring letter-writing or telegram campaigns	82	83	84
13. Entering into coalitions with other groups	79	93	90
14. Talking to media	73	74	86
15. Serving on advisory commissions and boards	58	76	76
16. Making monetary contributions to candidates	--	45	58
17. Attempting to influence appointment to public office	44	42	53
18. Doing favors for officials who need assistance	41	36	56
19. Filing suit or otherwise engaging in litigation	36	40	72
20. Working on election campaigns	--	29	24
21. Endorsing candidates	--	24	22
22. Running advertisements in media about position	18	21	31
23. Engaging in protests or demonstrations	13	21	20

Sources: State-Based Groups: Anthony J. Nownes and Patricia Freeman, "Interest Group Activity in the States," *Journal of Politics* 60 (1998): 92. Washington, DC-Based Groups: Kay Lehman Schlozman and John Tierney, "More of the Same: Washington Pressure Group Activity in a Decade of Change," *Journal of Politics* 45 (1983): 358.

Simulation

You Are a Lobbyist

Timeline

Interest Groups and Campaign Finance

group, individual letters from interested constituents, campaign contributions, trips, speaking fees, or the outright payment of money for votes. Of course, the last item is illegal, but there are numerous documented instances of money changing hands for votes. Because lobbying plays such an important role in Congress, many effective lobbyists often are former members of that body, former staff aides, former White House officials or Cabinet officers, or Washington insiders.

Attempts to Reform Congressional Lobbying. In 1946, in an effort to limit the power of lobbyists, Congress passed the Federal Regulation of Lobbying Act, which required anyone hired to lobby any member of Congress to register and file quarterly financial reports. Few lobbyists actually filed these reports. For years, numerous good government groups argued for the strengthening of lobbying laws. Civil liberties groups such as the ACLU, however, argue that registration provisions violate the First Amendment's freedom of speech and the right of citizens to petition the government.

But, public opinion polls continued to reveal that many Americans believed that the votes of numerous members of Congress were often available to the highest bidder. In late 1995, after nearly fifty years of inaction, Congress passed the first effort to regulate lobbying since the 1946 act. The Lobbying Disclosure Act employs a strict definition of lobbyist (one who devotes at least 20 percent of a client's or employer's time to lobbying activities). It also requires lobbyists to: (1) register with the clerk of the House and the secretary of the Senate; (2) report their clients and issues and the agency or house they lobbied; and, (3) estimate the amount they are paid by each client.

These reporting requirements make it easier for watchdog groups or the media to monitor lobbying activities. In fact, the first comprehensive analysis by the Center for Responsive Politics revealed that by June 1999, 20,512 lobbyists were registered. The number of organizations that reported spending more than one million dollars a year on lobbying also jumped dramatically. In 2004, nearly $4 million was spent on lobbying for every member of Congress.[31] (See Analyzing Visuals: Top Lobbying Expenditures.)

Lobbying the Executive Branch.   Groups often target one or more levels of the executive branch because there are so many potential access points including the president, White House staff, and the numerous levels of the executive branch bureaucracy. Groups try to work closely with the administration to influence policy decisions at their formulation and implementation stages. Like the situation with congressional lobbying, the effectiveness of a group often depends on its ability to provide decision makers with important information and a sense of where the public stands on the issue.

An especially strong link exists between interest groups and regulatory agencies (see chapter 8). Although these agencies are ostensibly independent of Congress and the president, interest groups often have clout there. Because of the highly technical aspects of much regulatory work, many groups employ Washington attorneys and lobbying firms to deal directly with the agencies. So great is interest group influence in the decision-making process of these agencies that many people charge that the agencies have been captured by the interest groups.

Lobbying the Courts.   The courts, too, have proved a useful target for interest groups.[32] Although you might think that the courts decide cases that affect only the parties involved or that they should be immune from political pressures, interest groups for years have recognized the value of lobbying the courts, especially the Supreme Court, and many political scientists view it as a form of political participation.[33] As shown

Analyzing Visuals
TOP LOBBYING EXPENDITURES

For most interest groups, lobbying is their most important activity. Successful lobbying efforts require spending large amounts of money, as shown in the bar graph. Based on the narrow definition of lobbying used under the Lobbying Disclosure Act, the reported expenditures account for money spent to contact members of Congress and executive-branch officials but do not include money spent for state-level lobbying, public relations work, legal work, or congressional testimony. Interest groups also supplement their lobbying efforts with campaign contributions to congressional candidates. After studying the bar graph, answer the following critical thinking questions: What is the correlation, if any, between an interest group's expenditures for lobbying and its expenditures for campaign contributions? Which interest groups are most likely to contribute to Republican candidates? Which interest groups are most likely to contribute to Democratic candidates? What do you think explains the differences in these groups' contribution tendencies?

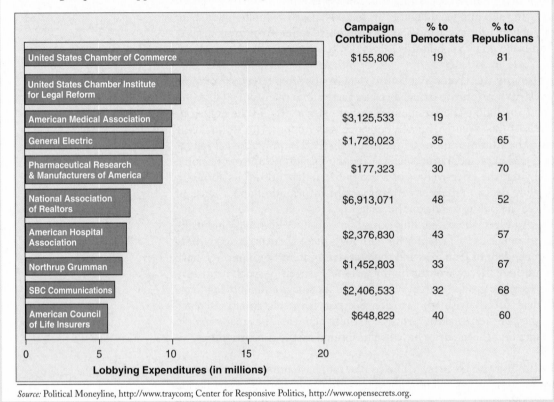

	Campaign Contributions	% to Democrats	% to Republicans
United States Chamber of Commerce	$155,806	19	81
United States Chamber Institute for Legal Reform			
American Medical Association	$3,125,533	19	81
General Electric	$1,728,023	35	65
Pharmaceutical Research & Manufacturers of America	$177,323	30	70
National Association of Realtors	$6,913,071	48	52
American Hospital Association	$2,376,830	43	57
Northrup Grumman	$1,452,803	33	67
SBC Communications	$2,406,533	32	68
American Council of Life Insurers	$648,829	40	60

Lobbying Expenditures (in millions)

Source: Political Moneyline, http://www.traycom; Center for Responsive Politics, http://www.opensecrets.org.

in Table 11.3, 72 percent of the Washington-based groups surveyed participated in litigation as a lobbying tool.

Generally, interest group lobbying of the courts can take two forms: direct sponsorship or the filing of *amicus curiae* briefs. Most major cases noted in this book either have been sponsored by an interest group or one or both of the parties in the case have been supported by an *amicus curiae* brief (discussed in chapter 9).

Grassroots Lobbying.   As the term implies, grassroots lobbying is a form of pressure-group activity that attempts to involve individuals who contact their representatives directly in an effort to affect policy.[34] Although it often involves door-to-door informational or petition drives—a tried and true method of lobbying—the term also encompasses more modern forms such as fax and Internet lobbying of lawmakers.

Interest groups regularly try to inspire their members to engage in grassroots activity, hoping that lawmakers will respond to those pressures and the attendant publicity. In essence, the goal of many organizations is to persuade ordinary voters to serve as their advocates. In the world of lobbying, there are few things more useful than a list of committed supporters. Other interest groups now run carefully targeted and costly television advertisements pitching one side of an argument. Some of these undefined masses, as they join together on the Internet or via faxes, may be mobilized into one or more groups.

Protest Activities.   Most groups have few members so devoted as to put everything on the line for their cause. Some will risk jail or even death, but it is much more usual for a group's members to opt for more conventional forms of lobbying or to influence policy through the electoral process. When these forms of pressure-group activities are unsuccessful or appear to be too slow to achieve results, however, some groups (or individuals within groups) resort to more forceful legal as well as illegal measures to attract attention to their cause. Since the Revolutionary War, violent, illegal protest has been one tactic of organized interests. The Boston Tea Party, for example, involved breaking all sorts of laws, although no one was hurt physically. Other forms of protest, such as Shays's Rebellion, ended in tragedy for some participants. Much more recently, anti-war protestors have been willing to march and risk detention and jail in the United States.

During the civil rights movement, Reverend Martin Luther King Jr. and his followers frequently resorted to nonviolent marches to draw attention to the plight of African Americans in the South. These forms of organized group activity were legal. The groups obtained proper parade permits and notified government officials. The protesters who tried to stop the freedom marchers, however, were engaging in illegal protest activity. Today, protesters regularly try to picket or protest meetings of the International Monetary Fund or the World Bank. Political conventions as well as inaugurations also routinely are targeted by protesters. (See Politics Now: The March for Women's Lives.)

Simulation

You Are the Leader of Concerned Citizens for World Justice

THE MARCH FOR WOMEN'S LIVES

On Sunday, April 25, 2004, women and men from all over the United States gathered in Washington, D.C., to show support for abortion rights and to highlight what march organizers called the Bush administration's "war against reproductive rights and health." It was the largest women's rights march in history and came at a time when many were doubting the current vitality of the women's movement and effectiveness of individual women's rights groups. The event also marked a new effort by women's groups to place the abortion rights issue in a wider context, equating it with the need to improve access to reproductive education and health care, access to emergency contraception, and affordable prenatal care.

Photo courtesy: Krista Kennell/Zuma/Corbis

March organizers, who had requested a permit for at least 750,000 people, estimated that more than 1 million attended. This peaceful march was the culmination of months of planning and the concerted activity of several pro-choice organizations, including NARAL Pro-Choice America, the National Organization for Women, the Planned Parenthood Federation of America, the Feminist Majority, the American Civil Liberties Union, the Black Women's Health Imperative, and the National Latina Institute for Reproductive Health. There was a donor gathering at the home of House Minority Leader Nancy Pelosi (D–CA), an afternoon tea highlighted by singer and songwriter Carole King, and a breakfast sponsored by Senator Hillary Rodham Clinton (D–NY). Attracting additional media attention to the event, actresses Whoopi Goldberg, Cybill Shepherd, and Ashley Judd and singers Ani DiFranco and Moby joined the marchers, along with members of Congress and former executive-branch officials such as former Secretary of State Madeleine Albright, for a day of speeches on the Mall.

As they attempted to expand the agenda from abortion rights to a wider array of reproductive rights, organizers had especially targeted young, college-age women and were heartened that busloads of students from many colleges and universities attended. In addition to student groups, more than 1,400 groups nationwide signed on to send members to Washington, D.C. Longtime abortion rights advocates, many of them now in their late fifties and early sixties, are particularly conscious of the need to recruit and energize new members. Interest groups and social movements cannot maintain themselves without new recruits, and the march, while demonstrating the ability of a wide array of organized interests to come together, also attracted a new cohort of reproductive rights activists who, organizers hope, not only will spread the word around the nation, but also will become the next generation of leaders of myriad pro-choice, reproductive rights organizations.

1. How did efforts made by interest groups to engage young people translate into an energized youth vote?
2. How effective is the use of celebrity advocates as a strategy in helping an interest group achieve its goals?

418

Election Activities

In addition to trying to achieve their goals (or at least draw attention to them) through the conventional and unconventional forms of lobbying and protest activity, many interest groups also become involved more directly in the electoral process.

Candidate Recruitment and Endorsements.   Many groups claim to be nonpartisan, that is, nonpolitical. But, some interest groups recruit, endorse, and/or provide financial or other forms of support for political candidates. For example, EMILY's List (EMILY stands for "Early Money Is Like Yeast—it makes the dough rise") was founded to support pro-choice Democratic women candidates, especially during party primary election contests. However, like its Republican counterpart the WISH List (WISH stands for Women in the Senate and House), it now recruits and trains candidates in addition to contributing to their campaigns. Some organizations take a more grassroots approach to their electoral activities.

Getting Out the Vote.   Many interest groups believe they can influence public policy by putting like-minded representatives in office. To that end, many groups on both sides of the ideological spectrum launch massive get out the vote (GOTV) efforts. These include identifying

TABLE 11.4   Interest Group Ratings of Selected Members of Congress

Member	ACU	ACLU	ADA	AFL-CIO	CC	CoC	LCV
Senate							
Dianne Feinstein (D-CA)	20	60	80	92	20	55	80
Bill Frist (R-TN)	100	20	0	15	100	100	0
Kay Bailey Hutchinson (R-TX)	100	25	5	23	100	95	4
Ted Kennedy (D-MA)	0	60	100	100	0	29	84
House							
Mary Bono (R-CA)	71	27	10	11	75	95	9
John Conyers (D-MI)	0	93	100	100	14	21	91
Tom DeLay (R-TX)	92	7	0	0	100	95	0
Shelia Jackson Lee (D-TX)	4	93	100	100	0	26	68

Key
ACU = American Conservation Union
ACLU = American Civil Liberties Union
ADA = Americans for Democratic Action
AFL-CIO = American Federation of Labor—Congress of Industrial Organizations
CC = Christian Coalition
CoC = Chamber of Commerce
LCV = League of Conservation Voters
Members are rated on a scale from 1 to 100, with 1 being the lowest and 100 being the highest support of a particular group's policies.

prospective voters and getting them to the polls on Election Day. The Christian Coalition, for example, organizes voter registration drives in churches across the country and distributes voter guides that illuminate candidates' positions on issues they view as important. Well-financed interest groups, such as MoveOn.org, often produce issue-oriented ads for newspapers, radio, and television designed to educate the public as well as increase voter interest in election outcomes.

Rating the Candidates or Office Holders.   Many liberal and conservative ideological groups rate candidates to help their members (and the general public) evaluate the voting records of members of Congress. The American Conservative Union (conservative) and the Americans for Democratic Action (liberal)—two groups at ideological polar extremes—routinely rate candidates and members of Congress based on their votes on key issues (see Table 11.4). These scores help voters to know more about their representatives' votes on issues that concern them.

Political Action Committees.   In 1974, Congress passed legislation to allow corporations, labor unions, and interest groups to form political action committees (PACs) (see Figure 11.6). PACs allow these interests to raise money to contribute to political candidates in national elections. In 2002, campaign finance law was changed dramatically, as discussed earlier in this chapter. One of the unintended consequences

FIGURE 11.6 The Number of Political Action Committees

Created in the early 1970s, political action committees (PACs) allow individuals to collect money and contribute to political campaigns. PACs saw explosive growth in the 1980s and, after a period of decline, have recently stabilized in numbers. ■

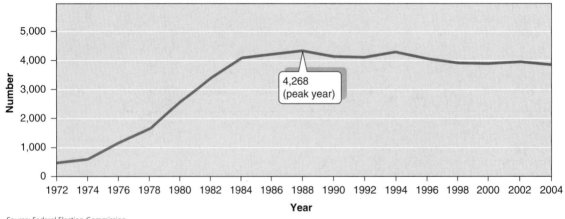

Source: Federal Election Commission.

of the changes was the creation of the 527 groups discussed in the chapter opening vignette and in chapter 12.

The new Bipartisan Campaign Reform Act continued to mandate that contributions to PACs are not tax deductible, unlike some contributions to interest groups. And, PACs generally don't have members who call legislators; instead, PACs have contributors who write checks specifically for the purpose of campaign donations. PAC money plays a significant role in the campaigns of many congressional incumbents, often averaging over half a House candidate's total campaign spending. PACs generally contribute to those who have helped them before and who serve on committees or subcommittees that routinely consider legislation of concern to that group.

SUMMARY

POLITICAL PARTIES AND INTEREST GROUPS play very important roles in the American political system. Political parties have been a key method of selecting candidates, organizing Congress, and other elected bodies, and setting policy agendas since the 1800s. They still are powerful predictors of voting—especially in terms of how elected officials vote. Both major political parties are similarly organized at the local, state, and national levels. Their ability to incorporate ideas of fledgling parties, historically, has made it more difficult for third parties to flourish as they do in other nations.

Interest groups are involved in activities including lobbying all three branches of government, stirring up grassroots efforts for policy change, and all sorts of legal and illegal protest activities. They also often play key roles in the election process by providing endorsements, volunteers, and funds, often in the form of contributions from political action committees or 527s.

KEY TERMS

civic virtue, p. 403
civil service laws, p. 390
coalition, p. 398
collective good, p. 405

direct primary, p. 389
disturbance theory, p. 405
free rider problem, p. 408
interest group, p. 385
issue-oriented politics, p. 390
lobbying, p. 412
machine, p. 389
national convention, p. 392
party identification, p. 393
party platform, p. 392
patron, p. 405
political party, p. 385
public interest group, p. 410
social capital, p. 403
third-partyism, p. 390
ticket-split, p. 390

SELECTED READINGS

Aldrich, John Herbert. *Why Parties? The Origin and Transformation of Political Parties in America*. Chicago: University of Chicago Press, 1995.

Baumgartner, Frank, and Beth Leech. *Basic Interests*. Princeton, NJ: Princeton University Press, 1998.

Beck, Paul Allen, and Marjorie Randon Hershey. *Party Politics in America*, 10th ed. New York: Pearson Longman, 2002.

Berry, Jeffrey M. *The Interest Group Society*, 4th ed. New York: Addison Wesley, 2001.

Cigler, Allan J., and Burdett A. Loomis, eds. *Interest Group Politics*, 6th ed. Washington, DC: CQ Press, 2002.

Herrnson, Paul S., Ronald G. Shaiko, and Clyde Wilcox. *The Interest Group Connection*, 4th ed. Washington, DC: CQ Press, 2005.

Key, V. O., Jr. *Politics, Parties, and Pressure Groups*, 5th ed. New York: Crowell, 1964.

Kollman, Ken. *Outside Lobbying: Public Opinion and Interest Group Strategies*. Princeton, NJ: Princeton University Press, 1998.

Maisel, L. Sandy, ed. *The Parties Respond*, 4th ed. Boulder, CO: Westview, 2002.

McGlen, Nancy E., et al. *Women, Politics, and American Society*, 4th ed. Upper Saddle River, NJ: Prentice Hall, 2004.

Olson, Mancur, Jr. *The Logic of Collective Action: Public Good and the Theory of Groups*. Cambridge, MA: Harvard University Press, 1965.

Patterson, Kelly D. *Political Parties and the Maintenance of Liberal Democracy*. New York: Columbia University Press, 1996.

Reichley, James. *The Life of the Parties: A History of American Political Parties*. Lanham, MD: Rowman and Littlefield, 2000.

Riordan, William L., ed. *Plunkitt of Tammany Hall*. New York: Dutton, 1963.

Sabato, Larry J., and Bruce A. Larson. *The Party's Just Begun: Shaping Political Parties for America's Future*, 2nd ed. New York: Longman, 2002.

Schattschneider, E. E. *Party Government*. New York: Holt, Rinehart and Winston, 1942.

Sifry, Micah L. *Spoiling for a Fight: Third-Party Politics in America*. New York: Routledge, 2002.

Sundquist, James L. *Dynamics of the Party System*, rev. ed. Washington, DC: Brookings Institution, 1983.

Wattenberg, Martin P. *The Decline of American Political Parties, 1952–1996*. Cambridge, MA: Harvard University Press, 1998.

WEB EXPLORATIONS

To evaluate how Republicans and Democrats portray their platform issues and use political language to present their policies, go to www.democrats.org/ and www.rnc.org

To explore the ideological agendas of unaffiliated think tanks and search for connections to specific parties or politicians, go to

www.heritage.org/

www.cato.org/

www.brookings.org/

To learn about the informal factions and interest groups that strive for influence with the major parties, go to

www.adaction.org/

www.cc.org

To compare the planks of several minor parties and find one that represents your views, go to

www.reformparty.org/

www.greens.org/gpusa/

www.lp.org/

www.natural-law.org/

For more on NOW and the NRA, see

www.now.org/

www.nra.org/

For more about Common Cause and Public Citizen, Inc., see www.commoncause.org

www.publiccitizen.org/

For more on the Christian Coalition of America and other conservative groups, see

www.cc.org/

www.heritage.org/

www.cbn.com/

For more on the AFL-CIO, see

www.aflcio.org/

For information on interest groups that watch over lobbyists' activities, see

www.comoncause.org/special/pisites.htm#3

To experience how the lobbying process works, go to

www.meyersandassociates.com/lobbyist.html

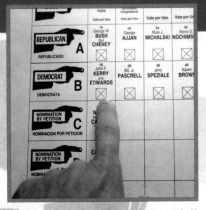

Photo courtesy: Najlah Feanny/Corbis

12

Campaigns, Elections, and Voting

CHAPTER OUTLINE

- Types of Elections
- Presidential Elections
- Congressional Elections
- Campaign Finance
- Voting Behavior
- Bringing It Together: The 2004 Presidential Campaign and Election

DURING THE MONTHS LEADING UP TO the 2004 presidential election, no one doubted that the election between Republican President George W. Bush and the Democratic challenger, Massachusetts Senator John Kerry, would be close. The question everyone wanted answered was exactly how close it would be. Although the presidential election is national, both candidates focused on specific states that showed either narrow margins or even ties. Many of these so-called "battleground states" were located in the Rust Belt—Wisconsin, Michigan, Ohio, and Pennsylvania; however, others were spread across the country, such as Minnesota, Iowa, Florida, New Hampshire, New Mexico, and even Hawaii.

Of these several battleground states, three stood out as the most valuable because of their razor-thin margins of victory in 2000 and their large number of electoral votes. The first was Pennsylvania, a state the 2000 Democratic Candidate Al Gore had won narrowly with 220,000 votes, with 21 electoral votes. Second, Florida, with the miniscule and heavily contested 537 vote margin for Bush in 2000, had 27 electoral votes up for grabs. Finally, there was Ohio with 20 electoral votes, a state no Republican candidate has been able to lose and still go on to win the presidency. By Election Day, it was conventional wisdom that either candidate had to win at least two of these three states if he was going to win the election. By early evening, it was clear that Bush would take Florida by a much wider margin than in 2000, and Kerry would narrowly win Pennsylvania. This left the election down to Ohio, which both candidates had visited

423

more than twenty-five times in 2004. Throughout the night, Bush appeared to hold a 2% voter margin over Kerry, leading some television stations—Fox News and NBC—to call the state for Bush, while others—like ABC, CBS, and CNN—left it too close to call. However, fears that Ohio might become the 2004 version of Florida quickly abated when it became clear that Kerry could not rely on the provisional and absentee ballots to overtake Bush's voter lead. By the morning after Election Day, Bush took Ohio.

Ohio alone would not have been enough for Bush to win the election. To push his vote count over the 270 needed for victory, Bush also won New Mexico and Iowa (states Gore carried in 2000), but he lost New Hampshire to Kerry. The remaining battle-ground states also went to Kerry, but they did not collectively have enough electoral votes for him to win. When looking at a 2004 Electoral College map of the United States, one can see that the division of coastal "blue" (Democratic) states and the "red" (Republican) states is clear. Like the Pacific states (except Alaska), New England is now completely Democratic, while the South from Florida to Arizona is solidly Republican. Because of these geographical differences, many students of politics raise questions about whether blue and red Americans see America the same way and respond differently or if America is actually two nations fighting a cultural war within the midwest battlegrounds, a question the 2008 presidential elections may help to answer.

Comparing Voting and Elections

EVERY FOUR YEARS, ON THE TUESDAY following the first Monday in November, a plurality of voters, simply by casting ballots peacefully across a continent-sized nation, reelects or replaces politicians at all levels of government—from the president of the United States, to members of the U.S. Congress, to state legislators. A number of other countries do not have the luxury of a peaceful transition of political power. We tend to take this process for granted, but in truth it is a marvel. American political institutions have succeeded in maintaining peaceful elections, even when they are as closely contested as the high-stakes 2000 presidential election. Fortunately, most Americans, though not enough, understand why and how elections serve their interests. Elections take the pulse of average people and gauge their hopes and fears.

Today, the United States of America is a democratic paradise in many respects, because it probably conducts more elections for more offices more frequently than any other nation on earth. Moreover, in

NATIONAL ELECTIONS 2004

In 2004 Americans voted in two national elections. Both were held the same day, November 2. One election was for president. In the other, voters elected members to Congress. These were only two of one hundred national elections scheduled to take place in 2004 around the world. This number is up only slightly from previous years.

Across the world, there were ninety-seven national elections held in 2003 and ninety-three in 2002. There were also eight national referenda, something that does not happen in the United States.

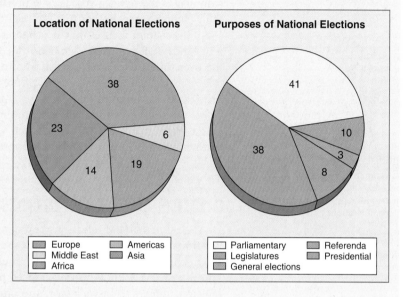

Location of National Elections

38
23
6
14
19

Europe
Middle East
Africa
Americas
Asia

Purposes of National Elections

41
10
38
3
8

Parliamentary
Legislatures
General elections
Referenda
Presidential

Referenda generally address three different issues. One is constitutional reform, such as amending an election system. A second set of issues deals with allowing provinces to have more autonomy or joining a federation or international organization such as the European Union. The third set of issues involves moral questions such as permitting divorce or legalizing abortion.

In some countries, no national elections were held; in others, citizens went to the polls for more than one.

Voters in France went to the polls the most often in any single year. Because of the way in which their national elections are set up, they voted four times in 2002. Voters in Serbia, a country that emerged out of the break-up of Yugoslavia, went to the polls most frequently between 2002–2004. They voted in the following:

- First-round presidential election in September 2002.
- Second-round presidential election in October 2002.

- Presidential rerun election in December 2002.
- First-round presidential election in early November 2003.
- Second-round presidential election in late November 2003.
- Parliamentary elections in December 2003.
- Presidential election in June 2004.

What is not clear is whether these frequent elections signal that democracy is strong in Serbia or if they are a sign that not all is well and that democracy is in danger because political institutions are weak. Concerns have been raised as well about the use of referenda. Are they ways for the public to express its voice, or do referenda short circuit the process of government by taking power away from elected representatives?

Questions

1. How often should elections be held? Can they be held too frequently?
2. Should the United States make use of national referenda?

Source: http://www.ifes.org/eguide.

recent times, the U.S. electorate (those citizens eligible to vote) has been the most inclusive in the country's history; no longer can one's race or sex or creed prevent participation at the ballot box. But, challenges still remain. After all the blood spilled and energy expended to expand the suffrage (as the right to vote is called), little more than half the potentially eligible voters bother to go to the polls.

This chapter focuses on the purposes served by elections, the various kinds of elections held in the United States, and patterns of voting over time. After an examination of the types of elections, we will take a closer look at the elements of presidential elections, including primaries, conventions, and delegates, followed by a look at congressional elections. We then will explore the controversial topic of campaign finance. Finally, we will discuss voting behavior, focusing on distinct patterns in voter turnout and vote choice.

primary election
Election in which voters decide which of the candidates within a party will represent the party in the general election.

closed primary
A primary election in which only a party's registered voters are eligible to vote.

open primary
A primary in which party members, independents, and sometimes members of the other party are allowed to vote.

TYPES OF ELECTIONS

IN THE U.S. SYSTEM, elections come in many varieties. In **primary elections,** voters decide which of the candidates within a party will represent the party's ticket in the general elections. There are different kinds of primaries. For example, **closed primaries** allow only a party's registered voters to cast a ballot, and **open primaries** allow independents and sometimes members of other parties to participate. Closed primaries are considered healthier for the party system because they prevent members of one party from influencing the primaries of the opposition party. On the one hand, studies of open primaries indicate that

Photo courtesy: Sylvia Johnson/Woodfin Camp & Associates

■ Controversy over vote counting in the 2000 presidential election brought people to West Palm Beach, Florida, to protest on behalf of Al Gore and George W. Bush.

IS CALIFORNIA THE NEW FLORIDA?

During the Florida vote recount of the 2000 presidential election, average Americans learned an unsettling truth: the technology they use to vote affects the likelihood that their vote will be counted. One technology in particular, the punch-card ballot, contributed to the confusion over who would be our president, George W. Bush or Al Gore. Politicians, pundits, and voters called for improving voting technology, but which technology a county should pick became a difficult question. The two leading electronic choices were optical scanning technology, the same kind employed on standardized tests, and Digital Recording Electronic devices (DREs), computers that use a touchscreen or keypad interface and record ballots on a hard drive.

Many counties chose DREs. Not only did they fit in with the American love of the "new" and the digital technology boom, but DREs, it was argued, would avoid the perils of punch-card ballots: over-voting and undervoting. DRE software would reject any mistaken attempt to vote for two candidates for the same office, thus preventing overvoting. And, since the machines do not use paper, they would have no risk of "hanging chads" (the bits that adhere to ballot cards when voters don't completely punch out their selections), thus eliminating undervoting. Advocates also argued that the arrangement of candidate names in a big font on a bright screen would make the ballot easier to read than on a punch-card ballot. They also noted that counting votes would take less time than in many other voting systems, since the DRE operator merely dials into a central server and transfers ballots digitally in a matter of seconds. Once all the votes are in, the server instantly has the error-free results.

However, during the 2004 California primaries, DREs were put to the test throughout the state and failed. San Diego County was the most extreme case. One-third of the machines failed

when the batteries powering the DREs ran out of juice the night before the election. When the DREs would not turn on the morning of the primaries, officials were a loss since they had no backup plan. It also turned out that many of the DRE manufacturers were "rejigging and patching their software without heed to the lengthy certification process prescribed by law."[a]

Optical scanning technology, the road not taken in voting technology reform, may actually be preferable to DREs. Researchers from Caltech and MIT tested all existing voting technology and discovered that optical scanning technology recorded votes correctly all but 1.6 percent of the time. Astonishingly, punch-card ballots and DREs both scored a 3 percent error-rate, meaning that counties that exchanged punch-cards for touch-screen systems spent a bunch of taxpayer money to miscount the same number of votes. However, optical scanning is not perfect; the researchers found "in Hawaii in 1998, 7 out of the 361 optical scanners failed to operate properly."[b]

As with any technology, however, it may simply take time for DREs to be perfected and for Americans to get used to them. In the meantime, if you use a punch-card ballot, check the back for hanging chads, and if you're an election official in charge of DREs, please check the batteries the night before the election!

What method of voting do you consider the most error-free? Why? What do you foresee will be the dominant method five or ten years from now?

---

[a] Andrew Gumbel, "Out of Touch," *Los Angeles City Beat*, April 29, 2004, http://www.lacitybeat.com/article.php?id=863&IssueNum=47.

[b] Caltech/MIT Voting Technology Project, "Residual Votes Attributable to Technology: An Assessment of the Reliability of Existing Voting Equipment," Version 2, March 30, 2001.

427

crossover voting
Participation in the primary of a party with which the voter is not affiliated.

raiding
An organized attempt by voters of one party to influence the primary results of the other party.

runoff primary
A second primary election between the two candidates receiving the greatest number of votes in the first primary.

nonpartisan primary
A primary used to select candidates regardless of party affiliation.

general election
Election in which voters decide which candidates will actually fill elective public offices.

initiative
An election that allows citizens to propose legislation and submit it to the state electorate for popular vote.

referendum
An election whereby the state legislature submits proposed legislation to the state's voters for approval.

recall
Removal of an incumbent from office by popular vote.

crossover voting—participation in the primary of a party with which the voter is not affiliated—occurs frequently.[1] On the other hand, the research shows little evidence of **raiding**—an organized attempt by voters of one party to influence the primary results of the other party.[2]

If none of the candidates in the initial primary secures a majority of the votes, some states have a **runoff primary,** a contest between the two candidates with the greatest number of votes. One final type of primary, used in Nebraska and Louisiana (in statewide, nonpresidential primaries), and in hundreds of cities large and small across America, is the **nonpartisan primary,** which is used to select candidates without regard to party affiliation. A nonpartisan primary could produce two final candidates of the same party from a slate of several candidates from many parties.

Once party members vote for their party candidates for various offices, each state holds its general election. In the **general election,** voters decide which candidates will actually fill the nation's elective public offices. These elections are held at many levels, including municipal, county, state, and national. Whereas primaries are contests between the candidates within each party, general elections are contests between the candidates of opposing parties.

Three other types of elections are the initiative, the referendum, and the recall. Used in twenty-four states and the District of Columbia, initiatives involve voting on issues (as opposed to voting for candidates). An **initiative** is a process that allows citizens to propose legislation and submit it to the state electorate for popular vote, as long as they get a certain number of signatures on petitions supporting the proposal. A **referendum** is an election whereby the state legislature submits proposed legislation to the state's voters for approval. The third type of election (or "deelection") found in many states is the **recall,** in which voters can remove an incumbent from office by popular vote.

PRESIDENTIAL ELECTIONS

VARIETY ASIDE, NO OTHER U.S. ELECTION can compare to the presidential contest. This spectacle, held every four years, brings together all the elements of politics and attracts the most ambitious and energetic politicians to the national stage. Voters in a series of state primary elections and caucuses select delegates who will attend each party's national convention. After the primary elections (or caucuses) held in the winter and spring and the national convention for each party held in mid and late summer, a final set of fifty separate state elections is held on the Tuesday after the first Monday in November to select the president. This lengthy process exhausts candidates and voters alike, but it allows the diversity of the United States to be displayed in ways a shorter, more homogeneous presidential election process could not.

Timeline

The Initiative and Referendum

The Living Constitution

No Person shall be a Representative who shall not have attained to the Age of twenty five Years.

—Article I, section 2

No Person shall be a Senator who shall not have attained to the Age of thirty Years.

—Article I, section 3

. . . neither shall any person be eligible to that Office [of the Presidency] who shall not have attained to the Age of thirty five Years.

—Article II, section 1

There was little debate among the Framers at the Constitutional Convention that elected officials should have enough experience in life and in politics before being qualified to take on the responsibility of representing the interests of the nation and of their district or state. However, a minor, who is not subject to the authority of the state in the same way as a full citizen, also could not possibly be qualified to possess it. Notice how the age limits scale upward according to the amount of deliberation and decision making that the position involves. House members only need to be twenty-five, but the president must be at least thirty-five, giving whoever would run for that office plenty of time to acquire the political experience necessary for the central role he or she will play.

State governments usually employ similar requirements. For instance, Virginia requires that candidates for the state's House of Delegates and Senate be at least twenty-one years old, while candidates for the state's three most powerful executive positions—governor, lieutenant governor, and attorney general—must be at least thirty years old. South Dakota, however, sets the minimum age limit for its most important executive officers—governor and lieutenant governor—at twenty-one.

Amazingly, the Framers did not impose an age limit on Supreme Court justices, not even the chief justice. Perhaps the Framers thought that the president was not likely to appoint minors to the bench, or at least that they would not be approved by the Senate. Looking at the nine justices today, it is obvious that the Framers were right not to worry.

The Nomination Campaign

nomination campaign
That part of a political campaign aimed at winning a primary election.

front-loading
The tendency of states to choose an early date on the primary calendar.

The **nomination campaign** is that part of a political campaign aimed at winning a primary election. Candidates for a party's presidential nomination try to get as many delegates as they can, as early as they can. The primary schedule has also been altered by a process called **front-loading,** the tendency of states to choose an early date on the primary calendar. Seventy percent of all the delegates to both party conventions are now chosen before the end of March. This trend is hardly surprising, given the added press emphasis on the first contests and the voters' desire to cast their ballots before the competition is decided.

Front-loading has also had other important effects on the nomination process. First, a front-loaded primary schedule generally benefits the front-runner, since opponents have little time to turn the contest around once they fall behind. Second, front-loading gives an advantage to the candidate who can raise the bulk of the money before the nomination season begins, since there will be little opportunity to raise money once the primaries begin and since candidates will need to finance campaign efforts simultaneously in many states. In 2004, Internet fund-raising emerged as a means to soften this advantage; its use will continue and expand in future elections. This trend, however, did not help Howard Dean, the early front-runner and major fundraiser in the 2004 Democratic primaries. Finally, front-loading has amplified the importance of the "invisible primary"—the year or so prior to the start of the official nomination season when candidates begin raising money and unofficially campaigning.[3]

Photo courtesy: Matt York/AP/Wide World Photos

■ Democratic presidential candidates are introduced to the audience prior to an October 2003 debate in Phoenix, Arizona.

Selecting the Delegates.   Every four years, Americans not only get to vote for the president, but they also get to participate in the selection of candidates. Each state has its own laws concerning the nomination of presidential candidates, but basically, there are two methods: primaries and caucuses. Primaries are like general elections. Caucuses, in contrast, are small conventions where party members meet, listen to candidates or their representatives, and then vote for delegates to represent them at the national convention. Because only a small proportion of delegates are selected in these state caucuses, most states use presidential primaries, be they open or closed.

Who Are the Delegates?.   In one sense, party conventions are microcosms of the United States: every state, most localities, and all races and creeds find some representation there. (For some historic "firsts" for women at the conventions, see Table 12.1.) Yet, delegates are an unusual and unrepresentative collection of people in many ways. It is not just their exceptionally keen interest in politics that distinguishes delegates. These activists also are ideologically more to the right or left than most Americans and financially better off than most.

The delegates in each party clearly exemplify the philosophical gulf separating the two parties. Democratic delegates are well to the left of their own party's voters on most issues, and even farther away from the opinions held by the nation's electorate as a whole. Republican delegates are a mirror image of their opponents—considerably to the right of GOP voters and even more so of the entire electorate. Although it is sometimes said that the two major parties do not present U.S. citizens with a clear choice of candidates, it is possible to argue the contrary. Our politics are perhaps too polarized, with the great majority of Americans, overwhelmingly moderates and pragmatists, left underrepresented by parties too fond of ideological purity.

TABLE 12.1 Historic Moments for Women at the Conventions

Since 1980, Democratic Party rules have required that women constitute 50 percent of the delegates to its national convention. The Republican Party has no similar quota. Nevertheless, both parties have tried to increase the role of women at the convention. Some "firsts" and other historic moments for women at the national conventions include:

1876	First woman to address a national convention
1890	First women delegates to conventions of both parties
1940	First woman to nominate a presidential candidate
1951	First woman asked to chair a national party
1972	First woman keynote speaker
1984	First major-party woman nominated for vice president (Democrat Geraldine Ferraro)
1996	Wives of both nominees make major addresses
2000	Daughter of a presidential candidate nominates her father
2004	Both candidates introduced by their daughters

Source: Center for American Women in Politics.

■ President George W. Bush and Vice President Dick Cheney. In 2004, Bush faced no national opposition for the Republican Party presidential nomination. This allowed Bush and Cheney to begin preparing for the general election campaign in early 2004.

Photo courtesy: M. Spencer Green/AP/Wide World Photos

The Party Conventions.   The seemingly endless nomination battle does have a conclusion: the national party convention held in the summer of presidential election years. The out-of-power party traditionally holds its convention first, in late July, followed in mid-August by the party holding the White House. Preempting an hour or more of prime-time network television for four nights and monopolizing the cable networks such as CNN, Fox News, and C-SPAN, these remarkable conclaves are difficult for the public to ignore, giving the civically engaged viewer a chance to learn about the candidate and the apathetic viewer something to complain about.

The conventions once were much more. They were composed of party members that made actual decisions, where party leaders held sway and deals were sometimes cut in "smoke-filled rooms" to deliver nominations to little-known contenders called "dark horses." This era predated the modern emphasis on reform, primaries, and proportional representation, all of which have combined to make conventions the place where parties choose one of several nominees who has been preselected through the various primaries and caucuses.[4]

The General Election Campaign

general election campaign
That part of a political campaign aimed at winning a general election.

After earning the party's nomination, candidates embark on the **general election campaign.** They must seek the support of groups and voters and decide on the issues they will emphasize. When courting interest groups, a candidate seeks both money and endorsements, although the results mainly are predictable: liberal, labor, and minority groups usually back Democrats, whereas conservative and business organizations support Republicans. The most active groups often coalesce around emotional issues such as abortion and gun control, and these organizations can produce a bumper crop of money and activists for favored candidates.

Virtually all candidates adopt a brief theme, or slogan, to serve as a rallying cry in their quest for office. Most slogans can fit many candidates ("She thinks like us," "He's on our side," "She hears you," "You know where he stands"). Candidates try to avoid controversy in their selection of slogans, and some openly eschew ideology. (An ever-popular one of this genre is "Not left, not right—forward!") The clever candidate also attempts to find a slogan that cannot be easily lampooned.

Comparative
Comparing Political
Campaigns

The Personal Campaign

In the effort to show voters that they are hardworking, thoughtful, and worthy of the office they seek, candidates try to meet personally as many citizens as possible in the course of a campaign. To some degree, these **personal campaign** events are symbolic, especially for presidential candidates, since it is possible to have direct contact with only a limited number of people.

In a typical campaign, a candidate for high office maintains an exhausting schedule. The day may begin at 5 a.m. at the entrance gate to an auto plant with an hour or two of handshaking, followed by similar glad-handing at subway stops until 9 a.m. Strategy sessions with key advisers and preparation for upcoming presentations and forums may fill the rest of the morning. A luncheon talk, afternoon fundraisers, and a series of television and print interviews crowd the afternoon agenda. Cocktail parties are followed by a dinner speech, perhaps telephone or neighborhood canvassing of voters, and a civic-forum talk or two. More meetings with advisers and planning for the next day's events can easily take a candidate past midnight. Following only a few hours of sleep, the candidate starts all over again. After months of this grueling pace, the candidate may be functioning on automatic pilot and sometimes momentarily may be unable to think clearly.

Beyond the strains this fast-lane existence adds to a candidate's family life, the hectic schedule leaves little time for reflection and long-range planning. Is it any wonder that under these conditions many candidates commit gaffes?

personal campaign
That part of a political campaign concerned with presenting the candidate's public image.

The Organizational Campaign

The **organizational campaign** is the behind-the-scenes business effort that funds and supports the candidate. It raises money from supporters, which is then spent on the campaign infrastructure: a staff, offices,

organizational campaign
That part of a political campaign involved in fund-raising, literature distribution, and all other activities not directly involving the candidate.

television advertising production and airing, direct mail, fund-raising dinners, and public opinion polling that helps reveal to campaign managers which issues the public cares about.

Also, volunteers walk the streets of their neighborhoods, going door to door to solicit votes, while other volunteers use computerized telephone banks to call targeted voters with scripted messages. Both contact methods are termed **voter canvass.** Most canvassing, or direct solicitation of support, takes place in the month before the election, when voters are paying attention. Close to Election Day, the telephone banks begin vital **get out the vote (GOTV)** efforts reminding supporters to vote and arranging for their transportation to the polls if necessary. As the media become less effective in encouraging political education and participation, candidates increasingly realize the value of identifying base voters and getting them to the polls.

Depending on the level of the office sought, the organizational staff can consist of a handful of volunteers or hundreds of paid specialists supplementing and directing the work of thousands of volunteers. Presidential campaign organizations have the most elaborate structure. At the top of the chart is the **campaign manager,** who coordinates and directs the campaign. The campaign manager is the person closest to the candidate, the person who delivers the good news and the bad news about the condition of the campaign and makes the essential day-to-day decisions, such as whom to hire and when to air which television ad.

Campaign consultants are the private-sector professionals and firms who sell to a candidate the technologies, services, and strategies required to get that candidate elected to his or her office of choice. Their numbers have grown exponentially since they first appeared in the 1930s, and their specialties and responsibilities have increased accordingly, to the point that they are now an obligatory part of campaigns at almost any level of government. Candidates hire generalist consultants to oversee their entire campaign from beginning to end. Alongside the generalist consultant are more specialized consultants who focus on the new and complex technologies for only one or two areas, such as fund-raising, polling, mass mailings, media relations, advertising, and speech writing. Key positions include the **finance chair,** who is responsible for bringing in the large contributions that fund the campaign, the **pollster,** who takes public opinion surveys to learn what issues voters want candidates to address in speeches, and the **direct mailer,** who supervises direct-mail fund-raising.

Many critics claim that consultants strip campaigns of substance and reduce them to a clever bag of tricks for sale. Others insist that despite the prevalence of consultants, running for office is still the bread and butter of campaigns: shaking hands, speaking persuasively, and listening to the voters. Voters, they say, are smart enough to tell the difference between a good candidate and a bad one, regardless of the smoke and mirrors erected by their consultants. Nevertheless, consul-

voter canvass
The process by which a campaign reaches individual voters, either by door-to-door solicitation or by telephone.

get out the vote (GOTV)
A push at the end of a political campaign to encourage supporters to go to the polls.

campaign manager
The individual who travels with the candidate and coordinates the many different aspects of the campaign.

campaign consultants
Private sector professionals and firms that sell to a candidate the technologies, services, and strategies required to get that candidate elected to office.

Simulation
You Are a Presidential Campaign Consultant

finance chair
A professional who coordinates the fund-raising efforts for the campaign.

pollster
A professional who takes public opinion surveys that guide political campaigns.

direct mailer
A professional who supervises a political campaign's direct-mail fund-raising strategies.

tants do make a difference. In campaigns for the U.S. House of Representatives, for example, the use of professional campaign consultants has been shown to have a positive impact on candidates' fund-raising ability[5] and on candidates' final vote shares.[6]

The Media Campaign

The media campaign is as complex as it is essential for a candidate to win election. The various elements that make up the media (television, radio, the Internet, newspapers, and magazines) are the best methods available to candidates to get their message to every potential voter. Candidates employ a network of staff to manage the different kinds of media.

The **communications director** develops the overall media strategy for the candidate, carefully blending press coverage with paid TV, radio, and mail media. A candidate cannot merely buy an election by blasting major media markets with political advertising. That is both an inefficient and extremely expensive method. A candidate cannot rely entirely on the attention of the press, since the press interests are capricious and never align with those of the candidate. The communications director develops a strategy of using both paid and free media to market a candidate most effectively to voters, such as airing negative ads in areas recently visited by the competing candidate.

The **press secretary** is charged with interacting and communicating with journalists on a daily basis. We are all familiar with the campaign press secretary, since it is his or her job to be quoted in the newspapers or on TV, explaining the candidate's positions or reacting to the actions of the opposing candidate. Good news is usually announced by the candidate. Bad news, including attacks from the other side, is the preserve of the press secretary—better to have someone not on the ballot doing the dirty work of the campaign.

Media consultants are outside contractors who design TV and radio and mail advertisements. Candidates and their media consultants decide on how to use the **paid media** (such as television advertising) that the campaign creates and pays to have disseminated, and the **free media** (such as newspaper articles) that result from stories about the campaign that the media choose to broadcast. **Positive ads** stress the candidate's qualifications, family, and issue positions with no direct reference to the opponent. These are usually favored by the incumbent candidate. **Negative ads** attack the opponent's character and platform and may not even mention the candidate who is paying for the airing—except for the candidate's brief, legally required statement that he or she approved the ad. **Contrast ads** compare the records and proposals of the candidates, with a bias toward the sponsor. Most paid advertisements are short **spot ads** that range from ten to sixty seconds long, though some may run as long as thirty minutes and take the form of documentaries.

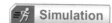

Simulation

You Are a Professional Campaign Manager

Simulation

You Are a Media Consultant to a Political Candidate

communications director
This person develops the overall media strategy for the candidate, carefully blending the free press coverage with the paid TV, radio, and mail media.

press secretary
The individual charged with interacting and communicating with journalists on a daily basis.

media consultant
A professional who produces political candidates' television, radio, and print advertisements.

paid media
Political advertisements purchased for a candidate's campaign.

free media
Coverage of a candidate's campaign by the news media.

positive ad
Advertising on behalf of a candidate that stresses the candidate's qualifications, family, and issue positions, without reference to the opponent.

negative ad
Advertising on behalf of a candidate that attacks the opponent's platform or character.

contrast ad
Ad that compares the records and proposals of the candidates, with a bias toward the sponsor.

spot ad
Television advertising on behalf of a candidate that is broadcast in sixty-, thirty-, or ten-second duration.

■ Right-wing 1964 Republican candidate Barry Goldwater's famous slogan, "In your heart, you know he's right," was quickly lampooned by incumbent Democratic opponent President Lyndon B. Johnson's campaign as "In your guts, you know he's nuts."

Photo courtesy: Bettmann/Corbis

inoculation ad

Advertising that attempts to counteract an anticipated attack from the opposition before the attack is launched.

Although negative advertisements have grown dramatically in number during the past two decades, they have been a part of American campaigns for some time. In 1796, for example, Federalists portrayed presidential candidate Thomas Jefferson as an atheist and a coward. Before the 1980s, well-known incumbents usually ignored negative attacks from their challengers, believing that the proper stance was to be above the fray. But, after some well-publicized defeats of incumbents in the early 1980s in which negative television advertising played a prominent role,[7] incumbents began attacking their challengers in earnest. The new rule of politics became "An attack unanswered is an attack agreed to." In a further attempt to stave off brickbats from challengers, incumbents began anticipating the substance of their opponents' attacks and airing **inoculation ads** early in the campaign to protect themselves in advance from the other side's spots. (Inoculation advertising attempts to counteract an anticipated attack from the opposition before such an attack is launched.)

During the campaign season, the news media constantly report political news. What they report is largely based on news editors' decisions of what is newsworthy, what is "fit to print." Often, the press will simply report what candidates are doing, such as giving speeches, holding fundraisers, or meeting with party leaders. Even better, the news media can report on a candidate's success, perhaps giving that candidate the brand of a "winner," making him or her that much more difficult to beat. On the other hand, the reporters may run stories on a candidate's darker past, such as run-ins with the law or a failed marriage.

Many analysts observe that not all media practices in campaigns are conducive to fair and unbiased coverage. For example, the news media often regard political candidates with suspicion—looking for possible deception even when a candidate is simply trying to share his or her message with the public. This attitude makes it difficult for candidates to appear in a positive light or to have a genuine opportunity to explain their basic ideas via the news media without being on the defensive. In addition, many studies have shown that the media are obsessed with the horse-race aspect of politics—who's ahead, who's behind, who's gaining—to the detriment of the substance of the candidates' issues and ideas. Public opinion polls, especially tracking polls, many of them taken by the news outlets themselves, dominate coverage, especially on network television, where only a few minutes a night are devoted to politics.

The Electoral College: How Presidents Are Elected

The campaign for the presidency has many facets, but the object of the exercise is clear: winning a majority of the **Electoral College.** This uniquely American institution consists of representatives of each state who cast the final ballots that actually elect a president (see Table 12.2). The total number of **electors**—the members of the Electoral College—for each state is equivalent to the number of senators and representatives that state has in the U.S. Congress. And, the District of Columbia is accorded three electoral votes.

Electoral College
Representatives of each state who cast the final ballots that actually elect a president.

elector
Member of the Electoral College chosen by methods determined in each state.

■ Presidential debates have come a long way—at least in terms of studio trappings—since the ill-at-ease Richard M. Nixon was visually bested by John F. Kennedy in the first televised debate. John Kerry's strong performances in the three presidential debates of 2004 helped him stay within striking distance of President George W. Bush's lead going into the final weeks of the campaign.

Photos courtesy: left, Bettmann/Corbis; right, Rick Wilking/Reuters/Corbis

The Electoral College was the result of a compromise between Framers such as Roger Sherman and Elbridge Gerry, who argued for selection of the president by the Congress, and those such as James Madison, James Wilson, and Gouverneur Morris, who favored selection by direct popular election. Since there were no mass media in those days, most citizens were unlikely to know much about candidates for national election. But, the electors would be men of character with a solid knowledge of national politics who were able to identify, agree on, and select prominent national statesmen.

There are three essentials to understanding the Framers' design of the Electoral College. The system was constructed: (1) to work without political parties; (2) to cover both the nominating and electing phases of presidential selection; and, (3) to produce a nonpartisan president.

The Electoral College machinery was somewhat complex. Each state designated electors. Each elector had two votes to cast in the Electoral College's selection for the president and vice president, although electors could not vote for more than one candidate from their state. The rules of the college stipulated that each elector was allowed to cast only one vote for any single candidate, and by extension obliged each elector to use his second vote for another candidate. There was no way to designate votes for president or vice president; instead, the candidate with the most votes (provided he also received votes from a majority of the electors) won the presidency and the runner-up won the vice pres-

Visual Literacy
American Electoral Rules: How Do They Influence Campaigns?

TABLE 12.2   How the Electoral College Works

1. Each state is allotted one elector for each U.S. representative and senator it has. Washington, D.C., receives three electors, the same number of electors as the least populous state. The total number of electoral votes is 538.

2. Mostly, electors are nominated at state party conventions. The electors' names are given to the state's election official.

3. On Election Day, voters in each state cast their ballot for the slate of electors representing their choice of presidential ticket. The electors' names do not usually appear on the ballot.

4. The slate of electors for the presidential ticket that receives the most votes is appointed, and all the electoral votes for that state go to those candidates. (Except for Maine and Nebraska, which each give two at-large delegates to whoever wins the state and the rest to whoever wins in each congressional district.)

5. A candidate needs to win a majority of electoral votes—270—to be elected president. If no candidate wins a majority of electoral votes, the House chooses the president and the Senate chooses the vice president.

6. In December, in a largely ceremonial gesture, the electors cast ballots for president and vice president and are expected to follow the popular vote of their state. On rare occasions, "faithless" electors have voted for another candidate.

7. The votes are counted at a joint session of Congress, and the president officially is elected.

FIGURE 12.1 The States Drawn in Proportion to Their Electoral College Votes

This map visually represents the respective electoral weights of the fifty states in the 2004 presidential election. For each state, the gain or loss of Electoral College votes based on the 2000 U.S. Census is indicated in parentheses. ■

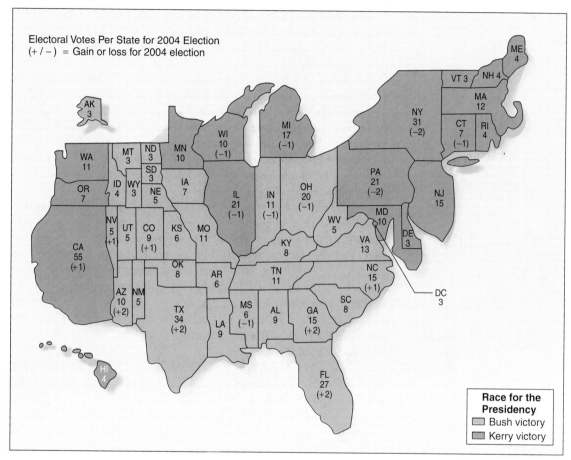

Source: *New York Times* 2004 Election Guide, http://www.nytimes.com.packages/html/politics/2004_ELECTION GUIDE_GRAPHIC/.

idency. If two candidates received the same number of votes and both had a majority of electors, the election was decided in the House of Representatives, with each state delegation acting as a unit and casting one vote. If no candidate secured a majority, the election also would be decided in the House, with each state delegation casting one vote for any of the top five electoral vote-getters. In both these scenarios, the candidate needed a majority of the total number of states for victory. (Figure 12.1 shows a map of the United States drawn in proportion to each state's 2004 Electoral College votes.)

Early Problems with the Electoral College.   The republic's fourth presidential election revealed a flaw in the Framers' Electoral College plan. In 1800, Thomas Jefferson and Aaron Burr were, respectively, the presidential and vice presidential candidates advanced by the Democratic-Republican Party, and supporters of the Democratic-Republican Party controlled a majority of the Electoral College. Accordingly, each Democratic-Republican elector in the states cast one of his two votes for Jefferson and the other one for Burr, a situation that resulted in a tie for the presidency between Jefferson and Burr, since there was no way under the constitutional arrangements for electors to earmark their votes separately for president and vice president. Even though most understood Jefferson to be the actual choice for president, the Constitution mandated that a tie be decided by the House of Representatives. It was, of course, and in Jefferson's favor, but only after much energy was expended to persuade lame-duck Federalists not to give Burr the presidency.

The Twelfth Amendment, ratified in 1804 and still the constitutional foundation for presidential elections, was an attempt to remedy the confusion between the selection of vice presidents and presidents that beset the election of 1800. The amendment provided for separate elections for each office, with each elector having only one vote to cast for each. In the event of a tie or when no candidate received a majority of the total number of electors, the election still went to the House of Representatives; now, however, each state delegation would have one vote to cast for one of the three candidates who had received the greatest number of electoral votes.

The Electoral College modified by the Twelfth Amendment has fared better than the college as originally designed, but it has not been problem free. For example, in the 1824 election between John Quincy Adams and Andrew Jackson, neither presidential candidate secured a majority of electoral votes, once again throwing the election into the House. Although Jackson had more electoral and popular votes than Adams, the House voted for the latter as president. On two other occasions in the nineteenth century, the presidential candidate with fewer popular votes than his opponent won the presidency. In the 1876 contest between Republican Rutherford B. Hayes and Democrat Samuel J. Tilden, no candidate received a majority of electoral votes; the House decided in Hayes's favor even though he had only one more (disputed) electoral vote and 250,000 fewer popular votes than Tilden. In the election of 1888, President Grover Cleveland secured about 100,000 more popular votes than did Benjamin Harrison, yet Harrison won a majority of the Electoral College vote, and with it the presidency (see Table 12.3).

Modern Problems with the Electoral College.   Several near crises pertaining to the Electoral College occurred in the twentieth century. The election of 1976 was almost a repeat of those nineteenth-century

TABLE 12.3   Close Calls in Presidential Elections

It is possible for the candidate who wins the popular vote to lose the election. This has happened four times, including in 1824, when the House decided the election because no candidate won a majority of Electoral College votes.

Election year/ candidates	Popular vote percentage	Electoral votes received	Electoral votes needed for majority
1824			131
John Quincy Adams	→ 30.92%	84	
Andrew Jackson	41.34	99	
Henry Clay	12.99	37	
William H. Crawford	11.17	41	
1876			185
Rutherford B. Hayes	→ 47.95%	185	
Samuel J. Tilden	50.97	184	
1888			201
Benjamin Harrison	→ 47.82%	233	
Grover Cleveland	48.62	168	
2000			270
George W. Bush	→ 47.87%	271	
Al Gore	48.38	266	

Sources: "How the Electoral College Works," *Washington Post* (November 19, 2000): A1. © 2000, Washington Post. Reprinted with permission.

contests in which the candidate with fewer popular votes won the presidency. Even though Democrat Jimmy Carter received about 1.7 million more popular votes than Republican Gerald Ford, a switch of some 8,000 popular votes in Ohio and Hawaii would have secured for Ford enough votes to win the Electoral College, and hence the presidency. Had Ross Perot stayed in the 1992 presidential contest, he could have thrown the election into the House of Representatives. His support had registered from 30 percent to 36 percent in the polls in early 1992. When he reentered the race, some of that backing had evaporated, and he finished with 19 percent of the vote and carried no states. However, Perot drained a substantial number of Republican votes from George Bush, thus splitting the GOP base and enabling Clinton to win many normally GOP-leaning states.

Throughout the 2000 presidential campaign, many analysts foresaw that the election would likely be the closest since the 1960 race between John F. Kennedy and Richard M. Nixon. Few realized, however, that the election would be so close that the winner would not be officially declared for more than five weeks after Election Day, and that a mere 500 votes in Florida would effectively decide the presidency of the United States.

Timeline

And the Winner Is . . .?
Close Calls in
Presidential Elections

Participation
The Electoral College

Given the periodically recurring dissatisfaction expressed by the public, especially in the wake of the 2000 election, reformers have seized the opportunity to suggest several proposals for improving the Electoral College system. Three major reform ideas have developed: (1) abolition (getting rid of the Electoral College completely and selecting the president by popular vote); (2) a congressional district plan in which candidates receive one electoral vote for each congressional district that they win in a state; and, (3) removal of all voting power from human electors but retention of the Electoral College in principle in an attempt to eliminate the problems caused by so-called faithless electors.

Patterns of Presidential Elections

The Electoral College results reveal more over time than simply who won the presidency. They show which party and which regions are coming to dominance and how voters may be changing party allegiances in response to new issues and generational changes.

party realignment
A shifting of party coalition groupings in the electorate that remains in place for several elections.

Party Realignments.   Usually such movements are gradual, but occasionally the political equivalent of a major earthquake swiftly and dramatically alters the landscape. During these rare events, called **party realignments,** existing party affiliations are subject to upheaval.[8] Many voters may change parties, and the youngest age group of voters may permanently adopt the label of the newly dominant party. The existing party cleavage fades over time, allowing new issues to emerge. Until recent times, at least, party realignments in the U.S. experience occurred about thirty-six years apart.

critical election
An election that signals a party realignment through voter polarization around new issues.

Preceding a major realignment are one or more **critical elections,** which may polarize voters around new issues and personalities in reaction to crucial developments, such as a war or an economic depression. With the aid of timely circumstances, realignments take place in two main ways.[9] Some voters are converted from one party to the other by the issues and candidates of the time. New voters may also be mobilized into action: immigrants, young voters, and previous nonvoters may become motivated and then absorbed into a new governing majority, especially if they have been excluded previously.

However vibrant and potent party coalitions may be at first, as they age, tensions increase and grievances accumulate. The majority's original reason for existing fades, and new generations neither remember the traumatic events that originally brought about the realignment nor possess the stalwart party identifications of their ancestors. New issues arise, producing conflicts that can be resolved only by a breakup of old alignments and a reshuffling of individual and group party loyalties. Viewed from historical perspective, party realignments ensure stability by adapting to changes in American politics.

In the entire history of the United States, there have been six party realignments. Three tumultuous eras in particular have produced significant elections. First, during the period leading up to the Civil War, the Whig Party gradually dissolved and the Republican Party developed and won the presidency in 1860. Second, the populist radicalization of the Democratic Party in the 1890s enabled the Republicans to greatly strengthen their majority status and make lasting gains in voter attachments. Third, the Great Depression of the 1930s propelled the Democrats to power, causing large numbers of voters to repudiate the GOP and embrace the Democratic Party. Each of these cases resulted in fundamental and enduring alterations in the party equation.

The last confirmed major realignment, then, happened in the 1928–1936 period, as Republican Herbert Hoover's presidency was held to one term because of voter anger about the Depression. In 1932, Democrat Franklin D. Roosevelt swept to power as the electorate decisively rejected Hoover and the Republicans. This dramatic vote of no confidence was followed by substantial changes in policy by the new president, who demonstrated in fact or at least in appearance that his policies were effective. The people responded to his success, accepted his vision of society, and ratified their choice of the new president's party in subsequent presidential and congressional elections.

A critical realigning era is not the only occasion when changes in partisan affiliation are accommodated. In truth, every election produces realignment to some degree, since some individuals are undoubtedly pushed to change parties by events and by their reactions to the candidates. Research has suggested that partisanship is much more responsive to current issues and personalities than had been believed earlier, and that major realignments are just extreme cases of the kind of changes in party loyalty registered every year.[10]

Secular Realignment.   Although the term realignment is usually applied only if momentous events such as war or economic depression produce enduring and substantial alterations in the party coalitions, political scientists have long recognized that a more gradual rearrangement of party coalitions can occur.[11] Called **secular realignment,** this piecemeal process depends not on convulsive shocks to the political system, but on slow, almost barely discernible demographic shifts—the shrinking of one party's base of support and the enlargement of the other's, for example— or simple generational replacement (that is, the dying off of the older generation and the maturing of the younger generation). According to one version of this theory, termed "rolling realignment,"[12] in an era of weaker party attachments (such as we currently are experiencing), a dramatic, full-scale realignment may not be possible. Still, a critical mass of voters may be attracted for years to one party's banner in waves or streams, if that party's leadership and performance are consistently exemplary.

secular realignment
The gradual rearrangement of party coalitions, based more on demographic shifts than on shocks to the political system.

The decline of party affiliation has in essence left the electorate dealigned and incapable of being realigned as long as party ties remain tenuous for so many voters.[13] Voters shift with greater ease between the parties during dealignment, but little permanence or intensity exists in identifications made and held so lightly. If nothing else, the calendar may indicate the error in realignment theory; if major realignments occur roughly every thirty-six years, then we are long overdue. The last major realignment took place between 1928 and 1936; thus, the next one might have been expected in the late 1960s and early 1970s.

As the trends toward ticket-splitting, partisan independence, and voter volatility suggest, there is little question that we have been moving through an unstable and somewhat dealigned period at least since the 1970s. The foremost political question today is whether dealignment will continue (and in what form) or whether a major realignment is in the offing. Each previous dealignment has been a precursor of realignment,[14] but realignment need not succeed dealignment, especially under modern conditions.

CONGRESSIONAL ELECTIONS

MANY SIMILAR ELEMENTS are present in different kinds of elections. Candidates, voters, issues, and television advertisements are constants. But, there are distinctions among each kind of election as well. Compared with presidential elections, congressional elections are a different animal.

Unlike major-party presidential contenders, most candidates for Congress labor in relative obscurity. There are some celebrity nominees for Congress, but the vast majority of party nominees are little-known state legislators and local office holders who receive remarkably little coverage in many states and communities. For them, just getting known, establishing name identification, is the biggest battle.

The Incumbency Advantage

incumbency
The condition of already holding elected office.

The current circumstances enhance the advantages of **incumbency** (that is, already being in office), and a kind of electoral inertia takes hold: Those people in office tend to remain in office. Reelection rates for sitting House members range well above 90 percent in most election years, and research shows that district attentiveness is at least partly responsible for incumbents' electoral safety.[15]

Frequently, the reelection rate for senators is as high, but not always. In a bad year for House incumbents, "only" 88 percent will win (as in the Watergate year of 1974), but the senatorial reelection rate can drop much lower on occasion (to 60 percent in the 1980 Reagan landslide, for example). There is a good reason for this lower senatorial reelection rate. A Senate election is often a high-visibility contest; it receives much more publicity than a House race. So, while House incumbents remain protected and insulated in part because few voters pay attention to their little-known challengers, a Senate-seat challenger can become well known more easily and thus be in a better position to defeat an incumbent.

The 2004 congressional elections provided evidence of the tremendous power of incumbency. Although not as turbulent an election as the Republican takeover of Congress in 1994, the results illustrate the disadvantage faced by challengers. Only one incumbent senator, Democrat Tom Daschle from South Dakota, lost a reelection bid, and just seven incumbent House members were ousted. Four of these representatives were defeated in Texas, the result of a redistricting plan.

It is almost foolhardy to challenge a House incumbent unless his or her district has been redrawn. Open seats that occur through resignation, the creation of a new district, or death, however, offer one of the few ways for those with political aspirations to get into the House of Representatives.

Redistricting.   The U.S. Constitution requires that a census, which entails the counting of all Americans, be conducted every ten years. After each U.S. Census, all congressional district lines are redrawn so that every legislator represents about the same number of citizens.

This process of redrawing congressional districts to reflect increases or decreases in seats allotted to the states, as well as population shifts within a state, is called **redistricting.** When shifts occur in the national population, states gain or lose congressional seats through a process called reapportionment. For example, in the 2000 Census, many northeastern states showed a population decline and lost congressional seats, whereas states in the South, Southwest, and West showed great population growth and gained seats.

Through redistricting, which has gone on since the first U.S. Census in 1790, the political party in each statehouse with the greatest number of members tries to ensure that the maximum number of its party members can be elected to Congress. Redistricting often involves what is called **gerrymandering,** a process in which partisan legislators draw oddly shaped districts to achieve their goals. Gerrymandered redistricting plans routinely meet with court challenges across the country. Over the years, the Supreme Court has ruled that:

- Congressional as well as state legislative districts must be apportioned on the basis of population.[16]
- Purposeful gerrymandering of a congressional district to dilute minority strength is illegal under the Voting Rights Act of 1965.[17]
- Race can be a factor in redrawing district lines.[18]

redistricting
The redrawing of congressional districts to reflect increases or decreases in seats allotted to the states, as well as population shifts within a state.

Simulation
You Are Redrawing the Districts in Your State

gerrymandering
The legislative process through which the majority party in each statehouse tries to assure that the maximum number of representatives from its political party can be elected to Congress through the redrawing of legislative districts.

Analyzing Visuals
CONGRESSIONAL ELECTION RESULTS, 1948–2004

Take a few moments to study the table, which indicates whether or not the president's party gained or lost seats in each election since 1948, and then answer the following critical thinking questions: Are there any striking patterns in the outcomes of congressional elections that occur in presidential election years? Are there any striking patterns in the outcomes of congressional elections that occur in nonpresidential (midterm) election years? Drawing on what you've learned from this chapter, how might you explain the patterns in midterm elections?

GAIN (+) OR LOSS (–) FOR PRESIDENT'S PARTY

PRESIDENTIAL ELECTION YEARS			NONPRESIDENTIAL ELECTION YEARS		
President/Year	House	Senate	Year	House	Senate
Truman (D): 1948	+76	+9	1950	−29	−6
Eisenhower (R): 1952	+24	+2	1954	−18	−1
Eisenhower (R): 1956	−2	0	1958	−48	−13
Kennedy (D): 1960	−20	−2	1962	−4	+3
Johnson (D): 1964	+38	+2	1966	−47	−4
Nixon (R): 1968	+7	+5	1970	−12	+2
Nixon (R): 1972	+13	−2	Ford (R): 1974	−48	−5
Carter (D): 1976	+2	0	1978	−15	−3
Reagan (R): 1980	+33	+12	1982	−26	+1
Reagan (R): 1984	+15	−2	1986	−5	−8
G. Bush (R): 1988	−3	−1	1990	−9	−1
Clinton (D): 1992	−10	0	1994	−52	−9[a]
Clinton (D): 1996	+10	−2	1998	+5	0
G. W. Bush (R): 2000	−2	−4	2002	+6	+2
G. W. Bush (R): 2004	+3	+4			

[a]Includes the switch from Democrat to Republican of Alabama U.S. Senator Richard Shelby.

Scandals, Coattails, and Midterm Elections. Scandals may drive an incumbent out of office or make him or her more vulnerable to challengers for the party's nod or in the general election. Moreover, the presidential coattail effect may give a challenger an advantage over an incumbent: successful presidential candidates usually carry into office congressional candidates of the same party in the year of their election. There has been an overall decline in the strength of the coattail effect in modern times, however, as party identification has weakened and the powers and perks of incumbency have grown. (See Analyzing Visuals: Congressional Election Results, 1948–2004.)

Midterm elections, too, present a threat to incumbents. This time it is the incumbents of the president's party who are most in

midterm election
Election that takes place in the middle of a presidential term.

jeopardy. Just as the presidential party usually gains seats in presidential election years, it usually loses seats in off years. The problems and tribulations of governing normally cost a president some popularity, alienate key groups, or cause the public to want to send the president a message of one sort or another. An economic downturn or a scandal can underline and expand this circumstance, as the Watergate scandal of 1974 and the recession of 1982 demonstrated. The 2002 midterm elections, however, marked the first time since 1934 that a first-term president, George W. Bush, gained seats for his party in a midterm election.

Senate elections are less inclined to follow these off-year patterns than are House elections. The idiosyncratic nature of Senate contests is due to their intermittent scheduling (only one-third of the seats come up for election every two years) and the existence of well-funded, well-known candidates who can sometimes swim against whatever political tide is rising.

Also worth remembering is that midterm elections in recent history have a much lower voter turnout than presidential elections. A midterm election may draw only 35 percent to 40 percent of adult Americans to the polls, whereas a presidential contest usually attracts between 50 percent and 55 percent.

CAMPAIGN FINANCE

CAMPAIGN FINANCE REFORM has been a major source of discussion among politicians and pundits in recent years. For the past thirty years, campaign finance has been governed by the provisions of the Federal Election Campaign Act (FECA). The most recent bout of reforms, the Bipartisan Campaign Reform Act of 2002 (BCRA), was sponsored by Senators John McCain (R–AZ) and Russ Feingold (D–WI) in the Senate. The bills passed on Valentine's Day and, in March, President George W. Bush signed BCRA, or what is also called the McCain-Feingold Act, into law. This act has altered the campaign finance landscape in ways we perhaps have yet to discover (see Table 12.4).

Participation

The Debate over Campaign Finance Reform

Included within BCRA was a fast-track provision that any suits challenging the constitutionality of the reforms would be immediately placed before a U.S. district court, and giving appellate powers to the U.S. Supreme Court. The reason for this provision was simple: to thwart the numerous lobbying groups and several high-profile elected officials who threatened to tie up BCRA in the courts until they could find a judge who would kill it. No sooner did Bush sign BCRA than U.S. Senator Mitch McConnell (R–KY) and the National Rifle Association separately filed lawsuits claiming that BCRA violated free speech rights, specifically by equating financial contributions with symbolic political speech.

TABLE 12.4 Contribution Limits for Congressional Candidates Before and After Bipartisan Campaign Reform Act, 2002

Contributions from	Given to Candidate (per election)[a] Before/After	Given to National Party (per calendar year) Before/After	Total Allowable Contributions (per calendar year) Before/After[e]
Individual	$1,000/$2,000	$20,000/$25,000	$25,000/$47,500 each year per two-year cycle
Political action committee[b]	$5,000/$5,000	$15,000/$15,000	No limit/No Limit
Any political party committee[c]	$5,000/$10,000	No limit/No limit	No limit/No limit
All national and state party committees taken together	To House candidates: $30,000 plus "coordinated expenditures"[d] To Senate candidates: $27,500 plus "coordinated expenditures"[d]		

Note: The regulations under the Bipartisan Campaign Reform Act did not take effect until after the 2002 election.
[a]Each of the following is considered a separate election: primary (or convention), runoff, general election.
[b]Multicandidate PACs only. Multicandidate committees have received contributions from at least fifty persons and have given to at least five federal candidates.
[c]Multicandidate party committees only. Multicandidate committees have received contributions from at least fifty persons and have given to at least five federal candidates.
[d]Coordinated expenditures are party-paid general election campaign expenditures made in consultation and coordination with the candidate under the provisions of section 441(a)(d) of the Federal Code.
[e]Some individual contribution limits were indexed for inflation for 2005–06. They will be indexed again in future cycles.

In May 2003, a three-judge panel of the U.S. District Court for the District of Columbia found that the BCRA restrictions on soft money donations violated free speech rights, although the BCRA restrictions on political advertising did not. The decision was immediately appealed to the Supreme Court, which stayed the district court's decision. After oral arguments in September, the Court handed down its 5–4 decision, *McConnell* v. *FEC*, in December, concluding that the government's interest in preventing political party corruption overrides the free speech rights to which the parties would otherwise be entitled. In other words, the Supreme Court very narrowly upheld the BCRA measures restricting speech both in the form of political contributions and in political advertising. There are some serious questions about whether the Court has really solved the problem of campaign finance reform, since the attempt to avoid the corruption that so often plagues a democracy necessarily means limiting the political speech necessary to sustain democracy.

Sources of Political Contributions

In 2004 alone, the Center for Responsive Politics estimates that more than $3.9 billion was spent on the presidential and congressional elections, a 30 percent increase on the $3 billion spent in 2000. The congressional elections account for $2.7 billion, with the majority going to incumbents. As of the last filing before the 2004 election, Democratic incumbents in the House spent an average of nearly $918,879. Republican incumbents in the House spent an average of $1,086,616. Their challengers, in contrast, spent an average of $299,328. These figures exclude money not subject to FEC regulations and independent expenditures, so the amounts are underestimates. (See Table 12.5.)

Given the cash flow required by a campaign and the legal restrictions on political money, raising the funds necessary to run a modern campaign is a monumental task. (Figure 12.2 shows campaign amounts for the 2004 presidential election; see page 450.) Consequently, presidential and congressional campaigns have squads of fundraisers on staff. These professionals rely on several standard sources of campaign money.

Individual Contributions.   Individual contributions are donations from individual citizens. Citizens typically donate because they like the candidate or party or a particular stand on issues they care about, or like to feel involved in the political process, or want access to the candidate.

The maximum allowable contribution under federal law for congressional and presidential elections is $2,000 per election to each candidate, with primary and general elections considered separately. Individuals are also limited to a total of $45,750 in gifts to all candidates combined in each calendar year. Most candidates receive a majority of all funds directly from individuals, and most individual gifts are well below the maximum level.

Finally, individuals who spend over $10,000 to air "electioneering communication," that is, "any broadcast, cable, or satellite communication which refers to a clearly identified candidate for Federal office" that airs within sixty days of a general election or thirty days of a primary election, is now subject to strict disclosure laws. The rationale behind the last regulation is that spending any more on an ad favoring a candidate is effectively the same as a contribution to the candidate's campaign and requires the same scrutiny as other large donations.

Political Action Committee (PAC) Contributions.   When interest groups such as labor unions, corporations, trade unions, and

---

TABLE 12.5   Average Campaign Funds Raised, Spent, and Contributed in 2004 Congressional Races

	Party	No. of Candidates	Average Raised	Average Spent	Average Cash on Hand	Average from PACs	Average from Individuals
Senate	All	192	$2,319,609	$2,100,856	$539,459	$322,257	$1,549,560
	Democrats	79	$2,866,436	$2,611,234	$693,716	$359,463	$1,946,322
	Republicans	96	$2,267,888	$2,047,296	$500, 682	$348,586	$1,482,921
House	All	1216	$512,347	$419,004	$193,979	$168,089	$295,597
	Democrats	555	$484,941	$402,169	$187,423	$162,675	$286,580
	Republicans	618	$570,712	$461,518	$212,262	$184,459	$322,894

Note: All figures are based on FEC reports filed by all candidates through November 2, 2004.

Source: Center for Responsive Politics, www.opensecrets.org.

FIGURE 12.2 Presidential Campaign Funds, 2004 Election. ■

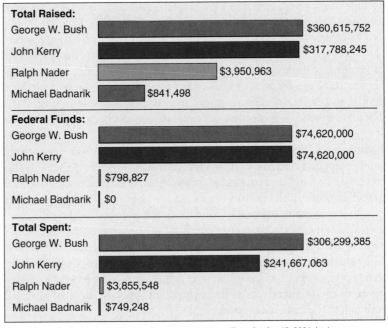

Source: Center for Responsive Politics, http://www.opensecrets.org. (From October 13, 2004 data)

political action committee (PAC)
Federally mandated, officially registered fund-raising committee that represents interest groups in the political process.

Visual Literacy
PACs and the Money Trail

ideological issue groups seek to make donations to campaigns, they must do so by establishing **political action committees (PACs).** PACs are officially recognized fund-raising organizations that are allowed by federal law to participate in federal elections. (Some states have similar requirements for state elections.) Approximately 4,000 PACs are registered with the FEC.

In 2004, PACs contributed $266 million to Senate and House candidates, while individuals donated $657 million. On average, PAC contributions account for 36 percent of the war chests (campaign funds) of House candidates and 18 percent of the treasuries of Senate candidates. (See Figure 12.3.) Incumbents benefit the most from PAC money; incumbents received $233 million, much more than the $33 million given to challengers during the 2004 election cycle. By making these contributions, PACs hope to secure access to the candidate after he or she has been elected in order to influence them on issues important to the PAC, since a candidate might reciprocate campaign donations with loyalty to the cause. Therefore, PACs give primarily to incumbents because incumbents tend to win.

Because donations from a small number of PACs make up such a large proportion of campaign war chests, PACs have influence disproportionate to that of individuals. Studies, in fact, have shown that PACs effectively use contributions to punish legislators and affect policy, at least in the short run.[19] Legislators who vote contrary to the wishes of a PAC see their donations withheld, but those who are suc-

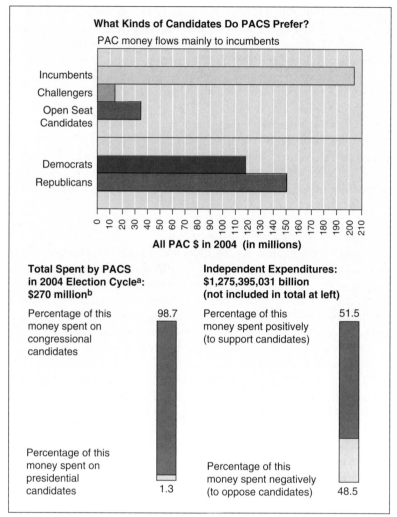

What Kinds of Candidates Do PACS Prefer?

PAC money flows mainly to incumbents

All PAC $ in 2004 (in millions)

Total Spent by PACS in 2004 Election Cycle[a]: $270 million[b]

Percentage of this money spent on congressional candidates — 98.7

Percentage of this money spent on presidential candidates — 1.3

Independent Expenditures: $1,275,395,031 billion (not included in total at left)

Percentage of this money spent positively (to support candidates) — 51.5

Percentage of this money spent negatively (to oppose candidates) — 48.5

[a]The amount is the total from January 1, 2003 to June 30, 2004.
[b]Total amount spent by PACs does not include $21 million in independent expenditures.

Source: Federal Election Commission.

FIGURE 12.3 Expenditures by PACs in the 2004 Election Cycle

Most PAC expenditures support congressional candidates. A majority of the money is spent positively, to support candidates. Only a small fraction is used to attack opponents in presidential campaigns. Notice that PAC spending has a slight bias toward Republican candidates and a strong bias toward incumbents. ■

cessful in legislating in the PAC's wishes are rewarded with even greater donations.[20] (Interest groups are treated in more detail in chapter 11.)

In an attempt to control PACs, BCRA has a limit on the way PACs attempt to influence campaigns. The law strictly forbids PACs from using corporate or union funds for the electioneering communications discussed earlier. PACs can only use corporate or labor contributions for administrative costs. The purpose of the limit is to prevent corporations or unions from having an undue influence on the outcome of elections, as they have in the past, by heavily advertising toward specific audiences in the weeks leading up to elections.

Political Party Contributions.   Candidates also receive donations from the national and state committees of their parties. As mentioned in chapter 11, political parties can give substantial contributions to their congressional nominees. In 2004, the national committees of the two major parties spent over $875 million to support their candidates. In competitive races, the parties may provide 15 to 17 percent of their candidates' total war chests. In addition to helping elect party members, campaign contributions from political parties have another, less obvious benefit: helping to ensure party discipline in voting. One study of congressional voting behavior in the 1980s, for instance, found that those members who received a large percentage of their total campaign funds from their party voted with their party more often than they were expected to.[21]

Member-to-Candidate Contributions.   In Congress and in state legislatures, well-funded, electorally secure incumbents often contribute campaign money to their party's needy incumbent and nonincumbent legislative candidates.[22] This activity began in some state legislatures (notably California), but it is now well established at the congressional level.[23] Generally, members contribute to other candidates in one of two ways. First, some members have established their own PACs—informally dubbed "leadership" PACs—through which they distribute campaign support to candidates. Second, individual members can give up to $2,000 per candidate per election and $10,000 per candidate for each cycle: $5,000 for the primary election and $5,000 for the general election from a leadership PAC.

Candidates' Personal Contributions.   Candidates and their families may donate to the campaign. The Supreme Court ruled in 1976 in *Buckley* v. *Valeo* that no limit could be placed on the amount of money candidates can spend from their own families' resources, since such spending is considered a First Amendment right of free speech.[24] For wealthy politicians, this allowance may mean personal spending in the millions. In 2004, twenty-one candidates for House or Senate seats spent over $1 million of their own money to finance their campaigns; only one of the candidates, Michael McCaul (R–TX), was victorious. The biggest spender by far was Democrat Blair Hull, who invested $28.7 million in his losing efforts against Barack Obama in the Illinois primary. While self-financed candidates often garner a great deal of attention, most candidates commit much less than $100,000 in family resources to their election bids.

public funds
Donations from the general tax revenues to the campaigns of qualifying presidential candidates.

Public Funds.   **Public funds** are donations from general tax revenues. Only presidential candidates (and a handful of state and local contenders) receive public funds. Under the terms of the FEC (which first established public funding of presidential campaigns), a candidate for president can become eligible to receive public funds during the nominating contest by raising at least $5,000 in individual contributions of $250 or less in each of twenty states. The candidate can apply for federal **matching funds,** whereby every dollar raised from individuals in amounts less than $251 is matched by the federal treasury on a dollar-for-dollar basis. Of course, this assumes there is enough money in the Presidential Election Campaign Fund to do so. The fund is accumulated by taxpayers who designate $3 of their taxes for this purpose each year when they send in their federal tax returns. (Only about 20 percent of taxpayers check off the appropriate box, even though participation does not increase their tax burden.)

For the general election, the two major-party presidential nominees can accept a $75 million lump-sum payment from the federal government after the candidate accepts his or her nomination. If the candidate accepts the money, it becomes the sole source for financing the campaign. A candidate could refuse the money and be free from the spending cap the government attaches to it. John Kerry considered doing just that in order to help finance general election campaign operations. Because the Democratic convention, during which Kerry accepted his nomination, occurred five weeks before the Republican convention, Kerry actually had five more weeks than Bush during which he had to stretch out the $75 million the government provided.

matching funds
Donations to presidential campaigns from the federal government that are determined by the amount of private funds a qualifying candidate raises.

Independent Expenditures.   Because of two Supreme Court decisions, individuals, PACs, and now political parties may spend unlimited amounts of money directly advocating the election or defeat of a candidate as long as these expenditures are not made in coordination with the candidate's campaign.[25] For example, a group may create and run television advertisements urging voters to support or defeat its candidate. However, because independent expenditure advertisements expressly advocate the election or defeat of a specific federal candidate, they must be paid for with **hard money**—that is, with money raised under the FECA guidelines.

hard money
Legally specified and limited contributions that are clearly regulated by the Federal Election Campaign Act and by the Federal Election Commission.

The Internet.   The Internet, like campaign finance reform, has the potential to alter radically the way candidates raise funds for their campaigns. After all, making an online appeal for campaign contributions costs significantly less than raising funds through expensive direct-mail campaigns or pricey fund-raising events. Nevertheless, the potential weaknesses of Internet fund-raising are unlikely to stop candidates from experimenting with it. Former Republican presidential candidate John McCain became the first political candidate to raise over $1 million online in forty-eight hours after his victory in the New Hampshire primary in 2000. The Internet converted McCain's momentum into

Participation
Democracy and the Internet

money and volunteers virtually overnight. McCain eventually took in over $5 million online—nearly 25 percent of his total contributions.

The Internet also promises to create headaches for the Federal Election Commission. The FEC had to rule on issues such as whether a business site link to a campaign site constitutes in-kind contribution from the business to the campaign, and whether funds raised online by presidential candidates are eligible to be matched with public funds from the Presidential Election Campaign Fund. (In the first case, the FEC ruled yes; in the second case, it ruled no.) Clearly, these issues are only the beginning of a seemingly limitless plethora of concerns regarding the Internet and campaign finance which the FEC will be asked to address. Campaign finance experts question whether the agency has the resources to regulate and monitor the newly unfolding campaign activity on the Internet.[26]

soft money
The virtually unregulated money funneled by individuals and political committees through state and local parties.

Soft Money and Issue Advocacy Advertisements.   Soft money is campaign money raised and spent by political parties to pay for expenses—such as overhead and administrative costs—and grassroots activities such as political education and GOTV efforts. Soft-money donations are now prohibited under BCRA. The last election cycle for the parties to use soft money was 2001–2002, and the amount raised, nearly $430 million for Republican and Democrats combined, highlights why the reform seemed necessary. Republicans raised $219 million in soft money from pharmaceutical, insurance, and energy companies. Democrats came in just under $211 million in soft money from unions and law firms.[27] With soft money banned, wealthy donors and interest groups now lack the privileged and potentially corrupting influence on parties and candidates. Like every other citizen, they must donate within the hard money limits placed on individuals and PACs.

Future Campaign Finance Reform

Despite the overblown promises of campaign finance nirvana by some of those pushing the McCain-Feingold Bipartisan Campaign Reform Act, many problems remain in this complicated area of politics and constitutional law. For example, much of the money once given as soft money has shown up in the new **527 political committees** (the number 527 comes from the provision of the Internal Revenue tax code that gives life to these committees).

527 political committee
A group that organizes for political fund-raising; named after the provision of the tax code that permits their creation.

The 527s exist on all sides of the political fence, though the Democrats aggressively pursued them in 2004. Two of the largest Democratic committees are the Media Fund and Americans Coming Together (ACT), both run by allies of presidential nominee John Kerry and raising millions of dollars from people, such as billionaire George Soros, who desired to see President George W. Bush defeated. These committees bought TV, radio, and print advertising to sell their message, focusing on the battleground or "swing" states that were not firmly in the Bush or Kerry camps.

Even though most political observers predicted that President Bush would easily outspend his Democratic rival in the presidential contest, 527s helped Senator Kerry spend more than the president and also air more TV ads, a stunning development that considerably aided the Democratic campaign. As fund-raising records in almost every category were shattered in 2004, the campaign reform law clearly had no effect on overall spending.

It is easy to see that reformers will once again attempt to reform their reforms. The next target may well be the 527s. Their abolition is highly unlikely—and the money supporting them would simply reappear in some other forum—but there is a need for greater transparency. The 527s are required to have far less disclosure than other forms of finance committees, and that does cry out for a legislative fix. Overall, however, the lesson of McCain-Feingold is obvious. No amount of clever legislating will rid the American system of campaign money. Interested individuals and groups will always give lots of cash. The challenge is to find a way to get that cash disclosed in a timely fashion for the press and the public. As always, disclosure and its sunshine are the ultimate check on potential misbehavior in the realm of political money.

VOTING BEHAVIOR

WHETHER THEY ARE CASTING BALLOTS in congressional or presidential elections, voters behave in certain distinct ways and exhibit unmistakable patterns to political scientists who study them.

Patterns in Voter Turnout

Turnout is the proportion of the voting-age public that votes (see Figure 12.4). About 40 percent of the eligible adult population in the United States votes regularly, whereas 25 percent are occasional voters. Thirty-five percent rarely or never vote. (For the various methods citizens use once they turn out to vote, see Table 12.6.) Some of the factors known to influence voter turnout include education, income, age, race and ethnicity, and interest in politics. (Figure 12.5 shows percentages of registered and nonregistered members of the voting-age public.)

turnout
The proportion of the voting-age public that votes.

**Voting Turnout:
Who Votes?**

Education.   People who vote are usually more highly educated than nonvoters. People with more education tend to learn more about politics, are less hindered by registration requirements, and are more self-confident about their ability to affect public life. Therefore, one might

FIGURE 12.4　Voter Turnout in Presidential and Midterm Elections. ■

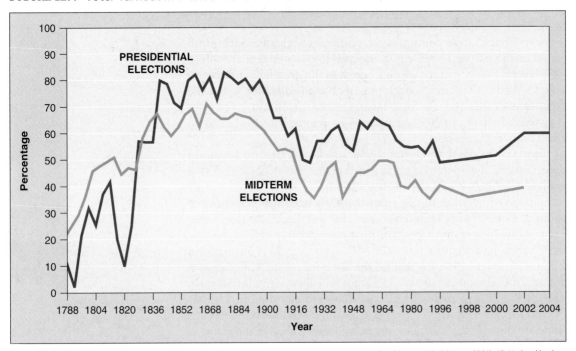

Source: Adapted from Harold W. Stanley and Richard G. Niemi, *Vital Statistics on American Politics,* 2001–2002 (Washington, DC: CQ Press, 2001), 12. Updated by the authors.

TABLE 12.6　How America Votes

The U.S. voting system relies on a patchwork of machines to tally voters' choices, with different methods used even within each state. The following table illustrates the type of voting machines used in each of the ten largest counties in Ohio, one of the important battleground states of the 2004 election.

County	Registered Voters	Equipment
Cuyahoga	861,113	Punch card
Franklin	706,668	Electronic
Hamilton	522,307	Punch card
Montgomery	334,787	Punch card
Summit	334,515	Punch card
Lucas	281,500	Optical scan
Stark	246,562	Punch card
Mahoning	177,445	Electronic
Lorain	166,092	Punch card
Lake	150,137	Electronic

Source: "The e-Book on Election Law," Moritz College of Law at Ohio State University, November 2004, http://moritzlaw.osu.edu/electionlaw/.

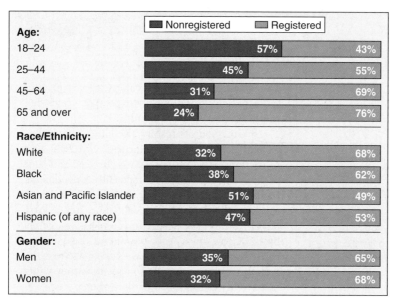

Age:	Nonregistered	Registered
18–24	57%	43%
25–44	45%	55%
45–64	31%	69%
65 and over	24%	76%
Race/Ethnicity:		
White	32%	68%
Black	38%	62%
Asian and Pacific Islander	51%	49%
Hispanic (of any race)	47%	53%
Gender:		
Men	35%	65%
Women	32%	68%

FIGURE 12.5 Nonvoters
Note the number of nonvoters who are registered but do not vote. ◼

Source: U.S. Census Bureau, Current Population Survey, July 2004.

argue that institutions of higher education provide citizens with opportunities to learn about and become interested in politics.

Income. There is also a relationship between income and voting. A considerably higher percentage of citizens with annual incomes over $40,000 vote than do citizens with incomes under $10,000. Income level, to some degree, is connected to education level, as wealthier people tend to have more opportunities for higher education, and more education also may lead to higher income. Wealthy citizens are more likely than poor ones to think that the "system" works for them and that their votes make a difference.

By contrast, lower-income citizens often feel alienated from politics, possibly believing that conditions will remain the same no matter for whom they vote. American political parties may contribute to this feeling of alienation. Unlike parties in many other countries that tend to associate themselves with specific social classes, U.S. political parties do not attempt to link themselves closely to one major class (such as the "working class"). Therefore, the feelings of alienation and apathy about politics prevalent among many lower-income Americans should not be unexpected.

Age. A strong correlation exists between age and voter participation rates. The Twenty-Sixth Amendment, ratified in 1971, lowered the voting age to eighteen. While this amendment obviously increased the

SHOULD THE VOTING AGE BE LOWERED TO SIXTEEN?

OVERVIEW: In Baltimore, Maryland, hundreds of sixteen- and seventeen-year-olds have registered to vote. Laws governing elections require only that voters be eighteen the day of the election and not when they register. Interestingly, the addition of these young voters could potentially affect the city's future council elections, which have been historically narrow contests: "in 1979, Kweisi Mfume, now president of the National Association of Colored People, was elected to the city council by three votes."[a]

In California, some legislators have proposed giving partial voting rights to teens; fourteen-year-olds would receive a one-quarter vote and sixteen-year-olds would receive a half vote. Internationally, Germany and Austria have already lowered their voting ages to sixteen. The Electoral Commission in Great Britain recommended in April 2004 that the voting age for British citizens be lowered from eighteen to sixteen. Students and elected officials in Tanzania have made demands to lower the voting age from eighteen, both because

Tanzanians finish their education at fourteen and, sadly, because of falling life expectancy rates due to the African AIDS epidemic.

Throughout its history, the United States has expanded voting rights, starting with removing restrictions based on property ownership and later passing the Fifteenth and Nineteenth Amendments to grant suffrage respectively to African American men and all women. The Civil Rights Act of 1964 put an end to racial restrictions imposed on voters by Jim Crow laws. And, passage of the Twenty-Sixth Amendment lowered the voting age to eighteen. Should we continue to expand voting rights by lowering the voting age still further?

Arguments for Lowering the Voting Age to Sixteen

■ **The government must represent the interests of all Americans, but we cannot guarantee that it will if we do not lower the age limit.** There are issues that uniquely affect young voters that the government can overlook unless teens hold it accountable.

number of *eligible* voters, it did so by enfranchising the group that is least likely to vote. A much higher percentage of citizens age thirty and older vote than do citizens younger than thirty, although voter turnout decreases over the age of seventy, primarily because of physical infirmity, which makes it difficult to get to the polling location. Regrettably, less than half of eligible eighteen- to twenty-four-year-olds are even registered to vote. However, record numbers voted in 2004.

Race and Ethnicity.   Another pattern in voter turnout is related to race: whites tend to vote more regularly than do African Americans. This difference is due primarily to the relative income and educational levels of the two racial groups. African Americans tend to be poorer and have less formal education than whites; as mentioned earlier, both of these factors affect voter turnout. Significantly, though, highly educated

- **There is no magical transformation one undergoes when one turns eighteen.** By sixteen, a person has more or less developed intellectually, and some sixteen-year-olds have more maturity than some adults, so they should not be bound by an arbitrary date.
- **The earlier young people are exposed to politics, the more likely they will participate when they're older.** We should socialize American youth into better citizens by introducing them to the great ceremony of democracy, the election, to try to raise future turnout.

Arguments Against Lowering the Voting Age to Sixteen

- **An ABCNEWS/*Washington Post* poll showed that young voters overwhelmingly favored George W. Bush for the 2004 presidential election.**[b] Thus either young voters strongly favor Republicans, or, more likely, they prefer the incumbent. The last thing we need is to give more advantages to the incumbent.
- **Because voters under eighteen are very likely still dependent on their parents, parents will hold undue influence over their children's votes.** Parents could possibly threaten or bribe their children to vote a certain way and disguise it as everyday parenting.
- **Lowering the voting age will not make a bit of difference in the outcomes of elections.** Most sixteen-year-olds are not interested in politics and would not vote. It likely might be worse if they did, since they would not have a very good idea of what they were doing.

Selected Readings

Patricio Aylwin Azocar, et al., *Youth Voter Participation: Involving Today's Young in Tomorrow's Democracy.* Stockholm: International IDEA, 1999.

Henry A. Giroux, *The Abandoned Generation: Democracy Beyond the Culture of Fear.* New York: Palgrave Macmillan, 2003.

---

[a] Robert Redding Jr., "Baltimore 16-year-olds to Vote," *Washington Times,* August 21, 2003, http://www.washtimes.com/metro/20030820-094324-4992r.htm.

[b] http://abcnews.go.com/sections/politics/US/youth_voters_poll_040315.html.

and wealthier African Americans are as likely to vote as whites of similar background, and sometimes more likely.

Like any voting group, Hispanics and Latinos are not easily categorized and voting patterns cannot be neatly generalized. However, several major factors play out as key decision-making variables: one's point of origin, length of time in the United States, and income levels. Although Hispanics and Latinos share a common history of Spanish colonialism and similar nation building, they differ in political processes and agendas. Despite having U.S. citizenship, Puerto Ricans can vote in a presidential election only if they live on the mainland and establish residency. Cuban Americans are concentrated in south Florida and tend to be conservative and vote for GOP candidates. Mexican American voting patterns are very issue-oriented, divided according to income levels and generation.[28]

Interest in Politics.   Although socio-economic factors undoubtedly influence voter participation rates, an interest in politics must also be included as an important factor for voter turnout. Many citizens who vote have grown up in families interested and active in politics, and they in turn stimulate their children to take an interest. Conversely, many nonvoters simply do not care about politics or the outcome of elections, never having been taught their importance at a younger age.

People who are highly interested in politics constitute only a small minority of the United States. For example, the most politically active Americans—party and issue-group activists—make up less than 5 percent of the country's more than 285 million people. Those who contribute time or money to a party or a candidate during a campaign make up only about 10 percent of the total population. On the other hand, although these percentages appear low, they translate into millions of Americans who contribute more than just votes to the system.

Why Is Voter Turnout So Low?

The United States has one of the lowest voter participation rates of any nation in the industrialized world. In 1960, 62 percent of the eligible electorate voted in the presidential election, but by 2000, despite the closeness of the race and the consequent importance of a single vote, participation only touched 51 percent. In 2004, participation climbed to 60.7 percent. Figure 12.6 shows the most common reasons given for not voting. A number of contributing factors are discussed below.

Too Busy.   According to the U.S. Census Bureau, 21 percent of registered nonvoters surveyed said that they did not vote because they were too busy or had conflicting work or school schedules. Another 15 percent said that they did not vote because they were ill, disabled, or had a family emergency. Although these reasons seem to account for a large portion of the people surveyed, they may also reflect the respondents' desire not to seem uneducated about the candidates and issues or apathetic about the political process.

The Prepared Voter Kit

Difficulty of Registration.   Of those citizens who are registered, the overwhelming majority vote. The major reason for lack of participation in the United States seems to be that a relatively low percentage of the adult population is registered to vote. There are several reasons for the low U.S. registration rates. First, while nearly every other democratic country places the burden of registration on the government rather than on the individual, in the United States the registration process requires individual initiative—a daunting impediment in this age of political apathy. Thus, the cost (in terms of time and effort) of registering to vote is higher in the United States than it is in other industrialized democracies. Second, many nations automatically register all of their citizens to

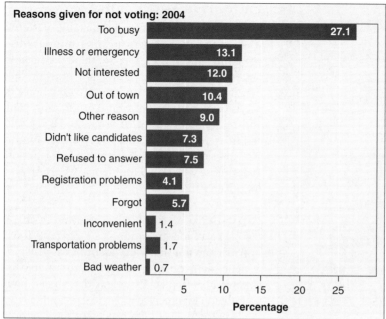

Reasons given for not voting: 2004

Reason	Percentage
Too busy	27.1
Illness or emergency	13.1
Not interested	12.0
Out of town	10.4
Other reason	9.0
Didn't like candidates	7.3
Refused to answer	7.5
Registration problems	4.1
Forgot	5.7
Inconvenient	1.4
Transportation problems	1.7
Bad weather	0.7

Source: U.S. Census Bureau, Current Population Survey, July 2004.

FIGURE 12.6 Why People Don't Vote. According to the U.S. Census Bureau's *Current Population Survey,* "too busy" was the single biggest reason Americans gave for not voting on Election Day. Anger toward politicians and disenchantment with the current political system also drove Americans away from the polls, but critics were heartened by strong 2004 turnout. ∎

vote. In the United States, however, citizens must jump the extra hurdle of remembering on their own to register. Indeed, it is no coincidence that voter participation rates dropped markedly after reformers pushed through strict voter registration laws in the early part of the twentieth century. Correspondingly, several recent studies of the effects of relaxed state voter registration laws show that easier registration leads to higher levels of turnout. When states adopted Election Day registration of new voters, large and significant improvements in turnout occurred among younger voters and the poor.[29]

Difficulty of Absentee Voting.   Stringent absentee ballot laws are another factor in low voter turnout for the United States. Many states, for instance, require citizens to apply in person for absentee ballots, a burdensome requirement given that one's inability to be present in his or her home state is often the reason for absentee balloting in the first place.

Number of Elections.   Another explanation for low voter turnout in the United States is the sheer number and frequency of elections, which few if any other democracies can match. Yet, an election cornucopia is the inevitable result of federalism and the separation of powers, which result in layers of often separate elections on the local, state, and national levels.

Photo courtesy: Ron Edmonds/AP/Wide World Photos

■ Citizen Change was one of many organizations that endeavored to educate, register, and turn out young voters in 2004. Here, Sean "P. Diddy" Combs is seen wearing a shirt featuring the group's much-publicized slogan.

Patterns in Vote Choice

Just as there are certain predictable patterns when it comes to American voter turnout (discussed previously), so, too, are there predictable patterns of vote choice. One of the most prominent and consistent correlates of vote choice is partisan identification. Some other consistent and notable correlates of vote choice include candidate evaluation and issue voting. Figure 12.7 presents some demographic information about those who voted for George W. Bush and John Kerry in 2004.

Party Identification.   As discussed in chapter 11, party identification is a long-term force in American politics. Party identification, which is dependent on a variety of factors noted in chapter 11, often acts as a lens that shapes how an individual perceived a particular candidate.[30] It also affects how one processes information about candidates and political issues.

Candidate Evaluations.   As American elections are increasingly portrayed as horse races with a focus on the candidate and not necessarily the party, individual evaluations of candidates, regardless of their party affiliation, are becoming more and more important. The rise of what many analysts term the candidate-centered campaign has facilitated the importance of the candidate over the party—at least in the minds of some voters.

Voters evaluate candidates in a variety of ways. Often, their family's, friends', or neighbors' appraisals of candidates are key. Of course, the media often are critical in helping voters shape their evaluations of candidates.[31] For others, the race, gender, or ethnicity of a candidate is important, particularly for those concerned with descriptive representation. There have been elections, for example, where gender was a factor, although precise data are not always available to prove the conventional wisdom. Journalists in 1920 claimed that women—in their first presidential election after the passage of the Nineteenth Amendment granted women suffrage—were especially likely to vote for

FIGURE 12.7   Exit Poll Results for the 2004 Election. ■

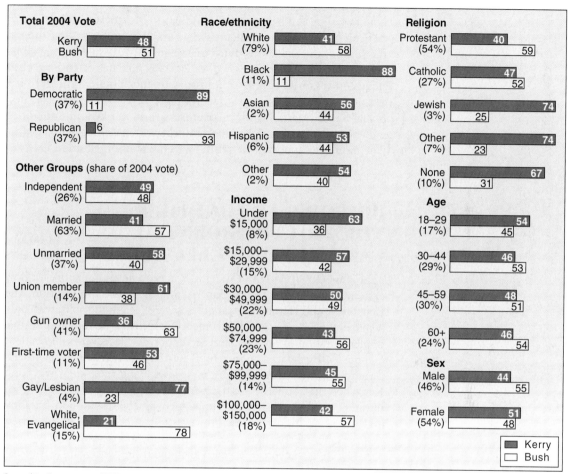

Source: http://www.cnn.com/ELECTION/2004.

Republican presidential candidate Warren G. Harding. In the sexist view of the day, women were supposedly taken in by the handsome Harding's charm. Recent evidence indicates that women act and react differently from men to some candidacies, including those of other women. Since 1980, the so-called gender gap (the difference between the voting choices of men and women) has become a staple of American politics.

Issue Voting.   Many voters are moved by a particular candidate's views on a certain issue or set of issues. However, clear differences are not always present between two candidates. Moreover, it sometimes is difficult to find out a candidate's view on a particular issue, although the Internet has made this much easier. Some issues such as war, abortion, and gun control are easy ones where candidates often have clear stands on yes or no issues. Other issues are much more difficult to use as a means for candidates to attract (or repel) voters. Complex tax issues, Social Security, and health care reform are so murky and difficult to understand that, although important, they often do not help a candidate mobilize supporters or get them to the polls on Election Day.

BRINGING IT TOGETHER: THE 2004 PRESIDENTIAL CAMPAIGN AND ELECTION

THE 2004 PRESIDENTIAL CAMPAIGN may go down in history for how extremely it divided the nation. A month before the election, the Republican and Democratic candidates were even in the polls, with only 3 percent of Americans undecided. Despite his incumbent status, implementation of tax cuts, and reputation for decisiveness, President George W. Bush faced an incredibly heated race against Massachusetts Senator John Kerry. At the most basic level, Americans knew that John Kerry had the knowledge and experience to serve in the highest office in the nation. Many were also unhappy with the situation in Iraq, job losses, and health care costs. However, Americans were casting their first presidential vote in the post-9/11 world, and they had reservations about electing someone whose leadership during a national security crisis had not yet been proven.

The Party Nomination Battle

Any speculation that Senator John McCain, Bush's 2000 Republican primary rival, might challenge the president in 2004 was silenced in May by a Bush campaign ad that featured the Arizona senator praising the president's leadership. Without any significant Republican activity, the Democrats were the focus of media attention for the primary season.

Although some had assumed that Al Gore would make a second attempt at winning the White House, the former vice president announced in December 2002 that he had no intention to do so. The media were fixated on the prospect of a run by Senator Hillary Rodham Clinton (D–NY), but her insistence to the contrary left the field wide open for 2000 vice presidential nominee Senator Joseph Lieberman (D–CT) and three other political veterans: Representative Dick

Gephardt (D–MO), Senator Bob Graham (D–FL), and Senator John Kerry (D–MA).

Early in the primary, the other candidates appeared marginal. Senator John Edwards (D–NC) threw his hat into the ring before even completing his first term in the Senate. Former Senator Carol Moseley Braun (D–IL), the first African American woman in the Senate, had been absent from the national political stage for several years. Former Governor Howard Dean came from the small state of Vermont and had done little during his term as governor to attract national attention. Representative Dennis Kucinich (D–OH) held extreme political beliefs and appeared to be running more to get across an ideological message than with the hope of winning. The Reverend Al Sharpton, an African American activist from New York, appeared primarily interested in gaining national fame rather than winning over primary voters. Retired General Wesley Clark entered late in the race, after being drafted by supporters who believed that his military credentials would render him the best candidate to compete in the fall of 2004.

The ten Democratic candidates spent the spring and summer of 2003 in the typical primary season fashion: fund-raising, debating, giving speeches, and concentrating on the key states of Iowa and New Hampshire. By autumn, Senator Graham had dropped out of the race, citing fund-raising problems. Autumn also brought the unexpected rise of Howard Dean. His solid stance against the invasion of Iraq and harsh criticism of President Bush appealed to Democratic partisans, providing Dean with impressive grassroots support and a large war chest. Although in the spring of 2003 Democratic insiders were predicting John Kerry would emerge as the front-runner, the fall brought Howard Dean the endorsements of party leaders such as Iowa Senator Tom Harkin and former Vice President Al Gore.

Initially, the Democrats' campaigns were focused on contrasting themselves with President Bush. However, as Dean emerged as the apparent front-runner, his rivals began aiming many of their attacks in his direction rather than at the president. The former governor's third-place finish in the Iowa caucuses, behind both John Kerry and John Edwards, may have been partly attributable to these attacks. Others blamed the Iowa upset on the Dean campaign's mismanagement of resources—not spending enough on ads and appearances and over-spending on other items. Perhaps also fatal to Dean's translating partisan excitement into caucus and primary victories was his reputation as having a short temper.

The appeal of Gephardt, Lieberman, and Clark proved narrow, and the poll numbers of Moseley Braun, Sharpton, and Kucinich never reached double digits. After Iowa, the race centered on Kerry and Edwards, with Kerry winning most of the primaries. Edwards dropped out of the race in March, leaving Senator John Kerry of Massachusetts the presumptive Democratic candidate. Democrats appeared united in their determination to defeat George W. Bush in the general election. For this reason, many suggest, they quickly settled on a candidate and channeled their energies toward winning in the fall.

The impact of third parties on the 2004 presidential election was insignificant compared to their effect in 2000. In 2000, Green Party candidate and consumer advocate Ralph Nader gathered 3 percent of the national vote, playing the spoiler in key states, including Florida and New Hampshire. However, Nader's vote totals were 2 percent short of the number needed for the Green Party to receive federal funding for the 2004 election season. Nader sought the presidency again in 2004, but this time he was not the Green Party nominee. The Green Party nominated its own general counsel, David Cobb, for president, while Nader ran as an independent and received the endorsement of the Reform Party. Despite his efforts, by October Nader was officially on the ballot in only the District of Columbia and thirty-four states, nine fewer than in 2000.

Members of the two major parties—not quick to forget Nader's impact on the 2000 presidential election—took part in some highly controversial campaign tactics. It was reported that Republicans donated to his campaign and assisted him in his efforts to get on ballots, with the goal of reducing the vote count for John Kerry. Similarly, there were accusations of obstruction on the part of Democrats, who would most likely benefit from Nader's absence from the ballot.

The Democratic Convention

Twenty days before the start of the Democratic National Convention, Senator John Kerry made public his selection of a vice presidential running mate: North Carolina Senator John Edwards, Kerry's most persistent rival in the Democratic primaries. Not since Ronald Reagan in 1980 had a nominee picked a primary rival as a running mate. This choice also was notable as the earliest vice presidential selection in a modern presidential campaign, which may have been a strategic move by the Kerry campaign to demonstrate party unity and to get the charismatic Edwards on the campaign trail as much as possible.

Whereas other vice presidential hopefuls might have carried a particular state for the Democrats, the choice of John Edwards was viewed as a classic attempt to balance the ticket. When detractors characterized Kerry as a blue-blooded, northeastern liberal, Edwards, a more moderate southern Democrat of humble beginnings, would stand by his side. Edwards was serving only his first term in the U.S. Senate (prior to his presidential bid he had gained prominence as a highly successful trial lawyer); in light of Kerry's long tenure of public service, he was not viewed as bringing particular experience or expertise to the ticket. However, his energy and skill at connecting with voters were thought to be significant assets in the campaign.

With Kerry entering the national convention virtually tied in the polls with George W. Bush, he and Edwards would take this opportunity to define their candidacy, woo new voters, and rally their party faithful at the July 26–29 Democratic National Convention. The convention was held in Boston, Massachusetts, Kerry's home state and solid Democratic territory.

The overarching theme of the Democrats' convention was "Respected Abroad, Stronger at Home." This emphasis on national security was most prominent on the final night of the convention, which featured testimonials from Vietnam War veterans including former Senator Max Cleland (D–GA) and Kerry's swiftboat crewmates. Kerry opened his speech with a salute and the words "I am John Kerry, and I am reporting for duty." In Kerry's speech, foreign affairs and his personal biography vastly overshadowed other topics. The biographical portion was most likely in response to polls that showed Kerry had not yet established a personal connection with Americans. Strategists hoped that his other focus, national security, would convince Americans that he would handle threats of terrorism and the unrest in Iraq and Afghanistan better than President Bush. "In these dangerous days, there is a right way and a wrong way to be strong," Kerry said. "Strength is more than tough words."

Kerry also countered GOP accusations that he was a flip-flopper. "Now, I know that there are those who criticize me for seeing complexities," he said. "And I do, because some issues just aren't all that simple. Saying there are weapons of mass destruction doesn't make it so. Saying we can fight a war on the cheap doesn't make it so. And proclaiming 'mission accomplished' certainly doesn't make it so." In one of his most direct attacks on the integrity of President Bush, Kerry pledged that his leadership would "start by telling the truth to the American people."

Despite what most analysts considered a solid performance, the Kerry-Edwards ticket did not receive any significant post-convention bounce. The Kerry campaign argued that challengers historically run behind incumbents by about 15 points heading into a convention, whereas Kerry entered the convention already polling neck and neck with Bush. John Kerry and John Edwards left Boston with an energized (and financially generous) base, increased familiarity to the electorate, and a *very* close race.

The Republican Convention

It came as no surprise that incumbent President George W. Bush was running for reelection, but there was some pre-convention debate regarding whether Dick Cheney would run as his vice president. Cheney had significantly lower approval ratings with voters than did the president, and some analysts doubted Cheney's objectivity in the

Iraq rebuilding efforts because of his connections to oil company Halliburton. Rumors flew that Secretary of State Colin Powell or Arizona Senator John McCain might be asked to take over Cheney's job. Other speculation centered on Secretary of Homeland Security Tom Ridge, the former governor of Pennsylvania. The Bush campaign, however, continuously affirmed that Cheney would remain on the ticket and that he was viewed as an asset to the campaign and administration. Cheney, a conservative from Wyoming who had served in the U.S. House of Representatives and in previous Republican administrations, was thought to bring vast foreign and domestic policy experience and a certain *gravitas* to the administration. McCain, Powell, or Ridge might win some moderates' votes or even a key state, but to change vice presidents between terms would have been shocking and politically risky.

The Republican National Convention was held from August 30 to September 2 in New York City, one of the most heavily liberal, Democratic locales in the nation and most certainly Kerry territory. It was clear that the GOP picked New York City not to win over its residents, but to use the symbolism of the 9/11 terrorist attacks to their advantage. By bringing voters back to a time when they gave President Bush enormously high approval ratings, and reminding them of the post-9/11 era of heightened homeland security, the Republican Party hoped to build on its perceived strength in issues relating to national defense.

Under the theme "A Nation of Courage," the convention showcased moderate Republicans. The right-wing branch of the Republican Party that had captured the stage at past conventions—Pat Buchanan, Jerry Falwell, Pat Robertson, and Ralph Reed—would stand aside as the more moderate Arnold Schwarzenegger, Rudy Giuliani, and John McCain spoke on behalf of their party and President Bush. The convention would be a delicate balancing act between reaching out to swing voters (who were charmed in 2000 by Bush's "compassionate conservative" agenda) without alienating the socially conservative Republican base.

In his speech accepting the party's nomination, George W. Bush vowed to stay the course on terrorism. More specifically, Bush said that his second term would prioritize simplifying the federal tax code, reducing federal regulations, revamping labor laws, providing incentives for small businesses to provide health care, increasing funding for job training, revamping Social Security, and placing limits on lawsuits. Although he highlighted these types of issues—those which would be most salient with moderate and independent voters—he was careful to assure his conservative base that he would be uncompromising on social issues such as abortion and same-sex marriage. Bush also took advantage of his location to reawaken the emotion, unity, and fear surrounding the 9/11 attacks and remind voters of his handling of the crisis. "My fellow Americans, for as long as our country stands, people will look to the resurrection of New York City and they will say: here buildings fell, and here a nation rose," he said. "Having come this far, our tested and confident nation can achieve anything." Perhaps the most effective aspect of the president's speech was its simple patriotic appeal. "I will never relent in defending America," he said. "Whatever it takes."

The convention was not only a depiction of the Republican Party's agenda and campaign strategy, but also a vivid demonstration of how polarized the nation had become this election season. Bush's speech was interrupted twice by hecklers, who were removed by security guards. Thousands of New Yorkers and protesters from other states took to the streets during the convention for primarily peaceful protests against Bush, the Iraq War, and the Republican Party. One such protest included a three-mile-long symbolic unemployment line, in which each individual held a pink slip, as an expression of anger over the job losses during Bush's presidency. Over 1,700 individuals were arrested for reasons related to their protesting during the convention, and accusations of police misconduct abounded.

Still, the GOP had reason to be pleased with its convention performance, and Bush left New York with a modest 2 percent postconvention bounce in public opinion polls. With only two months left before Election Day, some polls showed Bush had the support of 52 percent of likely voters.

The Presidential Debates

Conventional wisdom suggests that presidential debates rarely alter the complexion of a contest, but with such a tight election, the three meetings between President George W. Bush and Senator John Kerry offered the prospect of a rare decisive event. The weeks preceding these face-offs were filled with traditional jockeying and posturing by the Democrats and Republicans, with much of this back-and-forth activity reported by the media. With suggestions from the nonpartisan Commission on Presidential Debates, the candidates agreed to three presidential debates as well as one vice presidential debate between Vice President Dick Cheney and Senator John Edwards. Each debate lasted ninety minutes and was presented in a different format.

Timeline

Television and
Presidential Campaigns

The first debate took place on September 30, 2004, in Coral Gables, Florida, and focused on foreign policy. The event featured questions posed by the moderator, PBS host Jim Lehrer, with responses and rebuttals by the candidates. Bush hammered at Kerry's inconsistent statements and policies throughout the ninety minutes, while Kerry stressed the failure of the Bush administration to prove that Iraq posed a large enough threat to the United States to have warranted invasion. Television ratings were exceptionally high; the first debate was watched by 62.5 million viewers, the most since 1992. Viewers generally found that Kerry won the debate, and many pundits commented on Bush's lack of energy and focus.

Senator John Edwards and Vice President Dick Cheney faced off in a heated debate on October 5, managing very high television ratings despite airing alongside major league baseball playoffs. When talking about his stance on same-sex marriage, Edwards created some controversy by highlighting the fact that Cheney's daughter Mary was a lesbian, which Kerry also mentioned during his final debate with Bush. Some commentators took this as an attempt to diminish support for Bush among religious conservative voters, but opinion polls showed that almost two-thirds of the public thought Kerry and Edwards' comments were "inappropriate."

A town hall format was used for the second presidential debate, wherein voters found to be undecided by the Gallup polling organization were allow to ask questions of each candidate. Reacting against the criticism that he had seemed tired and unfocused during the earlier debate, Bush was extremely forthright and energetic. Bush even talked over moderator Charlie Gibson of ABC News, who was attempting to ask a follow-up question. Debate questions were selected to give more weight to the Iraq War, but little new emerged about either candidate's positions.

The candidates met for the last time on October 13 in Tempe, Arizona, with the candidates standing behind podiums and answering questions from CBS News anchor Bob Schieffer. For the first time during the debates, the questions were geared toward domestic issues. Bush worked hard to portray Kerry as a liberal, pointing to his voting record on taxes and defense. Kerry attacked the president's record on health care, education, and tax policy. The last debate was considered a win for Kerry by the public and media commentators. With his debate performances, Kerry seemed to even the playing field going into the final days of the campaign. He had entered the debate season down in the polls, and he finished virtually tied with Bush.

The Fall Campaign and General Election

In the final weeks of the campaign, public opinion was deadlocked, and many Americans began to fear that the closeness and uncertainty of 2000 was again possible in 2004. There was even the real possibility of a tie in the Electoral College, which would throw the election into the House of Representatives. The election was especially close in the key battleground states of Ohio, Florida, Pennsylvania, New Mexico, Iowa, and Wisconsin.

Bush stayed on message during the last days of the campaign, emphasizing the need to continue the effort in Iraq and to strongly prosecute the war on terrorism. Kerry continued to hack away at the president's choice to invade Iraq as misguided and without a plan for victory. Kerry especially criticized Bush's handling of foreign relations, mentioning the bad blood in Europe and around the world created out of his Iraq policy. Kerry promised a change in international relations in which the United States would be more attuned to the concerns of allies and would expend more effort building alliances to fight the global war on terrorism. Bush fought back, attempting to paint Kerry as a flip-flopper who constantly switched his positions to better fit public opinion. Despite the efforts of each campaign, public opinion remained very divided in key states like Ohio and Florida.

Election Results

With the painful memories of 2000 still fresh in their minds, network and cable news bureaus proceeded with caution on Election Night. Exit polling in 2000 had proved unreliable, leading many networks to incorrectly call an early victory for Al Gore in Florida. Wary of causing another election debacle, the networks were reluctant to declare an early winner in 2004. As CNN vice president David Bohrman said of the media the day of the election, "I think we're all pretty much in a race not to be first."

For 2004, the major broadcast and cable networks created the National Election Pool (NEP) to gather polling information. Despite the vows of the media to keep a lid on early exit polling, rumors began leaking on the Internet, primarily on Web logs and political sites, of a Kerry lead across the country. By the time polls closed in the eastern states, many thought a Kerry victory to be the result. When the first precincts began reporting, anxiety spread through the Bush campaign. Virginia, which Bush had won by eight points in 2000, seemed initially too close to call. This seemed to confirm the strong Kerry numbers in the exit polling.

As the night wore on, Bush began to show a convincing lead in key battleground states. However, the networks remained extremely cautious, only calling the states that had given a clear and commanding victory to either candidate. By midnight, Bush had won Florida and was ahead in Ohio, but neither candidate had captured the necessary 270 electoral votes. Around 2:00 a.m., Edwards addressed the expectant crowd at the Kerry headquarters in Boston to say that they were not conceding the election. Appearing confident and energetic, Edwards said, "It's been a long night but we've waited four years for this victory, and we can wait one more night." Despite a lead of over 100,000 votes for Bush in Ohio, the Kerry campaign believed there might be enough late votes to turn the tide. Nearly 200,000 provisional ballots had been cast, and the Kerry campaign held on through the night, convinced that these might push them to victory.

Wednesday morning, however, the Bush campaign was confident that they had carried the election, and they informed the Kerry campaign that they would be declaring victory. In his formal concession speech later that day, Kerry emphasized the need for unity after such a divisive campaign. When Bush gave his victory speech, he also spoke of the need for unity, but he emphasized that he considered his victory a ratification by the people of his policies.

Turnout in the 2004 Election

The 2004 election had the highest voter turnout rate since 1968, with 60.7 percent of eligible citizens participating, or an estimated 120 million votes. Fifteen million more Americans voted in 2004 than in 2000, despite long lines that kept some voters waiting for over seven hours. Not surprisingly, the largest turnouts occurred in swing states, where a majority of campaign time and resources were spent. Alabama, Georgia, Florida, South Carolina, Tennessee, Virginia, and the District of Columbia had record turnouts. According to the Committee for the Study of the American Electorate (CSAE), the highest turnout overall for the presidential vote was in Minnesota, where 76.2 percent of eligible voters cast ballots; Wisconsin, New Hampshire, and South Dakota followed closely. Only one state, Arizona, appeared to have a lower turnout in 2004 than in 2000.

The major partisan divide is seen as a primary cause for such high numbers. Emotions about the presidency of George W. Bush made the campaign more bitter and vicious than any election in recent memory but also spurred people to vote. Both parties fielded strong get out the vote efforts, but the Republicans' centralized voter drive bested the Democrats' decentralized activities, which had been farmed out to other groups.

Despite the highly publicized youth vote campaign on both sides, increases among college-attending youth were seen only in the battleground states, and there only slightly. Across the board, young people accounted for 17 percent of the overall turnout, the same percentage as in 2000.

Because of such a polarized election, the third-party factor was almost completely nonexistent in 2004. A little over 1 million votes went to the four minor-party candidates. If the nearly even political division between Republicans and Democrats continues, the role of minor parties will decline. However, the polarization that brought about such large turnouts may prove to be temporary.

The Next Four Years

George W. Bush won the 2004 election with 51 percent of the national vote. His victory, complete with increased Republican majorities in the House of Representatives and the Senate, presents the question "What next?" for several players in American politics. The first is President Bush himself. Although he is the first president to win a majority (rather than a plurality) of the popular vote since his father in 1988, he has inherited a deeply divided electorate. Bush could be a uniter, moderating his positions to bring in lawmakers from the Democratic Party and build a consensus. Or, he could spend the political capital that he has earned to assert conservative policy initiatives that he kept on the back burner during his first term: Social Security reform, medical liability and health care reform, and permanent tax cuts. At the time of this writing, it appears very likely that one of Bush's first efforts will be to make an appointment to the Supreme Court, which will undoubtedly generate intense discussion of divisive social issues such as abortion and same-sex marriage. After an ugly election season, Bush has several reasons to reach out to moderates and liberals, but he also feels buoyed by the GOP's gains in the White House and Congress and would like to take advantage of that mandate and momentum.

Four years are an eternity in politics. President George W. Bush and the Republican majorities in Congress will have to decide how much they want to push through their agenda and make a legacy for themselves, versus how much they want to reach out to lawmakers across the aisle. This balancing act will be based not only on principle—whether it is better to reconcile the country or pass policies that conservatives believe in—but also on electoral self-interest: a desire to expand the GOP's appeal and the need to keep together the conservative base that pushed President Bush to victory in 2004.

As the Democrats emerge from the 2004 defeat, the party finds itself grappling with disappointment and self-doubt, as well as needing to reevaluate its fundamental message and overhaul its leadership. The party is divided over whether to move further left, in the spirit of Howard Dean, the new chair of the Democratic National Committee, or move closer to the middle of the political spectrum in a country that has proven to be more center-right than the Democrats had anticipated. There is further debate over whether the basic political philosophy of the Democrats is out of touch with mainstream America, or if this cycle's leadership failed to articulate a potentially successful ideology. Either way, the Republicans won this battle of the culture war, and the Democrats must hone a message that resonates with the masses of southern and midwestern Americans who decided to keep the president and the GOP in power.

SUMMARY

THERE ARE VARIOUS TYPES of primary elections in the country, as well as general elections, initiatives, referenda, and recall elections. In presidential elections, primaries are sometimes replaced by caucuses, in which party members choose a candidate in a closed meeting, but recent years have seen fewer caucuses and more primaries.

No U.S. election can compare to the presidential contest. This spectacle, held every four years, brings together all the elements of politics and attracts the most ambitious and energetic politicians to the national stage. No longer closed affairs dominated by deals cut in "smoke-filled rooms," today's conventions are more open made-for-television events in which the party platform is drafted and adopted, and the presidential ticket is formally nominated.

Compared with presidential elections, which are played out on the national stage, congressional elections are a different animal. Most candidates for Congress labor in relative obscurity.

Since the 1970s, campaign financing has been governed by the terms of the Federal Election Campaign Act (FECA). Because of the rise of soft money, the FECA was amended in 2002 by the Bipartisan Campaign Finance Reform Act, which was promptly challenged by opponents in the courts.

Whether they are casting ballots in congressional or presidential elections, voters behave in certain distinct ways and exhibit unmistakable patterns to political scientists who study them.

A very competitive Democratic primary season, which had Howard Dean leading for much of the winter, ended in victory for John Kerry in Iowa. Kerry's momentum carried him on to a quick primary victory, and began the unofficial general campaign far in advance of the summer. Public opinion remained extremely close until the conventions, where President Bush benefited from a well-orchestrated effort by the Republicans. Bush's slight lead over Kerry was diminished by a lackluster performance during three televised debates and the end of the race was a photo finish. Turnout was very brisk, and President Bush managed a close but convincing win in both the Electoral College and the popular vote.

KEY TERMS

campaign consultants, p. 434
campaign manager, p. 434
closed primary, p. 426
communications director, p. 435
contrast ad, p. 435
critical election, p. 442
crossover voting, p. 428
direct mailer, p. 434
elector, p. 437
Electoral College, p. 437
finance chair, p. 434
527 political committee, p. 454
free media, p. 435
front-loading, p. 430
general election, p. 428
general election campaign, p. 432
gerrymandering p. 445
get out the vote (GOTV), p. 434
hard money, p. 453
incumbency, p. 444
initiative, p. 428

inoculation ad, p. 436
matching funds, p. 453
media consultant, p. 435
midterm election, p. 446
negative ad, p. 435
nomination campaign, p. 430
nonpartisan primary, p. 428
open primary, p. 426
organizational campaign, p. 433
paid media, p. 435
party realignment, p. 442
personal campaign, p. 433
political action committee (PAC), p. 450
pollster, p. 434
positive ad, p. 435
press secretary, p. 435
primary election, p. 426
public funds, p. 452
raiding, p. 428
recall, p. 428
redistricting, p. 445
referendum, p. 428
runoff primary, p. 428
secular realignment, p. 443
soft money, p. 454
spot ad, p. 435
turnout, p. 455
voter canvass, p. 434

SELECTED READINGS

Abramson, Paul R., John H. Aldrich, and David W. Rohde. *Change and Continuity in the 2000 and 2002 Elections*. Washington, DC: CQ Press, 2003.

Ansolabehere, Stephen, and Shanto Iyengar. *Going Negative: How Political Ads Shrink and Polarize the Electorate*. New York: Free Press, 1997.

Berelson, Bernard R., Paul F. Lazarsfeld, and William N. McPhee. *Voting: A Study of Opinion Formation in a Presidential Campaign*, reprint ed. Chicago: University of Chicago Press, 1986.

Burnham, Walter Dean. *Critical Elections and the Mainsprings of American Politics*. New York: Norton, 1970.

Campbell, Angus, Philip E. Converse, Warren E. Miller, and Donald E. Stokes. *The American Voter*, reprint ed. Chicago: University of Chicago, 1980.

Fenno, Richard F., Jr., *Senators on the Campaign Trail: The Politics of Representation*. Norman: University of Oklahoma Press, 1998.

Fiorina, Morris P. *Retrospective Voting in American National Elections*. New Haven, CT: Yale University Press, 1999.

Herrnson, Paul S. *Congressional Elections: Campaigning at Home and in Washington*, 4th ed. Washington, DC: CQ Press, 2003.

Holbrook, Thomas M. *Do Campaigns Matter?* Thousand Oaks, CA: Sage, 1996.

Jacobson, Gary C. *The Politics of Congressional Elections*, 5th ed. New York: HarperCollins, 2000.

Key, V. O., Jr., with Milton C. Cummings. *The Responsible Electorate*. Cambridge, MA: Harvard University Press, 1966.

Nie, Norman H., Sidney Verba, and John R. Petrocik. *The Changing American Voter*. Cambridge, MA: Harvard University, 1980.

Patterson, Thomas E. *The Vanishing Voter: Public Involvement in an Age of Uncertainty*. New York: Vintage, 2003.

Sabato, Larry J. *Midterm Madness: The Elections of 2002*. Lanham, MD: Rowman and Littlefield, 2003.

Sabato, Larry J. *Overtime! The Election 2000 Thriller*. New York: Longman, 2001.

Sabato, Larry J., Howard R. Ernst, and Bruce A. Larson. *Dangerous Democracy?: The Battle Over Ballot Initiatives in America*. Lanham, MD: Rowman and Littlefield, 2001.

Sabato, Larry J., and Glenn R. Simpson. *Dirty Little Secrets: The Persistence of Corruption in American Politics*. New York: Random House, 1996.

Sundquist, James L. *Dynamics of the Party System: Alignment and Realignment of Political Parties in the United States*. Washington, DC: Brookings Institution, 1983.

Teixeira, Ruy. *The Disappearing American Voter*. Washington, DC: Brookings Institution, 1992.

Thurber, James A., and Candice J. Nelson. *Campaign Warriors: Political Consultants in Elections*. Washington, D.C.: Brookings Institution, 2000.

Verba, Sidney, Kay Lehman Schlozman, and Henry E. Brady. *Voice and Equality: Civic Voluntarism in American Politics*. New York: Belknap, 1996.

Wayne, Stephen J. *The Road to the White House*, 6th ed. New York: Wadsworth, 2003.

WEB EXPLORATIONS

To see how presidential candidates presented themselves in the technology age of the 2004 race, see the official sites of some of the past, and possibly future, candidates.
http://www.johnkerry.com/
http://www.gop.com/

To learn about the functions of the Federal Election Commission, the government agency that monitors and enforces campaign finance and election laws, see
http://www.fec.gov/

To access the most up-to-date, high-quality data on voting, public opinion, and political participation, go to
http://www.gallup.com/

To learn more about the Electoral College, go to
http://www.fec.gov/pages/ecmenu2.htm

To learn more about candidates you have supported in the past or to familiarize yourself with other political candidates so you can make informed choices, go to
http://www.vote-smart.org/

To find out about money and finance in politics, go to
www.opensecrets.org

To look at what voters said before going to the polls and whom they actually voted for, go to
http://www.pollingreport.com/

To get involved and find out what you can do about campaign reform, go to
http://www.house.gov/shays/reform/cfr3526-sum.htm
http://www.cnn.com/2004/ALLPOLITICS/02/24/elec04.prez.bush.marriage/index.html

13

Social and Economic Policy

Photo courtesy: Alex Wong/Corbis

IN 2003, THE UNITED STATES federal government assumed a new major responsibility in the area of health care for its citizens. Following years of agitation and national debate over the high cost of prescription drugs, President George W. Bush signed into law the Medicare Prescription Drug, Improvement, and Modernization Act. Hotly debated in Congress because of its expensive price tag and its controversial aspects, the legislation was hailed by President Bush as "the greatest advance in health care coverage for America's seniors since the founding of Medicare."[1] Seniors choosing to participate received drug discount cards in 2004; the more extensive subsidized prescription benefit would take effect in 2006. The estimated cost for the first ten years of this new government benefit was originally projected at $400 million, but shortly after the legislation was signed, the cost was recalculated to be significantly higher.

This was not the first time the federal government took on health care responsibilities. In 1965, the expensive new programs of Medicare (for the elderly) and Medicaid (for the poor) were established as part of an overall expansion of the governmental programs to promote social welfare. Medicare became a sacred program in the decades that followed, and it achieved considerable success in improving the health of the nation's senior citizens.

However, the absence of a drug benefit as part of Medicare left many older Americans with decreased ability to pay for the prescription drugs they depend on to maintain their well-being. Prescription drug costs rose at double-digit rates in the late 1990s, and it was estimated in 2002 that approximately two-fifths of American retirees were without insurance to help pay for the escalating cost of essential medicine. This led to increasing demand for government action. Letters, calls, and petitions from constituents pressed members of Congress to act on the high cost of prescription drugs. Media stories about older Americans going bankrupt to pay for needed medications pushed the issue further onto center stage, and public hearings by Congress provided an additional spotlight. President Bush signed the prescription drug benefit into law in December 2003.

Does establishing such an expensive new government program serve the national interest? For many seniors—some of whom remained skeptical about the specifics of this new legislation—the answer was "yes": it appeared that the passage of this new benefit meant that Congress and the president finally were addressing a serious concern in their lives. Other observers, however, were more skeptical: where will the money come from to pay the hundreds of billions of dollars this prescription drug benefit will cost just over its first ten years? According to one critic, "The drug benefit is a blatant pitch for the votes of the elderly that worsens the long-term budget outlook and will be paid for by the young."[2] Some opponents of the program argued that the new drug benefit was really a boon to pharmaceutical and insurance companies, and didn't provide enough help to seniors. Was the government being responsible or irresponsible in establishing this new program? What obligation does the government owe to promoting the social welfare of its people?

PUBLIC POLICY IS A PURPOSIVE COURSE of action followed by government in dealing with some problem or matter of concern.[3] Public policies are governmental policies based on law; they are authoritative and binding on people. Individuals, groups, and government agencies that do not comply with policies can be penalized through fines, loss of benefits, or even jail terms. As the phrase "course of action" implies, policies develop or unfold over time. They involve more than a legislative decision to enact a law or a presidential decision to issue an executive order. Also important is how the law or executive order is carried out. Whether a policy is vigorously enforced, enforced in only some instances, or not enforced at all helps determine its meaning and impact.

public policy
An intentional course of action followed by government in dealing with some problem or matter of concern.

In this chapter, we will discuss social and economic policy. Policies in both areas follow similar patterns, in what is called the policy-making process. After considering the nature of the policy-making process, we will examine social welfare policy and the government's involvement in the economy. Finally, we will examine the government's role in stabilizing the economy.

THE POLICY-MAKING PROCESS

POLITICAL SCIENTISTS AND OTHER SOCIAL SCIENTISTS have developed many theories and models to explain the formation of public policy.[4] Here, we present a widely used model (see Figure 13.1) of the policy-making process that views it as a sequence of stages of functional activities. Public policies do not just happen; rather, they are typically the products of a predictable pattern of events. Models for analyzing the policy-making process do not always explain *why* public policies take the specific forms that they do, however. That depends on the political struggles over particular policies.[5] Nor do models necessarily tell us *who* dominates or controls the formation of public policy. The model in Figure 13.1 can be applied and used to analyze any of the public policies discussed throughout this book.

Despite the limitations of models, however, public policy making frequently does follow the sequence of stages. Sometimes some of the stages may merge, such as the policy formulation and adoption stages. Another instance of stages merging occurs when administrative agencies like the Occupational Safety and Health Administration (OSHA) make policy through rule making at the same time that they implement it. Finally, we need to recognize that what happens at one stage of the policy-making process affects action at later stages, and sometimes such action is done deliberately in anticipation of these effects. Thus, particular provisions may be included in a law either to help or hinder its implementation, depending on the interests of the provisions' proponents.

Stages of the Policy Process

Basically, the policy process has seven stages: (1) A *problem* that disturbs or distresses people gives rise to demands for relief, often through governmental action. Individual or group efforts are then made to get the problem (2) placed on a governmental *agenda*.[6] If successful, this step is followed by (3) the *formulation* of alternatives for dealing with the problem. (4) *Policy adoption* involves the formal enactment or approval of an alternative. (5) *Budgeting* provides financial resources to carry out the approved alternative, which can now truly be called a policy. (6) *Policy implementation*, the actual administration or application

FIGURE 13.1 Stages of the Policy-making Process. ■

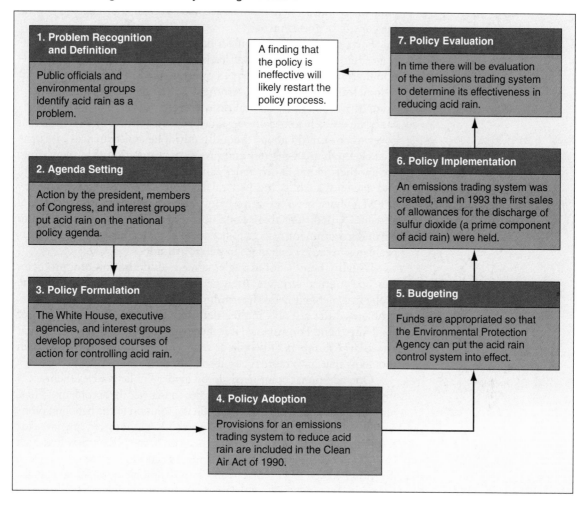

1. **Problem Recognition and Definition**

Public officials and environmental groups identify acid rain as a problem.

2. **Agenda Setting**

Action by the president, members of Congress, and interest groups put acid rain on the national policy agenda.

3. **Policy Formulation**

The White House, executive agencies, and interest groups develop proposed courses of action for controlling acid rain.

4. **Policy Adoption**

Provisions for an emissions trading system to reduce acid rain are included in the Clean Air Act of 1990.

A finding that the policy is ineffective will likely restart the policy process.

7. **Policy Evaluation**

In time there will be evaluation of the emissions trading system to determine its effectiveness in reducing acid rain.

6. **Policy Implementation**

An emissions trading system was created, and in 1993 the first sales of allowances for the discharge of sulfur dioxide (a prime component of acid rain) were held.

5. **Budgeting**

Funds are appropriated so that the Environmental Protection Agency can put the acid rain control system into effect.

of the policy to its targets, may then be followed by (7) *policy evaluation* to determine the policy's actual accomplishments, consequences, or shortcomings. Evaluation may restart the policy process by identifying a new problem and touching off an attempt to modify or terminate the policy.

Problem Recognition and Definition

At any given time, there are many conditions that disturb or distress people: polluted air, outsourcing of jobs overseas, earthquakes, hurricanes, tsunamis, childhood obesity, the rising cost of college tuition, lewdness on television, too few dedicated public officials, or possible terrorist attacks. All disturbing conditions do not automatically become problems; some of them may be accepted as trivial, inevitable, or beyond the control of government.

For a condition to become a problem, there must be some criterion—standard or value—that leads people to believe that the condition does not have to be accepted or acquiesced to and, further, that it is something with which government can deal effectively and appropriately. For example, natural disasters such as earthquakes or hurricanes are unlikely to become a policy problem because there is little that government can do about them directly. The consequences of earthquakes, the human distress and property destruction that they bring, are another matter. Their relief can be a focus of government action, and agencies such as the Federal Emergency Management Agency (FEMA) have been set up to reduce the hardships caused by natural disasters. Conditions that at one time are accepted as appropriate and beyond government responsibility may at a later time be perceived as problems because of changes in public attitudes.

Usually there is not a single, agreed-on definition of a problem. Indeed, political struggle often occurs at this stage because how the problem is defined helps determine what sort of action is appropriate. Problems differ not only in their definitions but also in the difficulty of resolving them. For instance, it is more difficult to tackle problems that affect large numbers of people or that require behavioral change than problems that have more focused solutions.

One additional point needs to be made. Public policies themselves frequently are viewed as problems or the causes of other problems. Thus, for some people, gun control legislation is a solution to the handgun problem. To the National Rifle Association (NRA), however, any law that restricts gun ownership is a problem because of the NRA's view that such laws inappropriately restrict an individual's right to keep and bear arms. To conservatives, legal access to abortion is a problem; for social liberals, laws restricting the right to abortion fall into the problem category.

Agenda Setting

Once a problem is recognized and defined by a significant segment of society, it must be brought to the attention of public officials and it must secure a place on an **agenda,** a set of problems to which policy makers believe they should be attentive. Political scientists have identified two basic agenda types in the area of public policy: the systemic agenda and the governmental or institutional agenda.[7] The **systemic agenda** is essentially a discussion agenda; it comprises "all issues that are commonly perceived by the members of the political community as meriting public attention and as involving matters within the legitimate jurisdiction" of governments.[8] Every political community—national, state, and local—has a systemic agenda.

agenda
A set of issues to be discussed or given attention.

systemic agenda
All public issues that are viewed as requiring governmental attention; a discussion agenda.

A **governmental** or **institutional agenda** includes only problems to which legislators or other public officials feel obliged to devote active and serious attention. Not all the problems that attract the attention of officials are likely to have been widely discussed by the general public, or even the attentive public—those who follow certain issues closely. Problems or issues (an issue emerges when disagreement exists over what should be done about a problem) may move onto an institutional agenda, whether from the systemic agenda or elsewhere, in several ways. These include crisis situations, political campaigns, and interest group lobbying, among many others.

governmental (institutional) agenda
The changing list of issues to which governments believe they should address themselves.

Policy Formulation

Policy formulation involves the crafting of appropriate and acceptable proposed courses of action to ameliorate or resolve public problems. It has both political and technical components. The political aspect of policy formulation involves determining generally what should be done to reduce acid rain, for example—whether standard setting and enforcement or emissions testing should be used. The technical facet involves correctly stating in specific language what one wants to authorize or accomplish, so as to adequately guide those who must implement policy and to prevent distortion of legislative intent. Formulation may take different forms.[9]

policy formulation
The crafting of appropriate and acceptable proposed courses of action to ameliorate or resolve public problems.

1. *Routine formulation* is the continuous process of formulating policy proposals within a well-established issue area. For instance, the formulation of policy for veterans' benefits represents a standard process of drafting proposals similar to those established in the past.

2. *Analogous formulation* handles new problems by drawing on experience with similar problems in the past. What has been done in the past to cope with the activities of terrorists? What has been done in other states to deal with child abuse or divorce law reform?

3. *Creative formulation* involves attempts to develop new or unprecedented proposals that represent a departure from existing practices and that will better resolve a problem. For example, plans to develop an anti-missile defense system to shoot down incoming missiles represents a departure from previous defense strategies of mutual destruction.

Policy formulation may be undertaken by various players in the policy process—the president, presidential aides, agency officials, specially appointed task forces and commissions, interest groups, private research organizations (or think tanks), and legislators and their staffs. The people engaged in formulation are usually looking ahead toward policy adoption.

SHOULD THE FEDERAL GOVERNMENT REGULATE MARRIAGE AND FAMILY?

OVERVIEW: Historically, the states have been chiefly responsible for social policy. Since the New Deal of the 1930s and the Great Society programs of the 1960s, however, the American people have decided it is proper for the federal government to engage in social policy within defined limits such as Social Security. With President Bill Clinton's signing of the Defense of Marriage Act (DOMA) in 1996, the launching of President George W. Bush's Healthy Marriage Initiative (HMI) in 2002, and his administration's support in 2004 of an amendment to the Constitution to bar same-sex marriage, the institutions of marriage and family have been put at the vanguard of social policy debate. In particular, the Bush administration's HMI requested $1.5 billion over five years in the welfare reform authorization bill to promote research and fund programs to give those receiving social welfare the counseling and tools to keep their marriages together. The basic assumption is that two-parent households are less likely to go or stay on social welfare and that a stable marriage fosters self-sufficiency and improves emotional well-being.

In order for all Americans to enjoy the rights and liberties offered by life in the United States, most believe government has a role in helping those who are somehow disadvantaged. Americans generally accept the fact that government programs are necessary to provide social welfare and to help secure the well-being of citizens. Many Republicans and Democrats believe that in order to secure this well-being, the traditional male father/female mother family structure should be protected. It is believed those who grow up within this structure are less likely to commit violent crimes, abuse drugs, or engage in prostitution and are more likely to finish high school and college. The Bush administration framed this debate in such a way that those who are opposed to its policy initiative (particularly Democrats) are seen as being opposed to family responsibility and accountability. Many Republicans (especially those who believe in limited government) find themselves opposed to these initiatives because they understand that the federal government should not fund these programs or violate the states' right to determine family law.

Is legislation defining or helping marriage a proper duty of government? It is undeniable that familial and marriage institutions are currently in a state of change. The Healthy Marriage Initiative is an attempt to encourage social and individual responsibility by attempting to lower rates of illegitimacy and the number of single-parent households. Social research reveals that the vast majority (approximately 80 percent) of children living below the poverty line come from single-parent households. What is to be done?

At what point should the federal government be permitted or barred from entering the very private sphere of marriage? Where does the proper constitutional authority for family and marriage law lie—with the people, the states, or the federal government? Should the American people have the final say in what defines a marriage or family? Are acts of government in the social arena—such as the Defense of Marriage Act, the Healthy Marriage Initiative, and the proposed amendment to the Constitution to bar same-sex marriage—legitimate in a society that still advocates a uniquely American form of freedom? On the other hand, the crime, poverty, illiteracy, and lack of opportunity linked to broken and single-parent families are destructive not only for the individuals who must endure them, but for American society as a whole. Is it not then the proper place of the federal government to ensure that those who are disadvantaged have the tools through which to succeed?

Arguments in Favor of Federal Family Policy

- **Research from those at both ends of the political spectrum suggests children and parents benefit from the institution of marriage.** Social studies from both liberal and conservative groups suggest that two-parent households are less likely to go onto, or remain on social welfare. Furthermore, children in single-parent households are seven times more likely to live in poverty than those who live with two parents. Studies show that children in two-parent households are more likely to do better in school, and they have higher graduation rates as well.

- **The Healthy Marriage Initiative is cost effective.** According to the Heritage Foundation, a conservative think tank, research indicates the benefits from funding HMI programs outweigh the projected costs of traditional welfare programs such as Temporary Aid to Needy Families and food stamps. The end result will be lowered federal expenditures for social welfare programs while increasing parental responsibility and familial self-sufficiency.

- **The Healthy Marriage Initiative is voluntary.** Supporters of HMI argue that it does not constitute an impermissible government intrusion into the private lives of those receiving social welfare because it is a purely voluntary program. Proponents say it is designed for those who desire a strengthened marriage as a means to extricate the family from government and social dependence.

Arguments Against Federal Family Policy

- **HMI does not address the true needs of social welfare recipients.** Opponents of HMI argue that most families do not need counseling, but rather they need education, jobs and job programs, day care, and low-cost transportation. In addition, stricter enforcement of childcare laws would help relieve the economic burden on those receiving social welfare.

- **Social policy regarding families and marriage is the constitutional responsibility of the states.** Many conservatives and liberals argue that marriage and family policy belongs to the proper authority of state governments. When discussing the federal marriage amendment before Congress, former Republican congressman Bob Barr argued that to interfere with the states' right to regulate marriage is to sacrifice the Constitution to social engineering.

- **The Healthy Marriage Initiative does not address the evolving nature of the family structure.** HMI assumes the two-parent household of a married man and woman is the norm. Though the benefits of a two-parent, husband and wife household are desirable, social and historical change, the growing number of same-sex unions, and high divorce and illegitimacy rates make it unreasonable to assume that HMI can ultimately be as effective as its adherents claim.

Questions

1. Will HMI be as effective as its proponents claim? If so why? If not, why not?
2. Which level of government—local, state, or federal—is best suited to address family needs, and why?

Selected Readings

Mary Jo Bane. *Lifting Up the Poor: A Dialogue on Religion, Poverty, and Welfare Reform.* Washington, DC: Brookings Institution Press, 2003.

Randy Albelda. *Lost Ground: Welfare Reform, Poverty and Beyond.* Cambridge, MA: South End Press, 2002.

Policy Adoption

policy adoption
The approval of a policy proposal by the people with the requisite authority, such as a legislature.

Policy adoption involves the approval of a policy proposal by the people with requisite authority, such as a legislature or chief executive. This approval gives the policy legal force. Because most public policies in the United States result from legislation, policy adoption frequently requires the building of majority coalitions necessary to secure the enactment of legislation.

In chapter 6, we discuss how power is diffused in Congress and how the legislative process comprises a number of roadblocks or obstacles—House subcommittee, House committee, House Rules Committee, and so on—that a bill must successfully navigate before it becomes law. A majority is needed to clear a bill through each of these obstacles; hence, not one majority but a series of majorities are needed for congressional policy adoption. To secure the needed votes, a bill may be watered down or modified at each of these decision points. Or, the bill may fail to win a majority at one of them and die, at least for the time being.

The adoption of major legislation, such as the Medicare Prescription Drug, Improvement, and Modernization Act of 2003, requires much negotiation, bargaining, and compromise. In some instances, years or even decades may be needed to secure the enactment of legislation on a controversial matter. Congress considered federal aid to public education off and on over several decades before it finally won approval in 1965. At other times, the approval process may move quickly.

Not all policy adoption necessitates formation of majority coalitions. Presidential decision making on foreign affairs, military actions, and other matters is often unilateral. Although a president has many aides and advisers and is bombarded with information and advice, the final decision rests with him. Ultimately, too, it is the president who decides whether to veto a bill passed by Congress. Sometimes a president can get concessions from Congress by threatening to veto legislation. For example, George W. Bush was able to secure some changes to a post-9/11 spending bill by simply raising the specter of a veto.

Budgeting

Visual Literacy
Where the Money Goes . . .

Most policies require money in order to be carried out; some policies, such as those providing income security, essentially involve the transfer of money from taxpayers to the government and back to individual beneficiaries. Funding for most policies and agencies is provided through the budgetary, or appropriations, process. Whether a policy is well funded or poorly funded has a significant effect on its scope, impact, and effectiveness.

A policy can be nullified by an absence of funding or refusal to fund. Other policies or programs often suffer from inadequate funding. For example, in 1999 the Federal Aviation Administration admitted that long recommended security measures were yet to be implemented at national airports because of underfunding. This problem continues in the wake of the 9/11 terrorist acts. In spite of new legislation creating the Transportation Security Agency and requiring it to supervise security for the nation's airlines, funding problems caused the agency to miss several mandated deadlines. The No Child Left Behind Act is another example of a widely supported yet dramatically underfunded program, which has made its implementation difficult.

The budgetary process also gives the president and the Congress an opportunity to review the government's many policies and programs, to inquire into their administration, to appraise their value and effectiveness, and to exercise some influence on their conduct. Not all of the government's hundreds of programs are fully examined every year. But, over a period of several years, most programs come under scrutiny.

Policy Implementation

Policy implementation is the process of carrying out public policies, most of which are implemented by administrative agencies. Some, however, are enforced in other ways. Product liability and product dating are two examples. Product liability laws such as the Food and Drug Act of 1906, the National Traffic and Motor Vehicle Safety Act of 1966, and the Consumer Product Safety Act of 1972 typically are enforced by lawsuits initiated in the courts by injured consumers or their survivors. In contrast, state product-dating laws are implemented more by voluntary compliance when grocers take out-of-date products off their shelves or by consumers when they choose not to buy food products after the use dates stamped on them. The courts also get involved in implementation when they are called on to interpret the meaning of legislation, review the legality of agency rules and actions, and determine whether institutions such as prisons and mental hospitals conform to legal and constitutional standards.

Administrative agencies may be authorized to use a number of techniques to implement the public policies within their jurisdictions. These techniques can be categorized as authoritative, incentive, capacity, and hortatory techniques, depending on the behavioral assumptions on which they are based.[10]

Authoritative techniques for policy implementation rest on the notion that people's actions must be directed or restrained by government in order to prevent or eliminate activities or products that are unsafe, unfair, evil, or immoral. Consumer products must meet certain safety regulations, and radio stations and television networks can be fined heavily or even have their broadcasting licenses revoked if they broadcast obscenities.

Many governmental agencies have authority to issue rules and set standards to regulate such matters as meat and food processing, the

policy implementation
The process of carrying out public policy through governmental agencies and the courts.

discharge of pollutants into the environment, the healthfulness and safety of workplaces, and the safe operation of commercial airplanes. Compliance with these standards is determined by inspection and monitoring, and penalties may be imposed on people or companies that violate the rules and standards set forth in a particular policy. For example, under Title IX, the federal government can terminate funds to colleges or universities that discriminate against female students. Its detractors sometimes stigmatize this pattern of action as command and control regulation, although in practice it often involves much education, bargaining, and persuasion in addition to the exercise of authority. In the case of Title IX, for instance, the Department of Education will try to negotiate with a school to bring it into compliance before funding is terminated for violating the act.

Incentive techniques for policy implementation encourage people to act in their own best interest by offering payoffs or financial inducements to get them to comply with public policies. Such policies may provide tax deductions to encourage charitable giving, or award grants to companies to install pollution control equipment. Farmers receive subsidies to make their production (or nonproduction) of wheat, cotton, and other commodities more profitable. Conversely, sanctions such as high taxes may discourage the purchase and use of such products as tobacco or liquor, and pollution fees may reduce the discharge of pollutants by making this action more costly to businesses.

Capacity techniques provide people with information, education, training, or resources that will enable them to participate in desired activities. The assumption underlying the provision of these techniques is that people have the incentive or desire to do what is right but lack the capacity to act accordingly. Job training may enable able-bodied people to find work, and accurate information on interest rates will enable people to protect themselves against interest-rate gouging. Financial assistance can help the needy acquire better housing and warmer winter coats and perhaps lead more comfortable lives.[11]

Hortatory techniques encourage people to comply with policy by appealing to people's better instincts in an effort to get them to act in desired ways. In this instance, the policy implementers assume that people decide how to act according to their personal values and beliefs on matters such as right and wrong, equality, and justice. During the Reagan administration, Nancy Reagan implored young people to "Just say no" to drugs. Hortatory techniques also include the use of highway signs that tell us "Don't Be a Litterbug" and "Don't Mess with Texas" to discourage littering. Slogans such as "Only You Can Prevent Forest Fires" are meant to encourage compliance with fire and safety regulations in national parks and forests.

The capacity of agencies to administer public policies effectively depends partly on whether an agency is authorized to use appropriate implementation techniques. Many other factors also come into play, including the clarity and consistency of the policies' statutory mandates, adequacy of funding, political support, and the will and skill of agency personnel. There is no easy formula that will guarantee successful policy implementation; in practice, many policies only partially achieve their goals.

Policy Evaluation

Practitioners of **policy evaluation** seek to determine what a policy actually is accomplishing. They may also try to determine whether a policy is being fairly or efficiently administered. In the case of welfare programs, official evaluators have often been more interested in evidence of waste, fraud, and abuse than in assessing the effectiveness of the programs in meeting the needs of the poor.

policy evaluation
The process of determining whether a course of action is achieving its intended goals.

Policy makers frequently make judgments on the effectiveness and necessity of particular policies and programs. These evaluations often are based mostly on anecdotal and fragmentary evidence rather than on solid facts and thorough analyses. Sometimes a program has been judged to be a good program simply because it is politically popular. In recent decades, however, policy evaluation has taken a more rigorous, systematic, and objective form. Social scientists and qualified investigators design studies to measure the societal impact of programs and to determine whether these programs are achieving their specified goals or objectives. The national executive departments and agencies often have officials and units responsible for policy evaluation; so do state governments.

Policy evaluation may be conducted by a variety of players: congressional committees, through investigations and other oversight activities; presidential commissions; administrative agencies themselves; university researchers; private research organizations, such as the Brookings Institution and the American Enterprise Institute; and the Government Accountability Office (GAO). Evaluation research and studies can stimulate attempts to modify or terminate policies and thus restart the policy process. Legislators and administrators may formulate and advocate amendments designed to correct problems or shortcomings in a policy. In 1988, for example, legislation was adopted to correct weaknesses in the enforcement of the Fair Housing Act of 1968, which banned discrimination in the sale or rental of most housing. However, some people may decide that the best alternative is simply to eliminate the policy. For example, through the Airline Deregulation Act of 1978, Congress eliminated the Civil Aeronautics Board and its program of economic regulation of commercial airlines. This action was taken on the assumption that competition in the marketplace would better protect the interests of airline users. Competition has indeed reduced the cost of flying on many popular routes, but it also has contributed to the financial woes of many airlines. On December 31, 1995, the Interstate Commerce Commission expired after almost a century of regulating railroads and other modes of transportation. The demise of programs is rare, however; more often, a troubled program is modified or allowed to limp along because it is doing something that some people strongly want done, even if the program is not doing it well.

SOCIAL WELFARE POLICY

social welfare policy
Government programs designed to improve quality of life.

SOCIAL WELFARE POLICY IS A TERM that designates a broad and varied range of government programs designed to provide people with protection against want and deprivation, improve their health and physical well-being, provide educational and employment training opportunities, and otherwise enable them to lead more satisfactory, meaningful, and productive lives. The issue of who is deserving and what they deserve is at the heart of the debate over social welfare programs. Over time, the focus of social welfare programs has expanded from providing minimal assistance to the destitute to helping the working poor attain a degree of security and provide for their health, nutrition, income security, employment, and education needs.

The Roots of Social Welfare Policy

Most social welfare programs in the United States are largely a product of the twentieth century, although their origins can be traced far into the nation's past. As U.S. society became more urban and indus-

Photo courtesy: Bettmann/CORBIS

■ The Great Depression, beginning in late 1929 and continuing throughout the 1930s, dramatically pointed out to average Americans the need for a broad social safety net and gave rise to a host of income, health, and finance legislation.

trial, self-sufficiency declined and people became more interdependent and reliant on a vast system of production, distribution, and exchange. The Great Depression of the 1930s reinforced the notion that hard work alone would not provide economic security for everyone, and showed that the state governments and private charities lacked adequate resources to alleviate economic want and distress.

Income Security.   Passage of the **Social Security Act** in 1935 represented the beginning of a permanent welfare state in America and a dedication to the ideal of greater equity. The act consisted of three major components: (1) old-age insurance (what we now call Social Security); (2) public assistance for the needy, aged, blind, and families with dependent children (later, people with disabilities were added); and, (3) unemployment insurance and compensation.

Social Security Act
A 1935 law that established old-age insurance (Social Security) and assistance for the needy, children, and others, and unemployment insurance.

The core of the Social Security Act was the creation of a compulsory old-age insurance program funded equally by employer and employee contributions. The act imposed a payroll tax, collected from the employer, equal to 1 percent from both employee and employer starting in 1937. The Social Security Act also addressed the issue of unemployment, requiring employers to pay 3 percent of a worker's salary into an insurance fund. If workers became unemployed, they could draw from this fund for a given period of time. During the time laid-off workers drew from the insurance fund, they were required to seek other jobs. This component of the Social Security Act served two basic purposes. On the individual level, it provided income to laid-off workers, expanding the social safety net; on the broader economic level, it acted as an automatic stabilizer, increasing payments to the system when the economy slowed.

Timeline

The Evolution of Social Welfare Policy

Social Security is credited with replacing a piecemeal collection of local programs with a national system. This national system was widely praised but also was perceived to contain two basic flaws: the payroll tax was regressive (the tax fell disproportionately on lower-income contributors) and some workers were excluded from the program.

National health insurance was considered at the time Social Security legislation was passed. Because of the strong opposition from the American Medical Association (AMA), which was the dominant force in American medicine at the time, health insurance was omitted from Social Security legislation. It was feared that mention of this concept would jeopardize adoption of other important elements of the program. Health insurance remained on the back burner for many years.

Health Care.   Governments in the United States have long been active in the health field. Local governments began to establish public health departments in the first half of the nineteenth century, and state health departments followed in the second half. Knowledge of the bacteriological causes of diseases and human ailments discovered in the late-nineteenth and early twentieth centuries led to significant advances in improving public health. Public sanitation and clean-water programs, pasteurization of milk, immunization programs, and other activities reduced greatly the incidence of infectious and communicable diseases. The increase in American life expectancy from forty-seven in 1900 to seventy-eight in 2004 is linked to public health programs.

Beginning in 1798, with the establishment of the National Marine Service (NMS) for "the relief of sick and disabled seamen," which was the forerunner of the Public Health Service, the national government has provided health care for some segments of the population. Efforts have been made over the years to expand coverage of health care to more and more Americans. The current Medicare and Medicaid programs that provide hospital benefits for all aged people covered by Social Security (Medicare) and medical costs for the poor (Medicaid) were first passed by Congress in 1965. With the enactment of the Medicare and Medicaid programs, the share of health care expenditures financed by public spending rose from under 25 percent in 1960 to almost 40 percent in 1970. During this time, public expenditures on health care as a percent of total gross domestic product (GDP) rose by more than 100 percent.

Social Welfare Policies Today

Income security and health care encompass many complex policies and programs. While all levels of government (national, state, and local) are involved with the development and implementation of social welfare policies, we emphasize the national government's role. However, new programs are giving states greater control over public welfare and health care programs.

Income security programs protect people against loss of income because of retirement, disability, unemployment, or death or absence of the family breadwinner. Although cases of total deprivation are now rare, many people are unable to provide a minimally decent standard of living for themselves and their families. They are poor in a relative if not an absolute sense. In 2004, the poverty threshold for a four-person family unit was $18,810.[12]

Income security programs fall into two general categories. Social insurance programs are **non-means-based programs** that provide cash assistance to qualified beneficiaries. **Means-tested programs** require that people must have incomes below specified levels to be eligible for benefits. Benefits of means-tested programs may come either as cash or in-kind benefits, such as food stamps.

non-means-based program
Program such as Social Security where benefits are provided irrespective of the income or means of recipients.

means-tested program
Income security program intended to assist those whose incomes fall below a designated level.

Non-Means-Based Programs. Non-means-based social insurance programs operate in a manner somewhat similar to private automobile or life insurance. Contributions are made by or on behalf of the prospective beneficiaries, their employers, or both. When a person becomes eligible for benefits, the monies are paid as a matter of right, regardless of how much wealth or unearned income (for example, from dividends and interest payments) the recipient has. For Social Security, a limit is imposed on earned income.

Old Age, Survivors, and Disability Insurance.   This program began as old-age insurance, providing benefits only to retired workers. Its coverage was extended to survivors of covered workers in 1939 and to the permanently disabled in 1956. Customarily called Social Security, it is not, as many people believe, a pension program that collects contributions from workers, invests them, and then returns them with interest to beneficiaries. Instead, current workers pay taxes that directly go toward providing benefits for retirees. In 2004, an employee tax of 7.65 percent was levied on the first $87,900 of wages or salaries and placed into the Social Security Trust Fund. An equal tax was levied on employers. Nearly all employees and most of the self-employed (who pay a 15.3 percent tax) are now covered by Social Security. People earning less than $87,900 pay a greater share of their income into the Social Security Fund, since wages or salaries above that amount are not subject to the Social Security tax. The Social Security tax therefore is considered a regressive tax because it captures larger proportions of incomes from lower and middle-income individuals than from high-wage earners.

People born before 1938 are eligible to receive full retirement benefits at age sixty-five. The full retirement age gradually rises until it reaches sixty-seven for persons born in 1960 or later. Individuals can opt to receive reduced benefits as early as age sixty-two. In 2002, the average monthly Social Security benefit for all retired workers was $936, while in 2004, the maximum monthly benefit was $1,825. Social Security is the primary source of income for many retirees and keeps them from living in poverty. However, eligible people are entitled to Social Security benefits regardless of how much *unearned* income (for example, dividends and interest payments) they also receive. As of 2004, there was no limit on the amount of income recipients older than sixty-five could earn without penalty. For Social Security recipients between the ages of sixty-two and sixty-four, one dollar for every two dollars earned was withheld after a specific amount of earnings was reached. One dollar for every three dollars earned was withheld from a sixty-five-year-old recipient's earnings.[13]

The Trustees of the Social Security Trust Funds predicted in 2002 that, starting about 2010, Social Security Fund expenditures will begin to increase rapidly as the Baby Boom generation reaches retirement age. It was estimated that by 2018, payments would exceed revenues collected (see Figure 13.2). Viewing costs and revenues as a proportion of taxable payrolls (to correct for the value of the dollar over time), one

FIGURE 13.2 Social Security Costs and Revenues, including Projections, 1970–2080. ■

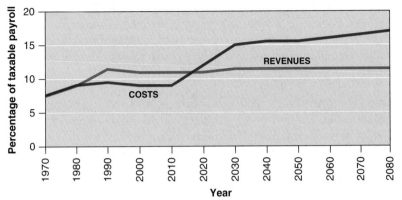

Source: Status of the Social Security and Medicare Programs, A Summary of the 2004 Annual Reports, http://www.ssa.gov/OACT/TRSUM/trsummary.html.

can see that projected revenues remain relatively constant over time, while costs are projected to rise substantially. Aside from the retirement of Baby Boomers, other factors pressuring the fund include increased life expectancies and low fertility rates.

After George W. Bush was elected in 2000, he created a President's Commission to Strengthen Social Security. This panel consisted of sixteen members, with the former Democratic senator from New York Daniel Patrick Moynihan and Richard Parsons, co-chief operating officer of AOL Time Warner, serving as co-chairs. By the end of 2001, the panel disappointed proponents of privatization with their set of recommendations. The panel provided three options: (1) allowing workers to invest up to 2 percent of their payroll tax in personal accounts; (2) allowing workers to invest up to 4 percent of their payroll tax in personal accounts, to a maximum of $1,000 per year; and, (3) allowing workers to invest an additional 1 percent of their earnings in a personal account. Proponents of privatization had hoped for a single recommendation. Congress ignored the recommendations, no doubt influenced by the slump in the stock market and unpopular panel observations. The panel noted it believed that ultimately benefits would have to be cut or more money would have to be assigned to the program. Following his reelection in 2004, Bush reaffirmed his support for Social Security privatization.

Most Americans remained unconvinced about such privatization, particularly given the volatility of the stock market in 2000–2002. Many approaching retirement age were even less enthused when Alan Greenspan, chair of the Federal Reserve Board of Governors, in a 2004 speech, restated his long-held belief that more painful changes in the program—including delay of eligibility—were needed to keep Social Security (and Medicare) solvent in the decades ahead.[14] (See Politics Now: The Politics of Social Security Reform.)

THE POLITICS OF SOCIAL SECURITY REFORM

In his State of the Union Address in January 2005, President George W. Bush reiterated his support for partial privatization of Social Security. The president had campaigned for office advocating such a reform, and he remained committed to the idea of allowing younger workers the option of using some of their Social Security payroll taxes for private investments. His advocacy of this position after the steep stock market decline in 2001 and 2002 was characteristic of an administration that prized consistency in its policy positions, in contrast to holding one's finger in the air to see which way the political wind was blowing.

Republicans in Congress who may have been influenced by polling data did not universally embrace Bush's position on Social Security. Polls showed that the public was growing more skeptical about the wisdom of investing Social Security funds in the stock market. In a *Wall Street Journal*/NBC poll taken in July 2002, 55 percent of Americans said they would oppose partial privatization of Social Security, while 41 percent supported the idea. This represented a sharp drop in support from December 2001, when 48 percent opposed the idea and 46 percent were in favor. In April 1998, 41 percent of those polled said they opposed privatization, while 52 percent were in favor. The performance of the stock market likely had an impact on opinion. A report issued by the Center for Economic and Policy Research, a liberal think tank, documented that workers who invested in the stock market between 1998 and 2002 would have lost considerable sums of money.

House Republicans tried to distance themselves from the president by passing a bill that promised not to privatize the retirement system. While many agreed in principle with the president, they worried about giving the Democrats an emotional issue to raise with retirees and those near retirement age. Many Republicans advocated pushing the timetable back further by deferring debate on Social Security until after the 2004 presidential election. Consultants had urged Republican candidates to avoid the word "privatization" and to challenge opponents to be specific about how they would keep Social Security solvent. A nationwide series of polls and focus groups about Social Security convinced Republicans that they were vulnerable to accusations that they planned to cut Social Security benefits. A series of Capitol Hill briefings by a GOP polling firm recommended that Republican candidates communicate messages about Social Security that included the word "control" rather than "privatization." The firm further recommended emphasizing that the individual citizen and not the government should be in control of Social Security funds.

Democrats tried to raise the looming threat of privatization as an issue in the 2002 midterm election, but with little success. They contended that Republicans were committed to creating private investment accounts that would lead to cuts in benefits and an unraveling of the system. Democrats cast themselves in their familiar role of guardians of Social Security in order to attract elderly voters. The elderly were perceived to be a critical voting bloc because of their high rate of voting, especially in midterm elections. Republican congressional strategists who were worried about the impact of privatization schemes on the elderly vote sought to "inoculate" their candidates from Democratic attacks. They claimed that the long-term health of Social Security warranted "sober debate." Republican candidates began to list three principles for any revamping of Social Security: no benefit cuts, no rise in the retirement age, and no increase in the payroll tax. Republicans apparently won the argument, as the GOP added seats to its House majority and regained control of the Senate in 2002.

Sources: Amy Goldstein, "Bush Continues to Back Privatized Social Security," *Washington Post* (July 25, 2002): A6; Robin Toner, "Social Security Issue Is Rattling Races for Congress," *New York Times* (June 4, 2002): A1; Mike Allen and Juliet Eilperin, "Wary Words on Social Security: GOP Shunning Use of Privatization," *Washington Post* (May 11, 2002): A1; and Greg Hitt, "Social Security Plan Stalls: Stock Market's Slide Undermines Support for Privatization," *Wall Street Journal* (July 23, 2002): A4.

Unemployment Insurance. As mentioned earlier, unemployment insurance is financed by a payroll tax paid by employers. The program pays benefits to workers who are covered by the government plan and are unemployed through no fault of their own. The Social Security Act provided that if a state set up a comparable program and levied a payroll tax for its support, most of the federal tax would be forgiven (not collected). The states were thus accorded a choice: either set up and administer an acceptable unemployment program, or let the national government handle the matter. Within a short time, all states had their own programs.

Unemployment insurance covers employers of four or more people, but not part-time or occasional workers. Benefits are paid to unemployed workers who have neither been fired for personal faults, nor quit their jobs, and who are willing and able to accept suitable employment. State unemployment programs differ considerably in levels of benefits, length of benefit payment, and eligibility for benefits. For example, in 2002, average weekly benefit payments ranged from $401 in Arizona and $354 in Massachusetts to $167 in Alabama and $168 in Mississippi.[15] In general, less generous programs exist in southern states, where labor unions are less powerful. Nationwide, only about half of the people who are counted as unemployed at any given time are receiving benefits.

In November 2004, the national unemployment rate stood at 5.4 percent. (See Analyzing Visuals: Unemployment Rates by State.) Some states, such as Oregon, California, Texas, the Carolinas, and New York, had especially high rates of unemployment. A loss of confidence in the stock market, uncertainty about the fight against terrorism and the developments in postwar Iraq, fallout from the bankruptcies of large corporations (such as Enron), the outsourcing of white-collar jobs to foreign countries, and slow economic growth all contributed to a lack of hiring. There were signs of economic recovery, but it did not seem to be offering the robust increase in jobs that usually accompanied such an upswing.

Social Insurance: Means-Tested Programs. Means-tested income security programs are intended to help the needy, that is, individuals or families whose incomes fall below specified levels, such as a percentage of the official poverty line. Included in the means-tested categories are the Supplemental Security Income (SSI), Temporary Assistance for Needy Families (TANF), and food stamp programs.

Supplemental Security Income. This program began under the Social Security Act as a grant-in-aid program to help the needy aged or blind. Grants were financed jointly by the national and state governments from general revenues, but the states played a major role in determining standards of eligibility and benefit levels. In 1950, Congress extended coverage to needy people who were permanently and totally disabled.

Analyzing Visuals

UNEMPLOYMENT RATES BY STATE

This map shows the rates of unemployment across the United States in the late fall of 2004. According to the Bureau of Labor Statistics, the U.S. unemployment rate was 5.4 percent in November 2004, down from a high of 6 percent in 2003. Nevertheless, the rate is substantially higher than the 4 percent annual rate in 2000, and certain states and regions have rates far higher than the national average. Based on your analysis of this map and your understanding of the chapter discussion, answer the following critical thinking questions: Which states are currently suffering from the highest levels of unemployment, and why do you think that is so? Why do you think unemployment rates vary substantially from state to state? Do you detect any similarities among states with the lowest rates of unemployment? What role do you think the unemployment rate played in President Bush's reelection?

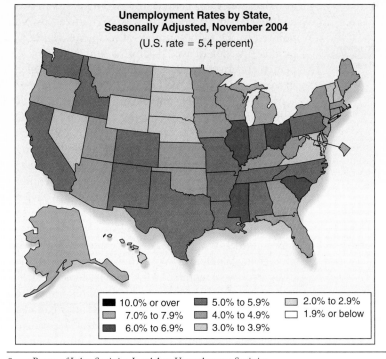

Unemployment Rates by State,
Seasonally Adjusted, November 2004
(U.S. rate = 5.4 percent)

- ■ 10.0% or over
- ■ 7.0% to 7.9%
- ■ 6.0% to 6.9%
- ■ 5.0% to 5.9%
- ■ 4.0% to 4.9%
- ■ 3.0% to 3.9%
- □ 2.0% to 2.9%
- □ 1.9% or below

Source: Bureau of Labor Statistics, Local Area Unemployment Statistics.

With the support of the Nixon administration, Congress reconfigured the grant programs into the Supplemental Security Income (SSI) program in 1974. Primary funding for SSI is provided by the national government, which prescribes uniform benefit levels throughout the nation. To be eligible, beneficiaries can own only a limited amount of possessions. In 2004, monthly payments were about $564 for an individual, $846 for a married couple.[16] The states may choose to supplement the federal benefits, and forty-eight states do. For years, this program generated little controversy, as modest benefits go to people who obviously cannot provide for themselves. However, in 1996, access to SSI and other programs was limited by legislation.

Personal Responsibility and Work Opportunity Reconciliation Act (PRWORA) of 1996.

Participation

Making a Difference: Welfare Reform

In 1950, Aid to Families with Dependent Children (AFDC) was broadened to include not only dependent children without fathers but also mothers or other adults with whom dependent children were living. The AFDC rolls expanded greatly since 1960 because of the increasing numbers of children born to unwed mothers, the growing divorce rate, and the migration of poor people to cities, where they were more likely to apply for and be provided with benefits.

Because of its clientele, the AFDC program was the focus of much controversy and frequently was stigmatized as welfare. Critics who pointed to the rising number of recipients claimed that it encouraged promiscuity, out-of-wedlock births, and dependency, which resulted in a permanent class of welfare families. In what was hailed as the biggest shift in social policy since the Great Depression, a new welfare bill, the Personal Responsibility and Work Opportunity Reconciliation Act (PRWORA) of 1996, created the Temporary Assistance for Needy Families (TANF) program to replace AFDC. The shift from AFDC to TANF was meant to foster a new philosophy of work rather than welfare dependency. The most fundamental change enacted in the new law was the switch in funding for welfare from an open-ended matching program to a block grant to the states. PRWORA also gave states more flexibility in reforming their welfare programs toward work-oriented goals.

Significant features of the welfare plan included: (1) a requirement for single mothers with a child over five years of age to work within two years of receiving benefits; (2) a provision that unmarried mothers under the age of eighteen were required to live with an adult and attend school to receive welfare benefits; (3) a five-year lifetime limit for aid from block grants; (4) a requirement that mothers must provide information about a child's father in order to receive full welfare payments; (5) cutting off food stamps and Supplemental Security Income for legal immigrants; (6) cutting off cash welfare benefits and food stamps for convicted drug felons; and, (7) limiting food stamps to three months in a three-year period for persons eighteen to fifty years old who are not raising children and not working.[17]

In 2002, the George W. Bush administration released a detailed plan for TANF reauthorization. The plan proposed to strengthen work rules to ensure that all welfare families were engaged in meaningful activities that would lead to self-sufficiency. The administration proposed increasing the proportion of TANF families that would have to participate in work activities and increasing the number of hours of

The Living Constitution

We the People of the United States, in Order to form a more perfect Union, establish Justice, insure domestic Tranquility, provide for the common defence, promote the general Welfare, and Secure the Blessings of Liberty to ourselves and our Posterity, do ordain and establish this Constitution for the United States of America.

—Preamble

The Preamble of the U.S. Constitution lets posterity know the purpose and ends of the Constitution, and Supreme Court Justice Joseph Story—who served on the Court from 1812 to 1845, during its formative years—held that the Preamble also provides the "best key to the true interpretation" and spirit of the United States' fundamental law. Though the seemingly austere Preamble is not a source of rights or powers for the federal government, its inclusion in the Constitution was not without comment. Story, an Anti-Federalist, argued that the language of the Preamble could allow for an expansive judicial interpretation of the Constitution, and could do so in such a manner that the federal government would be given the authority of "general and unlimited powers of legislation in all cases."

It is true that the extent and authority of both the federal and state governments have increased, but the Preamble is understood to declare that "the People" are the source of all constitutional authority, and it is they, through constitutional institutions, who determine what constitutes justice and the "general Welfare." Constitutional government, it may be said, should strive to secure the well-being and happiness of all citizens, and it is to this end that social policy in the United States is directed.

The federal government is the only American government with the authority and means to ensure that social policy is fairly applied across the states, and it does faithfully attempt to pursue social policy that reflects the prevailing sentiments of the American people. For example, in 1996, social welfare in the United States was radically transformed to reflect a new understanding of how best to help the unfortunate, and it was done so with the intent to promote the general welfare of all Americans—to balance the interests not only of those whose taxes support the social welfare, but also of those for whom public support is necessary. Thus understood, the Preamble gives expression and guidance to the desires and will of the American people.

■ Food stamps remain an important component of the federal government's safety net for low-income Americans.

required work.[18] As of February 2005, the legislation reauthorizing TANF was still pending in Congress.

Food Stamp Program.   The initial food stamp program (1939–1943) was primarily an effort to expand domestic markets for farm commodities. Food stamps provided the poor with the ability to purchase more food, thus increasing the demand for American agricultural products. Attempts to reestablish the program during the Eisenhower administration failed, but in 1961, a $381,000 pilot program began under the Kennedy administration. It was made permanent in 1964 and extended nationwide in 1974. Although strongly opposed by the Republicans in Congress, Democrats put together a majority coalition when urban members agreed to support a wheat and cotton price support program wanted by rural and southern Democrats in return for their support of food stamps.

In the beginning, recipients had to pay cash for food stamps, but this practice ceased in 1977. Benefiting low-income families, the program has helped to combat hunger and reduce malnutrition. Food stamps went to more than 21 million beneficiaries in 2003 at a cost of $23.9 billion. The average participant received $84 worth of stamps per month. In 2003, families of four earning less than $1,961 per month qualified for food stamps.

The national government operates several other food programs for the needy. These include a special nutritional program for women, infants, and children (WIC); a school breakfast and lunch program; and an emergency food assistance program.

The Effectiveness of Income Security Programs

entitlement program
Income security program to which all those meeting eligibility criteria are entitled.

Many of the income security programs, including Social Security, Supplemental Security Income, and food stamps, are **entitlement programs.** That is, Congress sets eligibility criteria—such as age, income level, degree of disability, or unemployment—and those who meet the criteria are legally entitled to receive benefits. Moreover, unlike such programs as public housing, military construction, and space exploration, spending for entitlement programs is mandatory. Year after year, funds must be provided for them unless the laws creating the programs are changed. This feature of entitlement programs has made it difficult to control spending for them.

Income security programs have not eliminated poverty and economic dependency. Income security programs, however, have improved the lives of large numbers of people. Millions of elderly people in the United States would be living below the poverty line were it not for Social Security. Income security programs alleviate the problem of poverty, but they do not attack its cause. Poverty and economic dependency will not be eradicated as long as the conditions that give rise to them persist. There will probably always be people who are unable to provide adequately for themselves, whether because of old age, mental or physical disability, adverse economic conditions, or youth. A panoply of income security programs is a characteristic of all democratic industrial societies.

Health Care

Currently, many millions of people receive medical care through the medical branches of the armed forces, the hospitals and medical programs of the Department of Veterans Affairs, and the Indian Health Service. The government spends billions of dollars for the construction and operation of facilities and for the salaries of the doctors and other medical personnel, making the government's medical business truly a big business.

Most medical research is financed by the national government, primarily through the National Institutes of Health (NIH). The National Cancer Institute, the National Heart, Lung, and Blood Institute, the National Institute of Allergy and Infectious Diseases, and the other NIH institutes and centers spend more than $10 billion annually on biomedical research. NIH scientists and scientists at universities, medical schools, and other research facilities receiving NIH research grants conduct the research. Most Americans accept and support extensive government spending on medical research. Congress, in fact, often appropriates more money for medical research than the president recommends.

The United States spends significant sums of money on public health, a larger proportion of its gross domestic product than most industrialized democracies. In 2002, the United States spent $5,440 per person on health, more per person on health care than any other country. While these sums were being spent, the United States ranked only thirty-seventh in quality of health care, according to a World Health Organization analysis. Canada, Japan, and France far surpassed the United States in such measures as how long their citizens live in good health.[19]

Much of the increase in funding for health care has gone to the Medicare and Medicaid programs. Reasons for growth in medical spending include the public's increased expectations, increased demand for services, advances in health care technology, the perception of health care as a right, more citizens living longer, and the third-party payment system.[20]

Medicare.   Medicare, which covers persons over age sixty-five who receive Social Security benefits, is administered by the Center for Medicare and Medicaid Services in the Department of Health and Human Services. Medicare coverage has two components, Parts A and B. Benefits under Part A come to all Americans automatically at age sixty-five, when they qualify for Social Security. It covers hospitalization, some skilled nursing care, and home health services. Individuals have to pay about $700 in medical bills before they are eligible for Part A benefits. Medicare is financed by a payroll tax of 1.45 percent paid by both employees and employers on the total amount of one's wages or salary.

Part B, which is optional, covers payment for physicians' services, outpatient and diagnostic services, X-rays, and some other items not covered by Part A. Excluded from coverage are eyeglasses, hearing aids, and dentures. This portion of the Medicare program is financed partly by monthly payments from beneficiaries and partly by general tax revenues.

As noted in the opening vignette for this chapter, a new Medicare benefit will provide some prescription drug coverage to those who opt to participate. Started in 2004 with a discount card that lowered prices for many seniors from 10 to 25 percent, the full program goes into effect in 2006 and will provide an estimated 40 million seniors the opportunity to get some federal help to pay for prescriptions. Those who choose to participate will pay a monthly premium of approximately $35. After a $250 annual deductible, 75 percent of their prescription costs will be covered. For those whose annual prescription drug costs exceed $5,100, the new program will pay 95 percent of prescription costs over that amount. There are some odd gaps in coverage, however. Many congressional Democrats found the bill too weak to help the average senior citizen and claimed its primary beneficiaries would be the pharmaceutical and insurance industries. But, even some Democrats voted for its final passage, as they agreed with the leaders of the American Association of Retired Persons (AARP) that it was time to do something, and this seemed the only plan with a chance to pass.[21]

The addition of the prescription drug benefit troubled many budget conservatives because of the added costs it is projected to impose on a system that, whatever its merits, is extraordinarily expensive. The actual costs of this new program were seriously understated during the debate, and that leads many to wonder how the burgeoning federal budget can withstand such new pressure. Medicare itself has become a costly program because people live longer, the elderly need more hospital and physicians' services, and medical care costs are rising rapidly. Attempts to limit or cap expenditures for the program have had only marginal effects. With millions of Baby Boomers set to retire in the next fifteen years, the system will be under even greater strain.

Medicaid.   Enacted into law at the same time as Medicare, the Medicaid program provides comprehensive health care, including hospitalization, physician services, prescription drugs, and long-term nursing home care (unlike Medicare) to all who qualify as needy under TANF and SSI. In 1986, Congress extended Medicaid coverage to low-income families (less than 133 percent of the official poverty level) for pregnant women and children. The states were also accorded the option of extending coverage to all pregnant women and to all children under one year of age in families with incomes below 185 percent of the poverty level. Nursing facility services, in-patient general hospital services, home health services, and prescription drugs represented major categories of spending within the Medicaid program.

Medicaid is jointly financed by the national and state governments. The national government pays 50 to 79 percent of Medicaid costs, based on average per capita income, which awards more financial support to poor than to wealthy states. Each state is responsible for the administration of its own program and sets specific standards of eligibility and benefit levels for Medicaid recipients within the boundaries set by national guidelines. Nearly all needy people are covered by Medicaid in some states; in others, only one-third or so of the needy are protected. Some states also award coverage to the "medically indigent," that is, to people who do not qualify for welfare but for whom large medical expenses would constitute a severe financial burden.

Although the average amount paid for by the states varies, the portion of state budgets going to Medicaid is similar—ever upward. If Medicaid expenditures continue to grow at their present rate, the proportion of funding that is available for other programs will be reduced.

The Cost of Health Care.   The costs of Medicare and Medicaid, which vastly exceed early estimates, have been major contributors to the ballooning costs of health care and the budget deficit. In 2003, national expenditures for both the Medicare and Medicaid programs were $438 billion. Projected increases are expected to grow between 2003 and 2009 at a faster pace than increases in Social Security, defense, and discretionary nondefense spending.[22] In 2005, Medicare, along with its new prescription drug benefits, was expected to cost $540 billion.

A number of factors have contributed to the high and rising costs of health care. First, more people are living longer and are requiring costly and extensive care in their declining years. Second, the range and sophistication of diagnostic practices and therapeutic treatments, which are often quite expensive, have increased. Third, the expansion of private health insurance, along with Medicare and Medicaid, has reduced the direct costs of health care to most people and increased the demand for services. More people, in short, can afford care. They may also be less aware of the costs of care. Fourth, the costs of health care have also increased because of its higher quality and because labor costs have outpaced productivity in the

Timeline

The Growth of the Budget and Federal Spending

provision of hospital care. Fifth, U.S. medicine focuses less on preventing illnesses and more on curing them, which is more costly.

Public opinion polls indicate that most people are satisfied with the quality of health care services provided by physicians and hospitals, but a substantial majority express dissatisfaction over the costs and accessibility of health care.[23] There is, as a consequence, a strong belief in the need to improve the nation's health care system.

ECONOMIC POLICY

DURING OUR NATION'S FIRST CENTURY, the states were responsible for managing economic affairs. The national government defined its economic role narrowly, although it did collect tariffs, fund public improvements, and encourage private development. Congress became active in setting economic policy and enacting economic regulation only after people realized that the states alone could not solve the problems affecting the economy.

The Roots of Economic Policy

Although the U.S. economic system is a mixed free-enterprise system characterized by the private ownership of property, private enterprise, and marketplace competition, the national government has long played an important role in fostering economic development through its tax, tariff, public lands disposal, and public works policies, and also through the creation of a national bank. For much of the nineteenth century, however, national regulatory programs were few and were restricted to such tasks as steamboat inspection and the regulation of trade with the Native American tribes.

Following the Civil War, however, the United States entered a period of rapid economic growth and extensive industrialization. Small business owners, reformers, and farmers in the Midwest pressured the national government to control these new forces. After nearly two decades of agitation, in 1887, Congress finally adopted the Interstate Commerce Act to regulate the railroads. The act, to be enforced by the new Interstate Commerce Commission (ICC), required that railroad rates should be "just and reasonable."[24]

Three years later, Congress dealt with the problem of "trusts," the name given to large-scale, monopolistic businesses that dominated many industries, including oil, sugar, whiskey, salt, cordage, and meatpacking. The Sherman Antitrust Act of 1890 prohibits all restraints of trade and all monopolization or attempts to monopolize. The Interstate Commerce Act and the Sherman Antitrust Act constitute the nineteenth- and early twentieth-century response of the national government to the new industrialization.

THE BOSSES OF THE SENATE.

Photo courtesy: Bettmann/CORBIS

■ Here, a political cartoonist depicts how the U.S. government was perceived by some as being dominated by various trusts, during the Progressive era.

The Progressive Era

The Progressive movement drew much of its support from the middle class and sought to reform the political, economic, and social systems of U.S. society. There was a desire to bring corporate power fully under the control of government and make it more responsive to democratic ends. Progressive administrations under presidents Theodore Roosevelt and Woodrow Wilson established or strengthened regulatory programs to control railroads, business, and banking and to protect consumers.

Consumer protection legislation came in the form of the Pure Food and Drug Act and the Meat Inspection Act, both enacted in 1906. These statutes marked the beginning of consumer protection as a major responsibility of the national government. The Meat Inspection Act was passed partly in response to publication of Upton Sinclair's novel *The Jungle*, which described the unsavory and unsanitary conditions in Chicago meatpacking plants. The Pure Food and Drug Act prohibited the adulteration and mislabeling of foods and drugs, which were common practices at this time.

The Depression and the New Deal marked a major turning point in U.S. history in general and in U.S. economic history in particular. During the 1930s, the *laissez-faire* state was replaced with the **interventionist state,** in which the government plays an active and extensive role in guiding and regulating the private economy.[25] The New Deal established the national government as a major regulator of private businesses, as a provider of Social Security, and as ultimately responsible for maintaining a stable economy. It brought about a number of reforms in almost every area, including finance, agriculture, labor, and industry.

laissez-faire
A French term literally meaning "to allow to do, to leave alone." It is a hands-off governmental policy that is based on the belief that governmental involvement in the economy is wrong.

interventionist state
Replacement for the laissez-faire state in which the government took an active role in guiding and managing the private economy.

Financial Reforms.   The major New Deal banking laws were the Glass-Steagall Act (1933) and the Banking Act (1935). The Glass-Steagall Act required the separation of commercial and investment banking and set up the Federal Deposit Insurance Corporation (FDIC) to insure bank deposits, originally for $5,000 per account. Although it had long been opposed by conservatives, bank deposit insurance has now become an accepted feature of the U.S. banking system. The Banking Act reorganized the Federal Reserve System, removed the secretary of the treasury as an ex-officio member, and formally established the Open Market Committee (discussed later in this chapter).

Legislation was also passed to control abuses in the stock markets. The Securities Act (1933) required that prospective investors be given full and accurate information about the stocks or securities being offered to them. The Securities Exchange Act (1934) created the Securities and Exchange Commission (SEC), an independent regulatory commission. The SEC was authorized to regulate the stock exchanges, to enforce the Securities Act, and to reduce the number of stocks bought on margin (that is, with borrowed money).

Agriculture and Labor.   During the New Deal, Congress passed several laws designed to help farmers who reduced their crop production to bring it into better balance with demand. These price support laws are still controversial today. At the same time, Congress passed the National Labor Relations Act (also known as the Wagner Act) that guaranteed workers' right to organize and bargain collectively through unions of their own choosing. A series of unfair labor practices, such as discriminating against employees because of their union activities, was prohibited. The National Labor Relations Board (NLRB) was created to carry out the act and to conduct elections to determine which union, if any, employees wanted to represent them. Unions prospered under the protection provided by the Wagner Act.

Participation
Farm Subsidies and
Domestic Policy

The last major piece of New Deal economic legislation was the Fair Labor Standards Act (FLSA) of 1938. Intended to protect the interests of low-paid workers, the law set twenty-five cents per hour and forty-four hours per week as initial minimum standards. Within a few years, wages rose to forty cents per hour, and hours declined to forty per week. The act also banned child labor.[26]

Industry Regulations.   Several industries were the subjects of new or expanded regulatory programs. The Federal Communications Commission (FCC) was created in 1934 to regulate radio, telephone, and telegraph industries. The Civil Aeronautics Board (CAB) was put in place in 1938 to regulate the commercial aviation industry. The Motor Carrier Act of 1935 put the trucking industry under the jurisdiction of the Interstate Commerce Commission (ICC). Regulation of industries such as trucking and commercial aviation, like railroad regulation, extended to such matters as entry into the business, routes of service, and rates.

Economic and Social Regulations

Economists and political scientists frequently distinguish between economic regulation and social regulation. **Economic regulation** focuses on such matters as control of entry into a business, prices or rates that businesses charge, and service routes or areas. Regulation is usually tailored to the conditions of particular industries, such as railroads or stock exchanges. "Economic regulation places government in the driver's seat with respect to the economic direction and performance of the regulated industry."[27] In contrast, **social regulation** sets standards for the quality and safety of products and the conditions under which goods are produced and services rendered. Social regulation strives to protect and enhance the quality of life. Regulation of product safety by the Consumer Product Safety Commission is an example of social regulation. Professor Michael Reagan, noted authority in the study of regulation, makes a helpful distinction: "Social regulation can generally be differentiated from economic regulation by the former's concern with harm to our physical (and sometimes moral and aesthetic) well-being, rather than harm to our wallets."[28]

Most of the regulatory programs established through the 1950s fell into the category of economic regulation. From the mid-1960s to the mid-1970s, however, the national government passed social regulatory legislation on such topics as consumer protection, health and safety, and environmental protection. Congress based this legislation on its commerce clause authority.

As a consequence of this flood of social regulation, many industries that previously had limited dealings with government found they now had to comply with government regulation in the conduct of their operations. For example, the automobile industry previously had been lightly touched by anti-trust, labor relations, and other general statutes. By the early 1970s, however, the quality of its products was heavily regulated by the Environmental Protection Agency (EPA) motor vehicle emissions standards and federally mandated safety standards. The automobile companies found this experience both galling and expensive. The chemical industry found itself in much the same situation.

Deregulation

Deregulation, which involves the reduction in market controls (such as controls on allowable rates or controls on who can enter the field), emerged as an attractive political issue even before the wave of social regulation began to wane. Deregulation, in theory, would increase market competition and lead to lower prices for consumers. The focus of the deregulation movement was on the economic regulatory pro-

economic regulation
Governmental regulation of business practices, industry rates, routes, or areas serviced by particular industries.

social regulation
Governmental regulation of the quality and safety of products as well as the conditions under which goods and services are produced.

deregulation
Reduction in market controls, such as controls on allowable rates or who can enter a field.

ECONOMIC FREEDOM AROUND THE WORLD

Globalization is blurring the territorial boundaries that separate countries. In the process, it is creating a single world economy. Significant differences still remain among countries, however, in regard to their political and economic systems. These differences are important to investors because they affect investors' ability to earn profits and their decisions on where to set up new businesses or expand existing ones. Important considerations include tax rates, communication and transportation systems, regulations governing investments, and labor costs. The last of these has been particularly influential for certain businesses. Between 2000 and 2003, the United States lost 455,000 jobs in the computer and electronic industry. It is not hard to understand why. Salaries for computer programmers in the United States, for example, ranged from $60,000 to $80,000 per year. In Ireland, the range was $23,000 to $34,000; in India, it was $5,880 to $11,000.

We can get a quick picture of how hospitable a country is to business by looking at its ranking on the *Economic Freedom of the World* index prepared by the Economic Freedom Network. In 2000, the group evaluated 123 countries on a 10-point scale, with 10 being the highest score. The measure scores a country's performance on thirty-seven different dimensions, including the existence of a legal system that protects an individual's private property, the existence of a stable currency, patent rights protections, the freedom to compete in labor and product markets, and tax policies that encourage investment. According to the authors of the study, economic freedom does not lead to greater income inequality and tends to appear where there are high individual income levels, high rates of economic growth, and long life expectancy. The 2000 report, the sixth edition of the survey, found that the average economic freedom score was 6.39—up from 5.99 in 1995. Overall, economic freedom declined during the 1970s and reached a low of 5.32 in 1980. Since then, economic freedom has been on the rise.

The graph shows that in 2000, Hong Kong, with a score of 8.8, had the highest economic freedom ranking. The United States ranked third (8.5). Mexico, just below the midpoint, was sixty-sixth (6.3). The highest-ranking South American country was Chile at fifteenth (7.5). African and Latin American countries as well as countries that emerged from the former Soviet Union tended to congregate at the bottom of the rankings. Botswana was the highest-ranking African country at thirty-eighth (7.0). The bottom five countries in the ranking were Ukraine, Algeria, Guinea-Bissau, Myanmar, and the Democratic Republic of the Congo. Because of the absence of data, Iraq, Saudi Arabia, Cuba, and North Korea were not evaluated or ranked.

grams for such industries as railroads, trucking, and commercial air transportation; most social regulatory programs continued to enjoy strong public support and were left largely alone by the deregulation movement.

Beginning in the 1950s and 1960s, economists, political scientists, and journalists began to point out defects in some of the economic regulatory programs.[29] They contended that regulation sometimes encouraged monopolistic exploitation, discrimination in services, and inefficiency in the operation of regulated industries. Moreover,

Comparing Economic Policy

Questions

1. What are some factors that might help a country—for example, Russia or Mexico—to raise its ranking?

2. What factors might cause the ranking of a country—for example, Hong Kong—to fall?

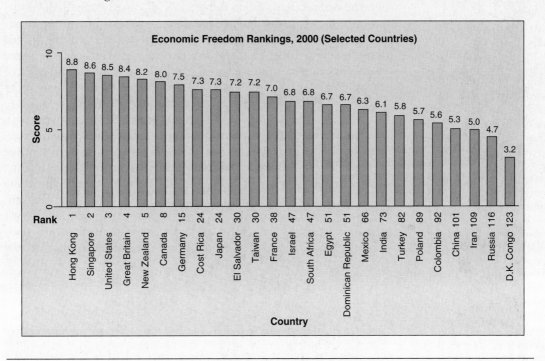

Economic Freedom Rankings, 2000 (Selected Countries)

Source: Economic Freedom Network, http://www.freetheworld.com.

regulated firms often had difficulty competing on the basis of prices and also discouraged the entry of new competitors.

For some time, nothing changed in the regulatory arena despite these criticisms. In the mid-1970s, however, President Gerald R. Ford decided to make deregulation a focal point of his administration. About this time, Senator Ted Kennedy (D–MA) became chair of a subcommittee of the Senate Judiciary Committee. Wanting to use his new position and acting on the advice of his staff, he decided to hold hearings on airline deregulation. The combined actions of Ford and Kennedy put deregulation on the national policy agenda. Democrats and Republicans, liberals and conservatives, all found deregulation to be an appealing political issue.

Only one deregulation act was passed during the Ford administration. However, deregulation picked up momentum after Jimmy Carter became president in 1977. Legislation that deregulated commercial airlines, railroads, motor carriers, and financial institutions was enacted during his term. Two additional deregulation laws were adopted in the early years of the Reagan administration.

An exception to the usual rules and regulations guiding deregulation was the Airline Deregulation Act of 1978 (discussed earlier in this chapter), which completely eliminated economic regulation of commercial airlines over several years. Although many new passenger carriers flocked into the industry when barriers to entry were first removed, they were unable to compete successfully with the existing major airlines. Most of the original new entrants have now disappeared, as have some of the major airlines that were operating at the time of deregulation.

The deregulation of the savings and loan business, coupled with the failure of the Reagan administration to enforce the remaining controls on savings and loans adequately, led in time to a costly instance of deregulatory failure. Poor management, bad commercial investments, and corruption forced hundreds of savings and loans, especially in the Southwest, into bankruptcy.[30] The Financial Institutions Reform, Recovery, and Enforcement Act (1989) revamped the regulatory system for savings and loans, provided for the liquidation of insolvent associations, and bailed out their depositors. Total direct costs to the taxpayers were over $500 billion.[31]

■ Stadium employees remove letters from one of the Enron Field signs in Houston, Texas. The Houston Astros paid $2.1 million to get back the naming rights to their stadium from the collapsed energy trader Enron.

Photo courtesy: James Nielsen/Getty Images

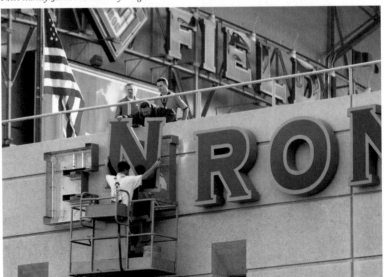

Strong public and governmental support continues to exist for social regulation dealing with consumers, workers, and the environment. But, in the wake of the savings and loan scandals of the 1980s, the more recent downturn of the stock market, and extensive corporate greed and fraud that has led to the collapse not only of the dot-com economy but also large corporations including Enron and WorldCom, the cry today is for more regulation of business, not less. Still, the Bush administration has been reticent to add more controls on business, although several members of Congress are clamoring for renewed oversight and accountability, whether through heightened enforcement of existing legislation and regulation or passage of new ones.

Stabilizing the Economy

Although there continues to be disagreement about the degree to which governments, especially the national government, should be involved, few question the important role that government plays in the economic stability in the nation, which is critical to the success of domestic and national policy. **Economic stability** is a condition in which there is economic growth, a rising national income, high employment, and a steadiness in the general level of prices. Conversely, economic instability involves either inflation or recession. **Inflation** occurs when there is too much demand for the available supply of goods and services, with the consequence that general price levels rise as buyers compete for the available supply. Prices may also rise if large corporations and unions have sufficient economic power to push prices and wages above competitive levels. A **recession** is marked by a decline in the economy. Investment sags, production falls off, and unemployment increases.

Typical tools by which government influences the economy include monetary policy (control of the money supply) and fiscal policy (spending and taxing decisions). Fiscal policy commitments as well as decisions related to the size of the deficit or surplus are observable in budget outputs. These outputs reflect the clash of various interest groups as they compete for advantage. The ultimate budget reflects the power of these groups as well as a mandate to stabilize the economy. Since the economy is not closed off from outside forces, national and global changes must be taken into account.

Monetary Policy: Regulating Money Supply.
The government conducts **monetary policy** by managing the nation's money supply and influencing interest rates. In an industrialized economy, all those making exchanges—consumers, businesses, and government—use money. That is, prices of goods and services are set in money units (dollars), and the amount of money in circulation influences the quantity of goods and services demanded, the number of workers hired, the decisions to

economic stability
A situation in which there is economic growth, rising national income, high employment, and steadiness in the general level of prices.

inflation
A rise in the general price levels of an economy.

recession
A short-term decline in the economy that occurs as investment sags, production falls off, and unemployment increases.

monetary policy
A form of government regulation in which the nation's money supply and interest rates are controlled.

Photo courtesy: Doug Mills/AP/Wide World Photos

■ Federal Reserve Board Chair Alan Greenspan helped shepherd the economy through one of its longest stretches of economic expansion, and in spite of recent economic downturns, was appointed by President George W. Bush to a new term.

Federal Reserve Board
A seven-member board that sets member banks' reserve requirements, controls the discount rate, and makes other economic decisions.

build factories, and so forth. Money is more than just the currency and coin in our pockets: it includes balances in our checkbooks, deposits in bank accounts, and the value of other assets. The Federal Reserve is responsible for changing the money supply. As it makes these changes, it attempts to promote economic stability.

The **Federal Reserve Board** has responsibility for the formation and implementation of monetary policy because of its ability to control the credit-creating and lending activities of the nation's banks. When individuals and corporations deposit their money in financial institutions such as commercial banks (which accept deposits and make loans) and savings and loan associations (S&Ls), these deposits serve as the basis for loans to borrowers. In effect, the loaning of money creates new deposits or financial liabilities—new money that did not previously exist.

The Federal Reserve System.   Created in 1913 to adjust the money supply to the needs of agriculture, commerce, and industry, the Federal Reserve System comprises the Federal Reserve Board (FRB) (formally, the Board of Governors of the Federal Reserve System; informally, "the Fed"), the Federal Open Market Committee (FOMC), and the twelve Federal Reserve Banks in regions throughout the country. The Fed represents a mixture of private interests and governmental authority.

The primary monetary policy tools are the setting of reserve requirements for member banks, control of the discount, and open market operations. Formally, authority to use these tools is allocated to the FRB, the Federal Reserve Bank boards of directors, and the FOMC, respectively. In actuality, however, all three are dominated by the FRB, which, in recent decades, has been under the sway of its chair. Arthur Burns and Paul Volcker (past chairs) and Alan Greenspan, the current chair, have been influential and respected policy makers. Public officials and the financial community pay great attention to the utterances of the Fed's chair for clues to the future course of monetary policy.

reserve requirements
Governmental requirements that a portion of member banks' deposits must be retained to back loans made.

Reserve requirements set by the Federal Reserve designate the portion of the banks' deposits that banks must retain as backing for their loans. The reserves determine how much or how little banks can lend to businesses and consumers. For example, if the FRB changed the reserve requirements and allowed banks to keep $10 on hand rather than $15 for every $100 in deposits that it held, it would free up some additional money for loans. Banks would have an extra $5 for every $100 deposited that they can use to stimulate economic activity. The **discount rate** is the rate of interest at which the Federal Reserve Board lends money to member banks. In **open market operations,** the FRB buys and sells government securities in the open market. The FRB can also use moral suasion to influence the actions of banks and other members of the financial community by suggestion, exhortation, and informal agreement. Because of its commanding position as a monetary policy maker, the media, economists, and market observers pay attention to verbal signals about economic trends and conditions emitted by the FRB and its chair.

How the FRB uses these tools depends in part on its views of the state of the economy. If inflation appears to be the problem, then the Fed would likely restrict or tighten the money supply. If a recession with rising unemployment appears to threaten the economy, then the FRB would probably act to loosen or expand the money supply in order to stimulate the economy.

discount rate
The rate of interest at which member banks can borrow money from their regional Federal Reserve Bank.

open market operations
The buying and selling of government securities by the Federal Reserve Bank in the securities market.

Fiscal Policy: Taxing and Spending.

Fiscal policy involves the deliberate use of the national government's taxing and spending policies to influence the overall operation of the economy and maintain economic stability. The president and Congress formulate fiscal policy and conduct it through the federal budget process. The powerful instruments of fiscal policy are budget surpluses and deficits. These are achieved by manipulating the overall or "aggregate" levels of revenue and expenditures.

fiscal policy
Federal government policies on taxes, spending, and debt management, intended to promote the nation's macroeconomic goals, particularly with respect to employment, price stability, and growth.

According to standard fiscal policy theory, there is a level of total or aggregate spending at which the economy will operate at full employment. Total spending is the sum of consumer spending, private investment spending, and government spending. If consumer and business spending does not create demand sufficient to cause the economy to operate at full employment, then the government should make up the shortfall by increasing spending in excess of revenues. This was essentially what John Maynard Keynes recommended for the national government during the Great Depression. If inflation is the problem confronting policy makers, then government can reduce demand for goods and services by reducing its expenditures and running a budget surplus.[32]

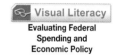

Visual Literacy
Evaluating Federal Spending and Economic Policy

Discretionary fiscal policy involves deliberate decisions by the president and Congress to run budget surpluses or deficits. This can be done by increasing or decreasing spending while holding taxes constant, by increasing or cutting taxes while holding spending stable, or by some combination of changes in taxing and expenditure. For example, President George W. Bush's 2003 tax cuts were attempts to stimulate the economy by putting more money into the hands of taxpayers in spite of a growing deficit.

Simulation
You Are Trying to Get a Tax Cut

SUMMARY

THIS CHAPTER EXAMINED the policy-making process, social welfare policies, and economic policies. The policy-making process can be viewed as a sequence of functional activities beginning with the identification and definition of public problems. Once identified, problems must get on the governmental agenda. Other stages of the process include policy formulation, policy adoption, budgeting for policies, policy implementation, and the evaluation of policy.

The origins of social welfare policy can be traced back to the early initiatives in the nation's history. Only after the Great Depression, however, was a public-sector role in the delivery of social services broadly accepted. Most income security programs generally take two forms: non-means-based programs and means-based programs, which indicate that all people who meet eligibility requirements are automatically entitled to receive benefits. Governments in the United States have a long history of involvement in the health of Americans. Most state and local governments have health departments, and the U.S. government has several public health and medical research divisions. Medicare and Medicaid are the two most prominent national programs. As the cost of health care has risen, however, new demands have been made to restrain the rate of growth in costs.

Efforts by the national government to regulate the economy began with anti-monopoly legislation during the Progressive era. Then, during the New Deal, a host of new programs were created by Congress and the president to correct the lingering effects of the Great Depression. Full employment, employee-employer relations, and social regulation became new concerns of government. Even before social regulation which involves the reduction in market controls, emerged as an attractive political issue.

The national government continues to shape monetary policy by regulating the nation's money supply and interest rates. Monetary policy is controlled by the Federal Reserve Board. Fiscal policy, which involves the deliberate use of the national government's taxing and spending policies, is another tool of the national government and involves the president and Congress setting the national budget.

KEY TERMS

agenda, p. 480
deregulation, p. 505
discount rate, p. 511
economic regulation, p. 505
economic stability, p. 509
entitlement program, p. 498
Federal Reserve Board, p. 510
fiscal policy, p. 511
governmental (institutional) agenda, p. 481
inflation, p. 509
interventionist state, p. 503
laissez-faire, p. 503
means-tested program, p. 490
monetary policy, p. 509
non-means-based program, p. 490
open market operations, p. 511
policy adoption, p. 484
policy evaluation, p. 487
policy formulation, p. 481
policy implementation, p. 485
public policy, p. 477
recession, p. 509
reserve requirements, p. 510
social regulation, p. 505
Social Security Act, p. 489
social welfare policy, p. 488
systematic agenda, p. 480

SELECTED READINGS

Chernow, Ron. *Alexander Hamilton*. New York: Penguin, 2004.

Derthick, Martha. *Agency Under Stress: The Social Security Administration in American Government*. Washington, DC: Brookings Institution, 1990.

Devine, Robert S. *Bush Versus the Environment*. New York: Anchor Books, 2004.

Gilens, Martin. *Why Americans Hate Welfare: Race, Media, and the Politics of Antipoverty Policy*. Chicago: University of Chicago Press, 2001.

Kettl, Donald F. *Deficit Politics: Public Budgeting in Its Institutional and Historical Context*. New York: Macmillan, 1992.

Krugman, Paul. *The Great Unraveling*. New York: W. W. Norton, 2003.

Levitan, Sar, Garth Mangum, and Stephen Mangum. *Programs in Aid of the Poor*. Baltimore, MD: Johns Hopkins University Press, 1998.

Lindbloom, Charles E., and Edward J. Woodhouse. *The Policy-Making Process*, 3rd ed. Englewood Cliffs, NJ: Prentice Hall, 1993.

Mann, Thomas, and Norman Ornstein, eds. *Intensive Care: How Congress Shapes Health Policy*. Washington, DC: American Enterprise Institute and Brookings Institution, 1995.

Mead, Lawrence M., ed. *The New Paternalism: Supervisory Approaches to Poverty*. Washington, DC: Brookings Institution Press, 1997.

Phillips, Kevin. *Wealth and Democracy: A Political History of the American Rich*. New York: Broadway Books, 2002.

Rubin, Robert E., with Jacob Weisberg. *In an Uncertain World: Tough Choices from Wall Street to Washington*. New York: Random House, 2003.

Skocpal, Theda. *The Missing Middle: Working Families and the Future of American Social Policy*. New York: Norton, 2000.

Thompson, Frank, and John DiIulio Jr. *Medicaid and Devolution: A View from the States*. Washington, DC: Brookings Institution Press, 1998.

Thurmaier, Kurt M., and Katherine G. Willoughby. *Policy and Politics in State Budgeting*. Armonk, NY: M. E. Sharpe, 2001.

Tonelson, Alan. *The Race to the Bottom: Why a Worldwide Worker Surplus and Uncontrolled Free Trade Are Sinking American Living Standards*. Boulder, CO: Westview, 2002.

Weil, Alan, and Kenneth Finegold, eds. *Welfare Reform: The Next Act*. Washington, DC: Urban Institute Press, 2002.

Wilsford, David. *Doctors and the State: The Politics of Health Care in France and in the United States*. Durham, NC: Duke University Press, 1991.

WEB EXPLORATIONS

To understand how public policies are prioritized and analyzed, go to www.ncpa.org

To see an overview of the legislative process for public policy, go to www.house.gov/houseTying_it_all.html

To understand how public policy laws are made, go to http://thomas.loc.gov/home/thomas.html

To learn more about how public policies are budgeted, go to www.cbpp.org

To learn about the research institutes and organizations that evaluate policies, go to http://www.aei.org www.brookings.org

To learn more about the most current Social Security benefits and statistics, go to http://www.ssa.gov/

For a progress report on welfare reform, go to www.progress.org

For other health care policy initiatives and consumer health information, go to www.nih.gov

To learn about other educational policies, go to http://nces.ed.gov/

To learn about the government Bureau for Economic Analysis, go to www.bea.doc.gov

To compare various business cycle indicators, go to http://www.tcb-indicators.org/

To access the most current labor and wages data for your state or region, go to http://www.bls.gov/ncs/

To learn about current economic policy, go to http://www.nber.org

To learn more about regulation of financial markets via the Federal Reserve Board, go to http://www.federalreserve.gov/

To learn about current fiscal policy, go to http://www.gpoaccess.gov/usbudget/index.html

To compare the current fiscal budget with budgets from prior years, go to http://www.whitehouse.gov/omb

To compare the federal budget with the national debt, go to http://www.gpoaccess.gov/usbudget/fy04/index.html

14

Foreign and Defense Policy

Photo courtesy: Mikhail Metzel/AP/Wide World Photos

WHEN THE UNITED STATES LAUNCHED its war against Saddam Hussein's Iraqi government in March 2003, it signaled a dramatic break in American policy. In most past conflicts of this magnitude, the United States had intervened militarily in response to a direct attack (such as Pearl Harbor) or to defend other countries that had been invaded (such as South Korea or Kuwait). The U.S. invasion of Iraq was part of a new strategy that sought to promote American security through aggressive new tactics, including preemptive strikes against potentially dangerous nations. Believing that the Hussein regime had been violating international law by secretly developing weapons of mass destruction, the United States government was willing to act even though the United Nations Security Council refused to endorse the recourse to war. This bold but controversial U.S. strategy is part of something called the Bush Doctrine.

Like other presidents before him, George W. Bush was putting his distinctive stamp on how the country should address threats to national security. Particularly after the terrorist attacks of September 11, 2001, Bush and his foreign policy team concluded that a more ambitious, "muscular" posture was needed to fight global threats to U.S. interests. By attacking Hussein's forces in Iraq, American resolve would provide an object lesson to other countries that were not behaving as the United States wanted. According to Richard Perle, a senior adviser to the Bush administration, "It's always been at the heart of the Bush Doctrine that a more robust policy would permit us to elicit greater cooperation from adversaries."[1] When

Libyan leader Muammar Qaddafi indicated his willingness to abandon the development of weapons of mass destruction in late 2003, it was viewed as proof that the Bush Doctrine worked.[2] Having seen what happened to Saddam Hussein when he failed to take the Americans seriously, Qaddafi was folding up rather than fight.

Critics, however, believe the Bush Doctrine is misguided for several reasons. They point to the frightening precedent of launching preemptive wars, and the dangerous lesson that might teach other countries (for instance, Pakistan and India) who fear and hate their adversaries. Critics also question the morality of invading another country based solely on what it *might* do. Senator Robert Byrd (D–WV), a staunch opponent of the Iraq War, referred to the U.S. action as "an unprovoked invasion of a sovereign nation."[3] Critics question whether such an aggressive strategy might actually lead to a backlash against the United States by our allies (the governments of Canada, Mexico, France, Germany, and Russia were among those who opposed the invasion of Iraq), and a deepening hatred of the United States by adversaries. By attacking an Arab government in Iraq, was the United States creating, as Egyptian President Hosni Mubarak warned, many more Osama bin Ladens?

I N THE 1990S, FOLLOWING THE END of the Cold War, the collapse of the Soviet Union, and the expulsion of Saddam Hussein from Kuwait in the 1991 Persian Gulf War, U.S. foreign policy—after a string of successes—was undergoing a transition. What role would the United States play in a very different post–Cold War world? Was China the next major adversary, or would the world be a safer one as the new millennium approached? It remained in transition when Democrat Bill Clinton was replaced by Republican George W. Bush in 2001. After the attacks on September 11, 2001, however, that transition period ended, and the United States had a new adversary: terrorism. More Americans began to pay attention to foreign policy and defense issues again. Many wondered how policy is made by the government and how the United States emerged as the last surviving superpower, only to be susceptible to a devastating series of terrorist attacks on one fateful day.

Like social and economic policy, U.S. foreign and defense policy has evolved. Today, the United States is the most powerful and influential country in the world. No other state has as large an economy, as powerful a military, or plays as influential a role as the United States. The U.S. economy is twice as large as that of Japan, the country with the second largest economy. The U.S. military is unrivaled in strength.

Photo courtesy: Dennis Brack

■ As national security adviser, Condoleezza Rice provided daily briefings to President George W. Bush about global threats. For his second term, President Bush selected Rice to be his secretary of state, replacing Colin Powell. Here, at the U.S. Senate, Rice testifies before the 9/11 Commission investigating the 2001 terrorist attack on the United States.

isolationism
A national policy of avoiding participation in foreign affairs.

unilateralism
A national policy of acting without consulting others.

moralism
The policy of emphasizing morality in foreign affairs.

pragmatism
The policy of taking advantage of a situation for national gain.

American culture, though often criticized, has swept the world, from music to movies to clothes to food. It was not always this way. When the United States was founded, it was a weak country on the margins of world affairs, its economy shattered by the Revolutionary War, its military composed of volunteers who had not been paid for years, and its culture regarded by European powers as backward and barbarian.

Even so, the United States was fortunate. Separated from Europe and Asia by vast oceans, it had abundant resources and industrious people. The United States often stood apart from world engagements, following a policy of **isolationism,** that is, avoiding participation in foreign affairs. However, isolationism was rarely total. Even in its early years, the United States engaged in foreign affairs, and it always was a trading nation. Another U.S. policy was **unilateralism,** that is, acting without consulting others. **Moralism** was also central to the U.S. self-image in foreign policy, with most Americans believing their country had higher moral standards than European and other countries. Many Americans were also proud of their **pragmatism,** that is, their ability to find ways to take advantage of a situation. Thus, when Europe was at war, Americans sold goods to both sides and profited handsomely. When land became available in North America, Americans found a way to get it.

In this chapter, we first will trace the roots of U.S. foreign and defense policy in the years since the United States became a world power. After studying the executive branch and foreign and defense policy making, we will discuss other shapers and influencers of foreign and defense policy. Finally, we will explore the challenge of balancing foreign and domestic affairs in the twenty-first century.

THE ROOTS OF CURRENT U.S. FOREIGN AND DEFENSE POLICY

WHEN JOHN F. KENNEDY became president in 1961, he brought a sense of optimism and activism to the United States that captivated many Americans. "Ask not what your country can do for you,"

Kennedy urged Americans in his inaugural address, "but what you can do for your country."

In foreign and defense policy, containing the Soviet Union while at the same time establishing cordial relations with it to lessen the peril of nuclear war was high on the agenda. Thus, in 1961, Kennedy met Soviet leader Nikita Khrushchev, in Vienna. The meeting did not go well. Both leaders returned to their respective countries and increased military spending. In 1962, the Soviet Union began to deploy intermediate-range ballistic missiles in Cuba, only ninety miles from Florida, leading to the **Cuban Missile Crisis.**[4] The United States reacted strongly, placing a naval blockade around Cuba and warning the Soviet Union to withdraw the missiles or suffer the consequences. After several days during which the world was close to nuclear war, Khrushchev backed down and withdrew the missiles. The Cuban Missile Crisis led to another period of improved U.S.-Soviet relations. During the crisis, the United States and the Soviet Union had marched to the edge of nuclear war, and neither liked what they had seen. Thus, in 1963, the two superpowers concluded a partial nuclear test ban treaty and installed a "hot line" between Washington and Moscow to allow the leaders of the two countries to talk directly during crises.

The Cuban Missile Crisis confirmed the need to contain the Soviet Union. The Soviet Union was an expansionist power, most Americans believed, as shown by the missile crisis. Despite its dangers, containment was the correct strategy, and the United States remained the moral defender of liberty and justice, acting pragmatically but always with restraint to prevent communist expansion. Few questioned the morality of containment, the necessity for pragmatism, or the need for internationalism and American-led multilateralism.

Then came the **Vietnam War.** The United States sought to contain communism from spreading from North Vietnam into South Vietnam starting in the 1950s, but it was in the mid-1960s that U.S. bombing and ground operations began, and they escalated quickly. While many in South Vietnam were grateful for U.S. assistance, others were actively supporting the communists. The United States eventually found itself in the midst of a civil war in which it was difficult to determine friend from foe. Eventually, the U.S. presence in Vietnam grew to over 500,000 troops, more than 58,000 of whom ultimately were killed. As deaths mounted and costs grew, many Americans asked questions they had rarely asked before. Was the United States on the side of justice in Vietnam, or had it only replaced France there as a colonial power? Was the United States pursuing an honorable objective with dishonorable means? How much killing and how great a cost would the United States bear to prevent the expansion of communism? Was communism still the enemy it had been? Increasingly, U.S. citizens became less persuaded that their mission in Vietnam was moral or that communism was dangerous.

Timeline

From Stand-Alone to Superpower: The Evolution of U.S. Foreign Policy

Cuban Missile Crisis

The 1962 confrontation that nearly escalated into war between the United States and Soviet Union over Soviet deployment of medium-range ballistic missiles in Cuba.

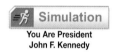

Simulation

You Are President John F. Kennedy

Vietnam War

Between 1965 and 1973, the United States deployed up to 500,000 troops to Vietnam to try to prevent North Vietnam from taking over South Vietnam; the effort failed and was extremely divisive within the United States.

Participation

Economic Sanctions and Cuba

■ Many Americans continue to visit the Vietnam War Memorial in Washington, D.C., to grieve for those in the U.S. military who gave their lives during the conflict in Southeast Asia.

Photo courtesy: Bachman/The Image Works

U.S. economic preeminence also declined in the 1960s, and Vietnam, in part, was to blame. Billions of dollars were spent there. But, other causes also existed for reduced U.S. economic preeminence. Other nations had rebuilt their economies following World War II, often with technologies more advanced than those of the United States. In addition, U.S. investment lagged as excessive consumerism began to take its toll.

By the end of the 1960s, U.S. optimism waned as the American century appeared to have become the American decade. Militarily and economically, the United States had no equal, but the optimism that had marked the U.S. world outlook for much of the 1950s and 1960s had faded.

Détente, Human Rights, and Renewed Containment: 1969–1981

When Richard M. Nixon was inaugurated as president in 1969, he declared it was time to move from "an era of confrontation" to "an era of negotiation" in relations with the Soviet Union. Recognizing that nuclear war would destroy life as it existed, searching for a way to exit Vietnam, and trying to improve East–West relations without conceding international leadership or renouncing containment, Nixon undertook policies that began this transformation. The improvement in U.S.–Soviet relations was called **détente**.[5]

d'etente
The relaxation of tensions between the United States and the Soviet Union that occurred during the 1970s.

As Nixon calculated how to achieve these objectives, some criticized his approach as cynical. Emphasizing pragmatism to the virtual exclusion of moralism, Nixon's approach reminded many of old-style

European power politics that the United States had rejected since its earliest days. Critics pointed to the **Nixon Doctrine** (that the United States would provide military aid to countries but not do the fighting for them) as evidence of this cynicism. Under the Nixon Doctrine, the United States expanded military aid to South Vietnam and accelerated bombing even as negotiations for American withdrawal proceeded. To many, this showed that Nixon ignored morality. Others supported Nixon's approach, arguing that it would get the United States out of Vietnam, open relations with China, and improve relations with the Soviet Union.

The changed nature of U.S.-Soviet relations brought about by détente was best illustrated by the frequency of summit meetings. From 1972 to 1979, American and Soviet leaders met six times, but détente was more than summitry. It also included increased trade, arms control agreements such as the Strategic Arms Limitation Treaty and the Anti-Ballistic Missile Treaty, and cultural exchanges. Détente improved East–West relations in Europe as well. For example, the heads of government of almost every nation in Europe and North America attended a meeting in Helsinki, Finland, in 1975.

Détente was short lived. Even as leaders met in Helsinki, events unfolded that undermined détente. In 1975, civil war broke out in Angola as Portugal ended its colonial presence. The following year, the Soviet Union helped Cuba deploy 20,000 troops to Angola to swing the war toward the pro-Soviet faction. Replacing Nixon as president in 1974, Gerald R. Ford supported Nixon's foreign and military policy lines but criticized Soviet and Cuban actions in Angola. However, the United States did not respond after Congress, fearing another Vietnam, passed a bill that prevented the United States from providing aid.

When Jimmy Carter became president in 1977, he, too, intended to pursue détente. However, he rejected Nixon's foreign policy cynicism. Carter instead emphasized **human rights,** that is, the protection of people's basic freedoms and needs. This found a sympathetic ear among many Americans. Once again, they believed, the United States would emphasize morality in foreign policy. Some Americans wondered, however, if Carter's emphasis on human rights was misdirected and was weakening the United States.

Concern about American weakness grew in 1979 when radical Iranians, with the support of Iran's fundamentalist Islamic government, overran the U.S. embassy in Tehran and held the embassy staff captive. The Iranian hostage crisis eroded Carter's support in the United States. For over a year, the country was powerless to win the hostages' release. A failed rescue attempt added to American humiliation. The hostages were not released until the day that Carter left office in 1981.

Détente finally died in 1979 when the Soviet Union invaded Afghanistan. Described by Carter as "the most serious strategic challenge since the Cold War began," the Soviet invasion led to an immediate

Nixon Doctrine
The policy implemented at the end of the Vietnam War that the United States would provide arms and military equipment to countries but not do the fighting for them.

human rights
The belief that human beings have inalienable rights such as freedom of speech and freedom of religion.

Carter Doctrine
Policy announced after the 1979 Soviet invasion of Afghanistan that the Persian Gulf area was a vital U.S. interest and the United States would fight to maintain access to it.

increase in U.S. defense spending. Carter also adopted a more hard-line approach to foreign policy, announcing the **Carter Doctrine,** under which the United States would fight to prevent any further Soviet expansion toward the Persian Gulf and the nearby oilfields.

Containment Revisited and Renewed: 1981–1989

U.S.–Soviet relations were tense during Jimmy Carter's last year as president, but they became confrontational during Ronald Reagan's first term in office as Reagan accelerated the U.S. arms buildup and initiated an activist foreign policy in response to Soviet adventurism in developing countries. In addition, Reagan emphasized morality in American foreign policy and pushed to create an open international economic system.[6]

U.S–Soviet relations deteriorated rapidly during Reagan's first years in office. In 1983 alone, Reagan announced his "Star Wars" strategic defense plan; the Soviets destroyed a Korean airliner that flew into Soviet airspace; the United States invaded Grenada, a pro-Soviet state, and stepped up support for the Contras, an insurgency attempting to overthrow the pro-Soviet Sandinista government in Nicaragua; the Soviets used carpet bombing and chemical warfare in Afghanistan; and the **North Atlantic Treaty Organization (NATO)** deployed intermediate-range ballistic missiles in Europe, leading to a Soviet walkout from arms talks in Geneva. In superpower relations, 1983 was not a good year.

North Atlantic Treaty Organization (NATO)
The first peacetime military treaty the United States joined, NATO is a regional political and military organization created in 1950.

But, in 1984, relations improved as the United States and the Soviet Union upgraded the hotline and agreed to expand arms-control talks. Most importantly, the rhetoric from both capitals deescalated. What happened?

First, the 1984 U.S. presidential election constrained U.S. rhetoric. Although most Americans supported the arms buildup, they were concerned about confrontation with the Soviets. Thus, Reagan moderated his statements. Second, U.S. foreign and military policy initiatives had an impact on Moscow as, in addition to its arms buildup, the United States implemented the **Reagan Doctrine,** under which the United States provided arms to anti-Soviet movements fighting pro-Soviet governments in Afghanistan, Angola, Mozambique, and Nicaragua. These programs increased the cost of Soviet involvement there and led Soviet leaders to rethink their foreign policy. Finally, the Soviet Union had serious internal problems. Its economy was performing poorly and it had a leadership crisis, with three Soviet leaders dying between 1982 and 1985.

Reagan Doctrine
Policy that the United States would provide military assistance to anti-communist groups fighting against pro-Soviet governments.

Mikhail Gorbachev worked with Reagan to improve relations after Gorbachev became the Soviet leader in 1985. Gorbachev introduced reforms in domestic, foreign, and military policies that transformed the Soviet Union and U.S.–Soviet relations. Although the reforms were intended to address the serious problems that the Soviet Union faced, they eventually led to the end of the Cold War and the demise of the Soviet Union. Gorbachev and Reagan held five summits before Reagan left office. Significant changes in the U.S.–Soviet relationship began at the third summit when the two local leaders signed an agreement to destroy all intermediate nuclear forces. This was the first time that an entire class of nuclear weapons was eliminated. Changes in the U.S.–Soviet relationship became even more pronounced between 1988 and 1991 as Gorbachev redefined several long-held outlooks on international relations, arms control made steady progress, and several negotiations on developing-world conflicts achieved success.

Searching for a New International Order: 1989–2001

George Bush assumed the United States presidency in 1989 pledging to continue Reagan's foreign policy directions. However, the pace and scope of change in Eastern Europe and the Soviet Union raised questions about the entire direction of U.S. foreign policy. The first question came from Eastern Europe. In 1989, the people of many Eastern European states revolted against their governments. During previous rebellions, Soviet troops stationed in Eastern Europe subdued the rebellions. This time, Gorbachev ordered Soviet troops to remain in their barracks. The rebellions continued, and in every communist country in Eastern Europe, the government fell.

The United States was not quite sure what to do. The collapse of communism in Eastern Europe was unexpected, and the United States

Photo courtesy: AP Photo/Jeff Widener

■ A Chinese man stands alone to block a line of tanks in Tiananmen Square in June 1989. The man, calling for an end to the recent violence against pro-democracy demonstrators, was pulled away by bystanders, and the tanks continued on their way. The Chinese government crushed a student-led demonstration for democractic reform, killing hundreds, perhaps thousands, of demonstrators in the strongest anti-government protest since the 1949 revolution. Ironically, the name Tianamen means "Gate of Heavenly Peace."

had no policies ready to initiate. At first, Bush proceeded cautiously. As it became clear that the revolutions were irreversible, the United States and other democratic states helped the new noncommunist Eastern European states try to establish democratic political and free market economic systems. Bush's foreign policy challenges were not confined to Eastern Europe. He also had to deal with the Tiananmen Square massacre, in which the Chinese government brutally repressed pro-democracy demonstrators. Additional problems included an attempted military coup in the Philippines and an anti-American dictator, General Manuel Noriega, in Panama. The United States eventually suspended relations with China, supported the Philippine government, and invaded Panama. In the world that was emerging, military force still had utility.

The 1990 Iraqi invasion of Kuwait produced a new challenge. The Bush administration believed that the invasion threatened vital U.S. interests, and most Americans agreed. The United Nations passed a resolution authorizing the use of force to expel Iraqi forces from Kuwait, and shortly after Congress voted to support the use of military force against Iraq, the Persian Gulf War began in January 1991. Called **Operation Desert Storm,** the U.S. and allied forces defeated Iraqi forces in a matter of weeks. The objective was achieved with few U.S. casualties.[7]

Operation Desert Storm
The 1991 American-led attack against Iraq to expel Iraqi forces from Kuwait.

Meanwhile, startling events were unfolding in the Soviet Union. Weakened by a failed coup attempt against Mikhail Gorbachev in the summer of 1991, its economy in a shambles, and torn by internal dissent and the desires of nationalities for independence, the Soviet Union collapsed.[8] The Cold War was over, as was the need for containment. Once again Americans asked questions: What would U.S. strategy now be? With the Cold War over, should the United States cut defense spending, and if so, how much? How much aid should the United States send to its former enemy to help it survive its collapse? What would the new international order be?

By 1993, the United States had a multifaceted foreign and military policy agenda. While a need for military forces remained, it was not clear when they should be used. For example, in Somalia in 1992 and 1993, the United States acting under UN auspices used military force to try to restore order and distribute food. Conversely, in the former Yugoslavia, neither the United States nor any other country at first intervened to stop Serbia's ethnic cleansing campaign against Bosnian Muslims.

This was the complex world that Bill Clinton faced when he assumed the presidency in 1993. Defining the American role in this world presented a challenge. Clinton's agenda centered on implementing engagement and enlargement, shaping new international economic relationships, deciding when U.S. armed forces should be used overseas, and puzzling over what role the United States should play in the post–Cold War world.

Engagement meant that the United States would not retreat into isolationism as it did after World War I and for a short time after World War II. Engagement implied that the United States relied on negotiations and cooperation rather than confrontation and conflict, although it would use force when necessary. **Enlargement** meant that the United States would promote democracy, open markets, and other Western political, economic, and social values. In practice, engagement and enlargement led to the implementation of the Partnership for Peace program with former communist states in Eastern Europe and the former Soviet Union and the expansion of NATO.

International economic issues were one focus of Clinton's activities. With help from Republicans, he guided the **North American Free Trade Agreement (NAFTA)** into law, establishing the free flow of goods among Canada, Mexico, and the United States. The United States under Clinton also played a major role in initiating two other major free trade areas, the Free Trade Area of the Americas and the Asia-Pacific Economic Cooperation agreement, as well as creating the **World Trade Organization,** charged with overseeing world trade, judging trade disputes, and lowering tariffs.[9]

Deciding when to use U.S. armed forces overseas was a vexing problem for Presidents George Bush and Bill Clinton. As we have seen, from the end of World War II to the collapse of the Soviet Union, U.S. military intervention was usually tied to containing communism. With the Soviet Union gone, this easy benchmark for deciding when to intervene no longer existed. Thus, both the administrations had to clarify when and under what conditions the United States would intervene. In short order, crises developed in Somalia, Bosnia, North Korea, Rwanda, Haiti, Iraq, and Kosovo. Each crisis was different, and each had potential for armed U.S. intervention. The United States intervened militarily in Somalia, Bosnia, Haiti, Iraq, and Kosovo, but not in North Korea or Rwanda, always in different ways and usually with varied results. No pattern was evident about the use of U.S. military force overseas in these crises. In each case, different situations dictated different responses.

A New Order for the Twenty-First Century?

When George W. Bush became president in 2001, he faced the same range of issues with which his two predecessors grappled. How should the United States help Russia and other former communist states? How should the United States handle China's emergence as a world power? What could the United States do to promote peace in the Middle East? When should the United States intervene militarily overseas? When should the United States act unilaterally and when should it act multilaterally?

During his first months as president, Bush conducted an active foreign policy, traveling to other countries and ordering several changes to

engagement
Policy implemented during the Clinton administration that the United States would remain actively involved in foreign affairs.

enlargement
Policy implemented during the Clinton administration that the United States would actively promote the expansion of democracy and free markets throughout the world.

North American Free Trade Agreement (NAFTA)
Agreement that promotes free movement of goods and services among Canada, Mexico, and the United States.

World Trade Organization
International governmental organization created in 1995 that manages multilateral negotiations to reduce barriers to trade and settle trade disputes.

U.S. FOREIGN POLICY AND THE UNITED NATIONS

The George W. Bush administration has had what amounts to a love-hate relationship with the United Nations (UN). However, the tension present in the Bush administration's interaction with the UN is not unique. More than one U.S. administration has simultaneously been drawn to the UN and turned its back on it—in large part because of the different perspectives on U.S. foreign policy goals and the role of the UN. The United States sees itself as an international reformer and understands that the UN can be an important ally in its mission to change the world. And, as a key founder of the UN, the United States sees itself as a custodian or protector of the world organization. Tensions result because often the agenda that the United States sets for the UN differs from that which the UN as an institution sets for itself. Finally, the United States, like all other members of the UN, sees the UN as something to use to further its national interests. Viewed in this light, membership in the UN is no different from membership in the World Trade Organization, the Organization of American States, or the North Atlantic Treaty Organization.

The uncertainty produced by these competing strands in American thinking about where the UN fits into its foreign policy is particularly pronounced in one of the most visible and controversial tasks being undertaken by the UN today: peacemaking. The Bush administration, for example, turned to the UN for help with peacemaking in Iraq.

Peacemaking is a second-generation concept for the UN —the original concept was peacekeeping. The original hope was that permanent members of the Security Council (the United States, Great Britain, France, China, and the Soviet Union) would be able to work together to keep international peace. This hope was soon dashed by the outbreak of the Cold War, which placed some of these states on competing sides. In the mid 1950s, in an effort to lessen the intensity of the Cold War in the developing world and to reestablish a role for itself in settling international disputes, the UN moved forward with the twin ideas of preventive diplomacy and peacekeeping. Before a conflict turned into open fighting, the UN would try to mediate and settle the dispute. If its efforts failed, it could send UN peacekeeping forces to stabilize a situation. The presence of UN peacekeepers (known as "blue helmets") was governed by three rules. First, UN peacekeepers must be invited into a country by its government. Second, they must be neutral in the conflict. Third, they must leave when asked. Both the United States and the Soviet Union were willing to accept the presence of

Comparing Foreign and Security Policy

policy. As a Texan, Bush placed high priority on U.S. relations with Mexico and other Latin American states. Indeed, his first trip outside the United States as president was to Mexico to discuss immigration, anti-drug policies, economic development, and border issues. Bush also visited Europe twice, first going to NATO headquarters in Belgium and four other countries and next to Italy to the meeting of the heads of state of the world's eight leading industrial powers. On both trips, Bush met with Russian President Vladimir Putin.

Bush also made it clear that he intended to pursue ballistic missile defense and abandon the 1972 Anti-Ballistic Missile Treaty between the United States and Russia. This was one of the main issues that Bush and Putin discussed during their meetings. Bush also announced that the United States would not abide by the Kyoto environmental agree-

UN peacekeepers as a second-best solution in a conflict. It meant that although neither side had won, neither side had lost to the other.

With the end of the Cold War and the diminished U.S.–Soviet rivalry for influence around the world, the need for UN peacekeeping declined. Conflicts between states and within states, however, continued. In fact, we saw the emergence of "failed states"—states that are no longer capable of maintaining law and order within their boundaries or of providing the minimum level of social services to their citizens. Some states devolved into chaos, with citizens caught between warring factions. To address such crises, the UN reworked the concept of peacekeeping into peacemaking. Under it, UN blue helmets would not have to be invited into a country by the government or have to leave when asked. Once in a country, they are not expected to be neutral and stay above the conflict. They are there to help bring an end to it and reestablish peace and order.

As the table highlights, an inherent tension is built into UN peacekeeping efforts. The states that provide the most money for peacekeeping are not those who provide the most troops. Both sets of states believe they should have the major say in how these troops are used.

Largest Contributors to UN Peacekeeping Operations	
Financial	
United States	$674.5 million
Japan	541.6
France	295.9
Germany	198.9
Personnel	
Pakistan	13.6%
Bangladesh	10.3
Nigeria	7.3
Ghana	5.0
Nepal	5.0

Questions

1. Who should have the most say in UN peacekeeping operations, those who contribute the money for them or those who provide the personnel? Why?
2. Which of the competing strands of American orientation toward the UN discussed above should be given the most weight in U.S. foreign policy decisions? Why?

Source: Congressional Quarterly Researcher (February 27, 2004): 177.

ments, and he pushed Congress to expand presidential authority to negotiate preferential trade agreements.[10]

By September 2001, the Bush administration had a full foreign policy agenda. Relations with Latin America, Europe, Russia, and China all loomed large, as did security, international economics, immigration, drugs, and the environment. However, the new administration had not sorted through this considerable agenda to determine which items it considered most important. Suddenly and unexpectedly, however, the Bush administration's foreign and military priorities became clear.

On the morning of September 11, 2001, members of **al-Qaeda,** a terrorist network founded and funded by Muslim fundamentalist Osama bin Laden, hijacked four jetliners, flying two into the twin towers of New York's World Trade Center. The impact destroyed them and

al-Qaeda
Worldwide terrorist organization led by Osama bin Laden; responsible for numerous terrorist attacks against U.S. interests, including September 11, 2001, attacks against the World Trade Center and the Pentagon.

■ The south tower of the World Trade Center collapses September 11, 2001, after it was struck by a hijacked airplane. The north tower, also struck by a hijacked plane, collapsed shortly after. The tragic September 11 terrorist attacks caused enormous loss of life and had a profound impact on U.S. foreign and military policy.

Photo courtesy: Thomas Nilsson/Getty Images

killed almost 3,000 people. Another hijacked plane slammed into the Pentagon, killing 189. The fourth plane plummeted into a field in Pennsylvania after passengers charged the hijackers and forced them to lose control of the plane.[11]

After 9/11, President George W. Bush organized a coalition of nations to combat terrorism. He also demanded that Afghanistan's Taliban government, which had provided safe haven for bin Laden and al-Qaeda's terrorist training camps, turn bin Laden over to the United States. When the Taliban refused, the United States in October initiated air strikes against Taliban and al-Qaeda targets. By the end of 2001, the Taliban were overthrown and countries around the world were assisting in the fight to combat terrorism. Meanwhile, the international community pledged $1.8 billion in 2002 to help rebuild Afghanistan, with another $2.7 billion for subsequent years.

Outside Afghanistan, a broad war on terrorism began soon after the 9/11 attacks as many countries began to share intelligence about terrorists and as Interpol and other security agencies stepped up surveillance of terrorists. Albania, Belgium, France, Germany, India, Italy, Morocco, Singapore, Spain, the United Kingdom, the United States, and other countries detained suspected al-Qaeda members. Around the world, over a thousand people were detained because of ties to al-Qaeda, 500 in the United States alone.

Despite these efforts and increased security measures within the United States and abroad, the U.S. Central Intelligence Agency (CIA) estimated that five to ten thousand al-Qaeda operatives remained in sixty-eight countries, including the United States. U.S.-led anti-terrorist efforts

THE IMPACT OF 9/11 ON AMERICAN CAMPUSES

The September 11, 2001, terrorist attacks on the World Trade Center and the Pentagon had an immense impact on the United States. American colleges and universities were not immune from that impact.

Some effects of September 11 were predictable. Colleges and universities across the United States reported increased enrollment in courses on Islam, international affairs, and terrorism. ROTC programs on many campuses experienced renewed interest. Security at information technology facilities and other sensitive sites was increased on most campuses. A number of campuses worked with state police and aviation authorities to create no-fly zones near football stadiums. Unfortunately, a few campuses also experienced anti-Arab and anti-Islamic incidents.

American campuses also became a focus of the effort to improve homeland security, a part of the U.S. global war on terrorism. This was because even though most of the September 11 hijackers were on tourist or work visas, two were in the United States on student visas. Concern over terrorists on student visas increased more when, several months after the attacks, the Immigration and Naturalization Service (INS) admitted it had processed a pre–September 11 visa application from one of the hijackers and granted a student visa to him even after he had conducted one of the attacks and died.

The most notable impact on campuses of the effort to improve homeland security was the full implementation of the Student and Exchange Visitor Information System (SEVIS) required by the USA Patriot Act of 2001. SEVIS is a Web-based registration and tracking system operated by the INS to monitor foreign students and scholars on certain types of visas. SEVIS allows the INS to rapidly integrate information on foreign students and scholars with other information collected by the INS, U.S. intelligence agencies, and the Departments of State and Defense. Even so, SEVIS is no panacea. Only about 2 percent of the foreign nationals who enter the United States each year, or about 600,000 people, enter as scholars or students.

In 2002, the administration of President George W. Bush proposed the creation of an Interagency Panel for Science and Security that would "prohibit certain international students from receiving any training in sensitive areas, including areas of study with direct application to the development and use of weapons of mass destruction." The panel closely scrutinizes visa applications from prospective students from certain countries who are engaged in particularly sensitive fields of study.

Some efforts to improve homeland security on campuses had the potential to significantly alter campus life. For example, in Georgia, one legislator introduced a bill that would have required professors to report to the INS any foreign student who had missed class for two weeks. Although well intentioned, this would have converted professors into INS agents. Other legislators recognized this, and the bill died in committee. Other states had similar experiences.

Terrorism has had a major impact on twenty-first-century American life, and on American college and university campuses as well. Whether the steps taken to improve security in the United States or on campus will be sufficient to deter or end the terrorist threat remains to be seen.

therefore continued, with the United States providing anti-terrorist training to the military in Georgia, the Philippines, and Yemen. The Bush administration also declared that the United States would take the war to countries that aided or sheltered terrorists. Iraq, Iran, and North Korea

527

war on terrorism
Initiated by George W. Bush after the September 11, 2001, attacks to weed out terrorist operatives throughout the world, using diplomacy, military means, improved homeland security, stricter banking laws, and other means.

weapons of mass destruction (WMDs)
Biological, chemical, and nuclear weapons, which present a sizable threat to U.S. security.

■ George W. Bush aboard U.S.S. *Abraham Lincoln*, May 2003.

Photo courtesy: AP Photo/J. Scott Applewhite

dominated U.S. attention, with Bush calling these three nations the "axis of evil" in his 2002 State of the Union message.[12] Other officials charged that Cuba, Djibouti, Libya, Somalia, Syria, and Sudan also assisted or shielded terrorists.

The **war on terrorism,** then, was a multifaceted, global undertaking that included military action overseas, increased security measures at home, cooperative intelligence with allies, coalition diplomacy, and eliminating terrorist access to financial institutions. Of particular interest is the continued threat of nuclear, biological, and chemical weapons, known as **weapons of mass destruction (WMDs).**

In the summer of 2002, the Bush administration made it clear that it considered Iraqi leader Saddam Hussein a profound, immediate danger to the security of the United States and the world. U.S. officials claimed that Hussein was violating international law by continuing secret development of WMDs. The administration also viewed Iraq as a potential breeding ground for terrorists. The United States successfully pressured Hussein to allow into the country UN weapons inspectors, who had been denied free access to Iraq for some time. Teams of UN inspectors, led by Hans Blix, investigated scores of sites in Iraq and interviewed Iraqi scientists in late 2002 and early 2003, but could locate no solid evidence that Iraq either had or was developing WMDs.

President Bush and Britain's Prime Minister Tony Blair, however, did not believe the findings of the UN inspectors. Based on what proved to be faulty intelligence, Bush and Blair argued that Hussein was developing WMDs. Moreover, they asserted that Hussein posed a severe danger to the world and, given his long history of brutality, needed to be removed from power so Iraq could become a democratic nation. The United States and Britain convinced several other countries of the need for ousting Hussein but failed to convince the UN Security Council to authorize the use of force, largely due to the opposition of France and Russia. Frustrated that the UN would not offer its support, but resolute to proceed anyway, President Bush referred to those countries which did support war as "the coalition of the willing." Britain, Italy, Spain, Poland, Australia, Japan, and several other countries stood with the United States, while France, Russia, Germany, Canada, and Mexico were among those nations opposing this action. When Hussein refused to abdicate voluntarily when given a last-minute ultimatum, the war began.

The overthrow of Hussein's government in the spring of 2003 was relatively quick. The U.S.-led bombing campaign—dubbed "shock and awe" to capture its massive impact—quickly destroyed much of the military and governmental infrastructure in Iraq, and Hussein's forces seemed helpless and disorganized. Having severely softened the Iraqi resistance through the bombing, ground forces were then deployed and moved rapidly toward Baghdad, and the Hussein government fled in disarray. Some of Hussein's key officers and aides were killed, others were captured, and others went into hiding. Within weeks, the U.S.-led forces had entered Hussein's palaces, torn down statues of the dictator around the country, and were beginning their efforts to create a post-Saddam government in Iraq.

To commemorate the end of major combat operations, President Bush chose to speak to the country in early May 2003 aboard an aircraft carrier, the U.S.S. *Abraham Lincoln*, off the coast of southern California. Dressed in a flight suit, Bush co-piloted a Navy jet, making a tailhook landing on the deck of the *Lincoln*. With a sign proclaiming "Mission Accomplished" flying from the ship's tower in the background, the president stood on the deck and thanked those on board for their part in winning the Iraq conflict. "The transition from dictatorship to democracy will take time," the president told the nation, "but it will be worth every effort. Our coalition will stay until our work is done."[13]

Though the Hussein government was toppled, the situation in Iraq was far less secure than was hoped. In the months after declaring an end to the major combat, soldiers from the United States and its allies found themselves under attack from mortar fire, roadside bombings, and suicide missions. American war deaths and injuries by 2004 alarmed the American people, as the list of war dead topped 1,000, with about 8,000 injured. Many Iraqis, even those glad to be free of Hussein's tyrannical rule, were troubled by the lawlessness unleashed by Hussein's overthrow, resented the U.S. occupation, and demanded a more rapid transition to self-government. Bush administration and military officials had underestimated the difficulty of the postwar situation, and began to ask for assistance from the UN.

Following the transition to Iraqi self-government in June 2004, a new round of assassinations and attacks on softer targets by Iraqi militants caused tremendous instability. While some parts of Iraq were successfully rebuilding and remained relatively calm thanks to help from the United States and its allies, the overall situation was enormously volatile. Oil pipelines were sabotaged, Iraqi police stations were attacked, and Iraqis faced great uncertainty about the future. And, no evidence of weapons of mass destruction had been found in Iraq.

The Living Constitution

To provide for calling forth the Militia to execute the Laws of the Union, suppress Insurrections and repel Invasions;

To provide for organizing, arming, and disciplining, the Militia, and for governing such Part of them as may be employed in the Service of the United States, reserving to the States respectively, the Appointment of the Officers, and the Authority of training the Militia according to the discipline proscribed by Congress;

—Article I, Section 8

With the Constitution's Article I militia clauses, a significant defect of the Articles of Confederation was corrected. A fundamental weakness of the earlier document was that it did not grant the central government adequate means for national defense, and this defect was understood to hamper the Revolutionary War effort. In the view of the Framers, a government without the force to administer its laws or to defend its citizens was either a weak government or no government at all, and these clauses consequently give the federal government authority to call up the state militias in times of national emergency or distress.

Many Anti-Federalists were concerned that the federal government could use the state militias for unjust ends. They held that state governments should control their militias in order to prevent any perfidy on the part of the federal government. To this end, the states were given authority to name militia officers and train their forces. During the War of 1812—to the consternation of President James Madison—two state governments withheld their militias, because they believed it was the purview of the state to set the terms for the use of its guards. The Supreme Court has since held that, except for constitutional prohibitions, the Congress has "unlimited" authority over the state militias, and the National Defense Act of 1916 brought the state militias under the control of the national government.

The National Guard has proved effective and essential in defending the United States. With the extensive use of the National Guard to assist American efforts in Iraq and in the struggle against terrorism, its role has expanded. The militia clauses ensure the unity, effectiveness, and strength of the United States military not only during wartime, but also during other national emergencies.

The situation in Iraq was exacerbated when news sources revealed that some members of the U.S. military had committed brutal and inhumane acts against Iraqi detainees at Abu Ghraib prison. Prisoners were intimidated by dogs, beaten, forced to strip and engage in homosexual acts or pile together on the floor, and subjected to a variety of other acts that violated the Geneva conventions of warfare. The U.S. Army, which had been slow to investigate claims by the Red Cross and others about Abu Ghraib, issued a classified report in late February 2004 that cited rampant examples of "sadistic, blatant, and wanton criminal abuses."[14] Not only had the abuse been frequent, but there were photos of U.S. soldiers smiling and giving the thumbs-up sign while standing next to piles of naked Iraqi prisoners, or intimidating a hooded prisoner by pretending to be about to torture him. The abuses at Abu Ghraib were an extreme embarrassment to the United States, and the photos incensed many in Iraq and the Arab world, who argued that the cruelty depicted made a lie out of the U.S. claim of superior morality in deposing Saddam Hussein. President Bush and Secretary of Defense Donald Rumsfeld denounced the prisoner abuse, but Congress investigated whether the prisoner intimidation might have been encouraged by those high in the chain of command.

Iraq remains an unfinished piece of business. An uneasy coalition of Iraqis had taken control of the government, but violence continued, and it was unclear how long the United States would need to station troops or how many more Americans would die in the struggle to make post-Hussein Iraq a democratic haven in the Arab world. President Bush continued to defend the war even though the cost had been very high (in dollars and casualties), and no weapons of mass destruction were discovered. Would the United States go to war in such a preemptive strike again, given the high cost and the damage done to relations with many allies?

THE EXECUTIVE BRANCH AND FOREIGN AND DEFENSE POLICY MAKING

THE EXECUTIVE BRANCH PLAYS the most important role in creating and implementing U.S. foreign and defense policy, and within the executive branch, the president is the most important individual. Among executive departments, the Department of State obviously plays a major role in foreign and defense policy. So, too, does the Department of Defense, the Central Intelligence Agency, and the National Security Council. These institutions and agencies, with only a few additions such as the newly created Department (and other new offices) of Homeland Security, remain the core of U.S. foreign and defense policy making and implementation.

THE UNITED STATES AND THE INTERNATIONAL CRIMINAL COURT

In 1998, a United Nations conference finalized a treaty establishing an International Criminal Court (ICC) that would have jurisdiction over crimes against humanity, war crimes, and genocide once sixty states ratified it. By 2001, 139 states had signed the treaty. The United States was not one of them.

The United States opposes crimes against humanity, war crimes, and genocide. In the mid-1990s, it deployed thousands of troops to Bosnia to help prevent genocide. In the late 1990s, it supported the creation of a UN tribunal that indicted Yugoslav President Slobodan Milosevic for war crimes and convicted other Serbs of crimes against humanity for their ethnic-cleansing campaign against Bosnian Muslims. In 1999, the United States contributed most of the armed forces for NATO's military operation against ethnic cleansing in Kosovo.

Why then did the United States not support the ICC? Some conservative Americans believed that the powers the ICC statutes gave the court might lead to politically motivated prosecutions of U.S. military personnel involved in peacekeeping missions, fearing that frivolous charges might be made against U.S. personnel engaged in legitimate activities. For example, Senator Jesse Helms (R–NC) argued that a government that committed human rights abuses against its citizens might charge that a member of the U.S. armed forces trying to prevent such abuses was violating the rights of its citizens and bring charges against him or her in the ICC. Defend-

ers of the ICC asserted that this could not occur, because the ICC statutes allowed the United States and other peacekeeping states to preempt the ICC by first trying anyone so accused in their own national courts.

The United States under President Bill Clinton signed the treaty in 2000, but the Senate never ratified it. When George W. Bush took office in 2001, he renounced the treaty. As the International Criminal Court neared operational status in 2002, Bush threatened to oppose all UN peacekeeping missions if the ICC began operations, to refuse to provide U.S. funding for such operations if approved, and to refuse to have U.S. forces participate in any peacekeeping efforts.

The Bush administration also initiated an extensive diplomatic offensive designed to conclude one-on-one agreements with other countries that they would not prosecute or bring changes against U.S. peacekeepers. By late 2002, at least twelve countries had signed such agreements, but most were close U.S. allies such as Israel, small countries such as Micronesia and the Marshall Islands, or countries strongly influenced by U.S. preferences, such as Tajikistan and Honduras.

The U.S. diplomatic effort was widely criticized outside the United States as an attempt to circumvent the ICC. For example, the European Union and many of its members chastised the United States, and Amnesty International called the effort an attempt to undermine the ICC. By early 2003, the future of U.S. participation in the ICC remained unclear.

The Role of the President

The president is preeminent in foreign and defense policy making, for several reasons. The president alone is in charge of all the resources that the executive branch can apply to foreign and defense policy. The president has greater access to and control over information, and the president alone can act with little fear that his actions will be countermanded.

The president has exclusive sources of information—Department of State diplomats, military attaches working for the Department of Defense, CIA agents, and national technical means of gathering information, such as satellites—that others do not have. Private citizens, companies, interest groups, Congress, and the media cannot match the president's sources for such information as the whereabouts of Osama bin Laden and other al-Qaeda operatives. Unfortunately, however, sometimes even the president does not have enough information.

The willingness of most people to listen to the president alone about foreign and defense affairs adds to presidential power. Ironically, the media are the group outside of government most likely to be in a position to counter what the president may say about foreign and defense affairs, but the media are also the group that the president uses to communicate with the American people. It is a curious relationship.

The Departments of State, Defense, and Homeland Security

The Departments of State and Defense have responsibility for implementing U.S. foreign and defense policy. The 22,000 Department of State personnel gather information on foreign political, economic, social, and military situations, represent the United States in negotiations and international organizations, and provide services such as processing visa applications. U.S. interests are served by U.S. embassies and consulates of the Department of State in over 160 countries. In 1999, the Department of State expanded its role by absorbing two independent agencies: the Agency for International Development and the Arms Control and Disarmament Agency.

The Department of Defense provides the forces to undertake military operations. It was created after World War II when Congress consolidated the Departments of War, Army, Navy, and Air Force into a single

■ Former secretary of state Colin Powell speaks at the United Nations, in 2003, to ask other nations to support the invasion of Iraq.

Photo courtesy: Kathy Wilkens/AP/Wide World Photos

department. Under the secretary of defense and other appointed civilian officials, the Department of Defense directs U.S. forces from the Pentagon, a complex across the Potomac River from Washington, D.C. With thousands of officials overseeing its operations, the Department of Defense is among the most influential executive departments.

Following the 9/11 terrorist attacks on the United States, President George W. Bush created the Office of Homeland Security. With Executive Order 13228, he tasked it to coordinate the executive branch's efforts to "detect, prepare for, prevent, protect against, respond to, and recover from terrorist attacks against the United States." In late 2002, the U.S. Congress enacted legislation to convert the Office of Homeland Security into the **Department of Homeland Security.** This conversion was the largest reorganization of the federal government since the creation of the Department of Defense in 1947. Underlining both the importance of and the threat to homeland security, the new department merged twenty-two agencies and employs over 170,000 people. Its responsibilities include detecting and identifying threats against the United States, devising ways to defend against emerging threats, implementing whatever defense measures it decides on and for which it can obtain presidential approval, and ultimately preventing terrorist attacks against the American homeland.

Department of Homeland Security

Cabinet department created after September 11, 2001, to coordinate domestic U.S. security efforts against terrorism.

The Central Intelligence Agency and National Security Council

The **Central Intelligence Agency (CIA)** and the **National Security Council (NSC)** were established by Congress in 1947 respectively to collect, collate, and analyze information necessary to meet national security requirements and to advise the president on foreign and defense affairs. The CIA, the primary agency in the world's largest and most expensive intelligence community, consists of thirteen agencies, including the Defense Intelligence Agency, the National Security Agency, four armed services intelligence groups, the National Imagery and Mapping Agency, the National Reconnaissance Office, and other agencies.

During the Cold War, the CIA ran covert operations to try to alter political events in many countries.[15] At times, these operations undermined broader U.S. objectives by supporting assassinations, corruption, and other scandalous activities. In the 1970s, Congress criticized the CIA and mandated changes in procedures to provide more congressional oversight to its secret operations. In the 1990s, the end of the Cold War and the penetration of the CIA by foreign agents raised congressional interest in reforming the CIA. To a certain extent, this happened even before September 11, 2001.

However, after 9/11, the CIA and the rest of the intelligence community were criticized for failing to identify clues that could have prevented the attacks and for relying too heavily on electronic means of

Central Intelligence Agency (CIA)

Executive agency responsible for collection and analysis of information and intelligence about foreign countries and events.

National Security Council (NSC)

Executive agency responsible for advising the president about foreign and military policy and events.

gathering intelligence and not heavily enough on human sources. The CIA and other agencies respond both that there was insufficient evidence to conclude that attacks were imminent and that more funds are required to hire human intelligence sources and analysts. There is also evidence that the FBI and CIA failed to inform each other of evidence that suggested a terrorist plot involving airplanes was being planned by al-Qaeda. Faulty intelligence also apparently led President Bush into believing that Iraq had weapons of mass destruction in 2003. The CIA director at the time, George Tenet, reportedly told the president that evidence of Iraq's WMDs was a "slam dunk case."[16] Later it was argued that the CIA had relied heavily on Iraqi exiles who had fabricated WMD evidence against Hussein in order to encourage U.S. action.[17]

The NSC was set up to institutionalize the system by which the U.S. government integrated foreign and military policy and to coordinate U.S. activities on a range of foreign policy and military issues. The NSC includes the president, the vice president, the secretaries of state and defense, the chair of the Joint Chiefs of Staff, and the director of Central Intelligence. The NSC provides advice on foreign and defense affairs directly to the president. The special assistant for national security affairs runs the NSC and is often one of the president's closest advisers.

OTHER SHAPERS AND INFLUENCERS OF FOREIGN AND DEFENSE POLICY

EVEN THOUGH THE EXECUTIVE BRANCH is the most powerful branch of government in the formulation and implementation of U.S. foreign and defense policy, other groups influence and shape American foreign and defense policy. We turn now to these other groups: Congress, the military-industrial complex, the news media, and the public.

Congress

The Constitution gave Congress fewer responsibilities in foreign and defense policy than the president, but it often plays a significant role. Most would agree that Congress is the second most important body in shaping American foreign and defense affairs.[18] Congress influences foreign and defense policy through its congressional leadership; congressional oversight; approval of treaties, executive agreements, and appointments; appropriations; and the War Powers Act—all facets of congressional power discussed in greater detail in earlier chapters of this book.

Congress's other oversight powers include the ability to conduct hearings on foreign and military policy and to have the president and

War Powers Act
Passed by Congress in 1973; the president is limited in the deployment of troops overseas to a sixty-day period in peacetime (which can be extended for an extra thirty days to permit withdrawal) unless Congress explicitly gives its approval for a longer period.

executive agreement
Formal government agreement entered into by the executive branch that does not require the advice and consent of the U.S. Senate.

CIA inform congressional committees about covert operations. From World War II until the late 1960s, Congress deferred to the president and the military on foreign and military issues and rarely exercised its oversight responsibilities outside appropriations. The Vietnam War changed this. Thus, in 1973, Congress passed the **War Powers Act** to try to prevent future interventions overseas without specific congressional approval. Under the act, the president can deploy troops overseas for sixty days in peacetime unless Congress gives explicit approval for a longer period. If Congress does not give explicit approval within sixty days, the president then has thirty days to withdraw troops. Under the act, the president could respond to an emergency such as rescuing endangered Americans but could not engage in a prolonged struggle without congressional approval.

The Constitution gives the Senate explicit power to approve treaties, but the Senate has rejected treaties only sixteen times in U.S. history. The Senate's power to approve treaties is not inconsequential, however. Presidents want to avoid the embarrassment of Senate rejection of a treaty, the delay of a filibuster, or senatorial refusal to consider a treaty, and they often adjust treaties accordingly. Presidents can avoid the treaty process by using **executive agreements,** which unlike treaties do not require Senate ratification. Table 7.2, in chapter 7, illustrates how frequently presidents use executive agreements, often thwarting congressional power.

Congress has a key role in shaping foreign and military policy through its power to appropriate funds. Congress can influence when and where the United States fights through its control of the budget. While the power to go to war is shared by the executive and legislative branches of government, the power to appropriate funds belongs to the legislature alone. Congress has been careful about using this power. For example, in 1982, Congress used its appropriation power to limit U.S. involvement in Nicaragua. In 1979, a revolutionary group called the Sandinistas came to power in Nicaragua. By 1982, the Sandinistas received aid from Cuba and the Soviet Union, usually siding with the Soviet Union on international issues. The Reagan administration therefore provided military aid to the Contras, a group of Nicaraguans fighting the Sandinistas. Many U.S. citizens opposed funding the Contras. After much debate, Congress voted to cut appropriations to the Contras.

The Contra example also shows how the executive branch's ability to act can limit the impact that congressional control of appropriations may have on the conduct of U.S. foreign and military policy. After Congress cut funding for the Contras, some people in senior positions in the Reagan administration felt so strongly about funding the Contras that they contacted foreign nations to provide funds to purchase weapons for the Contras. In addition, they arranged arms sales to Iran, overcharging Iran for the weapons and using the surplus funds to buy weapons for the Contras.

Analyzing Visuals

U.S. Defense Spending

Since World War II, U.S. defense spending has risen and fallen, mirroring the prevailing state of tension and conflict in world affairs. Driven by World War II and its aftermath, U.S. defense expenditures totaled nearly $1 trillion in 1945 and about half that in 1946. By 1947, the United States had begun to enjoy the dividends of peace as defense spending sunk to lower levels.

As U.S.–Soviet tensions began to escalate in the late 1940s, defense spending rose. More spending was driven by the 1951–1954 Korean War. Throughout the Cold War until the early 1990s when the Soviet Union broke up, U.S. defense spending fluctuated widely, following the rise and fall of tensions in U.S.–Soviet relations detailed in this chapter. Examine the bar graph, which shows the U.S. defense expenditures in billions of constant 1996 dollars, and answer the following critical thinking questions: What trends do you observe in defense spending during the 1960s and 1970s? What factors might explain these trends? What happened to defense spending in the last year of the Carter administration and during the Reagan presidency (see Appendix V for the dates of their terms)? Why? After the Cold War ended in the early 1990s, U.S. defense spending declined but remained surprisingly high. Why? What trend do you see in defense spending in the twenty-first century? What factors might explain this trend?

Note: Figures for 2002 and after do not include spending for Department of Homeland Security. Budgeted estimates for defense spending in 2005–2006 have risen considerably, as a result of the war in Iraq.

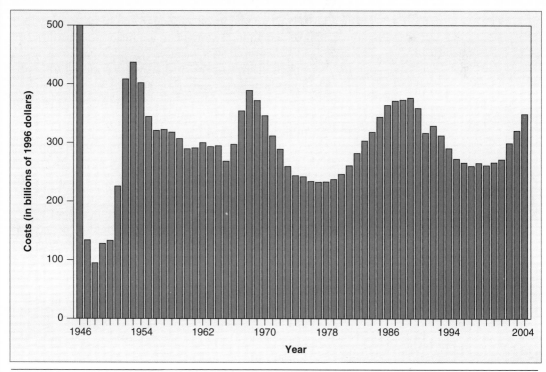

Sources: Department of Defense, Center for Defense Information, and Congressional Budget Office.

The Military-Industrial Complex

In his 1961 farewell address, President Dwight D. Eisenhower, a general who commanded allied forces during World War II, warned that the United States had developed a **military-industrial complex** that included the military and defense industries. This complex, Eisenhower feared, could become an increasingly dominant factor in U.S. politics with "potential for the disastrous rise of misplaced power."[19]

The military-industrial complex has potential to acquire power for several reasons. First, it has economic clout. During the Cold War, as much as 7 percent of the U.S. gross national product was spent on defense. (See Analyzing Visuals: U.S. Defense Spending.) Second, it has access to technical expertise and political information. Third, the military and defense industries share many interests. For example, both benefited economically when tensions between the United States and Soviet Union increased. Fourth, personal and professional relationships between the military and defense industries are close, with many military officers on retirement going to work for defense industries. Finally, the military and defense industry officials work closely with legislators and their staffs. Planned or unplanned, undue influence can accompany close working relations.

military-industrial complex
The grouping of the U.S. armed forces and defense industries.

Evaluating Defense Spending

The News Media

The news media play a major role in foreign and defense policy formulation and implementation. Investigation is a major news media activity. The news media claim to have a balanced perspective in investigations, but most presidents claim that the media are too critical. Other people argue that the news media are too willing to accept government statements. For example, the media were initially hesitant to criticize U.S. actions in Afghanistan or any aspect of the war on terrorism.

The government uses the news media to help achieve its foreign and defense policy goals. During the 1991 Persian Gulf War, the military provided the media extensive access to marines in landing ships off the shore of Kuwait. The Pentagon hoped that Iraq would monitor the broadcasts and that the news coverage would convince Iraq to keep its best divisions on the Kuwaiti coast, waiting for the landing that never came. The assault far inland went perfectly. The U.S. government had used the media to gain a military advantage.

The media also put issues on the foreign policy agenda. For example, in 2004, journalists learned of the abuse of Iraqi detainees by U.S. soldiers at Baghdad's Abu Ghraib prison and pursued the story vigorously. Their focus on this issue led to congressional hearings into how such abuse had occurred, and Bush administration denun-

■ Prisoner abuse at Abu Ghraib prison in Iraq.

Photo courtesy: The New Yorker Magazine

FIGURE 14.1 The Most Important Problem: Domestic or Foreign, 1947–2002. ■

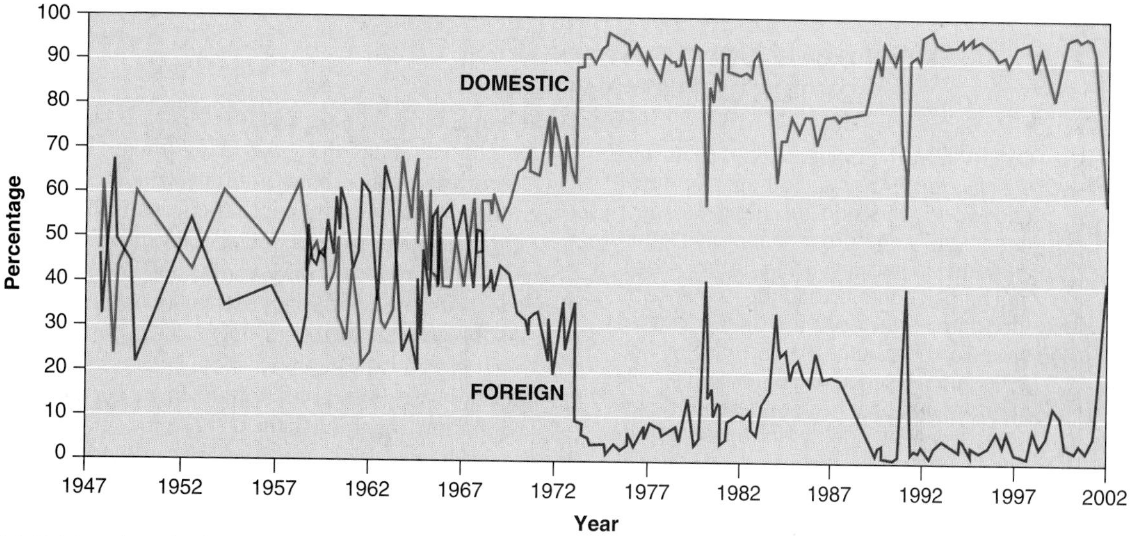

Note: Typical question: "What do you think is the most important problem facing this country today?"

Sources: Harold W. Stanley and Richard G. Niemi, eds., *Vital Statistics on American Politics*, 2001–2002 (Washington, DC: CQ Press, 2001). Reprinted by permission. Updates from Roper and Gallup Polls.

ciations of the abuse. Complex issues such as international trade or third world debt, which take time to explain and offer little opportunity for startling footage, receive less media coverage than stories about war and disasters, even though their overall impact may be greater.

The media are influential as agenda setters, but they do not determine policy. The media's ability to influence public opinion is closely related to their agenda-setting role. Media coverage of the Vietnam War is a good example of the media's ability to influence public opinion. It is often said that Vietnam was the first TV war, with footage of battles and deaths broadcast into living rooms the same day that they occurred. Most analysts agree that these reports reduced public support for the conflict, just as media coverage of escalating violence in Iraq deflated support for that U.S.-led war.

The media can also assist in building public support for a war or for a foreign policy initiative. For example, in the war against Iraq, journalists were embedded with troops, giving them direct access to the frontlines of the conflict. Reports from the front contributed to popular support for the war, at least in the first year.

The Public

Public opinion also influences U.S. foreign and defense policy. However, as revealed in Figure 14.1, unless are very salient foreign policy issues, most Americans are far more interested in domestic affairs.

SHOULD THE UNITED STATES PULL OUT OF THE UNITED NATIONS?

OVERVIEW: The United Nations came into existence in 1945 as an institution borne of two world wars and the desire of most nations for an international organization dedicated to pursuing global justice, peace, and human rights. To back up its mandate, the United States and the United Nations have worked together to help maintain relative global security. For example, UN member nations helped defend South Korea from invasion by North Korea, provided a blueprint to help mediate peace in the Middle East, and voted for sanctions against South Africa to help end racial apartheid. The UN has also helped millions living in famine, as well as aided countless refugees fleeing war and natural disasters by providing food, shelter, clothing, and medical relief. The World Health Organization—a UN establishment—is considered a model of success.

Nevertheless, although having 191 members, the United Nations relies disproportionately on the United States for monetary, material, and military support. Moreover, since the end of the Cold War, the United States and UN have developed competing and antagonistic views in regard to the UN's mandate and global role. The primary problem has to do with legitimacy and sovereignty. In 1992, the UN released a bold initiative—the Agenda for Peace—to recast the UN's peacekeeping role, but the move seemed an attempt to give the UN control over U.S. military and foreign policy resources. The consequence of this initiative was peacekeeping failures in Somalia, Rwanda, and Bosnia, in which over one million have been killed. The Agenda for Peace advocates peacekeeping, yet the UN does not have the requisite forces to carry out this agenda. Only the United States has the sufficient force to carry out this mandate.

Furthermore, due to disagreements with the United States over its military and foreign policy role

in Iraq and the Middle East, the UN voted to eject the United States from the UN Human Rights Commission. This action infuriated the U.S. government because countries that engage in human rights violations, such as Sudan, Libya, and Cuba, retained their seats on the commission. The United States walked out of the UN conference on racism in 2001 because the focus was singularly on perceived Israeli racism instead of racism in general. Finally, after thwarting U.S. policy toward Iraq prior to the U.S.-led invasion in 2003, the UN became embroiled in a major financial scandal involving its Oil for Food program. This program was created during Saddam Hussein's regime in order to give the Iraqi people humanitarian aid while sanctions against Hussein's government were in place. Nearly $1 billion disappeared into hidden bank accounts and fake corporations, and the U.S. Congress launched an investigation into where the money went.

Should nations such as the United States cede control of their militaries to the United Nations? Since the United States provides the bulk of military force and funding for UN programs (though the United States is consistently in arrears in paying its dues), should not the United States have a dominant role in determining UN policy and actions?

Arguments in Favor of the United States Pulling Out of the United Nations

- **The United Nations is incapable of enforcing its own resolutions.** As the run-up to the U.S.-led invasion of Iraq demonstrates, the UN is incapable of enforcing its own declarations and resolutions. Saddam Hussein and his regime violated sixteen UN resolutions created to prevent the development of weapons of mass destruction (WMDs) and enforce human rights. During this period, tens of thousands of Iraqis were killed by the Hussein government, and the Hussein regime hid programs to develop and build WMDs—fooling UN weapons inspectors.

- **The United States is not accountable to international organizations when pursuing its own interests.** The United States and United Nations have divergent interests and understandings of international law and diplomacy. To put American armed forces under UN command is to possibly give control of the military to those who oppose U.S. interests. Once the United States loses control of its armed forces command structure, it cedes control of the military to an organization that has demonstrated it will act against U.S. defense interests, as in the UN Security Council's attempt to stop the U.S.-led invasion of Iraq in 2003.
- **Many Americans believe that adhering to UN resolutions is to give up American sovereignty.** Many Americans believe there is an attempt to create a "world government" and that to accede to UN mandates and resolutions is to relinquish U.S. sovereignty and U.S. control over its own citizens. Many see the UN as a stepping stone to this end. For example, many nations want the United States to join and abide by the new International Criminal Court (ICC) in which defendants are denied basic U.S. constitutional protections, such as the prohibition against *habeas corpus*, or illegal imprisonment. This is considered yet one more instance of the international community trying to institute international government.

Arguments Against the United States Pulling Out of the United Nations

- **The UN engages in peacekeeping and nation building when the United States will not.** The UN is currently engaged in fifteen peacekeeping operations. There are currently 44,000 military personnel from member nations in operations in places such as Bosnia, Sierra Leone, and East Timor. The UN can provide peacekeeping support when the United States is either unable or unwilling, thus preventing humanitarian disaster and conflict. This is an essential function if global security and stability are to be maintained.
- **The United States must lead by example.** Because the United States has a unique world, military, and economic position, it can use its various strengths and principles to promote global peace and justice. Why should other nations respond to UN resolutions and decrees when the United States does not? By acceding to UN requests, the United States can set an example for other nations to follow, and this may help facilitate other nations' compliance with UN wishes to ensure global security.
- **International institutions provide global stability and promote peaceful conflict resolution.** Since the establishment of the United Nations, there have been no worldwide wars. The UN was able to provide security for South Korea and it acts as an international forum for conflict mediation. Though imperfect, the UN affords a medium in which human rights policy is debated and developed and international security and stability discussed. For example, the UN has taken on the cause of disarmament and elimination of WMDs and thereby provides legitimacy in this policy domain, whereas the United States cannot. Because the United States is a world power, its membership in the UN gives the organization credibility and validity.

Questions

1. Does adhering to UN mandates mean giving up national sovereignty?
2. What can be done to reconcile U.S. and UN interests? Do the United States and United Nations have similar interests? If not, what is to be done?

Selected Readings

Thomas Weiss, ed. *United Nations and Changing World Politics.* Boulder, CO: Westview, 2004.
Dennis Jett. *Why Peacekeeping Fails.* New York: Palgrave Macmillan, 2001.

In the United States and other democracies, foreign policy or defense crises generally increase presidential popularity, but sometimes the increase is temporary. President George W. Bush's approval ratings skyrocketed to unprecedented highs in the weeks after the 9/11 disaster, and remained at high levels during the war in Afghanistan. They fell somewhat at the beginning of the war against Iraq in 2003, then began to recede significantly only when the situation in Iraq remained unstable many months after the Hussein government had toppled. As a rule, the American public affects the formulation and implementation of foreign and military policy in three ways: in elections, via public opinion, and via public action. Political activists especially affect U.S. policy when they join or work with international **nongovernmental organizations (NGOs),** international organizations that have members from several countries who seek a set of objectives but are not formally connected to a government.

nongovernmental organization (NGO)

An organization that is not tied to a government.

THE CHALLENGE OF BALANCING FOREIGN AND DOMESTIC AFFAIRS

TO A CERTAIN EXTENT, THE DIVISION OF U.S. policies into foreign affairs and domestic affairs is artificial. It is only rarely possible to concentrate on domestic issues to the exclusion of international issues. Nevertheless, except for homeland defense and the war on terrorism, many Americans believe the United States should concentrate on solving its domestic problems, minimizing U.S. involvement in other foreign and military issues.

Even after 9/11, finding the appropriate balance between domestic and foreign affairs is difficult for the president and other policy makers. Scarce national resources and scarce presidential time must be parceled out as competition for resources and time emerges between foreign and domestic issues. Striking the appropriate balance between foreign and domestic affairs so that American interests and objectives are achieved and the American public is satisfied is thus a continuing challenge for the president and others involved in the foreign and defense policy process.

Following the 9/11 terrorist attacks, there was widespread agreement within the United States that America's grand strategy should cen-

■ At a ceremony in the White House Rose Garden on April 10, 2004, President George W. Bush announces his selection of Representative Porter Goss (R–FL), chair of the House Select Committee on Intelligence, to become the new Director of the Central Intelligence Agency.

Photo courtesy: Mannie Garcia/Reuters/Corbis

ter on homeland defense and the war on terrorism. This view is understandable, but it overlooks a broader point that first requires discussion of the meaning of grand strategy.

Grand strategy refers to the choices a government makes to apply economic, military, diplomatic, and other resources to preserve the country's people, territory, economy, and values.[20] Building a grand strategy has three components.

The first component is answering the question, "What should grand strategy be?" For the United States, should it be restricted to homeland defense and the war on terrorism? These are two critical policy areas, but are they too limited by themselves to be grand strategy? For example, should the United States adopt a "close-out strategy" in which it attempts to prevent any other country or group from developing the ability to challenge it economically or militarily? Or, should the United States use its power and wealth to try to create a cooperative multilateral world in which policies are made on the basis of the greatest good for the greatest number?

The second component in building a grand strategy is answering the question, "How can we develop consensus for a grand strategy?" Sometimes, a grand strategy is obvious and consensus develops easily. This was the case early in American history when George Washington argued that America should steer clear of entangling alliances, and it was the case after World War II when the Soviet threat made containment of communism the obvious grand strategy. It appears to be the case again today following al-Qaeda's assault on America. But, are homeland defense and the war on terrorism, even though important, too limited to qualify as grand strategy?

The third component is leadership, required so appropriate policies can be implemented. Since conflicting viewpoints and interests lead different people and interest groups to have different views about appropriate grand strategy, leadership, usually provided by the president, is a requisite element of grand strategy. Once a grand strategy has been identified and consensus developed, policies in keeping with the grand strategy must be implemented. Even when consensus exists, there will be debate over specific policies. Even in the absence of a consensus, foreign and defense policies must be put in place.

grand strategy
The choices a government makes to balance and apply economic, military, diplomatic, and other resources to preserve the nation's people, territory, and values.

SUMMARY

FOREIGN AND MILITARY POLICY are important functions of the U.S. government. From the earliest days, isolationism, unilateralism, moralism, and pragmatism were central elements of U.S. foreign and military policy. After World War II, foreign and military policy often dominated the American political agenda, and defense spending became one of the biggest items in the national budget. Foreign and military policy became major concerns, especially issues such as U.S.–Soviet relations, nuclear weapons, and the Vietnam War. Despite debate, an underlying consensus existed that American policy should focus on containing the Soviet Union. After the Soviet Union collapsed, no immediate consensus emerged on the direction of U.S. foreign policy until the 9/11 attacks elevated homeland defense and the global war on terrorism to the top of the U.S. foreign and defense policy agenda.

Balances found in other parts of the U.S. political system are generally absent in foreign and military policy. The executive branch of government dominates foreign and military policy, with the Departments of State and Defense being particularly important. Within the executive branch, the president predominates.

Institutions outside the executive also play a role in U.S. foreign and military policy. These include Congress, the military-industrial complex, the news media, and the public.

The United States faces major challenges in foreign and military policy during the twenty-first century, especially homeland defense, the global war on terrorism, and building a grand strategy.

KEY TERMS

al-Qaeda, p. 525
Carter Doctrine, p. 520
Central Intelligence Agency (CIA), p. 534
Cuban Missile Crisis, p. 517
Department of Homeland Security, p. 534
détente, p. 518
engagement, p. 523
enlargement, p. 523
executive agreement, p. 536
grand strategy, p. 543
human rights, p. 519
isolationism, p. 516
military-industrial complex, p. 538
moralism, p. 516
National Security Council (NSC), p. 534
Nixon Doctrine, p. 519
nongovernmental organization (NGO), p. 542
North American Free Trade Agreement (NAFTA), p. 523
North Atlantic Treaty Organization (NATO), p. 520
Operation Desert Storm, p. 522

pragmatism, p. 516
Reagan Doctrine, p. 520
unilateralism, p. 516
Vietnam War, p. 517
war on terrorism, p. 528
War Powers Act, p. 536
weapons of mass destruction (WMDs), p. 528
World Trade Organization, p. 523

SELECTED READINGS

Allison, Graham F., and Philip Zelikow. *Essence of Decision: Explaining the Cuban Missile Crisis,* 2nd ed. New York: Pearson, 1999.

Ambrose, Stephen, and Douglas Brinkley (contributor). *Rise to Globalism: American Foreign Policy Since 1938,* 8th ed. New York: Penguin, 1997.

Axelrod, Alan. *American Treaties and Alliances.* Washington, DC: CQ Press, 2000.

Boot, Max. *The Savage Wars of Peace: Small Wars and the Rise of American Power.* New York: Basic Books, 2002.

Byman, Daniel, and Matthew C. Waxman. *The Dynamics of Coercion: American Foreign Policy and the Limits of Military Might.* Cambridge: Cambridge University Press, 2002.

Clarke, Richard A. *Against All Enemies: Inside America's War on Terror.* New York: Free Press, 2004.

Eckes, Alan E., Jr. *Opening America's Markets: U.S. Foreign Trade Policy Since 1776.* Chapel Hill: University of North Carolina Press, 1995.

Friedman, Thomas L. *The Lexus and the Olive Tree: Understanding Globalization.* New York: Anchor Books, 2000.

Goldstein, Joshua S. *International Relations,* 5th ed. New York: Longman, 2005.

Halberstam, David. *War in a Time of Peace: Bush, Clinton, and the Generals.* New York: Scribner's, 2001.

Hook, Steven W., and John Spanier. *American Foreign Policy Since World War II,* 15th ed. Washington, DC: CQ Press, 2000.

Huntington, Samuel P. *The Clash of Civilizations and the Remaking of World Order.* New York: Touchstone Books, 1998.

Johnson, Chalmers. *Blowback: The Costs and Consequences of American Empire.* New York: Owl Books, 2001.

Kennan, George F. *American Diplomacy, 1900–1950.* Chicago: University of Chicago Press, 1951.

Kissinger, Henry. *Diplomacy.* New York: Touchstone Books, 1995.

Mann, Robert A. *A Grand Delusion: America's Descent into Vietnam.* New York: Basic Books, 2001.

Mead, Walter Russell. *Special Providence: American Foreign Policy and How It Changed the World*. New York: Knopf, 2001.

Mearsheimer, John J. *The Tragedy of Great Power Politics*. New York: Norton, 2001.

Nye, Joseph S., Jr. *The Paradox of American Power: Why the World's Only Superpower Can't Go It Alone*. New York: Oxford University Press, 2002.

Papp, Daniel S. *Contemporary International Relations*, 6th ed. New York: Longman, 2002.

Papp, Daniel S. *The Impact of September 11 on Contemporary International Relations*. New York: Longman, 2003.

Parenti, Michael. *The Terrorism Trap: September 11 and Beyond*. San Francisco: City Light Books, 2002.

Patterson, Thomas G., et al. *American Foreign Relations: A History to 1920,* 4th ed. New York: D. C. Heath, 1995.

WEB EXPLORATIONS

To see the reach and worldwide involvement of the United Nations, go to www.un.org

To learn about the specific workings of the IMF and World Bank, go to www.imf.org www.worldbank.org

To learn more about NATO's peacekeeping operations in Kosovo, go to www.nato.int

To learn more about U.S. military operations around the globe, go to www.defenselink.mil

To learn more about the National Security Council and the CIA, go to http://www.cia.gov/

To learn more about key congressional committees in military and foreign affairs, go to
http://www.house.gov/hasc
http://www.senate.gov/~armed_services/
http://www.house.gov/international_relations
http://www.senate.gov/~foreign

For a world map of countries that have ratified the Chemical Weapons Convention, go to
http://projects.sipri.se/cbw/docs/cw-cwc-mainpage.html

The Context for Texas Politics and Government

THE FACE OF TEXAS IS CHANGING. By the time you read this, Anglos may no longer constitute a majority of Texans for the first time since the early 1800s. As a result of immigration trends and differential birthrates among the ethnic groups in Texas, Hispanics, African Americans, and Asian Americans will make Texas a majority–minority state (a state in which ethnic and racial minorities form the majority of the state's population). The changing Texas demographics will probably produce other changes in Texas as well—social, economic, and political.

The demographic history of Texas involves growth, but the 1990s were exceptional for several reasons. First, the growth of Texas's population by nearly 3.9 million was the largest decade increase in population in the state's history. Second, the population growth occurred in all twenty-seven of Texas's metropolitan areas, in 73 percent of its counties, and in 74 percent of its towns and cities. Third, the population became even more ethnically diverse. During the 1990s, the Anglo population increased by only 7.6 percent while the Hispanic population increased by 53.7 percent and the African American population increased by 22.5 percent. According to state demographer Steve Murdock, "For the State of Texas as a whole and pervasively across the state, population change has come to be increasingly determined by change in non-Anglo populations."[1] Finally, Texas's population, like the population of the rest of the United States, is aging, a result of increasing life expectancy and the aging of the Baby Boomers.

As these trends continue in the twenty-first century, what effects will the changing demography of Texas have on the economic, social, and political characteristics of Texas? During the first four decades of the twenty-first century, the labor force will grow significantly. With the changing ethnic composition and the aging of Texas workers, the Texas workforce will be less educated than in 2000, unless ethnic differences in education levels are addressed quickly. Demographer Steve Murdock states, "If differentials in the socioeconomic characteristics of the labor force do not change, the state's future labor force will be less well educated, less skilled, earn lower salaries and wages, and thus be in greater need of labor force training."[2]

Increases in the demand for education will also be substantial. Enrollment in public education institutions at all levels will increase by 79 percent by 2040. Community college and university enrollments will also increase dramatically—by 102 percent and 82 percent, respectively. As a result, the cost of providing an education to Texans will increase substantially.

In human services, the changes in Texas's population produce an anticipated percentage increase in Temporary Assistance for Needy Families (TANF) recipients, an even greater percentage increase in Medicaid recipients, and the greatest percentage increase in food stamp recipients. As the recipients increase, there is an associated cost to the state to meet the human services needs of Texans.[3]

These demographic, economic, and social changes will produce a form of politics that is different from what existed at the close of the twentieth century. They will also affect what it means to be a Texan.

WHAT DOES IT MEAN to be a Texan? The beliefs that Texans hold are a product of Texas's roots—its land, its people, and its history. The politics and government of a state are shaped by its inhabitants' ideas about politics and government, by the social and ethnic composition of its population, by its history, and by its economy. These factors, along with its constitution (see chapter 16) and its relationship with the national government (see chapter 3), provide the context for politics and government, as well as the continuity and changes.

In this chapter, we describe the ideological, social, historical, and economic context for Texas politics and government. By placing Texas in context, we gain an appreciation for the unique and the common characteristics of Texas politics and government.

- First, we will look at *the roots of Texas politics and government*, focusing on the land and people of Texas.
- Second, we will analyze *the ideological context* for Texas politics and government, noting how a set of ideas has been modified by Texas's unique experiences.
- Third, we will examine *the economy of Texas*, focusing on the evolution of Texas's economy from a colonial, land-based economy to a modern, information-based economy.
- Finally, we will analyze *wealth and poverty in Texas*, indicating how the distribution of wealth and poverty influences politics and government in the Lone Star State.

THE ROOTS OF TEXAS POLITICS AND GOVERNMENT

THE ROOTS OF TEXAS politics and government are found in the early settlers of Texas and in the type of society and government they created. But, even before people inhabited Texas, there was the land. With an area of 267,339 square miles, Texas is larger than most nations and contains every major landform: mountains, plains, plateaus, and hills. In far West Texas are the Chisos and Davis Mountains. Plains constitute the major landform in Texas, covering much of West Texas, North Texas, the Gulf Coast, and northwestern Texas. The Edwards Plateau is the major plateau, or tableland, in Texas. Hills are found in many parts of Texas, but they are especially prominent in the German Hill Country. The variety of landforms and the geographical size of Texas has an effect on its inhabitants. Taming a land of such great size and variety is not accomplished easily, but many different peoples have tried.

With its 22.1 million residents in 2003, Texas is the second largest state in population and in territory.[4] Texas's population is almost as diverse as its geography. Whereas the United States in 2002 was 68 percent Anglo, 13 percent Hispanic, and 12 percent African American, Texas, in the same year, was 51 percent Anglo, 34 percent Hispanic, and 11 percent African American.[5] The Institute of Texan

Photo courtesy: Laurence Parent
■ In the Texas Panhandle, Palo Duro Canyon creates magnificent views that rival those of the Grand Canyon.

Cultures identifies twenty-seven ethnic groups in contemporary Texas. From the beginning, Texas's population was diverse. The first inhabitants, of course, were the American Indians, or Native Americans.

Native Americans

There are few Native American tribes in present-day Texas. However, from prehistoric times, Native Americans representing four different cultural traditions established permanent residence in Texas, and members of many more tribes and nations, some of whom are still present in Texas, were brief inhabitants.

In the coastal areas of the state and extending into all of South Texas, the Coahuiltecan and Karankawan tribes maintained an imperiled existence in a harsh environment by hunting and gathering. In central Texas, scattered bands of Native Americans established themselves during the 1500s. By the eighteenth century, they had become a buffalo-hunting, tepee-using, horse-riding Plains people. Plains tribes associated with Texas in those early days were the Lipan and Kiowa Apache, Kiowa, and especially Comanche.[6] The Jumano, related to the Puebloan culture of the American Southwest, were present from historical times. Spanish Fort on the Red River was the headquarters for a group of semi-sedentary tribes, known today as the Wichita, who extended to Waco in central Texas. In eastern and northeastern Texas, tribes of Caddo, joined together in confederacies, possessed a complex culture built around intensive farming and agriculture.

The Native American legacy in Texas is substantial. The Caddo established economic and cultural patterns—involving farming, trading, and trotline fishing—on which subsequent inhabitants of Texas expanded. The Caddo also greeted early Spanish explorers as *Tayshas,* meaning "friends." The term was subsequently Hispanicized to *Tejas,* and then Anglicized to *Texas.* Similarly, the most feared and respected Native Americans in Texas, the Comanche, displayed many of the characteristics of individualism that Anglo Texans on the frontier most admired.[7] Also, their resistance to Anglo expansion forced the farmers and ranchers to become horsemen and to adapt to the challenges of existence on the frontier.

By the late 1800s, few Native Americans remained in Texas, a result of epidemics of diseases such as cholera and smallpox, military campaigns, and their forced removal to reservations in other states. Native Americans constitute a small percentage of Texas's population, and their political influence reflects their small numbers. Currently, there are only three Native American tribes on reservations in Texas: the Alabama-Coushatta in Polk County (in East Texas), the Kickapoo near Eagle Pass (in South Texas, on the Rio Grande River), and the Tigua near El Paso (in far West Texas). The oldest, the Alabama-Coushatta reservation, was established in 1854.

The Tigua first became embroiled in Texas politics when they opened their Speaking Rock Casino in 1993. In 1987, Congress recognized the Tigua, and in exchange, the tribe agreed to prohibit gambling in all forms and to obey Texas laws. Nevertheless, the tribe filed a lawsuit, which they lost, attempting to force the state to negotiate a casino compact with the tribe under the 1988 Indian Gaming Regulatory Act. In 1999, Texas Attorney General John Cornyn sought an injunction to halt gambling on tribal property. In 2001, a federal district court granted a permanent injunction against the tribe's casino and ordered it to close by November 30, 2001. The Tigua appealed his ruling. In February 2002, the casino was forced to close.

Other tribes in Texas have tried to establish gambling operations. In 1999, the Alabama-Coushatta tribe voted to bring gambling to its Texas reservation and opened a casino in November 2001. In July 2002, a federal district court ordered it to close. The tribe also joined the Tigua in lobbying the Texas legislature to authorize casinos on their reservations.[8] In Eagle Pass, the Kickapoo's Lucky Eagle Casino has been offering bingo, card games, and video games since 1996.

Hispanics

Spaniards explored Texas in the sixteenth century, but only by the early eighteenth century did they establish permanent settlements. An early colony in Nacogdoches was followed by a *presidio*, San Antonio de Bexar, and a mission, San Antonio de Valero, along the San Antonio River. A colony in La Bahia (Goliad) followed. Only in the 1740s and 1750s did Spaniards colonize the Rio Grande, although these were some of their most successful settlements.

The mainstays of Spanish colonization included four institutions: (1) the mission, which performed civilian as well as religious functions; (2) the *presidio*, which provided frontier defense; (3) the *rancho*, which sustained civilian life; and, (4) towns or civilian settlements. By the end of the eighteenth century, only about 5,000 *pobladores* (settlers) inhabited Texas.[9] Nonetheless, their legacy far exceeds what their numbers suggest. They created a culture that valued "egalitarianism, a sense of duty, and a respect for physical prowess and gallantry in the face of adversity."[10] They also provided cultural norms for ranchers, sheep herders, and goat raisers. In addition, Spanish legal traditions, such as those pertaining to women's property rights, endured, as did customs protecting debtors.[11]

Photo courtesy: Joel Salcido/Bob Daemmrich Photography, Inc.

■ Tigua Indians are one of only three Native American tribes on reservations in Texas. Located in El Paso, the tribe operated the Speaking Rock Casino, which was closed in 2002 as a result of a federal lawsuit filed by Texas Attorney General John Cornyn. When operating, the casino earned the 1,200-member tribe $60 million annually, allowing the tribe to build houses for its members, provide social and health programs, and provide annual cash payments of $15,000 to each tribe member.

After Mexico's independence from Spain in 1821, Mexican colonialization of Texas was no more successful. In 1836, when Texas became an independent republic, no more than 7,000 or 8,000 Spaniards, Christianized Native Americans, and mestizos (people of mixed European and Native American ancestry) resided in Texas. In 1850, the U.S. Census revealed a Hispanic population of only 14,000—less than 7 percent of Texas's population. As late as 1887, the state Census counted only 83,000 Hispanics, only 4 percent of the Texas population. Concentrated in the border counties along the Rio Grande, Hispanics were outnumbered even by German Americans. However, between 1890 and 1910, a major influx of Mexicans occurred, resulting in a doubling of the Hispanic population of 1887. Between 1910 and the 1980s, the Hispanic population in Texas grew tenfold, caused largely by an explosive birthrate in Mexico and the steady industrialization of Texas. During the late 1940s, Hispanics displaced African Americans as the largest ethnic minority in Texas.[12]

By 2003, Hispanics had achieved considerable political clout in Texas. In 2004, 37 Hispanics served in the Texas Legislature, 261 were county

Photo courtesy: Bob Daemmrich/Bob Daemmrich Photography, Inc.
■ These Ballet Folklorico dancers are representative of many performers who appear annually at the Texas Folklife Festival. The festival draws thousands to San Antonio every June to sample the crafts, foods, music, storytelling, and dances of the diverse people who are Texans.

officials, 580 were municipal officers, 375 held judicial posts, 759 served on elected school boards, and 56 were special district officials.

Currently, almost all Hispanic elected officials are Democrats (97 percent); however, the Republican Party made a concerted effort to attract Hispanic voters in recent elections, appealing to Hispanics' desires for educational advancement, personal responsibility, and economic opportunity.[13]

African Americans

African Americans have inhabited Texas since Spanish rule but probably made up no more than 12 percent of the population in Texas prior to 1836. This was due to the Mexican government's opposition to slavery, and most early settlers in Texas came from the southern mountain states, where slavery was less common. In the late 1830s, however, an influx of African Americans accompanied Anglo planters from coastal southern states. With slavery legalized in the Republic of Texas, the number of African Americans increased rapidly, composing 20 percent of the population by 1840. The growth of the African American population in Texas was effectively halted by the Civil War. Between 1865 and 1880, only 6 percent of immigrants were African American, and the percentage of African Americans has continued to decline since 1865, the year in which nearly one-third of Texas's population was African American.[14]

The bulk of the settlement by African Americans in Texas occurred between 1836 and 1865. The area of greatest settlement for African Americans lay east of a line connecting Texarkana and San Antonio. By 1860, thirteen Texas counties had African American majorities. All of these counties were located along the major rivers of eastern and southeastern Texas. In 1887, twelve counties had African American majorities. In 1930, only four counties had African American majorities, and by 1980, there were none.[15]

African Americans in Texas held fewer elected offices in 2001 than they did in 1993.[16] In 2001, 460 African Americans held elective office. Among the elected officials, two African Americans were U.S. Representatives, two were state senators, fourteen were representatives, twenty were county officials, 282 were municipal officials, forty-three were judicial or law enforcement officials, and ninety-five

Photo courtesy: Erich Schlegel/Dallas Morning News

■ In 2003, Edward D. Garza was elected to a second term as mayor of San Antonio. During his first term, Garza ensured that San Antonio, long known as "Military City USA," continued its close relationship with the military and defense contractors. In February 2003, Garza helped San Antonio secure a Toyota manufacturing facility, resulting in 2,000 high-wage jobs for the city.

were elected to school boards and other elected education positions. In early 2003, three African Americans (all Republicans)—Railroad Commissioner Michael Williams and Texas Supreme Court Justices Wallace Jefferson and Dale Wainwright—held statewide elective offices. In 2004, Perry appointed Jefferson chief justice of the Texas Supreme Court.

Asian Americans

The first permanent resident Asian Americans in Texas were probably Chinese immigrants who arrived in Houston in 1869 to clear land for the Houston and Texas Central Railway. In the early 1900s, a distinguished Japanese businessman, Seito Saibara, was invited to the United States to help develop the rice industry on the Gulf Coast. In 1903, Harris County officials invited him to start a colony in Webster, just south of Houston. Saibara bought 304 acres and began bringing families from Japan. During the 1970s, thousands of Vietnamese immigrants came to Texas when the South Vietnamese government neared collapse and ultimately fell to North Vietnam.

In 2000, there were 562,319 Asian Americans in Texas, primarily of Vietnamese, Chinese, Indian, Filipino, Korean, and Japanese ethnicity. The larger cities in Texas contain Asian neighborhoods. In 2003, few Asian Americans held elective political office in Texas. The offices held were mostly at the county or municipal level.[17] Martha Wong won election to the Texas House in 2002, becoming the first Asian American woman and the second Asian American elected to the Texas legislature. In 2004, Hubert Vo was elected to the Texas House.

Anglos

As the term is used in Texas, **Anglos** are non-Hispanic whites. During the early period of Anglo settlement in Texas, 1815 to 1836, the Anglo immigrants to Texas were predominantly upper Southerners from Tennessee, Kentucky, Arkansas, and North Carolina. By 1820, these people had firmly established themselves in northeast Texas. Missouri, Kentucky, Tennessee, and Arkansas provided most of these settlers.

In the southeastern border area of Texas, known as the Atascosita District, Anglos began

Anglos
Non-Hispanic whites.

■ In Houston, Bellaire Boulevard hosts signs in Chinese, Japanese, Vietnamese, and other Asian languages.

Photo courtesy: John Everett/Houston Chronicle

drifting in after 1819. These settlers were lower Southerners, mostly poor whites from Louisiana, Mississippi, and Alabama.

North of the Big Thicket, between the Trinity and Sabine Rivers, a few small Anglo settlements developed. Most of these settlers were upper Southerners, although many slave-owning planters were attracted by the fertile Redlands area. Thus, by 1836, more than 60 percent of Anglos in Texas were from the upper South, about 25 percent were from the lower South, and about 10 percent were New Englanders.[18]

From Texas's independence to the Civil War, Anglo immigration increased, drawing more heavily from the lower South. The legalization of slavery in the Texas Republic resulted in the first major wave of lower Southerners, primarily from Alabama, Georgia, Mississippi, and Louisiana. According to the 1850 Census, lower Southerners had become almost as numerous as the upper Southerners. The two groups, however, occupied different areas of Texas. Most of eastern and southeastern Texas was successfully settled by lower southern planters, and the continuing waves of upper Southerners were directed to the western interior of Texas.

In the post–Civil War period, upper and lower southern immigration continued in roughly equal proportions. The western expansion to the New Mexico border by 1880 was primarily an achievement of upper Southerners, who settled most of West Texas, and lower Midwesterners (Illinois, Kansas, and Iowa), who dominated the upper Panhandle.

Anglos have dominated politics and government in Texas since its independence from Mexico in 1836. Since statehood, Anglos have provided all of Texas's governors and lieutenant governors, almost all of its statewide elected officials, an overwhelming majority of its legislators, and almost all of the members of its administrative boards and commissions. However, the changing composition of Texas's population presages a likely challenge to the Anglo dominance in politics and government.

The Contemporary Population of Texas

The patterns of settlement established by Texas's first residents are still evident today, providing a measure of continuity, but new patterns are emerging as Texas becomes more heavily populated, more urbanized, and more diverse ethnically. The 2000 Census tallied 20,851,820 residents of Texas. By 1994, Texas's population size had surpassed New York's, making Texas the second most populous state in the nation. Between 1990 and 2000, Texas added more than 3.8 million people to its population. Texas's population growth during the period was the result of natural increase (49.7 percent) and immigration from other states and from other nations (50.3 percent). This balance between the components of population growth combined with a relatively constant rate of growth through natural increase makes continued population growth in Texas likely.[19]

The urbanization of Texas also continued during the 1990s, and the rural population of Texas fell below 16 percent by 2000. Despite the rural image frequently associated with Texas, a majority of Texans have lived in urban areas since the 1940s. In 2000, Texas had twenty-seven metropolitan areas, ranging in size from Victoria, with 84,000 people, to Houston, with 4 million people. Central Texas and the lower Rio Grande Valley area were the fastest-growing regions of Texas during the 1990s.[20] Three Texas cities (Dallas, Houston, and San Antonio) are among the ten most populous cities in the United States.

Probably the most important demographic change in Texas between 1990 and 2000 involves the ethnic composition of the population. Texas's minority populations have increased much more rapidly than the Anglo population. Hispanics, the largest minority group, made up 32 percent of the population, increasing by 54 percent during the decade. African Americans, who composed about 11.5 percent of the population, increased by 19 percent. In 2000, Anglos, who still constituted a majority with 52.4 percent of the population, increased only slightly.[21] However, population projections for Texas anticipate that Anglos will cease to be the majority by early 2005, and sometime during the 2020s, Hispanics will probably outnumber Anglos in Texas (see Analyzing Visuals: Population Trends in Texas).

Timeline

Texas's Evolving Demographic Makeup

As Hispanics become the principal ethnic group and Anglos lose their majority status, politics and government will change. First, the continued growth in the Hispanic population will result in greater political clout for Hispanics. In partisanship, Hispanics are more likely to be Democrats than Republicans. In ideology, Hispanics divide about equally among liberals, conservatives, and moderates in self-identification.[22]

Given the policy preferences of Hispanics and presuming an increase in their political influence, several policy changes can be anticipated. The tax structure in Texas, which takes 17 percent of the income of poorest Texans (incomes less than $20,999 annually) and only 5 percent of the income of richest Texans (incomes greater than $84,453 annually), will likely be revised to become less regressive. State spending for elementary and secondary education will probably increase, given the need for a better-educated workforce. Furthermore, spending on health care will probably increase.

In subsequent chapters, we return frequently to the topic of Texas's people; however, we now shift our focus to the ideological context for Texas politics and government.

Analyzing Visuals
POPULATION TRENDS IN TEXAS

Population projections for the next thirty-five years indicate that the demographic trends established during the 1990s will continue in Texas. The Hispanic and Asian American populations will continue to grow faster than the Anglo and African American populations. After reviewing the figure and reading the material in this chapter on population trends, answer the following critical thinking questions: How will the changing composition of Texas's population affect partisan electoral politics in Texas? What economic and social policy changes do you think the changing composition of the population will produce?

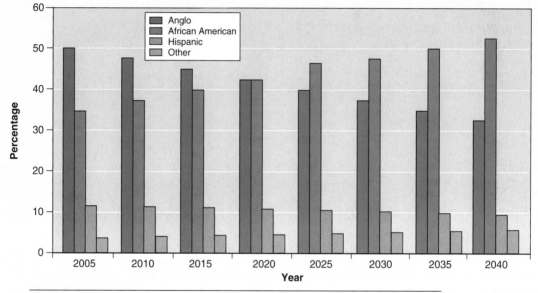

Source: Texas State Data Center, *2004 Population Projections—State of Texas*, recommended scenario, June 2004, http://txsdc.utsa.edu/tpepp/2004projections/2004_txpopprj_txtotnum.php.

THE IDEOLOGICAL CONTEXT

THE IDEOLOGICAL CONTEXT for Texas politics and government centers on a Texan Creed. The Texan Creed incorporates many of the same ideas that were influential for other Americans—individualism, liberty, constitutionalism, democracy, and equality. The features that distinguish the Texan Creed from the ideas held by other Americans arise from the unique historical experiences of Texas and Texans, especially

Photo courtesy: David Woo

■ Austin is a central component of the core economic triangle that also includes Dallas, Houston, and San Antonio. Austin is a center for high-tech industries in contemporary Texas.

between the 1820s and 1880s. Texas has changed substantially since the late 1800s, but the repetition of the prior historical experiences, whether mythical or not, keeps the creed alive and perpetuates it in each new generation. Consequently, we first explore how these experiences have shaped the five ideas of the Texan Creed.

The Texan Creed

Texan Creed
A set of ideas—primarily individualism and liberty—that shape Texas politics and government.

The **Texan Creed** consists of a set of ideas that identify Texans and provide the basis for their politics and government. For a majority of Texans, there is a consensus on the importance of the five ideas of the Texan Creed. Contemporary Texas is more heterogeneous than nineteenth-century Texas, but the ideas that were established during that century are still important today. Among the five ideas, individualism holds a special place for most Texans.

individualism
The belief that each person should act in accordance with his or her own conscience.

Individualism.   For most Americans, **individualism,** which stresses the primacy of the individual conscience as the basis for behavior, is the product of seventeenth-century Protestantism. Historian T. R. Fehrenbach cites individualism as the reason that early Anglo settlers came to Texas in the first place:

The early Texans descended from clans and families, heavily Scotch Irish, who deserted the panoply of Europe, despising its hierarchies and social organism . . . and who plunged into the wilderness. These folk sought land and opportunity, surely—but they were also consciously fleeing something: a vision of the world in which community and state transcended the individual family and its personal good.[23]

Coming to Texas in the late-eighteenth century, these people created a society dedicated to individualism. According to the ideal, the individual is responsible for the benefits that she or he receives in life and in the hereafter. For Texans, land possesses both a symbolic and a practical meaning. During the nineteenth century, Texans created a social environment in which every person could be a landowner, independent and supreme over his or her "country." The landowners' ethos remains in contemporary Texas, a legacy of early Texas individualism. For most Texans, the landowner remains the ideal.[24]

The individualism created in Texans' attachment to the land was nurtured by the frontier experience. For most Americans, the frontier era was short lived. Civilization advanced rapidly. For Texans, however, the **frontier era** lasted four decades (1830s to 1870s) and involved three distinct challenges: a battle with Mexico for cultural and political dominance, a more dangerous conflict for survival with a Native American population, and a struggle to conquer a difficult land. The frontier era had an enormous impact on Texans.

frontier era
The period when Texas constituted a border between American civilization and an area inhabited by a hostile, indigenous population.

For Texans, the most dangerous frontier was the western, Native American frontier. By 1834, Texan colonists had placed themselves within range of the Comanche. Previous wars between Native Americans and Anglos followed a common pattern: Anglo encroachment engendered Native American retaliation, which incited a military response that subdued the Native Americans. The Plains Indians, such as the Comanche, were not stationary, agricultural peoples. They were nomads who followed the bison herds over the seemingly boundless prairie. Thus, the conflict involved an Anglo farming population and powerful, warlike Native Americans. The Comanche were defending their territory from intruders and their raids exacted a terrible toll. As historian T. R. Fehrenbach notes, "Between 1836 and 1860, 200 men, women, and children were killed each year by Indians on the Texas border; between 1860 and 1875 at least 100 died or were carried off annually. The trek through central Texas cost seventeen white lives per mile."[25]

In order to survive on the frontier, Anglo farmers and ranchers had to adapt. They became true horsemen, they learned to survive in Native American country, and they adapted their agriculture to raising stock. The most important adaptation, however, involved frontier defense—the creation of the **Texas Rangers**. The rangers were composed of

Texas Rangers
A mounted militia formed to provide order on the frontier.

farmers and ranchers threatened by the native population; they were young, adventuresome, courageous volunteers. Though moral and ethical questions surround their tactics, few have questioned their success in seeking out their enemies' weakness and then attacking it without mercy. These characteristics and the use of Samuel Colt's revolving pistol, which gave each ranger the firepower of six, enabled the rangers to subdue their enemies.[26] However, as Fehrenbach admits,

> The Rangers never halted all the lawlessness and violence, of course, and the Army, not they, waged all the final campaigns against the Indians . . . . But Texans applauded their efforts . . . . For Rangers, born of the frontier, embodied many of the bedrock values of the frontier. They were brutal to enemies, loyal to friends, courteous to women, kind to old ladies; they never gave up, claiming that no power on earth could stop the man in the right who kept "a-coming." These were male values, warrior values.[27]

The final contribution to individualism came from the cowboy, who experienced the closing of the frontier and its way of life. Similar to the ranger in many of his values, the cowhand adopted a semifeudal notion of loyalty to his boss and brand, taken from the Mexican cattle-ranching culture. To herd half-wild cattle over thousands of miles required physical courage, but not recklessness. However, no respectable cowboy backed away from a fight that was forced upon him.[28] In all its manifestations, individualism has produced in Texans "a hard pragmatism and absence of ideology, a worship of action and accomplishment, a disdain for weakness and incompetence, and a thread of belligerence—and finally, a natural mythology stemming from the Alamo."[29] (The Alamo is discussed in the next section on liberty.)

Liberty.   Closely related to individualism and nearly as important to the Texan Creed is the idea of liberty. **Liberty** ensures that a person's inherent rights are free from government infringement. For Texans, a passion for liberty has additional sources: it was the reason for Texas's revolt against Mexico and the battle for the Alamo.

The decision by Texans to declare their independence from Mexico in 1836 had many causes, but the most important ones involved Mexico's attempts to exert greater control over Texas and Texans. Minor problems—religious requirements imposed on the settlers and Mexican opposition to slavery—offered potential areas of greater conflict, but a more serious concern involved the lack of an adequate local government through which the settlers could exercise a voice in the administration of their own affairs and the maintenance of order.[30] This grievance and Mexican suspicions of Anglo motives led the Mexicans to ban further immigration in 1830 and, two years later, to enforce the collection of tariff duties. In response to these Mexican actions, the colonists dispatched Stephen F. Austin to request separate statehood for Texas and other reforms. Until 1835, Texans considered themselves

liberty
The belief that government should not infringe upon a person's individual rights.

loyal Mexican citizens and were attempting to uphold the principles of the liberal, federal Mexican constitution of 1824. Only when the futility of such a position became evident were the "Texians," as they called themselves, willing to revolt against Mexico itself.[31]

In October 1835, Mexican President Antonio López de Santa Anna replaced the federal constitution of 1824 with the *Siete Leyes* (the "Seven Laws"), which established a centralized government under the president's control. The *Siete Leyes* signaled the end of republicanism in Mexico, converted the states into departments under the central government, and replaced the elected governors with appointed ones. At the same time, Mexican troops took up positions in Texas. When Mexican troops attempted to take a cannon in Gonzales, a skirmish ensued, and Texians prepared for war. A summons to arms in 1835 appealed to the Texians: "Fellow citizens, Your cause is a good one, none can be better; it is republicanism in opposition to despotism; in a word it is liberty in opposition to slavery. You will be fighting for your wives and children, your homes and firesides, for your country, for liberty."[32] With the adoption of this declaration, Texas established the right to revolution and laid the foundation for its subsequent government.

More than any historic event, **the Alamo,** a former Spanish mission in the heart of San Antonio that separated Mexican forces from Anglo settlements, exemplifies Texans' passion for liberty. In February and March of 1836, Lieutenant Colonel William Barret Travis and his band of about 180 volunteers fought to their deaths against a Mexican army of more than 5,000. The Alamo defenders lost the battle, but historian Joe Frantz contends that they "set the stage for ultimate Texas unification and victory"[33] and created a legacy that inspires and defines Texans more than a century and a half later. Over the years, fact and legend have intertwined so that the real story of the Alamo is impossible to discover. However, the true story is unimportant, for the power of the Alamo as a symbol of Texan independence and liberty transcends any measure of the truth. To a significant degree, the importance of the Alamo is embodied in the statements and the alleged actions of its heroes: David Crockett, William Barret Travis, and Jim Bowie.

Upon his arrival in Texas in 1836, David Crockett was administered the oath of allegiance by Judge John Forbes, who was forced to pause during his reading. Crockett had "noticed that he was required to uphold 'any future government' that might be established. That could mean a dictatorship. He refused to sign until the wording was changed to 'any future *republican* government.'"[34] Similarly, when he reached the Alamo, Crockett, noted for his verbal excesses, announced that "all the honor that I desire is that of defending as a high private, in common with my fellow citizens, the liberties of our common country."[35] For Crockett and others of his generation, the defining historical event was the American Revolution. To these men, the similarities between the American Revolution and the revolt by Texans were overpowering.

the Alamo
A San Antonio mission that was defended by Texans during their war for independence.

THE HEROES OF THE ALAMO

THE ALAMO COULD be viewed as a disastrous military defeat. After all, the more than 180 defenders of the Alamo died either in the battle or in subsequent executions by the victorious Mexican Army. For most Texans, however, the Alamo represents Texas's founding myth, indicating who Texans are and the values they embrace. Three heroes of the Alamo—James Bowie, David Crockett, and William Barret Travis—are responsible for many of the myths relating to the Alamo. Who were these men?

James Bowie was born in Kentucky but spent most of his childhood in Louisiana. Before entering Texas in the 1830s, Bowie had been a slave trader and land speculator in Louisiana. In Texas, he speculated in land, became a Mexican citizen, and married. In January 1836, Bowie arrived in San Antonio de Bexar with approximately thirty men.

Before arriving at the Alamo, David Crockett had established himself as a politician in Tennessee. Crockett was first elected to the U.S. House of Representatives in 1827 and reelected in 1829, but he lost his reelection bid in 1831. He returned to Congress in 1833 and was touted by Whig Party politicians as a possible anti-Jackson candidate for the presidency in 1836. However, Crockett lost his congressional election in 1835 and became disenchanted with his constituents and politics. As he had threatened, Crockett decided to explore Texas. Viewing Texas as an opportunity to rejuvenate his political career, he joined the volunteers and set out for San Antonio de Bexar.

Of the three Alamo heroes, William Barret Travis was the least well known. Born in South Carolina, Travis practiced law and started a newspaper in Alabama before he decided to abandon his pregnant wife and son and move to Texas early in 1831. Practicing law in Texas, Travis associated with a group of militants. In January 1836, after Travis was commissioned a

lieutenant colonel of cavalry, Governor Henry Smith ordered him to recruit one hundred men and reinforce Colonel James Neill at the Alamo. Travis arrived at the Alamo with only thirty recruits and reported to Neill, who soon left the fort, leaving Travis in command. Because the volunteers wanted Bowie to command and the regulars wanted Travis, they agreed to share the command. In late February, however, Bowie became ill, and Travis took sole command of the Alamo. Travis is best known for his reply to Santa Anna's demand that he surrender (he replied with a cannon ball), his letters requesting reinforcements, and the commitment to liberty and freedom they expressed.

Travis, shot in the head on the north bastion, was among the first to die. Bowie died in the Long Barracks, where he was shot several times in the head. Controversy still surrounds Crockett's death, although many historians now consider Mexican Lieutenant José Enrique de la Pena's diary an accurate account. Pena contends that Crockett and several other survivors were taken prisoner. Santa Anna ordered them executed immediately, and they were bayoneted and then shot. Nevertheless, the legend that Crockett died on the Alamo walls swinging Betsy, his rifle, when he ran out of ammunition dies hard, but his execution and Pena's description of the survivors' deaths "without complaining and without humiliating themselves" actually underscores the survivors' bravery.[a]

According to historian Stephen L. Hardin, "Even stripped of chauvinistic exaggeration, . . . the battle of the Alamo remains an inspiring moment in Texas history. The sacrifice of Travis and his command animated the rest of Texas and kindled a righteous wrath that swept the Mexicans off the field at San Jacinto."[b]

---

[a]See William R. Williamson, "Bowie, James"; Michael A. Lofaro, "Crockett, David"; Archie P. McDonald, "Travis, William Barret," *The Handbook of Texas Online*. Accessed January 4, 2001, http://www.tsha.utexas.edu/handbook/online/index.html.

[b]Stephen L. Hardin, "Alamo, the Battle of the," *The Handbook of Texas Online*. Accessed January 4, 2001, http://www.tsha.utexas.edu/handbook/online/articles/AA/qea2.html.

William Barret Travis, the youthful commander of the Alamo, probably best exemplifies the ideal of individual liberty and freedom. In his appeal for assistance, which was addressed "To The People of Texas & All Americans in the World," Travis pledged never to surrender or retreat and called on Americans everywhere "in the name of liberty, of patriotism & everything dear to the American character, to come to our aid."[36] In a letter to a friend, Travis explained his stand at the Alamo: "he felt the spirit of the times—the conviction that liberty, freedom and independence were in themselves worth fighting for; the belief that a man should be willing to make any sacrifice to hold these prizes."[37]

Whether Travis really drew a line in the dirt is disputed. Nevertheless, his speech in which he gave his men three choices—surrender, escape, or fight to the end—is a cornerstone of the Alamo legacy. Travis urged his men to fight with him, but he left the choice to each individual. Aware that no reinforcements were coming, all but one man crossed the line, choosing to fight and die with Travis. Jim Bowie, confined to a cot by typhoid-pneumonia, allegedly said, "Boys, I am not able to go to you, but I wish some of you would be so kind as to remove my cot over there."[38]

■ The Alamo, where more than 180 Texians fought to their deaths for freedom and liberty, provides a backdrop for the Texas livestock show parade in San Antonio.

Photo courtesy: Bob Daemmrich/Bob Daemmrich Photography, Inc.

Tejanos
Native Texans of Mexican descent.

The symbolic power of the Alamo reaches all Anglo Texans, regardless of political ideology. To a conservative, the Alamo symbolizes rugged individualism on the frontier and the need to defend liberty. A liberal sees in the Alamo the struggle for a sense of community, justice, and civil liberties.[39] Both visions offer insight into Texas and its politics. For *Tejanos* (native Hispanic inhabitants of Texas), the Alamo is an ambiguous symbol. Although Texas independence was the result of an alliance between Anglos and *Tejanos,* who played a crucial role, the ambivalence that *Tejanos* feel "stems from . . . the long use of the Alamo as an everyday symbol of conquest over Mexicans, as a vindication for the repressive treatment of Mexicans."[40]

constitutionalism
Limits placed on government through a written document.

Constitutionalism and Democracy.   Texans grant nearly equal status to the ideas of **constitutionalism** and democracy (see chapter 1). Following a tradition established in the United States, Texas has, for each of its governments, adopted a formal, written constitution, which clearly and distinctly limits the authority of government. In fact, from their first constitution in 1836, Texans created what historian T. R. Fehrenbach considers a "state that did not and could not plan society—they saw this as an immoral intrusion upon personal liberty—and in fact had almost no control over society in general."[41] Further support for the constitutionalism is seen in the inclusion, in all of Texas's constitutions, of an extensive Bill of Rights (we will examine the constitutions of Texas and their provisions in detail in chapter 16). Texans' desire for democracy was reflected in their commitment to creating an Athenian or Jeffersonian democracy—that is, a male, slave-owning democracy of property holders.

equality
The belief that all individuals should be treated similarly, regardless of socio-economic status.

Equality.   The idea of **equality** that developed in Texas during the nineteenth century was a product of the social system. Although there were substantial differences in social and economic statuses of Anglo males, no rigid social or political hierarchy existed. The commitment to social and political equality reflected a society based on land ownership, and land was a plentiful commodity. However, the equality accorded Anglo males did not extend to other members of the society. For non-Anglos, the inequality was palpable and perverse. Historian T. R. Fehrenbach describes slavery for African American Texans as "a system of the entrepreneurial exploitation of labor for profit, based on a law and society that was explicitly racist, in that the servitude of black people was justified by their racial inequality with whites."[42] The end of slavery was followed by the legal segregation of African Americans. The Anglo response to Hispanics has been similar, and Mexican Americans have been subjected to segregation and discrimination as well.

American Creed
Set of ideas that provide a national identity, limit government, and structure politics in America.

The Texan Creed is similar to the American Creed. According to political scientist Samuel Huntington, the **American Creed** consists of five ideas—individualism, equality, liberty, constitutionalism, and democracy—that provide Americans with a national identity, limit government authority, and are the foundation for American politics.[43] Like the American Creed, the Texan Creed provides the ideas that are the foundation for politics and government. Though similar to the American Creed, the Texan Creed has been shaped by historical events to place more emphasis on individualism and liberty than does the American Creed. If the Texan Creed is to endure, it must be transmitted from generation to generation, and Texans make a concerted effort to ensure its transmission.

As people acquire additional knowledge about politics and government, there is a growing need to organize that information and make it meaningful. For those who are most involved and active in politics, it means the development of a political ideology. As we noted in chapter 1, a political ideology is a consistent set of beliefs and attitudes concerning the scope and purpose of government. People who possess an ideology are called ideologues.

Political Ideologies in Texas

Politics, as we explained in chapter 1, involves conflicts over different ideas about the proper scope and purpose of government. If everyone agreed about what government should do and to what extent it should do it, there would be no need for politics. However, there is no agreement. The Texan Creed allows different conceptions of government's role. Some people may want the government to regulate individual behavior so that greater liberty is enjoyed by all; others may claim that the individual's right should be supreme and absolute.

Figure 15.1 illustrates the kinds of conflict that occur in Texas concerning the proper role of government. The choices that a person makes on these issues indicate his or her idea of the scope of government (how much government should do) and the purpose of government (what goals are legitimate for government). Those choices also determine the person's political ideology: libertarian, populist, conservative, or liberal.[44]

Photo courtesy: Lowell Georgia/CORBIS Images

■ The Alamo Cenotaph, erected on Alamo Plaza in 1939, honors the heroes of the Alamo. At the east panel, depicted in the photo, are statues of James Bowie and James B. Bonham. Statues of William B. Travis and David Crockett stand in front of the west panel.

THE TEXAS MYSTIQUE

For most Texans, Texas is special. To most non-Texans, Texas and Texans embody a set of stereotypes: big, brash, boastful, and boisterous. When President George W. Bush uses phrases such as "Bring 'em on," "Mission accomplished," and "America will never seek a permission slip," the stereotypes are reinforced, and Texans react as they have always reacted when they consider themselves and their state under attack—they fight back.[a]

The feelings that Texans have for their state result from the state's history and a mythology that has developed about that history. The mythology has many sources. Texas won its independence from a foreign power and maintained itself as a sovereign nation for nearly a decade. Many of these myths were created and perpetuated by Texas historians.[b]

During its struggle for independence, Texas produced a number of heroes who stood for the values that Texans admire, despite their past failures and idiosyncrasies. For Texans, the message is that a person is not judged by his past but by his present accomplishments. John Bainbridge described Texas as the frontier of America—"the land of the second chance, the last outpost of individuality, the stage upon which the American Drama . . . is being performed with eloquence and panache, as if for the first time."[c]

Other nineteenth- and early twentieth-century experiences and heroes bolstered the naive optimism and penchant for risk-taking shared by Texans. The frontier, the cowboy, and the independent oil producer hold a special attraction for Texans. In each case, the honest, hard-working individual succeeds against overwhelming odds. Self-reliance is the trademark of the Texas mystique. Conversely, depending on government to solve problems is a sign of weakness and the failure of individual initiative. Historian Randolph Campbell notes that the key to Texas's image of uniqueness is the way that "the Lone Star State embodies in an exaggerated way so many of the ideals and emotions shared by citizens of the United States."[d]

Since the 1980s oil bust, however, Texas has changed, becoming more like the rest of the United States in many respects. The economy has diversified, becoming more dependent on technology and services.

The economic changes have resulted in social changes. The new immigrants to Texas demand a healthy environment and adequate social services. As a result, Texans appear more willing to turn to government to solve social and environmental problems.[e]

Finally, the ethnic composition of the population in Texas has changed. The myths and legends that form the Texas identity were created and perpetuated by Anglos. As people of color replace Anglos as the largest ethnic group in Texas, the foundation for the Texas identity will have to change.

During the twenty-first century, Texans will either adapt their traditional identity and mythology to accommodate the economic and social changes or will seek a new identity and a new mythology. Regardless, that identity will have to incorporate all elements of a multiethnic and multicultural society, urban in residence and diverse economically. There are signs that the accommodation has begun in the growing recognition of the *Tejano* contribution to Texas's revolution and the acknowledgement of the role of Juan Seguín, José Antonio Navarro, and the *Tejanos* who died at the Alamo. As Historian Andrés Tijerina notes, "The myth is that Anglos brought liberty to Texas, when in reality *Tejanos* initiated the struggle with the authoritarian government of Santa Anna in Mexico."[f] Of course, this accommodation supports the legend of the Texans' quest for autonomy and local control.

[a]Mimi Swartz, "Them's Fightin' Words!" Texas Monthly (July 2004): 80.
[b]Laura Lyons McLemore, *Inventing Texas: Early Historians of the Lone Star State* (College Station: Texas A&M University Press, 2004).
[c]John Bainbridge, *The Super-Americans* (New York: Holt, Rinehart and Winston, 1972), 379–80.
[d]Randolph B. Campbell, *Gone to Texas: A History of the Lone Star State* (New York: Oxford University Press, 2003), 471.
[e]Benjamin Soskis, "Lone Star Joining: Why Texas Looks Like America," *New Republic* (18 September 2000): 23–7.
[f]Stefan Lovgren, "Alamo's Unsung Heroes—Remembering the Tejanos," *National Geographic News*, April 12, 2004, accessed August 4, 2004, http://news.nationalgeographic.com/news/2004/04/0412_040412_alamotejano.html.

Libertarians.   Libertarianism is "a highly individualistic extension of classical liberalism . . . . Libertarians emphasize very strongly the autonomy of the individual and the minimal role required of government."[45] Compared to conservatives, who view government as a necessary evil, libertarians see government as an evil, limiting the ability of individuals to make choices and achieve their own destinies.

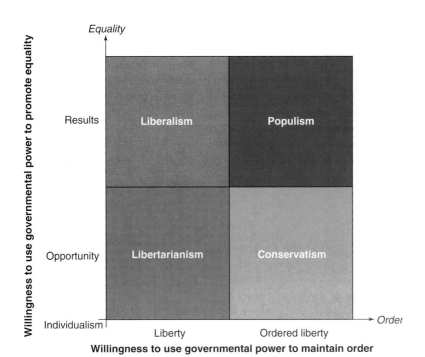

FIGURE 15.1 The Four Ideologies

The axes represent people's attitudes concerning the use of government to achieve certain goals. The horizontal axis represents a person's willingness to use governmental power to limit personal freedoms in order to maintain order. The vertical axis represents a person's willingness to use governmental power to promote equality. Each ideology reflects a choice between conflicting values. For example, liberals oppose the use of governmental power to limit personal freedoms in order to maintain order, but liberals support the use of governmental power to promote equality over protecting personal freedoms. On the other hand, conservatives support the use of governmental power to maintain order over protecting personal freedoms, but conservatives support the protection of personal freedom over the use of governmental power to promote equality. Libertarians support the protection of personal freedom over the use of governmental power either to promote equality or to maintain order. Populists support the use of governmental power to maintain order and to promote equality over the protection of personal freedom. ■

THE CIVICS EDUCATION REQUIREMENT
IN TEXAS COLLEGES AND UNIVERSITIES

The Texas legislature requires every student enrolled in a public institution of higher education in Texas to complete six semester hours of instruction in government or political science as a graduation requirement. How did this requirement come about? Who was responsible for the legislation? What was the legislature's intent?

The current requirement that you are obliged to follow was created in fits and starts and has evolved a great deal since the late 1920s. In 1929, the 41st Texas Legislature passed a bill that established 6th- and 7th-grade history and civil-government courses on patriotism and the duties of citizenship. The bill also required courses in the U.S. Constitution and the current Texas Constitution for high school and college students and exams on both constitutions. In its final version—the one that actually passed the legislature—the requirement for studying "patriotism and the duties of a citizen" was deleted.

The law must have created a storm of controversy because the legislature revisited the issue three times during the next year. Each change in the legislation involved the effective date of the requirement so that students who had already started their college educations were not prevented from graduating on schedule.

For several years, there were no more changes or amendments, and the issue seemed resolved. However, in 1937, the legislature passed another bill, sponsored by Representative A. P. Cagle, who was also chair of the Baylor University Political Science Department, which specified that *any* six semester hours of study in American government would fulfill the college requirement. The bill was amended so that no student could graduate without a total of six semester hours in Texas and American government. Again, the law resulted in problems for many students, forcing the legislature to adopt a measure ensuring that the bill would not apply to students who had enrolled prior to September 1, 1937.

More changes followed. In 1939, students were allowed to substitute Reserve Officer Training Corps (R.O.T.C.) for one of the two required courses. In 1995, students were allowed to meet the requirement by passing an examination rather than taking government classes.

Thus, an initial attempt to provide citizenship training in the public schools was expanded numerous times over many years to include six semester hours of government.

Not surprisingly, this requirement creates concerns for some students. Although the law may seem straightforward or obvious, it has been interpreted historically in two different ways, both of which meet the obligations of the law. At about half of the state's universities and colleges, the requirement is met by offering students one three-hour course in Texas state and local government and a second three-hour course in United States government—a format commonly called the "Texas A & M method." The other half of the universities and colleges offer six semester hours of instruction, usually in two courses, covering United States government and Texas state and local government in both classes—a format called the "University of Texas method." Unfortunately, some students run into problems because of these two interpretations.

For many students, the government requirement is met during the first two years of college. Increasingly, students in Texas and other states are beginning their college careers in community or junior colleges and then transferring to four-year institutions. Thus, if you take one government course at one institution, transfer to a different institution, and then take a second government course, you may find, when applying for graduation, that you have not met the legislative requirement and cannot graduate because the second school interpreted the law differently than the first. You are then stuck fulfilling the second school's requirement.

Populists.   In contrast to libertarians, **populists** favor government intervention both to promote equality and to establish or maintain an ordered liberty. Populists support the greatest scope of government action. Populism swept the nation in the 1880s and 1890s, becoming one of the largest social movements in American history. Texas has a strong populist tradition. Started in Comanche County by Thomas Gaines in 1886 as a protest against its Democratic Party's leaders, the People's Party led the political struggle for the ideas promoted by the Farmers' Alliance. The fundamental value championed by the People's Party was the equality of humankind. Thus, the People's Party sought government intervention to regulate or, if necessary, to control the economy. The economic issues of greatest concern to the populists involved land, transportation, and money.[46]

Concerning the conflict between individualism and an ordered liberty, the People's Party showed less tolerance for diversity and individual choice in matters of morality. The People's Party had a strong Protestant religious flavor. The populist movement was essentially a native Anglo movement, which was unsuccessful with foreign-born Texans and ignored Mexican Americans. For example, Germans, who were courted by the populists, viewed the movement as anti-alien, anti-Catholic, anti-liberal, and prohibitionist.[47]

Conservatives.   As we explained in chapter 1, conservatives believe that government should not promote equality, but they support government regulation of individual behavior in order to ensure an ordered liberty. The contradiction that conservatives exhibit in terms of the scope of government action can be explained by American conservatism's view of human nature. According to this view, humans are selfish, flawed by original sin, and in need of moral guidance. Thus, American conservatism believes in the necessity for moral principles to guide human behavior and allows government, through legislation and other devices, to apply those principles. Similarly, doubts about the capabilities of humans lead to a reluctance to allow government tampering with natural economic and social laws.

In contemporary Texas, self-identified conservatives are prominent in both of the major political parties and both state and local government, as well as the population generally.[48]

Liberals.   Liberalism (as you will remember from chapter 1) favors a government that uses its authority to promote equality but that leaves an individual free to make moral or personal decisions. Modern liberalism in Texas is traceable to the effects of industrialization and the economic and social dislocations associated with it. The events that define modern American liberalism are the Great Depression, which promoted the use of government authority to limit the economic effects of dramatic swings in the business cycle, and the civil rights movement, which promoted the use of government authority to ensure equality for all elements of society.

populists
People who support the promotion of equality and of traditional values and behaviors.

While favoring government's promotion of economic, political, and social equality, modern liberals oppose government infringement on each individual's freedom to make personal choices on moral issues, such as the decision by a woman to terminate a pregnancy. In Texas, liberals have always constituted a minority of the population.

As political scientist V. O. Key Jr. noted more than fifty years ago, Texas politics is about economics, and Texas "voters divide along class lines in accord with their class interests."[49] We will turn next to an examination of the evolving Texas economy.

THE ECONOMY OF TEXAS

UNTIL QUITE RECENTLY, the Texas economy was land based and colonial in structure. Texas produced, processed, and shipped its agricultural and mineral products to outside markets. Thus, the Texas economy was dependent on external demand and the prices paid for its cotton, cattle, or petroleum.

Cotton

The first real economy in Texas was created by southern planters and resembled the southern seaboard of the United States in prior centuries. In the 1830s, the economy was based on large slave plantations. The money crop, cotton, was barged down Texas rivers to the Gulf of Mexico because reefs prevented the development of ports at the mouths of Texas rivers. The cotton was then shipped to Europe or the United States, mostly through New Orleans. Later, Galveston was developed as a port, and it was the commercial center of Texas from the 1840s to the 1880s. During Texas's experience as a republic, and during its early statehood, cotton was the economic heart. Consequently, the region flourished during the cotton boom that preceded the Civil War. Cotton survived the Civil War, but the plantation system did not, and it was replaced by sharecropping. Nevertheless, Texas's annual cotton harvest accounts for a fourth of the total cotton production in the United States, providing $1.14 billion in receipts in 2000.[50]

Cattle

The cattle kingdom, inherited from the Mexicans, spread across the entire American West, capturing the fancy of Texas and the world in the late nineteenth century. Initially, the cattle business involved rounding up stray cattle and driving them to the Kansas railheads. The demand for beef created a link between the western frontier and the industrial marketplace. Like King Cotton, the cattle kingdom drew people and money from afar and involved agricultural products shipped to distant markets. For example, the largest ranch in Texas, the XIT, involved a Chicago syndicate, which was given 3 million acres in return for constructing the state capitol in 1881. Covering parts of nine counties in the Panhandle, the XIT ranch, which operated until the early 1900s, featured more than 1,500 miles of fence.[51]

Petroleum

For much of the twentieth century, petroleum was the basis for the Texas economy. From the first major oil discovery in 1901 at Spindletop, near Beaumont, by mining engineer Captain A. F. Lucas, Texas and the production of crude oil have been synonymous. Between 1900 and 1901, Texas oil production increased fourfold. In 1902, Spindletop alone produced 17 million barrels, 94 percent of the state's production. In 1923, the success of Santa Rita No. 1 ushered in the West Texas oil industry. The largest Texas oil field, the East Texas field, was discovered by C. M. "Dad" Joiner in 1930. However, the discovery of the East Texas field created a surplus of petroleum in a depressed economy. After World War II, the United States market sought cheaper oil in the Middle East. However, the oil embargo by the Organization of Petroleum Exporting Countries (OPEC) in 1973, a year after Texas reached its peak in oil production, caused an economic boom during the 1970s as prices were driven upward. This boom was followed by the bust of the 1980s when, in 1986, the price for West Texas crude fell below ten dollars a barrel. In 1981, the petroleum industry contributed 27 percent of the state's gross state product (GSP). Eighteen years later, in 1999, the industry contributed only 7.5 percent to the GSP, due to the lower price for crude oil and America's greater dependence on foreign oil.[52]

The Contemporary Economy

Since the 1980s, the Texas economy, which is projected to produce a GSP of $925 billion in 2005, has become more diverse, more nationalized, and more globalized than in the past. The diversity was thrust upon the Texas economy by the decline of the petroleum industry in the early 1980s. The importance of increased economic diversity is that it allows regions to withstand economic setbacks in one or more industries.[53] Currently, the greatest economic growth is occurring in a core area anchored by Houston, Dallas–Fort Worth, and San Antonio. According to former Comptroller John Sharp,

> This core triangle of high-growth industries and population tends to dominate the business sections of newspapers and to draw the most attention in plans for future development. Power is shared in a variety of ways by the three largest urban centers. Each is a distinct market and supply center, defining not only itself and the surrounding areas, but serving as a business link to the rest of the world, too . . . .
>
> With just 10 percent of the state's land mass, the core is home to 60 percent of Texans, less than two-thirds of whom were born in Texas . . . .

Economic characteristics draw the most vivid distinctions. With the obvious exceptions of agriculture, forestry, and fisheries, jobs are more plentiful in the central triangle, higher education more readily available and the growth of future industries more assured. The triangle cities are particularly strong in the financial, insurance and real estate sectors, in business and repair services, and in microelectronics, computer technology and biotechnology.[54]

Today, the Texas economy more closely resembles the national economy, although the Texas economy grew faster than the United States economy during the 1990s. During the 1990s, Texas led all states in net job creation.

The growth in jobs occurred in most sectors of the economy. Construction jobs increased by 5.7 percent, bolstered by low interest rates and increasing demand for residential and nonresidential construction. Growing by 30 percent during the 1990s, manufacturing jobs in Texas are concentrated in high-technology areas, primarily computers and electronics. The service-producing sectors of the economy accounted for the largest

Photo courtesy: David J. Sams/Bob Daemmrich Photography, Inc.

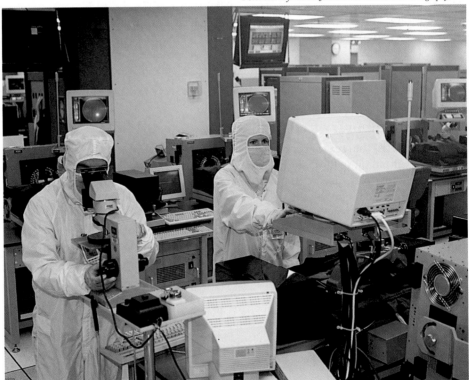

■ Workers in a Texas Instruments wafer-fabrication clean room demonstrate the effects of modern technology on jobs in the contemporary Texas economy.

TEXAS IN COMPARISON
The Socio-economic Context in the States

Texas in Comparison, a feature that appears in chapters 15–21, compares Texas with the three other most populous states—California, New York, and Florida—in terms of variables pertaining to the chapter's focus. During the 1990s, Texas replaced New York as the second most populous state in the United States. The four largest states vary in the percentage of ethnic minorities, with California having the largest percentage of Hispanics and New York having the largest percentage of African Americans. The four states also vary in poverty levels, with Texas having the largest percentage of population living below the poverty level and Florida having the smallest percentage below the poverty level.

State	Resident Population (2003)	African American Population (2002)	Hispanic Population (2002)	Population Below Poverty (2003)
Texas	22,118,509	11.2%	33.6%	16.3%
California	35,484,453	6.4%	33.9%	13.4%
New York	19,190,115	15.3%	16.0%	13.5%
Florida	17,019,068	15.0%	18.1%	13.1%

share of the growth in jobs during the decade. Leading the service-producing sectors were business services, engineering, accounting, research, consulting, and management services. Meanwhile, employment in public utilities and in government decreased as a percentage of the total.[55] In 2004, after three years of decline in Texas, the number of jobs finally surpassed the March 2001 peak of 9.5 million jobs.[56]

As the 1990s ended, the unemployment rate in Texas was 4.5 percent, the lowest rate in twenty years. The economic strength of the 1990s reduced the number of unemployed Texans by 15 percent. After reaching a peak in 1992, the unemployment rate and the number of unemployed Texans decreased each year during the decade,[57] but the recession of 2001 reversed that trend. By late 2003, the unemployment rate had reached 6.1 percent.[58]

The Texas economy became globalized during the 1990s, and Texas businesses compete throughout the world. In 2000, Texas exports reached $100 billion, growing by 66 percent since 1993 and accounting for 13.8 percent of Texas's gross product. Four industries—electronics, industrial machinery (which includes both computers and oil and gas field machinery), chemicals and petrochemicals, and transportation equipment—accounted for 66 percent of Texas's exports in 2000. In 2001, Texas export revenues declined to $95 billion. After 2001, Texas exports increased slowly until they exceeded $100 billion in 2004.[59]

For long-term, sustained economic growth, however, competition in the global market requires a commitment to developing a highly skilled, high-wage workforce supported by advanced technology, efficient telecommunications, strong research and development, and innovative marketing systems.[60] This is the economic challenge to Texas in the twenty-first century.

Join the Debate

SHOULD TEXAS ADOPT AN INCOME TAX?

OVERVIEW: Texas is one of only seven states that does not have a personal income tax. However, as the Texas legislature searches for a method of eliminating the current "share-the-wealth" or "Robin Hood" plan (as detractors call it) for equalizing funding for public education in Texas, the idea of an income tax loses some of its opposition.

In 1991, just as in 2004, the legislature met in the midst of a school finance crisis. Then Governor Ann Richards had expressed her support for a state lottery to raise new revenues during the gubernatorial campaign. Few public officials supported an income tax at that time (72 percent of House members and 77 percent of senators opposed an income tax), despite the fact that retiring Lieutenant Governor Bill Hobby announced his support for an income tax in 1989. When Richards's lottery plan failed, Lieutenant Governor Bob Bullock announced his support for an income tax, proposing a 5 percent tax on personal income and an 8 percent tax on corporate income.

Groups quickly took positions on Bullock's proposal. Common Cause and the Texas Trial Lawyers Association supported Bullock's proposal, but opposition from the Republican Party of Texas and the Texas Association of Business quickly surfaced.

In 1993, Bullock announced a change of heart, endorsing a constitutional amendment *banning* an income tax. However, as the saying goes, "The devil is in the details," and a closer reading of the proposed amendment indicated that the legislature *could* adopt an income tax, but the tax would not take effect until the measure was approved by a majority of voters in a statewide referendum *and* that at least two-thirds of any income derived from an income tax must go to reducing local property taxes for public education and the remaining revenues must be dedicated to public education. Voters overwhelmingly approved the constitutional amendment.

Read and think about the following arguments for and against an income tax. Then, join the debate concerning whether Texas should adopt an income tax by answering the series of questions posed.

Arguments in Favor of Adopting an Income Tax

- **An income tax is fairer than either a sales tax or a property tax.** Both the sales tax and the property tax, Texas's two major sources of revenue, are regressive.
- **An income tax can be deducted from an individual's federal income taxes.** Unlike the sales tax, which could not be deducted from an individual's federal income tax, tax payments under a state income tax are deductible for taxpayers who itemize their deductions.

WEALTH AND POVERTY IN TEXAS

IN DISTRIBUTION OF INCOME, Texas ranks among the most unequal states. Between 1998 and 2000, Texas ranked third among the fifty states in income inequality between rich and poor families, and fourth among the fifty states in income inequality between rich and middle-income families. In Texas, the richest 20 percent of families had aver-

- **An income tax raises additional revenues needed to fund adequately the state's social programs.** Texas spends very little money on programs to provide income assistance to the needy and health care for its less fortunate residents.

Arguments Against Adopting an Income Tax

- **An income tax would result in a higher tax burden for Texans.** States that adopted an income tax between 1957 and 1997 increased their overall tax burden three times as much as those states without an income tax.
- **An income tax would harm Texas's favorable business climate.** Businesses are attracted to Texas because of the low tax burden.
- **Texans oppose an income tax.** Surveys consistently show that a majority of Texans oppose an income tax.

Questions

1. What effect would an income tax have on personal income and businesses in Texas?
2. What effect would an income tax have on spending for social programs and education in Texas?

Selected Readings

Dave McNeely, "Senator Wading into Income Tax Waters," *Austin American-Statesman* (May 4, 2004), accessed June 10, 2004, http://www.statesman.com/metrostate/content/metro/mcneely/05/050404.html; Dave McNeely, "Senator Makes Case for Income Tax to Pay for Schools," *Austin American-Statesman* (May 5, 2004), accessed June 10, 2004, http://www.statesman.com/metrostate/content/metro/mcneely/05/050504.html.

Richard Vedder, "The Worst Tax for Texans? Comparing Income, Property, Sales and Corporate Taxes," *Taxing Texans: A Six-Part Series Examining Taxes in the Lone Star State.* Part 1 (Austin: Texas Public Policy Foundation, 2002), accessed June 10, 2004, http://www.texaspolicy.com/pdf/2002-02-28-tax-taxingtexans1.pdf.

Selected Web Sites

http://www.texastaxrelief.com/ This site, Texans for Lower Taxes, created by Representative Eddie Rodriguez, offers a calculator to demonstrate the effect that an income tax would have on an individual's taxes as well as information about Rodriguez's proposed income tax for Texas.

http://www.austinchamber.org The Austin Chamber of Commerce site includes a study of Texas taxes completed by Ray Perryman of the Perryman Group (http://www.austinchamber.org/The_Chamber/About_The_Chamber/What_We_Do/Education/SF/RPerryman.doc). The study analyzes various taxes in Texas, including the income tax.

age incomes that were triple the average incomes of middle-income families. Compared with families in the lowest 20 percent of income, the richest families had 11 times the average income (see Analyzing Visuals: Share of Income in Texas).[61]

Despite the unprecedented economic growth in Texas and other states, the gap between the rich and the poor has increased. Con-

Analyzing Visuals
SHARE OF INCOME IN TEXAS

Texas ranks among the most unequal states in terms of income distribution. During 1998–2000, Texas ranked third among the states in income inequality between rich and poor families. After viewing the pie chart and reading the material on wealth and poverty in Texas, answer the following critical thinking questions: Why is the distribution of income in Texas so unequal? What government policies contribute to the inequality? If Texans decided to reduce the inequality, what policies would be necessary?

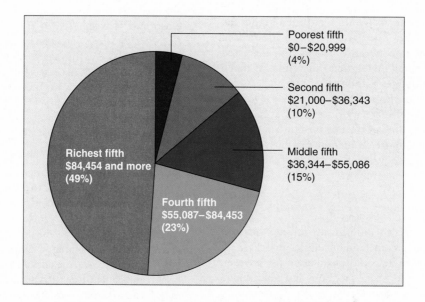

Poorest fifth
$0–$20,999
(4%)

Second fifth
$21,000–$36,343
(10%)

Middle fifth
$36,344–$55,086
(15%)

Richest fifth
$84,454 and more
(49%)

Fourth fifth
$55,087–$84,453
(23%)

Source: Center on Budget and Policy priorities, "Pulling Apart: A State-by-State Analysis of Income Trends," April 23, 2002, Accessed November 21, 2002, http://www.cbpp.org/4-23-02sfp.pdf.

tributing factors to the income disparity are that most new jobs are low-paying positions in the service sectors of the economy, incomes have risen fastest for people with the most education, and the minimum wage has not kept up with inflation. Texas ranked fortieth among the fifty states in percentage of high school graduates, which means that many Texans are ill prepared to qualify for better-paying jobs.[62]

Poverty is not only more pronounced in Texas than in the nation as a whole but is also more prevalent among certain ethnic groups, among children under eighteen years of age, and in certain areas of Texas. Among the major ethnic groups in Texas, Hispanics have the highest poverty rate, followed by African Americans, and Anglos. Twenty-one percent of children under eighteen years of age in Texas live in poverty; the national average is 16 percent. Also, the poverty rates for young children (under seven years of age) in Texas are higher than the national average.

Poor people do not usually participate actively and routinely in politics and government in Texas or in the other states, while the wealthy tend to be more active. Politics and government affect everyone in Texas, but the wealthy have the most to gain or lose through policy changes, so they actively protect their interests.

As we note in subsequent chapters, the economic leaders in Texas engage in many political activities. In the past, wealthy Texans influenced state politics either by recruiting and funding candidates for public office or by seeking public office themselves. In the 1940s and 1950s, Houston-area and statewide politics were heavily influenced by a group of millionaire executives. They recruited and designated candidates for office, and they raised money and business support for those candidates. One of the millionaires, George Brown, was crucial in the successful efforts in the 1950s to pass state laws limiting labor unions.[63]

Before becoming president in 1989, George Bush, a Midland and Houston oil millionaire, ran unsuccessfully for the U.S. Senate as a Republican in 1964. He won a U.S. House of Representatives seat in 1966 and 1968 before losing a U.S. Senate race again in 1970 to Democratic business millionaire Lloyd Bentsen.

Both Clayton Williams and Bill Clements—a frequent Republican nominee for governor—were among the wealthiest Texans. Robert Mosbacher, another of the wealthiest Texans, served as President George Bush's secretary of commerce. Dallas billionaire H. Ross Perot contributed money to Clements's campaigns before running for president in 1992 and 1996.[64] Other examples of wealthy Texas businessmen taking the leap into electoral politics include Land Commissioner David Dewhurst, former Governor George W. Bush, and Democratic gubernatorial nominee Tony Sanchez.

SUMMARY

IN THIS CHAPTER, we examined the context for Texas politics and made the following points:

1. The Roots of Texas Politics and Government

The roots of Texas politics and government reside in the breadth of Texas's geography, in the variety of peoples who have inhabited Texas, and in the ideas that those people have held about the scope and purpose of government. Native Americans, Hispanics, African Americans, Asian Americans, and Anglos have contributed to Texas's political culture. As the composition of Texas's population has changed, different ideas about politics and government have emerged.

2. The Ideological Context

A Texan Creed provides the foundation for politics and government in Texas. The Texan Creed comprises five ideas: individualism, liberty, equality, constitutionalism, and democracy. In addition, four ideologies—libertarianism, populism, liberalism, and conservatism—influence the responses of Texas politicians and political activists to issues of public policy.

3. The Economy of Texas

The Texas economy evolved from a land-based, colonial economy to a modern industrial, service, and information-based economy. Dependent first on cotton, then on cattle, and finally on petroleum, the economy of Texas was controlled by external markets. The contemporary Texas economy closely mirrors the U.S. economy in terms of its structure and operation.

4. Wealth and Poverty in Texas

Texas has an image of great economic wealth, but poverty is more common in Texas than in the United States generally. The inequities in wealth in Texas are concentrated ethnically and geographically.

KEY TERMS

SELECTED READINGS

Barr, Alwyn. *Black Texans: A History of Negroes in Texas, 1528–1995,* 2nd ed. Norman: University of Oklahoma Press, 1996.

Campbell, Randolph B. *Gone to Texas: A History of the Lone Star State.* New York: Oxford University Press, 2003.

Fehrenbach, T. R. *Seven Keys to Texas,* rev. ed. El Paso: Texas Western Press, 1986.

Himmel, Kelly. *Conquest of the Karankawas and the Tonkawas, 1821–1859.* College Station: Texas A&M University Press, 1999.

Newcomb, W. W., Jr. *The Indians of Texas: From Prehistoric to Modern Times.* Austin: University of Texas Press, 1961.

Tijerina, Andres. *Tejanos and Texas Under the Mexican Flag, 1821–1836.* College Station: Texas A&M University Press, 1994.

WEB EXPLORATION

For more on the Institute of Texan Cultures, go to
   www.texancultures.utsa.edu/main/

For more information about Texas's population, go to the Texas State Date Center, http://txsdc.tamu.edu/

For more about Texas history and Texans go to The Handbook of Texas Online,
   http://www.tsha.utexas.edu/handbook/online/

For current information on the Texas economy, go to Business and Industry Data Center,
   www.bidc.state.tx.us/

For more on wealth and poverty in Texas go to the Center for the Public Policy Priorities, http://www.cppp.org

The Texas Constitution

THE CURRENT TEXAS CONSTITUTION is often criticized, and attempts to revise the document have been frequent. The constitution has provided the framework for Texas government since 1876, and to make the document applicable to solving contemporary problems, it has been amended 432 times since its adoption. With each amendment, the Texas Constitution has become longer, more detailed, and more confusing.

Between 1971 and 1976, the Texas legislature struggled to produce a new constitution that would meet the needs of Texans and provide an acceptable substitute for the current constitution. Their attempts failed miserably. For members of the legislature, who had served as the Constitutional Convention of 1974, there were few political benefits in advocating constitutional reform, especially when the political costs of their inability to produce a new constitution for the voters were calculated. Consequently, constitutional revision, except for the constant parade of constitutional amendments, was abandoned for nearly a quarter of a century.

In 1999, Representative Rob Junell and Senator Bill Ratliff proposed a new constitution reducing it from 376 sections and approximately 90,000 words to 150 sections and 19,000 words. Despite a public opinion poll that showed 49 percent of the population thought constitutional revision was a "very important" or "somewhat important" issue, the proposed new constitution never left committee. Senator Ratliff told the *Austin American-Statesman,* "[Voters know] . . . that any document that you have to amend 20 times every other year is broke. It's sort of a Texas tragedy, actually, that

CHAPTER OUTLINE

- **The Roots of the Texas Constitution**

- **The Current Texas Constitution**

- **Constitutional Revision**

we can't seem to come to grips with the fact that we need a new, basic document going into the next century and the next millennium."[1] Proponents of a new Texas Constitution will have to wait a little longer for that realization.

TEXAS HAS DRAFTED several constitutions since it declared its independence from Mexico in 1836. Each constitution has been written to deal with changing political conditions in Texas. First, Texas was an independent republic. Then Texas joined the United States as the twenty-eighth state, which required a new constitution. Next, Texas seceded from the United States in 1861 to join the Confederacy during the American Civil War. To reenter the union required two constitutions. Finally, after Reconstruction, Texas adopted its current constitution in 1876. Since then, attempts to modernize the Texas Constitution have represented a political struggle between continuity and change.

To understand the Texas Constitution and its evolution is the focus of this chapter.

- First, we will discuss *the roots of the Texas Constitution*, examining the legacies of Texas's first five constitutions.
- Second, we will discuss *the current Texas Constitution*, examining the convention that framed it, its provisions, and the criticisms that continue to dog the document.
- Finally, we will assess *constitutional revision* in Texas, considering both piecemeal change through constitutional amendments and comprehensive revision efforts.

THE ROOTS OF THE TEXAS CONSTITUTION

LIKE MOST OTHER STATES, Texas has had several written constitutions. Constitutions serve several purposes. A constitution specifies the civil liberties of individuals by placing limits on government's ability to restrict an individual's basic rights (see chapter 5). Constitutions also establish the structures of government and provide their powers. Finally, constitutions provide a method of constitutional change. We consider each Texas constitution in turn.

The 1836 Texas Constitution

Prior to its independence, Texas was governed as a part of Mexico under the Mexican Constitution of 1824, which established a federal republic and provided that each state should write its own constitution. Combined as a single state, Texas and Coahuila established a constitution in 1827. Because of escalating tensions between Mexicans and Texians (see chapter 15), Texas declared its independence in 1836, established the Republic of Texas, and adopted the constitution of 1836. The fifty-nine delegates who assembled at Washington-on-the-Brazos to draft the document borrowed heavily from the U.S. Constitution and contemporary state constitutions and were guided by their political experiences. They quickly produced a document because of the imminent threat of attack by Mexican cavalry troops.[2]

The 1836 Texas Constitution included typical American features: a preamble; the incorporation of a separation of powers combined with checks and balances; recognition of slavery; a definition of citizenship that precluded Africans, the descendents of Africans, and Indians; a bill of rights; adult male suffrage; and an amending process.

It also created a bicameral Congress, consisting of a Senate and House of Representatives, whose members were popularly elected and exercised powers similar to those of the U.S. Congress. The executive branch included a president and vice president, whose powers resembled the powers of the U.S. president and vice president. The judiciary consisted of courts at four levels: justice, county, district, and supreme courts.

Spanish Mexican law also found its way into the constitution. Community property rights were established; homesteads were protected and exempted from taxation; and Texas courts were not separated into distinct courts of law and equity. However, the delegates' preference for English common law prevailed when deciding all criminal cases.[3]

The 1845 Texas Constitution

When Texas ceased to be an independent republic and joined the United States, a new constitution was necessary. In June 1845, President Anson Jones called a convention to assemble in July, which approved the U.S. offer of annexation and drew up a constitution, which the voters ratified in October 1845. The U.S. Congress accepted the 1845 Texas Constitution on December 29, 1845, and Texas became the twenty-eighth state to join the United States in February 1846.

Often cited as among the best of all state constitutions of its time, the 1845 Texas Constitution was noted for its straightforward, simple form. It created a bicameral legislature consisting of a Senate and House of Representatives that met biennially (once every two years). The governor served a two-year term and was limited to serving no more than four years in any six-year period. The attorney general and secretary of state were appointed by the governor and confirmed by the Senate; the comptroller and treasurer were elected by the legislature biennially in a joint session of the legislature. Adopted in 1850, an amendment provided for the election of state officials who were originally appointed by the governor or the legislature. The governor could convene the legislature, was commander in chief of the state militia, granted pardons and reprieves, and could veto legislation, which could be overridden by a two-thirds vote of both chambers. The judiciary included a supreme court, district courts, and additional courts created by the legislature. The supreme court consisted of three judges, appointed by the governor for six-year terms. The constitution created district courts, whose judges were also appointed by the governor and which had a district attorney appointed by a joint session of the legislature for two-year terms.

The 1861 Texas Constitution

When Texas seceded from the United States in February 1861 at the beginning of the Civil War, the convention that had proposed secession reconvened to direct the transition of Texas into the Confederacy and replace the 1845 constitution. A provision in the 1845 constitution that provided for the emancipation of slaves was deleted, and the emancipation of slaves was prohibited. However, many changes that some secessionist leaders had advocated were not incorporated, such as legalizing the resumption of the African slave trade, taking an extreme position on states' rights, and making major changes in existing laws.[4]

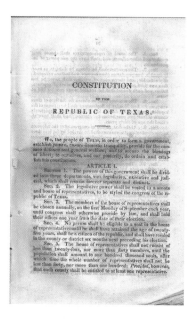
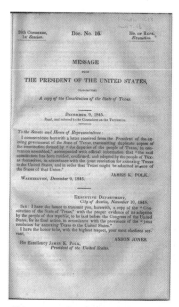
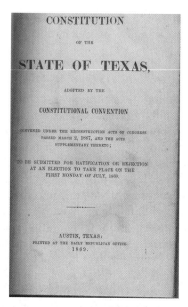

Photos courtesy: Rare Books and Special Collections, Tarlton Law Library, University of Texas at Austin

■ The collage depicts the original constitution of the Republic of Texas (1836), the transmittal letter that accompanied the 1845 Texas Constitution, and the cover page from the 1869 Texas Constitution.

The 1866 Texas Constitution

When Texas reentered the union after the Civil War, presidential Reconstruction required certain changes in the state's charter, such as the acceptance of the abolition of slavery. In addition to those changes, the constitutional convention of 1866 proposed a series of amendments, which were narrowly adopted in June 1866. In the executive branch, the governor's term was increased to four years, but the governor was prohibited from serving more than eight years in any twelve-year period. The governor was given a line-item veto over appropriations and had his salary increased from $3,000 to $4,000 annually. The attorney general, comptroller, and treasurer were also elected to four-year terms. The legislators' salaries were also increased significantly, although the structure and powers of the legislature changed only slightly. Only white men could serve as legislators. The state supreme court was increased to five judges, and they were elected for ten-year terms. Also elected were district judges, but their terms were shorter. The jurisdiction of each court was specified in detail.

An additional method of constitutional revision was adopted, which allowed the legislature by a three-fourths vote of each chamber and approval by the governor to call a convention to propose changes. Provisions of the constitution also called for internal improvements in the state and a system of public education, segregated by race and directed by a superintendent of public instruction. State land was set aside to support public education, to create and support a university, and for charitable institutions.[5]

Photo courtesy: Texas State Library and Archives Commission

■ Brigadier General Edmund J. Davis was elected governor of Texas in 1870. His administration was controversial because of the governor's programs, such as universal public education, and the taxes that were levied to support the programs.

The 1869 Texas Constitution

When the U.S. Congress ended presidential Reconstruction in 1867, additional requirements were placed on Texas's readmission to the union. Texas was required to have another constitutional convention. In what was called congressional Reconstruction, Congress required that the convention write a new state constitution that would provide for universal adult male suffrage. When the constitution had been written and the state had ratified the Fourteenth Amendment to the U.S. Constitution, Congress would consider the case for readmission to the union. The vote on holding the convention and electing delegates produced a lopsided victory for a convention, primarily due to an overwhelmingly favorable African American vote.

When the ninety delegates met in June 1868, they represented four different voting blocs, differentiated by geography, party, and issues. None of the four blocs was dominant, though each bloc pushed its own agenda. The delegates failed to consider the convention's principal task until the last month of the convention. In February 1869, the convention broke up in confusion. Forty-five of the ninety delegates signed a partially assembled constitution. Military officers gathered the materials together after the convention and, in July 1869, voters approved the convention's proposals as the 1869 constitution.[6]

The constitution met the requirements of congressional Reconstruction. In addition, it extended the term of senators to six years, increased the governor's salary, and allowed the governor to appoint the attorney general and secretary of state. The number of state supreme court justices and the length of their terms were reduced. All judicial offices were appointive. Overall, the constitution created a strong and expensive state government with annual legislative sessions, a system of centralized public education, higher salaries for public officials, and a lack of controls on state and local taxing powers.[7]

THE CURRENT TEXAS CONSTITUTION

THE ADOPTION OF A NEW CONSTITUTION for Texas was shaped by the effects of Reconstruction.[8] Governor Richard Coke and the legislature's Democratic leadership believed that only a document drafted by a legislative committee would ensure a short, liberal constitution and allow a more activist government. A majority of House members, however, considered anything but a convention "anti-democratic." A joint legislative committee produced a constitution that shared many similarities with its predecessors. However, the joint committee's proposed constitution failed when the Texas House rejected it. A special legislative session then called a constitutional convention in 1875.[9]

Of the ninety elected delegates to the convention, seventy-five were Democrats and fifteen were Republicans. However, one of the Republicans served a short time and was replaced by a Democrat. Thus, the convention actually included seventy-six Democrats and fourteen Republicans. Six African Americans, all Republicans, were originally elected as delegates, but one resigned after the first day and was replaced by an Anglo. Of the ninety delegates, thirty-eight identified themselves as members of the Patrons of Husbandry, or Grange, an organization of farmers created in response to the economic panic of 1873. Seventy-two delegates were immigrants from other southern states. Seven delegates were European immigrants. Only four were native Texans.

Averaging only forty-five years of age, the delegates had a wealth of political experience. Eleven delegates had been members of a previous Texas constitutional convention—most commonly the 1861 convention. At least thirty members had served at least one term in the Texas legislature. In addition, several delegates had served in other states' legislatures, the United States Congress, and the Congress of the Confederate States. Five delegates had been judges, and four had executive and administrative experience. Evaluating the delegates to the 1875 constitutional convention, political scientist Joe E. Ericson concluded, "The convention of 1875 was composed, therefore, of a much abler group of men on the basis of their previous experience and training than is generally conceded. Their background and training compares favorably with that of the delegates to any previous constitutional convention held in Texas. If their product is inferior, then the cause must lie elsewhere."[10]

Reasons for the 1876 Constitution

What accounts for the 1876 constitution, a constitution that is quite different from previous Texas constitutions and the U.S. Constitution? Three factors explain the adoption of an organic, restrictive Texas Constitution.

First, the 1876 constitution was, to some extent, a reaction to Reconstruction. Certainly the adoption of the 1869 constitution angered many Texans. To many, the 1869 constitution was an illegitimate constitution that Texas had been forced by the Reconstruction government to accept.

Second, the 1869 constitution had led to Governor E. J. Davis's regime. During that administration, power had been centralized in the state government. In all, Davis appointed more than 8,000 state and local officials. The legislature granted the governor extraordinary powers to maintain public order. For example, the governor controlled a state police that could operate anywhere in the state and could declare martial law in any Texas county, suspend the laws, and assess punishments for violators.

The legislature also adopted expensive programs that increased taxes dramatically. Universal, compulsory education for all children under the direction of a state superintendent of education was a progressive but expensive policy. In addition, the legislature provided bond subsidies to railroads. After only two years, state and county property tax rates in Texas had increased from fifteen cents on $100 property valuation to $2.18 on $100 property valuation. In addition, there were other taxes. Wanting to avoid similar governments in the future, the convention delegates of 1875 attempted to hobble government.

The third factor affecting the 1876 constitution was a movement that swept through the United States in the 1870s, calling for a politics of substantive issues and restrictive constitutionalism.[11] Using the ideological labels explained in chapter 15, the movement had both populist and libertarian elements.

In the 1875 Constitutional Convention, this movement took the form of "retrenchment and reform," the motto adopted by the members

Photo courtesy: Texas State Library and Archives Commission

■ Members of the Constitutional Convention of 1875, which drafted the current Texas Constitution, are evaluated more highly today than they were when the convention met.

GOVERNOR E. J. DAVIS AND THE ESTABLISHMENT OF AN ACTIVIST GOVERNMENT

REPUBLICAN GOVERNOR Edmund J. Davis was arguably the most controversial governor in the history of Texas because of his activist government under the 1869 constitution. Born in Florida in 1827, Davis moved with his parents to Galveston, Texas, in 1848. He worked there as a clerk in the post office and studied law, then moved to Corpus Christi where he worked in a store and continued his law studies. After his admission to the bar in 1849, Davis became an inspector and deputy collector of customs in Brownsville. In 1853, he became district attorney in Brownsville, and three years later, Governor Elisha M. Pease appointed him a district judge in Brownsville.

A member of the Democratic Party, Davis supported Sam Houston and opposed Texas's secession from the Union in 1861. Refusing to take an oath to the Confederacy, Davis lost his judgeship and fled the state in 1862. Later that year, Davis received a colonel's commission and recruited members for the First Texas Cavalry (U.S.). Davis and his unit were involved in several campaigns in Texas during 1863. In late 1864, Davis was promoted to brigadier general and spent the remainder of the war in Mississippi, although he returned to Texas for the surrender of Confederate forces in Texas in 1865.

After the Civil War, Davis participated in Texas politics as a Republican. He was a member of the 1866 Constitutional Convention, ran unsuccessfully for the Texas Senate, and was president of the Constitutional Convention in 1869. In 1869, Davis narrowly defeated another Republican for governor. Taking office in 1870, Governor Davis, supported by a Radical Republican legislature, established an activist government that promoted controversial policies such as the creation of a state police to establish law and order, an education policy that required mandatory, integrated education for children and an expansion of taxes to fund those programs.

The state police created by Davis in 1870, justified by increasing lawlessness in Texas and inadequate law enforcement, was composed of African Americans, Hispanics, and Anglos, most of whom were Republicans. Despite their general effectiveness, the force was unpopular because it included African Americans and was under Governor Davis's control. When the Democrats gained control of the Texas legislature in 1873, the Police Act was repealed and the force disbanded.[a]

In 1873, Davis sought reelection against Democrat Richard Coke, who defeated Davis by a two-to-one margin. Republicans claimed that the election was unconstitutional because the election was held on one day rather than over a four-day period as required by the 1869 constitution. Although Davis was prepared to accept the election results, the Texas Supreme Court ruled the election invalid, leaving Davis in an awkward situation. After consulting with other Republicans, Davis appealed to President Ulysses S. Grant to send troops to allow Davis to remain in office until the legal issue was resolved. As he wrote President Grant, Davis did not object to the election but did not see how he could disregard the Texas Supreme Court's decision. When President Grant refused to send assistance, Davis resigned on January 19, 1874.

From 1875 until his death in 1883, Davis led the Republican Party in Texas as chair of the state executive committee. He unsuccessfully sought the governorship in 1880 and a seat in the U.S. House of Representatives in 1882. Davis is buried in the State Cemetery in Austin.[b]

[a] John G. Johnson, "State Police," *The Handbook of Texas Online,* accessed November 26, 2000, http://www.tsha.utexas.edu/handbook/online/articles/view/SS/jls2.html.

[b] Carl H. Moneyhon, *Republicanism in Reconstruction Texas* (Austin: University of Texas Press, 1980), 183–96; Carl H. Moneyhon, "Edmund Jackson Davis," *The Handbook of Texas Online,* accessed November 26, 2000, http://www.tsha.utexas.edu/handbook/online/articles/view/DD/fda37.html.

of the Grange and their allies, who were anti-Coke Democratic delegates. For these delegates, the 1869 constitution had violated important Texas ideals, including a belief that government should be limited in its purpose. Historian Patrick Williams disputes this emphasis: "There were distinct patterns to their [the delegates] votes, especially when it came to government promotion of economic growth and social welfare."[12] The division among Democrats at the convention was more complex than support or opposition to government activism; it also involved the *way* that government should be active, and it resulted in four distinct groupings. One group supported rapid commercial and agricultural growth and believed that the government's principal role was to nurture private enterprise, but that otherwise government's role should be limited. A second group also supported economic growth and assistance to private enterprise, but they further believed that government should invest in Texas's human resources, such as schools. A third group wanted government's role to be almost exclusively the promotion of those activities that private enterprise would not or could not accomplish, such as education and frontier defense. A fourth group favored less government generally, whether the purpose of government was economic assistance to private enterprise or to the state's social welfare.[13]

The provisions of the 1876 constitution, therefore, are not only a reaction to Reconstruction and the Davis regime but also the product of a national movement and a complex mix of motives among the convention delegates.

Provisions of the 1876 Constitution

The current Texas Constitution has seventeen numbered articles (see Table 16.1). Article 13, Spanish and Mexican Land Titles, was deleted by amendment in 1969.[14] Consequently, the constitution currently has sixteen operable articles. Many of the provisions of the constitution are nearly identical to the way they were written when ratified in 1876, but others have been amended extensively. Like the U.S. Constitution, the Texas Constitution incorporates many principles of American constitutional theory. However, because the U.S. Constitution is a **liberal constitution**—establishing the basic structure and principles of government—and the Texas Constitution is a **statutory constitution**—creating the structure and powers of government in great detail—the two are quite different.

Article 1 of the Texas Constitution contains the Texas Bill of Rights. Many of its provisions are similar to the U.S. Constitution's Bill of Rights, but the Texas Bill of Rights is longer and in some respects more extensive. Because of the framers' experience during the Davis administration, the Texas Bill of Rights contains provisions that state that the "writ of *habeas corpus* is a writ of right, and shall never be suspended" and that the Bill of Rights "is excepted from the general powers of government, and shall forever remain inviolate."[15] Amendments incorporating equal rights for women and ensuring rights for victims of violent crimes were added later.

liberal constitution
Constitution that incorporates the basic structure of government and allows the legislature to provide the details through statutes.

statutory constitution
Constitution that incorporates detailed provisions in order to limit the powers of government.

The Living Constitution

Article 7, section 1: A general diffusion of knowledge being essential to the preservation of the liberties and rights of the people, it shall be the duty of the legislature of the state to establish and make suitable provision for the support and maintenance of an efficient system of free public schools.

In the Constitutional Convention of 1875, no issue was more vigorously debated as the delegates represented differing views on public education. In the end, Article 7, section 1, reflects the majority's opinion that "an elaborate and expensive system [of public education] like the one devised by the hated Republicans" should be prevented.[a] The initial result was a return to education as it had existed in Texas in the 1850s.

In cases from the early 1900s, Texas courts have interpreted the terms "suitable," "free," and "public" in such a way as to allow the legislature great latitude in providing a public education to Texas residents.

Texas courts began to interpret Article 7, section 1, differently in the late 1980s and early 1990s. In 1987, a state district court judge, Harley Clark, ruled that the Texas system of funding public education violated Article 1, section 3, and Article 7, section 1, of the Texas Constitution. Article 1, section 3, declares that all people in Texas have equal rights. Additionally, Judge Clark ruled that "under our state constitution[,] education is a fundamental right for each of our citizens."[b] When the state appealed, the 3rd Texas Court of Appeals reversed Judge Clark. Viewing the issue as a political question, the court eschewed its ability to interpret Article 7, section 1.

TABLE 16.1 Articles of the Texas Constitution

Preamble

Article	1	Bill of Rights	Article	11	Municipal Corporations
Article	2	The Powers of Government	Article	12	Private Corporations
Article	3	Legislative Department	Article	13	Spanish and Mexican Land (repealed August 5, 1969)
Article	4	Executive Department			
Article	5	Judicial Department			
Article	6	Suffrage	Article	14	Public Lands and Land Office
Article	7	Education	Article	15	Impeachment
Article	8	Taxation and Revenue	Article	16	General Provisions
Article	9	Counties	Article	17	Mode of Amending the Constitution of This State
Article	10	Railroads			

Edgewood Independent School District appealed that decision to the Texas Supreme Court. In 1989, the court unanimously reversed the 3rd Court of Appeals, ruling, in *Edgewood* v. *Kirby,* that Article 7, section 1, "imposes . . . an affirmative duty to establish and provide for the public free schools."[c] Furthermore, the Texas system of funding public education violated Article 7 because the system "is neither financially efficient nor efficient in the sense of providing for a 'general diffusion of knowledge' statewide"[d] and relies too heavily on local property taxes. Because the value of property varies widely from school district to school district, the state did not make the most efficient use of the state's resources in funding public education.

Over the next four years, the legislature struggled to develop a system that created a more equal distribution of money among the state's more than 1,000 school districts. Finally, in 1993, the legislature developed a plan that met the court's requirement.[e]

But the quest for an efficient system of financing public education in Texas continues. New court challenges claim that the cap on local property taxes constitutes a statewide property tax, which Article 8, section 1e, of the Texas Constitution prohibits.

Question

If a statewide property tax violates the Texas Constitution, what alternatives for funding public education should Texas consider?

---

[a]George D. Braden, *The Constitution of the State of Texas: An Annotated and Comparative Analysis,* Vol. 2 (Austin: 1977), 506.

[b]Harley Clark, District Judge, 250th District Court, *Edgewood Independent School District, et al.* v. *William Kirby, et al.,* written opinion, April 29, 1987, 2, Travis County Courthouse, Austin, Texas.

[c]*Edgewood* v. *Kirby,* 777 S.W.2d 394. 397 (Tex. 1989).

[d]*Edgewood* v. *Kirby,* 777 S.W.2d 397 (Tex. 1989).

[e]*Edgewood* v. *Meno,* 893 S.W.2d 450 (Tex. 1995).

Article 2 of the Texas Constitution establishes a separation of powers among the legislative, executive, and judicial branches in Texas government and prohibits an individual from holding positions in more than one branch simultaneously.

Article 3 establishes the legislative branch, specifying its structure and powers. Article 3's provisions also include legislative procedures, such as a requirement that a bill's title clearly indicate its content. Other provisions place limits and requirements on the legislature, such as specifying, in great detail, the purposes for which the legislature can levy taxes. Another provision of Article 3 specifies that the legislature is prohibited from passing special or local legislation for certain purposes, such as creating offices and assigning duties for counties, cities, and other local governments.

Analyzing Visuals

VOTER TURNOUT FOR CONSTITUTIONAL AMENDMENTS

The Texas legislature schedules the popular vote to ratify proposed constitutional amendments during either a general election or a special election. Starting in the 1980s, almost all of the votes to ratify constitutional amendments occurred in special elections. After reviewing the data in the table, answer the following critical thinking questions: What do you notice about the difference in voter turnout between general elections and special elections? Which type of election resulted in the greatest percentage of amendments being adopted during the 1980s, 1990s, and 2000s? If you were a member of the Texas legislature, during which type of election would you schedule the popular vote for most constitutional amendments (assuming that you favor the adoption of the amendments)?

Source: Secretary of State, Election Results, Turnout and Voter Registration Figures (1970–present), accessed June 17, 2004, http://www.sos.state.tx.us/elections/historical/70-92.shtml. Texas Legislative Library, Constitutional Amendments, updated February, 2004, accessed June 17, 2004 http://www.lrl.state.tx.us/legis/constAmends/lrlhome.cfm.

Decade	Type of Election	Voter Turnout[a]	Considered Amendments	Adopted Amendments	% Adopted
1970s	General—Presidential	45.52	15	12	80.0
	General—Gubernatorial	25.47	16	12	75.0
	Special	5.42	26	16	61.5
1980s	General—Presidential	45.81	20	16	80.0
	General—Gubernatorial	29.44	10	10	100.0
	Special	10.23	77	65	84.4
1990s	General—Presidential	45.31	0	0	0.0
	General—Gubernatorial	30.41	1	1	100.0
	Special	9.47	91	63	69.2
2000s	General—Presidential	44.30	0	0	0.0
	General—Gubernatorial	19.80	1	1	100.0
	Special	7.45	41	41	100.0

[a]Voter turnout indicates the percentage of voting-age people who voted. For the 1970s, special election turnout figures are only for the 1977 and 1979 special elections (no figures were available for 1971, 1973, or 1975).

Article 4 establishes the executive branch. The governor's term was reduced to two years (it was reinstated to four years only in 1974), and the governor's salary was reduced. To ensure the independence of other executive officers from the governor's control, the major executive officers—lieutenant governor, attorney general, comptroller, treasurer, and land commissioner—were elected independently. The addition of numerous elected and appointed boards and commissions in Texas by constitutional amendment and legislation has further diminished the governor's control over the executive branch. A seeming anomaly to the reduction of the governor's powers was the retention of the governor's line-item veto. However, the framers probably viewed the line-item veto as another check on the legislature's spending powers.[16]

Analyzing Visuals

AMENDMENTS TO THE TEXAS CONSTITUTION

Amendments to the 1876 Texas Constitution grew slowly during the first five decades of the constitution's existence. The 1980s was the decade in which the greatest number of amendments was adopted. After reviewing the chart, answer the following critical thinking questions: What events are associated with peri-ods of increased constitutional amendments (1930s, 1960s, and 1980s)? What does the number of amendments adopted between 2001 and 2003 suggest about the current decade's future? What does the increasing number of amendments suggest about the viability of the Texas Constitution?

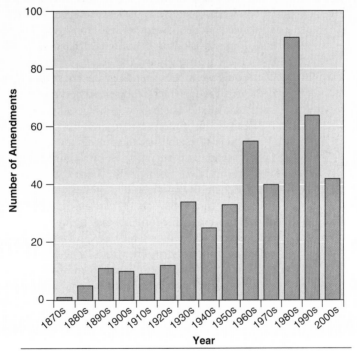

Note: The 2000s cover only three years, 2001 to 2003.

Source: Texas Legislative Reference Library, *Amendments to the Texas Constitution.* N.d. Accessed August 11, 2002, http://www.lrl.state.tx.us/legis/amendments/mainpage.html.

In Article 5, the constitution created a judicial system that included a supreme court (the highest state court for civil matters), a court of appeals (the highest state court for criminal matters), district courts, county courts, commissioners courts, and justice of the peace courts. The judicial branch was also subject to popular control. The article also specifies in detail the qualifications of judges, the jurisdiction of the courts, and even the operation of the courts.

Article 7, the education article, created a public school system that differed dramatically from the system that the Davis administration had created. The superintendent of public instruction's position and compulsory school attendance were eliminated, schools were segregated by race, and the constitution made no provision for local school taxes. The constitution funded public education through a poll tax, general funds, and interest earned on the principal in the Permanent School Fund.

Constitutional provisions relating to local governments are found in several articles. In fact, Article 9, which is entitled "Counties," provides no information about the structure of county government and its officials. That information is contained in Article 5, the Judicial Article. In all, four articles must be consulted to find all of the constitutional provisions relating to counties.

In several articles, the 1876 constitution limits the legislature's discretion in enacting fiscal policies—taxing and spending. First, it mandates a balanced budget. Except for war or insurrection, debt is prohibited. Seventy-four provisions in the original 1876 constitution related to taxation, spending state money, and the use of private property.[17] As an additional check on government spending, the constitution contains provisions for dedicated funds, which require that certain tax moneys be deposited in particular funds. The balanced-budget and dedicated-fund provisions of the Texas Constitution serve to limit the discretion of the legislature.

Article 17 establishes the process for amending the Texas Constitution. Amendments are proposed by a joint resolution, which must receive a two-thirds majority vote of the Texas House of Representatives and the Texas Senate. Ratification of a proposed amendment requires a simple majority of those who actually cast ballots in an election. The ratification of constitutional amendments may occur in a general election, which is conducted in even-numbered years in November, or in special elections, which are conducted at other times. The legislature determines when the election to ratify a constitutional amendment will be held.

Having a statutory constitution that requires constitutional amendment to make major and even minor changes in government also means that the constitution has been amended many times. The United States Constitution has survived since 1789 with only twenty-seven amendments. Because the first ten amendments, the Bill of Rights, were necessary to achieve ratification and because the Twenty-first Amendment repeals the Eighteenth Amendment, there have been only fifteen actual changes to the U.S. Constitution in more than 200 years. In contrast, the Texas Constitution has been amended 432 times in only 128 years (see Analyzing Visuals: Amendments to the Texas Constitution).

Criticisms of the 1876 Constitution

With so many amendments, one might think that Texans would have been able to make a nineteenth-century constitution applicable to the twenty-first century. In many respects, however, the constitutional amendments have

TEXAS IN COMPARISON
State Constitutions

State constitutions are frequently revised. All four of the largest states have adopted several constitutions. Florida has adopted the most constitutions since statehood, but Texas has the longest constitution. The California Constitution has been amended most frequently.

State	Number of Constitutions Since Statehood	Number of Words in Constitution (2004)	Number of Amendments (2004)
Texas	5	80,000	submitted 605, ratified 432
California	2	54,645	submitted 848, ratified 507
New York	4	51,700	submitted 290, ratified 216
Florida	6	51,456	submitted 127, ratified 96

not fundamentally changed the basic structure of Texas government. For many Texans, the 1876 constitution does not provide an adequate foundation for governing in the twenty-first century. With the addition of so many amendments, Texas has earned the distinction of having one of the longest constitutions in the United States (almost 90,000 words). Only Alabama's constitution contains more words. The amendments have also exacerbated the disorganization that originally plagued the 1876 constitution. The length and disorganization of the Texas Constitution, however, is far less serious than other concerns.

Some of the most serious concerns relate to the three branches of Texas government. The plural executive has been criticized because it limits the executive power of the governor to implement public policy. By dividing the executive authority among several officials, who are elected statewide, the constitution makes these officials the co-equals of the governor. Though the constitution declares that the governor is the state's chief executive, it also denies him or her the powers necessary to perform that role. The governor's executive authority is further diminished by the numerous agencies, boards, and commissions that make up a substantial portion of the executive branch of Texas government. Political scientist and Texas Constitution expert Janice May has stated: "Texas has probably the most disintegrated and fragmented administrative organization in the country."[18] Despite efforts in the 1990s to transfer more control to the governor, the executive branch remains badly fragmented.

In the legislative branch, the most important criticisms relate to the constitutional provisions that make the legislature a part-time, citizen legislature. Among these provisions are the requirement for 140-day biennial sessions and the low, constitutionally mandated salary for legislators. Meeting every two years for such a short time makes governing a large urban state difficult. Particularly burdensome is the need to prepare a budget for a two-year period, anticipating economic conditions so that revenues will cover appropriations and the next legislature will not face a large deficit. A legislator's salary of $7,200 per year, which has not changed since 1975, plus a per diem for expenses, affects who can financially afford to serve and who can afford the time away from their primary occupation to attend regular and special sessions. Restrictions on the legislature, such as dedicated funds and specific prohibited activities, have been criticized because they limit the legislature's ability to react to social and economic changes in a modern, urban state. Perhaps the restrictions were more reasonable when Texas was a rural, agricultural state.

The structure of the Texas judiciary and the method of selecting judges are also frequently criticized. The court system in Texas consists of a bewildering number of courts, divided into several levels, many with overlapping jurisdictions. The Texas Constitution creates most of these courts. Capping the court system are two supreme courts: the Texas Supreme Court, which is the highest state court for civil cases, and the Texas Court of Criminal Appeals, which is the highest state court for criminal cases. Each court has nine members, elected on a partisan ballot, as are almost all members of Texas courts. Many political scientists, attorneys, and even Texas judges have questioned whether partisan election is the best way to select judges (see chapter 20).

The 1876 constitution places severe restrictions on local governments. First, the structure of county government is established in the constitution, which means that the smallest and the largest counties in Texas have a commissioners court, a county judge, and a number of independently elected officials to run the various county departments. Although the structure may be effective in rural Texas counties, urban counties, where more than 80 percent of Texans currently reside, find the structure inefficient and unable to adapt to the changes that have occurred in their counties. Also, counties are limited in their ability to raise revenue and provide needed services. The restrictions placed on county and city government in Texas have resulted in the creation of thousands of special districts across Texas (see chapter 17).

With all the criticisms of the 1876 constitution, legislators and citizens have often called for revisions to the document, which is the topic of the next section.

CONSTITUTIONAL REVISION

CONSTITUTIONAL REVISION in Texas can occur through two methods. First, the constitution can be updated through amendments intended to remove obsolete portions, clarify ambiguous sections, or consolidate sections that pertain to a single topic. This is usually referred to as **piecemeal revision.** The other method involves a new constitution for Texas, such as the revision suggested by the students at Angelo State University (see On Campus: Angelo State University's Texas Constitution) or Representative Junell and Senator Ratliff's proposal during the 76th Legislature in 1999. This is usually called **comprehensive revision.**

piecemeal revision
Constitutional revision through constitutional amendments that add or delete items.

comprehensive revision
Constitutional revision through the adoption of a new constitution.

On Campus

ANGELO STATE UNIVERSITY STUDENTS' TEXAS CONSTITUTION

When Professor Edward C. Olson, Government Department head at Angelo State University, received a telephone call from Representative Rob Junell inviting him to lunch, he could not have anticipated the reason for the invitation. Olson had known Junell for several years and had managed Junell's first campaign for the Texas House of Representatives. Over lunch, Junell asked Olson if it would be possible to create a course on revising the current Texas Constitution. After discussing the proposal with his dean, Olson informed Junell that the course would be offered.

Under the direction of several Angelo State University professors, students in a combined undergraduate and graduate government class rewrote the Texas Constitution as a class project. Conducted during the spring semester of 1998, and meeting once a week for sixteen weeks, the students were divided into groups to study the Texas and other state constitutions and to present their proposals for a portion of a new constitution for Texas. The members of each group were carefully selected to ensure that there would be different opinions represented in the group, promoting lively discussions and vigorous debates during the weekly class meetings when the students presented their proposals. After each group's presentation had been discussed, the class voted on the constitution's provisions; the vote of at least nine of the fourteen regular participants in the class was required for the adoption of a provision. During the last few weeks of the semester, the class held longer sessions to draft the final document. Representative Junell attended all of the class sessions, offering his expertise and recruiting additional experts to speak to the class, including 3rd Court of Appeals Chief Justice Marilyn Aboussie, attorney Tom Luce, Texas Tech University Chancellor John Montford, and Senator Bill Ratliff.

Photo courtesy: Tina Miller/Angelo State University Photo

Edward Olson's Government 6391 class at Angelo State University drafted a new constitution for Texas that was introduced by Representative Rob Junell (D–San Angelo) in 1999.

The Angelo State University proposal would have preserved many essential features of the current constitution, such as the Bill of Rights, but it would have also made several substantial changes. According to Professor Olson, the most significant changes proposed by the students included:

- **Eliminating the "deadwood" in the current constitution.**
- **Eliminating most partisan elections of judges.**
- **Streamlining the plural executive.**
- **Consolidating and simplifying the local government provisions.**

The Angelo State University students' proposal provided the basis for House Joint Resolution (HJR) 1, which Representative Junell introduced during the 76th Legislature in 1999.

Piecemeal Revision Efforts

The first amendment to the Texas Constitution was proposed in 1877. Since then, amendments have been considered by every legislature, but the addition of amendments accelerated in the 1930s and again in the 1980s (see Analyzing Visuals: Amendments to the Texas Constitution).

Ironically, many piecemeal changes in the Texas Constitution have resulted from attempts to produce comprehensive reform. For example, in 1957, the League of Women Voters was successful in getting the legislature to direct the Legislative Council to study each section of the constitution and make recommendations. The legislature also created a Citizens Advisory Committee. In its report, the Legislative Council found that the 1876 constitution, "despite its age and alleged deficiencies, is still overall a sound document and generally reflects the governmental philosophy of the people of Texas for their government."[19] The Citizens Advisory Committee disagreed, seeking a constitutional commission to study the need for constitutional revision.

Similarly, between 1966 and 1969, Governor John Connally led an effort to revise the Texas Constitution. Although Connally's efforts to call a constitutional convention failed, the legislature did create a Texas Constitutional Revision Commission to study the constitution and make recommendations to the legislature in 1969. The commission's proposed constitution was disregarded by the legislature, but the commission provided momentum for the earlier Citizens Advisory Committee's proposal to eliminate the "deadwood" provisions of the Texas Constitution through a single amendment. The amendment, which removed fifty-two provisions including Article 13 on Spanish Land Titles and reduced the constitution's length by 10 percent, was passed by the legislature and adopted by the voters in August 1969.[20]

More recently, Representative Anna Mowery led an attempt to revise the Texas Constitution. As a modest beginning, Mowery introduced a constitutional amendment in 1997 that changed the wording in several articles of the constitution. In the next legislative session, Mowery's proposal amended sixty-four provisions of the constitution and repealed seventeen provisions. Seventeen sections of the amendment merely modernized the language. Several sections eliminated provisions that allowed only property owners to vote in certain elections, a restriction that was not enforced and has been held unconstitutional in most elections. The legislative article was the focus for most of the proposed revisions. None of the proposed changes significantly altered the powers of government, the rights of individuals, or the structure of Texas state and local government.[21] In November 1999, voters approved Mowery's amendment. In 2001, another amendment by Mowery

You Are Attempting to Revise the Texas Constitution

■ Representative Anna Mowery, who introduced constitutional amendments to modernize the Texas Constitution, discusses legislation with Representative Kenny Marchant.

Photo courtesy: Bob Daemmrich/Bob Daemmrich Photography, Inc.

Politics Now

THE TEXAS SODOMY LAW

In 1972, Texas voters approved an equal rights amendment to the Texas Constitution. The amendment states that "Equality under the law shall not be denied or abridged because of sex, race, color, creed, or national origin." The amendment is usually considered an attempt to ensure that women enjoy the same rights as men, but two Houston men found that it also offered them protection against a conviction under a Texas sodomy law.

In 1860, Texas adopted a sodomy law that prohibited certain sex acts between consenting adults, regardless of the gender of the participants. Under that law, sodomy was a felony, punishable by imprisonment. In 1973, the Texas legislature downgraded sodomy to a class "C" misdemeanor, punishable only by a fine, and redefined the offense as anal or oral sex between members of the same gender.

In September 1998, John Geddes Lawrence and Tyron Garner were arrested in Houston for sodomy. Police entered their Houston apartment in response to a complaint of an "armed intruder" in the apartment but found only Lawrence and Garner engaging in sodomy. The men were arrested, charged with sodomy, and convicted. The men appealed the decision. The 14th Texas Court of Appeals ruled 2–1 that the Texas sodomy law, because it applied only to anal and oral sex between individuals of the same gender, violated the Texas Equal Rights Amendment. According to Justice John S. Anderson, the author of the majority opinion, "The simple fact is, the same behavior is criminal for some but not for others, based solely on the sex of the individuals who engage in the behavior. . . . We hold that section 21.06 of the Texas Penal Code violates the Texas Equal Rights Amendment's guarantee of equality under the law."

The state's justification for the law was the state's legitimate interest to enforce principles of morality and family values. The court of appeals majority wrote that "it does not follow that simply because the Texas Legislature has enacted as law what may be a moral choice of the majority, the courts are, thereafter, bound to acquiesce. Our Constitution does not protect morality; it does, however, guarantee equality to all persons under the law."

The state asked for a rehearing by all nine members of the court. In 2001, the 14th Texas Court of Appeals voted 7–2 to uphold the Texas sodomy law, reversing the earlier ruling. In 2002, the Texas Court of Criminal Appeals refused to grant a petition for discretionary review, and Lawrence and Garner appealed to the U.S. Supreme Court, claiming that their rights under the U.S. Constitution's Fourteenth Amendment had been violated.

In June 2003, the Supreme Court declared the Texas sodomy law a violation of the Fourteenth Amendment's "due process" clause and the privacy protections that the amendment provides and, in the process, overturned *Bowers* v. *Hardwick* (1986), which had upheld Georgia's ban on sodomy. The 6–3 decision sparked a vigorous dissent from Justice Antonin Scalia, who characterized the majority opinion as paving the way for same-sex marriages: "Today's opinion dismantles the structure of constitutional law that has permitted a distinction to be made between heterosexual and homosexual unions, insofar as formal recognition in marriage is concerned."

Sources: Arthur S. Leonard, "Texas Appeals Court Strikes Down Sodomy Law—Again," Lgny.comnews, accessed November 18, 2000, http://www.lgny.com/issue_135/pages_135/news_texassodomy_135.html. Lambda Legal, Cases, "Lawrence and *Garner* v. *Texas*," updated May 14, 2002, accessed August 11, 2002, http://www.lambdalegal.org/cgi-bin/iowa/cases/record?record-93. The quotations are from *John Geddes Lawrence and Tyron Garner* v. *State of Texas*, 14th Court of Appeals, June 8, 2000, 14-99-00109, 14-99-00111-CR, accessed November 19, 2000, http://www.14thcoa.courts.state.tx.us/Opinions/060800/opinions.html; *Lawrence* v. *Texas* (2003). Legal Information Institute, Supreme Court Collection, accessed June 17, 2004, http://supct.law.cornell.edu/supct/html/02-102.ZS.html.

that eliminated duplication and clarified provisions of the constitution won legislative approval and was ratified by voters.

Despite these recent changes, many Texans believe that only a thorough rewriting of the Texas Constitution will make it applicable to modern Texas. Professor Dick Smith's observations, made nearly forty years ago, seem especially prophetic today: "Even if, in due time, many nonsubstantive changes are made, through the overworked amending process, it will still be an inadequate, outdated fundamental law for the state."[22]

Comprehensive Revision Efforts

The legislature's first attempt to call a constitutional convention for a comprehensive revision occurred in 1877. It was the first in a long series of such attempts. Between 1919 and 1949, the legislature regularly considered proposals for a constitutional convention. None of the resolutions calling for a constitutional convention or creating a revision commission was approved by the legislature. In 1949, Governor Beauford Jester's Citizens Committee on the Constitution requested the legislature to form a Commission on the Texas Constitution. The resolution to create the commission received an unfavorable committee report and was never considered by the House.[23]

When the legislature failed to consider the constitution produced by the 1967–1968 Constitutional Revision Commission and voters ratified the 1969 amendment to eliminate the "deadwood" in the 1876 constitution, most political observers expected constitutional revision to wane in importance. However, the 62nd Legislature, meeting in 1971, created the first constitutional convention in Texas in nearly a century.

■ The Constitutional Revision Commission, chaired by Robert Calvert and co-chaired by Beryl Buckley Milburn, prepared a draft constitution for the Constitutional Convention of 1974.

Photo courtesy: Texas State Library and Archives Commission

The 1974 Constitutional Convention. In 1971, a group of recently elected representatives proposed a constitutional amendment that called for the Texas legislature of 1973 to sit as a constitutional convention in 1974 and required the legislature to establish a Constitutional Revision Commission to draft a new constitution prior to the constitutional convention. The voters approved the amendment in November 1972 by almost a two-to-one margin (61 percent to 39 percent). The only substantive limitation on the legislature involved Article 1—the Bill of

Rights—which could not be changed. There was also a time limit on the convention. The convention would automatically end on May 31, 1974, unless the convention voted to adjourn earlier or to extend the session for not more than sixty days after the May deadline.

In 1973, the legislature quickly adopted a resolution establishing the **Constitutional Revision Commission.**[24] The commission's membership was finalized in March 1973, and the commission began meeting immediately. From April through June, the commission held nineteen public hearings across the state, meeting with citizens and local advisory committees. On November 1, 1973, the commission submitted a draft constitution to the members of the legislature.

The convention started with great expectations. The 181 members of the 1973 legislature (150 state representatives and thirty-one state senators) met as a constitutional convention on January 8, 1974. The Constitutional Revision Commission had prepared a draft constitution from which the convention could begin its work. The convention only had to make whatever modifications it desired to the commission's draft and submit it to the voters for ratification. Most political observers expected a revised constitution to be presented to Texas voters at the 1974 general election. However, the convention adjourned on July 30, 1974, without producing a new constitution. The final vote fell three short of the two-thirds vote necessary to submit a revised constitution to the voters.

How can the failure of the constitutional revision effort be explained? According to political scientist Janice May, a member of the Constitutional Revision Commission, there are several reasons:

First, the legislature was the constitutional convention. The legislature as a constitutional convention may bring too much of the politics from the legislative arena into the convention. The delegates were influenced by reelection considerations, institutional and personal rivalries between the chambers, pressure from lobbyists, and partisan and ideological differences. The general practice among the states had been to have delegates to a constitutional convention elected by the people. If the convention had been made up of citizen delegates whose political careers might have ended with the adjournment of the convention, the final result might have been different.

The second reason for failure involved the decision rules used in the convention, especially the two-thirds rule. The convention delegates were divided into several substantive and procedural committees (see Table 16.2). Once the committee reported out a section, the section was then debated and voted on by the entire convention. For a particular article to be approved by the convention, a simple majority vote was required. However, the final document, made up of all previously approved sections and articles, required a two-thirds majority vote for submission to the voters. This was a rare rule in the history of constitutional conventions. On ten resolutions representing a final document, a simple majority of the delegates voted to submit the document to the voters.

Constitutional Revision Commission
Group established to research and draft a constitution for a constitutional convention.

TABLE 16.2	Committees of the 1974 Constitutional Convention	
Substantive Committees	*Procedural Committees*	
Finance	Rules	
Local Government	Administration	
Education	Submission and Transition	
Legislature	Style and Drafting	
Judiciary	Public Information	
General Provisions		
Executive		
Rights and Suffrage		

The third reason for failure, and the single most important policy issue, was right-to-work. (A right-to-work provision states that membership or nonmembership in a union cannot be a condition of employment.) The Taft-Hartley Act of 1947 allowed states to establish a right-to-work law, and the Texas legislature passed one in that year. As we noted in chapter 13, labor union leaders considered the Taft-Hartley Act a "slave labor" law. Delegates supported by business interests came to the 1974 constitutional convention determined to place a right-to-work provision in the Texas Constitution, which would have made it more difficult to repeal. On the other hand, labor unions refused to support any constitutional revision that contained a right-to-work provision. The issue dragged long-standing partisan, faction, and labor-management battles into the convention.

The fourth reason for the convention's failure was the lack of exceptional political leadership. As president of the convention, Speaker Price Daniel Jr. probably bears most of the responsibility for the lack of leadership. Daniel's committee appointments included many freshmen appointments and not enough experienced legislators. Furthermore,

■ Members of the 1973 legislature met as a constitutional convention in 1974. They adjourned without producing a new constitution for Texas.

Photo courtesy: Texas State Library and Archives Commission

Daniel did not attempt to compromise on the right-to-work issue early in the convention. Having announced before the convention that he would not seek another term as House speaker in 1975, Daniel was a lame-duck speaker, which reduced his ability to influence members of the convention. Of course, other politicians, such as Governor Dolph Briscoe, could have provided leadership, but Briscoe decided to take a neutral public stand on constitutional revision.

The final reason involves "cockroaches" and revisionists. In the jargon of constitutional revision, a **cockroach** is an obstructionist who opposes any revision of the constitution. About twenty members of the constitutional convention were cockroaches. In addition, several members were **revisionists,** who opposed the constitutional revision effort because the legislature was the convention and the proposed revision did not go far enough toward giving Texas a good constitution. Together, these two groups were large enough to prevent the adoption of a final resolution.[25]

cockroach
A member of a constitutional convention who opposes any changes in the current constitution.

revisionist
A member of a constitutional convention who will not accept less than a total revision of the current constitution.

■ Senator Bill Ratliff, known as "Obi Wan" by his colleagues, holds up a Star Wars light saber, presented by Representative Rob Junell (standing at the podium). In 1999, Ratliff and Junell proposed a comprehensive revision of the Texas Constitution.

The 1975 Constitutional Amendments.   In 1975, the legislature rewrote the constitution that the 1974 convention had failed to adopt the previous summer as eight amendments, each dealing with a particular portion of the constitution, and presented them to the voters. But, on November 4, 1975, Texas voters rejected all eight amendments by a two-to-one margin. Several explanations account for the amendments' defeat. First, the constitutional revision efforts of 1974 and 1975 were preceded by the Sharpstown political scandal in Texas (see chapter 18) and the Watergate scandal at the national level. Both scandals affected the public's trust in government. Second, many Texans feared that the new constitution would make the government too powerful. Third, although Lieutenant Governor Bill Hobby and House Speaker Bill Clayton threw their support behind the new constitution, Governor Dolph Briscoe announced his opposition to the document less than a month before the election. Finally, several groups, representing

Photo courtesy: Bob Daemmrich/Bob Daemmrich Photography, Inc.

Join the Debate

SHOULD TEXAS ADOPT THE INITIATIVE PROCESS?

OVERVIEW: Texas does not allow citizens to propose legislation or constitutional amendments through initiative petitions. Currently, twenty-four states employ some form of the initiative process, which allows citizens to propose public policies for a state. In some states, citizens can propose laws or constitutional amendments, either *directly* or *indirectly*. In the *direct initiative process,* proposed legislation or constitutional amendments are placed on a ballot for popular approval without going through the state legislature. In the *indirect legislative process,* proposed legislation or constitutional amendments must first be submitted to the state legislature during a regular session.

Since the first statewide initiative appeared on the ballot in Oregon in 1904, the use of the initiative has waxed and waned. A populist idea that was implemented during the Progressive era, the initiative was used with increasing frequency until 1920, when its use fell dramatically until the late 1970s. Between 1981 and 1990, 286 measures were placed on ballots through the initiative process. From 1991 to 2000, 389 initiatives were on statewide ballots. In 2004, only 59 initiatives appeared on statewide ballots.

Read and think about the following arguments for and against adopting the direct or indirect initiative process in Texas. Then, join the debate concerning whether Texas should adopt an initiative process by answering the questions posed after the arguments.

Arguments in Favor of Adopting an Initiative Process

- **Adopting the initiative process, either direct or indirect, increases the involvement of citizens in government and politics.** When the initiative is available to the people, they use it to make public policies that they favor by signing petitions and other forms of political involvement.
- **Adopting the initiative process reduces the power of special interests in politics and government.** When people are empowered,

interests that benefited from provisions of the present constitution, actively campaigned against at least some of the amendments. In the end, voters were not convinced that the proposed amendments justified replacing the existing constitution.

The 1999 Constitutional Revision Effort.

The constitution introduced by Representative Rob Junell and Senator Bill Ratliff, two of the legislature's more powerful members, proposed major substantive changes in the structure and operation of Texas government. In the legislative branch, the proposal increased House and Senate members' terms to four and six years respectively, placed term limits on House and Senate members, and created veto sessions, an opportunity for the legislature to call itself into session to override gubernatorial vetoes.

Under the proposal, the governor would become a true chief executive, heading a Cabinet of nine appointed department heads. Cabinet members would be confirmed by the Senate and serve at the governor's

special interests lose out to majoritarian democratic movements.

- **Adopting the initiative process makes government more responsive to the people.** When people are able to effect policy changes directly, the government is more likely to heed the voice of the people.

Arguments Against Adopting an Initiative Process

- **Adopting the initiative process increases the power of special interests.** Initiatives can be sponsored by special interests through paid signature collectors and media advertisements.
- **Adopting the initiative process subjects the minority to the tyranny of the majority.** A pluralistic society needs to safeguard minorities from emotional and misguided majorities.
- **Adopting the initiative process reduces the power of the legislature and the deliberation and compromise that occur in the legislative process.** Politics involves deliberation and compromise. Too frequently, the initiative process involves little deliberation and allows for no compromise.

Questions

1. What effect would the adoption of an initiative process have on political participation and democracy in Texas?
2. What effect would the adoption of an initiative process have on the power of special interests in Texas?

Selected Readings

David S. Broder. *Democracy Derailed: Initiative Campaigns and the Power of Money.* New York: Harcourt, Inc., 2000.

M. Dane Waters, ed. *The Battle over Citizen Lawmaking: A Collection of Essays.* Durham, NC: Carolina Academic Press, 2001.

Selected Web Sites

http://www.iandrinstitutute.org This is the Web site of the Initiative and Referendum Institute at the University of Southern California.

http://www.ncsl.org/programs/legman/irtaskfc/IandR_report.pdf This National Conference of State Legislatures Web site reports on the problems associated with special-interest influence in the initiative process.

pleasure. Although the lieutenant governor, comptroller of public accounts, and attorney general would remain as independently elected executive officers, the executive branch would be consolidated and placed under much greater gubernatorial control.

The judiciary would be simplified into fewer courts. A merit system—incorporating nominating commissions, gubernatorial appointments, and nonpartisan retention elections—would be used to select judges for district courts, courts of appeals, and a single supreme court. The supreme court would consist of fourteen justices, divided into seven-member civil and criminal divisions, and a chief justice, who could sit with both divisions, and would replace the current two supreme courts.

The legislature, however, never considered the proposed 1999 constitution. Instead, the House Select Committee on Constitutional Revision reported favorably on Representative Mowery's proposal for nonsubstantive changes, which were described earlier in the chapter. The Texas Constitution remained substantially unchanged.

SUMMARY

IN THIS CHAPTER, we discussed the constitutions of Texas and made the following points:

1. **The Roots of the Texas Constitution**
   Texas adopted five successive constitutions to reflect Texas's changing status from an independent nation (1836), to a state in the United States (1845), to a state in the Confederacy (1861), to a state readmitted into the union (1866 and 1869). Each of these documents shaped the current Texas Constitution.

2. **The Current Texas Constitution**
   The provisions of the 1876 Texas Constitution are a product of the constitution of 1869, the E. J. Davis administration from 1870 to 1874, and a national movement toward substantive and restrictive constitutions. The current constitution has been criticized because of its disorganization, the limits to executive and legislative powers, the structure of the judiciary, and the limits on local government.

3. **Constitutional Revision**
   Most changes to the Texas Constitution have resulted from piecemeal efforts to adapt the constitution to changing economic and social conditions in the state. The result has been the adoption of 432 constitutional amendments, a longer and more confusing document, and an impetus for comprehensive constitutional change through a constitutional convention.

KEY TERMS

cockroach, p. 601
comprehensive revision, p. 594
Constitutional Revision Commission, p. 599
liberal constitution, p. 587
piecemeal revision, p. 594
statutory constitution, p. 587
revisionist, p. 601

SELECTED READINGS

Angell, Robert H. *A Compilation and Analysis of the 1998 Texas Constitution and the Original 1876 Text.* Lewiston, NY: E. Mellen Press, 1998.

Braden, George D. *Citizens' Guide to the Texas Constitution.* Austin: Institute of Urban Studies, University of Houston, 1972.

Cornyn, John. "The Roots of the Texas Constitution: Settlement to Statehood." *Texas Tech Law Review* 26 (1995): 1089–1218.

May, Janice C. *The Texas Constitutional Revision Experience in the 1970s.* Institute for Urban Studies, University of Houston. Austin: Sterling Swift, 1975.

May, Janice C. *The Texas State Constitution: A Reference Guide.* Greenwood, CT: Greenwood Press, 1996.

Tarr, G. Alan. *Understanding State Constitutions.* Princeton, NJ: Princeton University Press, 1998.

WEB EXPLORATIONS

To read the 1845 Texas Constitution, go to
http://www.wepin.com/rotsstuff/Texas%20Constitution%20of%201845.htm

To read the 1869 Texas Constitution, go to
http://tarlton.law.utexas.edu/constitutions/text/1869index.html

To learn more about amendments to the Texas Constitution, go to
http://www.lrl.state.tx.us/legis/amendments/mainpage.html

To find out more about voter turnout in constitutional elections, go to
http://www.sos.state.tx.us/elections/historical/index.shtml

To learn more about Representative Junell and Senator Ratliff's proposal, go to
http://www.capitol.state.tx.us/cgi-bin/tlo/textframe.cmd?LEG=76&SESS=R&CHAMBER=H&BILLTYPE=JR&BILLSUFFIX=00001&VERSION=1&TYPE=B

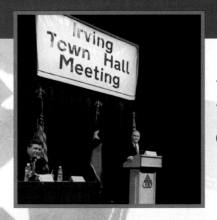

17

Local Government and Politics in Texas

SANTA FE, TEXAS, is a small community located between Galveston and Houston. In the 1990s, the Santa Fe Independent School District—a local government—took a school prayer dispute all the way to the U.S. Supreme Court. By school policy, a high school student delivered a prayer over the public address system before each football game. Two families filed suit in federal court, alleging that the school district had promoted attendance at a revival meeting, chastised children who held minority religious beliefs, allowed teachers to promote their own religious views in the classroom, distributed Bibles, allowed verbal harassment of students who declined to accept Bibles or objected to prayers in school, and allowed students to deliver Christian messages at graduation ceremonies and football games.[1]

The court found the school district in violation of the U.S. Constitution. The school trustees then adopted a policy, titled "Prayer at Football Games," authorizing a student election to determine whether "invocations" should be delivered, and a second election to select the student to deliver any message so authorized. In 1999, an appeals court ruled against the school district. The student elected to deliver the prayer then persuaded a new judge that not allowing students to pray publicly at football games amounted to "state-sponsored atheism." The judge ordered the school district to allow her to deliver a prayer, which she did over the loudspeaker system, to rousing applause.[2]

605

It was all to no avail. In 2000, the U.S. Supreme Court handed down its unequivocal answer: "Simply by establishing this school-related procedure, which entrusts the inherently nongovernmental subject of religion to a majoritarian vote, a constitutional violation has occurred." In *Santa Fe Independent School District* v. *Jane Doe et al.,* the Court warned that school-sponsored prayers encourage "divisiveness along religious lines in a public school setting, a result at odds with the Establishment Clause [of the First Amendment]."

Thus, a local government in Texas pursued a public policy that was ultimately declared by the U.S. Supreme Court to be in violation of the U.S. Constitution. Battles over school prayer, though, are not likely to end, as evidenced by subsequent school prayer cases in Louisiana, Florida, and other states.

M OST PEOPLE KNOW LESS about their local governments than they do those farther away, and they do not even bother to express their will by voting in local elections. Yet, people come into contact with their local governments every day. Texas has three basic categories of political subdivisions that can be characterized as local governments. There are 1,196 city governments, 254 county governments, and 3,334 "special district" governments, including 1,089 school districts.[3] Some are established directly in the Texas Constitution, while some are established in statute. The voluminous Local Government Code creates some political subdivisions and establishes rules for all of them.

In this chapter, we will discuss the forms and roles of local government and politics in Texas:

- First, we will examine *the roots of local government in Texas,* including historical and constitutional influences.
- Second, we will describe the structure, role, and function that *counties* play as local governments and administrative arms of the state government in Texas.
- Third, we will look at the governance of *cities* in Texas and how forms, powers, and politics of city government have changed.
- Finally, we will explore the myriad *special districts* in Texas, with an emphasis on water districts and school districts.

THE ROOTS OF LOCAL GOVERNMENT IN TEXAS

THE ROOTS OF GOVERNANCE for counties, cities, and schools in Texas go back to the colonial period. Few people lived in Texas when Spain and then Mexico governed the area, and there certainly were no settlements of any size. Thus, local governments that were created were expected to govern vast rural territories. Each of twenty-three large districts, or municipalities, was governed by a council, a judge, an attorney, a sheriff, and a secretary.[4] The 1827 Constitution of the State of Coahuila y Tejas also directed these local governments to establish schools to educate the young.[5]

When the Republic of Texas was formed, it continued using the local districts (municipalities) that Mexico had established, but it called them *counties*. In nineteenth-century rural America, including Texas, counties were the governmental point of contact for most people.[6] The Congress of the Republic also enacted laws creating cities as **municipal corporations.** By the end of the republic, Congress had created thirty-six counties and incorporated fifty-three cities. These county and city governments became involved in protracted battles over the politics of education.

When Texas joined the United States, the form of government for counties was brought forward with few changes from the Republic. The legislature carved the large counties that had originated with Spanish and Mexican governments into smaller counties. By 1861, there were 122 counties.[7] During those early days of statehood, the legislature continued to incorporate cities.[8]

Texas's early state constitutions carried forward the Republic's constitutional support for public education through local governments, though with varying degrees of support. In 1854, the legislature made state funds available to local (mostly private) schools. The 1869 constitution mandated a strong public education system, but the taxes levied to support the system generated intense opposition, fueling the fires against the Reconstruction constitution.[9]

The constitution of 1876 continued the basic form of county government but increased the number of county officers. The legislature continued to expand the number of counties until 1931, when Loving County (along the New Mexico border) was organized as the 254th county. As the number of counties grew, disputes over boundaries inevitably arose, pitting one county against another. The legislature responded by passing specific bills affixing the boundaries of counties in dispute and by passing new laws in an attempt to avoid future boundary disputes.[10]

Photo courtesy: Brett Coomer Stringer/AP/Wide World Photos

■ Santa Fe High School Senior Marian Ward delivers a prayer before a football game. In 2000, the Supreme Court ruled that student-led prayer at high school football games violated the establishment clause of the U.S. Constitution.

municipal corporation
A city.

Roots of Government

HOME RULE COMES TO TEXAS CITIES

A S AMERICANS MOVED off the farms and into cities in the late nineteenth and early twentieth centuries, burgeoning cities found it difficult to manage the new growth and to respond to social, economic, and infrastructure problems that the growth brought. They turned to state legislatures for new authority. As rural populations dwindled, rural-dominated legislatures sometimes violated requirements to redistrict, thus keeping themselves in power. Cities often could not get what they wanted from hostile state legislatures.

In 1875, Missouri decided to allow cities to adopt their own charters and decide how to govern themselves, thus triggering a movement across the nation for municipal home rule. Home-rule proposals became a part of the agenda of the Progressive movement in the early 1900s.

In nineteenth-century Texas, the Congress of the Republic, the state legislature, began granting "special charters" to a few cities, with powers that other cities did not have. Soon, the legislature was spending a great deal of time granting special municipal charters and amending those charters to add new provisions. The effort to liberalize special charters, and the burden that local matters placed on the legislature, then fueled the call for municipal home rule. In 1911, the legislature proposed a constitutional amendment for municipal home rule, and voters approved it in 1912. In 1913, the legislature passed a law implementing home rule, stipulating generally that home-rule cities may adopt any provisions that are not inconsistent with the state constitution or statutes.[a]

Within a year, twenty-three of the forty Texas cities that were eligible to convert to home-rule status had done so.[b] By 2000, 304 Texas cities had home rule,[c] with only about twenty eligible cities declining to convert to home rule.

By the 1980s, the federal Advisory Commission on Intergovernmental Relations ranked Texas first in the nation in the level of freedom the state constitution and legislature gives to its cities through home rule.[d] However, such freedom is not uniform for all cities.

[a]Terrell Blodgett, "Municipal Home Rule Charters," *Public Affairs Comment* (University of Texas, 1996), 1–7; Blodgett, "Home Rule Charters," *The Handbook of Texas Online*, last updated July 23, 2001, accessed July 12, 2002, http://www.tsha.utexas.edu/handbook/online/articles/view/HH/mvhek.html.

[b]Delbert Taebel, Susan Horton, and Jay Stanford, *A Citizen's Guide to Home-Rule Charters in Texas Cities* (Arlington: University of Texas at Arlington Institute of Urban Studies, 1985).

[c]Dale Krane, Platon Rigos, and Melvin Hill Jr., *Home Rule in America: A Fifty-State Handbook* (Washington, DC: CQ Press, 2000), 401.

[d]Terrell Blodgett, "Texas Cities: The Bulwark of Democracy," 1999 William P. Hobby Jr. Distinguished Lecture, Southwest Texas State University, accessed January 4, 2001, http://www.swt.edu/cpm/lectures/blodgett_txt.html.

home rule
The right and authority of a local government to govern itself, rather than have the state govern it.

Under the constitution of 1876, a general state law still allowed local incorporation of small cities, but the legislature found itself writing numerous municipal charters for growing cities. As a result of a nationwide municipal **home rule** movement, Texas adopted a constitutional amendment in 1912 that allowed some cities to decide their own structure and, with some limits, their powers (see Roots of Government: Home Rule Comes to Texas Cities).[11] In 1933, the constitution was amended to allow counties home-rule authority also, but the conditions under which a county could qualify for home-rule status were so stringent that no county successfully converted to home-rule status (see The Living Constitution). The provision was repealed from the constitution as "deadwood" in 1969.[12]

Finally, the 1876 constitution (Article 7, section 1) requires the legislature to "establish and make suitable provision for the support and maintenance of an efficient system of public free schools." When Texas embraced the concept of public schools in the late nineteenth century, first county commissioners were empowered to run the schools, then cities, then separate school districts. What resulted was a patchwork of systems around the state. In 1900, the legislature required that independent school districts be governed by seven-member boards of trustees, whose members must be elected in at-large elections.[13]

COUNTIES

TEXAS HAS BY FAR THE LARGEST number of counties of any state: 254. Brewster County, the largest, with 6,200 square miles of territory, is larger than Connecticut, Delaware, or Rhode Island. Harris County is the most populous, with nearly 3.6 million people. It also is the third most populous county in the nation—behind Los Angeles County, California, and Cook County (Chicago), Illinois. Loving County is the least populous, with an estimated population of only sixty-five residents in 2003 (see Analyzing Visuals: Texas Counties and Population). Texas's counties have formed the **Texas Association of Counties,** with headquarters in Austin, to provide information, training, and other services for Texas county officials. The group also lobbies the legislature on behalf of county governments.

Photo courtesy: Bob Daemmrich/Bob Daemmrich Photography, Inc.

■ The Texas Association of Counties represents county governments at the state capitol and provides professional services to them and their employees. Its headquarters is located just blocks from the capitol.

The Living Constitution

Structure and Powers of County Government in Texas

Article 5, section 18: Each county shall...be divided into four commissioners precincts in each of which shall be elected by the qualified voters thereof one County Commissioner, who shall hold office for four years.... The County Commissioners..., with the County Judge as presiding officer, shall compose the County Commissioners Court, which shall exercise such powers and jurisdiction over all county business, as is conferred by this Constitution and the laws of the State, or as may be hereafter prescribed.

The Texas Constitution provides the structure for county government and its powers in Article 5. The principal problems for counties are their constitutionally mandated structure and their lack of powers. As professor Braden notes, "Notwithstanding several constitutional provisions concerning powers of counties . . . , numerous statutes spelling out county powers, and a great many court cases, it is easy to explain the constitutional powers of counties: there are hardly any."[a] The answer to these problems is home rule for Texas counties.

In 1933, the legislature proposed a constitutional amendment to Article 9 to allow county home rule, and a majority of citizens supported the amendment. Purportedly adopted during the Great Depression to reduce the cost of government, the amendment proved unworkable. In practice, the requirement that a county home-rule charter be adopted by *a majority of qualified electors in the county, a majority of those voting in the incorporated areas of the county,* and *a majority of those voting in the unincorporated areas of the county* made the county home rule impossible.[b] In El Paso County, shortly after the amendment's adoption, a group pushed for a home-rule charter. They produced a charter that most considered an improvement over the current structure of

County governments are multifunctional. Their primary areas of responsibility include roads, public safety, jails, public health, and elections. In Texas, counties are both administrative arms of the state govern-

county government. The proposal was endorsed by the *El Paso Herald-Post*, which ran a series of articles preceding the charter election. In the only proposal to reach the voters, the voters in the City of El Paso approved the charter by a 1,143 vote margin in the May 1934 election, but voters outside the City of El Paso defeated the charter by a margin of 848 votes. Although the countywide margin for approval was 295 votes, the charter was defeated because the charter failed to receive a majority of rural El Paso County votes.

Also in 1934, Travis County initiated a home-rule campaign, but legal questions about the charter commission's authority ended the campaign. The third county to attempt home rule in 1934 was Tarrant County, which failed because the county commissioners court ignored the home-rule charter convention's proposal. Home rule movements in Bexar, Dallas, and Harris Counties in 1934 failed for various reasons.[c] In 1969, the home-rule amendment was removed from the Texas Constitution.

Home rule for Texas counties would permit each county's residents to create a government that would fit the residents' specific needs. A merger of county and city governments and offices could occur. Counties also could make and enforce local ordinances, as home-rule cities do now. As a result, the legislature would no longer be required to solve individual county problems with amendments to the Texas Constitution or state laws.[d]

Questions

1. If a workable amendment allowing Texas counties to establish home rule were adopted, what changes would you anticipate in your county? Would governments (city, county, and special districts) be merged?
2. What problems would your county face in establishing a home-rule charter? Explain your answer.

[a]George D. Braden, *The Constitution of the State of Texas: An Annotated and Comparative Analysis*, vol. 1 (Austin: Texas Legislative Council, 1977), 448.

[b]Braden, *The Constitution of the State of Texas*, 652.

[c]Robert E. Norwood, *Texas County Government: Let the People Choose* (Austin: Texas Research League, 1970), 72–4.

[d]Braden, *The Constitution of the State of Texas*, 652.

ment and locally elected governmental bodies. The state needs to perform some functions—such as elections, public health initiatives, and automobile registration—throughout the state but cannot staff state offices all

Analyzing Visuals
TEXAS COUNTIES AND POPULATION

In Texas, all county governments share the same structure, regardless of their size. Some governments serve counties with very large populations, while others serve counties with very small populations. Some county governments must respond to explosive population growth, while others grapple with significant drops in population and economic activity. After studying the map depicting the counties and reading the material in this chapter on the structure of county government, answer the following critical thinking questions: Where are the counties with the greatest percentage increase in population located? Where are the counties with the largest percentage loss in population located? What effect do you think these differences in populations and growth or loss rates have on the ability of a county government to meet the needs of the residents? What changes in structure would allow counties to operate more effectively?

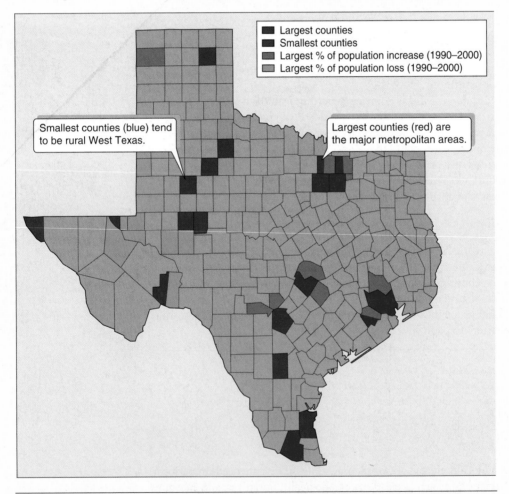

Largest counties
Smallest counties
Largest % of population increase (1990–2000)
Largest % of population loss (1990–2000)

Smallest counties (blue) tend to be rural West Texas.

Largest counties (red) are the major metropolitan areas.

Source: U.S. Census Bureau, Census 2000 PHC-T-4, Ranking Tables for Counties: 1990 and 2000, accessed April 20, 2001, http://www.census.gov/population/cen2000/phc_;4/tab01.pdf.

across this large state. So, counties serve as local offices to administer some programs for the state government. At the same time, counties perform many functions that are strictly local, so their officers are selected locally.

Structure of County Government

When delegates met in the constitutional convention in 1875, a primary goal was to limit government's power. County authority is fragmented into offices consisting of a county judge, commissioners, county attorney, district attorney, sheriff, treasurer, auditor, tax assessor-collector, county clerk, judges, district clerk, justices of the peace, constables, and other offices.

County officers (except for the auditor) are elected to four-year terms. The county runs the state's elections, so county offices are on the general election ballot at the same time as state elections, with officials elected in partisan elections. All are elected countywide, except for the four commissioners, the justices of the peace, and constables.

County Commissioners Court. The primary governing entity for the county is the commissioners court,[14] whose form is prescribed by the constitution as consisting of one county judge

Photo courtesy: CORBIS

■ The Ellis County courthouse, in Waxahachie, is one of the grandest courthouses in Texas. Designed by noted architect J. Riely Gordon, the courthouse was built in 1897. In 2002, the courthouse was rededicated after a complete restoration funded by the Texas Historical Commission and the county.

and four county commissioners (see The Living Constitution). The **county judge** is formally the judge for court cases heard in the county (through the "constitutional county court"). Some county judges, primarily in rural counties, retain nonlitigation judicial matters, such as wills. Despite the name, though, today's county judge is actually the chief executive officer of the county. He or she also serves as a voting member and the chair of the commissioners court.

The **commissioners court,** as the legislative body for the county, is responsible for adopting the budget for all county offices, setting tax rates, overseeing county programs, and redistricting. The four **county commissioners** perform both legislative and executive functions and are elected from single-member districts called precincts. Commissioners serve four-

county judge
Elected official who is the chief administrative officer of county government, serves on the commissioners court, and may also have some judicial functions.

commissioners court
The legislative body of a county in Texas.

county commissioner
Elected official who serves on the county legislative body, the commissioners court.

year, staggered terms. Throughout much of the twentieth century, the commissioners' primary job was to provide roads for farmers to get to and from town. In fact, they are still known in some areas as "road commissioners."

The commissioners court must perform redistricting functions for county commissioner precincts.Commissioners courts often drew precinct district lines to produce four districts that were geographically fairly equal sized. After the U.S. Supreme Court declared in 1963 and 1964 that congressional and state legislative district lines must be drawn to produce equal population districts,[15] a resident of Midland County, Texas, sued the county, arguing that equal representation should also apply to this local legislative body. In 1968, the U.S. Supreme Court agreed, in *Avery* v. *Midland*,[16] declaring that the one-person, one-vote standard applied to counties as well. As a result, in Texas's metropolitan areas, county commissioners courts are now elected by the majority urban residents, rather than by rural residents.

District Attorneys and County Attorneys.   Counties elect district attorneys, county attorneys, and criminal district attorneys. The chief prosecutors for violations of state laws are usually district attorneys. A **district attorney (DA)** or a **criminal district attorney** may be elected from and serve one county, but in areas of small population, the DA may be elected from and serve a judicial district that encompasses more than one county. Most counties also elect a county attorney. The **county attorney** provides legal advice and services to the county government and may also prosecute some criminal cases.

Sheriff.   The **sheriff** serves as chief law enforcement officer in the county, generally operating in the unincorporated areas of the county while leaving law enforcement in the cities to municipal police departments. The sheriff hires deputies, and together they provide general public safety protection for citizens, serve warrants and civil papers, conduct criminal investigations, arrest offenders, and operate the county jail.

County Clerk and District Clerk.   The **county clerk** keeps records for the county commissioners court and for county courts. He or she is also the official keeper of records such as real estate titles and marriage licenses and is responsible for conducting county and state elections, except where the county has a separate elections administrator. **District clerks** keep records for district courts. In some small counties, one clerk may perform the duties of the county and district clerk.

Judges and Constables.   District judges, county court-at-law judges, justices of the peace, and constables provide judicial and court services. The number of each varies from county to county, as the legislature has adopted a crazy-quilt pattern of institutions and officials, county by county, depending on population size and on local initiatives asking the legislature for special consideration. (These officials are discussed more in chapter 20.)

---

district attorney (DA)
Elected official who prosecutes criminal cases.

criminal district attorney
Elected official who prosecutes criminal cases.

county attorney
Elected official serving as the legal officer for county government and also as a criminal prosecutor.

sheriff
Elected official who serves as the chief law enforcement officer in a county.

county clerk
Elected official who serves as the clerk for the commissioners court and for county records.

district clerk
Elected official who is responsible for keeping the records for the district court.

County Tax Assessor-Collector. The **county tax assessor-collector** is responsible for registering voters, collecting local property taxes, registering automobiles, and collecting motor vehicle sales taxes and registration fees. Because the legislature created county central appraisal districts in the 1970s, tax assessor-collectors do not actually assess property values anymore. Instead, the central appraisal district assesses the value of property for all taxing entities in the county and the tax assessor-collector collects the taxes.

Treasurer and Auditor. The **county treasurer** is the county's money manager. All but the smallest counties are also required to have a **county auditor.** The auditor audits records of all county officers and departments, helps prepare the county budget, and sets up and administers the accounting systems. Unlike other county officials, the auditor is appointed for a two-year term by the district court judge or judges. Because auditor and treasurer functions are similar, several counties have asked the legislature for constitutional amendments to abolish the requirement that they have a treasurer. The legislature and voters have obliged—amending the constitution to repeal the requirement for some specific counties but not for others.[17]

Authority of County Governments

County authority is established in the Texas Constitution and in statute. Article 9 of the constitution is devoted to counties, and other articles also address county structure and power. The **Local Government Code** devotes Chapters 71–87 to counties, plus scattered provisions in other chapters.

Texas counties do not have **general ordinance-making authority,** the legal right to adopt ordinances covering a wide array of subject areas—an authority that cities have. Counties are limited to the specific grants of power and areas of responsibility spelled out in the constitution and statutes. Consequently, when new problems arise, or when counties have difficulty administering existing laws, they must seek new or clarified authority from the legislature. For instance, the constitution requires counties to provide health care for those who cannot afford to pay for it themselves. As health care costs soared, counties had more and more difficulty in meeting this obligation. In 1985, the legislature responded with a major initiative for indigent health care, providing expanded authority for counties to

county tax assessor-collector
Elected official who collects taxes for the county (and perhaps for other local governments).

county treasurer
Elected official who serves as the money manager for county government.

county auditor
Official appointed by a district judge to audit county finances.

Local Government Code
The Texas statutory code containing state laws about local governments.

general ordinance-making authority
The legal right to adopt ordinances covering a wide array of subject areas, authority that cities have but counties do not.

■ Each county in Texas is required by the state constitution to provide medical care for those who cannot afford it. Counties choose to perform this duty in different ways. In the Houston area, the Harris County Hospital District makes its services available to all residents of the county. The district runs three hospitals, including Ben Taub General Hospital.

*Photo courtesy: Carrie Elizabeth Tucker/*Houston Chronicle

TEXAS IN COMPARISON
Local Government in the States

Texas does not have some local governments, such as townships, that a number of other states have. But, states can be compared on the basic forms of local governments—cities, counties, and special districts. The level of public services provided by local governments is often measured by looking at the number of governmental employees.

State	Number of Cities	Number of Counties	Number of Special Districts	City Employees (full-time, per 10,000 population, 2002)	County Employees (full-time, per 10,000 population, 2002)
Texas	1,196	254	3,334	139 (Houston)	61 (Harris)
California	475	57	3,877	134 (Los Angeles)	102 (Los Angeles)
New York	1,545	57	1,808	579 (New York)	82 (Suffolk)
Florida	404	66	721	140 (Jacksonville)	163 (Dade)

address the problem. In May 2004, Travis County, in which Austin is located, joined other large urban counties in Texas by creating a county hospital district to provide mandated indigent care and other services approved by the district's board.

Of course, another method of responding to county-level problems would be to grant them general ordinance-making authority, as cities have. The Texas Association of Counties has lobbied the legislature in favor of expanded authority numerous times, but developers and realtors have opposed the counties, and the legislature has repeatedly defeated the effort. In 1999, however, in the wake of the boom of suburban and rural development and the court decision in *Elgin Bank* v. *Travis County*, the legislature approved a new law (Chapter 232 of the Local Government Code) that allows counties significant authority to regulate subdivisions. The law requires platting and drainage in new subdivisions and gives counties authority to enforce those requirements.[18] Since then, numerous counties have begun using the new powers.[19]

A key function of county governments is administering elections. Counties have independent authority to make many election decisions, and uniform election procedures do not always exist from county to county. Following the 2000 Florida election fiasco, in which confusing butterfly ballots and faulty punch-card systems made some votes invalid, the Texas legislature in 2001 revamped county election authority and procedures. Punch-card ballots will be phased out in counties where they are still used; any new voting system must meet accessibility needs of disabled voters; butterfly ballots are prohibited; ballots must be hand inspected; and ineligible-voter lists must be verified by the county.[20] In response to the Help America Vote Act (HAVA) of 2002, the legislature adopted additional measures in 2003 to ensure compliance with the act by January 1, 2006, including the creation of a statewide voter registration list and the provision of at least one direct recording electronic (DRE) voting device at each polling place.[21]

Finances of County Governments

Counties must perform a myriad of functions for state government, yet they must raise their own money for most of those services. Historically, counties have relied heavily on the property tax. In 1987, the legislature also allowed counties to collect a sales tax, but only if the county is not part of a metropolitan area with a metropolitan transit authority that collects a sales tax.

In recent years, counties have increased their reliance on fee revenues. Some fee revenues (for instance, motor vehicle registration fees) are pass-through: counties simply collect the state-imposed fees and send the money on to Austin, retaining only a small portion allowed for county overhead. Counties are authorized to collect other fees that are totally county revenues. The legislature has created numerous new fees in recent years, especially in the area of criminal justice. The collection and distribution system for these fees is complicated and confusing for offices throughout the courthouse.[22] Counties collect thirty-three different fees for state government, plus up to thirty fees for local services. In 2001, voters approved a constitutional amendment to consolidate local fees, with implementation left to the legislature.[23]

In the 2003 legislative session, with the state facing a $10 billion deficit, the legislature cut services, increased fees, and passed the costs of programs to the counties. In response, county officials pushed for a

■ Skyline of Houston, Texas. With a population of 2 million, Houston ranks as the largest city in Texas and fourth largest in the nation. It uses a strong mayor form of government.

Photo courtesy: Paul S. Howell

constitutional amendment to prohibit the state from imposing under-funded or unfunded mandates on the counties.[24]

CITIES

TEXAS HAS 1,196 CITIES. Houston is the largest, with 2 million citizens. Most cities, however, are small. When the municipal home-rule amendment was added to the constitution in 1912, it authorized cities with more than 5,000 people to write their own city charter and decide what structure and authority to give their city government. Today, about 300 cities are home-rule cities. The others are called **general-law cities**, because they are governed by the general state laws regarding municipalities, rather than by a locally adopted charter.[25] For the small general-law cities, the Local Government Code spells out the form and powers of the city government, and even specific actions that the city must follow.

The idea behind home rule is that city leaders need tools to address their local problems and that one-size-fits-all state provisions deny cities the flexibility they need. For any city that qualifies for home rule, the Local Government Code stipulates that the city "may adopt and operate under any form of government" and that "the municipality has full power of local self government." Thus, some home-rule cities decide, for instance, to operate their own electric company, while others do not; some allow citizens to recall city officials from office, while others do not.

Even home-rule municipalities sometimes have state laws passed just to restrict their authority to govern themselves or to give them special authority. For instance, the Local Government Code stipulates that if the city of Houston does not adopt a voter-approved local ordinance providing for some single-member districts, then it must follow a specific form spelled out in the statute. (The city responded to the pressure and adopted its own system.) The legislature, however, must be careful. Laws aimed at one specific local government are unconstitutional,[26] so legislators devise laws that apply to cities in a particular population bracket. Of course, they can try to create a population bracket that encompasses only one city, so long as no one challenges it in court.

Forms of City Governments

For most general-law cities, the Local Government Code mandates a mayor–council or commission form of government.[27] Figure 17.1 shows the organizational scheme for Waller, a general-law city in Waller County, outside of Houston.

For home-rule cities able to decide their own form of government, what are the options available? The four general types are **weak mayor–council**, **strong mayor–council**, **council–manager**, and **city commission.** The details of these forms, however, vary from city to city. About 290 Texas home-rule cities have chosen the council–manager form of government, fifteen have chosen weak mayor–council, and four

general-law cities
Cities with fewer than 5,000 residents, governed by a general state law rather than by a locally adopted charter.

weak mayor–council
A form of city government in which the mayor has no more power than any other member of the council.

strong mayor–council
A form of city government in which the mayor has strong powers to run the city by hiring, managing, and firing staff and controlling executive departments; the mayor also serves on the council.

council–manager
A form of city government in which the city council and mayor hire a professional manager to run the city.

city commission
A form of city government in which elected members serve on the legislative body and also serve as head administrators of city programs.

Analyzing Visuals

TYPE OF GOVERNMENT AND ELECTION SYSTEMS IN TEXAS'S TOP TEN CITIES

Texas home-rule cities may choose any form of city government. A city's election system, however, must conform to the requirements of U.S. and Texas constitutions and laws. Since the 1970s, many Texas cities have been sued under the federal Voting Rights Act to force changes in the manner of election of city officials. After studying the table and the material in this chapter, answer the following critical thinking questions: Which form of city government is most popular among the ten largest cities in Texas, and why do you think most cities employ that form? How do the following factors affect the selection of an election system by a city: population of the city, ethnic diversity of the city, membership on the city council, political influence in the city? Which method of electing city council members would you favor? Explain your choice.

City	Type of Government	City Council Election System	Estimated Population 2003 (thousands)
Houston	Strong Mayor–Council	9 single-member districts, 5 at-large, plus mayor at-large	2,010
San Antonio	Council–Manager	10 single-member districts, mayor at-large	1,215
Dallas	Council–Manager	14 single-member districts, mayor at-large	1,208
Austin	Council–Manager	7 at-large-by-place	672
Fort Worth	Council–Manager	8 single-member districts, mayor at-large	585
El Paso	Council–Manager	8 single-member districts, mayor at-large	584
Arlington	Council–Manager	5 single-member districts, 3 at-large, plus mayor at-large	355
Corpus Christi	Council–Manager	5 single-member districts, 3 at-large, plus mayor at-large	279
Plano	Council–Manager	4 single-member districts, 3 at-large, plus mayor at-large	242
Garland	Council–Manager	8 single-member districts, mayor at-large	218

FIGURE 17.1 Organizational Chart: City of Waller (General Law)

Waller, Texas, is an incorporated city with about 2,000 residents, requiring it to be a general-law city. ■

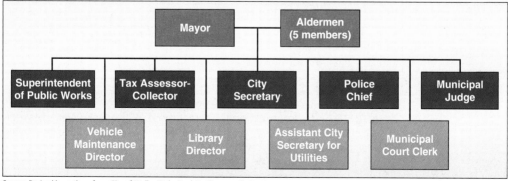

Source: Derived by authors from City of Waller Web site, http://www.wallertexas.com.

have chosen strong mayor–council.[28] (See Analyzing Visuals: Type of Government and Election Systems in Texas's Top Ten Cities.)

Weak Mayor–Council.   The mayor could be elected at large, or by the city council from among their members. The mayor has authority to preside over city council meetings and is the symbolic head of government, but is essentially equal in power to other city council members. The collective council hires, manages, and fires city staff. Figure 17.2 shows the city organizational chart for White Oak, a weak-mayor home-rule city in Gregg County, bordering Longview.

Strong Mayor–Council.   The strong mayor is distinguished from a weak mayor by his or her executive powers. The mayor is elected citywide, presides at city council meetings, hires, manages, and fires city staff, and may have the power to veto actions of the city council. Most large American cities have strong mayors. Among Texas's ten largest cities, only Houston utilizes the strong mayor–council form. Figure 17.3 shows the city organizational chart for the city of Houston.

Council–Manager.   Progressive-era reformers promoted a system that empowers a professional manager, hired by the city council, to run the city (hire, manage, and fire staff), while the city council and mayor set policy, adopt budgets and tax rates, and oversee the manager. Most home-rule cities in Texas have city managers. Figure 17.4 shows the city organizational chart for Austin, a council–manager system.

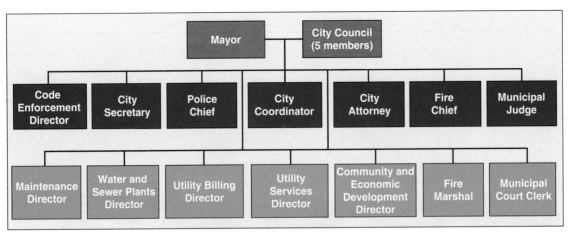

FIGURE 17.2 Organizational Chart: City of White Oak (Weak Mayor)
White Oak, Texas, is an incorporated city that grew to just over 5,000 residents in the 1990 Census and converted to home-rule status. So far, it has retained a weak mayor–council structure. ■

Source: Derived by authors from City of White Oak Web site, http://www.cityofwhiteoak.com.

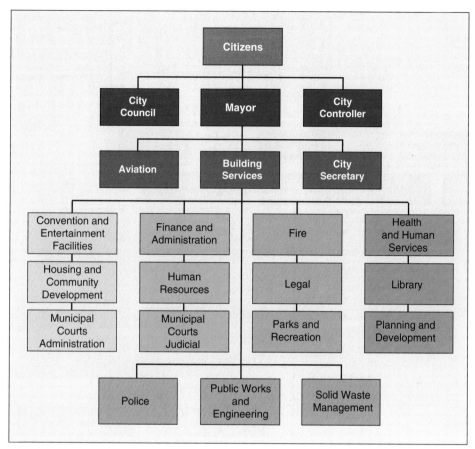

FIGURE 17.3 Organizational Chart: Houston (Strong Mayor). ■

Source: City of Houston.

City Commission.   On September 8, 1900, the deadliest natural disaster in U.S. history devastated Galveston, the wealthiest city in Texas at the time. A hurricane killed an estimated 8,000 to 10,000 people and wiped out three-fourths of the city. In attempting to cope with the disaster, the legislature allowed Galveston to revamp its city government, giving authority to specific individuals (commissioners) to govern particular policy areas (such as public health, public safety, public improvements). The city managed to build a major sea wall, prop up houses and buildings, and clean up and rebuild the city.[29] In this form of government, the commissioners meet as a body to adopt budgets, set tax rates, and perform other communal functions, but each individual member has authority in the specified functional area. After Galveston's experience, the commission form of government spread quickly to nearly 500 cities across the nation, but the form has since fallen into disuse amid charges of turf battles and lack of coordination among the officials. Today, no Texas city

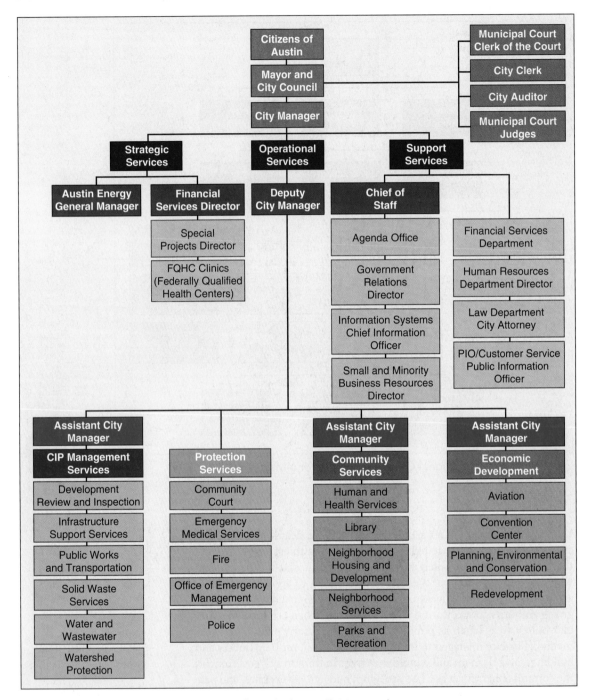

FIGURE 17.4 Organizational Chart: City of Austin (Council–Manager). ■

Source: City of Austin Web site, http://www.ci.austin.tx.us/help/orgchart.htm.

uses the commission form of government.[30] Some cities use the term "commission" rather than "council" for the governing body, but they do not have the commission form of government.

Authority and Functions of City Governments

Cities are multifunctional governments, providing police, fire, public works, recreation, health, and other services. Cities have wide authority to provide services directly to citizens. Some decide to give franchises to private companies to provide services in the city (such as the garbage pickup service).

Municipalities have broad regulatory authority. When cities use regulatory authority in the areas of zoning, buildings, signs, nuisances, and subdivision development, public needs and private property rights often collide. The **Texas Municipal League** serves as the voice of cities in the capital, lobbying to defend cities' authority and powers. Sometimes, of course, cities do not agree with each other. Other times, cities and their association fight battles against counties and the Texas Association of Counties.

Texas Municipal League
Professional association and lobbying arm for city governments.

Finances of City Governments

Cities raise revenues from several sources, including the municipal sales tax, property taxes, occupation taxes, fees, state and federal revenues, and borrowing (bond sales). If a city has chosen to provide its citizens services such as electricity, water, and garbage collection, fees for these services can be a significant portion of the budget, making it difficult to compare municipal budgets around the state. Most Texas cities use both capital budgeting and operating budgeting as

■ A skyline of Big Spring, Texas, the county seat of Howard County in West Texas. Big Spring is a home-rule city with a population of about 25,000. It uses a council–manager form of government.

Photo courtesy: Bob Daemmrich/Bob Daemmrich Photography, Inc.

Join the Debate

SHOULD TEXAS CITIES BE ALLOWED TO PHOTOGRAPH RED-LIGHT RUNNERS?

OVERVIEW: Running red lights is a national problem. In 2002, as many as 207,000 crashes, 178,000 injuries, and 921 fatalities in the United States were attributed to red-light running.[a] The problem is particularly acute in Texas. Between 1992 and 1998, Texas had the second highest total of fatalities attributed to running red lights, and five Texas cities were among the top thirty cities in the nation in red-light-running fatalities. According to Texas Department of Public Safety crash records, the number of people killed or injured in crashes attributable to red-light running increased from about 10,000 in 1975 to about 25,000 in 1999.[b] Many cities have adopted one method to combat the problem: photographing red-light runners with automated cameras. As of June 2004, more than one hundred communities had installed cameras at traffic lights to record the license plates of red-light runners, most extensively in California, Maryland, and North Carolina. At that time, only one Texas city—Garland—employed the cameras, although several cities were contemplating their use.[c]

The application of this new technology to apprehend red-light runners has been controversial. Some argue that such "big brother" government techniques are dangerous to civil liberties. Lobbyists for cities, uncertain about the status of state law over this new policy area, have tried unsuccessfully to get explicit authorization from the Texas legislature for traffic camera systems. Opponents in Texas have blocked legislative efforts to explicitly authorize cities to use photographs of red-light runners as evidence in legal proceedings against the drivers.

Read and think about the following arguments for and against using cameras at traffic lights to apprehend red-light runners. Then, join the debate by answering the questions posed after the arguments.

Arguments in Favor of Using Red-light Cameras

- **Red-light cameras reduce the number of fatalities resulting from vehicles running red lights.** Several cities using red-light cameras have experienced a significant reduction in intersection crashes and fatalities.
- **Red-light cameras allow law enforcement personnel to concentrate on other matters.** Freed from the necessity of watching for red-light runners, police can concentrate on other serious threats to public safety, such as rapes and murders.
- **Red-light cameras are a constitutional method of enforcing traffic codes.** When operating a motor vehicle in open view of the public, one cannot expect privacy. No constitutional guarantee is being violated by the use of red-light cameras.

tools for long-range planning and management of debt and revenues. Sewage and water treatment are the highest priority in capital budgeting.[31]

In the 1980s and 1990s, to attract development, Texas cities turned to innovative policies involving tax incentives, such as tax increment financing, reinvestment zones, tax abatement agreements, and economic development corporations. These policy initiatives can result in decreases in tax revenues, though the intent is to use those tax breaks

Arguments Against Using Red-light Cameras

■ **Red-light cameras violate an individual's right to privacy protected by several amendments to the U.S. Constitution and the Texas Constitution.** These concerns are based on constitutional protections afforded by the Fourth Amendment (protection against unreasonable searches and seizures), the Fifth Amendment (the right to remain silent), the Sixth Amendment (the right to confront accusers), and the Fourteenth Amendment (due process and equal protection of the law).

■ **Red-light cameras are used by cities to generate income and not to achieve safety goals.** In Garland, Texas, over a nine-month period, 30,000 drivers were photographed running red lights at four intersections. Garland will take in $2.25 million if everyone pays the $75 fine.

■ **Red-light running can be reduced through methods that do not infringe on individual liberties.** Traffic safety engineers note that redesigning intersections, synchronizing traffic signals, larger traffic signal heads, and longer yellow lights reduce red-light running.

Questions

1. Do you favor or oppose the use of red-light cameras? What other methods might curtail the problem of red-light running?

2. Is the invasion of one's privacy created by red-light cameras an acceptable cost to save lives and reduce the number and cost of intersection crashes? Why or why not?

Selected Readings

Tara Di Trolio, "Red-light Cameras Slow Yield on Red," *Governing* 17 (November 2003), accessed July 5, 2004, http://www.governing.com/archive/2003/nov/redlight.txt.

Sean C. Stevens, "Benefits from Camera Technology Outweigh Privacy Issues," *Journal of Science, Technology and International Affairs* 2 (1999), accessed July 5, 2004, http://www.georgetown.edu/sfs/programs/stia/students/vol.02/stevens.htm.

Selected Web Sites

http://www.stopredlightrunning.com/ The National Campaign to Stop Red-Light Running.

http://www.aclu.org The American Civil Liberties Union.

[a]National Campaign to Stop Red-Light Running, "The Problem," accessed July 2, 2004, http://www.stopredlightrunning.com/html/problem.htm.

[b]Cesar Quiroga, Edgar Kraus, Ida van Schalkwyk, and James Bonneson, "Red Light Running: A Policy Review," Texas Transportation Institute, Texas A&M University, Report No. CTS-02/150206-1, March 2003, accessed June 30, 2004, http://tti.tamu.edu/cts/reports/cts-02.pdf.

[c]National Campaign to Stop Red-Light Running, "Red Light Cameras," June 2004, accessed July 2, 2004, http://www.stopredlightrunning.com/html/redlight.htm.

to stimulate economic activity that would not otherwise occur, and to then recoup tax revenues from the new activity.

Municipal Annexation

One of the most complicated, controversial, and convoluted areas of municipal government and politics is the issue of municipal boundaries and **annexation** of territory to expand those boundaries. Absent any state

annexation
Enlargement of a city's corporate limits by incorporating surrounding territory into the city.

extraterritorial jurisdiction (ETJ)
The area outside a city's boundaries over which the city may exercise limited control.

restrictions, home-rule cities could decide on their own whether and how to grow. In 1963, the legislature passed the Municipal Annexation Act to restrict home-rule cities' leeway in annexing. The 1963 act is an arena for legislative battles nearly every session. The most significant areas of controversy in annexation policies include how the annexation occurs, services that cities must provide in newly annexed areas, and the status of areas beyond the city limits known as **extraterritorial jurisdictions (ETJs).**

Under the Municipal Annexation Act, a city may expand its municipal boundaries by an area up to 10 percent of its geographic area in any one year.[32] The city is not required to obtain the consent of anyone for annexation, though it must hold public hearings. A city also controls an ETJ of up to five miles from its city limits, depending on its population size.[33] The act states that the purpose of limited municipal controls in areas beyond city limits is "to promote and protect the general health, safety, and welfare."[34] When a city decides to annex territory, it may not include any area within the existing ETJ of another municipality. When cities annex territory, they must provide services to those areas within timelines specified in the act.

To complicate matters, some cities use what is called limited-purpose annexation. A home-rule municipality with a population greater than 225,000 may annex an area for the limited purposes of applying its planning, zoning, health, and safety ordinances in the area, without the consequences of full annexation. Still another variant is called strip annexation. Some cities have used annexation powers to annex narrow strips along highways, in order to extend city boundaries (and ETJs) to outlying areas rapidly. In 1973, the act was amended to prohibit the annexation of strips less than 500 feet, and in 1987 the minimum permissible width was increased to 1,000 feet.[35]

In 1998, a Senate interim committee made several recommendations for amendments to the Municipal Annexation Act.[36] The 1999 legislature amended numerous provisions of the proposal, then passed it. As a result of those 1999 amendments, in order to annex, a city must now take the following steps:

- Develop a three-year plan for annexation, and not annex the targeted area during that three-year period.
- Make an inventory of the current services in the area.
- Provide to the annexed area all services currently provided in its full-purpose boundaries no later than two and one-half years (or four and one-half years in some circumstances) after annexation.
- Require negotiations and arbitration regarding services.
- Conduct at least two public hearings.
- Not reduce level of services in the area from what they were before annexation.

If a court finds that the service plan is not being implemented, it must provide an option of disannexation, or it must order compliance, a refund of taxes, or civil penalties. The law grandfathers existing land uses or planned land uses at the time of annexation.[37]

Politics and Representation in City Governments

Unlike county elections, municipal elections in Texas are nonpartisan, and they are held on election dates separate from state and county elections. With political parties absent from the nominating process, who then is influential in the socialization, recruitment, and financing of city candidates? The answer to that question is different today from what it was up to the 1970s.

Traditionally, city council elections in Texas have tended to be at-large or **at-large-by-place** elections, where all candidates had to run for office across the entire city. The general pattern of competition was that the business community in the city would coalesce, plan strategy for the elections, recruit candidates, keep other candidates out of the race if possible, and fund the candidates.[38] Because it was difficult to mount a serious campaign across an entire large city without substantial resources, these business coalitions held nearly monopoly power on municipal politics for decades. Not surprisingly, the candidates that they recruited to fill city council and mayoral seats typically came from the business community and reflected business community leadership: They were white, male, and conservative politically.

It was the coming of single-member districts in the 1970s that weakened the business monopoly over municipal politics in Texas. The

at-large-by-place
An election system in which all positions on the council or governing body are filled by city-wide elections, with each position designated as a seat, and candidates must choose which place to run for.

Photo courtesy: Eduardo Verdugo/AP/Wide World

■ San Antonio Mayor Ed Garza (left) meets with Mexican President Vicente Fox in Mexico City.

League of United Latin American Citizens (LULAC), the Mexican American Legal Defense and Educational Fund (MALDEF), the National Association for the Advancement of Colored People (NAACP), and Texas Rural Legal Aid began using the federal Voting Rights Act (see chapter 12) as a basis for lawsuits challenging the validity of at-large municipal elections that usually resulted in all-white city councils. As courts handed down decisions overturning at-large elections, most large cities in Texas abandoned at-large elections in favor of either single-member districts or a mixed system of some single-member districts and some at large. A variety of systems are demonstrated in Analyzing Visuals: Type of Government and Election Systems in Texas's Top Ten Cities.

With the advent of single-member districts, candidates who previously could not mount an effective campaign throughout the entire city became viable. The most visible result of the change in election systems has been the ethnic and racial make-up of city governments. By the 1990s, African Americans and Mexican Americans constituted majorities or near majorities of the city councils in some of the largest cities.[39] The best known of the local officials has been Henry Cisneros, who served as mayor of San Antonio in the 1980s and 1990s and then served in President Bill Clinton's Cabinet. Recent Mexican American mayors include Ed Garza (San Antonio), Gus Garcia (Austin), and Raymond Caballero (El Paso). Former Houston Mayor Lee Brown, former Dallas Mayor Ron Kirk, and former Arlington Mayor Elzie Odom are African American.

Additionally, women have won considerable support in recent city elections. Women winning mayoral elections in recent decades include current Dallas Mayor Laura Miller,[40] Houston's Kathy Whitmire, Dallas's Annette Strauss, San Antonio's Lila Cockrell, Austin's Carole Keeton Strayhorn (now state comptroller), and Fort Worth's Kay Granger (now U.S. Representative).

Of course, the selection of single-member districts as a means of addressing imbalance in city politics is not the only option. **Cumulative voting** allows a voter in a multimember or at-large system to cast a number of votes equal to the number of seats being filled; the voter may cast his or her votes all for one candidate or split them among candidates in various combinations.

cumulative voting
A method of voting in which voters have a number of votes equal to the number of seats being filled, and voters may cast their votes all for one candidate or split them among candidates in various combinations.

Photo courtesy: Richard Michael Pruitt/Dallas Morning News

■ When Dallas Mayor Ron Kirk resigned to run for the U.S. Senate in 2002, council member Laura Miller won the mayor's race. Before running for office, she was an investigative reporter.

GETTING STUDENTS INVOLVED IN POLITICAL CAMPAIGNS

The Annette Strauss Institute for Civic Participation was founded in 2000 at the University of Texas at Austin "to respond to growing political cynicism and disaffection in the United States." Among the projects of the Institute is participation in the Campaign for Young Voters.

Guided by the goal of increased youth participation in politics, the Strauss Institute initiated a research effort to discover why young people do not vote and what would cause them to vote. Armed with the research results, the Campaign for Young Voters, assisted by the Strauss Institute, created a toolkit that was distributed to candidates for public office. The toolkit provided information about the issues that excite today's youth, their worries, and methods to involve them in politics.

The campaign to involve young people involved three phases: Phase I involved the development of the toolkit[a], Phase II involved a number of youth-oriented activities designed to acquaint candidates with strategies for reaching young people; Phase III involved congressional campaigns in California, Iowa, Arkansas, Pennsylvania, and Texas, where candidates were encouraged to run youth-centered campaigns. During this phase, the Strauss Institute conducted several studies that assessed the effects of their efforts.

The research produced several surprising findings and observations:

- Youth are complex. Young people perceive themselves as observers of politics and government rather than participants. Similarly, they are "bewildered" by politics, not "uninformed" about politics. In addition, youth are hopeful about politics and can, given the right stimulus, be drawn into civic participation.
- Incorporating young people in American politics requires an understanding of local youth cultures. Greater differences existed among the five states than among the youth within each of the states. For example, Des Moines,

Iowa, youth were diffident, "least willing to discuss leadership characteristics or to imagine specific political solutions, and least able to see the relevance of governance as a problem-solving tool." The youth of El Paso, Texas, were "least likely to notice the impact of the State on their lives and least likely to prize the right to vote." El Paso youth were also most likely to see political leaders in a negative light and to claim that all politicians do not care what the people think. On the other hand, Little Rock youth "sounded like the League of Women Voters. . . . They sounded like model citizens—hopeful but not naïve, intelligent about politics but not cerebral about it.[b]

What was learned from Phase III of the project? Although mobilizing youth in political campaigns requires several techniques, the most significant involved mobilization efforts: "community group support may well turn out to be the key ingredient in increasing mobilization among young people." Additionally, efforts to involve youth should "work with local candidates (mayors, state representatives, state senators). Work with local, youth-oriented community groups. Work with non-chain local newspapers and non-network local television stations."[c] With additional mobilization efforts by the Annette Strauss Institute and the Campaign for Young Voters, perhaps the decline in political participation by America's youth will be reversed in the future.

---

aThe toolkit is available at http://www.campaignyoungvoters.org/.

bThe information and quotes from this section on observations come from Jay Childers and Roderick Hart, "Report #8: Focus Group Study of Youth and Politics," August 8, 2003, accessed June 30, 2004, http://communication.utexas.edu/strauss/
pdf/report_eight_focus_group_study_of_youth_and_politics.pdf.

cPhilip Paolino, Sharon F. Jarvis, and Roderick P. Hart, "Report #5: Survey of Youth Attitudes," February 5, 2003, accessed June 30, 2004, http://communication.utexas.edu/
strauss/pdf/report_five_survey_of_youth_attitudes.pdf.

proportional representation
A voting system that apportions legislative seats according to the percentage of the vote won by a particular political party.

Some small Texas cities and some school districts are experimenting with cumulative voting (see the discussion of school districts). **Proportional representation** awards seats based on the proportion of the vote that a political party receives for a legislative body. Since Texas cities are nonpartisan, cumulative voting, rather than other types of proportional representation, is used to address imbalances.

SPECIAL DISTRICTS

NOT ONLY DOES THE TEXAS Constitution set up the state, county, and city governments; it also sets up some political subdivisions of the state that are collectively known as special districts. The constitution also allows the legislature, counties, and cities to set up additional special districts. Texas has more than 3,000 special districts. Whereas state, county, and city governments are multifunctional, a special district usually performs just one function. Table 17.1 lists some of the types of special districts.

TABLE 17.1 Special Districts in Texas

The Texas Constitution creates some special districts. It also authorizes the legislature, counties, and cities to create some special districts. Following is a list of some types of special districts, with an example of each.

Constitutional Special Districts	Example
Road district	Travis County Road District No. 1
School district	Lubbock Independent School District
Junior college district	North Harris Community College District
Hospital district	Tarrant County Hospital District
Airport authority	Dallas–Fort Worth Airport Authority
Tax appraisal district	Erath County Appraisal District
Conservation and reclamation district	Southeast Texas Agricultural Development District

Statutory Special Districts	Example
Sports facility district	Nueces County Sports Facility District
Crime control and prevention district	Fort Worth Crime Control and Prevention District
Municipal utility district (MUD)	Circle C MUD No. 3
Metropolitan transit authority	Dallas Area Rapid Transit Authority
Soil conservation district	Webb County Soil and Water Conservation District
Waste disposal authority	Gulf Coast Waste Disposal Authority
Municipal power agency	Texas Municipal Power Agency
Groundwater subsidence district	Harris–Galveston Coastal Subsidence District
River authority	Brazos River Authority
Underground water district	High Plains Underground Water Conservation District
Water conservation and improvement district (WCID)	Harris County WCID No. 91
Flood control district	Harris County Flood Control District

Source: Authors; Virginia Marion Perrenod, Special Districts, *Special Purposes: Fringe Government and Urban Problems in the Houston Area* (College Station: Texas A&M Press, 1984).

Water Districts

Growing population pressures and recurrent droughts make water management a hot potato in Texas politics and policy. The constitution authorizes the legislature to create special districts for water management (Article 3, section 52) and for conservation and development of natural resources (Article 16, section 59). The legislature also creates other types of water districts. For instance, in 1999 alone, the legislature created thirteen water districts.[41] The Water Code regulates the creation of groundwater conservation districts and the election of their local boards. In cases where there is no local election to create a district, the Texas Commission on Environmental Quality (TCEQ) can designate a priority groundwater management area and force hearings and elections to create a district.[42] Since 1990, for instance, the TCEQ has designated part of Comal County as a priority area.[43]

School Districts

The most common type of special district is a school district. Texas has 1,040 local school districts, more than any other state in the nation.[44] Elected school trustees are unpaid government officials. They set the policies for the districts, set the district property-tax rate, decide where and when to build new schools, and hire the superintendents to run the schools.

All of Texas is divided among the school districts. Some districts are small—San Vicente Independent School District in Brewster County had twenty students in 2002—while the largest, Houston Independent School District in Harris County, had 210,670 students.[45] Texas has more than 7,600 public elementary and secondary schools, second in the nation to California.[46] The State Board of Education, the commissioner of education, and the Texas Education Agency (TEA) have some jurisdiction over school districts. In 1995, the Texas legislature enacted an entirely new education code, abolishing some state policies and allowing school districts more leeway in deciding policies.

The 1995 act also set out a process for creating home-rule school districts, free from many state requirements and TEA guidance, if local voters so choose. So far, no districts have attempted to convert to home rule. However, the act also authorized the creation of **charter schools,** which are public schools operating under a contract granted by the

charter school
Public school sanctioned by a specific agreement that allows the program to operate outside the usual rules and regulations.

■ In 1983, Dallas area voters approved creation of a new special district, the Dallas Area Rapid Transit Authority (DART). In 1990, DART began construction of a light-rail system and inaugurated it with its first run in 1996.

Photo courtesy: Chuck Pefley/Stock Boston, Inc.

Politics Now

SLOW ROADS, TOLL ROADS, OR NO ROADS

According to studies of traffic congestion in the United States, Austin, Texas, ranks at the top for medium-sized cities. Urban sprawl, fast-growing suburbs, limited public transportation, and roadway construction delays placed Austin in that unenviable position. The methods of dealing with congestion are limited, and many are controversial.[a]

In 2001, the Texas Constitution was amended to create the Texas Mobility Fund, a revolving bond fund to finance transportation projects.[b] In addition, the legislature authorized the creation of Regional Mobility Authorities to construct, operate, and maintain turnpike projects. Travis and Williamson counties created the Central Texas Regional Mobility Authority (CTRMA) in 2002. CTRMA is a special district governed by a seven-member board (three board members are appointed from each of the counties, and the governor appoints the presiding member). Although CTRMA has no taxing authority, it can undertake a myriad of transportation projects, issue bonds, condemn land and take it for public use, and convert roads to toll roads through its expanded authority granted by the Texas legislature in 2003.

CTRMA analysis resulted in a toll-road plan that converts ten existing or planned roads into toll roads. The CTRMA board adopted the plan in early April 2004, after conducting more than fifty community meetings. Despite those efforts, opposition to the plan developed quickly. Many Austin residents believed that the members of CTRMA board were not accountable to the public, that they would have to pay tolls to use existing roads, that additional roads were not being built as a result of this plan, and that they were being taxed twice because roads already being constructed were being converted to toll roads. CTRMA maintained that using tolls allows the leveraging of available funds in the bond market. Faced with a

legislature that is unwilling to increases motor fuel taxes to provide more funds for roads, the Texas Transportation Commission maintained that the only options for congested urban areas are "slow roads, toll roads, or no roads."

On July 12, 2004, the Capitol Area Metropolitan Planning Organization (CAMPO), whose twenty-three members are elected officials from Travis, Williamson, and Hays counties, met to approve CTRMA's toll-road plan. Before a mostly anti–toll-road audience, CAMPO board members ultimately approved most of CTRMA's plan by a 16–7 vote. CAMPO board members who voted for the plan were not enthusiastic, but they believed that the area would lose Texas Mobility Fund money and that the roads would not be completed quickly enough to ease congestion without the tolls. Shortly after the CAMPO vote, People for Efficient Transportation, a political action committee, started a petition drive to recall two Austin city council members who had voted for the toll plan.[c]

Although few Austinites are in favor of continued congestion and transportation woes, they are not convinced that CTRMA has the solution. The events surrounding the creation and adoption of the toll-road plan for Austin illustrate the problems inherent in special districts: they are obscure to most people, and they are easily created by other levels of government that are unable or unwilling to provide services.

aAnthony Downs, "Traffic: Why It's Getting Worse, What Government Can Do," Brookings Institution, Policy Brief, No. 128, January 2004, accessed August 14, 2004,
http://www.brookings.edu/comm/policybriefs/pb128.pdf.

bHouse Research Organization, "Major Issues of the 77th Legislature, Regular Session," *Focus Report* (July 2, 2001), 174–5.

cStephen Scheibal, "Group Signs Up Veteran Petitioner for Recall," *Austin American-Statesman* (August 7, 2004): B1, B5.

state (with the intention of trying different educational methods) rather than under the control of the local school district. By 2002, there were 241 public charter schools with 46,979 students, receiving nearly $276 million in state funds.[47] In the years after 1995, more than a dozen charter schools failed, some were experiencing rapid teacher turnover, and some were operating with no school transportation and no school lunches. As a consequence, in 2001 the legislature limited the number of charter schools and mandated management and financial controls over charter schools.

In 1900, the legislature mandated at-large elections for school districts. Later, it began authorizing at-large-by-place elections, and as early as 1950, it authorized the Dallas Independent School District to elect some trustees from single-member districts.[48] Just as at-large elections in cities have been challenged under the Voting Rights Act, so have at-large elections in school districts. Litigation began in the 1970s, and more than one hundred school districts were sued or threatened with a suit in a twelve-year period in the 1980s and 1990s. By 1997, 135 school districts elected at least some trustees from single-member districts.[49]

On being challenged, some districts entered into negotiated agreements with plaintiffs, and some of those districts approved cumulative voting systems rather than single-member districts. As a result of lawsuits and negotiated settlements, Texas has more governments that use cumulative voting systems than any other state in the nation. By 2004, forty school districts had held elections with cumulative voting.[50] When the legislature redrafted the Education Code in 1995, after an intense House floor fight, it specifically authorized the use of cumulative voting in conjunction with at-large elections, and additional lawsuits since then have been settled using cumulative voting.

For more than three decades, the big policy issue in Texas concerning school districts has been school finance. Texas relies heavily on the local property tax collected by school districts to fund public education, with additional money from the state. As a result of this heavy reliance, in some recent years, Texas led the nation in local property tax increases. After protracted court battles, the legislature adopted a revised school finance system in 1993.

The 1993 school-finance reform *recaptures* and *redistributes* school tax revenues by limiting school district revenues, capping tax rates in districts, and adjusting the state aid formula to guarantee a specified yield per tax effort for districts. The bill capped taxable wealth in a school district. The cap forces richer districts to choose from among five methods to reduce their wealth:

1. Consolidate with a lower-wealth district.

2. Detach some property and transfer it to another district.

3. Send money directly to the state.

4. Pay for the education of some students in another district.

5. Consolidate tax bases with another district.

In the few years since adoption of the system, districts with wealth higher than the maximum allowed have tended to choose options 3 and 4; only in the first year did any district choose to consolidate with another district, consolidate tax bases, or detach property. In 2003–2004, 134 districts had to reduce their wealth by choosing from those options.[51]

In 1997 and 1999, because the budget surpluses were so high, the legislature used them to increase state spending for education and thus to encourage local school districts to lower their property tax rates. Still, after the 1999 session, half the districts planned to raise taxes.[52] By 2004, nearly one-half of Texas's school districts had reached or were near the maximum local property tax rate.

SUMMARY

THIS CHAPTER has examined local governments and politics in Texas.

1. The Roots of Local Government in Texas

Spain and Mexico established what are now known as counties in Texas. The Republic of Texas and the state of Texas carried forward counties in the series of Texas constitutions. The legislatures also created municipalities. The constitution of 1876 was written to include counties and municipalities and eventually included school districts and other special districts.

2. Counties

County governments are both local governments and administrative arms of state government. Their form is spelled out in the constitution. Counties are limited to exercising the authority granted them by the state.

3. Cities

Cities with fewer than 5,000 residents are limited to exercising the authority granted them by the state, while the constitution grants larger cities home-rule authority. Home-rule cities choose their form of government. Texas cities vary in the type of election systems they use, though federal Voting Rights Act lawsuits have forced many cities to adopt single-member districts, with a resulting diversification of city government.

4. Special Districts

The constitution, the legislature, and other local governments have created more than 3,000 special districts in Texas. Special districts perform a single function, providing services in areas as diverse as water conservation, health, and rapid transit. The best-known type of special district is the school district.

KEY TERMS

annexation, p. 625
at-large-by-place, p. 627
charter school, p. 631
city commission, p. 618
commissioners court, p. 613
council–manager, p. 618
county attorney, p. 614
county auditor, p. 615
county clerk, p. 614

SELECTED READINGS

Blodgett, Terrell. *Texas Home Rule Charters*. Austin: Texas Municipal League, 1994.

Brischetto, Robert, and Richard Engstrom. "Cumulative Voting and Latino Representation: Exit Surveys in Fifteen Texas Communities." *Social Science Quarterly* 78 (December 1997): 973–91.

House Research Organization. "Managing Groundwater for Texas's Future Growth." *Focus Report* (March 23, 2000).

Jones, Laurence F., Edward C. Olson, and Delbert A. Taebel. "Change in African American Representation on Texas City Councils: 1980–1993," *Texas Journal of Political Studies* 18 (Spring/Summer 1996): 70.

Olson, Edward C., and Laurence F. Jones. "Change in Hispanic Representation on Texas City Councils Between 1980–1993," *Texas Journal of Political Studies* 18 (Spring/Summer 1996): 53–74.

Perrenod, Virginia Marion. *Special Districts, Special Purposes: Fringe Governments and Urban Problems in the Houston Area*. College Station: Texas A&M Press, 1984.

WEB EXPLORATIONS

To learn more about counties in the United States, go to
http://www.naco.org/
To learn more about Texas counties, go to
http://www.county.org/
To learn more about local prosecutors, go to
www.tdcaa.com/
To learn more about municipal politics and government in Texas and around the nation, go to
http://www.nlc.org
To learn more about governing localities, go to
www.txregionalcouncil.org/

18

The Texas Legislature

REPRESENTATIVE JIM DUNNAM was elected chair of the Democratic Caucus in the Texas House of Representatives at a very inauspicious time.[1] In 2003, for the first time in more than a century, Democrats constituted a minority of House members. Still, Dunnam was able to forge an alliance that included nearly all the Democrats in the Texas House to thwart the intentions of Texas Congressman and U.S. House Majority Leader Tom DeLay, the Texas legislature's Speaker Tom Craddick, and Governor Rick Perry to redraw the district lines during the regular session of the 78th Legislature in order to gain between four and seven Republican seats in Congress.

Realizing that redistricting plans were soon to come to the House floor, Dunnam assembled a core of House Democratic leaders. They discussed legislative maneuvers to keep the measure from coming to the House floor and the alternative of doing nothing and hoping to prevail in a court challenge to the bill under the Voting Rights Act or hoping that the bill would fail in the Senate. The final option was breaking a quorum (the required minimum of two-thirds of the members that must be present to conduct business), a tactic that was last employed in 1979 by twelve Texas senators, known as the "Killer Bees." Slowly, support for the final option grew, reaching more than fifty Democrats, which was the number necessary to prevent a quorum.

The group decided to leave Texas so that they were beyond the jurisdiction of Texas law enforcement officials, who would be ordered to arrest the absent members and return them to the capitol. After conversations with Oklahoma's Democratic governor and attorney general, Dunnam chose Ardmore, Oklahoma.

On May 11, 2003, forty-seven House Democrats boarded two buses, knowing that four additional representatives would join them in Ardmore, ensuring that they would have the fifty-one members necessary to prevent a quorum. For the next four days, the representatives stayed at the Ardmore Holiday Inn, meeting to discuss strategy and issues and holding press conferences to counter press conferences held by Governor Perry and Speaker Craddick, who referred to the Democrats as the "Chicken Ds." In their press conferences, the Democrats targeted Tom DeLay. As Representative Steve Wolens stated, "We will not be accomplice to a partisan, gerrymandered, Washington, D.C., plan." On May 16, when House rules prevented the redistricting bill from being considered during the regular session, the Democrats returned to Austin.

The reaction to the Democrats' walkout was mixed. Republicans vilified the "Ardmore 51" for shirking their duties as legislators, but Democrats praised them as heroes. Indeed, legislative politics may never be the same in Texas. According to political scientist Tucker Gibson, "Texas has been held up as a kind of model of bipartisanship, with legislators organized not on the basis of party lines but on the basis of political philosophy. Now there appears to be this development of partisanship within the legislature. And we haven't had that up to now."

T HE TEXAS LEGISLATURE serves the following functions: to represent the people in government; to legislate, budget, and tax; to perform constituent casework; to oversee the bureaucracy (see chapter 19); to consider **constitutional amendments** (proposed changes) for the Texas and U.S. constitutions; to confirm the governor's appointees; to **redistrict** (redraw election-district boundaries) itself and the U.S. congressional districts in Texas; and to **impeach** (accuse) and remove from office corrupt officials.

There is much to learn about the Texas legislature's structure and procedures, but were we to study the legislature alone, we would not

constitutional amendment
A change, addition, or deletion to a constitution.

redistrict
Redraw election-district boundaries.

impeach
A vote by the House to formally accuse a government official of official wrongdoing.

fully understand its place in the political system. We must also look at external forces that influence its actions—such as elections, lobbyists, governors, and the media.

In this chapter, we will discuss the following:

- . First, we will examine the historical and constitutional *roots of the legislative branch,* focusing on the evolution of the Texas legislature from its roots in Mexico to its contemporary structure.

- Second, we will look at the *state constitution and the legislative branch of government,* indicating how the Texas Constitution affects legislators and how they perform their duties.

- Third, we will focus on *legislative membership: representing the public,* describing the election of legislators and their personal and political characteristics.

- Fourth, we will explore *how the Texas legislature is organized,* including ways in which legislative leadership and legislative opposition organize and operate.

- Fifth, we will study the *law-making and budgeting function of the legislature,* describing the stages of the legislative and budgeting process in the legislature.

- Sixth, we will examine *how legislators make decisions,* focusing on the interactions between legislators and the people who influence their voting decisions.

- Finally, we will look at the relationship between *the legislature and the governor,* indicating how the governor wields influence with legislators.

THE ROOTS OF THE LEGISLATIVE BRANCH

THE PREDECESSORS TO THE TEXAS LEGISLATURE were Mexican legislatures, a series of elected conventions, and the Congress of the Republic of Texas. Mexico won its war of independence from Spain in 1821, and by 1824 it adopted a constitution that provided for a federal republic. The provinces of Tejas and Coahuila were joined together. The State of Coahuila y Tejas drafted a constitution in 1827 and organized a legislature. Texians grew disenchanted with their representation and with Mexican policies, and they convened conventions in 1832, 1833, and 1835 that called for separate statehood and a separate state legislature. Another convention assembled in 1836 and, with a new civil war erupting, declared Texas's independence.[2]

The Constitution of the Republic of Texas provided for a bicameral Congress (two chambers). The first Congress convened in 1836, and each Congress lasted one year. The Republic of Texas had nine congresses.[3] When Texas joined the United States in 1846, the Congress of the Republic dissolved and the 1st Legislature of the State of Texas convened. A legislature sat for a two-year period. The numbering of the legislative sessions was not changed when new constitutions were later adopted. Thus, the first legislature to meet under the current constitution (in 1876) was the 15th Legislature.

In the 1830s, Anglo immigrants from the United States dominated the series of conventions, even though *Tejanos* were in the official government of Coahuila y Tejas. Some *Tejanos* were leaders in the 1830s conventions, most notably Lorenzo de Zavala, who then served as interim vice president of the Republic of Texas.[4] After the Civil War, African Americans were a vital part of the Texas political process. During Reconstruction, African Americans were elected to the Constitutional Convention of 1868 and to the Texas legislature from 1869 to 1874, then in reduced numbers up to the 1890s. The end of Reconstruction brought about the end of representation for African Americans when white supremacists regained power. The Constitutional Convention of 1875 included a small number of African American delegates, and a few African Americans won election to the legislature into the 1890s; 1895 was the last year that an African American served in the legislature until 1967.[5] The nine African American representatives and two African American senators in the 1871–1872 legislature were not surpassed in number until 1977.

Photo courtesy: Bob Daemmrich/Corbis Sygma

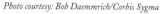 Representative Pete Gallego, surrounded by other members of the "Ardmore 51," thanks the crowd that gathered to welcome them back to Austin.

ROTTEN BOROUGHS IN TEXAS

"ROTTEN BOROUGHS" were parliamentary districts in England that sustained their historical representation in Parliament even though most of the rural residents had long abandoned the countryside for London. A similar phenomenon occurred in American state legislatures, including Texas, in the late nineteenth and early twentieth centuries.

At the turn of the twentieth century, when the rural-dominated Texas legislature was called on to redistrict itself, it faced a dwindling rural population and a burgeoning urban population. Rural legislators did not wish to cede power by transferring seats to the urban areas and, for a while, they had a safety valve for the House. The Texas Constitution of 1876 allowed the House to increase its size, up to a maximum of 150. Rural House members kept their number of seats approximately even, while adding new seats to urban areas. That strategy worked up through 1921, when the House reached its cap of 150 seats. When it came time to redistrict in 1931 and again in 1941, rural legislators simply could not or would not do it, since redistricting meant giving up seats (and incumbent legislators) to urban areas. In 1936, rural legislators even got the constitution amended to place a cap on urban representation.[a]

By not redistricting in 1931, House districts ranged from 52 percent under the ideal equalized size up to 158 percent over the ideal. Population disparities worsened throughout the decade. The 1941 House districts, using the 1921 redistricting scheme, ranged from 55 percent under the ideal to 210 percent over. Once again, those disparities worsened throughout the decade, becoming so extreme that the legislature

was forced to act. In 1947, the legislature proposed a constitutional amendment to establish a Legislative Redistricting Board, with the power to act if the legislature ever again failed to pass a redistricting bill after the U.S. Census. Voters approved the amendment in 1948. The amendment had its intended effect. In 1951, the legislature approved the redistricting bills, rather than let the board redistrict it. Yet, House districts still ranged from 43 percent under to 96 percent over the ideal. In 1961, the legislature redistricted and improved House equality. The new districts ranged from 47 percent under to 66 percent over the ideal.[b] The 1936 amendment, which passed with the support of 59 percent of the voters, had a pronounced effect on representation in the Texas House, as the table for Harris County (which contains the city of Houston) indicates.

This provision "greatly magnified the strength of rural Texas at the expense of urban areas and heavily diluted minority voting power in the state."[c] In the 1960s, it was the U.S. Supreme Court that finally ended rotten boroughs in states by making courts watchdogs over legislative redistricting, to assure equalization. The Texas legislature was compelled to redistrict in 1966 under the new standards and has adhered more closely to equal representation in recent redistrictings. In 2003, it was partisanship, rather than rural/urban legislative gridlock, that triggered action by the Legislative Redistricting Board. Though the board's 2003 plans were heavily criticized for their partisan gerrymandering, they adhere closely to the principle of equally populated districts.

aSee Wesley Chumlea, "The Politics of Legislative Apportionment in Texas 1921–1957," Ph.D. diss., University of Texas, 1959.
bData from James R. Jensen, "Legislative Apportionment in Texas," *Social Studies* 2, University of Houston Public Affairs Research Center, 1964.
cDavid Richards, "So Long, Oscar," *Texas Observer* (November 17, 2000):11.

Year	Texas Population	Ideal House District Population	Harris County Population	Number of Representatives (Number of Representatives if apportioned equally)
1940	6,414,824	42,765	528,961	7(12)
1950	7,711,194	51,407	806,701	8 (15)
1960	9,579,677	63,864	1,243,158	12 (19)

THE STATE CONSTITUTION AND THE LEGISLATIVE BRANCH OF GOVERNMENT

THE **BICAMERAL TEXAS LEGISLATURE** consists of a Senate of thirty-one members, ranking fortieth in size among the states, and a House of Representatives of 150 members, ranking eighth.[6] The 1876 constitution set the size of the Senate but allowed the House to grow to a maximum of 150, which it reached in 1921.

Both the House and the Senate must pass a bill for it to become law. Nonetheless, there are a few differences in the duties of the two chambers. The House has the responsibility of initiating action to raise state revenue. The Senate has the responsibility of confirming the governor's appointees to many state offices. Article 15 of the Texas Constitution allows the House to impeach public officials and the Senate to try and, if convicted, to remove impeached officials from office.[7] Impeachment requires a majority vote in the House, and conviction requires a two-thirds vote in the Senate.

bicameral Texas legislature
The legislature has two bodies, a House of Representatives and a Senate.

Constitutional Provisions Affecting Legislators

The Texas Constitution sets out the length of legislators' terms of office, requirements that a person must meet to serve as a legislator, provisions for legislators' pay, and provisions limiting what a legislator may do in office. These requirements are shown in Table 18.1. It also includes numerous rules governing the legislative process.

Length of Terms.   Representatives are elected for two-year and senators for four-year terms, with no limit on the number of terms they may serve. Senate elections are staggered—fifteen seats are up for election, then two years later, the other sixteen are up for election. In the first election after redistricting, all senators must run because new district boundaries are drawn. Senators then draw lots to see who serves a two-year term and who gets a four-year term, so that membership terms return to a staggered system.

Compensation.   Legislative salaries are established in the constitution at $600 per month for each month of the term of office, or $7,200 per year. Legislators also get a **per diem**, a per day allowance to cover room and board expenses when they are in session. Texas legislators' pay was last raised, by constitutional amendment, in 1974. In 1991, voters amended the constitution to allow the new Ethics Commission to propose a higher salary, subject to approval by the voters. The commission may also propose higher salaries for the speaker and the lieutenant governor. The commission has taken no action under this new authority. The 1991 amendment allows the Ethics Commission to set the per diem rate at an amount no higher than the maximum federal

per diem
Legislators' per day allowance covering room and board expenses while on state business.

TABLE 18.1   Constitutional Requirements Affecting Texas Legislators

	Senate	House
Residency	5 years in Texas, 1 year in district	2 years in Texas, 1 year in district
Minimum age	26 years	21 years
Term of office	4 years	2 years
Citizenship	United States	United States
Voting status	Qualified (registered) voter	Qualified (registered) voter
Salary	$600 per month	$600 per month
Conflict of interest	Must disclose any personal interest in a bill; may not hold any other state office or contract	Must disclose any personal interest in a bill; may not hold any other state office or contract

Source: Texas Constitution, Article 3.

tax deduction for business expenses. The commission adopted the rate of $125 per day for 2003–2004.

Sessions of the Legislature

Texas has a **biennial legislature**—it meets regularly once every two years. Biennial state legislatures were common in the nineteenth and into the twentieth century. Today, forty-four states have annual sessions, and Texas is the only large, urban state that uses biennial sessions.[8] The constitution calls the biennial session of the legislature a **regular session.** In 1960, voters approved an amendment establishing a 140-day limit for regular sessions. The constitution also allows the governor to call **special (called) sessions** of the legislature lasting up to thirty days each.

biennial legislature
A legislative body that meets in regular session only once in a two-year period.

regular session
The biennial 140-day session of the Texas legislature, beginning in January of odd-numbered years.

special (called) session
A legislative session of up to thirty days, called by the governor, during an interim between regular sessions.

LEGISLATIVE MEMBERSHIP: REPRESENTING THE PUBLIC

MEMBERS OF THE TEXAS LEGISLATURE *represent* the public in government. It is the members of the legislature who make the institution work, and thus it is important to examine qualifications and characteristics of the membership and what influences the selection of those particular members.

Variables Affecting Members' Elections

Two election variables are significant in determining who the members of the legislature are. First, members run from districts, so we examine how the lines for those districts are drawn. Second, members may run for reelection to an unlimited number of terms, so we examine the stability or turnover in legislative membership.

single-member district
An election system for legislative bodies in which each legislator runs from and represents a single district, rather than the entire geographic area encompassed by the government.

Redistricting.   Legislators are chosen in **single-member districts,** where each legislator represents a separate, distinct election district.

TEXAS IN COMPARISON
Legislatures in the United States

American state legislatures vary considerably, as allowed in a federal system. While only Nebraska varies from the bicameral norm, states do vary on other legislative attributes.

State	Regular Legislative Sessions	Special Legislative Sessions	Size of the State House of Representatives	Size of the State Senate	Annual Legislative Salaries (2003)	Women As Percentage of the Legislature (2004)
Texas	140 calendar days, biennial	30-day limit, called only by the governor	150 (8th)	31 (40th)	$7,200 (39th)	19.3 (33rd)
California	285 days	no limit, called only by the governor	80 (36th)	40 (19th)	99,000 (1st)	30.0 (5th)
New York	no limit on length	no limit, called by 2/3 of legislators	150 (8th)	62 (2nd)	79,500 (2nd)	21.2 (24th)
Florida	60 calendar days extended by 3/5 vote	20-day limit (extended by a 3/5 vote), called by legislative leaders, both houses, or by petition through Dept. of State, 3/5 members of both chambers	120 (16th)	40 (19th)	27,900 (19th)	25.0 (21st)

Because districts become unequal in population size over time, the U.S. and the Texas constitutions require that the district lines be redrawn every decade to assure citizens equal representation, regardless of where they live.[9] The legislature redistricts in the year after the U.S. Census, so redistricting was done in 2001 following the 2000 Census.

The goal of redistricting is to create districts with equal-sized populations. Based on the 2000 Census of 20.9 million Texans, the ideal Senate district size is 672,639 constituents and the ideal House district size is 139,012 constituents. Reaching that goal of equality is a process laden with political intrigue and hidden traps. Political parties, incumbents running for reelection, courts, the U.S. Department of Justice, and racial and ethnic groups are the primary players in redistricting, and their goals are often at odds. Legislators often *gerrymander* districts (see Table 18.4 on page 654 for a Glossary of Legislative Lingo), drawing the lines to enhance or diminish the power of one group.

In the 1991 redistricting, Democratic incumbents wanted to protect their seats but knew that if they protected themselves too strongly, the courts could reject their plan and write their own plan. That is exactly what happened. The new districts drawn by the courts for 1993 resulted in an increase for Republicans in the Texas Senate and for minorities in both chambers. In 1995, a group of Republican voters sued the state to overturn the House plan. The House negotiated with the plaintiffs and redrew some districts in metropolitan areas, and the U.S. Department of Justice and a federal court panel approved the new plan. The 1990s redistricting

The Living Constitution

The Basis for Representation in the Texas Senate

Article 3, section 25: The State shall be divided into Senatorial Districts of contiguous territory according to the number of qualified electors as nearly as may be, and each district shall be entitled to elect one Senator; and no single county shall be entitled to more than one Senator.

The basis for representation in the Texas Senate has changed over time. The Texas Constitution of the Republic (1876) based representation in the Senate on "free population (free negroes and Indians excepted)" and entitled each district to only one senator. The 1845 Constitution based representation on the "number of qualified electors." No change in the provision occurred until the 1876 Texas Constitution, which retained the "number of qualified electors" as the basis for representation but also limited a county, regardless of its population, to one senator.[a]

During the 1960s, the U.S. Supreme Court and lower federal courts issued several opinions that affected Texas. In *Reynolds* v. *Sims* (1964), the U.S. Supreme Court decided that the equal protection clause of the Fourteenth Amendment to the U.S. Constitution requires that both chambers of a bicameral legislature be apportioned solely on the basis of population. In *Kilgarlin* v. *Martin* (1966), a U.S. federal district court, applying the standards set in *Reynolds* v. *Sims,* declared the 1961 Texas Senate redistricting unconstitutional because it limited a single county to one senator, regardless of the county's population. However, basing representation in the Senate on "qualified voters" rather than the "total population" was not affected by the ruling. As Justice William J. Brennan, writing for the majority in *Burns* v. *Richardson* (1966), noted, "We start with the proposition that the Equal Protection Clause does not require the States to use total population figures derived from the federal census

skirmishes led to increased Republican representation, including Republican majority Senates in 1997, 1999, and 2001.

In 2001, the Democratic House, Republican Senate, and Republican Governor Perry did not reach an accommodation on redistricting during the regular session, so the Legislative Redistricting Board (with four Republicans and one Democrat) approved Senate and House plans

as the standard by which this substantial population equivalency is to be measured."[b] Continuing, Justice Brennan stated, "Neither in *Reynolds* v. *Sims* nor in any other decision has this Court suggested that the States are required to include aliens, transients, short-term or temporary residents, or persons denied the vote for conviction of crime, in the apportionment base by which their legislators are distributed and against which compliance with the Equal Protection Clause is to be measured."[c] Despite the fact that Texas was not required to use the total population as the basis for representation in the Senate, the legislature employed that figure during redistricting in the 1960s and 1970s, primarily because it was more readily available.

The issue was settled in 1981 when Comptroller Bob Bullock asked Attorney General Mark White whether the legislature was required by the Texas Constitution to use "qualified electors" for redistricting. Attorney General White responded that "The section 25 requirement that the state be divided into senatorial districts on the basis of qualified electors is unconstitutional on its face as inconsistent with the federal constitutional standard."[d] General White cited *Kilgarlin* v. *Martin* (1966) as the basis for his assertion. Unless challenged in court and overturned, the attorney general's opinion stands. Nevertheless, the Texas Constitution was not changed until 2001. The section now reads: "The state shall be divided into Senatorial Districts of contiguous territory, and each district shall be entitled to elect one Senator."[e]

Questions

1. If the basis for representation in the Texas Senate were "qualified voters" rather than the "total population," which groups would benefit?
2. Which groups would be disadvantaged? Explain your responses.

---

[a]George D. Braden, *The Constitution of the State of Texas: An Annotated and Comparative Analysis*, vol. 1 (Austin: Texas Legislative Council, 1977), 147.

[b]*Burns* v. *Richardson*, 384 U.S. 73 (1966).

[c]*Burns* v. *Richardson*.

[d]Mark White, Attorney General Opinion, Opinion No. MW-320, May 30, 1981, accessed May 29, 2004, http://www.oag.state.tx.us/opinions/op46white/mw-350.htm.

[e]Texas Constitution, Article 3, section 25, amended November 6, 2001, accessed May 29, 2004, http://www.capitol.state.tx.us/txconst/sections/cn000300-002500.html.

(by 3 to 2 votes) that distinctly favored Republicans. A three-judge federal panel in Tyler approved the board's Senate plan, then approved its House plan with modifications requested by the Department of Justice.

The 2001 legislature also failed to redistrict the congressional lines, leaving that task to the courts. A state district court in Austin established a congressional redistricting plan, but the Texas Supreme Court threw it out. Then the federal judges in Tyler drew their own plan, using as criteria historic district locations, compactness and contiguity of the districts (following city and county boundaries where possible), and protection of incumbents,[10] and in 2002 the U.S. Supreme Court approved the plan. During the regular session of the 78th Legislature, the Republican-controlled legislature tried to redistrict Texas's congressional district, only to have their plans thwarted by Democrats in the House as we described in the chapter's opening vignette. Later, Senate Democrats fled to New Mexico when Lieutenant Governor Dewhurst announced that he would not observe the traditional calendar rule during the second called session. Finally, Senator John Whitmire (D–Houston) broke with his fellow Democrats and returned to Austin, ensuring the existence of a quorum and new congressional districts. The remaining Democratic senators then left New Mexico and returned for the remainder of the third called session.[11]

Reelection Rates and Turnover of Membership.   In the early years of the Texas legislature, more than four-fifths of the legislators served a single term and did not seek reelection.[12] Now, most incumbents seek reelection, and most are successful. The turnover rates for the Texas House were 7 percent in 2000, 23 percent in 2002, and 11 percent in 2004; the turnover rates for the Texas Senate were 6 percent in 1998, 3 percent in 2000, 23 percent in 2002, and 6 percent in 2004. The election after redistricting is often the most volatile; incumbents must run in reconfigured districts, with new voters, and the districts may be drawn in ways to alter party balance in the district. The 2002 turnover rates confirm this volatility.

Today, many legislators make a career of politics. In 2003, the average tenure of incumbents was nearly nine years in the Texas Senate and nearly ten years in the House. Across the United States, frustration, born out of a sense that the system of representation and election is biased in favor of incumbents staying in office, fueled a new political movement for **term limits**. However, Texas does not have the systems of initiative and referendum (see chapter 12)—the methods used to force term limits in most states—and it is unlikely that Texas legislators will approve limits for themselves.[13]

term limits
Restrictions that exist in some states about how long an individual may serve in state and/or local elected offices.

Personal and Political Characteristics of Members

An examination of member characteristics such as party affiliation, ideology, occupation, race, gender, and age can reveal who represents Texans in the legislature and can show whether there are distinctive patterns to that representation. Figures 18.1 and 18.2 present membership characteristics for the past thirty years.

Occupation, Education, and Religion.   In Texas, in 2004, 52 percent of senators and 33 percent of representatives were businesspeople, while 23 percent of senators and 31 percent of representatives were attorneys. Also,

FIGURE 18.1 Texas House Membership, 1975–2005. ■

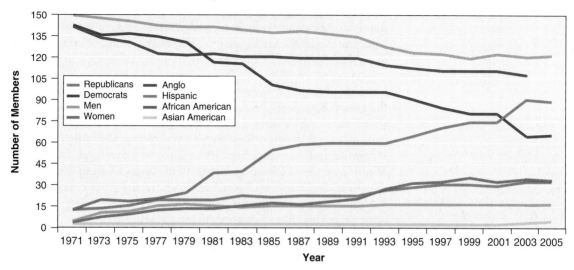

18 percent of House members and 16 percent of senators are professionals, a category that includes many business-related activities.[14] The increasing number of Republicans in both chambers reduces the percentage of attorneys and increases the percentage of professionals and businesspersons.

In 2004, every senator and all but six House members had attended some college, and a majority of legislators had graduate degrees. Understandably, more Texas legislators have law degrees than any other type of graduate degree, with master's degrees second.

FIGURE 18.2 Texas Senate Membership, 1975–2005. ■

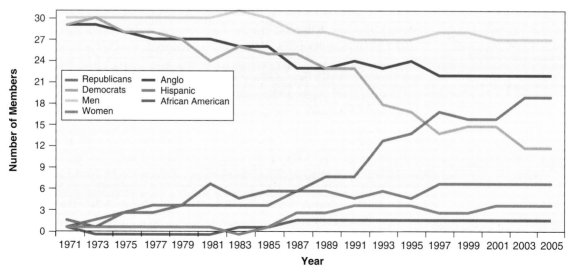

With the diversification of the legislature since the 1970s has come a broadening of the representation of religious denominations. While Baptists traditionally had the highest number of members in the legislature, by the 1990s, Catholics were the largest group, followed by Baptists, Methodists, and Episcopalians.

Gender, Race, and Age.   Historically, most state legislators across the nation have been Anglo males. The recent trend in legislatures is an increase in minorities and women. In the 2005 Texas House membership, of eighty-seven Republicans, eighty-five were Anglo, one was Hispanic, and one was Asian American; of sixty-three Democrats, twenty-nine were Hispanic, nineteen were Anglo, fourteen were African American and one was Asian American. In the Senate, all nineteen Republicans were Anglo. Of Senate Democrats, seven were Hispanic, three were Anglo, and two were African American.

Most Texas legislators are in their forties or fifties in age. House members tend to be young to middle-aged, while senators tend to be middle-aged to older. In 2003, the average House member was fifty-one; the youngest House member was twenty-four, and the oldest was seventy-eight. The average Senate member was fifty-four; the youngest senator was forty, and the oldest was sixty-eight.

Political Party.   Historically, Democrats have won far more seats in the Texas legislature than have Republicans. Republicans only had a legislative majority in 1870, until winning a majority of the Senate in 1996, 1998, 2000, and 2002, and House majorities in 2002 and in 2004. This Democratic dominance in Texas is overwhelming but also reflects that in the twentieth century, Democrats typically controlled about two-thirds of *all* state legislative chambers. Figures18.1 and 18.2 demonstrate the growth of the Republican Party in the Texas legislature.

Ideology.   The four kinds of ideology described in chapter 15 can be useful in analyzing legislative voting patterns in Texas. It is difficult to find analyses of voting patterns that take into account populism and libertarianism. Recall from chapter 15 that we focused on differences in *equality* and *liberty* in our definitions of ideology. For the 2003 session, we identified for each session five votes in the House on equality and five on liberty measures, based on the description of those ideologies we presented in chapter 20, to measure the four-part ideological framework. This analysis reveals an ideologically divided House. Analyzing Visuals: Ideological Voting Patterns in the Texas House of Representatives presents the data for the 2003 regular legislative session. In that session, the House was predominantly conservative in ideology. There were ninety-six conservatives, thirty-three liberals, eleven populists, and eight libertarians.

Liberals, populists, and libertarians were Democrats; with few exceptions, conservatives and libertarians were Republicans. The cen-

Analyzing Visuals

IDEOLOGICAL VOTING PATTERNS IN THE TEXAS HOUSE OF REPRESENTATIVES

The members of the Texas House of Representatives are usually considered conservative in terms of political ideology. The chart depicts the placement of each member of the Texas House based on their roll call votes on ten issues during the 2003 regular legislative session, selected because they either offered a choice between equality and opportunity or between individual liberty and order. After studying the chart, answer the following critical thinking questions: Which ideologies are most common among the members? What is the ideological difference between members of the Democratic Party in the House and members of the Republican Party in the House? Is the difference what you expected based on your understanding of Democrats and Republicans? Explain your answer.

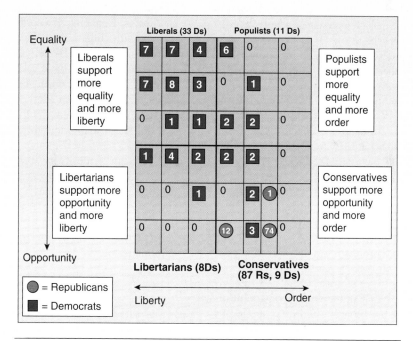

Source and Methodology: An ideological voting pattern was identified from five roll call votes in the 2003 regular session selected on equality/opportunity and five roll call votes selected on liberty/order. *House Journal* record votes 42, 74, 367, 699, and 935 were used to measure legislators' placement on the equality/opportunity axis. Record votes 385, 404, 501, 762, and 801 were used to measure legislators' placement on the liberty/order axis. For instance, on Record Vote 42, an aye vote was a vote for limits on medical liability; it was categorized as a vote for "equality" and against "opportunity." On Record Vote 385, an aye vote was a vote for informed consent before an abortion is performed and a twenty-four-hour waiting period before an abortion may be performed; it was categorized as a vote for "order" and against "liberty." Each legislator was then placed on the thirty-six-point grid based on the thirty-six possible combinations of scores, from 0–0 to 5–5.

On Campus

YOUNG CONSERVATIVES OF TEXAS

The Young Conservatives of Texas (YCT) describes itself as "an independent, non-partisan youth organization dedicated to the preservation of individual liberties and freedoms through limited government." Furthermore, "YCT is an organization that enables college students the opportunity to participate in the political process. YCT believes that there is no better way to educate and train young citizens as to the working of our government than to have them directly involved."[a] Currently, YCT has chapters at eleven Texas colleges and universities.

YCT chapters have engaged in a number of activities on college campuses:

- **Rating members of the Texas legislature.** Since the 1975 legislative session, YCT has published ratings of members of the Texas House and Senate. These ratings, according to the group, have been "utilized by numerous candidates in their races, . . . have exposed candidates and politicians who claim to be conservative but yet vote a different way[,] . . . get widespread publicity and have been very effective."

- **Publishing a professor watch list.** In 2003, the University of Texas at Austin chapter of YCT published a list of professors who, according to the group, "push an ideological viewpoint on their students through oftentimes subtle but sometimes abrasive methods of indoctrination." According to the group, professors on the list are not cited for expressing their opinions: "What is considered is whether the professor respects and strives for intellectual honesty in his or her classroom through presenting a fair and balanced delivery of information that is not

crafted to produce a certain mindset within the receiving student." Among the professors on the list were three government professors. The group's honor roll recognizes professors that "embody intellectually honest classroom or teach a subject we feel is important in higher education but is oftentimes downplayed, shunned or forgotten about by largely liberal campuses."[b] Other chapters of YCT plan similar watch lists for their campuses.

- **Bake sales.** Engaging in a controversial activity to call attention to their opposition to affirmative action, YCTs on several college campuses have held bake sales that involve different prices based on the buyer's ethnicity or gender. At Southern Methodist University (SMU), YCT members charged white males one dollar for a cookie, white women were charged 75 cents, Hispanics paid 50 cents, and African Americans were charged 25 cents. After a complaint by an African American student, SMU officials halted the event, citing the "potentially unsafe situation for students."[c] A similar event at Texas A&M University resulted in no action by the university's administration.[d]

[a]Young Conservatives of Texas Web site, accessed June 5, 2004, http://www.yct.org.

[b]Young Conservatives of Texas, University of Texas Chapter, "Professor Watch List," accessed June 5, 2004, http://studentorgs.utexas.edu/yct/watchlist.html; Sharon Jayson, "Group's Ideology Watch List Singles Out 10 UT Professors," *Austin American-Statesman* (October 31, 2003): B1.

[c]"SMU Bake Sale Offends Some," *Houston Chronicle* (September 26, 2003): A27.

[d]"Bill of Goods: Cookie Sale Was Half-Baked Affirmative Action Protest," *Houston Chronicle* (November 21, 2003): A46.

ter of the House Democratic party is liberal, leaning populist, while the center of the House Republican party is solidly conservative. The Republican center has become overwhelmingly conservative, and contains no liberals, populists, or libertarians; the Democratic center is predominantly liberal but must accommodate members of the other three ideologies.

HOW THE TEXAS LEGISLATURE IS ORGANIZED

CHAPTER 6 HIGHLIGHTS the key role that political parties play in the organization of the U.S. Congress. While parties are present in the Texas legislature, they have not played the dominant role that they do in Congress (though with the recent Republican surge, that appears to be changing). Rather, the institutional leaders and the committees are the key organizational units.

Leaders

The constitution declares that the lieutenant governor shall serve as the **president of the Texas Senate** and that the Senate shall elect a president **pro-tempore** (or **pro-tem**) to serve in the absence of the lieutenant governor. The constitution states that the House of Representatives shall choose its leader, the **speaker of the Texas House,** from among its members. At the beginning of each regular session, the House elects a speaker for the biennium. The speaker appoints a speaker pro-tem.

Committees

The legislature works through a system of committees. A **committee** is a subunit of the legislature appointed to work on designated subjects. Committees help legislators develop subject specialties and, presumably, to then make better-informed public policies. Table 18.2 defines the types of committees. At the beginning of a regular session, the House and Senate create standing committees, and the chairs of those committees appoint ad hoc subcommittees for specific bills.

president of the Texas Senate
The lieutenant governor of Texas, serving in his constitutional role as presiding officer of the Senate.

pro-tempore (pro-tem)
A legislator who serves temporarily as legislative leader in the absence of the Senate president or House speaker.

speaker of the Texas House
The state representative who is elected by his or her fellow representatives to be the official leader of the House.

committee
A subunit of the legislature, appointed to work on designated subjects.

TABLE 18.2   Types of Legislative Committees

Standing Committee
A committee created at the beginning of a legislative biennium, which continues in existence throughout the biennium.

Substantive Committee
A committee that considers legislation as its primary duty; most are standing committees.

Procedural Committee
A committee that has jurisdiction over such things as legislative rules and calendars and administration of the House or Senate.

Special (or Ad Hoc) Committee
A committee created to study a specific problem or policy area; the committee is given a certain amount of time to complete its work, then it goes out of existence.

Interim Committee
A standing committee (or a commission, including some nonlegislative members), charged by the speaker and lieutenant governor to study high-profile issues during the interim between sessions; for instance, the House Select Committee on Child Welfare and Foster Care reported to the legislature in 2005.

Joint Committee
A committee created by both the House and the Senate, with members from both chambers, for a specific duty; examples include the Legislative Budget Board, the Legislative Council, and the Legislative Reference Library Board.

Conference Committee
A joint committee appointed by the House and the Senate for one specific bill passed by both chambers but with different provisions; it writes a common version of the bill and reports back to both chambers.

TABLE 18.3   Legislative Committees of the 79th Legislature, 2005–2006

House Committees (number of members)		Senate Committees (number of members)
Substantive Committees:	Juvenile Justice and Family Issues (9)	*Substantive Committees:*
Agriculture and Livestock (7)	Land and Resource Management (9)	Business and Commerce (9)
Appropriations (29)	Law Enforcement (7)	Subcommittee on Emerging Technologies (5)
Border and International Affairs (7)	Licensing and Administrative Procedures (9)	Criminal Justice (7)
Business and Industry (9)	Local Government Ways and Means (7)	Education (9)
Civil Practices (9)	Natural Resources (9)	Subcommittee on Higher Education (6)
Corrections (7)	Pensions and Investments (7)	Finance (15)
County Affairs (9)	Public Education (9)	Government Organization (7)
Criminal Jurisprudence (9)	Public Health (9)	Health and Human Services (9)
State Culture, Recreation, and Tourism (7)	Regulated Industries (7)	Intergovernmental Relations (5)
Defense Affairs and State-Federal Relations (9)	State Affairs (9)	International Relations and Trade (7)
Economic Development (7)	Transportation (9)	Jurisprudence (7)
Elections (7)	Urban Affairs (7)	Natural Resources (11)
Energy Resources (7)	Ways and Means (9)	Subcommittee on Agriculture (3)
Environmental Regulation (7)	*Procedural Committees:*	State Affairs (9)
Financial Institutions (7)	Calendars (11)	Transportation and Homeland Security (9)
Government Reform (7)	General Investigating and Ethics (5)	Veterans Affair and Military Installations (5)
Higher Education (9)	House Administration (11)	Subcommittee on Base Realignment and Closure (3)
Human Services (9)	Local and Consent Calendars (11)	*Procedural Committees:*
Insurance (9)	Redistricting (15)	Administration (7)
Judiciary (9)	Rules and Resolutions (11)	Nominations (7)

Some Senate committees also have permanent subcommittees. Table 18.3 lists the standing committees and the number of members of each one for the 2003–2004 biennium. House members typically serve on two or three committees. Senators serve on three or four standing committees and subcommittees.

Two of the most significant powers of the speaker and the lieutenant governor are the powers to appoint legislators to committees and to appoint the committee chairs. In the 1970s, the House created a weak seniority system for assignment to substantive committees. Each member selects one committee that he or she wants to serve on, but the speaker does not have to honor every seniority request—a maximum of one-half of a committee's members (excluding the chair and vice chair) may be determined by seniority, with the other half completely within the power of the speaker to name. House committee chairs appoint subcommittee members and chairs; in the Senate, the lieutenant governor appoints chairs of the standing subcommittees.

Organizing for Power and Influence in the Legislature

legislative party caucus
An organization of legislators who are all of the same party, and which is formally allied with a political party.

An organization of legislators who are all affiliated with the same political party is called a **legislative party caucus** (e.g., the House Republican Caucus). In the absence of parties, strong factions and strong leaders rule. There were no party caucuses in Texas until the 1980s. The result is that a strong party system is now antithetical to the system of strong speakers and lieutenant governors that has evolved in its absence.[15] It remains to be seen whether party caucuses will merely coexist in a subservient position with the leadership or will manage to become a new power center.

Leadership and Opposition in the House

In the 1800s, by custom, a House speaker would serve one two-year term. A few served two terms, and one served three nonconsecutive terms. By the middle of the twentieth century, two terms was the norm.

Today, legislators vote publicly on a speaker who is seeking reelection—with the fear of retaliation from a newly reelected speaker and his or her allies against any who opposed them. So, few do. Since the change to open balloting in 1973, we have witnessed the longest speakerships in Texas history. Bill Clayton served four terms (1975–1982). Gib Lewis followed with five terms (1983–1992). Pete Laney (1993–2002) served five terms and sought a sixth term. With Representative Tom Craddick's announcement that he had enough pledges of support to become the new House speaker in 2003, Laney's tenure was ended. Craddick is the first Republican speaker in more than 130 years; it remains to be seen whether the partisan leadership change will also mean a change in the tenure pattern for speakers.

Photo courtesy: Bob Daemmrich/Bob Daemmrich Photography, Inc.

■ Texas legislative committees typically meet in rooms assigned to them in the capitol or the underground capitol extension. Here, the Senate Redistricting Committee meets in May 2001 on the Senate floor.

The Speaker's Race.   The campaign to determine who shall be speaker for the biennium, called the **speaker's race,** is the cornerstone of the legislative process in the House. A representative who wishes to be speaker announces his or her intentions and asks legislators to sign "pledge cards" of support. Victorious candidates raise (typically from lobbyists) and spend huge amounts of money to get the required seventy-six votes. Much of the campaign money is spent to help elect legislators who will be pledged to the speaker candidate; thus, the speaker's campaign becomes a quasi-party organization.

The Texas House speaker's race really never ends; instead, it becomes the center for organizing the leadership team, known as the **speaker's lieutenants** and the **speaker's team,** and wielding influence within the House. A speaker who is running for reelection relies on help from lieutenants in circulating pledge cards and persuading legislators to support him or her. When a speaker retires, the lieutenants vie among themselves for the office. Savvy lieutenants will seek pledge

speaker's race
The campaign to determine who shall be the speaker of the Texas House for a given biennium.

speaker's lieutenants
House members who make up the speaker's team, assisting the speaker in leading the House, either informally, or in a role as a committee chair or other institutional leader.

speaker's team
The leadership team in the House, consisting of the speaker and his or her most trusted allies among the members, most of whom the speaker appoints to chair House committees.

TABLE 18.4	A Glossary of Legislative Lingo

Legislators often use colorful words and phrases in their debates—terms that may be unfamiliar or confusing to casual observers.

Backscratching: Helping another legislator with a vote, with the expectation that he or she will return the favor.

Carrying water: Sponsoring a bill or an amendment at the request of a lobbyist.

Cockroach: A legislator known as an obstructionist, opposing any significant change.

Dog-and-pony show: Lengthy committee hearings, featuring scores of witnesses who tell emotional and personal stories to persuade the legislators to vote a bill out of committee or to kill it.

Gerrymandering: Drawing redistricting lines to help or hurt either an incumbent or a group of voters, such as Democrats, Republicans, Anglos, or Mexican Americans.

Gutting: Amending a bill in such a way that it severely weakens the bill or changes its original purpose.

Keying (or cueing): Watching another legislator to see which way he or she is voting before deciding how to vote. Floor leaders extend an arm with one finger held high to indicate that followers should vote "aye" or with two fingers held high to indicate that followers should vote "nay."

Lite guv: The term lieutenant governor is often abbreviated as "lt. gov." In a verbal takeoff of this abbreviation, the office is humorously abbreviated, in comparison to the governor, of course, as the "lite guv."

Logrolling: Supporting and voting for another member's "local" bill (affecting only the author's district), with the assumption that he or she will then support you when you have a bill coming up.

Pork barrel: Appropriations of money to a project in a single legislative district.

Sine die: Legislators use this Latin phrase to describe the 140th day (the last day) of a regular legislative session.

Taking a walk: Leaving a committee hearing or the floor to avoid voting on a controversial bill if such a vote would hurt the legislator with one group or another.

That dog won't hunt: A debating point suggesting that the legislator does not believe another member's argument.

Photo courtesy: AP/Wide World

■ Representative Tom Craddick at a news conference on November 7, 2002. Craddick won election as House speaker for 2003–2004 and for 2005–2006.

cards for the speaker who is running for reelection and simultaneously for themselves for the future.

House Leadership and the Political Parties. Until 2003, Republicans controlled the House during only one session, in 1870. There have not been party nominees for speaker, and parties have not been the basis of the competition. Personal and factional groupings have dominated the selection process, with the conservative Democratic faction almost always winning. House Democratic leaders often supported bipartisanship and eschewed efforts to create party caucuses. Speaker Laney was more open to party organization, especially after some Republicans organized an effort to defeat him in 1998.

THE RISE OF PARTISANSHIP IN THE TEXAS HOUSE

From the 1870s until 2003, Democrats controlled the Texas House. Conflicts in the Texas House involved the speaker and his team versus those members who opposed the speaker. The factions contained members of both parties. However, by the 78th Legislature, when Republicans gained control of the House, Speaker Tom Craddick appointed a disproportionate percentage of Republican committee chairs. Partisan differences became more evident, leading to the Democrats' breaking the quorum in May 2003 to prevent adoption of a partisan redistricting plan for Texas's congressional districts. A trend emerged earlier in the legislative session when Republicans pushed budget cuts for health and human services and for education.[a] The differences between Republican and Democratic Party members are greatest on government regulation of business, taxing and spending, and social issues (such as abortion and same-sex marriage). The table demonstrates the party unity on selected bills in 2003 that involve these issues. Democratic House members show less cohesiveness than Republicans on nearly all of the votes in the table.

Additional evidence of increased partisanship is the willingness of Democratic Party leaders to campaign actively in primary elections against Democratic incumbents who have been too supportive of the Republican leadership. Eighteen Democratic House incumbents were challenged in the March 2004 primary elections; seven lost their primary contest either in the first primary election or a runoff election who had supported Republican Speaker Tom Craddick and the Republican redistricting effort.

According to political scientists Malcolm Jewell and Marcia Lynn Whicker, "strong party cohesion in the legislature depended on polarization of the state party: the two legislative parties should represent distinctly different types of constituencies with different interests."[b] The number of Republican legislators in Texas is growing, and Democrats are less likely to draw their votes from conservative, rural voters and more likely to draw their votes from lower-income African American and Anglo voters. If this trend continues, bipartisanship in the Texas House will cease to exist, and partisanship will increasingly provide the basis for political power and conflict.

---

[a]Michael King, "The House Adjourns to Oklahoma," *Austin Chronicle* (May 16, 2003), accessed May 18, 2004, http://www.austinchronicle.com/issues/dispatch/2003-05-16/pols_capitol.html.

[b]Malcolm E. Jewell and Marcia Lynn Whicker, *Legislative Leadership in the American States* (Ann Arbor: University of Michigan Press, 1994), 79.

Bill Number	Explanation	Percent Republican Unity	Percent Democratic Unity
HB 1	Amendment to the general appropriations bill to increase funding for CHIP by $250 million.	99	85
HB 15	Informed consent for abortion bill. Required 24-hour wait and pamphlet explaining abortion procedure.	100	74
SB 7	Defense of Marriage Act that prohibits recognition of same-sex marriages and civil unions from other states.	100	34
SB 14	Amendment to prohibit insurers from raising premiums without prior approval from the insurance commissioner.	84	91
SB 285	Amendment that would prohibit the DHS from denying medical care to any person who is eligible for financial assistance, even if the individual refuses to cooperate with the agency.	96	93

Source: Computed from Young Conservatives of Texas, 78th Legislative Ratings, accessed May 15, 2004, http://www.uct.org/yct-2003-ratings.pdf.

The Speaker's Influence over Committees.   Speakers have the ability to stack important committees with legislators from the faction that controls the House. Historically, there were no restraints on the speaker's powers to assign representatives to their committees. Because of the perception that speakers used these assignments to reward their friends (with appointment to the most important committees) and to punish their enemies (with appointment to the least desired committees), reformers in the mid-1970s won a limited seniority system that the speaker must consider in some appointments. Before the reforms, conservatives (reflecting the ideology of the speakers) were substantially overrepresented on key committees. Since the reforms, conservatives have still been overrepresented on those committees, but to a lesser degree.[16]

House Opposition and the Political Parties.   Opposition to the speaker and the speaker's team has not organized along party lines, though that is changing now. Indeed, since the mid-1970s, the Democratic speakers relied on Republicans as a part of their coalition to win office and rewarded them with committee chair positions. In 2003, Speaker Craddick followed that tradition, appointing twenty-nine loyal Republicans and eleven Democrats, who had expressed their support for Craddick shortly after the November elections, as chairs.

Even Republicans long resisted organizing, gaining greater leverage by being part of the conservative leadership coalition. In the early 1980s, Republican Representative Tom Craddick stated, "it's more to [our] benefit for us not to have" a caucus. One Republican said that a caucus would "polarize the members on party rather than on philosophy and issues."[17] A House Republican Caucus was not formally organized until 1989, with Craddick as its chair.

Organizing in the House Through Nonparty Caucuses.   A **nonparty legislative caucus** is a group of legislators organized around some attribute other than party affiliation. In the absence of strong parties, opposition is usually ad hoc, with legislators who oppose the speaker on one issue supporting him or her on others. In some sessions, nonparty caucuses (including county and regional delegations, ad hoc issue groups, racial and ethnic groups, and ideological groups) have served as opposition vehicles.

A caucus called the House Study Group (HSG) formed in 1975 in opposition to Speaker Bill Clayton's team. The result was warfare between the two camps. For twenty years, the speakers' teams tried to eliminate the HSG. While the repeated attempts failed, they did succeed in changing it from an opposition caucus to a staff-research office named the House Research Organization (HRO), which now serves all House members.

In 1985, Republicans and a few conservative Democrats formed the Texas Conservative Coalition (TCC). It helped defeat a health care proposal in 1985, triggering a special session to pass it. By 1993, the TCC

nonparty legislative caucus
An organization of legislators that is based on some attribute other than party affiliation.

was using parliamentary points of order and staff research to effectively promote and oppose legislation. In 1994, moderate and liberal Democrats formed a new caucus, the Legislative Study Group, to counter the influence of the Conservative Coalition. By 2004, the TCC membership included eighty legislators, and the LSG membership included forty-five Texas legislators.

Leadership and Opposition in the Senate

The constitution says that the lieutenant governor shall serve as the president of the Senate (though he or she is not a member of the Senate and may not vote except in the case of a tie vote). In 1999, anticipating George W. Bush's run for the presidency, legislators and voters approved a constitutional amendment requiring the Senate, in the case of a vacancy in the office of lieutenant governor, to elect a lieutenant governor (and Senate president) from among its members until the next general election. When Rick Perry ascended to the governorship and vacated the lieutenant governorship in December 2000, the Senate convened a special session and elected Republican Senator Bill Ratliff as lieutenant governor. He served through 2002 but did not seek reelection. Voters elected Republican David Dewhurst to the office, effective January 2003.

The Role of the Lieutenant Governor.   The lieutenant governor of Texas is one of the most powerful lieutenant governors in the states. Across the nation, twenty-six lieutenant governors preside over their

Photo courtesy: Dallas Morning News

■ State 2002 GOP Convention delegates listen to Republican lieutenant governor nominee David Dewhurst, whose image is projected on a giant screen. Dewhurst defeated Democratic nominee John Sharp in the general election and won a four-year term as lieutenant governor.

senates, twenty-five can vote only in the case of a tie, and seven appoint committees.[18] The Texas lieutenant governor has all those powers and appoints the committee chairs. The senators themselves have written the rules to give the lieutenant governor real power over them—the power to appoint committee chairs, assign members to committees, and refer bills. In the absence of a majority party leader in the Texas Senate, the Senate president is the most powerful force.

Coalition Building in the Senate.   In the small Senate, especially with weak political parties, leadership and opposition are typically organized on an ad hoc basis and are heavily influenced by the personal relationships the senators and the lieutenant governor establish with each other. Lieutenant governors are responsible for guiding legislation through the Senate, and they must appoint allies as key committee chairs, place allies on the important committees, and build a leadership coalition.

Partisanship was never a factor in this coalition building because there were few Republicans, and there was not a Republican lieutenant governor in the twentieth century until Rick Perry in 1999. As Republicans gained in numbers, Lieutenant Governor Bill Hobby included them in his coalition. In 1991, Lieutenant Governor Bob Bullock adopted a more partisan approach, stripping Republicans of their committee chair positions. In 1993, when Republicans for the first time gained more than one-third of the Senate, Bullock reversed himself and appointed Republicans as committee chairs. In 2005, Republican David Dewhurst appointed nine Republicans and six Democrats to chair standing committees. Lieutenant governors know that their legislative powers depend on senators voting them those powers, and that they cannot afford to have a large bloc of senators opposed to them.

As in the House, a conservative faction has typically dominated the Senate. The current manifestation of this leadership faction is a Republican–conservative Democratic combination. Liberal Democrats have typically been the opposition. Unlike in the House, though, the opposition in the Senate has a strong protector—the **Senate two-thirds rule.** As a means of controlling the flow of legislation, the Senate requires every bill to win a vote of two-thirds of the senators before it can be considered. So if an opposition bloc has at least one-third of the senators, the leadership bloc must bargain with it to get the bill passed. This rule makes the leadership-opposition blocs more fluid in the Senate.

Senate two-thirds rule
The rule in the Texas Senate requiring that every bill win a vote of two-thirds of the senators present to suspend the Senate's regular order of business, so that the bill may be considered.

THE LAW-MAKING AND BUDGETING FUNCTION OF THE LEGISLATURE

legislative process
The process the legislature follows in considering and enacting legislation.

THE **LEGISLATIVE PROCESS** is the method that the legislature follows in passing legislation. We look at the different kinds of legislative documents known as bills and resolutions, the significance of legislative rules, the step-by-step process in how a bill becomes a law, and special issues concerning the budgeting process.

What Is a Bill? What Is a Resolution?

When the legislature adopts or amends a state law, it is through a document called a *bill*. Other adoptions by the legislature are called *resolutions*. There are different kinds of resolutions. Thus, anything that the legislature considers will be labeled a bill, a joint resolution, a simple resolution, or a concurrent resolution.

When the legislature wants to create a new law (called a *statute*) or amend an existing one, it must do so by passing a **bill.** The constitution specifies the form that every bill must take. A **joint resolution** either proposes an amendment to the Texas Constitution or ratifies an amendment to the U.S. Constitution. A **simple resolution** goes through only one chamber (such as the resolution to adopt House rules or a resolution commending a citizen). A **concurrent resolution** expresses the will of both chambers, though there is no authority of the force of law behind it.

bill
A proposed law.

joint resolution
A legislative document that either proposes an amendment to the Texas Constitution or ratifies an amendment to the U.S. Constitution.

simple resolution
A legislative document proposing an action that affects only the one chamber in which it is being considered, such as a resolution to adopt House rules or to commend a citizen.

concurrent resolution
A legislative document intended to express the will of both chambers of the legislature, even though it does not possess the authority of law.

Rules, Procedures, and Internal Government

The rules adopted by the House and the Senate embody the constitutional limitations, plus more specific rules needed for smooth working (or for power wielding) in the legislature.[19] The House and Senate also adopt "housekeeping" resolutions setting members' office budgets, employees policies, administrative authority, and the governing of caucuses.

How a Bill Becomes Law

The constitution requires that a bill must be read on three separate days in each chamber of the legislature. It must also pass both chambers in the exact same form. Analyzing Visuals: Basic Steps in the Texas Legislative Process summarizes the basic steps by which a bill is enacted into law in the Texas legislature.

Most committees get more bills referred to them than they can reasonably consider. Even when a legislator requests a hearing, there is no requirement that the chairperson schedule the bill for one. So, when does a committee chair decide to let the committee consider a bill or decide to kill the bill by not setting it on the agenda? Such decisions are usually made privately, with no public discussion, and are influenced by the position (if any) of the speaker of the House or the Senate president, by the lobbying of interest groups, and by the political needs of the chair and the bill's author.

Analyzing Visuals

BASIC STEPS IN THE TEXAS LEGISLATIVE PROCESS

The graphic displays the sequential flow of a bill. After studying the graphic and reading the material on how a bill becomes a law, answer the following critical thinking questions: What differences do you note between the House procedures and the Senate procedures? What is the effect of such requirements as a two-thirds vote for amendments on third reading in both chambers and a two-thirds vote to suspend the rules for a bill to be brought to the floor of the Senate? Do you consider the legislative process too complicated and cumbersome, or do you favor requiring a bill to gain support repeatedly before it becomes law? Explain your answer.

Source: Legislative Budget Board, Texas Legislative Council, *Texas Fact Book, 2000* (January 2000): 10–11. Revised by the authors.

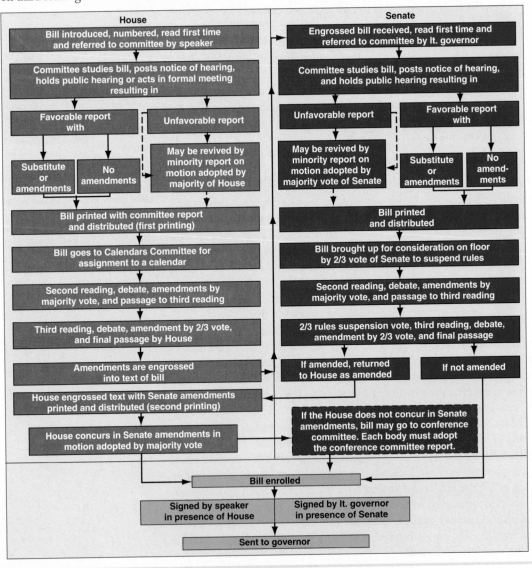

Most bills are considered in *public hearings*, in which citizens may testify for or against the bill, but House committees may consider bills in *formal meetings*, in which testimony is usually not accepted. If the chair or committee refers a bill to a subcommittee, the subcommittee chair decides whether to have a public hearing or a formal meeting. Often, subcommittee meetings are brief huddles at the floor desk of the chair. There is little discussion, and the members often simply ratify decisions made in private meetings of legislators and lobbyists. Action by the subcommittee is in the form of recommendations by majority vote to the full committee, which usually adopts them as drafted.

At this point in the legislative process, the House and the Senate diverge considerably. In both chambers, all bills reported from committee are referred to a procedural committee. Bills in the House go to the Calendars Committee or, if the substantive committee requests it, to the Local and Consent Calendars Committee.[20] In the Senate, bills reported from committee are referred to a procedural committee, but it is an informal process that determines the fate of legislation in the Senate.

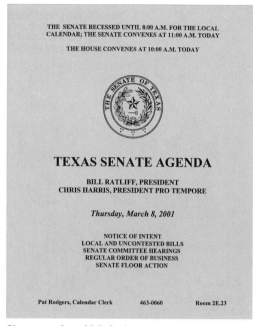

THE SENATE RECESSED UNTIL 8:00 A.M. FOR THE LOCAL CALENDAR; THE SENATE CONVENES AT 11:00 A.M. TODAY

THE HOUSE CONVENES AT 10:00 A.M. TODAY

TEXAS SENATE AGENDA

BILL RATLIFF, PRESIDENT
CHRIS HARRIS, PRESIDENT PRO TEMPORE

Thursday, March 8, 2001

NOTICE OF INTENT
LOCAL AND UNCONTESTED BILLS
SENATE COMMITTEE HEARINGS
REGULAR ORDER OF BUSINESS
SENATE FLOOR ACTION

Pat Rodgers, Calendar Clerk   463-0060   Room 2E.23

Photo courtesy: Senate Media Services

■ The Texas Senate Agenda is a daily publication informing senators and the public of the day's actions. Note that the "Regular Order of Business" is printed each day, but the real daily calendar consists of those bills listed under "Notice of Intent".

The House Calendars Committee.   The Calendars Committee sets the daily calendar for the House.[21] Under 1993 reforms the committee is required to distribute the daily calendar to each representative at least thirty-six hours in advance, and the committee has complied with the rule. Other reforms include requirements of advance public posting of the meetings and opening the meetings to the public and other members. Another reform requires the committee to take a public vote on each bill, within thirty days of receiving it, on whether to place it on a calendar. The committee circumvents this requirement by setting the bills that it wishes to set, then adopting a universal motion to not set all other bills on a calendar. Our review of the committee's minutes since 1993 revealed that the committee went through the formal procedures required to meet the new rules without changing the real decision-making process. The meetings typically lasted one to five minutes, as the members quickly ratified the list of bills brought in by the committee chair. Clearly, the real decision making was done in the behind-the-scenes process.

The Senate Calendaring Function.   The Senate Administration Committee sets a Local and Uncontested Calendar to consider noncontroversial bills, but for significant bills, the process that is used to winnow down the number of bills is a rule requiring a two-thirds vote

"SHOW 'EM WHO'S BOSS," YOU SAID ---- "A SLAP IN TH' MOUTH, THAT'S THE ONLY LANGUAGE THESE KILLER BEES UNDERSTAND," YOU SAID ---- LOOKS LIKE THEY UNDERSTOOD, ALL RIGHT ----

BEN SARGENT ---
©1979 The Austin American-Statesman

Photo courtesy: Ben Sargent, Austin American-Statesman. By permission.
■ The 1979 Texas Senate "Killer Bees" stung the Senate and Lieutenant Governor Bill Hobby, preserving the traditional calendaring system.

intent calendar
The Senate calendar listing bills on which the author or sponsor has given notice of intent to move to suspend the regular order of business in order that the Senate may consider them.

quorum
The minimum number required to conduct business (as in a legislative body).

first reading
The Texas Constitution requires three readings of a bill by the legislature; first reading is when the bill is introduced, its caption is read aloud, and it is referred to committee.

third reading
The Texas Constitution requires three readings of a bill by the legislature; third reading is the final reading in a chamber, unless the bill returns from the other chamber with amendments.

second reading
The Texas Constitution requires three readings of a bill by the legislature; the second reading is when debate and consideration of amendments occur before the whole chamber.

to consider any bill out of its regular order. A senator whose bill has been approved by committee must give written *notice of intent* to move to suspend the regular order of business. This daily listing of notices is called the **intent calendar.**

By tradition, at the beginning of each legislative session, a senator will introduce a frivolous bill with no intention of ever asking for a vote on it in the full Senate. The bottleneck bill is the first bill to be approved by any committee, so it is then placed at the top of the order of business. Thus, *every* bill except that one is always out of order, so long as the author of that bill does not request a vote on it. Thus, before any other bill can be considered, the Senate must first vote to suspend the rule governing the regular order of business. That motion requires a two-thirds vote and must be made for each and every bill, both on second reading and on third reading.

The 1979 Killer Bees incident provides a colorful example of what can happen when that norm is violated.[22] More recently, in 2003, eleven of twelve Democratic Senators fled to Albuquerque, New Mexico, to prevent the consideration of a congressional redistricting bill that would increase the number of Republicans in the U.S. House of Representatives. Like the Ardmore 51 described in the chapter's opening vignette, the Democratic senators hoped to prevent a congressional redistricting bill.

Lieutenant Governor Dewhurst called the two-thirds rule merely a Senate "tradition" that is followed or abandoned at the will of the lieutenant governor. When Senator John Whitmire decided to return to Texas, he ensured an end to the Democratic senators' holdout in New Mexico and the ultimate passage of the Republican-sponsored redistricting bill.[23]

The Bill Reaches the Floor.   At the beginning of each legislative day, the speaker or president calls the members to order and the roll is called to ascertain whether a **quorum,** a required minimum of two-thirds of the members, is on the floor. After housekeeping measures (such as a prayer, announcements, introductions) and **first reading** of bills, the members consider the bills on **third** (final) **reading** (i.e., bills that have already been approved on second reading and require only the usually perfunctory final vote), then bills on **second reading** (when the real debate occurs).

In the Senate, the president recognizes a senator to suspend the regular order of business so that the Senate may consider a bill on second reading. Unlike the House, the Senate has no time limits on debate, creating the **filibuster** as a tactical tool. A senator may hold the floor for an unlimited amount of time and thus can try to kill a bill by refusing to allow a vote on it.

An amendment must be **germane** to the bill—that is, related to the topic. Amendments can drastically alter a bill and thus become powerful tools in the hands of opponents. The consideration of amendments is a critical part of the legislative process for both sides, and a controversial bill has the potential of lengthy debate and twists and turns in tactical victories and defeats.

In the chamber in which the bill originated, when the final vote on a bill on third reading is favorable, the bill is considered to be an **engrossed bill** and is then sent to the other chamber by a staff messenger. It then goes through the referral and committee process and may or may not ever make it to the floor of the second chamber.

Two Bills into One: The Final Stages

The Texas Constitution requires that, in order to become law, a bill must be adopted by both houses in exactly the same form. Many bills are amended in the second chamber, so an additional step is required to meet this requirement. The original chamber could simply vote to *concur* with the amendments placed on the bill by the other chamber,

filibuster
A formal way of halting action on a bill by means of long speeches or unlimited debate in the Senate.

germane
Related to the topic.

engrossed bill
A bill that has been given final approval on third reading in one chamber of the legislature.

Photo courtesy: Alex Labry/Texas House of Representatives

■ House clerks go through a stack of bills ready for first reading. They simply read the bill number, author, and bill caption, then announce the committee to which the speaker refers the bill. That is the extent of a bill's first reading.

Join the Debate

ARE CHARTER SCHOOLS A GOOD ALTERNATIVE FOR TEXAS STUDENTS?

> **OVERVIEW:** The "school choice" movement has suggested several vehicles for opening educational opportunities beyond the traditional public and private school options. In 1995, the Texas legislature approved the establishment of charter schools—public schools given a charter by the state, rather than being part of a local school district. They are paid for with public funds, but they are free from many school-district or state-mandated requirements, with the goal of fostering innovative and successful approaches to education.

After the 1995 legislation, several schools were quickly chartered in Texas, and school choice advocates came back to the legislature for authorization for more schools in the ensuing sessions. Yet, in 2001, in the wake of several Texas charter school closings, the legislature tightened controls and limited the number of new charter schools. By January 2004, 190 state-approved charter schools were educating more than 60,000 Texas children.

Read and think about the following arguments for and against charter schools. Then, join the debate over charter schools by answering the questions posed after the arguments.

Arguments in Favor of Charter Schools

- **Charter schools have more autonomy and flexibility than traditional public schools.** Charter schools have more opportunity for innovative and better instruction and curriculum as well as school organization and governance. Students who remain in charter schools should therefore experience strong academic gains.

- **Charter schools are more accountable than traditional public schools because they must meet the needs of parents and students as well as performance standards established by state agencies.** Charter schools engage in more collaborative efforts, which lead to internal accountability.

- **Autonomy, innovation, and accountability lead to improved student performance and increased parent and teacher satisfaction.** Charter school autonomy, innovation, and accountability should produce higher parental

or it may vote to *not concur* and request a conference committee to adjust the differences between the two versions of the bill.

Conference committees have five House members appointed by the speaker and five senators appointed by the lieutenant governor. If conferees cannot reach a compromise, the bill is dead. If they do reach a compromise, this new version of the bill is presented to each chamber, which must approve it with no further amendments, by majority vote.[24]

Approval of the Final Document. If a bill achieves final approval, it is then an **enrolled bill** and is sent to the governor. The governor may sign the bill into law, ignore it (in which case it goes into effect without his or her signature), or veto it.

enrolled bill
A bill that has been given final approval in both chambers of the legislature and is sent to the governor.

and student satisfaction, higher teacher/employee satisfaction and empowerment, and greater equity in education, including better services for at-risk students.

Arguments Against Charter Schools

- **Charter schools take the more affluent students and those with higher academic skills, leaving public schools bereft of resources, yet responsible for educating the high-risk, high-cost students.** Charter schools will drain resources from public schools, and leave them responsible for educating students with lower academic skills.
- **Charter schools are less accountable than traditional public schools.** Because they are relieved of many of the reports required of public schools, charter schools are less accountable than public schools.
- **Charter school teachers are not as well qualified as public school teachers.** Teachers at charter schools usually do not have as much education as teachers in public schools and are usually paid less than teachers at public schools, so charter schools would not attract the best teachers.

Questions

1. Do you support or oppose charter schools as an alternative for Texas students? Explain your answer.
2. If charter schools and public schools compete for students and resources, how would this competition affect Texas education?

Selected Readings

Matt Moore, "Texas Charter Schools: Do They Measure Up?" National Center for Policy Analysis, Brief Analysis No. 403, June 25, 2002, accessed June 2, 2004, http://www.ncpa.org/pub/ba/ba403/.

Timothy J. Gronberg and Dennis W. Jansen, "Navigating Newly Chartered Waters: An Analysis of Texas Charter School Performance," Texas Public Policy Foundation, April 2001, accessed June 2, 2004, http://www.ncpa.org/pub/ba/ba403/.

Selected Web Sites

http://www.tea.state.tx.us/charter/ Texas Education Agency, Texas Charter Schools.

http://www.charterstexas.org Charter School Resource Center of Texas.

The Budgeting Process

Biennial legislative sessions necessitate biennial budgets. Thirty states prepare annual budgets, while twenty, including Texas, have biennial budgets.[25] The budgeting process is complex, largely because many of the numbers used to create the budget are projections and estimates, and constitutional requirements limit what the legislature can do in Texas.

The Legislative Budget Board (LBB) and the Governor's Budget Office prepare budgets for the legislature to consider. Before a regular session begins, the two offices hold joint hearings for state agencies to present their requests and for the public to comment. In the end, however, each prepares a separate budget proposal to submit to the legislature. For

■ The new Robert E. Johnson State Office Building (named after a former legislator and longtime House parliamentarian) houses legislative support offices and staff, such as the Legislative Budget Board and the Sunset Advisory Commission.

Photo courtesy: Bob Daemmrich/Bob Daemmrich Photography, Inc.

balanced budget
A budget in which the legislature balances expenditures with expected revenues, with no deficit.

deficit spending
Government spending in the current budget cycle that exceeds government revenue.

debt
The total outstanding amount the government owes as a result of borrowing in the past.

budget execution authority
The authority to move money from one program to another program or from one agency to another agency.

instance, for the 2004–2005 biennium, Governor Perry submitted a "zero-based budget," urging lawmakers to scrutinize every program and expenditure during the budgeting process.

In the budgeting process, legislators must adhere to a constitutional requirement for a **balanced budget**—balancing spending with expected revenues (as estimated by the comptroller of public accounts), and thus avoiding deficit spending. **Deficit spending** is spending in the current budget cycle (in Texas's case, the biennium) above and beyond incoming revenue, while **debt** is the total outstanding amount owed from past borrowing. Forty states, including Texas, have a balanced-budget requirement.[26] In 1978, Texas adopted an additional constitutional spending limit. Article 8, section 22, of the constitution now imposes a limit on state spending, calculated by a complex formula. The LBB is to determine the spending limit by estimating the rate of growth of the state's economy. The LBB established the estimated rate of growth of the Texas economy at nearly 12 percent for 2004–2005.[27]

In 1985, voters approved a constitutional amendment (Article 16, section 69) creating **budget execution authority**. During an interim, the governor and the LBB are authorized to move money from one program to another or even from one agency to another. Because the lieutenant governor is the chair and the speaker the vice chair of the LBB (and they appoint the members), this budget execution authority, in essence, allows the governor, lieutenant governor, and speaker the flexibility to handle some budget crises without having to call the legislature into special session.

HOW LEGISLATORS MAKE DECISIONS

IN MAKING DECISIONS on how to vote, legislators interact with executive branch officials, judges, voters, lobbyists, reporters, staff members, party officials, and officials from the federal government and from other states. The legislature is also a social system and must be understood in the context of the norms of behavior and roles that legislators take with each other, from "backscratching" to "logrolling" (see Table 18.4 on legislative lingo).

Staffing for Technical Assistance, Specialized Information, and Political Assistance

Early efforts at increasing legislative information were aimed at establishing state libraries, interim committees to gather information between sessions, and legislative councils. The councils were centralized staffing operations to provide bill drafting, policy research, and program evaluation services.

The Texas legislature created its **Legislative Council** in 1949. It is a joint committee chaired by the lieutenant governor. The council operates only during the interims, though its staff operates year-round. The Legislative Council has ten representatives, five senators, and the lieutenant governor and speaker as members. The council's attorneys and other staff members draft bills, conduct policy studies during the interim between sessions, produce documents such as committee schedules, legislative calendars, and bill-status information, and manage the legislature's computer systems.

Legislative Council
A joint legislative committee (with a large staff) that provides legal advice, bill drafting, copyediting and printing, policy research, and program evaluation services for members of the legislature.

The legislature also established the **Legislative Budget Board (LBB)** in 1949. The LBB has four representatives, four senators, and the lieutenant governor and speaker as members. The LBB's staff analysts prepare the state budget and conduct evaluations of agencies' programs.

Legislative Budget Board (LBB)
A joint legislative committee (with a large staff) that prepares the state budget and conducts evaluations of agencies' programs.

By the 1970s, committees in the Texas legislature were typically served by two or three staff members, hired by the committee chairperson. The expertise and duties of committee staff members vary considerably, with each chair having different priorities. In 2003, new Speaker Craddick abolished the four-year-old House Bill Analysis Office and returned to the committee staff members the job of analyzing bills.

Individual representatives did not have staff members—or offices—until the 1960s. Before then, they used a common pool of secretaries. Now legislators receive a monthly account to pay for office expenses, including staff. A typical representative hires three to five staff members in Austin, plus one or two district staff members. Senators hire about five to ten capitol staff members, plus district staff. The staff provides constituent services (casework), administrative support, and assistance drafting legislation, negotiating with staff and lobbyists, and preparing support materials.

Relations with Lobbyists

A recurring issue in public policy is the proper role of lobbyists and their relationship with legislators. In the 1960s and 1970s, state legislatures passed many "open-government" measures, including stricter requirements for lobbyists to register, so that the public would know who was seeking to influence state government. In 2003, 1,578 lobbyists registered with the Texas Ethics Commission—about nine for every legislator—representing more than 2,000 clients.

Lobbyists legitimately approach the legislature to protect the interests of the members of their group through public-policy changes. In trying to persuade legislators, they provide information that legislators need to evaluate—and thus lobbyists can be an invaluable resource to legislators in their quest for deliberative democracy. That role as an information source also makes lobbyists power players, and they can become protective of their influence with legislators by monopolizing access to legislators. One lobbyist justified his opposition to a stronger legislative staff by saying: "as long as the representative has analysis, he abdicates [decision-making responsibility] and doesn't need to talk to me." Party caucuses and leaders can also present competition for lobbyists. Upon the formation of the Senate Democratic Caucus in 1983, a senator said: "when the party starts taking positions on issues, lobby influence will be diminished."[28]

■ No one likes to pay higher taxes. When legislators consider tax proposals, lobbyists from the businesses that would be taxed are usually strong opponents of the proposals. They are often able to block the tax increases.

Photo courtesy: Sargent © Austin American-Statesman. *Reprinted with permission of Universal Press Syndicate. All rights reserved.*

The Ethics of Lobbying

While most lobbyist–legislator contact happens with complete legitimacy, there are so many questionable contacts and practices that an element of continuity in legislative politics is recurring questions about ethics.[29] Exposure of Frank Sharp's bribery of legislators in 1971 led to the largest wave of Texas government reforms in modern times. Since the Sharpstown scandal, Texas has experienced the federal government's attempt to ensnare corrupt legislators through its "Brilab" sting operation (Speaker Clayton was accused of accepting a bribe but was acquitted in 1980), stories of outlandish spending by lobbyists on the "wining and dining" of legislators, a chicken magnate, Lonnie "Bo" Pilgrim, walking around the Senate floor in 1989 handing out checks to senators after talking with them about his support of Governor Clements's workers' compensation proposals, legislators creating and maintaining for political and personal expenses privately funded "officeholder accounts," and Speaker Lewis's misdemeanor convictions for failure to report all his private financial holdings.

Often, the questionable activities concern the blurring of the line between lobbying activities and election and campaign activities. The same individuals who are the most successful lobbyists (primarily business representatives) are also deeply involved in raising and contributing money for legislative campaigns. Questions recur about whether campaign finances, wining and dining, and officeholder accounts taint public policy and political equality. In the wake of repeated news stories about lobby-paid junkets, stories about legislators paying their mortgages or buying their cars with political funds, demands from public-interest groups for limits on lobbyists' expenditures, and Governor Ann Richards's successful 1990 campaign that capitalized on perceived unethical conduct, the 1991 legislature passed an ethics reform bill. The new law restricted the amount of money that lobbyists can spend, increased their reporting requirements, and established the Texas Ethics Commission.

Photo courtesy: Bob Daemmrich/Stock Boston, Inc.

■ Lobbyists, citizens, and government officials descend on the state capitol during legislative sessions to interact with legislators and influence public policy making. The new underground Capitol Extension Building houses legislators' offices, committee offices, and committee hearing rooms.

THE LEGISLATURE AND THE GOVERNOR

GOVERNORS HAVE LEVERAGE to push their agenda through the give-and-take of legislative politics because they have some things that legislators want—such as an emergency declaration for their bills

■ Governor Rick Perry holds a press conference after signing Senate Bill 1948 in 2003 (the Tulia bill), which allowed fourteen Tulia, Texas residents to be released on bond while they awaited action by the Board of Pardons and Paroles. The defendants were convicted in a drug bust in 1999, but a trial court review discovered that the key witness was not credible and withheld evidence from the defense. Acting on the recommendation of the Board of Pardons and Paroles, Perry pardoned the convicted Tulia residents in August 2003.

Photo courtesy: Bob Daemmrich/Corbis Sygma

(which allows the bills to be heard early in a legislative session), adding their bills to a call for a special session, or signing their bills into law.

Except for unusual circumstances, only the governor may call the legislature into special session.[30] This is a significant power of the governor because he or she may call one at any time for any purpose. The governor must specify what issues the legislature is being called to consider. A special session may last no longer than thirty days. However, there is no limit on how many sessions a governor may call, and indeed they have been called back to back.

Party loyalty is a new factor in gubernatorial-legislative relations. During the long speakership of Gib Lewis (1983–1992), opposition virtually disappeared except when Republicans left the leadership coalition on selected issues. When the legislature was fighting Republican Governor Bill Clements on tax or school-finance issues, Republican legislators would oppose the speaker's bills. It put a strain on Lewis's leadership coalition because seven committee chairs were Republicans.

At the end of the legislative process, the governor may sign the bill into law, **veto** the bill (nullify its passage), or ignore it, in which case it becomes law without his or her signature. In chapter 19, we examine governors' vetoes more closely. If the governor vetoes a bill, the legislature may consider a motion to override the veto, which requires a two-thirds vote. However, most vetoes happen late in the session or after the legislature has adjourned, so there is no chance to attempt an override. Vetoes of regular-session bills may not be overridden by a subsequent special session.

veto
The formal, constitutional authority of the chief executive to reject bills passed by both houses of the legislative body, thus preventing their becoming law without further legislative action.

SUMMARY

THE TEXAS LEGISLATURE performs several functions: representing citizens, making laws, performing casework for constituents, and overseeing the bureaucracy. In this chapter, we described and analyzed:

1. **The Roots of the Legislative Branch**
   The Texas legislature evolved from roots in Mexico and the United States as a bicameral institution that met annually in the Republic of Texas to its current structure.

2. **The State Constitution and the Legislative Branch of Government**
   The Texas Constitution places limits on the legislature by setting the structure of the two chambers, establishing specific rules for the legislative sessions, prescribing the members' qualifications and salary, and limiting the legislature's power.

3. **Legislative Membership: Representing the Public**
   Members of the Texas legislature do not accurately reflect the demographic composition of Texas. Legislators are more likely than the general population to be Anglos, male, lawyers and businesspeople, middle-aged, and well educated. They are also conservative in political ideology. However, the composition of the legislature is changing to include more Hispanics, African Americans, and women.

4. **How the Texas Legislature Is Organized**
   Unlike most states, the Texas legislature does not choose its leaders or create its committees in a partisan fashion. Consequently, conflicts are between the legislative leaders' teams and their opposition rather than between political parties. Nonparty caucuses are also influential in the Texas legislature.

5. **The Law-making and Budgeting Function of the Legislature**
   The Texas legislature makes laws and establishes the state budget during each biennial session. The legislative process involves several stages, all of which provide an opportunity to halt or modify legislative proposals.

6. **How Legislators Make Decisions**
   Texas legislators are influenced by several sets of political actors, including staff members, lobbyists, and members of the executive branch.

7. **The Legislature and the Governor**
   The powers of the Texas governor include legislative powers and dictate that the governor and the legislature interact frequently and regularly during legislative sessions.

KEY TERMS

balanced budget, p. 666
bicameral Texas legislature, p. 641
biennial legislature, p. 642
bill, p. 659
budget execution authority, p. 666
committee, p. 651
concurrent resolution, p. 659
constitutional amendment, p. 637
debt, p. 666
deficit spending, p. 666
engrossed bill, p. 663
enrolled bill, p. 664
filibuster, p. 663
first reading, p. 662
germane, p. 663
impeach, p. 637
intent calendar, p. 662
joint resolution, p. 659
Legislative Budget Board (LBB), p. 667
Legislative Council, p. 667
legislative party caucus, p. 652
legislative process, p. 658
nonparty legislative caucus, p. 656
per diem, p. 641
president of the Texas Senate, p. 651
pro-tempore (pro-tem), p. 651
quorum, p. 662
redistrict, p. 637
regular session, p. 642

second reading, p. 662
Senate two-thirds rule, p. 658
simple resolution, p. 659
single-member district, p. 642
speaker of the Texas House, p. 651
speaker's lieutenants, p. 653
speaker's race, p. 653
speaker's team, p. 653
special (called) session, p. 642
term limits, p. 646
third reading, p. 662
veto, p. 670

SELECTED READINGS

Brewer, J. Mason. *Negro Legislators of Texas,* 2nd ed. Austin: Jenkins, 1970 (1st ed., 1935).

Ivins, Molly. *Molly Ivins Can't Say That, Can She?* New York: Random House, 1991.

Moncrief, Gary F., Peverill Squire, and Malcolm E. Jewell, *Who Runs for the Legislature?* Upper Saddle River, NJ: Prentice Hall, 2001.

Monmonier, Mark. *Bushmanders and Bullwinkles: How Politicians Manipulate Electronic Map and Census Data to Win Elections.* Chicago: University of Chicago Press, 2001.

Pittman, H. C. *Inside the Third House: A Veteran Lobbyist Takes a 50-Year Frolic Through Texas Politics.* Austin: Eakin Press, 1992.

Vega, Arturo. "Gender and Ethnicity Effects on the Legislative Behavior and Substantive Representation of the Texas Legislature," *Texas Journal of Political Studies* 19(2) (1997): 1–21.

WEB EXPLORATIONS

To learn more about the National Conference of State Legislatures, go to
http://www.ncsl.org
To learn more about the Texas legislature, go to
http://www.capitol.state.tx.us
To learn more about the House Research Organization, go to http://www.capitol.state.tx.us/hrofr.htm
To learn more about the Texas Conservative Coalition, go to http://www.txcc.org
To learn more about the Texas Legislative Council and Redistricting, go to http://www.tlc.state.tx.us

The Governor and Bureaucracy in Texas

"I CANNOT REMEMBER FEELING SO ANGRY. I cannot remember feeling so insulted," claimed State Senator Judith Zaffirini after Governor Rick Perry's record-breaking seventy-eight vetoes on a single day.[1] Two weeks after the 2001 legislative session had adjourned, on a Father's Day Sunday just before the deadline for signing or vetoing bills, Perry vetoed seventy-eight bills, for a total of eighty-two vetoes, a new record for one session.[2] Perry's vetoes quickly became known as the "Father's Day Massacre."

While gubernatorial vetoes are a long-standing tradition in the American states as a policy and political tool, vetoes come with a price. A governor has to hope that those who benefit from the vetoes will outnumber those who object to them. Governor Perry's seventy-eight Father's Day vetoes came with the price of alienating legislators, interest groups, and the media.

For example, Senator Zaffirini and others who worked long and hard on Medicaid issues during the legislative session could not understand how the governor could veto a bill that would allow the state to gain $417 million in federal funds over five years. And, the Texas Medical Association (TMA), always a staunch supporter of conservatives and Republicans such as Governor Perry, had already endorsed Perry for reelection. Yet, his veto of the TMA's legislative centerpiece prompted one prominent member to decline an appointment from Governor Perry to the Texas Board of Health and then triggered a withdrawal of the election

673

endorsement and a TMA endorsement of Democrat Tony Sanchez for governor.

The media's reaction included a *Dallas Morning News* objection to Perry's veto of a bill to ban execution of mentally retarded criminals. The newspaper entitled its editorial "Perry's Mistake" and wrote that "It is deeply disappointing that Gov. Perry vetoed a bill that would have provided justice for families of the victims while allowing Texans to show they are civilized."[3] Perry's veto ended up being wasted, as the U.S. Supreme Court declared such executions unconstitutional in 2002.

Texas Monthly's Paul Burka was particularly caustic in his assessment of the Father's Day Massacre. He argued that "the vetoes were Perry's first indication of the kind of governor he intends to be. And the news is not good: one whose notion of leadership is negative rather than positive, 'you can't' rather than 'we can.'. . . He chose to be an outsider, chose to play gotcha with the Legislature rather than to work with it, chose to snipe from ambush rather than engage in the open. . . . The staff churned out its objections to bills, and there was nobody with the experience or wisdom to see the big picture—including Perry himself."[4]

plural executive
An executive branch in which power and policy implementation are divided among several executive agencies rather than centralized under one person; the governor does not get to appoint most agency heads.

THE TOP POLITICAL LEADER and top official of the executive branch of Texas state government is the governor. However, power and policy implementation are not centralized in the Texas governor's office; rather, Texas has a **plural executive**, with power divided among several independently elected officials, appointed officials, and more than one hundred executive boards and commissions. The governor has little direct power over state agencies. Because Texas governors are not assured of control of state government, they must build strong outside support. That could consist of support from the economic powers, popular support among the voters, or both. In this chapter, we will explore the governorship and the executive branch, or bureaucracy, in Texas:

- First, we will examine the *roots of the executive in Texas*, indicating how the Texas governorship and division of executive authority developed.
- Second, we will describe the *constitutional roles of the governor*, emphasizing the roles of chief of state, chief executive, and commander in chief.

- Third, we will look at the *development of gubernatorial power*, comparing the powers of the Texas governor with those of other state governors and describing the powers of the Texas governor in political roles.

- Fourth, we will assess the *governor as policy maker and political leader*, describing how Texas governors use personal and political skills to achieve their policy goals.

- Fifth, we will explore the *plural executive in Texas*, describing the elected officials that make up the plural executive and their duties.

- Sixth, we will look at the structure of the *modern Texas bureaucracy*, examining the organization and operation of Texas's executive boards and commissions.

- Finally, we will discuss *making agencies accountable*, describing the methods that the legislature and executive use to ensure bureaucratic accountability.

*Photo courtesy: Brad Loper/*Dallas Morning News

■ Governor Rick Perry addresses the 2002 state Republican convention.

THE ROOTS OF THE EXECUTIVE IN TEXAS

IN 1691, THE SPANISH KING DESIGNATED the first *Governador de Tejas*—Don Domingo Teran de los Rios—who, in addition to governing, drove cattle from interior Mexico and established the first herds in Texas.[5] After the Mexican Revolution against Spain, the Mexican Constitution of 1824 and the 1827 Constitution of the State of Coahuila y Tejas established a governor and an executive council and gave the governor the power to rule by decree.

From President of the Lone Star Republic to Governor of Texas

After the Texas Revolution against Mexico, from 1836 to 1845, under the Republic of Texas, the chief executive was the president, who ruled with a Cabinet (top officials appointed by and responsible to the chief executive). When Texas joined the United States in 1845, it was with a relatively powerful governor. The governor, who was elected to a two-year term of office, appointed almost all state officials, including judges. By 1850, the constitution was amended to provide for the direct election of judges, the attorney general,

Photo courtesy: © CORBIS

■ Sam Houston served as commander in chief of the Texas armies during the Texas Revolution. He then served as the first president of the Lone Star Republic. When Texas joined the United States, he served as U.S. senator from Texas. Finally, he served as governor of Texas.

comptroller, treasurer, and land commissioner. The state's Confederate constitution of 1861 was similar to the 1845 one in terms of the governor's powers.[6]

The 1866 constitution included a four-year term of office for the governor, with a limit of two consecutive terms, and gubernatorial (meaning of or by the governor) appointment of all officials but the comptroller and the treasurer. A new power for the governor was the line-item veto, which had been used in the Confederacy. The 1869 constitution retained a four-year term and allowed the governor to appoint local officials and state police and impose martial law. However, as one scholar of the Texas governorship wrote, "more disintegration of the executive power than ever was effected." The lieutenant governor, comptroller, treasurer, land commissioner, and public-instruction superintendent were all elected to four-year terms.[7]

The 1876 constitution further decentralized and limited state government, as we note in chapter 16. The governor's term was reduced to two years and the salary was reduced from $5,000 to $4,000. While Texans have amended this constitution many times since its adoption, the basic structure of executive power remains the same: a weak governor, who must share power both with others in the executive branch and with a strong legislature. Texas has had thirty-one governors under this constitution (see Table 19.1).

Terms of Office

The constitution sets the length of the term of office for the governorship, methods for removing a governor from office, and the line of succession in the event of a vacancy in the office. The constitution originally set the governor's salary, though the legislature now does so.

Length and Number of Terms.   The length of the term of office for the governor is four years. It was established as a two-year term in the original 1876 constitution and remained two years until it was amended, effective with the 1974 election.[8] Twelve states, including Texas, have no limit on the number of terms of office their governors may serve.[9]

Until the 1940s, no Texas governor served more than two terms (see Table 19.1). Then, from the 1940s to the 1970s, a three-term tradition (six years) was maintained. Ann Richards served a single four-

TABLE 19.1 Texas Governors, 1876–2004

Number	Governor	Party	Terms	Years Served	Birthdate	Age	Left Office By	Occupation
1	Richard Coke	D	1	2+ (1874–1876)	3-13-1829	43	resigned	lawyer/farmer
2	Richard B. Hubbard	D	1+	3+ (1876–1879)	11-1-1832	44	defeated	lawyer
3	Oran M. Roberts	D	2	4 (1879–1883)	7-9-1815	63	retired	lawyer/educator
4	John Ireland	D	2	4 (1883–1887)	1-1-1827	56	retired	lawyer
5	Lawrence Sul Ross	D	2	4 (1887–1891)	9-27-1838	48	retired	farmer/soldier
6	James S. Hogg	D	2	4 (1891–1895)	3-24-1851	39	retired	lawyer/editor
7	Charles A. Culberson	D	2	4 (1895–1899)	6-10-1855	39	retired	lawyer
8	Joseph D. Sayers	D	2	4 (1899–1903)	9-23-1846	57	retired	lawyer
9	Samuel Lanham	D	2	4 (1903–1907)	7-4-1846	56	retired	lawyer
10	Thomas M. Campbell	D	2	4 (1907–1911)	4-22-1856	50	retired	lawyer/railroad exec.
11	Oscar B. Colquitt	D	2	4 (1911–1915)	12-16-1861	49	retired	lawyer/editor
12	James E. Ferguson	D	1+	2+ (1915–1917)	8-31-1871	43	impeached	banker/lawyer/farmer
13	William P. Hobby	D	1+	2 (1917–1921)	3-26-1878	39	retired	editor
14	Pat M. Neff	D	2	4 (1921–1925)	11-26-1871	49	retired	lawyer/educator
15	Miriam A. Ferguson	D	1	2 (1925–1927)	6-13-1875	49	defeated	housewife
16	Dan Moody	D	2	4 (1927–1931)	6-1-1893	33	retired	lawyer
17	Ross Sterling	D	1	2 (1931–1933)	2-11-1875	55	defeated	president of Mobil Oil
	Miriam A. Ferguson[a]	D	1	2 (1933–1935)	6-13-1875	57	retired	housewife
18	James V. Allred	D	2	4 (1935–1939)	3-2-1899	35	retired	lawyer
19	W. Lee O'Daniel	D	1+	2+ (1939–1941)	3-11-1890	48	resigned	businessperson/ salesperson
20	Coke Stevenson	D	2+	5+ (1941–1947)	3-20-1888	53	retired	lawyer/banker/rancher
21	Beauford Jester	D	1+	2+ (1947–1949)	1-12-1893	54	died	lawyer
22	Allan Shivers	D	3+	7+ (1949–1957)	10-5-1907	41	retired	lawyer
23	Price Daniel	D	3	6 (1957–1963)	10-10-1910	46	defeated	lawyer/educator/rancher
24	John Connally	D	3	6 (1963–1969)	2-27-1917	45	retired	lawyer/rancher
25	Preston Smith	D	2	4 (1969–1973)	3-8-1912	56	defeated	businessperson
26	Dolph Briscoe	D	2[b]	6 (1973–1979)	4-23-1923	49	defeated	rancher/banker
27	Bill Clements	R	2[c]	4 (1979–1983)	4-13-1917	61	defeated	oilman
28	Mark White	D	1[c]	4 (1983–1987)	3-17-1940	42	defeated	lawyer
	Bill Clements[a]	R	1[c]	4 (1987–1991)	4-13-1917	69	retired	oilman
29	Ann Richards	D	1[c]	4 (1991–1995)	9-1-1933	57	defeated	teacher/campaigner
30	George W. Bush	R	1+[c]	6 (1995–2000)	7-6-1946	48	resigned	oilman/businessperson
31	Rick Perry	R	1+[c]	(2000–?)	3-4-1950	50	—	farmer

[a]Miriam Ferguson and Bill Clements served nonconsecutive terms as governor.
[b]Briscoe served one two-year term and one four-year term.
[c]Served four-year terms.

Sources: Authors; Garland Adair, *Texas Pictorial Handbook* (Austin: Texas Memorial Museum, 1957); William Atkinson, *James V. Allred: A Political Biography* (Ph.D. diss., TCU, 1978); Biographical Files—Governors of Texas (Austin: Center for American History, University of Texas); Robert A. Calvert and Arnoldo DeLeon, *The History of Texas* (Arlington Heights, IL: Harlan Davidson, 1990); Council of State Governments, *The Governors of the States, Commonwealths, and Territories 1900–1980* (Lexington, KY: Council of State Governments, 1981); *Dallas Morning News* (March 7, 1991); Fred Gantt Jr., *The Chief Executive in Texas: A Study in Gubernatorial Leadership* (Austin: University of Texas Press, 1964), appendix 3; Ross Phares, *Governors of Texas* (Gretna, LA: Pelican, 1976); *Texas Almanac* (Dallas: A. H. Belo Corp., 1992); Marquis Who's Who, *Who's Who in the South and Southwest,* 16th ed., 1978–1979, and 18th ed., 1982–1983 (Chicago: Marquis Who's Who).

year term, then, in 1994, lost her race for reelection. George W. Bush beat her and then won reelection in 1998. He is the first governor to win back-to-back four-year terms, though he did not serve out his second term, as he resigned to become president.

Salary.   In all of Texas's constitutions until 1954, the governor's salary was set in the constitution. Voters repeatedly defeated salary increases before a $12,000 salary was approved in 1935. In 1953, the constitution was amended to allow the legislature to set the governor's salary. It quickly became one of the highest governor's salaries in the nation. The salary level stagnated in the 1990s, and the comparative ranking slipped. In 2003, the governor was paid $115,345, which ranked fifteenth in the nation; the highest governor's salary was New York's, at $179,000.[10] In 2005, the Texas governor's salary was still $115,345.

Impeachment.   Texas executive officials, like federal officials, are subject to impeachment by the legislative branch. One Texas governor has been impeached, convicted, and removed from office. In 1917, Jim Ferguson angered legislators and University of Texas (UT) alumni by vetoing UT appropriations. Legislators resurrected old allegations that he had misused public money, impeached him, and convicted him. He was removed from office and barred from holding office again. Later, his wife Miriam successfully ran for governor under the slogan "Two Governors for the Price of One."

succession
The constitutional declaration that the lieutenant governor succeeds to the governorship if there is a vacancy.

Succession.   Article 4, section 17, of the constitution provides for **succession.** The lieutenant governor succeeds to the governorship if there is a vacancy. Since 1876, five lieutenant governors have succeeded to the governorship. In 2000, George W. Bush was elected president; he then resigned his governorship in midterm, and Lieutenant Governor Rick Perry became governor. Perry served out Bush's term and then successfully ran for a term of his own in 2002 (see chapter 21). Should he seek and win reelection in 2006, he would become the longest-serving Texas governor.

THE CONSTITUTIONAL ROLES OF THE GOVERNOR

chief of state
The governor in his or her role as the official head representing the state of Texas in its relationships with the national government, other states, and foreign dignitaries.

chief executive officer
The governor, as the top official of the executive branch of Texas state government.

commander in chief
The governor in his or her role as head of the state militia.

THE ROLES THAT THE GOVERNOR PLAYS are set by constitutional and legislative mandates and by custom. Some of these roles encompass real powers and functions of the governorship, while others appear to be little more than ceremonial.

The Texas Constitution designates the governor as the **chief of state, chief executive officer,** and **commander in chief** of Texas. The fragmented organization of executive power, however, makes the position of chief executive officer one that depends largely on the political and personal skills of the governor.

The governor plays other roles that are alluded to in the constitution but not spelled out specifically. Article 4, section 9, requires the governor to "present estimates of the amount of money required to be raised by taxation for all purposes." In 1931, the legislature institutionalized this role

■ Governor Rick Perry addresses a joint session of the Texas Legislature in 2001, in the House chambers.

by designating the governor as the state's **chief budget officer**. Because of the governor's limited constitutional powers over judicial vacancies (Article 5, section 28) and pardons, parole, and clemency (Article 4, section 11), he or she has a limited role in law enforcement. The original 1876 constitution gave the governor almost absolute power in **clemency,** the power to reduce prison terms. The legislature created a Board of Pardons and Paroles in 1929, thus reducing the governor's powers, as well as the pressure on governors.[11] Article 4, section 11, gives the governor the power to grant reprieves and commutations of punishment and pardons "on the written signed recommendation and advice of the Board of Pardons and Paroles." The governor has also become a powerful figure in legislative politics. Article 4 of the constitution gives the governor the authority to call the legislature into special sessions, set the agenda for those sessions, deliver **governor's messages** to the legislature, veto acts of the legislature, and sign bills and resolutions. These constitutional powers, plus the ability to *threaten* to veto bills (and thus gain a seat in negotiations over bills), make the governor an ever-present force in legislative affairs.

chief budget officer
The governor, who is charged with preparing the state budget proposal for the legislature.

clemency
The governor's authority to reduce the length of a person's prison sentence.

governor's message
Message that the governor delivers to the legislature, pronouncing policy goals, budget priorities, and authorizations for the legislature to act.

THE DEVELOPMENT OF GUBERNATORIAL POWER

HOW MUCH POWER and what kinds of power a governor has depend on constitutional provisions, the era and political times in which a governor serves, and the relative power of other governmental officials.

Regardless of how these factors have changed, Texas governors have always been weaker than governors in most other states.

Restriction of Governors' Powers

Nationwide, distrust of government and governors in the eighteenth and nineteenth centuries led to restrictions on the power that governors could wield and on their terms of office. Gradually, throughout the twentieth century, states lifted many of the gubernatorial restrictions and empowered their governors. At the start of the twenty-first century, most governors possess significant powers.

Texas was a practitioner of restrictions on gubernatorial power, especially in reaction to the strong government set up during Reconstruction. Under the 1869 constitution, the governor had complete control over voter registration, the militia, and the state police, and could appoint the governing bodies of towns and cities. In 1872, voters rebelled and elected an anti-administration legislature, which triggered adoption of a new constitution. The desire to punish Davis and to prohibit future governors from becoming powerful led constitutional convention delegates in 1875 to adopt provisions that reduced the governor's salary, elected a plethora of other officers independent from the governor, and restricted the governor's appointment and removal powers.[12]

Comparing the Texas Governor with Other Governors

Today, a comparison of the fifty governors around the United States reveals substantial differences among them. Whereas forty-one states have some kind of Cabinet system in which the major agency directors are selected by and responsible to the governor, Texas does not.[13] Rather, Texas has a plural executive: most agency directors are appointed by boards, rather than directly by the governor; some agency directors are elected; there is no systematic, ongoing process for the governor to coordinate executive policies; and it is virtually impossible for the governor to fire a board member or an agency head.

On political scientist Joseph Schlesinger's 1960–1961 scale, the Texas governor tied for the weakest of the forty-eight governors when the variables of tenure, appointments, budget, and signing and vetoing bills were combined (see Table 19.2). When he updated his scale using 1968–1969 data, Texas ranked fiftieth, leading Schlesinger to comment that "Texas is the only populous state where the governor's formal strength is low."[14] Political scientist Thad Beyle has updated the rankings numerous times since then; in his rankings, Texas always ranked forty-eighth or forty-ninth, until he changed the variables in 1999 (Texas ranked twenty-eighth).[15]

TEXAS IN COMPARISON
Governors and the Executive Branch

State governments grew considerably throughout the twentieth century, and most of the growth was in the executive branches. States vary considerably, though, in the attributes and powers of the chief executive—the governor—and in the relative size of the executive agencies under the governor.

State	Governor's Salary, 2003	Frequency of Meetings of Governor's Cabinet	Governors Who Became President of the United States	Maximum Number of Terms Allowed	Joint Election of Governor/ Lieutenant Governor	Number of Full-time Equivalent (FTE) State Employees (2002)	Number of State Employees per 10,000 Population
Texas	$115,345 (15th)	(no Cabinet)	George W. Bush	unlimited	no	269,674 (2nd)	124
California	175,000 (2nd)	Every 2 weeks	Ronald Reagan	2	no	378,362 (1st)	108
New York	179,000 (1st)	Governor's discretion	Martin Van Buren Grover Cleveland Theodore Roosevelt Franklin D. Roosevelt	unlimited	yes	252,512 (3rd)	132
Florida	120,121 (12th)	Every 2 weeks	none	2	yes	184,793 (4th)	111

Constitutionally, it is apparent that the Texas governor is weak. Governors may be able to amass and exercise more strength, though, in the political arena, where appearance, charisma, and bluff may count more than constitutional reality. In 1994 and 1999, Beyle compared "personal power" of the governors. Texas's governor ranked significantly higher on personal power than on the institutional powers rankings. Further, the legislature and the voters have strengthened the Texas governorship in recent years. Today, the governor can appoint more high-level positions than ever before, and he or she has (limited) budget execution authority. Also, a 1980 amendment (Article 15, section 9) allows the governor, for the first time under the current constitution, to remove from office gubernatorial appointees—but only with a two-thirds vote of the Senate, and only his or her own appointees, not previous governors' appointees. No governor has yet used this power.

The Governor's Power to Appoint Executive Officials

The governor appoints more *agency heads* today than ever before (see Table 19.3). Recent additions to the governor's appointment powers include education commissioner, health and human services commissioner, and transportation director. However, most appointments are to *boards, commissions,* and *advisory panels.* The governor makes several hundred appointments a year.[16]

TABLE 19.2	Powers of the Texas Governor Compared to Other Governors			

Four snapshots of governors in the United States show that Texas governors have long been weaker than governors in other states.

	Number of Points (and Comparative Rank)			
Characteristics	*1960–1961*	*1968–1969*	*1990*	*2002*
Tenure	2 (33rd)	2 (41st)	5 (1st)	5 (1st)
Appointments	1 (38th)	1 (41st)	2 (46th)	1.5 (46th)
Budget	1 (41st)	1 (45th)	1 (50th)	2 (49th)
Veto	3 (14th)	3 (41st)	5 (1st)	5 (1st)
Budget changing			1[a]	
Legislative strength			2 (33rd)	
Separately elected officials				1 (41st)
Gubernatorial party control				4 (3rd)
Combined	7 (48th)	7 (50th)	16 (49th)	18.5 (38th)

[a]For 1990, Beyle added a new category comparing the governor's power with respect to legislative budget-changing power. He found only four states where the governor had any significant power over the legislature, and forty-three states, including Texas, where the governor was "very weak."

Sources: Joseph Schlesinger, "Politics, the Executive," in Herbert Jacob and Kenneth Vines, eds. *Politics in the American States: A Comparative Analysis* (Boston: Little, Brown, 1965), 220–9, and 2nd ed., 1971, 225–34; Thad L. Beyle, "Governors," in Virginia Gray, Herbert Jacob, and Robert Albritton, eds., *Politics in the American States,* 5th ed. (New York: HarperCollins, 1990), 574; Thad L. Beyle, "The Governors," in Virginia Gray and Russell Hanson, eds., *Politics in the American States,* 8th ed. (Washington, DC: CQ Press, 2003).

A 1933 court case determined that the legislature may designate someone other than the governor to make an appointment, and no Senate confirmation would be required. However, if the legislature does not provide an alternative means, the governor appoints.[17] While presidential appointment requires only a simple majority confirmation in the U.S. Senate, Texas gubernatorial appointments require consent of the Texas Senate in a vote of at least two-thirds of those present (Article 4, section 12c). **Senatorial courtesy** is a norm that requires the governor to preclear a nominee with the senator in whose district the nominee resides. Senatorial courtesy and the recent growth of a two-party legislature mean that a governor must be sensitive to senatorial concerns or risk either embarrassment or a political battle.

senatorial courtesy
A process by which a governor, when selecting an appointee, defers to the state senator in whose district the nominee resides.

Analysis of appointees reveals that governors tend to appoint people like themselves and their allies. Because all but two governors have been male, all but three have been Democrats, and all have been Anglo, it should not be surprising that Anglo, male Democrats historically dominated state boards and commissions. **Overrepresentation and underrepresentation** are higher and lower numbers, respectively, than would be expected based on the group's numbers in the general population. For governors' appointees, those who have been overrepresented in appointments are Anglos and males, while women, African Americans, and Mexican Americans have been underrepresented.

overrepresentation and underrepresentation
Higher and lower numbers, respectively, than would be expected from a group in comparison with that group's numbers in the general population.

Analyzing Visuals: Analysis of Gubernatorial Appointments shows that the pattern of appointments has changed only marginally in the past

---

TABLE 19.3 State Agency Heads Appointed by the Governor

As recently as the 1970s, Texas governors appointed only a handful of the heads of executive agencies. While most agency heads are still not appointed by the governor, the list of those who are appointed by the governor is growing longer.

Adjutant General

Chief Administrative Law Judge

Executive Director, Children's Trust Fund of Texas Council (nomination by Commissioners of Health and Human Services, Health, and Mental Health/Mental Retardation)

Executive Director, Texas Council on Alcohol and Drug Abuse (nomination by Commissioner of Health and Human Services)

Executive Director, Criminal Justice Policy Council

Commissioner of Education

Fire Fighters Pension Commissioner (nomination by State Firemen's and Fire Marshals' Association and Texas State Association of Fire Fighters)

Executive Commissioner of Health and Human Services Commission

Executive Director, Department of Housing and Community Affairs (nomination by Board of Housing and Community Affairs)

Chair, Regional Mobility Authorities

Insurance Commissioner

Executive Director, Interagency Council on Early Childhood Intervention (nomination by Commissioner of Health and Human Services)

Presiding Officer, Private Sector Prison Industries Oversight Authority

Public Insurance Counsel

Public Utility Counsel

Secretary of State

Executive Director, Office of State–Federal Relations

Source: Marilyn Duncan and Shirley Beckwith, *Guide to Texas State Agencies,* 11th ed. (Austin: LBJ School of Public Affairs, 2001); author.

three decades, with the significant exception of Ann Richards. She is the only governor to appoint numbers of women and racial and ethnic minorities in approximate proportion to their presence in the population. By the end of her term, 45 percent of her appointees were women, 19 percent were Mexican American, and 14 percent were African American. Governor Bush did not appoint as many women and minorities; at the end of his first term, 37 percent of his appointees were women, 13 percent were Mexican American, and 9 percent were African American. In his first year of office, Governor Perry appointed fewer women than Governor Bush, but more minorities—though still fewer than Governor Richards: 33 percent of his appointees were women, 16 percent Mexican American, and 11 percent African American.

In addition to the significance of homogeneity or diversity of appointees, another issue has dominated analysis of gubernatorial appointees: the role of campaign donations. Often, key appointments go to the governor's largest campaign contributors. In his gubernato-

Analyzing Visuals

ANALYSIS OF GUBERNATORIAL APPOINTMENTS

Historically, governors' appointees to state offices have been Anglo males. Recent data indicate more diversity in gubernatorial appointments; however, Anglo males are still overrepresented. After studying the table depicting the appointments by five Texas governors and reading the material in this chapter on the governor's power to appoint executive officials, answer the following critical thinking questions: Which governor's appointees were most diverse ethnically and in gender? Is there a difference between the appointments of Democratic governors White and Richards and Republican governors Clements, Bush, and Perry? How would you explain the trend toward the appointment of more females and ethnic minorities by governors?

| | Texas | Appointees of Governor: | | | | |
	Population 2000	White	Clements	Richards	Bush	Perry
Gender						
Male	49.5%	78%	82%	55%	63%	67%
Female	50.5	22	18	45	37	33
Race/ethnic group						
White	52.4	82	89	65	77	73
Mexican American	32.0	12	7	19	13	16
African American	11.5	6	3	14	9	11
Other	4.1	n/a	n/a	2	n/a	n/a

Sources: Clements, White, and Bush appointees from Peggy Fikac, "Bush Appointing Many Females, Minorities," *San Antonio Express-News* (July 9, 2000); Richards appointees from list supplied by Office of Governor Ann Richards, October 13, 1994; Governor Perry's appointees from Peggy Fikac, "Race Looms as Issue in Race," *San Antonio Express-News* (October 7, 2001).

rial campaigns, Bush collected about $2.4 million in contributions from people that he appointed to state positions.[18] Of Governor White's early appointments, 27 percent were campaign contributors.[19] Governor Richards appointed her largest contributor to the Parks and Wildlife Board. Another large contributor was appointed chair of the UT Board of Regents. George W. Bush kept this tradition alive by appointing big contributors to key posts.

The Power of Staff and Budget

The responsibilities of the governor's staff are broad: developing the governor's budget proposal and policy recommendations; performing public relations; serving as liaison with local, state, and federal agencies and with the legislature and party officials; answering correspondence and visiting with citizens who call on the governor; contacting and negotiating with lobbyists. These duties change with the priorities and organizational preferences of each governor. Since the 1950s, the governor's staff size has grown tremendously. Recent governors have had about 200 staff members.

The amount of money that the legislature appropriates for the operations of the Office of the Governor depends on what functions the legislature and the governor choose to place under the office. While the governor's appropriations may exceed $100 million a year, usually less than $10 million of that is for the narrower Governor's Office, and the remainder is for discretionary funds and the suboffices included in the governor's budget.

THE GOVERNOR AS POLICY MAKER AND POLITICAL LEADER

AS POLITICAL SCIENTIST FRED GANTT points out in his study of the Texas governorship through the middle of the twentieth century, "Instead of the 'Chief Executive of Texas,' under existing laws he might more accurately be labeled the 'Chief Persuader of Texas.'"[20] In more recent years, an analysis of Ann Richards's governorship concluded that she "pushed the powers of a weak office to their limits,"[21] and George W. Bush was perceived as a governor with strong personal skills that made him a strong governor. The political leadership that a governor is able to provide flows from the governor's skills and previous experience, as well as similarity in party, philosophy, and ideology with other decision makers.

These skills must be honed in the electoral arena in order to win the governorship. All Texas governors have sought reelection; governors must, then, maintain those electoral connections while in office. These electoral linkages help build the visibility of the governor as well as an image of strength—which in turn helps him or her in wielding governmental power in battles with other officials and private interest groups.

Public-Opinion Leadership

Because of their weak constitutional powers, Texas governors resort to public-opinion leadership to increase their power with other office holders. Governors have sometimes had their own television shows. Governor White ran television commercials to build support for higher teacher salaries. Governors hold news conferences either on a regular basis or whenever they believe such conferences would be beneficial to them. Sometimes they go outside Austin to try to stir up public support for their policies. Governor Richards tried a "tour of state government" to promote dialogue between state officials and citizens in several locations across the state. Governor Bush spoke around the state about his tax and education proposals.

Analyzing Visuals

IDEOLOGY AND GOVERNORS

Governors' speeches, messages to the legislature, vetoes, and general philosophy about government and its role suggest where they might best fit in the grid of the four ideologies. After viewing the chart and reading the material in the chapter on Texas's governors, answer the following critical thinking questions: What does the location of most recent Texas governors in the conservative ideological category suggest about the people who seek the office? What does it suggest about Texans' views of the governor's role? What national historical event would you associate with the election of James Allred, classified as a populist, as governor?

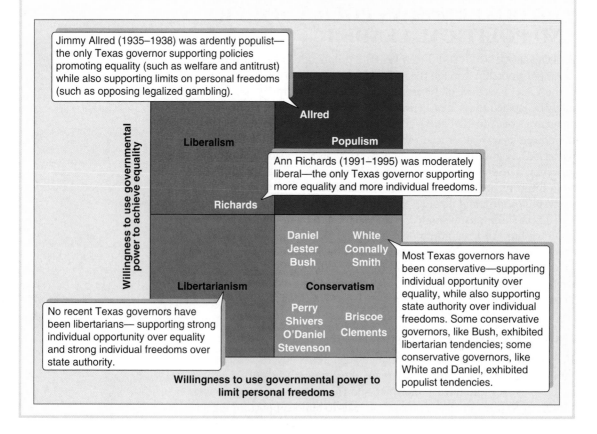

Jimmy Allred (1935–1938) was ardently populist—the only Texas governor supporting policies promoting equality (such as welfare and antitrust) while also supporting limits on personal freedoms (such as opposing legalized gambling).

Ann Richards (1991–1995) was moderately liberal—the only Texas governor supporting more equality and more individual freedoms.

No recent Texas governors have been libertarians— supporting strong individual opportunity over equality and strong individual freedoms over state authority.

Most Texas governors have been conservative—supporting individual opportunity over equality, while also supporting state authority over individual freedoms. Some conservative governors, like Bush, exhibited libertarian tendencies; some conservative governors, like White and Daniel, exhibited populist tendencies.

Liberalism

Populism

Allred

Richards

Daniel   White
Jester   Connally
Bush   Smith

Conservatism

Perry
Shivers   Briscoe
O'Daniel Clements
Stevenson

Libertarianism

Willingness to use governmental power to achieve equality

Willingness to use governmental power to limit personal freedoms

Relationship with the Legislature

To be a successful governor, one must succeed in pushing a program through the legislature and in killing unwanted legislative measures. To do so, a governor must develop good personal or working relationships

House Speaker Pete Laney, Governor George W. Bush, and Lieutenant Governor Bob Bullock seemed to work together skillfully, despite Laney and Bullock being Democrats and Bush being a Republican. In his 2000 campaign for the presidency, Bush touted his relationship with Bullock (by then deceased) as evidence of his ability to work in a bipartisan fashion.

Photo courtesy: Bob Daemmrich/Bob Daemmrich Photography, Inc.

with key legislators and must use the powers of the governorship to assist the legislative process and, sometimes, to thwart it.

A governor uses a grab bag of tools to win his or her legislative agenda, including direct appeals to voters, pleas from citizen study groups, pressure from lobbyists, breakfasts for legislators, entertainment (including evenings at the governor's mansion), individual legislative conferences, floor leaders, and staff representatives working the floor.[22] The "state of the state" message and budget message are the formal vehicles governors use to convey their wishes to the legislature. Governors also make "emergency proclamations," which serve to put governors' favored bills ahead of others on the legislative schedule.

A key power of all U.S. governors is the ability to call special sessions of the legislature and to set the agenda for the special session (governors of fourteen states, including Texas, can set the agenda).[23] The Texas governor's ability to control the agenda of special sessions extends only to regular legislative acts and not to appointments or impeachments.

The veto—the power to nullify bills passed by the legislature—is one of a governor's most potent legislative weapons, as we saw in this chapter's opening scenario. All of Texas's constitutions have given the governor the veto power, with the condition that the legislature may override (cancel) the veto by a vote of two-thirds in each chamber.[24] When the governor receives a bill passed by the legislature, he or she has ten days in which to sign or veto the bill. However, if the end of the legislative session occurs in that ten-day period, the governor then has twenty days from adjournment to consider the bills.

At the national level, if the U.S. Congress passes a bill and adjourns, and the president does not sign the bill, it dies (see chapter 6). This is called a "pocket veto" (the president just pockets the bill and ignores it). In Texas, if the governor does not sign a bill, it becomes law anyway—Texas does not have the pocket veto.[25]

In Texas, most bills are passed in the last ten days of the session. Consequently, most vetoes occur after adjournment, as did Governor Perry's Father's Day vetoes, and the legislature has no chance to vote to override. There have been only seventy-six veto override attempts under the current constitution, and only twenty-six of these have been successful. Governor Clements had one veto overridden in 1979, and there have been no override attempts since then.[26]

A variation of the veto authority is the line-item veto. For bills that appropriate money, this power allows the governor to select one or more lines of appropriations and veto them, while signing the rest of the bill into law. Line-item veto authority has been in the Texas constitutions since 1866. Forty-three governors now have this power.[27] In some legislative sessions, the governor vetoes only a handful of line items; in others, governors have vetoed up to twenty-six items. In 2003, Governor

■ The Texas Capitol. The "capitol complex" consists of all the state office buildings in the area around the capitol. In the distance is the campus of the University of Texas at Austin.

Photo courtesy: Bob Daemmrich/Bob Daemmrich Photography, Inc.

Perry vetoed $81.2 million through line-item vetoes, including $7.4 million for the State Aircraft Pooling Board, which effectively eliminated the agency, $22.5 million for the Texas Excellence Fund, and $22.5 for the University Research Fund.[28]

Because the major appropriations bill is always passed at the end of a session, the legislature adjourns and then has no chance to override any line-item vetoes. Thus, the line-item veto can be a powerful weapon, and every recent governor has used it. However, the legislature has learned to mitigate against it by organizing material in the appropriations bills in such a manner as to limit the usefulness of such a veto (by lumping programs together and by using "riders" to describe programs and funding levels, rather than line items for those programs).

THE PLURAL EXECUTIVE IN TEXAS

AMERICANS PLACE A HIGH VALUE ON ELECTIONS. We assume that elected officials are more responsive to citizens, and thus more democratic, than nonelected officials. Elected officials may not have any more authority than appointed officials, but election seems to give them more legitimacy in the eyes of citizens—and certainly being a part of the electoral process gives them more political power than appointed officials. The median number of statewide elected officials for the fifty states is six. Texas ranks seventh among the states, electing nine statewide officials plus the State Board of Education, whose fifteen members are elected from districts.[29] Nearly half the states have reduced the number of elected state officials in recent decades. Texas joined this trend in 1995, abolishing the position of state treasurer.

Comparative

Comparing Executive Branches

While most agency directors cooperate with the governor in policy implementation, there have been hostilities (see Roots of Government: Struggles over Cabinet Government). Elected agency heads can often present difficulties for governors. Attorneys general are often seen as "governors-in-waiting," and many of them have feuded publicly with a governor, then run against the governor in the next election. Executive feuds are not limited to those with the attorney general.

Attorney General

Next to the governor and the lieutenant governor, the **attorney general** is the most significant elected state official. The attorney general serves as the chief counsel for the state of Texas. Because the attorney general is elected, he or she is independent from the governor (and, indeed, the governor has his or her own legal adviser). In about half of the years since 1978, governors and attorneys general have even been from different parties. Often, attorneys general have ambitions to run for governor, which can impede cooperation.

attorney general
The elected official who is the chief counsel for the state of Texas.

The Living Constitution

The Texas Governor's Veto Power

Article 4, section 14: Every bill which shall have passed both houses of the Legislature shall be presented to the Governor for his approval. If he approve he shall sign it; but if he disapprove it, he shall return it, with his objections. . . . If . . . two-thirds of the members present agree to pass the bill, it shall be sent . . . to the other House . . . and, if approved by two-thirds of the members of that House, it shall become a law. If any bill shall not be returned by the Governor . . . within ten days . . . the same shall be a law . . . unless the Legislature, by its adjournment, prevent its return, in which case it shall be a law. . . . If any bill presented to the Governor contains several items of appropriation he may object to one or more of such items, and approve the other portion of the bill.

The Texas Constitution provides for gubernatorial vetoes in Article 4, section 14. The 1836 constitution of the Republic of Texas is the basis for this provision. The provision has remained largely intact through the various Texas constitutions, with several notable exceptions. First, until the constitution of 1876, the governor was allowed only five days to return vetoed bills. Second, under the constitution of the Republic, the president could exercise a pocket veto (if the legislature adjourned during the five days allotted the president to sign or veto a bill, then the Texas president, by refusing to sign the bill, could exercise a veto). None of the constitutions of statehood have allowed the pocket veto. Furthermore, the constitutions of 1845, 1861, 1866, and 1869 did not allow post-adjournment vetoes. The current constitution extended the time to return objectionable bills to ten days and permitted the post-adjournment veto, giving the governor twenty

While election campaigns for attorney general often focus on criminal issues, the attorney general has little authority in the field of criminal law and focuses instead on civil law. As chief counsel to state agencies, the attorney general and the hundreds of assistant attorneys general also represent most agencies in litigation. When an agency sues a private individual or organization to force compliance with a state law or agency regulation, the attorney general's office usually provides the attorney for the agency.

days from adjournment to sign or veto bills. The line-item veto for appropriations measures originated with the 1866 constitution.[a]

If the governor vetoes a bill and the legislature is in session, the provision requires that the chamber of origin must first consider the bill and that a two-thirds majority of the members present is necessary to send the bill to the other chamber. However, because the constitution does not specify whether the vote in the second chamber must be two-thirds of the members present or of the members elected, the chambers differ on their interpretations. According to Senate Rules, "A vote of two-thirds of all members elected to the Senate shall be required for the passage of House bills that have been returned by the Governor with his objections, and a vote of two-thirds of the members of the Senate present shall be required for the passage of Senate bills that have been returned by the Governor with his objections."[b] In the House, on the other hand, a two-thirds vote of the members present is required, regardless of the bill's chamber of origin. The constitution is clear that on line-item vetoes, a two-thirds vote of the members present in each chamber is required.

Other states' veto provisions vary greatly. Some states require only a majority vote to override a veto, others require a three-fifths majority, and some require a three-fourths majority. Many states allow the governor a pocket veto. Some states allow an "amendatory" veto, which allows the governor to return an objectionable bill to the legislature with suggested changes that would make the bill acceptable. If the legislature agrees, the bill is returned for the governor's signature.

The veto is the Texas governor's most significant constitutional power. The line-item veto, because the governor's budgetary powers are weak, is almost the only power that the governor has over the amounts and purposes of expenditures by the state.

Question

1. Should the governor's veto power be enhanced through the "amendatory" veto, or does the Texas governor have sufficient veto powers currently? Explain your answer.

---

[a]George D. Braden, *The Constitution of the State of Texas: An Annotated and Comparative Analysis*, vol. 1 (Austin: Legislative Council, 1977), 333.
[b]Texas Senate, Rules of the 78th Legislature, Rule 6.20.

As the state's chief lawyer, the attorney general may issue advisory opinions to state and local officials on the legality of their actions, as Attorney General Dan Morales did in response to the *Hopwood* decision, forbidding colleges and universities from enforcing some affirmative action plans, and as Attorney General John Cornyn did in 2000, forbidding local governments from using public funds to provide health services to undocumented immigrants. Attorney General Opinions

Roots of Government

STRUGGLES OVER CABINET GOVERNMENT

AS PRESIDENT OF the Republic of Texas, Sam Houston governed with a Cabinet. In the ensuing decades, governors maintained significant control over the executive branch of state government in Texas, but the 1876 constitution then stripped the governor of many powers, including controls over the executive branch. Attempts since then to reconvene Cabinet-style executive authority have been short lived, often accompanied by high-profile clashes among executive officials. While fifteen states give constitutional authority to the governor—as chief executive—to reorganize the executive branch without having to get legislative approval (subject only to legislative veto), Texas has never given that much authority to the governor.[a]

Sometimes appointed officials have opposed increased gubernatorial influence, sometimes elected executive officers have done so, and sometimes the legislature has blocked governors' initiatives. Governor Oscar Colquitt (1911–1915) feuded with Attorney General Jewel Lightfoot, and the attorney general resigned. Governor Jim Ferguson (1915–1917) met with state boards, ordered them to act according to his wishes, and threatened the removal of board members if they did not comply. Governor Miriam Ferguson (1925–1927) feuded with Attorney General Dan Moody, and Moody defeated her in the next election for governor. In 1931, the legislature created a committee to reorganize state government. Its reorganization plan suggested a Cabinet-style

government to strengthen executive coordination, but the Cabinet proposal was killed.[b] Governor W. Lee O'Daniel (1939–1941) complained about the lack of gubernatorial control over boards, particularly the staggered terms of members. Governor Beauford Jester (1947–1949) invited elected heads and some appointed heads to join a Cabinet; the effort was short lived, as he died in office.[c] Texas's longest serving governor, Allan Shivers (1949–1957) waited until his final inauguration in 1955 to proclaim:

> I believe we should begin giving serious thought to reorganizing the executive branch. If the governor is to be held accountable for the conduct of the executive branch, future governors should have direct authority over—as well as responsibility for—the performance of administrative functions which are not policymaking in character, [including] appointment and removal.[d]

The idea of a more unified executive in Texas, possibly with a governor's Cabinet, is not dead—but such proposals have been defeated for more than a century, and their chances do not seem to have improved.

[a]Larry Sabato, *Goodbye to Good-Time Charlie: The American Governorship Transformed*, 2nd ed. (Washington, DC: CQ Press, 1983), 62.

[b]Joint Advisory Committee on Government Operations, "Final Report to the Governor of Texas and Members of the 65th Texas Legislature," January 1977.

[c]Fred Gantt Jr., *The Chief Executive in Texas: A Study in Gubernatorial Leadership* (Austin: University of Texas Press, 1964), 111 and 122.

[d]Gantt, *The Chief Executive in Texas*, 136, from *House Journal*, 54th legislature, 70.

have the force of law for agency officials, until or unless a court rules otherwise.

The attorney general has continuous opportunities to provide public-policy leadership by deciding what kinds of cases to emphasize and by being pulled into public-policy areas. Jim Mattox (1983–1991) sued numerous companies to force compliance with consumer safety, anti-fraud, and environmental statutes. Dan Morales (1991–1999) sued tobacco companies on health-related issues, winning a huge settlement for the state. Mattox and Morales devoted a massive amount of staff time to resolving the *Ruiz* v. *Estelle* case concerning prison management, and to a new policy area, child-support collection. Also, Morales staff members spent much time on redistricting issues, as a result of numerous lawsuits over the legislature's 1990s redistricting plans for the U.S. Congress and the Texas legislature (see chapters 7 and 23).

In 1998, Jim Mattox won the Democratic nomination for attorney general in a comeback attempt but lost the general election to John Cornyn, the first Republican so elected. Cornyn served on the Texas Supreme Court from 1990 to 1998. In 1999, Attorney General Cornyn attacked the tobacco settlement that Morales had agreed to. He also issued an opinion rescinding Morales's *Hopwood* opinion. Cornyn served only one term, choosing in 2002 to run for the U.S. Senate. Republican Greg Abbott, also a former Texas Supreme Court Justice, won the office of attorney general in 2002.

Comptroller of Public Accounts

The **comptroller of public accounts** is the state's tax collector. As of 1996, with the constitutional amendment abolishing the office of state treasurer, the comptroller is also the state's money manager. What makes the comptroller a powerful statewide official, though, is that he or she is responsible for estimating the amount of revenue that the state will have coming in, and the legislature may not appropriate more than that amount (except by a four-fifths vote). Thus, the comptroller becomes a significant legislative player.

comptroller of public accounts
The elected official who is the state's tax collector.

Photo courtesy: Bob Daemmrich/Bob Daemmrich Photography Inc.

■ Carole Keeton Strayhorn is the first Republican to be elected comptroller of public accounts. Here, she holds a capitol news conference on the state budget.

The revenue-forecasting function requires the comptroller to have a sophisticated economic-analysis capability. The agency includes a large economic and policy research staff, which has become one of the state's most respected economic forecasting centers. Still, part of the comptroller's power in the legislative process is that the forecasts are built on assumptions, and those assumptions can be changed. For instance, the comptroller can increase or decrease the projected state revenues by increasing or decreasing the assumed price of a barrel of oil. Thus, if the comptroller wants to influence the amount of money available to the legislature, the revenue estimating process can accommodate those tactics.

In 1998, Republican Carole Keeton Rylander narrowly defeated Democrat Paul Hobby (son of former Lieutenant Governor Bill Hobby) to become the first Republican comptroller. She rose from local politics, having served on the Austin school board and as mayor of Austin. She lost a race for Congress, was appointed to the Insurance Board, then won a seat on the Railroad Commission. As comptroller, she emphasized the school district audits that the office is now responsible for. In 2002, Rylander easily won reelection as comptroller and is seen as a likely candidate for higher office in the 2006 elections. After her reelection, she married and changed her name to Strayhorn.

Land Commissioner

land commissioner
The elected official responsible for managing and leasing the state's property, including oil, gas, and mineral interests.

The **land commissioner** is more significant in Texas than in most states because the state owns so much land. The 1845 terms of annexation to the United States gave to the state "all the vacant and unappropriated lands lying within its limits."[30] The land commissioner is responsible for managing and leasing the property.

As oil was discovered in the early twentieth century, the land commissioner enjoyed newfound importance—oil revenues from state-owned land pumped up funds for schools and universities, to which the land-generated revenues are constitutionally committed. Also, the land commissioner was given responsibility for the new Veterans Land Program in 1946, a program that loans money to veterans for the purpose of buying a homestead. Now the program includes loans for houses as well as land.

In 1999, David Dewhurst became the first Republican to win the office. Dewhurst had served in the Air Force, Central Intelligence Agency, and State Department, then founded a Houston energy and investments company. He had not previously held an elective office. Dewhurst served as head of Governor Perry's Task Force on Homeland Security in 2001–2002 and was also instrumental as a member of the Legislative Redistricting Board that redrew state legislative district lines in 2001. Dewhurst served only one term, choosing to run for lieutenant governor in 2002. He was replaced as land commissioner by fellow Republican Jerry Patterson, who won the office in 2002. Patterson had earlier been a state senator and in 1998 had lost to Dewhurst in the Republican primary for land commissioner.

Agriculture Commissioner

The **agriculture commissioner** is the only one of the statewide elected officials whose job was created by the legislature instead of by the constitution. The job of the commissioner is to promote and regulate agricultural interests. The Texas Department of Agriculture administers promotion campaigns for Texas commodities and encourages use of Texas products through labeling them Texas-made. Traditional regulatory programs include monitoring the accuracy of weights and measures, regulating the safety of grain warehouses, and ensuring compliance with pest-control regulations and egg- and seed-labeling requirements.

In 1982, Jim Hightower defeated the incumbent commissioner in the Democratic primary and won the general election. Hightower had been head of an agricultural-policy think tank in Washington, then had been editor of the *Texas Observer*, putting a definite populist voice to its coverage. Hightower was reelected in 1986. He was narrowly defeated by Rick Perry in the general election in 1990—the first time that a Democrat other than governor had lost an executive office to a Republican.

Perry, a Democratic state representative who had led an effort to limit Hightower's powers and his pesticide regulatory authority, switched to the Republican Party to run against Hightower. Perry deemphasized Hightower's new programs and reemphasized the traditional role of the department. He won reelection easily in 1994. In 1998, Perry was elected lieutenant governor, and in 2000, he succeeded to the governorship upon George W. Bush's resignation.

Perry was succeeded as agriculture commissioner by Republican Susan Combs, a lawyer-rancher who served in the Texas House from 1993 through 1996 from Austin. She co-authored the state's private property rights act. Combs then served as U.S. Senator Kay Bailey Hutchison's state director. She is the first woman to hold the post of agriculture commissioner. Combs sought and won reelection in 2002. In 2004, she announced that she would seek the comptroller's office in 2006.

Railroad Commissioners

The three railroad commissioners are elected in statewide elections. Whereas other state officials are elected to four-year terms, railroad commissioners are elected to six-year **staggered terms,** where one seat is up for election every two years. The **Railroad Commission** was the highest achievement of populists in the 1890s. Populists demanded regulation of railroads, and they insisted that the people have direct control over those regulators by electing them. Over the years, other regulatory duties have been added to the agency's responsibilities. In the early twentieth century, it was given authority over the oil and gas

Photo courtesy: Harry Cabluck/AP/Wide World Photos

■ Susan Combs is the first woman and second Republican to serve as Texas agriculture commissioner. Here, she speaks at a capitol news conference during the 2001 legislative session.

agriculture commissioner
The elected state official in charge of regulating and promoting agriculture.

staggered terms
Terms of office for members of boards and commissions that begin and end at different times, so that a governor is not usually able to gain control of a majority of the body for a long time.

Railroad Commission
A full-time, three-member paid commission elected by the people to regulate oil and gas and some transportation entities.

Photo courtesy: Bob Daemmrich

■ Members of the The Texas Railroad Commission are, from left to right, Michael Williams, Victor Carrillo, and Charles Matthews. The commission was created to regulate railroad rates during the late nineteenth century, but the commission's principal task currently involves regulation of the oil and gas industry.

industry. Regulation of trucking and mining came later. Today, the federal government has usurped much of the agency's regulatory responsibilities for railroads and trucking, leaving oil and gas regulation as its primary function. As the Politics Now: The Texas Railroad Commission: Watchdog or Lapdog? feature highlights, it is the oil and gas industry that has the most influence at the agency.

After the 1994 elections, for the first time in Texas history, all three railroad commissioners were Republicans, and that has remained the case since then. In 2002, the commission included Charles Matthews, Michael Williams, and Tony Garza. President Bush then appointed Garza as U.S. Ambassador to Mexico. Matthews had been mayor of Garland and had served on a power authority board. Williams is the first African American to serve as railroad commissioner. Governor Bush appointed him in 1998 and, with his election to an unexpired term in 2000, he is the first African American elected to statewide executive office in Texas. In 2002, he won election to a full term. Williams had served President George Bush as assistant secretary of education for civil rights, and had served as general counsel to the Texas Republican

Governor Rick Perry meets with other governors in 2001 in an El Paso meeting of the Western Governors Association. To Governor Perry's right is Utah Governor Mike Leavitt, and to his left, the chair of the association, Arizona Governor Jane Dee Hull.

Photo courtesy: J.R. Hernandez/AP/Wide World

Party. Garza served as the first Republican county judge in Cameron County, then Governor Bush appointed him secretary of state. In 1998, he became the first Republican Mexican American to win statewide office. In 2003, Governor Perry appointed Victor Carrillo to the commission. Carrillo won a full term in 2004.

State Board of Education

The **State Board of Education** (SBOE) is an excellent example of the fragmentation of institutions and authority in Texas state government. Public education is governed by the elected fifteen-member SBOE, a commissioner of education appointed by the governor, a large bureaucracy called the **Texas Education Agency** (TEA), and local and regional entities. In the 1990s, those entities sometimes warred with each other, with the legislature, and with interest groups.

Although the state has always had a presence in education, the nature of state leadership has evolved.[31] In 1995, the governor was given sole authority to appoint the commissioner, with Senate confirmation.

The SBOE became a lightning rod for public attention in the 1990s as elections to the board became a battleground between religious right and traditional public education forces. Those differences carried over into policy battles over curriculum standards, sex education, phonics, public vouchers for private school education, creationism, and textbook content. The controversy was heightened in the 1990s when San Antonio millionaire businessman James Leininger helped fund and elect religious right candidates to the board.

State Board of Education
The fifteen-member elected body that sets some education policy for the state and has limited authority to oversee the Texas Education Agency and local school districts.

Texas Education Agency
The state agency that oversees local school districts and disburses state funds to districts.

THE DEREGULATION OF TEXAS
PUBLIC COLLEGE AND UNIVERSITY TUITION

During the waning hours of the 78th legislature's regular session, advocates of deregulation of public college and university tuition secured the votes necessary to pass Republican Representative Geanie Morrison's bill. As amended by the Senate, the bill allows the governing boards of public higher education institutions to set tuition amounts necessary for the effective operation of the institution. A portion of the tuition increase must be set aside for financial assistance, which may take the form of grants, scholarships, work-study programs, student loans, and student repayment assistance. Supporters of the bill claimed that the deregulation was necessary to allow the institutions to respond to budget cuts without increasing class size, offering fewer classes, cutting salaries, or limiting access to a college education. Opponents of the bill, on the other hand, argued that public colleges and universities should first seek other methods of balancing their budgets before they increase the financial burden on students and their families. They also noted that the members of the governing boards are appointed and thus are not directly accountable to the students or to the voters.[a]

Shortly after the bill's passage, University of Texas at Austin President Larry Faulkner stated that students could expect a tuition increase for the spring 2004 semester. Sly Majid, vice president of student government, expressed a concern that "deregulation will create a two-tiered educational system. The students who can afford to go to UT will go to UT, and other students will go to satellite schools, less prestigious ones that are more affordable."[b] Other colleges and universities also contemplated changes for the spring semester. The University of Houston anticipated a 21 percent increase. Texas A&M University prepared for a 21 percent increase by fall semester 2004. Smaller universities, such as Stephen F. Austin State University, also anticipated tuition increases.[c] As tuition costs increase, students are borrowing more money to finance their college educations; nonfederal loans increased by 41 percent nationally in 2003.[d]

To consider the amount of tuition increase at the University of Texas at Austin, a committee was formed composed of four students, a faculty member, and four officers of the university. Brian Haley, student government president and member of the committee, praised the establishment of the committee, noting that it is unique to the University of Texas at Austin campus and provides students with "unprecedented involvement in the tuition-setting process."[e]

In subsequent legislative sessions, the legislature will be forced to balance the increasing demand for a college-educated workforce with the demands from Texas colleges and universities for more money to provide that education. Meeting those demands while equitably sharing the burden between taxpayers and students will not be easy.

[a]House Research Organization, "Major Issues of the 78th Legislature, Regular Session," *Focus Report* (August 6, 2003), 122–3.

[b]Delaney Hall, "Legislature Deregulates Tuition," *Daily Texan Online*, June 1, 2003, accessed August 13, 2004, http://www.dailytexanonline.com/news/2003/06/01/News/Legislature.Deregulates.Tuition-493895.shtml.

[c]Nicolas Brulliard, "State Colleges Increasing Tuition Rates," *Daily Texan Online*, August 11, 2003, accessed August 13, 2004, http://www.dailytexanonline.com/news/2003/08/11/TopStories/State.Colleges.Increasing.Tuition.Rates-450029.shtml; Tessa Moll, "Texas A&M to Increase Tuition by 21 Percent," *Daily Texan Online*, August 11, 2003, accessed August 13, 2004, http://www.dailytexanonline.com/news/2004/03/30/University/Texas.Am.To.Increase.Tuition.By.21.Percent-645037.shtml.

[d]Tessa Moll, "Students Borrow More as Education Costs Increase," *Daily Texan Online*, June 15, 2004, accessed August 13, 2004, http://www.dailytexanonline.com/news/2004/06/15/TopStories/Students.Borrow.More.As.Education.Costs.Increase-687695.shtml.

[e]Delaney Hall, "Tuition Policy Committee's Duties Outlined," *Daily Texan Online*, August 6, 2003, accessed August 13, 2004, http://www.dailytexanonline.com/news/2003/08/06/News/Tuition.Policy.Committees.Duties.Outlined-492980.shtml.

In 2002, with newly redistricted lines, Republicans increased their number on the board to ten, which they retained after the 2004 elections..

MODERN TEXAS BUREAUCRACY

Simulation

You Are a Governmental Affairs Consultant

THE PURPOSE OF GOVERNMENT bureaucracy is implementation—to put into effect, to *execute* legislative policy, hence the term *executive* branch. Legislatures are chiefly responsible for creating public policies (policy making). Bureaucracies are supposed to translate legislative intent into actual, working public policy—that is, to implement the wishes of the legislature. Agencies do so by rule making (adopting standards and processes by which they operate and make decisions), regulation of private activities, and provision of services and products. However, as they attempt to understand and to implement legislative intent, agency officials often must fill out the details that are missing in legislation and thus sometimes also *make* policy. Texas's rule-making process, spelled out in the **Administrative Procedures Act,** requires agency officials to seek written public comments, and agencies sometimes have public hearings before adopting rules and regulations.

Administrative Procedures Act
A statute containing Texas's rule-making process.

Legislatures create executive agencies to respond to particular problems. How they organize the agencies is determined by the nature of the problem, the personalities and political dynamics at work, and the organizational structure that is in vogue at the time. Texas executive agencies are organized in a host of ways, but there are two basic patterns (see Figure 19.1).

FIGURE 19.1 **Texas State Agency Organizational Leadership Schemes**
State agencies have different leadership structures and different ways of being authorized. Two basic patterns are shown here. ■

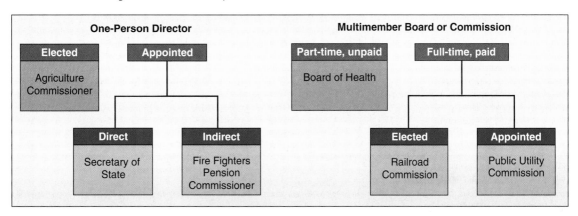

First, there are those agencies headed by one person. Eight are appointed by the governor, such as the secretary of state; six are elected by the people, as noted earlier. The governor appoints few directors of state agencies (see Table 19.3), though the number has grown in recent years.

Second, there are agencies run by multimember boards or commissions.[32] Ninety-six agencies are run by a part-time, unpaid board or commission. (Those two terms are used interchangeably.) The members of most governing boards are appointed by the governor. In most cases, the board hires a person to run the agency. The Texas State Board of Medical Examiners is an example of such an agency. The commission's members, appointed by the governor, make policy and hire an administrator.

Five agencies are run by a full-time, paid commission. These include the governor-appointed Public Utility Commission (PUC), Texas Commission on Environmental Quality (TCEQ), Texas Workforce Commission, Board of Pardons and Paroles, and the elected Railroad Commission. Commission members usually hire an executive director to assist them in running the agency. Table 19.4 highlights Texas's fifteen largest state agencies by appropriations and by employment level.

TABLE 19.4   Top 15 State Agencies; Ranked by Appropriations and by Employment

While Texas has more than 200 state agencies, most of them are small. Generally, the largest agencies in appropriations are also large in numbers of employees.

Agency (excludes universities)	2004–2005 Appropriation (All Funds)		2003–2004 FTE[a]	
	In millions	Rank	Number	Rank
Texas Education Agency	$30,070.6	1	806	—[b]
Health and Human Services Commission	19,367.7	2	1,044	—
Department of Transportation	10,635.3	3	14,815	3
Department of Human Services	9,125.4	4	13,688	4
Department of Criminal Justice	4,909.3	5	40,760	1
Teacher Retirement System	4,051.7	6	438	—
Department of Mental Health/Mental Retardation	3,996.0	7	19,945	2
Department of Health	3,593.1	8	4,866	7
Employees Retirement System	2,380.5	9	286	—
Texas Workforce Commission	2,085.4	10	3,689	10
Department of Protective and Regulatory Services	1,732.1	11	6,802	6
Office of Attorney General	852.7	12	4,110	9
Department of Public Safety	797.1	13	7,554	5
Commission on Environmental Quality	689.5	14	3,045	11
Rehabilitation Commission	591.4	15	2,603	14

[a]FTE—Full-time equivalent employees, 2003–2004.

[b]Blanks indicate agencies not ranked in top 15.

Sources: Legislative Budget Board, *Texas Fact Book,* 44, 47; State Auditor, *A Quarterly Report on Full-time Equivalent State Employees for the Quarter Ending August 31, 2003,* December 2003, Report No. 04–702.

Secretary of State

The first appointment made by an incoming governor, and a key one, is the **Texas secretary of state.** This officer is literally the secretary for the state of Texas—the keeper of the records. Election data and filings, state laws and regulations, public notifications through the *Texas Register,* and corporate charters are examples of records managed by the secretary of state.

The secretary of state serves as the state's chief elections officer—registering voters, making sure that counties conduct the elections properly, and collecting and certifying election results. In this capacity, the secretary is one of the most important political officials inside state government. The secretary is a key liaison between the governor and both the political party and elected officials across the state.

Secretaries of state have a golden opportunity to create a statewide political base. In fact, many secretaries run for statewide elective office after serving the governor.

Governor Bush appointed Tony Garza as his secretary of state, the second Mexican American appointed to the post. Garza was the only Republican county judge in South Texas, and in 1994 had run unsuccessfully for the Republican nomination for attorney general. Garza resigned in 1997, then won election as railroad commissioner in 1998. Bush appointed Alberto Gonzales as his new secretary of state. Gonzales served until 1999, when Bush appointed him to the Texas Supreme Court to fill a vacancy there (he later became President Bush's counsel and U.S. Attorney General). In February 1999, Bush appointed Elton Bomer as secretary of state. Bomer was his insurance commissioner and had previously been a Democratic state representative. Even before he was sworn in as governor, Rick Perry announced his selection of seven-term Democratic State Representative Henry Cuellar to be his secretary of state. When Cuellar resigned to run for Congress, Perry appointed former State Representative Gwyn Shea. In 2003, Shea resigned, and Perry selected Geoffrey Connor, her assistant, to replace her. In 2004, Roger Williams succeeded Connor.

Public Utility Commissioners

The **Public Utility Commission** (PUC) has jurisdiction over telephone and electric power companies, while the Railroad Commission retains authority over gas companies. The three members of the PUC are appointed to staggered six-year terms by the governor. The public utility commissioners have a role that is largely **quasi-judicial.** The agency was created in 1975 in a storm of public sentiment to limit rapidly rising utility rates. But, the governor did not support utility regulation, and the early commissioners were generally perceived as sympathetic to utility companies.

Texas secretary of state
The state official appointed by the governor to be the keeper of the state's records, such as state laws, election data and filings, public notifications, and corporate charters.

Public Utility Commission
A full-time, three-member paid commission appointed by the governor to regulate public utilities in Texas.

quasi-judicial
A government commission receiving petitions from companies or individuals, hearing evidence in a hearing similar to a judicial proceeding, and ruling on the petition.

In 1995, the legislature redrafted the PUC's statute. Technological developments and congressional support for deregulation framed the debate. In 1995, the legislature passed a bill deregulating telecommunications, and in 1997 passed a bill deregulating public utilities. Under the 1997 bill, most monopoly electric utilities split into transmission and distribution companies, power generating companies, retail providers, and independent system operators. One goal is to guarantee residential customers choice of providers (though the PUC must maintain a no-call list for customers who don't want telephone solicitation about electric service). The PUC will still regulate transmission and distribution, but rates for power generating and retail were deregulated as of January 1, 2002. (Glitches in tryouts of the system became apparent in 2001, which delayed full implementation of deregulation.) After 2004, the PUC's role is to monitor abuses of market power, provide remedies, and oversee and review power grid procedures. The 2001 California energy crisis and the 2002 Enron and other energy-trading scandals may still impact Texas's deregulation.

Texas Commission on Environmental Quality

Texas Commission on Environmental Quality
A full-time, three-member paid commission appointed by the governor to administer the state's environmental programs. (Formerly the Texas Natural Resource Conservation Commission.)

In 1991, the legislature combined many of the state's environmental programs into a new agency, the Texas Natural Resource Conservation Commission (TNRCC), and abolished the Air Control Board and the Water Commission. In 2002, the agency assumed a new name, the **Texas Commission on Environmental Quality** (TCEQ). The three commissioners are appointed by the governor to staggered six-year terms. Commissioners have a quasi-judicial role in contested cases, but they have significant policy roles that make them the real powers in running the agency.

Businesses that will be emitting pollutants into the air or water must seek permits from the commission and must comply with regulations to limit the amount of those emissions. Thus, the commission becomes a lightning rod for conflicts between environmental and neighborhood groups seeking to restrict activities that could pollute, and businesses seeking to keep costs down while using modern industrial techniques and expanding or beginning new operations supplying products to the marketplace.

In 2001, TNRCC was recreated through the sunset process (described below) and in 2002 renamed the Texas Commission on Environmental Quality. The biggest controversy in the legislative debate was over the long battle to end the "grandfathered" status of several facilities in the state that emit air pollutants but have not had to comply with the state's air quality law. Those who wanted to end the grandfather status lost in 1997 and 1999 battles with Governor Bush but won in 2001. Another significant change in legislative policy is that the agency must now consider not just the environmental impacts of a specific business that is applying for a permit, but also the cumulative impacts of concentrated facilities in an area.

Insurance Commissioner

Because of the need to know whether insurance companies have assets sufficient to pay their claims, and because out-of-state companies proved difficult to pursue if customers had complaints of fraud, Texas has long had a public official or public body to oversee or regulate the insurance industry. The legislature has periodically reorganized the state agency, sometimes having a multimember body of commissioners and sometimes a single commissioner. Today, the **insurance commissioner** runs the Department of Insurance and is one of the few single executive heads appointed directly by the governor—though, again, the commissioner has a high level of independence because the governor could remove the commissioner only under extraordinary circumstances. The commissioner's job is to monitor the health of the insurance industry and, within new confines voted in by the legislature, to regulate insurance rates.

insurance commissioner
The official appointed by the governor to direct the Department of Insurance and regulate the insurance industry.

Between 1997 and 2002, homeowner's insurance premiums increased by more than 100 percent. In 2003, the legislature passed SB 14, which authorized the insurance commissioner to force insurance companies to lower their rates on homeowners' insurance. However, two of the largest insurers in Texas, State Farm and Farmers, fought the commissioner's attempt to lower their rates 12 percent and 17.5 percent respectively. The companies insisted that their rates were fair and contested the commissioner's attempt to force lower rates in court. In December 2004, after extended negotiations with the Texas Department of Insurance, Farmers agreed to lower its future rates.

Health and Human Services Commission

Health and human service programs are administered in Texas by numerous state agencies.

In 1991, the legislature created the commissioner of health and human services to *oversee* the massive health and human services programs scattered across the agencies. In 2003, the legislature completely reorganized the health and human services agencies to create a new system. The legislation merges twelve agencies into four new departments under the Health and Human Services Commission (HHSC), which is headed by an executive commissioner (appointed by the governor and confirmed by the Senate). The HHSC is also given additional duties, such as centralizing eligibility requirement for several programs, including Medicaid, Temporary Assistance for Needy Families, and the Children's Health Insurance Program. In addition, HHSC is responsible for consolidating administrative services for all health and human

executive commissioner of Health and Human Services Commission
The official appointed by the governor to oversee the state's multi-agency health and human service programs.

services agencies. The four new departments, each headed by a commissioner selected by the **executive commissioner of Health and Human Services Commission** with the governor's approval, are:

- Department of Family and Protective Services, which reconstitutes the Department of Protective and Regulatory Services.
- Department of Assistive and Rehabilitative Services, which assumes the powers and duties of the Texas Rehabilitation Commission, Commission for the Blind, Commission for the Deaf and Hard of Hearing, and Interagency Council on Early Childhood Intervention.
- Department of Aging and Disability Services, which consolidates mental retardation and state school programs of the Department of Mental Health and Mental Retardation (MHMR), community care and nursing home services programs of the Department of Human Services, and aging services programs of the Texas Department of Aging.
- Department of State Health Services, which takes over programs from the Texas Department of Health, the Texas Commission on Alcohol and Drug Abuse, and the Health Care Information Council. It also assumes the community and state hospital programs from MHMR.

All of the new departments were to provide consolidated operations by September 2004, but the consolidation will spread into 2005. By merging the agencies, the legislature hopes to improve service, enhance accountability, increase efficiencies, and reduce costs.

Public Counsels

captured agency
A government regulatory agency that consistently makes decisions favorable to the private interests that it regulates.

public counsels
Officials appointed by the governor to represent the public before regulatory agencies.

In recent years, as conflicts grew over regulatory policies, public-interest groups charged that regulatory agencies had become **captured agencies.** They were seen as consistently making decisions favorable to business interests and not adequately protecting consumers. A concept that gained some acceptance is that of **public counsels** to serve as advocates for the public before governmental agencies. The legislature gave the governor power to appoint a public insurance counsel and a public utility counsel. The counsels and their staffs examine rate-hike requests and other regulatory matters, then they go before the regulators to argue for their position, which is usually for rate reductions or for lower rate increases than the private companies have requested or the regulatory agency staff has recommended.

Boards and Commissions

Most state agencies are organized with a multimember policy-making body and a staff under the direction of the volunteer, part-time policy-making body. Some of these bodies are called boards, some are called commissions, and a very few are called councils or authorities. Collectively, these bodies are often referred to as the "board and commission" system of government. Some boards or commissions govern more than one agency. For instance, the ten boards of trustees of the state's colleges and universities run thirty-seven general academic institutions, nine medical schools, and nine major services.

In almost all cases, members of these policy-making bodies are appointed by the governor, with Senate confirmation. (A few have statutorily designated membership from agency heads or elected officials.) These appointments to boards and commissions constitute the bulk of the governor's appointments. However, for most boards, the terms of members are six years, and the terms are staggered, so a governor is not usually able to gain control of a majority of a board until late in his or her term of office. Even then, there is no assurance that members will do as the governor wishes because the governor may not fire the members. The governor may request the removal of an official that he or she appointed, but it requires approval of two-thirds of the Senate, and no such removal has ever occurred.

MAKING AGENCIES ACCOUNTABLE

IN CREATING AGENCIES AND PROGRAMS, and in delegating authority to agencies, legislatures do not wash their hands of responsibility for those programs. Rather, they have a duty to oversee what they have created and delegated. Legislative oversight of the bureaucracy includes review of expenditures, review of rules and regulations, performance reviews, audits, sunset review (in which the continuing need for an agency is evaluated), review of staff sizes and functions, and response to constituent complaints about agencies.

The Sunset Process

A **sunset law** establishes a date for programs or regulations to expire (the *sun* will *set* on them) unless the legislature renews them. The sunset concept is used in Texas to force a review of executive agencies and programs. The Texas Sunset Act was adopted in 1977. The Sunset Advisory Commission consists of five state senators, five state representatives, one public member appointed by the lieutenant governor, and one public member appointed by the House speaker. Under the Texas system, each state agency is given a twelve-year life span. If the commission recommends continuation of an agency, it drafts legislation, always with changes in the structure or procedures of the agency.

In addition to agency-specific recommendations, the first commission adopted a set of across-the-board **good government** recom-

Photo courtesy: Texas Sunset Advisory Commission

■ The Sunset Advisory Commission meets during the interim between legislative sessions to develop recommendations on abolishing, continuing, or changing state agencies up for sunset review.

sunset law
A law that sets a date for a program or regulation to expire unless reauthorized by the legislature.

good government
A term used for policies that open up agencies to public participation and scrutiny and that minimize conflicts of interest.

SHOULD TEXAS LOCK THE REVOLVING DOOR?

Government service at the highest levels is usually a temporary endeavor. People come from the private sector into policy leadership positions in regulatory agencies, then return to the private sector.

Critics point to the revolving door phenomenon as the key to private interests capturing public policy for their benefit. They argue that officials who come from private industry, or who are likely to turn to private industry for employment after leaving public service, are not likely to make the hard decisions required of public servants, but are more likely to serve the needs of private interests at the expense of the public interest.

Many people in both government and the private sector argue that such exchanges assure knowledgeable policy making. They say it is essential for those who impose requirements on business to understand the dynamics of the industry, so that regulations are effective and sensible.

Read and think about the following arguments for and against allowing the revolving door between the public and private sectors. Then, join the debate over the revolving door by answering the questions posed after the arguments.

Arguments in Favor of Allowing the Revolving Door

- **The ability of people to move back and forth between government and private industry allows the government to access the expertise of people in the private sector.** Most people who have highly technical knowledge do not want a career as a public servant, and locking the revolving door would make any public service less appealing.
- **Locking the revolving door would make it unlikely that people with technical and arcane knowledge would work for government.** Where would the government find people with the knowledge necessary to make public policy in highly technical or arcane areas if moving from the public sector to the private sector is prohibited?
- **Most people who leave government positions to work in the private sector are ethical and do not misuse the experience that they gained as public servants.** The problem is exaggerated by proponents of locking the revolving door.

mendations for all agencies to open themselves up to public participation and scrutiny and to minimize conflicts of interest.

By 2003, 346 agencies had been reviewed through the sunset process. Of those agencies, 282 (81 percent) were continued; 31 (9 percent) were abolished; 16 (5 percent) were abolished and had their functions transferred; 11 (3 percent) were combined; and 2 (1 percent) were separated.

Staff Size and Pay

A favorite method of legislative review and control of agencies is to monitor and then to increase or reduce staff size. Legislators and governors often vow to cut the number of state employees as a way of reducing the budget and as a way of controlling bureaucracy. Governor Clements

Arguments Against Allowing the Revolving Door

- **The failure to lock the revolving door allows former public officials to take advantage of their government contacts.** Former officials will use their government contacts to lobby for the benefit of industries rather than the public. They will also enrich themselves at the expense of the public interest.
- **The existence of a revolving door causes citizens to lose faith in their government and its accountability to them.** If citizens believe that government decisions are not made in their best interest, citizens are less likely to trust their government and less willing to abide by the government's decisions.
- **The revolving door provides an incentive for top-level officials to leave government service.** Government officials at the highest levels can earn much more from private industries that hire them for their government contacts. That provides an incentive for them to leave public service.

Questions

1. Do you favor or oppose locking the revolving door in Texas? Explain your answer.

2. What would be a compromise between allowing or completely closing the revolving door in Texas between public and private sectors?

Selected Readings

Betsy Russell. "State Urged to Restrict 'Revolving Door,'" *The Spokesman-Review.com,* July 18, 2004, accessed August 13, 2004, http://www.spokesmanreview.com/idaho/story.asp?ID=16272.

Peggy Kerns. "Revolving Door Laws," National Conference of State Legislators, Eye on Ethics, Briefing Papers on the Important Ethics Issues, accessed August 13, 2004, http://www.ncsl.org/programs/ethics/legisbrief-revolving.htm.

Selected Web Sites

http://www.govexec.com/ Government Executive Magazine.

http://www.tpj.org/index.jsp Texans for Public Justice.

vowed to cut 25 percent of the state workforce; when he left office, it was larger than when he took office. More recently, the legislature has adopted caps on numbers of employees that the agency may employ. (One result of this policy is increased contracting for services—the state is currently contracting with nearly 30,000 contractors.)

Numbers of employees are usually measured in units known as **full-time equivalent (FTE)** workers. That is, if you have five full-time employees and two half-time employees, then you have six FTEs. In 2002, the number of FTE state workers in Texas was approximately 269,674.[33] Another measure used to compare government employees across states is to modify the figures for the population in the state. In 2002, the number of FTE state workers per 10,000 population in Texas was 124.

The legislature adopts pay scales, titled the Classification Salary Schedule and the Exempt Salary Schedule, as a part of the appropria-

full-time equivalent (FTE)
A unit of measurement for number of employees.

tions bills. The bottom of the salary schedule for fiscal year 2004–2005 is $14,376, while the top is $190, 380. Some top officials, however, are also allowed to accept private pay supplements.

Regulating the Revolving Door

One practice that tends to reinforce close relations between private interests and public regulators, and thus to influence the direction of change, is the **revolving door,** the ongoing exchange of personnel between the two. Most often, employees of the agency quit and go to work for the industry that they had regulated; then they often turn around and lobby the agency for their new private employer. Sometimes it happens in reverse, or even in a revolving fashion. Industry and many agency officials argue that such exchanges help to ensure that regulators know the industry they are regulating. Critics charge it is a key method that private groups use to capture agencies: employees hoping to get better-paying jobs with the industry will be tempted to make decisions for personal or industry benefit, not for public benefit. Also, businesses have ready access to decision makers if their lobbyists are former agency officials.

The revolving door periodically becomes a public issue, particularly when an explicit decision benefiting a private interest can be tied to the role of one individual, first as a regulator, then as a representative of private industry. Governor Richards and numerous state officials proposed to "lock" the revolving door at most agencies, as it was already locked at the PUC, by prohibiting officials from working for a regulated industry for a period after leaving the agency. The legislature extended the revolving door lock to TCEQ and the Department of Insurance. Then the legislature applied a limited revolving door restriction to all regulatory agencies. The general revolving door statute applies only to officers and employees with exempt or high-end pay classifications.

Regulating the Relationship Between Agencies and Private Interests

Executive agencies have the primary role of implementing decisions made by the legislature. However, they also play key policy-making roles, and their freedom to interpret legislative intent makes them policy powerhouses. The iron triangle (see chapter 9 and Figure 9.4) is a model that includes the role that agencies play in the policy process. The closeness of private interests in Texas to legislators (through lobbying and campaign contributions) and to executive agencies (through influence on gubernatorial appointments and through the revolving

revolving door
An exchange of personnel between private interests and public regulators.

THE TEXAS RAILROAD COMMISSION: WATCHDOG OR LAPDOG?

"ARE YOU NUTS?" So read a letter from an oil industry representative to Texas Railroad Commissioner Tony Garza in reaction to his 2001 proposal to require stricter cleanup standards for oil spills.[a] At issue was environmental protection policy, as well as the standing of the Railroad Commission (RRC) with the general public and with the industry that it regulates.[b]

In 1999, the RRC staff began developing new oil spill guidelines. The staff and Garza proposed uniform methods of cleanup (with higher standards), required oil producers to generate a plan for cleanup, and required operators to notify surface landowners of spills and cleanup plans. The *Austin American-Statesman* wrote at the time: "the proposed rule could be viewed as a move to change the culture and outlook of an agency seen as a lapdog of the oil industry."[c]

Traditionally, the oil industry has been the biggest player in RRC elections. In the 1990s, the industry contributed more than $1 million to the winning Republican campaigns of Tony Garza, Charles Matthews, and Michael Williams. Yet, there were strained relations on the Republican panel. In June 2001, Garza proposed to begin an informal public comment period on the oil spill rule change and won Williams's vote, against Matthews.

Matthews reacted by sending out thousands of letters encouraging oil producers to express their opposition. He called Garza's proposal "the most liberal, onerous, unrealistic and unsound environmental rule in the history of the commission. . . . This cannot be allowed to stand."[d] The industry dutifully sounded the alarm and flooded the commission with phone calls and more than 1,000 letters. In July, at the Railroad Commission's annual "state of the industry" meeting, the Texas Independent Producers and Royalty Owners Association (TIPRO) led a delegation opposing the rule.

By August, RRC Chair Michael Williams had changed his mind about the rule, and proposed to shut off the comment period before any formal hearing was held. A TIPRO representative stated to the press that without the reversal of position, Williams would have had problems getting political support in the next election. Garza protested Williams's about face, saying, "we have only heard from the insiders of the industry."[e] But, this time Garza lost, on a 2–1 vote. He vigorously dissented, stating: "what we've said is that we are very comfortable with the status quo and we have a fear of embracing discussion and dialogue."[f]

The *Corpus Christi Caller-Times* wrote that the decision had perpetuated an "image of an agency that can't decide if its job is to be the watchdog over oil polluters and irresponsible producers, or an agency that walks hand in hand with the oil industry."[g] The *Austin American-Statesman* wrote that the effort "to change the culture of the commission was received with undisguised hostility by the petroleum industry. . . . [By this vote, the] Railroad Commission cemented its reputation as little more than an arm of the oil and gas industry."[h]

---

[a]Editorial Board, "Commission Again Sides with Industry," *Austin American-Statesman* (August 8, 2001): A14.

[b]This feature also draws on Ralph K. M. Haurwitz, "Oil, Gas Pipe Leaks in Countryside Break No Rules: Comprehensive Regulation Unlikely for Rural Pipelines," *Austin American-Statesman* (November 18, 2001): A1; Ralph K. M. Haurwitz, "Lawmakers Poised to Study Rural Pipelines: Damage Prevention," *Austin American-Statesman* (December 4, 2001): A1; and Editorial Board, "Railroad Commission Again Fails to Protect Texas," *Austin American-Statesman* (August 25, 2001): A10.

[c]Editorial Board, "Commission Again Sides with Industry."

[d]Editorial Board, "Commission Again Sides with Industry."

[e]Claudia Grisales, "Agency Drops Bid to Tighten Oil Spill Rules: Railroad Commission Chairman Says Pleas from Oil Industry Changed His Mind on Toughening Law," *Austin American-Statesman* (August 7, 2001): A1.

[f]Claudia Grisales, "Oil Spills Cleanup Proposal Quashed: Railroad Commission Rejects Toughened Rules After Industry Outcry," *Austin American-Statesman* (August 22, 2001): D1.

[g]Editorial Board, "Agency Folds on Vital Clean-Water Issue," *Corpus Christi Caller-Times* (August 10, 2001).

[h]Editorial Board, "Railroad Commission Again Fails to Protect Texas."

door) lends strength to the iron-triangle model. Political scientist Marver Bernstein described the evolution of agencies, from their creation in an atmosphere of public outrage at perceived abuses at the hands of private industry to their original role as independent watchdogs over the industry, to an unintended role as an agency captured by the private interests, consistently making decisions favorable to those interests.[34]

The Texas Railroad Commission fits Bernstein's model (see Politics Now: The Texas Railroad Commission: Watchdog or Lapdog?). Born as the fruit of populists' anger at railroad company rates and practices, the commission at first responded to the public's demand for lower rates. By the time the agency's largest role was to regulate the oil and gas industry, it was so fully captured by that industry that it ran an ad (sponsored by two industry associations) claiming that "Since 1891 the Texas Railroad Commission has served the oil industry."[35]

The PUC has had a history similar to that of the Railroad Commission. Attempts at creating a new state agency had stalled for years. In the 1970s, the populace was stirred up over high utility rates and the appearance of favoritism to utility companies by government institutions. This popular participation, triggered by economic crisis, brought about political change and the creation of the PUC. However, key state leaders still opposed an adversarial regulatory relationship with the industry, governors appointed commissioners sympathetic to the industry, and the agency quickly became captured by the industry.

SUMMARY

TEXAS GOVERNORS ARE WEAK, compared with other governors, and they must share political power with other executive leaders and with the legislature.

1. The Roots of the Executive in Texas
The powers held by Texas governors and other executive officials fluctuated considerably with changes of constitutions in the nineteenth century. This history has influenced the array of elected and appointed executive officials, the terms of office for the governorship, and the governor's salary.

2. The Constitutional Roles of the Governor
The constitution and the legislature have created gubernatorial roles, including chief of state, chief executive officer, commander in chief, chief budget officer, and more informal roles in law enforcement and in legislative politics.

3. The Development of Gubernatorial Power
Texas governors have always been weaker than governors in other states. Governors may be able to amass and exercise more strength, though, in the political arena, where appearance, charisma,

and bluff may count more than constitutional reality. Texas gubernatorial power, however, has increased over the past two decades.

4. The Governor As Policy Maker and Political Leader

The political and policy leadership that a governor is able to provide flows from the governor's skills, previous experience, and similarity in party, philosophy, and ideology with other decision makers. At the base of that leadership is electoral skill. Texas's governors resort to public-opinion leadership to increase their power with other office holders. Still, to be successful, a governor must succeed in pushing a program through the legislature and in killing unwanted legislative measures.

5. The Plural Executive in Texas

Texas elects nine statewide executive officials—more than most states—as well as fifteen education board members elected from districts. There are frequent clashes between governors and other executive officials.

6. Modern Texas Bureaucracy

Texas executive agencies are organized in two basic patterns. First, there are those agencies headed by one person; second, there are those agencies run by a board or commission.

7. Making Agencies Accountable

Legislatures have a duty of legislative oversight of executive agencies and programs. Oversight tools include review of expenditures, review of rules and regulations, performance reviews, audits, sunset review, and review of staff sizes and functions.

KEY TERMS

SELECTED READINGS

Comptroller of Public Accounts. *Challenging the Status Quo: Toward Smaller, Smarter Government*, 1999.

Duncan, Marilyn, and Shirley Beckwith. *Guide to Texas State Agencies*, 11th ed. Austin: LBJ School of Public Affairs, 2001.

Gantt, Fred, Jr. *The Chief Executive in Texas: A Study in Gubernatorial Leadership*. Austin: University of Texas Press, 1964.

Lauderdale, Michael. *Reinventing Texas Government*. Austin: University of Texas Press, 1999.

Prindle, David. *Petroleum Politics and the Texas Railroad Commission*. Austin: University of Texas Press, 1981.

Sunset Advisory Commission. *Guide to the Texas Sunset Process*, 2001.

WEB EXPLORATIONS

To learn more about the Texas governor's office, go to
   http://www.governor.state.tx.us

To learn more about governors' organizations, go to
   http://www.nga.org

To learn more about the Texas executive branch, go to
   http://www.www2tsl.state.tx.us/trail/agencies.jsp

To learn more about services provided by the comptroller
   and other state programs, go to
   http://www.window.state.tx.us

To learn more about the sunset process in Texas, go to
   http://www.sunset.state.tx.us

20

The Texas Judiciary

FOR MANY OF THE REPORTERS in attendance, a feeling of déjà vu must have pervaded the room. A Texas Supreme Court chief justice was announcing his resignation, and several groups were criticizing members of the Texas Supreme Court for taking campaign contributions from groups representing litigants before the court. It must have seemed like 1988 all over again. In 1988, Chief Justice John Hill resigned his position halfway through his term, claiming that he wanted to devote all his attention to ending the "money-driven, partisan system" for selecting judges in Texas. In 2004, Chief Justice Thomas R. Phillips, whom Governor Bill Clements had appointed to replace Hill, was also stepping down in the middle of his term after presiding over the state's highest court for civil cases for sixteen years. Phillips was also critical of Texas's partisan system for selecting judges and had campaigned for a merit system, or Missouri Plan, for selecting judges, a selection process that entails bipartisan nominating commissions, gubernatorial appointments, and retention elections. Both chief justices failed to convince the legislature to change judicial selection in Texas.[1]

John Hill's Committee of 100—established in 1986 and composed of citizens appointed by Hill, the speaker of the Texas House, and the lieutenant governor—proposed the "Texas Plan," which closely resembled the Missouri Plan. The Committee of 250 provided organized opposition to the Texas Plan. Later, organized labor and plaintiff lawyers joined the opposition to the Texas Plan. The opposition favored the retention of partisan judicial elections.[2]

CHAPTER OUTLINE

- The Roots of the Texas Judiciary
- The Structure of the Texas Judiciary
- Judges and Judicial Selection
- Criticisms of the Texas Judicial Branch
- The Judicial Process in Texas

713

Chief Justice Phillips fared no better than his predecessor. In 2000, he led a conference on judicial selection that was coordinated by the National Center for State Courts (NCSC). The conference resulted in several recommendations. In a series of State of the Judiciary addresses to the Texas legislature, Phillips called for judicial selection reform. In his most recent address, Phillips stated, "I have saved for last the issue which is most critical for our courts—the question of how we elect our judges. Our partisan, high-dollar judicial selection system has diminished public confidence in our courts, damaged our reputation throughout the country and around the world, and discouraged able lawyers from pursuing a judicial career."[3] He then made his case for an appointive, retention election method of judicial selection. In 2003, the Senate passed a constitutional amendment on judicial selection, but the House let it die in committee.

Texas is one of only four states that still choose all of their trial and appellate judges, both initially and for subsequent terms, in partisan elections. The Texas judiciary faces other challenges as well. As Chief Justice Phillips noted in his resignation statement, "Of course, the Texas judiciary is far from perfect. Many of its problems may be traced to the structure of our judicial system, which is essentially a relic of the nineteenth century."[4]

THE ONGOING EFFORT to reform judicial selection in Texas demonstrates one of two respects in which the judiciary differs from the other branches of Texas government—the legislature and the executive. First, the judiciary is the least familiar branch of Texas government. Most Texans have little knowledge of the structure and operation of the courts and even less knowledge of the judges who hold positions on them. Second, unlike the other branches, the judiciary cannot initiate action. It must wait for an individual or group to seek its assistance by initiating a lawsuit. Even then, the court must determine whether it is an issue that can be settled by the application of state law or is a matter that must be considered by another branch of government.

As in other states, the principal function of courts in Texas is to settle disputes by applying the law. The dispute may involve the state's acting on behalf of the community to prosecute suspected criminals or it may involve individuals who disagree about the terms of a contract. In both kinds of disputes, the courts examine the facts, interpret the law, and attempt to settle the conflict.

In this chapter, we will examine the Texas judiciary to understand how the courts apply and interpret the law to settle disputes.

- First, we will examine the *roots of the Texas judiciary*, describing how the structure and operation of the judiciary evolved since the early 1800s.

- Second, we will describe the *structure of the judiciary* in contemporary Texas, indicating the various types of courts and their responsibilities.

- Third, we will describe *judges and judicial selection* in Texas, indicating who settles disputes in Texas and how they are chosen.

- Fourth, we will assess the *criticisms of the Texas judicial branch,* analyzing persistent problems that affect the ability of the judiciary to settle disputes fairly and impartially.

- Finally, we will describe the *judicial process in Texas.*

THE ROOTS OF THE TEXAS JUDICIARY

THE FIRST COURTS IN TEXAS were established in the Austin colony when Stephen F. Austin appointed a provisional justice of the peace for the province of Texas in 1822. Since Texas was a part of Mexico, the Mexican governor subsequently replaced the justice of the peace with three elected officials who applied Spanish law in Austin's colony. The judiciary was a point of contention between the Anglo settlers and the Mexican government.

As an independent republic, Texas created a judiciary that primarily reflected English tradition although some features of Spanish law were retained. Under the 1836 constitution, the Republic of Texas created a supreme court, which had appellate jurisdiction only, and allowed Congress to create inferior courts. Judges were elected by Congress. Counties also had county and justice of the peace courts, whose judges were popularly elected.

In subsequent constitutions, Texas retained the basic judicial structure established in the 1836 constitution. Almost every constitution provided for the popular election of judges. As caseloads increased, additional courts were created, especially at the appellate level. In the 1876 constitution, the judiciary consisted of the supreme court, with appellate civil jurisdiction; the court of appeals, with criminal jurisdiction and limited civil jurisdiction; and an array of district, county, and justice of the peace courts. In 1891, the constitution was amended to provide an intermediate level of courts of civil appeal. The amendment also changed the name of the court of appeals to the court

Photo courtesy: Bob Daemmrich/Bob Daemmrich Photography, Inc.

■ Governor Bill Clements originally appointed Thomas Phillips to the position of chief justice in 1988, when John Hill resigned. Phillips has worked diligently, but unsuccessfully, to change the method of judicial selection in Texas. He resigned in 2004, and Governor Perry appointed Justice Wallace Jefferson to replace him.

Roots of Government

JUDGE ROY BEAN: THE LAW WEST OF THE PECOS

NINETEENTH-CENTURY RURAL TEXANS had little government to interfere with their chosen way of life, which meant they also had little government to enforce the law. Television and movie westerns are rife with stories of lawless towns and outgunned sheriffs. Texas has its own version of the story, personified by the most famous justice of the peace in American history, Pecos County Justice of the Peace Roy Bean.

Citizen Bean had been no saint: From the 1840s to the 1880s, he had been a trader and saloonman. Despite questionable business dealings, Bean managed to stay one step ahead of the law and angry customers, eventually arriving at a railroad camp just west of the Pecos River in West Texas in 1882.

Bean set up a saloon in a tent, attracting thirsty—and mischievous—railroad workers. The railroad camp was lawless and violent, attracting the attention of the Texas Rangers. The rangers needed a justice of the peace, and county commissioners appointed Bean. He held the post for most of the next twenty years. Twice he was defeated for reelection but won back the seat both times.

Judge Bean was known to intimidate and cheat people. At the same time, he was humorous, dramatic, and shrewd, gaining a reputation far and wide.

Photo courtesy: Bettmann/CORBIS

Judge Roy Bean dispensing justice at the "Jersey Lilly." As the sign indicates, Judge Bean constituted the law west of the Pecos in Texas.

Judge Bean died shortly after retiring from the bench in 1902, but his legacy lives on. Two biographies and a movie chronicle the legend of the Law West of the Pecos.

Sources: "Roy Bean," "Langtry, Texas," and "Woodrow Wilson Bean Sr.," *The Handbook of Texas Online*, last updated July 23, 2001, accessed June 10, 2002, http://www.tsha.utexas.edu/handbook/online/articles/print/BB/fbe8.html; http://www.tsha.utexas.edu/handbook/online/articles/view/LL/hll17.html; http://www.tsha.utexas.edu/handbook/online/articles/view/BB/fbeay.html. Everett Lloyd, *Law West of the Pecos* (San Antonio: University Press, 1931; rev. ed., San Antonio: Naylor, 1967); C. L. Sonnichsen, *Roy Bean, Law West of the Pecos* (New York: Macmillan, 1943; reprinted Albuquerque: University of New Mexico Press, 1986).

of criminal appeals and limited its jurisdiction to criminal cases. With the addition of the intermediate courts, the Texas Supreme Court was allowed to exercise discretion in accepting appeals. However, the additional civil appeals courts did not affect a growing caseload for the Texas Court of Criminal Appeals. In 1980, the courts of civil appeals became courts of appeals and their jurisdiction was extended to criminal cases.[5]

Over the years, constitutional amendments and legislative acts have added courts and changed the structure of the Texas judiciary, creating a system that is among the most complicated and confusing in the United States. In the next section, we describe the current array of courts and their responsibilities.

THE STRUCTURE OF THE TEXAS JUDICIARY

THE TEXAS JUDICIARY incorporates five levels of courts, some created by the constitution and others created by the legislature. Figure 20.1 illustrates the courts at each level.

Local Trial Courts

At the lowest level are local trial courts of limited jurisdiction, which include municipal courts and justice of the peace courts. By statute, the legislature allows each incorporated city in Texas to create a municipal court. Some larger cities are allowed several courts. In 2003, 882 cities had established municipal courts, employing approximately 1,325 judges. **Municipal courts** exercise original jurisdiction over traffic misdemeanors, such as speeding, failure to wear a seat belt, and parking on a sidewalk. The maximum penalty in these cases is a fine or sanction that does not include confinement to jail or imprisonment. Municipal courts also have original jurisdiction over Class C misdemeanors, such as public intoxication and simple assault. The penalty in these cases cannot exceed $500. Violations of city ordinances, which may include a maximum fine of $2,000 for violations of fire safety, zoning, and public heath ordinances, are also handled by municipal courts. Finally, municipal courts exercise civil jurisdiction in cases involving dangerous dogs, and municipal judges perform magistrate functions. Magistrate duties include conducting examining trials (preliminary hearings for county and district courts to determine whether sufficient evidence exists to hold someone for trial), issuing search and arrest warrants, and providing statutory warnings.

municipal court
City court with limited criminal jurisdiction.

In 2003, more than 8 million new cases were filed in Texas municipal courts. Of those cases, nearly 82 percent involved traffic violations—thus, the name "traffic courts" given to municipal courts. Fifty-three percent of the cases disposed in 2003 involved a trial and a decision by a judge or jury, and fewer than 1 percent of those cases were appealed.[6]

The other local trial court in Texas is the justice of the peace court. Most states have eliminated justice courts, but there were 835 justice of the peace courts in Texas in 2003. Each of Texas's 254 counties,

FIGURE 20.1 The Court Structure of Texas

This figure shows the jurisdictions, levels, and different courts in the Texas judiciary. ■

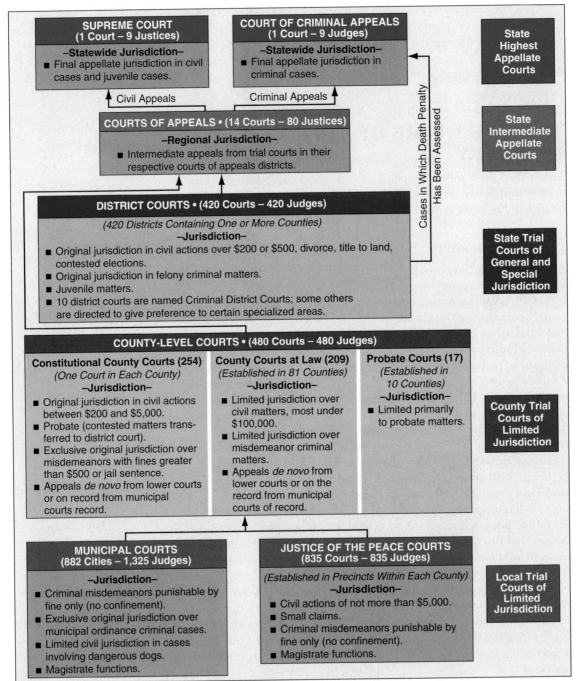

Note: Some municipal courts are courts of record—appeals from those courts are taken on the record to the county-level courts. All justice of the peace courts and most municipal courts are not courts of record. Appeals from these courts are by trial de novo in the county-level courts, and in some instances in the district courts. An offense that arises under a municipal ordinance is punishable by a fine not to exceed: (1) $2,000 for ordinances that govern fire safety, zoning, and public health, or (2) $500 for all others.

Source: Office of Court Administration, Austin, Texas, 2003.

depending on its population, must create between one and eight justice precincts. Depending on the population of the precinct, each justice precinct in a county has one or two judges.

Justice of the peace courts have both civil and criminal jurisdiction. They exercise exclusive original jurisdiction in civil cases involving less than $200, and concurrent original jurisdiction with district and county courts in civil cases involving less than $5,000. The justice of the peace courts function as small claims courts: the parties in a civil suit present their sides in the case before a judge, who decides the case based on the evidence and testimony provided by the parties. Neither party needs to be represented by an attorney. Because small claims courts provide an inexpensive method of resolving disputes involving small amounts of money, they are often called the "people's courts."

justice of the peace court
Local county court for minor crimes and civil suits.

Justice of the peace courts have original jurisdiction over Class C misdemeanors throughout the county. However, if municipalities within a county have municipal courts, the justice courts usually only hear cases that occur within the unincorporated areas of the county. Justices of the peace also perform magistrate duties—such as issuing search and arrest warrants, conducting preliminary hearings, performing marriages—and have jurisdiction over forcible entry and detainer actions, which are usually attempts by landlords to remove tenants. In 2003, nearly 3 million new cases were filed in justice of the peace courts. Of those, 90 percent were criminal cases. The remaining 10 percent were civil cases, of which more than half involved forcible entry and detainer suits. Small claims suits constituted 22 percent of the civil cases.

County Courts

At the next level of the Texas judiciary are county courts of limited jurisdiction. There are two major categories of county courts: constitutional county courts and county courts at law.

The Texas Constitution establishes a constitutional county court in each of the state's 254 counties. **Constitutional county courts** have concurrent original jurisdiction in civil matters with justice of the peace courts (suits between $200 and $5,000) and with district courts (suits between $200.01 and $5,000). They also have jurisdiction over probate cases (legal matters primarily involving wills and estates), unless the probate is contested, in which case they are transferred to a district court. Constitutional county courts exercise criminal jurisdiction over Class A and B misdemeanors, which carry penalties of a fine greater than $500 and/or a jail sentence.

constitutional county court
Constitutionally mandated court for criminal and civil matters.

Constitutional county courts also exercise appellate jurisdiction over cases from municipal and justice of the peace courts. Since few municipal courts and no justice of the peace courts are courts of record, there is no transcript of the trial. Without a transcript, there is no record of the proceedings for the county court to review for procedural errors. Consequently, appeals from most municipal courts and

DRIVING WHILE INTOXICATED IN TEXAS

Texas leads the nation in alcohol-related traffic deaths. According to the National Highway Traffic Safety Administration (NHTSA), 1,745 people were killed in alcohol-related crashes in Texas in 2002. The Texas Department of Public Safety reported that alcohol-related crashes caused 25,142 injuries in 2001, and more than 96,000 arrests for driving while intoxicated are made annually. Adults between the ages of twenty-one and thirty-four are more likely to be involved in alcohol-related crashes or to be arrested for driving while intoxicated (DWI) than people in other age categories. Despite zero-tolerance laws for under-age drinking and driving, it is a serious problem in Texas. In 2001, alcohol was involved in 25,490 crashes and took the lives of 303 young people between the ages of fifteen and twenty-four.

In recent legislative sessions, the penalties for DWI have been increased. For persons under twenty-one years old, any blood alcohol concentration (BAC) while driving violates the law. For those between seventeen and twenty-one years of age, the penalty for the first offense includes a sixty-day driver's license suspension, a maximum fine of $500, twenty to forty hours of community service, and mandatory attendance in alcohol-awareness classes. For those with a BAC exceeding .08, the penalty for the first offense is seventy-two hours to 180 days in jail, a maximum fine of $2,000, and a ninety-day to one-year suspension of your driver's license.[a]

On college campuses in Texas, activities have been developed to educate students about DWI and to change social norms in an effort to reduce DWI in the state. Three programs have received recognition for excellence:

- In 2002, the University of Texas at Austin received a $5,000 grand prize for its wide-ranging Longhorns Against Drunk Driving program to change campus norms. The program included several components: development of an online student alcohol and drug use survey that was used to conduct pre- and post-assessment of campus norms; coordination of campus activities through the UT Campus/Austin Community Advisory Committee; and a broad-scale media outreach program with stickers, posters, radio public service announcements, T-shirts, Web site, newspaper ads, on-campus TV announcements, and mall displays.[b]

- In 2003, Texas A&M University won a $1,000 state prize for "The Choice Is Up to You: Make Responsible Decisions," a broad-scoped campaign initiated for the campus and surrounding community to emphasize responsible decision making. Training was conducted with numerous campus individuals and groups, including residence hall directors and advisers, the judicial board, off-campus resident advisers, freshman orientation counselors, designated-driver program staff, and teaching assistants for athlete life-skills classes. "Bee a good neighbor" neighborhood walks provided local students with information about state alcohol laws.[c]

- In 2000, Texas State University and the University of Texas at Austin produced "A Night to Remember: The Truth About DWI," a film depicting the consequences of driving while intoxicated. The film was mentioned in a booklet by the Automobile Club of Southern California describing "best practices" for preventing drinking and driving on college campuses.[d]

[a]The facts are from Texas DWI Web site, accessed August 7, 2004, http://www.texasdwi.org/.

[b]Automobile Association of America Web site, Higher Education Center Drinking and Driving Prevention Awards, 2001–2002 Awards, accessed August 7, 2004, http://www.csaa.com/global/articledetail/0,1398,1004040000%257C2877,00.html.

[c]Automobile Association of America Web site, Higher Education Center Drinking and Driving Prevention Awards.

[d]Automobile Club of Southern California, "Reducing Drinking and Driving on Campus: Best Practices from the College and University Drinking and Driving Prevention Awards Program," January 2003, accessed August 7, 2003, http://www.aaa-calif.com/corpinfo/guides/drinking-prevention-booklet-3.pdf.

all justice of the peace courts take the form of a completely new trial—termed a **trial *de novo.***

Statutory county courts—**county courts at law**—were created to relieve county judges in urban counties of their judicial functions so that they could concentrate on their duties as presiding officer of the commissioners court (see chapter 17). In 2003, there were 209 county courts at law in eighty-one counties. Some counties have several county courts at law.

The state legislature has created county courts at law to meet the needs of each county's court system. Since the courts cost the state nothing, if the state legislators from a county want a court at law created, the legislature will probably accommodate them. Since each court is established by statute, a county court at law may have concurrent jurisdiction with other statutory county courts or may exercise original subject matter jurisdiction in a limited field—such as civil, criminal, or probate—or appellate jurisdiction. Sixteen probate courts, whose jurisdiction is limited to probate, have been established in eight counties in Texas. The original civil jurisdiction of these courts varies greatly, although most exceed the $5,000 limit placed on the constitutional county courts, and at least one court has no limit.[7]

The effect of these statutes is a bewildering array of county courts at law, making meaningful generalizations about these courts and their jurisdictions difficult. Nevertheless, most county courts at law have limited original jurisdiction in civil cases, usually in those cases that involve less than $100,000. They also have limited original jurisdiction in criminal cases involving Class A and B misdemeanors. Most county courts at law have the same appellate jurisdiction as constitutional county courts.

County courts of all types added nearly 800,000 cases to their dockets in 2003. Of that number, 69 percent were criminal cases. Among the criminal cases, 23 percent of the new cases and appeals were for theft or worthless checks, and 18 percent were for driving while intoxicated or under the influence of drugs (DWI/DUID). Of the remaining cases, civil cases accounted for 19 percent, and probate cases represented 7 percent.

District Courts

The state courts of general and special jurisdiction are the district courts, which numbered 420 in 2003. The **district courts** have original civil jurisdiction in cases involving more than $200 or $500, all suits over the title to land, divorce proceedings, election contests, and contested probate matters. The district courts also have original criminal jurisdiction in all felony cases.

Most district courts exercise both criminal and civil jurisdiction. However, in metropolitan areas, the district courts tend to specialize in criminal, civil, juvenile, or family matters.

District courts added more than 800,000 new cases to their dockets during 2003. Of that total, 66 percent were civil cases, 30 percent

trial *de novo*
New trial, necessary for an appeal from a court that is not a court of record.

county court at law
Statutory county court to relieve county judge of judicial duties.

district court
Court of general jurisdiction for serious crimes and high-dollar civil cases.

were criminal cases, and 5 percent were juvenile cases. The largest category of criminal case offenses involved drug-related offenses. Among civil cases, the largest category was divorce.

Intermediate Courts of Appeal

court of appeals
Intermediate appellate court for criminal and civil appeals.

There are fourteen **courts of appeals** in Texas and a total of eighty justices. Other than the 1st and 14th Courts of Appeals, which are located in Houston and serve the same area, each court serves a distinct geographic region. Each court includes a chief justice, who is elected as chief justice by the voters in a general election, and between two and twelve justices. Cases are usually heard by a panel of three justices. Certain cases, however, are heard *en banc*, which means that all of the justices assigned to the particular court of appeals participate. Since the courts are reviewing the record of the trial court, no testimony is taken, and no juries are involved. Decisions are rendered by a majority of the justices participating in the case. These courts exercise appellate jurisdiction over civil and criminal appeals from district and county courts in their respective regions. Only death penalty cases, which go directly from a district court to the court of criminal appeals, escape the courts' jurisdiction.

More than 10,000 new cases were filed in the courts of appeals during 2003. Of those cases, 54 percent were criminal cases, and 46 percent were civil cases. To equalize the number of cases heard by each court, the Texas Supreme Court transfers cases between the courts. In 2003, 251 civil cases and 612 criminal cases were transferred.

Comparative
Comparing Judicial
Systems

Photo courtesy: Bob Daemmrich

■ The Texas Supreme Court in late November 2004. Pictured, from left to right, are Dale Wainwright, Harriet O'Neill, Nathan L. Hecht, Chief Justice Wallace B. Jefferson, Priscilla R. Owen, Steven W. Smith, Scott A. Brister, and David Medina.

The members of the Texas Court of Criminal Appeals in 2005. Front row: Paul Womack, Lawrence E. Meyers, Sharon Keller, Tom Price, Cheryl Johnson. Back row: Charles Holcomb, Michael Keasler, Barbara Hervey, Cathy Cochran.

Photo courtesy: Bob Daemmrich/Bob Daemmrich Photography, Inc.

The Supreme Courts

The state's highest appellate courts include the **Texas Supreme Court,** for civil matters, and the **Texas Court of Criminal Appeals,** for criminal matters. Both courts have limited original jurisdiction, but most of their cases involve appeals from the courts of appeals. Both are courts of last resort, meaning that they are the last state courts to which a person can appeal a case. Of course, a person who claims that a "federal question" is involved may petition the U.S. Supreme Court for a writ of *certiorari* (see chapter 10).

The Texas Supreme Court includes a chief justice and eight justices. The Texas Court of Criminal Appeals also has nine members, a presiding judge and eight judges. The Texas Supreme Court always hears cases *en banc,* with all nine justices participating in the case. The constitution allows the Texas Court of Criminal Appeals to sit in panels of three judges, except for capital murder cases, but it almost never does. For both courts, decisions are reached by a majority vote. Both courts are located in Austin, but they are allowed to hear cases in other locations in Texas.

The operations of the two highest state courts in Texas are similar. Each court exercises some discretion in reviewing cases, although the Texas Court of Criminal Appeals is required to review all capital cases from the district courts. To secure a review by the Texas Supreme Court, a party in a suit files a **petition for review**—a request for the Supreme Court to review the decision of the court of appeals. In conference, the nine justices consider the request, and if four justices agree, the petition is granted. The case is then scheduled for oral argument

Texas Supreme Court
Court of last resort in civil and juvenile cases.

Texas Court of Criminal Appeals
Court of last resort in criminal cases.

petition for review
Request for Texas Supreme Court review, which is granted if four justices agree.

application for discretionary review
Request for Texas Court of Criminal Appeals review, which is granted if four judges agree.

before the court, and the parties to the suit submit legal briefs.[8] In 2003, the Texas Supreme Court considered 968 petitions for review and granted 112 (12 percent) of them. A refusal to grant a petition for review allows the ruling of the lower court to stand. The Texas Court of Criminal Appeals reviews **applications for discretionary review,** following the same procedure as the Supreme Court in reviewing its petitions for review. If four judges concur, the petition is granted. In 2003, the Texas Court of Criminal Appeals considered 1,742 petitions for discretionary review and granted 111 (6 percent).

After the courts hear the oral arguments in a case, they decide the case in conferences. Once the court has reached a decision, one of the justices is assigned the task of writing the court's opinion. The Texas Supreme Court justices wrote 128 opinions in 2003. Of those opinions, eighty-nine (70 percent) were deciding opinions, including sixty majority opinions, and twenty-nine *per curiam* (see chapter 10). The remaining opinions were concurring opinions, dissenting opinions, or concurring and dissenting opinions. During that same period, the Texas Court of Criminal Appeals judges wrote 612 opinions, of which 473 were deciding opinions. Of the 473 deciding opinions, 186 were signed opinions and 287 were *per curiam*. The remaining opinions were concurring and dissenting opinions.

The Texas Supreme Court performs several administrative duties in addition to its judicial responsibilities. It is responsible for establishing the rules and procedures that govern trials and appeals in civil and juvenile cases in Texas. It also establishes the rules for the operation of state agencies in the judicial branch, such as the Office of Court Administration, Commission on Judicial Conduct, and State Bar of Texas.

JUDGES AND JUDICIAL SELECTION

THERE ARE MORE THAN 3,100 JUDGES in Texas. Except for municipal judges, they are selected in partisan elections. Trial judges—justices of the peace, constitutional and statutory county court judges, and district court judges—serve four-year terms, while appellate judges and justices—courts of appeals, supreme court, and court of criminal appeals—serve six-year terms. After describing the qualifications for Texas judges, we will examine judicial selection.

Judicial Qualifications and Personal Characteristics

The Texas Constitution establishes the qualifications for most Texas judges, which vary by judicial office (see Table 20.1). Consequently, Texas judges vary greatly in education and training. In personal characteristics, however, the judges are quite similar.

TABLE 20.1 Judicial Qualifications

Court	Term of Office	Salary, 2003	Qualifications
Municipal courts	2 or 4 years, varies by city	Set by city, highly variable	Determined by the city
Justice of the peace courts	4 years	Set by county, highly variable	None
Constitutional county court	4 years	Set by county, highly variable	Must be "well informed in the law"
County courts at law	4 years	Set by county, highly variable	25 years of age, county resident for 2 years, licensed attorney in Texas, served as judge or practiced law for 4 years
District courts	4 years	$101,700 ($0–$23,300 supplement provided by the county)	Citizen, district resident for 2 years, licensed attorney in Texas, practicing lawyer or judge for 4 years
Courts of appeals	6 years	Chief justice: $107,850 Justices: $107,350 ($3,551–$4,650 supplement provided by counties in the district)	Citizen, 35 years of age, practicing attorney or judge of a court of record for at least 10 years
Texas Court of Criminal Appeals	6 years	Presiding judge: $115,000 Judges: $113,000	Same as courts of appeals
Texas Supreme Court	6 years	Chief justice: $115,000 Justices: $113,000	Same as courts of appeals

Source: Office of Court Administration, fiscal year 2003.

For municipal courts, the municipality's legislative body or the city charter establishes the qualifications for its judges. These qualifications vary widely among the municipalities in Texas. In 2003, nearly one-half were graduates of law schools, and nearly one-third were licensed to practice law. In ethnicity, 85 percent were Anglo, 12 percent were Hispanic, and 2 percent were African American. Sixty-nine percent of the judges were males.

Justices of the peace are required to be registered voters, but there are no educational, age, or experience requirements. As a result, in 2003, few had graduated from law school, and even fewer were licensed attorneys. Eighty-one percent of the judges were Anglos, 15 percent were Hispanic, and 3 percent were African American. Sixty-nine percent of the justices of the peace were males.

The Texas Constitution requires constitutional county judges to be "well informed in the law of the State," but no law degree or license to practice law is required. However, county judges who perform judicial duties are required to complete at least thirty hours of instruction. Among the county court judges in 2003, 14 percent had graduated from law schools, and 12 percent were licensed attorneys. Almost all of the judges were Anglo males.

A statutory county court judge must be at least twenty-five years old and a licensed attorney with a minimum of four years' experience either as a judge or a practicing attorney. Because of the qualifications, nearly all of the judges in 2003 had graduated from law school and were licensed attorneys. In ethnicity, 78 percent of the judges were Anglos, 18 percent were Hispanic, and 3 percent were African American. Seventy percent were males.

A district court judge must have resided in the judicial district for two years and have been a licensed attorney in Texas or judge for four years. Almost all of the district judges are licensed attorneys. In 2003, 83 percent of the judges were Anglos, 12 percent were Hispanic, 3 percent were African American, and 74 percent were males.

The constitution requires all appellate court judges—those on the courts of appeals, supreme court, and court of criminal appeals—to be at least thirty-five years of age and have been a practicing attorney or a judge of a court of record for at least ten years. In 2003, judges for Texas's fourteen courts of appeals were predominately middle-aged, Anglo males. The judges had served on the court for an average of nearly six years, and a majority had been lawyers in private practice before becoming a judge on the court. Nearly one-fifth had previously served as a judge on a trial court.

The members of the state's two highest courts also share similar personal characteristics. In 2004, there were six males and two females on the Texas Supreme Court, five males and four females on the Texas Court of Criminal Appeals, their average age was nearly fifty-five, and the members were overwhelmingly Anglos. Supreme Court Justices Dale Wainwright and David Medina and Chief Justice Wallace Jefferson were the only ethnic minorities on the state's higher courts.

Judicial Selection

For more than a century, Texas has chosen its judges in partisan elections and is currently one of only eight states that elect all or most of their judges through partisan elections. There are two exceptions to partisan elections: municipal judges, and filling vacancies in other judicial offices. Municipal judges may be elected or appointed by the city council. If vacancies occur in statutory county judgeships, the county commissioners court appoints a judge. For district courts, courts of appeals, and the Texas Supreme Court and Texas Court of Criminal Appeals, vacancies are filled by gubernatorial appointment. In 2003, four of the nine supreme court justices were initially appointed to the court, as were 47 percent of the eighty court of appeals judges and 41 percent of the 420 district court judges.

Most of the time, however, potential judges have to compete in partisan contests. Opinion polls indicate that a majority of Texans favor an electoral system and the accountability of judges that it promotes. They

Politics Now

STOKING THE FIRES FOR
JUDICIAL CAMPAIGN FINANCE REFORM

Judicial reform has been a subject of some controversy in Texas since the airing of the CBS *60 Minutes* segment "Is Justice for Sale?" in 1987. Most reform advocates have championed proposals to change the method of selection of judges, while others have tried to change the way campaigns are financed. One such proposal was the 1995 Judicial Campaign Fairness Act that limited contributions from law firms and lawyers. In 1997, Texans for Public Justice (TPJ), a self-proclaimed judicial watchdog group, formed to spotlight the role of money in Texas judicial campaigns and to press for stronger campaign finance reforms.

To influence public opinion, TPJ analyzes public campaign finance reports and unleashes high-profile press releases. In 2000, TPJ's "Checks and Imbalances" focused on the concentration of judicial campaign contributions in the legal community and energy and natural resource companies.[a] TPJ also initiated a monthly series of press releases, "Dollar Docket," that examines Texas Supreme Court decisions and campaign contributions to the justices by parties to the suit or their attorneys.

By 2000, each successful incumbent justice had spent more than $1 million to win or retain the seat. TPJ charged that "the appearance that justice is for sale in Texas is mushrooming."[b] Republican Chief Justice Tom Phillips adopted voluntary campaign contributions limits in 1990 and still spent $2.6 million in his successful cam-

paign. In 1998, Republican Justice Craig Enoch raised $1.5 million.[c]

Meanwhile, TPJ continued its campaign to convince citizens and policy makers that stricter limits are necessary to ensure justice in the courts. In one of its "Dollar Docket" analyses, TPJ cited a case decided by the Texas Supreme Court in 2000, noting that the Texas Farm Bureau had given two justices contributions in February and March of 2000. In April, the court voted unanimously for the Farm Bureau in a pending case. Of course, seven judges that ruled in favor of the Texas Farm Bureau did not receive contributions in the two months preceding the hearing, and it is difficult to prove that money buys votes. Still, cases such as the above raise questions.[d]

As a result of such cases, many attempts have been made to reform the way judges are elected or chosen. For example, in 2001, Representative Pete Gallego introduced a bill to change Texas's judicial election system by prohibiting contributions to unopposed candidates. It failed.

[a]Texans for Public Justice, "Checks and Imbalances: How Texas Supreme Court Justices Raised $11 Million," accessed January 14, 2001, http://www.tpj.org/reports/checks.

[b]Texans for Public Justice, news release, April 3, 2000.

[d]Texans for Public Justice, "Supreme Court Fundraising Tops $11 Million," news release, April 11, 2000.

[d]The case was *Henson v. Texas Farm Bureau Mutual Insurance.* Texans for Public Justice, "Court Quickly, Unanimously Goes with Cash: Insurance Industry Wins Big, Texas Consumers Suffer," news release, April 13, 2000, http://www.tdi.uregina.ca/~ursc/internet/history.html.

believe that they should be able to choose the people who make decisions that affect their life, liberty, and property.

Over the last two decades, several incidents have raised questions about to whom the judges are accountable and whether judges who depend on campaign contributions to get elected can remain fair and impartial. Since the early 1970s, when the Texas legislature passed a strong Deceptive Trade Practices–Consumer Protection Act, a battle for control of the Texas Supreme Court has raged between plaintiffs' lawyers, who represent injured parties in civil suits, and defense lawyers, who defend businesses, doctors, and insurance companies. During the late 1970s and early 1980s, plaintiffs' lawyers and their association, the Texas Trial Lawyers Association, were the presumptive winners. In 1985 for example, the Supreme Court decided for the plaintiffs in 69 percent of the court's cases and for the defendants in only 28 percent of the cases.[9]

The Texas Supreme Court received national attention in 1987 when journalist Mike Wallace devoted a segment of *60 Minutes* to examine the question "Is Justice for Sale?" Wallace focused on the campaign contributions of Houston trial lawyer Joe Jamail, who won an $11 billion settlement against Texaco for interfering with Pennzoil's attempt to purchase Getty Oil Company in 1984. Jamail, who contributed $10,000 to the district court judge who tried the case shortly before the trial began, gave thousands more to supreme court justices. Wallace questioned the ethics of a judicial system that allowed lawyers to contribute to the political campaigns of judges before whom they appear. Later in 1987, Democratic Chief Justice John Hill and Democratic Justices Robert Campbell and James Wallace resigned from the supreme court. Republican Governor William Clements appointed three Republicans to fill the vacancies on the court, including Thomas R. Phillips as chief justice.

With six supreme court positions on the ballot in 1988, business interests saw an opportunity to reverse the supreme court's preference for plaintiffs, and judicial campaigns became more expensive as the competition increased. Twenty candidates seeking the six positions on the supreme court in 1988 raised more than $10 million for their primary and general election campaigns. Two supreme court candidates raised more than $2 million.[10] Also, nonlawyer special-interest groups, especially the Texas Medical Association, became major contributors to judicial candidates through their political action committees (see chapter 21). The Texas Medical Association supported a slate of four Republicans and two conservative Democrats. Only one candidate, Paul Murphy, was defeated by a plaintiff-backed candidate, Lloyd Doggett.

During the early 1990s, the cost of judicial elections continued to rise. In 1990, six candidates for three seats on the court spent $6 million. A study of fund-raising by Texas Supreme Court justices during the 1994 and 1996 election cycles indicated that a significant percentage of campaign contributions came from lawyers, law firms, and PACs with interests before the court. The report concluded that "today's justices continue to sully the court's reputation by raising millions of dollars from parties and lawyers who have business before the court."[11] In 1998, three Republican incumbent justices raised an average of $1 million to their Democratic opponents' average of $96,000. Incumbent Democratic Justice Rose Spector raised $563,931 to her Republican opponent's $1,214,450.[12] (See Politics Now: Stoking the Fires for Judicial Campaign Finance Reform.)

As Republicans replaced Democrats on the Texas Supreme Court, the court became more likely to rule in favor of defendants. Between 1995 and 1998, 70 percent of the supreme court cases that pitted consumers, patients, and crime victims as plaintiffs against corporate, professional, and government defendants were won by the defendants. In 2002–2003, defendants won 79 percent of the cases. With Republicans holding all nine supreme court seats and more firmly in control of conservatives led by Nathan Hecht and Priscilla Owen, the court in 2002–2003 reached a zenith in its support of insurance companies and other defendants in civil suits.[13]

The large sums of money necessary to compete in judicial races and the sources of those contributions have created an image problem for Texas judges. As Chief Justice Thomas R. Phillips told the Texas legislature in 1999, "Neither party label nor campaign war chests necessarily compromise a judge's ability to be fair and impartial . . . . But these attributes of Texas justice *do* compromise the *appearance* of fairness."[14]

Indeed, in a poll of Texans, 83 percent thought that campaign contributions have a significant effect on judges' decisions. Only 7 percent stated that the contributions have no effect on their decisions. Furthermore, nearly half of the state judges and 79 percent of Texas attorneys stated that campaign contributions have a significant influence on judicial decisions. Only 14 percent of the judges and 1 percent of the attorneys believed that campaign contributions have no influence on judicial opinions.[15]

CRITICISMS OF THE TEXAS JUDICIAL BRANCH

THE TEXAS COURT SYSTEM has been criticized on several grounds. Each of these criticisms has resulted in attempts to reform that aspect of the judiciary. We consider each criticism and the possible reforms in turn.

Reforming the Court Structure

As indicated earlier, the judicial system is complex and confusing, consisting of five layers of courts. Simplification and unification of the court structure has been the goal of numerous proposals for judicial reforms.

Because of the addition of courts over the years, Texas trial courts present a tangle of mixed jurisdictions where overlapping jurisdiction is the

Join the Debate

SHOULD TEXAS ELECT ITS JUDGES?

OVERVIEW: Judges are expected to be well qualified, fair in making their decisions, and independent from political and public pressures. In a democratic system, we also expect some degree of judicial accountability to the public. Texas selects its judges in partisan elections—a system intended to stress accountability. Judicial campaigns have become high-dollar affairs, requiring judicial candidates to solicit funds. But, some campaign contributions raise concerns about future undue influence. These concerns have fueled movements in Texas, as well as across the nation, to reform state-level judicial selection processes in an attempt to increase judicial independence.

Arguments in Favor of Judicial Elections

- **Texans favor the election of judges.** In public opinion polls in Texas, 70 percent of those polled want to continue to elect their judges.
- **Electing judges promotes democracy.** Texans mistrust government and favor popular control. Keeping the partisan election of judges promotes government by the people.
- **Elected judges are as competent and qualified as judges selected by other methods.** There is no empirical evidence to indicate that any method of judicial selection results in more competent and better qualified judges.

Arguments Against Judicial Elections

- **Judicial elections are costly.** In 2002, a political consultant estimated that a statewide judicial contest would cost a candidate $2 million.
- **Judicial elections turn judges into partisan politicians rather than impartial judges.** The judiciary is supposed to be fair and

rule rather than the exception. This allows an attorney to "shop" for justice, seeking a judge that is more likely to decide favorably for a client.

The constitutional revision efforts in 1974 and 1975 (see chapter 16) included a proposal for a new structure for the court system.[16] In the early 1990s, the Texas Research League studied the Texas judiciary and published a rather extensive report with recommendations for a new court structure.[17] The constitutional revision efforts of Representative Junell and Senator Ratliff in 1999 also included changes in the Texas judiciary, which were endorsed by Chief Justice Phillips.

Although the proposals vary, all simplify and unify the court structure. Figure 20.2 illustrates such a proposal.

The district courts would be the state's only trial courts, except for the specific jurisdiction assigned to justice of the peace courts. The state would be divided into judicial districts. Specialization could be retained so that some district judges could handle specific cases. The courts of appeals would be retained, but the geographic districts would be redrawn to equalize the courts' caseloads.

impartial in their decisions about cases and controversies. As a result of the U.S. Supreme Court decision in *Republican Party of Minnesota* v. *White* (2002), the Texas Supreme Court repealed the canon in its Code of Conduct that prevented judges or judicial candidates from commenting on issues that might come before their courts. If judges conduct issue-oriented campaigns, they become politicians rather than fair and impartial jurists.

- **Judicial candidates funded by special interests are less likely to be independent as judges.** In a 1998 Texas public opinion poll, 83 percent of those polled stated that judicial decisions were "very significantly" or "fairly significantly" affected by campaign contributions.

Questions

1. Do you think judges in Texas should be elected? Why or why not?

2. What can be done to reduce the possibility that elected judges will show favoritism toward lawyers and their clients who contributed to the judges' political campaigns?

Selected Readings

Tom James. "Reforming Judicial Elections: The Case for Judicial Elections in Texas" *Veritas* 3 (March 2002), accessed May 13, 2004, http://www.texaspolicy.com/pdf/2002-3-2-veritas-judgelect.pdf.

Anthony Champagne. "Interest Groups and Judicial Elections," *Loyola of Los Angeles Law Review* 34 (June 2001), accessed May 13, 2004, http://llr.lls.edu/volumes/v34-issue4/champagneinterestgroups.pdf.

Selected Web Sites

http://www.fed-soc.org/ The Federalist Society.
http://www.tpj.org/index.jsp Texans for Public Justice.

Most reforms recommend the merger of the two supreme courts, the Texas Supreme Court and the Texas Court of Criminal Appeals, into one supreme court. The proposal by Junell and Ratliff contemplated one supreme court consisting of a chief justice and fourteen justices, who would be divided equally between a civil division and criminal division. The chief justice could, by court rule, sit with either or both divisions.

Reforming Judicial Selection

Since at least 1946, various groups, have recommended that Texas adopt a merit system for selecting judges. In 1994, Lieutenant Governor Bob Bullock appointed a committee of state senators and judges to study judicial selection and make a recommendation for reform. After many meetings, the committee produced a compromise that called for the governor to appoint appellate judges. Trial judges in urban counties would be elected from county commissioner precincts. After serving for a period of time, they would have to run in countywide retention elections. Later, they would have

FIGURE 20.2 Proposal for a Unified, Simplified Texas Judiciary. ■

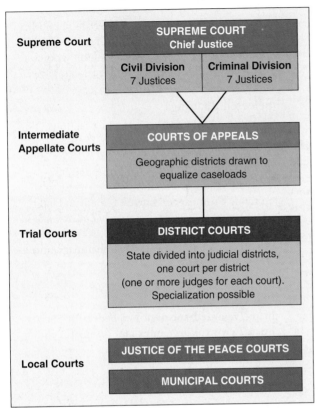

to be reelected from county commissioner precincts. The elections would be nonpartisan. The Texas Senate easily passed the proposal in 1995, but opposition in the House surfaced from Hispanics and Republicans, who had the support of Governor Bush.

In 1996, the Texas Supreme Court appointed several task forces to develop proposals for improving the Texas courts. The task forces considered judicial selection, but they were unable to agree on a substitute for the current system. In every legislative session since 1997, legislators have considered major proposals for judicial selection reform. In every session, the proposed legislation passed the Senate but failed to win House approval. A compromise that accommodates the varied interests in judicial selection has not proven possible so far.[18]

Reforming Campaign Finance

Faced with the cost of judicial campaigns and its effect on the judiciary's imputed fairness, the legislature enacted a Judicial Campaign Fairness Act in 1995. The act limits contributions to judicial candidates, depending on the judicial office sought. For supreme court justices, individuals can contribute $5,000 per election. However, a candidate who is unopposed either in the primary or in the general election faces reduced contribution limits. Law firms and their political action committees can contribute $30,000 to a supreme court candidate, which includes individual contributions from the firm's attorneys. Candidates are also limited in the amount of contributions that they can accept from general political action committees not affiliated with law firms. Voluntary expenditure limits are also established for judicial campaigns. In addition, judicial candidates must file disclosure reports with the Texas Ethics Commission. Failure to comply with the law results in civil and possibly criminal penalties.

There are several loopholes in the act. Most importantly, there is no requirement that a judge who has received a large contribution from a lawyer or party to a suit before the court recuse himself or herself from the case. Incumbent judges who face little or no opposition in primary or general elections can still amass large war chests that intimidate potential candidates in future elections.[19]

Increasing Minority Representation on the Bench

Hispanics and African Americans have never been represented on the Texas courts in proportion to their percentages of the population. The high cost of judicial campaigns, racially polarized voting in statewide and countywide contests, and the small numbers of Hispanics and African Americans who are licensed attorneys have limited their success. With increasing Republican strength in judicial elections, minority candidates, who almost always are Democrats, are even less likely to win judicial contests today.

Xavier Rodriguez's case illustrates a problem that minorities face in judicial elections even when they are members of the Republican Party. Governor Rick Perry appointed Rodriguez to the Texas Supreme Court in 2001. In the 2002 Republican primary election, he had the support of state Republican leaders, endorsements from major newspapers, and a $700,000 warchest; yet he lost to a little-known Anglo lawyer, Steven Wayne Smith. As political scientist Richard Murray noted, "In a primary where there are so many white voters who know little about either candidate, the default goes to the Anglo over the Hispanic . . . . He might have survived if his parents had named him Billy Bob."[20]

The effect of partisan preferences has been dramatic. In 1997, among the eighty judges on the courts of appeals, forty-four were Republicans and thirty-six were Democrats. Of the fourteen courts of appeals, six courts had a Republican majority, six courts had a Democratic majority, and two courts were evenly divided. On the state's top courts, seven of the nine supreme court justices were Republican, and six of the nine court of criminal appeals judges were Republicans. In January 2003, all eighteen members of the two highest courts were Republicans, and sixty-two of the eighty courts of appeals judges were Republicans. As a result, ten courts had Republican majorities, two courts had Democratic majorities, and two courts were evenly divided.[21]

THE JUDICIAL PROCESS IN TEXAS

MOST TEXANS WILL EXPERIENCE the judicial system as a potential juror or in municipal court for a traffic offense. Others, however, may experience the criminal or civil justice process as a plaintiff or defendant. For every Texan, a general understanding of the judicial process is helpful. We start by describing the criminal justice process and then consider the civil justice process.

The Criminal Justice Process

In Texas, the legislature has established a graded penalty system, classifying criminal offenses into eight categories: capital murder, four degrees of felonies, and three classes of misdemeanors (see Table 20.2 on page 737). The legislature also adopts the code of criminal procedure, which regulates how criminal trials are conducted.

The Living Constitution

The Texas Supreme Courts

Article 5, section 1: The judicial power of this State shall be vested in one Supreme Court, in one Court of Criminal Appeals, in Courts of Appeals, in District Courts, in County Courts, in Commissioners Courts, in Courts of Justices of the Peace, and in such other courts as may be provided by law.

The Texas judicial system reflects both Spanish and Anglo-American traditions. The earliest courts were based on Spanish traditions. The constitution of the Republic of Texas (1836) provided for a Supreme Court, which consisted of a chief justice and all of the district judges, who served as associate justices. Subsequent constitutions, including the 1876 constitution, provided for one Supreme Court. However, the 1876 constitution, unlike other constitutions, stripped all criminal jurisdiction from the Supreme Court and gave it to a Texas Court of Appeals. In 1891, an amendment created an intermediate court of civil appeals and a separate court of criminal appeals with criminal jurisdiction. The court of criminal appeals, which originally consisted of three judges, was enlarged to five members in 1966 and to nine members in 1977. In 1980, a constitutional amendment extended intermediate appellate jurisdiction in criminal cases to the

Arrest and Searches. In many cases, an individual will be arrested after an arrest warrant has been issued by a magistrate. To issue the warrant, a magistrate will require sufficient information in the form of a complaint. The officer seeking the arrest warrant must satisfy the requirements of probable cause: tangible evidence that a crime was committed and that the person named in the complaint committed the offense. In most cases, however, police officers arrest an individual without a warrant but based on probable cause because the officer sees an offense being committed or receives a credible report of the commission of a felony and the officer does not have time to procure a warrant. Upon arrest, a person and his or her possessions may be searched. Again, a search warrant is usually necessary, but there are conditions under which a warrantless search is reasonable and evidence seized may be admissible in court. In Texas, search warrants

734

courts of civil appeal and renamed them courts of appeals. Only one other state, Oklahoma, has two Supreme Courts.[a]

There are several criticisms of Texas's system of two Supreme Courts. Some critics stress the inefficiency of having two highest state courts and the possibility of conflicting rulings from the courts. Others argue that judges who deal exclusively with either civil or criminal law are unlikely to possess the broad perspective that judges who deal with both types of law develop. Some critics note the tendency for the court of criminal appeals to overturn convictions based on "technicalities" or procedural matters that have no bearing on the convicted person's guilt or innocence. Supporters of the two Supreme Courts counter that the two courts have rarely disagreed or issued conflicting opinions, that specialization in criminal or civil law is a benefit because judges cannot be experts in both types of law, and that what critics call "technicalities" are really constitutional and statutory rights that protect all citizens from abuses by the judicial system.[b]

Questions

1. Are two Supreme Courts necessary and advisable, or would the merger of the two courts into one Supreme Court, exercising both criminal and civil jurisdiction, be better?
2. What problems might result from the merger of the courts? Explain your answer.

---

[a] George D. Braden, *The Constitution of the State of Texas: An Annotated and Comparative Analysis* (Austin: 1977), 363–8; "Texas Court of Criminal Appeals," *The Handbook of Texas Online*, accessed July 21, 2004, http://www.tsha.utexas.edu/handbook/online/articles/view/TT/jpt1.html.

[b] See William L. Willis, "The Evolution of the Texas Court of Criminal Appeals," *Texas Bar Journal* (September 1966); and Paul Burka, "Trial by Technicality," *Texas Monthly* (April 1982).

are not required for searches pursuant to a lawful arrest and for seizures of evidence in plain view of an officer. Of course, searches conducted with the consent of the person under arrest are considered reasonable.

Booking.   Booking establishes an administrative record of a suspect's arrest. At this time, the suspect is usually fingerprinted and photographed, has the charges explained, and is allowed to make a phone call.

Magistrate Appearance.   If the district or county attorney decides to charge the suspect, he or she becomes a defendant and is brought before a magistrate. The magistrate informs the defendant of the charges, his or her rights under *Miranda* v. *Arizona* (1966), and his or her right to an examining trial. An examining trial is conducted by a

Analyzing Visuals

IS JUSTICE FOR SALE IN THE STATE OF TEXAS?

In early November 1998, CBS's *60 Minutes* reporter Mike Wallace produced a second segment on judicial selection in Texas (his first investigative report on Texas judges, which aired in 1987, is discussed briefly in this chapter). The Ben Sargent cartoon reprinted here first appeared in the *Austin American-Statesman* in November 1998, days after the *60 Minutes* segment aired. Analyze the cartoon by answering the following critical thinking questions: What political event, situation, or politicians are depicted? What message is conveyed by the images? What message do the words in the speech bubble and labels in the cartoon convey? What position does the cartoonist appear to take on the issue? Which effect is the cartoonist attempting to achieve: exaggeration, irony, or juxtaposition? How does the cartoon achieve that effect?

magistrate to determine if there is sufficient evidence to continue the criminal proceedings. If the magistrate decides that there is not sufficient evidence, the defendant is released.

Grand Jury Indictment.   Unless defendants waive their right, a grand jury review will be held. In Texas, grand juries consist of twelve

TABLE 20.2   The Texas System of Graded Penalties

Offense	Maximum Punishment	Examples
Capital felony	Execution	Capital murder
First-degree felony	5–99 years or life; $10,000 fine	Aggravated sexual assault; theft of property valued at $200,000 or more
Second-degree felony	2–20 years; $10,000 fine	Tampering with a consumer product; theft of property valued at $100,000 or more but less than $200,000
Third-degree felony	2–10 years; $10,000 fine	Drive-by shooting without injury; theft of property valued at $20,000 or more but less than $100,000
State jail felony	180 days to 2 years; $10,000 fine	Credit-card or debit-card abuse; theft of property valued at $1,500 or more but less than $20,000
Class A misdemeanor	1 year; $4,000 fine	Burglary of a vehicle; abuse of a corpse; theft of property valued at $500 or more but less than $1,500
Class B misdemeanor	180 days; $2,000 fine	Silent or abusive calls to a 911 service; DWI; theft of property valued at more than $20 but less than $500
Class C misdemeanor	$500 fine	Assault without bodily injury; attending a dog fight; theft of property valued at less than $20

TEXAS IN COMPARISON
Crime, Courts, and Judges

Over the past decade, criminal justice has been the fastest growing area of state governments. The largest states have prison populations that dwarf the number in the federal system. Three of the four largest states practice capital punishment. In June 2004, the New York Court of Appeals declared the New York death penalty statute unconstitutional; there were four men on death row at that time. The structure of the state court systems, method of judicial selection, and compensation of judges vary considerably, with Texas having the lowest salaries.

State	Number of Prisoners on Death Row (2004)	Courts of Last Resort (2003)	Compensation of Judges (2003)	Prison Population (2003)
Texas	454	2, Supreme Court and Court of Criminal Appeals, 9 justices each, partisan election	Supreme Courts, $113,000; district courts, $101,700	164,222
California	635	1, Supreme Court, 7 justices, appointed by governor, retention election	Supreme Court, $162,409; superior courts, $133,052	163,361
New York	0	1, court of appeals, 7 justices, appointed by governor from Judicial Nomination Commission, senate confirmation	court of appeals, $151,200; Supreme Courts, $136,700	65,914
Florida	381	1, Supreme Court, 7 justices, appointed by governor with nomination commission	Supreme Court, $150,000; circuit courts, $130,000	80,352

people. The prosecutor presents the evidence to the grand jury, and if nine members are convinced that sufficient evidence exists to justify a trial, the grand jury issues a "true bill." In that case, an indictment accusing the defendant is prepared by the prosecutor. Otherwise, the defendant is released.

Arraignment.   After an indictment in felony cases and in misdemeanor cases that can result in a jail sentence, an arraignment is required. If the defendant is indigent and requires a court-appointed attorney, the judge will either appoint one or a public defender will be provided. After the defendant is represented by counsel, the judge will again read the charge and take the defendant's plea. At this time, the defendant may plead guilty as a result of a plea-bargain agreement. The prosecutor provides the court with a victim's impact statement, which may be used by the judge or jury during sentencing.

Pretrial Motions.   Pretrial motions establish the scope of the trial. Pretrial motions can also be used by the defense attorney to request a jury trial or bench trial, request a continuance, determine if the defendant is competent to stand trial, change the trial's location, or discover evidence held by the prosecution that could prove the defendant's innocence.

Jury Selection.   Defendants have a right to a jury trial but can waive that right unless the charge is capital murder. If either the prosecution or defense requests a jury trial, a group of potential jurors, known as the *venire* or jury pool, is assembled. The potential jurors are assigned numbers randomly and seated in the courtroom. The prosecution and the defense question the potential jurors in a process known as *voir dire*. Each side gets a number of peremptory challenges, which allow the attorneys to dismiss jurors without cause. Neither side may use its peremptory challenges to exclude potential jurors based on their race or gender. Any potential juror may be challenged for cause. After *voir dire*, if the case involves a felony, the first twelve potential jurors will constitute the jury; if the case involves a misdemeanor, the first six will form the jury. Jury verdicts must be unanimous.

Trial.   In Texas, trials are conducted in two distinct phases—a guilt determination phase and a sentencing phase. There are seven stages in the guilt determination phase. First, the prosecution reads the indictment or information. Then the defense attorney, acting for the defendant, responds by entering a plea. Second, the prosecution provides opening remarks. The defense attorney may deliver opening remarks or wait until the prosecution has presented its case to make remarks. Third, the prosecution presents the state's case, attempting to prove the defendant guilty beyond a reasonable doubt. Fourth, the defense presents its case. In rebuttal, the

Analyzing Visuals

UNITED STATES AND TEXAS EXECUTIONS

Texas leads the nation in the number of executions and is second to California in the number of inmates on death row. The chart indicates the number of executions annually in the United States and in Texas from the reinstatement of the death penalty by the U.S. Supreme Court in 1976 to the end of 2004. By the end of 2004, 944 persons had been executed in the United States. In 2000, Texas set a record with forty executions, nearly half of all executions in the nation. After studying the chart, answer the following critical thinking questions: What factors do you think explain the low number of executions annually between 1976 and 1991? What factors account for the rapid increase after the mid-1990s? What effect do you think the increased number of executions will have on public support for the death penalty in Texas?

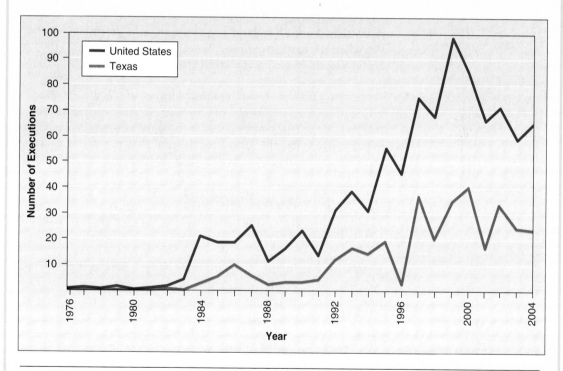

Sources: U.S. and Texas data from the Death Penalty Information Center Web site, Executions by year, updated November 17, 2004, accessed December 15, 2004, http://www.deathpenaltyinfo.org/article.php?scid=8&did=146. Earlier Texas data from the Texas Department of Criminal Justice Web site, Statistics, Texas Annual Executions, updated July 4, 2004, accessed August 7, 2004, http://www.tdcj.state.tx.us/stat/annual.htm.

prosecution can call additional witnesses to discredit the defense's witnesses. The defense is also given an opportunity to rebut the state's rebuttal witnesses. Fifth, the judge reads the jury its charge, a set of instructions for reaching a verdict. Sixth, the prosecution and defense deliver their final arguments. Finally, the jury retires to the jury room to deliberate and reach a verdict. If the jury cannot reach a unanimous verdict, the judge may declare a mistrial. If the jury finds the defendant not guilty, he or she is released from custody. If the defendant is found guilty, the second phase begins—the sentencing phase.

During the sentencing phase, the defendant's prior convictions are admitted as evidence. The stages are similar to the guilt phase but abbreviated into five steps. In capital murder cases, the sentencing phase involves the jury considering whether the defendant is likely to commit further violent crimes and is a threat to society and whether the defendant actually caused, intended, or anticipated that a human life would be taken. If the jury answers both questions affirmatively, then the jury must consider whether mitigating circumstances warrant a sentence of life imprisonment rather than the death penalty. The jury's responses determine whether the defendant receives life in prison or death by lethal injection.[22] (See Analyzing Visuals: United States and Texas Executions.)

Appeals.   Except in capital murder cases, which are automatically reviewed by the Texas Court of Criminal Appeals, convicted criminals may appeal the trial court's decision to a court of appeals. The court of appeals will review the records of the trial to determine if a reversible error was committed.

The Civil Justice Process

The Texas Supreme Court establishes civil procedures, which tend to be less formal than criminal procedures.

Pretrial Procedures.   To initiate a civil suit, the plaintiff, the person who has been injured, files a petition with the clerk of the court that will hear the case. The petition indicates the plaintiff's complaints against the defendant and the remedy sought in the case. The court clerk informs the defendant of the charges filed and indicates that the defendant can provide a written answer to the complaint. Before the judge sets a trial date, the parties file their petitions, answers, and other documents pertinent to the case. Either party to the suit may request a jury trial.

Trial.   As in a criminal trial, a civil trial begins with the plaintiff's attorney presenting the evidence and witnesses. The defendant's attorney may challenge the evidence presented and cross-examine the plaintiff's witnesses. The defendant's attorney then presents evidence, which may be challenged by the plaintiff's attorney, and witnesses, who may be questioned by the plaintiff. If a jury is deciding the case, the judge will issue a charge to the jury. After the charge, the lawyers make their final arguments. The judge then issues the jury a set of questions that the jury will answer. The jury's answers will provide the basis for the judgment in the case. In district courts, ten of the twelve jurors must agree on the answers. In county and justice of the peace courts, five of the six jurors must agree. Based on the jury's answers or verdict, the judge issues a judgment, indicating the remedy to the complaint.

Appeals.   Appeals in civil cases, as in criminal cases, involve the record from the trial court, written briefs by the attorneys, and oral arguments before the judges. Appeals from district and county courts are reviewed by a court of appeals and possibly by the Texas Supreme Court.

SUMMARY

THE TEXAS JUDICIARY is probably the least familiar of the three governmental branches to most Texans. The system is complex, disorganized, and caters to attorneys. In describing and analyzing the judiciary, we have made the following points:

1. **The Roots of the Texas Judiciary**
   Texas's first courts were established in the Austin colony. Over the years, the court system has evolved through several constitutions. In most cases, there were few courts, and judges were elected by popular vote. The establishment of additional courts and adjustments to the courts' jurisdictions created the complex and confusing court system of today.

2. **The Structure of the Texas Judiciary**
   Five levels of courts make up the Texas judiciary. At the lowest level are local courts of limited jurisdiction. The trial courts of general and special jurisdiction have original jurisdiction in serious criminal cases and higher-dollar civil suits. The courts of appeals are intermediate appellate courts for criminal and civil cases. Texas has two courts of last resort: a Supreme Court for civil cases and a Court of Criminal Appeals for criminal cases.

3. **Judges and Judicial Selection**
   The qualifications necessary to be a judge vary by court. The qualifications for justice of peace and constitutional county courts are minimal. For appellate courts, a license to practice law and experience as an attorney or judge is required. Most judges in Texas are middle-aged, Anglo males. Texas uses partisan elections to select most of its judges.

4. **Criticisms of the Texas Judicial Branch**
   There are many criticisms of the Texas judiciary, and many groups and individuals have proposed reforms to address the criticisms. Many proposals suggest that the judicial structure could be unified and simplified. The Texas legislature has considered several plans to reform judicial selection. Several groups representing minorities have sought reforms to increase the number of Hispanic and African American judges in Texas.

5. **The Judicial Process in Texas**
   For most Texans, the operation of the judicial process in Texas is obscure and unfamiliar. The procedures in a criminal case are more formal and rigorous than in a civil case, but the process is similar. Criminal cases proceed through several identifiable stages from arrest to trial. In

civil cases, which usually take longer to resolve, the process follows similar stages that lead to a settlement and possible award of damages.

KEY TERMS

application for discretionary review, p. 724
constitutional county court, p. 719
county court at law, p. 721
court of appeals, p. 722
district court, p. 721
justice of the peace court, p. 719
municipal court, p. 717
petition for review, p. 723
Texas Court of Criminal Appeals, p. 723
Texas Supreme Court, p. 723
trial *de novo,* p. 721

SELECTED READINGS

Anderson, Ken. *Crime in Texas.* Austin: University of Texas Press, 1997.

Champagne, Anthony, and Judith Haydel, eds. *Judicial Reform in the States.* New York: University Press of America, 1993.

Champagne, Anthony, and Edward J. Harpham, eds. *Texas Politics: A Reader,* 2nd ed. New York: Norton, 1998.

Horton, David M., and Ryan Kellis Turner. *Lone Star Justice.* Austin: Eakin Press, 1999.

Texans for Public Justice. *Checks and Imbalances: How Texas Supreme Court Justices Raised $11 Million.* Austin: Texans for Public Justice, 2000.

Texas Research League. Texas Courts: A Study by the Texas Research League. 3 Reports. Austin: Texas Research League, 1990–1992.

WEB EXPLORATIONS

To learn more about the Texas Supreme Court, go to http://www.supreme.courts.state.tx.us/

To learn more about the Texas Court of Criminal Appeals, go to http://www.cca.courts.state.tx.us/

To learn more about the Texas Civil Justice League and Texans for Lawsuit Reform, go to http://www.tcjl.com

To learn more about Texans for Public Justice, go to http://www.tpj.org

To view a report on the Texas Supreme Court's decisions in 1999–2000, go to http://www.findlaw.com/llstategov/tx//txca.html

21

Political Parties, Interest Groups, Elections, and Campaigns in Texas

THE EVENT IN TEXAS THAT TRIGGERED the contest for what many political observers consider the most powerful position in Texas government—lieutenant governor—occurred in 2000 when Governor George W. Bush was elected president of the United States. When Bush resigned the governorship and Lieutenant Governor Rick Perry became governor, Bill Ratliff was elected by the Senate to replace Perry. Former Comptroller of Public Accounts John Sharp, who had announced his intention to seek the lieutenant governorship earlier, was unopposed in the Democratic primary. Lieutenant Governor Bill Ratliff and several other Republicans announced their intentions to seek the Republican nomination but later dropped out, perhaps influenced by David Dewhurst's decision to seek the nomination. Dewhurst, who had been elected land commissioner in 1998, has a large personal fortune and appeared willing to spend as much of it as necessary to win the nomination.

David Dewhurst's strengths are his good looks and wealth. As journalist S. C. Gwynne noted, "He is a large, strikingly handsome man, six feet five inches tall, and has a lean muscled body of someone thirty years younger."[1] His fortune resulted from the sale of two electricity-producing cogeneration plants in 1996 for more than $200 million. On the other hand, John Sharp's strength is his knowledge of government and his ability

743

to turn a speech into a conversation. When the same audience heard Sharp and Dewhurst, Sharp usually got the better reviews.[2] But, record and experience do not ensure one's election to statewide office.

In contemporary Texas, Republican candidates are close to holding the partisan advantage that Democrats held from the 1870s to the 1970s. Throughout the campaign, public opinion polls indicated that the election results would be very close. Despite Sharp's advantage in endorsements by newspapers and by interest groups, many of whom traditionally support Republican candidates, Dewhurst's fund-raising advantage—$16.3 million to Sharp's $8.7 million—and his support from Republican Party identifiers kept the contest close. Throughout the campaign, both candidates sought an advantage by running advertisements that attempted to characterize their opponents. Dewhurst attempted to paint John Sharp as a tax-and-spend liberal who favored tax increases, including an income tax. Sharp, on the other hand, portrayed Dewhurst as an extreme conservative. During the final weeks of the campaign, Dewhurst appeared with Governor Rick Perry and U.S. Senator Phil Gramm, emphasizing his party affiliation and indicating that his election would ensure that Governor Perry, who held a commanding lead over Democrat Tony Sanchez in public opinion polls, would be able to pursue his agenda. Dewhurst suggested that Sharp would wake up every morning thinking of ways to thwart Governor Perry's policy initiatives.

Dewhurst's 52–46 percent election victory, according to most analysts, was the result of a heavy Republican voter turnout and straight-ticket voting. Sharp had depended on heavy Hispanic and African American turnout, which did not provide sufficient votes to overcome the Republican advantage in voter turnout statewide.

THE SHARP–DEWHURST CONTEST for lieutenant governor illustrates a number of points about political parties, interest groups, campaigns, and elections in contemporary Texas. Interest groups and political parties represent the interests of their members and promote the adoption of certain government policies, but the activities of interest groups focus on *influencing* government, while the activities of political parties focus on *controlling* government. For example, interest groups made contributions to Sharp and to Dewhurst. Elections provide the mechanism by which parties gain control of government, and campaigns create a link among the political parties, their candidates, interest groups, and the public.

In this chapter, we will examine political parties, interest groups, campaigns, and elections in Texas and consider them from several vantage points.

- First, we will consider the *roots of political parties, interest groups, elections, and campaigns in Texas,* noting how these institutions and processes developed in Texas history.

- Second, we will examine *political parties in Texas.* Political parties consist of a party organization, a party in the electorate, and a party in government. We will describe and analyze how these components operate in Texas.

- Third, we will explore *interest groups in Texas,* describing the types of interest groups and the activities that groups employ to influence public policy.

- Finally, we will examine *elections and political campaigns in Texas,* indicating the types of elections and the extent of electoral participation. We will also describe and analyze political campaigns and voting behavior.

THE ROOTS OF POLITICAL PARTIES, INTEREST GROUPS, ELECTIONS, AND CAMPAIGNS IN TEXAS

POLITICAL PARTIES AND INTEREST GROUPS developed slowly in Texas. As noted in chapter 20, early Anglo settlers in Texas were from the upper and lower South, and many brought their Democratic Party attachments with them. But, until the late 1840s, personality was the dominant force in electoral politics. In 1848, the Democratic Party emerged as a formal organization that actively participated in elections. Until the end of the Civil War in 1865, personalities still strongly influenced party politics in Texas, providing the basis for factions within the dominant Democratic Party. In 1867, in response to congressional Reconstruction, the Republican Party of Texas formed and took control of Texas politics and government from 1868 to 1874 (see chapter 16). After Reconstruction, the Democratic Party, though challenged occasionally by third parties such as the Greenback Party and People's Party (see Roots of Government: The Populist Challenge to Democratic Party Dominance), controlled Texas government, making Texas a one-party state.

The era of one-party Democratic dominance (1874–1986) was filled with feuds between contending factions within the party. In the

Roots of Government

THE POPULIST CHALLENGE TO DEMOCRATIC PARTY DOMINANCE

FOR MUCH OF ITS HISTORY, Texas was a one-party, Democratic state. However, being a one-party state did not mean that the Democratic Party's dominance went unchallenged. One of those challenges occurred during the late-nineteenth century, in a period of passionate political involvement.

In the last quarter of the nineteenth century, as the United States began its transition from an agrarian to an urban society, Texas felt the dislocation acutely. In the 1870s, nearly 70 percent of Texans were employed in agricultural pursuits, and cotton was the principal crop. In 1875, the price of cotton fell from about 15 cents to 11 cents a pound, where it remained until the end of the century. Because the cost of producing cotton was nearly 8 cents a pound, the farmers' situation was dire. The crop-lien system, in which a merchant or landlord gave the farmer financial assistance in return for a lien on the farmer's crop, compounded the farmers' problem. The effect of this system was to force many farmers into a condition of near slavery to merchants or landlords.[a]

Responding to these conditions, farmers in Texas initially formed an interest group, the Farmers' Alliance, and later a political party, the People's Party. In 1877, a group of farmers met at the Lampasas County farm of J. R. Allen to form the "Knights of Reliance," which was later changed to the Farmers' Alliance. The alliance's membership grew rapidly, primarily because the alliance identified the sources of the farmers' plight and proposed measures to correct these problems.[b] In these early efforts, the alliance was acting as a self-help organization for farmers and was not involved in politics.

In 1886, the Farmers' Alliance discussed sixteen "demands" addressed to the governments of Texas and the United States. The narrow adoption of the demands reflected a split in the alliance between delegates who wanted to remain a self-help organization and the majority who favored an activist political organization. Despite the split, the alliance's factions worked together to promote the alliance's growth.[c]

Photo courtesy: Wisconsin Historical Society

This Lampasas County farmhouse was the site of the first meeting of the Farmers' Alliance in Texas. The house was later dismantled and reassembled at the Chicago Exposition of 1893.

With the endorsement of political activism in 1886, the alliance was forced to choose between two political options: becoming an interest group or a political party. The alliance chose to enter politics as an interest group, focusing its efforts on influencing public officials. The alliance demonstrated perhaps its greatest influence in 1890 when the Democratic Party nominated James Stephen Hogg, who supported the alliance's goals, for governor.

The movement to form a political party began in the late 1880s, when some alliance members urged the creation of a new political party to advance the class interests of farmers and laborers. In 1891, the People's Party of Texas was created, candidates were nominated for public office, and a party organization was formed. The People's Party was competitive with the Democratic Party in Texas during the 1890s, but after 1904, the party failed to field candidates for public office.

[a]Donna A. Barnes, *Farmers in Rebellion: The Rise and Fall of the Southern Farmers Alliance and People's Party in Texas* (Austin: University of Texas Press, 1984), 1–3.
[b]Barnes, *Farmers in Rebellion*, 6.
[c]Lawrence Goodwyn, *The Populist Moment: A Short History of the Agrarian Revolt in America* (New York: Oxford University Press, 1978), 44–54.

1930s, the Great Depression and President Franklin Roosevelt's New Deal created a split over economic policy that resulted in the development of liberal and conservative factions, which would battle for control of the party until the end of the one-party era.

Like political parties in Texas, interest groups developed slowly. The most influential interest groups in the nineteenth century represented agrarian interests, and the influence of the Grange, though not monolithic, was evident in the constitutional convention of 1875. Groups representing oil and gas interests supplanted agrarian groups during the early twentieth century. However, economic interests, especially those representing businesses, maintained their preeminence.

Campaigns and elections, which originally were centered on personal loyalties to candidates, became partisan or factional contests. Until the early 1960s, the most important elections were the Democratic primaries, which featured candidates of the contending factions. Democratic candidates always won the general elections, and voter turnout, because of the lack of competition, suffered. Voter turnout was also hampered by legal impediments to voting, some of which persisted until the 1970s.

POLITICAL PARTIES IN TEXAS

POLITICAL PARTIES IN TEXAS perform the same functions as the national parties. The parties perform these functions through their three components: party organization, party in the electorate, and party in government.

*Photo courtesy: Brad Loper/*Dallas Morning News

■ Delegates to the 2002 Republican state convention in Dallas demonstrate their support for Governor Rick Perry during his address to the convention.

Party Organization

The party organization consists of the structures that constitute the party organization and the party activists who occupy positions in the party structure. The party organization includes both a formal organization, established in state law, and a functional organization, which describes how the party actually operates.

Formal Organization.　Texas state law establishes the formal organization for political parties. There is both a temporary and a permanent party organization for each political party.

temporary party organization
Party organization that exists for a limited time and includes several levels of conventions.

The **temporary party organization** consists of conventions at the precinct, the county or state senatorial district, and the state levels. Held every two years, party conventions are attended by party activists and last only a short period of time. The conventions meet to select delegates to subsequent party conventions, choose party leaders, and establish party policies.

Every two years, the first party convention occurs at the voting-precinct level. Election precincts are voting districts that usually contain fewer than 3,000 registered voters. On the date of the primary election (currently the second Tuesday of March in even-numbered years) after the polls have closed, the parties hold their **precinct conventions.** The political parties conduct primary elections to select their nominees for elected public office—governor, state senator, state representative, and county judge, for example. Participation is open, but only about 1 percent of the voters in the party's primary election actually attend the precinct conventions. Even in presidential election years, attendance rarely exceeds 10 percent of the eligible participants.

precinct convention
Precinct party meeting to select delegates and adopt resolutions.

The precinct convention's principal task is to select delegates to the party's **county convention** or, in those counties that are in more than one state senatorial district (which included fifteen counties in 2004), to the **state senatorial district convention.** In both the Democratic and the Republican Parties, each precinct in the county or senatorial district is allocated delegates based on the number of votes cast in the precinct for the party's gubernatorial nominee in the most recent gubernatorial election. After delegates to the county or senatorial district convention have been chosen, the precinct convention debates and then either adopts or rejects resolutions; the resolutions that are adopted are forwarded to the county or senatorial district convention.

county convention
County party meeting to select delegates and adopt resolutions.

state senatorial district convention
Party meeting held when a county is a part of more than one senatorial district.

On the third Saturday after the primary election, each party holds its county and senatorial district conventions. The delegates and alternates who were selected in the precinct conventions attend the county and senatorial district conventions.

The principal purpose of the county or senatorial district conventions is to select delegates to the party's state convention. Like the precincts, each county or senatorial district is allocated delegates based on its support for the party's gubernatorial nominee in the most recent general election. Also, the conventions consider resolutions adopted in the precinct conventions; if these resolutions are adopted at the county or senatorial district level, the resolutions are sent to the state convention for possible incorporation in the party's platform.

In June, on a date selected by the state executive committee of each party, the delegates assemble for the party's **state convention.** The state convention certifies the results of the party's primary (which nominates the party's candidates for public office), drafts and adopts the party's platform, and selects the party's state executive committee, including the state party chairperson and vice chairperson. In presidential election years, the state convention also selects the party's slate of presidential electors, nominates the state's members for the party's national committee, and selects the state's delegates to the party's national convention. The Republican Party allocates all of its national convention delegates based on the presidential primary results, and delegate selection committees, whose members are chosen by the presidential candidates, provide lists of delegates for the state convention to select. In the Democratic Party, delegates are allocated on the basis of the presidential primary results (75 percent of the allotted delegates) and on the basis of support for the candidates at the precinct, county or state senatorial, and state conventions (25 percent of the allotted delegates).

The **permanent party organization** consists of the party chairpersons and committees, which purportedly work throughout the year performing party-building and electoral functions. Because of their principal activities, the parties' permanent organizations are tied to electoral districts. Each electoral unit, from the smallest (the precinct) to the largest (the state) is represented in the permanent organization. The political party appears hierarchical in structure, with power concentrated at the top, but party organizations are more accurately described as stratarchies—organizations with power distributed in layers or strata.[3] Consequently, each level of party organization is relatively independent of the other levels and concentrates on electoral activities within its level or strata.

Each precinct in Texas has a **precinct chairperson** who represents the party in that electoral district. The chairperson is elected for a two-year term in the party's primary election. The chairperson is responsible for informing members of the party's activities and issue positions, getting party members to the polls on election days, and serving on the party's county executive committee.

Each county in Texas has a **county chairperson** and a **county executive committee.** The county chairperson is elected in the party's primary for a two-year term. At the county level, the county chairperson conducts the party's primary elections, arranges for the county convention, raises funds for the county organization, campaigns for party candidates, and promotes precinct organization efforts.

state convention
Party meeting held to adopt the party's platform, elect the party's executive committee and state chairperson, and in a presidential election year, elect delegates to the national convention and choose presidential electors.

permanent party organization
Party organization that operates throughout the year, performing the party's functions.

precinct chairperson
Party leader in a voting precinct.

county chairperson
Party leader in a county.

county executive committee
Precinct chairpersons in a county that assist the county chairpersons.

The Living Constitution

Article 6, section 1: (a) The following classes of persons shall not be allowed to vote in this State:

(1) persons under 18 years of age;

(2) persons who have been determined mentally incompetent by a court, subject to such exceptions as the Legislature may make; and

(3) persons convicted of any felony, subject to such exceptions as the Legislature may make.

(b) The legislature shall enact laws to exclude from the right of suffrage persons who have been convicted of bribery, perjury, forgery, or other high crimes.

The Texas Constitution establishes the exclusions from the right to vote in Article 6, section 1. Of the various disqualifications, the provisions relating to convicted criminals have the greatest impact. The prohibitions on voting by criminals have appeared in every Texas constitution. In 1836, the constitution of the Republic disqualified persons "convicted of bribery, perjury, or other high crimes and misdemeanors." The 1845 constitution changed the language slightly to prohibit voting by persons "convicted of bribery, perjury, forgery, or other high crimes." The same language appeared in the Texas constitutions of 1861, 1866, and 1869. The constitution of 1869 also disqualified all felons. Although the convention delegates in 1875 debated which crimes should result in disqualification, they retained the felony disqualification. However, they did allow the legislature to make exceptions.[a]

state executive committee
Sixty-two-member party committee that makes decisions for the party between state conventions.

state party chairperson
Party leader for the state.

Formally, the supreme unit of the party's permanent organization is the **state executive committee,** composed of a chairperson and a vice chairperson (state law requires that the chairperson and vice chairperson not be of the same gender) and one man and one woman from each of the state's thirty-one senatorial districts. The representatives from the senatorial districts are elected at the state convention for two-year terms. The **state party chairperson** and vice chairperson are chosen by the entire convention. The state executive committee's duties include certifying the party's candidates for the general election, conducting the

The legislature originally allowed no exceptions, and convicted felons were barred from voting for life. However, in 1983, the legislature allowed convicted felons to vote five years after completing their sentences. Later, the waiting period was reduced to two years. In 1997, the legislature adopted the current provision, which excludes from the disqualification anyone who has not been convicted of a felony, or if convicted, has completed any sentence resulting from the conviction, which includes any incarceration, probation, parole, or supervision. Also, a person is not disqualified if he or she has been pardoned or "otherwise released from the resulting disability to vote." Consequently, without a pardon, a convicted felon must complete the sentence imposed by the court for his or her crime before he or she is eligible to vote.[b]

In Texas, the number of convicted felons who are disenfranchised approaches 500,000 adults. According to political scientist Michael McDonald of George Mason University, there were 164,222 prisoners, 431,989 probationers, and 102,271 parolees in Texas in 2004. Of those, McDonald estimates that 482,488 are ineligible felons, the largest number in any state in the United States.[c]

Question

1. Should Texas, like some states, prohibit convicted felons from voting for life? Or should Texas, like Maine and Vermont, allow convicted felons to vote? Explain your answer.

---

[a]George D. Braden, *The Constitution of Texas: An Annotated and Comparative Analysis*, vol. 2 (Austin: Texas Legislative Council, 1977), 483.

[b]Juan Castillo, "Did Your Time? Groups Want You to Vote," *Austin American-Statesman* (April 26, 2004): A1.

[c]Michael McDonald, "2004 Voting-Age and Voting-Eligible Population Estimates and Voter Turnout," United States Elections Project, George Mason University, accessed August 10, 2004, http://elections.gmu.edu/Voter_Turnout_2004.htm.

state convention, and promoting the party's candidates and issue positions. The formal party organization is depicted in Figure 21.1.

Functional Organization

The formal organizational chart of any organization may not provide the real story of how well the organization functions and where decisions are made. The formal organization provides a skeleton for the party organization, but its performance is determined by the effective-

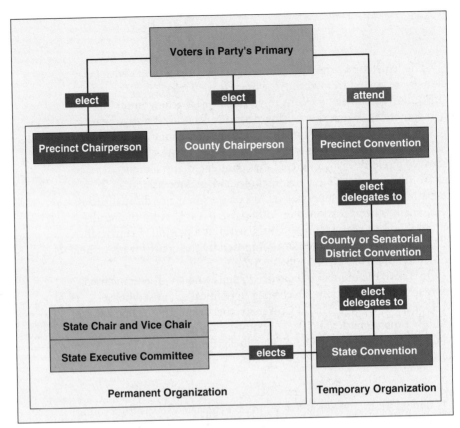

FIGURE 21.1 Party Organization in Texas. ■

ness of the people who occupy those positions and who use those positions to further the party's political goals. Thus, in this section, we describe and assess the party organizations in Texas in terms of their unity and effectiveness in performing the party's functions.

Democratic Party Unity.   Since 1976, control of the Democratic Party organization in Texas has been in ideological liberals' hands. Their control has affected the number of liberals among Democratic candidates for statewide office, their electoral success, and the party's platform. During the 1950s and 1960s, the only liberal Democrat elected to statewide office in Texas was U.S. Senator Ralph Yarborough. However, in 1982, four liberal Democrats—Jim Mattox, Jim Hightower, Garry Mauro, and Ann Richards—were elected to statewide executive offices. All won reelection in 1986, and Ann Richards was elected governor in 1990. In recent elections, however, liberal Democrats have not fared as well. Republicans replaced the liberal class of 1982 in statewide elective offices during the 1990s.

■ Tina Benkiser (left) and Charles Soechting (right), who were elected in 2004, are state chairs of the Texas Republican Party and Democratic Party, respectively.

The success of liberal Democrats in the 1980s and early 1990s also had an effect on the Republican Party, as conservative Democrats, having lost control of the Democratic Party, increasingly abandoned the Democratic Party for the Republican Party. By the 1990s, Democratic Party leaders were overwhelmingly liberal or moderate ideologically. A recent study of Democratic Party activists indicated that 60 percent were self-described liberals, 25 percent were moderates, and 15 percent were conservatives.[4]

Republican Party Unity.   The Republican Party has always been conservative ideologically. Though more cohesive ideologically than the Democratic Party, the Republican Party in Texas also has its intraparty conflicts. Republican Party activists are overwhelmingly conservative (91 percent), with few moderates (7 percent) and even fewer liberals (2 percent).[5] Republican conflicts typically are over goals and policies. Republican *pragmatists* or *economic conservatives* emphasize the party's role in elections and governing and its economic policies. The pragmatists seek to expand the party's membership, reaching out to people who have not traditionally been members of the Republican coalition, and to pursue policies that advance the economic well-being of its members. Republican *ideologues* or *social conservatives* emphasize the party's representation function, stressing the party's conservative political ideology over winning elections and controlling the government, and social conservatism. The ideologues are more interested in promoting conservative social policies, especially anti-abortion, than electing Republican candidates to office.

The clash between the factions has been evident in every Republican state convention since 1994, when a coalition of religious conservatives and anti-abortion activists dominated the party's state convention and elected their candidate state party chair. The Christian

TEXAS IN COMPARISON
Political Parties, Interest Groups, and Elections in the States

Political parties in the four largest states vary considerably in the degree of party competition in which party controls the legislature. New York has the largest number of registered lobbyists, and California has the fewest lobbyists.
The states also vary greatly in the percentage of registered voters.

States	Rank Among the Fifty States in Interparty Competition (1995–1998)	Party Composition in the Legislature (2005)	Registered Lobbyists (2001)	Voting-Age Population (2004)	Percentage of Registered Voters (2004)
Texas	1st (tied with Washington)	Texas House of Representatives: 87 Republicans, 63 Democrats Texas Senate: 19 Republicans, 12 Democrats	1,512	16,236,943	81
California	6th	California Assembly: 48 Democrats, 32 Republicans California Senate: 25 Democrats, 15 Republicans	1,021	26,647,974	62
New York	9th (tied with South Carolina)	New York Assembly: 104 Democrats, 46 Republicans New York Senate: 34 Republicans, 27 Democrats	2,930	14,790,563	80
Florida	3rd	Florida House of Representatives 84 Republicans, 36 Democrats Florida Senate: 26 Republicans, 14 Democrats	2,000	13,441,589	77

Coalition extended its control by electing the party vice chair, Susan Weddington, and a majority of the state executive committee.[6] In 1996, the issue that divided the convention was abortion.

In 1997, when Susan Weddington was elected state chair, she pledged to unify the party's factions. She reached out to the party's moderates and economic conservatives, many of whom supported abortion rights. However, the election of David Barton, a social conservative like Weddington, as state vice chair raised concerns among some moderate Republicans. Nevertheless, Weddington declared a new leadership and focus for the state party.[7] In 1998, social conservatives proposed and adopted a provision denying party funding and support to any candidates who refused to endorse a ban on the late-term abortion procedure that social conservatives term "partial-birth abortion." In 2002, the social conservatives pushed the Republican platform even further, calling for the deportation of immigrants who do not carry the required ID, stricter requirements for voter registration, and the termination of bilingual education programs in Texas.[8] In 2004, state convention delegates adopted a platform that declares that "the United States is a Christian nation" and that the Ten Commandments "are the basis of our basic freedoms and the cornerstone of our Western tradition."[9]

Party Effectiveness: What's at Stake?   Assessing party organizational effectiveness requires us to examine different factors, depending on the level of party organization being assessed. Consequently, we consider each level of party organization—statewide, county, and precinct—in turn.

At the state level, party effectiveness is related to the complexity of the party's organization and the capacity of the party's organization to perform its party-building functions. Indicators of organizational complexity include an accessible party headquarters, a complex division of labor, a substantial party budget, and a professional leadership. In Texas, both parties maintain fairly complex organizations. A state party's ability to perform its party-building duties is calculated in two areas: (1) institutional support activities such as fund-raising, electoral mobilization programs, and publication of a newsletter; and, (2) candidate-centered activities such as contributions to candidates, and recruitment of candidates. A comparison of the contemporary Democratic and Republican Parties in Texas reveals that an advantage in both measures of party building is enjoyed by the Republican Party.

At the county and precinct levels, the party organization's primary task is campaigning for the party's candidates and getting voters to the polls. County and precinct chairpersons are most influential in determining the party's effectiveness at this level.[10] Studies of party activities at these levels reveal that Republican Party activists are more likely to involve their members in party and political activities.

There is also a substantial difference between Republican chairpersons and Democratic chairpersons in their perceptions of changes in their party's organizational strength and effectiveness. A large percentage of Republican county and precinct chairpersons (more than three-fourths on most measures) viewed their organizations as more effective in 2001 than they had been in 1981, 1986, or 1991. On the other hand, few Democratic chairpersons (about one-fourth or fewer on most measures) viewed their organizations as stronger during the same period.[11]

How does the examination of the parties' functional organizations help us understand party politics in Texas? The lack of unity in both parties detracts from their effectiveness as organizations and from their ability to represent a majority of Texans.

Party in the Electorate

The most important function for the party organization is winning elections, which means mobilizing interest in the party's goals and candidates among the voters—the electorate. The party in the electorate consists of those people who identify with a political party and consider themselves members (see chapter 11). In slightly more than half of the states—not including Texas—voters register as members of a particular political party or as independents.

Analyzing Visuals

PARTY IDENTIFICATION IN TEXAS, SELECTED YEARS 1952–2003

The chart depicts party identification of Texans in selected years between 1952 and 2003. The chart shows the changes that have occurred in party identification, reflecting the rise of Republicans in Texas. After examining the chart and reading the relevant sections in the chapter on political parties in the electorate, answer the critical thinking questions presented in the balloon captions below.

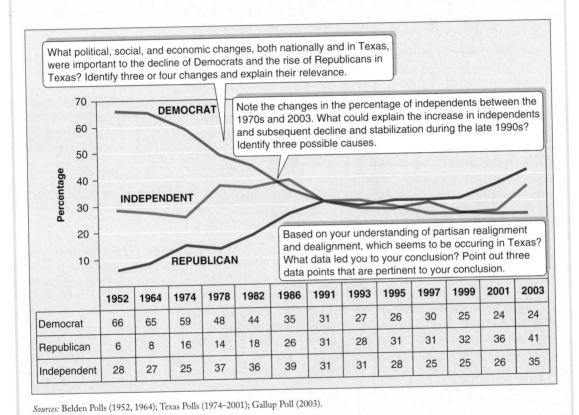

What political, social, and economic changes, both nationally and in Texas, were important to the decline of Democrats and the rise of Republicans in Texas? Identify three or four changes and explain their relevance.

Note the changes in the percentage of independents between the 1970s and 2003. What could explain the increase in independents and subsequent decline and stabilization during the late 1990s? Identify three possible causes.

Based on your understanding of partisan realignment and dealignment, which seems to be occuring in Texas? What data led you to your conclusion? Point out three data points that are pertinent to your conclusion.

	1952	1964	1974	1978	1982	1986	1991	1993	1995	1997	1999	2001	2003
Democrat	66	65	59	48	44	35	31	27	26	30	25	24	24
Republican	6	8	16	14	18	26	31	28	31	31	32	36	41
Independent	28	27	25	37	36	39	31	31	28	25	25	26	35

Sources: Belden Polls (1952, 1964); Texas Polls (1974–2001); Gallup Poll (2003).

Because Texans don't register by political party, opinion polls are used to determine the party identifications of Texans.[12] As explained in chapter 11, party identification is a psychological attachment that is formed early in life but can be altered by events, issues, and political personalities. Partisan attachments are considered important in determining a party's chances for electoral victory and, consequently, its ability to control government.

Distribution of Party Attachments. In 1952, when survey research began measuring party identification, only 6 percent of Texans identified themselves as Republicans, and 66 percent identified themselves as Democrats. Since 1952, however, the percentage of Democrats has steadily declined, and the percentage of Republicans has steadily increased. In 1991, the percentage of Republicans and Democrats were identical. In public opinion surveys conducted since 1999, there have been more Republicans than Democrats in Texas. In 2003, 41 percent of Texans identified with the Republican Party, and 25 percent identified with the Democratic Party. The Republican rise and Democratic decline is depicted in Analyzing Visuals: Party Identification in Texas, Selected Years 1952–2003.

The recent changes in party affiliation among Texans involve more than just a decrease in Democrats and an increase in Republicans. The percentage of independents—individuals who identify with neither major political party—has also increased in Texas. In fact, independents constituted the second most numerous category in 2003. Thus, whereas 72 percent of the population in Texas identified with one of the major political parties in 1952, only 65 percent did in 2003. Consequently, people with attachments to the Democratic or the Republican Party constitute a smaller percentage of the electorate now than in 1952. This is not a good sign for supporters of strong political parties or for the view that strong parties are essential to democracy.

Party Realignment in Texas.   Realignments, triggered by critical elections, produce profound changes in the distribution of partisan attachments (see chapter 12). According to some political scientists, Texas has experienced an attenuated realignment (or secular realignment). They offer the following evidence:

- Young voters were more likely to identify with the Republican Party than the Democratic Party during the 1980s and 1990s. Among party identifiers, young people (age eighteen to twenty-nine) were much more likely to identify with the Republican Party than were older people. Consequently, generational replacement favored the Republicans.

- Some Democrats switched to the Republican Party. These conversions were most likely among conservative Democrats of an upper-level socio-economic status who were bringing their party identification into line with their ideology and status.

- New residents of Texas were more likely to identify with the Republican Party than were native Texans or long-term residents. Between 1970 and 2000, when Texas experienced an influx of immigrants, most of the new residents brought an identification with the Republican Party, which they kept.

- Party identification, especially among Republicans, is important in determining vote choices in elections. Between 80 and 90 percent of Republicans voted for Republican candidates in recent elections.

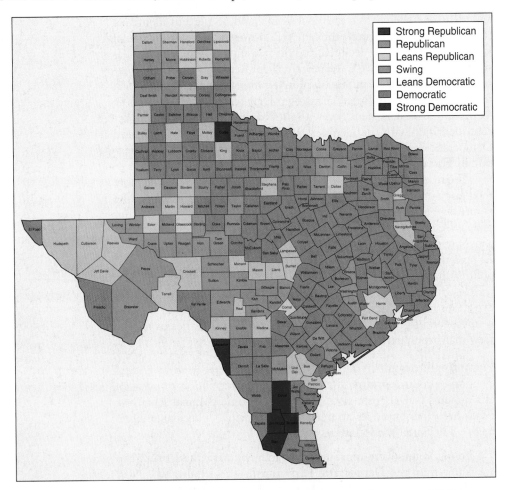

FIGURE 21.2 Republican and Democratic Party Strength in Texas by County (1970s)
The map reflects the strength of the Texas Republican and Democratic Parties based on votes for Republican and Democratic candidates in selected general election contests during the 1970s. ∎

Sources: Based on county election results from the 1972 presidential election, 1974 gubernatorial election, 1976 presidential election, 1978 gubernatorial election, 1978 lieutenant governor election, and the 1978 attorney general election. Mike Kingston, Sam Attlesey, and Mary G. Crawford, *The Texas Almanac's Political History of Texas* (Austin: Eakin Press, 1992); *Texas Almanac, 1980–1981* (Dallas: A. H. Belo Corporation, 1979).

Also, in the two largest counties of Texas, a majority of voters cast straight-ticket ballots, voting for all candidates of one party.

■ Republican candidates won more counties (especially the most populous counties) than Democrats in recent presidential, gubernatorial, and other statewide elections. Indeed, a map of voting trends in the 1970s (Figure 21.2) is dramatically different from a map of voting trends from the 1990s (Figure 21.3).[13]

■ In 2000, Republican candidates won every statewide election, continuing their hold on all twenty-nine statewide elected officials.

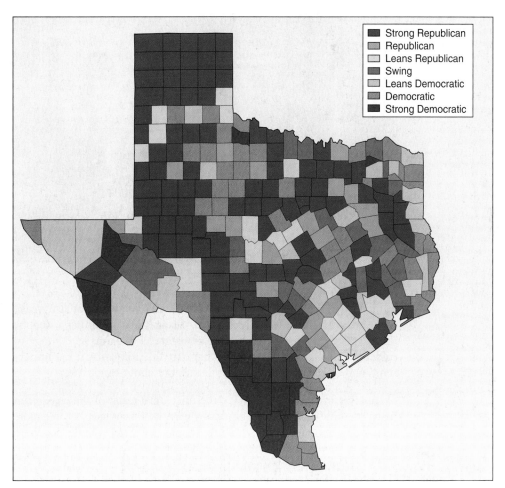

FIGURE 21.3 Republican and Democratic Party Strength in Texas by County (1990s)
The map reflects the strength of the Texas Republican and Democratic Parties based on votes for Republican and Democratic candidates in selected general election contests during the 1990s. ■

Sources: Based on county election results from the 1992 presidential election, 1994 gubernatorial election, 1996 presidential election, 1998 gubernatorial election, 1998 lieutenant governor election, and the 1998 comptroller election. Texas Almanac, 1996–1997 (Dallas: Dallas Morning News, 1995); Texas Almanac, 1998–1999 (Dallas: Dallas Morning News, 1997); Texas Almanac, 2000–2001 (Dallas: Dallas Morning News, 1999); Texas Secretary of State Web site, Historical Election Results, accessed February 18, 2001, http://204.65.104.19/elchist.exe.

Republicans also retained control of the Texas Senate, which they controlled since 1997, and in 2002 won control of the Texas House. The total number of Republican elected officials increased to approximately 1,966.[14]

Another possible interpretation of the surveys on party identification in Texas is that Texans are not realigning but dealigning. In a dealignment, party affiliations weaken, and the importance of party

■ Senator Letica Van de Putte (with microphone) addresses the press as chair of the Democratic caucus. Caucus members were instrumental in delaying the congressional redistricting bill during the second called session of the 78th Legislature. Despite the Democrats' efforts, the bill passed during the third called session.

Photo courtesy: CORBIS

affiliation to the population's political attitudes and behavior also weakens. According to this interpretation, Texas is not becoming a Republican state; it is becoming a no-party state. The large percentage of independents is cited as evidence that party identification is less important, and elections are not about parties but about candidates.

The Contemporary Party Coalitions. As a result of the changes in party identification among Texans, the party coalitions have become more like their national counterparts (see chapter 11). Increasingly, people in the upper income categories identify with the Republican Party; people in the lower income categories identify with the Democratic Party. Also, the Democratic Party is the party of liberals and populists, African Americans and Hispanics, and women; the Republican Party is the party of conservatives and libertarians, Anglos, males, and the Christian Right.

The Party in Government

As noted in chapter 11, the party in government is a political party's mechanism for establishing cooperation among the separate branches of government. In theory, all public officials who are appointed or elected under the same party label work together to establish and implement public policies that represent the party's positions on issues. How strong is the party in government in Texas, and how well does it perform this unifying function?

In the Executive Branch. For members of the executive branch in Texas, the Texas Constitution establishes several impediments to cooperation. Foremost is the independent election of the most important executive officers in Texas. Even the governor and lieutenant governor do not run as a team on the ballot (see chapter 19). Consequently, the relationship between the governor and lieutenant governor, even when they are members of the same political party, may be strained. Also, because the Texas attorney general's office has often been used as a stepping stone by politicians who aspire to be governor, the relationship between those two officials may not be the most cordial, even when they are members of the same political party. Other statewide elected officials in the executive branch may also harbor such ambitions. For example, Republican Texas Comptroller Carol Keeton Strayhorn has done everything but formally announce her intention to challenge Republican Governor Rick Perry for the party's gubernatorial nomination in 2006.

Because the executive officers are elected independently, candidates of the same political party have little incentive to campaign together or even to coordinate their campaigns for public office. Typically, each office-seeker establishes his or her campaign organization. This practice further reduces the likelihood of cooperation after the election. In 1982, faced for the first time with Republican opposition in all major executive races, the Democratic candidates showed a greater degree of cooperation than normal and even coordinated portions of their campaigns.

In the Legislative Branch.   In the Texas legislature, as noted in chapter 18, partisan considerations are usually minimized. Until recently, Texas was one of only five states that did not hold inclusive party caucuses, elect party leaders, or create party committees. Party caucuses and committees are formed to provide information to party members on policy issues and to formulate the party's position on issues. In 1981, a group of Democratic members of the Texas House of Representatives formed a Democratic caucus. By 1987, the caucus included all Democrats, including the speaker of the House and all Democrats on his team, a practice that has continued in subsequent sessions. By 1989, the speaker's team and the caucus began to work together, reducing the tension that had characterized the earlier years.[15] From 1993 to 2003, while Pete Laney was House speaker, the Democratic caucus was not very active. In 2003, when Republicans gained control of the House and elected a Republican speaker, the caucus became more active (see chapter 18). Similarly, since 1999, Senate Democrats, faced with a Republican governor and lieutenant governor, decided to give the caucus a more prominent role. Caucus chairs called frequent meetings, discussed policy and strategy, and held press conferences to publicize the Democrats' position on issues before the legislature.

Prior to 1989, the Republicans avoided party organization in the House, preferring to work with the speaker and conservative Democrats through the Texas Conservative Coalition. However, in 1989, the Republicans organized a caucus, "formed a policy committee to screen suggested legislation before it went to the full caucus for endorsement, and maintained a political arm called the Republican Campaign Legislative Committee."[16] Also, Governor Bill Clements, who had opposed a Republican organization in the House in 1979, now endorsed it during his second term (1987–1991).

Despite predictions to the contrary, the Texas legislature continues to operate with strong institutional leaders, eschewing the opportunity to build strong party organizations.[17]

In the Judicial Branch.   In Texas, all judges, except municipal court judges, are elected on a partisan ballot. Consequently, a reluctance to politicize the judiciary, which is evident in some states, is less pronounced in Texas. However, candidates for legislative and executive positions rarely team with members of their party seeking judgeships in a coordinated campaign. Thus, the elections are usually conducted independently.

The influence of party is often dominant in the appointment of judges when a vacancy occurs either through a judge's death, resignation, retirement, or removal. Because a large percentage of judges are initially appointed to their positions by the governor, he or she has many opportunities to reward party members with judicial appointments. A comparison of judicial appointments by Governor Clements during his last term (1987–1991) and Governor Richards during her term (1991–1995) indicates that each appointed an overwhelming majority of judges who shared the governor's party affiliation.[18] More recently, when Governor Rick Perry was given the opportunity to fill vacancies on the Texas Supreme Court, he chose Republicans.

Appointments of judges by governors could also be viewed as an attempt to fill the courts with judges who share the governor's political ideology. This assumes that judges, in interpreting the law, can exercise some discretion and that Republican judges and Democratic judges differ in how they interpret the law and decide cases. For example, during the 2002–2003 term, the Texas Supreme Court, on which Republicans held all of the seats, decided for the defendant in 79 percent of its cases. In 1985, when Democrats controlled the Supreme Court, defendants won only 28 percent.[19]

INTEREST GROUPS IN TEXAS

RECALL THAT WHEN PEOPLE FORM GROUPS, they must decide whether to act as a political party or as an interest group. We now turn from parties to interest groups, considering first the types of interest groups and then their political activities.

Types of Interest Groups

Usually, political scientists classify interest groups according to the type of interest that the group represents. We have adopted a classification that focuses on the policy goals of the group: business groups and trade associations, professional associations, labor groups, racial and ethnic groups, and public-interest groups.

Business Groups and Trade Associations.   Interest groups representing businesses in Texas are diverse, but business groups and trade associations generally agree that their primary goal is to maintain a favorable climate for businesses in Texas. More specifically, these groups attempt to ensure that business taxes remain low, that labor union influence is restricted, and that favorable business regulations exist. Some *business interest groups* (e.g., Texas Association of Business, and Texas Association of Taxpayers) represent business interests generally. Others, known as *trade associations*, represent specific industries and their interests. Among the more influential trade associations are the Texas Automobile Dealers Association, and the Texas Bankers Association. To increase their influence, many corporations (Southwestern Bell and AT&T, for example) also hire their own lobbyists when the legislature is considering a matter of particular importance to their interests.

Professional Associations.   Some of the most influential interest groups in Texas represent professional associations, such as trial lawyers, physicians, teachers, and realtors. The Texas Trial Lawyers Association (TTLA) represents the interests of lawyers who make their living representing people in personal-injury lawsuits or product-liability suits. The Texas Medical Association (TMA) represents physicians, and the Texas State Teachers Association (TSTA), the Texas Federation of Teachers (TFT), the Association of Texas Professional Educators (ATPE), and the Texas Classroom Teachers Association (TCTA) compete to represent public-school teachers. The Texas Association of Realtors (TAR) works for realtors in Texas. All of these groups attempt to influence regulations and public policies that affect their professions.

Labor Groups.   Although labor groups have never been strong in Texas, their influence is greatest in the Golden Triangle area of Beaumont, Port Arthur, and Orange. Labor unions attempt to establish rights for their members to collective bargaining, occupational safety, and increased wages. The membership of the American Federation of Labor–Congress of Industrial Organizations (AFL-CIO) has declined since the 1980s. Within the AFL-CIO, the more influential unions are the Texas Oil, Chemical, and Atomic Workers Union (OCAW), the American Federation of State, County, and Municipal Employees (AFSCME), and the Communication Workers of America (CWA).

Racial and Ethnic Groups.   Racial and ethnic groups promote political, economic, and social equality for their members, freedom from discrimination, and representation in public offices. Because they are the largest ethnic minorities in Texas, Hispanics and African Americans have the greatest number of groups representing their interests. The oldest and largest Hispanic group, the League of United Latin American Citizens (LULAC), is involved in efforts to change the method of selecting judges in Texas (see chapter 20), and the Mexican American Legal Defense and Educational Fund (MALDEF) was instrumental in the lawsuit that led to greater equality in funding for public education in Texas. The National Association for the Advancement of Colored People (NAACP) supported the challenge to the Democratic Party's white primary, fought to end segregation in public education, and continues to fight for increased economic and social opportunities for African Americans.

Public-Interest Groups.   Public-interest groups advocate public policies intended to benefit the public interest. Among the more active groups in Texas are the Baptist Christian Life Commission, Common Cause, Clean Water Action, the Sierra Club, Public Citizen, Texans for Public Justice, Texas Alliance for Human Needs, Texas Citizen Action, and Americans Disabled for Attendant Programs Today (ADAPT). These groups seek public policies that protect consumers, the environment, the poor, the elderly, the young, and the disabled.

Political Activities of Interest Groups

Interest groups usually engage in three distinct, but related, types of political activities: lobbying, electioneering, and litigation. In this section, we identify and explain each of these activities.

Lobbying.   When most people think of interest group activities, lobbying is probably the first thing that comes to mind. Indeed, lobbying may be the universal activity of interest groups. Most groups practice direct and indirect lobbying.

■ Kwame Walker, a Senate staff member for thirteen years, became a "hired gun" in 1999, lobbying the Texas legislature for his clients.

Photo courtesy: Tom Lankes/Austin American-Statesman

Attempting to influence public officials through direct contacts defines direct lobbying. Because public officials reside in all three branches of government (legislature, executive, and judiciary) and at all levels of government (national, state, and local), we would expect lobbyists (the people who lobby) to attempt to influence all of them. Indeed, lobbyists are evident wherever public policy and political decisions are made.

In 1987, there were approximately 800 lobbyists in Texas. In 2003, there were 1,578 lobbyists registered with the Texas Ethics Commission. Those lobbyists were paid somewhere between $132 million and $276 million for their services.[20] Even so, those figures do not indicate the more than 2,000 interest groups with lobbyists working in Austin during the regular legislative session in 2003. The discrepancy between registered lobbyists and the number of interest groups with lobbyists is partially due to the legal requirements for registration in Texas. However, much of the discrepancy arises because many lobbyists have more than one client. In 1987, 80 percent of the registered lobbyists represented only one client, but nearly 11 percent represented four or more clients.[21]

Texas laws requiring lobbyist registration and placing restrictions on lobbying activity were passed in several legislative sessions since the 1950s. In some respects, the laws are broad and encompassing. Lobbying is defined as efforts to influence the legislative and the executive branches, and the law applies even when the legislature is not in session. Furthermore, individuals who register as lobbyists must indicate their employers, provide information about their expenditures, and indicate the bills or regulations about which they are concerned. In 1991, the legislature limited the annual amount that a lobbyist could spend on a public official to $500. Pleasure trips and honoraria paid for by lobbyists were also prohibited. In 2001, the legislature established new conflict-of-interest rules for registered lobbyists.

In the late 1980s, two trends characterized lobbyists in Texas. First, there was an increase in the number of contract lobbyists ("hired guns") who work for more than one client. Many of these contract lobbyists were former members of the legislative or executive branches. In the 1990s, that trend continued, as more former legislators and bureaucrats took positions representing interest groups. The second trend involved greater ethnic and gender diversity among lobbyists. By 1999, the number of women, Hispanics, and African Americans had increased significantly.[22] This trend reflects the changing ethnic and gender composition of government, as well as the tendency for interest groups to assemble a team of lobbyists who are individually assigned to specific legislators or bureaucrats, based on a number of shared characteristics.

According to lobbyists, their principal job involves access to public officials and presenting information about their issues. To present information to legislators or administrators though, lobbyists first need to gain access to public officials. Access comes from the lobbyist's reputation and from the interest group's contributions to the legislator's campaign (a technique that we discuss more fully in the next section of this chapter). Consequently, many lobbyists are former public officials who have established personal relationships with the people to whom they now want access. Furthermore, their previous experience in public office increases their credibility with current legislators and bureaucrats. As lobbyist and former legislator Bill Messer states, "The real job is to articulate a position and to state a constituency. If you don't have a constituency, then you don't have any influence."[23]

Currently, lobbyists must rely on their information and integrity. As Bill Clayton, former Texas House speaker and current lobbyist, stated, "Integrity is the one thing that counts more than anything. If you lie to one of the members, you won't ever get a job again."[24] Despite the personal friendships that many lobbyists have cultivated with legislators and administrators, lobbyists have to make their case on its merits.

The information provided by lobbyists can be substantive (usually technical) or political. Substantive information provides details about the content of the legislation. Political information indicates how the legislation will affect the legislator's constituents and supporters. Furthermore, lobbyists can provide experts to testify at legislative hearings. Probably the most persuasive information provided by lobbyists involves what other states have done concerning a particular issue and the effects of those measures. Although the lobbyists represent particular interests, the case for or against a bill must be made in terms of good social policy, not the benefits to the particular interest.[25]

From legislative session to session, the interests that lobbyists represent vary according to the legislative agenda, but some interests are always present. Most prevalent are business interests. In 2003, the Texas businesses that employed the greatest number of lobbyists were energy and natural resource companies, establishing more than 900 contracts worth up to $42 million to the lobbyists that they employed. In second place among businesses was the health industry, with 822 contracts worth up to $32 million, and third place belonged to the miscellaneous businesses, which included alcohol and gambling interests and which spent up to $29 million on 694 contracts.[26]

The individuals targeted by lobbyists vary. Some lobbyists pursue a "top-down" strategy, concentrating their efforts on the leadership. Because the Texas speaker of the House and president of the Senate (lieutenant governor) have considerable powers, lobbying the leadership can be productive. However, most lobbyists focus their efforts on the committees with jurisdiction over legislation that affects the interests of the group. As their numbers have increased, legislative staff members are also among the lobbyists' targets, particularly those members who are considered influential with the legislator. Finally, on the House and Senate floors, lobbyists concentrate their efforts on legislators who are undecided, rather than those who have committed to vote for or against a given measure.[27]

Lobbyists do not confine their activities to the legislature. Interactions between lobbyists and administrators of state agencies and departments are frequent in Texas. A 1982 study of executive agencies in Texas indicated that interest-group-initiated contacts with agencies occurred frequently or very frequently and that half of the contacts were administration initiated. These contacts usually involve an exchange of information or an attempt to influence policies. Administrative agencies contact interest groups to ascertain the effects of their programs on group members and to solicit input on proposed regulations. Interest groups, on the other hand, contact agencies to obtain information about their programs and to influence the agencies' rules and regulations.

In addition to direct lobbying, interest groups also engage in a form of lobbying called indirect or "grassroots" lobbying. There are actually two forms of indirect lobbying. In the first form, interest groups attempt to activate their members, urging them to contact their representatives or

THE CAMPAIGN TO LIMIT MEDICAL LIABILITY

During much of the 1980s, Texas was known as the lawsuit capital of the nation. Trial lawyers were influential in the selection of Texas Supreme Court justices, and judgments in cases before the courts favored the plaintiffs over defendants. In the 1990s, groups representing businesses focused their efforts on the legislature, encouraging them to pass tort reform measures, and on the courts, where they supported candidates who were supportive of business interests. In 2003, the legislature was disposed toward extending tort reforms.

Charles W. Bailey Jr.—president of the Texas Medical Association (TMA) —described the TMA's activities in the nineteen months preceding the regular session of the Texas legislature in 2003 as crucial. According to Bailey, "We've learned that our success in the legislature is directly related to how well the medical community executes on some basics during the interim.[a] During the interim, then Lieutenant Governor Bill Ratliff created an interim Senate Select Committee on Liability Reform. At hearings held by the committee, physicians testified about the effects of lawsuits on physicians' malpractice insurance premiums and the availability of health care services. Meanwhile, TMA lobbyists arranged meetings with incumbent legislators. In addition, the TMA's political action committee—TEXPAC—provided campaign assistance to candidates who supported the TMA's position on liability reform and health care issues. These efforts, involving members of the TMA and their spouses, emphasized a form of grassroots lobbying.[b]

The TMA's efforts during the legislative session focused on legislation that included sweeping medical liability reforms and a constitutional amendment that would cap noneconomic damages for physicians, institutions. Under the law, noneconomic damages—for pain, suffering, loss of companionship, disfigurement, or physical impairment—would be limited to $750,000. Of the damages, $250,000 could come from physicians or medical personnel, and $250,000 could come from each hospital or nursing home, but a person could only collect from two medical facili-

ties. Although the noneconomic damage limits were included in the medical liability law, the constitutional amendment was deemed necessary to prevent a court from finding that the limits violated Article 1, section 13, of the Texas Constitution (know as the "open courts provision"). In 1988, the Texas Supreme Court had used that provision to declare a $500,000 liability limit unconstitutional.[c] The medical liability law passed the House and Senate in different forms. The differences were resolved in conference. The constitutional amendment also passed both chambers and was set for voter approval in a September 2003 special election.

The efforts surrounding the adoption of the constitutional amendment (proposition 12) by Texas voters pitted trial lawyers and consumer groups against tort reformers, business groups, insurance companies, hospitals, physicians, and other health care providers. The battle was waged on television, in newspapers, and through mailings to Texas households. On one side, Save Texas Courts, argued that a basic constitutional right to have courts, judges, and juries decide damages in civil trials was being handed over to the legislature. On the other side, Yes on 12 argued that limiting medical liability would allow physicians to continue to practice medicine by reducing the cost of medical malpractice insurance, thereby insuring access to quality health care.[d] In all, nearly $13 million was spent by both sides to influence voters.

On September 13, 2003, nearly 1.5 million voters went to the polls or had voted during early voting. The amendment barely passed.

[a]Christopher Guadagnino, "The Story Behind Tort Reform Success in Texas," *Physician's News Digest,* Spotlight, September 2003, accessed August 11, 2004, http://www.physiciansnews.com/spotlight/903.html.

[b]Guadagnino, "The Story Behind Tort Reform Success."

[c]*Lucas* v. *United States,* 757 S.W. 2d 687 (Tex. 1988).

[d]Darrin Schlegel, "Insurers Share Blame for Rise in Malpractice Rates, Some Say," *Houston Chronicle* (August 27, 2003); Jane Elliott, "Amendment Pits Powerful Lobbies," *Houston Chronicle* (August 30, 2003); James Pinkerton, "Valley at Epicenter of Debate on Malpractice Caps," *Houston Chronicle* (August 30, 2003).

executive officials to influence public policy. The second form attempts to change the climate of public opinion, largely through television advertising. Political activists have termed some of these lobbying efforts "Astroturf" because although they look like grassroots political efforts, they are actually manufactured by interest groups. Despite their artificial quality, they offer a semblance of popular support for a position. In 2003, Astroturf interest groups led the efforts to limit tort liability for doctors, hospitals, and insurance companies (see Politics Now: The Campaign to Limit Medical Liability).

Electioneering.   Electioneering has become a major political activity of interest groups since the mid-1970s. Interest groups maintain that their involvement in political campaigns is to ensure access to public officials. As one lobbyist notes, the price of access is a $1,000 contribution to a senator's campaign and a $250 contribution to a representative's campaign.[28]

Like most states, Texas has experienced a boom in the activity of political action committees (PACs), which are groups formed to solicit funds and then to use those funds to help elect or defeat candidates for public office. In 2002, there were 964 general-purpose PACs registered in Texas. There were ninety-nine more PACs in 2002 than in 2000, and PAC spending increased by 57 percent during the period, from $54 million in 1999–2000 to $85 million in 2001–2002. Of the 2001–2002 spending by PACs, business PACs contributed the most money to candidates, ideological and single-issue PACs contributed considerably less money, and labor PACs contributed the least money.[29] Table 21.1 provides a list of the top fifteen general PACs in 2002.

A study of campaign contributions by twenty-two Texas PACs that are interested in protecting businesses from civil lawsuits for personal injuries (torts) demonstrated how PACs target their contributions. Although the twenty-two PACs contributed to all but one of the 181 legislators in the House and Senate in 1995 and 1996, the principal beneficiaries of the PACs' largess were legislators involved in close elections, freshmen legislators, Republicans, and the leadership in both chambers. In all, the twenty-two PACs contributed $3.1 million to winning legislative candidates between January 1995 and December 1996.[30]

Litigation.   Practiced extensively by civil rights and environmental groups in the 1950s and 1960s, litigation recently has become a more common weapon in the arsenal of interest group activities. Much of the increased use of litigation can be attributed to the new judicial federalism, which has made state courts more likely to entertain such lawsuits (see chapter 16). The purpose of litigation is to effect or prevent changes in public policy. Litigation can also be used as a delaying tactic to slow change.[31] However, because litigation is expensive, the

TABLE 21.1 Top General-Purpose PACs, 2002

Rank 2002	Rank 2000	Political Action Committee	2002 Spending	Interest Category
1	1	Texas Democratic Party	$15,041,055	Democratic Party
2	2	Republican Party of Texas	6,725,988	Republican Party
3	9	Texas Trial Lawyers Association	2,862,549	Lawyers
4	5	Texas for Lawsuit Reform	2,447,618	Business
5	4	Texan Assoication of Realtors	2,149,380	Business
6	26	Duke Energy Corporation	1,785,449	Business
7	8	Texas Medical Association	1,663,027	Profession
8	3	Texas 2000	1,500,132	Lawyers
9	7	Vinson and Elkins	1,376,153	Lawyers
10	14	Compass Bancshares	1,146,650	Business
11	11	Texas Partnership PAC	955,102	Democractic Party
12	41	Valero Refining and Marketing	895,661	Business
13	—*	Texans for a Republican Majority	800,441	Republican Party
14	19	Fullbright and Jaworski	760,131	Lawyers
15	12	SBC Communications	746,242	Business

*Texans for a Republican Majority did not exist in 2000.

Source: Texans for Public Justice, :"The 100 Biggest PACs in Texas." *Texas PACs: 2002 Election Cycle,* November 2004, accessed December 13, 2004. http://www.tpj.org/reports/txpacs02/bycycle.html.

groups that are most likely to pursue litigation are those who are prosperous enough to afford the expense.

ELECTIONS AND POLITICAL CAMPAIGNS IN TEXAS

THIS SECTION DISCUSSES the various types of elections that are conducted in Texas—primary elections, special elections, general elections, and local elections—and examines political campaigns and voting behavior.

Types of Elections

In Texas, elections are frequent, and the ballot tends to be longer than in other states. The legislature has established uniform dates (first Saturday in February, first Saturday in May, second Saturday in September, and first Tuesday after the first Monday in November) for general and special elections, but elections can occur much more frequently.

Primary Elections.   By Texas law, any party whose candidate for governor receives more than 20 percent of the vote must hold a primary election to nominate candidates. Parties whose gubernatorial candidate receives less than 20 percent of the vote can nominate their candidates in primary elections or in party conventions.

Primaries were established in Texas in 1905 with the passage of the Terrell Election Law, which required a combination of the primary election and a state convention to determine the party's nominees. In 1907, the law was amended to establish a direct primary election, with a plurality vote necessary to secure the nomination. In 1918, the legislature adopted a majority vote requirement to win the primary and established a second, or runoff, primary between the first- and second-place vote-getters if no candidate received a majority of the vote in the first primary.[32]

Although primary elections in Texas are supposedly closed elections (see chapter 13), voters can still choose to participate in the opposition party's primary election, making them operate more like open primaries.

Participation in primary elections is usually low in Texas, especially in runoff primaries. However, between 1906 and 1962, a larger percentage of Texas voters participated in the Democratic primary than participated in the general election. Participation in the Democratic primaries was high because they often included contests reflecting the ideological split in the party, making the results more important than the general elections, which were almost always won by the Democratic candidates. In 1962, for the first time in Texas history, the number of voters in the general election in a nonpresidential election year exceeded the number of voters in the Democratic primary election. Since then, as participation in the general election has increased, participation in the Republican primary has increased while participation in the Democratic primary has decreased. This change reflects the rise of the Republican Party in Texas and the resulting increase in the importance of the general election.[33] In 2004, 5.2 percent of the voting-age population voted in the Democratic primary, and 4.3 percent voted in the Republican primary. Only about 5 percent of the voting-age population participated in the parties' runoff primaries in that year.

Because primary elections are party elections, each party is responsible for administering its own primary election, which includes preparing the ballots, conducting the elections, tabulating and certifying the results, and financing the election.

special election
Election held at a time other than general or primary elections.

Special Elections.   **Special elections** are held in Texas to fill vacancies in state legislative and U.S. congressional offices, to approve local bond proposals, and if the legislature chooses, to approve amendments to the Texas Constitution (see chapter 16). Executive and judicial vacancies are filled by gubernatorial appointment. The dates for special elections are set by the legislature for amendments to the Texas Constitution, by the governor to fill legislative and congressional vacancies, and by the local government to approve bond proposals. The parties do not hold primaries to nominate candidates for special elections; thus, access to the ballot for legislative or congressional vacancies is through filing fees or signatures on petitions. Consequently, the number of candidates in special elections tends to be large. Candidates who seek an office in special elections are identified by political party on the ballot, and they must receive a majority of the votes cast to win the office. If no candidate receives a majority of the vote, a runoff election between the top two vote-getters is held one month after the first election.

General Elections.   General elections are interparty contests to determine which candidates will hold public office. In Texas, as in most states, the general election is held on the first Tuesday after the first Monday in November of even-numbered years. Since 1974, when Texas adopted a four-year gubernatorial term, the governor and other statewide elected executive officials who also serve four-year terms are elected in nonpresidential years. In elections for state, district, and county offices, the person who receives the most votes—a plurality—wins the election.

General elections are administered and funded by the state. The secretary of state, the state's chief election official, is responsible for certifying state and district candidates, ensuring that the county clerks certify local candidates and that the county commissioners court appoints the necessary officials to administer the election, and reporting and maintaining the election results.

Local Elections.   **Local elections** are conducted to elect city councils, mayors, school-board members, and special district boards. (In chapter 17, we discussed the unique role of counties as both local governments and administrative arms of state government; county elections are part of the state electoral system.) Cities and special districts may conduct their elections in odd-numbered years, and some cities require a majority vote to win, necessitating a runoff election if no candidate receives a majority. These elections are nonpartisan and are usually conducted in May.

local election
Election conducted by local governments to elect officials.

Political Campaigns in Texas

As noted earlier, there are ample (some say too many) opportunities to vote in Texas. How do Texans find out about the candidates, their party affiliations, and their positions on issues of public policy in all of these elections? Political campaigns are supposed to perform that function.

Ideally, election campaigns should offer the electorate an opportunity to compare the candidates and their views on the major issues of public policy. Then, armed with this knowledge, voters should choose among the competing political views and, thereby, determine public policy. Unfortunately, contemporary political campaigns do not meet this standard. As political scientist W. Lance Bennett has noted, contemporary political campaigns are about the three M's—money, media, and marketing.[34] We will consider the influence of these factors in Texas campaigns before analyzing voters' decisions in recent gubernatorial campaigns.

Money: The Mother's Milk of Politics.   Everyone knows that contemporary political campaigns are expensive. In the 2002 gubernatorial campaign in Texas, incumbent Governor Rick Perry spent nearly $28 million, and his challenger, Tony Sanchez, spent slightly more than $76 million in the general election. In 1998, candidates who won in contested House contests raised an average of $190,173 in campaign contributions to the losers' average of $90,038.[35] In 2002, incumbent Texas senators raised an average of $523,857 to their challengers' average of $50,479.[36] Money does not guarantee electoral success, but winning candidates generally outspend their opponents. Why are election campaigns so expensive in Texas, and how do the candidates raise the money necessary to be competitive?

The geographic size of Texas makes money important in electoral campaigns. As journalist Kaye Northcott noted, "Money doesn't just talk in Texas elections: it does tap dances and sings the state anthem in three-part harmony."[37] The key to name recognition is television advertising. After spending nearly ten months campaigning, Buddy Temple had raised his name recognition from 5 to 12 percent. When his television advertising campaign started, two days yielded an increase from 12 to 24 percent. As Temple noted, "That made a believer out of me. If you don't have the money to make a good showing on television, you don't have a chance in Texas."[38]

Individual contributions provide the majority of campaign contributions in Texas, but increasingly, contributions from groups, through their PACs, have become more important, especially to incumbents in state legislative contests. In 2002, of the $21.4 million raised by candidates for the Texas Senate, PACs contributed 52 percent, and individuals contributed 48 percent. Of the $33.1 million raised by Texas House candidates, individuals contributed 53 percent, and PACs contributed 47 percent. During the 2002 gubernatorial campaign in Texas, Tony Sanchez funded his campaign primarily from his personal fortune, contributing nearly $57 million and loaning himself another $22 million. On the other hand, Rick Perry received the largest percentage of his contributions from individuals (74 percent). PACs provided the remaining 26 percent. Perry's contributions averaged slightly more than $2,000; the greatest number of contributions were in amounts of $500 or less.[39]

Not only is political money important in Texas, but there are also few restrictions placed on its use in political

■ Byron LeMasters, a senior at the University of Texas at Austin in 2005, started the Burnt Orange Report Web log with Jim Dallas, also a student at UT, in April 2003. Byron was among the bloggers selected to attend the Democratic National Convention at Boston in 2004.

Photo courtesy: Byron LeMasters

BLOGGING AT BURNTORANGE.COM

Byron LaMasters is a senior majoring in government at the University of Texas at Austin. He is also one of four University of Texas at Austin students and former students who maintain a Web log or, as they are commonly called, a blog on local Austin, state, national, and University of Texas politics. LaMasters and Jim Dallas, who graduated from UT recently, started the blog, the Burnt Orange Report, in April 2003. In June of that year, Andrew Dobbs, a current UT student who interned with the Dean campaign and worked for Representative Jim McReynolds during the 78th Legislature, joined as a contributor. The final contributor, and the youngest at nineteen years old, is Karl-Thomas Musselman, who joined the group in October 2003. All four are Democrats and are, or have been, active in the University Democrats at the University of Texas at Austin.

Covering all types of politics, burntorangereport.com gets between 600 and 1,000 hits daily. When they started, they were only receiving between 500 and 700 hits daily. However, when LaMasters decided to openly discuss a rumor about Governor Rick Perry that was circulating in the capital, the hits skyrocketed to 25,000 a day. As result of the coverage and other blogs picking up the rumor, Governor Perry "felt compelled to deny the unsubstantiated rumors."[a] In early 2004, LaMasters urged blog visitors to help defeat long-time Democratic Representative Ron Wilson, the only Democrat in the Texas House to vote for the Republican-backed congressional redistricting bill that endangered several incumbent House Democrats, by contributing to his opponent in the party's primary. His appeal raised several thousand dollars for Alma Allen, who won the primary elec-

tion and subsequently called LaMasters on his mobile phone to thank him for his assistance.

In many ways, this typifies blogs, bloggers, and the blogosphere. LaMasters, Dallas, Dobbs, and Musselman are not reporters. They blog about whatever interests them. They cover what the mainstream media do not. Furthermore, they make no pretense of being fair or balanced. But, for young people, they are frequently the source for political news. Most young Americans get their news from friends, from e-mails, and from links to Web sites provided by their friends. As political scientist Gary Chapman notes, "The hyper-linked character of e-mail and the Web lead heavy Internet users to a diversity of information sources that older people find difficult to grasp."[b] Joe Trippi, former Howard Dean campaign manager, sees bloggers as having arrived: "I really think the power of the Internet to democratically let people come together and link together is going to change everything. And I think bloggers are a big piece of that. It will alter how we consume all media."[c]

In 2004, both major political parties acknowledged the impact of bloggers by credentialing between twenty and forty of them to their national conventions. In July 2004, Byron LaMasters attended the Democratic National Convention in Boston and reported on convention activities. Being selected to cover the Democratic National Convention is a tribute to LaMasters and the other contributors to the Burnt Orange Report.[d]

[a]Patrick Beach, "Conventions Ask Bloggers to Join the Convention," *Austin American-Statesman* (July 25, 2004): H4.

[b]Gary Chapman, "Make Way for the Bloggers—They Give Us News with Attitude," *Austin American-Statesman* (July 23, 2004): A13.

[c]Quoted in Beach, "Conventions Ask Bloggers to Join," H1.

campaigns. In Texas, campaign finance regulation has usually come as a response to blatant, both legal and illegal, excesses by campaign contributors. A major reform was passed in 1973 in the wake of the Sharpstown scandal (see chapter 18). However, even the scandal did not produce strong legislation. The law merely required candidates to designate a campaign treasurer and to report contributions and expenditures. There were numerous loopholes in the legislation, such as the requirement that only "opposed" candidates must report contributions and expenditures.[40] After Lonnie "Bo" Pilgrim passed out checks for $10,000 to Texas senators in an attempt to influence workers' compensation legislation in 1989, the legislature, at the urging of Governor Richards, attempted to strengthen the regulation of campaign finance in 1991. The legislature created the Ethics Commission, which now receives the contribution and expenditure reports for candidates for state office, and it did close some of the loopholes in the previous law. In 1999, the legislature adopted a law requiring candidates for statewide offices, the state legislature, and many district offices to file their contribution and expenditure reports electronically. Since the 2000 elections, the information has been available on the Ethics Commission's Web site. However, there are still no limits on contributions by individuals or PACs to legislative and executive candidates in Texas.

Media: Linking the Candidates and the Voters.   Although politicians once believed that campaigning should be conducted personally and should involve face-to-face contacts with the voters at campaign rallies, technology has made personal contacts less effective. As noted in chapter 12, campaign communications are now conducted through the media. This is especially true for statewide political campaigns, but it is also becoming more common in district and local campaigns. In a state the size of Texas, the only way to effectively reach potential voters is through the state's nineteen media markets. As political consultant Mark McKinnon noted, "It's impossible to effectively communicate with voters in Texas any other way but television. TV is the next best thing to being there. TV allows the candidate to be in everybody's living room, up close and personal."[41]

This reliance has spawned a new industry composed of experts adept at developing and producing political appeals for the media. As more people have become detached from their partisan affiliations, party leaders have lost the skills necessary to organize campaigns capable of electing candidates to public office. Thus, candidates have turned to *political consultants,* specialists in the modern campaign technology, to plan and organize their campaigns.[42] The specialized knowledge possessed by campaign consultants has led to the third component of contemporary campaigns—marketing.

Marketing: Selling the Candidate.   The transition from party-centered to candidate-centered campaigns was facilitated by political consultants. At first, political consultants offered candidates only their technical expertise, probably gained from experience in commercial marketing or advertising. However, as candidates' dependence on media and the techniques of commercial advertising increased, political consultants expanded their influence in the campaign. Despite the proliferation of consultants and their specialization, the most important consultants operate in the area of opinion polling and media services.

Candidates use several techniques to assess the public's concerns and desires, but public opinion polls have become the most commonly used technique. The earliest and most comprehensive opinion survey is the benchmark poll. Conducted a year or more before the election, the benchmark poll is a planning document. The poll typically includes a large number of questions to assess the public's general mood and perception of the candidate's strengths and weaknesses, as well as the strengths and weaknesses of the candidate's likely opponent or opponents. The results of the benchmark poll are used to design the campaign's main themes and to establish the candidate's image.

In 1994, a poll conducted for George W. Bush indicated that the primary concern of voters was crime. According to Micheline Blum, president of Blum and Weprin Associates, "We had done a poll early in the year about issues, and exactly what voters wanted done . . . . On crime, they needed to feel that once a criminal was put away for a really serious offense, he was going to stay away. There were certain safety issues people wanted to hear about and Bush addressed them."[43] Bush made crime and citizen safety a centerpiece of his gubernatorial campaign.

During the campaign, the most important polls are tracking polls (see chapter 10). Conducted over a period of two or three weeks, the tracking polls are used to determine the effectiveness of the campaign's theme and advertising, to detect shifts in voters' preferences among various segments of the population, and to evaluate the changing image of the candidate.

ARE ELECTRONIC VOTING SYSTEMS BETTER THAN PAPER BALLOTS?

Texas, like other states, is eliminating punch-card voting systems and lever machines to comply with the Help America Vote Act (HAVA) of 2002. By 2006, there will also be one direct recording electronic (DRE) voting system at each polling place to accommodate disabled voters. However, some experts have raised questions about the security of DRE voting.

In the 2000 election, Texas's 254 counties employed five election systems for voting. The largest number of counties, 150, employed optical-scan ballots, which are paper ballots that can be scanned and tallied using an optical scanner. Ninety counties used paper ballots, which are marked by the voter and must be tallied manually by individuals. Fourteen counties used punch-card ballots, such as those used in Florida. Three counties used lever-machine voting systems, and four counties used DREs. Under Texas's plan to comply with the HAVA, the lever-machine voting systems and the punch-card ballots will be replaced by January 1, 2006.

The trend among the states is to adopt some form of electronic voting. However, as more states have adopted electronic voting, problems have surfaced. In Muscogee, Georgia, touch-screen voting machines registered "yes" when voters voted "no."

In Maryland, a team of computer experts from Johns Hopkins University showed how hackers could determine the password needed to access the Diebold voting machines, break into the results, and program the software to change votes. These problems have caused many states to rethink their plans to adopt electronic voting.

Read and think about the following arguments for and against electronic voting systems. Then, join the debate concerning whether Texas should acquire electronic voting systems by answering the questions posed after the arguments.

Arguments in Favor of Electronic Voting Systems

- **Electronic voting systems allow disabled voters to cast secret ballots.** Electronic voting systems can be equipped with audio systems that allow visually impaired and blind voters to hear ballot options and select their vote without human assistance, ensuring that their vote is secret.

- **Electronic voting systems eliminate some of the problems associated with other voting methods.** For example, electronic voting systems can prevent overvoting (voting for more

To assess the emotional state of the electorate, pollsters employ focus groups, which include a small, not necessarily representative, sample of voters. According to pollsters, these sessions are useful in finding the public's hot-button issues, which evoke the most emotional and intense responses. These groups are also employed to test campaign commercials before the ads are aired on television.[44]

The most important campaign consultants provide media services to their candidates. As noted in chapter 12, media consultants furnish a number of campaign services, such as the creation of the media messages and the coordination of those messages with the campaign theme. The importance of media messages, particularly negative ads, was demonstrated in the 1990 gubernatorial campaign between Ann Richards and Clayton Williams, and, as noted in the chapter vignette, in the Sharp–Dewhurst race for lieutenant governor in 2002.

than one candidate for an office) and warn voters of undervoting (not voting for a candidate for an office).

- **Electronic voting systems are easy to use and allow the results to be tabulated quickly.** Diebold's electronic voting system uses a touch-screen computer, similar to an automated teller machine (ATM), which is easy to use and familiar to most people. Also, results from electronic voting machines are available faster than from other voting methods, such as optical scan systems.

Arguments Against Electronic Voting Systems

- **Electronic voting systems do not provide paper tallies of the votes, which are necessary for a recount.** Unless votes can be verified, there is the possibility of another disputed election as in the Florida debacle of 2000.
- **Electronic voting is not secure.** Computer experts have demonstrated that at least some of the current voting systems can be compromised.
- **Electronic voting systems are prone to viruses and glitches, just like any computer.** Just like any computer, electronic voting systems can freeze up, crash, or lose data.

Questions

1. Can electronic voting systems be made secure and reliable enough to ensure that votes are accurately counted? Explain your answer.
2. Do you think that using electronic voting systems will solve the problems associated with other voting systems, such as "hanging chads" or poorly designed ballots, which result in overvoting or undervoting? Explain your answer.

Selected Readings

Kavan Peterson. "Integrity of Electronic Voting Questioned," *Stateline.org*, May 3, 2004, accessed August 14, 2004, http://www.stateline.org/stateline/?pa=story&sa=showStoryInfo&id=368968.

Mike Langberg. "Opponents of Change a Threat to Electronic Voting," *San Jose Mercury News*, February 13, 2004, accessed August 14, 2004, http://www.mercurynews.com/mld/mercurynews/business/7945076.htm.

Selected Web Sites

http://www.verifiedvoting.org Verified Voting Foundation.

http://www.diebold.com/dieboldes/default.htm Diebold Election Systems.

The ultimate goal in a political campaign is winning, which requires that eligible voters who support the candidate participate in the election and vote for the candidate in the election. Thus, our attention in the next section shifts to the factors that influence the voters' decisions during an election.

The Voters' Decisions

In an election, the potential voter really faces two decisions. The first decision involves whether to participate. The second decision, which applies only if the person has chosen to participate in the election, involves which candidates to support. In Texas, fewer than half of those age-eligible (people eighteen years of age and older) voters decide to participate in presidential elections, and fewer than one-third decide to participate in gubernatorial elections. Why is voter turnout—the percentage of voting-age people who vote—so low in Texas, ranking forty-ninth among the fifty states in 2004?

Voter Turnout.   Like most decisions concerning political participation, the decision to vote is the result of a calculation that weighs the costs of voting against the benefits of voting. People vote when they believe that voting will yield benefits.

Voting is generally perceived as requiring little effort, but it does involve costs. For example, a voter must find out when the election is held and where the polling place is located, take the time to travel to the polling place, and most importantly, meet the legal requirements to vote. Until the mid-1960s, a number of legal restrictions in Texas, including a poll tax and a white-only Democratic primary, made voting costly, especially for particular groups or categories of Texans. The legal restrictions fell most heavily on the poor, the uninformed, Hispanics, and African Americans.

In contemporary Texas, the legal requirements for voting are minimal. The nominal requirements include U.S. citizenship, being eighteen years of age or older, residency in the state, and registration. The only people who are prohibited from voting are the "mentally incompetent" (as declared by a court of law) and convicted felons who have not completed their sentence, including any term of incarceration, parole, supervision, or probation. Thus, the only real legal barrier to voting is registration, which, in Texas, is relatively easy. A person who wishes to vote must register at least thirty days prior to the election. Once registered, a person is permanently registered and will receive a new registration certificate every two years unless he or she moves during that period. Forms are readily available and are printed in both Spanish and English on postage-free postcards. In 1991, the Texas legislature adopted a motor-voter registration system, which allows a person who is obtaining a driver's license or a Department of Public Safety (DPS) identification card to be registered to vote. The effect of the motor-voter registration system has been to increase significantly the percentage of the population that is registered to vote—from 65 percent before motor-voter in the 1980s to a high of 85 percent in 2000. Since then, registration has fluctuated between 75 and 80 percent.

The Texas legislature reduced the cost of voting with the adoption of early voting. Presently, early voting extends over a two-week period, commencing seventeen days before the election and continuing through the fourth day prior to the election.

The effect of early voting on turnout has been negligible. Early voting has had an impact on the political parties' get-out-the-vote efforts, moving the start of activities to an earlier date and requiring an adjustment in organization and volunteer-recruitment schedules.[45] In the 2002 gubernatorial election, 36 percent of the votes were cast during the early voting period. A comparison of early voters and Election Day voters indicated that early voters are more partisan, older, more conservative, more likely to be male, and require less mobilization than Election Day voters. Candidates can allocate their resources so as to turn out their core supporters early and then concentrate their campaign efforts on those voters who require stronger issue and candidate appeals to obtain their votes on Election Day.[46]

The costs of voting have been reduced significantly in Texas over the past thirty years, but a large percentage of Texans still fail to vote. To complete an explanation of voter turnout, we need to consider the benefits of voting.

The most obvious benefit of voting involves election outcomes—the party and candidates that win the offices contested in the election. Although the results of elections have significant effects on people's lives, an individual person does not have to vote in an election to receive the benefits. The benefits, in terms of the election outcomes, are collective and thus are available to nonvoters as well as to voters. Consequently, the value of a person's vote is not equal to the benefits derived from a given election outcome but to the probability that his or her individual vote will decide a given election. Therefore, the value of voting in most elections is quite small, and it raises questions about why anyone would bother to vote, since there are some costs involved. Apparently, the answer lies in the fact that people derive benefits from voting that are not dependent on deciding the outcome of an election.

In other words, there are selective benefits associated with voting. According to political scientist Ruy Teixeira, the selective benefits are basically expressive, which means that the person must find his or her vote meaningful.[47] For some people, voting expresses a general commitment to a political party, a social category (ethnicity, gender, or social class), or society in general. These benefits are largely symbolic because they are not directly connected to which candidate wins the election. For other people, voting expresses a concern about the election's effect on who holds public office and public policy. These benefits are instrumental because they express a desire to achieve certain results through the election of a particular candidate or political party. An individual who votes because he or she strongly supports the policy goals of a certain candidate would be an example.

A connection to politics—which is achieved through an identification with a political party, through an involvement in public affairs, and through a sense that government is responsive to people's demands—makes voting meaningful and influences the decision to vote. Many Texans lack a strong connection to politics.

Voter turnout in gubernatorial elections in nonpresidential years over the past century has exhibited several trends. After reaching its zenith in the 1890s, when more than 75 percent of the eligible voters voted, voter turnout in Texas fell precipitously for the next decade, finally stabilizing

Analyzing Visuals

Voter Turnout in Texas, 1958–2004

Voter turnout is the proportion of the voting-age public that votes. In Texas, voter turnout during much of the twentieth century remained well below the national average. The chart displays voter turnout in presidential, congressional, gubernatorial, and primary elections between 1958 and 2004. After studying the chart and reading the material on voter turnout in this chapter, answer the following critical thinking questions: What explains the fact that until 1962, voter turnout in the Democratic Party's primary election exceeded voter turnout in the general election for governor? What does the increase in voter turnout in the Republican Party's primary election and decreasing voter turnout in the Democratic Party's primary election suggest? What do you think explains the general increase in voter turnout in gubernatorial general elections since 1972? Why do you think voter turnout was greater in the 1994 gubernatorial election than in the 1998 gubernatorial election?

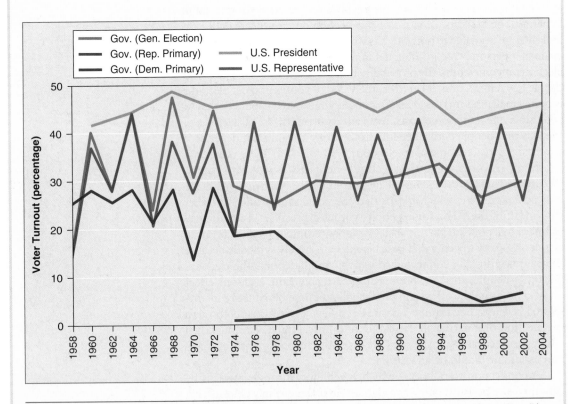

Sources: For 1958–1968, Clifton McCleskey, Allan K. Butcher, Daniel E. Farlow, and J. Pat Stephens, *The Government and Politics of Texas,* 7th ed. (Boston: Little, Brown, 1982), 41; for 1970–2004, Secretary of State, "Turnout and Voter Registration, 1970–current," accessed December 15, 2004, http://www.sos.state.tx.us/elections/historical/70-92.shtml.

at approximately 24 percent of the eligible voters by 1910. In the 1920s, voter turnout dipped again, falling into the low teens and remaining there for the next two decades. During the 1950s and 1960s, voter turnout rose to a twentieth-century high of nearly 35 percent in 1970, before falling into the low 20 percent range during the 1970s. Voter turnout increased during the 1980s, but it never exceeded 30 percent until the 1990s (see Analyzing Visuals: Voter Turnout in Texas, 1958–2004).

Undoubtedly, making voting easier increases voter turnout, but high rates of turnout cannot be achieved solely by minimizing the effort required to vote; people must be motivated by the benefits of voting. During the 1890s, political campaigns in Texas were party centered. Party workers and their supporters marched strong partisans to the polls. The parties were supported by a partisan press, and they distributed campaign literature to a politically active citizenry. Partisan politics occupied a central role in people's lives, both as a social activity and as a statement of personal identity. Obviously, one cannot recreate the society or the politics of the late nineteenth century, but efforts can be made to connect people with politics by providing the institutional means for people to find meaning in political participation. On the other hand, because of attempts to reduce the effort required to vote in Texas, the percentage of Texans who are registered to vote has increased. However, early voting procedures have not increased turnout, as only 46.1 percent of the age-eligible Texans voted in the 2004 presidential election.

The Vote Choice: Parties, Issues, and Candidates.

During the entire nineteenth and first part of the twentieth century, the vote choice was party oriented. Most voters practiced straight-ticket voting, voting for the same party's candidates for all national, state, and local offices. Currently, the vote choice is more office oriented and person oriented, meaning that the basis for the vote choice varies by political office and is more dependent on issues and candidates. Thus, more voters engage in split-ticket voting, voting for some candidates from one party and some from another.

Most explanations of the vote choice focused on three psychological factors: party identification, issues, and candidate characteristics. Party identification was seen as providing stability in the voter's choice, and assessments of candidate characteristics were considered primarily responsible for the variation in the voter's choice. Issues were considered less important. Based on an analysis of voters' choices in presidential elections, the authors of *The American Voter* study implied that vote choices in other elections were motivated by the same factors. However, recent changes in electoral behavior indicate that partisanship is no longer able to structure the vote because of declining partisanship in the electorate and declining strength of partisanship among those members of the electorate who are partisan.[48] Because of the electorate's greater volatility, predicting and explaining the vote choice have become more difficult. Nonetheless, a comparison of the 1986 and 2002 gubernatorial elections in Texas helps clarify the relative importance of the factors.

In 1986, an incumbent Democratic governor, Mark White, was seeking a second term as Texas's governor. In the Republican primary, despite facing a credible challenge, Bill Clements won the first primary handily, avoiding a divisive and expensive runoff election. Meanwhile, in the Democratic primary, White faced five unknown and poorly financed opponents. Winning the first primary with only 53 percent of the vote, White barely escaped a runoff and was embarrassed.

In 1986, party identification favored the Democratic candidate (see Analyzing Visuals: Party Identification in Texas). Nevertheless, among Democratic Party identifiers, White won only 82 percent of the vote, whereas Clements won 92 percent of the Republican vote. Also, among those demographic categories that traditionally support Democratic candidates (low- and moderate-income voters, African Americans, and Hispanics), voter turnout was lower, and support was less enthusiastic than in the gubernatorial election of 1982.[49] Finally, among reasons given for their vote, 20 percent of White's voters and a mere 4 percent of Clements's voters noted party loyalty.

For a large number of voters in 1986, the most important factor in their vote choice pertained to the candidates. The largest percentage of Clements's voters (38 percent) indicated that they voted for Clements as a vote against Mark White. Almost a fifth (19 percent) of White's voters indicated that they voted against Clements.[50] As one study demonstrated, there are several dimensions to candidate characteristics: personal qualities, integrity, reliability, charisma, and competence.[51] Of these dimensions, competence is usually the most important and was the basis for the vote against White. Of course, the judgments of the candidates' competence included some issue content. Voters seemed less confident in Mark White's ability to deal with the fiscal situation, which included an estimated $5.3 billion revenue deficit for the next biennium, especially because he had presided over large tax and fee increases during his tenure. Also, the education reforms that White had championed, especially the "no pass, no play" requirements and the tests for public school teachers, and his inability to get the pay raises that he had promised educators hurt White in many areas of the state, especially in rural West Texas and the Texas Panhandle. More than anything else, the 1986 election demonstrated that although party labels were still important to at least a portion of the electorate, "the better candidate with the better issues and the better campaign can win in most areas regardless of party label."[52]

In 2002, Rick Perry was seeking election as governor after succeeding George W. Bush, who resigned as governor to become U.S. president. Perry was unopposed in the Republican gubernatorial primary. In the Democratic primary, Tony Sanchez, a wealthy Laredo businessman, expected no opposition, but at the last minute, former Texas Attorney General Dan Morales decided to file for the gubernatorial nomination rather than for the U.S. Senate nomination. As a result, Sanchez had to spend more than $20 million in a highly charged, negative primary election campaign. In the end, Sanchez won handily, with more than 60 percent of the vote.

In 2002, the Republican Party held an advantage among Texans in party identification, and the advantage was even greater among voters. Among their respective party identifiers, both candidates did well, but many more Democrats than Republicans defected to the opposition candidate. Sanchez received 78 percent of the Democratic identifiers' votes and Perry received 92 percent of the Republican identifiers' votes. Among independents, Perry received 49 percent of the vote to Sanchez's 33 percent. Sanchez won majorities from several groups that traditionally support Democratic candidates (83 percent of the African American vote, at least 65 percent of the Hispanic vote, and 68 percent of self-identified liberals). Perry won an overwhelming majority of the vote from Anglos; rural, suburban, and small city dwellers; voters thirty years old and older; voters whose income exceeded $35,000 annually; and Protestants.[53]

Perry and Sanchez voters differed on the issues that were most important to them. Perry voters were more likely to be concerned about taxes than Sanchez voters, who were more concerned about the state of the economy, education, and health care. According to Fox News Election Day polls, Texas voters were equally divided on the factor that most determined their vote choice for governor (47 percent cited positions on the issues, and 47 percent cited personal character and experience). Only 23 percent identified political party as the basis for their vote choice. Regardless of the basis for the vote choice, Perry received an overwhelming majority of the votes.[54]

SUMMARY

IN THIS CHAPTER, we described and analyzed political parties, interest groups, elections, and political campaigns in Texas.

1. **The Roots of Political Parties, Interest Groups, Elections, and Campaigns in Texas**
   Political parties developed slowly in Texas, following a period of factional politics based on personalities. With the exception of Reconstruction, the Democratic Party dominated Texas politics until the mid-1980s. Interest groups also developed as economic, social, and ethnic groups organized to influence government.

2. **Political Parties in Texas**
   The party organizations in Texas include a formal organization and a functional organization. At all levels, the Republican Party's organization is stronger than the Democratic Party's organization. Since 1952, the party in the electorate has become more Republican, less Democratic, and more independent in its party attachments. Partisan changes in the

1980s and 1990s made the parties in Texas more like their national counterparts. While some political scientists maintain that Texas has experienced a partisan realignment, others claim that Texans have dealigned. The party in government in Texas is very weak.

3. Interest Groups in Texas
In Texas, interest groups—representing business groups and trade associations, professional associations, labor groups, racial and ethnic groups, and public-interest groups—engage in a variety of political activities such as direct and indirect lobbying, electioneering, and litigation. The most powerful groups represent business and professional interests.

4. Elections and Political Campaigns in Texas
Primary elections, general elections, special elections, and local elections are conducted to nominate candidates, select public officials, fill vacancies, and select local officials. Contemporary political campaigns in Texas are candidate-centered affairs, dominated by the three M's—money, media, and marketing. Voting decisions include a decision to vote, which requires registration, and a choice among candidates, which requires some information about the candidates. Although the costs of voting have been reduced significantly over the last twenty-five years, voter turnout remains low in Texas. Vote choices are less predictable in contemporary Texas than in the past.

KEY TERMS
county chairperson, p. 749
county convention, p. 748
county executive committee, p. 749
local election, p. 771
permanent party organization, p. 749
precinct chairperson, p. 749
precinct convention, p. 748
special election, p. 770
state convention, p. 749
state executive committee, p. 750

state party chairperson, p. 750
state senatorial district convention, p. 748
temporary party organization, p. 748

SELECTED READINGS

Black, Earl, and Merle Black. *The Rise of Southern Republicans*. Cambridge, MA: Harvard University Press, 2002.

Dryer, James A., Jane E. Leighley, and Arnold A. Vedlitz. "Party Identification and Public Opinion in Texas, 1984–1994: Establishing a Competitive Two-Party System," in Anthony Champagne and Edward J. Harpham, eds., *Texas Politics: A Reader*, 2nd ed., 108–22. New York: Norton, 1998.

Goodwyn, Lawrence. *Texas Oil, American Dreams: A Study of the Texas Independent Producers and Royalty Owners Association*. Austin: Texas State Historical Association, 1996.

Hadley, Charles D., and Lewis Bowman, eds. *Southern State Party Organizations and Activists*. Westport, CT: Praeger, 1995.

Martin, Roscoe. *The People's Party in Texas: A Study in Third-Party Politics*. Austin: University of Texas Press, 1970.

Murray, Richard, and Sam Attlesey. "Texas: Republicans Gallop Ahead," in Alexander P. Lamis, ed., *Southern Politics in the 1990s*, 305–42. Baton Rouge: Louisiana State University Press, 1999.

Stein, Robert M. "Early Voting." *Public Opinion Quarterly* 62 (Spring 1998): 57–69.

Thomas, Clive S., and Robert J. Hrebenar. "Interest Group Power in the Fifty States: Trends Since the Late 1970s." *Comparative State Politics* 20(4) (1999): 3–16.

WEB EXPLORATIONS
To learn more about Texas Democrats, go to
http://www.txdemocrats.org/
For more about Texas Republicans, go to
http://www.texasgop.org
To learn about the Texas AFL-CIO, go to
http://www.texasaflcio.org/
To learn more about lobbying in Texas, go to
http://www.ethics.state.tx.us/guides/LOBBY%20guide.htm
To access the contribution and expenditure reports of Texas PACs, see
http://www.ethics.state.tx.us/
For Texas voter turnout and election results, go to
http://www.sos.state.tx.us/elections/historical/index.shtml

The Declaration of Independence

In Congress, July 4, 1776
The Unanimous Declaration of the Thirteen United States of America

When in the Course of human events it becomes necessary for one people to dissolve the political bands which have connected them with another, and to assume, among the powers of the earth, the separate and equal station to which the Laws of Nature and of Nature's God entitle them, a decent respect to the opinions of mankind requires that they should declare the causes which impel them to the separation.

We hold these truths to be self-evident, that all men are created equal, that they are endowed by their Creator with certain unalienable Rights, that among these are Life, Liberty and the pursuit of Happiness. That to secure these rights, Governments are instituted among Men, deriving their just powers from the consent of the governed. That whenever any Form of Government becomes destructive of these ends, it is the Right of the People to alter or to abolish it, and to institute new Government, laying its foundation on such principles and organizing its powers in such form, as to them shall seem most likely to effect their Safety and Happiness. Prudence, indeed, will dictate that Governments long established should not be changed for light and transient causes; and accordingly all experience hath shewn that mankind are more disposed to suffer, while evils are sufferable, than to right themselves by abolishing the forms to which they are accustomed. But when a long train of abuses and usurpations, pursuing invariably the same Object evinces a design to reduce them under absolute Despotism, it is their right, it is their duty, to throw off such Government, and to provide new Guards for their future security.—Such has been the patient sufferance of these Colonies; and such is now the necessity which constrains them to alter their former Systems of Government. The history of the present King of Great Britain is a history of repeated injuries and usurpations, all having in direct object the establishment of an absolute Tyranny over these States. To prove this, let Facts be submitted to a candid world.

He has refused his Assent to Laws, the most wholesome and necessary for the public good.

He has forbidden his Governors to pass Laws of immediate and pressing importance, unless suspended in their operation till his Assent should be obtained; and when so suspended, he has utterly neglected to attend to them.

He has refused to pass other Laws for the accommodation of large districts of people, unless those people would relinquish the right of Representation in the Legislature, a right inestimable to them and formidable to tyrants only.

He has called together legislative bodies at places unusual, uncomfortable, and distant from the depository of their Public Records, for the sole purpose of fatiguing them into compliance with his measures.

He has dissolved Representative Houses repeatedly, for opposing with manly firmness his invasions on the rights of the people.

He has refused for a long time, after such dissolutions, to cause others to be elected; whereby the Legislative Powers, incapable of Annihilation, have returned to the People at large for their exercise, the State remaining in the mean time exposed to all the dangers of invasion from without, and convulsions within.

He has endeavored to prevent the population of these States; for that purpose obstructing the Laws of Naturalization of Foreigners; refusing to pass others to encourage their migration hither, and raising the conditions of new Appropriations of Lands.

He has obstructed the Administration of Justice, by refusing his Assent to Laws for establishing Judiciary powers.

He has made Judges dependent on his Will alone, for the tenure of their offices, and the amount and payment of their salaries.

He has erected a multitude of New Offices, and sent hither swarms of Officers to harass our people, and eat out their substance.

He has kept among us, in times of peace, Standing Armies without the Consent of our legislatures.

He has affected to render the Military independent of and superior to the Civil power.

He has combined with others to subject us to a jurisdiction foreign to our constitution, and unacknowledged by our laws, giving his Assent to their Acts of pretended Legislation:

For quartering large bodies of armed troops among us:

For protecting them, by a mock Trial, from punishment for any Murders which they should commit on the Inhabitants of these States:

For cutting off our Trade with all parts of the world:

For imposing Taxes on us without our Consent:

For depriving us in many cases, of the benefits of Trial by Jury:

For transporting us beyond Seas to be tried for pretended offences:

For abolishing the free System of English Laws in a neighboring Province, establishing therein an Arbitrary government, and enlarging its Boundaries so as to render it at once an example and fit instrument for introducing the same absolute rule into these Colonies:

For taking away our Charters, abolishing our most valuable Laws, and altering fundamentally the Forms of our Governments:

For suspending our own Legislatures, and declaring themselves invested with power to legislate for us in all cases whatsoever.

He has abdicated Government here, by declaring us out of his Protection and waging War against us.

He has plundered our seas, ravaged our Coasts, burnt out towns, and destroyed the lives of our people.

He is at this time transporting large Armies of foreign Mercenaries to compleat the works of death, desolation and tyranny, already begun with circumstances of Cruelty and perfidy scarcely paralleled in the most barbarous ages, and totally unworthy the Head of a civilized nation.

He has constrained our fellow Citizens taken Captive on the high Seas to bear Arms against their Country, to become the executioners of their friends and Brethren, or to fall themselves by their Hands.

He has excited domestic insurrections amongst us, and has endeavored to bring on the inhabitants of our frontiers, the merciless Indian Savages, whose known rule of warfare, is an undistinguished destruction of all ages, sexes and conditions.

In every stage of these Oppressions We have Petitioned for Redress in the most humble terms: Our repeated Petitions have been answered only by repeated injury: A Prince, whose character is thus marked by every act which may define a Tyrant, is unfit to be the ruler of a free people.

Nor have We been wanting in attention to our British brethren. We have warned them from time to time of attempts by their legislature to extend an unwarrantable jurisdiction over us. We have reminded them of the circumstances of our emigration and settlement here. We have appealed to their native justice and magnanimity; and we have conjured them by the ties of our common kindred to disavow these usurpations, which would inevitably interrupt our connections and correspondence. They too have been deaf to the voice of justice and consanguinity. We must, therefore, acquiesce in the necessity, which denounces our Separation, and hold them, as we hold the rest of mankind, Enemies in War, in Peace Friends.

We, therefore, the Representatives of the United States of America, in General Congress, Assembled, appealing to the Supreme Judge of the world for the rectitude of our intentions, do, in the Name, and by Authority of the good People of these Colonies, solemnly publish and declare, That these United Colonies are, and of Right ought to be Free and Independent States; that they are Absolved from all Allegiance to the British Crown, and that all political connection between them and the State of Great Britain, is and ought to be totally dissolved: and that as Free and Independent States, they have full power to levy War, conclude Peace, contract Alliances, establish Commerce, and to do all other Acts and Things which Independent States may of right do. And for the support of this Declaration, with a firm reliance on the protection of Divine Providence, we mutually pledge to each other our Lives, our Fortunes and our sacred Honor.

JOHN HANCOCK

NEW HAMPSHIRE
Josiah Bartlett
William Whipple
Matthew Thornton

MASSACHUSETTS BAY
Samuel Adams
John Adams
Robert Treat Paine
Elbridge Gerry

RHODE ISLAND
Stephen Hopkins
William Ellery

CONNECTICUT
Roger Sherman
Samuel Huntington
William Williams
Oliver Wolcott

NEW YORK
William Floyd
Philip Livingston
Francis Lewis
Lewis Morris

NEW JERSEY
Richard Stockton
John Witherspoon
Francis Hopkinson
John Hart
Abraham Clark

PENNSYLVANIA
Robert Morris
Benjamin Rush
Benjamin Franklin
John Morton
George Clymer
James Smith
George Taylor
James Wilson
George Ross

DELAWARE
Caesar Rodney
George Read
Thomas McKean

MARYLAND
Samuel Chase
William Paca
Thomas Stone
Charles Carroll

VIRGINIA
George Wythe
Richard Henry Lee
Thomas Jefferson
Benjamin Harrison
Thomas Nelson, Jr.
Francis Lightfoot Lee
Carter Braxton

NORTH CAROLINA
William Hooper
Joseph Hewes
John Penn

SOUTH CAROLINA
Edward Rutledge
Thomas Heyward, Jr.
Thomas Lynch, Jr.
Arthur Middleton

GEORGIA
Button Gwinnett
Lyman Hall
George Walton

Federalist No. 10

November 22, 1787
James Madison

TO THE PEOPLE OF THE STATE OF NEW YORK.

Among the numerous advantages promised by a well constructed Union, none deserves to be more accurately developed than its tendency to break and control the violence of faction. The friend of popular governments, never finds himself so much alarmed for their character and fate, as when he contemplates their propensity to this dangerous vice. He will not fail therefore to set a due value on any plan which, without violating the principles to which he is attached, provides a proper cure for it. The instability, injustice and confusion introduced into the public councils, have in truth been the mortal diseases under which popular governments have every where perished; as they continue to be the favorite and fruitful topics from which the adversaries to liberty derive their most specious declamations. The valuable improvements made by the American Constitutions on the popular models, both ancient and modern, cannot certainly be too much admired; but it would be an unwarrantable partiality, to contend that they have as effectually obviated the danger on this side as was wished and expected. Complaints are every where heard from our most considerate and virtuous citizens, equally the friends of public and private faith, and of public and personal liberty; that our governments are too unstable; that the public good is disregarded in the conflicts of rival parties; and that measures are too often decided, not according to the rules of justice, and the rights of the minor party; but by the superior force of an interested and over-bearing majority. However anxiously we may wish that these complaints had no foundation, the evidence of known facts will not permit us to deny that they are in some degree true. It will be found indeed, on a candid review of our situation, that some of the distresses under which we labor, have been erroneously charged on the operation of our governments; but it will be found, at the same time, that other causes will not alone account for many of our heaviest misfortunes; and particularly, for that prevailing and increasing distrust of public engagements, and alarm for private rights, which are echoed from one end of the continent to the other. These must be chiefly, if not wholly, effects of the unsteadiness and injustice, with which a factious spirit has tainted our public administrations.

By a faction I understand a number of citizens, whether amounting to a majority or minority of the whole, who are united and actuated by some common impulse of passion, or of interest, adverse to the rights of other citizens, or to the permanent and aggregate interests of the community.

There are two methods of curing the mischiefs of faction: the one, by removing its causes; the other, by controlling its effects.

There are again two methods of removing the causes of faction: the one by destroying the liberty which is essential to its existence; the other, by giving to every citizen the same opinions, the same passions, and the same interests.

It could never be more truly said than of the first remedy, that it is worse than the disease. Liberty is to faction, what air is to fire, an aliment without which it instantly expires. But it could not be a less folly to abolish liberty, which is essential to political life, because it nourishes faction, than it would be to wish the annihilation of air, which is essential to animal life, because it imparts to fire its destructive agency.

The second expedient is as impracticable, as the first would be unwise. As long as the reason of man continues fallible, and he is at liberty to exercise it, different opinions will be formed. As long as the connection subsists between his reason and his self-love, his opinions and his passions will have a reciprocal influence on each other; and the former will be objects to which the latter will attach themselves. The diversity in the faculties of men from which the rights of property originate, is not less an insuperable obstacle to a uniformity of interests. The protection of these faculties is the first object of Government. From the protection of different and unequal faculties of acquiring property, the possession of different degrees and kinds of property immediately results: and from the influence of these on the sentiments and views of the respective proprietors, ensues a division of the society into different interests and parties.

The latent causes of faction are thus sown in the nature of man; and we see them every where brought into different degrees of activity, according to the different circumstances of civil society. A zeal for different opinions concerning religion, concerning Government and many other points, as well of speculation as of practice; an attachment to different leaders ambitiously contending for pre-eminence and power; or to persons of other descriptions whose fortunes have been interesting to the human passions, have in turn divided mankind into parties, inflamed them with mutual animosity, and rendered them much more disposed to vex and oppress each other, than to cooperate for their common good. So strong is this propensity of mankind to fall into mutual animosities, that where no substantial occasion presents itself, the most frivolous and fanciful distinctions have been sufficient to kindle their unfriendly passions, and excite their most violent conflicts. But the most common and durable source of factions, has been the various and unequal distribution of property. Those who hold, and those who are without property, have ever formed distinct interests in society. Those who are creditors, and those who are debtors, fall under a like discrimination. A landed interest, a manufacturing interest, a mercantile interest, a monied interest, with many lesser interests, grow up of necessity in civilized nations, and divide them into different classes, actuated by different sentiments and views. The regulation of these various and interfering interests forms the principal task of modern Legislation, and involves the spirit of party and faction in the necessary and ordinary operations of Government.

No man is allowed to be a judge in his own cause; because his interest would certainly bias his judgment, and, not improbably, corrupt his integrity. With equal, nay with greater reason, a body of men, are unfit to be both judges and parties, at the same time; yet, what are many of the most important acts of legislation, but so many judicial determinations, not indeed concerning the rights of single persons, but concerning the rights of large bodies of citizens, and what are the different classes of legislators, but advocates and parties to the causes which they determine? Is a law proposed concerning private debts? It is a question to which the creditors are parties on one side, and the debtors on the other. Justice ought to hold the balance between them. Yet the parties are and must be themselves the judges; and the most numerous party, or, in other words, the most powerful faction must be expected to prevail. Shall domestic manufactures be encouraged, and in what degree, by restrictions on foreign manufactures? are questions which would be differently decided by the landed and the manufacturing classes; and probably by neither, with a sole regard to justice and the public good. The apportionment of taxes on the various descriptions of property, is an act which seems to require the most exact impartiality; yet, there is perhaps no legislative act in which greater opportunity and temptation are given to a predominant party, to trample on the rules of justice. Every shilling with which they over-burden the inferior number, is a shilling saved to their own pockets.

It is in vain to say, that enlightened statesmen will be able to adjust these clashing interests, and render them all subservient to the public good. Enlightened statesmen will not always be at the helm: Nor, in many cases, can such an adjustment be made at all, without taking into view indirect and remote considerations, which will rarely prevail over the immediate interest which one party may find in disregarding the rights of another, or the good of the whole.

The inference to which we are brought, is, that the *causes* of faction cannot be removed; and that relief is only to be sought in the means of controlling its *effects*.

If a faction consists of less than a majority, relief is supplied by the republican principle, which enables the majority to defeat its sinister views by regular vote: It may clog the administration, it may convulse the society; but it will be unable to execute and mask its violence under the forms of the Constitution. When a majority is included in a faction, the form of popular government on the other hand enables it to sacrifice to its ruling passion or interest, both the public good and the rights of other citizens. To secure the public good, and private rights, against the danger of such a faction, and at the same time to preserve the spirit and the form of popular government, is then the great object to which our enquiries are directed: Let me add that it is the great desideratum, by which alone this form of government can be rescued from the opprobrium under which it has so long labored, and be recommended to the esteem and adoption of mankind.

By what means is this object attainable? Evidently by one of two only. Either the existence of the same passion or interest in a majority at the same time, must be prevented; or the majority, having such co-existent passion or interest, must be rendered, by their number and local situation, unable to concert and carry into effect schemes of oppression. If the impulse and the opportunity be suffered to coincide, we well know that neither moral nor religious motives can be relied on as an adequate control. They are not found to be such on the injustice and violence of individuals, and lose their efficacy in proportion to the number combined together; that is, in proportion as their efficacy becomes needful.

From this view of the subject, it may be concluded, that a pure Democracy, by which I mean, a Society, consisting of a small number of citizens, who assemble and administer the Government in person, can admit of no cure for the mischiefs of faction. A common passion or interest will, in almost every case, be felt by a majority of the whole; a communication and concert results from the form of Government itself; and there is nothing to check the inducements to sacrifice the weaker party, or an obnoxious individual. Hence it is, that such Democracies have ever been spectacles of turbulence and contention; have ever been found incompatible with personal security, or the rights of property; and have in general been as short in their lives, as they have been violent in their deaths. Theoretic politicians, who have patronized this species of Government, have erroneously supposed, that by reducing mankind to a perfect equality in their political rights, they would, at the same time, be perfectly equalized and assimilated in their possessions, their opinions, and their passions.

A republic, by which I mean a government in which the scheme of representation takes place, opens a different prospect, and promises the cure for which we are seeking. Let us examine the points in which it varies from pure democracy, and we shall comprehend both the nature of the cure and the efficacy which it must derive from the union.

The two great points of difference, between a democracy and a republic, are, first, the delegation of the government, in the latter, to a small number of citizens, elected by the rest; secondly, the greater number of citizens, and greater sphere of country, over which the latter may be extended.

The effect of the first difference is, on the one hand, to refine and enlarge the public views, by passing them through the medium of a chosen body of citizens, whose wisdom may best discern the true interest of their country, and whose patriotism and love of justice, will be least likely to sacrifice it to temporary or partial considerations. Under such a regulation, it may well happen, that the public voice, pronounced by the representatives of the people, will be more consonant to the public good, than if pronounced by the people themselves, convened for the purpose. On the other hand the effect may be inverted. Men of factious tempers, of local prejudices, or of sinister designs, may by intrigue, by corruption, or by other means, first obtain the suffrages, and then betray the interest of the people. The question resulting is, whether small or extensive republics are most favorable to the election of proper guardians of the public weal, and it is clearly decided in favor of the latter by two obvious considerations.

In the first place, it is to be remarked that, however small the republic may be, the representatives must be raised to a certain number, in order to guard against the cabals of a few; and that however large it may be, they must be limited to a certain number, in order to guard against the confusion of a multitude. Hence, the number of representatives in the two cases not being in proportion to that of the constituents, and being proportionally greatest in the small republic, it follows, that if the proportion of fit characters be not less in the large than in the small republic, the former will present a greater option, and consequently a greater probability of a fit choice.

In the next place, as each Representative will be chosen by a greater number of citizens in the large than in the small Republic, it will be more difficult for unworthy candidates to practise with success the vicious arts, by which elections are too often carried; and the suffrages of the people being more free, will be more likely to center on men who possess the most attractive merit, and the most diffusive and established characters.

It must be confessed, that in this, as in most other cases, there is a mean, on both sides of which inconveniences will be found to lie. By enlarging too much the number of electors, you render the representatives too little acquainted with all their local circumstances and lesser interests; as by reducing it too much, you render him unduly attached to these, and too little fit to comprehend and pursue great and national objects. The Federal Constitution forms a happy combination in this respect; the great and aggregate interests being referred to the national, the local and particular, to the state legislatures.

The other point of difference is, the greater number of citizens and extent of territory which may be brought within the compass of Republican, than of Democratic Government; and it is this circumstance principally which renders factious combinations less to be dreaded in the former, than in the latter. The smaller the society, the fewer probably will be the distinct parties and interests composing it; the fewer the distinct parties and interests, the more frequently will a majority be found of the same party; and the smaller the number of individuals composing a majority, and the smaller the compass within which they are placed, the more easily will they concert and execute their plans of oppression. Extend the sphere, and you take in a greater variety of parties and interests; you make it less probable that a majority of the whole will have a common motive to invade the rights of other citizens; or if such a common motive exists, it will be more difficult for all who feel it to discover their own strength, and to act in unison with each other. Besides other impediments, it may be remarked, that where there is a consciousness of unjust or dishonorable purposes, communication is always checked by distrust, in proportion to the number whose concurrence is necessary.

Hence it clearly appears, that the same advantage, which a Republic has over a Democracy, in controlling the effects of faction, is enjoyed by a large over a small Republic—is enjoyed by the Union over the States composing it. Does this advantage consist in the substitution of Representatives, whose enlightened views and virtuous sentiments render them superior to local prejudices, and to schemes of injustice? It will not be denied, that the Representation of the Union will be most likely to possess these requisite endowments. Does it consist in the greater security afforded by a greater variety of parties, against the event of any one party being able to outnumber and oppress the rest? In an equal degree does the increased variety of parties, comprised within the Union, increase this security? Does it, in fine, consist in the greater obstacles opposed to the concert and accomplishment of the secret wishes of an unjust and interested majority? Here, again, the extent of the Union gives it the most palpable advantage.

The influence of factious leaders may kindle a flame within their particular States, but will be unable to spread a general conflagration through the other States: a religious sect, may degenerate into a political faction in a part of the Confederacy but the variety of sects dispersed over the entire face of it, must secure the national Councils against any danger from that source: a rage for paper money, for an abolition of debts, for an equal division of property, or for any other improper or wicked project, will be less apt to pervade the whole body of the Union, than a particular member of it; in the same proportion as such a malady is more likely to taint a particular county or district, than an entire State.

In the extent and proper structure of the Union, therefore, we behold a Republican remedy for the diseases most incident to Republican Government. And according to the degree of pleasure and pride, we feel in being Republicans, ought to be our zeal in cherishing the spirit, and supporting the character of Federalists.

PUBLIUS

Federalist No. 51

February 6, 1788
James Madison

TO THE PEOPLE OF THE STATE OF NEW YORK.

To what expedient then shall we finally resort for maintaining in practice the necessary partition of power among the several departments, as laid down in the Constitution? The only answer that can be given is, that as all these exterior provisions are found to be inadequate, the defect must be supplied, by so contriving the interior structure of the government, as that its several constituent parts may, by their mutual relations, be the means of keeping each other in their proper places. Without presuming to undertake a full development of this important idea, I will hazard a few general observations, which may perhaps place it in a clearer light, and enable us to form a more correct judgment of the principles and structure of the government planned by the convention.

In order to lay a due foundation for that separate and distinct exercise of the different powers of government, which to a certain extent, is admitted on all hands to be essential to the preservation of liberty, it is evident that each department should have a will of its own; and consequently should be so constituted, that the members of each should have as little agency as possible in the appointment of the members of the others. Were this principle rigorously adhered to, it would require that all the appointments for the supreme executive, legislative, and judiciary magistracies, should be drawn from the same fountain of authority, the people, through channels, having no communication whatever with one another. Perhaps such a plan of constructing the several departments would be less difficult in practice than it may in contemplation appear. Some difficulties however, and some additional expense, would attend the execution of it. Some deviations therefore from the principle must be admitted. In the constitution of the judiciary department in particular, it might be inexpedient to insist rigorously on the principle; first, because peculiar qualifications being essential in the members, the primary consideration ought to be to select that mode of choice, which best secures these qualifications; secondly, because the permanent tenure by which the appointments are held in that department, must soon destroy all sense of dependence on the authority conferring them.

It is equally evident that the members of each department should be as little dependent as possible on those of the others, for the emoluments annexed to their offices. Were the executive magistrate, or the judges, not independent of the legislature in this particular, their independence in every other would be merely nominal.

But the great security against a gradual concentration of the several powers in the same department, consists in giving to those who administer each department, the necessary constitutional means, and personal motives, to resist encroachments of the others. The provision for defense must in this, as in all other cases, be made commensurate to the danger of attack. Ambition must be made to counteract ambition. The interest of the man must be connected with the constitutional right of the place. It may be a reflection on human nature, that such devices should be necessary to control the abuses of government. But what is government itself but the greatest of all reflections on human nature? If men were angels, no government would be necessary. If angels were to govern men, neither external nor internal controls on government would be necessary. In framing a government which is to be administered by men over men, the great difficulty lies in this: You must first enable the government to control the governed; and in the next place, oblige it to control itself. A dependence on the people is no doubt the primary control on the government; but experience has taught mankind the necessity of auxiliary precautions.

This policy of supplying by opposite and rival interests, the defect of better motives, might be traced through the whole system of human affairs, private as well as public. We see it particularly displayed in all the subordinate distributions of power; where the constant aim is to divide and arrange the several offices in such a manner as that each may be a check on the other; that the private interest of every individual, may be a sentinel over the public rights. These inventions of prudence cannot be less requisite in the distribution of the supreme powers of the state.

But it is not possible to give to each department an equal power of self defense. In republican government the legislative authority, necessarily, predominates. The remedy for this inconveniency is, to divide the legislature into different branches; and to render them by different modes of election, and different principles of action, as little connected with each other, as the nature of their common functions, and their common dependence on the society, will admit. It may even be necessary to guard against dangerous encroachments by still further precautions. As the weight of the legislative authority requires that it should be thus divided, the weakness of the executive may require, on the other hand, that it should be fortified. An absolute negative, on the legislature, appears at first view to be the natural defense with which the executive magistrate should be armed. But perhaps it would be neither altogether safe, nor alone sufficient. On ordinary occasions, it might not be

exerted with the requisite firmness; and on extraordinary occasions, it might be prefidiously abused. May not this defect of an absolute negative be supplied, by some qualified connection between this weaker department, and the weaker branch of the stronger department, by which the latter may be led to support the constitutional rights of the former, without being too much detached from the rights of its own department? If the principles on which these observations are founded be just, as I persuade myself they are, and they be applied as a criterion, to the several state constitutions, and to the federal constitution, it will be found, that if the latter does not perfectly correspond with them, the former are infinitely less able to bear such a test.

There are moreover two considerations particularly applicable to the federal system of America, which place that system in a very interesting point of view.

First. In a single republic, all the power surrendered by the people, is submitted to the administration of a single government; and usurpations are guarded against by a division of the government into distinct and separate departments. In the compound republic of America, the power surrendered by the people, is first divided between two distinct governments, and then the portion allotted to each, subdivided among distinct and separate departments. Hence a double security arises to the rights of the people. The different governments will control each other; at the same time that each will be controlled by itself.

Second. It is of great importance in a republic, not only to guard the society against the oppression of its rulers; but to guard one part of the society against the injustice of the other part. Different interests necessarily exist in different classes of citizens. If a majority be united by a common interest, the rights of the minority will be insecure. There are but two methods of providing against this evil: The one by creating a will in the community independent of the majority, that is, of the society itself, the other by comprehending in the society so many separate descriptions of citizens, as will render an unjust combination of a majority of the whole, very improbable, if not impracticable. The first method prevails in all governments possessing an hereditary or self appointed authority. This at best is but a precarious security; because a power independent of the society may as well espouse the unjust views of the major, as the rightful interests, of the minor party, and may possibly be turned against both parties. The second method will be exemplified in the federal republic of the United States. While all authority in it will be derived from and dependent on the society, the society itself will be broken into so many parts, interests and classes of citizens, that the rights of individuals or of the minority, will be in little danger from interested combinations of the majority. In a free government, the security for civil rights must be the same as for religious rights. It consists in the one case in the multiplicity of interests, and in the other, in the multiplicity of sects. The degree of security in both cases will depend on the number of interests and sects; and this may be presumed to depend on the extent of country and number of people comprehended under the same government. This view of the subject must particularly recommend a proper federal system to all the sincere and considerate friends of republican government: Since it shows that in exact proportion as the territory of the union may be formed into more circumscribed confederacies or states, oppressive combinations of a majority will be facilitated, the best security under the republican form, for the rights of every class of citizens, will be diminished; and consequently, the stability and independence of some member of the government, the only other security, must be proportionally increased. Justice is the end of government. It is the end of civil society. It ever has been, and ever will be pursued, until it be obtained, or until liberty be lost in the pursuit. In a society under the forms of which the stronger faction can readily unite and oppress the weaker, anarchy may as truly be said to reign, as in a state of nature where the weaker individual is not secured against the violence of the stronger: And as in the latter state even the stronger individuals are prompted by the uncertainty of their condition, to submit to a government which may protect the weak as well as themselves: So in the former state, will the more powerful factions or parties be gradually induced by a like motive, to wish for a government which will protect all parties, the weaker as well as the more powerful. It can be little doubted, that if the state of Rhode Island was separated from the confederacy, and left to itself, the insecurity of rights under the popular form of government within such narrow limits, would be displayed by such reiterated oppressions of factious majorities, that some power altogether independent of the people would soon be called for by the voice of the very factions whose misrule had proved the necessity of it. In the extended republic of the United States, and among the great variety of interests, parties and sects which it embraces, a coalition of a majority of the whole society could seldom take place on any other principles than those of justice and the general good; and there being thus less danger to a minor from the will of the major party, there must be less pretext also, to provide for the security of the former, by introducing into the government a will not dependent on the latter; or in other words, a will independent of the society itself. It is no less certain that it is important, notwithstanding the contrary opinions which have been entertained, that the larger the society, provided it lie within a practicable sphere, the more duly capable it will be of self government. And happily for the *republican cause*, the practicable sphere may be carried to a very great extent, by a judicious modification and mixture of the *federal principle*.

PUBLIUS

Appendix IV

Presidents, Congresses, and Chief Justices: 1789–2005

Term	President and Vice President	Party of President	Congress	Majority Party House	Majority Party Senate	Chief Justice of the United States
1789–1797	**George Washington** John Adams	None	1st 2nd 3rd 4th	(N/A) (N/A) (N/A) (N/A)	(N/A) (N/A) (N/A) (N/A)	John Jay (1789–1795) John Rutledge (1795) Oliver Ellsworth (1796–1800)
1797–1801	**John Adams** Thomas Jefferson	Federalist	5th 6th	(N/A) Fed	(N/A) Fed	Oliver Ellsworth (1796–1800) John Marshall (1801–1835)
1801–1809	**Thomas Jefferson** Aaron Burr (1801–1805) George Clinton (1805–1809)	Democratic-Republican	7th 8th 9th 10th	Dem-Rep Dem-Rep Dem-Rep Dem-Rep	Dem-Rep Dem-Rep Dem-Rep Dem-Rep	John Marshall (1801–1835)
1809–1817	**James Madison** George Clinton (1809–1812)[a] Elbridge Gerry (1813–1814)[a] (VP vacant, 1815–1817)	Democratic-Republican	11th 12th 13th 14th	Dem-Rep Dem-Rep Dem-Rep Dem-Rep	Dem-Rep Dem-Rep Dem-Rep Dem-Rep	John Marshall (1801–1835)
1817–1825	**James Monroe** Daniel D. Tompkins	Democratic-Republican	15th 16th 17th 18th	Dem-Rep Dem-Rep Dem-Rep Dem-Rep	Dem-Rep Dem-Rep Dem-Rep Dem-Rep	John Marshall (1801–1835)
1825–1829	**John Quincy Adams** John C. Calhoun	National-Republican	19th 20th	Nat'l Rep Dem	Nat'l Rep Dem	John Marshall (1801–1835)
1829–1837	**Andrew Jackson** John C. Calhoun (1829–1832)[b] Martin Van Buren (1833–1837)	Democrat	21st 22nd 23rd 24th	Dem Dem Dem Dem	Dem Dem Dem Dem	John Marshall (1801–1835) Roger B. Taney (1836–1864)
1837–1841	**Martin Van Buren** Richard M. Johnson	Democrat	25th 26th	Dem Dem	Dem Dem	Roger B. Taney (1836–1864)
1841	**William H. Harrison**[a] John Tyler (1841)	Whig				Roger B. Taney (1836–1864)

1841–1845	**John Tyler** (VP vacant)	Whig	27th 28th	Whig Dem	Whig Whig	Roger B. Taney (1836–1864)
1845–1849	**James K. Polk** George M. Dallas	Democrat	29th 30th	Dem Whig	Dem Dem	Roger B. Taney (1836–1864)
1849–1850	**Zachary Taylor**[a] Millard Fillmore	Whig	31st	Dem	Dem	Roger B. Taney (1836–1864)
1850–1853	**Millard Fillmore** (VP vacant)	Whig	32nd	Dem	Dem	Roger B. Taney (1836–1864)
1853–1857	**Franklin Pierce** William R. D. King (1853)[a]	Democrat	33rd 34th	Dem Rep	Dem Dem	Roger B. Taney (1836–1864)
1857–1861	**James Buchanan** John C. Breckinridge	Democrat	35th 36th	Dem Rep	Dem Dem	Roger B. Taney (1836–1864)
1861–1865	**Abraham Lincoln**[a] Hannibal Hamlin (1861–1865) Andrew Johnson (1865)	Republican	37th 38th	Rep Rep	Rep Rep	Roger B. Taney (1836–1864) Salmon P. Chase (1864–1873)
1865–1869	**Andrew Johnson** (VP vacant)	Republican	39th 40th	Union Rep	Union Rep	Salmon P. Chase (1864–1873)
1869–1877	**Ulysses S. Grant** Schuyler Colfax (1869–1873) Henry Wilson (1873–1875)[a]	Republican	41st 42nd 43rd 44th	Rep Rep Rep Dem	Rep Rep Rep Rep	Salmon P. Chase (1864–1873) Morrison R. Waite (1874–1888)
1877–1881	**Rutherford B. Hayes** William A. Wheeler	Republican	45th 46th	Dem Dem	Rep Dem	Morrison R. Waite (1874–1888)
1881	**James A. Garfield**[a] Chester A. Arthur	Republican	47th	Rep	Rep	Morrison R. Waite (1874–1888)
1881–1885	**Chester A. Arthur** (VP vacant)	Republican	48th	Dem	Rep	Morrison R. Waite (1874–1888)
1885–1889	**Grover Cleveland** Thomas A. Hendricks (1885)[a] (VP vacant, 1886–1889)	Democrat	49th 50th	Dem Dem	Rep Rep	Morrison R. Waite (1874–1888) Melville W. Fuller (1888–1910)
1889–1893	**Benjamin Harrison** Levi P. Morton	Republican	51st 52nd	Rep Dem	Rep Rep	Melville W. Fuller (1888–1910)
1893–1897	**Grover Cleveland** Adlai E. Stevenson	Democrat	53rd 54th	Dem Rep	Dem Rep	Melville W. Fuller (1888–1910)
1897–1901	**William McKinley**[a] Garret A. Hobart (1897–1899)[a] Theodore Roosevelt (1901)	Republican	55th 56th	Rep Rep	Rep Rep	Melville W. Fuller (1888–1910)
1901–1909	**Theodore Roosevelt** (VP vacant, 1901–1905) Charles W. Fairbanks (1905–1909)	Republican	57th 58th 59th 60th	Rep Rep Rep Rep	Rep Rep Rep Rep	Melville W. Fuller (1888–1910)

1909–1913	**William Howard Taft** James S. Sherman (1909–1912)[a]	Republican	61st 62nd	Rep Dem	Rep Rep	Melville W. Fuller (1888–1910) Edward D. White (1910–1921)
1913–1921	**Woodrow Wilson** Thomas R. Marshall	Democrat	63rd 64th 65th 66th	Dem Dem Dem Rep	Dem Dem Dem Rep	Edward D. White (1910–1921)
1921–1923	**Warren G. Harding**[a] Calvin Coolidge	Republican	67th	Rep	Rep	William Howard Taft (1921–1930)
1923–1929	**Calvin Coolidge** (VP vacant, 1923–1925) Charles G. Dawes (1925–1929)	Republican	68th 69th 70th	Rep Rep Rep	Rep Rep Rep	William Howard Taft (1921–1930)
1929–1933	**Herbert Hoover** Charles Curtis	Republican	71st 72nd	Rep Dem	Rep Rep	William Howard Taft (1921–1930) Charles Evans Hughes (1930–1941)
1933–1945	**Franklin D. Roosevelt**[a] John Nance Garner (1933–1941) Henry A. Wallace (1941–1945) Harry S Truman (1945)	Democrat	73rd 74th 75th 76th 77th 78th	Dem Dem Dem Dem Dem Dem	Dem Dem Dem Dem Dem Dem	Charles Evans Hughes (1930–1941) Harlan F. Stone (1941–1946)
1945–1953	**Harry S Truman** (VP vacant, 1945–1949) Alben W. Barkley (1949–1953)	Democrat	79th 80th 81st 82nd	Dem Rep Dem Dem	Dem Rep Dem Dem	Harlan F. Stone (1941–1946) Frederick M. Vinson (1946–1953)
1953–1961	**Dwight D. Eisenhower** Richard M. Nixon	Republican	83rd 84th 85th 86th	Rep Dem Dem Dem	Rep Dem Dem Dem	Frederick M. Vinson (1946–1953) Earl Warren (1953–1969)
1961–1963	**John F. Kennedy**[a] Lyndon B. Johnson (1961–1963)	Democrat	87th	Dem	Dem	Earl Warren (1953–1969)
1963–1969	**Lyndon B. Johnson** (VP vacant, 1963–1965) Hubert H. Humphrey (1965–1969)	Democrat	88th 89th 90th	Dem Dem Dem	Dem Dem Dem	Earl Warren (1953–1969)
1969–1974	**Richard M. Nixon**[c] Spiro Agnew (1969–1973)[c] Gerald R. Ford (1973–1974)[d]	Republican	91st 92nd	Dem Dem	Dem Dem	Earl Warren (1953–1969) Warren E. Burger (1969–1986)
1974–1977	**Gerald R. Ford** Nelson A. Rockefeller[d]	Republican	93rd 94th	Dem Dem	Dem Dem	Warren E. Burger (1969–1986)
1977–1981	**Jimmy Carter** Walter Mondale	Democrat	95th 96th	Dem Dem	Dem Dem	Warren E. Burger (1969–1986)
1981–1989	**Ronald Reagan** George Bush	Republican	97th 98th 99th 100th	Dem Dem Dem Dem	Rep Rep Rep Dem	Warren E. Burger (1969–1986) William H. Rehnquist (1986–)

1989–1993	**George Bush** Dan Quayle	Republican	101st 102nd	Dem Dem	Dem Dem	William H. Rehnquist (1986–)
1993–2001	**Bill Clinton** Al Gore	Democrat	103rd 104th 105th 106th	Dem Rep Rep Rep	Dem Rep Rep Rep	William H. Rehnquist (1986–)
2001–2005	**George W. Bush** Dick Cheney	Republican	107th 108th	Rep Rep	Dem Rep	William H. Rehnquist (1986–)

[a]Died in office.
[b]Resigned from the vice presidency.
[c]Resigned from the presidency.
[d]Appointed vice president.

Selected Supreme Court Cases

- *Agostini* v. *Felton* (1997): The Court agreed to permit public school teachers to go into parochial schools during school hours to provide remedial education to disadvantaged students because it was not an excessive entanglement of church and state.

- *Ashcroft* v. *Free Speech Coalition* (2002): The Court ruled that the Child Online Protection Act of 1998 was unconstitutional because it was too vague in its reliance on "community standards" to define what is harmful to minors.

- *Barron* v. *Baltimore* (1833): Decision that limited the application of the Bill of Rights to the actions of Congress alone.

- *Benton* v. *Maryland* (1969): Incorporated the Fifth Amendment's double jeopardy clause.

- *Board of Regents* v. *Southworth* (2000): Unanimous ruling from the Supreme Court that stated that public universities could charge students a mandatory activities fee that could be used to facilitate extracurricular student political speech as long as the programs are neutral in their application.

- *Bowers* v. *Hardwick* (1986): Unsuccessful attempt to challenge Georgia's sodomy law.

- *Boy Scouts of America* v. *Dale* (2000): The Court ruled that the Boy Scouts could exclude gays from serving as scoutmasters because a private group has the right to set its own moral code.

- *Brandenburg* v. *Ohio* (1969): The Court fashioned the direct incitement test for deciding whether certain kinds of speech could be regulated by the government. This test holds that advocacy of illegal action is protected by the First Amendment unless imminent action is intended and likely to occur.

- *Brown* v. *Board of Education* (1954): U.S. Supreme Court decision holding that school segregation is inherently unconstitutional because it violates the Fourteenth Amendment's guarantee of equal protection; marked the end of legal segregation in the United States.

- *Brown* v. *Board of Education II* (1955): Follow-up to *Brown* v. *Board of Education* (1954), this case laid out the process for school desegregation and established the concept of dismantling segregationist systems "with all deliberate speed."

- *Brown University* v. *Cohen* (1997): Landmark Title IX case that put all colleges and universities on notice that discrimination against women would not be tolerated, even when, as in the case of Brown University, the university had tremendously expanded sports opportunities for women.

- *Buckley* v. *Valeo* (1976): The Court ruled that money spent by an individual or political committee in support or opposition of a candidate (but independent of the candidate's campaign) was a form of symbolic speech, and therefore could not be limited under the First Amendment.

- *Bush* v. *Gore* (2000): Controversial 2000 election case that made the final decision on the Florida recounts, and thus, the result of the 2000 election. The Rehnquist Court broke from tradition in this case by refusing to defer to the state court's decision.

- *Cantwell* v. *Connecticut* (1940): The case in which the Supreme Court incorporated the freedom of religion, ruling that the freedom to believe is absolute, but the freedom to act is subject to the regulation of society.

- *Chicago, B&O R.R. Co.* v. *Chicago* (1897): Incorporated the Fifth Amendment's just compensation clause.

- *Civil Rights Cases* (1883): Name attached to five cases brought under the Civil Rights Act of 1875. In 1883, the Supreme Court decided that discrimination in a variety of public accommodations, including theaters, hotels, and railroads, could not be prohibited by the act because it was private and not state discrimination.

- *Clinton* v. *City of New York* (1998): The Court ruled that the line-item veto was unconstitutional because it gave powers to the president denied him by the U.S. Constitution.

- *Colorado Republican Federal Campaign Committee* v. *Federal Election Commission* (1996): The Supreme Court extended its ruling in *Buckley* v. *Valeo* (1976) to include political parties.

- *Cooper* v. *Aaron* (1958): Case wherein the Court broke with tradition and issued a unanimous decision against the Little Rock School Board, ruling that the district's evasive schemes to avoid the *Brown II* (1955) decision were illegal.

- *Craig* v. *Boren* (1976): The Court ruled that keeping drunk drivers off the roads may be an important governmental objective, but allowing women aged eighteen to twenty-one to drink alcoholic beverages while prohibiting men of the same age from drinking is not substantially related to that goal.

- *DeJonge* v. *Oregon* (1937): Incorporated the First Amendment's right to freedom of assembly.

- *Dred Scott* v. *Sandford* (1857): Concluded that the U.S. Congress lacked the constitutional authority to bar slavery in the territories; this decision narrowed the scope of national power while it enhanced that of the states. This case marks the first time since *Marbury* v. *Madison* (1803) that the Supreme Court found an act of Congress unconstitutional.

- *Duncan* v. *Louisiana* (1968): Incorporated the Sixth Amendment's trial by jury clause.

- *Furman* v. *Georgia* (1972): The Supreme Court used this case to end capital punishment, at least in the short run. (The case was overturned by *Gregg* v. *Georgia* in 1976.)

- *Garcia* v. *San Antonio Metropolitan Transport Authority* (1985): In this case the Court ruled that Congress has the broad power to impose its will on state and local governments, even in areas that have traditionally been left to state and local discretion.

- *Gibbons* v. *Ogden* (1824): The Court upheld broad congressional power over interstate commerce.

- *Gideon* v. *Wainwright* (1963): Granted indigents the right to counsel.

- *Gitlow* v. *New York* (1925): Incorporated the free speech clause of the First Amendment, ruling that the states were not completely free to limit forms of political expression.

- *Grutter* v. *Bollinger* (2003): The Court voted to uphold the constitutionality of the University of Michigan's law school policy, which gave preferences to minority students.

- *Gregg* v. *Georgia* (1976): Overturning *Furman* v. *Georgia* (1972), the case ruled that Georgia's rewritten death penalty statute was constitutional.

- *Griswold* v. *Connecticut* **(1965):** Supreme Court case that established the Constitution's implied right to privacy.

- *Klopfer* v. *North Carolina* **(1967):** Incorporated the Sixth Amendment's right to a speedy trial.

- *Korematsu* v. *U.S.* **(1944):** In this case, the Court ruled that the internment of Japanese Americans during World War II was constitutional.

- *Lawrence* v. *Texas* **(2003):** The Supreme Court reversed its 1986 ruling in *Bowes* v. *Hardwick* by finding a Texas statute that banned sodomy to be unconstitutional.

- *Lemon* v. *Kurtzman* **(1971):** The Court determined that direct government assistance to religious schools was unconstitutional. In the majority opinion, the Court created what has become known as the *Lemon* Test for deciding if a law is in violation of the establishment clause.

- *Malloy* v. *Hogan* **(1964):** Incorporated the Fifth Amendment's self-incrimination clause.

- *Mapp* v. *Ohio* **(1961):** Incorporated a portion of the Fourth Amendment by establishing that illegally obtained evidence cannot be used at trial.

- *Marbury* v. *Madison* **(1803):** Supreme Court case in which the Court first asserted the power of judicial review in finding that a congressional statute extending the Court's original jurisdiction was unconstitutional.

- *McConnell* v. *FEC* **(2003):** The government's interest in preventing political party corruption overrides the free speech rights to which the parties would otherwise be entitled.

- *McCulloch* v. *Maryland* **(1819):** Supreme Court upheld the power of the national government and denied the right of a state to tax the bank. The Court's broad interpretation of the necessary and proper clause paved the way for later rulings upholding expansive federal powers.

- *Miller* v. *California* **(1973):** Case wherein the Supreme Court began to formulate rules designed to make it easier for states to regulate obscene materials and to return to communities a greater role in determining what is obscene.

- *Miranda* v. *Arizona* **(1966):** The Fifth Amendment requires that individuals arrested for a crime must be advised of their right to remain silent and to have counsel present.

- *Muller* v. *Oregon* **(1908):** Case that ruled Oregon's law barring women from working more than ten hours a day was constitutional; also an attempt to define women's unique status as mothers to justify their differential treatment.

- *Near* v. *Minnesota* **(1931):** By ruling that a state law violated the freedom of the press, the Supreme Court incorporated the free press provision of the First Amendment.

- *New York Times Co.* v. *Sullivan* **(1964):** Supreme Court decision ruling that simply publishing a defamatory falsehood is not enough to justify a libel judgment. "Actual malice" must be proved to support a finding of libel against a public figure.

- *New York Times Co.* v. *U.S.* **(1971):** Also called the Pentagon Papers case; the Supreme Court ruled that any attempt by the government to prevent expression carried "a heavy presumption" against its constitutionality.

- *In re Oliver* (1948): Incorporated the Sixth Amendment's right to a public trial.

- *Palko v. Connecticut* (1937): Set the Court's rationale of selective incorporation, a judicial doctrine whereby most but not all of the protections found in the Bill of Rights are made applicable to the states via the Fourteenth Amendment.

- *Parker v. Gladden* (1966): Incorporated the Sixth Amendment's right to an impartial trial.

- *Planned Parenthood of Southeastern Pennsylvania v. Casey* (1992): An unsuccessful attempt to challenge Pennsylvania's restrictive abortion regulations.

- *Plessy v. Ferguson* (1896): Plessy challenged a Louisiana statute requiring that railroads provide separate accommodations for blacks and whites. The Court found that separate but equal accommodations did not violate the equal protection clause of the Fourteenth Amendment.

- *Pointer v. Texas* (1965): Incorporated the Sixth Amendment's right to confrontation of witnesses.

- *Quilici v. Village of Morton Grove* (1983): The Supreme Court refused to review a lower court's ruling upholding the constitutionality of a local ordinance banning handguns against a Second Amendment challenge.

- *Regents of the University of California v. Bakke* (1978): A sharply divided Court concluded that the university's rejection of Bakke as a student had been illegal because the use of strict affirmative action quotas was inappropriate.

- *Reno v. American Civil Liberties Union* (1997): The Court ruled that the 1996 Communications Decency Act prohibiting transfer of obscene or indecent materials over the Internet to minors violated the First Amendment because it was too vague and overbroad.

- *Reynolds v. Sims* (1964): In this case, the Court decided that every person should have an equally weighted vote in electing governmental representatives.

- *Robinson v. California* (1962): Incorporated the Eighth Amendment's right to freedom from cruel and unusual punishment.

- *Roe v. Wade* (1973): The Supreme Court found that a woman's right to an abortion was protected by the right to privacy that could be implied from specific guarantees found in the Bill of Rights and the Fourteenth Amendment.

- *Romer v. Evans* (1996): A Colorado constitutional amendment precluding any legislative, executive, or judicial action at any state or local level designed to bar discrimination based on sexual preference was ruled not rational or reasonable.

- *Tennesse v. Lane* (2004): The Court ruled that disabled persons could sue states that failed to make reasonable accommodations to assure that courthouses are handicapped accessible.

- *Texas v. Johnson* (1989): Case in which the Court overturned the conviction of a Texas man found guilty of setting fire to an American flag.

- *U.S. v. Miller* (1939): The last time the Supreme Court addressed the constitutionality of the Second Amendment; ruled that the Amendment was only intended to protect a citizen's right to own ordinary militia weapons.

- *U.S.* v. *Morrison* **(2000):** The Court ruled that Congress has no authority under the commerce clause to enact a provision of the Violence Against Women Act providing a federal remedy to victims of gender-motivated violence.

- *U.S.* v. *Nixon* **(1974):** In a case involving President Richard M. Nixon's refusal to turn over tape recordings of his conversations, the Court ruled that executive privilege does not grant the president an absolute right to secure all presidential documents.

- *Webster* v. *Reproductive Health Services* **(1989):** In upholding several restrictive abortion regulations, the Court opened the door for state governments to enact new restrictions on abortion.

- *Weeks* v. *U.S.* **(1914):** Case wherein the Supreme Court adopted the exclusionary rule, which bars the use of illegally obtained evidence at trial.

- *Wolf* v. *Colorado* **(1949):** The Court ruled that illegally obtained evidence did not necessarily have to be eliminated from use during trial.

- *Zelman* v. *Simmons-Harris* **(2002):** The Court concluded that governments can give money to parents to allow them to send their children to private or religious schools.

Glossary

A

administrative adjudication: A quasi-judicial process in which a bureaucratic agency settles disputes between two parties in a manner similar to the way courts resolve disputes.

administrative discretion: The ability of bureaucrats to make choices concerning the best way to implement congressional intentions.

Administrative Procedures Act: A statute containing Texas's rule-making process.

advisory referendum: A process in which voters cast nonbinding ballots on an issue or proposal.

affiliates: Local television stations that carry the programming of a national network.

affirmative action: Policies designed to give special attention or compensatory treatment to members of a previously disadvantaged group.

agenda: A set of issues to be discussed or given attention.

agenda setting: The constant process of forming the list of issues to be addressed by government.

agriculture commissioner: The elected state official in charge of regulating and promoting agriculture.

the Alamo: A San Antonio mission that was defended by Texans during their war for independence.

al-Qaeda: Worldwide terrorist organization led by Osama bin Laden, responsible for numerous attacks against U.S. interests, including 9/11 attacks against the World Trade Center and the Pentagon.

American Creed: Set of ideas that provide a national identity, limit government, and structure politics in America.

American dream: An American ideal of a happy, sucessful life, which often includes wealth, a house, a better life for one's children, and, for some, the ability to grow up to be president.

amicus curiae: "Friend of the court"; a third party to a lawsuit who files a legal brief for the purpose of raising additional points of view in an attempt to influence a court's decision.

Anglos: Non-Hispanic whites.

annexation: Enlargement of a city's corporate limits by incorporating surrounding territory into the city.

Anti-Federalists: Those who favored strong state governments and a weak national government; opposed the ratification of the U.S. Constitution.

appellate court: Court that generally reviews only findings of law made by lower courts.

appellate jurisdiction: The power vested in an appellate court to review and/or revise the decision of a lower court.

application for discretionary review: Request for Texas Court of Criminal Appeals review, which is granted if four judges agree.

apportionment: The proportional process of allotting congressional seats to each state following the decennial census.

allotment: The proportional process of allotting congressional seats to each state following the decennial census.

Articles of Confederation: The compact among the thirteen original states that was the basis of their government. Written in 1776, the Articles were not ratified by all the states until 1781.

at-large-by-place: An election system in which all positions on the council or governing body are filled by city-wide elections, with each position designated as a seat, and candidates must choose which place to run for.

at-large election: Election in which candidates for office must compete throughout the jurisdiction as a whole.

attorney general: The elected official who is the chief counsel for the state of Texas.

B

balanced budget: A budget in which the legislature balances expenditures with expected revenues, with no deficit.

Barbary Wars: Conflicts the United States fought in the early eighteenth century with North African states against their piracy.

bicameral legislature: A legislature divided into two houses; the U.S. Congress and the state legislatures are bicameral except Nebraska, which is unicameral.

bicameral Texas legislature: The legislature has two bodies, a House of Representatives and a Senate.

biennial legislature: A legislative body that meets in regular session only once in a two-year period.

bill: A proposed law.

bill of attainder: A law declaring an act illegal without a judicial trial.

Bill of Rights: The first ten amendments to the U.S. Constitution, which largely guarantee specific rights and liberties.

Black Codes: Laws denying most legal rights to newly freed slaves; passed by southern states following the Civil War.

blanket primary: A primary in which voters may cast ballots in either party's primary (but not both) on an office-by-office basis.

block grant: Broad grant with few strings attached; given to states by the federal government for specified activities, such as secondary education or health services.

Bretton Woods Agreement: International financial agreement signed shortly before the end of World War II that created the World Bank and the International Monetary Fund.

brief: A document containing the legal written arguments in a case filed with a court by a party prior to a hearing or trial.

***Brown v. Board of Education* (1954):** U.S. Supreme Court decision holding that school segregation is inherently unconstitutional because it violates the Fourteenth Amendment's guarantee of equal protection; marked the end of legal segregation in the United States.

budget execution authority: The authority to move money from one program to another program or from one agency to another agency.

bureaucracy: A set of complex hierarchical departments, agencies, commissions, and their staffs that exist to help a chief executive officer carry out his or her duties. Bureaucracies may be private organizations of governmental units.

business cycles: Fluctuation between expansion and recession that is a part of modern capitalist economies.

C

Cabinet: The formal body of presidential advisers who head the fifteen executive departments. Presidents often add others to this body of formal advisers.

campaign consultant: The private-sector professionals and firms who sell to a candidate the technologies, services, and strategies required to get that candidate elected.

campaign manager: The individual who travels with the candidate and coordinates the many different aspects of the campaign.

candidate debate: Forum in which political candidates face each other to discuss their platforms, records, and character.

captured agency: A government regulatory agency that consistently makes decisions favorable to the private interests that it regulates.

Carter Doctrine: Policy announced after the 1979 Soviet invasion of Afghanistan that the Persian Gulf area was a vital U.S. interest and the United States would fight to maintain access to it.

categorical grant: Grant for which Congress appropriates funds for a specific purpose.

Central Intelligence Agency: Executive agency responsible for collection and analysis of information and intelligence about foreign countries and events.

charter: A document that, like a constitution, specifies the basic policies, procedures, and institutions of a municipality.

charter school: Public school sanctioned by a specific agreement that allows the program to operate outside the usual rules and regulations.

checks and balances: A governmental structure that gives each of the three branches of government some degree of oversight and control over the actions of the others.

chief budget officer: The governor, who is charged with preparing the state budget proposal for the legislature.

chief executive officer: The governor, as the top official of the executive branch of Texas state government.

chief of state: The governor in his or her role as the official head representing the state of Texas in its relationships with the national government, other states, and foreign dignitaries.

citizen: Member of the political community to whom certain rights and obligations are attached.

city charter: A document similar to a constitution, setting out city government structure and powers and its political processes.

city commission: A form of city government in which elected members serve on the legislative body and also serve as head administrators of city programs.

city council: The legislature in a city government.

civic virtue: The tendency to form small-scale associations for the public good.

civil law: Codes of behavior related to business and contractual relationships between groups and individuals.

civil liberties: The personal guarantees and freedoms that the federal government cannot abridge by law, constitution, or judicial interpretation.

civil rights: The government-protected rights of individuals against arbitrary or discriminatory treatment by governments or individuals based on categories such as race, sex, national origin, age, religion, or sexual orientation.

Civil Rights Act of 1964: Legislation passed by Congress to outlaw segregation in public facilities and racial discrimination in employment, education, and voting; created the Equal Employment Opportunity Commission.

***Civil Rights Cases* (1883):** Name attached to five cases brought under the Civil Rights Act of 1875. In 1883, the Supreme Court decided that discrimination in a variety of public accommodations, including theaters, hotels, and railroads, could not be prohibited by the act because it was private, not state, discrimination.

civil service laws: These acts removed the staffing of the bureaucracy from political parties and created a professional bureaucracy filled through competition.

civil service system: The system created by civil service laws by which many appointments to the federal bureaucracy are made.

civil society: Society created when citizens are allowed to organize and express their views publicly as they engage in an open debate about public policy.

clear and present danger test: Test articulated by the Supreme Court in *Schenck* v. *U.S.* (1919) to draw the line between protected and unprotected speech; the Court looks to see "whether the words used…" could "create a clear and present danger that they will bring about substantive evils" that Congress seeks "to prevent."

clemency: The governor's authority to reduce the length of a person's prison sentence.

closed primary: A primary election in which only a party's registered voters are eligible to vote.

cloture: Mechanism requiring sixty senators to vote to cut off debate.

coalition: A group of interests or organizations that join forces for the purpose of electing public officials.

coattail effect: The tendency of lesser-known or weaker candidates lower on the ballot to profit in an election by the presence on the party's ticket of a more popular candidate.

cockroach: A member of a constitutional convention who opposes any changes in the current constitution.

collective good: Something of value that cannot be withheld from a non-member of a group, for example, a tax write-off or a better environment.

collective security: The concept that peace would be secured if all countries collectively opposed any country that invaded another.

commander in chief: The governor in his or her role as head of the state militia.

commission: Form of local government in which several officials are elected to top positions that have both legislative and executive responsibilities.

commissioners court: The legislative body of a county in Texas.

committee: A subunit of the legislature, appointed to work on designated subjects.

Committees of Correspondence: Organizations in each of the American colonies created to keep colonists abreast of developments with the British; served as powerful molders of public opinion against the British.

communications director: The person who develops the overall media strategy for the candidate, blending the free press coverage with the paid TV, radio, and mail media.

commute: The action of a governor to cancel all or part of the sentence of someone convicted of a crime, while keeping the conviction on the record.

compact: A formal, legal agreement between a state and a tribe.

comprehensive revision: Constitutional revision through the adoption of a new constitution.

comptroller of public accounts: The elected official who is the state's tax collector.

concurrent powers: Authority possessed by both the state and national governments that may be exercised concurrently as long as that power is not exclusively within the scope of national power or in conflict with national law.

concurrent resolution: A legislative document intended to express the will of both chambers of the legislature, even though it does not possess the authority of law.

confederation: Type of government where the national government derives its powers from the states; a league of independent states.

conference committee: Joint committee created to iron out differences between Senate and House versions of a specific piece of legislation.

congressional review: A process whereby Congress can nullify agency regulations by a joint resolution of legislative disapproval.

congressionalist: One who believes that Article II's provision that the president should ensure "faithful execution of the laws" should be read as an injunction against substituting presidential authority for legislative intent.

conservative: One thought to believe that a government is best that governs least and that big government can only infringe on individual, personal, and economic rights.

Constitution: A document establishing the structure, functions, and limitations of a government.

constitutional amendment: A change, addition, or deletion to a constitution.

constitutional county court: Constitutionally mandated court for criminal and civil matters.

constitutional courts: Federal courts specifically created by the U.S. Constitution or by Congress pursuant to its authority in Article III.

Constitutional Revision Commission: Group established to research and draft a constitution for a constitutional convention.

constitutionalism: Limits placed on government through a written document.

containment: Strategy to oppose expansion of Soviet power, particularly in Western Europe and East Asia, with military power, economic assistance, and political influence.

content regulation: Governmental attempts to regulate the electronic media.

contrast ad: Ad that compares the records and proposals of the candidates, with a bias toward the sponsor.

cooperative federalism: The relationship between the national and state governments that began with the New Deal.

council–manager: A form of city government in which the city council and mayor hire a professional manager to run the city.

county: A geographic district created within a state with a government that has general responsibilities for land, welfare, environment, and, where appropriate, rural service policies.

county attorney: Elected official serving as the legal officer for county government and also as a criminal prosecutor.

county auditor: Official appointed by a district judge to audit county finances.

county chairperson: Party leader in a county.

county clerk: Elected official who serves as the clerk for the commissioners court and for county records.

county commissioner: Elected official who serves on the county legislative body, the commissioners court.

county convention: County party meeting to select delegates and adopt resolutions.

county court at law: Statutory county court to relieve county judge of judicial duties.

county executive committee: Precinct chairpersons in a county that assist the county chairpersons.

county judge: Elected official who is the chief administrative officer of county government, serves on the commissioners court, and may also have some judicial functions.

county tax assessor–collector: Elected official who collects taxes for the county (and perhaps for other local governments).

county treasurer: Elected official who serves as the money manager for county government.

court of appeals: Intermediate appellate court for criminal and civil appeals.

criminal district attorney: Elected official who prosecutes criminal cases.

criminal law: Codes of behavior related to the protection of property and individual safety.

critical election: An election that signals a party realignment through voter polarization around new issues.

crossover voting: Participation in the primary of a party with which the voter is not affiliated.

Cuban Missile Crisis: The 1962 confrontation that nearly escalated into war between the United States and Soviet Union over Soviet deployment of medium-range ballistic missiles in Cuba.

cumulative voting: A method of voting in which voters have a number of votes equal to the number of seats being filled, and voters may cast their votes all for one candidate or split them among candidates in various combinations.

D

de facto **discrimination:** Racial discrimination that results from practice (such as housing patterns or other social factors) rather than the law.

de jure **discrimination:** Racial segregation that is a direct result of law or official policy.

debt: The total outstanding amount the government owes as a result of borrowing in the past.

Declaration of Independence: Document drafted by Thomas Jefferson in 1776 that proclaimed the right of the American colonies to separate from Great Britain.

deep background: Information provided to a journalist that will not be attributed to any source.

deficit spending: Government spending in the current budget cycle that exceeds government revenue.

delegate: Role played by elected representatives who vote the way their constituents would want them to, regardless of their own opinions.

democracy: A system of government that gives power to the people, whether directly or through their elected representatives.

departments: Major administrative units with responsibility for a broad area of government operations. Departmental status usually indicates a permanent national interest in a particular governmental function, such as defense, commerce, or agriculture.

Department of Defense: Chief executive-branch department responsible for formulation and implementation of U.S. military policy.

Department of Homeland Security: Cabinet department created after 9/11 to coordinate domestic U.S. security efforts against terrorism.

Department of State: Chief executive-branch department responsible for formulation and implementation of U.S. foreign policy.

détente: The relaxation of tensions between the United States and the Soviet Union that occurred during the 1970s.

Dillon's Rule: A court ruling that local governments do not have any inherent sovereignty but instead must be authorized by state government.

direct democracy: A system of government in which members of the polity meet to discuss all policy decisions and then agree to abide by majority rule.

direct incitement test: A test articulated by the Supreme Court in *Brandenburg* v. *Ohio* (1969) that holds that advocacy of illegal action is protected by the First Amendment unless imminent lawless action is intended and likely to occur.

direct initiative: A process in which voters can place a proposal on a ballot and enact it into law without involving the legislature or the governor.

direct mailer: A professional who supervises a political campaign's direct-mail fund-raising strategies.

direct (popular) referendum: A process in which voters can veto a bill recently passed in the legislature by placing the issue on a ballot and expressing disapproval.

direct primary: The selection of party candidates through the ballots of qualified voters rather than at party nomination conventions.

discharge petition: Petition that gives a majority of the House of Representatives the authority to bring an issue to the floor in the face of committee inaction.

discount rate: The rate of interest at which member banks can borrow money from their regional Federal Reserve Bank.

district attorney (DA): Elected official who prosecutes criminal cases.

district-based election: Election in which candidates run for an office that represents only the voters of a specific district within the jurisdiction.

district clerk: Elected official who is responsible for keeping the records for the district court.

district court: Court of general jurisdiction for serious crimes and high-dollar civil cases.

disturbance theory: Political scientist David B. Truman's theory that interest groups form in part to counteract the efforts of other groups.

divided government: The political condition in which different political parties control the White House and Congress.

domestic dependent nation: A type of sovereignty that makes an Indian tribe in the United States outside the authority of state governments but reliant on the federal government for the definition of tribal authority.

dual federalism: The belief that having separate and equally powerful levels of government is the best arrangement.

due process clause: Clause contained in the Fifth and Fourteenth Amendments. Over the years, it has been construed to guarantee to individuals a variety of rights ranging from economic liberty to criminal procedural rights to protection from arbitrary governmental action.

due process rights: Procedural guarantees provided by the Fourth, Fifth, Sixth, and Eighth Amendments for those accused of crimes.

E

economic interest group: A group with the primary purpose of promoting the financial interests of its members.

economic regulation: Governmental regulation of business practices, industry rates, routes, or areas serviced by particular industries.

economic stability: A situation in which there is economic growth, rising national income, high employment, and steadiness in the general level of prices.

Eighth Amendment: Part of the Bill of Rights that states: "Excessive bail shall not be required, nor excessive fines imposed, nor cruel and unusual punishments inflicted."

elector: Member of the Electoral College chosen by methods determined in each state.

Electoral College: Representatives of each state who cast the final ballots that actually elect a president.

electorate: Citizens eligible to vote.

electronic media: The broadcast and cable media, including television, radio, and the Internet.

Embargo Act: Passed by Congress in 1807 to prevent U.S. ships from leaving U.S. ports for foreign ports without the approval of the federal government.

engagement: Policy implemented during the Clinton administration that the United States would remain actively involved in foreign affairs.

engrossed bill: A bill that has been given final approval on third reading in one chamber of the legislature.

enlargement: Policy implemented during the Clinton administration that the United States would actively promote the expansion of democracy and free markets throughout the world.

enrolled bill: A bill that has been given final approval in both chambers of the legislature and is sent to the governor.

entitlement program: Income security program to which all those meeting eligibility criteria are entitled.

enumerated powers: Seventeen specific powers granted to Congress under Article I, section 8, of the U.S. Constitution; these powers include taxation, coinage of money, regulation of commerce, and the authority to provide for a national defense.

Equal Employment Opportunity Commission: Federal agency created to enforce the Civil Rights Act of 1964, which forbids discrimination on the basis of race, creed, national origin, religion, or sex in hiring, promotion, or firing.

equal protection clause: Section of the Fourteenth Amendment that guarantees that all citizens receive "equal protection of the laws."

Equal Rights Amendment: Proposed amendment that would bar discrimination against women by federal or state governments.

equal time rule: The rule that requires broadcast stations to sell air time equally to all candidates in a political campaign if they choose to sell it to any.

equality: The belief that all individuals should be treated similarly, regardless of socio-economic status.

establishment clause: The first clause in the First Amendment; it prohibits the national government from establishing a national religion.

ex post facto **law:** Law passed after the fact, thereby making previously legal activity illegal and subject to current penalty; prohibited by the U.S. Constitution.

exclusionary rule: Judicially created rule that prohibits police from using illegally seized evidence at trial.

executive agreement: Formal government agreement entered into by the president that does not require the advice and consent of the U.S. Senate.

executive commissioner of Health and Human Services Commission: The official appointed by the governor to oversee the state's multi-agency health and human service programs.

Executive Office of the President (EOP): Establishment created in 1939 to help the president oversee the executive branch bureaucracy.

executive order: A rule or regulation issued by the president that has the effect of law. All executive orders must be published in the *Federal Register*.

executive privilege: An implied presidential power that allows the president to refuse to disclose information regarding confidential conversations or national security to Congress or the judiciary.

exit polls: Polls conducted at selected polling places on Election Day.

extradite: To send someone against his or her will to another state to face criminal charges.

extraterritorial jurisdiction (ETJ): The area outside a city's boundaries over which the city may exercise limited control.

F

fairness doctrine: Rule in effect from 1949 to 1985 requiring broadcasters to cover events adequately and to present contrasting views on important public issues.

Federal Employees Political Activities Act: 1993 liberalization of the Hatch Act. Federal employees are now allowed to run for office in nonpartisan elections and to contribute money to campaigns in partisan elections.

Federal Reserve Board: A seven-member board that sets member banks' reserve requirements, controls the discount rate, and makes other economic decisions.

federal system: System of government where the national government and state governments derive all authority from the people.

federalism: The philosophy that describes the governmental system created by the Framers; see also **federal system**.

The Federalist Papers: A series of eighty-five political papers written by John Jay, Alexander Hamilton, and James Madison in support of ratification of the U.S. Constitution.

Federalists: Those who favored a stronger national government and supported the proposed U.S. Constitution; later became the first U.S. political party.

Fifteenth Amendment: One of the three Civil War amendments; specifically enfranchised newly freed male slaves.

Fifth Amendment: Part of the Bill of Rights that imposes a number of restrictions on the federal government with respect to the rights of persons suspected of committing a crime. It provides for indictment by a grand jury, protection against self-incrimination, and prevents the national government from denying a person life, liberty, or property without the due process of law. It also prevents the national government from taking property without fair compensation.

fighting words: Words that, "by their very utterance inflict injury or tend to incite an immediate breach of peace." Fighting words are not subject to the restrictions of the First Amendment.

filibuster: A formal way of halting action on a bill by means of long speeches or unlimited debate in the Senate.

finance chair: A professional who coordinates the fund-raising efforts for the campaign.

First Amendment: Part of the Bill of Rights that imposes a number of restrictions on the federal government with respect to the civil liberties of the people, including freedom of religion, speech, press, assembly, and petition.

First Continental Congress: Meeting held in Philadelphia from September 5 to October 26, 1774, in which fifty-six delegates (from every colony except Georgia) adopted a resolution in opposition to the Coercive Acts.

first reading: The Texas Constitution requires three readings of a bill by the legislature; first reading is when the bill is introduced, its caption is read aloud, and it is referred to committee.

fiscal policy: Federal government policies on taxes, spending, and debt management, intended to promote the nation's macro-economic goals, particularly with respect to employment, price stability, and growth.

Fourteenth Amendment: One of the three Civil War amendments; guarantees equal protection and due process of the laws to all U.S. citizens.

Fourth Amendment: Part of the Bill of Rights that reads: "The right of the people to be secure in their persons, houses, papers, and effects, against unreasonable searches and seizures, shall not be violated, and no Warrants shall issue, but upon probable cause, supported by Oath or affirmation, and particularly describing the place to be searched, and the persons or things to the seized."

free exercise clause: The second clause of the First Amendment. It prohibits the U.S. government from interfering with a citizen's right to practice his or her religion.

free media: Coverage of a candidate's campaign by the news media.

free rider problem: Potential members fail to join a group because they can get the benefit, or collective good, sought by the group without contributing to the effort.

frontier era: The period when Texas constituted a border between American civilization and an area inhabited by a hostile, indigenous population.

front-loading: The tendency of states to choose an early date on the primary calendar.

full faith and credit clause: Portion of Article IV of the Constitution that ensures judicial decrees and contracts made in one state will be binding and enforceable in any other state.

full-time equivalent (FTE): A unit of measurement for number of employees.

fundamental freedoms: Those rights defined by the Court to be essential to order, liberty, and justice.

G

General Agreement on Tariffs and Trade: Devised shortly after World War II as an interim agreement until a World Trade Organization could be created to help lower tariffs and increase trade.

general election: Election in which voters decide which candidates will actually fill elective public offices.

general election campaign: That part of a political campaign aimed at winning a general election.

general-law cities: Cities with fewer than 5,000 residents, governed by a general state law rather than by a locally adopted charter.

general ordinance-making authority: The legal right to adopt ordinances covering a wide array of subject areas, authority that cities have but counties do not.

germane: Related to the topic.

gerrymandering: The legislative process through which the majority party in each statehouse tries to assure that the maximum number of representatives from its political party can be elected to Congress through the redrawing of legislative districts.

get-out-the-vote (GOTV): A push at the end of a political campaign to encourage supporters to go to the polls.

Gibbons v. *Ogden* **(1824):** The Court upheld broad congressional power over interstate commerce. The Court's broad interpretation of the Constitution's commerce clause paved the way for later rulings upholding expansive federal powers.

good government: A term used for policies that open up agencies to public participation and scrutiny and that minimize conflicts of interest.

government: A collective of individuals ad institutions, the formal vehicles through which policies are made and affairs of state are conducted.

government corporations: Businesses established by Congress that perform functions that could be provided by private businesses (such as the U.S. Postal Service).

governmental (institutional) agenda: The changing list of issues to which governments believe they should address themselves.

governmental party: The office holders and candidates who run under a political party's banner.

governor: Chief elected executive in state government.

governor's message: Message that the governor delivers to the legislature, pronouncing policy goals, budget priorities, and authorizations for the legislature to act.

grand strategy: The choices a government makes to balance and apply economic, military, diplomatic, and other resources to preserve the nation's people, territory, and values.

grandfather clause: Voting qualification provision in many Southern states that allowed only those whose grandfathers had voted before Reconstruction to vote unless they passed a wealth or literacy test.

Great Compromise: A decision made during the Constitutional Convention to give each state the same number of representatives in the Senate regardless of size; representation in the House was determined by population.

gross domestic product (GDP): The total market value of all goods and services produced in a country during a year.

H

hard money: Legally specified and limited contributions that are clearly regulated by the Federal Election Campaign Act and by the Federal Election Commission.

Hatch Act: Law enacted in 1939 to prohibit civil servants from taking activist roles in partisan campaigns. This act prohibited federal employees from making political contributions, working for a particular party, or campaigning for a particular candidate.

hold: A tactic by which a senator asks to be informed before a particular bill is brought to the floor. This stops the bill from coming to the floor until the hold is removed.

home rule: The right and authority of a local government to govern itself, rather than have the state govern it.

human rights: The belief that human beings have inalienable rights such as freedom of speech and freedom of religion.

I

impeach: A vote by the House to formally accuse a government official of official wrongdoing.

impeachment: The power delegated to the House of Representatives in the

Constitution to charge the president, vice president, or other "civil officers," including federal judges, with "Treason, Bribery, or other High Crimes and Misdemeanors." This is the first step in the constitutional process of removing such government officials from office.

implementation: The process by which a law or policy is put into operation by the bureaucracy.

implied powers: Powers derived from the enumerated powers and the necessary and proper clause. These powers are not stated specifically but are considered to be reasonably implied through the exercise of delegated powers.

impressment: The British practice in the early eighteenth century of stopping ships at sea to seize sailors suspected of having deserted the Royal Navy.

inclusion: The principle that state courts will apply federal laws when those laws directly conflict with the laws of a state.

incorporation doctrine: An interpretation of the Constitution that holds that the due process clause of the Fourteenth Amendment requires that state and local governments also guarantee those rights.

incumbency: The fact that being in office helps a person stay in office because of a variety of benefits that go with the position.

incumbency factor: The fact that being in office helps a person stay in office because of a variety of benefits that go with the position.

independent executive agencies: Governmental units that closely resemble a Cabinet department but have a narrower area of responsibility (such as the Central Intelligence Agency) and are not part of any Cabinet department.

independent regulatory commission: An agency created by Congress that is generally concerned with a specific aspect of the economy.

indirect initiative: A process in which the legislature places a proposal on a ballot and allows voters to enact it into law, without involving the governor or further action by the legislature.

indirect (representative) democracy: A system of government that gives citizens the opportunity to vote for representatives who will work on their behalf.

individualism: The belief that each person should act in accordance with his or her own conscience.

inflation: A rise in the general price levels of an economy.

information warfare: Attacks against information and communication systems, which present a sizeable threat to U.S. security.

inherent powers: Powers of the president that can be derived or inferred from specific powers in the Constitution.

initiative: A process that allows citizens to propose legislation and submit it to the state electorate for popular vote.

inoculation ad: Advertising that attempts to counteract an anticipated attack from the opposition before the attack is launched.

insurance commissioner: The official appointed by the governor to direct the Department of Insurance and regulate the insurance industry.

intent calendar: The Senate calendar listing bills on which the author or sponsor has given notice of intent to move to suspend the regular order of business in order that the Senate may consider them.

interagency councils: Working groups created to facilitate coordination of policy making and implementation across a host of governmental agencies.

interest group: An organized group that tries to influence public policy.

international governmental organization (IGO): An organization created by the governments of at least two and often many countries that operates internationally with the objectives of achieving the purposes that the member countries agree on.

International Monetary Fund: International governmental organization created shortly before the end of World War II to stabilize international financial relations through fixed monetary exchange rates.

interstate compacts: Contracts between states that carry the force of law; generally now used as a tool to address multistate policy concerns.

interventionist state: Alternative to the laissez-faire state; the government takes an active role in guiding and managing the private economy.

Iranian hostage crisis: Crisis during the Carter administration when Iranian students with support of the Iranian government took over the U.S. embassy in Tehran, holding all the personnel hostage.

iron triangles: The relatively stable relationships and patterns of interaction that occur among an agency, interest groups, and congressional committees or subcommittees.

isolationism: A national policy of avoiding participation in foreign affairs.

issue networks: The loose and informal relationships that exist among a large number of actors who work in broad policy areas.

issue-oriented politics: Politics that focuses on specific issues rather than on party, candidate, or other loyalties.

J

Jim Crow laws: Laws enacted by southern states that discriminated against blacks by creating "whites only" schools, theaters, hotels, and other public accommodations.

joint committee: Includes members from both houses of Congress, conducts investigations or special studies.

joint resolution: A legislative document that either proposes an amendment to the Texas Constitution or ratifies an amendment to the U.S. Constitution.

judicial activism: A philosophy of judicial decision making that argues judges should use their power broadly to further justice, especially in the areas of equality and personal liberty.

judicial implementation: Refers to how and whether judicial decisions are translated into actual public policies affecting more than the immediate parties to a lawsuit.

judicial restraint: A philosophy of judicial decision making that argues courts should allow the decisions of other branches of government to stand, even when they offend a judge's own sense of principles.

judicial review: Power of the courts to review acts of other branches of government and the states.

Judiciary Act of 1789: Established the basic three-tiered structure of the federal court system.

jurisdiction: Authority vested in a particular court to hear and decide the issues in any particular case.

justice of the peace court: Local county court for minor crimes and civil suits.

K

Kyoto Conference on Global Climate Change: 1997 international conference to develop agreements to reduce the emission of greenhouse gases that contribute to global warming.

L

laissez-faire: A French term literally meaning "to allow to do, to leave alone." It is a hands-off governmental policy that is based on the belief that governmental involvement in the economy is wrong.

land commissioner: The elected official responsible for managing and leasing the state's property, including oil, gas, and mineral interests.

League of Nations: Created in the peace treaty that ended World War I, it was an international governmental organization dedicated to preserving peace.

Legislative Budget Board (LBB): A joint legislative committee (with a large staff) that prepares the state budget and conducts evaluations of agencies' programs.

Legislative Council: A joint legislative committee (with a large staff) that provides legal advice, bill drafting, copyediting and printing, policy research, and program evaluation services for members of the legislature.

legislative courts: Courts established by Congress for specialized purposes, such as the Court of Military Appeals.

legislative party caucus: An organization of legislators who are all of the same party, and which is formally allied with a political party.

legislative process: The process the legislature follows in considering and enacting legislation.

libel: False written statements or written statements tending to call someone's reputation into disrepute.

liberal: One considered to favor extensive governmental involvement in the economy and the provision of social services and to take an activist role in protecting the rights of women, the elderly, minorities, and the environment.

liberal constitution: Constitution that incorporates the basic structure of government and allows the legislature to provide the details through statutes.

libertarian: One who favors a free market economy and no governmental interference in personal liberties.

liberty: The belief that government should not infringe upon a person's individual rights.

line-item veto: The authority of a chief executive to delete part of a bill passed by the legislature that involves taxing or spending. The legislature may override a veto, usually with a two-thirds majority of each chamber.

lobbying: The activities of a group or organization that seeks to influence legislation and persuade political leaders to support the group's position.

lobbyist: Interest group representative who seeks to influence legislation that will benefit his or her organization through political persuasion.

local election: Election conducted by local governments to elect officials.

Local Government Code: The Texas statutory code containing state laws about local governments.

logrolling: Vote trading; voting yea to support a colleague's bill in return for a promise of future support.

Louisiana Purchase: The 1803 land purchase authorized by President Thomas Jefferson, which expanded the size of the United States dramatically.

M

machine: A party organization that recruits its members with tangible incentives and is characterized by a high degree of control over member activity.

majority leader: The elected leader of the party controlling the most seats in the House of Representatives or the Senate; is second in authority to the speaker of the House and in the Senate is regarded as its most powerful member.

majority party: The political party in each house of Congress with the most members.

majority rule: The central premise of direct democracy in which only policies that collectively garner the support of a majority of voters will be made into law.

manager: A professional executive hired by a city council or county board to manage daily operations and to recommend policy changes.

mandate: A command, indicated by an electorate's votes, for the elected officials to carry out their platforms.

manifest destiny: Theory that the United States was divinely mandated to expand across North America to the Pacific Ocean.

***Marbury* v. *Madison* (1803):** Supreme Court first asserted the power of judicial review in finding that the congressional statute extending the Court's original jurisdiction was unconstitutional.

margin of error: A measure of the accuracy of a public opinion poll.

Marshall Plan: European Recovery Program, named after Secretary of State George C. Marshall, of extensive U.S. aid to Western Europe after World War II.

matching funds: Donations to presidential campaigns from the federal government that are determined by the amount of private funds a qualifying candidate raises.

mayor: Chief elected executive of a city.

***McCulloch* v. *Maryland* (1819):** The Supreme Court upheld the power of the national government and denied the right of a state to tax the bank. The Court's broad interpretation of the necessary and proper clause paved the way for later rulings upholding expansive federal powers.

means-tested program: Income security program intended to assist those whose incomes fall below a designated level.

media campaign: That part of a political campaign in which the candidate reaches out to the voters, in person or via the media, to create a positive impression and gain votes.

media consultant: A professional who produces political candidates' television, radio, and print advertisements.

media effects: The influence of news sources on public opinion.

Medicaid: An expansion of Medicare, this program subsidizes medical care for the poor.

Medicare: The federal program established in the Lyndon B. Johnson administration that provides medical care to elderly Social Security recipients.

mercantilism: An economic theory designed to increase a nation's wealth through the development of commercial industry and a favorable balance of trade.

merit system: The system by which federal civil service jobs are classified into grades or levels, to which appointments are made on the basis of performance on competitive examinations.

midterm election: Election that takes place in the middle of a presidential term.

military-industrial complex: The grouping of the U.S. armed forces and defense industries.

minority leader: The elected leader of the party with the second highest number of elected representatives in the House of Representatives or the Senate.

minority party: The political party in each house of Congress with the second most members.

Miranda **rights:** Statements that must be made by the police informing a suspect of his or her constitutional rights protected by the Fifth Amendment, including the right to an attorney provided by the court if the suspect cannot afford one.

Miranda **v.** *Arizona* **(1966):** A landmark Supreme Court ruling that held the Fifth Amendment requires that individuals arrested for a crime must be advised of their right to remain silent and to have counsel present.

Missouri (Merit) Plan: A method of selecting judges in which a governor must appoint someone from a list provided by an independent panel. Judges are then kept in office if they get a majority of "yes" votes in general elections.

monarchy: A form of government in which power is vested in hereditary kings and queens who govern in the interests of all.

monetary policy: A form of government regulation in which the nation's money supply and interest rates are controlled.

money: A system of exchange for goods and services that includes currency, coins, and bank deposits.

Monroe Doctrine: President James Monroe's 1823 pledge that the United States would oppose attempts by European states to extend their political control into the Western Hemisphere.

moralism: The policy of emphasizing morality in foreign affairs.

muckraking: A form of journalism, in vogue in the early twentieth century, concerned with reforming government and business conduct.

multilateralism: The U.S. foreign policy that actions should be taken in cooperation with other states after consultation.

municipal corporation: A city.

municipal court: City court with limited criminal jurisdiction.

municipality: A government with general responsibilities, such as a city, town, or village government, that is created in response to the emergence of relatively densely populated areas.

N

national convention: A party conclave (meeting) held in the presidential election year for the purposes of nominating a presidential and vice presidential ticket and adopting a platform.

national party platform: A statement of the general and specific philosophy and policy goals of a political party, usually promulgated at the national convention.

National Security Council: Executive agency responsible for advising the president about foreign and defense policy and events.

natural law: A doctrine that society should be governed by certain ethical principles that are part of nature and, as such, can be understood by reason.

necessary and proper clause: The final paragraph of Article I, section 8, of the U.S. Constitution, which gives Congress the authority to pass all laws "necessary and proper" to carry out the enumerated powers specified in the Constitution; also called the elastic clause.

negative ad: Advertising on behalf of a candidate that attacks the opponent's platform or character.

network: An association of broadcast stations (radio or television) that share programming through a financial arrangement.

New Deal: The name given to the program of "Relief, Recovery, Reform" begun by President Franklin D. Roosevelt in 1933 to bring the United States out of the Great Depression.

New Federalism: Federal/state relationship proposed by Reagan administration during the 1980s; hallmark is returning administrative powers to the state governments.

New Jersey Plan: A framework for the Constitution proposed by a group of small states; its key points were a one-house legislature with one vote for each state, the establishment of the acts of Congress as the "supreme law" of the land, and a supreme judiciary with limited power.

New York Times Co. **v.** *Sullivan* **(1964):** The Supreme Court concluded that "actual malice" must be proved to support a finding of libel against a public figure.

Nineteenth Amendment: Amendment to the Constitution that guaranteed women the right to vote.

Ninth Amendment: Part of the Bill of Rights that reads "The enumeration in the Constitution, of certain rights, shall not be construed to deny or disparage others retained by the people."

Nixon Doctrine: The policy implemented at the end of the Vietnam War that the United States would provide arms and military equipment to countries but not do the fighting for them.

nomination campaign: That part of a political campaign aimed at winning a primary election.

nongovernmental organization (NGO): An organization that is not tied to a government.

non-means-based program: Program such as Social Security where benefits are provided irrespective of the income or means of recipients.

nonpartisan election: A contest in which candidates run without formal identification or association with a political party.

nonpartisan primary: A primary used to select candidates regardless of party affiliation.

nonparty legislative caucus: An organization of legislators that is based on some attribute other than party affiliation.

North American Free Trade Agreement (NAFTA): Agreement that promotes free movement of goods and services among Canada, Mexico, and the United States.

North Atlantic Treaty Organization (NATO): The first peacetime military treaty the United States joined, NATO is a regional political and military organization created in 1950.

O

off the record: Information provided to a journalist that will not be released to the public.

off-year election: Election that takes place in the middle of a presidential term.

Office of Management and Budget (OMB): The office that prepares the president's annual budget proposal, reviews the budget and programs of the executive departments, supplies economic forecasts, and conducts detailed analyses of proposed bills and agency rules.

oligarchy: A form of government in which the right to participate is conditioned on the possession of wealth, social status, military position, or achievement.

on background: Information provided to a journalist that will not be attributed to a named source.

on the record: Information provided to a journalist that can be released and attributed by name to the source.

one-person, one-vote: The principle that each legislative district within a state should have the same number of eligible voters so that representation is equitably based on population.

open market operations: The buying and selling of government securities by the Federal Reserve Bank in the securities market.

open primary: A primary in which party members, independents, and

sometimes members of the other party are allowed to vote.

Operation Desert Storm: The 1991 American-led attack against Iraq to expel Iraqi forces from Kuwait.

organizational campaign: That part of a political campaign involved in fund-raising, literature distribution, and all other activities not directly involving the candidate.

organizational party: The workers and activists who staff the party's formal organization.

original jurisdiction: The jurisdiction of courts that hear a case first, usually in a trial. Courts determine the facts of a case under their original jurisdiction.

overrepresentation and underrepresentation: Higher and lower numbers, respectively, than would be expected from a group in comparison with that group's numbers in the general population.

oversight: Congressional review of the activities of an agency, department, or office.

P

package or general veto: The authority of a chief executive to void an entire bill that has been passed by the legislature. This veto applies to all bills, whether or not they have taxing or spending components, and the legislature may override this veto, usually with a two-thirds majority of each chamber.

paid media: Political advertisements purchased for a candidate's campaign.

pardon: The authority of a government to cancel someone's conviction of a crime by a court and to eliminate all sanctions and punishments resulting from conviction.

parole: The authority of a governor to release a prisoner before his or her full sentence has been completed and to specify conditions that must be met as part of the release.

party caucus or conference: A formal gathering of all party members.

party identification: A citizen's personal affinity for a political party, usually expressed by his or her tendency to vote for the candidates of that party.

party in the electorate: The voters who consider themselves allied or associated with the party.

party realignment: A shifting of party coalition groupings in the electorate that remains in place for several elections.

patrons: Persons who finance a group or individual activity.

patronage: Jobs, grants, or other special favors that are given as rewards to friends and political allies for their support.

Pearl Harbor: Naval base in Hawaii attacked by Japan on December 7, 1941, initiating U.S. entry into World War II.

Pendleton Act: Reform measure that created the Civil Service Commission to administer a partial merit system. The act classified the federal service by grades, to which appointments were made based on the results of a competitive examination. It made it illegal for federal political appointees to be required to contribute to a particular political party.

per diem: Legislators' per day allowance covering room and board expenses while on state business.

permanent party organization: Party organization that operates throughout the year, performing the party's functions.

personal campaign: That part of a political campaign concerned with presenting the candidate's public image.

personal liberty: A key characteristic of U.S. democracy. Initially meaning freedom from governmental interference, today it includes demands for freedom to engage in a variety of practices free from governmental discrimination.

petition for review: Request for Texas Supreme Court review, which is granted if four justices agree.

piecemeal revision: Constitutional revision through constitutional amendments that add or delete items.

***Plessy v. Ferguson* (1896):** Plessy challenged a Louisiana statute requiring that railroads provide separate accommodations for blacks and whites. The Court found that separate but equal accommodations did not violate the equal protection clause of the Fourteenth Amendment.

plural executive: An executive branch in which power and policy implementation are divided among several executive agencies rather than centralized under one person; the governor does not get to appoint most agency heads.

pocket veto: If Congress adjourns during the ten days the president has to consider a bill passed by both houses of Congress, without the president's signature, the bill is considered vetoed.

policy adoption: The approval of a policy proposal by the people with the requisite authority, such as a legislature.

policy evaluation: The process of determining whether a course of action is achieving its intended goals.

policy formulation: The crafting of appropriate and acceptable proposed courses of action to ameliorate or resolve public problems.

policy implementation: The process of carrying out public policy through governmental agencies and the courts.

political action committee (PAC): Federally mandated, officially registered fund-raising committee that represents interest groups in the political process.

political culture: Commonly shared attitudes, beliefs, and core values about how government should operate.

political ideology: The coherent set of values and beliefs about the purpose and scope of government held by groups and individuals.

political machine: An organization designed to solicit votes from certain neighborhoods or communities for a particular political party in return for services and jobs if that party wins.

political party: A group of office holders, candidates, activists, and voters who identify with a group label and seek to elect to public office individuals who run under that label.

political socialization: The process through which an individual acquires particular political orientations; the learning process by which people acquire their political beliefs and values.

politico: Role played by elected representatives who act as trustees or as delegates, depending on the issue.

politics: The study of who gets what, when, and how—or how policy decisions are made.

pollster: A professional who takes public opinion surveys that guide political campaigns.

popular consent: The idea that governments must draw their powers from the consent of the governed.

popular sovereignty: The right of the majority to govern themselves.

populists: People who support the promotion of equality and of traditional values and behaviors.

pork: Legislation that allows representatives to bring home the bacon to their districts in the form of public works programs, military bases, or other programs designed to benefit their districts directly.

positive ad: Advertising on behalf of a candidate that stresses the candidate's qualifications, family, and issue positions, without reference to the opponent.

pragmatism: The policy of taking advantage of a situation for national gain.

precedent: Prior judicial decision that serves as a rule for settling subsequent cases of a similar nature.

precinct chairperson: Party leader in a voting precinct.

precinct convention: Precinct party meeting to select delegates and adopt resolutions.

preemption: A concept derived from the Constitution's supremacy clause that allows the national government to override or preempt state or local actions in certain areas.

president of the Texas Senate: The lieutenant governor of Texas, serving in his constitutional role as presiding officer of the Senate.

presidentialist: One who believes that Article II's grant of executive power is a broad grant of authority allowing a president wide discretionary powers.

press briefing: A relatively restricted session between a press secretary or aide and the press.

press conference: An unrestricted session between an elected official and the press.

press release: A document offering an official comment or position.

press secretary: The individual charged with interacting and communicating with journalists on a daily basis.

primary election: Election in which voters decide which of the candidates within a party will represent the party in the general election.

print press: The traditional form of mass media, comprising newspapers, magazines, and journals.

prior restraint: Constitutional doctrine that prevents the government from prohibiting speech or publication before the fact; generally held to be in violation of the First Amendment.

privilegs and immunites clause: Part of Article IV of the Constitution guaranteeing that the citizens of each state are afforded the same rights as citizens of all other states.

Progressive movement: Advocated measures to destroy political machines and instead have direct participation by voters in the nomination of candidates and the establishment of public policy.

progressive tax: The tax level increases with the wealth or ability of an individual or business to pay.

proportional representation: A voting system that apportions legislative seats according to the percentage of the vote won by a particular political party.

prospective judgment: A voter's evaluation of a candidate based on what he or she pledges to do about an issue if elected.

pro-tempore (pro-tem): A legislator who serves temporarily as legislative leader in the absence of the Senate president or House speaker.

public corporation (authority): Government organization established to provide a particular service or to run a particular facility that is independent of other city or state agencies is to be operated like a business. Examples include a port authority or a mass transit system.

public counsels: Officials appointed by the governor to represent the public before regulatory agencies.

public funds: Donations from the general tax revenues to the campaigns of qualifying presidential candidates.

public interest group: An organization that seeks a collective good that will not selectively and materially benefit the members of the group.

public opinion: What the public thinks about a particular issue or set of issues at any point in time.

public opinion polls: Interviews or surveys with samples of citizens that are used to estimate the feelings and beliefs of the entire population.

public policy: An intentional course of action followed by government in dealing with some problem or matter of concern.

Public Utility Commission: A full-time, three-member paid commission appointed by the governor to regulate public utilities in Texas.

push polls: "Polls" taken for the purpose of providing information on an opponent that would lead respondents to vote against that candidate.

Q

quasi-judicial: A government commission receiving petitions from companies or individuals, hearing evidence in a hearing similar to a judicial proceeding, and ruling on the petition.

quorum: The minimum number required to conduct business (as in a legislative body).

R

raiding: An organized attempt by voters of one party to influence the primary results of the other party.

Railroad Commission: A full-time, three-member paid commission elected by the people to regulate oil and gas and some transportation entities.

random sampling: A method of poll selection that gives each person in a group the same chance of being selected.

Reagan Doctrine: Policy that the United States would provide military assistance to anti-communist groups fighting against pro-Soviet governments.

recall: A process in which voters can petition for a vote to remove office holders between elections.

recession: A short-term decline in the economy that occurs as investment sags, production falls off, and unemployment increases.

redistrict: Redraw election-district boundaries.

redistricting: The redrawing of congressional districts to reflect increases or decreases in seats allotted to the states, as well as population shifts within a state.

referendum: An election whereby the state legislature submits proposed legislation to the state's voters for approval.

regional primary: A proposed system in which the country would be divided into five or six geographic areas and all states in each region would hold their presidential primary elections on the same day.

regressive tax: The tax level increases as the wealth or ability of an individual or business to pay decreases.

regular session: The biennial 140-day session of the Texas legislature, beginning in January of odd-numbered years.

regulations: Rules that govern the operation of a particular government program that have the force of law.

republic: A government rooted in the consent of the governed; a representative or indirect democracy.

reserve (or police) powers: Powers reserved to the states by the Tenth Amendment that lie at the foundation of a state's right to legislate for the public health and welfare of its citizens.

reserve requirements: Governmental requirements that a portion of member banks' deposits must be retained to back loans made.

reservation land: Land designated in a treaty that is under the authority of an Indian nation and is exempt from most state laws and taxes.

restrictive constitution: Constitution that incorporates detailed provisions in order to limit the powers of government.

retrospective judgment: A voter's evaluation of the performance of the party in power.

revisionist: A member of a constitutional convention who will not accept less than a total revision of the current constitution.

revolving door: An exchange of personnel between private interests and public regulators.

right-of-rebuttal rule: A Federal Communications Commission regula-

tion that people attacked on a radio or television broadcast be offered the opportunity to respond.

right to privacy: The right to be let alone; a judicially created doctrine encompassing an individual's decision to use birth control or secure an abortion.

Roe v. Wade (1973): The Supreme Court found that a woman's right to an abortion was protected by the right to privacy that could be implied from specific guarantees found in the Bill of Rights applied to the states through the Fourteenth Amendment.

Roosevelt Corollary: Concept developed by President Theodore Roosevelt early in the twentieth century that it was the U.S. responsibility to assure stability in Latin America and the Caribbean.

rule making: A quasi-legislative administrative process that has the characteristics of a legislative act.

Rule of Four: At least four justices of the Supreme Court must vote to consider a case before it can be heard.

runoff primary: A second primary election between the two candidates receiving the greatest number of votes in the first primary.

S

sampling error or margin of error: A measure of the accuracy of a public opinion poll.

Second Continental Congress: Meeting that convened in Philadelphia on May 10, 1775, at which it was decided that an army should be raised and George Washington of Virginia was named commander in chief.

second reading: The Texas Constitution requires three readings of a bill by the legislature; the second reading is when debate and consideration of amendments occur before the whole chamber.

secular realignment: The gradual rearrangement of party coalitions, based more on demographic shifts than on shocks to the political system.

segregated funds: Money that comes in from a certain tax or fee and then is restricted to a specific use, such as a gasoline tax that is used for road maintenance.

select (or special) committee: Temporary committee appointed for specific purpose, such as conducting a special investigation or study.

selective incorporation: A judicial doctrine whereby most but not all of the protections found in the Bill of Rights are made applicable to the states via the Fourteenth Amendment.

Senate two-thirds rule: The rule in the Texas Senate requiring that every bill win a vote of two-thirds of the senators present to suspend the Senate's regular order of business, so that the bill may be considered.

senatorial courtesy: A process by which a governor, when selecting an appointee, defers to the state senator in whose district the nominee resides.

seniority: Time of continuous service on a committee.

separation of powers: A way of dividing power among three branches of government in which members of the House of Representatives, members of the Senate, the president, and the federal courts are selected by and responsible to different constituencies.

Seventeenth Amendment: Made senators directly elected by the people; removed their selection from state legislatures.

Shays's Rebellion: A 1786 rebellion in which an army of 1,500 disgruntled and angry farmers led by Daniel Shays marched to Springfield, Massachusetts, and forcibly restrained the state court from foreclosing mortgages on their farms.

sheriff: Elected official who serves as the chief law enforcement officer in a county.

simple resolution: A legislative document proposing an action that affects only the one chamber in which it is being considered, such as a resolution to adopt House rules or to commend a citizen.

single-member district: An election system for legislative bodies in which each legislator runs from and represents a single district, rather than the entire

geographic area encompassed by the government.

Sixteenth Amendment: Authorized Congress to enact a national income tax.

Sixth Amendment: Part of the Bill of Rights that sets out the basic requirements of procedural due process for federal courts to follow in criminal trials. These include speedy and public trials, impartial juries, trials in the state where crime was committed, notice of the charges, the right to confront and obtain favorable witnesses, and the right to counsel.

slander: Untrue spoken statements that defame the character of a person.

social capital: The myriad relationships that individuals enjoy that facilitate the resolution of community problems through collective action.

social contract: An agreement between the people and their government signifying their consent to be governed.

social contract theory: The belief that people are free and equal by God-given right and that this in turn requires that all people give their consent to be governed; espoused by John Locke and influential in the writing of the Declaration of Independence.

social regulation: Governmental regulation of the quality and safety of products as well as the conditions under which goods and services are produced.

Social Security Act: A 1935 law that established old-age insurance (Social Security) and assistance for the needy, children, and others, and unemployment insurance.

social welfare policy: Government programs designed to improve quality of life.

soft money: The virtually unregulated money funneled by individuals and political committees through state and local parties.

solicitor general: The fourth-ranking member of the Department of Justice; responsible for handling all appeals on behalf of the U.S. government to the Supreme Court.

sovereign immunity: The right of a state to be free from lawsuit unless it gives permission to the suit. Under the Eleventh Amendment, all states are considered sovereign.

Spanish-American War: Brief 1898 war against Spain because of Spanish brutality in Cuba and U.S. desire to attain overseas territory.

speaker of the House: The only officer of the House of Representatives specifically mentioned in the Constitution; elected at the beginning of each new Congress by the entire House; traditionally a member of the majority party.

speaker of the Texas House: The state representative who is elected by his or her fellow representatives to be the official leader of the House.

speaker's lieutenants: House members who make up the speaker's team, assisting the speaker in leading the House, either informally, or in a role as a committee chair or other institutional leader.

speaker's race: The campaign to determine who shall be the speaker of the Texas House for a given biennium.

speaker's team: The leadership team in the House, consisting of the speaker and his or her most trusted allies among the members, most of whom the speaker appoints to chair House committees.

special district: A local government that is responsible for a particular function, such as K–12 education, water, sewerage, or parks.

special election: Election held at a time other than general or primary elections.

special (called) session: A Texas legislative session of up to thirty days, called by the governor, during an interim between regular sessions.

spoils system: The firing of public-office holders of a defeated political party and their replacement with loyalists of the newly elected party.

spot ad: Television advertising on behalf of a candidate that is broadcast in sixty-, thirty-, or ten-second duration.

staggered terms: Terms of office for members of boards and commissions that begin and end at different times, so that a governor is not usually able to gain control of a majority of the body for a long time.

Stamp Act Congress: Meeting of representatives of nine of the thirteen colonies held in New York City in 1765, during which representatives drafted a document to send to the king listing how their rights had been violated.

standing committee: Committee to which proposed bills are referred.

stare decisis: In court rulings, a reliance on past decisions or precedents to formulate decisions in new cases.

State Board of Education: The fifteen-member elected body that sets some education policy for the state and has limited authority to oversee the Texas Education Agency and local school districts.

state constitution: The document that describes the basic policies, procedures, and institutions of the government of a specific state, much as the U.S. Constitution does for the federal government.

state convention: Party meeting held to adopt the party's platform, elect the party's executive committee and state chairperson, and in a presidential election year, elect delegates to the national convention and choose presidential electors.

state executive committee: Sixty-two-member party committee that makes decisions for the party between state conventions.

state party chairperson: Party leader for the state.

state senatorial district convention: Party meeting held when a county is a part of more than one senatorial district.

statutory constitution: Constitution that incorporates detailed provisions in order to limit the powers of government.

stewardship theory: The theory that holds that Article II confers on the president the power and the duty to take whatever actions are deemed necessary in the national interest, unless prohibited by the Constitution or by law.

Strategic Offensive Arms Reduction Treaty: 2002 U.S.-Russian treaty that reduced the number of nuclear warheads in each side's arsenal respectively to about 1,700 and 2,200, the lowest total in decades.

stratified sampling: A variation of random sampling; Census data are used to divide a country into four sampling regions. Sets of counties and standard metropolitan statistical areas are then randomly selected in proportion to the total national population.

straw polls: Unscientific surveys used to gauge public opinion on a variety of issues and policies.

strict constructionist: An approach to constitutional interpretation that emphasizes the Framers' original intentions.

strict scrutiny: A heightened standard of review used by the Supreme Court to determine the constitutional validity of a challenged practice.

strong mayor–council: A form of city government in which the mayor has strong powers to run the city by hiring, managing, and firing staff and controlling executive departments; the mayor also serves on the council.

substantive due process: Judicial interpretation of the Fifth and Fourteenth Amendments' due process clause that protects citizens from arbitrary or unjust laws.

succession: The constitutional declaration that the lieutenant governor succeeds to the governorship if there is a vacancy.

suffrage movement: The drive for voting rights for women that took place in the United States from 1890 to 1920.

sunset law: A law that sets a date for a program or regulation to expire unless reauthorized by the legislature.

superdelegate: Delegate slot to the Democratic Party's national convention that is reserved for an elected party official.

supremacy clause: Portion of Article VI of the U.S. Constitution mandating that national law is supreme to (that is, supercedes) all other laws passed by the states or by any other subdivision of government.

suspect classification: Category or class, such as race, that triggers the highest standard of scrutiny from the Supreme Court.

symbolic speech: Symbols, signs, and other methods of expression generally also considered to be protected by the First Amendment.

systemic agenda: All public issues that are viewed as requiring governmental attention; a discussion agenda.

T

Taftian theory: The theory that holds that the president is limited by the spe-

cific grants of executive power found in the Constitution.

Taliban: Fundamentalist Islamic government of Afghanistan that provided terrorist training bases for al-Qaeda.

tariffs: Taxes on imports used to raise government revenue and to protect infant industries.

Tejanos: Native Texans of Mexican descent.

temporary party organization: Party organization that exists for a limited time and includes several levels of conventions.

Tenth Amendment: The final part of the Bill of Rights that defines the basic principle of American federalism in stating: "The powers not delegated to the United States by the Constitution, nor prohibited by it to the States, are reserved to the States respectively, or to the people."

term limits: Restrictions that exist in some states about how long an individual may serve in state or local elected offices.

term limits: Restrictions that exist in some states about how long an individual may serve in state and/or local elected offices.

Texan Creed: A set of ideas—primarily individualism and liberty—that shape Texas politics and government.

Texas Association of Counties: Professional association and lobbying arm for county governments.

Texas Commission on Environmental Quality: As of 2002, the new name for the Texas Natural Resource Conservation Commission.

Texas Court of Criminal Appeals: Court of last resort in criminal cases.

Texas Education Agency: The state agency that oversees local school districts and disburses state funds to districts.

Texas Municipal League: Professional association and lobbying arm for city governments.

Texas Natural Resource Conservation Commission: A full-time, three-member paid commission appointed by the governor to administer the state's environmental programs.

Texas Rangers: A mounted militia formed to provide order on the frontier.

Texas secretary of state: The state official appointed by the governor to be the keeper of the state's records, such as state laws, election data and filings, public notifications, and corporate charters.

Texas Supreme Court: Court of last resort in civil and juvenile cases.

third-partyism: The tendency of third parties to arise with some regularity in a nominally two-party system.

third reading: The Texas Constitution requires three readings of a bill by the legislature; third reading is the final reading in a chamber, unless the bill returns from the other chamber with amendments.

Thirteenth Amendment: One of the three Civil War amendments; specifically bans slavery in the United States.

Three-Fifths Compromise: Agreement reached at the Constitutional Convention stipulating that each slave was to be counted as three-fifths of a person for purposes of determining population for representation in the U.S. House of Representatives.

ticket-split: To vote for candidates of different parties for various offices in the same election.

Title IX: Provision of the Educational Amendments of 1972 that bars educational institutions receiving federal funds from discriminating against female students.

totalitarianism: An economic system in which the government has total control over the economy.

town meeting: Form of local government in which all eligible voters are invited to attend a meeting at which budgets and ordinances are proposed and voted on.

tracking polls: Continuous surveys that enable a campaign to chart its daily rise or fall in support.

trade associations: A group that represents a specific industry.

trial court: Court of original jurisdiction where a case begins.

trial *de novo*: New trial, necessary for an appeal from a court that is not a court of record.

Truman Doctrine: U.S. policy initiated in 1947 of providing economic assistance and military aid to countries fighting against communist revolutions or political pressure.

trust land: Land owned by an Indian nation and designated by the federal Bureau of Indian Affairs as exempt from most state laws and taxes.

trust relationship: The legal obligation of the United States federal government to protect the interests of Indian tribes.

trustee: Role played by elected representatives who listen to constituents' opinions and then use their best judgment to make final decisions.

turnout: The proportion of the voting-age public that votes.

Twenty-Fifth Amendment: Adopted in 1967 to establish procedures for filling vacancies in the office of president and vice president as well as providing for procedures to deal with the disability of a president.

Twenty-Second Amendment: Adopted in 1951, prevents a president from serving more than two terms or more than ten years if he came to office via the death or impeachment of his predecessor.

U

unfunded mandates: National laws that direct states or local governments to comply with the federal rules or regulations (such as clean air or water standards) but contain no federal funding to defray the cost of meeting these requirements.

unilateralism: A national policy of acting without consulting others.

unitary system: System of government where the local and regional governments derive all authority from a strong national government.

unit rule: A traditional party practice under which the majority of a state delegation can force the minority to vote for its candidate.

United Nations: An international governmental organization created shortly before the end of World War II to guarantee the security of nations and to promote global economic, physical, and social well-being.

U.S. v. Nixon (1974): Key Supreme Court ruling on power of the president, finding that there is no absolute constitutional executive privilege to allow a president to refuse to comply with a court order to produce information needed in a criminal trial.

V

veto: The formal, constitutional authority of the chief executive to reject bills passed by both houses of the legislative body, thus preventing their becoming law without further legislative action.

veto power: The formal, constitutional authority of the president to reject bills passed by both houses of Congress, thus preventing their becoming law without further congressional action.

Vietnam War: Between 1965 and 1973, the United States deployed up to 500,000 troops to Vietnam to try to prevent North Vietnam from taking over South Vietnam; the effort failed and was extremely divisive within the United States.

Virginia Plan: The first general plan for the Constitution, proposed by James Madison. Its key points were a bicameral legislature, an executive chosen by the legislature, and a judiciary also named by the legislature.

voter canvass: The process by which a campaign gets in touch with individual voters, either by door-to-door solicitation or by telephone.

W

War of 1812: Fought between the United States and Great Britain over impressment and U.S. territorial designs on Canada.

war on terrorism: Initiated by George W. Bush after the 9/11 attacks to weed out terrorist operatives throughout the world, using diplomacy, military means, improved homeland security, stricter banking laws, and other means.

War Powers Act: Passed by Congress in 1973; the president is limited in the deployment of troops overseas to a sixty-day period in peacetime (which can be extended for an extra thirty days to permit withdrawal) unless Congress explicitly gives its approval for a longer period.

Washington's Farewell Address: Washington's 1796 final address as president in which he declared that the

United States should avoid becoming involved in foreign alliances.

weak mayor–council: A form of city government in which the mayor has no more power than any other member of the council.

weapons of mass destruction: Biological, chemical, and nuclear weapons, which present a sizeable threat to U.S. security.

whip: One of several representatives who keep close contact with all members and take nose counts on key votes, prepare summaries of bills, and in general act as communications links within the party.

wire service: An electronic delivery of news gathered by the news service's correspondents and sent to all member news media organizations.

World Bank: International governmental organization created shortly before the end of World War II to provide loans for large economic development projects.

World Trade Organization: International governmental organization created in 1995 that manages multilateral nego-tiations to reduce barriers to trade and settle trade disputes.

writ of *certiorari:* A request for the Court to order up the records from a lower court to review the case.

Y

yellow journalism: A form of newspaper publishing in vogue in the late-nine-teenth century that featured pictures, comics, color, and sensationalized, over-simplified news coverage.

Notes

CHAPTER 1

1. Thomas Byrne Edsall, "The Era of Bad Feelings," *Civilization* (March/April 1996): 37.
2. Jack C. Plano and Milton Greenberg, *The American Political Dictionary,* 6th ed. (New York: Holt, Rinehart and Winston, 1982).
3. The United States Agency for International Development, "Agency Objectives: Civil Society."
4. See William Strauss and Neil Howe, *Generations: The History of America's Future, 1984–2069* (New York: William Morrow, 1991), and Fernando Torres-Gil, *The New Aging: Politics and Generational Change in America* (New York: Auburn House, 1992).
5. William R. Buck and Tracey Rembert, "Not Just Doing It: Generation X Proves That Actions Speak Louder than Words," *Earth Action Network* (September 19, 1997): 28.
6. *Public Opinion Online,* Question Number 27, September 15–17, 2001.
7. Jack C. Plano and Milton Greenberg, *The American Political Dictionary,* 9th ed. (Fort Worth, TX: Harcourt Brace, 1993), 16.
8. Philip E. Converse, "The Nature of Belief Systems in Mass Publics," in David E. Apter, ed., *Ideology and Discontent* (New York: Free Press, 1964), 206–21.

CHAPTER 2

1. See Richard B. Bernstein with Jerome Agel, *Amending America* (New York: New York Times Books, 1993), 138–40.
2. *Oregon* v. *Mitchell,* 400 U.S. 112 (1970).
3. Bernstein, *Amending America,* 139.
4. For an account of the early development of the colonies, see D. W. Meining, *The Shaping of America,* vol. 1: *Atlantic America, 1492–1800* (New Haven, CT: Yale University Press, 1986).
5. For an excellent chronology of the events leading up to the writing of the Declaration of Independence and the colonists' break with Great Britain, see Calvin D. Lonton, ed., *The Bicentennial Almanac* (Nashville, TN: Thomas Nelson, 1975).
6. See Garry Wills, *Inventing America: Jefferson's Declaration of Independence* (New York: Random House, 1978). Wills argues that the Declaration was signed solely to secure foreign aid for the ongoing war effort.
7. For more about the Articles of Confederation, see Merrill Jensen, *The Articles of Confederation* (Madison: University of Wisconsin Press, 1940).
8. For more on the political nature of compromise at the convention, see Calvin C. Jillson, *Constitution Making: Conflict and Consensus in the Federal Constitution of 1787* (New York: Agathon, 1988).
9. Bernard Bailyn, *The Ideological Origins of the American Revolution* (Cambridge, MA: Belknap, 1967).
10. Richard E. Neustadt, *Presidential Power: The Politics of Leadership from FDR to Carter* (New York: Macmillan, 1980), 26.
11. Charles A. Beard, *An Economic Interpretation of the Constitution of the United States,* reissue edition (New York: Free Press, 1996).
12. John Patrick Diggins, "Power and Authority in American History: The Case of Charles A. Beard and His Critics," *American Historical Review* 86 (October 1981): 701–30; Robert Brown, *Charles Beard and the Constitution: A Critical Analysis of An Economic Interpretation of the Constitution* (Princeton, NJ: Princeton University Press, 1956).

13. Jackson Turner Main, *The Anti-Federalists* (Chapel Hill: University of North Carolina, 1961).
14. Gordon S. Wood, *Creation of the American Republic, 1776–1787,* reissue ed. (New York: Norton, 1993).
15. Federal Republicans favored a republican or representative form of government (do not confuse this term with the modern Republican Party, which came into being in 1854; see chapter 12). Ultimately, the word federal came to mean the form of government embodied in the new Constitution, just as confederation meant the league of states under the Articles, and later came to mean the Confederacy of 1861–1865.
16. See Ralph Ketcham, ed., *The Anti-Federalist Papers and the Constitutional Debates* (New York: New American Library, 1986).
17. See Herbert J. Storing, *What the Anti-Federalists Were For* (Chicago: University of Chicago Press, 1981), for a fuller discussion of Anti-Federalist views.
18. See Alan P. Grimes, *Democracy and the Amendments to the Constitution* (Lexington, MA: Lexington Books, 1978).
19. See Jane J. Mansbridge, *Why We Lost the ERA* (Chicago: University of Chicago Press, 1986).
20. *Marbury* v. *Madison,* 5 U.S. 137 (1803).
21. Speech by Attorney General Edwin Meese III before the American Bar Association, July 9, 1985, Washington, DC. See also Antonin Scalia and Amy Gutman, eds. *A Matter of Interpretation: Federal Courts and the Law* (Princeton, NJ: Princeton University Press, 1998).
22. Speech by William J. Brennan Jr. at Georgetown University, Text and Teaching Symposium, October 10, 1985, Washington, DC.
23. Bruce Ackerman, *We the People: Foundations* (Cambridge, MA: Belknap, 1991).

CHAPTER 3

1. T. R. Reid, "States Feel Less Pinch in Budgets, Services," *Washington Post* (May 9, 2004): A3. This vignette draws heavily from this work.
2. Reid, "States Feel Less Pinch."
3. Reid, "States Feel Less Pinch."
4. Reid, "States Feel Less Pinch."
5. Alan Ehrenhalt, "Every Government's Mandate," *New York Times* (April 27, 2003): D13.
6. Kris Hundley, "Health Care Costs up 8.7%," *St. Petersburg Times* (January 3, 2003): E1.
7. Catherine F. Klein, "Full Faith and Credit: Interstate Enforcement of Protection Orders Under the Violence Against Women Act of 1994," *Family Law Quarterly* 29 (1995): 253.
8. Nancy Plevin, "Ohio Frees Indian-Rights Activist 'Little Rock' Reed," *Santa Fe New Mexican* (March 12, 1999): B1.
9. *New Mexico ex rel. Ortiz* v. *Reed,* 524 U.S. 151 (1998).
10. John Mountjoy, "Interstate Cooperation: Interstate Compacts Make a Comeback," Council of State Governments, available online at http://www.csg.org.
11. *McCulloch* v. *Maryland,* 17 U.S. 316 (1819).
12. *Gibbons* v. *Ogden,* 22 U.S. 1 (1824).
13. *Dred Scott* v. *Sandford,* 60 U.S. 393 (1857).
14. *Plessy* v. *Ferguson,* 163 U.S. 537 (1896).
15. *Panhandle Oil Co.* v. *Knox,* 277 U.S. 218, 223 (1928).
16. *Indian Motorcycle Co.* v. *U.S.,* 238 U.S. 570 (1931).
17. *Pensacola Telegraph* v. *Western Union,* 96 U.S. 1 (1877).

18. Christopher Cox, "The 16th Amendment Is the Most Invasive Intrusion by the Government into Citizens' Lives," *Los Angeles Times* (June 20, 1995): B7.
19. John O. McGinnis, "The State of Federalism," testimony before the Senate Government Affairs Committee, May 5, 1999.
20. *NLRB* v. *Jones and Laughlin Steel Co.*, 301 U.S. 1 (1937).
21. *U.S.* v. *Darby Lumber Co.*, 312 U.S. 100 (1941).
22. *Wickard* v. *Filburn*, 317 U.S. 111 (1942).
23. Morton Grodzins, "Centralization and Decentralization in the American Federal System," in Robert A. Goldwin, ed., *A Nation of States* (Chicago: Rand McNally, 1963), 3–4.
24. Alice M. Rivlin, *Reviving the American Dream* (Washington, DC: Brookings Institution, 1992), 92.
25. Rivlin, *Reviving the American Dream*, 98.
26. Richard P. Nathan et al., *Reagan and the States* (Princeton, NJ: Princeton University Press, 1987), 4.
27. "Devolutionary Thinking Is Now Part of a Larger Critique of Modern Governmental Experience," *Public Perspective* (April/May 1995): 28.
28. Richard Wolf, "States Bracing for Leaner Times," *USA Today* (July 10, 2000): 1A.
29. Reid, "States Feel Less Pinch."
30. David S. Broder, "So, Now Bigger Is Better?" *Washington Post* (January 12, 2003): B1.
31. Marianne Arneberg, "Cuomo Assails Judicial Hodgepodge," *Newsday* (August 15, 1990): 15.
32. *U.S.* v. *Lopez*, 514 U.S. 549 (1995).
33. *Seminole Tribe* v. *Florida*, 517 U.S. 44 (1996).
34. *Boerne* v. *Flores*, 521 U.S. 507 (1997).
35. *Printz* v. *U.S.*, 521 U.S. 898 (1997).
36. *Florida Prepaid* v. *College Savings Bank*, 527 U.S. 627 (1999).
37. Linda Greenhouse, "In a Momentous Term, Justices Remake the Law and the Court," *New York Times* (July 1, 2003): A18.
38. *Nevada Department of Human Resources* v. *Hibbs*, 538 U.S. 72 (2003).

CHAPTER 4

1. Janny Scott, "Protesters Are Denied Potent Tactic of the Past," *New York Times* (February 13, 2003): B1.
2. "Restrictions Overreach," *USA Today* (May 27, 2003): 14A.
3. Charles Lane, "Court Made Dramatic Shifts in Law," *Washington Post* (June 30, 2002): A6.
4. The absence of a bill of rights led Mason to refuse to sign the proposed Constitution, noting that he "would sooner chop off his right hand than put it to the Constitution as it now stands." Quoted in Eric Black, *Our Constitution: The Myth That Binds Us* (Boulder, CO: Westview, 1988), 75.
5. *Barron* v. *Baltimore*, 32 U.S. 243 (1833).
6. *Allgeyer* v. *Louisiana*, 165 U.S. 578 (1897).
7. *Gitlow* v. *New York*, 268 U.S. 652 (1925).
8. *Near* v. *Minnesota*, 283 U.S. 697 (1931). For more about *Near*, see Fred W. Friendly, *Minnesota Rag: The Dramatic Story of the Landmark Case That Gave New Meaning to Freedom of the Press* (New York: Random House, 1981).
9. *Palko* v. *Connecticut*, 302 U.S. 319 (1937).
10. *Zobrest* v. *Catalina Foothills School District*, 506 U.S. 813 (1992).
11. *Engel* v. *Vitale*, 370 U.S. 421 (1962).
12. *Lee* v. *Weisman*, 505 U.S. 577 (1992).
13. *Santa Fe Independent School District* v. *Doe*, 530 U.S. 290 (2000).
14. *Elk Grove* v. *Newdow*, 124 S.Ct. 2301 (2004).
15. *Lemon* v. *Kurtzman*, 403 U.S. 602 (1971).
16. "An Eternal Debate," *Omaha World-Journal* (November 27, 2002): B6.
17. *Widmar* v. *Vincent*, 454 U.S. 263 (1981).
18. *Lamb's Chapel* v. *Center Moriches Union Free School District*, 508 U.S. 384 (1993).
19. *Rosenberger* v. *University of Virginia*, 515 U.S. 819 (1995).
20. *Lamb's Chapel* v. *Center Moriches Union Free School District*, 508 U.S. 384 (1993).
21. *Agostini* v. *Felton*, 521 U.S. 203 (1997).
22. *Mitchell* v. *Helms*, 530 U.S. 793 (2000).
23. *Zelman* v. *Simmons-Harris*, 536 U.S. 639 (2002).
24. *Employment Division, Dept. of Human Resources of Oregon* v. *Smith*, 494 U.S. 872 (1990).
25. *Boerne* v. *Flores*, 521 U.S. 507 (1997).
26. Tony Mauro, "Stern's Raunch Is Better than Silence," *USA Today* (May 12, 2004): 13A.
27. *Ex parte McCardle*, 74 U.S. 506 (1869).
28. David M. O'Brien, *Constitutional Law and Politics*, vol. 2, *Civil Rights and Civil Liberties* (New York: Norton, 1991), 345.
29. See Frederick Siebert, *The Rights and Privileges of the Press* (New York: D. Appleton-Century, 1934), 886, 931–40.
30. *Schenck* v. *U.S.*, 249 U.S. 47 (1919).
31. *Brandenburg* v. *Ohio*, 395 U.S. 444 (1969).
32. *New York Times Co.* v. *Sullivan*, 403 U.S. 713 (1971).
33. *Nebraska Press Association* v. *Stuart*, 427 U.S. 539 (1976).
34. *Abrams* v. *U.S.*, 250 U.S. 616 (1919).
35. *Stromberg* v. *California*, 283 U.S. 359 (1931).
36. *Tinker* v. *Des Moines Independent Community School District*, 393 U.S. 503 (1969).
37. *Texas* v. *Johnson*, 491 U.S. 397 (1989).
38. *U.S.* v. *Eichman*, 496 U.S. 310 (1990).
39. Linda Greenhouse, "Supreme Court Roundup: Free Speech or Hate Speech: Court Weighs Cross Burning," *New York Times* (May 28, 2002): A18. *R.A.V.* v. *City of St. Paul*, 505 U.S. 377 (1992).
40. *Virginia* v. *Black*, 538 U.S. 343 (2003).
41. *Chaplinsky* v. *New Hampshire*, 315 U.S. 568 (1942).
42. *New York Times Co.* v. *Sullivan*, 376 U.S. 254 (1964).
43. *Chaplinsky* v. *New Hampshire*, 315 U.S. 568 (1942).
44. *Cohen* v. *California*, 403 U.S. 15 (1971).
45. *Regina* v. *Hicklin*, L.R. 2 Q.B. 360 (1868).
46. *Roth* v. *U.S.*, 354 U.S. 476 (1957).
47. *Miller* v. *California*, 413 U.S. 15 (1973).
48. *Barnes* v. *Glen Theater*, 501 U.S. 560 (1991).
49. *National Endowment for the Arts* v. *Finley*, 524 U.S. 569 (1998).
50. *Reno* v. *American Civil Liberties Union*, 521 U.S. 844 (1997).
51. *Ashcroft* v. *Free Speech Coalition*, 122 S.Ct. 1389 (2002).
52. David G. Savage, "Ban on 'Virtual' Child Porn Is Upset by Court," *Los Angeles Times* (April 17, 2002): A1.
53. Lyle Denniston, "Court Puts 2D Pornography Law on Hold: A Majority Doubt Giving Localities an Internet Veto," *Boston Globe* (May 14, 2002): A2.
54. Nick Anderson and Elizabeth Levin, "Crime Bill Passes Easily in Congress: Measure Includes Expansion of Amber Alert System," *Los Angeles Times* (April 11, 2003): A36.
55. *DeJonge* v. *Oregon*, 229 U.S. 353 (1937).
56. *Barron* v. *Baltimore*, 32 U.S. 243 (1833).
57. *Dred Scott* v. *Sandford*, 60 U.S. 393 (1857).
58. *U.S.* v. *Miller*, 307 U.S. 174 (1939).
59. *Quilici* v. *Village of Morton Grove*, 104 U.S. 194 (1983).
60. *Printz* v. *U.S.*, 514 U.S. 898 (1997).
61. *Wilson* v. *Arkansas*, 514 U.S. 927 (1995).
62. *U.S.* v. *Sokolov*, 490 U.S. 1 (1989).
63. *U.S.* v. *Knights*, 534 U.S. 112 (2001).
64. *U.S.* v. *Matlock*, 415 U.S. 164 (1974).
65. *Johnson* v. *U.S.*, 333 U.S. 10 (1948).
66. *Winston* v. *Lee*, 470 U.S. 753 (1985).
67. *South Dakota* v. *Neville*, 459 U.S. 553 (1983).
68. *Michigan* v. *Tyler*, 436 U.S. 499 (1978).
69. *Hester* v. *U.S.*, 265 U.S. 57 (1924).
70. *Carroll* v. *U.S.*, 267 U.S. 132 (1925).
71. *U.S.* v. *Arvizu*, 122 S.Ct. 744 (2002).
72. *Skinner* v. *Railway Labor Executives' Association*, 489 U.S. 602 (1989).

73. *Vernonia School District* v. *Acton*, 515 U.S. 646 (1995).
74. *Board of Education of Independent School District No. 92 of Pottawatomie County* v. *Earls*, 536 U.S. 822 (2002).
75. *Ferguson* v. *City of Charleston*, 532 U.S. 67 (2001).
76. *Counselman* v. *Hitchcock*, 142 U.S. 547 (1892).
77. *Brown* v. *Mississippi*, 297 U.S. 278 (1936).
78. *Dickerson* v. *U.S.*, 530 U.S. 428 (2000).
79. *Weeks* v. *U.S.*, 232 U.S. 383 (1914).
80. *Mapp* v. *Ohio*, 367 U.S. 643 (1961).
81. *Johnson* v. *Zerbst*, 304 U.S. 458 (1938).
82. *Gideon* v. *Wainwright*, 372 U.S. 335 (1963).
83. *Argersinger* v. *Hamlin*, 407 U.S. 25 (1972).
84. *Scott* v. *Illinois*, 440 U.S. 367 (1979).
85. *Alabama* v. *Shelton*, 535 U.S. 654 (2002).
86. *Strauder* v. *West Virginia*, 100 U.S. 303 (1880).
87. *Taylor* v. *Louisiana*, 419 U.S. 522 (1975).
88. *Batson* v. *Kentucky*, 476 U.S. 79 (1986).
89. *Maryland* v. *Craig*, 497 U.S. 836 (1990).
90. See Michael Meltsner, *Cruel and Unusual: The Supreme Court and Capital Punishment* (New York: Random House, 1973).
91. *Furman* v. *Georgia*, 408 U.S. 238 (1972).
92. *Gregg* v. *Georgia*, 428 U.S. 153 (1976).
93. *Olmstead* v. *U.S.*, 277 U.S. 438 (1928).
94. *Griswold* v. *Connecticut*, 381 U.S. 481 (1965).
95. *Eisenstadt* v. *Baird*, 410 U.S. 113 (1972).
96. *Roe* v. *Wade*, 410 U.S. 113 (1973).
97. *Webster* v. *Reproductive Health Services*, 492 U.S. 490 (1989).
98. *Planned Parenthood of Southeastern Pennsylvania* v. *Casey*, 502 U.S. 1056 (1992).
99. "House Sends Partial Birth Abortion Bill to Clinton," *Politics USA* (March 28, 1996): 1.
100. *Stenberg* v. *Carhart*, 530 U.S. 914 (2000).
101. *Bowers* v. *Hardwick*, 478 U.S. 186 (1986).
102. *Lawrence* v. *Texas*, 539 U.S. 558 (2003).
103. *Boy Scouts* v. *Dale*, 530 U.S. 640 (2000).
104. Charles Lane, "Poll: Americans Say Court Is 'About Right,'" *Washington Post* (July 7, 2002): A15.
105. Lane, "Poll: Americans Say Court Is 'About Right.'"
106. *Romer* v. *Evans*, 517 U.S. 620 (1996).
107. *Cruzan* v. *Director, Missouri Dept. of Health*, 497 U.S. 261 (1990).
108. *Vacco* v. *Quill*, 521 U.S. 793 (1997).
109. Office of the Attorney General, Memorandum for Asa Hutchinson, Administrator, the Drug Enforcement Administration, November 6, 2001.
110. William McCall, "Oregon Suicide Law Gets Longer Reprieve: Court Allows US Senate 5 Months to Ready Arguments," *Boston Globe* (November 21, 2001): A8.
111. *Oregon* v. *Ashcroft*, 192 F. Supp. 2d 1077 (2002); and Kim Murphy, "U.S. Cannot Block Oregon Suicide Law, Judge Rules," *Los Angeles Times* (April 18, 2002): A1.
112. *Bush* v. *Schiavo*, 885 S. 2d. 321 (Fla, 204), cert. denied

CHAPTER 5

1. Michael Cooper, "Officers in Bronx Fire 41 Shots, and an Unarmed Man Is Killed," *New York Times* (February 5, 1999): A1.
2. Amy Wilentz, "New York: The Price of Safety in a Police State," *Los Angeles Times* (April 11, 1999): M1.
3. N. R. Kleinfield, "Veterans of 60's Protests Meet the Newly Outraged in a March," *New York Times* (April 16, 1999): B8.
4. *Minor* v. *Happersett*, 88 U.S. 162 (1875).
5. *The Civil Rights Cases*, 109 U.S. 3 (1883).
6. *Plessy* v. *Ferguson*, 163 U.S. 537 (1896).
7. *Williams* v. *Mississippi*, 170 U.S. 213 (1898); *Cummins* v. *Richmond County Board of Education*, 175 U.S. 528 (1899).
8. *Missouri ex rel. Gaines* v. *Canada*, 305 U.S. 337 (1938).
9. *Sweatt* v. *Painter*, 339 U.S. 629 (1950), and *McLaurin* v. *Oklahoma*, 339 U.S. 637 (1950).
10. *Sweatt* v. *Painter*, 339 U.S. 629 (1950).
11. *Brown* v. *Board of Education*, 347 U.S. 483 (1954).
12. But see Gerald Rosenberg, *Hollow Hope: Can Courts Bring About Social Change* (Chicago: University of Chicago Press, 1991).
13. Quoted in Juan Williams, *Eyes on the Prize: America's Civil Rights Years, 1954–1965* (New York: Penguin, 1987), 10.
14. *Brown* v. *Board of Education II*, 349 U.S. 294 (1955).
15. Quoted in Williams, *Eyes on the Prize*, 37.
16. *Cooper* v. *Aaron*, 358 U.S. 1 (1958).
17. Jo Freeman, *The Politics of Women's Liberation* (New York: Longman, 1975), 57.
18. *Hoyt* v. *Florida*, 368 U.S. 57 (1961).
19. Betty Friedan, *The Feminine Mystique* (New York: Dell, 1963).
20. *Palko* v. *Connecticut*, 302 U.S. 319 (1937).
21. *Reed* v. *Reed*, 404 U.S. 71 (1971).
22. *Mississippi University for Women* v. *Hogan*, 458 U.S. 718 (1982).
23. *Craig* v. *Boren*, 429 U.S. 190 (1976).
24. *Orr* v. *Orr*, 440 U.S. 268 (1979).
25. *JEB* v. *Alabama ex rel. TB*, 440 U.S. 268 (1979).
26. *U.S.* v. *Virginia*, 518 U.S. 515 (1996).
27. *Rostker* v. *Goldberg*, 453 U.S. 57 (1981).
28. *Michael M.* v. *Superior Court of Sonoma County*, 450 U.S. 464 (1981).
29. *Rostker* v. *Goldberg*, 453 U.S. 57 (1981).
30. *U.S.* v. *Virginia*, 518 U.S. 515 (1996).
31. "How Much Will the Wage Gap Cost You?" http://www.aflcio.org/issuespolitics/women/equalpay/equalpay.cfm. Accessed May 18, 2004.
32. *Meritor Savings Bank* v. *Vinson*, 477 U.S. 57 (1986).
33. *Oncale* v. *Sundowner Offshore Services, Inc.*, 523 U.S. 75 (1998).
34. *Hishon* v. *King & Spalding*, 467 U.S. 69 (1984).
35. *Johnson* v. *Transportation Agency*, 480 U.S. 616 (1987).
36. *Davis* v. *Monroe County Board of Education*, 526 U.S. 629 (1999).
37. Joyce Gelb and Marian Lief Palley, *Women and Public Policies* (Charlottesville: University of Virginia Press, 1996).
38. Ernesto B. Virgil, *The Crusade for Justice* (Madison: University of Wisconsin Press, 1999).
39. *White* v. *Register*, 412 U.S. 755 (1973).
40. *Plyer* v. *Doe*, 457 U.S. 202 (1982).
41. "MALDEF 'Pleased' with Settlement of California Public Schools Inequity Case, *Williams* v. *California*," August 13, 2004, press release.
42. Rennard Strickland, "Native Americans," in Kermit Hall, ed., *The Oxford Companion to the Supreme Court of the United States* (New York: Oxford University Press, 1992), 579.
43. *Cobell* v. *Norton*, 204 F.3d 1081 (2001). For more on the Indian trust, see http://www.indiantrust.com/overview.cfm.
44. Richard Luscombe, "Tribes Go on Legal Warpath," *The Observer* (April 25, 2004): 20.
45. Diane Helene Miller, *Freedom to Differ: The Shaping of the Gay and Lesbian Struggle for Civil Rights* (New York: New York University Press, 1998).
46. Sarah Brewer, David Kaib, and Karen O'Connor, "Sex and the Supreme Court: Gays, Lesbians, and Justice," in Craig A. Rimmerman, Kenneth D. Wald, and Clyde Wilcox, *The Politics of Gay Rights* (Chicago: University of Chicago Press, 2000).
47. Evan Gerstmann, *The Constitutional Underclass: Gays, Lesbians, and the Failure of Class-Based Equal Protection* (Chicago: University of Chicago Press, 1999).
48. Deborah Ensor, "Gay Veterans Working for Change," *San Diego Union* (April 13, 2002): B1.
49. *Lawrence* v. *Texas*, 539 U.S. 558 (2003).
50. Joan Biskupic, "Court's Opinion on Gay Rights Reflects Trends," *USA Today* (July 18, 2003): 2A.
51. David Pfeiffer, "Overview of the Disability Movement: History, Legislative Record and Political Implications," *Policy Studies Journal* (Winter 1993): 724–42; and "Understanding Disability Policy," *Policy Studies Journal* (Spring 1996): 157–74.

52. Joan Biskupic, "Supreme Court Limits Meaning of Disability," *Washington Post* (June 23, 1999): A1.
53. *Tennessee* v. *Lane,* 2004 U.S. Lexis 3386 (2004).
54. *Regents of the University of California* v. *Bakke,* 438 U.S. 265 (1978).
55. *Grutter* v. *Bollinger,* 539 U.S. 306 (2003).
56. *Gratz* v. *Bollinger,* 539 U.S. 306 (2003).
57. Michael Markowitz, "Gay Rights: Shareholders' Power Is the New Weapon in the Fight for Workplace Equality," *Newsday* (January 4, 2004): F10.
58. Victoria Colliver, "Class Action Considered in Wal-Mart Suit," *San Francisco Chronicle* (September 25, 2003): B1.
59. "Wal-Mart's Immigrant Labor Problem," *Tampa Tribune* (November 14, 2003): 10.

CHAPTER 6

1. For an outstanding account of Pelosi's campaign for the whip post, see Juliet Eilperin, "The Making of Madam Whip: Fear and Loathing—and Horse Trading—The Race for the House's No. 2 Democrat," *Washington Post* (January 6, 2002): W27.
2. "Mother of All Whips," *Pittsburgh Post-Gazette* (February 9, 2002): A11.
3. Sue Thomas, *How Women Legislate* (New York: Oxford University Press, 1994); and Karen O'Connor, ed., *Women and Congress: Running, Winning and Ruling* (New York: Haworth, 2002).
4. Barbara Sinclair, "The Struggle over Representation and Law-making in Congress: Leadership Reforms in the 1990s," in James A. Thurber and Roger H. Davidson, eds., *Remaking Congress: Change and Stability in the 1990s* (Washington, DC: CQ Press, 1995), 105.
5. "What Is the Democratic Caucus?" http://dcaucusweb.house.gov/about/what_is.asp.
6. Woodrow Wilson, *Congressional Government: A Study in American Government* (New York: Meridian Books, 1956, originally published in 1885), 79.
7. Roger H. Davidson, "Congressional Committees in the New Reform Era: From Combat to the Contract," in Thurber and Davidson, *Remaking Congress,* 28.
8. For more about committees, see Christopher Deering and Steven S. Smith, *Committees in Congress,* 3rd ed. (Washington, DC: CQ Press, 1997).
9. Woodrow Wilson, *Congressional Government.* (New York: Houghton Mifflin, 1885).
10. Kenneth A. Shepsle, *The Giant Jigsaw Puzzle: Democratic Committee Assignments in the Modern House* (Chicago: University of Chicago Press, 1978).
11. Tim Groseclose and Charles Stewart III, "The Value of Committee Seats in the House, 1947–91," *American Journal of Political Science* 42 (April 1998): 453–74.
12. Richard F. Fenno Jr., "U.S. House Members in Their Constituencies: An Exploration," *American Political Science Review* 3 (September 1977): 883–917.
13. Gary W. Cox and Jonathan N. Katz, "Why Did the Incumbency Advantage in U.S. House Elections Grow?" *American Journal of Political Science* 40 (May 1996): 478–97; and Kenneth N. Bickers and Robert M. Stein, "The Electoral Dynamics of the Federal Pork Barrel," *American Journal of Political Science* 40 (November 1996): 1300–26.
14. Marjorie Randon Hershey, "Congressional Elections," in Gerald M. Pomper et al., *The Election of 1992: Reports and Interpretations* (Chatham, NJ: Chatham House, 1993), 159.
15. Alan I. Abramowitz, "Incumbency, Congressional Spending, and the Decline of Competition in House Elections," *Journal of Politics* 53 (February 1991): 34–56.
16. Mildred L. Amer, "Membership of the 108th Congress: A Profile." Congressional Research Service (March 20, 2003).
17. Amy Keller, "The Roll Call 50 Richest: For Richer or Poorer Thanks to Spouses, Kerry Keeps Top Spot and Clinton Joins List," *Roll Call* (September 9, 2002).
18. Amer, "Membership of the 108th Congress."
19. Warren E. Miller and Donald Stokes, "Constituency Influence in Congress," *American Political Science Review* 57 (March 1963): 45–57.
20. *Congressional Quarterly Weekly Report* (January 6, 2001).
21. Norman Ornstein, "GOP Moderates Can Impact Policy—If They Dare," *Roll Call* (February 12, 2003).
22. Byron York, "Bored by Estrada? Owen May Be a Reprise," *The Hill* (March 19, 2003): 43.
23. See L. Martin Overby, "The Senate and Justice Thomas: A Note on Ideology, Race, and Constituent Pressures," *Congress & the Presidency* 21 (Autumn 1994): 131–6.
24. Ken Kollman, "Inviting Friends to Lobby: Interest Groups, Ideological Bias, and Congressional Committees," *American Journal of Political Science* 41 (April 1997): 519–44. See also Marie Hojnacki and David C. Kimball, "Organized Interests and the Decision of Whom to Lobby in Congress," *American Political Science Review* 92 (December 1998): 775–90.
25. Barbara S. Romzek and Jennifer A. Utter, "Congressional Legislative Staff: Political Professionals or Clerks?" *American Journal of Political Science* 41 (October 1997): 1251–79; and Susan Webb Hammond, "Recent Research on Legislative Staffs," *Legislative Studies Quarterly* (November 1996): 543–76.
26. Keith Krehbiel, "Cosponsors and Wafflers from A to Z." *American Journal of Political Science* 39 (November 1995): 906–23.
27. Joel D. Aberbach, *Keeping a Watchful Eye: The Politics of Congressional Oversight* (Washington, DC: Brookings Institution, 1990).
28. William F. West, "Oversight Subcommittees in the House of Representatives, *Congress & the Presidency* 25 (Autumn 1998): 147–60.
29. This discussion draws heavily on Steven J. Balla, "Legislative Organization and Congressional Review," paper delivered at the 1999 meeting of the Midwest Political Science Association.
30. *Wall Street Journal* (April 13, 1973): 10.

CHAPTER 7

1. "Two Hundred Years of Presidential Funerals," *Washington Post* (June 10, 2004): C14.
2. Gail Russell Chaddock, "The Rise of Mourning in America," *Christian Science Monitor* (June 11, 2004): 1.
3. Richard E. Neustadt, *Presidential Power and the Modern Presidency* (New York: Free Press, 1991).
4. Winston Solberg, *The Federal Convention and the Formation of the Union of the American States* (Indianapolis, IN: Bobbs-Merrill, 1958), 235.
5. James P. Pfiffner, "Recruiting Executive Branch Leaders," *Brookings Review* 19 (Spring 2001): 41–3.
6. Benjamin I. Page and Mark P. Petracca, *The American Presidency* (New York: McGraw-Hill, 1983), 262.
7. "War Powers: Resolution Grants Bush Power He Needs," *Rocky Mountain News* (September 15, 2001): B6.
8. *Public Papers of the Presidents* (1963), 889.
9. Quoted in Neustadt, *Presidential Power,* 9.
10. Quoted in Page and Petracca, *The American Presidency,* 57.
11. See Louis Fisher, *Constitutional Conflicts Between Congress and the President,* 4th ed. (Lawrence: University Press of Kansas, 1997).
12. Franklin D. Roosevelt, Press Conference, July 23, 1937.
13. See Lance LeLoup and Steven Shull, *The President and Congress: Collaboration and Conflict in National Policymaking* (Boston: Allyn and Bacon, 1999).
14. See Cary Covington, J. Mark Wrighton, and Rhonda Kinney, "A 'Presidency-Augmented' Model of Presidential Success on House Roll Call Votes," *American Journal of Political Science* 39 (November 1995): 1001–24; and Wayne P. Steger, "Presidential Policy Initiation and the Politics of Agenda Control," *Congress & the Presidency* 24 (Spring 1997): 102–14.
15. Quoted in Thomas E. Cronin, *The State of the Presidency,* 2nd ed. (Boston: Little, Brown, 1980), 169.
16. Robert A. Caro, *Master of the Senate: The Years of Lyndon Johnson* (New York: Knopf, 2002).

17. Paul C. Light, *The President's Agenda: Domestic Policy Choice from Kennedy to Carter* (Baltimore, MD: Johns Hopkins University Press, 1983).

18. Mary Leonard, "Bush Begins Talks on Human Cloning," *Boston Globe* (January 17, 2002): A6.

19. Samuel Kernell, *New Strategies of Presidential Leadership*, 2nd ed. (Washington, DC: CQ Press, 1993), 3.

20. Jeffrey Cohen, "Presidential Rhetoric and the Public Agenda," *American Journal of Political Science* 39 (February 1995): 87–107.

21. Brian Kates and Kenneth R. Bazinet, "Crisis Forges a New Bush First-Year," *Daily News* (January 20, 2002): 9.

22. George Reedy, *The Twilight of the Presidency* (New York: New American Library), 38–9.

23. Reedy, *Twilight of the Presidency,* 33.

24. Neustadt, *Presidential Power,* 1–10.

25. Samuel Kernell, *Going Public: New Strategies of Presidential Leadership,* 3rd ed. (Washington, DC: CQ Press, 1996).

26. William E. Gibson, "Job Approval Ratings Steady: Personal Credibility Takes a Hit," *News and Observer* (August 19, 1998): A16.

27. Michael R. Kagay, "History Suggests Bush's Popularity Will Ebb," *New York Times* (May 22, 1991): A10.

CHAPTER 8

1. Thomas Frank, "Homeland Security: Terror Warnings Not Coordinated," *Newsday* (May 28, 2004): A4.

2. Harold D. Lasswell, *Politics: Who Gets What, When and How* (New York: McGraw-Hill, 1938).

3. H. H. Gerth and C. Wright Mills, *From Max Weber* (New York: Oxford University Press, 1958).

4. Office of Personnel Management, *The Fact Book,* available online at http://www.opm.gov/feddata/03factbk.pdf. The Postal Service, like the rest of the federal government, continues to downsize. "20,000 Job Cuts at Postal Service," *Newsday* (January 9, 2002): A38.

5. David Osborne and Ted Gaebler, *Reinventing Government* (Reading, MA: Addison-Wesley, 1992), 20–21.

6. Office of Personnel Management, *2003 Fact Book.* See also Julie Dolan, "The Senior Executive Service: Gender, Attitudes and Representative Bureaucracy," *Journal of Public Administration Research and Theory* 10(3) (2003): 513–29.

7. Stephen Barr, "Some Trainees Voice Frustration with Presidential Management Intern Program," *Washington Post* (November 26, 2001): B2.

8. A Report of the U.S. Merit Systems Protection Board, Executive Summary, http://www.mspb.gov/studies/rpt%2008-01%20pmi-program/pmi_program.pd8.

9. Kenneth J. Cooper, "U.S. May Repay Loans for College," *Washington Post* (December 13, 2001): A45.

10. "A Century of Government Growth," *Washington Post* (January 3, 2000): A17. On the difficulty of counting the exact number of government agencies, see David Nachmias and David H. Rosenbloom, *Bureaucratic Government: U.S.A.* (New York: St. Martin's Press, 1980).

11. For the EPA to become a department and its head a formal member of the president's Cabinet, Congress would have to act.

12. The classic work on regulatory commissions is Marver Bernstein, *Regulating Business by Independent Commission* (Princeton, NJ: Princeton University Press, 1955).

13. Karen DeYoung, "Saudis Detail Steps on Charities; Kingdom Seeks to Quell Record on Terrorist Financing," *Washington Post* (December 3, 2002): A1.

14. Michael Lipsky, *Street-Level Bureaucracy: Dilemmas of the Individual in Public Services* (New York: Russell Sage Foundation, 1980).

15. Cornelius M. Kerwin, *Rulemaking: How Government Agencies Write Law and Make Policy,* 2nd ed. (Washington, DC: CQ Press, 1999), xv.

16. David J. Lorenzo, "Countering Popular Misconceptions of Federal Bureaucracies in American Government Classes," *PS: Political Science and Politics* 4 (December 1999): 743–7.

17. George A. Krause, "Presidential Use of Executive Orders, 1953–1994," *American Politics Quarterly* 25 (October 1997): 458–81.

18. Irene Murphy, *Public Policy on the Status of Women* (Lexington, MA: Lexington Books, 1974).

19. Rosemary O'Leary, *Environmental Change: Federal Courts and the EPA* (Philadelphia: Temple University Press, 1993).

20. James F. Spriggs III, "The Supreme Court and Federal Administrative Agencies: A Resource-Based Theory and Analysis of Judicial Impact," *American Journal of Political Science* 40 (November 1996): 1122.

21. Wendy Hansen, Renee Johnson, and Isaac Unah, "Specialized Courts, Bureaucratic Agencies, and the Politics of U.S. Trade Policy," *American Journal of Political Science* 39 (August 1995): 529–57.

CHAPTER 9

1. *Marbury* v. *Madison,* 5 U.S. 137 (1803); *Martin* v. *Hunter's Lessee,* 14 U.S. 304 (1816).

2. Oliver Ellsworth served from 1796 to 1800.

3. *Marbury* v. *Madison,* 5 U.S. 137 (1803).

4. This discussion draws heavily on Jack C. Plano and Milton Greenberg, *The American Political Dictionary,* 10th ed. (Fort Worth TX: Harcourt Brace, 1996), 247.

5. Cases involving citizens from different states can be filed in state or federal court.

6. Quoted in Lawrence Baum, *The Supreme Court,* 3rd ed. (Washington, DC: CQ Press, 1989), 108.

7. See Barbara A. Perry, *A Representative Supreme Court? The Impact of Race, Religion, and Gender on Appointments* (New York: Greenwood, 1991).

8. Clarence Thomas was raised a Catholic but attended an Episcopalian church at the time of his appointment, having been barred from Catholic sacraments because of his remarriage. He again, however, is attending Roman Catholic services.

9. The Polling Company, accessed May 30, 2002, http://www.pollingcompany.com/News.asp?FormMode=ViewReleases&ID=50.

10. John Brigham, *The Cult of the Court* (Philadelphia: Temple University Press, 1987).

11. Stephen L. Wasby, *The Supreme Court in the Federal Judicial System,* 4th ed. (Chicago: Nelson-Hall, 1988), 199. Much of this change occurred as the result of an increase in state criminal cases, of which nearly 100 percent concerned constitutional questions.

12. Data compiled by authors for 2003–2004 term of the Court.

13. Justice Stevens chooses not to join this pool. According to one former clerk, "He wanted an independent review," but Stevens examines only about 20 percent of the petitions, leaving the rest to his clerks. Tony Mauro, "Ginsburg Plunges into the Cert Pool," *Legal Times* (September 6, 1993): 8.

14. Paul Wahlbeck, James F. Spriggs II, and Lee Sigelman, "Ghostwriters on the Court? A Stylistic Analysis of U.S. Supreme Court Opinion Drafts," *American Politics Research* 30 (March 2002): 166–92.

15. Richard A. Posner, *The Federal Courts: Crisis and Reform* (Cambridge, MA: Harvard University Press, 1985), 114.

16. Edward Lazarus, *Closed Chambers: The First Eyewitness Account of the Epic Struggles Inside the Supreme Court* (New York: Random House, 1998).

17. "Retired Chief Justice Warren Attacks…Freund Study Group's Composition and Proposal," *American Bar Association Journal* 59 (July 1973): 728.

18. Kathleen Werdegar, "The Solicitor General and Administrative Due Process," *George Washington Law Review* (1967–1968): 482.

19. Rebecca Mae Salokar, *The Solicitor General: The Politics of Law* (Philadelphia: Temple University Press, 1992), 3.

20. Richard C. Cortner, *The Supreme Court and Civil Liberties* (Palo Alto, CA: Mayfield, 1975), vi.

21. Gregory A. Caldeira and John R. Wright, "*Amicus Curiae* Before the Supreme Court: Who Participates, When and How Much?" *Journal of Politics* 52 (August 1990): 803.

22. See also John R. Hermann, "American Indians in Court: The Burger and Rehnquist Years," Ph.D. dissertation, Emory University, 1996.

23. Donald L. Horowitz, *The Courts and Social Policy* (Washington, DC: Brookings Institution, 1977), 538.

24. *Webster* v. *Reproductive Health Services,* 492 U.S. 518 (1989).

25. See, for example, Tracy E. George and Lee Epstein, "On the Nature of Supreme Court Decision Making," *American Political Science Review* 86 (1992): 323–37; Melinda Gann Hall and Paul Brace, "Justices' Responses to Case Facts: An Interactive Model," *American Politics Quarterly* (April 1996): 237–61; Lawrence Baum, *The Puzzle of Judicial Behavior* (Ann Arbor: University of Michigan Press, 1997); and Gregory N. Flemming, David B. Holmes, and Susan Gluck Mezey, "An Integrated Model of Privacy Decision Making in State Supreme Courts," *American Politics Quarterly* 26 (January 1998): 35–58.

26. Jeffrey A. Segal and Harold Spaeth, *The Supreme Court and the Attitudinal Model* (New York: Cambridge University Press, 1993).

27. Gerard Gryski, Eleanor C. Main, and William Dixon, "Models of State High Court Decision Making in Sex Discrimination Cases," *Journal of Politics* 48 (1986): 143–55; and C. Neal Tate and Roger Handberg, "Time Binding and Theory Building in Personal Attribute Models of Supreme Court Voting Behavior, 1916–1988," *American Political Science Review* 35 (1991): 460–80.

28. Donald R. Songer and Sue Davis, "The Impact of Party and Region on Voting Decisions in the U.S. Courts of Appeals, 1955–86," *Western Political Quarterly* 43 (1990): 830–44.

29. See, generally, Lee Epstein and Jack Knight, "Field Essay: Toward a Strategic Revolution in Judicial Politics: A Look Back, a Look Ahead," *Political Research Quarterly* 53 (September 2000): 663–76.

30. Thomas R. Marshall, "Public Opinion, Representation and the Modern Supreme Court," *American Politics Quarterly* 16 (1988): 296–316.

31. Curtis J. Sitomer, "High Court to Rethink Abortion?" *Christian Science Monitor* (September 16, 1988): 3.

32. *U.S.* v. *Korematsu,* 323 U.S. 214 (1944).

33. *Youngstown Sheet & Tube Co.* v. *Sawyer,* 343 U.S. 579 (1952). The Supreme Court ruled that President Truman's seizure and operation of U.S. steel mills in the face of a strike threat were unconstitutional, because the Constitution implied no such broad executive power. See Alan Westin, *Anatomy of a Constitutional Law Case* (New York: Macmillan, 1958); and Maeva Marcus, *Truman and the Steel Seizure Case* (New York: Columbia University Press, 1977).

34. *U.S.* v. *Nixon,* 418 U.S. 683 (1984).

35. Gallup Poll, Public Opinion Online (May 21–24, 2004).

36. Timothy R. Johnson and Andrew D. Martin, "The Public's Conditional Response to Supreme Court Decisions," *American Political Science Review* 92 (June 1998): 299–309.

37. "Supreme Court Cases Overruled by Subsequent Decision," U.S. Government Printing Office, accessed online at http://www.gpoaccess.gov/constitution/pdf/con041.pdf.

38. *Lee* v. *Weisman,* 505 U.S. 577 (1992).

39. *Reynolds* v. *Sims,* 377 U.S. 533 (1964).

40. *Mississippi University for Women* v. *Hogan,* 458 U.S. 718 (1982).

CHAPTER 10

1. Allan M. Winkler, "Public Opinion," in Jack Greene, ed., *The Encyclopedia of American Political History* (New York: Charles Scribner's Sons, 1988), 1038.

2. *Literary Digest* 122 (August 22, 1936): 3.

3. *Literary Digest* 125 (November 14, 1936): 1.

4. Robert S. Erikson, Norman Luttbeg, and Kent Tedin, *American Public Opinion: Its Origin, Contents, and Impact* (New York: Wiley, 1980), 28.

5. Richard Dawson et al. *Political Socialization,* 2nd ed. (Boston: Little, Brown, 1977), 33.

6. Robert D. Hess and David Easton, "The Child's Changing Image of the President," *Public Opinion Quarterly* 14 (Winter 1960): 632–42; and Fred I. Greenstein, *Children and Politics* (New Haven, CT: Yale University Press, 1965).

7. James Simon and Bruce D. Merrill, "Political Socialization in the Classroom Revisited: The Kids Voting Program," *Social Science Journal* 35 (1998): 29–42.

8. Simon and Merrill, "Political Socialization in the Classroom Revisited."

9. *Statistical Abstract of the United States, 1997* (Washington, DC: Government Printing Office, 1997), 1011.

10. Princeton Research Survey Associates Poll, accessed through LEXIS, Question ID USPSRA.011104, R19, December 19, 2003–January 3, 2004.

11. Princeton Research Survey Associates Poll, accessed through LEXIS, Question ID USPSRA.032504, RIT06B, March 17–21, 2004.

12. Steven M. Cohen and Charles S. Liebman, "American Jewish Liberalism," *Public Opinion Quarterly* 61 (1997): 405–30.

13. Cable News Network, CNN.com.

14. Edward S. Greenberg, "The Political Socialization of Black Children," in Edward S. Greenberg, ed., *Political Socialization* (New York: Atherton, 1970), 181.

15. Elaine J. Hall and Myra Marx Ferree, "Race Differences in Abortion Attitudes," *Public Opinion Quarterly* 50 (Summer 1986): 193–207; and Jon Hurwitz and Mark Peffley, "Public Perceptions of Race and Crime: The Role of Racial Stereotypes," *American Journal of Political Science* 41 (April 1997): 375–401.

16. Elaine S. Povich, "Courting Hispanics: Group's Votes Could Shift House Control," *Newsday* (April 21, 2002): A4.

17. Alejandro Portest and Rafael Mozo, "The Political Adaptation Process of Cubans and Other Ethnic Minorities in the United States: A Preliminary Analysis," in F. Chris Garcia, ed., *Latinos and the Political System* (Notre Dame, IN: University of Notre Dame Press, 1988), 161.

18. Pamela Johnson Conover and Virginia Sapiro, "Gender, Feminist Consciousness and War," *American Journal of Political Science* 37 (November 1993): 1079–99.

19. Margaret Trevor, "Political Socialization, Party Identification, and the Gender Gap," *Public Opinion Quarterly* 63 (Spring 1999): 62–89.

20. Alexandra Marks, "Gender Gap Narrows over Kosovo," *Christian Science Monitor* (April 30, 1999): 1.

21. Pew Research Center for the People and the Press (2002).

22. Pew Research Center for the People and the Press, "Iraq Prison Scandal Hits Home, But Most Reject Troop Pullout," released May 12, 2004, http://people-press.org/reports/display.php37REportID=213.

23. Tanya Bricking, "Young Voters May Not," *Cincinnati Enquirer* (October 19, 1996): A1.

24. Susan A. MacManus, *Young* v. *Old: Generational Combat in the 21st Century* (Boulder, CO: Westview, 1995).

25. Richard Morin, "Southern Exposure," *Washington Post* (July 14, 1996): A18.

26. "Church Pews Seat More Blacks, Seniors, and Republicans," http://www.gallup.com/POLL_ARCHIVES/970329.html.

27. Suzanne Soule, "Will They Engage? Political Knowledge, Participation and Attitudes of Generations X and Y," paper prepared for the 2001 German and American Conference, 6.

28. Soule, "Will They Engage?" quoting Richard G. Niemi and Jane Junn, *Civic Education* (New Haven, CT: Yale University Press, 1998).

29. Tamara Henry, "Kids Get 'Abysmal' Grade in History," *USA Today* (May 10, 2002): 1A.

30. "Don't Know Much About…" *Christian Science Monitor* (May 16, 2002): 8.

31. Quoted in Everett Carl Ladd, "Fiskin's 'Deliberative Poll' Is Flawed Science and Dubious Democracy," *Public Perspective* (December/January 1996): 41.

32. V. O. Key Jr., *The Responsible Electorate: Rationality in Presidential Voting, 1936–1960* (Cambridge, MA: Belknap Press of Harvard University, 1966).

33. Gerald M. Pomper, *The Performance of American Government* (New York: Free Press, 1972); and Benjamin I. Page, *Choices and Echoes in Presidential Elections* (Chicago: University of Chicago Press, 1978).

34. Norman H. Nie, Sidney Verba, and John Petrochik, *The Changing American Voter* (Cambridge, MA: Harvard University Press, 1976).

35. Richard Nodeau et al., "Elite Economic Forecasts, Economic News, Mass Economic Judgments and Presidential Approval," *Journal of Politics* 61 (February 1999): 109–35.

36. Michael Towle, review of *Presidential Responsiveness and Public Policy-making: The Public and the Policies* by Jeffrey E. Cohen, *Journal of Politics* 61 (February 1999): 230–2.

37. John E. Mueller, *War, Presidents, and Public Opinion* (New York: Wiley, 1973), 69.

38. Francis J. Connolly and Charley Manning, "What 'Push Polling' Is and What It Isn't," *Boston Globe* (August 16, 2001): A21.

39. Michael W. Traugott, "The Polls in 1992: Views of Two Critics: A Good General Showing, but Much Work Needs to Be Done," *Public Perspective* 4 (November/December 1992): 14–16.

40. See Mitchell Stephens, *A History of News: From the Drum to the Satellite* (New York: Viking, 1989).

41. Charles Press and Kenneth VerBurg, *American Politicians and Journalists* (Glenview, IL: Scott, Foresman, 1988), 8–10.

42. For a delightful rendition of this episode, see Shelley Ross, *Fall from Grace* (New York: Ballantine, 1988), ch. 12.

43. Doris A. Graber, *Mass Media and American Politics*, 3rd ed. (Washington, DC: CQ Press, 1989), 12.

44. See Thomas C. Leonard, *The Power of the Press: The Birth of American Political Reporting* (New York: Oxford University Press, 1986), ch. 7.

45. Richard L. Rubin, *Press, Party, and Presidency* (New York: Norton, 1981), 38–9.

46. Stephen Bates, *If No News, Send Rumors* (New York: St. Martin's Press, 1989), 185.

47. Data complied by the Newspaper Association of America at http://www.naa.org/marketscope/pdfs/DailyReadership1964-Present.pdf.

48. *PR Newswire* "NAA Finds Newspaper Readership Steady in Top 50 Markets" May 3, 2004.

49. Pew Research Center for the People and the Press, "Cable and Internet Loom Large in Fragmented Political News Universe," January 11, 2004.

50. Katy Bachman "Direct Broadcast Satellite Gains Users; Cable Wanes," mediaweek.com, April 7, 2004.

51. Andrew Kohut, *The Biennial Pew Media Survey: How News Habits Changed in 2004,* Brookings/Pew Research Center Forum, Washington, DC, June 8, 2004, http://www.brookings.edu/dybdocroot/comm/events/20040608.pdf.

52. This was the fundamental conclusion of Shanto Iyengar and Donald R. Kinder, *News That Matters* (Chicago: University of Chicago Press, 1987).

53. M. Just, T. Buhr, and A. Crigler, "Voice, Substance, and Cynicism in Presidential Campaign Media," *Political Communication* 16 (January 1999): 25–44.

54. Political Communications Study, January 11, 2004, http://people-press.org/reprots/dispky.php3?PageID=77.

55. Pew Research Center, "Cable and Internet Loom Large."

56. UCLA Center for Communication Policy, "The UCLA Internet Report: Surveying the Digital Future," January 2003; PEJ Research.

57. Thomas Patterson, *Out of Order* (New York: Vintage, 1994).

58. Mike Allen, "Bush's Isolation from Reporters Could Be a Hindrance," *Washington Post* (October 8, 2004): A9.

59. Larry Sabato. *Feeding Frenzy: Attack Journalism and American Politics* (Baltimore: Lanahan, 2000).

60. *New York Times Co. v. Sullivan,* 376 U.S. 254 (1964). See also Steven Pressman, "Libel Law: Finding the Right Balance," *Editorial Research Reports* 2 (August 18, 1989): 462–71.

61. *Curtis Publishing Co. v. Butts,* 388 U.S. 130 (1967); *Associated Press v. Walker,* 388 U.S. 130 (1967).

62. American Society of Newspaper Editors, *The Changing Face of the Newsroom* (Washington, DC: ASNE, 1989), 33; William Schneider and I. A. Lewis, "Views on the News," *Public Opinion* 8 (August/September 1985): 6–11, 58–59; and S. Robert Lichter, Stanley Rothman, and Linda S. Lichter, *The Media Elite* (Bethesda, MD: Adler and Adler, 1986).

63. National Survey of the Role of Polls in Policymaking, Kaiser Family Foundation, http://www.kff.org/content/2001/3146/toplines.pdf.

64. See Dom Bonafede, "Crossing Over," *National Journal* 21 (January 14, 1989): 102; Richard Harwood, "Tainted Journalists," *Washington Post* (December 4, 1988): L6; Charles Trueheart, "Trading Places: The

Insiders Debate," *Washington Post* (January 4, 1989): D1, 19; and Kirk Victor, "Slanted Views," *National Journal* 20 (June 4, 1988): 1512.

65. http://www.stateofthenewsmedia.org/narrative_overview_audience.asp?media=1.

66. Pew Research Center, "Cable and Internet Loom Large."

67. David Domke, David P. Fan, Dhavan V. Shah, and Mark D. Watts, "The Politics of Conservative Elites and the 'Liberal Media' Argument," *Journal of Communication* 49 (Fall 1999): 35–58.

68. Benjamin I. Page, Robert Y. Shapiro, and Glenn R. Dempsey, "What Moves Public Opinion?" *American Political Science Review* 81 (March 1987): 23–44.

69. Fox News/Opinion Dynamic Poll, conducted June 18–19, 2002.

70. Pew Research Center for the People and the Press, "Internet News Takes Off: Event Driven News Audiences," June 8, 1998, http://people-press.org.

71. Pew Research Center, "Cable and Internet Loom Large."

72. Pew Research Center, "News Media's Improved Image Proves Short-Lived."

73. Christopher Stern, "FCC Chairman's Star a Little Dimmer," *Washington Post* (July 25, 2003): E01, http://www.washingtonpost.com/ac2/wp-dyn?pagename=article&contentId=A43044-2003Jul24&notFound=true.

74. *New York Times Co. v. U.S.,* 403 U.S. 713 (1971).

CHAPTER 11

1. Howard Kurtz, "MoveOn.org's Swift Boat Response to Anti-Kerry Ad," *Washington Post* (August 17, 2004): A8.

2. Kurtz, "MoveOn.org's Swift Boat Response."

3. "Campaign Finance Reform Led to Birth of 527s," *Seattle Times* (July 25, 2004): A18.

4. Graham Wilson, *Interest Groups in the United States* (New York: Oxford University Press, 1981), 4.

5. V. O. Key Jr., *Politics, Parties, and Pressure Groups* (New York: T. J. Crowell, 1942), 23.

6. John H. Aldrich, *Why Parties? The Origin and Transformation of Party Politics in America* (Chicago: University of Chicago Press, 1995).

7. By contrast, Great Britain did not develop truly national, broad-based parties until the 1870s.

8. See *Historical Statistics of the United States: Colonial Times to 1970,* part 2, series Y-27-28 (Washington, DC: Government Printing Office, 1975), based on unpublished data prepared by Walter Dean Burnham.

9. Frank J. Sorauf, *Party Politics in America,* 5th ed. (Boston: Little, Brown, 1984), 22.

10. See V. O. Key Jr., *American State Politics: An Introduction* (New York: Knopf, 1956).

11. Christian Collet and Martin P. Wattenberg, "Strategically Unambitious: Minor Party and Independent Candidates in the 1996 Congressional Elections," in John C. Green and Daniel M. Shea, eds., *The State of the Parties: The Changing Role of Contemporary American Parties,* 3rd ed. (Lanham, MD: Rowman and Littlefield, 1999).

12. Marc J. Heatherington, "The Effect of Political Trust on the Presidential Vote, 1968–1996," *American Political Science Review* 93 (1999): 311–26.

13. See Steven E. Finkel and Howard A. Scarrow, "Party Identification and Party Enrollment: The Difference and the Consequence," *Journal of Politics* 47 (May 1985): 620–42.

14. Senator George J. Mitchell (D–ME), as quoted in the *Washington Post* (February 9, 1986): A14.

15. Janet M. Box-Steffensmeier, "A Dynamic Analysis of the Role of War Chests in Campaign Strategy," *American Journal of Political Science* 40 (May 1996): 352–71.

16. See David E. Price, *Bringing Back the Parties* (Washington, DC: CQ Press, 1984), 284–8.

17. See, for example, Sarah McCally Morehouse, "Legislatures and Political Parties," *State Government* 59 (1976): 23.

18. David W. Rohde, *Parties and Leaders in the Postreform House* (Chicago: University of Chicago Press, 1991); and John A. Aldrich and David W. Rohde, "The Transition to Republican Rule in the House: Implications for Theories of Congressional Politics," *Political Science Quarterly* 112 (1997–1998): 541–67.

19. Robert D. Putnam, "Bowling Alone: America's Declining Social Capital," *Journal of Democracy* 6 (1995): 650–65; and Putnam, *Bowling Alone: The Collapse and Revival of American Community* (New York: Simon and Schuster, 2000).

20. Everett Carll Ladd, quoted in Richard Morin, "Who Says We're Not Joiners," *Washington Post* (May 2, 1999): B5.

21. John Brehm and Wendy Rahn, "Individual-Level Evidence for the Causes and Consequences of Social Capital," *American Journal of Political Science* 41 (July 1997): 999.

22. Mark Schneider et al., "Institutional Arrangements and the Creation of Social Capital: The Effects of Public School Choice," *American Political Science Review* 91 (March 1997): 82–93.

23. Nicholas Lemann, "Kicking in Groups," *Atlantic Monthly* (April 1996): NEXIS.

24. Robert D. Putnam et al., *Making Democracy Work: Civic Traditions in Modern Italy* (Princeton NJ: Princeton University Press, 1994).

25. David B. Truman, *The Governmental Process: Political Interests and Public Opinion* (New York: Knopf, 1951), 33.

26. Truman, *The Governmental Process*, ch. 16.

27. Robert H. Salisbury, "An Exchange Theory of Interest Groups," *Midwest Journal of Political Science* 13 (1969): 1–32.

28. Mancur Olson Jr. *The Logic of Collective Action: Public Goods and the Theory of Groups* (Cambridge, MA: Harvard University Press, 1965).

29. Jeffrey M. Berry, *Lobbying for the People: The Political Behavior of Public Interest Groups* (Princeton, NJ: Princeton University Press, 1977), 7.

30. Jack L. Walker, "The Origins and Maintenance of Interest Groups in America," *American Political Science Review* 77 (June 1983): 390–406.

31. The Center for Responsive Politics, http://www.opensecrets.org.

32. Some political scientists speak of "iron rectangles," reflecting the growing importance of a fourth party, the courts, in the lobbying process.

33. Clement E. Vose, "Litigation as a Form of Pressure Group Activity," *Annals* 319 (September 1958): 20–31.

34. Robert A. Goldberg, *Grassroots Resistance: Social Movement in Twentieth Century America* (Belmont, CA: Wadsworth, 1991).

CHAPTER 12

1. Paul Allen Beck, *Party Politics in America*, 8th ed. (New York: Longman, 1998); David Adamany, "Cross-over Voting and the Democratic Party's Reform Rules," *American Political Science Review* 70 (1976): 536–41; Ronald Hedlund and Meredith W. Watts, "The Wisconsin Open Primary: 1968 to 1984," *American Politics Quarterly* 14 (1986): 55–74; and Gary D. Wekkin, "The Conceptualization and Measurement of Crossover Voting," *Western Political Quarterly* 41 (1988) 105–14.

2. Beck, *Party Politics in America*; Alan Abromowitz, John McGlennon, and Ronald Rapoport, "A Note on Strategic Voting in a Primary Election," *Journal of Politics* 43 (1981): 899–904; and Gary D. Wekken, "Why Crossover Voters Are Not 'Mischievous' Voters," *American Politics Quarterly* 19 (1991): 229–47.

3. Larry J. Sabato, "Presidential Nominations: The Front-loaded Frenzy of 1996," in Larry J. Sabato, ed., *Toward the Millennium: The Elections of 1996* (New York: Allyn and Bacon, 1997).

4. Byron Shafer, *Bifurcated Politics: Evolution and Reform in the National Party Convention* (Cambridge, MA: Harvard University Press, 1988).

5. Paul S. Herrnson, "Campaign Professionalism and Fundraising in Congressional Elections," *Journal of Politics* 54 (1992): 859–70.

6. Stephen K. Medvic and Silvo Lenart, "The Influence of Political Consultants in the 1992 Congressional Elections," *Legislative Studies Quarterly* 22 (February 1997): 61–77.

7. Five liberal Democratic U.S. senators, including George McGovern of South Dakota, were defeated in this way in 1980, for example.

8. On the subject of party realignment, see Walter Dean Burnham, *Critical Elections and the Mainsprings of American Politics* (New York: Norton, 1970); Kristi Andersen, *The Creation of a Democratic Majority* (Chicago: University of Chicago Press, 1979); and John R. Petrocik, "Realignment: New Party Coalitions and the Nationalization of the South," *Journal of Politics* 49 (May 1987): 347–75.

9. Barbara Farah and Helmut Norpoth, "Trends in Partisan Realignment, 1976–1986: A Decade of Waiting," paper prepared for the annual meeting of the American Political Science Association, Washington, DC, August 27–31, 1986.

10. Morris P. Fiorina, *Retrospective Voting in American National Elections* (New Haven, CT: Yale University Press, 1981); and Charles H. Franklin and John E. Jackson, "The Dynamics of Party Identification," *American Political Science Review* 77 (1983): 957–73.

11. See, for example, V. O. Key Jr., "A Theory of Critical Elections," *Journal of Politics* 17 (February 1955): 3–18.

12. The less dynamic term "creeping realignment" is also sometimes used by scholars and journalists.

13. Everett Carl Ladd, "Like Waiting for Godot: The Uselessness of 'Realignment' for Understanding Change in Contemporary American Politics," in Byron Shafer, ed., *The End of Realignment? Interpreting American Electoral Eras* (Madison: Wisconsin, 1991).

14. See Paul Allen Beck, "The Dealignment Era in America," in Russell J. Dalton et al., *Electoral Change in Advanced Industrial Democracies: Realignment or Dealignment?* (Princeton, NJ: Princeton University Press, 1984), 264. See also Philip M. Williams, "Party Realignment in the United States and Britain," *British Journal of Political Science* 15 (January 1985): 97–115.

15. Glenn R. Parker and Suzanne L. Parker, "Correlates and Effects of Attention to District by U.S. House Members," *Legislative Studies Quarterly* 10 (May 1985): 223–42.

16. *Wesberry* v. *Sanders,* 376 U.S. 1 (1964).

17. *Thornburg* v. *Gingles,* 478 U.S. 30 (1986).

18. *Shaw* v. *Reno,* 113 S.Ct. 2816 (1993).

19. Steven T. Engel and David J. Jackson, "Wielding the Stick Instead of Its Carrot: Labor PAC Punishment of Pro-NAFTA Democrats," *Political Research Quarterly* 51 (September 1998): 813–28.

20. Janet M. Box-Steffensmeier and J. Tobin Grant, "All in a Day's Work: The Financial Rewards of Legislative Effectiveness," *Legislative Studies Quarterly* 24 (November 1999): 511–23.

21. Kevin M. Leyden and Stephen A. Borrelli, "An Investment in Goodwill: Party Contributions and Party Unity Among U.S. House Members in the 1980s," *American Politics Quarterly* 22 (October 1994): 421–52.

22. Amy Keller, "Helping Each Other Out: Members Dip Into Campaign Funds for Fellow Candidates," *Roll Call* (June 15, 1998): 1.

23. For member contribution activity at the state level, see Jay K. Dow, "Campaign Contributions and Intercandidate Transfers in the California Assembly," *Social Science Quarterly* 75 (1994): 867–80. For member contribution activity at the congressional level, see Bruce A. Larson, "Ambition and Money in the U.S. House of Representatives: Analyzing Campaign Contributions from Incumbents' Leadership PACs and Reelection Committees" (Ph.D. dissertation, University of Virginia, 1998). For a briefer account, see Paul S. Herrnson, "Money and Motives: Spending in House Elections," in Lawrence C. Dodd and Bruce I. Oppenheimer, eds., *Congress Reconsidered*, 6th ed. (Washington, DC: CQ Press, 1997).

24. *Buckley* v. *Valeo,* 424 U.S. 1 (1976).

25. *Buckley* v. *Valeo,* 424 U.S. 1 (1976); *Colorado Republican Federal Campaign Committee* v. *Federal Election Commission,* 116 S.Ct. 2309 (1996).

26. Amy Keller, "Experts Wonder About FEC's Internet Savvy: Regulating Web Is a Challenge for Watchdog Agency," *Roll Call* (May 6, 1999): 1, 21.

27. http://www.commoncause.org/laundromat/stat/topdonors01.htm.

28. League of United Latin American Citizens, http://www.lulac.org.

29. Stephen Knack and J. White, "Election-Day Registration and Turnout Inequality," *Political Behavior* 22 (March 2000): 29–44.

30. Charles E. Smith Jr et al., "Party Balancing and Voting in Congress in the 1996 National Election," *American Journal of Political Science* 43 (July 1999): 737–64.

31. Russell J. Dalton, Paul A. Beck, and Robert Huckfeldt, "Partisan Cues and the Media: Information Flows in the 1992 Presidential Election," *American Political Science Review* 92 (March 1998): 111–26.

CHAPTER 13

1. "President Signs Medicare Legislation," White House News Release, December 8, 2003, www.whitehouse.gov/news/releases/2003/1220031208-2.html.

2. Robert J. Samuelson, "Medicare as Pork Barrel," *Newsweek* (December 1, 2003): 47.

3. James E. Anderson, *Public Policymaking: An Introduction,* 4th ed. (Boston: Houghton Mifflin, 2000). This discussion draws on Anderson's study.

4. Anderson, *Public Policymaking;* Thomas R. Dye, *Understanding Public Policy,* 10th ed. (Upper Saddle River, NJ: Prentice Hall); and Charles E. Lindbloom and Edward J. Woodhouse, *The Policy-Making Process,* 3rd ed. (Upper Saddle River, NJ: Prentice Hall, 1992).

5. Karen O'Connor, *No Neutral Ground: Abortion Politics in an Age of Absolutes* (Boulder, CO: Westview, 1996); and Randy Shilts, *And the Band Played On: Politics, People, and the AIDS Epidemic* (New York: St. Martin's Press, 2000).

6. Roger W. Cobb and Charles D. Elder, *Participation in American Politics: The Dynamics of Agenda Building,* 2nd ed. (Baltimore, MD: Johns Hopkins University Press, 1983).

7. Cobb and Elder, *Participation in American Politics,* ch. 5.

8. Cobb and Elder, *Participation in American Politics,* 85.

9. Charles O. Jones, *An Introduction to the Study of Public Policy,* 3rd ed. (Monterey, CA: Brooks/Cole, 1984), 87–9.

10. This discussion draws on Anne Schneider and Helen Ingram, "Behavioral Assumptions of Policy Tools," *Journal of Politics* 52 (May 1990): 510–29.

11. Schneider and Ingram, "Behavioral Assumptions of Policy Tools."

12. U.S. Census Bureau, Office of Management and Budget.

13. Fact Sheet, Social Security, http://www.sss.gov/cola2002.htm, accessed July 13, 2002.

14. William Branigin, "Greenspan Urges Lawmakers to Consider Entitlement Cuts," *Washington Post* (February 25, 2004): A1.

15. Summary Data for State Programs by State, https://www.ows.doleta.gov/unemploy/txdocs/sumapr02.html, accessed July 14, 2002.

16. http://ssa-custhelp.ssa.gov.

17. Steven G. Koven, Mack C. Shelley II, and Bert E. Swanson, *American Public Policy: The Contemporary Agenda* (Boston: Houghton Mifflin, 1998), 271.

18. Nanette Relave, "TANF Reauthorization and Work Requirements," The Reauthorization Resource (February 2002), https://www.welfareinfo.org/workrequirements_trn.asp, accessed July 11, 2002.

19. *USA Today,* http://www.usatoday.com/news/health/2004-01-08-health-care_x.htm.

20. Mark Rushefsky and Kant Patel, *Politics, Power, and Policy Making* (Armonk, NY: M. E. Sharpe, 1998), 27.

21. John F. Dickerson, "Can We Afford All This?" *Time* (December 8, 2004): 48–51; Edward Walsh and Bill Brubaker, "Drug Benefits Impact Detailed," *Washington Post* (November 26, 2003): A10.

22. U.S. Department of Health and Human Services, Centers for Medicare and Medicaid Services, "Report Details."

23. Marilyn Werber Serafina, "Medicrunch," *National Journal* 27 (July 29, 1995): 1937.

24. After 108 years of operation, the ICC expired at the end of 1995 as part of the effort by congressional Republicans to reduce federal regulations and allow market forces more freedom in which to operate.

25. Ludwig Von Mises, *Critique of Interventionism* (Hudson, NY: Foundation for Economic Education, 1996).

26. William G. Whittaker, *The Fair Labor Standards Act* (Hauppauge, NY: Nova, 2002).

27. Larry N. Gerston, Cynthia Fraleigh, and Robert Schwab, *The Deregulated Society* (Pacific Grove, CA: Brooks/Cole, 1988), 27.

28. Quoted in Gerston, Fraleigh, and Schwab, *The Deregulated Society,* 27.

29. Martha Derthick and Paul J. Quirk, *The Politics of Deregulation* (Washington, DC: Brookings Institution, 1985).

30. Martin Mayer, *The Greatest-Ever Bank Robbery: The Collapse of the Savings and Loan Industry* (New York: Scribner's, 1990).

31. L. William Seidman, *Full Faith and Credit: The Great S&L Debacle and Other Washington Sagas* (New York: Times Books, 1993). Seidman was in charge of the Resolution Trust Corporation during the early years of the S&L bailout.

32. James D. Savage, *Balanced Budgets and American Politics* (Ithaca, NY: Cornell University Press, 1988), 176–9.

CHAPTER 14

1. Dana Millbank, "The 'Bush Doctrine' Experiences Shining Moments," *Washington Post* (December 21, 2003): A26.

2. Millbank, "The 'Bush Doctrine' Experiences Shining Moments."

3. Robert C. Byrd, "The Truth Will Emerge," Senate Speeches, United States Senate, May 21, 2003; see http://byrd.senate.gov.byrd_speeches/byrd_speeches.html.

4. See Graham Allison, *Essence of Decision: Explaining the Cuban Missile Crisis* (Boston: Little, Brown, 1971).

5. Michael Froman, *The Development of the Idea of Détente* (New York: St. Martin's Press, 1982).

6. See Colin S. Gray, "Strategic Forces," in Joseph Kruzel, ed., *American Defense Annual 1986–87* (Lexington, MA: Lexington Books, 1986). For a discussion of Reagan's early international economic policies, see Jeffrey E. Garten, "Gunboat Economics," *Foreign Affairs* 63 (1985): 538–99.

7. See William Head and Earl H. Tilford Jr., eds., *The Eagle in the Desert: Looking Back on U.S. Involvement in the Persian Gulf War* (Westport: CT: Praeger, 1996).

8. For good discussions of the events that led to the decline and fall of the Soviet Union, see Geoffrey Hosking, *The Awakening of the Soviet Union* (Cambridge, MA: Harvard University Press, 1990); David Remnick, *Lenin's Tomb: The Last Days of the Soviet Empire* (New York: Random House, 1993); and Jeffrey T. Checkel, *Ideas and International Political Change: Soviet/Russian Behavior and the End of the Cold War* (New Haven, CT: Yale University Press, 1997).

9. Jeffrey J. Schott, *The WTO After Seattle* (Washington, DC: Institute for International Economics, 2000); and Bhagirath L. Das, *World Trade Organization: A Guide to New Frameworks for International Trade* (New York: St. Martin's Press, 2000).

10. "Statement on an International Trade Agenda," White House, May 10, 2001.

11. See Dan Papp, *The Impact of September 11 on Contemporary International Relations* (New York: Pearson, 2003).

12. George W. Bush, "State of the Union Message," *New York Times* (January 2002): NEXIS.

13. "Commander in Chief Lands on USS Lincoln," CNN.com, May 2, 2003.

14. Seymour M. Hersh, "Torture at Abu Ghraib," *New Yorker* (May 10, 2004): 10.

15. See Loch K. Johnson, *America's Secret Power: The CIA in a Democratic Society* (New York: Oxford University Press, 1989).

16. Zachary Coile, "Tenet's Emotional Farewell to CIA Staff," *San Francisco Chronicle* (June 4, 2004): A20.

17. Jane Mayer, "The Manipulator," *New Yorker* (June 3, 2004): 58–72.

18. James M. Lindsay, "Congress, Foreign Policy, and the New Institutionalism," *International Studies Quarterly* 38 (June 1994): 281–304.

19. For Eisenhower's thoughts on the subject, see Dwight D. Eisenhower, *The White House Years* (Garden City, NY: Doubleday, 1963–1965).

20. Richard Rosecrance and Arthur A. Stein, "Beyond Realism: The Study of Grand Strategy," in Richard Rosecrance and Arthur A. Stein, eds., *The Domestic Bases of Grand Strategy* (Ithaca, NY: Cornell University Press, 1993), 1–21.

CHAPTER 15

1. Steve H. Murdock et al., *The New Texas Challenge: Population Change and the Future of Texas* (College Station: Texas A&M University Press, 2003), 19.
2. Murdock, *The New Texas Challenge,* 140.
3. The data for this section is from Murdock, *The New Texas Challenge.*
4. During 1994, Texas passed New York in population, replacing it as the second largest state in population. The 2000 Census officially established Texas as the second largest state. California, with 35.5 million residents, remains the most populous state in 2003.
5. U.S. Census Bureau, *State Characteristic Estimates,* Table ST-EST2002-ASRO-03, September 18, 2003, accessed June 10, 2004, http://eire.census.gov/popest/data/states/ST-EST2002-ASRO-03.php.
6. W. W. Newcomb Jr., *The Indians of Texas: From Prehistoric to Modern Times* (Austin: University of Texas Press, 1961), 22.
7. Newcomb, *The Indians of Texas,* 180–5.
8. Andrew Mollison, "Life Without Casino Isn't Easy for Alabama-Coushatta Indians," *Lufkin Daily News* (April 27, 2003).
9. Arnoldo De Leon, *Mexican Americans in Texas: A Brief History* (Arlington Heights, IL: Harlan Davidson, 1993), 7–19.
10. De Leon, *Mexican Americans in Texas,* 20.
11. Donald E. Chipman, *Spanish Texas, 1519–1821* (Austin: University of Texas Press, 1992), 242–60.
12. Terry G. Jordan, "A Century and a Half of Ethnic Change in Texas, 1836–1986," *Southwestern Historical Quarterly* 89 (April 1986): 392–4.
13. "Hispanics Key in '98 Vote, Both Parties Say," *Corpus Christi Caller-Times Interactive* (September 22, 1998), accessed October 19, 1999, http://corpuschristionline.com/texas98/texas20612.html; Lomi Kriel, "Dems, GOP Vie for Sought-After Hispanic Vote," *Daily Texan Online* (October 16, 2003), accessed June 10, 2004, http://www.dailytexanonline.com/news/2004/06/03/TopStories/Gop-Convention.To.Rejuvenate.Support-684288.shtml; Will Krueger, "Hispanic Leaders Looking Ahead," *Daily Texan Online* (October 17, 2003), accessed June 10, 2004, http://www.dailytexanonline.com/news/2003/10/17/TopStories/Hispanic.Leaders.Looking.Ahead-531638.shtml; *2004 National Directory of Latino Elected Officials* (Los Angeles: NALEO Education Fund, 2004); 116.
14. Jordan, "A Century and a Half of Ethnic Change," 400–1; Terry G. Jordan, John L. Bean Jr., and William M. Holmes, *Texas: A Geography* (Boulder, CO: Westview, 1984), 79.
15. Jordan, "A Century and a Half of Ethnic Change," 402, 404; Jordan, Bean, and Holmes, *Texas,* 79.
16. David A. Bositis, "Black Elected Officials, 1994–1997," *Focus Magazine* (September 1998); Joint Center for Political and Economic Studies Web site, accessed October 29, 1999, http://www.jointctr.org/focus/issues/sep98.html; David A. Bositis, *Black Elected Officials: A Statistical Summary 2001* (Washington, DC: Joint Center for Political and Economic Studies, 2003), 14–15.
17. Comptroller of Public Accounts, "Lone Star Asians," *Fiscal Notes* (November 1997): 3–5; *2003–04 National Asian Pacific American Political Almanac* (Los Angeles: UCLA Asian American Studies Center, 2003), 300–2.
18. Jordan, Bean, and Holmes, *Texas,* 71, 73.
19. Steve H. Murdock et al., "Dynamic Population Change in Size and Diversity," *Texas Almanac, 2002–2003* (Dallas: Dallas Morning News, 2001), 286.
20. Murdock, "Dynamic Population Change in Size and Diversity," 286–9.

21. Steve H. Murdock, Md. Nazrul Hoque, and Beverly A. Pecotte, "Texas Population: Historical Patterns and Future Trends," *Texas Almanac, 1994–1995* (Dallas: Dallas Morning News, 1993), 303–4; Texas State Data Center, *Population Projections for Texas,* February 1998; U.S. Census Bureau, Basic Facts, Quick Tables, QT-PL, Race, Hispanic and Latino, and Age: 2000, accessed April 4, 2001, http://factfinder.census.gov/bf/.
22. See Pew Hispanic Center, "Latinos in California, Texas, New York, Florida, and New Jersey," Survey Brief, March 2004, accessed June 16, 2004, http://www.pewhispanic.org/site/docs/pdf/LATINOS%20IN%20CA-TX-NY-FL-NJ-031904.pdf; Tamar Jacoby, "A Voting Bloc Without a Party," *New York Times* (October 28, 2002): A25.
23. T. R. Fehrenbach, *Seven Keys to Texas,* rev. ed. (El Paso: Texas Western Press, 1986), 3–4.
24. T. R. Fehrenbach, "Seven Keys to Understanding Texas," *Atlantic Monthly* (March 1975): 123–4.
25. Fehrenbach, *Seven Keys to Texas,* 22.
26. T. R. Fehrenbach, *Lone Star: A History of Texas and the Texans* (New York: Macmillan, 1968), 472–6.
27. Fehrenbach, *Seven Keys to Texas,* 29.
28. Fehrenbach, *Seven Keys to Texas,* 24–5.
29. Fehrenbach, *Seven Keys to Texas,* 76.
30. Alwyn Barr, *Texans in Revolt: The Battle for San Antonio, 1835* (Austin: University of Texas Press, 1990), 1–4.
31. William C. Brinkley, *The Texas Revolution* (Austin: Texas State Historical Association, 1952).
32. Quoted in Mark E. Nackman, *A Nation Within a Nation* (Port Washington, NY: Kennikat Press, 1975), 27.
33. Joe B. Frantz, *Texas: A Bicentennial History* (New York: Norton, 1976), 69.
34. Walter Lord, *A Time to Stand: The Epic of the Alamo* (Lincoln: University of Nebraska Press, 1961), 54.
35. Lord, *A Time to Stand,* 82.
36. Paul Andrew Hutton, "The Alamo: An American Epic," *American History Illustrated* (March 1986): 24.
37. Lord, *A Time to Stand,* 142.
38. Lon Tinkle, *The Alamo* (New York: McGraw-Hill, 1958), 118.
39. Gilbert M. Cuthbertson, "Individual Freedom: The Evolution of a Political Ideal," in Robert F. O'Connor, ed., *Texas Myths* (College Station: Texas A&M University Press, 1986), 179.
40. David Montejano, *Anglos and Mexicans in the Making of Texas, 1836–1986* (Austin: University of Texas Press, 1987), 305.
41. Fehrenbach, *Seven Keys to Texas,* 95.
42. Fehrenbach, *Seven Keys to Texas,* 128.
43. Samuel P. Huntington, *American Politics: The Promise of Disharmony* (Cambridge, MA: Harvard University Press, 1981), 13–60.
44. William S. Maddox and Stuart A. Lilie, *Beyond Liberal and Conservative: Reassessing the Political Spectrum* (Washington, DC: Cato Institute, 1984), 7–21.
45. Maddox and Lilie, *Beyond Liberal and Conservative,* 14–5.
46. Roscoe Martin, *The People's Party in Texas* (Austin: University of Texas Press, 1970), 31–52.
47. Martin, *The People's Party in Texas,* 82–112.
48. *Texas Poll Report* (January–March 1994): 6.
49. V. O. Key Jr., *Southern Politics* (New York: Vintage Books, 1949), 261.
50. Fehrenbach, *Seven Keys to Texas,* 50–2; *Texas Almanac, 2002–2003* (Dallas: Dallas Morning News, 2001), 596.
51. Fehrenbach, *Seven Keys to Texas,* 52–4; *Texas Almanac, 1986–1987* (Dallas: Dallas Morning News, 1985), 212.
52. Fehrenbach, *Seven Keys to Texas,* 58–60; Donald A. Hicks, "Advanced Industrial Development," in Antony Champagne and Edward J. Harpham, eds., *Texas at the Crossroads: People, Politics, and Policy* (College Station: Texas A&M University Press, 1987), 49–50; *Texas Almanac, 1994–1995,* 608; Comptroller of Public Accounts, *Fiscal Notes,* (January 1994): 1, 14; "The Texas Economy Online," Texas Department of Economic Development Web site, October 26, 1999, accessed October 29, 1999, http://www.bidc.state.tx.us/overview/2-2te.html.

53. Comptroller of Public Accounts, "The Texas Economies: What Makes Them Tick," *Fiscal Notes* (December 1993): 7–10.

54. Comptroller of Public Accounts, *Fiscal Notes* (January 1994): 16–7.

55. Comptroller of Public Accounts, "Texas Economic Update: Looking 10 Years Back and 10 Years Forward" (Winter 2000), accessed December 12, 2001, http://www.window.state.tx.us/ecodata/teu00_1.html.

56. Comptroller of Public Accounts, "The Necessary Ingredient Is Jobs," *Texas Economic Update* (Summer 2003), accessed June 15, 2004, http://www.window.state.tx.us/ecodata/teusum03/.

57. "Texas Economy: Employment Growth and Low Inflation," *Texas Almanac, 2000–2001,* 577–9; Comptroller of Public Accounts, *Fiscal Notes* (July 1999): 10–1; Comptroller of Public Accounts, "Texas Economic Update."

58. "Overview of the Texas Economy," Texas Business and Industry Data Center, accessed June 15, 2004, http://www.bidc.state.tx.us/overview/2-2te.htm.

59. Comptroller of Public Accounts, "The Texas Economy: Employment Growth Continues"; *Texas Almanac, 2002–2003* (Dallas: Dallas Morning News, 2001), 547; Overview of the Texas Economy.

60. Comptroller of Public Accounts, *Fiscal Notes* (January 1994): 12–3.

61. Economic Policy Institute/Center on Budget and Policy Priorities, "Pulling Apart: A State-by-State Analysis of Income Trends," April 23, 2002, accessed August 11, 2002, http://www.cbpp.org/4-23-02sfp.pdf.

62. Dick Lavine, "Income Gap Continues to Grow Despite Strong Economy," Center for Public Policy Priorities, news release, January 18, 2000, accessed July 24, 2000, http://www.cppp.org/products/media/pressreleases/PR11800.html; Jay P. Greene, "High School Graduation Rates in the United States," Manhattan Institute for Policy Research, revised April 2002, accessed June 17, 2004, http://www.manhattan-institute.org/html/cr_baeo.htm.

63. George Norris Green, *The Establishment in Texas Politics* (Westport, CT: Greenwood, 1979), 17; Chandler Davidson, *Race and Class in Texas Politics* (Princeton, NJ: Princeton University Press, 1992), 105.

64. See Christine Carroll, "The 100 Richest People in Texas," *Texas Monthly* (September 1992): 118–43.

CHAPTER 16

1. Juan B. Elizondo Jr., "Ratliff: Time to Rewrite Constitution: Lawmaker Joined by Watchdog Group in Effort to Update State Document," *Austin American-Statesman* (October 28, 1999); Bill Ratliff and Rob Junell, "A New Constitution for the New Millennium," *Austin American-Statesman* (December 9, 1998); Osler McCarthy, "Poll Shows Support for New Constitution," *Austin American-Statesman* (February 13, 1999).

2. Ralph W. Steen, "Convention of 1836," *The Handbook of Texas Online,* accessed September 9, 2000, http://www.tsha.utexas.edu/handbook/online/articles/view/CC/mjc12.html.

3. Joe C. Ericson, "Constitution of the Republic of Texas," *The Handbook of Texas Online,* accessed September 9, 2000, http://www.tsha.utexas.edu/handbook/online/articles/view/CC/mhc1.html.

4. Walter L. Buenger, "Constitution of 1861," *The Handbook of Texas Online,* accessed September 9, 2000, http://www.tsha.utexas.edu/handbook/online/articles/view/CC/mhc4.html.

5. S. S. McKay, "Constitution of 1866," *The Handbook of Texas Online,* accessed September 9, 2000, http://www.tsha.utexas.edu/handbook/online/articles/view/CCmhc5.html.

6. Claude Elliott, "Constitutional Convention of 1869," *The Handbook of Texas Online,* accessed September 9, 2000, http://www.tsha.utexas.edu/handbook/online/articles/view/CC/mjc4.html.

7. S. S. McKay, "Constitution of 1869," *The Handbook of Texas Online,* accessed September 9, 2000, http://www.tsha.utexas.edu/handbook/online/articles/view/CC/mhc6.html.

8. Seth S. McKay, *Seven Decades of the Texas Constitution of 1876* (Austin: University of Texas Press, 1930), 47–143.

9. John Walker Mauer, "State Constitutions in a Time of Crisis: The Case of the Texas Constitution of 1876," *Texas Law Review* 68 (June 1990): 1638–9.

10. J. E. Ericson, "The Delegates to the Convention of 1875: A Reappraisal," *Southwestern Historical Quarterly* 67 (1963/1964): 22–7. Ericson's reappraisal of the delegates is based on Nat Q. Henderson's *Directory of the Officers and Members of the Constitutional Convention of the State of Texas, A.D. 1875* (Austin: n.p., 1875).

11. Mauer, "State Constitutions," 1646–7.

12. Patrick G. Williams, "Of Rutabagas and Redeemers: Rethinking the Texas Constitution of 1876," *Southwestern Historical Quarterly* 106 (October 2002): 250.

13. Williams, "Of Rutabagas and Redeemers," 250–3.

14. Although the content of the section was deleted, the title remains to prevent confusion with the numbering of the remaining articles.

15. *Texas Constitution,* Article 1, sections 12 and 29, respectively.

16. Donald S. Lutz, "The Texas Constitution," in Kent L. Tedin, Donald S. Lutz, and Edward P. Fuchs, eds., *Perspectives on American and Texas Politics,* 5th ed. (Dubuque, IA: Kendall/Hunt, 1998), 45.

17. Lutz, "The Texas Constitution."

18. Janice C. May, "Constitutional Revision in Texas," in Richard H. Kraemer and Philip W. Barnes, eds., *Texas: Readings in Politics, Government, and Public Policy* (San Francisco: Chandler, 1971), 318.

19. Dick Smith, "Constitutional Revision, 1876–1961," in Fred Gantt Jr., Irving O. Dawson, and Luther G. Hagard Jr., eds., *Governing Texas: Documents and Readings* (New York: Crowell, 1966), 53.

20. The amendment accounts for sections and articles of the current constitution that have only the title or section number appearing in the text. For example, Article 3, section 3a (repealed August 5, 1969).

21. Legislative Council, Analysis of Proposed Constitutional Amendments, November 2, 1999, Election (Austin: Legislative Council, 1999).

22. Smith, "Constitutional Revision," 55.

23. Informational Booklet on the Proposed 1976 Revision of the Texas Constitution, 64th Legislature, 1975, 3–7; Janice C. May, *The Texas Constitutional Revision Experience in the 1970s* (Austin: Sterling Swift, 1975), 25–30; Dick Smith, "Constitutional Revision," 51–5.

24. See Texas Advisory Commission on Intergovernmental Relations, *The Texas Constitutional Revision Commission of 1973* (Austin: Texas Advisory Commission of Intergovernmental Relations, 1972), on the importance of the commission to the convention's success.

25. Janice May, *The Texas Constitutional Revision Experience,* 160–200.

CHAPTER 17

1. Supreme Court of the United States, *Santa Fe Independent School District v. Jane, Jane, and John Doe et al.,* No. 99-62, June 19, 2000; American Civil Liberties Union Freedom Network, "In the Courts: *Santa Fe v. Jane Doe et al.,* Brief for Respondents," accessed September 25, 2000, http://www.aclu.org/court/santafe.html.

2. Associated Press, "Texas Student Says Pre-Game Prayer After Federal Judge Clears Way," September 7, 1999, accessed September 25, 2000, http://www.freedomforum.org/religion/1999/9/7prayer.asp; "Teen Says Pre-Game Prayer After Court Order Clears Way," *Dallas Morning News* (September 4, 1999): A31.

3. U.S. Census Bureau, "2002 Census of Governments," GC02-1(P), issued July, 2002, accessed June 24, 2004, http://ftp2.census.gov/govs/cog/2002COGprelim_report.pdf.

4. Texas State Historical Association, "County Organization," *The Handbook of Texas Online,* last updated July 23, 2001, accessed June 7, 2002, http://www.tsha.utexas.edu/handbook/online/articles/view/CC/muc10.html.

5. George Braden, *The Constitution of the State of Texas: An Annotated and Comparative Analysis,* vol. 2 (Austin: Texas Advisory Commission on Intergovernmental Relations, 1977), 505.

6. See Dick Smith, "The Development of Local Government Units in Texas" (Ph.D. diss., Harvard University, 1938). See also Herman

James and Irvin Stewart, "County Government in Texas," *University of Texas Bulletin,* No. 2525 (July 1, 1925).

7. Texas Association of Counties, "About Counties—County Government History," accessed June 7, 2002, http://www.county.org/counties/history.asp; and "About Counties—County Government: Some Facts About Texas Counties," accessed June 7, 2002, http://www.county.org/counties/facts.asp.

8. Terrell Blodgett, "Texas Cities: The Bulwark of Democracy," 1999 William P. Hobby Jr. Distinguished Lecture, Southwest Texas State University, accessed September 17, 2000, http://www.swt.edu/cpm/lectures/blodgett_txt.html.

9. Braden, *The Constitution of the State of Texas,* 505.

10. Today, those boundary disputes continue. In 2000, a court declared in favor of Denton County in its boundary dispute with Tarrant County over the now lucrative real estate between the Dallas–Fort Worth area and Denton.

11. Texas State Historical Association, "City Government," *The Handbook of Texas Online,* last updated July 23, 2001, accessed June 11, 2002, http://www.tsha.utexas.edu/handbook/online/articles/view/CC/mvc2.html. See also Egbert Cockrell, "Municipal Home Rule with Special Reference to Texas," *Southwestern Social Sciences Quarterly* 1 (1920/1921): 147; and "Do Statewide Planning and the Consistency Concept Infringe on Home Rule Authority," *Journal of Planning Literature* 11 (May 1997): 564–74.

12. See Roscoe C. Martin, "County Home Rule Movement in Texas," *Southwestern Social Science Quarterly* (March 1935): 1–11; John P. Keith, "City and County Home Rule in Texas," University of Texas Institute of Public Affairs, 1951; Braden, *The Constitution of the State of Texas,* 652; and W. E. Benton, "The County Home Rule Movement in Texas," *Southwestern Social Science Quarterly* 31 (1950): 108.

13. Steve Bickerstaff, "Voting Rights Challenges to School Boards in Texas: What Next?" *Baylor Law Review* 49 (Fall 1997): 1017.

14. While the correct punctuation for this term would be commissioners' court, constitutional and legal references designate it as commissioners court, with no apostrophe, so we will use the official method throughout this chapter.

15. *Gray* v. *Sanders,* 372 U.S. 368 (1963), *Wesberry* v. *Sanders,* 376 U.S. 1 (1964), and *Reynolds* v. *Sims,* 84 S.Ct. 1362 (1964).

16. *Avery* v. *Midland County, Texas, et al.,* 390 U.S. 474 (1968).

17. The office of county treasurer has been abolished for Tarrant, Bee, Bexar, Collin, Andrews, Gregg, El Paso, Fayette, and Nueces counties.

18. Judon Fambrough, "County Regulation of Rural Subdivisions," Land Development, Publication 1195, October 1997 (rev. 2000), accessed June 29, 2004, http://recenter.tamu.edu/pdf/1195.pdf; "Counties Achieve 'Sea Change' on Development Authority," *County* 11 (July/August 1999), accessed June 11, 2002, http://www.county.org/resources/library/county_mag/county/114/issue.html.

19. Paul Sugg, "Last Year, Counties Were Granted Greater Authority to Address Unbridled Development. So What Happened?" *County* 12 (November/December 2000), accessed June 11, 2002, http://www.county.org/resources/library/county_mag/county/126/issue.html.

20. Jim Lewis, "Election Reform: Will the Prayers Be Answered?" *County* 13 (July/August 2001), accessed June 11, 2002, http://www.county.org/resources/library/county_mag/county/134/issue.html.

21. 78th Texas Legislature, HB 1549, Regular Session, 2003, accessed June 29, 2004, http://www.capitol.state.tx.us/cgi-bin/tlo/textframe.cmd?LEG=78&SESS=R&CHAMBER=H&BILLTYPE=B&BILLSUFFIX=01549&VERSION=5&TYPE=B.

22. "Are Legislators Too 'Fee Bill' Minded?" *County* 9 (January/February 1997), accessed June 11, 2002, http://www.county.org/resources/library/county_mag/county/091/issue.html.

23. House Research Organization, "Constitutional Amendments proposed for November 2001 Ballot," *Focus Report* (August 13, 2001): 55.

24. See Elna Christopher, "Unfunded Mandates: County Officials Uniting Behind Initiative," *County* 16 (March/April 2004): 32–5.

25. Almost all general-law cities have fewer than 5,000 people. However, even a few home-rule cities have fewer than 5,000 people. At one time, those cities had more than 5,000 people and achieved home-rule status.

26. Article 3, section 53, of the constitution prohibits the legislature from passing "any local or special law . . . regulating the affairs of counties, cities, towns, wards or school districts."

27. For Type A and Type B general-law cities, the Local Government Code specifies an aldermanic form of government. However, cities are allowed to change their charters and could adopt the council–manager form of government. Also, in 2003, the legislature changed the Local Government Code to allow cities to assign duties to city officials, a provision that allows cities to create a city administrator, who performs the functions that a city manager performs in the council–manager form of government. Type C general-law cities are required to incorporate with the commission form of government. In practice, Texas cities do not incorporate as Type C cities.

28. Dale Krane, Platon Rigos, and Melvin Hill Jr., *Home Rule in America: A Fifty-State Handbook* (Washington, DC: CQ Press, 2000), 401; Blodgett, "Texas Cities."

29. "Hurricane That Wrecked Galveston Was Deadliest in U.S. History," CNN (September 8, 2000), accessed September 8, 2000, http://www.cnn.com/2000/WEATHER/09/07/galveston.backgrounder/index.html.

30. Blodgett, "Texas Cities"; Bradley R. Rice, "Commission Form of City Government," *The Handbook of Texas Online,* last updated July 23, 2001, accessed June 11, 2002, http://www.tsha.utexas.edu/handbook/online/articles/view/CC/moc1.html.

31. Laurence F. Jones, Nirmal Goswami, and Ralph Warren, "An Assessment of Capital Budgeting in Texas Cities: A Research Note," *Texas Journal of Political Studies* 19 (Spring/Summer 1997): 54–7.

32. A city may carry over some of this allowance from one year to another but may expand no more than a total of 30 percent of its area in one year.

33. The ETJ ranges from one-half mile for those cities with fewer than 5,000 citizens, up to five miles from the corporate limits for cities with more than 100,000 citizens.

34. Local Government Code, chapter 42.

35. Local Government Code, section 43.121 Limited Purpose Annexation (planning, zoning, health, and safety). Section 43.130 states that citizens in a limited-purpose annexation area may vote in city council races but not bond elections. Section 43.122 limits strip annexation to at least 1,000 feet wide and no more than three miles, in most cases.

36. Senate Interim Committee on Annexation Interim Report, 76th Legislature, October 1998.

37. Local Government Code, chapters 41–43.

38. See, for instance, Craig Smyser, "Houston's Power: As It Was," *Houston Chronicle* (June 27, 1977): 6.

39. In 2004, Houston had eight Anglos, three African Americans, two Hispanics, and two Asian Americans serving as city council members and mayor; Dallas had seven Anglos, four African Americans, and four Hispanics; San Antonio had six Hispanics, four Anglos, and two African Americans; Fort Worth had seven Anglos and two African Americans.

40. For a profile of Miller, see John Nichols, "The Online Beat: From Muckraker to Mayor," *The Nation Online,* February 18, 2002, accessed June 20, 2002, http://www.thenation.com/thebeat/index.mhtml?bid=1&pid=18.

41. "State Buffs Up County Statutes," *County* 11 (July/August 1999), accessed September 17, 2000, http://www.county.org/publications/county/archiveindex.html.

42. Bill D. Dugatt III, "How to Create a Groundwater Conservation District," Bickerstaff, Heath, Smiley, Pollan, Kever, and McDaniel, April 8, 1999, accessed September 17, 2000, http://www.bickerstaff.com.

43. Sugg, "Last Year, Counties Were Granted Greater Authority."

44. Texas Education Agency, *Snapshot 2001–2002,* accessed July 6, 2004, http://www.tea.state.tx.us/perfreport/snapshot/2002/pdf/snap022.pdf; National Center for Education Statistics, U.S. Department of Education, Digest of Education Statistics 2001, Table 91, accessed July 23, 2002, http://www.nces.ed.gov/pubs2002/digest2001/tables/dt091.asp.

45. Texas Education Agency, *Snapshot 2001–2002.*

46. Texas Education Agency, *Snapshot 2001–2002;* National Center for Education Statistic, U.S. Department of Education, Digest of Education Statistics 2001, Table 99, accessed July 23, 2002, http://www.nces. ed.gov/pubs2002/digest2001/tables/dt099.asp.

47. Texas Education Agency, *Snapshot 2001–2002.*

48. Bickerstaff, "Voting Rights Challenges," 1021.

49. Bickerstaff, "Voting Rights Challenges," 1024 and 1056, fn 49.

50. "Cumulative Voting in Texas City Councils and School Districts," Center for Voting and Democracy, May 2004, accessed October 22, 2004, http://www.fairvote.org/cumulative/texas.htm.

51. Texas Education Agency, *School Finance: List of Chapter 41 Districts for 2003–2004,* updated July 31, 2003, accessed July 6, 2004, http://www. tea.state.tx.us/school.finance/funding/ch41/ch41_04_lst.xls.

52. House Research Organization, "The Tax System and Public School Financing in Texas," *Session Focus* (March 24, 1999): 2; "Texas Budget Highlights, Fiscal 2000–01," *State Finance Report* 76-3 (October 21, 1999): 10.

CHAPTER 18

1. Material for this vignette was taken from Jake Bernstein, "Remember the Holiday Inn," *Texas Observer* (June 6, 2003); Jim Henderson, "Furtive Plan Was 'Only Alternative,'" *Houston Chronicle* (May 14, 2003); Kris Axtman, "A Texas Standoff That's Crossed State Lines," *Christian Science Monitor* (May 16, 2003); and James W. Riddlesperger Jr. "Redistricting Politics in Texas 2003," paper presented at the Annual Meeting of the Southern Political Science Association, New Orleans, January 8–10, 2004.

2. Texas State Historical Association, "Convention of 1833" and "Republic of Texas," *The Handbook of Texas Online,* updated July 23, 2001, accessed June 10, 2002, http://www.tsha.utexas.edu/handbook/online/ articles/view/CC/mjc10.html and http://www.tsha.utexas.edu/ handbook/online/articles/view/RR/mzr2.html.

3. Texas State Historical Association, "Congress of the Republic of Texas," *The Handbook of Texas Online,* updated July 23, 2001, accessed June 10, 2002, http://www.tsha.utexas.edu/handbook/online/articles/ view/CC/mkc1.html.

4. Texas State Historical Association, "Lorenzo de Zavala," *The Handbook of Texas Online,* updated July 23, 2001, accessed June 10, 2002, http:// www.tsha.utexas.edu/handbook/online/articles/view/ZZ/fza5.html.

5. See J. Mason Brewer, *Negro Legislators of Texas,* 2nd ed. (Austin: Jenkins, 1970).

6. Kendra A. Hovey and Harold A. Hovey, *Congressional Quarterly's State Fact Finder 2004: Rankings Across America* (Washington, DC: CQ Press, 2004), 103.

7. There are several ways that state officials may be removed from office. See Article 15 of the Texas Constitution.

8. National Conference of State Legislatures. "2004 State Legislative Session Calendar," updated May 10, 2004, accessed May 17, 2004, http:// www.ncsl.org/programs/legman/about/sess2004.htm.

9. The Texas Constitution actually allowed for unequal population in Senate districts, but in 1964, the U.S. Supreme Court declared in *Reynolds* v. *Sims* that both chambers in states with bicameral state legislatures must be apportioned according to population.

10. House Research Organization, "New Districts in Place for 2002 Elections," *Interim News,* no. 77-4 (January 14, 2002).

11. See Jim Riddlesperger, "Redistricting Politics in Texas 2003," paper prepared for presentation at the Southern Political Science Association Convention, New Orleans, January 8–10, 2004, accessed February 18, 2004, http://www2.gasou.edu/spsa/conference.htm.

12. Ralph A. Wooster, "Membership in Early Texas Legislatures, 1850–1860," *Southwestern Historical Quarterly* 69 (October 1965): 163–73.

13. For more information on initiative and referendum, see Shaun Bowler, Todd Donovan, and Caroline Tolbert, eds., *Citizens as Legislators: Direct Democracy in the United States* (Columbus: Ohio State University Press, 1998).

14. Calculated by the author based on biographical profiles provided by senators (http://www.senate.state.tx.us/78r/senate/Members.htm) and House biographical data provided to the Chief Clerk's Office (http://www.house.state.tx.us/members/pdf/biodata.pdf).

15. For a description of this nonparty speaker system and the current birthing of parties that threatens to undo that system, see Keith Hamm and Robert Harmel, "Legislative Party Development and the Speaker System: The Case of the Texas House," *Journal of Politics* 55 (November 1993): 1140–51.

16. Gary Moncrief, "Committee Stacking and Reform in the Texas House of Representatives," *Texas Journal of Political Studies* 2(1) (1979): 47.

17. *Dallas Times-Herald* (December 1, 1980); *San Angelo Standard Times* (February 13, 1983); *Austin American-Statesman* (January 11, 1981).

18. Council of State Governments, *Book of the States 2004,* vol. 36 (Lexington, KY: Council of State Governments, 2004), 191.

19. For more detailed information, see House Research Organization, "How a Bill Becomes Law: 79th Legislature," *Focus Report* (January 28, 2005); and Rules and Housekeeping Resolutions, *Daily Floor Report* (January 12 and 13, 2005).

20. The Local and Consent Calendar is supposed to be reserved for noncontroversial bills (though sometimes a controversial matter will be sneaked through on it). Bills on this calendar are not usually debated; if they are contested, they will be pulled from this calendar.

21. This daily calendar actually includes several calendars. Bills are considered on Major State, General State, Emergency, Resolutions, Constitutional Amendments, Local and Consent, or Senate Calendars.

22. For an account of the incident, see Robert Heard, *The Miracle of the Killer Bees* (Austin: Honey Hill, 1981).

23. See Clay Robison, "Texas Democrats Bolt Again," *Houston Chronicle* (July 28, 2003), accessed May 18, 2004, http://www.chron.com/cs/ CDA/printstory.mpl/topstory2/2015694; Michael King, "Albuquerque or Bust!" *Austin Chronicle* (August 8, 2003), accessed May 18, 2004, http://www.austinchronicle.com/issues/dispatch/2003-08-08/ pols_capitol.html; Gary Scharrer, "Demo Breaks Ranks: Senator's Return Could End Standoff," Elpasotimes.com (September 3, 2003), accessed May 18, 2004, http://www.borderlandnews.com/stories/ borderland/20030903-16807.shtml.

24. Technically, the rules only require that a majority of members of the conference committee from each chamber sign the report. This loophole allows "phantom" meetings—some conference committees never meet. The chairs simply negotiate the language behind closed doors, then present it to the others for their signatures.

25. House Research Organization, "Writing the State Budget," *State Finance Report,* no. 77-1 (February 1, 2001).

26. Council of State Governments, *Book of the States 1998–99,* vol. 32 (Lexington, KY: Council of State Governments, 1998), 234–5.

27. Legislative Budget Board staff interview, November 26, 2002.

28. *Fort Worth Star-Telegram* (January 13, 1983).

29. See, for instance, Texans for Public Justice, "Austin's Oldest Profession: Texas' Top Lobby Clients and Those Who Service Them," July 2002, accessed July 3, 2002, http://www.tpj.org/reports/lobby02/ index.html.

30. A 1999 constitutional amendment allows the Senate president pro tem, in the event of a vacancy in the office of lieutenant governor, to call the Senate into special session for the sole purpose of electing a lieutenant governor. The December 2000 special session of the Senate was called in this fashion.

CHAPTER 19

1. Associated Press, "Texas Governor Vetoes Record Number of Bills," *USA Today* (June 20, 2001), accessed July 5, 2002, http://www.usatoday.com/news/politics/2001-06-20-texas.htm.

2. House Research Organization, "Vetoes of Legislation—77th Legislature," *Focus Report* (June 26, 2001).

3. "Perry's Mistake," *Dallas Morning News* (June 19, 2001): 14A.

4. Paul Burka, "No! No! No! Rick Perry's Veto Binge Was the First Sign of the Kind of Governor He Wants to Be," *Texas Monthly* (August 2001), accessed July 5, 2002, http://www.texasmonthly.com/mag/issues/2001-08-01/.

5. Fred Gantt Jr., *The Chief Executive in Texas: A Study in Gubernatorial Leadership* (Austin: University of Texas Press, 1964), 15–16. Charles Polzer lists thirty-one Spanish governors of Texas from 1717 to 1823. *Documentary Relations of the Southwest*, in Biographical Files—Governors of Texas (Austin: Center for American History, University of Texas, 1977).

6. See constitution of 1845 and amendment of 1850. Also see Gantt, *The Chief Executive in Texas*, 20–27.

7. Gantt, *The Chief Executive in Texas*, 30–1.

8. The 1827 constitution included a four-year term, with a one-term limit. The constitution of the Texas Republic limited the president to a single three-year term (Sam Houston served two nonconsecutive terms). The 1845 and 1861 constitutions included a two-year term, with a limit of no more than four years in a six-year period. The 1866 constitution included a four-year term, with a limit of no more than eight years in a twelve-year period. The 1869 constitution had the most liberal provisions—a four-year term of office, with no term limits. Gantt, *The Chief Executive in Texas*, 335.

9. Council of State Governments, *Book of the States 2004*, vol. 36 (Lexington, KY: Council of State Governments, 2004), 173.

10. Gantt, *The Chief Executive in Texas*, 38; Council of State Governments, *The Governor: The Office and Its Powers* (Lexington, KY: Council of State Governments, 1972); Council of State Governments, *Book of the States 2000–01*, 39.

11. Gantt, *The Chief Executive in Texas*, 151–2.

12. See Gantt, *The Chief Executive in Texas*, 29–33; and Seth McKay, "Making the Texas Constitution of 1876," Ph.D. diss., University of Pennsylvania, 1924.

13. In Maine, New Hampshire, New Jersey, and Tennessee, the governor is the *only* statewide elected official and names all other officials. Council of State Governments, *Book of the States 2000–01*, 25–6, 31–2.

14 Joseph Schlesinger, "Politics, the Executive," in Herbert Jacob and Kenneth Vines, eds., *Politics in the American States: A Comparative Analysis* (Boston: Little, Brown, 1965), 225–34 (quotation at 231).

15. Virginia Gray, Herbert Jacob, and Robert Albritton, *Politics in the American States*, 5th ed. (New York: HarperCollins, 1990), appendices 6.1–6.7; Thad L. Beyle, "Governors: The Middlemen and Women in Our Political System," in Virginia Gray and Herbert Jacob, eds., *Politics in the American States: A Comparative Analysis*, 6th ed. (Washington, DC: CQ Press, 1996); Thad L. Beyle, "The Governors," in Virginia Gray and Russell Hanson, eds., *Politics in the American States: A Comparative Analysis*, 8th ed. (Washington, DC: CQ Press, 2003).

16. It is not clear exactly how many appointments a governor makes. A 1982 analysis states that there are about 4,000 appointments, with about 2,000 subject to confirmation. Yet, a 1989 Senate study counted only 1,389 appointees. Governor George W. Bush made about 3,400 appointments in just over four years in office. See Senate Nominations Committee, "Analysis of Gubernatorial Appointees to Agencies, Boards and Commissions," December 8, 1989, 1; Charles Wiggins, Keith Hamm, and Howard Balanoff, "The 1982 Gubernatorial Transition in Texas," in Thad L. Beyle, ed., *Gubernatorial Transitions: The 1982 Elections* (Durham, NC: Duke University, 1985), 396; Wayne Slater, "Bush Steps Up Number of Hispanic Appointees," *Dallas Morning News* (October 12, 1999): A1.

17. The case is *Denison v. State*. Texas Legislative Council, "Staff Memo to Senate Committee on State Affairs, Subcommittee on Nominations," January 26, 1981.

18. Slater, "Bush Steps Up Number of Hispanic Appointees."

19. Wiggins, Hamm, and Balanoff, "The 1982 Gubernatorial Transition," 398.

20. Gantt, *The Chief Executive in Texas*, 327.

21. Richard Murray and Gregory Weiher, "Texas: Ann Richards, Taking On the Challenge," in Thad L. Beyle, ed., *Governors and Hard Times* (Washington, DC: CQ Press, 1992), 186.

22. For descriptions and examples of governors' legislative prowess, see Gantt, *The Chief Executive in Texas*, 42, 237–8, 244–54.

23. Council of State Governments, *Book of the States 2000–01*, 66–8.

24. Gantt, *The Chief Executive in Texas*, 39. Most states require a two-thirds vote to override, but seven require three-fifths and six others require a simple majority. Council of State Governments, *Book of the States 2000–01*, 101. The Texas Constitution is confusing in its language about overrides of vetoes. It says that an override requires a vote of two-thirds of the members present in the chamber that passed the bill first, and two-thirds of the elected members of the chamber that passed the bill last—or, if it is a line-item veto, two-thirds of the members present in each chamber.

25. The president of the Republic of Texas had pocket-veto authority—if he refused to sign a bill passed in the last five days of a session, the bill died. No constitution since statehood has included pocket-veto authority. Braden, *The Constitution of the State of Texas*, 333.

26. Texas Legislative Council, "Gubernatorial Veto: Powers, Procedures, and Override History," staff memorandum, May 22, 1990. See also Fred Gantt Jr., "The Governor's Veto in Texas: An Absolute Negative?" *Public Affairs Comment* 15 (March 1969), University of Texas Institute of Public Affairs.

27. See Gantt, *The Chief Executive in Texas*, 39; Council of State Governments, *Book of the States 2004*, 162–3.

28. House Research Organization, "Texas Budget Highlights Fiscal 2004–05," *State Finance Report*, 78-3 (November 17, 2003): 5.

29. Council of State Governments, *Book of the States 2004*, 175.

30. How much land this represented is uncertain, since even the boundaries of the state were in dispute.

31. For a more detailed analysis of the SBOE, see House Research Organization, "State Board of Education: Controversy and Change," *Focus Report* (January 3, 2000).

32. These figures do not include regional agencies, such as river authorities, or local agencies created or funded by the state, such as the fifty community college districts.

33. Kathleen O'Leary Morgan and Scott Morgan, eds., *State Rankings 2004: A Statistical View of the 50 United States*, 15th ed. (Lawrence, KS: Morgan Quinto Press, 2004), 338–9.

34. Marver Bernstein, *Regulating Business by Independent Commission* (Princeton, NJ: Princeton University Press, 1955), 90.

35. *Texas Almanac 1972–73* (Dallas: A. H. Belo, 1971), 397.

CHAPTER 20

1. Clay Robison, "Different Chief Justice, but Same Story," *Houston Chronicle* (May 1, 2004).

2. American Judicature Society, *Judicial Selection in the States: Texas, History of Judicial Selection*, accessed July 8, 2004, http://www.ajs.org/js/TX_history.htm.

3. Chief Justice Thomas R. Phillips, State of the Judiciary, March 4, 2003, accessed July 7, 2004, http://www.supreme.courts.state.tx.us/Advisory/SOJ.pdf.

4. Thomas R. Phillips, Statement by Chief Justice Thomas R. Phillips, April 29, 2004, accessed July 7, 2004, http://www.supreme.courts.state.tx.us/advisory04.29.04.asp.

5. Paul Womack, "Judiciary," *The Handbook of Texas Online*, accessed November 15, 2000, http://www.tsha.utexas.edu/handbook/online/articles/view/JJ/jzj1.html.

6. Figures for all of the courts in the chapter are from the Office of Court Administration, *Annual Report of the Texas Judicial System, Fiscal Year 2003* (Austin: Office of Court Administration, 2003).

7. Texas Research League, "The Texas Judiciary: A Structural-Functional Overview," *Texas Courts: A Study by the Texas Research League*, Report 1 (Austin: Texas Research League, 1990), 41.

8. The operation of the supreme court is described in James A. Vaught, "Internal Procedures in the Texas Supreme Court," *Texas Tech Law Review* 26(3) (1995): 935–58.

9. Walt Borges, "The Court's Bill Chill," *Texas Lawyer* (September 4, 1995): 1.

10. Anthony Champagne, "Judicial Reform in Texas," in Anthony Champagne and Judith Haydel, eds., *Judicial Reform in the States* (New York: University Press of America, 1993), 107.

11. Texans for Public Justice, "Payola Justice: How Supreme Court Justices Raise Money from Court Litigants," Conclusion, February 1998, accessed November 8, 1998, http://www.tpj.org/reports/payola/conclusions.html.

12. Texans for Public Justice, "Checks and Imbalances: How Texas Supreme Court Justices Raised $11 Million," The Justices' War Chests, April 2000, accessed November 8, 2000, http://www.tpj.org/reports/checks/warchests.html.

13. Texas Watch Foundation, *Shifting Sands for Consumers: 2002–2003 Texas Supreme Court Year-in-Review*, October 30, 2003, accessed July 8, 2004, http://www.txwfoundation.org/courtwatch/Review_2002_2003.pdf.

14. Thomas R. Phillips, "State of the Judiciary," Supreme Court Web site, March 29, 1999, accessed December 2, 2000, http://www.supreme.courts.state.tx.us/soj99.html.

15. Office of Court Administration, *Public Trust and Confidence in the Courts and Legal Profession in Texas* (Austin: Office of Court Administration, 1998); Office of Court Administration, *The Courts and the Legal Profession in Texas—An Insider's Perspective: A Survey of Judges, Court Personnel, and Attorneys* (Austin: Office of Court Administration, 1998).

16. Texas Chief Justice's Task Force on Judicial Reform, *Justice at the Crossroads: Court Improvement in Texas* (Austin, 1972).

17. Texas Research League, *Texas Courts: A Study by the Texas Research League*, 3 Reports (Austin: Texas Research League, 1990–1992).

18. For an overview of revision attempts, see American Judicature Society, *Judicial Selection in the States*, Texas, History of Judicial Selection Reform, accessed July 8, 2004, http://www.ajs.org/js/TX_history.htm.

19. Supreme Court of Texas Judicial Campaign Finance Committee, "Report and Recommendations," Office of Court Administration Web site, February 23, 1999, accessed December 3, 2000, http://www.supreme.courts.state.tx.us/JCFSC/campaign1.htm.

20. John Williams, "Name Game Cost GOP Candidate," *Houston Chronicle* (March 25, 2002), accessed November 27, 2002, http://www.chron.com/cs/CDA/story.hts/metropolitan/williams/1307892.

21. Pamela Fridich et al., *Lowering the Bar: Lawyers Keep Texas Appeals Judges on Retainer.* (Austin: Texans for Public Justice, 2003), 2.

22. David M. Horton and Ryan Kellus Turner, *Lone Star Justice* (Austin: Eakin Press, 1999), 169–205; Ken Anderson, *Crime in Texas* (Austin: University of Texas Press, 1997).

CHAPTER 21

1. S. C. Gwynne, "Lonesome Cowboy," *Texas Monthly* (June 2002): 110.

2. Gwynne, "Lonesome Cowboy," 205.

3. Samuel J. Eldersveld and Hanes Walton Jr., *Political Parties in American Society*, 2nd ed. (New York: Bedford/St. Martin's, 2000), 106.

4. Frank B. Feigert, Dawn Miller, Kenda Cunningham, and Rachel Burlage, "Texas: Incipient Polarization?" *American Review of Politics* 24 (Summer 2003): 192–3.

5. Feigert et al., "Texas: Incipient Polarization."

6. Paul Lenchner, "The Party System in Texas," in Anthony Champagne and Edward J. Harpham, eds., *Texas Politics: A Reader*, 2nd ed. (New York: Norton, 1998), 165–7.

7. A. Phillips Brooks, "GOP Lieutenant Gets Close Look," *Austin American-Statesman* (August 9, 1997): B1, B7.

8. Jake Bernstein, "Elephant Wars: The Christian Right Flexes Its Muscle at the Republican Convention," *Texas Observer* (July 5, 2002): 8–9, 19, 29.

9. Jake Bernstein and Dave Mann, "In Search of the Next Crusade," *Texas Observer* (June 18, 2004).

10. Barbara Norrander, "Determinants of Local Party Campaign Activity," *Social Sciences Quarterly* 67 (September 1986): 567.

11. Frank B. Feigert and Nancy L. Williams, "Texas: Yeller Dogs and Yuppies," in Charles D. Hadley and Lewis Bowman, eds., *Southern State Party Organizations and Activists* (Westport, CT: Praeger, 1995), 84–5; Feigert et al., "Texas: Incipient Polarization," 193–4.

12. The Scripps-Howard Texas Poll question is: "Generally speaking, do you usually think of yourself as a Democrat, a Republican, an Independent, or something else?" According to state law in Texas, a party member is anyone who participates in the party's primary election.

13. James A. Dryer, Arnold Vedlitz, and David B. Hill, "New Voters, Switchers, and Political Party Realignment in Texas," *Western Political Quarterly* 41 (March 1988): 155–67; Kent L. Tedin, "The Transition of Electoral Politics in Texas: 1978–1990," in Kent L. Tedin and Donald S. Lutz, eds., *Perspectives on American and Texas Politics: A Collection of Essays*, 3rd ed. (Dubuque, IA: Kendall/Hunt, 1992), 129–51; James A. Dyer, Jan E. Leighley, and Arnold Vedlitz, "Party Identification and Public Opinion in Texas, 1984–1994: Establishing a Competitive Party System," in Anthony Champagne and Edward J. Harpham, eds., *Texas Politics: A Reader*, 2nd ed. (New York: Norton, 1998), 108–22.

14. "Republican Party of Texas Growth Chart," Texas Republican Party Web site, accessed December 22, 2001, http://www.texasgop.org/library/growth.asp.

15. Keith E. Hamm and Robert Harmel, "Legislative Party Development and the Speaker System: The Case of Texas," *Journal of Politics* 55 (November 1993): 1145–6.

16. Hamm and Harmel, "Legislative Party Development and the Speaker System," 1146.

17. See R. Bruce Anderson, "Party Caucus Development and the Insurgent Minority Party in Formerly One-Party State Legislatures," *American Review of Politics* 19 (Fall 1998): 191–216.

18. *Texas Lawyer* (May 1994): 1, 28.

19. Paul Allen Beck and Frank J. Sorauf, *Party Politics in America*, 7th ed. (New York: HarperCollins, 1992), 420; Walt Borges, "The Court's Big Chill," *Texas Lawyer* (September 4, 1995): 1; Walt Borges, "The Texas Supreme Court in 1998–1999: Moderating the Counter-Revolution," A Report of Court Watch, A Project of Texas Watch, accessed October 31, 1999, http://www.texaswatch.org/cwreview.htm; "Shifting Sands for Consumers," Court Watch 2002–2003 Annual Report. October 30, 2003, accessed August 10, 2004, http://www.txwfoundation.org/courtwatch/Review_2002_2003.pdf.

20. Because lobbyists are only required to report their income to the Texas Ethics Commission in broad categories (e.g., $10,000–24,999), the exact amount paid to lobbyists for their services is unknown. Figures from Texans for Public Justice, "Austin's Oldest Profession: Texas' Top Lobby Clients and Those Who Service Them," 2004 edition, August 4, 2004, accessed August 10, 2004, http://www.tpj.org/docs/2004b/08/lobby04/index.html.

21. Keith E. Hamm and Charles W. Wiggins, "Texas: The Transformation from Personal to Informational Lobbying," in Ronald J. Hrebenar and Clive S. Thomas, eds., *Interest Group Politics in the Southern States* (Tuscaloosa: University of Alabama Press, 1993), 163.

22. Osler McCarthy, "Minority Lobbyists Increase Their Presence at Legislature," *Austin American-Statesman* (April 12, 1999): A1, A12.

23. Quoted in Robert Bryce, "Access Through the Lobby," *Texas Observer* (February 24, 1995): 16.

24. Quoted in Bryce, "Access Through the Lobby," 16.

25. Alan Rosenthal, *The Third House: Lobbyists and Lobbying in the States* (Washington, DC: CQ Press, 1993), 190–9.

26. Texans for Public Justice, "Austin's Oldest Profession."

27. Rosenthal, *The Third House*, 182–90.

28. Bryce, "Access Through the Lobby," 16.

29. Personal correspondence, Andrew Wheat, Texans for Public Justice, October 25, 2004.

30. Lynn Tran and Andrew Wheat, *Tort Dodgers: Business Money Tips Scales of Justice* (Austin: Texans for Public Justice, 1997).

31. Jeffrey M. Berry, *The Interest Group Society,* 2nd ed. (New York: HarperCollins, 1989), 154–7.

32. Fred Gantt Jr., *The Chief Executive in Texas: A Study in Gubernatorial Leadership* (Austin: University of Texas Press, 1964), 269–71.

33. Richard Murray, "The 1982 Texas Election in Perspective," *Texas Journal of Political Studies* 5 (Spring/Summer 1983): 49–50; Paul Burka, "Primary Lesson," *Texas Monthly* (July 1986): 104–5.

34. W. Lance Bennett, *The Governing Crisis: Media, Money, and Marketing in American Elections* (New York: St. Martin's, 1992), 84–111.

35. Texans for Public Justice, *The Gated Community: How Texas House Incumbents Locked Out Challengers in 1998* (Austin: Texans for Public Justice, 1999).

36. Texans for Public Justice, *Money in Politex: A Guide to Money in the 2002 Texas Elections* (Austin: Texans for Public Justice, 2003), 14.

37. Kaye Northcott, "Getting Elected," *Mother Jones* (November 1982): 18.

38. Quoted in Northcott, "Getting Elected," 19.

39. Texans for Public Justice, *Money in Politex,* 19, 31, 35.

40. See Jon Ford, "Texas: Big Money," in Herbert E. Alexander, ed., *Campaign Money: Reform and Reality in the States* (New York: Free Press, 1976), 78–109.

41. Quoted in David Elliot, "Image Is Everything: How TV Has Reshaped Campaigning," *Austin American-Statesman* (October 16, 1994): A1, A8.

42. For an excellent article on Texas campaign consultants, see Juan B. Elizondo Jr., "Political Consultants: How They Do It," *Austin American-Statesman* (October 18, 1998): H1, H5.

43. Everett Carll Ladd, ed., *America at the Polls, 1994* (Storrs, CT: Roper Center for Public Opinion Research, 1995), 78.

44. Jerry Hagstrom and Robert Guskind, "Calling the Races," *National Journal* (July 30, 1988): 1972–5; Elliot, "Image Is Everything," A8.

45. Delbert A. Taebel, Nirmal Goswami, and Laurence Jones, "The Politics of Early Voting in Texas: Perspectives of County Party Chairs," *Texas Journal of Political Studies* 16 (Spring/Summer 1994): 43–4.

46. Robert M. Stein, "Early Voting," *Public Opinion Quarterly* 62 (Spring 1998): 57–69.

47. Ruy A. Teixeira, *The Disappearing American Voter* (Washington, DC: Brookings Institution, 1992), 12–3.

48. Morris P. Fiorina, "The Electorate at the Polls in the 1990s," in Sandy Maisel, ed., *The Parties Respond: Changes in American Parties and Campaigns,* 2nd ed. (Boulder, CO: Westview, 1994), 124–5. Angus Campbell, Philip E. Converse, Warren E. Miller, and Donald E. Stokes, *The American Voter* (Chicago: University of Chicago Press, 1960), 523–31, provides the classic statement of the influence of these factors.

49. *Texas Poll Report* (Fall 1986): 4; Kent L. Tedin, "The 1982 Election for Governor of Texas," *Texas Journal of Political Studies* 5 (Spring/Summer 1983): 29.

50. John C. Henry, "Poll Shows Anti-White Sentiment," *Austin American-Statesman* (December 5, 1986): B2.

51. Arthur H. Miller, Martin P. Wattenberg, and Oksana Malanchuk, "Schematic Assessments of Presidential Candidates," *American Political Science Review* 80 (June 1986): 521–40.

52. Thomas L. Whatley, ed., *Texas Government Newsletter* (November 17, 1986): 2.

53. Zogby Ten-State Post Election Poll: Texas, November 11, 2002.

54. Fox News Election Day Poll: Texas (Governor), November 8, 2002, accessed November 26, 2002, http://www.foxnews.com/story/0,2933,69201,00.html.

Index